STALIN'S AGENT

Books by the Same Author

Nikolai Khokhlov ('Whistler'): Self-Esteem with a Halo (2005)
The KGB's Poison Factory: From Lenin to Litvinenko (2009, 2010)
El caso Orlov: Los servicios secretos soviéticos en la guerra civil española, 1936–1939 (2013)

STALIN'S AGENT

THE LIFE AND DEATH OF
ALEXANDER ORLOV

BORIS VOLODARSKY

OXFORD
UNIVERSITY PRESS

OXFORD
UNIVERSITY PRESS

Great Clarendon Street, Oxford, OX2 6DP,
United Kingdom

Oxford University Press is a department of the University of Oxford.
It furthers the University's objective of excellence in research, scholarship,
and education by publishing worldwide. Oxford is a registered trade mark of
Oxford University Press in the UK and in certain other countries

Published in the United States of America by Oxford University Press
198 Madison Avenue, New York, NY 10016, United States of America

British Library Cataloguing in Publication Data
Data available

Library of Congress Control Number: 2014934427

ISBN 978–0–19–965658–5

Printed in Great Britain by
Clays Ltd, St Ives plc

Links to third party websites are provided by Oxford in good faith and
for information only. Oxford disclaims any responsibility for the materials
contained in any third party website referenced in this work.

For Valentina

Acknowledgements

I wish first of all to thank my wife, Valentina. Through the thirty-six years of our marriage she has unfailingly supported everything I have done. Throughout this exciting and demanding project, which has been a long time in the making, she helped to research archives, generate ideas, navigate through the murky world of Russian espionage and deception—and enabled us to finance it. Without her this book would not and could not have been written.

I could not have carried out the work without the friendly and professional advice of Dr Tennent H. ('Pete') Bagley, former tough intelligence operator, knowledgeable expert on Soviet intelligence history, and author of several important books on the KGB. Dr Warren W. 'Bud' Williams, an outstanding former intelligence officer, decorated US Ranger, and an academic historian with special interest in Austria, gave important advice.

It was difficult to gain access to so many archival sources in different parts of the world, so I am particularly grateful to Jorge Saenz Carbonell, Ambassador and Research Director for Diplomatic History in Costa Rica, who provided important documents never before studied by historians. I was greatly helped by Gail Malmgreen, Associate Head of Archival Collections, Tamiment Library, Robert F. Wagner Labor Archives, New York University, New York; Anatol Shmelev, Project Archivist, RFE/RL Collection, Hoover Institution, Stanford University, California; Martin F. Russell of the National Archives in College Park (NARA), Maryland; Russell A. Nichols, chief of the Freedom of Information Privacy Office of the US Army Intelligence and Security Command, Fort George G. Meade, Maryland; Celia Ashworth of The National Archives, Kew, Richmond; Anthony Tedeschi of the Lille Library, Bloomington, Indiana; Hans Landauer, founder and supervisor of the Document Archives of the Austrian Resistance (DÖW), Vienna; Teun van Lier of the International Institute of Social History in Amsterdam; and Fra' Elie de Comminges, at the time of writing Curator of the Magistral Archives and Libraries of the Order of Malta,

Rome. I also benefited from the most welcome and friendly assistance from archivists of the City of Vienna and others in the USA, France, Belgium, Germany, Russia, and Britain.

Among my academic colleagues, the outstanding Spanish scholar and diplomat Professor Ángel Viñas gave me invaluable advice and even editing help, although he was himself busy at the time writing five important volumes on the history of the Spanish Civil War. I am grateful and proud to call him my friend.

I owe particular thanks to another good friend, the renowned Spanish scholar Professor Paul Preston of the London School of Economics and Political Science. Paul not only gave me many hours of his valuable time but also agreed to supervise my doctorate on a related subject. Professor Preston read all chapters dealing with the Spanish Civil War with hawk-eyed precision and saved me from many errors. Other academics contributed knowledge and personal experience, among them Christopher Andrew, Hugh Thomas (Lord Thomas), Helen Graham, and Richard Baxell in Britain, Professors Stanley S. Payne, Robert H. Whealy, and George R. Esenwein in the United States, Peter Huber and Ralph Hug in Switzerland, Jesús F. Salgado Velo and Antonio M. Díaz Fernández in Spain, Reiner Tosstorff in Germany, and Nikita Petrov in Russia.

I must also thank Maria Dolors Genovés, director and author of the Catalonian Television documentary entitled *Especial A. Nin: Operació Nikolai*, a great film that is unfortunately little known to the English-speaking public. I got valuable insights from the material she gave me from her team's filming of Oleg Tsarev in his KGB office in Moscow. Great thanks, too, to John Hilton of the *Ann Arbor Observer* in Michigan, for his help, advice, and the rare documents that he kindly sent me.

Perhaps the most valuable documentary support came from declassified KGB, CIA, FBI, and French DST files kindly provided by Professor Hayden B. Peake, a US expert in intelligence documentation.

Gary Kern, the author of several important works on the history of Soviet intelligence, found time to advise me and to discuss the Krivitsky case, which he had written about with impressive research based on a large collection of documentary evidence.

During my research of this book I have studied a great number of secondary sources in many languages, but no books were more valuable to me than those written by the eminent intelligence historian Christopher Andrew. Professor Andrew also demonstrates his great knowledge and sophistication in his excellent Intelligence Seminar at Corpus Christi College, which brings together a remarkable group of postgraduates from around the world, and where I was privileged to lecture.

I would like to thank Mark Seaman, former official historian at the Imperial War Museum in London and expert on military intelligence, for reviewing my manuscript in its early stages. I am also grateful to Alex Goldfarb, an author and a former Soviet dissident, for his efforts to make this book appear earlier. My special thanks to Paolo Guzzanti, an Italian politician, journalist, and author, for his great help and support.

It is impossible not to mention the staff of the Cañada Blanch Centre for Contemporary Spanish Studies at the LSE, all of whom were most helpful.

Finally, I must thank Luciana O'Flaherty of Oxford University Press for her painstaking, insightful, and sympathetic reading of all the chapters.

So great was the contribution of these many fine scholars, intelligence professionals, archivists, and librarians that 'my' book might also be considered a collective work. I am deeply grateful. At the same time, I remain solely responsible for any errors herein.

Boris Volodarsky,

London

May 2014

Contents

PART II. IN SPAIN

PART III. THE ORLOV LEGACY

List of Plates

Abbreviations and Acronyms

AFP	Agence France-Press
AMAE	Archivio de Ministerio de Asuntos Exteriores
Amtorg	American–Soviet Trading Corporation, first Soviet trade representation established in New York
AOU	Administrative–Organizational Directorate
ARC	American Refrigerator Company
Arcos	All-Russian Cooperative Society, Anglo-Russian trade organization
AVO	Allamvedelmi Osztaly, the Hungarian secret police
BCEN	Banque Commerciale pour l'Europe du Nord
BKP	Bulgarian Communist Party
BNFMRA	British Non-Ferrous Metals Research Association
BOAR	British Army of the Rhine
BRD	Bundesrepublik Deutschland (Federal Republic of Germany), West Germany
BKP	Balgarska Komunisticheska Partiya (Bulgarian Communist Party)
CBA	Círculo de Bellas Artes
CCG	Control Commission for Germany
CEDA	Confederación Española de Derechas Autónomas (Confederation of the Autonomous Right), Spain
Centre	HQ of the KGB, its predecessors and its successor, SVR, previously Lubyanka, now Yasenevo a.k.a. Les ('Forest')
Cheka	Chrezvychainaya Komissiya (All-Russian Extraordinary Commission for Combating Counter-Revolution and Sabotage)
CIA	Central Intelligence Agency, the Agency, USA
CID	Criminal Investigation Department
CNT	Confederación Nacional del Trabajo (National Confederation of Labour)
Comintern	Communist International
CPGB	Communist Party of Great Britain

CPSU	Communist Party of the Soviet Union
CPUSA	Communist Party of the USA
DAIA	Delegacion de Asociaciones Israelitas Argentinas
DDR	Deutsche Demokratische Republik (German Democratic Republic), East Germany
DEDIDE	Departamento Especial de Información del Estado (a Spanish Republican intelligence service)
DGS	Dirección General de Seguridad (General Directorate of Security), Spain
DGSE	Direction Générale de la Sécurité Extérieure (General Directorate for External Security), foreign intelligence agency, France
DLB	dead letter box
DRG	diversionno-razvedyvatelnaya gruppa (sabotage and reconnaissance group), USSR/RF
DST	Direction de la Surveillance du Territoire (Directorate of Territorial Surveillance), French security service
ECCI	Comintern Executive Committee
EKU	Economic Directorate
EM	Estado Mayor (General Staff), Spain
FAI	Federación Anarquista Ibérica (Iberian Anarchist Federation)
FAPSI	Federalnoe Agentstvo Pravitelstvennoi Svyazi i Informatsyi
FBI	Federal Bureau of Investigations, the Bureau, USA
FCD	First Chief Directorate, KGB's foreign intelligence branch
FO	Foreign Office, UK
FOIA	Freedom of Information Act
FPA	Federated Press of America
FSB	Federalnaya Sluzhba Bezopasnosti (Federal Security Service), Russian security service
FSK	Federalnaya Sluzhba Kontrrazvedki, predecessor of the FSB
FSO	Federalnaya Sluzhba Okhrany (Federal Protective Service)
FUE	Federación Universitaria Escolar
GC&CS	Government Code and Cipher School, UK
GCHQ	Government Communications Headquarters, UK
GD	Generaldirektion für die öffentliche Sicherheit (Austrian Counter-Intelligence Service)
GPU	Gosudarstvennoe Politicheskoe Upravlenie (State Political Directorate), USSR

GRU	Glavnoe Razvedupravlenie, Soviet and Russian Military Intelligence
GUGB	Glavnoe Upravlenie Gosudarstvennoi Bezopasnosti (Chief Directorate of State Security), USSR
Gulag	Glavnoe Upravlenie Lagerei (Chief Directorate for Forced Labour Camps)
GUPVO	Glavnoe Upravlenie Pogranichnoi i Vnutrennei Okhrany (Chief Directorate of the Border Guards and Internal Troops)
HUMINT	Human Intelligence (obtained from human sources)
ILS	International Lenin School
IMEMO	Institute for the World Economy and International Relations
INO	Inostrannyi Otdel (Foreign Intelligence Department), USSR
INS	Immigration and Naturalization Service, USA
IO	Inzhenernyi Otdel (Engineering Department)
ISH	International of Seamen and Harbour Workers
ISU	International Seamen's Union
ITF	International Transport Workers' Federation
IWW	Industrial Workers of the World
JARE	Junta de auxilio a los republicanos españoles
JIC	Joint Intelligence Committee, UK
JSU	Juventudes Socialistas Unificadas (Unified Socialist Youth)
Kempeitai	Military Police Corps, Japanese intelligence and counter-intelligence service
KGB	Komitet Gosudarstvennoi Bezopasnosti (Committee for State Security), USSR
KI	Komitet Informatsyi (Committee of Information), Soviet foreign intelligence agency
KIM	Kommunisticheskii International Molodyozhy (Communist International of Youth)
KJVD	Kommunistischer Jugend Verband Deutschlands (Young Communist League of Germany)
KPD	Kommunistische Partei Deutschlands (German Communist Party)
KPÖ	Kommunistische Partei Österreichs (Communist Party of Austria)
KRO	Kontr-razvedyvatelnyi otdel (Counter-Intelligence Department)
KSČ	Komunistická strana Československa (Czech and Slovak Communist Party)
KUNMZ	Kommunistichesky Universitet Natsionalnykh Menshinstv Zapada (Communist University of the National Minorities of the West)

MBP	Ministerstwo Bezpieczeństwa Publicznego (Ministry of Public Security), Poland
MGB	Ministerstvo Gosudarstvennoi Bezopasnosti (Ministry of State Security), USSR
MI5	British security service
MI6	alternative designation for SIS, British foreign intelligence service
MI1c	Secret Intelligence Service, predecessor of MI6
MID	Military Intelligence Division
MOPR	Mezhdunarodnaya Organizatsyia Pomoschi Rabochim (International Workers' Aid Organization), better known as International Red Aid, Comintern/USSR
MOTsR	Monarkhicheskaya Organizatsyia Tsentralnoi Rossii (Monarchist Association of Central Russia)
MVD	Ministerstvo Vnutrennikh Del (Ministry of Internal Affairs), USSR
NKGB	Narodnyi Komissariat Gosudarstvennoi Bezopasnosti (People's Commissariat for State Security)
NKID	Narodnyi Komissariat Inostrannykh Del (People's Commissariat for Foreign Affairs)
NKVD	Narodnyi Komissariat Vnutrennikh Del (People's Commissariat for Internal Affairs)
NKVT	Narodnyi Komissariat Vneshnei Torgovli (People's Commissariat for Foreign Trade)
NSA	National Security Agency, USA
ÖGB	Österreichischer Gewerkschaftsbund (Austrian Trade Union Federation)
OGPU	Ob'edinennoe Glavnoe Politicheskoe Upravlenie (Joint State Political Directorate), Soviet intelligence and security service
OKDVA	Osobaya Krasnoznamyonnaya Dalnevostochnaya Armiya (Special Red-Banner Far Eastern Army)
Okhrana	Tsarist security service, Russian Empire, 1881–1917
OKW	Oberkommando der Wehrmacht (Supreme Command of the German Armed Forces)
OMS	Otdel Mezhdunarodnykh Svyazei (International Liaison Department), the intelligence branch of the Comintern
OMSBON	Otdelnyi Motostrelkovyi Batalion Osobogo Naznacheniya (Special Motorized Battalion)
OO	Osoby Otdel
OSS	Office of Strategic Services, USA

OVRA	Organizzazione per la Vigilanza e la Repressione dell'Antifascismo (Organization for Vigilance and Repression of Anti-Fascism), Italy
OUN	Organization of Ukrainian Nationalists
PCA	Partido Comunista de la Argentina (The Communist Party of Argentina)
PCC	Partido Communista de Chile (Chilean Communist Party)
PCE	Partido Comunista de España (Spanish Communist Party)
PCF	Parti communiste français (French Communist Party)
PCM	Partido Comunista Mexicano (Mexican Communist Party)
PCP	Palestine Communist Party
PCO	passport control officer
PCO	Passport Control Organization
PLN	Partido Liberación Nacional (National Liberation Party), Costa Rica
POUM	Partido Obrero de Unificación Marxista (Workers' Party of Marxist Unification), Spain
POW	Polish Military Organization
PSOE	Partido Socialista Obrero Español (Spanish Socialist Workers' Party)
PSUC	Partit Socialista Unificat de Catalunnya (United Socialist Party of Catalonia)
RAF	Royal Air Force, UK
RGVA	Rossiisky Gosudarstvenny Voennyi Arkhiv (Russian State Military Archive)
RIS	Russian Intelligence Services
RKKA	Raboche-Krestyanskaya Krasnaya Armiya (The Workers–Peasants Red Army)
RMCP	Royal Mounted Canadian Police
ROP	Russian Oil Products
ROVS	Rossiisky Obschevoiskovoi Soyuz (Russian Combined Services Union)
RF	Russian Federation
RSDRP	Russian Social Democratic Labour Party
RSHA	Reichssicherheitshauptamt (Chief Directorate of Security of the Third Reich)
RU	Razvedupr, Soviet military intelligence, later GRU
SAC	Special Agent in Charge
SAJ	Sozialistische Arbeiter-Jugend (Socialist Workers Youth)
SAP	Sozialistische Arbeiterpartei

SB	Służba Bezpieczeństwa, Polish Security and intelligence service
SBP	Sluzhba Bezopasnosti Presidenta (Presidential Security Service), Russia
SBU	Sluzhba Bezpeky Ukrayiny (Security Service of Ukraine)
SCD	Second Chief Directorate, KGB's internal security branch
SD	Siecherheitsdienst
SDAPÖ	Sozialdemokratische Arbeiterpartei Österreich (Social Democratic Workers' Party of Austria)
SDECE	Service de Documentation Extérieure et de Contre-Espionnage (External Documentation and Counter-Espionage Service), French foreign intelligence service
SGON	Spetsialnaya Gruppa Osobogo Naznacheniya (Special Tasks Force)
SHAT	Service Historique de l'Armée de Terre
SHON	Shkola Osobogo Naznacheniya (Special Purpose School)
SIAM	Servicio de Información de Acción Militar
SIDE	Servicio de Información Diplomática Especial
SIEP	Servicio Especial de Información Periferico, Republican army's secret service, Spain
SIGINT	signal intelligence (derived from interception and analysis of signals)
SII	Servicio de Información e Investigación
SIM	Servicio de Investigación Militar (Spanish Republican military counter-intelligence service)
SIS	Secret Intelligence Service, UK
SIT	Servicio de Información Técnico
SOE	Special Operations Executive, UK
SOU	Secret Operational Directorate
SNK	Sovet Narodnykh Komissarov (Council of People's Commissars)
SPEKO	Spetsyalnyi kriptograficheskii otdel OGPU (Special Cryptographic Department)
Spetsnaz	Special Forces, USSR/RF
SR	Service de Renseignements
SR	Socialist Revolutionary
S&T	Scientific & Technical Intelligence
SS	Sluzhba Svyazi (Communication Service), predecessor of the OMS

SSOD	Soyuz Sovetskikh Obshchestv Druzhby i Kulturnoi Svyazi s Zarubezhnymi Stranami (Union of Soviet Societies for Friendship and Cultural Relations with Foreign Countries)
Stapo	Staatspolizei, Austrian security police
Stasi	common name for Ministerium für Staatssicherheit (MfS) (Ministry for State Security), DDR
StB	Czechoslovak security and intelligence service
SVR	Sluzhba Vneshnei Razvedki (Foreign Intelligence Service of Russia)
TUC	Trade Union Congress, UK
UD	Upravlenie Delami
UGT	Unión General de Trabajadores (General Union of Workers)
ULTRA	wartime signals intelligence obtained by breaking high-level encrypted enemy radio and teleprinter communications, GC&CS/UK
UME	Unión Militar Española (Spanish Military Union)
UMRA	Unión Militar Republicana Antifascista (Republican Antifascist Military Union)
UPA	Ukraińska Powstańcza Armia (Ukrainian Insurgent Army)
VChKa	Vserossiiskaya Chrezvychainaya Komissiya (All-Russian Cheka, immediate successor of the Cheka and predecessor of the OGPU)
VOKS	Vsesoyuznoe Obschestvo Kulturnoi Svyazi (s zagranitsei) (All-Union Society for Cultural Relations (with foreign countries)
WEB	West European Bureau
WOSTWAG	West-Osteuropäische Warenaustausch AG (West–East European Trade Exchange Joint Stock Society, legitimate trade organization and Soviet military intelligence front with head office in Paris and affiliates in Berlin, New York, Ulan Bator, Guangzhou, and Tientsin (Tianjin)

Chronology: The Evolution of the KGB, 1917–2012

December 1917   **Cheka and VeCheka**
Chrezvychainaya Komissiya (Cheka), Extraordinary Commission for Combating Counter-Revolution and Sabotage, and from 1918 VeCheka—All-Russian Extraordinary Commission for Combating Counter-Revolution, Profiteering, and Corruption.

February 1922   **GPU and OGPU**
Gosudarstvennoe Politicheskoe Upravlenie (GPU), State Political Directorate, part of the *Narodnyi Komissariat Vnutrennikh Del* (NKVD), People's Commissariat for Internal Affairs, and from November 1923 *Ob'edinennoe Glavnoe Politicheskoe Upravlenie* (OGPU), Joint State Political Directorate under direct control of the Council of People's Commissars (Sovnarkom).

July 1934   **GUGB**
Glavnoe Upravlenie Gosudarstvennoi Bezopasnosti (GUGB), Chief Directorate for State Security, again part of the NKVD.

February 1941–April 1943   **NKGB**
Narodnyi Komissariat Gosudarstvennoi Bezopasnosti (NKGB) People's Commissariat for State Security. During this period the GUGB was briefly transferred into a separate ministry (Commissariat), then was placed again under the NKVD, and finally from 14 April 1943 became NKGB.

March 1946   **MGB**
On 18 March 1946 all People's Commissariats were renamed Ministries and accordingly NKGB became *Ministerstvo Gosudarstvennoi Bezopasnosti* (MGB)

May 1947–November 1951 **KI**
Komitet Informatsyi (KI), Committee of Information. Both political intelligence (MGB) and military intelligence (GRU) were united in one service; in the summer of 1948 all military personnel were returned back to the General Staff of the Red Army; branches dealing with the new East Bloc countries and émigrés were returned to the MGB in late 1948; the KI was dismantled in 1951.

March 1953 **MVD**
Ministerstvo Vnutrennikh Del (MVD), Ministry for Internal Affairs. On 5 March 1953 the Service again became part of the enlarged MVD.

March 1954–November 1991 **KGB**
Komitet Gosudarstvennoi Bezopasnosti (KGB), Committee for State Security

December 1991 **SVR**, **FSK,** and **FAPSI**
The KGB was dismantled into several independent departments in September 1991. After the collapse of the Soviet Union, two former chief directorates of the KGB were reorganized into two different services *Sluzhba Vneshnei Razvedki* (SVR) for intelligence operations abroad, similar but not equal to MI6 and CIA; *Federalnaya Sluzhba Kontrrazvedki* (FSK), for counter-intelligence operations inside Russia and former Soviet republics; and two former KGB directorates— 8th (Government communications) and 16th (ELINT or Electronic intelligence) formed the *Federalnoe Agentstvo Pravitelstvennoi Svyazi i Informatsyi* (FAPSI), Federal Agency for Government Communication and Information under the President of the Russian Federation.

August 1992 Law on Foreign Intelligence
The SVR leadership compiled and the Russian parliament adopted the Law on Foreign Intelligence.

April 1995–March 2003 **SVR** and **FSB**
In April 1995 the FSK was renamed and reorganized into the *Federalnaya Sluzhba Bezopasnosti* (FSB), the Federal Security Service. A new Law on the Foreign Intelligences Services was passed by the Federal Assembly in late 1995 and signed by

the Russian President in January 1996. According to the law and its later amendments, the Russian President can personally issue any secret orders to the SVR without informing the lawmakers (i.e. the State Duma and Federation Council). In March 2003 FAPSI was reorganized into the *Spetzsviaz* (Service for Special Communications and Information), part of the FSB. In August 2004 it became one of the subunits of the Federal Guard Service (FSO), which was established in May 1996.

May 2000

SBP

Sluzhba Bezopasnosti Presidenta (SBP), the Presidential Security Service, is the successor of the 9th Chief Directorate of the KGB. Since May 2000 it has been the most powerful and secretive secret service of Russia. Although formally it is responsible to the Federal Guard Service, its head reports personally to the current Russian President.[1]

May 2012

Vladimir Putin, a former officer of KGB's First Chief Directorate and former Director of the FSB, became the President of the Russian Federation for the third time.

Foreword
by Tennent H. Bagley

This book sends a resounding warning to anyone who would write or study the history of Soviet espionage. It confronts and exposes the falsity of 'facts' that for two generations have been recorded by respected writers, documented by governments, and accepted as truth by Western intelligence communities. Applying an insider's specialized knowledge and perception onto a vast and original research, the former Soviet intelligence officer Boris Volodarsky demonstrates how easily myth and purposeful deceit can become respected history.

Dredging up any hidden events anywhere poses a daunting challenge to would-be historians. Secrets are, after all, meant to be kept secret and none more tightly than the genuine facts about Soviet secret operations, protected as they are by obsessive Russian suspiciousness and 'To Be Preserved Forever' in locked vaults, not in history books. Anyone who would delve into the secrets of Soviet State Security (called NKVD for most of the period covered in this book, but better known by its later appellation, KGB) must thrash through a jungle full of pitfalls and false guideposts that had been planted since the very beginnings of Soviet rule. The masters of the KGB have spent decades busily laying these traps to mislead and confuse and weaken and beat off those whom they are incurably convinced are trying to surround and put them down.

It would be hard to think of any case in which those pitfalls and false signposts have more effectively trapped and misled historians than the one described in this book. Astonishingly, it is only now—seventy years later—that a path is cleared through the jungle of lies that have surrounded a 'major figure' of Soviet intelligence history and the Spanish Civil War.

But even this late, Volodarsky's work is fresh and pertinent. While correcting the story of Alexander Orlov (to use one of the many names the man assumed), Boris offers unique insight into the methods and the mindset of those murderous and deceptive men who, with Orlov, staffed the NKVD/KGB—and whose FSB/SVR successors rule Russia today, with those methods and mindset little changed.

This is a complex story full of new details that will be precious for future researchers in this occult field. But that should not put off non-professional readers. Even if they do not care to follow all the details in their twists and turns, they will find in this book a treasure of spy intrigues, subtle deceptions, vile betrayals, astonishing careers, and unbelievable events. As Winston Churchill said of this high range of secret service work, 'the actual facts in many cases were in every respect equal to the most fantastic inventions of romance and melodrama. Tangle within tangle, plot and counterplot, ruse and treachery, cross and double-cross, true agent, false agent, double agent, gold and steel, the bomb, the dagger and the firing party were interwoven in many a texture so intricate as to be incredible and yet true.'[1] Here are murders in many forms and, in some chapters, on almost every page. Here are astounding careers like that of Iosif Grigulevich, Orlov's NKVD colleague, multiple murderer, saboteur, and spy—and also distinguished professor, author, and senior diplomat for Costa Rica. Here are new insights on well-known spy cases of the cold war like that of the infamous mole Kim Philby. In fact, had Orlov—Philby's NKVD supervisor in the 1930s—really defected and told the truth when he came out in 1938, the West would have been spared the deaths and debacles that this British traitor later caused.

The Spanish Civil War is the centrepiece of this book. Orlov headed the NKVD there, and Volodarsky offers new light and massive corrections to the history of Soviet involvement in that crucial episode of the twentieth century. For this alone the real story of 'Alexander Orlov' had to be told.

Here, then, is an important corrective to history and a useful reminder for those who seek to understand and cope with the eternal Russia that Alexander Orlov's story so vividly illustrates.

Tennent H. Bagley
Former deputy chief of the CIA's Soviet Bloc Division, Brussels 2013

Foreword
by Paul Preston

Lev Lazarevich Nikolsky was a middle-rank Russian agent who, under his pseudonym of Aleksandr Orlov, managed to turn himself into one of the most famous defectors of all time. What is known of his career is fascinating, but infinitely more intriguing are the versions thereof that he peddled himself and that were produced by his first biographers. The deconstruction of the reality and the subsequent versions is the object of this important study by Boris Volodarsky, himself an ex-officer of Russian military intelligence.

After serving in Berlin, Paris, Geneva, Vienna, Copenhagen, and London, without any special distinction, holding the rank of Major of State Security from December 1935, the dapper Orlov was sent to Spain in mid-September 1936 as an NKVD liaison to the Republican Ministry of Interior. There, he was involved in the operation to send Spain's gold reserves to Russia, albeit not, as he claimed to the US Congress, CIA, and FBI, as the prime mover but merely as the man responsible for security arrangements during the loading of the 'golden crates'. The most lasting legacy of his time in Spain—something that was not revealed in his post-defection publications—was the murderous pursuit of members of Trotsky's Fourth International. The most lasting repercussions of this derived from the successful operation to eliminate Andreu Nin, the leader of the anti-Stalinist Partido Obrero de Unificación Marxista. During his years in Moscow from 1921 until his expulsion in 1930, Nin had become a friend of Leon Trotsky and an important member of the anti-Stalinist Left Opposition. Orlov choreographed the complex process whereby Nin was first smeared as a fascist collaborator and then assassinated. For a brief period of several months Orlov also acted as NKVD case officer to Kim Philby, who was in Spain creating the right-wing image that subsequently smoothed his way into the British Secret Intelligence Service.

Fearing that he might himself become a victim of the massive terror operations being carried out by the vicious NKVD chief Nikolai Ivanovich Yezhov in Moscow, Orlov defected from Spain in 1938 after lengthy and meticulous preparation. Fully aware of what was happening during the Yezhovschina, Orlov had embezzled operational funds to the tune of $90,800. When he and his wife reached the United States via Canada (with a sum equivalent to $1,500,000 in 2014), they were able to live well. Unlike most defectors, Orlov did not immediately offer his secrets to Western security services. Initially, he had enough money not to need to do so. He also evaded almost certain retaliation by promising his NKVD superiors that he would not reveal any secrets. He did so with an emollient letter to the cruel and malevolent Yezhov, nicknamed 'my blackberry' (*Yezhevika*) and 'my little hedgehog' (*Yezhik*) by Stalin, 'the poison dwarf' by others. After declaring that his life had been one of 'irreproachable' service to the Soviet Union, the Communist Party, and the NKVD, he went on to describe a series of operations in which he had been 'heroically' involved. As Dr Volodarsky demonstrates, this constituted blackmail that, against all odds, worked.

Its implicit threat was that, if measures were taken against himself or his family, it would lead to revelations about the NKVD's activities and the exposure of Philby and other Soviet agents. The letter ended with what turned out to be a successful plea: 'If you leave me alone, I will never embark on anything harmful to the Party or the Soviet Union. I have not committed, nor will I commit, anything damaging to the Party and our country. I solemnly swear to the end of my days not to utter a word that may harm the Party that brought me up or the country, in which I grew up.' After an appendix listing forty-six operations including numerous assassinations, he wrote: 'All this will never see the light of the day!'

Orlov kept his promise, and, with his wife, he lived in hiding until a shortage of funds led to him initiating a process that would see him lauded as the highest-ranking Soviet intelligence defector. Having decided in early 1953 that he could make money by selling his story, he seems to have been emboldened to go public by the death of Stalin on 5 March. He approached *Life* magazine with a proposal to sell his memoirs for a small fortune. It was a well-calculated move—just a month before, in February 1953, a few weeks after leaving office, former US President Harry Truman had announced that *Life* magazine would publish his memoirs. The managing editor of the magazine was Edward Kramer Thompson, who in 1949 had succeeded

Whittaker Chambers, the one-time Communist writer and Soviet spy, now fervent anti-Communist. Ironically, Thompson would eventually marry Lee Eitingon, a relative of Leonid Eitingon, Orlov's deputy in Spain and the man who masterminded the assassination of Trotsky. Thompson and Henry Luce, the founder and owner, before parting with the money, wanted proof that Orlov really was the former NKVD general that he said he was.

Orlov's first choice to vouch for him was Ernest Hemingway, whose *The Old Man and the Sea* had recently appeared in *Life*, but he was in Cuba out of contact. So he turned to Louis Fischer, an immensely distinguished journalist then working for the *New York Times*. They had met in Madrid in September 1936, having been introduced by the Russian ambassador Marcel Rosenberg, and then again in November when the Republican government and most of the personnel of the Soviet Embassy had left the capital for Valencia. The only senior figures to remain behind, each with their own staffs, were Orlov and Brigadier Vladimir Gorev, who was officially the military attaché but actually Madrid Station Chief of Soviet Military Intelligence (RU, the future GRU). On 17 March 1953, Orlov telephoned Fischer, saying only that he was 'a friend from Spain' and requesting a meeting. Although Orlov had not identified himself, Fischer seemed to recognize him and invited him to his apartment. When he arrived, Fischer greeted him as 'my old friend Orlov' and quickly agreed to vouch for him to *Life* magazine. Orlov asked him to come to his lawyer's office, where he confirmed the former agent's identity, if not rank, to Luce and Thompson.

What *Life* published was a serialization of the memoirs in the form of five largely fictional articles, four in 1953 under the general heading '*Stalin's Secrets*' and a fifth, strangely entitled 'The Sensational Secret behind Damnation of Stalin' in April 1956. Together with his testimonies to the US Congress, all five were combined into a booklet issued by the official US Government Printing Office in 1973 with the title *The Legacy of Alexander Orlov*. Describing Orlov as 'the highest ranking officer of the Soviet State Security ever to come over to the side of the Free World', Senator James O. Eastland announced that Orlov had left behind him 'a priceless legacy— in the form of his testimony about the inner workings and objectives of the Communist conspiracy and about the activities of the Communist apparatus in the related fields of espionage and subversion'.

Shortly after the first four articles came out, a book was published in the United States: *The Secret History of Stalin's Crimes*. It swiftly became an international bestseller, translated into many languages including Chinese. Former US President Herbert Hoover and the first US ambassador to the Soviet Union William Bullitt sent personally signed letters to the author. Inevitably, the resulting furore brought Orlov to the attention of both the FBI and the CIA. The Director of the FBI, J. Edgar Hoover, was furious to learn from *Life* magazine that a senior Soviet agent had lived in America undetected for nearly fifteen years. Orlov was first handled by the Immigration and Naturalization Service (INS) and the FBI—both controlled by the Department of Justice, and then later by the CIA. All three agencies, the CIA with some subtlety and the FBI/INS perhaps with more rigour, interrogated Orlov. On 19 May 1953, FBI investigators also questioned Louis Fischer about Orlov's role in Spain. Under fierce FBI questioning, Orlov attempted to divert attention from his own real activities by pointing the finger at others. Despite having just been the beneficiary of Fischer's help, he claimed that the journalist had once been a Soviet intelligence agent. This was untrue. Fischer was never anything more than a Communist sympathizer. Accordingly, it appears that Orlov was falsely accusing Fischer to cast doubt on general allegations in his book *Men and Politics* about the murderous activities of the Russian security services in Spain.

During lengthy interviews, Orlov mixed harmless fact with misleading fiction and betrayed no Soviet secrets. Hoover was even more outraged to discover that the CIA had beaten him to the recruitment of Orlov, who became a well-paid consultant for the CIA Counter-Intelligence Staff and even lectured to the US intelligence personnel who were going to be posted to Warsaw Bloc countries under diplomatic cover. The main fruit of that collaboration was a CIA commission, *The Handbook of Intelligence and Guerrilla Warfare* (1963), a wildly inaccurate article 'How Stalin Relieved Spain of $600,000,000' (*Reader's Digest*, November 1966), and the ambitious survey 'The Theory and Practice of Soviet Intelligence', published in the classified CIA journal *Studies in Intelligence* (1963).

Taken together, not only did all of his publications managed to hoodwink the FBI and the CIA, but they have also significantly distorted subsequent writing about Orlov himself, about the activities of Soviet intelligence agencies in Western Europe before 1938, and, perhaps most damagingly, about the Spanish Civil War. In these writings, Orlov presented himself as a much-loved and admired friend of Stalin, who 'had often invited Orlov into his Kremlin office to consult him on details of operational intelligence work' and sent him to Spain as his personal envoy with special powers. He claimed to be 'the chief of the NKVD in Spain' and gave himself the rank of NKVD General, a rank that did not exist until the end of the Second World War. These claims, and numerous other subsequent ones, such as that he recruited Philby, Maclean, Burgess, and Blunt as well as members of the Oxford Spy Ring, are convincingly disproved by Dr Volodarsky's meticulous research.

Boris Volodarsky has produced the first full, critical biography of this extraordinary character. It is based on exhaustive use of a mass of very rare new documentation, including all available CIA, FBI, MI5, and French DST files dealing with Orlov's case as well as Orlov's personal papers. Dr Volodarsky has also used a daunting amount of material in several languages both on the Soviet services and on the Spanish Civil War. Throughout, the author painstakingly dismantles the various publications by 'Orlov' himself, including the even more fanciful posthumous memoirs *The March of Time* published in 2004. He also deconstructs subsequent partisan accounts of Orlov's life, written from the standpoints of the FBI and the KGB. In *Stalin's Agent*, Volodarsky demonstrates that the KGB regarded the record of Orlov's life as something meriting a disinformation operation. He provides an intriguing and critical account of those OGPU operations in Europe (France, Austria, Germany, and Britain) in which Orlov took part. In contrast to previous works, Volodarsky demonstrates that these operations were largely unsuccessful, as a result of which, in 1935, Nikolsky (who was not yet 'Orlov') was demoted to the OGPU transport department and lost his job in foreign intelligence. He shows that, in 1936, Nikolsky's mistress shot herself in front of the Lubyanka because he refused to leave his family, which would certainly have led to his disgrace had the outbreak of the Spanish Civil War not intervened, which permitted his friend Abram Sloutsky, the head of Soviet foreign intelligence, to send him to Madrid.

Volodarsky's account is placed in a wider context of a whole series of hitherto little-known Soviet intelligence operations in Europe and also in the USA. Similarly novel and of immense interest to a British audience is his reconstruction of the process of the recruitment and initial handling of the 'Cambridge Five'. This is based on the KGB documents that were made available to the British author John Costello, but were either not used or else misinterpreted. One intriguing claim made by Volodarsky is that there was no Cambridge Spy Ring as has been widely assumed but rather a process of recruitment of individual agents, like Burgess and Blunt, but also of more than 100 other British agents/collaborators. In a substantial appendix, the book provides the only existing biographical essay on their real recruiter, the Viennese Dr Arnold Deutsch. Another fascinating appendix provides a list of agents and suspected agents recruited in the UK before the war according to their KGB personal file numbers, which reveal the order and sometimes the date of their recruitment. Considerable new light is also shed on the case of two other famous pre-war defectors: Ignatz Reiss and Georges Agabekov. Dr Volodarsky thus illuminates well-known cases of the cold war, notably that of the infamous mole Kim Philby. As he demonstrated, had Orlov—Philby's NKVD supervisor in 1935—really defected and told the truth when he came out of Spain in 1938, the West would have been spared the problems that this traitor later caused.

For the interested in the Spanish Civil War, an invaluable part of this book is the account of Orlov's activities in Spain, which permitted his eventual defection and later sale of his fictional self to the Americans. This contributes utterly new material on at least two of the most crucial incidents of the war—the massacre of right-wing prisoners at Paracuellos del Jarama outside Madrid, from 6 November to 4 December 1936, and the kidnap and murder of the POUM leader, Andreu Nin, in June 1937. As a result of Volodarsky's work, the political history of the Republican zone in the Spanish conflict will never be the same again. Especially important in this regard is Volodarsky's account of Orlov's collaborator in Spain, the extraordinary professional assassin, Josip Grigulevich. A Spanish-speaking Lithuanian, Grigulevich belonged to the NKVD Administration for Special Tasks (assassination, terror, sabotage, and abductions) commanded by Yakov Isaakovich Serebryansky. Grigulevich acted in Spain as a multiple murderer, saboteur, and spy, was involved in assassination attempts against Trotsky, then later morphed into a distinguished professor, author, and (while still a Soviet intelligence operator) senior diplomat for Costa Rica. It is worthy of note that Volodarsky's remarkably thorough research includes full use of the Diplomatic Archive of Costa Rica.

Dr Volodarsky also provides the reader with a riveting account of Orlov's life in the USA. It is a dissection of the great deception whereby Orlov managed, through his contacts with the FBI, the CIA, and the French DST, to make a comfortable life for himself and his family and also remain safe from the revenge of the Russian services. As far as I know, Volodarsky is the first scholar to use all of Orlov's writings and interviews as well as the information about him now available in MI5 files at The National Archives. The advance on earlier accounts, in terms of accuracy and insight, is considerable. Dr Volodarsky is able to show that MI5, because of lack of experience (and because they 'missed' Orlov), failed to expose the numerous moles in British secret services, the Foreign Office, and parliament.

One mystery remains, concerning Orlov's ultimate relationship with the KGB. In the summer of 1971, the KGB invited him to return to Russia and be hailed as a hero. It has been suggested that his response was that he and his wife appreciated the offer but 'there were just too many factors that weighed against their being able to accept'. Perhaps because he concluded that it was a trick to get him back, Orlov said he was too old for the upheaval of the move. Nevertheless, his earlier biographers claim, he gave the emissary, Mikhail Feoktistov, a long list of names and positions of US officials who he said 'could be interesting for the Soviet intelligence service'. However, they provide no reference to this document from the archives of the KGB, refering solely to their interview with Feoktistov in his Moscow flat more than twenty years after the events, in February 1992. Yet Dr Volodarsky writes:

Surprisingly, when offered the chance to return to Moscow after more than thirty years of self-exile, Orlov agreed. At that time Oleg Kalugin, who would soon be promoted to head KGB foreign counter-intelligence operations, was deputy head of station in Washington, DC. He recalled in his memoirs: 'Shortly afterward, I returned to Moscow on vacation and asked my superiors what had happened with the Orlov case. They said the decision on his fate had been kicked all the way up to the Politburo, whose members finally decided that the old defector wasn't worth the fuss. The Politburo said it would be foolish to treat a traitor as a hero, and he was too old and the case too stale to trick him into coming back and then put him on trial. No, our leaders said, leave him alone. And so we did, after wasting an enormous amount of time and money hunting for the Stalin-era spy.'

There is no way of knowing the exact nature of Orlov's later relationship with the KGB. What Dr Volodarsky's work makes clear is that the much-vaunted 'defector' served his own interests until his death, remaining true to his oath taken in 1924 not to reveal information about Stalin's secrets.

Paul Preston
Director of the Cañada Blanch Centre for Contemporary Spanish Studies
London School of Economics

I, the undersigned, an official of the Economic Directorate of the GPU, Nikolsky, Lev Lazarevich, being in the service, commit myself by this to keep in strict secrecy all the information and data about the work of the GPU and its organs, under no pretext or in no form to make it public or share it, even with my close relatives and friends. Any non-fulfilment, non-compliance or breach of this commitment subjects me to the penalties . . .

([Signed] L. Nikolsky [Dated] 1 April 1924)
(Personal File SCHWED, No. 32476, vol. 1)

Always remember that I am not a traitor to my Party or my country. No one and nothing will ever make me betray the cause of the proletariat and the Soviet power. I did not want to leave my country any more than a fish wants to leave water, but delinquent activities of criminal people have thrown me in at the deep end . . . From my knowledge of other cases I know that your apparatus will concentrate all their reserves on my physical liquidation. Put a stop to your people! It suffices to say that they have caused me extreme misery by depriving me of the right to live and fight within the ranks of the Party to enjoy the just rewards of long years of unselfish service. I have not only been deprived of my country, but of the right to live and breathe the same air as the Soviet people.

If you leave me alone, I will never embark on anything harmful to the Party or the Soviet Union. I have not committed, nor will I commit anything damaging to the Party and our country.

I solemnly swear to the end of my days not to utter a word that may harm the Party that brought me up or the country, in which I grew up.

([Signed] L. Nikolsky, 23 July 1938)
(Operational Record File No. 76659, vol. 1, pp. 245–58)

To an advanced organism duplicity is, at worst, an option; for a lower one, however, it is the means of survival.

(Joseph Brodsky, Collector's Item)

And if all others accepted the lie which the Party imposed—if all records told the same tale—then the lie passed into history and became truth.

(George Orwell, *Nineteen Eighty-Four*)

Introduction

Two decades after the collapse of the Soviet Union and the end of the cold war, the history of Soviet intelligence and its many actors and assets remains essentially secret. A considerable number of books and academic (and non-academic) articles published in the West and Russia since the early 1990s have greatly improved our knowledge of Russian Intelligence Services (RIS), but still leave a lot of questions unanswered. Unsurprisingly, after some name-changing and organizational tinkering, the Soviet-era services for espionage and subversion abroad—mainly, the Komitet Gosudarstvennoi Bezopasnosti (KGB) (Committee for State Security) and Glavnoe Razvedupravlenie (GRU) (Soviet and Russian Military Intelligence)—remain essentially intact and their archives inaccessible. There is no Freedom of Information Act in Russia, and secret files are not routinely declassified and sent to the State Archives. The historical facts that Moscow has put into the public domain so far not only are incomplete, but are selected and structured to impress the world with the secret services' past cunning, to extol their already known spies and secret agents abroad and to hide their past, as well as ongoing activities that have not yet been exposed. Over this material hangs the shadow of purposeful deception, concealment, and distortion. Amazingly, modern Russian history is still a subject of fierce debate among scholars, politicians, and journalists.

Many books have appeared in Britain and the USA that portray Stalin's former secret police officer Alexander Orlov, who deserted his post and went into hiding in the United States, as the 'brightest of all the trophies that Stalin's reign of terror presented to the West', the defector, and a 'three-star KGB general, who outranked all others'.[1] In their turn, publications in Russia praise Orlov as one of the greatest spymasters of the twentieth century. Oleg Kalugin, the youngest general in KGB history and today an

American citizen, recalled in his memoirs how the Soviet Politburo considered inviting Orlov back to the USSR. It seems both sides vied to extol the man.

It took me thirteen years to research and write an entirely new and different biography of Orlov based on the original documents from the KGB archives. I also used all available declassified files from the Central Intelligence Agency (CIA), the Federal Bureau of Investigations (FBI), the MI5 (the British Security Service), and the Direction de la Surveillance du Territoire (DST) dealing with Orlov's case, an innumerable number of Spanish documents, photos, and films, as well as several hundred books in many languages. Basing my work on this huge collection of primary and secondary sources, I aim to prove that 'Orlov' was not in fact Orlov; that he was not a defector, and had never been a general. He did not recruit Burgess, Philby, Maclean, and Blunt, or any member of the Oxford Spy Ring, as widely believed.

In this book, readers will find updated information about both Cambridge and Oxford spy networks as well as other Soviet agents and collaborators. Among those who also figure in this narration, although they have never been identified as spies, agents, or collaborators, are personalities such as Christopher Hill, a former master of Balliol College, Oxford, and wartime head of the Russian desk at the Foreign Office, as well as Sir Roger Hollis of MI5. In this area, the figure of the long-time MI5 Director General stands alone.

When the Soviet cipher clerk Igor Gouzenko defected in Ottawa in September 1945, he declared that there was a GRU mole at a high level in the British Security Service with the code name ELLI. From the documents, we know that on 24 November 1945 the People's Commissar for State Security, Vsevolod Merkulov, sent a personal message to Stalin and Beria confirming that Gouzenko had betrayed the existence of 'the GRU agent inside British intelligence, Elli'.[2] Several authors argue that Hollis mixed in communist circles at Oxford in the 1920s and then covered up his links with the likes of Claud Cockburn, after joining MI5 in 1938, although Cockburn was listed at MI5 as a 'dangerous communist' by then. Peter Wright, chairman of the joint MI5/MI6 committee, codenamed FLUENCY, was appointed to find a traitor and investigate a whole history of Soviet penetration of Britain.[3] He found that Hollis had spent nine years in China (1927 to 1936) mixing in communist circles in Shanghai and Beijing with Agnes Smedley and Rewi Alley as well as important agents of Soviet military intelligence Arthur Ewert and Richard Sorge. The Trend Committee under Lord Trend, entrusted with the matter of investigating Hollis and Soviet penetration of MI5 in general, noted that Hollis returned to England via Moscow in both 1934 and 1936, always obscuring both the fact of those visits and their duration. Among those whom he may have met through Ewert or Sorge in China was Ursula Hamburger (née Kuczynski), who went on to become an important Soviet intelligence operator with the cover name 'Sonia' decorated multiple times by the Soviet government and cited, after her death in 2002, by the Russian President himself, as a super agent of Russian military intelligence. 'In Britain,' one recent researcher notes,

Sonia was based outside Oxford very close to the MI5 wartime headquarters at Blenheim Palace, where Hollis worked during the years 1941–45. During those years, by her own later account, she felt she had a protective hand inside the Security Service. At that time Hollis headed F Division of MI5—Soviet counter-espionage—while Kim Philby headed the corresponding section in MI6. And, finally, reports by the Radio Security Service (RSS) in those years of illegal radio transmissions from the Oxford area, later found to be Sonia's, were invariably returned to the RSS by both Hollis and Philby marked 'No Further Action'.[4]

It transpired that as soon as Roger Hollis became Deputy Director General of MI5 in 1953, he was personally in charge of assessing the Orlov material that had started to leak from the USA. Sir Roger continued to monitor it until 1956, when he was appointed Director General. At that point all MI5 interest in Orlov was suddenly stopped. One of the greatest authorities on intelligence history, Cambridge professor Christopher Andrew, claims in his *Authorized History of MI5* that he has proved conclusively Hollis was not a double agent. So let us accept it as an official view of the British government, though the informed opinion suggests that this is something that can never be proved conclusively.

Those interested in intelligence matters will find details of many other cases that do not figure in the authorized and official histories of MI5 and MI6.[5] (Finally, this book contains two important appendices, one with a new biography of perhaps the most productive Soviet recruiter of all times, the Austrian Dr Arnold Deutsch, and another with a list of the Soviet agents, suspected agents, and collaborators in Britain with some details of their recruitment and, where possible, their KGB personal file numbers. Present-day Russian intelligence assets and those fellow travellers who still live in Britain or the USA do not need to worry: it is a historical account that ends with the death of Orlov in 1973.

A considerable part of this book is devoted to Soviet intelligence operations in Spain during the Civil War because Orlov served as the NKVD head of station there until he deserted his post in the summer of 1938. This research took a great deal of time and required consultations with the leading experts in Britain, USA, Spain, Russia, Germany, Italy, Austria, and Switzerland; their names are in the Acknowledgements. Occasionally, I found the commitment and responsibility daunting, as it was also necessary to work with the archives of all those countries, and many others, fishing out nuggets of useful information. As a result, this is the fullest account to date of the Soviet intelligence involvement in the Spanish Civil War covering both the Narodnyi Komissariat Vnutrennikh Del (NKVD), predecessor of the KGB, and the Razvedupr (RU), the Soviet military intelligence directorate of the Red Army, as well as the little-known intelligence section of the Communist International known to the experts as the OMS—the Otdel Mezhdunarodnykh Svyazei.

A conclusion that I came to after my extensive research is that the KGB successfully hoodwinked many researchers and historians as to the true role of Orlov, his activities, and even his books. Fortunately, it is now possible not only to extend what John Costello praised as the 'new precedent for openness and objectivity in the study of intelligence history'[6] (set by the KGB and its successors), but also to expose some previously unknown Soviet intelligence operations carried out in the interwar period and during the Spanish Civil War—the secrets that the Russian government does not want anybody to know about.

PART
I

Feldbin, aka Nikolsky,
aka Nikolaev, aka
Goldin, aka Orlov

I

Bobruisk and Moscow

Leiba Lazarevich Feldbin was born on 21 August 1895 to a very religious Jewish family in the small town of Bobruisk in Byelorussia. Over the years he would adopt various other names, including, in 1936, the one by which he was to become famous: 'Alexander Orlov'.

In 1915, he moved to Moscow and studied briefly at the Lazarevsky Institute of Oriental Languages,[1] but left after two semesters to enrol at Moscow University's Faculty of Law. In 1916, Feldbin, along with his cousin Zinovy Katznelson,[2] was drafted into the Tsar's army. Both managed to avoid action, being relegated to the reserves behind the Urals instead of going to the front. In the autumn of 1917, Feldbin graduated as a junior officer from the 2nd Warrant Officer School, and a former classmate met him in the glamorous Moscow GUM department store wearing the uniform of a sub-lieutenant,[3] or *podporúchik* in Russian. The department store, then known as the Upper Trading Rows, had opened before the Revolution (and before the Selfridges store in London), and when the two classmates from Bobruisk met there, it hosted more than 1,200 departments. Shopping there was a fun adventure.

Soon after the Bolsheviks[4] had taken power in Russia, Feldbin joined the Communist Party. His sponsor (all new candidates needed a recommendation from an existing party member) was a veteran Marxist from Armenia who had become his friend and political mentor. Ten years later, this Armenian called for Stalin's removal and went on a hunger strike.

Several of Orlov's biographers claim that he 'picked up a sound knowledge of English, German and French'[5] at the Lazarevsky Institute. In reality, it is unlikely that two semesters were enough to teach Orlov sound knowledge of anything. Poor command of foreign languages, especially English and French (speaking Yiddish, Feldbin probably thought that he could easily master German), was this future spy's Achilles' heel. Even after living in the United States for years, he was told in 1942 that his English-language skills did not meet the requirements of the Berlitz School of Languages where he wanted to teach his native Russian. Naturally, as with all immigrants, after several decades in the USA his English did improve considerably.

Against a backdrop of anti-Semitism, Feldbin changed his name to the less Jewish-sounding 'Lev Nikolsky'. As the Russian Civil War ensued and the economy of the new regime became even more chaotic, he returned to civilian life and found a job amid tumbling incomes and rocketing prices.

Several months later, in February–March 1918, the Central Powers, including the German Empire, the Austro-Hungarian Empire, the Ottoman Empire, and the Kingdom of Bulgaria, used the right to self-determination of all nations, a fundamental principle of international law, in the peace negotiations of Brest–Litovsk as a pretext for the separation of the Kingdom of Poland. The Chełm province was apportioned to the Ukrainian Soviet Republic. In late October, three days before the official dissolution of the Dual Monarchy of Austria–Hungary as a result of military defeat in the First World War, a Polish Liquidation Commission was formed. In a few days, it succeeded in disarming the Austrian forces using members of the secret Polish Military Organization (POW), as well as legionnaires and the patriotic youth.

With the collapse of the German Reich in November, General Józef Piłsudski was freed from internment in Germany[6] and returned to Warsaw to take control of Poland. On 11 November, Piłsudski was appointed Commander-in-Chief of Polish forces and was entrusted with creating a national government for the newly independent country. Eleven days later he was head of state. The Treaty of Versailles, between the Allied and Associated powers (Britain, France, and the Russian Empire, which the Revolution transformed into the Soviet Empire), on the one side, and Germany, on the other, was signed on 28 June 1919. This Treaty ended the war and awarded Poland the desired direct access to the Baltic Sea through the Danzig (now the Polish town of Gdańsk) corridor dividing the bulk of Germany from the province of East Prussia. The ill-advised Polish advance against Kiev in June 1920 led to the Polish–Soviet war that had been brewing for the previous year and a half. Under the command of Mikhail Tukhachevsky, the young Red Army advanced, reaching the vicinity of Torún, Warsaw, and Lwów by July and August 1920. However, between 16 and 28 August, the Polish forces, led by Piłsudski, defeated the

Red Army decisively in a battle on the Vistula. This victory ended the Bolsheviks' last chance to foment widespread revolution in Central and Western Europe.

Vladimir Ilyich Ulyanov, the Bolshevik leader who after the revolution became head of state and is better known by his underground alias 'Lenin', had a plan not only to gain a victory over Poland, but also to spark a series of communist uprisings in Europe and to clear the way for the Red Army in the wake of the German proletarian revolution. Earlier, Lenin and his followers had set up a satellite Soviet republic in Hungary (headed by Béla Kun with a gang of Red Terror activists), rapidly moving over to Austria. During the summer of 1919, a lawyer from Budapest named Ernö Bettelheim gained the approval and funding of the recently founded Communist International, then known as the Third International and abbreviated as Comintern,[7] to organize a communist revolt in spite of the little influence of the Kommunistische Partei Österreichs (KPÖ) (the Communist Party of Austria). Meanwhile Kun sent the Hungarian Red Army to the Austrian border, only a two-hours march from Vienna, ready to invade and support the insurgents. Fortunately, the night before the planned rising, on 19 June 1919, the Austrian police arrested the entire KPÖ leadership except for Bettelheim.

Nikolsky (Orlov's name at the time), his wife, and daughter would spend many days in the Austrian National Library in the Vienna's Hofburg Palace reading about these events. Unbeknownst to him, many of his State Security colleagues did the same long before and long after him.

The Soviets carried out a military offensive against Poland between February and May 1920 as part of a long-term plan that could have placed a large part of Europe into the hands of extreme revolutionary communists. In September, Nikolsky was again summoned for service and posted to the 12th Red Army. Here he served with the so-called special assignment cavalry and was actively engaged in guerrilla warfare against the Polish army by stealing documents, blowing up bridges, power stations, and post offices, cutting telegraph lines, and capturing 'tongues' (enemy personnel with important information). Among his reported successful captures were Colonel Senkowski, commander of the Polish guerrilla forces, and Ignaty Sosnowski, an officer of Polish Military Intelligence.[8] However, this is quite certainly an invention. Sosnowski joined the State Security before Nikolsky, later became its Commissar 3rd Rank, and was shot in the Great Terror campaign in November 1937, together with Gleb Ivanovich Boky,[9] an old

Bolshevik with an exemplary revolutionary record who had been head of the top-secret Special Department or 'Spetsotdel' (interception of communications) for sixteen years.

A May 1920 decree 'On Measures against Polish Offensive' restored the right to impose the death penalty to revolutionary tribunals. During his service at the Polish front, Nikolsky was personally responsible for the executions of 'counter-revolutionary' formations operating behind the 12th Army lines. Eighty years after the events, Nikolsky's American friend and biographer wrote: 'Orlov admitted that his service with the 12th Red Army and the Border Guards was one of the most fruitful periods of his career.'[10]

The Polish army reconquered Central Lithuania with Vilnius (ceded to the Lithuanians by the Red Army), western White Ruthenia, western Wolhynia, and eastern Galicia, before the armistice of October 1920. The Soviet government finally recognized this border unconditionally in the Peace of Riga a few months later. At the beginning of 1921, Nikolsky was posted to the counter-intelligence section, known as the Osoby Otdel (OO) or Special Section, of the Soviet Border Guard troops in the city of Archangel. Here he married Maria Vladislavovna Rozhnetskaya, also a member of the Communist Party and a service woman, on 1 April 1921. In the summer, Nikolsky and his wife were both released from military service and returned to Moscow, where he entered the law school attached to the university to study part-time. In January 1922, Nikolsky became assistant prosecutor at the Criminal Court of Appeals, which was a low-level job, and on 1 September 1923, their daughter was born. She was named Vera and was their only child.

That autumn, the Soviet leadership was deeply concerned about increasing the productivity of their country's economy. Lenin was still alive. However, he was mute, paralysed on his right side, and bed-ridden. The characteristically Leninist approach was to increase discipline and compulsion, and its main enforcer—the Cheka under the 'Iron Felix', heir to the noble Polish szlachta family Dzierżyński—would play an important role. Since March 1922, the service had been planning considerable expansion of its Economic Directorate, the EKU, where top Cheka functionaries often served as heads of its principal departments.[11]

By the beginning of 1924, Dzierżyński and his deputies had completely restructured the Economic Department of what was first the Chrezvychainaya Komissiya (Cheka), then the Gosudarstvennoe Politicheskoe Upravlenie

(GPU), and finally the Ob'edinennoe Glavnoe Politicheskoe Upravlenie (OGPU), the Joint State Political Directorate under the Council of People's Commissars, a new repressive machine created to help command and control Russian's failing economic system.[12] Nikolsky's cousin Zinovy Katznelson was one of its top brass. Thanks to his protection and patronage, Nikolsy joined the OGPU in a lowly post in the financial section; he was later promoted to section chief.

Nikolsky's service record in the first volume of his NKVD personal file No. 32476 shows that, after taking his oath and signing his declaration on 1 April 1924, he was accepted as a junior officer of the 6th Section (finances) of the Economic Directorate (EKU). The documents from the KGB archives published by Russian historians Nikita Petrov and Alexander Kokurin clearly demonstrate that, when Nikolsky joined the OGPU, his uncle Katznelson headed that very EKU and that Nikolsky was promoted to head its financial section on 1 May.[13]

At the end of 1925, having served at the Lubyanka OGPU headquarters in Moscow for about a year, Nikolsky was sent to command a small unit of the OGPU Border Guards stationed in Tiflis, a job similar to the one he had had before on the Polish border and had liked.[14] That was not an occasional transfer either.

At the end of March 1925, the chairman of the Transcaucasian OGPU, Solomon Mogilevsky, was killed in a plane crash. A month later Katznelson vacated his EKU post and left for the ancient city of Tiflis. On 5 May he was officially appointed as Mogilevsky's replacement, the chairman of the Transcaucasian Cheka and plenipotentiary of the OGPU in the Caucasus. However, only half a year later, in December 1925, Katznelson returned to Moscow as Chief Inspector of the OGPU Troops and head of its Border Guards Directorate.[15] With this new power, he immediately arranged for his cousin's transfer to Georgia, the best, warmest, and most comfortable part of what became the Transcaucasian Soviet Republic with its sulphur baths, friendly folk, and abundant fruit. Nepotism has always been very strong in the KGB.

In Tiflis, Nikolsky's daughter Vera contracted a rheumatic fever infection and was later diagnosed as suffering from rheumatic heart disease. In order to secure proper medical treatment for Vera, Nikolsky asked Meer Trilisser, head of the INO ('Foreign Intelligence Department') to send him abroad. Shortly after, using the alias of 'Leo Nikolaev', Nikolsky and his family arrived in Paris.

Days before the Nikolskys left Moscow, on 20 July 1926, Dzierżyński died. His chosen successor, Mienżyński, was more pliant than his 'iron' predecessor (he was sometimes described as 'a pince-nez among leather jackets'). Otherwise, the two men had a good deal in common. Both were old Bolsheviks of well-to-do Polish ancestry who came to head the Cheka from its first days and were loyal to Stalin. At that time, many OGPU officers were of Polish descent. Ten years later, the successor of both Dzierżyński and Mienżyński, Nikolsky's boss Nikolai Yezhov would undertake to eliminate almost all of them.[16]

Already in 1933, a group of Poles had been arrested for alleged membership in the 'espionage and sabotage organizations of the Polish Military Organization' (POW), which had been set up in 1915 under General Piłsudski in the struggle for independence from Austria–Hungary and Germany, as well as from the Russian Empire. It was the onset of the anti-Polish campaign launched by Stalin and supported by his secret police chiefs, Yezhov and Beria.[17]

When Sergey Kirov, the Leningrad Party boss, was assassinated in December 1934, the first official announcement attributed this murder to some terrorists who allegedly stole into the Soviet Union from Poland.[18] The Katyn massacre would be a logical next step in this campaign. Although several of Nikolsky's colleagues from the INO would take part in the shootings, Nikolsky and his family were already far away. Their thirteen-year-long trip began in Paris.

2

Paris: August 1926–December 1927

Apart from his guerrilla raids into Polish territory during the Polish–Soviet war (February 1919–March 1921), Paris was Nikolsky's first trip as well as his first posting abroad. He was totally inexperienced in intelligence work and knew little, if anything, about the tricks of the trade. In Paris he used the name 'Nikolaev', serving under Yakov Davtyan (alias 'Davydov'). Davtyan was the founder and first head of the Inostrannyi Otdel (INO) (Foreign Intelligence Department) and now the OGPU head of station—'legal resident', in Russian intelligence parlance—in France. (The difference between 'legal' and 'illegal' residents is that the former work under diplomatic cover at the embassy or Trade Delegation and therefore enjoy diplomatic immunity, while the latter operate 'in black'—that is, without any official state protection and can be arrested and jailed.)

Unlike his new subordinate, Davtyan knew Europe well. From 1907 he had lived in Belgium, where he earned his university diploma as an engineer. In the course of his work with the Belgian Socialist Party, Davtyan became acquainted with Inessa Armand, a French communist who allegedly had an affair with Lenin. Together with Lenin and twenty-six other revolutionaries, she returned to Russia in April 1917 in what has since been described as the 'sealed train'. The German authorities provided a diplomatically sealed train to secure a safe passage for Lenin and his entourage to Petrograd amid growing unrest, in the expectation that he would bring the war on the Eastern Front to an end. After the October Revolution, Armand served as an executive member of the Moscow Economic Council (Gubsovnarkhoz), where Davtyan was her deputy after his return to Russia in August 1918. Together with Armand, he visited France as part of the Red Cross delegation. In September 1920, Armand advised Dzierżyński to invite

Davtyan to head the newly established INO. Later that month, she died in the Caucasus, having contracted cholera.

In November 1920 Dzierżyński asked the Central Committee to transfer Davtyan from the Narodnyi Komissariat Inostrannykh Del (NKID) (People's Commissariat for Foreign Affairs), where he headed a department, to the Cheka. Under the alias 'Davydov', Davtyan served as chief of Soviet foreign intelligence from December 1920 until January 1921 and then again from April to August 1921. From February 1922 he formally returned to the NKID, serving in Lithuania, China, and, from May 1925, in France, first as councillor and then as plenipotentiary. Davtyan was in Paris until September 1927 and then also worked in Persia, Greece, and Poland before his arrest in October 1937. During his interrogation at the Lubyanka internal prison Davtyan confessed to having been a spy for Britain.[1] Several decades later it was established that he had not been. In July 1938 Davtyan was executed.

This handsome Armenian not only taught his subordinate the rules of *konspiratsiya* (the main elements of intelligence trade) but was also a model of good manners and European sophistication.[2] Nikolsky enjoyed life in France. He could not fail to see the striking difference between poor post-revolutionary Russia, where the famine of 1921–2 had killed an estimated five million, and a great European power. His salary in US dollars and his status as an official Soviet representative were valuable perks. When Davtyan was appointed Soviet envoy to Persia in September 1927,[3] the new head of station arrived from Moscow, given a post as 'Second Secretary' at the Soviet Embassy.

During his testimonies before the US Senate in the 1950s and his debriefing by the CIA in the 1960s, Nikolsky/Orlov claimed that he had been head of station in Paris and that one Dmitri Mikhailovich Smirnov had been his assistant. As one of the CIA directors, Richard Helms, put it rather coyly later: 'Orlov provided only a superficial glimpse of the data he might have been persuaded to offer.'[4] In 1927, Smirnov, posing as 'Second Secretary' of the Soviet Embassy, was the OGPU 'legal' resident in Paris.[5] Nikolsky was only one of his subordinates. Smirnov was soon succeeded by Zakhar Volovich,[6] whose secret offices consisting of four rooms were on the third floor of the Soviet Embassy building. Nikolsky was attached to the Trade Delegation, most certainly reporting to one of the deputy residents. Smirnov was transferred from Paris to Berlin that same autumn, and Nikolsky followed him there after a few months.

Basing their comments on Orlov's own exaggerated claims, some of his biographers wrote that, after Davtyan had left Paris, 'Orlov commanded one of the largest Soviet intelligence networks in Europe'.[7] This deliberate disinformation was intended to boost his status. It was simply not possible, and for a good number of reasons.

First and foremost, Nikolsky had no operational experience either as a case officer or in any undercover work. He did not know Europe, could not speak any foreign language, and his main aim in going abroad had been to take care of his ailing daughter. He was neither skilled nor trained for directing any network. In 1927, as in later years, Nikolsky was no match for best-in-class Soviet intelligence personnel operating in Europe. Also his position as 'adjoint au représentant commercial' was too low for the station head, who always occupied a political post at the embassy. An OGPU resident agent could even sometimes be appointed ambassador, but he or she could never be lower in rank than attaché. In the case of Nikolsky, he did not even have a diplomatic passport—an absolutely necessary prerequisite for a head of station at any time.

Secondly, when Nikolsky was on his first assignment in France, the INO's priorities did not include intelligence collection. In 1926 the main target of its foreign operations, as formulated by its chief, Meer Trilisser, who succeeded Davtyan, was 'the identification on the territory of each state of counter-revolutionary groups operating against the Russian Socialist Federal Soviet Republic; the thorough study of all organizations engaged in espionage against our country [. . .] the acquisition of documentary material on all the above requirements'.[8] The struggle against anti-Bolshevik opposition abroad, known as the 'White Line', was considered the top priority by the leadership of Soviet intelligence. The situation did not change much, even when the Spanish Civil War broke out.

As well as engaging in permanent conflict with counter-revolutionaries, who were relentlessly exterminated in Russia and abroad, Soviet intelligence between the wars also became quite successful in penetrating the leading European powers: Great Britain, France, and Germany as well as Japan, its main Asian rival, following the Politburo's quest for political information. At the time, it had a number of operational advantages over Western intelligence agencies. As correctly noted by Christopher Andrew, while security in Moscow turned into an obsession, much of Western security remained lax. Besides, the Communist parties and their 'fellow travellers' in the West through the widespread Comintern network provided Soviet intelligence with a major source of ideological recruits, of which it took increasing advantage.[9] And, finally, Soviet intelligence often used the services of the 'illegals', while Western intelligence agencies in their operations always relied on 'official' representatives, with a sufficiently good cover of military attachés, consular employees, journalists, and, in the British case, passport control officers (PCOs).

The Soviet system of covert communist propaganda—its intelligence, counter-intelligence, and other clandestine operations in the West before the Second World War—was rather complex. Separately and independently, though often intertwining with each other, the system was operating along several major lines. The Comintern, which was directed theoretically by the Soviet Communist Party leadership but practically by Stalin himself, primarily collected political intelligence and provided recruits for Russian intelligence services. Its agents operated both with and without the help of the OGPU and RU. Sometimes various Comintern officials, Russian or foreign, were simultaneously staff officers of either political or military intelligence. At an early period, two OGPU departments—both economic (EKU) and foreign (INO)—separately collected intelligence abroad. Three Soviet intelligence services—OGPU, RU, and the Sluzhba Svyazi (SS), the Communication Service of the Comintern (later the OMS) had 'legal' and 'illegal' residences in the West. In the case of the Comintern, the residency was known as Communication Point (*tochka svyazi*) and differed from the Comintern's foreign bureaus and sub-bureaus. As a rule, during a foreign posting, officers were assisted by the so-called co-optees, civilian employees of the Narodnyi Komissariat Inostrannykh Del (NKID) (People's Commissariat for Foreign Affairs), the Narodnyi Komissariat Vneshnei Torgovli (NKVT) (People's Commissariat for Foreign Trade), or the Comintern's representatives. These were not necessarily agents, but if they were not happy to collaborate voluntarily they were forced to do so. As in the case of Davtyan or his INO successor Trilisser, these people often served either in the OGPU or in army intelligence as well as filling vacancies in both commissariats, NKID and NKVT, and in the Comintern Executive Committee (ECCI). Communications for the government and all its intelligence agencies were originally conducted by the Special Department ('Spetsotdel') of the OGPU before the army and the Comintern set up their own communication networks.

Vienna, the Austrian capital where the Nikolsky family would soon arrive (to remain there for quite a while), can serve as a showcase of covert operations conducted by various Soviet intelligence agencies from one operational base at that time.

In 1925, under the recently arrived plenipotentiary Jan Berzin,[10] the third Soviet envoy in less than two years, Benjamin Jakovenko-Chodkiewicz was the RU head of station working as 'First Secretary'. Dr Ephraim Goldenstein posing as 'Second Secretary' was in reality in charge of the OGPU Balkan operations. After the departure of Mieczyslaw Loganowski, the OGPU Vienna chief, Goldenstein took responsibility for both Austria and the Balkans.[11] Yakov Rudnik, a 'temporary' editor at the press section (he had arrived as a courier on a transit visa on 25 May 1925 and been 'held' at the embassy to allow the editor to take a holiday until 2 November 1927),[12] was an old Chekist who was sent to Vienna by the Comintern/OMS using the cover names 'Marin' and 'Luft'. This was probably a compensation for his earlier troubles (three years before Rudnik had been arrested in Paris and expelled from the country after spending two years behind the bars).[13] Rudnik and his 'wife', Tatiana Moiseenko, passing themselves off as Hilaire Noulens and Madam M. Motte, would be arrested again in Shanghai on 15 June 1931. The 'Noulens's Affair' became a *cause célèbre* in the foreign community of China as well as in Europe and North America. Gyula ('Julius') Alpari, a Hungarian communist and a former Commissar for Foreign Affairs in Béla Kun's government, was employed as an 'office clerk' while secretly working for both the Comintern and the OGPU. Another 'office clerk' was Karl Volk, former political commissar of the underground Military–Political Organization (the so-called MP-Apparat) in Lower Saxony during the Hamburg uprising of 1923. The 'uprising' had been prepared and directed by the Red Army intelligence directorate assisted by the Comintern and the Kommunistische Partei Deutschlands (KPD) (German Communist Party).[14] Future Spanish Civil War generals Manfred Stern (General Kléber) and Wilhelm Zaisser (General Gomez), the Austrian Otto Steinbrück, future defectors Ignatz Reiss and Walter Krivitsky, all of whom played a role in Orlov's life, took an active part in the training of the German militants, many of whom would meet again in Spain.

Yet another employee of the Soviet Embassy was Liza Gorskaya, better known as Elizaveta Zarubina, the future wife of Vasili Zarubin, who, unlike Orlov, was a real KGB general (and personally took part in the Katyn massacre). In Vienna Liza's role was a courier for Rudnik, Loganowski, Goldenstein, and, later, Ivan Zaporozhets. Zaporozhets, who would prominently figure in the Kirov murder case a decade later, served as the OGPU station head in Vienna from 1925 to 1927 after Goldenstein left for Turkey. (What has remained totally unknown until this day is that Liza was at that time married to the Austrian named Julius Hutschnecker, codenamed HOFMAN, who would later work for the OGPU in Berlin and London.) Liza was registered in Vienna as Elsa Hutschnecker and officially employed as secretary at the Soviet Embassy. There, one of her co-employees was Georg Killich. Killich, a skilful documentary forger known in Moscow as 'Georg Miller', would make a good career becoming head of the passport and documentary section of the OGPU. In the list of the embassy staff, he was modestly registered as courier and Liza as secretary,[15] while in fact she was a real courier and he collected and sent to Moscow various Austrian documents for use in forgeries. All these people were only a part of the intelligence personnel based at the Soviet legation in Vienna in 1925. As archival documents demonstrate,[16] some but not all of them were known to the Austrian security police. Eight years after the revolution, the number of spies working under diplomatic cover and of genuine diplomats was approximately equal. Two decades after the collapse of the Soviet Union, this balance remained the same, only the numbers doubled and tripled.

When Nikolsky was still a young intelligence operative, the Administration for Special Tasks then headed by Yakov ('Yasha') Serebryansky became another important element of the OGPU's activity abroad. Serebryansky joined the Communist Party in October 1923. The following month he was recruited by the INO and soon sent as an 'illegal' to Palestine. In the Middle East he managed to recruit a group of agents that later formed the basis of the 'Serebryansky's Service', or 'Yasha's Group', as it used to be called internally. Based in Paris and Brussels, from 1926 this group acted as an independent unit reporting only to the OGPU chief and primarily responsible for sabotage, abduction, and assassination operations on foreign soil.[17] In July 1934 it was reorganized into a special group for special purposes, known as Spetsialnaya Gruppa Osobogo Naznacheniya (SGON) (Special Tasks Force) in Russian. Serebryansky later worked in China and Japan and during the Spanish Civil War was in France training guerrilla groups and individual saboteurs. In summer 1938, Serebryansky was recalled to Moscow and in November was arrested. Broken by torture, he spat out whatever names came to his mind, falsely implicating others of being British and French spies. Naturally, he was sentenced to death (and his wife to ten years in the Gulag for failing to report on her husband), but luckily for him it was

July 1941 and Hitler's troops had already invaded the Soviet Union, so it was decided that Yasha would be more valuable alive than dead. He was quickly pardoned and readmitted to both the party and the secret service.

During the Spanish Civil War, Serebryansky and Nikolsky would work together on several sensitive cases, with Nikolsky coming to Paris quite regularly using his diplomatic passport in the name of 'Alexander Orlov'. But in 1927 Nikolsky was in Paris for the first time, officially serving as one of the assistants to Mikhail Lomovsky, head of the Soviet Trade Delegation. As such, he could have been involved in security matters concerning Soviet personnel in France having little or nothing to do with real operational work. Soon he was transferred to a similar post in Berlin.

The year 1927 was not the most fruitful one for Soviet intelligence. It began with sensational revelations about Soviet espionage in several European countries and in China. In April, the French Sûreté arrested eight members of a Soviet spy ring run by Jean Cremet, aliases 'l'Hermine rouge' and 'Le petit rouquin', one of the top functionaries of the Parti communiste français (PCF) (French Communist Party).[18] David J. Dallin, an American journalist and writer, revealed some remarkable details about Cremet's organization in his famous book devoted to Soviet espionage in the interwar period.[19] Cremet and his two mistresses, sisters Louise and Madeleine Clarac, who assisted in his espionage activities, managed to escape arrest and flee to the Soviet Union. Another member of the Cremet spy ring, a Russian émigré Lydia Stahl, fled to the USA. In Moscow, Cremet was appointed PCF representative to the ECCI. Dmitry Manuilsky, then in charge of the Comintern's clandestine operations, regularly sent Cremet on special missions abroad. The last trips were to China, Japan, and Indochina to help organize Communist parties there. Among others, he worked with Nguyen Ai Quoc, the future Ho Chi Minh, Zhou Enlai, and Deng Xiaoping. When Comintern networks were dismantled in Shanghai, Hong Kong, and Singapore in 1931, he disappeared. Jean Cremet was presumed dead by many historians, and David Dallin wrote that he disappeared in Macao, most probably liquidated by the Soviets, after 1936.[20] Following this myth, Pavel Sudoplatov, an NKVD assassin who served with Nikolsky in the same department and later headed its Special Tasks Division, claimed that Cremet was assassinated in 1938 for his open opposition to Stalin and support of Trotsky. However, the French authors Roger Faligot and Rémi Kauffer conducted a six-year investigation that led them to discover—thanks to many witnesses and newly opened archives—that

the famous French writer André Malraux (who would be made Squadron
Leader during the Spanish Civil War and would become France's first
Minister of Cultural Affairs) had saved Cremet's life by providing him
with false identity papers and helping him settle in Europe.[21] According
to their version, Cremet participated in the Spanish Civil War together with
Malraux, and then lived under an assumed name until the 1970s, when he
died in Brussels as 'Gabriel Peyrot'.

   As we have seen, the first Soviet 'illegal' resident in France representing
the Red Army intelligence directorate was Yakov Matveyevich Rudnik,
who, with the help of the Comintern representative in Paris, the Bulgarian
Stoyan Minev, succeeded in recruiting one Joseph Tommasi, an official in
the Car Aviation Union. In December 1921 the Deuxième Bureau, which
was one of several French military intelligence services, began to receive
reports from Switzerland indicating that Soviet agents were targeting
French armaments facilities. Rudnik was arrested and put into prison, but
Tommasi skipped to Moscow one step ahead of the Sûreté detectives
commanded by Louis Ducloux. Tommasi was given an apartment at the
Comintern hotel Lux and continued working for Soviet intelligence. But
he did not live long, passing away suddenly in 1926.[22]

   When Nikolsky arrived in Paris three years after Lenin's death, opposition to Stalin was still possible. A power struggle had begun involving a
group of perhaps not the most prominent but still highly placed old
Bolsheviks, including Lev Kamenev and Alexey Rykov, Lenin's deputies;
Mikhail Tomsky, member of the Central Committee; and Grigory Zinoviev, a long-time head of the Comintern and full member of the Politburo,
a governing body that was taking complete control over the party. The
group also included Nikolai Bukharin, another member of the Politburo,
Zinoviev's successor in the Comintern and editor-in-chief of the two
leading Soviet newspapers, *Pravda* and *Izvestia*; and, of course, Stalin and
Trotsky. Of these, Lenin thought Trotsky was 'the most able man', referring
to Trotsky's 'exceptional abilities' in his testament.[23] It turned out that
Stalin outwitted them all. After the 14th Party Congress in December
1925, the newly elected Central Committee demoted Kamenev to a non-
voting member, in April 1926 Zinoviev was expelled from the Politburo,
and at the end of the year Trotsky was ousted. At the 15th Party Congress in
December 1927, none of the members of the so-called anti-Stalinist United
Left Opposition headed by Trotsky was elected to the Central Committee.[24] In January 1928 Trotsky was sentenced to internal exile in a remote

corner of Kazakhstan, and Stalin became the undisputed leader of the Soviet Union for two-and-a-half decades.

While the OGPU and the Red Army servicemen in Russia were still choosing which leader to follow and Nikolsky was still in Paris taking care of his sick daughter, another Soviet 'illegal' with a 'Vienna connection' was arrested in France: Abram Bernstein, whom the security service suspected of being a high-ranking officer in the intelligence directorate (Razvedupr) of the Red Army. Bernstein, posing as an artist, together with his assistant Stephan Grodnicki, posing as a student, controlled Cremet's agents, who helped them to steal military secrets. It was also discovered that Bernstein distributed so-called intelligence questionnaires indicating what specific information Moscow sought. This activity could not escape the attention of the French Security Service. After receiving tips from various sources, a Sûreté team, led by Louis Ducloux, who had smashed the spy network of Rudnik–Tommasi, and Captain Eugène Josset, head of the Russian desk at the Service de Renseignements (SR), one of the country's military intelligence services, managed to feed false reports to the spy network, until finally, on 9 April 1927, Bernstein was arrested 'red-handed' in the process of receiving classified information.[25] As expected, his real name was not Bernstein. That was one of the many aliases of Stephan Uzdanski-Elensky, who three years previously had been expelled from Poland, where he was collecting intelligence using the legal cover of the attaché at the Soviet Embassy in Warsaw. Uzdanski then briefly worked, again 'from the legal positions', at the Soviet legation in Vienna under Plenipotentiary Adolf Joffe,[26] before moving to Paris as one of the 'illegal' residents, documented as 'Bernstein'. His contacts with the Soviet legation were through his wife, who was a member of Plenipotentiary Rakovsky's staff in Paris. Several months after their arrest, a French court sentenced Grodnicki to three years and 'Bernstein' to five years in jail.[27] In the meantime, another prison sentence, this one totalling forty-seven years and 32,000 francs in fines, was handed down to Jacques Duclos, then a member of the PCF Central Committee, who would become the chief coordinator of the party's 'special services' and play an important role in Spanish events from as early as 1930.[28] According to an undocumented source, it was around this time that he and another fanatical Stalinist, André Marti, became the main contacts for Soviet intelligence in the PCF.[29] Twenty years later, Duclos would be instrumental in eliminating Marti from the Party leadership. In 1927, however, it was Henri Barbé who was assigned to be the liaison between the PCF leadership and Soviet military intelligence. His contact with the Soviets was a successor of Uzdanski-Elensky, an officer known in the West as 'General Muraille', whose real name was Pavel Stuchevsky.[30] He was a former commissar in the Soviet–Polish war of 1920, and in Paris managed to expand the remnants of Cremet's intelligence network. According to the CIA files, Stuchevsky's assistant in France was Henry Robinson, who also worked for the OMS.[31]

As in the good old days, when the Tsarist Okhrana had a Foreign Branch named the Zagranichnaya Agentura, also known as the Paris centre, from where it directed all its foreign operations (with the second base in Berlin),[32] their Soviet successors used agents who could travel regularly between the two capitals and were always ready to switch identities and combine overt and covert operations. By the time the Nazis came to power, Berlin had become the largest foreign base used by the Soviets and was the spy capital of Europe. It also housed the underground West European Bureau (WEB) of the Comintern headed by Georgi Dimitrov, whose secretary was Arthur Illner, better known as 'Richard Stahlmann', a man with a twenty-year-long career in Soviet military intelligence.[33] Expecting problems from the all-seeing and all-knowing Gestapo agents, both Soviet intelligence and communist propaganda European headquarters moved temporarily to Copenhagen. After the Second World War, the operational base was again established in Germany, this time in Berlin-Karlshorst, while Vienna started to play an increasingly important role in the intelligence operations of the Soviet, and later the Russian, Ukrainian, Kazakh, and Chechen special services. By the time he was sent to Spain, Nikolsky/Orlov knew Berlin, Vienna, and Paris pretty well.

Understandably, Nikolsky was unable to boast of any operational success during his first year in Paris. He was learning French, studying the city, and trying to master bits and pieces of the profession of a case officer. He and his wife also had to spend a considerable amount of time with their ailing daughter. Besides, he should have been quite busy with routine work, because at this time the Soviet Trade Delegation in France, according to Alexander Barmin,[34] was placing huge orders for aeroplanes, spare parts, and some important equipment for military factories. When Barmin came there, shortly after Nikolsky had left, it had nine import departments. But Berlin, where Nikolsky arrived in January 1928, was a completely different kettle of fish.

3

Berlin: January 1928–April 1931

In January 1928 Nikolsky was transferred to Berlin after only seventeen months in France. Berlin was huge. At that time it was the most industrialized city of the continent and in its heyday. The Soviet Trade Delegation was housed in an ornate commercial building on Lindenstrasse, not far away from the diplomatic legation, headed at the time by chargé d'affairs Nikolai Krestinsky, who succeeded Adolf Ioffe in 1921. The post was an important and sensitive one because of Soviet Russia's crucial and delicate relationship with Germany at the time, but not nearly as important as his previous posts as a member of the Politburo and the Central Committee Secretariat. It was well known that Krestinsky supported Trotsky and lost all his high posts after Lenin's victory over Trotsky at the X Party Congress in March 1921. Since 1832 the Russian Embassy in Berlin had been located at Nos 63–65 Unter den Linden, one of the best-known and fashionable venues of the German Reichshauptstadt. Later, this former palace of Princess Amalie housed the Russian consulate.

Soon after Nikolsky had left Paris, the French capital became the centre of several important intelligence operations. In August 1928 the OGPU 'legal' resident Volovich,[1] who at that time reported not to Moscow but to the head of station in Berlin, though making a bad mistake about a 'walk-in'—a stranger who came straight to the embassy offering to provide Italian diplomatic ciphers for a fee—was commended for obtaining them at no cost to the OGPU.[2] On the same day the very next year, there was a similar walk-in at the Paris Embassy. On that occasion, the visitor was a cipher clerk from the British Foreign Office Communications Department.[3] These activities started a series of successful penetrations of Western intelligence services. When Nikolsky was in Berlin, General Kutepov, a leader of the anti-Bolshevik Rossiisky Obschevoiskovoi Soyuz (ROVS) (Russian Combined Services Union), was abducted in Paris by three operatives of the Serebryansky group. Two diplomats from the Soviet legation, Ivan Arens and Lev Helfand, were almost certainly part of the operation providing diplomatic cover.[4] However, in Nikolsky's KGB file there is no evidence of any of his intelligence successes at the time.

In July 1929, having made a successful career in the EKU, where Nikolsky had started his OGPU career, Abram Sloutsky, a friendly Jew who would soon be placed at the helm of Soviet foreign intelligence only to be murdered by his own subordinates three years later, was sent to Berlin and at the same time appointed assistant to the INO chief, Stanislaw Messing. In Berlin, Nikolsky was one of his junior subordinates. However, Sloutsky did not stay in Germany long, as on 1 January 1930 he was promoted to deputy chief, together with Mikhail Gorb,[5] who headed the Berlin residency until 1927. By that time Artur Artuzov, an experienced counter-intelligence officer, had succeeded Messing as the INO chief. When Stalin transferred Artuzov to the RU, an intelligence directorate of the Red Army, Sloutsky became chief of Soviet foreign intelligence and remained at this post until February 1938. In Berlin, Nikolsky worked as assistant to the 'legal' resident Nikolai Samsonov.[6] Orlov's biographers claim that in the Soviet Trade Delegation he was rubbing shoulders with Pavel Alliluyev, the elder brother of Stalin's second wife, Nadezhda. For example, Gazur writes that 'Orlov and Alliluyev had first met in early 1929, when the latter was assigned to the Soviet Trade Delegation in Berlin as a subordinate to Orlov'.[7] And, according to Costello and Tsarev, 'Stalin's decision to dispatch his brother-in-law to work under Orlov in Berlin was an indication of the importance he gave to the clandestine cooperation which brought the Soviet armed forces access to German weapons technology'.[8]

Orlov himself invented his friendship with Alliluyev for one of his *Life* articles published in April 1953, soon after Stalin's death.[9] Twenty years later it was mentioned again in Orlov's anonymous 'Brief Biography', claiming that the Soviet Commissar of Defence Voroshilov had sent Alliluyev to Berlin, where he was 'co-opted to Orlov's State Control unit, and they worked together closely for two years'.[10] This is sheer speculation.

In reality, Army Commissar Pavel Sergeyevich Alliluyev, one of the founders and leaders of the Red Army Armoured Corps, was a very high-ranking officer of the General Staff at the time when Nikolsky was a junior OGPU snooper in Berlin. Stalin's brother-in-law was sent to Germany as a member of the Red Army Purchasing Commission to control the quality of the military aeroplanes and powerful engines that had been purchased from

Germany within the framework of a secret Soviet–German (later Soviet–Nazi) cooperation agreement. Orlov himself wrote, this time correctly, that he 'met Paul Alliluyeva [*sic*] for the first time early in 1929 at the Soviet Trade Delegation in Berlin, where he had been sent to supervise the inspection of airplanes, aviation motors and other kinds of military equipment being purchased in Germany'.[11]

Their second meeting in Paris 'in the fall of 1937', however, is pure invention. Contrary to what Orlov claimed, Alliluyev never worked in the Soviet pavilion of the International Exposition dedicated to Art and Technology in Modern Life, where Nazi and Soviet pavilions were deliberately placed directly across from each other, with the Eiffel Tower optically sandwiched between the two. Ironically, architects of both pavilions were awarded gold medals. All that time Pavel Alliluyev was in Moscow, leaving only for a short holiday in Sochi on the Black Sea in October 1938. Orlov was also lying when he wrote in the same article that one day in 1939, when he was already in the United States, he was 'passing a newspaper stand which displayed a Russian newspaper and read, either in *Izvestiya* or *Pravda*', a short obituary of Alliluyev.[12] As a matter of fact, Alliluyev died on 2 November 1938, and the Soviet newspapers were not on sale in the USA until much later.

On 29 October 1929, the stock market crashed on Wall Street, an event that signalled the onset of what quickly became a worldwide depression. The crash had an immediate effect in Germany, as American investors, anxious about their finances, began withdrawing their loans. By 1929, German indebtedness had reached nearly 15 billion marks. Values on the German stock exchanges fell drastically during the last month of the year. Failures of business ventures multiplied. Early in 1930, Germany's second-largest insurance firm collapsed. Unemployment rose to three million during the course of the year. By the winter of 1931–2, when Alliluyev returned to Moscow after two years in Berlin, it had reached six million. Germany's industry was working at no more than 50 per cent of its capacity, and the volume of German foreign trade fell by two-thirds between 1929 and 1932.[13] In the next two years the two countries' economic relationship continued to deteriorate, and by 1934 Soviet imports from Germany had fallen from 430.6 million in 1930 to 63.3 million (while exports to Germany were reduced to 223 million Reichsmarks to compare with 426 million in 1929).[14]

Nikolsky's time in Berlin, however, coincided with the most intensive period of Soviet military collaboration with Weimar Germany. When he was working there, the Soviet Handelsvetretung (Trade Delegation) employed some colourful personalities of the former Hungarian Soviet Republic of Béla Kun. Former commissar Julius (Gyula) Lengyel worked shoulder to shoulder with former Interior Commissar Béla Vago, and Tibor Szamuely, former Commissar for Military Affairs. Szamuely's 'Lenin Boys' were widely feared for their random killings. All these former commissars, Nikolsky's Trade Delegation colleagues, were responsible for the bloody Red Terror in their native country.[15] In Berlin, Vago sat on the board of *Die Rote Fahne,* the all-German communist newspaper. Zoltan Lippay, another Trade Delegation employee travelling on a forged passport in the name of 'Aribert Bürgler', soon moved to Vienna, ostensibly to help Daniel Petrovsky, the *représentant commercial* according to his business card, but in reality to assist Igor Vorobyov, the OGPU station head,[16] about whom more shall be heard later.

Notably, the bulk of secret information in Germany at the time was collected neither by the OGPU nor from the Trade Delegation quarters. The main Soviet espionage agency operating there was the RU, acting through its 'illegal' residents and commercial fronts. One such front was a joint-stock import–export company known to SIS and MI5 as WOST-WAG (West-Osteuropäische Warenaustausch AG),[17] and the most important recruitment pool of new agents was the staff of the many underground 'Apparats' of the KPD.[18] Talent-spotters, recruiters, and case officers operating from both 'legal' and 'illegal' positions were actively assisted by the KPD functionaries.

Traditionally, the OGPU and its successor, even abroad, acted as a secret police force rather than an intelligence agency. From February 1929 onwards Stalin became increasingly preoccupied with the opposition to him within the Communist Party, which both he and Lenin before him had tried to control so much that they hardly slept at all. After Trotsky had been removed from the Soviet Union and deported to Turkey, Yakov Blyumkin, Trotsky's former bodyguard, sympathizer, and in 1929 chief 'illegal' resident in Turkey, not only visited the disgraced Communist leader during his exile but also agreed to take his letter to Moscow. Esther Rosenzweig, better known as Liza Gorskaya, the future wife of General Zarubin and at the time Blyumkin's mistress, betrayed him to the OGPU. Blyumkin was recalled to Moscow, arrested, and shot. After that episode, Stalin began to fear that there were other, undiscovered Blyumkins within the INO. Soon mass purges within the Soviet intelligence services began and continued almost without interruption until Stalin's death in 1953.

The activities of Soviet agents in Berlin also included industrial espionage, a concerted assault on the technological secrets of German industry. David Dallin devoted a separate chapter of his book *Soviet Espionage* to the work of the Trade Delegation.[19] He named many 'Gretha' (GPU) and 'Klara' ('Krasnaya Armiya'—i.e. Red Army) officers who were actively involved in Soviet industrial espionage in Germany in the 1930s. Dallin's list contains plenty of well-known and less well-known names. But this important and generally reliable account did not mention Nikolsky/Nikolaev/Orlov. (This could have been why, when speaking to the CIA in April 1965, Orlov insisted that Dallin 'at least in Berlin was a Soviet agent'.[20] But the six decades that have passed since this statement, together with a mass of documents that surfaced after the collapse of the Soviet Union, have proved that Dallin was not.)

'In those tumultuous days before Hitler's rise to power,' writes one of Orlov's biographers trying to justify the reason his friend was sent to Berlin, 'the Soviets focused on obtaining Western technological and industrial secrets both by legitimate means and any other way they could'.[21] Indeed, at the Soviet Trade Delegations, there was a special Engineering Department (Inzhenernyi Otdel (IO)) staffed by Red Army personnel, both civil and military, which was tasked with supplying Moscow with all-important foreign products, from the newest military equipment to household items. According to the recently unclassified files, in 1929–30 in Berlin there were more than 250 'illegals' in the Red Army intelligence directorate alone. The operational budget was $750,000 plus 515,000 roubles, with extra sums allocated for specialized trips abroad for scientists who worked in military research and production, and for the staff of Soviet military and naval attachés.[22]

Unlike their army colleagues, who before the war still had some last remnants of moral principles and tradition, for which many of them were cruelly purged during the Great Terror, the OGPU used all sorts of dirty tricks in their work. According to Sudoplatov, while he was in Berlin, Nikolsky, together with his friend and boss Sloutsky, met the Swedish 'Match King', Ivar Kreuger, and, by threatening him that the Soviet Union would kill the market by flooding it with cheap Soviet matches, extorted $300,000.[23] The trick hit paid dirt. In spite of several errors in Sudoplatov's books, the old general would not write about what he did not know. Needless to say, Nikolsky/Orlov himself never mentioned the episode, either in his writings or in personal 'friendly and confidential' discussions with his FBI minder.

The Kreuger group (Aktiebolaget Kreuger & Toll) and its successor firm Swedish Match (Svenska Tändsticks Aktiebolaget) had grown throughout the 1920s thanks to a series of successful acquisitions.[24] In the mid-1930s, it was a group of seventy manufacturing companies in thirty-one countries. Just a few years later, it accounted for approximately 60 per cent of the world's exports of matches and 20 per cent of world sales. The remaining market was controlled indirectly through cartel agreements.[25] If we bear this in mind, and also recall the fact that during the Stalin era Soviet production potential and export possibilities of anything that was not oil or gas or raw materials was not competitive in the world market, it is hard to imagine that the 'Match King' would give into blackmail. It is possible, however, that Nikolsky was indeed somehow involved in the operation against the Swedish tycoon, because after that time the code name SCHWED ('Swede') stuck to him.

In January 1931, when Nikolsky was still in Berlin, Iliya Ehrenburg, the leading Soviet foreign correspondent, arrived there. He then travelled through the whole of Germany and everywhere observed the same problems: five million unemployed, nervous and angry people, and street battles between Nazis and Communists. But he also noticed wealthy Kurfürstendamm with pink parrots in cosy cafés and oysters with champagne served in the KaDeWe food hall. Ehrenburg did not like what he saw in Germany.[26] Whether he really believed it or not, he wrote that back in October 1923 German history could have taken the right course, but now it was too late.

Despite this seemingly pessimistic mood, Ehrenburg, like Nikolsky, was a lucky man, because they were among the select few allowed to travel abroad from Russia. And, before the Nazis came to power, Berlin was perhaps the most modern capital of Europe, with wonderful theatres, cabarets, and elegant food markets.

It was also a true paradise for secret agents, who flooded the city. By that time Moscow had decided to shift the main responsibility for intelligence collection from 'legal residencies'—that is, stations within the embassies and trade delegations—to 'illegal residencies'—small undercover groups that operated independently of official Soviet missions and were controlled by 'illegal residents'—that is, case officers operating under cover. Later, the establishment of a new group of 'illegals' became an immensely time-consuming operation that involved years of detailed training and the painstaking construction of 'legends'. These 'legends' are false life stories tailor-made for each individual 'illegal'. That largely improvised attempt in the 1930s rapidly to expand the 'illegal' network brought into the OGPU's foreign operations, in the words of Christopher Andrew, 'both unconventional talent and a number of confidence tricksters'.[27] But, even if this was occasionally the case, it is hard to agree with Andrew's characterization of the spy ring of Berthold Ilk (codenamed BEER, BEYER, and HIRT)[28] and his deputy Moritz Weinstein (codenamed JULIUS) as a 'plain bluff'. Ilk, who can justifiably be counted among the Great Soviet 'Illegals' (Andrew's expression), set up a spy network that proved to be extremely effective and by the end of 1929 had acquired ten valuable sources, seven of whom provided documentary information, and thirty sub-agents, who also made important contributions. The large number of agents was necessary because the area of operations extended beyond Germany to Poland and the Baltic republics, including France and Britain. Between them Ilk and Weinstein could not cope with such a vast geographical area and they set up sub-stations in Warsaw, the Free City of Danzig (now Gdańsk), Breslau (now Wrocław), and Riga. Apart from receiving valuable political and technical information, Ilk reportedly organized supplies of passports both for his own people and for the Moscow Centre.[29] When his network was split into a few smaller groups, Ilk continued personally to control agents in Britain and France.[30] Julius Hutschnecker, alias 'Vasili L. Spiru', one of the husbands of Liza Gorskaya, was part of the Ilk–Weinstein spy ring and was sent to Berlin in August 1930.[31] Soon Ilk would arrange for Hutschnecker and his wife to be sent to London.

In Moscow, the early 1930s proved to be a period of great changes for the leadership of the OGPU. First of all, Zinovy Katznelson, head of the Chief Directorate of Border Guards and commander of the OGPU troops (and Nikolsky's uncle), was dismissed from his high posts. Ignaty Sosnowski, whom Nikolsky claimed to have personally recruited (which, as shown in Chapter 1, was not true), was transferred from Moscow to Minsk. Meer Trilisser, Nikolsky's foreign intelligence chief and a fierce critic of the 'right-wing deviation from the party line', had to leave the OGPU and was soon placed in the Workers' and Peasant's Inspection. Apart from Blyumkin, who was executed in November 1929, two other high-ranking OGPU officers, B. L. Rabinovich and G. A. Basov were shot in 1930 for 'Trotskyism'. Ivan Zaporozhets, chief OGPU resident in Vienna in 1925, was promoted to head the information and political control section that would soon be transformed into the secret political department. One of its divisions (4th section) was to conduct 'operational work' among writers, actors, and other representatives of the Soviet intelligentsia. In other words, secret police were spying on the country's intellectual elite, recruiting informants and agents within their ranks. Those who were allowed to travel abroad were 'co-opted' first of all. Unsurprisingly, some of them, like the virtuoso pianist Mikhail Kedrov,[32] would themselves become civil servants.

In April 1931, the EKU, where Nikolsky began his OGPU career, was reduced to only five sections (from ten in 1929). Stalin also decided to tighten control over his secret police, and in July the newly established Department of Personnel was placed under a trusted former functionary from the Central Party Committee. Genrikh Yagoda, first deputy chairman of the OGPU, was demoted to second deputy, and Ivan Akulov from the Workers' Control became first deputy. By the end of July, Messing, the INO chief who had succeeded Trilisser, was sacked from the OGPU and transferred to the People's Commissariat for Foreign Trade. He later headed the Trade Chamber. Job rotation under Stalin became a rule. Six years later it would be replaced by a firing squad.

Unlike the OGPU, the Red Army intelligence directorate under Jan Karlovich Berzin resisted restructuring. Berzin was fully aware that military intelligence appears in three basic forms: strategic, operational, and tactical, but from his first days in office his priority was technical intelligence—that is, intelligence about weapons and equipment used by the armed forces of other nations. To provide timely intelligence products and assessments, Berzin argued, and to inform Soviet defence research and equipment programmes, a stable organization was needed.

In terms of military collaboration, Germany was the most important partner.[33] From the very beginning, the whole work was under the personal control of Arvid Zeibot, Berzin's predecessor as the chief of the RU. From 1924 to 1935, when Berzin as the RU chief was responsible for the overall coordination of defence intelligence, he was the most informed person regarding secret Soviet military contacts with Germany, especially its operational, tactical, and technical aspects.[34] This was certainly one of the reasons he was chosen as the first Chief Military Adviser and Head of the Soviet Military Mission in Spain when the Civil War broke out there.

In March 1930 a special secret conference took place in Moscow devoted to technical intelligence. It was decided that the RU must be given additional financing in hard currency 'to buy samples of necessary equipment, full sets of technical documentation, important formulas, etc., while the consumers [government departments and R&D facilities] should provide extra sums for specific purchases in addition to the above-mentioned funds'.[35] Already, then, Stalin's military doctrine encompassed the possibility of future major conflict and Soviet military leaders wanted to equip their 'invasion armies', in the words of Marshal Tukhachevsky,[36] to be ready for an offensive.

Under Berzin, the structure of military intelligence as an integral part of the Defence Commissariat remained unchanged.[37] In February 1931 a new cipher department was added. Simultaneously, a signal intelligence unit was established within this cipher department.[38] As a means of collecting intelligence, signals intelligence was starting to play a more and more important role.

Berzin's claim to fame within Soviet intelligence was his part in adapting the techniques of agent penetration developed by both the Tsarist Okhrana and the OGPU after the revolution (principally against the émigré groups) to infiltrate foreign governments, army units, and intelligence services during the 1930s. While the INO's chief targets remained the counter-revolutionary White Guards, soon followed by the Trotskyists, Berzin was more interested in using agents to obtain Western codes and ciphers as well as some pieces of technology that could be applied to military needs.[39] Despite this difference in priorities, main areas of interest to both services were economic, logistic, scientific, and technical intelligence. Berzin was removed from his post in 1935 after a series of failures on the part of his officers in Europe.

In their writings, both Orlov and Krivitsky claimed that the OGPU and RU increasingly took over the intelligence networks of the Comintern. However, in the mid-1920s the Politburo banned the use of foreign communists as agents.[40] The reason was a chain of failures of RU agents in Europe and the Far East. As early as August 1925, Vladimir Antonov-Ovseyenko, Soviet consul in Prague, had insisted on a special meeting between the Comintern/OMS, the RU, and OGPU to sort out the problem. The meeting, following three major intelligence failures in a short period of time, took place in Moscow on 14 August. It was during this meeting that Iosif Pyatnitsky, the head of the OMS, Berzin, and Trilisser decided to shift the main responsibility for intelligence collection from 'legal' to 'illegal' networks and to use local Communist parties and their members but only after getting permission from the Comintern's leadership.

In spite of the ban, some RU station chiefs in Europe continued to use local communists. As a result, in November 1925 the Soviet vice-consul 'Khristofor Ivanovich Dymov' (the RU resident Bulgarian Hristo Boyev operated under this cover) was expelled from Czechoslovakia, and members of his spy ring, all local communists and one fellow Bulgarian, were arrested. In April 1927, 'Abram Bernstein' (Stefan Uzdanski-Elensky) was arrested in Paris, and his agents, French communists Pierre Dadot, Georges Ménétrier, Pierre Provost, Sergent, and Depuoilly, were locked up in La Santé prison.[41] In spring 1930, another Bulgarian RU officer, Ivan Vinarov (code-named MART), was sent to Vienna as chief RU resident. Before he left Moscow, he had been personally instructed by Berzin to avoid contacts with communists and rather to rely 'on honest, progressive people'. But, according to Vinarov's memoirs, he immediately got in touch with Austrian and Bulgarian Communist Party members.[42] In May, yet another Bulgarian, Ivan Krekmanov (SCHWARZ), an 'illegal' RU resident in Prague, actively used Czech communists, including Klement Gottwald—by that time Secretary General of the Komunistická strana Československa (KSČ) (Czech and Slovak Communist Party) and member of the parliament—in his clandestine work.[43] In Krekmanov's network there was also an Austrian communist Peter Stahl, a safe-house keeper and the secretary of the Bulgarian communists' cell in Vienna, Mincho Marinov. Thus, many RU residents continued using communists as agents, couriers, talent-spotters, or in other roles. And intelligence failures continued.

Amid considerable turmoil at the headquarters, Nikolsky returned to Moscow in April 1931. His successor in Berlin had been in place since March of that year. He was a 33-year-old Armenian named Gaik Badalo-vich Ovakimyan, who would remain there until August of the following year. When Nikolsky reported to the OGPU headquarters, Stanislaw Mes-sing still headed its foreign branch.[44] Nikolsky was one of his ninety-four subordinates with the modest rank of 'operative 7th category', equal to lieutenant. He had certainly never been the chief of 'the economic intelli-gence department of the INO', as Nikolsky/Orlov claimed,[45] for the simple reason that such a department never existed. Aged 36, he was still a very junior officer.

Several authors have suggested that Nikolsky had been sent to Berlin as 'an accredited diplomat' or 'an accredited trade counsellor', using 'the fictitious identity of Lev Lazarevich Feldel, a name he had no problem remembering as it was so similar to his real name'[46]—that is, Leiba Feldbin. However, Nikolsky was not an 'accredited diplomat', and before his posting to Spain had never had a diplomatic passport. Nikolsky's dark blue service passport, which he used for foreign travel at the time, identified its holder not as 'Feldel' but as 'Lev Leonidovich Nikolaev'.[47] With the same passport in the name of 'Nikolaev', Nikolsky returned to Berlin in August 1932, again as a Soviet Trade Delegation official temporally replacing Ovakimyan, who would soon be posted to New York. His return, one should add, had nothing to do with Soviet strategic interests or the role played by Germany, as some have claimed,[48] or even with the work of the Trade Delegation. No, Nikolsky came to Berlin with an entirely different agenda that summer.

As regards the place of Germany in Soviet intelligence priorities, by the time Nikolsky returned to Berlin, this had shifted slightly. Poland had again become the 'main adversary', and a great effort was put into collecting intelligence from there and other countries that had shared borders with the USSR. As for the other targets that figured in the intelligence reports— Germany, Italy, France, Britain, and the USA—Soviet intelligence services were criticized by the military commanders, and in particular by Mikhail Tukhachevsky, who would soon become a Marshal of the Soviet Union aged only 42, for not providing good intelligence for the last two. In those last days of August, as reported to Stalin, Trotsky wrote about the 'German puzzle', when two extreme wings of the Reichstag, the National Socialists and the Communists, representing the majority of voters, were fighting for power. Soviet intelligence was also aware of the fact that a book came out in London fully exposing details of secret military collaboration between Germany and Russia.[49] The United States came into focus only because it had a new president; economic indicators showed that the American economy reached its nadir and that the unemployment rate was hitting its highest level. At the same time, it boasted outstanding successes in engineering and applied sciences and a wonderful absence of a counter-espionage experience. The FBI, which is older than MI5, and the US Secret Service, one of the oldest law enforcement agencies in the world, were almost exclusively devoted to anti-violence and crime. J. Edgar Hoover headed the Bureau from May 1924, when Nikolsky arrived to spend his first day at a cramped Lubyanka office, until the early 1970s, when they both passed away. When the Bureau's name officially became the FBI in 1932, no one there had heard of, or even cared to learn about, Soviet penetration until much later. The FBI's Scientific Crime Detection Laboratory, which officially opened in 1932, was to provide forensic analysis. But they started investigating cases of espionage only in the 1940s.

With this favourable backdrop, operative 7th category Nikolsky, as was his official OGPU rank, once again documented as 'Leo Nikolaev', arrived in Berlin in August 1932 to prepare for his first undercover operation against the United States.

Interlude 1
First American Adventure: September–November 1932

On 25 August 1932 the Soviet Legation in Vienna asked the Austrian Foreign Ministry (Bundeskanzleramt, Auswärtige Angelegenheiten) to issue a one-month visa for 'Lev Leonidovich Nikolaev', an employee of the Soviet Trade Delegation in Berlin.[1] Permission was granted, and Nikolsky soon arrived in Vienna. Here he was greeted by his colleagues, OGPU officers Adolf Chapsky (alias Anton Schuster, codenamed KLIM), 2nd Secretary; Nikolai Fedorov,[2] deputy chief of the consular section, and Nikolai Popov, the trade representative. Popov had a spacious office at the embassy in Reisnerstrasse, but was also using another office at No. 9 Wallnergasse in the I District, metres away from the famous Café Central. Nikolsky/Nikolaev stayed in Vienna until 14 September, when he left by train for Berlin.[3] Before his departure, he telephoned Edward Winter, the representative of General Motors in Germany, telling him that he had just had a discussion with Mr Popov, who was as enthusiastic as himself about the idea of purchasing GM cars for the Soviet government. They arranged to meet in Berlin in two days' time. During the meeting, the American, anticipating possible lucrative business deals, gave 'Herrn Nikolaev' a letter of introduction to General Motors in New York and on the same day supported his visa application at the Consular Section of the US Embassy in Berlin.

A day before, on 15 September, after Nikolsky had successfully left Vienna, 'Legationssekretar Schuster' (that is, Chapsky) drove to the Foreign Ministry again and personally handed over another verbal note asking for a new visa to be issued to 'Nikolaev' for a business trip to Vienna for a period of two weeks.[4] That was a trick aimed to distract attention and, if necessary, confuse the security services of Austria and Germany. Schuster/Chapsky was well informed about his friend's real plans. Indeed, as soon as he obtained his American visa, Nikolsky took a train heading to Hamburg and from there went on to the port of Bremerhaven, where he boarded the SS *Europe* bound for the United States.

After a journey of about a week, Nikolsky arrived in the USA late one evening. In accordance with the US immigration procedures, he, together with other aliens, was taken to Ellis Island. In his declaration to the Immigration and Naturalization Service (INS), Nikolsky gave a false name, supplied fabricated personal information, lied about his membership of the Communist Party, and announced that he had no relatives in the United States.[5] (According to his last FBI minder: 'In 1975 the probating of Orlov's estate dragged on for almost two and a half years after his death. This was due to the large number of heirs who eventually surfaced. In September 1975 there were fifty-four heirs to Orlov's estate in the US alone. Some of them he contacted immediately upon arrival in 1932.')[6] As it was an undercover mission, he obviously also misinformed the authorities about the aim of his visit.

A Special Immigration Board of Inquiry was convened on Monday morning, 26 September, as it was necessary to establish this alien's eligibility for entry. Nikolsky was sworn in and testified under oath through an interpreter, because he did not speak English. Following his 'legend', he also testified that he had come to the USA to inspect GM automobile plants. He said that he was authorized to negotiate the purchase of 150 cars for various Soviet government agencies.[7] It was all a lie, but they believed him because between 1930 and 1932 Henry Ford sent 450 of his Detroit employees plus their families to live in Gorky, Russia, as part of a Ford Motor Company plan to assist the Soviet Union.[8] Nikolsky was admitted as a visitor for four months.

One can only speculate about the reasons for sending him across the ocean. As with many other Soviet Jews, Nikolsky/Feldbin had many relatives in the United States about whom he was only too well informed and who could be useful in the future. At a time when there were no diplomatic relations between the USA and Russia, such contacts were not simply tolerated but even encouraged, and being Jewish was considered as an advantage. (Naum Eitingon, another OGPU officer and also a Jew, visited the United States several times during the same period, and so did Yakov Serebryansky.)[9] Nikolsky's remit in America was to study the country, learn the language, and obtain a genuine American passport that would allow its holder free and unrestricted travel in Europe. Nikolsky succeeded in at least two of these tasks. He travelled the country and successfully established contacts with his relatives from Bobruisk who had immigrated there. With the help of another Soviet 'illegal' of Jewish heritage named Abram Einhorn (codenamed TARAS and HARDY),[10] Nikolsky also managed to get a US passport using the false name 'William Goldin'. Before coming to New York in early 1930, Einhorn had operated under-cover in Turkey, France, Germany, and Palestine and was then posted in Italy as a diplomat. In 1927 he was at the Moscow OGPU headquarters supervising operations in Iran and India and later, in 1928–9, he was an 'illegal' station chief in Iran. Georges Agabekov, one of the first Soviet defectors who, like Einhorn, worked at the OGPU's Oriental Section and also operated undercover in Iran and Turkey, must have known Einhorn very well. Surprisingly, there is no mention of him in Agabekov's MI5 file, now at The National Archives. On the other hand, much of what Agabe-kov knew and was eager to share with MI5 is missing, which demonstrates how inexperienced the Service used to be in working with defectors in those early years.

In 1931 Einhorn recruited Catherine ('Kitty') Harris, who would become a secret courier of the OGPU–NKVD foreign intelligence during the 1930s and 1940s. We shall hear a lot more about her later. Another very useful contact of Einhorn in New York was 'Jacob Golos' (codenamed ZVUK or SOUND), whose real name was Yakov Naumovich Reisen.[11] Golos was the source of genuine American documents that were used as cover for Soviet 'illegals'. At the time, fake passports based on such documents were known as 'books' in Soviet intelligence correspondence. No doubt with his help, in November 1932 Nikolsky became a happy owner of US passport No. 566042, which he would later use in London. A week later Nikolsky/ Goldin left the United States, unnoticed by anyone, on board the SS *Bremen* heading for Europe.

In Berlin, Nikolsky deposited his new 'book' at the Soviet Embassy and promptly departed for Russia. His two-month-long mission had been accomplished.

4

Vienna: April–July 1933

In the period between the wars, a number of 'legal' and 'illegal' Soviet networks operated simultaneously out of various countries against Britain and France, quickly restoring positions Soviet intelligence had lost during the 1927 exposures of several spy rings. Ignatz Reiss (RAYMOND), Walter Krivitsky (WALTER), Dmitry Bystroletov (ANDREI and HANS), Fyodor Karin (JACK), Vasili Zarubin (BETTI) and his wife Elisaveta Zarubina (VARDO, ERNA), Arnold Deutsch (ARNOLD, STEFAN), Theodor Maly (MANN, PAUL, THEO), Henri Christiaan Pieck (COOPER)—to name only a few rather successful and often highly productive OGPU residents, recruiters, and agent–runners—were collecting important intelligence for Moscow at the same time as acquiring new sources. Two additional channels of information for the Kremlin were its military intelligence and the Comintern/OMS networks, which had even more assets with access to secrets that the Soviet leadership was eager to know.

As early as 1930 in the the interwar period, a Polish Jewess and member of the Communist Party of Palestine named Sophia ('Zosha') Poznánska moved from Tel Aviv to Paris.[1] There she settled with her lover Shmuel Cinnamon in an attic in the Quartier Latin on the right bank, not far from the home of Leiba and Luba Trepper. Leiba, better known as Leopold, and Cinnamon had been expelled from Palestine some months before, when the British police had intensified persecutions of the Communists. Poznánska had first met Trepper in her kibbutz and then worked for him in Tel Aviv. It was Leopold Trepper who gave Zosha her first important field assignment. Another two friends of theirs, Polish Jews Alter Strohm and Isaiah Bir, also lived in the neighbourhood.[2] Theirs was only one of many Soviet spy networks in France.

While the roles of Trepper and Poznánska in this operation remain unclear, Bir and Strohm were instrumental in running a sophisticated RU network that grew out of the Rabkor ('worker–correspondent') movement. This movement originated in Russia after the Bolshevik revolution. There, factory workers were encouraged to write letters describing local affairs that could then be published in newspapers. In fact, the aim was to turn 'correspondents' into informants. The Rabkor experiment was repeated by communist parties in several countries, but it was only in France that the worker–correspondent movement became a major source of intelligence. A special committee at *l'Humanité*, the official newspaper of the PCF, presided over by Jacques Duclos, coordinated all activities. Reports suitable for propaganda purposes but useless for Soviet intelligence were published in *l'Humanité* or in a *Bulletin d'information* edited by a committee member named Riquier. Claude Liogier, a journalist and writer who wrote under the pseudonym 'André Philippe', led the group of such 'correspondents', primarily young trade unionists from defence-related industries, who sent 'letters to the editor' that often contained excellent information, which could be turned into high-grade intelligence reports. Behind Liogier stood Isaiah Bir, assisted by Alter Strohm, who acted as cut-outs or mutually trusted intermediaries between the RU resident Sergey Markovich and the committee.[3] In the French newspapers Bir was referred to as 'The Phantom', because of his ability to elude the police, and the whole Rabkor affair became known as *l'affaire Fantômas* after a fictional character created by French writers Marcel Allain and Pierre Souvestre. As if by design, in 1932, when la Sûreté investigated the case, the film *Fantômas*, directed by Paul Féjos with Jean Galland in the leading role, was hitting French movie screens.

When Bir, his assistant, and five French communists were arrested for conspiracy to commit espionage, witty journalists quickly labelled the affair 'The Fanto-Marx Conspiracy', writing: 'The police exposed a Soviet spy ring operating out of a Paris apartment arresting its leader, Isaiah Bir, nicknamed Fantômas, and his deputy, Alter Strohm. Both are members of the Communist Party.'[4] Quite possibly Strohm brought Leopold Trepper and Sophia Poznánska into the network. When in 1932 several of its members were arrested, Duclos, Trepper, and Markovich, the Soviet controller, managed to flee to Moscow. Poznánska fled to Brussels. Cinnamon and Luba Trepper remained in Paris. From Moscow, Duclos moved to Berlin, where, using the alias 'Lauer', he started working in the underground West European Bureau (WEB) of the Comintern headed by Dimitrov.[5] One day Duclos would become acting Secretary General of the PCF, later running for his country's presidency. He managed to score over 21 per cent of the vote, the highest ever for a Communist candidate in French history.

'In December 1936,' writes the Israeli journalist Neri Livneh, reviewing the only book about Poznánska recently published in Israel,

Trepper was sent from Moscow to Paris in order to discover who had betrayed the Fantomas network [in his memoirs *The Great Game*, published in 1977, Trepper devoted the whole chapter to the Fantômas case]. On the way to Paris, Trepper dropped in to visit Zosha in Antwerp, and suggested that she return to Paris. She agreed, despite the fact that this meant the end of her affair with Kenarek, one of her lovers in Belgium. In Paris she returned to the arms of Cinnamon, had an intimate relationship with another man, Jasha Aharonovitch, lived with yet another man, Benek Katz, and once again returned to Cinnamon, who was destined to be her most steadfast lover.[6]

Leopold Trepper was soon to become 'Le Grand Chef' and Sophia Poznánska one of the cipher experts of a legendary GRU network covering all Europe, Britain, and the USA that is now known as the 'Rote Kapelle' ('Red Orchestra'). Perhaps she realized that she did not have long to live and decided to live life to the full.

There are two versions of who betrayed the Fantômas ring. The Western version, presented by the American military historian Douglas Porch, suggests that it was Riquier, 'apparently struck with a case of bad conscience', who revealed the Rabkor network to a Sûreté agent.[7] The Russian version, first put forward by Trepper and later promoted by the intelligence historian Alexander Kolpakidi, implies that Bir and Strohm came to Moscow in 1936 insisting that Trepper should go to France to investigate the situation, because they refused to believe that Riquier had been a traitor. As a result, Trepper found out, and was able to prove with documents, that the traitor had actually been 'a Dutchman named Svitz', a wealthy American convert to communism.[8] The correct name of the then 30-year-old native of East Orange, New Jersey, was Robert Gordon Switz. The espionage case involving Switz and Lydia Stahl became the major media event in France in 1933.

In the meantime, in Russia, the first collectivization campaign brought a human catastrophe even before the terrible famine of 1932–3. Stalin insisted on forcing the tempo of grain exports 'to establish our position on the international market'. 'From a starving countryside,' notes Donald Rayfield, 'over five million tonnes of grain was being exported to pay for turbines, assembly lines, mining machinery and the funding of communist parties all over Europe, Asia and America'.[9] According to Rayfield:

The silence of the West, which emerged from its economic depression at least partly as a result of orders from the Soviet Union paid for by the blood of millions of peasants, is a blot on our civilization. Diplomats and journalists may well have shared Stalin's view that the Russian peasant was a subhuman brute; Western businessmen were eager for the contracts that Soviet industrialization was bringing their way. As the late British historian Christopher Hill said seventy years later of the Ukraine in 1933: 'I saw no famine.'[10]

Modern estimates of the death toll, based on documents declassified by the first non-biased chief of the Sluzhba Bezpeky Ukrayiny (SBU) (Security Service of Ukraine),[11] give the figure of about 10 million in Ukraine alone, including about 4 million famine deaths and a 6.1 million birth deficit.

Soviet industrialization also brought further changes to the OGPU. In October 1932 the Economic Directorate again grew to eleven sections. By March 1933 the INO had a staff of 110 operational officers.[12] At the same time, the OGPU's interest in France in terms of technical intelligence about weapons and equipment used by the armed forces of foreign nations decreased, because US military technology was now considered to be more modern and to be advancing more quickly. Although military matters were never completely ignored, none of INO's eight sections specialized in information relating to them.[13]

Under these circumstances, it is unclear why Nicolsky's chiefs should send him to France again, as his KGB-sponsored biography claims, to penetrate the legendary Deuxième Bureau, the military intelligence service, one of six French intelligence organizations. It is hard to say who came up with this idea, but it was probably Nikolsky himself, because he desperately needed to take his sick daughter to Western Europe for treatment.

Possibly from his direct boss, Otto Steinbrück, who was Austrian, Nikolsky had learned that a famous doctor, Karl von Noorden, had recently moved to Austria from Germany and had even been awarded the title of Honourable Citizen of Vienna. Dr Noorden's clients were rich and well placed, and many Soviet officials, including Yagoda's deputy, Yakov Agranov, and later Commissar Nikolai Yezhov himself, were among his patients.

The story goes that Nikolsky managed to persuade his bosses that he would be able to find and recruit a French officer of the Deuxième Bureau about whom Steinbrück and Maly had learned from an unnamed defector.

Soon a group was formed that included Nikolsky (codenamed SCHWED), assisted by a very young and entirely inexperienced junior operative named Alexander Korotkov (DLINNY),[14] and a courier using the alias 'Arnold Finkelberg' (codenamed EXPRESS). Contrary to what is claimed in some biographies,[15] Nikolsky's wife, Maria, was never part of the group and never reached Geneva, its final destination. Together with Vera, their daughter, she went only as far as Vienna, where they remained all the time under the care of Dr Noorden.[16] However, a person described as 'technical assistant and local courier codenamed JEANNE'[17] was not a complete invention.

To be accepted to the elite of the INO operational staff, poorly educated Korotkov, who had worked at the Lubyanka as a technician servicing several lifts that remained from the good old days when the building had housed an insurance company, had to do something extraordinary— something that would get him into the *nomenklatura*. Should he get there, he was pretty sure that he would then move up the career ladder at least as fast as his lifts did. Young, tall, and good-looking, Korotkov reached his goal by marrying Maria Wilkowyska who was teaching foreign languages to the INO officers. Thus Korotkov and Korotkov's wife, whose father, according to Sudoplatov, was a close friend of Nikolsky,[18] both became part of Operation EXPRESS. And Maria Korotkova, not Maria Nikolskaya, became the local courier codenamed JEANNE.

Remarkably, while Maly debriefed the defector in Moscow, Dmitri Bystroletov had already been cultivating a Deuxième Bureau officer named Rodolphe Lemoine, codenamed JOSEPH by the OGPU. (Born Rudolf Stallmann, the son of a wealthy Berlin jeweller, he had acquired French citizenship and taken the name of his wife.) Lemoine began working for the Deuxième Bureau in 1918. In the 1920s he recruited Ludwig Maringer, who had an antique business in London and Düsseldorf and later lived in The Hague and Paris. But his greatest coup was the recruitment in 1931 of a German cipher and signal intelligence specialist, Hans-Thilo Schmidt. Although some historians note that for the next decade Schmidt (codenamed H.E. and ASCHE by the French) was the Deuxième Bureau's most important foreign agent because the intelligence he provided laid the foundations for the breaking of the German Enigma machine,[19] French cryptanalysts themselves were unable to do it. Finally, they had to share their information with Polish colleagues. As a result of the efforts of several gifted Polish mathematicians, by 1932 a slightly simpler version of the Enigma code had been cracked.[20] Later, British cryptologists at Bletchley Park managed to solve the problem once and for ever, thereby providing crucial assistance to the Allied war effort.

After Bystroletov had made his initial contact with Lemoine, he was instructed to hand the case over to Ignatz Reiss, one of the 'illegal' OGPU residents in France posing as 'Walter Scott', an officer of the US military intelligence. Basing his conclusions on the documents made available to Western historians thanks to the former KGB archivist Vasili Mitrokhin, Christopher Andrew wrote that 'Lemoine appeared anxious to set up an exchange on German and foreign cipher systems, and supplied a mixture of good and bad intelligence as evidence of the Deuxième Bureau's willingness to co-operate'. Mitrokhin's notes reveal that Reiss showed an interest in acquiring Italian, Czechoslovak, and Hungarian ciphers and was still meeting his contacts from the Deuxième Bureau (Lemoine and his boss, Gustave Bertrand) as late as 1935.[21] By that time the French already knew that their contact worked for the OGPU.

In the spring of 1933 Nikolsky was allegedly sent to Paris to acquire an additional source in the Deuxième Bureau. He had a variety of identity documents to choose from. The set included a Soviet passport valid for travel abroad issued in the name of 'Léon Nikolaeff' and signed by Yagoda; an Austrian passport identifying him as 'Leo Feldbiene' (Maria and Vera also had both sets, one for 'Maria and Veronika Nikolaeff', and another for 'Margareta and Veronika Feldbiene');[22] and a genuine American passport in the name of 'William Goldin'. By the time the operation was unfolding, Nikolsky was already 36 years old, had quite a low-level line officer 'position' (ranks were abolished after the Revolution and not reintroduced until 1935), and could not boast of any achievement at all.

From Moscow the Nikolskys went first to Prague under the names of Leo, Maria, and Vera Nikolaev—names they had used during their first posting to France. On 18 April the Soviet Embassy in Czechoslovakia asked the Austrian Embassy to grant an urgent visa for 'Nikolaev' and members of his family. The following day this request was supported by a verbal note from the Soviet Embassy in Vienna.[23] It stated that 'Nikolaev' was an official of the People's Commissariat for Foreign Trade and was travelling to Austria on business.[24] It should have invented a better pretext.

In the spring of 1933 political and economic relations between Austria and the USSR were at their lowest point, and the new Plenipotentiary Adolf Petrovsky, with his seriously reduced staff, knew this better than anyone else.[25] Just days before his arrival, on 4 March 1933, Chancellor Engelbert Dollfuss, leader of the Christian Socialists, suspended parliamentary government and prohibited political assemblies in Austria. On 8 March, the Chancellor suspended the freedom of the press. Less than two months after the Reichstag fire that had consolidated Hitler's power, Dollfuss and many at the Federal Chancellery were seriously afraid of the Anschluss, the German annexation of Austria that was preceded by massive Nazi provocations. In April 1933 Vice-Chancellor Richard Smitz commented on 'the pressure coming from Berlin and certain news about plans to flood Austria with National Socialist (Nazi) propaganda, to overthrow Dollfuss and make the Anschluss by peaceful means—all of this apparently with the knowledge and approval of Mussolini and the Vatican...'.[26] That April Stalin decided to place a number of qualified British engineers working in the Soviet Union on trial for sabotage. As usual (we have seen similar behaviour in Russia more recently), foreign specialists were arrested on trumped-up charges, and the controlled court, conducted in the military style of a court martial without a jury and defence, found them guilty. The British government protested and ordered an embargo prohibiting imports into the United Kingdom 'of all goods grown, produced or manufactured in the Soviet Union'.[27] Finally, the engineers were permitted to return home.

While Anglo-Soviet relations were deteriorating again, the Soviet Union remained neutral to Nazi Germany and even boosted its international recognition by renewing the Russo-German Treaties of 1926 and 1929. As a result, any relations between Russia and Austria, including mutual trade and all sorts of political contacts, were limited to an absolute minimum, and none of the parties involved sought to improve them. When Nikolsky/ Nikolaev finally arrived in Vienna, the OGPU station at the embassy on Reisnerstrasse consisted of only two officers, and they seemed to have plenty of free time. Clearly, Austria was not an intelligence priority then.

Unsurprisingly, the Intelligence Directorate of the Red Army had chosen it as a convenient operational base. Being officially unrepresented in the Alpine Republic (there was no military attaché there, and apparently no need of any), the RU maintained several 'illegal' *rezidenturas* in Austria. The chief resident was Ivan Vinarov. He controlled agents and sources in Poland, Czechoslovakia, Bulgaria, Yugoslavia, Greece, and Turkey.[28] After his recall to Moscow in 1933, Fyodor Gaidarov took his place. One of Gaidarov's agents in Vienna was Krstio Belev, a fellow Bulgarian communist and writer, later arrested in Romania.[29] Also arrested in Romania in 1930 was Karl Nebenführ, who headed a small group of the Austrian RU agents and of whom we shall hear much more.

Several other RU agents of various nationalities operated with Nebenführ in Bucharest at the time. One of them was the American communist Nicholas Dozenberg, recruited by Alfred Tilton in Chicago three years before. Dozenberg later testified that he had been dispatched to the Romanian capital to establish a motion picture company as a front for Soviet intelligence operations.[30] It was believed that a company making movies should have no problem surreptitiously filming ports, barracks, and military fortifications. At that time Romania, like Poland, was considered one of the main adversaries and an important British outpost on the Soviet borders. Others involved in the Romanian operation were Austrians Fritz Klauda and Cilly Ausländer, arrested together with Nebenführ, the Italian Arnaldo Silva, and the Bulgarian Ivan Mitsiyev.[31] Based in Moscow from 1922, Silva was imprisoned during the famous trial of Italian communists a year later and was renowned in the Italian milieu for managing to escape from the Regina Coeli prison by passing himself off as a lawyer visiting detainees.[32] Both Silva and Nebenführ were released in 1932 and returned to Moscow.

Krivitsky headed another group. According to his biographer, in 1933 'Krivitsky also scored an intelligence coup. Two of his agents in Germany managed to obtain the complete designs for a new airplane engine. The Red Army got the designs and Krivitsky got the credits but the agents got caught.'[33] At least, this is what Krivitsky related to British intelligence in 1940 during his London debriefings. Leonid Anulov, also based in Vienna, was controlling networks in Italy and Switzerland, a typical set-up for the Red Army Intelligence Directorate.[34] Another residency, known as the *rezidentura svyazi* (the joint communications unit), was activated in April 1931 in Baden bei Wien. It was designed to ensure interoperability of communication procedures and equipment and was to connect Moscow with all its military agent networks in Central Europe. The groups run by Leopold Trepper and Sándor Rado were later organized on the basis of experience gained in Vienna, using the sources previously recruited by Isaak Rosenberg (codenamed THEODOR),[35] who had been posing as a Soviet diplomat at the League of Nations in Geneva for four years since September 1934.

One short story about this period, reproduced by Krivitsky in his book and repeated by several historians,[36] deserves an explanation.

In December 1931, the Austrian security police arrested one of the RU operational groups in Baden commanded by Konstantin Basov (RICHARD).[37] Basov/Ābeltiņš was assisted by his wife, whether real or in the line of duty, 'Ruth Klein', who it was quickly established was Gertrude ('Trude') Braun, a KPD member and a former OMS courier. The group leader, posing as a Vienna University student, used two passports—one Latvian, and one German identifying him as 'Martin Klein'. Also detained with Basov and his wife were Karlis Mikhelson, Adam Meikies, and Karlis Afelds. Trude Braun was soon released, because she was pregnant. She quickly left the country, while the others remained in custody. A military intelligence veteran named Vasili (in Krivitsky's book 'Vladimir') Dedushok decided to save his friends and turned for help to Colonel Kurt von Bredow of the German military intelligence, Abwehr. Soon all members of the group were expelled from Austria and returned to Moscow, while Dedushok was arrested by the OGPU in 1933 and sentenced to ten years in a concentration camp on Solovetsky Islands. Neither Krivitsky nor later researchers could explain what was wrong in Dedushok's actions. His arrest had clearly nothing to do with purges in the Red Army that began later.

Kurt von Bredow, who soon became a general heading military intelligence for the Reichswehr, was an important link between German military intelligence and the Soviets. Bredow had regular contacts with the famous Guchkov circle, a White Russian organization in Paris penetrated by Soviet agents from top to bottom.[38] A senior intelligence officer, not a Nazi, and loyal first and foremost to the army, von Bredow had every reason to assist his colleagues from Moscow. This was extremely dangerous, and the situation was aggravated even more by Dedushok's brazen appeal for help. In his turn, the general probably did not realize how much he was risking. During what became known as the Night of the Long Knives, on 30 June 1934, General von Bredow walked home, perfectly at ease. On his doorstep he confronted several SS officers who drew their revolvers and, without a word, shot him dead.[39] Both the NKVD and the RU lost an invaluable contact within the German military leadership. As a result, Dedushok was arrested and sent to the Gulag on the White Sea.

Natalia Zvonaryova, an intelligence officer, was also in Vienna at that time, serving, as one Russian historian put it, 'under all three of the fore-named GRU residents'.[40] In reality, Zvonaryova had been in Vienna for only a few months in 1931–2. She was part of the embassy's technical staff. In February 1933 she was back in Moscow.[41]

The OGPU head of station Adolf Chapsky, better known at the Austrian Foreign Ministry as '2nd Secretary Anton Schuster', met Nikolsky and his family at the Vienna Ostbahnhof and chauffeured them to a beautiful place called Hinterbrühl, 18 kilometres away from the capital, geographically in Lower Austria, at the heart of the Wienerwald ('Vienna Woods') area. Here, at 27 Hauptstrasse, a comfortable apartment was booked at the best pension that the town could offer at the time, named Schloß. Nowadays, this state-protected historical building houses a veterinary practice and, just as in the 1930s, still looks like a small castle.

At this picturesque place, Nikolsky's biographers claim that he 'had to brush up his English and his French'.[42] But a remote little town in the Austrian countryside is hardly the right place for linguistic exercises. According to their official police registration, in Hinterbrühl Nikolsky, his wife, and their little girl lived as Soviet citizens and obviously communicated between themselves in Russian.[43] The real reason for choosing such a place as Hinterbrühl was undoubtedly that it was ideal for proper rest and recovery for Nikolsky's daughter.

Here in the Austrian province they were enjoying life and fresh air when something happened that remained unknown, even to the KGB, for years. On 26 April, slightly over a month after their arrival, 'Leo and Maria' (nothing is mentioned in the documents about Vera) were suddenly arrested and escorted to prison. In those years, as can be seen from the files, it was common practice for the Austrian police to harass foreigners, especially from Eastern Europe and Russia, and sometimes they even detained diplomats. It was usual for any alien to be arrested if he or she did not have a valid passport and could not speak German. The Nikolskys neither demanded a Soviet representative, nor filed a protest, but quietly allowed themselves to be interviewed by the detectives. After some time they were released. It seems that Nikolsky never reported the incident to Moscow. The Austrian archives, though carefully checked by Soviet collaborators after the war,[44] still contain clear evidence of this episode.[45] Had it become known at the time, Nikolsky's intelligence career would have been finished.

Three months passed. Finally, Nikolsky sent a telegram to Moscow that read: 'Change status on 1 July and leave for my place of work. SCHWED.'[46] It was time to say goodbye to the family.

While Nikolsky was entertaining himself rambling around the Hinterbrühl hills that inspired Beethoven's powerful music, a former lift man turned spy was not too far away. Alexander 'Sasha' Korotkov, together with his wife, stayed first in Prague, adapting to 'bourgeoise' life, and later moved to Geneva, which had been selected as an operational base for the EXPRESS group. He almost certainly had to keep a very low profile, as he did not know Europe and at least for some part of his trip used a Soviet passport, which, contrary to a popular dictum, did not elicit much respect. The document identified him as 'Vladimir Petrovich Korotin'. It was hoped that after 'acclimatization' he would be able to pass for a Czech student.

Relevant Austrian archival records show that 'Arnold Finkelberg', Nikolsky's courier, never visited Austria.[47] But someone else did. On 27 June Nikolsky went to Prague, where he collected his American passport at the Soviet Embassy. The document identified him as 'William Goldin' from New York. Then 'Mr Goldin' ordered a ticket to Geneva with a stopover in Berlin. Following his sojourn in the Austrian province, he was probably able to understand some very basic local phrases and, of course, he had become acquainted with the Austrian penitentiary system. Alas, such an experience would prove to be of little use on the banks of Lac Léman. It is, however, possible that Nikolsky was learning some American English, taking lessons from his own courier, who could have been an American communist, because we know that Nikolsky had been preparing for an undercover mission in the United States. There was a sufficient number of Americans working for Soviet intelligence at that time. (This explanation is at least more logical than the story of the 'British professor' invented by Nikolsky himself and supported by some reports.[48] British English was the last thing that 'Yankee' Nikolsky needed in Paris.)

A clue to the possible real identity of the American known only under the alias 'Arnold Finkelberg' comes from old investigation files. Steve Nelson, a CPUSA activist and an NKVD agent, stands out as a possible candidate. In the early 1930s, Nelson attended the International Lenin School in Moscow, and later American investigators found out that in July 1933 he renewed his passport at the US Consulate in Vienna. It was also established that during that period he 'resided in Germany, Austria and Switzerland'.[49] And Switzerland was exactly were Nikolsky and the rest of the EXPRESS group were now heading. But first they had to stop in Berlin.

5

Geneva and Paris: Operation
EXPRESS, July 1933–May 1934

Theodor Maly, a Hungarian and a former priest, started his OGPU career in Moscow at the Special Cryptographic Department (then known as Spetsyalnyi kriptograficheskii otdel OGPU (SPEKO), which specialized in the interception of the diplomatic correspondence of the foreign legations accredited in the Soviet capital. Vladimir and Evdokia Petrov, Soviet defectors both of whom worked there later, described Maly's colleagues as elderly gentlemen, mostly former Russian aristocrats, including members of the nobility, who were employed because of their knowledge of foreign languages. At that time the service was short of trained linguists and, as the Petrovs write, 'had not yet been able to dispense with the services of all politically questionable persons who had high professional qualifications'.[1] Alongside Russian counts and barons, there also worked some tested and trusted foreigners, and Maly was one of them. But by the time Petrov joined the OGPU in 1933, Maly had already been working at its foreign department, INO. He was probably attached to its 3rd section, under the Austrian Otto Steinbrück, which targeted 'capitalist countries of the West'. There, Maly took part in the debriefing of an NCO of the French Deuxième Bureau. This man allegedly defected to Moscow, telling his OGPU interrogators that he knew an officer at the Deuxième Bureau who would be happy to work for the Soviets.

Nikolsky, by this time back at the Lubyanka INO offices, learned about the debriefing. It probably did not take him long to persuade Naum Eitingon, a fellow Jew from Bobruisk and now head of INO's 1st section (the 'illegals'), that he should go to Paris immediately, while his wife and daughter would stay in Austria under the watchful eye of Dr Norden. This is how Operation EXPRESS was launched—an operation that, from its very first day, gradually developed into a farce, with Nikolsky often finding himself in ridiculous situations.

The first stop was in Berlin, a city Nikolsky knew and remembered well. Somewhat confusingly, his biographers claim that here he met 'an agent of the Berlin *rezidentura* who used the code name STAHL'.[2] This man allegedly also promised to find him a candidate for recruitment inside the Deuxième Bureau. It is not known how long Nikolsky stayed in the German capital. After his meeting with the agent, quite satisfied with what he thought was a good start, Nikolsky proceeded to Geneva. As planned from the very beginning, his wife and daughter remained in Vienna,[3] moving from one address to another until they settled at the Hotel Atlanta on Währinger Strasse. The hotel is still there.

It is possible that in helping Nikolsky with his daughter's health problems (Vera had been ill for a long time and needed proper medical care) by sending him abroad again, the OGPU was also responding to the ongoing large-scale RU operation in France, which ended badly with twenty-nine people, including, as mentioned above, Lydia Stahl, arraigned on espionage charges. Some of the arrested, such as Robert Gordon Switz and his wife, Marjorie Tilley, were American passport-holders.

According to the newspaper articles that covered the process in every detail, the investigators believed (erroneously) that Lydia Stahl, who had managed to escape to the USA after the Cremet scandal, was a central figure.[4] Stahl was born in Russia in 1890 as Lydia Chekalova and moved to the West after marrying Baron Stahl, a member of the Finnish aristocracy. Mme Stahl had been well known to the security services on both sides of the English Channel for over ten years.[5] Lydia's lover from 1923 on was the French professor Louis Pierre Martin, former attaché of the Naval Ministry and officer of the Légion d'Honneur.[6] Naturally, he helped her. Other sources of the GRU spy ring were the Bessarabian Vatroslav Reich, an employee of the government biological and chemical laboratory, the French engineer Aubry, an employee of the War Ministry, and his wife, who supplied information on gunpowder and explosives. Colonel Octave du Moulin ('Agent 624'), a military expert and editor of *Armée et démocratie*, was also part of the ring, which, according to MI5 files on Switz and Tilley, altogether had 250 men and women involved in some way in the case.

There are several versions of how the network was uncovered. According to one, the Finnish security police arrested a group of Soviet agents in Finland controlled by Maria Schul, alias 'Martin', the wife of Janis Alfred

Tilton.[7] Tilton was one of the experienced GRU officers who successfully operated in France, Germany, and the United States.[8]

One of his agents, Nicholas Dozenberg, an American communist born, like Tilton, in Latvia, later testified that Tilton was the chief RU resident in the USA and recruited him in late 1927 or early 1928.[9] At that time Tilton was living in New York using Canadian papers in the name of 'Joseph Paquette'. He later managed to obtain another set of Canadian documents for him and his wife, this time in the name of 'Martin'. Dozenberg usually received money for his expenses through seamen couriers, whom he met at the dental practice of Dr Philip Rosenbliett.[10] During 1928 Dozenberg became acquainted with Lydia Stahl, who was Tilton's assistant in copying secret documents. Tilton and Stahl used the photographic studios of Joseph Turin in New York City for their work. In early 1929 a man documented as 'Mark Zilbert' arrived in the USA and took over from Tilton all activities as chief resident of Soviet military intelligence.[11] Zilbert's real name was Manfred Stern, and he was to become a prominent figure in the early days of the Spanish Civil War. His predecessor in New York, Alfred Tilton, would also be sent to Spain, where he was on a one-year-long undercover mission until October 1937.[12]

Back in 1929, Tilton returned to Moscow to report to the RU director, and his wife was sent to Helsinki as 'Maria Martin', using her Canadian passport. After a while, Stahl was dispatched to Paris. In Finland 'Martin' was assisted by Arvid Werner Jacobsen, an American. When a Finnish General Staff officer, Lieutenant Villno Armas Pentikainen, defected to the Soviet Union, the Finnish police started to check all his contacts. They soon found out that the lieutenant had some dealings with one Einari Vaha, who was promptly arrested and who during the interrogation confessed that he had been spying for the Russians.[13] This case is not well known. Soon after the trial, the *Time* magazine correspondent reported:

The Finnish High Court last week passed sentence upon the spy ring of 28 men and women it had been trying behind locked doors for nine weeks. To a 27-year-old graduate of the University of Michigan and onetime schoolteacher in a Detroit suburb, Arvid Werner Jacobsen, the judges gave a sentence of five years of hard labor. In Michigan his wife Sally said: 'Arvid took a university fellowship in Finland and then found out he was expected to give dangerous information.' The Finnish police charged that Arvid had been the ring's paymaster and the final link between the spies and the Soviet Legation in Finland. To the ringleader, a Mrs Marie Louise Schul-Martin [*sic*], the judges gave eight years; to the others sentences ranging from the minimum two years to six years.[14]

From the Security Service (MI5) files it is unclear how the Schuhl-Martin lead brought investigators to Lydia Stahl in Paris, but Dallin notes that it was her best friend, Ingrid Bostrom, a member of the Helsinki ring, who was arrested and 'started to sing'. Bostrom told the authorities all she knew about Lydia, her life, and her work for the Soviets. 'Starting from this point,' according to Dallin, 'French counterintelligence investigated and discovered the large network of which Lydia Stahl was an important member.'[15] This turned out to be an exaggeration.

By the end of March 1934, the RU spy ring in France had been smashed. Switz and his wife confessed and 'were exempted from punishment' by the French government. He promptly started writing for the London *Daily Express*. Stahl got a maximum prison term of five years, which was reduced to four years by the court of appeal when it became clear that she was only a photographer sometimes acting as a cut-out between RU residents and their sources.[16] Madeleine Mermet, another photographer who worked as a schoolteacher, was sentenced to three years. Dallin's 1955 account of the case, which nevertheless remains the most detailed and is generally quite reliable, notes that the real spymasters controlling the ring were Sergey Markovich, Veniamin Berkovich, and Robert Gordon Switz (codenamed AVIATOR). Twenty-two years later, in his account of the Fantômas case, Leopold Trepper quite certainly relied on Dallin's book, stating that Moscow sent Switz 'to Paris to become the leader of the Soviet Intelligence group there'.[17] Trepper could not have known this himself and did not mention the other two.

The GRU, successor of the RU, seems to agree with Trepper, who called Switz the 'paragon of the double game'. According to one of their historians, in 1931 Switz, who, he claims, was not American by birth, was sent to the USA with an American passport, but the immigration authorities found out that the passport was forged, and Switz started collaborating with the US Army Military Intelligence Division (MID).[18] The whole story is definitely based on the allegations of Trepper, who, investigating the Fantômas affair, claimed that he found twenty-three letters that Switz had allegedly sent to the US military attaché in Paris and that were part of his court file. According to Trepper, it was by chance that these letters had not been mentioned at the trial. This version, however, does not seem plausible.

Switz, whose father was a Russian émigré,[19] wrote:

I am not, and never was, a Communist, I was interested in the Soviet experiment as
an idealist. My first contacts with the Soviet spy organization were in New York
and in Washington. They saw how keen I was and arranged for me to go to
Moscow in the guise of an aviation instructor. When I returned to America I met
my wife, Marjory Tilley. She was a student at Vassar. She was only 19. We got
married and she agreed to come to Europe and help me.[20]

He added that in France he became disillusioned with his work for Soviet
intelligence.

Switz's MI5 file reveals that he was most probably recruited as a Russian
agent in the United States in 1931. It is possible that his recruiter was
Vladimir Gorev (alias 'Gordon'), from January 1930 to May 1933 posted
as an 'illegal' Red Army Intelligence Directorate resident in New York
whom Switz later described to the FBI as 'Otto' and 'Karl Schmidt'.[21] It is
also known that Switz, together with Lydia Stahl and Leon Minster, was
part of the network controlled by Manfred Stern and Gorev that was later
taken over by Alexander Ulanovsky. Two other members of this network
were Robert Osman and Joshua Tamer. They used a safe house owned by
Paula Levine, later a member of the Paris ring, and a photographic studio on
Gay Street in Greenwich Village, where Minster, codenamed CHARLIE, used
to photograph stolen documents.[22] Switz was sent by his controllers to
London in 1931 and subsequently to Paris.[23] (In 1931–2 Tilley, who was
also an agent and a rather well-paid one, as was revealed during the trial, was
specifically trained for photographing documents in order to replace Lydia
Stahl, who was preparing to leave for France.) Switz arrived in Paris to
replace Markovich, and they were spotted together by the watchers from
the surveillance team. Nevertheless, Markovich managed to escape, while
all the rest, including Berkovich, were caught.

The Russians, of course, blame Switz for their failures, especially because
he made his disagreement with them public and started collaborating with
the Sûreté, while it is evident that such big networks of agents could not have
been controlled by one person. Neither could they have existed undetected
for too long. Even a very small group such as Nikolsky, Korotkov, his wife,
Maria, and their American courier was doomed from the start.

When the detectives of several European countries were closing in on the
RU spy rings, Nikolsky, posing as the American tourist 'Goldin', a well-to-
do gentleman spending his happy days in the wonderful parks and restaurants of Geneva, instead had to spend week after week in Paris in the hope of

finding his potential recruit. It was all in vain. To his total distress, nobody fitted the description provided by the defector in Moscow.

On 5 September 1933 Nikolsky, signing his telegrams by his usual code name SCHWED, sent a long and detailed report to Moscow Centre. He complained that because neither he, nor his assistants, spoke French, he urgently needed a Frenchman or a fluent French speaker to help him. Nikolsky wrote that he had 'not got a single genuine Frenchman for "breeding" [razvodka], through whom I could orient myself and seek to make new acquaintances without immediately scaring them off by my alien citizenship and foreign appearance... I'm trying to get close to some people, but without success.'[24] Although the report contained many 'operational' details, Nikolsky never mentioned anything related to his assignment at the Deuxième Bureau.

For the first, but not the last time, he asked his chiefs to recall him to Moscow, leaving the rest of the group to continue their work. He again asked that the group should be strengthened by the addition of a Frenchman from another 'illegal' network and suggested that the whole operation might perhaps be entrusted to one of Maly's agents. The dispatch shows that in September 1933 Maly was in Paris. At the end of his dispatch SCHWED suddenly proposed that his expenses budget should be reduced, so that, should his mission fail, the overall losses would not be too heavy. He was obviously paltering, because while he was travelling between Geneva and Paris, Maria and Vera had been living in Austria for eighteen months without feeling embarrassed about wasting operational funds.

Maly's man, whom Nikolsky mentioned in his letter, is not identified. Possibly, it was Han Pieck, a Dutch artist recruited in 1930 by Ignatz Reiss. Reiss was an experienced OGPU 'illegal' who, like his friend Krivitsky, had previously worked for military intelligence. Pieck, codenamed COOPER, later operated under Maly's control in Holland, Switzerland, France, and Britain.[25] His work is well covered is several good books and previously secret documents from his MI5 files are now available to the public in the National Archives. Soon Nikolsky was summoned to Moscow to report in person.

Using money from the OGPU cashbox, in October 1933 Maria and Vera moved from the Wienerwald area to Vienna and settled at the Hotel Atlanta in the IX district, where most of the city's medical practices, laboratories, and hospitals are located. (The hotel was still open in the early twenty-first century and by all accounts seems not to have changed much in the intervening decades.) At the end of October the Soviet Embassy in Vienna asked the Austrian Foreign Ministry for an urgent visa for 'Lev Nikolaev' (the alias of Nikolsky at the time), who was in Moscow.[26]

The following day, the Austrian Embassy in Moscow sent a radiogram informing their ministry that 'Nikolaev' intended to visit Vienna for consultations with Dr Noorden, his family doctor.[27] In reality, Professor Dr Karl von Noorden could not help Vera and quite certainly had never been personally involved, because his medical speciality was diabetes mellitus, metabolism, and dietetics,[28] but not the heart deceases and rheumatism from which Nikolsky's daughter suffered.

This time, the Austrian authorities did not react too quickly to the Soviet request. On 3 November a memo was filed mentioning that the application was still under consideration. A week later the Austrian Embassy in Moscow sent another radiogram insisting on an urgent resolution of the case.[29] Finally, the visa was granted, and Nikolsky arrived in Vienna for a family reunion. Much later Nikolsky/Orlov had to testify about this period before the US Senate Committee. This is what he said:

Mr. ORLOV. I know of another case when, on personal instructions of Stalin, the NKVD tried to bribe one of the most important members of Mussolini's Cabinet... Well, I do not know whether he is alive and I would not like to mention his name right here. That was in the early thirties, and it had been arranged through an NKVD representative in Italy that the Cabinet Minister should come to Berlin to accept his bribe.

He came to the then head of the Soviet trade delegation in Berlin and they had a talk, and the head of the trade delegation had an envelope for him. There was $15,000.[30]

But even Orlov, who had no scruples about inventing stories, did not dare to say that he was personally involved in that operation when giving testimony under oath. A decade later, writing his second book, Orlov changed the story fabricating the following plot:

In the 1930s, the NKVD resident who was directing the underground intelligence in France lived there on a Canadian passport. He left for Rome to supervise an interesting operation which was designed to turn one of the key members of Mussolini's government into a secret Soviet collaborator. When the time for offering a substantial bribe drew near, the resident wrote to the Foreign Department of the NKVD a complete report about the operation and asked for final instructions. While awaiting an answer from Moscow, where the NKVD had to obtain the personal approval of Stalin, the resident decided to go to Capri for a short rest.[31]

This unnamed 'NKVD resident' was, of course, Nikolsky himself and the mysterious 'key member of Mussolini's government' none other than Giuseppe Bottai, Italy's Minister of Education between 1936 and 1943. However, in reality it is very doubtful that Pavel Zhuravlev, the NKVD head of station in Rome at the time, not to mention Nikolsky, could have had anything to do with Bottai, who at that time was deputy secretary of the Corporations (the reshaped Chamber of Deputies). Interestingly, Bottai, an ardent supporter of Mussolini before the war, became increasingly disenchanted with the Duce's leadership during the Second World War and took part in July's 1943 move to oust Mussolini. Later, he joined the French Foreign Legion and took part in Allied campaigns in France and Germany, returning to Italy in 1948. A devoted family man and one of the most famous actors of the period, as is clear from his recently published biography and his diaries,[32] Bottai has never been accused of having any contacts with the Soviets. It is impossible to say for sure how the Italian minister caught Nikolsky's attention, but it may have been because in 1934 he wrote a 'warning foreword' to the only edition of the Soviet leaders' writings that was published in Italy before the war.[33]

After Christmas, Nikolsky returned to his daily chores in Paris, travelling there by train via Geneva. The response to his old report came from the Centre five months later. Moscow asked him not to think about money and reminded him about his assignment.

On 24 March 1934 SCHWED reported to Moscow that, following instructions received from Paris from the 'illegal' resident Karin (JACK), he had signed up two new agents into his group, one codenamed B-205 (unidentified), and a JOSEPH.[34] Though little is known about B-205, who, it seems, was a young Frenchman with Communist views, JOSEPH was a code name of Rodolphe Lemoine, an experienced officer of the Deuxième Bureau, whose controllers were Reiss and Bystroletov. It is hard to imagine Nikolsky in the role of Lemoine's handler, as the Frenchman was 'as hooked on espionage as a drunk is on alcohol',[35] and SCHWED was simply not qualified to work with him. There is a JOSEPH who figures in the group's financial report to Moscow,[36] but it was probably a coincidence of code names, as sometimes happened. Anyway, a short while later it was reported that '205' was already working under Maly.

The last attempt of Nikolsky's group in Paris to make a recruitment was associated with the activities of the former electrician, Korotkov alias 'Rožecký', now posing as a Czech student. Evidently assisted by Mark

Zborowski,[37] a student of anthropology, recruited by the 'legal' NKVD station in France some time before, Korotkov/Rožecký enrolled at the Faculty of Anthropology of the University of Paris. There he met a young man who claimed to have been working part-time at the Deuxième Bureau as a document photographer. Nikolsky was also informed that this man's bride's father was an official at the French War Ministry.

Terribly excited, SCHWED immediately asked the Centre's permission to recruit such a promising candidate. To his great good fortune, Theodor Maly, who was assigned to verify this information, quickly found out that the 'student' was a dangle planted by the DST (dangles are enticing intelligence targets that are brought to the attention of an opposition service in the hope that he or she will be considered a bona fide recruit). The French had blown Korotkov's simple cover and started a game to learn more about his contacts and possibly catch him red-handed. Following Maly's warning, Korotkov was immediately sent back to Moscow, together with his wife. In April, a fortnight after his report about the two new members that he had allegedly added to his group (source 205 and JOSEPH), Nikolsky abandoned the operation and left Paris.

Before he bade farewell to France, a sudden meeting took place on a busy street. Its description in *Deadly Illusions* was almost certainly inspired by Bulgakov's masterpiece *Master and Margarita*. Slightly to paraphrase Orlov's biographers:

At the hour of sunset, on a hot spring day, two citizens appeared on the Grands Boulevards. One, about forty, in a grey summer suit, was short, dark-haired and well fed, his clean-shaven face adorned by small moustache. The other was a broad-shouldered not-so-very-young man with a mop of shaggy red hair, crumpled white trousers, and long stubble.

The first was none other than Lev Lazarevich Nikolsky, 'illegal' *rezident* of a powerful organization in Moscow, known by its initials as OGPU. His companion was a former Soviet diplomat, Vernik, now a scorned traitor and émigré.

When they had reached the shade of the linden trees, which were just turning green, the former diplomat hurried forward and exclaimed: 'Lyova!', then asking: 'Don't you recognise me?'

They stopped in the shadows, drank some wine and Nikolsky retired, pretending to be very busy. It was an April day of the year 1934...[38]

Nikolsky reported the meeting to Moscow, boarded a train, and departed for Geneva. It was just days after an RU operation in Paris was rolled up with twenty-one defendants facing trial. (As a result, thirteen spies received sentences totalling forty-one years.)

It is quite obvious that Orlov probably invented this episode, just as he invented most of the stories that appeared in his three books, published in Europe and the USA. The reason was a total and complete failure of his mission, and he had to find a way out of an unpleasant situation. It is possible, however, that Nikolsky met or saw Grigory Besedovsky, who, being first posted in Paris in 1928 as an adjoint or deputy at the trade legation, had by this time become Soviet chargé d'affaires in France. In October 1929, accused of counter-revolutionary 'plotting', Besedovsky escaped over the embassy wall and a year later published a book revealing a number of OGPU secrets.[39] Besedovsky had been granted political asylum in France and became a prominent member of the Russian community there.

In the meantime, 'Vernik' was not a complete invention. He was certainly part of the EXPRESS group, probably a driver or courier, and his name is mentioned, together with others, in at least one of the reports[40] of the EXPRESS group to Moscow.

One year later, in London, Nikolsky repeated the same trick that he had used in Paris in April 1934 by claiming that he had met an old acquaintance who could blow his cover, which gave him a good pretext for leaving the operation for the second time.

On 8 May Nikolsky informed his chiefs that he was leaving Paris for Switzerland.[41] At approximately the same time Steve Nelson, a candidate for the mysterious 'Arnold Finkelberg', an American whom Soviet intelligence decided not to identify and who served as this group's courier, returned to the USA.[42] He and 'Orlov' would meet again in Spain.

Steve Nelson, born Stjepan Mesaros in Croatia, was recruited in Moscow in 1931 or shortly after, during his two-year studies at the International Lenin School. Before he was sent to Spain as the political commissar of the Abraham Lincoln Battalion, he was a courier for the Comintern and the NKVD and, as we shall see later, had been engaged in Soviet espionage activities in the USA during the war. In August 1950 he was arrested and charged for attempting to overthrow the government. In 1953 he and five others were prosecuted and convicted under the Smith Act. During the same year, Orlov surfaced in New York while his book was hitting the headlines. After Nikita Khrushchev's revelations about Stalin's crimes, Nelson left the Communist Party.

6

Enterprise 'O'

The part of Orlov's history that attracted most attention and provoked a lot of speculation is his alleged work as a 'spymaster' in Britain. In their effort to prove that he was 'the mastermind' responsible for the recruitment of the infamous Cambridge spy ring, those who stood behind this disinformation project sought not only to demonstrate the foolishness of Western security services by claiming that they had failed to unmask an important recruiter and agent-runner in London but also to praise their own operation and the superior qualities of their intelligence officer, albeit a deserter, who managed to take in MI5 and Special Branch,[1] and later both the CIA and FBI.

In reality, the man who became known as Alexander Orlov played only a very small part in the wide-scale Soviet intelligence operation in the ISLAND (as Britain was codenamed in the OGPU correspondence). The operation began soon after the Bolshevik revolution and made Guy Liddell, head of counter-espionage during the Second World War, note in his diary: 'I am perfectly certain that they [Russians] are well bedded down here and that we should be making more investigations.'[2] Nevertheless, for about four decades after the establishment of MI5, Soviet espionage (unlike Soviet subversion) was not identified as a significant threat.

A massive attack on British institutions (the Foreign Office, Scotland Yard, intelligence and security services, political parties, military production facilities, armed forces, media, and so on) started after the Bolsheviks under Lenin and Trotsky had taken power in Russia and recognized that the British Empire was the main adversary of the young Soviet empire. The ARCOS raid in 1927, in which Liddell was involved, was a major coup in an attempt to uncover Soviet espionage networks in Britain. ARCOS, the All-Russian Cooperative Society Ltd, a British-registered company with only Soviet stockholders that began operations in London in October 1920,[3] was responsible for trading with the Soviet government[4] at the same time as serving as a front for espionage and propaganda activities. The chairman of the board and managing director of ARCOS was one R. P. Avramov, a civilian who had previously served as deputy Soviet trade representative in France and Germany. He was later sentenced to death and shot in Moscow.

Among those active in London during that period was Yakov ('Jan') Zhilinsky, head of personnel at ARCOS. He was described by MI5 in 1927 as one of the principal Soviet espionage agents in Western Europe, responsible in the UK for collecting both military and industrial intelligence as well as sponsoring Communist subversion.[5] The Security Service's sources were quite right in his case, and, apart from collecting all sorts of intelligence, Zhilinsky was responsible for liaison with Communist parties of the English-speaking countries.

Another suspect, Leonid Vladimirov, was probably a Red Army intelligence officer attached to the ARCOS Steamship Company in the 1920s. Vladimirov was involved in the purchasing of aircraft. Thereafter he was posted to the United States and later made a number of visits to the UK. Though MI5's suspicions regarding his role were never confirmed, the Security Service kept a file on him.[6] Vladimirov's colleague Ivan Orekhov, an engineer, came to London in 1926 as an employee of the same ARCOS Steamship Company. He was reported to have been involved in destroying secret files at the time of the ARCOS raid in 1927 and later left the country. However, both he and his wife appear to have continued working for ARCOS between 1929 and 1933. MI5 thought Orekhov worked for the OGPU.[7] Vasili Barabanov, allegedly a military intelligence officer, who served as a bookkeeper in the ARCOS Steamship Company in London between 1925 and 1927,[8] was yet another suspect.

Like many other employees of the Soviet institutions or businesses abroad, Isaak Groushko was a Russian émigré. He came to Britain as a political refugee in 1914. By 1922 he had made a career serving as the general manager of the Soviet trade delegation, where he was engaged in the purchase of aircraft machine guns for the Red Army. Naturally, he was suspected of having links to Soviet intelligence, but these were never conclusively established;[9] nor were those of Nikolai Klyshko, who in some sources is named as the first Soviet intelligence resident in London,[10] which is incorrect. Although the head of the Russian section Captain Maurice Bray, one of MI5's Russian speakers, concluded in July 1918 that

Klyshko was the 'most dangerous Bolshevik here', he probably had in mind Klyshko's communist propaganda activities but not his espionage.

From 1907 until the Bolshevik revolution in 1917 Klyshko lived in exile in London, where he found well-paid work with the famous Vickers company, which went through several name changes during the first decades of the twentieth century as it developed into a major warship and aircraft manufacturer. Klyshko married an English woman named Phyllis, described as tall, red headed, and very beautiful.[11] After 1917 Klyshko was very close to Maxim Litvinov, the party alias of Meir Henoch Mojszewicz Wallach-Finkelstein (simplified to Meer or Max Wallach), who at that time was active in the International Socialist Bureau and was later known as an unofficial Bolshevik representative in London. In the West, Litvinov became known as the Soviet government's roaming ambassador, appointed by Stalin as People's Commissar for Foreign Affairs in 1930. Until his sudden detention in London in 1918 (to be exchanged for Robert Bruce Lockhart, the first British envoy to Bolshevik Russia), Litvinov even lived in Klyshko's house in Hampstead's High Street. Like Litvinov, Klyshko was interned as a hostage on 6 September 1918 and subsequently deported, before returning to London in May 1920 with the Russian trade delegation headed by Leonid Krasin. During this short spell in Moscow Klyshko served as first deputy director of the state publisher Gosizdat. In early February 1920 he was briefly posted to Estonia as the Russian envoy. He served in that position for little more than a week, being succeeded by Isidor Gukovsky on 11 February. The latter, in turn, was succeeded by Litvinov in December. Once back in the UK, Klyshko was kept under surveillance. As a result of Lord Curzon's Memorandum, Klyshko had to leave Britain again.[12] It was only later that MI5 started to suspect him of setting up a spy ring headed by the pro-Bolshevik editor of the *Daily Herald*, William Norman Ewer.[13] After Klyshko had returned to Moscow in May 1923, he was appointed to head the Export Department of the People's Commissariat for Foreign Trade. In 1924–6 he was Soviet trade representative in China and in 1930–1 worked as manager of the technical bureau of the metal department of the Soviet Trade Delegation in Berlin. In this capacity he visited Britain at least four times.[14] On 2 September 1937 Nikolai Klyshko, who had never served in Soviet intelligence, was arrested in Moscow and a month later shot.

In the meantime, Mikhail Borodin, a prominent Comintern agent, spent six months in Britain in 1922, although he was ultimately arrested and deported following a tip-off from an MI5 'mole' within the party.[15] Finally, Wilfred Frances Remington Macartney was identified as a Russian agent tasked to collect aircraft intelligence. He was arrested in 1927, brought to trial on espionage charges in 1928, found guilty, and sentenced to ten years' imprisonment. He later served with the International Brigades in Spain.[16] Although no documents to prove this have surfaced so far, there is no doubt that Macartney was recruited by a member of the organization headed by Rudolf Kirchenstein (KNYAZ or PRINCE), known to Scotland Yard as Jacob Kirchenstein or 'Johnny Walker'.[17] A career military intelligence officer, Kirchenstein had served as the RU's head of station in Britain from 1924, first under Plenipotentiary Christian Rakovsky, then under Leonid Krasin, and then, after the latter's death in late November 1926, under Arkady Rosengoltz, the last Soviet diplomatic representative in London before relations were interrupted for two years.[18] Kirchenstein's friend Stefan Żbikowski (ALOIS), with whom he had spent time in Germany during the Hamburg Uprising some months before moving to London, was controlling the undercover RU cell, which, as reported,[19] was not too productive before the raid on the headquarters of ARCOS and the Soviet Trade Delegation at 49 Moorgate on 12 May 1927. On that day police decided personally to search one Anton Miller, a cipher clerk at ARCOS. During the following parliamentary debates Anton Miller was described as 'one of the leaders of the Russian spy organisation, in the very closest touch with the actual leader of it'.[20] In reality, it was Anton's brother Peter Miller, a cipher clerk of the Trade Delegation, who served as Kirchenstein's assistant. Others were the German communist Karl Bahn, Robert Koling alias 'Kaulin' from Riga, Stepan Melnichuk, and the already mentioned Zhilinsky (spelt 'Jilinsky' by the Scotland Yard report writer).[21] They were all members of the Kirchenstein espionage organization. The authorities were not aware of Żbikowski and his undercover cell, as, at that time, they knew nothing about the 'illegals', but when Kirchenstein, who was tailed, made contact with two individuals from the Air Ministry, E. G. Barton and T. R. Fiddy, in April 1927, Scotland Yard became concerned. Soon the raid of the ARCOS headquarters followed, although Kirchenstein warned in one of his letters intercepted by the Government Code & Cipher School that it would be better 'not to bring ARCOS into this mess'.[22] Naturally, Soviet chargé d'affaires Rosengoltz sent a letter of protest, but in Moscow it was noted that among the employees of the Trade Delegation and ARCOS there were many British communists.[23] Remarkably, during the first year of its British operation, ARCOS alone made £1,970,000 worth of purchases and by the end of 1921 almost tripled this turnover.[24]

Apart from Borodin, Comintern agents in London were also quite active,[25] and the Special Branch was tasked to deal with the problem. However, as the recently declassified documents demonstrate,[26] the Comintern OMS operating together with the OGPU and RU continued to send its representative to Britain and recruit new members into its networks using the CPGB functionaries and even former Metropolitan Police officers such as Walter Dale, Arthur Francis Lakey, and Jack Hayes as talent-spotters. In 1928 Lakey (MI5 alias 'Albert Allen') told the Security Service that two Special Branch men had been working for Ewer since 1922. This led to the arrest of Inspector Gilhoven and Sergeant Jane, along with Dale, whose diary was seized, revealing some of his clandestine activities as well as those of his friends. This included 'unremitting surveillance' of the Secret Intelligence Service (SIS) and GC&CS premises and their personnel. It also became known that in 1923 an SIS secretary had been targeted by Ewer's agent, Rose Edwardes, who acted under 'the false flag'.[27] After all, the perceived threat from communist subversion (rather than Soviet espionage) within British institutions in the interwar period was justified.

The ARCOS affair brought the already strained relations between Britain and the Soviets to a halt. Since the British general strike in May 1926, pressure had been mounting on Stanley Baldwin's government to break off diplomatic relations with Bolshevik Russia, which by now had become the Soviet Union. New evidence of Soviet espionage in the armed services in the spring of 1927 came as the last straw. On 26 May 1927 Sir Austen Chamberlain, then Secretary of State for Foreign Affairs, informed Rosengoltz that His Majesty's Government was breaking off diplomatic relations because of 'anti-British espionage and propaganda'. Ironically, during the last of the Moscow show trials in 1938, Rosengoltz was himself forced to confess to having been a spy for the British government from 1926 onwards.[28] The 'confession' did not help him, and on 15 March he was shot at the 'special facility' ('spetsobiekt') Kommunarka, together with eighteen other former diplomats, party, and state leaders, and OGPU–NKVD officers.

Lenin, Stalin, and other Soviet leaders considered Britain to be their main adversary, but following the ARCOS affair OGPU activities in the ISLAND were reduced for some time. Soviet military intelligence never stopped its operations against Britain, but it was decided to set up an operational base in the Netherlands and from there to penetrate the ISLAND. Ignatz Reiss, who was then working for the Intelligence Directorate of the Red Army and had recently been decorated with the Order of the Red Banner, moved from Prague to Amsterdam to organize the work. Among his Dutch agents was Henri Christiaan Pieck, and he was using two young German communist women, Hede Massing and Gerda Frankfurter, as his couriers.[29] Pieck would soon become a productive recruiter and agent-runner.

Once the dust had settled down after the ARCOS raid, clandestine work against Britain, codenamed Enterprise 'O' ('O' for *ostrov*, which means 'island' in Russian) in operational correspondence, was reactivated by Brun Ilk (BEER). In addition to his wide network of agents around Europe and a few confidential contacts in London, a new 'illegal' was sent from Moscow in the summer of 1930 specifically to establish himself in Britain. The name of the agent was Julius Hutschnecker,[30] an Austrian and an active member of the Kommunistische Partei Österreichs (KPÖ) (Austrian Communist Party), who had first been engaged in 1924 to work for the Mezhdunarodnaya Organizatsyia Pomoschi Rabochim (MOPR) (the International Workers' Aid Organization). As so often happened, in 1927 he was recruited by and worked for the OGPU. Artuzov, then deputy chief of its foreign department, sent Hutschnecker to Ilk. His arrival was preceded by the following message:

Your new officer has left and you will see him on 13–15 [August 1930]. We shall from now on call him HOFMANN ... He creates a good impression and should develop into a fine operator. We have not equipped him here very well and you will have to get him ready for work by providing him with a good cover, boots [personal papers], etc., without, however, forcing the pace.[31]

Two months later, Artuzov informed Ilk that HOFMANN was supposed to work under Ilk's direction in Enterprise 'O'—that is, in Britain. The deputy chief of INO informed his Berlin resident that, although Hutschnecker was well educated politically, he had never been involved in intelligence work and was therefore quite inexperienced in tradecraft.[32]

Finally, in the first half of October, Ilk sent HOFMANN to London, having obtained for him an Austrian passport in the name of 'Josef Lahodny'. One of Ilk's agents codenamed OS/29 (unidentified) accompanied him on that trip, and they both reached the ISLAND by the usual route of Copenhagen–Esbjerg–Harwich, arriving in Britain on 12 October 1930 without attracting any attention from the Security Service or Special Branch.

Soon the agent managed to introduce 'Lahodny' to the London representative of the German publishing house Adalbert Schulz Verlag. He also
introduced him to Charles Duff, an officer from the intelligence division of
the Foreign Office, over a meal at the Scott's fish restaurant on Haymarket
(which in the early 1980s moved to Mount Street in Mayfair. 'You will
certainly meet an Ian Fleming crowd there now', one ad informed its
patrons many years later). In October 1930, with Duff's help, HOFMANN
made many useful contacts. Back in Berlin, he reported to Ilk that the best
cover for him in London would be as a literary agent.[33] For the time being,
all went well.

On his next visit to England in November, Hutschnecker was again
accompanied by OS/29, and this time allegedly met another agent, OS/42,
described as 'an English journalist'. As soon as the man heard that
'Mr Lahodny' would be the new director of the Correspondents' Bureau, a
small news agency used as a front, he was 'pleased to retain the job as London
editor and to know that henceforth all organizational and financial issues
would be settled on the spot by the new chief'.[34] All this is, sadly, impossible
to verify independently, as it was Oleg Tsarev, a late co-author of Orlov's
biography, who provided this information. According to Tsarev, this Englishman was

a professional journalist who was an unlikely candidate for further promotion. The
diplomatic correspondent of a London newspaper, he frequently visited Berlin,
Rome, Belgrade, Vienna and Budapest. OS/29 met him in Berlin through an
American journalist and although this American recommended OS/29 as 'abso-
lutely reliable and beyond all suspicion', OS/42 agreed to the creation of the
Correspondents' Bureau only after consultation with the Foreign Office.[35]

While the identity of the English journalist remains obscure, the American
was almost certainly Frederick Robert Kuh, who had worked for the Soviet
ROSTA news agency in Vienna together with Sándor Rado and Walter
Krivitsky, two well-known Soviet intelligence operators. The Correspondents' Bureau mentioned above was probably nothing more than a branch of
the Federated Press of America (FPA), an organization known to have been
closely allied with Soviet intelligence.[36] The Security Service was quite
obviously not informed about Kuh's activities in Vienna, but his involvement with the FPA in London and friendship with a number of Soviet
diplomats, including extremely warm relations with Soviet Ambassador
Ivan Maisky, caused suspicions. Despite heavy surveillance and the Home

Secretary's warrant authorizing his phone tap, the authorities did not find any evidence of criminal wrongdoing.

Soon HOFMANN reported to Ilk:

OS/42 is convinced to this day that the bureau has a German–American background. There is considerable evidence to this effect in his whole work and behaviour, but only his closest friend OS/46 [unidentified] knows about this 'American line'... For various reasons, mostly of a material nature, OS/42 has become a fanatic as far as the bureau is concerned; recently it has become virtually his only source of income. That is why he is so concerned about it.

All the same, two emotions live in his breast. On the one hand, he wants to remain a good patriot and in all respects be looked upon with favour by the Foreign Office while, on the other, he conceals from it the 'American line' and the fact that OS/43 [unidentified] and OS/44 [unidentified] are collaborating with the bureau, since they, as highly-placed civil servants, are virtually breaking the law.[37]

When Hutschnecker visited London again on 15 January 1931, he obtained an alien's permit, giving 58c Lexham Gardens, Kensington, as his permanent address. Ilk proudly telegraphed to Artuzov: 'A few days ago I received a communication from HOFMANN in which he reported that he had already received a residence permit, a development he is very pleased about. In addition, he has been accepted as a member of a very well known English writers' club thanks to the warm recommendations of Duff.'[38] So far, so good.

But in March 1931 the resident urgently summoned his new agent to Berlin. Ilk explained to the Centre:

HOFMANN, contrary to my instructions not to work with the OS/42 group, and in particular with OS/46, beyond the framework of present activities and only to intensify them in keeping with our instructions to create the necessary periphery, has, probably in pursuit of excessive personal ambitions, exceeded my directives and decided to speak with OS/46 in fairly open terms and suggest to him that he should provide documentary material. This caused a sharp rebuke on the part of OS/46. I saw in this certain signs, which may lead to the denunciation of HOFMANN. His position is much more dangerous than I originally thought. I heard about this only on Monday from HOFMANN himself.[39]

Three days before leaving London, Hutschnecker was invited to a party. In mid-evening, as in a bad movie, the door opened and the couple who entered turned out to be old friends from Vienna. Ilk reported: 'The husband was a Zionist from Lithuania who had studied at Vienna University and knew HOFMANN well as a communist. His wife had also been a good friend of HOFMANN's wife in Vienna, who was working legally in our interests [Soviet Embassy] at that time, and knew about her activities.'[40]

Oleg Tsarev of the KGB Press Bureau, who provided this information to his British co-author Nigel West, decided it would be prudent not to disclose the identity of 'HOFMANN's wife in Vienna'. The KGB certainly had their reasons.

HOFMANN's wife, Elsa Hutschnecker, had been a student at the Faculty of Philosophy of Vienna University for two semesters and on 27 June 1924 defended her diploma. Her selected thesis on 'The History of the Peasant Movement in Russia, 1861–1910' won her a satisfactory mark.[41] During her student days she was also known as Esther Rosenzweig. Actually, it was her maiden name, given to her in 1900, when she was born to a Jewish family in the village of Rzhaventsy (now in the Ukraine). In the OGPU registry she was known successively as Lisa Gorskaya, ERNA, VARDO, Elisabeth Zubilina, and Elizaveta Zarubina. In 1924–8, together with Boris Bazarov (then Schpak), Ivan Zaporozhets, Ignatz Reiss, and other prominent members of the RIS, she was an employee of the Russian Legation in Vienna, and took Soviet citizenship in 1925. In the Austrian Foreign Ministry rosters of the time she figured as Elisaweta Hutschnecker, a typist. Elsa lived in Vienna at No. 134 Hauptstrasse, III District, not far from the Soviet Embassy. In Vienna, Fraulein Hutschnecker was registered as 'Jewish, single, student'.[42] She met her future husband Julius Hutschnecker when, as a member of the Bureau of the Central Committee of the Komsomol, a communist youth organization, he worked in Romania, while she was active in its Bessarabian branch. Elsa joined the KPÖ in 1923 (her party name was 'Anna Deutsch').[43] After taking Soviet citizenship, she was recruited to work for the OGPU and OMS as a translater and courier. Whether it was a match of love or a marriage of convenience to get a genuine Austrian passport is hard to say, maybe a mixture of the two. But the KGB archives reveal that in 1928 Elsa was sent to Moscow, where she was commissioned as an OGPU operative and went through some elementary instruction. In Moscow she assumed a new Russian-sounding name of 'Liza Gorskaya'. She was soon sent to Istanbul, Turkey, on a sensitive mission, where her task was to seduce and expose Yakov Blyumkin, the chief 'illegal' resident there. Blyumkin was also one of Trotsky's many supporters at the time the leader of the Bolshevik revolution was deported from his own country and settled on Prinkipo, his first station in exile. Liza became Blyumkin's mistress, which was not too difficult, and lured him back to the USSR, where this legendary assassin of the German Ambassador Graf von Mirbach back in 1918 soon faced the firing squad—not for the murder of Mirbach but for his friendship with Trotsky.

According to his KGB file, Julius Hutschnecker had been arrested for the first time in Vienna in 1915 and subsequently a number of times in Romania. In 1927 he came to Moscow and in 1930 was already working for the INO. In October, with a forged Austrian passport in the name of 'Anton Tauber', he successfully crossed the German border, slipping past the security police.[44] Artuzov informed Ilk that Hutschnecker should be prepared for clandestine work in the UK.

After that unfortunate meeting with her old Vienna friends in London and following Hutschnecker's final recall to the Soviet Union, Gorskaya–Hutschnecker was sent to Copenhagen as a female assistant/companion to Vasili Zarubin (alias 'Kartuunen'). Zarubin had been serving as the 'illegal' OGPU resident there since August 1927 after about a year in Finland. Zarubin joined the GPU in Moscow in January 1921. By that time he had already been married and had a one-year-old daughter Zoya. In April 1922, Zarubin was transferred to the Far Eastern Military District where he was appointed deputy chief of the so-called Special Department (known in the Red Army as the OO)—an internal security service under the GPU control. In 1925 he was invited to the foreign intelligence (INO), accepted and was sent with the family to China. There, in Harbin, in 1926 Olga Zarubina met Naum Eitingon, another OGPU officer who just arrived after a mission in Shanghai. From his young years Eitingon was a great womanizer and heart breaker. Although she had been married with a now six-year-old daughter, Olga let herself be seduced by Eitingon and left her husband who was urgently transferred to Finland. Because in China Eitingon was using the alias 'Naumov', Olga, who was his second wife, became Naumova while her daughter would keep the name Zoya Zarubina all her life.

After a rather dull tour of duty in Finland, Zarubin was sent to Denmark where he was soon joined by Gorskaya. By that time INO was separated from the Operational Directorate (SOU) and brought under the direct control of the OGPU Collegium. Within the INO Mikhail Gorb was placed in charge of the European operations. Although there is no evidence of her divorce from Hutschnecker, such trifles as that do not count so she and Zarubin became lovers. Her Austrian husband Hutschnecker was dismissed from the service after the incident in London, arrest in Berlin and a full report by an OGPU mole high in the anti-espionage division of the Berlin police about the case. He was lucky enough to escape the purges. She remained in the ranks, lived a long life, and died in Moscow, aged 87, in a car accident.

But before it all happened, in January 1930 Zarubin was summoned to Switzerland where Gorb informed him that he was now sent to France with a Czech passport. In spite of his good position in Copenhagen and Lisa still there, Zarubin obeyed the orders and using the Czechoslovak passport in the name of 'Jaroslav Kočík', a businessman, settled in the resort town of Antibes in the Côte d'Azur. Here Zarubin was lucky enough to meet Maiya Nezhinskaya whom he used all his charm to win over because she was from Paris, Zarubin's next destination, and came from a well-to-do Russian émigré family. After a while the whole Nezhinsky family would be working for the OGPU. Zarubin remained in France until 1933. In Paris, he married Lisa Hutschnecker and they became Jaroslav and Marianna Kočík. In his situation report to Moscow, Ilk wrote about Hutschnecker:

The HOFMANN case will, in all probability, leave a trace that in time could have serious consequences. In any case, everything points to the fact that Berlin can no longer remain a base for work against the ISLAND. As long as three weeks ago I reached the conclusion that the time has come when it will have to be transferred to some other location in the West. I think Paris would be the best choice.[45]

Naturally, a large spy network covering many countries but without multiple levels of sources, support personnel, and supervisors, will one day be compromised. This indeed happened to the Ilk organization, and several agents were eventually arrested. Ilk's residency was shut down in February 1933.[46] Basing his conclusions on Mitrokhin's notes, Christopher Andrew has perhaps certain grounds for making a rather critical assessment of Ilk's work (and that of his deputy, Maurice Weinstein).[47] At the same time, the OGPU needed three case officers—Fyodor Karin (JACK), Ivan Kaminsky (MOND), and Boris Bazarov (KIN and NORD)—to take over the Ilk–Weinstein group of agents and confidential contacts. After the ARCOS raid, Ilk certainly tried to restore the OGPU work in Britain, but it was a new member of Bazarov's group, Dmitri Bystroletov (ANDREI, later HANS),[48] who was first able to recruit agents at the Foreign Office who could obtain secret and confidential information. They were not high-fliers but were important enough to provide high-grade intelligence.

His star agent at the Foreign Office was Captain Ernest Holloway Oldham (codenamed ARNO), who delivered FO secrets that were much praised by the Lubyanka. Oldham was a walk-in who offered his services to the Soviets in Paris in 1929. The OGPU head of station Volovich (alias 'Yanovich') at first refused to see him, believing the British had sent an agent-provocateur. But a month later Oldham called again, bringing some secret documents to which he had access. It was first arranged that ARNO would meet his Soviet handlers outside Britain—in Paris, Berlin, and Amsterdam, where he travelled regularly throughout 1932 and 1933. In 1933 Soviet intelligence lost him for a while, but Bystroletov succeeded in tracking him down in a Paris bar. After the contact had been re-established, Bystroletov, posing as an Italian artist Joe Pirelli, was sent to London to ensure close supervision of this valuable source. He quickly seduced Lucy Oldham, the agent's wife, who was fourteen years older than her husband. Mrs Oldham became Bystroletov's mistress, informer (henceforth codenamed MADAM), and helper. Unbeknownst to the OGPU, by mid-July Oldham was dismissed from the Foreign Office. The Security Service had become suspicious of him to the point that a phone intercept was placed to find out more about his possible links to a hostile power. At the end of July, Oldham checked into the nursing home at 31 Queens Gate, West London, where he was under constant surveillance from British agents. On 25 July he checked out briefly, returning home before flying the same day to Vienna in the company of his Soviet handler. Upon their return, Oldham moved out of the family home at 31 Pembroke Gardens, Kensington, and took up lodging in the Hotel Jules, formerly known as the Waterloo Hotel, at 85–86 Jermyn Street.

By September 1931 the Centre was praising Bazarov's group efforts: 'I consider it a brilliant move. Artur [Artuzov] also read your messages and asked me to inform you that he was very satisfied with your work. Once again, having read your report for the second time, I cannot but admire your exemplary operational accomplishment.'[49]

In November 1932, Bystroletov was awarded a gun with the inscription 'for the relentless struggle against the counterrevolution'.[50] The award was given because he had demonstrated outstanding abilities and exceptional persistence in operational work. In spite of his great achievements, he was arrested in September 1938, sentenced to a long term, but survived the Gulag, was exonerated after Stalin's death, and managed to write his memoirs, a large part of which remains secret even now.[51] Bystroletov, who had only been known to MI5 as 'John' with the family name 'Buis-troleto',[52] died in Moscow in May 1975. The Security Service learned his true story only in the 1980s.

Back in the 1930s, Bystroletov knew that Oldham (ARNO) was a heavy drinker. When in 1932 he arrived in London at Christmas time, he found ARNO in a poor state. This was partly a result of stress, as Oldham became increasingly nervous about the risks of selling British secrets to the Soviets. Sometimes, in order to put more pressure on him, Bystroletov invited Bazarov to their meetings, playing a soft man/hard man game, with Bazarov posing as 'a rather menacing Italian Communist named da Vinci'. Perhaps as a result, Oldham was unable to curb his drinking. Finally, Lucy told her lover that British intelligence was on her husband's trail and that Oldham believed that the permanent under-secretary at the Foreign Office, Sir Robert Vansittart, had personally put him under observation. Bytroletov left England by the first plane, as Bazarov reported to Moscow at the end of July 1933.[53] Before leaving he managed to get from his agent the names of five or six of his Foreign Office colleagues, together with details of their private lives.

On 21 September one of the 'Watchers' reported: 'This man is still living at Jules Hotel and there is no indication of him leaving. Most of his time, when away from the hotel, he spends at the Chequers Public House, Duke Street, and he is invariably there from 6.30 p.m. to the closing hour . . . In my opinion, Oldham is rapidly heading for a breakdown.'[54] He was right. In late September 1933, almost a year to the day after his resignation from the Foreign Office, Oldham was found unconscious in his house in Pembroke Gardens. He was promptly taken to the hospital and pronounced dead on arrival. The OGPU was sure that the British had physically eliminated the unmasked agent by making his death appear to be suicide. They even feared that ANDREI/Bystroletov would also be hunted and perhaps dealt with in a similar way. He was, therefore, advised not to go to the ISLAND again without specific instructions from Moscow. Eight decades later one of Oldham's distant relatives wrote:

It is difficult to know whether to feel sympathy or anger towards Oldham. His file reveals details of a weak and greedy man, ultimately broken by drink, drugs and personal failings. However, once he'd got himself into trouble, the tragic way his life unravelled under pressure from both the British and the Soviets left him feeling there was no way out. Either way, his case certainly shows that espionage was not the glamorous lifestyle depicted by Ian Fleming's tales of James Bond—it was far more sordid, damaging and amateurish than that.[55]

Ironically, for Oldham's Soviet controller, it was exactly the glamorous lifestyle described in Ian Fleming's books, written long after these events. Bystroletov was not unduly disturbed by the loss of Oldham when he heard about his agent's fate. He concluded that Geneva, where several of Oldham's former colleagues were working as cipher clerks with the British delegation to the League of Nations, would be a good place for recruiting new agents. Less than three months after his hurried departure from London, in December 1933, he made contact there with Raymond Oake, in the words of Christopher Andrew 'one of the most promising potential recruits in the Communications Department' despite his lowly position of 'temporary clerk'. Moscow decided to entrust the cultivation of Oake to Henri Christiaan Pieck,[56] another OGPU 'illegal' with a wide circle of friends and acquaintances among British representatives in Geneva. Oake was codenamed SHELLEY, but it remains unknown whether he was fully recruited and, if he was, what information he provided. It seems that his main service to the OGPU was to introduce Pieck to Captain John H. King.[57] King was another 'temporary clerk' who joined the same Communications Department as Oake in 1934. The cultivation of both of them must have been supervised by Reiss, since by the spring of 1934 Bazarov had already left for Moscow, where he was appointed section chief at the INO.[58] Gradually King, henceforth codenamed MAG, became one of the most important OGPU sources of secret intelligence in the Foreign Office.

Unsurprisingly, *The Authorized History of MI5* does not even mention Oake's name, nor does it describe a subsequent damage assessment. His file, if it exists, has never been released to The National Archives. The KGB archivists also chose not to disclose any pertinent information, pointing only to SHELLEY's reluctance to cooperate, which can be deduced from Bystroletov's correspondence with the Centre during 1934.[59] On 8 October, Bystroletov reported to Moscow:

In Geneva COOPER [Pieck] became acquainted with a cipher clerk named King. He is about fifty years old, an Irishman who lived in Germany for about ten years and learned to speak German perfectly. A lively and inquisitive person, not stupid and well educated. He draws a sharp distinction between himself with his cultured ways and the 'pompous fools' of Englishmen. He likes music and is knowledgeable, and is keen on the theatre. He is very eccentric and likes magic.[60]

So the origin of the cryptonym MAG given to King becomes clear.

Seven months after his first meeting with Pieck, as seen from the documents copied by Mitrokhin in the KGB archives, King began to hand over 'large amounts of classified material, including Foreign Office telegrams, ciphers and secret daily and weekly summaries of diplomatic correspondence'.[61] Thanks to a tip from Krivitsky, King was unmasked as a Soviet asset, confessed, and was sentenced to ten years' imprisonment.[62] But that would happen later.

Moscow concluded that about 30 per cent of King's material had been the same as that provided by Francesco Constantini (DUNCAN), its long-serving agent at the British Embassy in Rome. The overlap was regarded as useful for checking the authenticity of the documents received from both agents. So Sloutsky, INO's deputy chief and 'managing director of Enterprise "O"', decided to transfer DUNCAN from the legal station in Rome, headed by Zhuravlev, to one of the leading Soviet agent controllers, Moisey Markovich Akselrod (codenamed OST), who would be acting 'from the illegal positions'. In 1934 Akselrod was sent to Rome using an Austrian passport to act as Constantini's controller.[63] He was ordered to suspend his regular meetings with the agent and recalled to Moscow three years later when the Centre suspected that Francesco Constantini (as well as his brother Secondo, a servant in the same embassy) was working under British control, a very far-fetched idea, taking into account the amount of extremely valuable classified material corroborated by other sources that he and his brother (codenamed DUDLEY) were delivering.

After Krivitsky had tipped off the Security Service about King, he was invited to visit London, because MI5 was anxious to know more about possible Soviet spies operating against British interests. Although he knew nothing about the Constantini brothers, he was able to identify over seventy Soviet intelligence personnel and agents operating abroad, most of them previously unknown to the Security Service. As one of the reports acknowledged, Krivitsky provided MI5 'for the first time with an insight into the organization, methods and influence of the RIS'.[64] (The acronym RIS—Russian Intelligence Services—referred to all secret services of the Soviet Union, at the time the NKVD, Razvedupr (military intelligence), and Comintern/OMS.) With the advantage of hindsight, it is apparent that during his London debriefing Krivitsky was able to reveal only small nuggets of information, despite the fact that from 1921 he had been a civil employee of the Razvedupr and in October 1935 was sent to Holland as INO's resident.[65] His confused and misleading information was seriously garbled and he admitted that 'he had only a general knowledge of matters affecting those countries other than Germany', and that he 'left English affairs largely to his assistant, Parparoff'.[66] Unfortunately, although his material should not be regarded as an overall deliberate attempt at misinformation, deceit, or falsification, Krivitsky's information was wildly inaccurate, owing to strict compartmentalization and lack of access because of his lowly status, and because, like Orlov after him, he invented a lot. Thus, his whole story about the military intelligence directorate of the Red Army (for which he had worked for about twelve years), its personnel, general organization, and system of intelligence collection abroad, must be dismissed as pure invention. In reality, contrary to Krivitsky's claims, Fyodor Karpovich Parparov had never served in the Red Army intelligence but since 1930 had been the OGPU 'illegal' resident in Germany. That is, Parparov's position was higher than that of Krivitsky, first, because he was a commissioned officer and, secondly, because Germany was considered far more important than The Netherlands, especially after 1933. Parparov never had anything to do with 'English affairs'. He was recalled with his family to Moscow in the spring of 1938 in connection with Krivitsky's defection. He later operated in Iran, and from 1943 was a member of Sudoplatov's 4th Department (subversion and sabotage behind the enemy lines).[67] Miraculously, he managed to survive the purges.

Krivitsky could not know that the RU leadership, cautious after the ARCOS raid and the following interruption of diplomatic relations, decided not to set up a permanent residency in London. One of its experienced officers from Latvia named Kristofors (Kristaps) Salniņš (pronounced Sal-nyn-sh), who, like Lenin three years before him, lived in London in 1908 keeping a safe house for the Russian revolutionaries, visited Britain undercover in 1930–2 controlling agents. After graduating from the Frunze Military Academy, Brigade Commissar Mikhail Yakovlevich Weinberg, alias 'Sokolov', was sent to London in 1932 as the RU's 'legal' resident, posing as Manager of the Engineering Department of Arcos Ltd. After four years of successful work, military engineer 3rd grade A. F. Belikov succeeded him. The Security Service suspected Weinberg/Sokolov of having an intelligence function, because he was the actual receiver of aircraft plans that were passed over to the Russians by a Communist draftsman named Eric Camp. In 1936 Camp was bound over for an offence under the Official Secrets Act,[68] and Weinberg/Sokolov had to leave Britain. After his return to Moscow, Weinberg was promoted to acting chief of the 3rd Section, the work of which Krivitsky discussed at length during his interviews at the London Langham hotel,[69] albeit entirely incorrectly. In 1938 Weinberg was arrested, accused of spying, and shot.

Under Berzin or until November 1935, the structure of the Razvedupr did not change. It consisted of five departments and several supporting sections. Formally, its 3rd Department dealt with information and statistics, but actually its analysts were responsible for estimating all collected intelligence and its value to customers. It was headed by Alexander Matveyevich Nikonov, a very experienced intelligence officer. Krivitsky said about Nikonov:

Nikonov was an expert on the Near East, knew Arabic and other eastern languages and was head of the VNO, the Military Scientific Society. This Society though not part of the Fourth Department [sic, IV Directorate] worked closely with it. Many of the summaries compiled by the third section were submitted to Nikonov for his consideration and frequent debates and meetings with members of the Fourth Department were based thereon.[70]

In reality, Nikonov was one of the leaders of the Soviet military intelligence and his responsibilities were estimates and planning.

In the Intelligence Directorate of the Red Army (RU) under Berzin were 111 officers and 190 civilian employees in 1934.[71] At that time Krivitsky, according to his biographer, was serving a six-month term in the Austrian prison.[72] In October 1935, he joined the INO and was sent to Holland as the 'illegal' NKVD resident.[73] Naturally, his knowledge about both Soviet secret services was very limited.

Soon after Weinberg's departure, Nikolai Vladimirovich Aptekar arrived as a chauffeur at the Soviet Embassy in London, first to the Naval Attaché in 1937 and two years later to the Military and Air Attaché. From the VENONA intercepts MI5 knew that in reality Aptekar, codenamed IRIS, was an intelligence officer. From the same source they also knew that the Secretary to the Soviet Military Attaché by the name of Semyon Davydovich Kremer, who arrived together with Aptekar, was another RU officer. However, for a long time this information was classified as 'Top Secret'.

Based on the information provided by Krivitsky to MI5, Gary Kern writes:

The one person Krivitsky thought the British should keep their eyes on was Simon Kremer, Fourth Department [sic] rezident in London. He was a legal, working under cover of Secretary to the Military Attaché, hence could be located. Krivitsky asked to see photographs of the Soviet Embassy staff, as names might be changed, and when shown a photo of Kremer, who evidently used his real name, made a positive identification. Kremer, an early contact of Kim Philby [sic], had not been recalled, but had remained in London with his wife and two children since 1937.[74]

Writer Nigel West also mentions Kremer: 'Deutsch's decision to rent a flat in Lawn Road is curious, for as well as having Jurgen Kuczynski at No. 6 and Gertrude Sirnis [*sic*][75] as neighbours, others living in the same block included Simon Kremer, the GRU rezident at the Soviet embassy.'[76] In reality, Kremer, codenamed BARCH, had never been the RU resident in London, as the Security Service knew from the intercepted radio traffic. Kremer joined the Intelligence Directorate of the Red Army soon after the outbreak of the war in Spain. He could not and indeed never had any contact with Philby, who, in the first place, had been recruited and run by the NKVD and at the time of Kremer's arrival was in Spain. In London Kremer was one of the case officers working under Division Commander Arkady Kuzmich Sirkov. Interestingly, his name is not even mentioned in the GRU history. Sirkov succeeded Army Corps Commander Vitovt Kazimirovich Putna, who had served as the Soviet Military Attaché in London from 1934 to 1936, when he was suddenly recalled to Moscow only to be arrested and executed.[77] Both military attachés were much higher in rank and importance than Kremer, who successfully operated in Britain until August 1942, even serving as acting head of station between 3 March and 10 October 1940, when his new boss arrived. Colonel Ivan Andreyevich Sklyarov (BRION) graduated from the General Staff Academy in 1939 before he was sent to London as the new Soviet Military Attaché and at the same time, which is not a rule, as RU resident. From 1941, using SONIA and SERGEY as cut-outs,[78] Kremer was controlling Klaus Fuchs, one of the leading scientists working on 'Tube Alloys'—the British atomic bomb project. Krivitsky's information, of course, could not help here. But in the last interwar decade he was the only source who could tell the Security Service at least something about the Soviet intelligence plans regarding Enterprise 'O'.

7

Vienna, Copenhagen, and London: 19 June–25 July 1934

Yet another person who could help the Security Service unmask the most important Soviet spies in Britain but preferred to keep his mouth shut was Lev Lazarevich Nikolsky, who would become known to MI5 as 'Nikolsky, alias SCHWED, alias Lyova, alias Orlov'.[1] One day in 1934, three months after he had hastily left Paris, Nikolsky was enjoying a warm Viennese summer with his family when a telegram arrived from Moscow directing him to London without delay.

His new mission briefing was remarkable in many aspects. The KGB decided to release only two pages (1 and 3), deleting some important information from what remained and publishing an abridged version of the text.[2] The instruction from the Centre signed by Artuzov informed SCHWED (Nikolsky) that in London he should take over a group of sources previously handled by ANATOLY (Yevgeny Mitskewicz). His main priority was to arrange for 'uninterrupted and regular' communication with another 'illegal' on the ISLAND, codenamed MAR (Ignaty Reif), and with Moscow Centre. At the end, SCHWED was instructed to travel to Paris, where his meeting with MAR would be set up by PYOTR (Stanislaw Glinski), the legal station chief based at the embassy. The letter also provided details of how to contact MAR in London. The message read (verbatim):

1/ You are being assigned, as part of the reorganization, to direct the group previously controlled by comrade ANATOLY [Mitskewicz]. The tasks of the group: cultivation, development and infiltration [of agents] into British intelligence organizations in the centre /London/ and periphery—LATVIA, FINLAND and ESTONIA.

The principal task of the London part of the group is penetration of the [British] intelligence service for unmasking its operations on our territory.

GROUP's COMPOSITION: 1/ your assistant for the central group [London] is Comr. MAR [Reif], the officer of [Moscow] Centre personally known to you. 2/ Comr. ARNOLD [Arnold Deutsch], our employee who worked for JACK's [Fyodor Karin] residency, a member of our compatriots [Communist Party], a group leader and technical worker. As for his personal and operational qualifications, he can be used as controller of individual sources as well as personal assistant to MAR in communication matters. 3/ GRIMM [unidentified]—a former source of the Berlin residency /probably known to you/ [deleted]. You may use him to orient yourself in finding a cover.

TO CONTACT MAR: MAR's address in London: 16 Brixton Hill, S.W.2 Max Wolisch.

To contact MAR through ARNOLD: London, W14, Castleton Road, Leontine Williams für M-r Deutsch.

Through GRIMM: [deleted, end of page 1, paragraphs 2 and 3 missing]

[Page 3]...meeting with YEGOR [unidentified] in order to inform him about a meeting with you. The meeting place with YEGOR is known to MAR but just in case I repeat it [deleted].

4/ You must first of all arrange for uninterrupted and regular communication with MAR on the ISLAND and with us. In the past two months we received two letters from MAR in secret ink that we were unable to develop. Such communication can certainly not satisfy us in terms of its form and periodicity. You must therefore take care that we should be able to: 1/ receive mail from you and MAR regularly, 2/ send telegraph messages to you and receive telegrams from you reporting the progress of your work.

It does not exclude corresponding in secret ink but this channel may duplicate other means [of communication]. ARNOLD [Deutsch], as the member of MAR's group who is well versed in photographic and secret ink techniques, will help you to solve the problem. For control letters home [to the Centre], here is the direct address and a [chemical] recipe /known to ARNOLD / for you and MAR: Moscow, B[olshaya] Serpukhovka, 7 Serpukhovsky Lane, apartment 7, to M. F. POPOVA /the initials and the family name on the envelope should be underlined/.

5/ By return letter inform us about the cash balance with MAR and you. Draft a budget necessary for your group. It should include: a/ salaries of the group members /SCHWED, JEANNE,[3] MAR, ARNOLD etc; b/ payments to sources, operational expenses of the sources, operational expenses of the group, travel expenses of the group, costs of the cover [a small private business that Nikolsky/Goldin later registered in London].

6/ Before you submit your budget [proposal] and get our approval, we are bringing forward an advance of 100 pounds that you should confirm by a separate receipt.

7/ At the time of this letter dispatch we received from MAR [Reif], currently in Copenhagen, the following [deleted] information: 'The group has recruited the son of the Anglo-agent Philby, counsellor of Ibn Saud. Also recruited is a female employee [deleted, possibly Melita Norwood][4] who has materials [deleted].[5] MAR established contacts and started working with the sources 1/ INSPECTOR [unidentified, possibly George Whomack], 2/ GOT [Percy Glading] and 3/ PROFESSOR [unidentified, possibly Maurice Dobb]. There are also leads and reports. MAR is waiting to get in touch with ANATOLY [Mitskewicz] and be recalled home.' We informed MAR by telegraph that he should immediately travel to Paris to meet you and ANATOLY. His recall is not in the agenda at the moment. As soon as we get his answer, we shall inform you by a telegram about the date of his arrival in Paris, while PYOTR [Stanislaw Glinski, the NKVD station chief] will arrange for your meeting with him.

8/ By a return mail we are expecting yours and MAR's detailed report concerning the work already done and a prospective plan for the near future.[6]

MI5 seems to have been unaware of the presence of Mitskewicz in London. In 2009 his official SVR biography, proudly displayed on the SVR website, confirmed that Yevgeny Mitskewicz was sent to London in 1931 and remained there until 1933.[7] It gives no further details about his status in the UK, but, because his name is missing from the London Diplomatic List of the period, it is clear that he operated under cover. (In the spring of 1927, as an aftermath of the ARCOS affair, the Conservative British government broke off diplomatic relations with the Soviets, but they were permanently restored in 1929, when the Labour Party headed by Ramsey Macdonald came to power. Ambassador Grigory Sokolnikov presented his Letter of Credence on 20 December of the same year. His diplomatic staff included Counsellor Dmitry Bogomolov, 2nd Secretary David Oldfield, and Press Attaché Maximilian Joelson.)

From the very beginning Nikolsky's instruction from Moscow seems strange. It is mentioned that SCHWED was to take over a group 'previously controlled by ANATOLY' (Mitskewicz). Then, the 'group's composition' is given as Reif (MAR), Deutsch (ARNOLD), and an unidentified 'former source in Berlin' (GRIMM). But neither Deutsch nor Reif was in London when Mitskewicz left the ISLAND in early 1933, as both arrived there for the first time in 1934. And, as shall be seen, the sources allegedly run by ANATOLY in London were collecting military, scientific, and technical intelligence and had nothing whatsoever to do with 'penetrating British intelligence organizations'. This 'instruction to Orlov from the Centre' looks like an improved and corrected version of the original telegram produced to enhance his image and fool the readers about his real aims on the ISLAND, which were to relieve Mitskewicz and Reif and take control over the remaining group of agents.

Mitskewicz was informed about two groups of agents in England, neither of which was active, when he was leaving London in 1933. One, in the Woolwich Arsenal, consisted of Percy Glading, George Whomack, Albert Williams, Charles Munday, and perhaps one or two others. The first four were later arrested and went on trial. Glading, Whomack, and Williams were found guilty of espionage and sentenced to different prison terms, while Munday pleaded not guilty and was acquitted. About the second group nothing has been established so far, but it was probably affiliated to the Soviet trading organization Russian Oil Products (ROP), which was registered as a British limited-liability company in 1924. All its shareholders were Russian nationals, which did not go unnoticed by the Security Service. According to its *Authorized History*, 'MI5 and the Special Branch calculated in 1930 that ROP had almost a thousand employees, about one-third of whom were members of the CPGB, and had built up a network of thirty-three offices, depots and installations across the UK'. The service reported in 1932 that 'one of the principal comrades who acts as liaison between ROP and the Party' was Percy Glading. ROP provided a sophisticated front for the increasing Soviet scientific and technological intelligence operations of the 1930s.[8] All this makes perfect sense. But the instruction to Nikolsky, formulated as 'the principal task of the London part of the group is penetration of the [British] intelligence service for unmasking its operations on our territory', seems an entirely new and highly questionable endeavour. With all their paranoia, the Centre should have been aware that all these 'operations' were limited to the underfunded efforts of the official SIS stations in the form of the Passport Control Organization (PCO), whose officers were technically attached to the embassies and whose cover, some say, wore steadily thinner as the interwar decades dragged on.[9] Although it was only in 1932 that Compton Mackenzie disclosed in his *Greek Memories* that the SIS existed, it had never been a secret for the OGPU, which had watched every move of its officers in Russia.

In early 1933 Mitskewicz reported to Moscow:

There are two intelligence groups 'on ice' in England, one of which is the Arsenal group...made up of employees of 1) the Arsenal (testing shells and weapons); 2) Armstrong (tanks, guns, rifles); 3) Fürst-Brown (tanks and armoured steel). A negative feature of this group is that it is led by a prominent member of the local Communist Party [Glading]. The group itself consists of non-party people...[10] Reif could be sent to London (without his wife) as illegal *rezident* and only these two groups should be given to him.[11]

After he had read this report, Artuzov's first impulse was to send to London Vasili Zarubin (codenamed BETTI and MAKSIM), one of the 'illegal' residents in Paris. He was to be assisted by Deutsch (ARNOLD and STEFAN) and Reif (MAR). Deutsch was to operate under his own name as an agent-recruiter and technical assistant and Reif, alias 'Max Wolisch', was to be a group leader controlling existing sources.[12] But the penetration of either MI5 or SIS was not on the agenda.

From January 1933 Deutsch was in Paris helping Fyodor Karin (JACK), another supervisor of an undercover cell[13]—that is, like Zarubin, an 'illegal' resident. Deutsch had a great talent for intelligence work. He later wrote in his NKVD biography that he 'carried out technical tasks for him [Karin], photography, etc., and set up crossing points across the French frontier to Belgium, Holland and Germany'. Apart from this, he tried to establish contact with fishermen in France, Holland, and Belgium in order to use fishing boats to install radio equipment, in case of war.[14] During this time Deutsch recruited two young women for the OGPU,[15] one of whom, codenamed LUXI,[16] later joined him in London.

In October Deutsch was informed about his new assignment: he was going to the ISLAND. After a short meeting with Zarubin and his wife in Paris, he went to Austria, and, according to his own biography written in Moscow in December 1938, recruited PFEIL ('Arrow') and JOHN (unidentified) as new agents.[17] Previously in Vienna he had introduced Edith Suschitzky to his OGPU case officer, who went under the name of 'Igor Vorobyov' but whose real name was Lebedinsky (codenamed ZIGMUND). Vorobyov was accredited as 'chef-adjoint du service consulaire' of the Soviet Embassy at 45–47 Reisnerstrasse in the III district.[18] Deutsch wrote: 'In February 1934 I went to London where I recruited EDITH [Edith Suschitzky] whom I already knew in Vienna.'[19] He left Austria on 31 January 1934, informing the authorities that he was 'moving abroad'.[20] It was his duty to report his moves and he complied.

At the same time Zarubin was summoned to the Centre, where Artuzov received him, together with Otto Steinbrück, then chief of the INO department responsible for political intelligence 'in the capitalist countries of the West'.[21] Artuzov awarded BETTI with an important NKVD medal 'Honourable Chekist' and told him about his new mission in London. Zarubin was to travel there via Geneva, where he was to stay for a while preparing grounds for his undercover work in the UK and meeting Reif, his future assistant.[22]

Russian sources provide contradictory information about Reif/Wolisch. In the Russian-language version of *Deadly Illusions*, Tsarev and Costello state that 'Reif was travelling...on a stolen Austrian passport No. 468302 issued in Vienna in 1933'.[23] In the KGB-sponsored biography of the Zarubins, 'Ignaty Reif (MAR)...had a genuine Austrian passport in the name of Max Wolisch'.[24] Austrian archival documents do not specify when his passport was issued. They show only that Max Wolisch, born on 9 May 1902 in Lemberg (now Lwów), domiciled in Bad Vöslau, Baden bei Wien, Austrian, atheist, single, trader, came to Vienna on 29 August 1933, staying there for two weeks and residing at No. 19 Hegergasse in the 3rd District.[25] Then he checked out and, unlike Deutsch, disappeared. As the photo of Wolisch in the Austrian police archives has not been found, it is impossible to compare it with the one published by the RIS,[26] but there is little doubt that this 'Wolisch' was the Soviet 'illegal' Reif. It is also clear that his passport was genuine (as he had no problem registering with the Vienna police) although certainly obtained by fraudulent means.

In Geneva, Zarubin met Reif and instructed him to travel to London and establish contact with an Englishman whom Zarubin had recruited some time before in Paris. This was the editor of a British magazine, which Zarubin planned to use as cover for his espionage activities.[27] On the way to London Reif visited Copenhagen, his operational base.

On 15 April 1934 he duly registered in the UK as a business representative of a Scandinavian company with his address as No. 17 Talbot Square, close to London's Paddington Station. In the meantime, Zarubin went to Schwyz in Central Switzerland, half an hour's drive from Zug and Lucerne, where his son Peter attended a boarding school and where Zarubin spent two weeks. Reif/Wolisch met him there on the way back from London. He also brought new instructions received from Moscow. Instead of England, a telegram from the Centre ordered BETTI to go to Austria, where an important rendezvous was scheduled.[28] Even before the war, Austria was a convenient meeting point and supplied Soviet undercover operators with genuine passports for quick cash.

Zarubin was informed that in Austria he would see Boris Berman (code-named SEMYON), one of the INO chiefs. Before moving to foreign intelligence, together with Sloutsky, Nikolsky, and Reif, Berman had served in the EKU. His elder brother, Matvei, also a Chekist, assisted by Sloutsky, had helped the OGPU leadership make up a fake 'counter-revolutionary plot' that resulted in the infamous 'Shakhty Trial',[29] the first of Stalin's show trials ten years before the infamous Moscow Trials.

They met in a Vienna safe house, where Zarubin was told that his London assignment had been cancelled and that instead he was to relocate to Berlin as one of the 'illegal' residents, an extremely dangerous mission after the Nazis' election victory in March 1933. At the end of that year Boris Gordon, chief OGPU resident in Germany, arrived, remaining there until May 1937. Zarubin was informed that, instead of him, Nikolsky would be sent to London.[30] Communications of all groups with the Centre were to proceed as usual via Paris, where Stanislav Glinsky headed the legal OGPU station hidden inside the embassy.[31] By June 1934, with the arrival of Theodor Maly (codenamed MANN),[32] who took over most important intelligence sources in France, Holland, Switzerland, and the UK, Paris became the principal base of Soviet intelligence operations.

Zarubin and his wife, Liza Gorskaya-Zarubina, left Switzerland and headed for Berlin, equipped, as their biographer writes, with new Norwegian passports.[33] However, according to Zarubin's SVR biography, which seems more credible, he was actually travelling on a Czech document in the name of 'Jaroslaw Koćik', a talent scout for Paramount Pictures, and Liza posed as 'Mariana Koćik'. In Berlin Zarubin is credited with running Willi Lehmann, a very important source in the Gestapo (codenamed A-201 and later BREITENBACH) recruited in 1929.[34] Lehmann, deputy division chief of counter-espionage at the Berlin police, joined the Gestapo in 1933 and a year later entered the SS. In the crucially important year 1939 this allowed him to get a smooth transfer to Amt IV of the newly established Reichssicherheitshauptamt (RSHA) (Chief Directorate of Security of the Third Reich). Lehmann would not be unmasked as a Soviet mole until December 1942. Zarubin is also credited with recruiting an attractive American student named Jane Lucie Booker as a cut-out for meeting Lehmann. Upon her return to the USA in 1939, Booker was also involved in the Soble/Soblen espionage ring, working against the American Trotskyists. She later collaborated with the FBI, telling them in an interview that in Berlin in 1937 she had met as part of Zarubin's network Margaret Browder, the younger sister of Earl Browder of the Communist Party of the USA (CPUSA), whom she knew as 'Jean Montgomery'.[35] In her turn, Margaret knew Zarubin only by the name of 'Herbert' when they worked in Germany together.

Copenhagen, where Reif settled after leaving Vienna, was selected as an operational base for the new 'G' Group, which was probably named after

Percy Eded Glading (codenamed GOT),[36] from the Communist Party of Great Britain (CPGB), who organized the Woolwich Arsenal spy ring. Reif had been running the London 'illegal' residency when Nikolsky received Artuzov's letter in July 1934.

As mentioned, in February 1934 Deutsch went to London alone and Reif joined him there in April. They worked together until June, when Reif left for Copenhagen again. By the summer their network of agents, helpers, talent-spotters, and couriers already included Edith Suschitzky (alias 'Betty Grey'); her husband Alexander Ethel Tudor-Hart (alias 'Harold White'); Alice 'Litzi' Friedmann, the first wife of Philby, later recruited as agent MARY; Kim Philby himself, then only a candidate for recruitment; agents PFEIL (also GERTA or HERTA, in Russian STRELA, unidentified),[37] JOHN (unidentified), FRIEND (Brian Goold-Verschoyle); PROFESSOR, LUXI, GRIMM, and YEGOR. In August or September GOT (Glading) introduced Deutsch to ATILLA (unidentified), who later brought his son, adding another agent to the already impressive list. Deutsch explained how it happened:

Reif spoke English badly. On one occasion, ATILLA told Reif about his son and asked him if he should involve him in our work. Reif understood something quite different and answered 'yes'. So ATILLA brought his son with him to the next meeting. Reif got very worried when he saw him, and when he heard who he was, he upbraided ATILLA. I met the latter to find out what exactly had happened. It turned out that it was Reif's lack of knowledge of English, which was the cause of the incident. The son turned out to very useful to us, however, and we began to work with him.[38]

ATILLA's son was codenamed NACHFOLGER ('Heir'). Both remain unidentified. In October Philby (SÖHNCHEN) was instructed to arrange a meeting between his college friend Donald Maclean and Reif, who started to 'educate' (cultivate) him using the false-flag technique by introducing himself as a representative of an 'anti-fascist organization'.[39] Subsequently, the whole Cambridge Spy Ring would be recruited under a false flag.

Nikolsky's first 'maiden' voyage to London was combined with a courier job. According to the initial plan, he was to be based permanently in Copenhagen, from where he should have been directing the activities of Deutsch and Reif. After his recent failure in Paris, he had hardly any clue how to 'cultivate, develop and infiltrate agents into British intelligence organizations', as his mission briefing allegedly demanded. At the Centre, Nikolsky did his best to avoid the assignment.[40] It did not work, and he had to spend several unhappy months in London, interrupted by extensive travel through continental Europe and twenty-two nights in Copenhagen hotels.

Denmark and its capital have always played a special role in the history of Russian espionage.[41] The Austrian archives keep a special collection of documents (box number PA-I-832) labelled 'Russian Espionage in Copenhagen', which is a treasure trove of facts and trivia regarding several colourful personalities and their breathtaking adventures starting from the early years of the twentieth century. When Hitler came to power in Germany, Copenhagen became a temporary base for Soviet clandestine operations in Western Europe, Scandinavia, and the Baltic states.

After he had read and destroyed the letter from the Centre, Nikolsky left his American passport in the name of 'William Goldin' at the Soviet Embassy in Vienna to be sent by courier to Moscow, and boarded a night train that carried him through Czechoslovakia, Poland, and his native Byelorussia all the way back to the Soviet capital. While he was travelling, a former member of the Soviet legation in Vienna, Georg Killich, who had by then settled in Moscow as 'Georg Miller' and become head of the document (forgery) section of the INO, put a fake entrance stamp in the passport, showing that 'Goldin' had entered Sweden legally some time in early July 1934. On 11 July, Nikolsky arrived in Stockholm, took his American passport to the British Consulate, and applied for a British visa. Formalities over, he set off on a trip to Copenhagen. On 15 July 1934 Nikolsky/Goldin entered the UK via the eastern port of Harwich. In London he met Reif, picked up a parcel, and departed by ferry from Ramsgate to Ostend, Belgium. On Wednesday, 25 July, Nikolsky returned to the Lubyanka headquarters to report to Artuzov and Sloutsky.[42] He spent less than a week in England and returned to Moscow wishing never to come back again.

Interlude 2

London: September–December 1934

In Moscow, Nikolsky wrote a personal letter to Sloutsky, then deputy chief of the INO, begging his boss not to send him to Britain again. This important document, dated 17 August 1934, deserves to be quoted in full:

I am asking you not to send me again on any assignment abroad for the following reasons:

1. The group where I am supposed to work is adequately provided with the leadership: the experienced veteran operational officer MAR [Reif] and his well-qualified assistant ARNOLD [Deutsch]. Currently, they are not sufficiently occupied with work.

2. Leaving me here will save the department considerable hard currency expenses related to my trip to America that had been planned [pre-decided] earlier.

3. My child is suffering from an acute heart disease and rheumatism. For three years she had been confined to bed. It is very difficult for me to secure her treatment abroad. At the same time, the treatment in our [NKVD] medical facilities could be arranged.

4. I have not yet been directing this group therefore I have no cases or sources to hand over so a decision to send me abroad can neither be connected with nor complicated by these circumstances.[1]

This document has never been reproduced before. When on 26 August Reif, the 'illegal' resident, was reporting on his and Deutsch's successes with Philby and Maclean,[2] Nikolsky was still in Moscow, from where he travelled to join his family in Vienna, arriving in mid-September.[3] From Austria he went to France, where he was due to meet Maly, and on 18 September (two months after he had reported to Sloutsky about his first trip) he returned to London via Dieppe and Newhaven. Here Goldin/Nikolsky registered a small business that he called the American Refrigerator Company Limited and started to make arrangements for the arrival of Maria and Vera. In early October 1934 they both left Vienna and bade farewell to the city,[4] never to return there again.

However, something seemed to be missing in this otherwise well-fitting schedule. The answer came from Orlov Collection in H. Keith Melton's private spy museum in Boca Raton, Florida.[5] On the lower of three shelves, there is an enlarged framed photo of 'William Goldin' from Orlov's American passport with a personal signature. On the odd page opposite the photo one can read: 'This passport is valid for two years from the date of issue unless limited to a shorter period.' The passport was issued on 23 November 1932, and so was valid until October 1934. To be used after that date, either the passport had to be extended or a new one issued. Indeed, there is an INS stamp on the same page showing that 'Goldin' arrived in the United States for the second time on 25 September 1934. This must have been the trip that he had mentioned in his August appeal to Sloutsky. No one knew about his second trip to America and for obvious reasons Orlov never told the US authorities about his work in Britain or in America. It is also unknown how long he stayed in the United States, but from New York he certainly returned to France. On 16 November 'Goldin' entered Great Britain, again arriving by ferry from Cherbourg.

Reif was summoned to the Home Office in January 1935. And it was Reif, not Deutsch, who had just recruited and was running Maclean.

Because his stay permit was expiring, the acting 'illegal' resident Reif was summoned to the Home Office and advised that he should leave the country. After his departure, Nikolsky wrote a report to the Centre, in which, among other things, he mentioned: 'I have taken over [the control of] Sirota [WAISE/Maclean], Synok [SÖNNCHEN/Philby], BÄR [unidentified], and professor [characteristically written in lower-case letters, which suggests it was quite possibly not only a code name but an academic rank as well]. ARNOLD [Deutsch] still runs ATILLA[6] and *naslednik* [NACHFOLGER].'[7] It was already the end of February and the letter does not even suggest that by this time Nikolsky had actually met any of those agents, as he was writing from a hospital.

What happened in reality is described in detail in the memo written and signed by Deutsch when he returned to Moscow:

Spravka o 'Lirike' (Memo about LYRIC)
In London, I established contact with EDITH [Edith Suschitzky/Tudor Hart], whom I already knew from my time in Vienna. In the autumn of 1934 [a memory slip, must be spring] 'Synok' [SÖHNCHEN/Kim Philby] came to EDITH from Vienna with his Austrian wife. This Austrian girl [Litzi Friedmann-Philby] was an active [Communist] party worker and introduced 'Synok' to this work. 'Synok' and his wife told EDITH about their intentions to work for us. In this connection we instructed EDITH to keep them away from the party work in London. In May or June 1934 EDITH put me in touch with 'Synok', but at that time I did not mention our activities to him and only some time later finally recruited him to work for us.

'Synok' had two mates in Cambridge, both active [Communist] party members, both with excellent opportunities and connections. They were LYRIC [Maclean] and MÄDCHEN [Burgess]. As LYRIC seemed to us a better candidate, we asked 'Synok' carefully to study his opportunities and contacts while pulling him out of active party work. After all we had learned about LYRIC, we asked 'Synok' finally to recruit him. This is exactly what he did! In this connection 'Synok' arranged a meeting between Reif and LYRIC, and Reif was in touch with him from October to December 1934. After that [from February 1935] SCHWED was his controller until October 1935, after which I was running him until my departure [in September 1937, though Deutsch briefly came back in November to put agents 'on ice'].

LYRIC and MÄDCHEN were good friends, but we agreed with LYRIC not to give MÄDCHEN any indication about his contact with us. [Three lines deleted.] As, according to our instructions, LYRIC started to distance himself from MÄDCHEN and the Party, the latter became suspicious that LYRIC was involved in special work and by asking inquisitive questions and [deleted] he learned that he [LYRIC] was working for us.

In order to prevent MÄDCHEN deliberating about the matter, we decided to recruit him (he was a valuable person) as well, and to do the job we sent LYRIC, about whose collaboration [with us] he [MÄDCHEN] had already learned. LYRIC discussed the issue with him and arranged for a rendezvous with STEFAN [Deutsch]. In this way in January 1935 MÄDCHEN began working for us. [Last paragraph of about twelve lines deleted.][8]

Thus, SCHWED/Nikolsky had nothing to do with the first three Cambridge University agents when they were successfully recruited. And he certainly knew nothing about those who joined the list after he had left London and was dismissed from the foreign intelligence department.

Deutsch wrote in his NKVD biography that he had worked with SCHWED for only about a month in June–July 1935, after which he, Deutsch, left for Moscow.[9] But even when they were both in Britain, the Centre regularly sent instructions to Nikolsky not to have personal contact with his assistant,[10] so there is little doubt that the grand strategy that led to the targeting of many future British high-fliers was devised exclusively by Deutsch. It was another quarter of a century, however, before Deutsch was identified as the chief recruiter of what became known as the Cambridge Five, an extraordinary group of Soviet agents all of whom went on to get jobs within security and intelligence services or other important institutions.[11] But much of what these spies achieved was in spite of, rather than because of, their brief handling by 'Orlov'.

8

London: January–March 1935

The Moscow Centre finally approved SCHWED's permanent transfer to London in a telegram dated 7 January 1935.[1] With his genuine American passport, Nikolsky, posing as 'William Goldin', was obliged to register by filling in an alien registration form and getting it stamped by the Bow Street police station, which he did on or about 14 January.

At the end of the month, as part of the usual routine, SCHWED sent Moscow a list of Philby's Cambridge friends who might be suitable for cultivation.[2] Philby himself was of little interest to Nikolsky. Philby's unorthodox choice of wife dismayed his upper-class family. 'His mother couldn't stand me,' Litzi later recalled. 'She was horrified by our marriage, which in her eyes was a terrible misalliance. Her favourite and only son married a communist woman of Jewish descent—a nightmare!'[3] With such a wife, Kim had hardly any chance of getting a decent job. And of course, in spite of his father's prominence, he was an outsider, with few prospects of joining what two decades later became known as the Establishment, the term coiled by the British journalist Henry Fairlie. From the very beginning of his espionage career no one expected Philby to join the secret service. This cannot and could not have been planned. In seems that Philby was initially recruited because he wanted to join a London communist cell and was then spotted by Edith Tudor-Hart, who had the right contacts in the right places and knew Kim's communist wife. Another reason was that the INO became convinced—erroneously—that, since his father, Harry St John Bridger Philby, was a former British government adviser, he must have been a member of the SIS. What made them think so is unclear, but the author of a KGB-sponsored biography of Philby could not help but comment: 'I don't know if Kim thought back to his own first assignment for the Soviets—going through his father's personal papers, making copies of the interesting ones and sending them to Moscow "for study". That was not the most decent behaviour.'[4]

It has already been established that one of the reasons why Nikolsky was sent to London in January 1935 was that the 'illegal' resident MAR (Reif/Wolisch) had been summoned to the Home Office and advised that he should leave the country by 15 March.[5] The reason for this decision is unclear, as Reif's alien registration card has not survived, but it definitely had nothing to do with his passport, as Nikolsky claimed in one of his reports to Moscow: 'I think that his [Reif's] passport is not suitable for working in other countries.'[6] There were no grounds for this conclusion, because, as we have seen, Reif had a genuine Austrian document that successfully passed passport control on many borders, including in Britain. It would certainly have passed a check against the Austrian records, too.[7] In writing about Reif's problems with his Austrian passport, Nikolsky was no doubt looking for a pretext to get his family out of the country and thus shorten his own stay there, because he obviously did not feel at home in London. A few weeks after the arrival of Maria and Vera, he informed the Centre:

Your information that the network supplying us 'books' [passports], one of which MAR [Reif] had, has failed has made me very worried. As you know, my wife has a book of the same country that MAR had. My wife's book is registered at the appropriate organization [Aliens Registration Office] with all details. That is why I have decided to send my wife and daughter back home.[8]

The Austrian passport saga actually began in 1925, when Georg Killich was working for the Soviet Legation in Vienna as a diplomatic courier, and in his free time provided the 'Vienna Organization' (a euphemism for the OGPU residency) with various Austrian documents that could be of use—birth certificates, passports, personal papers, diplomas, and even private correspondence. They were obtained by different means, including direct purchase (especially from the homeless), larceny, and loans from Communist party members and sympathizers. This was the permanent order of the day, and many OMS, OGPU, and RU agents were always looking for documents. When Deutsch worked for the Comintern in Vienna before coming to London as an OGPU recruiter, he was also part of the passport supply network. These and other activities did not remain unnoticed by the Austrian police, in whose reports Deutsch was mentioned as one of the active Soviet agents.[9] Should MI5 have discovered the name of a person described by Olga Grey, their penetration agent, as 'another man short and rather bumptious in manner' who was working with Glading,[10] they would have had no problem in finding out everything else about the elusive Dr Deutsch. But they did have a problem, because the bumptious man turned out to be rather careful.

In 1932, two years before Reif arrived in London for the first time, an important case of document forgery was investigated by the Austrian police. Thousands of passports from different countries, some as remote as San Salvador, Palestine, Syria, and Lebanon, were found, in what became known as the 'Klose case'. Several people who would become famous in the annals of espionage history, such as Gerhard Eisler and Hede Massing, were also involved.[11]

Theodor Maly, the OGPU controller of important assets before the war, complained several times that he was not happy with his forged passports. In October 1934 he informed Moscow that he was travelling on a Yugoslav passport, adding half-jokingly that since the murder of the king of Yugoslavia he did not envy himself for having it.[12] When Maly went to Holland using an Austrian passport, he again mentioned that it too was 'not very satisfactory', just like his American passport. Maly wrote to the Centre in April 1935 explaining that his document contained errors. 'When travelling nowadays through Europe on dubious documents, I am perhaps getting excessively sensitive to these questions.'[13] But all this did not prevent him from visiting Britain in May to complete the recruitment of John King.

Having heard that Maly and other NKVD operatives had had problems in Europe,[14] Nikolsky exaggerated the danger and sent his family back to Moscow. Later, in America, he remembered that there had once been a problem with forged Austrian passports and described this in the book he wrote for the CIA.[15] Needless to say, everything that he wrote about Maly, his Paris adventures, and his alleged visits to the American Consulate, was pure invention.[16] And, of course, he forgot to mention his own forged Austrian passport in the name of 'Leo Feldbiene',[17] which, had he known French, would have worried him, because it too contained a very serious error. But Nikolsky did not speak French and never used this passport in France, so it was accepted without problem.

Nikolsky had already carefully raised the question of his replacement by the end of February. He wrote to the Centre:

My stay at hospital prevents me from telling you about everything that I want in detail, as I planned when I started writing this letter. But MAR's [Reif] return home makes it easier. He is fully apprised of all cultivations in which he took the most active and conscientious part.

His departure reduces the number of operational officers to two—me and ARNOLD [Deutsch]. To get from you an equally qualified officer familiar with our apparatus at the Centre, with operational experience, who knows England and, most important, the English language, I have certainly no hope.

Anyway, if you are not going to send any support to our station now and if our replacement has not yet been chosen, I strongly recommend starting looking for a [well-qualified] officer, like Grafpen, for work here.

What happened to MAR [the Home Office did not prolong his stay and advised him to leave the country] may happen to any of us (me or ARNOLD).[18]

He soon left for Copenhagen, as, according to the immigration stamps in his passport, on 13 March 1935 'Goldin' returned to the UK on one of the Scandinavian ferries travelling from Esbjerg, Denmark.[19]

Correspondence between the London station and Moscow Centre shows Nikolsky (SCHWED) and Deutsch (ARNOLD) making desperate but fruitless attempts to get a source of political intelligence. One of the reports describes how they tried to use an unidentified agent whom they called BRIDE (a so-called access agent, in intelligence lingo) to get acquainted with a Foreign Office diplomat.[20] Philby, at the time assistant editor of the small liberal newspaper *Review of Reviews*, was instructed to place advertisements for typists and/or stenographers. 'Out of the sea of responses taken out of the post box by us', SCHWED informed Moscow in April, 'a steno-typist from the central secretariat of the Admiralty seems the most suitable candidate. To become better acquainted with her, SÖHNCHEN [Philby] accepted her for evening work in his editorial office. Now we have before us the task of finding a "lover" for her. You will appreciate that the outcome of such an affair is always unpredictable.'[21]

That was Nikolsky's favourite ploy. In his *Handbook of Intelligence* he wrote about 'the constant efforts by the Soviet intelligence to enrol into its service young women who work as secretaries, stenographers, code clerks and administrative assistants in important departments of foreign governments'.[22] This strategy later became known as honey traps and sexpionage, but in reality such schemes were rather rare, especially before the war. This time SCHWED did not have to wait long for the Centre's response. In particular, the instructions regarding Philby were very clear: 'Using SÖHNCHEN for recruitment is categorically forbidden!'[23] However, Nikolsky did not intend letting a mishap jeopardize his career and was eager to give himself another try.

9

Copenhagen: Early 1935

The year 1935 began badly for Soviet intelligence. While the Home Office unwittingly packed the NKVD resident off to Moscow, and Nikolsky was ill and confined to his hospital bed, its base in Copenhagen signalled an alarm. A group of RU officers and agents was suddenly arrested in the Danish capital. The problems started on 19 February when the uniformed police force appeared at the hotel Nordland and detained the Lithuanian-born American Communist George Mink. He was initially accused of attempted rape,[1] but false passports in his possession pointed to espionage. On the next day a more careful search of Mink's room produced a great deal of incriminating material, including codes, wireless transmission schedules, and secret documents. In a police ambush that followed a large number of people were detained. Apart from Mink, there were two other Americans, Leon Josephson and Nicholas Sherman, who came to visit Mink during the police search. Then, based on the information from Mink's notebooks, several Danes who served as couriers were also arrested, including communists Harry Rasmussen and William Larsen. Finally, either by good luck or because the officers ignored their instructions, three ranking Soviet military intelligence officials fell into the trap. David Uger,[2] Max Maksimov,[3] and David Lvovich[4] were apprehended in Copenhagen on espionage-related charges by the inspectors of the Criminal Investigation Department (CID).

Uger was one of the residents in Germany. He had arrived there via Denmark, quickly taken up control of an undercover cell, and was returning to Moscow to make a personal report and receive further instructions. In Copenhagen he suddenly decided to visit his colleague and went to the Nordland.

Maksimov was also on his way to Moscow, but, unlike Uger, he was going after two successful years as chief resident in several European countries, where he controlled a network of agents that was later split between three different supervisors. He followed the usual route Berlin–Copenhagen–Stockholm–Moscow and should have had no contacts in Denmark. Needless to say, the first thing he did was to look up his old friends, among whom was Lvovich, another victim of muddle-headedness.

Lvovich had just arrived in Copenhagen. In November 1933 he returned to the headquarters from an assignment in Germany and was sent to Denmark to help set up reserve communication facilities. Lvovich went to a safe house without any 'dry-cleaning' (surveillance check), failed to notice the police watchers, and fell into the trap.

Josephson was soon released. Two other Americans remained in custody. Under CID interrogation, Rasmussen admitted he was a courier. 'I arrived from the USA in 1934 on board the *Frederik VIII*,' he told the police, 'and established contact with Larsen, who introduced me to Mink and Sherman'. On 30 July 1935 George Mink and Nicholas Sherman were found guilty of espionage against a neighbouring country (Germany) and sentenced to eighteen months in prison.[5] The identity of the man calling himself 'Sherman' remained a mystery for the next seventy years.

His name was Aleksandr Petrovich Ulanovsky. Born in 1891 in Odessa as Israel Pinkhusovich Haskelevich, he was converted to anarchism at the age of 18, arrested a year later, managed to avoid being imprisoned, and in 1913 emigrated abroad. He lived in Britain, France, and Germany. Then he returned to Russia and, after taking part in the Bolshevik revolution and the civil war, joined the INO. In 1921 Ulanovsky was sent to Berlin with an intelligence assignment. Back in Moscow a year later, he worked for the newly launched Red International of Labour Unions, commonly known as the Profintern, visiting Germany and China as its emissary. The idea behind the Profintern was the creation of a new revolutionary international union association on the eve of the European proletarian revolution. The president of the Profintern was Solomon Lozovsky, assisted by British trade unionist Tom Mann and Alfred Rosmer from France, an old friend of Trotsky. The revolution did not take place, and the Profintern was dissolved two years before the war. In 1928 Ulanovsky was invited to join the Red Army intelligence and soon became one of its resident agents (code-named ULRICH) in China. His tenure lasted less than twelve months, as it was marred by an intelligence failure. In 1930 he was again in Germany but became involved in a scandal that somehow reached the Kremlin. The problem was that Ulanovsky continued recruiting agents from the local

Communist cadres in spite of the absolute ban issued by the Politburo[6]—an instruction that had never been strictly followed. Stalin personally intervened, and a special commission was set up to investigate.[7] Jan Berzin, the military intelligence chief, had to recall his representatives from Germany.[8] Ulanovsky was reprimanded.

Nevertheless, he was sent to the United States, together with his wife Nadezhda (ELAINE). There, Mink (codenamed FRANK) became his best agent. In 1934 Ulanovsky invited Mink to Copenhagen, where his assignment was to establish a transit communication station to retransmit messages received from agents in Nazi Germany and Britain. As before, he continued working with communists, which had been forbidden.

The arrest of four officers and several agents signalled the end of Berzin's career as the director of Military Intelligence. On 5 April 1935, the Defence Commissar Voroshilov signed an administrative order following which Berzin was dismissed from his post and placed on the reserve active-status list.[9] After Spain he was reinstated as director, but he did not last long.

Moscow learned about the affair in Copenhagen after three months. On 10 May, the Government Code and Cipher School (GC&CS) in London intercepted a report sent by the Comintern radio transmitter:

Nos. 95, 96
To ABRAHAM [Alexander Abramov-Mirov, Pyatnitsky's deputy, OMS]
Just learned HARDY's [George Hardy] wife since September 1934 had been helping comrade called ALEX from COPENHAGEN [Alexander Ulanovsky] to establish WILSON apparatus [radio transmitter] here for special purposes. Private cover address for the correspondence had been visited by police who informed comrade that a man was arrested in COPENHAGEN on charge of espionage and then asked for HARDY's wife by her former name [Paddy Ayriss]. Consider matter very serious and suggest you call her to see you. Why should such operations be mounted without my foreknowledge?
WEST [unidentified, possibly Robert Stewart][10]

Jessie 'Paddy' Ayriss mentioned in the telegram was an attractive communist married to a much older man, a leading figure in the CPGB. She visited Moscow at the age of 24, worked at the Soviet Embassy in London between 1937 and 1944, and was in contact with Percy Glading before his arrest. Ayriss had been suspected by the Security Service of working for Soviet intelligence but never prosecuted.[11]

Investigating the arrest of the American citizens four years later, members of the US House of Representatives heard from a witness that George Mink was caught because he had become 'mixed up with a woman Gestapo agent who turned over the whole bunch to Danish and German authorities'.[12] Russian sources assert that it was a police informer named 'Nilsen', who knew Mink and turned him over to the Danish security police.[13] 'Nilsen' is probably identical with Ejnar Nielsen, a member of the Danish delegation to the congress of the International Seamen and Harbour Workers (ISH) held in Hamburg-Altona in 1932 and led by the Danish OMS/Comintern agent Richard Jensen, in which George Mink also took part.[14]

The affair—the arrest of a group of ranking RU officers and agents in Copenhagen—became known as the 'Conference of Residents' at both the NKVD and military intelligence headquarters. After serving most of their eighteen-month sentence, Ulanovsky/Sherman and Mink were expelled to the USSR. The Soviet Embassy in Stockholm provided them with the necessary travel papers. Soon Mink was sent to Spain, together with Macartney, the spy who had been arrested in London ten years earlier. Mink would meet Orlov in Barcelona during the civil war.

10

Comrade Resident:
June–September 1935

When his scheme of encouraging young communist agents to seduce
secretaries and typists from various Westminster offices was again
rebuffed by Moscow, Nikolsky thought of another plan involving Philby.
He reported to the Centre:

During recent months there has been the following new development regarding
SÖHNCHEN. Emir Saud, the heir to Ibn Saud (and the commander of his father's
troops), is in England now, as you know, [regularly] seeing SÖHNCHEN's father. He
is looking for an English teacher whom the Emir would like to take along with him
to the East. The Emir addressed his request to find such a teacher to SÖHNCHEN's
father and to his ambassador (illegible). This led me to the following idea ['legend'
in the original]. We can use this opportunity not only to turn SÖHNCHEN into a
talent-spotter and journalist, but to launch him into a more solid venture. Not a
great one for the time being, as, despite SÖHNCHEN's good [personal] qualities, he,
according to my estimates, still has limited possibilities.

Before this plan could be finally approved or rejected, it collapsed. The
Emir found himself another teacher.

In the same letter to Moscow, Nikolsky discussed Philby's prospects:

On my instructions he was pressing his father to help him obtain a better political
post [claiming] that he was sick and tired of being a journalist and would like to
study politics alongside a serious man—a politician. But his father is not helping
him and advises him to continue in journalism. To wait until SÖHNCHEN has
become a prominent journalist to collect some serious information for us is a
long way to go. It is also quite hopeless for him without his father's help to seek
government employment somewhere like the Foreign Office. [To apply for the
job], one needs to be extremely well prepared to be able to pass the Civil Service
qualifying tests.

His plans to nurture a relationship with ANNA [Lockhart, according to the KGB archivists' note on the document] slowly wither away. They work for the same newspaper but do not progress beyond a casual exchange of courtesies.

[At the same time], his cultivation of [deleted] is not going the way we want it to.[1]

As mentioned, Maly visited Britain to complete John King's recruitment in May 1935, and in July the Centre noted that Maly and Bystroletov had made very good progress and that King, codenamed MAG, promised 'to be very important and interesting in the future'.[2] In London, King was run by Pieck (COOPER), who, together with his business partner Conrad Parlanti, found an office in Buckingham Gate with the specific aim of photographing King's material. In early June, Maly recommended to the Centre that Nikolsky should run King, because Pieck was obviously too valuable as an agent and recruiter to continue using him for a routine job. But Moscow turned this suggestion down and appointed Krivitsky, who had by that time joined the NKVD.[3] This move from the Red Army Intelligence Directorate to the secret police was his only opportunity to remain in Europe. He was again posted to The Hague as the 'illegal' resident agent. Amazingly, Krivitsky's role and status in various Soviet intelligence organizations remains a point of controversy even today. This carousel began when his ghost writer, Isaac Don Levine, called Krivitsky the 'Chief of Soviet Military Intelligence in Western Europe'.

Later, during one of his interviews with the FBI, Orlov stated that 'the writer [Don Levine] who assisted Krivitsky and with whom Orlov spoke said that just before the articles were to be published in the *Saturday Evening Post*, Krivitsky came to the writer and told him that he could not permit the story to be published in the form in which it had been prepared because he, Krivitsky, had never been a general in the Red Army Intelligence', according to Krivitsky's FBI file. As Orlov testified, Don Levine (whose name Orlov declined to furnish but whose identity the agents of the New York Office easily established), told Krivitsky that he had to go ahead with the story as it was prepared because Krivitsky had signed a contract. Krivitsky finally agreed to let the story be published as it had been prepared by Don Levine.

During his long life in America, Nikolsky, who habitually introduced himself as 'General Orlov', had been questioned by many people and organizations on a wide range of topics regarding Soviet secret services, their operations and personnel. Answering one questionnaire, he said that Krivitsky was a non-commissioned officer in the NKVD who in 1935 had 'failed to qualify for a commission of senior lieutenant of State Security, a

special rank which corresponded to that of captain of the army'. Orlov
further stated that Krivitsky's post as described by Don Levine had never
existed. Krivitsky, according to Orlov, had served in The Hague 'as an
NKVD letter drop, the lowliest denomination on the operative scale'.[4] Alas,
such a thing also never existed.

It so happens that Gary Kern, the American biographer of Krivitsky,
developed a certain sympathy for the defector. Kern, who was the first
reader of this book's first draft, correctly states that Krivitsky worked during
this period with Theodor Maly, a senior NKVD officer. From this, however, Kern jumped to the conclusion that 'he [Krivitsky] was not "the
Chief" in the sense of directing every Fourth Department [sic][5] intelligence
operation in Western Europe, but was something more than rezident. He
enjoyed special powers.'[6] Regretfully, Krivitsky's biographer presents no
proof of such special powers.

Another fan, Earl M. Hyde Jr, writes that Krivitsky 'became a member of
Josef Stalin's foreign intelligence organization, the GRU (Military) and, in
1937, with the rank of general, was head of Soviet intelligence operations
in Western Europe'. Hyde then elevates Krivitsky to 'Chief of all KGB
intelligence operations in Western Europe and Eastern Europe'[7] and adds
that, as such, Krivitsky knew a great deal. Richard Helms, Hyde's former
boss, also thought that, 'had Reiss and Krivitsky been thoroughly interrogated, and if General Orlov had agreed to disclose what he knew, Western
counterintelligence would certainly have identified most of the cadre of spies
who were to number among the KGB's most precious sources'.[8] In reality,
Reiss had never been interrogated, because shortly after his defection he was
assassinated by the NKVD. Krivitsky, on the contrary, was very thoroughly
interviewed by MI5, and Orlov disclosed much of what he knew, while all
this produced no effect upon the number of Soviet spies in America.

As a matter of fact, Krivitsky was nothing more (or less) than an undercover
agent ('illegal' resident) in a small country of little importance. In December
1935, overlooking Maly's reservations, the NKVD decided to send him to
London to run Captain King, the Foreign Office cipher clerk, despite the fact
that Krivitsky spoke no English and had no knowledge of photography.
Photography was important, because all documents had to be photographed
before being sent to Moscow. On the way to London, Krivitsky and Maly
met Pieck, a Dutch artist who recruited King. After the meeting it was clear
that Krivitsky was unsuitable for work with MAG (King) and the Centre sent
him to Amsterdam,[9] while Pieck continued to run King. This went on until

April 1936, when MI5 enquiries compelled Moscow to break off all contacts with Pieck, and Maly took his place. After his defection, Krivitsky was interviewed by the Security Service at length, but his information was seriously garbled. He was unable to provide clear leads during his debriefing to any current Soviet agent or intelligence personnel in Britain with the exception of King, who was arrested and sentenced to ten years' imprisonment. Dick White, a future Director General of MI5, observed: 'I did not wholly trust Krivitsky. He wasn't using his real name and he wasn't a general. He hadn't mastered enough to give us a proper lead.'[10] Besides, at the time MI5 was seriously handicapped in its investigations of Soviet espionage by lack of resources.[11] What is more, by the time Krivitsky appeared in London, the service had itself been penetrated.

One of the reasons why 'Slavatinsky' (Abram Sloutsky), the controller of the whole British operation, did not agree to letting SCHWED run King in June 1935 was that Nikolsky, as an operational officer, was nowhere near as successful as Maly or the other 'illegals' operating in Europe. Besides, by that time Deutsch had recruited a sufficient number of sources who demanded attention while he was going to leave for an obligatory holiday in Russia. For a while Nikolsky's direction of the group was on and off, with himself, and occasionally Deutsch, each running two agents, three of whom were young probationers.[12] Then finally Nikolsky was instructed to settle in London permanently and to start working. His American passport was genuine and he had not been engaged in any intelligence or communist propaganda activities in England so far, which meant that MI5 and Special Branch did not have any information on 'William Goldin'.[13] Indeed, they learnt about him only sixty years later.

In the meantime another undercover agent with a genuine British passport and family moved to the Belgian ferry port of Ostend with the task of settling in London. William Fisher, accompanied by his wife Ellie and their daughter Evelyn, was, like Deutsch, travelling under his own name. However, Fisher was not sent to London to work for SCHWED, as some authors claim.[14] He had to stay in Ostend for quite a while, arriving in London only in the autumn of 1935, when Nikolsky had already left for Copenhagen. He took up residence at 56 Queensway, on the corner of Inverness Place, opposite Bayswater underground station. But this central London address was not the right place for his wireless operator work, and in early 1936 the Fishers moved to a much more suitable residence, a flat in the new Rivermead Court in Fulham close to the exclusive Hurlingham Club, which to this day remains a green oasis of tradition and international renown. By the middle of February the receiver was constructed. On 14 February, Deutsch reported to the Centre that Fisher was asking questions about money.[15] Three months later, Willie, Ellie, and Evelyn found themselves back in their Moscow apartment. His name or, rather, his alias, would not surface again until October 1957, when the newspapers reported the trial of a Soviet spy, 'Rudolf Ivanovich Abel', in New York. 'Abel' was Fisher. Orlov followed the story from his comfortable hideout in Manhattan.

The American Refrigerator Company (ARC), which Nikolsky/Goldin decided to register at 80–6 Regent Street, very near Piccadilly Circus, was to be used as a legal cover. Its first, very prestigious, Central London address was, however, ill chosen, as a one-person import–export company was clearly out of place among such neighbours as the *Encyclopædia Britannica*, Hollywood Casting Bureau, and Duckerfield Dancing School, or the historic Café Royal with its legendary Grill Room once frequented by luminaries such as Oscar Wilde, Aubrey Beardsley, George Bernard Shaw, and Virginia Woolf. Immediately after Nikolsky's departure, the ARC office was moved by Maly to 135–7 Queen Victoria Street, a small and quiet place away from the city centre. In February 1936, shortly after he had taken control of the London operation, Maly asked Moscow whether he might 'join the refrigerator business which Lev [Nikolsky] ran?' They did not let him. Remarkably, in 1938 ARC was still active and even opened a branch office in the City, at 59 Knight Rider Street, EC4, closing its business only in 1941.[16] It is not known who was running the company and how it had been used by Soviet intelligence for five years, but during his directorship Nikolsky/Goldin imported only one refrigerator, and even that was for his private use.

One of the most noteworthy documents of Nikolsky's time in London is a ledger sheet of June–July 1935 with all the financial records of his cell:

SCHWED [Nikolsky] paid himself £120 a month, while STEFAN [Deutsch] got £80 and PFEIL [unidentified] received £56. One of the agents, codenamed ATILLA [but also OTELLO in some reports, unidentified] received £36. [His son] a source codenamed NACHFOLGER [unidentified][17]—£15. MÄDCHEN [Burgess] was paid £12 10 s., SÖHNCHEN [Philby] got £11, while WAISE [Maclean] was remunerated £40 to for his work.

Actual operational expenses for Nikolsky and Deutsch were £14 and £17 18 s. 8 d. accordingly. PFEIL received £3 12 s. EDITH [Edith Tudor-Hart]—5 s. 6 d., ATILLA—4 s., and LUXI earned £10 3 s. 3 d. 'für Verbindung', i.e. for providing a useful contact. For return trips to Copenhagen spending twenty-two nights in hotels Nikolsky drew £10 12 s. 10 d. PFEIL, who must have made several round trips to Denmark, was reimbursed £30 12 s. 7 d. Payments for Nikolsky's business amounted to £36 18 s. 8½d. in one month, plus £8 customs duties for his refrigerator.[18]

From this document it is clear that the classic spy who collected intelligence was the mysterious ATILLA. Whether he was active and what intelligence he delivered remains unknown.[19] It is also clear that PFEIL and EDITH were couriers, with EDITH often acting as a talent-spotter. LUXI was an access agent who arranged the contact between the potential spy and the recruiter. In the above group Deutsch was the recruiter and Nikolsky the external case officer. What Philby, Maclean, and Burgess did at this stage is unclear, in spite of many books and articles written about each of them. But, as a supervisor of this clandestine cell, Nikolsky felt obliged to deliver results. In July he passed on Philby's information that SÖHNCHEN had renewed his friendship with Tom Wylie, an old Trinity College friend from Cambridge who was then the Resident Clerk in the War Office. SCHWED wrote: 'The thought flashed through my mind that possibly we could send MÄDCHEN [Burgess] to Wylie; he [MÄDCHEN] is also a cultured pederast and an adroit chap who would—according to the mysterious laws of sexual attraction in this country—conquer Wylie's heart.'[20]

SCHWED also reported that Philby thought there was an opportunity to cultivate Dennis Proctor, a fellow left-wing member of the Apostles. After graduating in 1931, Proctor entered the Civil Service and by 1935 was Private Secretary to the Prime Minister, working in Stanley Baldwin's office at 10 Downing Street. But the Centre was not inclined to share Nikolsky's optimism and promptly vetoed the proposed cultivation.[21] Nikolsky understood and quickly responded with a telegram addressed to 'Slavatinsky' (Sloutsky): 'Anticipating that, along with the secretary of B[aldwin], who is a great friend of MÄDCHEN, you would take the same view of Wylie's case, I will also ban his cultivation.'[22] Yet another mishap.

In July the Centre forbade SCHWED to proceed with the recruitment of Burgess,[23] who had already met Deutsch about half a year before. Invited, as Philby and Maclean before him, to join the Comintern's underground struggle against fascism, Burgess told Deutsch that he was 'honoured and ready to sacrifice everything for the cause'.[24] Although Deutsch assigned him a code name (MÄDCHEN), the Centre was confused and demanded explanations. Some days later Nikolsky reported:

You seem puzzled about MÄDCHEN (Guy) and order [us] to break with him until you get explanations [regarding who this MÄDCHEN is].

I have told STEFAN [Deutsch] over the phone to suspend contact with him according to your instructions.

But I am rather surprised that there has been some misunderstanding over the matter: I begin to suspect that not all our reports reach you or perhaps part of them was not developed in full.

We got interested in MÄDCHEN during my last visit to our city [Moscow]. I reported to you then that he [Burgess] was going to our country as a tourist and that he was a friend of [Prime] Minister Baldwin's secretary. A check through our 2nd Department [control of arrivals and departures of people to and from the USSR] established that he had already left our country, so it was decided to approach him on the ISLAND.

We were tipped off about him by SYNOK [Philby] and SIROTA [Maclean], who characterized him as a very gifted and adventurous chap for whom all doors were open. His friendship with the [Prime] Minister's secretary [Dennis Proctor] was also noted. I wrote to you about the plan to recruit B[aldwin]'s secretary (with the help of MÄDCHEN). You abstained from the recruitment [of Proctor] but never said a word about MÄDCHEN (Guy).

Further on, in one of our previous parcels we sent photos of the letters of recommendation given to MÄDCHEN by one of the prominent MPs . . . [25]

At about the same time as Nikolsky, Reif, who had returned to Moscow and was promoted to head the British desk, was also asked to prepare a memorandum about the young recruits from Cambridge. He wrote in the memo:

Through 'Synok' [Philby] we established (in 1934) that one of his closest friends, a member of a compatriot [Communist] organization in Cambridge, the son of the late Minister of Education Maclean, had excellent connections in political circles. His work in the compatriots' organization was known to a very limited group of individuals. In his nature M. (we gave him the code name 'Sirota' or WAISE) is reserved, exceptionally loyal, always willing and ready to help the compatriot movement.

We have drafted a plan to reintegrate 'Sirota' back into high society. Under the guise of an assignment of a compatriot organization [Comintern], 'Synok' suggested that 'Sirota' should discontinue his association with Cambridge compatriots [Communist Party cell] and tell his comrades that he was busy with his studies and therefore was not able or willing to do the party work. After 3–4 months of such inactivity the Cambridge compatriots wrote 'Sirota' off as their member. His renewal of old contacts in high society convinced those few compatriots who knew him that he had distanced himself completely from the movement. In October 1934 'Synok' [Philby] was asked to set up a meeting between 'Sirota' [Maclean] and me. On behalf of an 'anti-fascist organization' I started his education according to our work's requirements. As Baldwin is a personal friend of the Maclean family, 'Sirota's' mother managed to obtain a letter from him (I read it personally) in which he [Baldwin] writes that he will do his best to help 'Sirota' to embark on a diplomatic career. It was also mentioned that a responsible official in the FO had been informed by Baldwin that he was personally interested in 'Sirota's' advancement. As is well known, those who want to join the diplomatic service in the UK must pass the Foreign Office exams. 'Sirota' is attending training courses and will sit his exams this summer. At the same time 'Sirota' is engaged in cultivation of individuals that may be of interest to us.

In February '35 I passed the control of 'Sirota' to SCHWED [Nikolsky/Orlov].

'Sirota' is not getting any fixed salary from us. We give him money according to operational needs. The sum does not exceed £3–4 a month. 'Sirota' requires a lot of training. He fulfils our assignments with interest and great care. He is ready to sacrifice anything for our work. Lately, he realized that he is a Soviet agent and with even greater inspiration was giving himself to our work. Without doubt, a promising source.[26]

Nikolsky's own report about the situation with 'Sirota' (Maclean/WAISE) confirmed and added more details to what the former London case officer Reif had said earlier. He explained that at the end of August the results of his Foreign Office exams would be announced, stressing that the examinations were conducted impartially and democratically and the outcome would be decided by the candidate's knowledge and not by favouritism. At the same time, Nikolsky deliberated that the election of Stanley Baldwin as the Prime Minister was a good sign, because he personally knew the Maclean family, but the resignation of Sir John Simon as the Secretary of State for Foreign Affairs could influence WAISE's career chances, as Sir Simon was acquainted with Maclean's mother, Gwendoline, while the new Minister was not. 'Our task', he wrote, 'is not to secure "Sirota's" career but to thrust him into the FO!' This indeed happened, and Maclean became the first of the Oxbridge Group to penetrate the highest echelons of the British Establishment by entering the Foreign Office in October 1935. But by this time Nikolsky would be far away from London.

At the end of his long report of 12 July, he reminded his readers about Burgess (MÄDCHEN) again:

You know MÄDCHEN, we got him through 'Sirota' [Maclean] . . . [Six lines deleted obviously with explanations of how the candidate got recommended and possibly with the identification of PROFESSOR as a talent-spotter.] MÄDCHEN is a former compatriot [member of the Cambridge Communist cell], a very well-educated fellow with adventurous inclinations. Though I rate him lower than Synok

[Philby/SÖHNCHEN] and Sirota [Maclean/WAISE], I nevertheless believe that he may be of service to us. [Handwritten note: 'MÄDCHEN is a pederast but he works on both fronts.']

Your misunderstanding regarding MÄDCHEN is especially difficult to comprehend because responding to our plan to send Guy (MÄDCHEN) to Lisa [Elizabeth Hill] to study Russian, in your letter of 27 May see §5 you agreed with our proposal and thought that would be a good way to find out the names of [intelligence] officers who study Russian with her [according to a report by PROFESSOR].

By the way, the plan is being successfully implemented. MÄDCHEN went to the Institute [sic] of Slavonic Studies asking them to recommend him a teacher. The university luckily sent him to Hill, who gave him one lesson privately.

The next step will be to ask her to put him in a group or to pair with other pupils so that he may get a better ear for pronunciation and to make lessons livelier. Thus we count on approaching other pupils. And MÄDCHEN sure knows how to make friends![27]

With her unusual biography (she was born to an Anglo-Russian family in St Petersburg), her love for the Russian language and culture, her social activity, and her many friends among the Russian émigré community in London (Moura Budberg among them), Lisa Hill could not have escaped the notice of the RIS, although, contrary to what was assumed, she was not the sister of Brigadier George A. Hill, the celebrated intelligence officer who operated in Petrograd with Sidney Reilly, and she never worked for MI6.[28]

The historian Sir Bernard Pares, director of the School of Slavonic and East European Studies, was widely regarded as the leading British expert of his generation on all things Russian. At the outbreak of the First World War he was appointed official observer to the Russian army and later seconded to the staff of the British Embassy in Petrograd. Following the Bolshevik revolution, Pares moved to Siberia to support the White Army, and after the civil war was banned by the communist government from re-entering Russia. In 1919 Pares moved to the recently founded School of Slavonic and East European Studies, where he took up the posts of Professor of Russian Language, Literature and History, editor of the *Slavonic Review*, and Director of the School. He retired from this post in 1939. Interestingly, describing the Moscow show trials of 1936–8, Pares wrote: 'Nearly all [those condemned] admitted having conspired against the life of Stalin and others, and on this point it is not necessary to doubt them.'[29] Lisa Hill was one of his students who graduated with a first and stayed on to study for a Ph.D. Nevertheless, when the time came, Sir Bernard refused to support her application to the Cambridge University lectureship.[30]

Although she gave private lessons before she was accepted at Cambridge University in 1936, Hill did not teach at the School of Slavonic Studies and never recalled meeting Burgess. Before and even after her temporary employment by the Ministry of Information during the war, she lived in Cambridge.

As already explained, in spite of several amazing coincidences, Brigadier Hill was not her brother. He was born in Estonia, the son of a timber merchant whose business interests extended from Siberia to Persia.[31] She was born in St Petersburg and indeed her siblings (three elder brothers and two sisters) included one named George Hill. As Lisa later wrote: 'There was also Brigadier George A. Hill, a well-known intelligence officer, a distant relation from the Baltic, who was often confused with my brother, who was George Edward.'[32] Was it really Orlov, Deutsch, and Burgess who made such a mess in their reports? Or, as is more likely, was it the KGB 'historians' who did not do their homework properly?[33]

Some useful information about the School of Slavonic and East European Studies could have come to Deutsch from Dorothy Galton, an active Communist in 1932–6, who was, quite amazingly, the MI5 link to the School regarding the provision of Russian language courses for military service personnel. In her memoirs, Elizabeth Hill remembered Galton, the secretary of Professor Pares, as 'a genial, practical and competent person'. In spite of her role as a 'link', the Security Service had strong and continuing suspicions that Galton was 'snooping', either for the Communist Party or for the Soviet intelligence services.[34]

As it happens, Colonel (later Brigadier) George Hill became Philby's instructor and a colleague at Brickendonbury Hall in Hertfordshire, a stunning Jacobean building and a training school for the Special Operations Executive (SOE) in 1940, when Philby finally joined the SIS.

Yet another ingenious idea fabricated by the KGB was to attribute the report containing photos of a homosexual orgy involving some prominent figures to Nikolsky as his great operational achievement. In 1935 Burgess became personal assistant to the right-wing Conservative MP Captain John Robert Macnamara, with whom he went on a 'fact finding mission to Nazi Germany' the following spring. Their days there, according to Burgess, were largely devoted to sexual escapades with gay members of the Hitler Youth.[35]

The incriminating photographic material was later delivered by Burgess to Deutsch. Forgetting that Nikolsky/Goldin had hastily retreated from London in September 1935—that is, two months *before* Burgess got his PA job at Macnamara's office—Orlov's biographers reference this information, found in the MÄDCHEN (Burgess) file at the KGB archives, to 'Orlov's report to the Centre of 12 July 1935'.[36] In reality, it was Deutsch, not Nikolsky, who reported this information to the Lubyanka, attaching the photos. And he did so long after SCHWED had left the ISLAND.

Deutsch's major service to Soviet intelligence was the recruitment of graduate students from Oxford and Cambridge, two English universities that provided a disproportionate number of Whitehall's highest fliers.[37] Deutsch, with his flair for intelligence work, also used his natural cover as a postgraduate student of London University and his academic qualifications to meet other young people. KGB files credit Deutsch during his compara-tively short sojourn in Britain (from February 1934 to September and then November 1937) with the recruitment of twenty agents and several contacts, a total of twenty-nine in all,[38] many of whom remain unidentified. Without doubt, Edith Tudor-Hart, a photographer as well as talent-spotter and courier for the cell, used her closeness to the CPGB leadership and her many acquaintances among the exiled Austrian community in London to help Deutsch get new recruits. Although she was on the MI5 watch-list from 1930 (she first travelled to England in 1925 to attend some teaching courses), and the Security Service kept files on her and her English husband, as well as on several of their friends and visitors to their house, her contacts with Deutsch were never reported.[39] In the meantime, in October 1934, shortly after she had introduced Philby to his NKVD recruiter Deutsch, she helped Deutsch to recruit Arthur Wynn (SCOTT), then a radio specialist and a future senior civil servant. Edith also acted as a cut-out for Guy Burgess in Paris and for Anthony Blunt and Bob Stewart in London until the NKVD station at the Soviet Embassy in Kensington Gardens was temporarily closed in 1940.

In August 1935 Deutsch went to Moscow on leave and remained there until November 1935.[40] Philby was also away from London that summer, as he and Litzi decided to spend their holidays in Spain. Therefore there were no messages from SCHWED before 9 September, when he sent a letter to Sloutsky, the controller of group 'G', commenting on the latter's earlier message: 'I am very pleased that he [Deutsch] was of use to you and that you were attentive to him and treated him as a comrade.'[41] Soon after he arrived in Moscow, in August, Deutsch and his wife were sent to the NKVD sanatorium for prolonged holidays. Nine months later, in May 1936, their daughter was born in London. They named her Ninette Elizabeth, or simply Nina in Russian.

After Philby and his wife had returned to London, he received an unexpected job offer from his father's old employer, the Indian Civil

Service. It was proposed that Philby junior should become a press liaison officer in New Delhi. Nikolsky is quoted as reporting to the Centre: 'I instructed SÖHNCHEN to take up this position.'[42] His next dispatch, dated 12 September, seeking Moscow's approval for Philby to go to India, was the last thing that SCHWED sent from London.[43] Shortly afterwards he used the same trick that he had once used in Paris, claiming that his illegal cover had been broken by an accidental meeting with someone who knew him in Austria as a Soviet citizen. Therefore, he explained, he had to make a hasty exit from London to Copenhagen. Nikolsky realized that his days as the London 'illegal' resident were numbered and preferred to leave the battle-ground of his own volition. Besides, he was clearly no match for Deutsch, Maly, Pieck, and Bystroletov and his wretched operational ideas were regularly turned down by the Centre. When Deutsch took over the control of Philby in November, his first instruction to SÖHNCHEN was to forget the Indian appointment.

Under Deutsch's supervision, Philby, Maclean, and Burgess rapidly graduated from probationers to fully-fledged Soviet agents. They might not have been told explicitly at that stage that they were working for the NKVD and instead were persuaded to think they were assisting the Comintern in its anti-fascist struggle. But, as good students, they were learning fast. Later Deutsch wrote in a memo to the Centre that 'they all knew that they are working for the Soviet Union. This was absolutely understood by them. My relations with them were based upon our party membership.'[44] Philby said that, when the proposition was made to him, he did not hesitate. 'One does not look twice at an offer of enrolment in an elite force,' he said, adding that he was finally able to emerge 'in my true colours, the colours of a Soviet intelligence officer'.[45] What else could he say—a gambler, a womanizer, and a heavy drinker locked in the Soviet Union and never promoted to an officer's rank in spite of his thirty-odd years as a Soviet spy. And one needs quite an imagination to call Stalin's secret police 'an elite force'.

On 9 October the Centre received a message sent by SCHOR, a wireless operator based in Copenhagen. SCHOR reported Nikolsky's story that in London he had bumped into the man who used to give him English lessons in Vienna. SCHWED claimed that the meeting had destroyed his 'legend' as the American businessman Goldin. On the next day he received instructions from Moscow to pull out.[46]

But, despite SCHWED's travails, the future for Soviet espionage in Britain at the outbreak of war was brighter than it had ever been before.[47]

11

Home, Sweet Home: October 1935–September 1936

Captain of State Security Nikolsky retuned to his office at the now NKVD Lubyanka headquarters on Tuesday, 29 October 1935. He had only three days to update Deutsch on the situation before the latter left for the UK. Maly also happened to be in Moscow at the time, settling family affairs with his first wife. When he returned to London at the end of November to work with MAG, his able recruiter Bystroletov was getting ready to return home after his excessively long European tour of duty.[1] Although *The Authorized History of MI5* mentions several of Maly's and Deutsch's security lapses, the fact that Deutsch had remained undiscovered for three years and Maly managed to leave the country under the nose of the Security Service's Observation Section demonstrates that they were smart operators and took great precautions to evade MI5 and Special Branch surveillance.

Before preparing for a meeting with an agent, usually in London, Deutsch would be driven out of town, watching carefully to see if the car was being followed. Once satisfied that he was not being tailed, he returned to London by public transport, changing several times en route. During his travels Deutsch concealed film of secret documents inside hairbrushes, travel requisites and household utensils. Reports to the Centre were usually sent in secret ink to an address in Copenhagen for forwarding to Moscow.[2]

On Saturday, 2 November, immediately after Deutsch had left Moscow, Nikolsky was summoned to Sloutsky's office. Although, as those who knew them both confirm,[3] the chief of the Soviet foreign intelligence and his subordinate were good friends, Sloutsky demanded a detailed explanation from 'Lyova' regarding his poor performance in London. Nikolsky wrote a report that was intended to demonstrate that Maclean's position at the Foreign Office had been his achievement,[4] and claiming other equally dubious successes. It did not help. While Reif, his predecessor in London, had been promoted upon his return to become the chief of the INO's British section, Nikolsky was reprimanded and dismissed from foreign intelligence. He was demoted to the Transport Department as assistant to its chief, Alexander Shanin. Later, during his debriefing by the FBI, Orlov claimed that this transfer was the result of his 'attempt to distance himself from the centre of power in the NKVD'. And the chairman of the US senate internal security subcommittee, Senator James O. Eastland, believed it was Yagoda, the NKVD chairman, who was not well disposed towards 'General Orlov' and therefore played a role in his transfer.[5] In reality, Yagoda had almost certainly never personally met SCHWED before he was sent to Spain.

Another legend cultivated by Orlov's fans is his allegedly leading role in the handling of Maclean and his work with his 'product' at the Centre after his return from London. Specifically, the spy is praised for passing on the complete minutes of the Imperial Defence Committee meeting of 20 December 1936 attended by Prime Minister Baldwin, and Orlov is complimented for producing a brilliant analysis of this and other documents.[6] In reality, by the time the Imperial Defence Committee met in London, Nikolsky/Orlov had already been in Madrid *for four months* and had his hands full of Spanish gold, French croissants, and the Trotskyists of all nationalities, real or imagined. Maclean's reports from England could not have reached him, and they never did.

In the meantime, while Nikolsky was familiarizing himself with the Russian undeveloped road network and railway infrastructure, things began to look bright for Soviet intelligence in London, thanks to the efforts of Deutsch, Maly, and their numerous helpers.

This, however, did not happen until spring 1936. In March, Maly reported a rich harvest of secret documents received from the Foreign Office cipher clerk Jonh King,[7] but there seems to have been no information coming from Maclean during his first months in the Western Department. Upon his return from London, Nikolsky explained in his memo that 'Maclean was not to take out any materials at this stage from the Foreign Office, but advised to confine himself to supplying us with brief information about the character and contents of the papers passing through his hands ... The preceding months of preparation confirmed that WAISE

[Maclean] enjoys free access to all the documents that pass through his department.'[8]

In April, Maly became the supervisor of the network and henceforth shared with Deutsch the running of the earlier recruits while adding new assets. At the same time, Adolf Chapsky, an experienced NKVD officer who had previously operated in Vienna, was transferred to London as head of the 'legal' NKVD station in summer 1936. Chapsky, using the alias 'Anton Schuster', had the official cover of 2nd Secretary of the Soviet Embassy. He frequently engaged the services of his brother, Bernard Davidovich, whose fur boutique in London was a convenient front for secret meetings and financial transactions.[9] By the time they all returned to Moscow in 1937 and *before* Anthony Blunt (TONY) and John Cairncross (MOLIÈRE) became part of the Cambridge Spy Ring, the total NKVD agent network in Britain exceeded 100.[10] Among those were Norman John 'James' Klugmann (codenamed MER), one of Cambridge's most influential Marxists; Olga Neyman (JACK), the Russian-born wife of a leading theoretical statistician and professor of mathematics at the University of California, recruited in London in 1935;[11] and Arthur Wynn (SCOTT), a CPGB member recruited in January 1937, who would himself become an active recruiter in Oxford and then a distinguished civil servant. There was also his wife Margaret (BUNNY), plus a range of others. Blunt, considered to be the fourth member of the Cambridge Five, was recruited by Deutsch with the help of Burgess in January 1937, at the same time as Wynn, and four months later came Cairncross, who in 1934 entered Trinity at the age of 21 with a scholarship in modern languages.[12] However, according to their KGB files, 103 agents were recruited in the period between Burgess and Blunt.

In 1933, H. P. Smolka, an Austrian Jew from a well-to-do family, went to London as a correspondent for the Viennese newspaper *Neue Freie Presse*. The paper's owner and publisher, Ernst Benedikt, in fact had to sell it to the Austrian government a year later. Then, after the Anschluss of Austria, the newspaper, scornfully labelled the 'Judenblatt' by the Nazis, was closed down. It did not reappear until 1946, when its former editor-in-chief, Ernst Molden, gave it a new birth as *Die Presse*. Quite by chance, his son Fritz, an Austrian diplomat in New York after the war, married Joan Dulles, the daughter of Allen Welsh Dulles, the future first civilian CIA director.[13] In the same year Smolka returned to Vienna as the correspondent for *The Times* of London in Central Europe.

Smolka visited the Soviet Union in 1936 and later made his reputation in Britain with a series of well-written articles for *The Times* describing his travels in the first country of real socialism. In London, Smolka, described by one of his acquaintances as 'ebullient and buccaneering',[14] became a naturalized British subject, changing his name to Harry Peter Smollett. Soon he joined the Exchange Telegraph Company, heading its newly formed foreign department, and in 1941 he achieved the remarkable feat of becoming head of the Soviet section in the wartime Ministry of Information, thanks, some say, to his acquaintance with Brendan Bracken.[15] Bracken was considered an excellent minister, serving from 1941 to the end of the war in 1945. Before Smolka–Smollett succeeded in getting his high ministerial post, he was allegedly recruited as a Soviet agent (codenamed ABO) by Kim Philby, whose wife Litzi had known Smolka in Vienna. But this 'recruitment' remained unknown to Moscow until 1943. Noticeably, two years earlier the head of the 'legal' NKVD station at the Soviet Embassy, Anatoly Gorsky (alias 'Gromov'), had forbidden any use of ABO as an agent.[16] Nevertheless, as became known several decades later, in London and upon his return to Vienna, Smolka continued to function as an agent of influence. This is undoubtedly the reason why the Russian authorities in Austria returned his father's factory, which had once been confiscated by them, to him so promptly, while others had to wait for years to have their alleged 'German property's' status cleared.[17] In Vienna, Smolka's wife worked as the correspondent of the ill-famed Communist News Agency Telepress, whose headquarters was in Prague.

One of the Ministry of Information employees with whom Bracken was unpopular was George Orwell, who served there under his given name of Eric Blair. It has been suggested that Smolka–Smollett was almost certainly the MOI official on whose advice the London publisher Jonathan Cape turned down *Animal Farm* as a nasty anti-Soviet piece.[18] But this was certainly not the only achievement of ABO. According to Christopher Andrew:

By 1943 Smollett was using his position to organize pro-Soviet propaganda on a prodigious scale. A vast meeting at the Albert Hall in February to celebrate the twenty-fifth anniversary of the Red Army included songs of praise by a massed choir, readings by John Gielgud and Laurence Olivier, and was attended by leading politicians from all parties. The film *USSR at War* was shown to factory audiences of one and a quarter million. In September 1943 alone, the Ministry of Information organized meetings on the Soviet Union for 34 public venues, 35 factories,

100 voluntary societies, 28 civil defence groups, 9 schools and a prison; the BBC in the same month broadcast thirty programmes with a substantial Soviet content.[19]

Despite these gloomy statistics, Smolka was made an Officer of the British Empire (OBE).

Ironically, some of Smolka's short stories about post-war Vienna were heavily drawn upon by Graham Greene when he worked there on his famous film *The Third Man*, often sitting at a small round table in the Café Mozart just behind the State Opera. However, it is probably a joke that the 'Smolka' bar featured in the film is named after the man,[20] although it is a known fact that the two worked closely together during the making of the film. It was Elizabeth Montagu, the daughter of Lord Montagu, who met Greene at Vienna airport and introduced him to her friend, Smolka. It has frequently been asserted, following Greene's own account of events, that Charles Beauclerk, who was serving as an intelligence officer in Vienna,[21] supplied Greene with the insider's information about the penicillin racket and the sewer police that he subsequently used in his script, but it turns out it was Smolka.

George Weidenfeld (later Baron Weidenfeld), who was also born in Vienna and knew Smolka in London, recalled that after the war *The Times* was going 'through a period of acute Russophilia'. In his autobiography Weidenfeld noted that 'under the aegis of E. H. Carr it employed pro-Soviet correspondents in Budapest and Moscow [but also in Vienna] who doggedly wrote apologies for Soviet foreign policy'.[22] One of Smolka's close friends was Harry Pollitt, the CPGB leader. Sadly, in the Smolka–Smollett case, no one paid attention to the warnings against him, and, after having served *The Times* for many years, he was nominated for the presidency of the Association of Foreign Journalists in Vienna (which he rejected), and died with his reputation unsullied in 1980.[23]

Another friend of Smolka in London was the Marxist historian Christopher Hill. Hill became a crypto-Communist—that is, a member of the CPGB underground 'apparatus' while studying at Balliol College, Oxford. In 1935 he also visited the Soviet Union, but, unlike Smolka, remained there for almost a year learning Russian, studying Soviet history and Marxism-Leninism, and forming a lasting affection for Soviet life and Stalin's politics. Whether he was recruited in Moscow as a fully-fledged agent is not known, but there is no doubt that after his return to Britain he wittingly chose a role of the Soviet agent of influence. That does not necessarily mean that Hill worked for the NKVD, but he certainly used his position to influence public opinion or decision-making to produce results beneficial to the Soviet Union. And, paraphrasing an informed expert, the work of an agent of influence can be far more valuable, subtle, and dangerous than that of a spy.[24]

Hill had spent two years working as an assistant lecturer at University College, Cardiff, before returning to Balliol as a fellow and tutor in modern history. When the civil war in Spain broke out, Hill reportedly wanted to join the International Brigades, like many of his Party comrades, but for whatever reason it was decided he should stay in Britain. In 1940, Hill was commissioned as a lieutenant in the Oxford and Bucks Light Infantry, after briefly serving in the Field Security Police. He was soon recruited to the SOE, where he was eventually promoted to major. Thanks to his fluency in Russian, Hill worked first as a liaison officer with Soviet military engineers and, quite possibly, with what became known as 'Pickaxe parties' in SOE parlance after a secret agreement was reached in Moscow between the SOE and the NKVD on 30 September 1941.[25] Soon, NKVD Col. Ivan Chichayev arrived in London to carry out liaison with the SOE, accompanied by three assistants. Meanwhile, a liaison office (codenamed SAM) was also set up in Moscow, which was initially run by Lieutenant Colonel Guinness and later by Brigadier George A. Hill.

At least twenty-five trained NKVD agents were successfully dropped by the RAF between 1942 and 1944,[26] and Hill himself had been assigned to a small SOE unit preparing to be parachuted into one of the Baltic states, but the mission was shelved, and in 1943 he was seconded to the Foreign Office. Because of his first-hand knowledge of all things Russian, he was soon promoted to head the Soviet desk. Thus, in the middle of the war, two Soviet agents of influence, Smolka and Hill, were responsible for Soviet affairs in two important ministries developing the British government policy towards the Soviet Union. As *The Times* put it:

While in this key post Hill used his formidable energies to the full. He urged the government to sack all White Russian émigrés working in British schools and universities and replace them with Soviet-approved staff. He set up a Committee for Russian Studies including other Communists, notably the Soviet agent Peter Smollett (alias Smolka) [*sic*], to make it easier for Soviet citizens to come to Britain and to exchange intelligence with the USSR . . . And in face of all the evidence to the contrary, the Foreign Office remained strangely convinced that Stalin's intentions towards Eastern Europe were strictly benign.[27]

Moreover, while at the Foreign Office Hill wrote a book, *The Soviets and Ourselves: Two Commonwealths*, which he later published with the help of Smolka and under a pseudonym.[28] Among other things, he described the Stalinist purges as 'non-violent'. Now we know that nearly 700,000 people were executed during the Great Terror[29] and that Stalin personally signed 357 'proscription lists' that condemned to execution some 40,000 people.[30] This in no way stopped Hill from writing on Stalin's death: 'He was a very great and penetrating thinker. Humanity not only in Russia but in all countries will always be deeply in his debt.'[31]

Although Hill concealed his Communist Party membership when joining the secret service and the Foreign Office, his activities after the war were scarcely subterranean. In 1946 he was one of the founders of the Communist Party Historians' Group, an association that included, among others, Maurice Dobb, Eric Hobsbawm, and Dorothy Thompson, and that claimed to have redefined the study of history in Britain. A year later, Hill published his *Lenin and the Russian Revolution*, an example of Marxist-Leninist scholarship. Some say his life changed in 1956 when he became disenchanted with the Party and married his second wife. Hill left the CPGB in 1957, but in 1967 gave a radio talk marking the centenary of the publication of Karl Marx's *Capital*. He ended it by telling how, in old age, Marx argued that he had not become either less radical or less political. And nor, it seems he intended his listeners to understand, had Christopher Hill.[32]

The name of yet another Soviet agent came to light in October 2004. James MacGibbon, who had died four years previously, aged 88, admitted in a twelve-page affidavit that he had spied for the Russians while working in the War Office. James was recruited after he became a Communist in 1934. Information from a secret source in late 1937 indicated that MacGibbon had performed 'a service' for the Soviets, for which he was rewarded. He was investigated and eventually interviewed, but denied the allegation.[33] When the war broke out, he volunteered to join the Royal Fusiliers and was commissioned as a second lieutenant. Because of his knowledge of German, he was posted into the Intelligence Corps and later to the War Office Military Operations, Section 3, where he was involved in planning Operation 'Overlord', the Allied invasion of Normandy in June 1944. MacGibbon, whose son Hamish followed in his career footsteps, finally became a publisher, head of MacGibbon & Kee, who were the first to publish Philby's *My Silent War* in 1968.

Old sympathies die hard, and it is probably right that people do not become less politically tolerant as they age. In June 1987 the *London Review of Books* published an article on treason where the author remembered his Cambridge years with Guy Burgess, who was one of those—two others were James Klugmann and John Cornford—who helped to introduce him into the Communist Party. James MacGibbon immediately responded by writing to the editor:

SIR: V. G. Kiernan's contribution on treason states succinctly something that has long needed saying. When the spy-book boom was reaching its height A. J. P. Taylor wrote that it seemed to him these left-wing spies had not much of importance to tell. It is the traitors of the Right—Lord Halifax, the then Foreign Secretary, hobnobbing with Goering in the late thirties, Ribbentrop's social success in London 'society', support of Franco that culminated in the defeat of France, and so on and so on, up to the present with the Libyan bombings and military support for the rebels in Nicaragua (the list is endless)—who seriously threaten the free world.[34]

As so many other important British institutions both before but especially during the war, the War Office turned out to be well penetrated by the Soviet agents. Leonard Henry ('Leo') Long arrived at Trinity already a Communist, and in May 1937 Anthony Blunt wrote in one of his reports to Moscow: 'As you already know, the actual recruits whom I took were Michael Straight and Leo Long.'[35] Like MacGibbon, Long turned out to be extremely important during the war, when he joined the Directorate of Military Intelligence. According to his post-war interrogator, Peter Wright, he was posted to MI14, with responsibility for assessing the work of the Signal Intelligence Agency of the Supreme Command of the German Armed Forces (OKW/Chi; that is, Oberkommando der Wehrmacht Chiffrierabteilung) and hence military strength. Throughout the war he used to meet Blunt, handing over 'any intelligence he could lay his hands on'.[36] After the war, Blunt recommended Long (codenamed ELLI) for a senior post in MI5, but the selection board passed him over. Long moved to the British Control Commission for Germany, where he eventually became Deputy Director of Military Intelligence.[37] Over the winter of 1945–6, all MI6 personnel in Germany were placed under the command of Lieutenant Colonel Felix Cowgill, an army officer seconded to SIS, whom Philby succeeded as head of Section V in 1944. The whole German SIS station was eventually transformed into an element of the Intelligence Division of the Control Commission, of which it formed the Technical

Section.[38] Leo Long left his post in the Commission in 1952—a year after Maclean and Burgess had defected to Russia.

Philby's own lucky chance came in 1939 when a journalist colleague introduced him to Marjorie Maxse, who offered him to write an application to the War Office, where his friend Burgess was already working. Their time there, however, was short lived: Burgess was soon fired, and Philby transferred to one of the SOE's schools in Beaulieu, Hampshire.

With the exception of the first three members of the future Cambridge Ring of Five (Philby, Maclean, and Burgess), who were still probationers when he was in London, Nikolsky knew nothing of the above. And he certainly did not care to know. In the spring of 1936 Nikolsky was up to his neck in the current chores of his new Transport Department,[39] his personal affairs, and a new violent campaign unrolled by Stalin against the Trotsky-ists. Although he saw it, he probably did not pay attention to *Pravda*'s report of 12 March. A telegram from Germany informed its readers that the Spanish general named José Sanjurjo had visited Berlin to negotiate the purchase of weapons. The NKVD case officers in Berlin—'legal' Boris Gordon and 'illegal' Vasili Zarubin and Fyodor Parparov—without doubt reported details to Sloutsky, as did their military intelligence colleagues.

Nikolsky, who in September would be sent to Spain as 'Alexander Orlov', would not have known that from 1935 the chief RU resident and Soviet Military Attaché in Berlin was Alexander Grigorievich Orlov, whose name, biographical details, and general's rank Nikolsky would later borrow. Orlov was assisted by Pavel Fomenko, posing as a member of the Soviet Trade Legation and military engineer 3rd rank Konstantin Leontyev. For two years, from 1936, the 'illegal' RU resident in Berlin was Ivan Krekma-nov (SCHWARZ and JAN),[40] who ran several important sources.

Who of the RU personnel was personally assigned as the controller of Oskar von Niedermayer is not known, but it can now be revealed that this former Reichswehr liaison in Moscow was a Soviet agent.

Oskar Ritter von Niedermayer, a German nobleman, traveller, soldier, and academic born in 1885 in Regensburg, Bavaria, from December 1921 worked at the secret Soviet section of the Defence Ministry (Reichswehr-ministerium) of the Weimar Republic set up early that year. The section, known as Sondergruppe-R, where 'R' stood for 'Russia', was responsible for the likewise secret Soviet–German military collaboration that began in August 1920. When Germany approached Soviet Russia, which, like Germany and its allies after the First World War, was an outcast state after the Bolshevik revolution, its specific aims were the rearmament of the armed forces prohibited by the Treaty of Versailles, the prevention of the British–Soviet rapprochement, and an alliance against Poland, a traditional enemy of Germany. The Soviet leadership initially hoped that good relations with Germany might help to counter the crippling effects of the international trade blockade (which indeed happened with the signing of the Treaty of Rapallo in 1922). The young Red Army badly needed German state-of-the-art military technologies, equipment, and training programmes. In April 1920 the Soviets asked whether Germany was prepared for a joint military action against Poland. And, last but not least, Lenin and his followers hoped for a successful Bolshevik-style proletarian revolution in Germany that would 'sparkle' the world revolution. For several years until 1932 Oskar von Niedermayer had worked in the Reichswehr office in Moscow, entrusted with serving as a liaison between the German army and the Red Army (including its intelligence directorate), as well as between the Reichswehr and the OGPU. In the yellow Lubyanka building, the OGPU headquarters, where his biography should have been well known, Niedermayer was nevertheless considered to be a high Abwehr official, though he never served as an intelligence officer.

As soon as this liaison office was opened, in March 1924 the Soviets approached their German counterparts to ask how Germany could help the Soviet Union to develop its military capabilities. Could, for example, the Albatros Werke build aeroplanes in the Soviet Union; could Blohm and Voss build submarines; could Krupp build ammunition production plants.[41] This entirely clandestine military collaboration continued until December 1926, when the *Manchester Guardian* published several articles on the subject, causing a major scandal. By 1932, when von Niedermayer was leaving Moscow, where he was in regular contact with Marshall Tukhachevsky and other Soviet military leaders, the end of Soviet–German collaboration efforts was clearly in sight.

During the war, Niedermayer, who had to interrupt his academic career at Berlin University in 1939 and joined the army as colonel in the Oberkommando der Wehrmacht (OKW) (Supreme Command of the German Armed Forces), served in Ukraine, where he was responsible for the training of the so-called Ostlegionen. He was later moved to Italy and then back to Germany. However, in July 1944 two officers of his staff reported on him to the Gestapo, and Niedermayer was arrested and court-martialled for defeatism, narrowly escaping death thanks to the American troops. On 9 May

1945 he was released from the prison of Torgau and sent to his home town of Regensburg. Travelling through Czechoslovakia, Niedermayer was arrested by the Soviet military counter-spy organization Smersh and sent to Moscow. In Russia, he was sentenced to twenty-five years, which he was to serve in the infamous Vladimir prison, but after only a few days there he died, in September 1948,[42] allegedly from tuberculosis.

Niedermayer's name suddenly popped up again in 1957 when Marshal Tukhachevsky was officially exonerated by Soviet authorities after his execution twenty years previously. One of the counts of his indictment alleged that for approximately twelve years the Soviet marshal was in contact with 'O. V. Niedermayer, a German spy, who was his link to the German General Staff'. However, an official document provided to the Exoneration Commission by the USSR Ministry of Defence stated that in 1936, in Berlin, Niedermayer was known for his anti-Nazi views and was regularly meeting his RU case officer, who received important intelligence from Niedermayer[43] regarding German military doctrine and capabilities.

With Lehmann in the Gestapo, Schulze-Boysen in the communications department of the Reich Air Transport Ministry, Gerhard Kegel in the Foreign Ministry, and Niedermayer teaching military doctrine to the German army officer corps, it is unlikely that information about General Sanjurjo's visit to Berlin was missed at the Centre.

There are still debates as to whether Moscow was sufficiently informed about the situation in Spain in May, June, and July 1936. There is little doubt that it was. First of all, of course, one source of insider information was the Comintern/OMS representatives and the leaders of the Partido Comunista de España (PCE) (Spanish Communist Party).[44] Besides, in 1936 the RIS already had excellent sources, not only in France, Germany, Italy, Portugal, and Spain itself but, which is more important, at the top echelons of power in Britain and the USA, both of whom were not indifferent to the situation on the Iberian Peninsula. The Soviet leaders certainly sensed that something was boiling behind the Pyrenees, but Spain was low on the agenda. The highest priority was Stalin's campaign against 'Trotskyism', which at the time was reaching its climax.

On 20 May the Politburo issued a special decree 'On the Trotskyites'.[45] According to the decree, in the shortest possible time the NKVD was obliged (1) to transfer all previously exiled Trotskyites to the Gulag for the period of three to five years; (2) to arrest and send to the Gulag for the period of three to five years all the Trotskyites expelled from the Communist Party for taking part in 'hostile activities', who reside in the main cities such as Moscow, Leningrad, Kiev, Minsk, Baku, etc.; (3) to shoot all arrested Trotskyites accused of terrorism. Almost every day Stalin received reports from the NKVD about the unmasking of a new Trotskyist group or Polish and German spies.[46] As is well known, Stalin placed at the top of the Trotsky conspiracy old Bolsheviks Zinoviev and Kamenev, plus another fourteen to prove that Trotsky was a terrorist and a Gestapo agent. All co-defendants had to be broken and questioned relentlessly until full confessions were squeezed out of them. In July, Nikolsky's chief Yagoda and the chief prosecutor Andrey Vyshinsky asked Stalin to let them retry Kamenev and Zinoviev, who had received 'light' prison sentences in 1935. In August, Stalin was informed that the prosecutor Vyshinsky and Judge Ulrikh had fully rehearsed the trial for performance later that month and that all was ready, so Stalin could spend all August and September on holiday in Sochi. All the defendants received death sentences, and all were shot a few hours later.[47] It was the first Moscow show trial and two more were still to follow.

On 24 May, Maly informed Moscow:

Tonight WAISE [Maclean] arrived with an enormous bundle of dispatches, of which MAG [King] had supplied only a few. Only some of them, which we have marked with a W, have been photographed, because we have run out of film and today is Sunday—and night time at that. We wanted him [Maclean] to take out a military intelligence bulletin, but he did not manage to do that. On Saturday he has to stay [on duty] in London and we hope that he will be able to bring out more, including those, which he had not managed to get out yet.[48]

Maclean was a rising star of the Foreign Office's Western Department, which followed the situation in the Iberian Peninsula with great attention from 1931. Nevertheless, it was only from February 1936, with the coming to power of the Popular Front government, that a precise interpretation of the Spanish crisis began to take shape at the Foreign Office. The conspirators informed the Foreign Office on 29 May, two weeks after General Sanjurjo's visit to Berlin to buy arms, of their intentions regarding a coup 'designed solely to restore order and to place in power a civilian, right-wing government'.[49] 'At the same time', notes the Spanish historian Enrique Moradiellos, 'the arrival in London of reliable reports informing of a military conspiracy aimed at the restoration of order, rather than being a fascist persuasion, suggested a denouement to the Spanish crisis, which would avoid repetition of the Russian revolutionary experience on the other side of Europe'.[50] As seen from Maly's report, Maclean duly copied all relevant Western Department documents for the NKVD. But the question is not whether Moscow was sufficiently informed; the key question is how, if at all, Maclean's (and others') intelligence influenced Soviet perception and its foreign policy.

By late spring 1936 Maclean became so valuable that the London residency advised Moscow to establish a special routine for handling him. 'I stress once again that WAISE should be transferred under a separate control,' Maly urged the Moscow Centre in a May report from London.[51] He insisted that the Centre should run Maclean through an exclusive and independent channel.

Such a channel was indeed established. The mission was entrusted to Bystroletov (HANS), who by that time had returned to Moscow. In the summer of 1936 Bystroletov travelled to Copenhagen and in all probability handled Maclean separately until the end of 1937 or early 1938, when Moscow learned that Maclean was being considered for his first diplomatic posting abroad as 3rd Secretary of the Paris Embassy. In March 1938 the Foreign Office personnel department warmly recommended him to the British ambassador to France,[52] Sir Eric Phipps. Thus, Maclean was able to provide his handlers with high-grade political intelligence from London during the crucial period of the Spanish Civil War.

Deutsch and Maly continued to run their ever-increasing group of agents together until June 1937, when Maly left for Paris. (Deutsch wrote in his NKVD biography: 'I returned to London and worked there: from November 1935 until April 1936 by myself, from April 1936 until the end of August 1936 with MANN [Maly], then up to January 1937 again by myself and till June 1937 again with MANN and later, till November 1937, again by myself.'[53]) Deutsch later mentioned that, together with his wife and daughter, born in London, he was compelled to leave England in September 1937 as his studies at London University had ended and all his attempts to get a work permit had failed. He settled in Paris and returned to London again in November for ten days in order to put his agent network on ice.[54] At the end of November he was recalled to Moscow, allegedly because of the defection of an important NKVD case officer in Paris.[55] His wife and their newly born child remained abroad for the next nine months.

In reality, the new head of the INO was mistaken about the defector. Ignatz Reiss, whom he had in mind, defected in July and was murdered by NKVD assassins on 4 September 1937. He had never worked with Deutsch and could hardly have known him. When writing about Reiss, Zalman Passov was probably thinking of Krivitsky (now codenamed GROLL), who defected on 6 October 1937 and knew both Deutsch and Maly.

Was it his good luck that Maly avoided arrest in London in June 1937 and managed to leave? After a short spell in Paris, he was recalled to Moscow, where he was subsequently arrested and sentenced to death as a 'German spy'.[56] Alas, the story of Maly's return to the USSR reproduced in *KGB: The Inside Story* and then in *The Mitrokhin Archive*, not to mention several other less important books, is not true. It says that Maly accepted the order to return to Moscow with an idealistic fatalism. 'I know that as a former priest I haven't got a chance,' he allegedly told Alexander Orlov—that is, Nikolsky—in Paris. 'But I have decided to go there,' Maly allegedly added, 'so that nobody can say: "That priest might have been a real spy after all."'[57] A nice story, but the point is that in June Maly could not have confided in Orlov in Paris, because Orlov was in Spain. And Maly had never been a priest.

Maly's successor as the Woolwich Arsenal cell controller was 'Willi Brandes' (not to be confused with Willi Brandt), who arrived with his French-speaking wife from North America in October 1937:

Nothing more was heard of Mally [*sic*], and in fact he was recalled to Moscow to perish in the purges. Similarly, Mikhail Borovoy, alias Willy Brandes, also disappeared, and his true identity did not emerge until the KGB's archives were opened [*sic*] and he was revealed as a member of the OGPU's [*recte* NKVD] new Scientific and Technical Section,[58] who had visited the United States under the alias Abraham Hoffman and during September and October 1936 had acquired naturalisation papers and obtained a marriage certificate in Montreal to apply for authentic Canadian passport in the name of Willy and Mary Brandes. Once back-stopped with this documentation, Borovoy had taken up residence in Fonset Court [*recte* Forset Court on Edgware Road], posing as a representative of a New York cosmetics company.[59]

When MI5 and Special Branch started to investigate the Woolwich Arsenal espionage case, they soon found out that Canadian passports for the members of the Brandes family had been obtained with the help of one Armand Labis Feldman. This lead got them nowhere until after the Second World War. But after the war the Royal Mounted Canadian Police (RMCP) located him in Canada, and, choosing between possible deportation and cooperation with the authorities, Feldman decided it would be in his best interest to cooperate.[60] As a result, he was allowed to settle in Montreal.

The man known as Feldman was a Soviet 'illegal' (codenamed BRIT), whose real name was Iosif Wolfovich Volodarsky (wrongly transliterated as 'Joseph Volkovich Volodarsky @ J. Olsen' in the MI5 files), the uncle of this writer. Volodarsky was born on 22 April 1903 in Kiev[61] and was educated as an oil engineer. Together with his first cousin, seven years his junior, Volodarsky moved to Moscow and was soon sent to New York, where he spent several years. He was almost certainly co-opted by the OGPU there. In or about 1930 Volodarsky arrived in London to work in the Russian Oil Products (ROP) company as manager and engineer, renting an apartment at 160 Highbury New Park, where other top managers of the ROP lived. In November 1932 he was arrested after an attempt to bribe a Shell-Mex employee, seeking to obtain industrial secrets while posing as a Romanian journalist 'J. Olsen'.[62] Volodarsky was found guilty and fined for an offence under the Corrupt Practices Act, but was actually suspected of being involved in commercial espionage by the Home Office. He left the United Kingdom within the same month, though his British visa was still valid until March 1933. Shortly after, now a commissioned OGPU officer, Volodarsky went to the United States again, this time with a fraudulent Canadian passport in the name of 'Armand Labis Feldman', to be engaged, as in Britain, in industrial espionage, but he was also running a source in the US Justice Department[63] and provided documentary support to other 'illegals'. One of them was 'Willi Brandes',[64] or, rather, Mikhail Borovoy.

After only a few weeks in the UK, the Brandes couple, who introduced themselves as Mr and Mrs 'Stevens', suddenly left the ISLAND in the direction of Paris. During their short stay in London they were observed by the Security Service watchers meeting George Whomack of the Woolwich Arsenal and by an MI5 agent photographing secret documents. What happened to them after their departure is unknown, but 'Willi Brandes' never surfaced again in the West.[65] He was reportedly arrested in Leningrad in February 1938 and, according to Tsarev, spent two years in Siberia.[66]

When Deutsch left London, all his agents there were put on ice and practically lost all contacts with their Soviet handlers. In January 1938, Bystroletov was suspended from duty pending investigation. He was transferred to the Chamber of Commerce in March and arrested on 17 September.[67] He managed to survive the Gulag.

Nikolsky's friend, the legal NKVD head of station in London, Adolf Chapsky, who in the previous four years had worked in Switzerland,

Austria, Czechoslovakia, Germany, and France, was like others recalled in 1937, arrested, and shot. The exact arrival date of his successor, Grigory Grafpen, codenamed SAM, a member of the Soviet Embassy staff posing as attaché 'Gregory Blank', is not clear from the Foreign Office records.[68] From 1927 to 1931 Grafpen had been employed by Amtorg in New York, where he worked together with his London predecessor, Chapsky, before returning to Moscow and joining the OGPU. By the time he arrived in London his smart American suits had certainly been worn out after years in the Lubyanka.

In February 1938 Deutsch wrote to Spiegelglass (codenamed DUCE and DOUGLAS):

Dear Comrade Spiegelglass,
   In early November [1937], when I went to London, I received instructions from you to put all our people on ice for a period of three months. I paid them all their salary up to 1 February [1938], and arranged with them that by that time somebody would get in touch with them. It is now already the end of February and as far as I know only PFEIL and JOHN have been contacted. For various reasons I consider it of great importance to renew contact with our comrades...[69]

The instructions to Grafpen were just to renew contact with Maclean, then the most productive of the Cambridge spies, who was able to smuggle large numbers of classified documents out of the Foreign Office. In connection with Maclean's planned foreign posting, the Centre wanted to replace him with John Cairncross (codenamed LIST or 'Leaf'), but Grafpen bungled the transition. In November he was recalled to Moscow, 'unmasked' as a Trotskyist, and on 29 December arrested and sentenced to five years of hard labour. He survived, and, after his sentence was overturned some three years after Stalin's death, Grafpen retired from his last job at the Pechora Railway in the Komi Republic in north-western Russia and moved to Leningrad. Particulars about his later life and death are unknown.

The story of agent NORMA, whom Grafpen introduced to Maclean as his new contact and courier, has been almost unanimously misinterpreted in many published works, as have her looks and age.[70] In reality, an experienced NKVD agent but not an officer, Katharine 'Kitty' Harris (codename NORMA and ADA), was about 40 at that time and thirteen years Maclean's senior.

Kitty was born on 24 May 1900 (possibly even 1899) in London in a Russian–Polish Jewish family and then went to Canada with her parents. Later she moved to the United States and took an active part in the workers' movement. Kitty met and became a mistress of Earl Russel Browder, a CPUSA functionary, and in 1923–8 was with him in China on a clandestine OMS mission. In 1931 she was an Amtorg employee, together with Grafpen. During the same year Abraham Einhorn recruited her as an OGPU agent. In 1937 Harris was in Moscow, waiting to be sent abroad. Both she and Krivitsky, who had come from Holland amd was shortly to return there for his last assignment, were staying at the Hotel Savoy, just a three-minute walk from the NKVD's Lubyanka headquarters. Harris had a genuine American passport, which was a great asset at the time. She left Moscow on 29 April. After Krivitsky defected, she worked for Zarubin in Germany, together with Margaret Browder, her former lover's younger sister. Before the contact with Maclean was renewed, Harris was recalled to the Centre, where she underwent special training, including mastering document photography. In March 1938 NORMA arrived in London and settled in a flat in Bayswater, north of Hyde Park, probably owned by the OGPU, where Nikolsky's family used to live.

On 4 April the Centre authorized Grafpen to arrange a meeting between NORMA (Harris) and LYRIC (Maclean). Six days later Harris met Maclean for the first time in Leicester Square and quickly became his mistress, violating all rules of undercover work. Harris was reprimanded but not recalled. Now she and Maclean were codenamed ADA and STUART. In September 1938 Maclean left for his first foreign posting in Paris, and in November Grafpen accompanied ADA to the French capital. He, in turn, was en route to Moscow and a labour camp.[71]

By then what used to be the legal INO station at the Soviet Embassy in London had been dramatically reduced and, with one exception, all of its case officers recalled to Moscow. The only remaining intelligence operator in London was Anatoly Veniaminovich Gorsky (codenamed KAP).[72] Sent to the UK in 1936, Gorsky had not had any higher education and worked as an assistant and cipher clerk to two successive residents, Chapsky and Grafpen. Naturally, he was poorly briefed. In the summer of 1939, when Philby, then a sort of intelligence probationer, as Philby called himself in his memoirs,[73] and still codenamed SÖHNCHEN, was due to return to London after the end of the Spanish Civil War, Gorsky asked the Centre: 'When you give us orders on what to do with SÖHNCHEN, we would appreciate some orientation on him, for he is known to us only in the most general terms.'[74] Though his official KGB/SVR biography credits Gorsky with running eighteen agents in London before his recall, the NKVD London station was shut down in February 1940 and a single short entry was made in the file: 'On the orders of People's Commissar Comrade Beria the *rezidentura* in London was closed down and KAP was recalled to the Soviet Union. The reason for closing the *rezidentura* was, allegedly, disinformation given by agents.'[75] Nevertheless, in November Gorsky (now codenamed VADIM) returned to the UK, and his name appeared in the London Diplomatic List, first as Attaché and then as 2nd Secretary, under the alias 'Anatoly Gromov'. During the first war years he was assisted by a cipher clerk and another two case officers. 'Initially a three-man operation,' his KGB biography states, 'Gorsky's London station numbered 12 operatives by early 1944'.[76] This, of course, is as misleading as anything else that originates in the KGB or its successor agencies.

To begin with, by April 1943 Gorsky had already been succeeded in London by Konstantin Kukin. Kukin remembered London well—from May 1931 to August 1932, then a young OGPU operative, he had been posted there under the cover of a position as department manager at ARCOS. Because the number one priority—intelligence work on the atomic problem—started in London and gradually moved to America, in September 1944 Gorsky was sent to the USA as head of station, posing as 1st Secretary of the Soviet Embassy in Washington. Because of the lack of personnel, he was also serving as the embassy's press officer and VOKS representative of the Vsesoyuznoe Obschestvo Kulturnoi Svyazi (VOKS) (s zagranitsei) (All-Union Society for Cultural Relations (with foreign countries)). VOKS was for cultural relations. Or so it claimed.

In August 1937 Kukin was posted to Washington as an attaché of the Soviet Embassy, and was soon promoted to Second Secretary. In late 1940 he returned to Moscow (leaving Michael Straight there without a Soviet controller), to continue working in the Anglo-American section. In 1943 Kukin succeeded Gorsky in London. He would soon be promoted to Soviet chargé d'affaires. In June 1947 Kukin returned to Moscow as head of the First (Anglo-American) Department of the Ministry of State Security.

His period in London was extremely busy as during his tenure both Soviet nuclear R&D facilities and Stalin's foreign ministry depended heavily on the intelligence supplied by Western agents.

From 11 September to 2 October 1945 the Council of Foreign Ministers of the five permanent members of the UN Security Council (the United States, Soviet Union, Britain, France and China) held its first meeting in London to discuss peace treaties with defeated enemy states and other post-war problems. The residency's penetration of the Foreign Office gave it an unusually important role. Throughout the meeting, according to KGB files, the Soviet Ambassador, Ivan Maisky, placed greater reliance on residency staff than on his own diplomats, forcing them to extend each working day into the early hours of the following morning. The Security Council meeting, however, was a failure, publicly exposing for the first time the deep East–West divisions which by 1947 were to engender the Cold War.[77]

Nikolsky's boss in Moscow, chief of the NKVD foreign intelligence Abram Sloutsky, would never know about the cold war. On 17 February 1938 Sloutsky was found dead in the office of the NKVD deputy commissar, allegedly from a heart attack. Sloutsky was almost certainly poisoned on Commissar Yezhov's orders[78] less than a month before the commissar's downfall began. Yezhov's first deputy later testified that, when Sloutsky was summoned to his office, Mikhail Alyokhin, deputy head of the operational techniques department, was hiding in the adjoining room. While Sloutsky was reporting, another of Yezhov's deputies entered the office, pretending to wait for the others to finish. Then he suddenly 'threw a mask with chloroform over Sloutsky's face'. After the victim had passed out, Alyokhin 'injected poison into the muscle of his right arm, as a result of which Sloutsky immediately died'. Subsequently, the first deputy summoned the doctor on duty, who certified Sloutsky's death.[79] However, contrary to what Orlov claimed in his book,[80] no hydrocyanic acid was used, as was later established.[81] And, as in many other cases, despite confessions, there is no other proof of Sloutsky's poisoning. After his chief's death, Spiegelglass was appointed acting head of Foreign Intelligence.[82]

During the spring and summer of 1936 Nikolsky was busy trying to put some order to his romance with a young NKVD operator, Galina Voitova. According to Sudoplatov, he finally refused to divorce his wife and left Voitova, who shot herself in front of the Lubyanka.[83] The date was 18 July 1936. Nikolsky would certainly have been dismissed from the NKVD had he failed to find a way out of the embarrassing situation.

'On 20 July, three days after Spain had become the cockpit of the European struggle between the forces of Fascism and the left, the Politburo approved sending Orlov to Spain.'[84] Remarkably, for many years no one seems to have noticed this glaring discrepancy between theory (or, rather, intentional deception) and reality.

To begin with, there was *no* Politburo meeting on 20 July. An informal meeting of 22 July, where the Spanish question was raised, only approved deliveries of fuel to the Republicans.[85] There was a session of the ECCI on 23 July, the first meeting after the rebel uprising. The ECCI had affirmed its general support of the Republic and on the next day, with Stalin's approval, agreed on instructions to the Spanish Communists,[86] but the details and dimensions of the Soviet or even the Comintern's international efforts would be fleshed out only in the weeks and months to come. Therefore, in July there was no talk of sending any Soviet representatives to Spain, with which the Soviet Union did not even have diplomatic relations.

However, in addition to the group of Comintern agents already there, who regularly reported personally and by radio, Stalin sent his most trusted journalists to Madrid, Valencia, and Barcelona. The *Pravda* editor Mikhail Koltsov arrived first, on 8 August. Another famous Soviet journalist and writer, Iliya Ehrenburg, had visited Spain before and was now in Paris preparing to go there again. On 15 August, the filmmakers Roman Karmen and Boris Makaseyev were summoned to the director of their film studio, who announced that the government had decided that they, too, should immediately be dispatched to the front line. They left Moscow for Paris four days later.[87] Ehrenburg, who was waiting there, briefed them regarding the situation on the fronts, and it was agreed that, after their first reconnaissance trip, they should come back to Paris, send all filmed material to Moscow, and then go to Barcelona together. On 21 August they were in Irún, the ancient Basque town on the French border, and two days later dispatched their first war chronicles to Moscow. After several days of preparation, accompanied by Ehrenburg,[88] they left for Catalonia.

Bill Williams, a young Canadian volunteer, was also there on that day. Having hunted all his life, Williams duly impressed the local Communist Party secretary with his sharp-shooting capabilities and was allowed to join a militia column preparing to march to battle:

On the third day of bombardment, the ships were joined in their attacks on San Sebastián by aerial bombers that continued to raid the city daily thereafter. Although Williams knew there was little likelihood of anyone proving that the Spanish ships had been supported in their shelling by a German battleship, there was no doubt whatsoever that the bombing raids were the work of foreign fascists. He clearly saw the Italian markings on the flanks of the aircraft.[89]

Williams could not know it of course, but in a few days the whole world would watch this attack and a young Canadian sniper shooting down the plane in the documentary chronicle filmed by Karmen and Makaseyev.

They were still filming as the Italian bombers, supported by the cruiser *Canaris*, strafed the civilians in Irún and San Sebastián, the capital of the province. Then, on 21 August the Politburo finally decided to send a small group that included diplomats, intelligence officers, and military advisers to Madrid.[90] Marcel Rosenberg, a veteran of the Soviet diplomatic corps, was appointed as ambassador.[91] Others who arrived together with him on 27 August were Counsellor Leonid Gaikis, who had grown up in Argentina and spoke Spanish. Tank Brigade Commander Vladimir Gorev, elegant, with perfect manners and a good command of English, was appointed military attaché. Besides, Josef Winzer, commercial attaché, Captain Nikolai Kuznetsov, naval attaché, one 'A. Kulov' and the technical staff[92] arrived together with the ambassador and took up residence in the Alfonso hotel. Soon the whole entourage moved to the luxurious Hotel Palace, located at Plaza de las Cortes, the cultural and political centre of the republic. But in the list of these new Russian guests there was no mention of 'Alexander Orlov'.

PART II

In Spain

12

The Backdrop: Spilling the Spanish Beans

In his 1937 essay, 'Spilling the Spanish Beans', George Orwell commented that 'there has been a deliberate conspiracy...to prevent the Spanish situation from being understood'. As the ongoing discussions demonstrate, myths about the Republic, the civil war, and the Francoist dictatorship continue and will continue to proliferate. Historians of the Spanish Civil War keep reminding us that the battle for the truth in what concerns the war and beyond is far from won.[1] Since 1936 the Spanish Civil War has been widely misinterpreted, and many would agree that we are still a long way from having a complete picture of how the political situation was viewed within its international context, especially before and immediately after the war broke out.[2]

When the Second Republic was established on 14 April 1931, people thronged the streets in an outburst of joy. King Alfonso XIII left the country following the municipal elections in which Republican candidates won the majority of votes. On the same Saturday night Monarchist conspirators met to lay down the foundations for subverting the Republic. They were unwilling to give it even a twenty-four-hour respite. The hopes of the people were soon blunted by the strength of the old order's defences.[3]

What constituted the real power—ownership of the land, the financial institutions, industry, and agriculture, as well as the media: major newspapers and radio stations—all remained in the same hands. And those who held that power united with the Church and the Army to defend what they considered as challenges to their property, religion, and national unity. For that purpose they used propaganda, political lobbying, and all other available means. Propaganda denounced the efforts at political and economic reform as the subversive work of the Communist International based in

Moscow. New right-wing political parties opposed to the Republic were founded and funded. Rural and industrial lock-out—in effect, strikes by the management to compel a settlement of disputes on terms favourable to the employer—became a regular response to the measures taken by the government in order to protect worker interests. By 1933 urgent and concerted actions by the right-wing opposition disillusioned the Socialists to the degree that they decided to leave their electoral alliance with the left-wing Republicans. In a system that favoured political coalitions, this led to the victory of the Right in the November 1933 elections.[4] The authoritarian Catholic party, the Confederación Española de Derechas Autónomas (CEDA), emerged as the largest single grouping in the Cortes.

Their day had come. Now employers and landowners started cutting wages, sacking workers, evicting tenants, and raising rents. Paul Preston has demonstrated how 'social legislation was dismantled and, one after another, the principal unions were weakened as strikes were provoked and crushed—notably a nation-wide stoppage by agricultural labourers in the summer of 1934. Tension was rising. The Left saw fascism in every action of the Right; the Right smelt revolution in every left-wing move.'[5]

In May 1934, Monarchists of the two dynastic branches, Alfonsine and Carlist, were able to cajole Mussolini into promising help for a future coup against the Republic. It happened months before the left-wing insurrection of October 1934.[6] On 6 October, three ministers from the CEDA party entered the government. Believing this to be the first step to the establishment of fascism, the Socialists responded by calling a general strike. This has subsequently been interpreted as a deliberate rejection by the Left of the rules of democratic coexistence. Martial law was swiftly declared, and the strike crushed. The bourgeois left-liberal government in Barcelona declared the independence of Spain's four Catalan provinces, but this federalist rebellion was short-lived. However, in Asturias, revolutionary miners, organized jointly by the Socialist Unión General de Trabajadores (UGT), the anarcho-syndicalist Confederación Nacional del Trabajo (CNT), and, belatedly, the Communists, fought a desperate battle against the Army for over two weeks. The Asturian workers were convinced that they were doing what other workers in Germany, Italy, Hungary, and other places had failed to do: taking up arms against fascism. Finally, they were reduced to submission by the joint action of the Army, Navy, and Air Force under the overall coordination of General Franco, who used brutal mercenaries from Spanish Morocco.[7] After the revolutionary uprising had been put down, Franco said: 'This was a frontier war and its fronts are socialism, communism and whatever attacks civilization in order to replace it with barbarism.'[8] Savage repression followed, including looting, rape, and summary executions. The government suspended constitutional guarantees and closed many left-wing newspapers. Torture in prisons was widespread. In the words of Paul Preston: 'It was to be the fire in which was forged the Popular Front, essentially a re-creation of the Republican–Socialist coalition.'[9]

When elections were called for mid-February 1936, it was now the Popular Front against the Right. The Popular Front campaign stressed the threat of fascism, demanding an end to detention and persecution of all those imprisoned after the October 1934 events. A well-financed right-wing campaign tried to convince the electorate that Spain was facing a life-or-death struggle between 'angels' and 'beasts', where the 'pervert Left' attempted to subvert the foundations of eternal Spain: the integrity of the Fatherland, the Army, Roman Catholicism, and the established social order. Spain was on the brink of revolution, they said. On 16 February the Popular Front gained a victory, albeit narrow, which shattered right-wing hopes of legally imposing an authoritarian state. According to Paul Preston:

Two years of aggressive rightist government had left the working masses, especially in the countryside, in a determined and vengeful mood. Having been blocked once in its reforming ambition, the Left was now determined to proceed rapidly with meaningful agrarian reform. In response, right-wing leaders provoked social unrest, then used it in blood-curdling parliamentary speeches and articles, to present a military rising as the only alternative to catastrophe.[10]

In spite of its victory, the Popular Front government was weak. Francisco Largo Caballero used his power in the Socialist Party to prevent the formation of a strong government by his Socialist rival Indalecio Prieto. At the same time, the Right prepared for war. During the spring of 1936 monarchist plotters negotiated the supply of modern Italian war materiel to assist the impending coup.[11] General Emilio Mola organized the military conspiracy. The parties of the Popular Front watched as the terror squads of the growing fascist party, the Falange Española, orchestrated a strategy of tension. As expected, its actions were provoking left-wing reprisals, thus creating disorder to justify the imposition of an authoritarian regime. One such reprisal—the murder of the monarchist leader José Calvo Sotelo—provided the signal for the conspirators.[12] These, in short, were the circumstances that led to the civil war that since its outbreak have been debated by various groups of historians.

To begin with, there are numerous falsifications about the origin of the conflict. As pointed out by Paul Preston, 'these derive from the initial lie that the Spanish Civil War was a necessary war fought to save the country from Communist take-over. The success of this fabrication influenced much writing on the Spanish Civil War to depict it as a conflict between two more or less equal sides.'[13] Another important matter that until recently has been given relatively little weight in the literature on the civil war in Spain is the extent to which the rebels' war effort was built on a prior plan of systematic mass murder.

The leaders of the rebellion, Generals Mola, Franco and Queipo de Llano, regarded the Spanish proletariat in the same way as they did the Moroccan, as an inferior race that had to be subjugated by sudden, uncompromising violence. Thus, they applied in Spain the exemplary terror they had learned in North Africa by deploying the Spanish Foreign Legion and Moroccan mercenaries.[14]

Long before the Spanish holocaust, Franco's war diary of 1922 approvingly described how Moroccan villages had been destroyed and their defenders decapitated by Franco's men. The future *Caudillo* (Franco's choice of title) himself led his legionaries on a raid from which they returned carrying as trophies the bloody heads of the local tribesmen.[15] The fact, hardly noticed before, is that from the very beginning the leaders of the military rebellion carefully planned mass destruction or, in the words of General Mola, elimination 'without scruple or hesitation of those who do not think as we do'.[16] Naturally, the Republican populace did not think as the rebels did. Thus, the bloody, prolonged, and uncompromising character of the conflict was predetermined.

Before we analyse the international context of the events preceding and following the night of 17–18 July 1936, it is necessary to understand that the Spanish Civil War was much more complex than simply a conflict between Fascism and Communism.[17] In the first place, polarization between opposing political forces ensued from the right's determination to block the reforming ambitions of the democratic regime established in April 1931, which in turn led to an ever more radicalized response by the left. Parallel to these processes, rightist theological and racial theories were elaborated to justify the destruction of the left by military intervention.[18]

The intention of forces that opposed the democratic reforms of the Second Republic was to ensure that the establishment interests summed up in the slogan of the right-wing CEDA party—'Religion, Fatherland, Family, Order, Work, Property', the untouchable elements of life in Spain—would never again be challenged as they had been from 1931 to 1936. Therefore, when the clergy justified the rebellion and the military rose, it was to implement General Mola's call for the elimination of the progressive liberal and left-wing 'thinkers', who questioned the central tenets of the right.[19] These narrow ambitions were presented to sympathetic foreign observers as part of a wider crusade against Communism. For different reasons in each case, both the declared and the real objectives of the military rebels ensured that Britain, France, Germany, Italy, and Russia would be deeply interested in Spanish situation. Thus, each would eventually be drawn into playing a role in the unfolding of events.

In the case of London, already after the elections of February 1936, political information from Spain began to flow to the Foreign Office and thus to Stanley Baldwin's cabinet by three channels: from the British diplomats, the existing SIS organization there, and the GC&CS, which intercepted communications between Spanish Communists, Comintern representatives, and Moscow. Therefore, the SIS was tasked with monitoring Communist activity in Spain and reporting on Soviet involvement. In the words of the Service's Official Historian, 'some of this was frustratingly imprecise'.[20] Because the documents remain classified, one has to believe the Official Historian. According to an independent researcher, the fourth channel of information was MI6's sources among the members of the so-called Spanish Committee in London,[21] a group that evolved into the Friends of Nationalist Spain.

In April 1936 a report from a Moroccan-based MI6 agent stated that a month previously—that is, in March—an unnamed Soviet ship had landed 'two large boxes containing rifles and small arms at Algeciras', an important international port in the south of Spain. How the agent learned about this shipment was not specified. The agent also reported that at about the same time the Soviet Union had provided 'a few million pounds' to the Partido Comunista de España (PCE) (Spanish Communist Party). At 54 Broadway, the offices of the SIS, those who received these reports thought the whole thing 'of little value', as the agent did not 'appear to have checked up his information' and did not mention its source. However, as the Service informed its Deuxième Bureau colleagues, London 'had not the slightest doubt that the Communist International, through its centre in Paris, is financing and controlling overt and subterranean activities in Spain'. The opinion of the French side on the matter was solicited, since 'the establishment of a Soviet regime in the Iberian Peninsula is hardly a happening which anyone can view with equanimity for military, political or economic reason'.[22] If there was a reply from the French, it did not survive. London's assurance that its information was correct was based on the fact that all its channels of information from Spain reported the same: that Soviet aid was on the horizon.

Both Europe and America saw the Soviet Union and the Moscow-based Comintern as menaces to stability. Some historians even think that this fear 'divided European opinion in the interwar years and paralysed the will to tackle the Nazi–Fascist threat'.[23] Because of Hitler's declared anti-communism, many hoped that Nazi Germany would destroy Soviet Russia and thereby destroy the Communist menace. They saw Spain as the defensive battleground against the invasion of Western Europe by the Soviet-style proletarian revolution.[24] Lacking reliable intelligence from Moscow,[25] many failed to realize that the USSR was actually quite weak, and world revolution was not on the Soviet agenda any more.

After Mussolini's successful expansion of Italy's African possessions, which already included Libya, Eritrea, Italian Somalia, and now Abyssinia, a tendency to exert influence over diplomacy-making lay at the heart of the democratic powers' appeasement agenda.[26] That means that British, American, and French diplomatic strategy 'was designed to leave the decision when or if to wage war to a time to be determined by them and not by the autocrats on the extreme political right and left'.[27] This diplomatic strategic thinking was formulated on the presumption that from the mid-1930s onwards the League of Nations—a body for resolving international disputes—was becoming impotent or, at least, had been severely undermined because of its failure to halt the Japanese in Manchuria and the Italians in Ethiopia earlier in the decade. By 1936 the League of Nations in Geneva had lost all credibility as an international arbitrator,[28] and the idea of collective security was fatally damaged. The effectiveness of international decisions now depended for the most part on the collaboration between Britain and France, with occasional American involvement, but also on the position of Germany and Italy, with the Soviet Union standing alone in the international diplomacy of the 1930s in spite of its mutual assistance treaty with France. Two decades after the Bolshevik revolution, the Soviet Union was still a pariah, 'barely tolerated by the international community',[29] in spite of a sudden change of Soviet foreign policy towards much greater cooperation with the West against the fascist threat.

The Italian invasion of Ethiopia and the Great Powers' inability to do anything about it also meant that the Final Declaration of the Stresa Conference, better known as the Stresa Front, an April 1935 agreement between Britain, France, and Italy, might not and would not be respected any more. That was a clear signal to dictators of all shades.

In Spain, the conspirators came to the conclusion that the planned spiral of provocation and reprisal had not persuaded public opinion to favour a military coup. It was necessary to raise the temperature. On 12 July four gunmen of the Falange[30] murdered a lieutenant of the Assault Guard, José del Castillo Sáenz de Tejada. Castillo was a member of the Unión Militar Republicana Antifascista (UMRA) (Republican Antifascist Military Union). Two months earlier Castillo's friend, a captain of the Guardia de Asalto, had been shot dead by a Falangist squad. His name was Carlos Faraudo de Miches. Three days after Captain Faraudo's murder, Santiago Casares Quiroga became the Prime Minister and Minister of War. After the assassination of Castillo, Casares showed one of his staff, Major of the Spanish Air Force Ignacio Hidalgo de Cisneros, a confiscated blacklist of fourteen UMRA members compiled by the Spanish Military Union—a clandestine association of army officers devoted to the overthrow of the Republic. Faraudo's name was number one on the list, Castillo's number two, and Hidalgo de Cisneros's number four.[31]

After the death of Castillo, who had recently been married, his close friend Captain Fernando Condés, together with several other police officers and leftist gunmen, decided to retaliate. In the early hours of the following day, at about 3 a.m., they went to the home of José Calvo Sotelo—one of the most important right-wing political figures in the country— kidnapped him in front of his wife and children, and, shortly after he got into a police truck, shot him. Later the perpetrator of the murder was identified as Luis Cuenca, the bodyguard of the Socialist leader Indalecio Prieto. The body of Calvo Sotelo was dropped at the entrance to the municipal cemetery, where it was discovered the next morning.[32] On the same day, 13 July, the Argentinean Vittorio Codovilla, codenamed LUIS, the Comintern representative in Spain, informed Moscow of what had happened and warned about the risk of fatal clashes.[33] For the right, he wrote to Moscow, it was the opportunity to launch their challenge to the Popular Front regime. The communists informed the government about their support but demanded 'energetic steps to stop the menace of the reactionaries'.[34] In the meantime, Gil-Robles declared that the parties of the Popular Front would be the first victims of the coming backlash.[35] 'Desgastar a las izquerdas,' was his famous phrase, 'wear down the left'. He probably knew what he was saying, although there is no documented evidence that the CEDA leader was kept informed of each stage of the plot.

Until this day there are no accurate figures for the number of outbreaks of violence or for the exact number of people killed and injured in the short period between February and July 1936. For all foreign observers, it was clear that the country was undergoing a serious crisis. This crisis was a result of several separate but interwoven and overlapping conflicts—among them, those between landless labourers and big landowners, between industrialists and urban workers, between military centralists and regional nationalists, between the Catholic Church and anticlerical elements, between anarchists and the state.[36] All these conflicts long pre-dated the February–July events, such that by that time they had created a tinder box that could be ignited into civil war by military rising. In these circumstances it was not surprising that the conspiracy that had been brewing behind the scenes since the early years of the Republic restarted with new vigour.[37] And it was not a purely domestic Spanish affair, because, even before the war broke out, it already had an international dimension. The conspiracy counted on fascist support and relied on an element of Western acquiescence, both of which had intensified since the Republican government resumed the 1931–3 policy reforms. In March preparations were well under way, with General José Sanjurjo visiting Berlin in an early and vain attempt to negotiate the purchase of weapons. On 1 July four contracts were signed in Rome detailing the supplies of arms (mostly modern bombers and fighters, including the Italian Savoia-Marchetti S.81 able to carry 500 kg bombs), ammunition, and fuel to the value of over 39 million lire (about 337 million euro in 2013) that Italy was prepared to provide.[38] It was previously believed that Italian aid was clinched in North Africa in the early days of the rebellion as a result of negotiations between Franco and the Italian military attaché in Tangiers. However, as a result of new research,[39] the story of when and how Mussolini was persuaded to intervene in the Spanish war on behalf of the conspirators, so dramatically related in many books and articles, should now be reconsidered.

That does not, of course, mean that the Italian or German agents were engaged in provoking disorders in Spain. On the contrary, neither the previous German ambassador, Johannes Graf von Welczeck, nor the newly appointed career German diplomat Eberhard von Stohrer (who did not arrive until late August 1937),[40] nor Orazio Pedrazzi, the Italian envoy, not to mention their staff, believed in the possibility of a successful coup. After the arrest of the Falangist leader José Primo de Rivera on 14 March 1936, for example, Pedrazzi dismissed altogether the possibility of a fascist uprising, reporting to Rome:

The only organization that had made a serious effort to oppose with force the lamentable social excesses, Falange Española, has been dissolved and its leaders, starting with Primo de Rivera, arrested. In any case, they were nothing more than sporadic manifestations . . . There was never any overall plan that might have eventually borne fruit. The present government has nothing to fear, at least for the moment, from its rightist opponents, who are for now politically impotent.

The German diplomatic documents also make it clear that the German Embassy in Madrid was in no way involved in the conspiracy. 'The documents examined in the archives of the German Foreign Ministry', their editors note, 'do not disclose evidence of German assistance to the Spanish rebels prior to the outbreak of hostilities'.[41]

Contrary to Pedrazzi's pessimistic forecast, preparations for the uprising had already been so serious that on 29 May the conspirators informed the British Foreign Office of their intentions 'to restore law and order' by placing in power 'a civilian, right-wing government'. A memorandum from the Western Department on 23 June warned that the chances of the Popular Front government survival 'are becoming very slight'. It also expressed concern that the Communists were 'arming themselves and strengthening their organization'. Secretary of State for Foreign Affairs Sir Anthony Eden spoke about the weakness of Spain in a meeting of the Cabinet on 6 July.[42] By that time plans had been made by the conspirators for a military coup between 10 and 20 July.[43] The fact that the British authorities were aware of what was about to happen does not mean that either MI6 or the Foreign Office was in any way involved in planning the military plot in Spain.

According to Michael Alpert, 'Foreign Office reactions to Spanish rumours were largely of the "wait and see" kind. Nevertheless, it was a military coup rather than a left-wing revolution that was expected. Thus

Mr Shuckburgh of the Foreign Office wrote on 6 April: 'There is now very much less chance of a Communist rising.' The burden of the comments was that the military coup would probably come and there was nothing to be done about it.[44]

Charles 'Evelyn' Shuckburgh was a young 27-year-old diplomat at the time and not a specialist in Spanish affairs. A more authoritative voice on this matter was R. A. J. Gascoyne-Cecil, better known as Viscount Cranborne. He had served as Under Secretary of State for Foreign Affairs from 1935 to 1938 and was informed about the situation in Spain on a regular basis by the SIS and GC&CS, both of which organizations knew perfectly well from the intercepts in the course of Operation MASK that no communist or left-wing rising was on the horizon in Spain.

In all three capitals, London, Paris, and Washington, there had been little sympathy for the Popular Front government in Spain. The three countries had the largest economic stake in Spain, and their ambassadors constantly warned of the dangerous instability there. For the British, the naval base at Gibraltar was of strategic importance and the territorial integrity of Spanish Morocco was essential to its colonial interests in North Africa. British holdings constituted 40 per cent of the total foreign investment in Spain. In 1935 Britain took 45 per cent of its imported iron ore and 66 per cent of all its imported pyrites from Spain.[45] The British owned various important businesses, including the Rio Tinto mining conglomerate, founded in 1873 when a group of investors bought ancient mines in the Andalusian province of Huelva, turning them into one of the largest industrial giants. The deeply conservative British ambassador in Madrid, Sir Henry Chilton, warned 'there will be hell to pay' should the extreme Left not be checked. 'If the military *coup d'état*, which it is generally believed is being planned, does not succeed, things will be pretty awful.'[46] In reality, whichever side won, Britain's stable position in Spain was pretty much guaranteed by two decisive elements: in the first place, British financial and economic strength was of crucial importance for the Spanish economy; secondly, the Royal Navy had absolute military supremacy in the area.[47] Chilton's warnings were, therefore, without foundation.

The Italian consul in Tangiers also heard the rumours of serious preparations. Towards the end of May he reported to his ministry about an impending uprising, but the ambassador in Madrid, Pedrazzi, dismissed this report, saying that the plans of any military revolt seemed 'destined for the moment to remain in the area of sterile recriminations, without ever leading to anything practical'.[48] It seems that, because their ties with German Nazis and Italian Fascists were so obvious, the conspirators decided to cut off all contacts with their diplomatic missions. Whatever contacts did take place, the German and Italian embassies in Spain knew nothing about them.

On 14 July a De Havilland Dragon Rapide plane arrived in Gando airport on Gran Canaria, from Casablanca, having started its journey at London Croydon. The plane's pilot was Captain Charles William Henry 'Cecil' Bebb, a former Royal Air Force officer renowned for his skill, and its passengers were a retired Army major and the sporting editor of *Country Life* Hugh Pollard, his 19-year-old daughter Diana, her friend Dorothy Watson, and one Luis Antonio Bolín. The party were intended to look like tourists, but they were not, and their mission was not to go sightseeing but to disguise the nature of the trip. The Spaniard Bolín had remained in Casablanca, but he left instructions to the party for the rest of their trip. They were instructed to arrive in Gran Canaria, take a steamer for Santa Cruz, the capital of Tenerife, and find a certain doctor. The doctor was forewarned about a possible visit.

Only a few days before, on 5 July, Bolín, then London correspondent for *ABC*, the Spanish monarchist newspaper, was advised by his friend Juan de la Cierva[49] to contact Captain Olley at Croydon and rent a suitable plane able to transport its passengers safely from the Canary Islands to Spanish Morocco. Then Bolín set off to arrange a lunch with Douglas Jerrold, editor of the right-wing Catholic *English Review* periodical published in London. The idea behind that lunch at Simpson's was to find a suitable group of passengers for the Dragon Rapide hired by Bolín from Olley Air Services with funds provided by a Spanish millionaire with an account at the Kleinwort Bank in London. Jerrold recommended his old friend Pollard.[50] Bolín's second lunch companion was the above-mentioned inventor Juan de la Cierva, whose father, also Juan, had been Spanish Minister of War under the monarchy. In 1925, during his time in office, France and Spain had agreed to combine forces against Abd-el-Krim in Morocco, and de la Cierva senior had placed Franco in command of the Spanish troops. King Alfonso XIII, in exile since 1931, had long been a friend of the family. Jerrold also knew the King, whom he interviewed after he vacated the throne.

Pollard's involvement in Franco's flight from his exile in the Canary Islands to Spanish Morocco, where he took control of the African army, is well known, but his MI6 personal file at The National Archives[51] and some recent publications[52] shed new light on the man and the circumstances surrounding this affair. Major Pollard, whose exploits earned him the appellation the 'Spanish pimpernel' from the *Life* magazine,[53] was an experienced British intelligence officer and firearms experts with a colourful past.[54] Jerrold decided he would be an ideal man for the job, not only because Pollard listed his hobbies in *Who's Who* as 'hunting and shooting' but because of his previous experience in the Mexican Revolution and in Morocco and a functional knowledge of Spanish. An additional plus for the operation was that Pollard was a staunch, fascist-sympathizing Roman Catholic and accordingly a convinced anti-communist.

There is little doubt that on the same day Pollard alerted his contacts in SIS or in the Directorate of Military Intelligence as to the nature of the operation in which he was about to get involved. He needed their urgent help, because three days before the departure, on 8 July, his daughter's friend Dorothy still did not have a passport.[55] But who informed the intelligence services does not really matter. As noted above, from the end of May telegrams started to arrive in London reporting on 'a military conspiracy aimed at the restoration of order to avoid repetition of the Russian revolutionary experience'.[56] Captain Bebb, the Dragon Rapide pilot, also remembered that, when he was waiting for his VIP passenger in Las Palmas, who at the very last moment turned out to be General Franco, the British consul arrived and 'passed very favourable comments on the mission I was about to take part in'.[57] It would be interesting to know what were the precise words that the British consul used, because before 18 July, when Captain Bebb flew Franco to Casablanca, he was led to believe that his passenger would be a rebel Rif leader who was to start another revolt in Morocco. But then again, even Bolín in his book quite openly admits that the consul was a friend of Franco, who met him regularly at the Golf Club.[58] This last statement, however, could hardly be true.

First of all, Franco's regular visits to the Las Palmas Golf Club, founded in December 1891, are not registered anywhere. Franco was appointed to his post as military commander of Tenerife only on 21 February 1936 and needed authorization to visit other islands.[59] That means that the general's visits to Las Palmas were at best limited. Secondly, the British consul in Las Palmas was Sydney Head, at the time 56, who was not a career diplomat. He had worked in the British company Grand Canary Coaling before joining the diplomatic service and in his free time played tennis. He probably did that better than anything else, because in 1907 he won the Spanish championship and received the cup from King Alfonso XIII.[60] Mr Head had been an honourable member and a star player of the Las Palmas Lawn Tennis Club, founded in March 1903, for more than three decades. The Club with its courts was situated in the grounds of the Hotel Metropol, the most luxurious local hotel and the one where the whole party of Bebb, Pollard, and the girls checked in on their arrival. If Bebb was right about the consul, then Head had probably heard about the planned uprising from his colleague in Santa Cruz, Tenerife: another British consul and a career diplomat Harold Patteson. Patteson arrived in June 1935 and was Head's liaison to the British Embassy and the Foreign Office.[61] He also had a wireless radio transmitter and a direct channel of communication to London.

Leaving the Canary Islands in the hands of the rebels and Pollard with his two blonde girls in the Metropol, Franco and the accompanying staff landed in Tetuán, which had already seized by the troops under the command of Colonel Sáenz de Buruaga, who met them at the airport on 19 July. It was the second day of the insurrection, and the only thing its leaders knew for sure was that there was an urgent need to ask for help from Germany and Italy and to send delegations to purchase aircraft and supplies in England.

A grateful Franco later awarded Pollard and his fellow passengers the Knights Cross of the Imperial Order of the Yoke and the Arrows (Encomienda de la Orden Imperial del Yugo y las Flechas). Diana and Dorothy received the same order of the lower class. They would not be the only Britons to receive an honourable Spanish decoration: Franco awarded Philby the Cross of Military Merit (Cruz del Mérito Militar con distintivo blanco) two years later. Shortly after the war broke out the SIS would approach Pollard, asking him if he would be prepared 'to go to Spain and personally put a long series of questions to Franco about his military plans, the external aid he was receiving and how he intended to use his air force', because the Service had 'unavoidably been somewhat slow in developing their organisation' in the Nationalist zone (the government side was better covered). But Pollard asked what seemed too much in return, and Frederick Winterbotham, his SIS contact, was told to drop the idea.[62] Nevertheless, according to Graham Macklin, formerly a Reader Advisor at The National Archives in Kew,[63] MI6 appointed Pollard head of its semi-autonomous 'Section D' in Madrid, with a remit to engage in clandestine sabotage across Europe. By that time Philby had already joined this section. In the section's name, 'D' stood for 'Destruction'. 'During May 1940,' Macklin writes,

Section D had what is described in the Special Operations Executive (SOE) in-house history as 'one small flirtation' with the idea of backing the monarchist (not republican) opposition in Spain as part of the British government's overarching strategy to keep the country out of the war. The plan was soon abandoned, however, once it was realised that it had absolutely no chance of success.[64]

Interestingly, Ángel Viñas carried out his own investigation, which led him to the conclusion that the story about Pollard's wartime involvement with the activities of Section D in Madrid is an exaggeration. It was discovered that Pollard entered active military service with the rank of lieutenant on 1 March 1940, that in June Alan Hillgarth,[65] the British Naval Attaché in Madrid, sent him on a short clandestine mission to Lisbon, and that in July he was transferred from the general list of the Intelligence Corps. In March 1942 Pollard was appointed Deputy Inspector of Armaments in the Ministry of Supply with the temporary rank of captain. Between October 1946 and June 1947 he was in Austria, 'on missions about which nothing is known'.[66]

From its very inception, the outbreak of hostilities in Spain elevated this local war to an international conflict. Several historians have even come to a conclusion that the war in Spain was in fact a European civil war, whose external participants, it was observed, were at least as important as the domestic combatants. While some of the countries involved in the conflict had similar agendas—for example, Italy and Germany—'none actively collaborated to form what could be described as a coherent, identifiable long-term strategy towards involvement in the war'.[67] This was also true of the democracies, and the failure of the Anglo-French-inspired Non-Intervention Committee vividly demonstrated it. Remarkably, the Spanish Civil War revealed that 'notions of diplomatic, let alone military alliances in Europe in 1936 were very tenuous indeed'.[68] It also revealed that it had the potential to undermine the Great Powers' strategy of applying some form of diplomatic control over matters of war and peace in Europe.

Were Britain, France, and the United States justified in abandoning the Spanish Republic? Their attitude, it was correctly noticed, was radically less proactive than it had been during the civil war in Russia. The Allied forces participated in the Russian Civil War when the British and French were exhausted in terms of material resources and manpower. No such constraints applied to them in 1936. And, thanks to the New Deal, the US economy was emerging from recession and could offer support in protecting democracy in Spain.[69] Nevertheless, the Great Powers stood back.

Some tend to believe that in 1936 and for the duration of the civil war in Spain

the stakes were too high for the British and French to offer direct intervention. There was their actual or perceived lack of preparedness for the war itself combined with the belief that the war might escalate into a wider European conflict. Furthermore, antagonising Franco by intervening in the war on the side of the democratic republic in Spain would also undermine the British government's wider agenda of appeasement of the fascist dictators.[70]

Hitler seems to have been more important to the British interests than Spain, and the Red threat more prevalent than the Nazi threat.

Lastly, the main reason why none of the powers involved in the Spanish Civil War viewed it as an opportunity to wage a war of conquest was that it was not in the interest of any of them to do so. The security of Gibraltar meant that it was in the interests of the British to be on good terms with the Spanish government, whatever its ideological identity, but it was a calculated gamble that if Franco won the war, then a diplomatic rapprochement could be reached after that event ... [The isolationism of the Americans was undoubtedly a factor.] In the case of the French, while France shared a frontier with Spain that could have come under threat by a Spanish nationalist regime bent on waging a war of aggression, this was not a major part of French military strategic planning. As far as the French were concerned, it was Germany and not Spain that posed the greatest threat to their security and from that to the remainder of Europe.[71]

Politically, and this can easily be inferred from the rebels' acts immediately after the coup, the real aim of the plotters was to do away with the economic, social, and cultural reforms of the biennium 1931–3 and their resumption after February 1936. Operationally, the civil war was, in the words of Ángel Viñas, 'the result of a semi-failed, semi-successful military uprising but also the consequence of three developments, two of which had been taken fully into account by the military and civilian plotters'. The first two were the hopes for assistance from Mussolini's Italy and the expectation that the British government, being properly advised, would not provide any assistance to the Republic. Only the third development feebly pursued by the nominal director of the rebellion, General Sanjurjo, in March 1936 exceeded all expectations. A week after the uprising, on 25 July, Hitler decided on the spur of the moment to come to Franco's aid. Immediate military assistance by the fascist powers and the decision not to intervene by the democracies changed the balance of forces in the theatre. Soviet help to the Republic was able to prevent defeat, as it did, but it was not long term and not sufficient in comparison with Italian and German involvement. 'The ins and outs of these developments', Professor Viñas writes, 'can be followed almost to the minute when one puts together the material available in Spanish, French, German, Italian, British and, crucially, former Soviet archives'.[72] Not too many have undertaken this daunting task.

Finally, a question that has occupied the minds of historians is the extent to which the Spanish Civil War was a 'dress rehearsal' for the Second World War.[73] 'The Spanish Civil War was not the first phase of the Second World War,' the Cambridge Professor Zara Steiner writes in her most recent volume on the European international history,[74] adding, however, that 'it was more than a sideshow'. This, and not the British or French policy of appeasement, seems to be the central question in the discussion of the importance of the Spanish Civil War in the international politics of the later 1930s. It is difficult not to agree with Michael Alpert of the University of Westminster that 'today it is easy to see that the behaviour of the Democracies over Spain could not have avoided sending a message to the Dictators that they would be able to do what they liked anywhere else'.[75] In this way, the Spanish Republic, before Austria or Czechoslovakia, became one of the first victims of fascism in Europe.[76]

As usual, even a definite answer to this important question cannot claim to help answering other important questions arising out of the immensely complex international context of the Spanish Civil War. However, the following chapters sketch out some human, political, military, and intelligence aspects reflecting the process of Soviet decision-making over Spain, which often remain unclear to many and to a large extent unknown to this day while the Soviet Union was, by far, the most mysterious and controversial participant in the Spanish Civil War and the Second World War.

13

Moscow, Madrid, and Valencia: August 1936–January 1937

S oon after the uprising, Moscow clearly demonstrated that the Soviet leadership knew what was going on in Spain and did care, but was not prepared to help at that stage. As the situation in Spain got worse, the Soviet Union was finding itself increasingly isolated. The international context was deteriorating, with all the hallmarks of a pre-war period. At the same time, entirely reliable intelligence directly from the Iberian Peninsula was missing. The concern of Stalin and the Politburo was fully comprehended at the intelligence headquarters and was followed by an array of desperate activities that began in August 1936 and continued long after Stalin had lost his interest in Spain.

It was perhaps not a coincidence that on the same day, Friday, 7 August, two sister organizations—the Comintern and the RU—presented their situation reports on Spain. There is little doubt that the two remaining intelligence agencies—the NKVD and Naval Intelligence—had prepared similar documents.[1] It is also clear that these reports covered all aspects of the conflict: political, economic, military, and technical. Remarkably, it was not Boris Melnikov, known in the Comintern as 'Miller',[2] head of its OMS, who was assigned to produce this document. Instead, Peter Shubin-Vilensky, deputy director of the ECCI information department, compiled the report, using the information both from the Comintern's bureau in Madrid headed by Vittorio Codovilla and surveys produced by its responsible functionaries, Palmiro Togliatti and Ernö Gerö, who since the October 1932 purge of the PCE leadership were personally involved in directing the PCE policy.[3] Accordingly, the RU chief, Solomon (Semyon) Uritsky, commissioned his deputy, Division Commander Alexander Nikonov, head of estimates and planning, to produce an evaluation of the Spanish situation based on all available sources.[4] In this job Nikonov was assisted by one of his best experts, Dr Evgeny Iolk.[5] The document went its usual way from Uritsky to the Chief of the Red Army General Staff Alexander Yegorov and then to Commissar of Defence Klim Voroshilov.

From these intelligence assessments the Soviet leadership could draw the following conclusions: that the situation in Republican Spain was not desperate from the military point of view; however, that without an external help the chances for victory were very unclear; and that it was necessary to open the embassy in Madrid as soon as possible to provide diplomatic cover for the Soviet political, military, and intelligence representatives who should be sent to observe and report. By the end of summer all this was done. On 21 August the Politburo met to name a career diplomat, Marcel Rosenberg, as Soviet Ambassador to the Spanish Republic.[6]

Two days later, on 23 August, Commissar for Foreign Affairs Maxim Litvinov wrote to the Soviet chargé d'affaires in France, Evgeny Hirschfeld, asking him to inform the Spanish ambassador that 'the Soviet leadership does not consider it possible to comply with requests to supply arms on the grounds that Spain is far away from Russia, such deliveries are expensive, arms cargo can be intercepted, and because the USSR is bound by its declaration of non-intervention and cannot violate it'. Earlier that day, the French chargé d'affaires in Moscow, Jean Payart, had handed Litvinov a note from his government regarding the Declaration of Non-Intervention into the Spanish Affairs.[7] A week later, in his letter to Ambassador Rosenberg in Madrid, Litvinov wrote that 'the question of assisting the Spanish government has been discussed by us several times, but we have come to the conclusion that it will be impossible to send anything from here'.[8] If the date of this letter is accurate, it leads to the conclusion that at the end of August Stalin was still hesitating in regard to full-scale Soviet military intervention in Spain. It is hardly surprising, because the Soviet dictator had more important things on his mind than Spain—the first show trial was staged in Moscow between 19 and 24 August, and we would assume that all his thoughts were there (even while his body was being pampered in Sochi).

Among the first official Soviet representatives who arrived in Madrid that August, only Rosenberg and Gaikis were career diplomats. The rest of the staff consisted of a group of Soviet intelligence operators. The 1st Secretary, A. Kulov, about whom nothing has become known so far, occupied the traditional slot of the NKVD head of station, assisted by L. Sokolov (a security officer) and Yu. Bondarenko (a cipher clerk). Gorev, a professional intelligence officer with several years' experience in China and the USA, represented the RU. In those early days, majors Iosif Ratner[9] and Hajji Umar Mamsurov[10] were his only assistants, and their first radio operator was Bruno Wendt,[11] a German communist who had worked with Richard Sorge in Japan. Wendt was recalled after several months and was succeeded by the Yugoslav Slavomir Vukelić,[12] the brother of Branko Vukelić (GIGOLO), Sorge's right-hand man in Japan in 1933. In Spain Vukelić was using the alias 'Vladimir Markovich'. The first Soviet commercial attaché in Spain was also an RU officer, the Bulgarian Ivan Vinarov (alias Winzer). We shall hear more about him. Two other officers who arrived in August were Nikolai Kuznetsov, the naval attaché, and Boris Sveshnikov, the air attaché.

In their response to the request for help from the Republican government, the Politburo and the Sovet Narodnykh Komissarov (SNK) (Council of People's Commissars) also sanctioned the establishment of the representation of the NKVD with the Spanish Ministry of Interior, headed from 4 September by the Socialist Ángel Galarza. Following this decree, Sloutsky, the foreign intelligence chief, nominated two candidates, both his friends, majors of state security, and the NKVD leadership issued an internal order No. V/832 appointing Lev Lazarevich Nikolsky (alias 'Alexander Mikhailovich Orlov', codenamed SCHWED) and Naum Markovich Belkin (alias 'Alexander Belyaev', codenamed KADI) as NKVD liaison in early September. Nikolsky collected his new diplomatic passport with exit and transit visas on 5 September. He and his family eventually crossed the Soviet–Polish border five days later, on 10 September.[13]

On 14 September 1936, an important meeting took place in Moscow. Krivitsky wrote:

Obedient to Stalin's orders, Yagoda called an emergency conference at his head-quarters, the Lubyanka, in Moscow. Frinovsky was present. Sloutsky, chief of the Foreign Division of the OGPU [recte NKVD], and General Uritsky of the General Staff of the Red Army were also present. From Sloutsky, whom I met frequently in Paris and elsewhere, I learned that at this conference a veteran officer of his department was detailed to establish the OGPU in Loyalist Spain. He was Nikolsky, alias SCHWED, alias Lyova, alias Orlov.[14]

In reality, Krivitsky could not and did not know this. But he and his ghost writer were writing the book after the war in Spain was over and at least some information became available thanks to the war correspondents. As a resident agent in The Hague at the time, Krivitsky could hardly be aware in what capacity Nikolsky was sent to Spain in 1936, but three years later he and Don Levine could both learn that Nikolsky was the NKVD chief there because it was not a secret. Many of those Americans who were in Spain knew it. Noticeably, although garbled, Krivitsky's account was not too far from what happened in Moscow on that day. Indeed, on 14 September there was a meeting of Soviet intelligence chiefs chaired by Vycheslav Molotov: Lazar Kaganovich, Andrey Andreyev (a former waiter whom Stalin had made a secretary to the Central Committee), Genrikh Yagoda, Abram Sloutsky, Mikhail Moskvin (*aka* Meer Trilisser, former head of INO now representing the Comintern intelligence department), Solomon Uritsky, and Georgi Dimitrov were invited to take part. They gathered in the Kremlin to discuss several important issues of Soviet foreign policy, among them organization of aid to the Spanish Republic.[15] It appears that Yagoda then invited Uritsky, Sloutsky, and Frinovsky, who at that time headed the Glavnoe Upravlenie Pogranichnoi i Vnutrennei Okhrany (GUPVO) (Chief Directorate of the Border Guards and Internal Troops) NKVD, to his Lubyanka office for more detailed professional talks, and that plans for some future NKVD activities in Spain were also discussed.

Thus, the plan to provide military assistance that would become known as Operation X was sketched out by the Kremlin officials and representatives of all intelligence services on 14 September. This plan would be the backbone of the Politburo decree of 29 September 1936 to go forward with the military operation in Spain.[16] But the decision to send Nikolsky, alias Orlov, as an NKVD liaison was an internal NKVD decision taken sometime before the meeting on 14 September, as by that day Orlov had already been on his way to Madrid.[17]

He and his family left Moscow travelling by train to France. In his pocket was a new diplomatic passport identifying its holder as an attaché of the Soviet embassy in Madrid. Similar documents in the names of 'Maria Orlova' and 'Vera Orlova' secured the family's free transit through Nazi Germany, whose authorities respected Soviet diplomats. Besides, diplomatic visas with black swastikas issued to them by the German Embassy in Moscow on the same day as their passports guaranteed their immunity on hostile territory.

In Paris the Orlovs were met by the legal NKVD resident Stanislav Glinsky[18] and accompanied to the hotel. The Paris station took care of Nikolsky's family until he found them comfortable accommodation in the Languedoc–Roussillon region of southern France, famous for its red wines as well as for fruit and vegetables, only 8 miles from the Mediterranean and 19 miles north of the French–Spanish border. They stayed in France until July 1938 (except for a short spell in a luxury residence in La Garriga near Barcelona).

Three days after receiving his Spanish entry visa, Orlov left Paris for Toulouse and from there departed to Barcelona by plane on 15 September. The next day he reported to Ambassador Rosenberg at the Hotel Palace in Madrid.

He was still on his way to Spain when, on 13 September, in absolute secrecy, the government decreed to transport the Spanish gold reserve to the Cartagena naval base. The first convoy departed from Madrid–Atocha railway station on 15 September carrying 800 cases filled with bags of gold coins. New shipments went out immediately. These totalled 10,000 cases transported under maximum security. After the gold had been sent, silver, banknotes, stocks, and bonds were also transferred to the port, where the treasure was guarded by a 300-men unit of the Fiscal Police under the command of Captain Jose Muñoz Vizcaino. In about a month's time, in connection with this operation, a new attaché would be introduced as 'Alexander Orlov' to several Spanish ministers, one of whom was to remember the episode in his memoirs.

Although Orlov certainly met Juan Negrín and other important Republican officials, his 'high-level position within the government'[19] should be discarded as a fairy tale based on Orlov's fantasies. Following Orlov's boasts, his American biographer cites Wednesday, 26 August 1936, as the day when Orlov was informed of his assignment to Spain.[20] That was just another of Orlov's inventions. The extraordinary Politburo meeting in Moscow at which the Comintern's direct involvement in the Spanish Civil War was first discussed took place on 28 August, after Ercoli (Togliatti) had returned from leave.[21] It was at that meeting that Georgi Dimitrov, secretary-general of the Comintern, and Dmitry Manuilsky, the ECCI secretary, were recommended by the *Instantsyia* (a Russian euphemism meaning the Party leadership but more often personally Stalin) to start an active campaign to lure international fighters to take part in the Spanish Civil War. It was perhaps not planned at the time, but in the course of war many of those fighters, and even their personal papers, would become an endless source of recruits for the Soviet intelligence services for years ahead. Remarkably, three days later, on 29 August 1936, the Politburo decided to ban all exports of arms, ammunition, and war planes to Spain following their decision to sign the Non-Intervention Declaration.[22]

Gazur writes about his Soviet friend:

Following long and frequent absences from his beloved Russia, Orlov felt that he deserved the promised assignment to the KGB Centre [sic] in Moscow . . . Orlov's desire to be posted to the KGB Centre in Moscow was based primarily on his concerns for his daughter's health and welfare. He reasoned that the medical facilities extended to him by virtue of his station in the hierarchy of the Communist Party [Nikolsky was a rank-and-file party member] would be superior and there- fore comparable to what was available in the West. Even more important, he felt that Vera's needs could be better nurtured by being in a family environment in which his parents and his wife's parents could provide her with loving care. An additional consideration and one of great importance was that an assignment to the KGB Centre would be less demanding of his time and thereby would afford him more opportunity to tend to the needs of the family at a very critical time.[23]

Bearing in mind Stalin's purges, which began in August 1936, taking the lives of hundreds of thousands of people including many NKVD officers and especially those who worked at the headquarters, Nikolsky would have had a very thin chance of survival had he remained in Moscow. Gazur's account should be tempered with the comments from Vladimir Petrov, who served with the OGPU–NKVD at the same time as Nikolsky, before he himself defected in Australia. Petrov recalled in this connection:

What emotions does a Soviet official feel when he is offered the opportunity of a posting to a foreign country? Whatever his feelings may be, if he is wise he keeps them severely in check and displays a certain calculated indifference to the prop- osition. On the one hand it is proper for him to show a readiness to serve in any capacity and in any situation where he may be of use to the Soviet Government. On the other hand he will be most unwise if he shows any undue enthusiasm at the prospect. Such enthusiasm, if reported, could be interpreted in the most dangerous light. Indeed, I knew of one official who lost his foreign appointment and his job because he showed himself too eager to go abroad.[24]

We cannot know what emotions were boiling inside Nikolsky, but we can assume that after a very stressful year in Moscow he was certainly happy to leave Russia.

By all measures, September 1936 was a very eventful month in terms of Soviet involvement in Spain. On 16 and 17 September, after the previous go-ahead from the Politburo, the ECCI Secretariat held meetings discussing the international help to the Spanish Republic. On the next day, 18

September, all member parties received their instructions.[25] The recruit-ment of volunteers proposed by the Comintern Executive was based largely on the initiatives that had been put forward by the KPD five weeks before the Politburo in Moscow had approved them on 20 September.[26] Imme-diately after the approval, two special couriers representing the KPD, Herbert Müller[27] and Hans Hausladen,[28] were sent to Europe to organize the mobilization, vetting, and transportation of volunteers for Spain. Müller was instructed to contact secret party cells in Prague, Zurich, Paris, and Brussels, and Hausladen in Copenhagen. At the same time, a mass solidarity campaign was to be launched in Europe and elsewhere. Later, the KPD would establish two branches in Paris to organize and coordinate all secret work in Spain. A special border crossing service (*Grenzdienst*) would be launched in the Pyrenees west of Andorra.[29] In Austria, an underground recruitment centre would be set up in Vienna.

After about a month in Spain, the NKVD liaison bureau sent its first report: 'There is no unified security service, since the government does not consider this to be very moral. Each party has therefore created its own security apparatus. In the present Government there are many former policemen with pro-Fascist sentiments. Our help is accepted politely, but the vital work that is so necessary for the country's security is sabotaged.'[30] Another pessimistic report followed some time later: 'All advice that we give to the leadership of the state security as well as all our assistance in the form of instructions and operational direction in the provinces leave the authorities quite unmoved. The political parties there establish their own counter-intelligence services under the command of the local committees of the Popular Front.'[31] Orlov's biographers noticed that his 'early reports to Moscow reflect his grave doubt about his mission, since his first impression of the military and political problems confronting the Republicans was not encouraging'.[32] In fact, it could have hardly been more pessimistic.

The Dirección General de Seguridad (DGS) (General Directorate of Security) was the only secret service that the Second Spanish Republic inherited from the old times. The Royal Decree of 12 November 1912 establishing the DGS stated that its jurisdiction extended to the whole national territory with an exclusive assignment in Madrid snatching from the Civil Governor responsibilities for and the control of the public order, meetings, demonstrations, shows, arms, passports, foreigners and their movements, hotels, travellers' inns, porters, public institutions, associations, vagrants and beggars, and prostitution. Another Royal Decree of 14 June

1921 substituted the DGS with the Chief Directorate of Public Order (Dirección General de Orden Público), which was again substituted by the DGS on 7 November 1923. Under the premiership of Miguel Primo de Rivera (September 1923–January 1930) it was established that the DGS, which had under its command the Corps of Vigilance and Security (Cuerpos de Vigilancia y Seguridad), would become the main law-enforcement agency where all information concerning public order as well as prevention and prosecution of crimes should be concentrated. The DGS was also given powers over the police, was responsible for the appointments and transfers of its personnel, their insignia, and identification, and named Inspectors General of Public Order in Madrid and Barcelona, who would appoint police chiefs (Jefes Superiores de Policía) with delegated powers of the Director General of the DGS. The DGS had always been part of the Ministry of Interior (Ministerio de Gobernación).[33]

The widescale persecution of dissidents, real or imaginary spies, and those who later became known as the fifth columnists[34] began on 4 August 1936 under the minister Ángel Galarza, the DGS chief Manuel Muñoz Martínez, and his deputy Vicente Girauta Linares by the creation of the so-called Comité Provincial de Investigación Pública in the Círculo de Bellas Artes (CBA) with representatives of all parties of the People's Front. This date seems to be the birthday of all subsequent *checas* (named after and modelled on the first secret police of the Soviet Russia, the Cheka). The committee had sections and tribunals and was initially situated in the cellars of the CBA, later moving to the calle de Fomento 9, where it became known as the Checa de Fomento, which operated until its dissolution in November 1936. Members of this *checa* were involved in repression, directly coordinating their activities with and sending reports to the DGS. There was also the 'Tribunal de Fomento', a committee of thirty people, which decided whom to release, whom to incarcerate, and who should be shot. If the verdict was death, the *checa* had a small *brigadilla* consisting of four members and commanded by an anarchist, Antonio Ariño Ramis, alias El Catalán. In its 'investigation' activities the *checa* used files and records provided by the DGS. Very soon in Madrid alone there were over 226 *checas* under the orders of the authorities as well as different political parties, trade unions, and other groups. Most of the agents had the warrant cards of the security services. In this early period of war, there also existed special units that manned random checkpoints, roadblocks, and street patrols, the so-called *Puestos especiales de vigilancia* under the Inspection General of Milicias

Populares, and 35 *checas* were affiliated with the militias of the rearguard (*milicias de vigilancia de retaguardia*) and often detained people on the orders of the DGS. The director-general decided what salaries should be paid to the judges, agents, and militiamen of the Checa de Fomento; those funds were usually formed from the confiscated valuables of private individuals and churches. The shootings and assassinations were carried out at night or early in the morning near cemeteries. According to one report, when this *checa* was closed down in November 1936 by the order of the Orden Público de Madrid, 472 cases of jewellery, gold, and platinum and other valuables were handed over to the government. The judges who worked at the Tribunal de Fomento then formed the Consejo de Policía, a special police council under Santiago Carrillo.[35]

Another checa affiliated with the DGS was the Checa de la Secretaría Técnica of the Director-General of Security and 'Escuadrilla del Amanecer' ('Dawn Patrol') located on Alcalá 82. Its primary task was to provide information from the police files to other *checas*, but it was also involved in arrests and assassinations. The *checa* was comprised of the members of the Assault Guard.

Yet another checa was under the sub-director of security, reporting first to Carlos de Juan Rodríguez, and then from October 1936 to Vicente Girauta. As its address was on Marqués de Cubas, it was known as the Checa de Marqués de Cubas. Its chief was Elviro Ferret Obrador, assisted by former policemen. The members of this *checa* were known for multiple assassinations and the shooting of prisoners at the Model Prison on 22 August 1936.

The Checa of Atadell, much hailed by the Republican press, was named after the militant socialist Agapito García Atadell. Many members of his *checa* were non-professionals—that is, they were members of the people's militia invited to join the Brigada de Investigación Criminal. It was also known under the name 'Milicias Populares de Investigación de García Atadell', whose staff was made of forty-eight agents. The second-in-command was Ángel Pedrero García, a former teacher, who became the Provisional Agent of the DGS in the first days of August 1936, and chiefs of its two groups were Luis Ortuño and Antonio Albiach Chiralt. The story of this *checa* is well known.[36] What may be less known is the fact that, when Atadell decided to escape but instead was arrested by the Nationalists and investigated in Las Palmas, the Jefatura Superior de Sevilla found documents throwing light on some vicissitudes of his life. Their report stated that he had belonged to the Juventud del Partido Comunista since 1922, and had been arrested ten times in 1924 and eight times in 1926. Atadell was later executed.

Also worth mentioning is the Checa Los Linces de la República ('The Wildcats of the Republic') located directly at the headquarters of the DGS. This *checa* was under the personal orders of the DGS director Muñoz, while searchers and arrests were carried out by the lieutenant of an assault unit Juan Tomás Estalrich and the captain of militia Emilio Losada, who was temporarily employed by the Bureau of Statistics (Estadística del Ayuntamiento de Madrid). This *checa* or *escuadrilla* coordinated its activities mainly with the Checa de Fomento and the Checa de Atadell.

The Checa de la Comisaría de Policía de Buenavista was led by a police professional, Luis Omaña, catapulted by the Popular Front from agent to Commissioner. However, its members included only a few police professionals; the majority of its staff were the militiamen and Assault Guards. Omaña's second-in-command was Santiago García Imperial, an outlaw who committed multiple murders and looting. Another member of this *checa*, also known as the Comisaría de Buenavista, was Fernando Valentí Fernández. In December 1936 Valentí was transferred to the Brigada Especial de Comisaría General (becoming its chief in May 1937).

The last *checa*, much feared in those days, was the Checa de la Agrupación Socialista de Madrid on the calle Fuencarral 103 in the palace of Count Eleta confiscated by the Partido Socialista Obrero Español (PSOE) (Spanish Socialist Workers' Party). Anselmo Burgos Gil, its chief, commanded the unit of guards providing security to the Soviet Embassy. The second chief was David Vázquez Baldominos, who will appear later in this story. Julio de Mora Martínez, another important member, was later to become one of the top officials of the Servicio de Investigación Militar (SIM) (Spanish Republican military counter-intelligence service), which is discussed in detail in the following chapters.

It is evident that in the early period of war the government did not trust the old police forces and quickly replaced the Corps of Vigilance and Security (Cuerpo de Vigilancia y Seguridad) and the Civil Guard (Guardia Civil) by the militias of the rearguard (Milicias de Vigilancia de la Retaguardia). Meanwhile, by October 1936,[37] Ángel Galarza, the Interior Minister, had already issued an order creating official rearguard brigades in the hope of ending 'uncontrollable activity' of various semi-partisan groups that operated under the cover of the *checas*.

There is little doubt that apart from his main mission—watch out and report—Nikolsky's remit in Spain was to help one of those semi-partisan groups that operated under the cover of the *checas*, and specifically the communists, to create their own security and intelligence service.[38] Long before his arrival, the PCE leadership together with their Comintern advisers were complaining about the Anarchists, POUMists (whom they labelled 'the Trotskyists'), and other parties of the government during visits to Moscow and in secret messages transmitted by radio (and intercepted by the British within the framework of Operation MASK).[39] The PCE needed its own professional and trained underground 'apparatus' modelled on those set up by the KPD to fight their enemies effectively. In Spain these were the rebels, their secret supporters the so-called fifth column, and all those who opposed the PCE in the Republican camp. That was well understood by Stalin and the Politburo because everyone remembered how effective the Communist *cheka* had been since the first days of the Bolshevik revolution. Stalin also quickly realized that the idea of the fifth column could well be used to justify the purges in his own country.

After less than a month in Spain, Nikolsky heard about new changes at the Moscow NKVD headquarters. On 11 October the Poliburo decided to dismiss Yagoda, the NKVD commissar. Nikolai Yezhov, Stalin's loyal lackey, was appointed,while at the same time remaining Secretary of the Central Committee and Chairman of the Control Commission. The leading body of the party ruled that he must 'devote nine-tenths of his time to the NKVD'.[40] This work was entirely new for Yezhov, and he needed time and fresh cadres. By the next spring Nikolsky would receive his new operational instructions. But for now, Matvei Berman and Mikhail Frinovsky became new deputies; Lev Mironov, Nikolsky's friend, was transferred from the Economic Department to counter-intelligence.[41] Though Yakov Agranov was still first deputy, he would not last long. Only Sloutsky, the INO chief, remained at his post, while in the spring Yezhov greeted 300 new young officers at the Lubyanka headquarters, recruited from the Party and the Komsomol to fill many important positions.

Because at that early stage of the war the role of the NKVD station was to advise the Interior Ministry, help the Communist Party, watch the arriving Soviet contingent, and observe and report to Moscow without any operational involvement, the KGB archivists who meticulously prepared documents for Orlov's 1993 biography failed to find a single intelligence report dating to his first months in Spain. But one phrase from the October 1936 telegram clearly demonstrates that the NKVD station was monitoring the situation and working in tune with the PCE leadership and the Comintern reps were preparing for an action against the 'enemies' in their own ranks. 'The Trotskyists organization POUM, active in Catalonia,' the report claimed, 'can easily be liquidated.'[42] That, however, was not going to happen until much later.

In the meantime, Moscow became more and more convinced that the British- and French-inspired policy of non-intervention, initially backed by the Soviet Union, was not working. Stalin realized that, unless something was done, the Republic was going to collapse under the onslaught of the rebel generals, generously (but not unselfishly) supported by direct state aid from both Fascist Italy and Nazi Germany, the most sophisticated military–industrial complex of its day. It was decided to risk British and French displeasure by secretly dispatching some military hardware, Soviet advisers, pilots, and tank crews.[43] The longer Nazi firepower was involved in the small conflict behind the Pyrenees, the more chance Stalin had to prepare for the big war. So, on 14 September, the very day Soviet diplomats were attending the second meeting of the Non-Intervention Committee on 14 September, Molotov was chairing a top secret Kremlin conference with the chiefs of all secret services to discuss Soviet help to the Republicans. The general blueprint of what later turned out to be a commercial business plan as well as an important political move was approved by the Politburo on 29 September. It became operative on the same day. To avoid accusations of violating the Non-Intervention Agreement certain precautions were worked out. Those included secrecy, delivery of second-hand and prefer-ably foreign weapons acquired elsewhere, outside help in the form of the International Brigades, and the direct sale of non-military equipment like trucks[44] and food supplies from Russia that could be considered as humani-tarian aid.

At the same time, the relevant documents in the *Rossiisky gosudarsvenny voyennyi arkhiv* (RGVA) (Russian State Military Archive) show that two days after the above-mentioned meeting, on 16 September, Operation X (where 'X' meant Republican Spain) was born, and Section X, consisting of a mixture of the NKVD and RU officers and representatives of the army, navy, air force, transport, and finance departments, was set up at the RU:

The officers submitted their lists of materials, personnel, costing, progress reports, recommendations and requests to do this or that to Uritsky [the RU director], who passed them to Voroshilov, the overall commander of the operation, who in turn passed them, with his own comments, suggestions and requests, to Stalin for approval or rejection. Indeed, one of the surprising revelations of these documents is the extent to which Stalin retained personal control over the whole operation, at least during its first year, for it seems that all decisions, even such minor ones as the withdrawal of quite small sums of money, were referred to him before being implemented.[45]

The operation began by a marked demonstration of the Kremlin's decision to support the Republicans, indicating that Moscow was really concerned and eager to help. At the same time, uneasy allies—the RU and NKVD—started collecting old military scrap to be sent to Spain on board the *Campeche*, which arrived in Cartagena on 4 October carrying 20,350 rifles of First World War vintage and some other historic weapons[46] of little use and almost without ammunition.

The Republican government was grateful, although its leaders fully realized that this was not enough and understood the danger of the situation. Besides political and military aspects, there was another problem that troubled them. Foreign Minister Álvarez del Vayo recalled in his memoirs:

In October of 1936 there was real danger that, once it became known the gold was in Cartagena, a sudden attempt would be made to seize it. We had to think of ways and means to protect it, while at the same time we had to be in a position to dispose of it without risk of a court embargo . . . There was nothing for it but to make use of the only state bank—that of Soviet Russia—disposed to grant facilities and guarantees when requested to serve as intermediary for the conversion of gold and currencies. The first overture regarding the possibility of using the Gosbank was made through the Soviet commercial attaché, M[onsier] Winzer. Later, negotiations were carried on by the ambassador, at that time M[onsieur] Rosenberg.[47]

Thus, the key Soviet representatives in all negotiations between Moscow and Madrid became Ambassador Marcel Rosenberg and commercial attaché Josef Winzer, better known at the Moscow RU headquarters as Ivan Vinarov.

Ivan Zolov Vinarov (codenamed MART) was born on 24 February 1896 to the family of a rich landowner in the town of Pleven in Bulgaria. In 1922 Vinarov escaped from arrest for illegal arms-smuggling for his party and came to Soviet Russia. In two years he was commissioned as an officer of the RU, the future GRU, and was again involved in secret arms supplies to the Balgarska Komunisticheska Partiya (BKP) (Bulgarian Communist Party) preparing a communist revolt. After graduating from a military intelligence course in Tambov, Vinarov was sent on clandestine missions to Bulgaria and Austria to help liquidate the consequences of the Soviet-sponsored attempt to overthrow the legitimate government of his own country.

On 16 April 1925 the Bulgarian communists under the leadership of the Comintern planted a bomb in the Sveta Nedelya cathedral in Sofia, aiming to eliminate the entire political leadership under Premier Alexander Tsankov in one blow.

Miraculously, with 123 dead and several hundred wounded, not a single government official appeared to have been hurt, and Tsankov started merciless purges of the members of the Peasants' and Communist parties. That was quite a surprise for Moscow, where it was expected that immediately after the explosion the communists would start an uprising and eventually seize power. The miscalculation led to a serious conflict. As a result, the diplomatic relations between Bulgaria and the Soviet Union were established only in 1934.

From January 1926 until February 1929 Vinarov was in China working under 'illegal' station chief Kristofors (Kristaps) Salniņš, whom he knew from the Bulgarian adventure and whom he would later meet again in Spain. Vinarov's wife, G. P. Lebedeva, was the group's cut-out, working as a cipher clerk in the Soviet legations in Beijing and Harbin. From 1930 till 1933 Vinarov was the most senior undercover RU agent ('illegal' resident), in Austria with wide responsibilities over Eastern Europe, the Balkans, Greece, and Turkey. (Krivitsky was also posted in Vienna at that time, reporting to Vinarov.) After Austria, Vinarov returned to Moscow and began his studies at the Special Faculty of the Frunze Military Academy, a rough equivalent of the British Army's Staff College, from which he graduated in July 1936. In August, Ambassador Rosenberg's small staff in Madrid included 'one commercial attaché Winzer'.[48] Actually, 'Winzer' is a German version of Vinarov's name, and both *Vinarov* and *Winzer* mean a 'winegrower' in English.

Some Russian intelligence historians[49] assert that from December 1936 to March 1938 Vinarov was the supervisor of an espionage network in Paris whose primary objective was Spain. Indeed, Vinarov himself mentioned it in his book.[50] But one has to take into account that, first, former intelligence officers never disclose all operational details in their books (quite often intentionally, sometimes because they simply forget them) and, secondly, there would be no contradiction, since many intelligence operators based in Spain, including Orlov, were at the same time quite active in

France, as will be seen below. Besides, after the fall of Bilbao, Vinarov had indeed moved to France, where he was certainly involved in some activity related to Spain until his recall to Moscow.

The idea of sending gold to the Soviet Union came to Juan Negrín, then the Finance Minister, who then consulted with the Prime Minister, Francisco Largo Caballero. Behind the decision, as can be concluded from del Vayo's words, were, among other factors, the experience of non-intervention, the difficulties in selling gold in Great Britain, the uproars that gold sales in France were causing, the need to keep international payments secret, and, last but not least, the anticipation of Soviet supplies. When the decision was ripe, both men informed Marcel Rosenberg, who reported the news to the Politburo. Whether this information was intercepted by the British remains unknown, but nothing was done to stop the shipment.

The decision to send some 500 tons of gold to Moscow as a deposit was not wholly precipitate. Historian Ángel Viñas, a leading authority on the subject, comments:

It had been ascertained during the first half of October that the Nationalists were continuously active in issuing accusations to the effect that the gold was being sold, and ad hoc legal provisions had been taken. Added to this was the impact of the Nationalists' representatives in Paris, a press campaign in France and, finally, a curious official statement by General Franco himself (4 October), which combined judicial arguments, appeals for non-intervention and veiled threats against recipients of the gold.[51]

Moreover, the Paris *Radio* telegraph agency's report of 9 October that certain British circles (including the City of London) were aware of the fact that the Republican government had decided to export part of the Bank of Spain reserves to Russia was an alarming proof that strictly confidential information was being leaked to the enemy.[52] A later FBI memo on the subject quoted the newspaper *Arriba* as reporting: 'A few days after Negrín had ordered the gold reserve of the Bank of Spain be sent to the USSR in 1936, *Radio Nacional* from Salamanca denounced this robbery perpetrated against the Spanish nation and tipped off the world to its illegitimacy.'[53]

All this was none of Orlov's business. But on 15 October 1936 the Prime Minister of the Republic officially announced to the Soviet ambassador that his government had decided to deposit the Spanish gold in the Russian State Bank (Gosbank). More than three decades after the events, Orlov wrote in his memoirs:

On 12 October [*sic*], when I had been at my Madrid post less than a month, my code clerk came into my office with the secret code book under his arm an a telegram in his hand...Telegram in hand I hurried to the Ambassador's rooms. I found Ambassador Rosenberg sweating over a similar message just received, in a different code. It was the first [*sic*] either of us had heard of the matter. Each of us knew what the other was thinking. Could it really be that Prime Minister Largo Caballero and his colleagues—honest, patriotic Spaniards—would consent to put their country's gold treasure in Stalin's greedy hands?[54]

In his book Orlov claimed that Stalin personally signed the telegram placing him, Orlov, in charge of this sensitive operation. Orlov's biographers also add that Orlov then summoned Negrín to the embassy to discuss the logistics.[55] No trace of Stalin's telegram has been found so far for the obvious reason that such a telegram never existed. Describing preparations for transporting Spanish gold to the Soviet Union, former Republican Foreign Minister Julio Álvarez del Vayo recalled that

on the Russian side there took part in the operation only an attaché from the embassy chosen by Ambassador Rosenberg, of whom all we knew was that he was to be called Blackstone. Negrín jocularly baptized him with this name when he was introduced by the Ambassador, who said in jest, 'Give him any name you wish!'...[He] had certainly been chosen by the imaginative Rosenberg because he would not attract too much attention among the mixed population of Cartagena, being able to pass for a British or American newspaper correspondent.[56]

It should be remembered that Nikolsky/Orlov stood about 5 feet 8 inches (173 cm) tall and in 1936 had black hair and moustache.

In spite of the plausible story that Orlov fed to the US Congress, CIA, and FBI, it is now apparent that Orlov's part in the operation was limited to the security arrangements during the loading of the 'golden crates'. In his turn, Winzer remained totally unnoticed by most scholars, who thought (erroneously) that the Soviet commercial attaché at the time was Artur Stashevsky, mentioning his involvement in the gold operation.[57] Remarkably, Krivitsky never mentioned his former chief Vinarov/Winzer in his own book or articles, or during his MI6 debriefing in London, which demonstrates that he was less than well informed about Spanish operations of both the NKVD and RU. With the advantage of hindsight, it is now possible to state with certainly that he was not informed at all.[58] His alleged personal involvement in the Spanish campaign, including his claims of purchasing of arms and other war materiel and even his visit to Spain, were probably invented by his ghost-writer, Isaac Don Levine.

By sheer coincidence, on the same very day, Thursday, 15 October 1936, when Largo Caballero announced that his government had decided to deposit the Spanish gold in Moscow, Stalin indicated his support of the Spanish communists by sending a personal telegram to José Diaz, leader of the PCE, saying: 'The workers of the Soviet Union are merely carrying out their duty in giving help within their power to the revolutionary masses of Spain. They are aware that the liberation of Spain from the yoke of fascist reactionaries is not a private affair of the Spanish people but the common cause of the whole advanced and progressive mankind.'[59] Stalin's telegram was preceded by only two days by a short coded instruction to the Partit Socialista Unificat de Catalunya (PSUC) (United Socialist Party of Catalonia) from the Comintern.[60] The last part read as follows: 'You are absolutely right: we should not participate in this government with the Trotskyite provocateurs, much less with the traitor Nin, Trotsky's agent in Spain, as criminal and murderous as he [Trotsky].'[61]

This was Moscow's response to the communists' complaints that the POUM was small and with little influence outside Catalonia. The POUM, one of whose leaders was Andreu Nin, was causing much anger in Moscow, because of its criticisms of the Show Trials as well as its denunciation of the Catalan government, the Generalitat, as counter-revolutionary. This coded instruction was written by Vittorio Codovilla, the long-term Comintern representative in Madrid. The communists considered Andreu Nin a traitor because in 1935, together with Joaquín Maurín, he had formed the POUM as a Bolshevik–communist alternative to the Comintern-loyal PCE. Nin was also close to Trotsky and the Left Opposition when he was in the Soviet Union. And, though he had broken with Trotsky on entering the Generalitat, the institutional system in which the self-government of Catalonia is organized, as Councillor of Justice, the POUM was a tight group of revolutionary Spanish Marxists, well led and independent of Moscow. This certainly upset the communists. Weeks of confrontation resulted in Nin's resignation. After a while, the chief of police in the Generalitat was replaced by a friend of its President, Lluís Companys, but soon gave way to a communist, Eusebio Rodríguez Salas, who would become PSUC Councillor for Public Order. But that was not all: encouraged by the first victory, the PCE began to call for the extermination of the POUM as 'Fascist spies' and 'Trotskyite Gestapo agents'.[62] But in October 1936 Orlov was far away from those party squabbles. Following Moscow's instructions, he spent two weeks in Cartagena guarding the gold, securing its reloading on the Soviet ships together with the Naval attaché Kuznetsov, and waiting for the news that the crates reached Moscow. Only then he did he return to Madrid, just in time to celebrate the 19th anniversary of the October Revolution with Gorev and others in the Gaylord Hotel.

While he was absent, a good friend of his arrived in Barcelona as head of the NKVD sub-station there. The real name of the officer, major of state security, was Naum Isaakovich Eitingon, but in Spain he would become known as 'Leonid Alexandrovich Kotov', political attaché of the Soviet consulate in Catalonia. Eitingon took with him to Spain Alexandra Kochergina, an attractive brunette, as Sudoplatov amiably remembered her,[63] and officer of the visa section, posing as his wife. Orlov's friend never bothered to register his marriages and in Moscow lived alternatively in two households.[64] Eitingon did not give up this lifestyle in Spain, either (old habits die hard), because together with him and Kochergina there also came a 30-year-old interpreter, Eugenia Puzyriova, another NKVD officer, who would later become his fourth wife.[65] So on or about 20 October the trio settled in the newly acquired spacious villa already occupied by the consul-general Vladimir Antonov-Ovseyenko, who had arrived earlier that month,[66] and soon started sending long political reports about the situation in Catalonia.

Eitingon (codenamed PIERRE and TOM) was born on 6 December 1899 in the Byelorussian town of Mogilev to the family of the papermill clerk from Shklov. Shklov is a small town not far from Bobruisk, Feldbin/Orlov's home town, in the Mogilev region. Eitingon completed just seven classes of the Mogilev School of Commerce (that is, he had no secondary education). Nevertheless, or, perhaps, because of this, he became a productive and ruthless intelligence operator.[67] Among his many exploits would be the assassination of Trotsky in Mexico, though it was his young Spanish agent, Ramón Mercader, who did the dirty work.

In October, soon after the first delivery of 'an assortment of old and ancient rifles and machine-guns of various nationalities', as Gerald Howson put it,[68] which the Spanish tanker *Campeche* had picked up at Feodosia in the Crimea, a group of military advisers arrived in Spain headed by the Chief of Military Mission Jan Berzin.[69] A former long-serving director of the intelligence directorate of the RU, he was now appointed Chief Soviet Military Adviser in Spain. Berzin was accompanied by his personal interpreter, Elena Konstantinovna Lebedeva (alias 'Lydia Mokretsova').[70] After the government had been evacuated from Madrid on 6 November, he established his headquarters in an old three-storey mansion on Calle de Alboraya in Valencia. His diplomatic passport identified him as 'Pavel

Ivanovich Grishin'. Berzin's office was on part of the ground floor and another part served as the officers' mess. Cipher clerks and W/T operators were on the first floor. Just like all the other Soviet intelligence chiefs in Spain (Gorev, Orlov, and Kotov), Berzin used the services of the German radio operators, while the KPD provided bodyguards recruited from its underground 'Apparatus', many if not all of whom were graduates from the ECCI military school or special RU courses. Berzin's radio operator was Hermann Siebler, who had joined the RU in 1927.[71] In his mission Berzin was surrounded by a formidable group of officers, all, except one, under 40 years of age, many of whom became marshals and generals during and after the Second World War.

As soon as the Soviet Military Mission had been established in Valencia in November, a group of Soviet sabotage and guerrilla warfare specialists arrived. On the military intelligence side, the deployment was personally supervised by Uritsky, the Director, with the everyday chores in the hands of Gaik Lazarevich Tumanyan, the brigade-commissar in charge of special section 'A' (active reconnaissance and special operations). Tumanyan had had some four years' experience in clandestine operations in China in 1930–4. He had come to Spain as the RU inspector in February 1937 accompanied by Iolk, leaving Spain, together with Ehrenburg, in May. Tumanyan went on for an important rendezvous with Vinarov in Paris and Ehrenburg returned to Moscow. Paulina Abramson, Mamsurov's wife, remembered that her husband had been a great friend of Tumanyan since 1924. Both survived the purges.

One of the first RU demolition specialists to arrive in Valencia was Major Ilya G. Starinov, alias 'Alexander Porokhnyak' (also known in Spain as Rudolf Wolf), who came together with his personal interpreter, Anna Obrucheva (alias Louise Kurting), and Artur Sprogis, accompanied by Elizaveta Parshina (alias Josefa Pérez Herrera). Berzin, who knew them all personally from his previous work as director of military intelligence, greeted them at his headquarters. Starinov and his interpreter were assigned to a small group of *guerrilleros* on the outskirts of Valencia, but soon, owing to the efforts of José Diaz and Dolores Ibárruri, a much better place was found in Benimàmet, a suburb north-west from the city, where a subversion and sabotage school was opened. It was later transformed into a fully functional base. The PCE sent Captain Domingo Ungría and twelve men under his command to form its core. Later they moved to the south, leaving the base to other trainees, and were headquartered in the city of Jaén in

Andalusia. With the help of the provincial party committee, a nondescript but comfortable two-storey house was found in the city centre. Soon the unit grew to a battalion, with Ungría as its commander, Antonio Buitrago as his assistant, Captain Francisco del Castillo Saez de Tejada as his deputy, Captain Lubo Ilič as chief of staff, and Augustin Fábregas as deputy commander for intelligence. The base was relocated to Villanueva de Cordoba in the north-eastern part of Cordoba province some 90 kilometres from Cordoba city. Starinov remained its chief adviser and demolition instructor until November 1937, when his tour of duty was over, and he returned to Moscow, handing over his duties to Kristofors (Kristaps) Salniņš (pronounced Sal-nyn-sh), a former deputy chief of Special Section 'A' at the headquarters. Brigade-commissar Salniņš was known in Spain as 'Victor Hugo'. The RU instructors gave instructions in how to use improvised explosives and sabotage technique, basic training in small arms and lessons in self-defence.

While the army provided a detachment called Special Operations Task Group of twenty-two personnel with substantial military skills, state security officers could not match them. On the NKVD side, senior major of state security Grigory Syroyezhkin, who had experience in counter-intelligence, was put in charge of guerrilla training. Syroyezhkin was a random choice; the NKVD had no appropriate specialists at the time and operated mainly as secret police, even abroad. He was also based in Valencia, together with his deputy, Lev Vasilevsky. Senior NKVD personnel travelled with diplomatic passports representing them as political attachés of the embassy, though in reality they were not members of the diplomatic staff.

Vladimir Petrov, who at that time worked as a cipher clerk at the *Spetsotdel* (special communications department), recalled:

Then came the Spanish Civil War. The Soviet's active intervention made it easy to infiltrate our agents there and to maintain excellent intelligence coverage; and I sweated until late into the night decoding lengthy cables reporting on the situation in Spain. I remember a whole series concerned with the shipping of arms to the Spanish Republican Army through Finland, where the arms were bought to conceal the extent of Soviet intervention.

The man in charge of this operation in Finland was Spiegelglass, deputy head of the OGPU [*sic*] Foreign Department. One night when I was on duty, I received a telephone call from Spiegelglass who asked if there was anything of particular interest to him; I knew that Spain was his special concern. Soon afterwards, he walked into the office—a rare thing for any chief of his rank to do. He was correct, polite, businesslike, and agile in movements and mind. Physically he was short of stature, sandy-haired and looked like a Russian though he was actually a Jew. He looked quickly through all the cables from Spain; they came from Madrid and Barcelona, where we had Residents working under legal cover.[72]

Petrov certainly describes the situation as it was in the autumn of 1936, as, apart from the NKVD station inside the Soviet Embassy in Madrid, where only mysterious 'A. Kulov' was working under legal cover, there was a sub-station in Barcelona, with Eitingon/Kotov also under the legal cover of political attachés. (In several published accounts Eitingon/Kotov is described as 'military attaché', which is wrong, because there was no such position in the consulate and because 'military attaché' is a legal cover for a RU officer. From October 1936 the RU station chief in Barcelona was Ivan Kuzmin, codenamed DIEGO, working undercover as trade representative.) Of the liaison officers at the Ministry of Interior, Orlov and Belyaev, neither was a member of the embassy.[73] A few months later the NKVD presence in Spain would increase, but not dramatically, as many commentators suggest, never exceeding ten people.

It is true that, about five months after his arrival in Spain, Major of State Security Nikolsky/Orlov would become a key figure in planning and carrying out all NKVD operations on the Republican territory. But the very facts that he came later than the rest of the embassy staff, including the RU resident Gorev, and especially that his name did not appear in the diplomatic list until a year later, make it possible to state with certainty that Orlov was neither Stalin's personal envoy with special powers, nor 'the chief of the NKVD in Spain', as some put it. And he could never be 'the NKVD General', because there were no such ranks there until long after he had disappeared from his post to surface in the United States.

As the British historian Helen Graham notes, by delaying the advance on the capital, Franco gave the Republicans vital time to organize the defence of Madrid.[74] On 4 November, with the Franco forces at the gates of the capital city, four representatives of the anarcho-syndicalist CNT joined the Popular Front government of Largo Caballero that included Communists, Socialists, and Republicans. Two days later, on 6 November, when by ironic coincidence the Soviet convoy with golden cargo reached Odessa, being quite convinced that Madrid would fall (though not all Cabinet members agreed), the Republican government left for Valencia and placed the protection of the city in the hands of General José Miaja.[75] The Soviet

Embassy and Military Mission hurriedly departed on the same night, together with the government, leaving Orlov the only NKVD representative in Madrid.[76]

In his book *Men and Politics*, Louis Fischer writes: 'I walked over to the Palace Hotel. If anybody knew the military situation the Russians would. The whole staff of the Soviet Embassy had left. The rooms were in disarray. Only Orlov had remained behind; the GPU would be the last to leave the post of duty. The members of the Spanish government, Orlov told me, had left the night before. I asked him what I ought to do'.[77]

But even Fischer, an eyewitness, was not entirely correct in his recollection. Apart from Orlov, at least part of the RU station, including military attaché Gorev, chief adviser for special operations Mamsurov, and Gorev's assastant Ratner, as well as their wireless operator Wendt, who was also a cipher clerk, remained in the Spanish capital. With the exception of Wendt, who was at his post, all other officers were as usual in civilian clothes preparing to celebrate the XIX anniversary of the Bolshevik Revolution, the biggest holiday in the Soviet Union. They all gathered in Gorev's spacious suite around the well-laid table in the company of Mikhail Koltsov, one of Russia's most successful writers and journalists, the famous Soviet documentary-maker Roman Karmen, Karmen's interpreter Lina (Paulina Abramson, the future wife of Mamsurov), Orlov and his Spanish interpreter Soledad Sancha,[78] and one very trusted Spanish comrade.

Just hours before the guests gathered at Gorev's hotel suite to celebrate, on 6 November the passenger ship *Manuel Arnuz* dropped anchor at the port of Veracruz, Mexico. Among those who disembarked there were two women, one of them named Caridad Mercader and another Lena Imbert, the girlfriend of Caridad's son, Ramón. They were accompanied by two communist teachers and were sent by the PCE to organize a solidarity campaign in Mexico City, where the Teachers' Union was very strong. They arrived with genuine Mexican passports but were immediately identified at the border crossing as Spaniards. This did not stop Caridad from freely entering Mexico and even addressing the members of the Mexican Congress. On 21 November she spoke on the Zócalo, the main plaza in the heart of the historic centre of Mexico City, in front of a huge audience. She said that Spain had become the battlefield where Communism and Fascism crossed their swords, and the world should now decide between one of them.[79] Four days later, on 25 November, Hitler's foreign minister Joachim von Ribbentrop, and the Japanese ambassador in Berlin, signed the

Anti-Comintern Pact. As Caridad predicted, for the time being Spain became the only battleground in the European war against Fascism, and the Comintern was determined to win this war. But to do it successfully, according to Stalin's logic, it was necessary to crush the 'enemy within'. Several Spanish women—Dolores Ibárruri, Margarita Nelken, Soledad Sancha, Caridad Mercader, and Lena Imbert (but also others, such as África de las Heras, Carmen Brufau Civit, and Elena Rodriguez Danilevskaya)— would take a very active part in this Stalinist campaign. Unsurprisingly, all of them would later meet in Moscow. Only Elena's sister, Julia Rodríguez-Danilevskaya, the wife of the NKVD agent Georges Soria, would settle in Paris. Thanks to her efforts, Elena was able to return to Madrid where she died in 1976.[80]

Documents about the period of the Great Terror and repression that became public after the collapse of the Soviet Union cover thousand of pages in many volumes. Thanks to the ground-breaking research of several prominent scholars published in the past few years,[81] many previously misinterpreted episodes of the Spanish Civil War have been dug out of obscurity and become clearer. It seems that Stalin was convinced that one of the main reasons the Republicans could be defeated was the presence of traitors in their camp. As in Russia, he demanded that traitors be dealt with decisively.[82] Obviously, his choice of the executioners of his will, in what concerned Spain, fell on the international Communists, first of all on the Germans, Swiss, and Austrians who had volunteered to defend the Republic, as constituting the most organized and disciplined group,[83] and also on the PCE militants. In several cases, the NKVD officers acted as instructors and supervisors.

In early December 1936, Jesús Hernández, one of the two Communist ministers in the Republican coalition government of the Popular Front, was allegedly invited to visit Ambassador Rosenberg, with whom he and other PCE leaders met regularly, in the Soviet Embassy in Valencia. The embassy was only minutes away from the headquarters of the Central Committee of the PCE, which occupied a huge rambling building on the Plaza de la Congregación. According to Hernández's recollections,[84] Rosenberg introduced the Spanish minister to Abram Sloutsky alias 'Marcos', who had been sent especially from Moscow to instruct 'Orlov' and 'Belyaev' (Nikolsky and Belkin) about the importance of their mission and to arrange for possible assistance.

The so-called recollections of Hernández regarding Sloutsky's visit and his views were based on the earlier writings of Krivitsky, and so must be taken with a pinch of salt. Hernández's book was written long after Krivitsky's articles had appeared in the *Saturday Evening Post*, and when he was working on his memoirs the former Republican minister without doubt consulted Krivitsky's book, which was based on those articles. According to Krivitsky, Sloutsky allegedly told him in Paris on the way back from Madrid that

we cannot allow Spain to become a free camping ground for all the anti-Soviet elements that have been flocking there from all over the world. After all, it is our Spain now, part of the Soviet front. We must take it solid for us. Who knows how many spies there are among those volunteers? And as for the anarchists and Trotskyites, even though they are anti-Fascist soldiers, they are our enemies. They are counter-revolutionists, and we have to root them out.[85]

For the very knowledgeable Isaac Don Levine, not only Krivitsky's ghost-writer but also editor of *Plain Talk*, a known anticommunist journal, it was not difficult to invent this dialogue. It is now documented that Sloutsky had never been sent to Spain.[86]

One of the first practical manifestations of the determination to eliminate the Trostyists in Spain came in the last week of November. After public criticism of the Soviet Union by the POUM, whose members were immediately labelled the 'Trotskyite–Fascist Gang', an attempt was made to mount pressure on the Catalan regional government, the Generalitat. On 24 November, Joan Comorera, the leader of PSUC in Catalonia, publicly demanded the removal of Andreu Nin as Councillor of Justice in the Catalan government, because of his supposed disloyalty and his repeated attacks on the great Soviet ally. Some commentators stress that the Soviet consul general made it perfectly clear to President of the Generalitat, Lluís Companys, that Catalonia could not expect to get further support from the Soviet Union unless the POUM members were expelled from the government.[87] However, as we now know from recently declassified documents,[88] relations between the Soviet representative in Catalonia and the local politicians have often been misunderstood or misinterpreted.

In the autumn of 1936 the feeling in Moscow was that, with Soviet help, the Republican government had a chance to win the war. Therefore, all information from Spain and especially from such a politically and industrially important region as Catalonia was of great interest to the Soviet leadership. Antonov-Ovseyenko was not alone in frequently sending long and detailed political reports addressed to the 'Instantsiya' (Politburo) from Barcelona. Iliya Ehrenburg, famous Soviet writer and NKVD collaborator, also went there in August–September to present his assessment of the situation. He later recalled his trip and his impressions in his articles and memoirs, boasting that he was the first Soviet there,[89] but his secret reports remained secret until quite recently.[90] Ehrenburg met Companys, the general secretary of the Comité Central de Milicias and councilor of the Generalitat Jaume Miravitles, and Buenaventura Durruti, a central figure of Spanish anarchism at the time. Ehrenburg sent several long letters to Ambassador Rosenberg, his old friend, reporting on the situation and giving details about his discussions with the Catalan leaders. Upon his return to Paris, Ehrenburg recalled, he met Antonov-Ovseyenko, who told him that his letters had been duly received in Moscow. Antonov-Ovseyenko also said that he had been appointed consul general because Moscow considered it was in the interest of Spain to bring together Catalonia and Madrid.[91] The first Soviet consul remained in Barcelona for about a year and, according to Ehrenburg, started to speak Catalan. Antonov-Ovseyenko, one of the military leaders of the October Revolution, party alias 'Bayonet', was arrested and shot in Moscow in February 1938.

Apart from journalists and diplomats who provided political intelligence, all Soviet intelligence services sent their officers and agents to Barcelona. In addition to two sub-stations (RU/Kuzmin, and NKVD/Kotov, with their radio operators and other support personnel), the military intelligence directorate of the Red Army regularly sent senior officers as observers who stayed in Catalonia for several months. Leonid Konstantinovich Bekrenev, alias 'Kilin' (codenamed KREMER),[92] arrived there in December 1936 as a representative of the Naval Intelligence Directorate, although like others he was listed as a 'technician'. Many OMS agents of various nationalities were permanently based in Barcelona, as well as 'illegals' from all Soviet intelligence organizations, which was a mixed group of Russians, Spaniards, Austrians, and Germans. 'The main task of the NKVD station in Spain, acting under the umbrella of the Soviet legation,' according to the Lubyanka directive, 'is to provide the Soviet leadership with the intelligence on the whole spectre of Spanish problems, including information dealing with counter-intelligence.'[93] Moscow's 'mission statements' for other services and agents must have been similar.

Between the wars, the NKVD could not compare its intelligence-gathering and analytical capabilities with those of the Intelligence Directorate of the Red Army—and Spain was no exception. But, preserving their traditional functions of a secret police organization and a disciplined enterprise for repression and preservation of power, the NKVD officers were more powerful in Spain and had a broader mandate to recruit agents wherever they could. That secured a considerable level of penetration, albeit, of course, not comparable with the situation in the Soviet Union, where virtually one in ten people was a secret police collaborator, especially in the urban areas (where the ambitious but frightening aim at the peak of the Great Terror was to make *every* Soviet citizen an NKVD agent).[94] High-level political penetration was certainly not on the agenda in Spain, though a lot of effort was spent finding useful contacts among its security organizations. A former chief of the SIM, Manuel Uribarri, even claimed, not quite accurately, that the SIM 'had to fight against the powerful Gestapo, the terrible Ovra, and the no less powerful and terrible GPU'.[95] Contrary to all previous instructions from Moscow, the NKVD was actively relying on the communists and sympathizers in the army and the police. Apart from those activities, there was a very small group of NKVD advisers who duplicated the work of Special Section 'A' of the military and instructed some separate guerrillas. As Helen Graham observes, they 'were keen to use the opportunity provided by the Spanish war to train their personnel and to test equipment and strategies in real and extended combat conditions'.[96] The results were immediately reported to the very top, because, as already noted, Stalin had become heavily embroiled in events on the Iberian Peninsula and 'practically not one document on the Spanish question escaped his attention'.[97] Unfortunately, for whatever reason, only very few of them have been declassified and published so far.

To obtain intelligence from Spain, the NKVD station had first of all to cultivate sources and run agents in such organizations as the DGS—a directorate within the Ministry of Interior with overall responsibility for state security, political police, and counterespionage service. Important was the Servicio de Información Técnico (SIT), a unit responsible for signals intelligence (sigint) and cryptography. Some *checas*, especially those controlled by the Communists, were penetrated and used. Considerable success was due to the fact that several Communists, mostly German, Austrian, and, of course, Spanish, managed to get employed by various services. The Republican government would later try to counter this penetration by establishing yet another secret service, the Departamento Especial de Información del Estado (DEDIDE),[98] but it did not last long, and only after a few months was incorporated into the SIM.

Stalin's keen attention to the events in Spain may be explained by the Russian history in general and the history of Bolshevism in particular. For them, from the very beginning, war was not just a threat from without; it was a time for social cataclysm and political upheaval. Because Bolshevik leaders themselves had achieved power as a result of war, they always believed that they might succumb to a combined effort by a foreign enemy and domestic anti-Bolshevik forces.[99] Stalin's speeches and writings of the period clearly demonstrate his preoccupation with the threat of a potential fifth column in his own country. 'To win a battle in wartime several corps of soldiers are needed,' Stalin explained during one of the Plenums. 'And to subvert this victory on the front, all that is needed are a few spies somewhere in the army headquarters or even division headquarters able to steal battle plans and give them to the enemy. To build a major railroad bridge, thousands of people are needed. But to blow it up, all you need are a few people. Dozens or even hundreds of such examples could be given.'[100] And Stalin's initial interest to Spain may be explained by his desire to prove to the world and to his own people, especially because Trotsky was still alive, that he, Stalin, was a great leader of a great country, and that he was right.

Trotsky and the Trotskyists were the biggest enemy of Stalin and therefore of Yezhov and his NKVD. So those who associated themselves with the Great Heretic were spies, fascists, wreckers, and enemies of the people. They had to be rendered harmless. In December 1936, the Presidium of the ECCI informed the PCE:

The Presidium considers as correct the struggle carried on by the Communist Party and supported by other organizations of the People's Front against the Trotskyites as agents of fascism, fulfilling provocative work in the interests of Hitler and General Franco, trying to split the People's Front, carrying on a counter-revolutionary campaign of slander against the USSR and using all means, all possible intrigues and demagogic methods to prevent the defeat of fascism in Spain. Recognizing that the Trotskyites are carrying on destructive work behind the lines of the Republican army in the interests of fascism, the Presidium endorses the line of the Party for the complete and final crushing of Trotskyism in Spain, which is necessary to obtain victory over fascism.[101]

'Were it only for the real forces of the Trotskyists,' wrote Franz Borkenau,

the best thing for the Communists to do would certainly be not to talk about them, as nobody else would pay any attention to this small and congenially sectarian group. But the Communists have to take account not only of the Spanish situation but of what is the official view about Trotskyism in Russia. Still, this is only one of the aspects of Trotskyism in Spain which has been artificially worked up by the Communists. The particular atmosphere which today exists about Trotskyism in Spain is created, not by the importance of the Trotskyists themselves, nor even by the reflex of Russian events upon Spain; it derives from the fact that the Communists have got into the habit of denouncing as a Trotskyist everybody who disagrees with them about anything. For in Communist mentality, every disagreement in political matters is a major crime, and every political criminal is a Trotskyist.[102]

The Spanish Communist Party, whose numbers began to grow rapidly in the course of the war, reaching those of the PCF, the largest Communist Party in Europe, was one of the factors that led to the defeat of the Spanish Republic. In 1936 Britain, France, and the United States were more afraid of the 'red menace' than of Fascism.

In the meantime another area of the activities of the Russian intelligence services was developing. Several hours before the Moscow Kremlin's Spasskaya Tower clock chimed midnight on 31 December, Louis Fischer, the roving correspondent of the *Nation* magazine, met Corps Commander Solomon Uritsky, the RU Director. Fischer was in the Soviet capital to see his Russian wife Markoosha and his two sons George and Victor, who lived there until the end of the Spanish Civil War. While there, he went on to check up on Luli Bolín de la Mora, the daughter of his friend Constancia de la Mora, who had been evacuated to the USSR and was staying at Uritsky's home. Having been, until a recent clash with André Marty, the Quarter Master of the International Brigades, Fischer was acutely aware of the deficiencies of the Internationalists. Accordingly, he suggested to Uritsky that foreign émigrés in the Soviet Union might be persuaded to volunteer for the Brigades.

Uritsky reported to the Politburo:

Fischer had returned from Spain, where he had taken an active part in the organization of the international units. I submit to you a shorthand report of his talk. FISCHER: [But] Now in the USSR there is another possibility. There are, first, foreign immigrants, who have foreign passports. Next, it's no secret to anyone that they're demoralized and that they don't have very sweet lives. It would be good for both sides if they went to Spain. So this needs to be speeded up.

Next—the second category of people consists of foreigners—Hungarians, Latvians, Poles, Germans and others. It is interesting to note: when a Hungarian comes from Paris or from Odessa to Spain, you soon can't tell which one came from Paris.

And here there must be hundreds, thousands, of comrades who speak foreign languages.[103]

The first group of about 500 international volunteers arrived in Albacete in mid-October 1936 (the exact number and date are debated). Perhaps as a result of Fischer's suggestion to Uritsky, on 19 January 1937, Stalin personally sanctioned the organized transportation of the émigrés from Russia and Europe to Spain.[104] Some of them would be recruited to Soviet intelligence services. Some of those who fought on the front would be allowed to return to the Soviet Union, only to be persecuted as 'traitors, spies, and enemies of the people'. Many, together with the Soviet officers, advisers, and technicians who were in Spain, would perish in the Gulag. In Stalin's Russia, there were no veterans of the Spanish Civil War. Remarkably, the conspiracy theories that were born in the Kremlin in the 1930s survived the end of the Soviet era.[105]

14

The Internationals

A fter 'Transport Organizations' had been established throughout continental Europe, the United Kingdom, and the the United States, thousands of volunteers reported to the recruitment centres. As Burt Cohen, an American senator, put it, 'they did it not for money, not for glory, but out of principle and idealism, and for that they deserve honour'.[1] Another reason was given by Hans Schafranek. 'From the summer of 1936,' Schafranek writes, 'revolutionaries weary of illegal political activity in their own country or the bitter experience of exhausting small group existence in the centres of emigration, poured into Spain from all corners of the world'.[2] For most, Spain offered a chance to fight back against fascism and presented the possibility of eventually being able to return to their homes.

Burt Cohen's letter was a response to a long article by Sam Tanenhaus on the Abraham Lincoln Battalion published in the same magazine in which he alleged that 'Soviet atrocities were not only committed against fictive "saboteurs" and "enemy agents" within the International Brigades. They were directed at the very foundations of the republic.'[3] Choosing the title 'Innocents Abroad' and quoting Gustav Regler and his expression 'the spy-disease, that Russian syphilis', Tanenhaus, however, does not bother to document those 'atrocities' and completely misses the fact that some of the American 'innocents' in Spain were actively recruited as informers, then cultivated and trained to become fully-fledged Soviet agents. His principal source for the article is the error-ridden work published in 2001.[4] It is the selection of documents from the Soviet archives that, in the words of one competent critic, the editors of this book 'have put together the way the House Un-American Activities Committee used to publish Soviet and Communist Party documents, using the sort of analytically biased descriptive commentaries that one usually finds from police agents'.[5]

A particularly prominent example of such recruitment was Morris Cohen (codenamed VOLUNTEER), who, together with his wife Lona, was involved in the Soviet atomic espionage network in the USA, later also helping to steal British naval secrets in England, where they were finally caught and imprisoned as part of the Portland Spy Ring.[6] Both were later given the title Hero of the Russian Federation. Other 'students' of the Barcelona spy school (codenamed CONSTRUCTION by the NKVD) completed their training and received orders to suspend all party work and lie low for further instructions. Even the Lincoln Brigade's loyal biographer, Peter Carroll, relates that after Spain a good number of American volunteers went to work for Soviet intelligence. Some Lincoln vets, such as Irving Raymond Schumann (VEIL) and Wally Amadeo Sabatini (NICK), were so much engaged with the NKVD during the civil war that in 1940 they would take part in the operation to murder defector Walter Krivitsky in their homeland.

Earl Browder, general secretary of the Communist Party of the USA and a long-time NKVD agent who figures in the operational correspondence as RULEVOI ('Helmsman'),[7] personally saw off the first contingent of plucky American volunteers sailing from New York Harbour on 26 December 1936. Browder's former wife Kitty Harris (ADA and NORA) was Donald Maclean's courier and mistress in London and Paris. His sister Margaret, codenamed ANNA, worked as a courier for the NKVD 'illegal' station in Berlin with Karin, Tacke, and the Zarubins;[8] and his cousin Helen Lowry (codenamed MADLEN, later NELLY), was married to Iskhak Abdulovich Akhmerov (YUNGA/JUNG), then deputy 'illegal' resident of the NKVD in the United States.

Morris Cohen, known in Spain as 'Israel Pickett Altman', was one of those who attended Communist propaganda gatherings in New York City's Madison Square Garden Arena, located at that time at Eighth Avenue and 50th Street. His father came from the Ukraine, where he was involved in political activities, and his mother was Lithuanian. In the United States, where they emigrated in 1905, their occupation was registered as produce-peddlers. In 1919, at the age of nine, Cohen and his parents attended a gathering in Tompkins Square Park in New York. The slogan was 'Hands off Revolutionary Russia'. From that time on Morris became a real patriot of his motherland and soon joined the Communist Party of the USA.

In his autobiography, written for the KGB, Cohen wrote that he enrolled on a postgraduate course at the University of Illinois, where he joined the Young Communist League, later becoming a party member. The party sent him to New York as a local organizer. His KGB memoirs are rather confusing, as he writes that he moved to the Big Apple in the autumn of 1936 and then the civil war in Spain broke out. When Cohen heard Phil Bard speak at a meeting of Bronx County functionaries, he decided that 'his duty lay where liberty was in greatest danger—in Spain'. He arrived there illegally with a group of seventeen American volunteers on 25 July 1937, and in early August was in a training camp in Terrazona, where he filled in a personal questionnaire. Answering question two, 'What do you intend to do after this war is finished?', Cohen wrote: 'When the war is finished, I would like to return to activity in the American Labor movement. However, if circumstances require my presence elsewhere, similar to the Spanish struggle against fascism, then I would go there.'[9]

Cohen's passport in the name of 'Altman' was supplied by the Soviet 'illegal' Yakov Golos, who in 1932 helped Nikolsky to obtain a genuine American passport. On the front lines, Cohen/Altman served as a political organizer for the Anglo-American Section III of Machine Gun Company 4 in the Mackenzie–Papineau or the Mac–Paps (Canadian) Battalion.[10] On 14 October 1937 he was wounded in both legs during the battle at Fuentes de Ebro, and in early 1938, together with Jack Bjoze and several others, was sent to the Barcelona reconnaissance and sabotage school commanded by a Latvian, Waldemar Ozols.[11] In April, a new entry was made in his personal file: 'Ahora presta servicio como guardia especial en Albacete' ('Now he serves in a special guard unit in Albacete').[12] That meant he had become a trusted member of the internal security service of the Internationals. Returning to the United States at the end of November 1938, Cohen, a young communist with war experience and special skills of a ranger fully dedicated to the Communist cause, could not find work. His friend Bjoze, at that time Executive Secretary of the VALB (Veterans of the Abraham Lincoln Brigade), recommended him to NKVD recruiters. However, in his KGB memoirs Cohen writes that he was recruited in Spain and 'became a Chekist-*razvedchik* (i.e. a Soviet intelligence operative) at a ceremony in one of the villas in Barcelona'.[13] In this manner he probably described his initial meeting with Eitingon, who 'initiated' him into the service of Stalin.

The man to whom Jack Bjoze introduced Morris Cohen was Semyon Semyonov (sometimes spelt 'Semen Semenov'), codenamed TWAIN, a member of the 'legal' NKVD station who was posing as an engineer in Amtorg. As Cohen later recalled, it was in early 1939, and indeed it should have been sometime before 30 April 1939, when the New York World's Fair had its grand opening and where he was sent as a guard to the Soviet delegation. Two years later, in 1941, Morris married Leontina ('Lona') Petka, daughter of the Polish immigrant Władyslaw Petka, whose family he had known even before he left for Spain, and soon he and Lona both started working for Moscow. Lona Cohen was codenamed LESLIE, and she and her husband also had a joint codename DACHNIKI.

In 1942 Morris Cohen was drafted to the US Army, and soon TWAIN introduced Lona to their new controller, Anatoly Yatskov (alias Yakovlev, codenamed ALEXEY), masquerading as Consul. Morris was demobilized in November 1945 and soon joined his wife in New York, becoming part of Yatskov's spy ring.[14] Following the defection of a well-informed courier, whose name was Elizabeth Bentley and who would play an important role in unmasking Soviet espionage in America, Moscow temporarily broke contact with the Cohens early in 1946, but renewed relations with them in Paris a year later and reactivated them in the United States in 1948.[15] The Cohens successfully worked in the USA for the next two years, when their operation was disrupted by the arrest of Julius (and Ethel) Rosenberg, for whom LESLIE had acted as a courier. They were quickly withdrawn to Mexico, where two Soviet agents—Sixto Fernández Doncel and Antonio Arjonilla Toribio, both Communists and members of the Junta de Auxilio a los republicanos españoles (JARE)—provided them with shelter until they could be moved to a safe place.[16] Later the Cohens, posing as 'Peter and Helen Kroger', operated in England as a support team of the Soviet 'illegal' 'Gordon Lonsdale' (Konon Molody) and his British sources. In 1961, the Special Branch arrested them on charges of espionage. After serving eight years in prison, the Cohens/Krogers were exchanged and in 1969 went to live in Moscow. Until her last days in 1992, Lona, now Yelena Cohen, together with Lisa Zarubina and Maria de las Heras, worked in the Directorate S ('Illegals') of the KGB training future undercover agents.

Among other colourful Anglo-Americans in the employ of Stalin's secret services in Spain were George Mink and Wilfred McCartney. (Long after the Spanish Civil War, MI5 informed the FBI liaison in London that Soviet intelligence representatives actively recruited from the International Brigades in Spain and that according to the Security Service about six American subjects had been recruited to spy in the USA. In the same note, MI5 also mentioned that, among the agents recruited in Spain were also 'certain British subjects who were sent to this country as the foundation of a special espionage organisation'.[17]) Among the suspects, the name of Wilfred McCartney, a convicted Soviet spy, still ranked rather high.[18]

McCartney, who has already been mentioned in connection with the ARCOS affair in London in 1927, was a flamboyant journalist of the Left, not a Communist. Like the Cohens many years later, he spent eight years behind bars charged with espionage for Russia. Already a rich man, he grew richer on the profits of a book he then wrote on his experiences after leaving prison, with an introduction by Compton Mackenzie.[19] In Spain, McCartney was the first commander of the British Battalion in training. 'He had to abandon command,' writes Hugh Thomas, 'because he was shot in the leg by Peter Kerrigan, Commissar of the British in Spain, who was apparently merely cleaning his gun'.[20] According to the latest research on the British volunteers in the Spanish Civil War, McCartney was due to return to London, and a farewell supper was held in his honour at the Albacete base. Apparently Kerrigan, the political commissar at the general headquarters of the International Brigades, was exchanging pistols with McCartney when his pistol went off, wounding McCartney in the arm.[21] Several studies raised the question of whether or not the shooting was an accident.

Douglas Frank Springhall, aliases 'Springy' and 'Peter', usually known as Dave, a prominent CPGB official, and Charles Oliver Green both served a prison term for espionage on behalf of the USSR. Springhall was involved in 'anti-military work' for the party and under the alias 'Dave Miller' attended a 'long course' in the ILS in Moscow between 1929 and 1931, when he was apparently recruited. Springhall was the first Briton to be appointed political commissar of the British Battalion, a position he held from December 1936 to February 1937. His good standing with the Soviets was also evident in a further tour of duty in Moscow in 1938–9. This time he arrived as the CPGB representative to the ECCI.[22] Springhall held various administrative positions in the party, culminating in a National Organizer role from 1940. He was arrested and convicted after an *in camera* trial in 1943 and sentenced to seven years' imprisonment for obtaining classified information for the Russians from Olive Sheehan, a clerk in the Air Ministry, who was the leader of a secret Communist group there. Subsequent enquiries showed that Springhall had also exploited the Communist convictions of Captain Desmond Uren, a Staff Officer in the SOE, to obtain classified information. Uren was court-martialled and also sentenced to seven years. Enquiries suggested that Springhall had been extensively involved in covert activities on behalf of the Party for many years.[23] After serving five years or so,

Springhall was released on parole on condition that he did not engage in political work in the United Kingdom. He died of cancer in Moscow in September 1953.[24] It was Springhall who recruited Alexander Foote as an agent of the Red Army intelligence. He was also instrumental in recruiting Bill Philips, who had worked with Foote in brigade transport in Spain. Both Foote (codenamed JIM) and Philips (JACK) would later meet in Germany as fellow-workers of Ursula Kuczynski's Rote Drei Swiss network. Foote knew her as 'Sonia' (it was actually her codename) and thought he learned her real name, 'Maria Schultz', and her nationality—a Russian or a Pole. She was German, a daughter of a famous Berlin economist, Robert René Kuczynski, and a Soviet agent of long standing. Ursula was one of Sorge's agents in China and before meeting Foote in Geneva had operated in London. Because she married another member of her network, the Briton Leonard Beurton,[25] she would move there again in 1941, carrying on her active work for the GRU for most of the decade. Based in Oxfordshire, she served as a channel of communication (a cut-out) between the GRU case officer at the London Embassy, Semyon Kremer, and atom spy Klaus Fuchs in Banbury. Fuchs came to Britain as a refugee from Nazi Germany in 1933. A year later the Germans slipped information to the Bristol police that Fuchs was an active Communist, but it was ignored. In September 1947, now Mr and Mrs Beurton, Ursula and her husband were interviewed by Jim Skardon and Michael Serpell of MI5, at which meetings she refused point blank to answer any questions. One of the final records in their MI5 file concerns their move to East Germany: 'The Beurtons left Britain for Berlin in December 1949 (Ursula) and June 1950 (Leonard) and Fuchs finally identified Ursula Beurton as his contact in November 1950.'[26] In East Berlin she retired from the GRU and began working for the government.

Yet another of Sonia's wireless operators in Switzerland was a German who had also fought with the Internationals in Spain and was sent by the GRU to Geneva to make a new transmitter as a stopgap in case her own set broke down or was seized. Franz Ahlmann (codenamed ALEX) later proved invaluable when it was necessary to carry the overflow of traffic. His only problem, according to Foote, was that Moscow sent Ahlmann on a Finnish passport allegedly issued in Canada, and he could speak neither Finnish nor English,[27] which the Swiss authorities quickly found out. Fortunately, this was in Switzerland and not Germany.

Charles Oliver Green arrived in Spain in the spring of 1937 and had two days of training before being sent to the front line. After about six months he

was promoted and became a sergeant. He was also recruited as an informer
for the NKVD to watch and write secret reports on other members of the
14th Battalion, where he served. After a while Green was suddenly asked
whether he would agree, as he said later, 'to undertake espionage against
Franco'. The young man agreed but instead was given money and advised
to return to Britain, where a Soviet representative would contact him. At
the end of 1937 Green was safely in London, but was 'reactivated' by a
member of the Soviet Trade Delegation, probably a GRU case officer, only
two years later. He was arrested in 1941 for petrol coupon forgery and
placed in Brixton prison, where he confessed to spying. Ironically, the
Security Service could not take any legal action against Soviet agents any
more, as Russia had become an ally.[28] Every detail of Green's case was duly
reported to the NKVD by Anthony Blunt,[29] a member of the Cambridge spy
ring who was recruited in London in 1937 and joined MI5 three years later.

Among other interesting personalities in Spain were Danny Gibbons, an
officer of the British Battalion and a brother of John Gibbons, an ILS
graduate and *Daily Worker* correspondent in Moscow—MI5 later tried to
cultivate members of the 'Robson–Gibbons' GRU spy ring. At the end of
the war in Spain, Danny was captured by the Italians and placed at the
detention centre at the Saragosa military academy, where the discipline was
hard and the sanitary conditions appalling. While there, the prisoners were
visited by several foreign correspondents. According to the official report,
among the visitors was *The Times* correspondent Kim Philby, 'a rather
conservative Englishman with leanings towards fascism', as one inmate, an
ex-metropolitan policeman from London, described him later.[30] Another
interesting personality among the British volunteers was Edward Smith, a
20-year-old carpenter from London who finished a special OMS course in
1936 and two years later turned up at the International Brigade base in
Figueras.[31]

This is but a short list. However, among all other nationalities, it was
German volunteers who provided the largest recruitment pool for the
Soviet services. Among many others, there were Communists Wilhelm
Zaisser, Erich Mielke, Heinz Hoffmann, Friedrich Dickel, Gustav Szinda,
Wilhelm Bahnik, Richard Staimer, Karl Kleinjung, Heinrich Fomferra,
Victor Priess, Richard Stahlmann (Artur Illner), Hans Schwarz, Wilhelm
Fellendorf, Alfred Schreiber, and Albert Hößler.

The success of agent recruitment belied the fact that the NKVD station in
Spain was a rather small organization in comparison, for example, with the

later cold war operation in such places as London, New York, East Berlin, or Vienna. Practically all recruitments were carried out on the so-called ideological principle, when agents and informants, both Spanish and foreign, agreed to collaborate because of their communist convictions and not for money. The choice of officers forming the residency was based on the geographical and national principle, typical of Stalinist Russia. Orlov/Nikolsky, Belyaev/Belkin, and Kotov/Eitingon were Jews from Byelorussia. Another colleague was Grigory Syroezhkin, who had served in Minsk.[32] In the history of Soviet intelligence he became rather famous for his role in Operation TRUST, one of the first successful deception operations of the Cheka. It was in Syroezhkin's Leningrad apartment that the 'ace of spies' Sidney Reilly was introduced to his future interrogator at the Lubyanka prison. Syroezhkin's deputy was Lev Vasilevsky (alias 'Grebetsky'). After Spain, Vasilevsky was the NKVD 'legal' resident in France (alias 'Lev Aleksandrovich Tarasov'), working under cover as the Soviet Consul General.[33] Eitingon would join him in Paris in March 1939. They would later serve together in Turkey, preparing the assassination of the German Ambassador Franz von Papen. Both Eitingon and Vasilevsky would also be involved in the operation against Trotsky in Mexico: one would organize the murder, and the other the release of the murderer. In Spain, Syroezhkin was officially assigned to the XIV Guerrilla Army Corps as senior adviser. In reality, together with Vasilevsky, he was mainly training volunteers in guerrilla tactics, sabotage, and espionage techniques (explosive devices, cryptography, radio transmission, secret writing) in a secret camp in the Sierra de la Mujer Muerta, not far from Madrid.

Stanislav Vaupshasov also came from Byelorussia and was also formally assigned to the XIV Cuerpo de Ejército Guerrillero as one of its advisers. He arrived in Spain, like many others, with a Soviet diplomatic passport identifying him as 'Stanislav Alexeyevich Dubovsky',[34] but this diplomat's only speciality was subversion, terror, and assassination. Together with Kyrill Orlovsky and Nikon Kovalenko, who were sent to Spain some months earlier than their friend, Vaupshasov spent five years fighting with the OGPU guerrillas in Poland and Western Byelorussia. Such clandestine operations were known in both OGPU and military intelligence as *aktivka* or 'active measures' (*aktivnye meropriyatiya*). This should not be confused with the term 'active measures' of the Soviet cold war propaganda, when it was a form of political warfare. Until after the death of Stalin, in both the OGPU–NKVD and GRU parlance, *aktivka* stood for assassination. This is the clue to understanding one particular passage from the book by the Communist minister Jesús Hernández, written long after the war:

Through the account of the man who had direct contact with Orlov, it was possible much later to reconstruct the facts. But the day after the consummation of the crime I was fully convinced that Andrés Nin had been assassinated. Comrade X let me know that she had transmitted a message to Moscow, which said: 'A.N. affair settled by method A'. The initials coincide with Andrés Nin's. What could 'method A' be? The absurd account of the 'abduction' by Gestapo agents pointed to the GPU's crime. Then 'A', in the Soviet delegation's code, stood for death. If this were not the case, the delegation—that is, Togliatti, Stepanov, Codovilla, Gueré, etc.—would have transmitted something less that 'affair settled'.[35]

Unfortunately, no copy of the mentioned telegram has been found to date. This is not entirely surprising, given the questionable nature of Jesús Hernández's 'memoirs'. As far as the intelligence jargon is concerned, Hernández was right: method A was 'active measure', i.e. murder, assassination, or liquidation, while 'D' stood for *diversiya* ('subversion') and DRG was the abbreviation for *diversionno-razvedyvatelnaya gruppa* (sabotage and reconnaissance unit).

Like Eitingon, Vaupshasov was born in 1899 and started his working life as a farm-labourer. Then he fought with the Red Army and in 1920 became a Cheka assassin and guerrilla fighter operating undercover. For his operations in his homeland Vaupshasov was awarded the Order of the Red Banner. In 1927 he finished short-term officers training courses. Vaupshasov/Dubovsky arrived in Spain in 1937, and it was in Barcelona that he met his old friends and compatriots: Kyrill Orlovsky,[36] Alexander Rabtsevich,[37] Nikon Kovalenko, Vasili Korzh,[38] Nikolai Prokopyuk,[39] and Artur Sprogis[40] from the RU. All of them were intelligence officers with long experience in guerrilla warfare and special operations.

Vaupshasov, who was known in Spain as 'camarado Alfred', later wrote in his book: 'Staff officers complained that I rarely visited the General Staff. Indeed, I was there only from time to time when there was a need to discuss specific tasks.'[41] This coincides almost word for word with what Division Commissar Mikhail Kachelin reported to Moscow: 'Dubrovin, as the adviser of the chief of the general staff, sees Rojos [recte Rojo] from time to time and is absolutely uninterested in the Staff's current work in all its aptitude.'[42] As the texts are almost identical, one may speculate that this report is about Vaupshasov and that Vaupshasov was in Spain under the alias 'Dubrovin' and not 'Dubovsky', as he claimed in his book.[43] Mitrokhin's notes reveal that

Vaupshasov was probably the Soviet Union's most profusely decorated intelligence hero. His murderous pre-war record, however, is still kept from public view in both Russia and his native Belarus, where a street is named after him. According to Mitrokhin, among his duties in Spain were the construction and guarding of a secret crematorium, which enabled the NKVD to dispose of its victims without worrying that their remains would ever be discovered.[44] Remarkably, this crematorium has not been found to date.

In charge of the crematorium was an NKVD agent, José Castelo Pacheco (codenamed JOSE, PANSO, and THEODOR). Pacheco was a Spanish Communist born in Salamanca in 1910 who was recruited by Eitingon in Barcelona in 1936.[45] Castelo's personal file, once in the custody of the KGB's Fifteenth Department (Registry and Archives), was transferred to the 8 Department of Directorate S (Illegals),[46] which was responsible for political assassination, terror, and subversion abroad. Castelo's file transfer could only have happened in the mid-1970s, when all functions of the former Department V (like 'victory') were transferred to the 8 Department. It is likely that, until ten to twelve years before Castelo's death in 1982, he was still in reserve as a KGB 'sleeper' with special skills to murder people.

The beginning of the Spanish Civil War and the struggle of the Republican government to defend itself against the nationalist rebellion led by General Franco fired the imagination of the whole international Left as a crusade against fascism. It also opened up a major new field of operations for Soviet intelligence. Mass recruitment of foreigners was to set an important precedent. In the first months of the Spanish Civil War the chief Soviet foreign intelligence priority remained intelligence collection. Gradually, all other operations were to be subordinated to 'special tasks'.[47]

15

JUZIK will be called ARTUR

Stanislav Vaupshasov, a Soviet intelligence hero who is said to have run a secret NKVD crematorium in Spain, was almost certainly lying when he wrote in his post-war memoirs[1] that in Spain he had heard about Grigulevich from General Walter (Karol Swierczewki), though Grig, as Grigulevich was known among his KGB friends, had indeed played a sinister role in the Spanish events, albeit for only a few months. The main reason why Swierczewki could not have known the man's real name was that during his career in the NKVD–KGB Grigulevich had been an 'illegal'—a deep-cover agent who operates on foreign territory under a false identity and without diplomatic protection. Throughout the whole history of the KGB, until the present day, the Illegals Directorate (the equivalent of the National Clandestine Service with its undercover operators) has been the most secret unit in the whole organization. And Grigulevich is considered to be one of its most successful stars.

Josifas Romualdovičius Grigulevičius, known in the Illegals Directorate of the NKVD–KGB as Iosif Romualdovich Grigulevich[2] for more than fifty years, was born on 5 May 1913 in Wilno (now Vilnius), Lithuania. His father was a Lithuanian Jew and his mother Russian. Josifas joined the Komsomol underground when he was only 13 years old and still a schoolboy. In 1929, because of his political activities, Grigulevičius was expelled from the gymnasium. Later, despite his Karaite upbringing,[3] he became a Communist and was quite active in the youth section of the Communist Party of Western Byelorussia, which had a special Lithuanian Bureau. Sudoplatov, his chief in the operation to assassinate Trotsky, recalled that, when a young man, Grigulevich had made a name for himself by liquidating Lithuanian police informers.[4] On 25 February 1932 he was arrested and spent more than a year in prison, in the infamous Lukiškės jail in Wilno, from which he was released on 13 May 1933. His mother, Nadezhda

Lavretskaya, had died one month previously. On 17 May, the *Vilniaus Rytojus* ('Vilnius Tomorrow') reported the trial of four pupils of the Vitaut gymnasium, among them D. Pumputis, J. Grigulevičius, J. Aidulis, K. Mackevičius, and a student by the name of I. Karosas. The first two received a two-year suspended sentence while others were acquitted. In August, Grigulevičius was summoned to police headquarters and ordered to leave Wilno, then a Polish city, within two weeks. He promptly left for Paris via Warsaw, where he was given money, contact addresses in the French capital, and documents to cross borders.

In Paris, Juzik (a short form of Josifas) was recruited by Iosif Friedgut,[5] a Soviet 'illegal' and then member of the Administration of Special Tasks. The Administration was a quasi-independent OGPU unit that at that time actively operated in Paris under the command of Yakov ('Yasha') Serebryansky. Assassination, terror, sabotage, and abductions were this group's primary pursuits. Serebryansky reported directly to the Chairman of the OGPU. Grigulevich had chosen the code name ARTUR[6] and started his long career as a Soviet 'illegal'.

In 1926 Romuald Grigulevičius, Juzik's father, was fired from the drug store in Panevėžys in central Lithuania, where he worked as chemist, and had to emigrate to Argentina to be able to support his family. There he opened a small drug store in a rural area. In August 1934, Grigulevičius junior arrived in Buenos Aires with orders to join the MOPR bureau in Argentina widely known there as el Socorro Rojo and to start looking for operational opportunities. The International Red Aid, commonly known by its Russian abbreviation MOPR (Mezhdunarodnaya Organizatsiya Pomoschi Rabochim), was a Comintern/OMS front founded in 1922 and now headed by Elena Stasova, a former Comintern representative to the German KPD, alias 'Herta'. In the OMS the clandestine work in Latin America was at that time controlled by Yu. A. Markov, who later worked in the NKVD. Juzik spent some weeks at his father's house in the village of La Clarita in Entre Ríos, studying Spanish and getting used to an entirely new environment. He turned out to be a very gifted chameleon, because later, in the intelligence reports about 'José Escoy' (one of Grigulevich's aliases), he would be called 'un agente soviético de origen brasileña'.[7] He evidently spoke Spanish well with a slight Slavic accent, which enabled him to pass himself off as a Brazilian.

Grigulevich very quickly found other gauchos judíos—Jewish wanderers, like himself—and began active assimilation with the Argentinean society. He soon received a telegram summoning him to the capital, where real underground work awaited him. Both Grigulevich himself and several Russian authors[8] mention that at that time he met Vittorio Codovilla[9] and Rodolfo Ghioldi,[10] the Latin American high-flyers of the Comintern. Almost certainly, this is an invention.

During the 1930s Codovilla worked for the Comintern, mainly outside Argentina. He was on a permanent mission in Spain from 1931 until 1937, and then in Paris but still occupied by the 'Spanish problem', returning to Argentina only in 1941.

At the time Grigulevich arrived in the Argentinean capital, Ghioldi was on his way to Moscow, from where he would be sent directly to Brazil. When the Comintern affair to organize a Communist revolution there in November 1935 failed and two of its leaders, Ghioldi and Luis Carlos Prestes,[11] were arrested.[12] During all this time, Grigulevich remained in Buenos Aires.

Several British historians and authors believe that the failure of the Communist putsch in Brazil was a British operation.[13] According to their version, Frank Foley, a British Passport Control Officer in Berlin (and an undeclared SIS officer), managed to recruit Johann de Graff, who worked for both the Comintern and the Red Army Intelligence Directorate. Inside MI6 the agent would become known only under his code name 'Jonny X'. Jonny was a German communist who took part in the mutiny on the battleship *Westfalen* in Wilhelmshaven in October 1917 and then escaped to Russia, where he underwent Communist indoctrination and learned the basics of clandestine work in the International Lenin School. There he was recruited by Soviet Military Intelligence and sent first to England and then to Germany. Jonny, however, became disillusioned with Communism and offered his services to the British by 'walking into' their Berlin Embassy, where Mr Foley was more than happy to see him. The intelligence writer Michael Smith claims that Jonny's recruitment and handling by Foley represents one of the most important cases in SIS history. Keith Jeffery, the Official Historian of the Service, devotes several pages of the book to 'The Jonny Case', giving credit for the agent's exemplary handling to Valentin Vivian and adding some colourful details to the story—needless to say, without any reference to primary sources. Among Jonny's important achievements, as stated in several published accounts, was information that de Graff allegedly provided to his handlers about the secret agents of the

Comintern in Britain and their attempted subversion of the armed forces, 'which was a decisive factor behind the fruitful co-operation on anti-communism between MI5 and SIS in the 1930s'.[14] This seems a little too far-fetched, as this future star agent was in Britain only once (before he visited Foley for the first time in February 1933), and for only a very short period of time, after which he worked elsewhere, including China and Brazil, so his knowledge and usefulness in what concerned the British operation would be at best minimal.

When de Graff was sent to Brazil to foment revolution there in 1935, the British SIS, according to Nigel West, played a key role in providing the Brazilian authorities with the detailed information they needed to suppress the uprising. When 'de Graff' was arrested in Brazil in 1940 and threatened with deportation to Germany, West writes, 'he was eventually captured in January 1940, and as soon as SIS learned of his arrest urgent representations were made in London to prevent his return to Germany, where he was wanted by the Gestapo as a senior KPD functionary. SIS succeeded in obtaining his release, and he was resettled in Canada where he became an adviser to the Royal Canadian Mounted Police on German espionage, and in 1943 participated in a double agent operation with a captured Abwehr agent, Waldemar von Janowsky, codenamed WATCHDOG.'[15] In Jeffery's version, Jonny briefed Vivian about his Brazil mission in Paris in November 1934. Then Vivian was personally running him in Rio, at the time the country's capital, until he entrusted this delicate mission to an unnamed British businessman. Jonny, who was a mercenary agent, 'reported over a few months on the progress of the conspiracy', until finally, on 20 June, the British ambassador himself warned Brazilian President Getulio Vargas. Further intelligence from Jonny led the Brazilian authorities 'to the Chief Communist representative' (who was Arthur Ewert but whose name is also not mentioned in the Official History). In January 1936 Jonny, together with all other Moscow agents, was arrested in Brazil for taking part in the attempted coup, but with the help of SIS managed to escape to Argentina. At the end of the year he was recalled to Moscow.

According to Jeffery, Jonny was soon sent to Brazil, where a SIS representative—again without any success—tried to use him as an agent provocateur against the local Nazi organization. As stated in the Official History, the Brazilian authorities arrested him for the second time in November (according to other sources, on 14 December) 1939 on charges of espionage, but the SIS intervened, and Jonny was released and brought to

Britain with his pregnant wife Gerti. The story ends by his being resettled to Canada, where he started to tell his tales to the Canadian press.[16]

Remarkably, many authors who write about Jonny and his adventures make no reference to the documentary sources, while the stories of real and bogus 'Jonny X' provide enough material for an exciting biography. And such a biography, entitled *Johnny: A Spy's Life*, was indeed written and published in America in 2010[17]—that is, in the same year that *The History of the Secret Intelligence Service* came out. Although this work is rather well documented, the author of *MI6* has not used it as his source, and the biographers of Johnny have not consulted Jeffery's book.

Johannes Heinrich De Graaf, also known as 'Ludwig Dinkelmeyer', 'Mattern', 'Franz Gruber', 'Pedro', and 'Richard Walter', indeed took part in the Comintern coup attempt in Brazil in 1935. According to William Waack, a Brazilian journalist who researched the Comintern archives in Moscow, De Graaf was recalled to the USSR and shot by the NKVD in 1938.[18] His German wife, Helena Kruger (alias 'Erna Gruber'), allegedly committed suicide in Buenos Aires when the family received the summons to go to Russia.

German historians Hermann Weber and Andreas Herbst believe there were two 'Jonnys'.[19] One, born on 11 May 1894 in Nordenham as Johann De Graaf, ran away from home and started his working career as a ship's boy on a merchant ship. He was first arrested in Amsterdam in 1914 for anti-war propaganda. Then, already a sailor of the German Kriegsmarine, De Graaf was arrested again three years later for taking part in the mutiny. Jonny, as was his lifelong nickname, joined the KPD from the first days of its foundation and later became a member of its underground *AM-Apparat* (literally, 'antimilitary department', but in reality an undercover party service for the subversion of the German police, army, navy, as well as 'hostile' paramilitary formations). A Communist candidate, he was elected deputy to the local Landtag in Westphalia in 1930, but had to leave Germany in the summer of that year, as the police started to investigate his (unspecified) activities on charges of high treason. Naturally, he went to Moscow. There Jonny was one of the politically active German Communists also attending one of the Comintern military school run by its Orgbureau, where, under the supervision of Pavel Vassiliev, he studied how to use explosives and launch subversive operations. After he had successfully learned his trade, Alexander Abramov-Mirov, at that time head of the OMS, then sent him to England, Manchuria, Shanghai, and in 1935 to Rio de Janeiro in a mixed group of OMS–RU agents to make a revolution. The group of 'revolutionaries' included Arthur Ewert and his wife Elisa, better known as Szabo posing as 'Harry Berger' and 'Machla Lenczycki';[20] Sofia and Pavel Stuchevsky, the latter a former RU resident in France still remembered there as 'General Muraille';[21] the Italian Amleto Locatelli;[22] the Argentinean Rodolpho Ghioldi with his wife Carmen Alfaya;[23] and also August Guralsky,[24] Boris Krayevsky, and Olga Benario.[25] Silo Meirelles, a trusted friend of Prestes, who had also been trained in Moscow, commanded the insurgent forces of Nordeste.[26] Jonny came to Brazil under the alias 'Franz Gruber', an Austrian businessman. He and his wife Helena ('Lena') Kruger arrived in Rio on board the French vessel *Florida* on 5 January 1935 and settled in a spacious apartment on Avenida NS de Copacabana, where 'NS' stands for Nossa Senhora, meaning Our Lady. On 10 January the Buenos Aires police issued an alien registration card to the US subjects 'Berger' and 'Lenczycki'. At about the same time, the Comintern-selected leader of the Brazilian revolution, Luis Carlos Prestes, with a Portuguese passport in the name of 'Antonio Vilar', and Olga Benario, documented as his German-born wife 'Maria Bregner-Vilar', left Moscow for Paris. After a week's stay, they moved to New York and arrived in Rio de Janeiro in April 1935.[27] It took the team seven months to mount a coup.

On 26 November Prestes called on his followers to take up arms, but the government was prepared. Hundreds of rebels were rounded up in Rio, Socorro, Natal, and Recife, and soon all prisons there were full. The British government communicated to the Vargas government their congratulations.

During the Second World War Jonny de Graaf was seconded to the RCMP in Canada but in early 1945 recalled to London and shortly assigned to MI6 head office. On 29 October 1945 he was naturalized as a British subject, John Henry De Graaf.[28] As expected, together with other men from the SIS who staffed various SIS units in Germany, he was then sent to his native Westphalia, where he was headquartered in Bad Oeynhausen. The town hosted the British military government of the British zone of occupation, officially, the Control Commission for Germany (CCG or British Element) and over the winter of 1945–6 the SIS representation in Germany was transferred into an element of the Intelligence Division of the CCG.[29] De Graaf, with German as his mother tongue, served there under

Major General John Sydney Lethbridgem who became Chief of Intelligence for the CCG headquartered in an impressive five-storey grey building
right in the town centre, which also housed the headquarters of the British
Army of the Rhine (BAOR). Jonny, his biographers write, was not very
happy there, and in August 1946 he retired from the Service, throwing a
party for his friends in London attended by Valentin Vivian and Frank
Foley.[30] Soon de Graaf, with his young wife Gerti, returned to Canada.
In 1972, Jonny accompanied by Neil Pollock, his case officer for ten years,
attended a party at the home of Ron Stewart in Washington, DC. During a
private conversation with Stewart, Jonny admitted killing Helena Krüger in
Argentina.[31] John Henry De Graaf—this is the right spelling of his name—
passed away on 2 December 1980.

De Graaf's son, also Jonny, was born in November 1919. The family
decided not to stay in Russia for long, and Maria De Graaf had returned to
Germany with the children returned to Germany by 1931. Then, on his
father's advice young, Jonny went to the Soviet Union, where he studied at
the famous Karl Liebknecht School for German-speaking children and then
attended a factory school at the Stalin Auto Works. In January 1938, at the
age of 19, De Graaf junior was arrested on suspicion of being a member of a
secret Hitler Jugend cell, but in May he was acquitted and released. During
all that time his father was in Brazil again, now trying to assemble a team
intended to take over a Comintern military network in Japan. Parallel to
that, an SIS representative in the region (based in Montevideo) tried to
employ Jonny 'as a sort of Nazi agent-provocateur' for which role he was ill
suited. 'In November 1939,' according to *M16*, the official history, 'he was
arrested for "espionage" and very roughly handled by the Brazilian police',
before London intervened, and Jonny was released and brought to Britain.[32]
Whether Moscow learned about his father's adventures is difficult to say,
but De Graaf junior was arrested again, and his fate remains unknown.[33]
The Austrian historian Hans Schafranek, who calls him 'Jonny De Graf', and
who was able to follow the life of De Graaf junior in the Moscow archives
from the Children's Home No. 6 to the Stalin Auto Works' professional
school, characterizes him as an 'inconveniently intelligent young man poorly
adjusted to demands and stresses of daily living'.[34] Schafranek, however, was
also not able to find out what happened to Jonny during the war, when the
last letter along with his photograph suddenly came to his sister in Germany.
The picture showed a good-looking young man, visibly well fed and wearing
a good suit and tie.

That there is not a single reference to a primary source in Jeffery's MI6 history is understandable, because the archives remain closed and secret. But surprisingly, considering the suggested level of cooperation between the SIS and the Security Service on Jonny's case, there seems to be no reference to him in the MI5 archives either. At least, *The Authorized History of MI5* as well as The National Archives in Kew keep silence about Jonny-the-Agent.

Instead, the unclassified MI5 files offer an amazing story of yet another 'Jonny'. His name was also Johannes De Graaf, but it was quite a different person, who was indeed an object of interest for the Security Service. MI5 and the Special Branch suspected that he had been a German spy![35] This Jonny collaborated with the authorities and, like his older namesake, was allowed to relocate from Britain to Canada in 1943. As he was born in November 1918, which makes him the same age as Jonny De Graaf junior, this incredible coincidence is particularly interesting.

Grigulevich, about whom both MI5 and the FBI knew nothing until quite recently, remained in Buenos Aires during and after the uprising in Brazil. Whether at that time he was indeed capable of getting Prestes and Ghioldi out of prison remains unanswered, but it is known that in 1935 in Argentina Juzik tried to make contacts among the intelligentsia and the Jewish community. He was welcomed especially cordially by Flora Toff, the secretary of the recently created Jewish organization Delegacion de Asociaciones Israelitas Argentinas (DAIA), which represented all Jewish associations of the country, and her brother Moses, also a DAIA official. Thanks to their help, Grigulevich established good relations with Miguel Finstein, the son of a rich chemist, at whose apartment he lived. 'Camarada Miguel', as Juzik was known among local communists, actively cultivated useful contacts whenever he could, and some of them, like the journalist and critic Ricardo Veles and the Marxist philosopher Emilio Troise, author of the Stalinist propaganda brochures *Materialismo dialectico* and *Los Germanos No Son Arios* (both 1938), and especially *Notas De Viaje a la URSS* (1953), would greatly help Grigulevich in his future clandestine operations.

One summer evening, Juzik was allegedly arrested while attending a youth party in the villa of Dr Augusto Bunje, leader of the Independent Socialist Party, at the Florida barrio in the northern suburbs of Greater Buenos Aires. According to one participant, Fanny Edelman, all the young people were detained on suspicion of Communist propaganda and subversive activities. After a night at the police station of La Plata, all were released, as the Communist lawyers managed to overrule police orders, though several compromising documents were seized.[36] Although Edelman never mentioned Grigulevich by name or by his alias, his Russian biographer claims that several decades later she confirmed to him personally that comrade 'Miguel' was there. In her memoirs Edelman writes only that after their release all the young *muchachas* and *muchahos* travelled by train back to the capital, where they learned about the right-wing insurrection in Spain. It was on the morning of 18 July 1936, she said—probably with tongue in cheek, because even with the five hours' difference the news from Spain could hardly have reached Argentina that Saturday morning. Anyway, it was decided that Juzik should leave the country as soon as possible. By September 1936, all necessary travel documents were obtained for him via the Comintern channels and he left for Spain via France.

Several KGB-related sources offer conflicting reports about Juzik's first days in Madrid. Some authors claim that Grigulevich was commissioned as Vidali's aide-de-camp at the Fifth Regiment,[37] while others suggest that he was first sent to Codovilla's Comintern office, which then directed him to the Soviet Embassy.[38] The semi-official KGB history, which is a half-fictional publication without any documental references, states only that, upon arriving in Madrid, MAKS (one of Grigulevich's many code names) immediately reported to the NKVD station. Grigulevich himself admitted, probably accurately, that he worked at the Soviet Embassy first as an interpreter, soon managing to become a close adviser of Santiago Carrillo, two years his junior and from 6 November an important member of the Junta de Defensa de Madrid as Councillor of Public Order.[39] Soon after they first met, Carrillo became such a close friend of the celebrated NKVD 'illegal', saboteur, and assassin that he subsequently chose Juzik as his son's secular 'godfather'.[40] However, it is hard to imagine when, where, and how the two could have met after Grigulevich had left Spain.

Even as a teenage militant, although mocked by his opponents as 'the chrysalis in spectacles', Carrillo had shown precocious leadership qualities. As secretary general of the Federación de Juventudes Socialistas, he had been one of the most militant advocates of the 'bolshevization' of the PSOE. He had been imprisoned after the miners' uprising in Asturias in October 1934. On his release after the elections of 16 February 1936, Carrillo immediately applied for a passport to travel to Russia, which was issued on 24 February 1936 in Madrid. Because he was watched, police and border guards of several countries immediately reported that Carrillo and his associates were going to Moscow as part of the Spanish youth delegation to the 'secret Communist congress'.[41] In reality, in March 1936 there was a Kommunisticheskii International Molodyozhy (KIM) (Communist International of Youth) conference in Moscow in preparation for several important international events that year, with KIM, the Soviet Komsomol, and the Spanish delegation taking an active part. These events were the World Youth Community for Peace, Freedom and Progress in Paris, the International Youth Conference for Peace, Liberty and Progress in Brussels, and, most importantly, the First World Youth Congress in Geneva. Both the Comintern and KIM, with their headquarters in Moscow and bureaus around the world, were firmly in the hands of the NKVD and the Red Army intelligence.

On his return to Spain, at the age of only 21, Carrillo had engineered the fusion between the Socialist and Communist youth movements, thus effectively putting young socialists into the Communist lap, and became secretary-general of the combined organization known as the Juventudes Socialistas Unificadas (JSU) (Unified Socialist Youth).[42] It was to be a Communist organization in all but name. The entire process seems to be the fruit of his stay in Moscow. Partly because one CARMEN,[43] a Soviet agent within the Spanish KIM Bureau, feared that Carrillo might end up in the Trotskyite Fourth International, he was thoroughly vetted and indoctrinated in Moscow. Like all prospective Communist leaders, young or old, Carrillo would have been obliged to convince his Comintern bosses that he would collaborate fully with the Soviet authorities. And Carrillo dutifully fulfilled this promise, later becoming the secretary-general of the PCE, a post that had been decided in Moscow for every Communist Party.[44] Eventually, the situation would change and in 1977 the Soviet magazine *New Times* would go as far as labelling Carrillo 'an enemy of socialism'.

All that, however, would be in the future. Now Carrillo was a faithful servant of the Kremlin. On 6 November 1936, when the Madrid front was close to breaking and the Republican government hastily retreated to Valencia, leaving the capital's defence in the hands of General Miaja, Carrillo was appointed to the post of Consejero de Orden Público in the hastily created Junta de Defensa de Madrid. (Another most important post, Councillor of Defence, was given to Antonio Mije, a Communist 'educated' in Moscow.) In other words, Santiago Carrillo became the chief of public security of the besieged capital. He immediately appointed five of his most trusted associates to the top positions in his department.[45] One of them, Federico Melchor, together with Carrillo, had spent three weeks in Moscow the previous March getting instructions. On the same night of 6–7 November, Carrillo also created a new organ, the Consejo de la Dirección General de Seguridad. This new council actually controlled all the activities of the DGS.

The honorary consul of Norway, who became the Norwegian chargé d'affaires when the consul left Spain, Felix Schlayer, described the situation of the security services in the autumn of 1936 as chaotic. Schlayer was a German engineer who had lived in Spain for about fifty years and died in Madrid. His book, first published in Nazi Germany in 1938 and translated into Spanish seven decades later, remains the object of fierce public debate.

The only existing Soviet intelligence history, in an article devoted to Grigulevich, gives the following version of how the events in Madrid developed at the time:

In the autumn of 1936 almost all diplomatic representations in Madrid demanded that the Republican government grant exterritorial status to many buildings where the embassy personnel as well as citizens of their respective countries lived. The inexperienced Spanish authorities agreed. The list contained about 70 houses flying the flags of different foreign states and decorated with their coats of arms. The *Seguridad* [DGS] leadership knew for sure that those residential buildings were in reality serving as hiding places for the so-called Fifth Column, as the secret supporters of Franco on the Republican territory became to be known. But they did not dare to search them since they were afraid of the diplomatic scandal.

In the first days of December 1936 [*sic*][46] a secret conference was convened at the *Seguridad* headquarters with Grigulevich present. It was decided that buildings and houses of the Finnish embassy should be stormed first. That was done on the night of 4 December. Among those arrested were 2,000 people, including 450 women and children. Huge arms caches and the workshop to manufacture hand grenades were found. All those arrested were escorted to prison by buses. It was discovered that Finnish diplomats were cashing between 150 and 1,500 pesetas per month for giving shelter to Franco's supporters. During the same night several houses of the Chilean embassy were taken over and many people arrested. The *Seguridad* seized important documents that compromised the Chilean embassy staff.

In spite of the fact that the *Seguridad* leadership took the law into their own hands and acted without any authorization from the government, let along any warrants or other legal papers, nothing was done to them and soon it was decided that all prisoners should be deported to France . . .

One of the Turkish embassy buildings was searched. One hundred crates with rifles, belonging to the fascist organisation, were seized . . .

The *Seguridad* forces also stormed the Consulate General of Peru and a five-storeyed house under the Peruvian flag. In one of the apartments a wireless transmitter was seized together with codes. The equipment belonged to the extreme nationalist *Falange Española*. About 800 people were arrested. Thanks to certain operative measures the diplomatic bags of the Czech chargé d'affaires were accessed [*sic*] and documentary proof retrieved which clearly pointed to his relations with Gestapo agents . . .[47]

Another account (which has to be read with some circumspection because of the author's self-censorship and overall demand for 'ideological correctness') belongs to Mikhail Yefimovich Koltsov, a famous *Pravda* correspondent in Spain. The main protagonist of Koltsov's famous *Spanish Diary*, Miguel Martínez (apparently not himself or another real person, but a collective figure based on several actors of the Spanish drama)[48] was on easy terms with many leaders of the Republican side. Koltsov states that, on 4 November 1936 (thereby corroborating a suspicion that the above quotation from the six-volume semi-official history of the Russian foreign intelligence should be considered as deliberate disinformation at least in what concerns the dates), Miguel started to worry about 'eight thousand fascists who are locked in several prisons around Madrid' and who threaten to become a real problem as a dangerous 'fifth column' fighting against the democratic republic. Later that day, during an important meeting 'at the commissariat general', Koltsov's hero raised the problem again, asking the Commissar General and Minister of Foreign Affairs, Julio Álvarez del Vayo, 'What's going to happen with the arrested [fascists]?' He was concerned because Ángel Galarza, the Minister of the Interior, had done nothing to resolve the problem.[49] 'There are eight thousand people. It is a big fascist column.' He received no definite answer.

Koltsov's diary entries dated 5 November, and the information from the chapter devoted to Grigulevich's exploits in Spain, coincide: foreign embassies are accused of giving 'shelter to fascists waiting for Franco' and were raided.[50] But where else could the author of the chapter on how Max fought his early battles (the chapter about Grigulevich) find a first-hand description of what happened in those days in Madrid? Naturally, from the *Pravda* correspondent who was present there.

On the next day, Koltsov made the following record: 'The Minister of Interior Galarza and his deputy, the director general of state security Muñoz, left the capital before anyone else. Out of eight thousand arrested fascists no one has yet been evacuated.'

Finally, on the anniversary of the Russian Bolshevik Revolution, 7 November (NS), Miguel Martínez asked the PCE Central Committee secretary, Pedro Checa, about the 'arrested fascists'. The latter explained that nothing had been done to date and that it was perhaps too late to do anything. 'To evacuate eight thousand people is a difficult task, requiring great resources,' Checa explained. No resources were available. Then, writes Koltsov, an idea came to Miguel Martínez that it was not necessary to 'evacuate' all fascists, but only the most hardened ones. According to him, 'anything should be done but these cadres must not be given to Franco'.[51] That was agreed upon by the Communist leaders, and 'three comrades were sent to two large prisons'. 'Fascists were brought out into the courtyard,' Koltsov noted, 'their names called out according to the lists. That surprised and shattered them. They thought they were going to be shot. They were sent in the direction of Arganda . . .'[52]

In reality, Koltsov was perfectly well informed about what happened to the prisoners on that day of the nineteenth anniversary of the October Revolution and that, instead of Arganda, they were transported in a different direction—to Torrejón de Ardoz—and massacred. It was not only Koltsov's professional duty to know and report to the Politburo about such cases—judging by his *Spanish Diary*, the *Pravda* correspondent fully approved of such crimes, because in his view every move against 'the fascists' was justified:

The actions of the 'Fifth Column' caused outbursts of terrible rage. People burst into the houses from where there were shots and not only thoroughly searched every apartment but killed many people, right and wrong, destroying and smashing everything at hand. One [multi-storey] house was even set on fire. Somebody was on the spot to broadcast that the same would happen with every other house and its inhabitants should fascist terrorists and saboteurs be found there. Those who lived in the houses must be vigilant—had mutual and personal responsibility.[53]

Two years before his death, MAKS/Grigulevich gave a revealing interview. He stated that in Madrid, where he had worked closely with Santiago Carrillo, he had a special unit of Socialist militants under him that he used in a 'great variety of operations'.[54] The elite police detachment called the Special Brigade (Brigada Especial) was formed from the agents who had been part of the police force in charge of the security of the Soviet Embassy in Madrid in late August 1936.[55] The date on which this ten-man unit was put under the command of Grigulevich it not known, but his testimony makes it clear that, in the autumn of 1936, he was already operating his small *brigadilla*, whose members knew Grigulevich as 'José Escoy'. The unit was made up of the so-called *especialmente elegidos* ('specially chosen'), normally recruited from among the militants of the JSU, the organization led by Santiago Carrillo after the merger of the Federación de Juventudes

Socialistas and the Juventud Comunista in the spring of 1936, when he came back from Moscow. Later, a member of perhaps the same, or a similar, Special Brigade (she does not provide any name or further details) told Katja Landau in a secret prison in Barcelona: 'No one knows where, or for whom we are working. And when our term is finished we have seen nothing and heard nothing. Yes, that's blind obedience if you like, but that is fitting for whoever agrees to become a convinced militant.'[56]

It is obvious that the opinion of Koltsov's 'Miguel Martínez' prevailed, because during the night of 7 November and on the next day collections (that became known as *sacas*) and transportation of prisoners continued. The evacuations would go on throughout most of November, until a new director general of Madrid's prisons, Melchor Rodríguez, took up his post on 4 December. All those *sacas* from the prisons in the autumn of 1936 were based on the lists issued from the department headed by Santiago Carrillo. Frequently, but not always, these were carried out by groups of las Milicias de Vigilancia de Retaguardia, small militia units that had been sanctioned by the Largo Caballero government. As already mentioned, according to his own words, until he left Spain in the summer of 1937, Grigulevich commanded one of the small *brigadillas* of the Republican security force. More importantly, he claimed later that he was 'the right hand of Carrillo' (who was only 21 then).[57] Remarkably, a staunch Stalinist and a militant PCE member Luis Lacasa also commanded a small unit of the Quinto Regimento, a Communist military formation very close to the young chief of public order in the capital. And, which was not a coincidence, Lacasa also left Spain in the summer of 1937, emigrating to the Soviet Union.

On 14 November, after the diplomatic corps had sent a joint protest to the Junta de Defensa de Madrid, the Republican press issued an ominous declaration 'Para deshacer una vil compaña': 'Neither the prisoners were victims of abuse, nor did they have any reason to fear for their lives.' They will all, it was said, be judged according to the law. Those who spread rumours about acts of cruelty risked the death penalty.[58] It was as simple and straightforward as that.

When the war was over, the victors initiated a massive state investigation of the repression throughout the entire Republican zone, including the murders of prisoners taken from Madrid to Paracuellos-Torrejón, known as the *Causa General*. Since then many experts in Spain and elsewhere have come to the conclusion that Santiago Carrillo had appointed those killers himself. At least one of his closest associates, Federico Melchor Fernández, was among those who accompanied him to Moscow in February–March 1936.[59] The names of the executioners are to be found in the transcripts of interrogations that were carried out in November 1939: Manuel Rascón Ramírez, Manuel Ramos Martínez, Agapito Sainz, Andrés Urresola Ochoa, and Lino Delgado. Some of them confessed and gave detailed testimonies. As is often the case, most of the main players managed to escape. Did Koltsov know who 'Miguel Martínez' really was? Vicente Rojo, the chief of staff of the Madrid front, in his memoirs referred to a foreign Communist, 'Miguel Martínez', who allegedly helped Vittorio Vidali organize the Fifth Regiment that later became the core of the Spanish Republican Army. But the memoirs were published in 1967, a year after Rojo's death, and memories do not always serve us well. Maybe the old general also read Koltsov's *Diario de la Guerra española* (1938). Noticeably, not a single Soviet or Comintern representative who was in Madrid in those days ever mentioned Paracuellos in his or her writings or interviews.

Serrano Poncela, another friend who, according to the testimonies, 'sorted out' the prisoners into categories ('military, aristocracy, workers, persons without occupation, etc.') was the editor of the socialist newspaper *Claridad*. After Carrillo had been made chief of the Madrid security, he appointed Serrano Poncela as his deputy with the title 'Delegado de Orden Público' (equivalent of the director general of security). It appears from all available documents and from a number of depositions that this man was the driving force behind many mass murders committed during the month of November. He was the one who gave the orders to the prison governors about releasing the prisoners, and he was the one who sent his subordinates to collect them.[60]

During the interrogations by the Nationalists, Ramón Torrecilla Guijarro told of how, on the night of 8 November 1936, together with five other militiamen sent by Serrano Poncela, he had arrived at Cárcel Modelo, Madrid's model jail. They demanded the card index and began sorting prisoners into categories. When, towards morning, they were halfway through the work, their chief Poncela appeared and ordered that all those in categories 1 and 2 (military and bourgeois) were to be prepared for transport in the waiting buses. He added that the man leading this expedition had already received instructions as to what was to be done with the prisoners. He also said that Ángel Galarza, the Interior Minister, had telephoned from Tarancón on his way to Valencia and instructed that it must be a 'definitive evacuation'.[61] Later, Serrano Poncela emigrated from Spain and lived for twenty-odd years in the Dominican Republic, where he became a well-known professor, author of a number of literary works. He never returned to Spain and died in exile.

Although possibly guilty of facilitating the massacres, Serrano Poncela was still a journalist and an intellectual, not a hands-on killer. Grigulevich, in contrast, was a member of the professional intelligence service—and, moreover, of its special branch, the Administration for Special Tasks, whose direct speciality was abduction and assassination on foreign soil. It is perhaps one of many ironies of life that after he had retired from active service (after returning from his last murderous mission in Italy and Yugoslavia), ARTUR also became a professor and presented a doctoral thesis in ethnography. Just like Poncela, Grigulevich wrote a number of literary works, including a series of biographies (in Russian): *The Shadow of the Cross over Cuba and the Congo* (1960), *Cardinals Go to Hell* and *Shadow of Vatican over Latin America* (both 1961), *Pancho Villa* (1962), *Miranda* (1965), *History of the Inquisition* (1970), *The Rebellious Church in Latin America* (1972), and (in Spanish) *La Iglesia a la Sociedad en América Latina* (1983). As seen from the titles, these books are directed against the Vatican and the Catholic Church's influence in Latin America, strictly according to the directions of the Politburo and the KGB. His other books—*Simon Bolivar, Che Guevara, Salvador Allende, David Siqueiros*—are biographies of those who, according to the author, devoted their lives to the revolution. What exactly he had in mind remains a mystery, but some of them he knew personally. Remarkably, Grig never wrote or said anything about his good old friend and Moscow neighbour, the Spanish architect Luis Lacasa.

Stalin's idea of how a Spanish 'problem' could be solved in a most effective way was the order to assassinate General Franco. Several groups were directed to the Nationalist side to fulfil the order.[62] Grigory Semyonov (codenamed ANDREI and GEORGES), a former Socialist Revolutionary terrorist but since 1920 an officer of the intelligence department of the Red Army General Staff, headed one of them. Together with Artur Stashevsky and Kristaps Salniņš, Semyonov operated in Germany in the early 1920s, and then in China, where Salniņš was his station chief. In 1929, after two years at the headquarters, Semenov was moved to administrative work, but in 1935 he was reinstated in the service and sent to Mongolia. When the war in Spain broke out, it was decided, according to the unofficial GRU history, to send him to the region of Rio Tinto and Aroche 'to liquidate several leaders of the fascist movement'.[63] Instead, he set out to organize guerrillas, whose mass actions he considered to be more productive than individual assassinations. In spite of the military success of his group, Semyonov and his second-in-command were recalled after three months, but he returned to Moscow alone, claiming that his subordinate had been killed when the group ran into an ambush. The story was later used by Orlov to enhance his own role as the guerrilla warfare organizer, and he described the episode using the invented names of 'Major Strik' and 'Captain Glushko'. As a matter of fact, 'Strik' was a pseudonym of a real guerrilla commander and NKVD officer Kirill Orlovsky.

Another officer whom the Russian sources say was sent behind the Nationalist line to assassinate Franco was Elli Bronina (née René Marceau), the wife of the former RU resident in Shanghai, Yakov Bronin.[64] This information, however, is contradicted by their son, Samuil Bronin, who describes Elli's mission to the Nationalist side using notes from her diaries.[65] According to the son's version, Uritsky, the RU chief, summoned Bronina to his office after her return from China, where her husband had been imprisoned as a Soviet spy, and explained that she would have to go to Spain to collect intelligence from the rebel zone and transmit it by radio to the RU station in Valencia (until October 1937 headed by Gorev). She was to assemble the transmitter herself from the spare parts that could be freely purchased in radio shops. In Copenhagen, Marceau-Bronina received a new British passport identifying her as a Canadian of French origin, named Martha Sunshine. Her legend suggested that she was looking for her fiancé, a German pilot, who had initially been stationed in Portugal for training and had then been transferred to Salamanca as an officer of the Condor Legion.[66] From Denmark, Ms Sunshine managed to get to Lisbon, and, as a rich, single, and good-looking young Canadian lady, quickly established the right contacts among the pro-Franco Portuguese officers. With their help she allegedly visited Salamanca and attended one of the fascist conferences, sitting in a box next to General Franco himself. She also managed to get an invitation to a reception held by the general. This was all, as, without any explanation, the Nationalist counter-intelligence became suspicious, searched her hotel room, and, having found nothing, nevertheless advised her to leave the country as soon as possible. She returned to Lisbon with her Portuguese friends, noticed that she was shadowed there too, and hurriedly left for Copenhagen and Moscow, arriving there in spring 1937.[67] According to her official GRU biography, in January Bronina was awarded the Order of Lenin for Spain. Her son relates that in the same year she retired from the service to start a new career as a doctor.[68] Though all protagonists are real and the GRU sources seem to confirm Bronina's assignment in Spain, it is difficult to accept this story at face value. As an experienced and trained radio operator, she could have been dispatched to Portugal to provide communication facilities to the undercover RU station. It is now known that the station chief was military engineer 3rd rank Bronislav Yanovich Ovsienko, assisted by an RU officer of Austrian descent, Karl Nebenführ,[69] and that they were controlling several agents. Therefore, it was necessary to communicate with Moscow, and it was easier to do via a powerful RU transmitter in Valencia. So Bronina could have been sent to Lisbon to secure radio communication between Portugal and Spain. But it is hard to believe that a young woman could have been given the almost impossible mission of assassinating General Franco. She was not a trained assassin, acted alone, and had no weapon. Another important argument is that in the inter-war period 'active measures' (abduction, assassination, sabotage, and other special operations) were part of the Section 'A' repertoire and were not entrusted to female radio operators.

The NKVD, in its turn, instructed its 'illegal' resident in London, Theodor Maly, to send Kim Philby, then codenamed SÖHNCHEN, as a war correspondent with Franco's forces. The agent was fully informed that his task was to find a way to approach the Generalissimo and kill him. Though Philby was quite enthusiastic, Maly reported to the Centre that SÖHNCHEN would not be able to fulfil the task.[70] In May, when Philby returned to London after his first three months in Spain, Maly reported to the Centre that Kim was certainly the wrong man for this 'special task'—that is to say, for the murder.[71]

Though Maly was ordered to continue preparing Philby for the mission and to intensify his efforts to get as close as possible to Franco's inner circle, it was clear that a reserve candidate was needed. By all measures, Grigulevich was an ideal choice. The only problem was to get him alongside the Caudillo.

Among those arrested by the Republicans was Raimundo Fernández-Cuesta y Merelo, an 'old shirt' and executor of José Antonio Primo de Rivera, the deceased leader of the fascist party Falange Española. Primo de Rivera was arrested on 14 March 1936. In November, after being transferred to a prison in Alicante, he was tried by a Popular Tribunal and sentenced to death. The story goes that Indalecio Prieto, Minister of Defence, personally met Fernández Cuesta through Ángel Baza, the first chief of the Republican SIM (according to Fernández Cuesta's *Testimonio*, he owned a restaurant in Bilbao). Prieto obviously knew from his own sources that there was some dissidence in the Franco camp. His idea, then, was to send Fernández-Cuesta into the rebel zone in the hope that he might lead Falangist opposition to Franco.[72] They met in July 1937, and, in return for a prisoner exchange for Justino de Azcárate, brother of the Republic's Ambassador in London, Fernández Cuesta quickly agreed to do what was requested of him, and, after Prieto's personal intervention, was released from prison and sent behind the lines. However, Sudoplatov recalled that 'Colonel Kotov' (Eitingon) managed to get Fernández-Cuesta's agreement to collaborate with the NKVD.[73] Sudoplatov claims, implausibly, that, with the help of Fernández-Cuesta and Grigulevich, Soviet intelligence managed to start secret negotiations with Franco in March 1937 to reach a compromise in the war. He further states that, although agreement with the Nationalist leadership could not be reached, several useful tips given by Fernández-Cuesta helped to recruit some unnamed 'high-ranking Franco's officials' as Soviet agents. (This, however, is even more implausible, not to say extremely far-fetched.)

In any event, diplomatic negotiations at a high level were the speciality neither of young Grigulevich nor of Eitingon. Both were men of action, not words. It is a possibility, albeit a remote one (as no documents will ever be made public even if they do exist), that it had been hoped to use the Fernández-Cuesta channel to get Grigulevich as close as possible to General Franco in order to assassinate the Nationalist leader. The same pattern was repeated in Yugoslavia in 1953 in an attempt against Marshal Tito, and again Grigulevich was selected as the assassin.[74]

However, a far greater priority than the death of Franco was the elimination of real or imaginable Trotskyists in Spain. Merciless destruction of their political opponents had been on the agenda of both the Soviet Communist Party under Stalin and the Nazi Party under Hitler. Psychopaths and tyrants usually belong to this destructive personality type. The term 'extermination' referred first of all to opposition among their own ranks. Both dictators were ruthless to those whom they considered their enemies, and it has been proved without any reasonable doubt that Trotsky was Stalin's Enemy Number One, a much more hated figure than Hitler, whom Stalin respected until he attacked the Soviet Union, let alone General Franco.

The animosity Stalin felt against Trotsky extended to all his followers and sympathizers, assistants, supporters in and outside Russia, and even relatives and members, albeit distant, of the Trotsky family. With very few exceptions, all of them were murdered or else perished in the Gulag. During the

Great Terror in the Soviet Union, which took place at the same time as the Spanish Civil War, anyone even remotely suspected of being a 'Trotskyite' was immediately considered to be a Gestapo spy, a wrecker, saboteur, and fifth columnist. To identify and eradicate them was the main task of Stalin's secret police. Therefore, the NKVD representative in Spain was a much more powerful figure than the head of Military Mission, the ambassador, or a Comintern emissary. Occupying this position in 1937–8, Orlov knew only too well what his priorities had to be.

In early December Ambassador Rosenberg arrived in Moscow to report on the situation in Spain. On 10 December he met Georgi Dimitrov.[75] On the next day, the ECCI reportedly informed the Spanish Communist Party: 'Whatever happens, the final destruction of the Trotskyites must be achieved, exposing them to the masses as a fascist secret service carrying out provocations in the service of Hitler and General Franco, attempting to split the Popular Front, conducting a slanderous campaign against the Soviet Union, a secret service actively aiding fascism in Spain.'[76]

This account is a loose interpretation of the telegram that was indeed sent on 11 December 1936:

From: MOSCOW
To: MADRID
No.:——
LUIS [Codovilla], PEPE [Diaz], PEDRO [Gerö]
Il faut prendre orientation à la liquidation politique des Trotskistes comme contre-révolutionnaires agents GESTAPO. Après campagne politique éloigner du gouvernement local et tous les organes. Supprimer presse, expulser tous éléments étrangers. Tachez de réaliser ces mesures en accord avec anarchistes.
RUDOLF [unidentified].[77]

For the sake of historical accuracy, it should be pointed out that the original Moscow telegram demanded 'the political liquidation' and not 'destruction' of the Trotskyists and that Moscow suggested the use of the anarchists as allies.

In one of his interviews Grigulevich recalled what happened after the news had reached the NKVD station about skirmishes in Barcelona (no date is given but it could hardly be before the afternoon of 3 May 1937). He said he had been immediately dispatched to the Catalan capital with his mobile squad to deal with the instigators. Fifty years after the events, Juzik invented an innocent-sounding story where, upon arrival in Barcelona, he met a group of merry anarchists who offered him vodka, caviar, and borscht; all this accompanied by Russian jokes mixed up with swear words. According to Grigulevich, these were the FAI members who had emigrated to

Moscow in the 1920s, married Russian and Ukrainian women, and after the revolution returned to Spain. Finally, still according to Grigulevich, he managed to arrest them and escorted the whole company to Antonov-Ovseyenko, the Soviet consul-general, who said that they were all drunk and refused to believe a word.[78] This, no doubt, was an entirely invented story, like very many other things that Grigulevich mentioned in his interviews or even in private discussions with friends.

In reality, the adventures of Grig in Barcelona were not as innocent as he painted them. Working in the Soviet intelligence archives, Vasili Mitrokhin noted that 'Grigulevich had taken a leading role in liquidating Trotskyists during the Spanish Civil War, as well as training saboteurs and arsonists to operate behind Franco's lines'.[79] This, of course, is an exaggeration taken from one of his 'heroic' biographies written for the KGB, but on 3 May 1937 Grigulevich (then codenamed MAKS) is said to have led his special unit to Catalonia.[80] This, again, may or may not be true, as the source of this information is highly unreliable. However, what is now known for sure is that he was in Barcelona in June, taking part in the crucial events that have remained an enigma for more than seventy years.

Many foreigners and anti-Stalinist militants were lodged at the Hotel Falcón. Paul Thalmann, a real Swiss Trotskyist, was also there at the time. He recalled that the hotel

buzzed with a swarm of journalists, politicians and exiles from the whole world, while several oppositional groups of Socialists and Communists met there. The SAP (Socialist Workers' Party), represented by Max Diamant and Willi Brandt, the activists of the KPD–Brandler tendency, Council Communists from Holland, Trotskyites from America, France, Britain and South America, Italian Maximalists, German Anarcho-Syndicalists and the Jewish Bund were all there. This was so much the case that some, such as the SAP and the Italian Maximalists, had their own distinct military units, which were a part of the POUM militia. Many of the revolutionaries had been soldiers during the First World War, and having military experience, they were determined to support the Spanish revolution both politically and military.[81]

Thalmann also mentioned that the POUM leaders were not interested in taking part in the political discussions and fractional intrigues of the Falcón inhabitants and left the organization of this motley crew in the hands of the Austrian Kurt Landau, the leader of the group 'Funke'.

The semi-official history of the Russian foreign intelligence states that Grigulevich and his people detained all residents and visitors of the Falcón.[82]

After a huge scandal, several foreign representatives, including the future chancellor of West Germany, were released.

The mystery of what really happened in Barcelona in July 1937 continued to intrigue many scholars and authors for decades. Helen Graham wrote in 2002:

The notorious case of the kidnapping and murder of POUM general secretary Andreu Nin remains a conundrum...A massive amount has been claimed and conjectured about this. But the fact remains that we still do not know exactly what happened to Nin or who was involved. To date nothing in the Comintern archives has shed any further light on the affair [which is quite normal and logical as, contrary to many published claims, the Comintern or its representatives had nothing at all to do with this case]. The NKVD material that has so far surfaced is less than conclusive, while the NKVD archives themselves are not on open access.[83]

In the meantime, as early as 1992 the Catalan television aired a brilliant documentary entitled *Especial Andreu Nin: Operació Nikolai* ('Operation "Nikolai"'), for the first time revealing what had been rumoured and suspected for years, and Costello with Tsarev published the appropriate KGB documents a year later in their biography of Orlov. However, until the present author started to explore the topic several years ago, little was known about the specific details of this operation and almost nothing about its participants. Though Operation NIKOLAI, as the abduction and murder of Nin was described in the NKVD telegrams, is analysed in detail in the following chapters, it seems justified to state here that Grigulevich was one of the leaders of this operation and almost certainly the executioner.

María Dolors Genovés, the author of the above-mentioned documentary, during a short interview with Oleg Tsarev, then an officer of the KGB Press Bureau, managed to film several previously secret documents and among them the personal file of SCHWED (Orlov), No. 32476. She shared her footage with this writer.

On page 101 there is a telegram:

4. About those involved in the NIKOLAI [Nin] case, the main participants are 1– L [deleted] and 2 – A[deleted]F[deleted]. I[deleted]M[deleted] was an indirect assistant. When he brought food to the place of detention and the gates were opened for him, our people entered the inner yard [twenty-one lines deleted]. Poltavsky was to report to you from Paris about the departure [for Moscow] of the last participant of the operation JUZIK. The main enciphered document, which is familiar to you, was written by his hand. He served as my interpreter in this case and was together with me in the car right near the premises from which the object [Nin] was brought out. (Eight lines deleted.)[84]

Cameraman Albert Arean shot a close-up of yet another document—an undated piece of paper marked as page 164 and stitched into the file. The handwritten text in Russian reads: 'N. from Alcalá de Henares in the direction of the Perales de Tajuña, half way, 100 metres from the road, in the field. BOM, SCHWED, JUZIK, two Spaniards. Signed PIERRE's driver Victor.'[85] Since the day of the murder, the puzzle of the code names has never been solved.

'Poltavsky' was almost certainly the senior major of state security Yakov Serebryansky, Juzik's former chief who at that time was in Paris leading the Spetsialnaya Gruppa Osobogo Naznacheniya (SGON) (the Special Tasks Force). Victor-the-driver who wrote this note was Victor Nezhinsky, an NKVD agent from a family of Russian émigrés, recruited by Zarubin in Paris. Victor was a former officer of the French army, a graduate from the military school in Saint-Céré. After the Spanish Civil War, he continued to work for Soviet intelligence in France just like his father (codenamed JEWELLER) and sister Maya. The family's collaboration with the KGB continued for over twenty years. PIERRE was not, as some of the commentators thought, Ernö Gerö, a high-ranking Comintern official and an NKVD collaborator from Hungary.[86] Gerö indeed had at one time had a pseudonym 'Pierre', but it was used only in Comintern correspondence and never in the NKVD exchanges. In reality, PIERRE was Naum Eitingon, chief of the NKVD sub-station in Barcelona, who, after Orlov's desertion, took up his post.

SCHWED was Nikolsky/Orlov; in the Spanish literature his code name is usually spelt as 'Xvied'. BOM was Erich Tacke, a German Communist who after the unsuccessful Hamburg uprising of October 1923 was recruited by the OGPU, predecessor of the NKVD, and became one of its 'illegals' operating in the USA, China, and then Europe. Before coming to Spain, Tacke was an 'illegal NKVD' resident agent in Berlin, working together with his Russian wife Yunona. Finally, as we know, JUZIK was Iosif Romualdovich Grigulevich.

The letter 'L' in Orlov's report may possibly stand for Luis Lacasa, a rather well-known Spanish architect at the time, but also a PCE activist and a member of the Fifth Regiment. From February till May 1937, Lacasa, together with another architect, Josep Lluis Sert, was busy designing and helping to erect the Spanish pavilion at the Paris World Exhibition. That, however, did not prevent him from attending a very privileged event in the Palace Hotel in Madrid. As a matter of fact, Lacasa, apart from Orlov's Spanish interpreter Soledad Sancha, was the only Spaniard who took part in the celebration of the Bolshevik Revolution on 7 November 1936 in the tight group of selected guests: Gorev, Ratner, Mamsurov, Paulina ('Lina') Abramson (all four RU), Orlov (NKVD), and Koltsov with Karmen. After the operation Lacasa emigrated to the USSR, where he lived in obscurity with Sancha until his death in 1966, having visited Spain only once, briefly, as a tourist in 1960.

In the NKVD document released to the joint publishing project of the KGB-sponsored biography of Orlov, all three Spanish names are carefully blackened, but by the letter count it may be possible to identify the second Spanish participant as Aurelio Fernández, though this is, of course, only a guess. He is probably not identical with Aurelio Fernández Sánchez, the FAI extremist who for a while headed the Investigation Department of the Comité Central de Milicias Antifascistas de Cataluña and later served as secretary of the Junta de Seguridad Interior responsible for public order. He later lived in exile in Mexico. About the third participant with initials (in Russian) I—M—, Orlov reported that he took only an indirect part.

Javier Jiménez Martin was a police officer assigned to the Special Brigade unit supervised by Grigulevich. In an interview with Catalan TV he recalled that José (Juzik/Iosif), whom he called 'un jefe de la GPU' and believed to be a Brazilian, was the real organizer of Nin's abduction and the one who stood behind the whole Operation NIKOLAI. As we now know, this is not entirely correct, though Juzik indeed played an important role in this provocation.

In late July 1937 Orlov reported to the Centre that 'the 'honeymoon' between the Socialists and Communists was over and that the Communists were banished from the government service, including the security police. Not only this telegram, but the real changes in the leadership of virtually all Republican special services where trusted PSOE members were placed in all important posts,[87] demonstrate that the NKVD grip on these services was not at all as tight as some authors asserted,[88] and that the NKVD station's successes heavily depended on the activity of the communists.

Grigulevich was the last of the assassins, except Nikolsky, to leave Spain in mid-summer 1937. He went to Moscow for special training. At the end of 1939 in a safe house Stalin's last hangman Beria introduced Grigulevich to Sudoplatov as the best candidate for the operation to murder Trotsky in Mexico.[89] Sudoplatov, himself an OGPU assassin and now the chief of the NKVD Special Tasks, had never heard about Juzik before.

16

NKVD and their 'Neighbours', 1937

Although Nikolsky/Orlov was sent to Madrid when the NKVD was under the leadership of Genrikh Yagoda, it was Nikolai Yezhov, the new People's Commissar of Internal Affairs, appointed on 26 September 1936, who put him in charge of the whole NKVD operation on the Iberian Peninsula. By the spring of 1937, 'Camarada Orlov'[1] had been promoted to become the NKVD chief resident agent in Spain, regularly sending situation reports to the Lubyanka headquarters. His information, however, only complemented what was received from sources 'close to Western governments', as the accompanying memos used to put it.

In early February 1937 Sergey Spiegelglass, the deputy head of Soviet foreign intelligence and Orlov's direct boss, forwarded to Stalin several 'special reports' (*spetzsoobscheniya*) all marked Top Secret. They seem to have been received from both the State Department in Washington, DC, and a source or sources in the Foreign Office, and reflected an Anglo-American view on how the Spanish conflict could be resolved. The British side thought that the only solution to the problem would be to agree with Germany and Italy to form a Spanish government that would be equally far from communism and fascism. It was thought that this agreement could be achieved by providing financial aid to both fascist states that were supporting the insurgents. The Foreign Office expected that Washington would be a partner in such a settlement, albeit unofficially.[2] Another special report described the Cabinet meeting at which Assistant Secretary of State Robert Walton Moore declared that, judging by all available information, it would be almost impossible to preserve world peace in 1937. Hitler demanded, and Mussolini agreed, that Franco's victory be hastened. Until the Spanish gold was returned to Spain, Germany and Italy would not agree to any negotiations, the document said.[3] There is little doubt that disturbing news from the NKVD stations abroad only fortified Stalin's conviction that, in the case of a world war, the Soviet Union would be alone without any ally, and that great Western powers were more interested in reaching an agreement with fascist states than with the Soviet Union.

Communications from the Soviet Embassy in Paris were no more encouraging than those from Berlin, London, Washington, or Tokyo. Only three months after the outbreak of the Spanish Civil War, Alexis Léger, secretary general of the Quai d'Orsay, complained to the French deputy chief of staff, General Victor-Henry Schweisguth, about the 'psychological disadvantages of the rapprochement with Russian communism [and] of the conspiracies which it plotted in every country'.[4] A fortnight later Léger warned the Soviet Ambassador Vladimir Potemkin that Soviet aid to the Republicans 'might well affect the whole future of relations between France and Russia and of the working of the Franco-Soviet Pact'.[5] British diplomats in Paris reported to Whitehall that many French officers hoped for a fascist victory in Spain.[6] Copies of these reports quickly found their way to Moscow, thanks to intelligence sources in both the French Cabinet Office and the British Foreign Office. But, while the Soviets still cherished hopes to strengthen the Mutual Assistance Pact through the development of military staff talks and Ambassador Potemkin lectured the Minister of State Camille Chautemps on the disadvantages of subordinating French policy to the British, the Foreign Office intervened heavily in April–May 1937 to bloc Franco-Soviet military negotiations.[7] In frustration, the Foreign Commissar Litvinov told Robert Coulondre, head of the Sous-Direction des Relations Commerciales, that he could do nothing to 'suppress the PCF [. . . but he] did not care in the least what the French government did to them. All that interested Russia was the military alliance with France.'[8] But all that interested the Quai d'Orsay was a hedge against Soviet–German reconciliation. Since in the spring of 1937 no one considered it a real possibility, there was no need for staff talks with the USSR. With the collapse of the staff talks, the last effort to achieve a big trade deal between the two countries also collapsed, to the chagrin of advocates of a Franco-Soviet alliance.

Under the circumstances, when all external diplomatic and political efforts as well as internal economic, agricultural, and even national policy measures were producing unsatisfactory results, Stalin was convinced he could rely *only* on the NKVD, which he thought would help him to overcome all problems. The culmination of the Great Terror campaign in 1937 coincided quite by chance with the civil war in Spain. Inevitably, these events would influence each other.

A serious reorientation of the Soviet foreign intelligence and internal security service, united under the roof of the NKVD, had been under way since Yezhov had become chief. For Yagoda, Yezhov's predecessor and one of the Service's founders, social disorder posed the greatest political danger to the state. Thus the struggle against social disorder became, for Yagoda, the equivalent of political struggle against counter-revolution.[9] While Stalin supported this line at first, his policy radically changed after the murder of Kirov (on 1 December 1934), and by late 1936 he was ready to oust Yagoda in favour of a tougher man with new ideas.

Yezhov's criticisms of the NKVD at the February–March 1937 Plenum of the CPSU Central Committee were in keeping with this turnabout. Yezhov sought to reorient the GUGB (Chief Directorate of State Security) towards the fight against political opposition, understood not as social disorder but as direct organized political subversion and espionage.[10] Orlov's reports from Spain demonstrate that new instructions reached him and that he followed strictly this policy line of his chief.

His NKVD colleagues in Spain had their own priorities. Major of State Security Naum Eitingon (alias Kotov), the resident in the sub-station in Barcelona, was overseeing agent recruitment operations and the 'illegals'. Captain of State Security Naum Belkin (alias Belyaev) acted as liaison/ adviser to the Republican police and security agencies. Senior Major of State Security Grigory Syroezhkin (alias 'Pancho', nicknamed Grande), based in Valencia, was in charge of Line D (sabotage and subversion). In his memoirs Orlov exaggerated his own significance by inventing several 'personal assistants', among them 'Colonel Tolin' and 'Colonel Gotzul'.[11] From the documents,[12] it can be stated with complete assurance that such 'colonels' never were in Spain.

Other NKVD operatives, such as Syroezhkin's deputy Vasilevsky (alias 'Grebetsky'), his old Leningrad pal Ivan Ozolin (codenamed KRAFT), Vaupshasov, Orlovsky (STRIK), Rabtsevich (VIKTOR),[13] Prokopyuk,[14] Kovalenko, and Korzh, were assigned as advisers to different reconnaissance and sabotage units. Still the main work of training demolition men and directing them behind the enemy lines was carried out by RU experts in special operations: senior adviser Hajji Umar Mamsurov (alias 'Alexander Ksanti'),[15] advisers Ilya Starinov (Rudolf and Rodolfo Wolf), Kristofors

Salniņš (Hugo, in Spanish coronel Víctor Jugos), who succeeded Mamsurov in 1937, Artur Sprogis, Grigory Kharitonenkov,[16] Alexander Rodimtsev, Nikolai Ostryakov, Ivan Skrebnyov (alias Pyotr Antonov), M. K. Kochegarov, Nikolai Patrakhaltsev (alias Pastukhov),[17] another senior adviser succeeded in June 1938 by Vasili Troyan (alias Solomin),[18] Andrey Zvyagin, Pyotr Gerasimov (alias Gankin), Andrei Emilev,[19] Alexander Kononenko, and others.

Their female comrades-in-arms were usually employed as interpreters, though some claim in their memoirs, probably not without ground, to have taken part in action. Among the known veterans are Maria Fortus,[20] Elisaveta Parshina,[21] Eugenia Ozolina, Anna Obrucheva, Paulina and Adelina Abramson (Kondratieva), Lyuba Mestón, Nora Chegodayeva, Lydia Kuper,[22] Maria Polyakova,[23] Irina Leitner,[24] Tatiana Ivanova, Olga Klimova, Daria Kravchenko, and Simona Grinchenko (Sima Krimker),[25] who served as Lister's translator. Many of these young women got married to the RU advisers they worked for. One of the interpreters, Maria Dobrova from Byelorussia, perhaps deserves a special mention.

She came from a poor working-class family and was 30 years old when she arrived in Spain as a volunteer for a one-year tour of duty in 1937.[26] Noticeably, she did not speak Spanish but was fresh from an English class. After Spain and another two years of studies at the Leningrad University, she began teaching there when the war broke out. Dobrova spent four years in Leningrad under siege and in 1944 was sent to Columbia as a member of the Consular Section of the Soviet Embassy, which, without doubt, was a cover for an intelligence assignment. She was commissioned as a staff officer in 1951 and sent for specialized training to a training centre where she was became accustomed to life in the West. There was also an advanced language course under the supervision of native speakers and profound tradecraft training supervised by experienced 'illegals'. After three years of such training, Dobrova was sent on a test run—a probationary period abroad—to Italy and France. In 1954 she successfully passed obligatory state examinations to a commission composed of the GRU Director Mikhail Shalin, who was posted to Japan during the war in Spain, the chief of the 1st Directorate (Illegals), Rear-Admiral Leonid Bekrenev, who served as an intelligence instructor attached to the Republican Fleet, and her personal supervisor, before travelling to the United States using a complex route. By the end of the year, Dobrova, alias 'Christina Macy', reached New York, where she opened a make-up studio. A high-ranking GRU officer by the

name of Dmitry Polyakov also served in New York as a Soviet representative to the Military Staff Committee of the United Nations twice at the time
that Dobrova was operating there undercover. During his second posting,
Polyakov's eldest son became seriously ill, but, because of the sensitivity of
Polyakov's mission, the new GRU leadership did not allow him to take the
boy to a New York hospital for treatment, so he died. Totally broken,
Polyakov approached the FBI and offered his services. In 1963 the FBI
started watching Dobrova/Macy, who noticed the surveillance and committed suicide to avoid detention. At the time, she was 56.

From the first weeks of the existence of the NKVD residency in Spain
there were several officers—Syroezhkin, Vasilevsky, Eitingon, and Orlovsky,
as well as at least three undercover agents, Grigulevich, Fortus, and another
'illegal', the German communist Erich Tacke—who could have been used
for 'special tasks'. According to Mitrokhin's notes, at certain times (in 1937)
Vaupshasov assisted in the 'liquidations', as the supervisor of a crematorium
where NKVD victims were literally turned to dust.

One has to say, however, that the 'direct action' (another KGB euphemism for assassination) was used very rarely and selectively, and was always
strictly coordinated by Moscow. As shall be seen from the following
chapters, the number of the NKVD victims almost certainly never exceeded
twenty or so, contrary to 'hundreds' and 'thousands' mentioned in many
printed sources,[27] just as the number of the NKVD officers in Spain at any
time remained limited to ten. Though people of different nationalities
volunteered as agents, informers, and collaborators, their number is greatly
exaggerated.

While Orlov concentrated on various tasks in Spain, Yakov ('Yasha')
Serebryansky organized training courses in Paris for saboteurs from the
International Brigades. But the main NKVD training grounds for guerrillas
and saboteurs were within Spain itself, at guerrilla training camps near
Valencia, Barcelona, and Bilbao, and in Archena (Murcia).[28] However,
contrary to Orlov's claims, the NKVD and especially Orlov himself had
very little to do with guerrilla operations in Spain.

In comparison with the NKVD, the Intelligence Directorate of the Red
Army General Staff had considerably more personnel who were fulfilling
different functions according to the requirements of its consumers and the
immediate war needs, including special operations behind the lines. Gorev,
the Soviet military attaché, described this work in detail in his reports to the
Director (Uritsky and then Berzin).[29] Another, less-well-known, role of the RU

advisers was to set up the Republican military intelligence, if not on the strategic, then at least on the front and division levels,[30] and the counter-espionage service. This service, which became know as the SIM, was established only in August 1937.

In most cases, nowadays, it is a mistake to think that a military attaché is a GRU resident in the country, though all members of the military attaché staff are part of the GRU residency. Traditionally, the GRU station chief is a deep-cover job, and he may be any member of the diplomatic staff. But, in wartime Spain, Brigadier Vladimir Efimovich Gorev (codenamed SANCHO) was both the Soviet military attaché and the legal RU resident, who also acted as a military adviser to Colonel Rojo, the chief of staff of the Madrid front.[31] Gorev was assisted by David Lvovich (codenamed LOTI)[32] and Iosif Ratner (codenamed JUAN), who was Gorev's secretary. His personal interpreter (and, some say, mistress) in Madrid was Emma Lazarevna Wolf, and his wireless operator and cipher clerk during the first months in Madrid was Bruno Wendt, a former German sailor and a communist who had served with the Red Army intelligence since 1929.[33] It is noteworthy that in January 1937, while in Spain, several senior RU officers, including both Gorev and Lvovich, were awarded the Order of Lenin, the highest Soviet decoration. Emma Wolf later remembered that her boss, who also served as counsellor of the Junta de Defensa de Madrid in those days, maintained especially close, 'direct and permanent' relations with Mikhail Koltsov, a person 'very well informed about everything that happened on the front lines and in the rearguard'.[34] Berzin, chief military adviser, who moved to Valencia with the Republican government, received his Order of Lenin upon his return to Moscow in May, and was promoted to Army Commander 2nd Rank—in modern terms he became a two-star general.

Lvovich was an experienced RU officer who nevertheless fell into a trap and was arrested in Copenhagen in 1935 when an RU network was rolled up by a counter-intelligence operation launched by the Danish security service.

Though, as seen from one of Gorev's earlier reports to the Director, there seemed to be a slight confusion about who should report to whom, all advisers/military specialists reported to Berzin, head of Military Mission, while Gorev's staff, formed according to the diplomatic protocol, directed military attachés (army, air, and navy), as well as military intelligence officers attached to different Republican formations, RU 'illegals', and selected agents. All Soviet military advisers, including Gorev's staff, were sent by the RU, though not all of them were intelligence officers. What is now called the 'defence department of the embassy' and was then known as the military attaché apparatus included Nikolai Kuznetsov (codenamed LEPANTO), naval attaché, assisted by Leonid Bekrenev (alias Kremer),[35] and Nikolai Annin (FRANÇOIS).[36] In his reports to the headquarters Gorev called his naval officers 'fishermen'. Several weeks after their arrival in Spain, he complained to the Director: 'The group of "fishermen" are in a difficult situation. None of them speak Spanish. FRANÇOIS is in the north; he has a translator, and [as one may conclude] from his dispatches, he is working, teaching people, things are happening. Two others are in Cartagena with LEPANTO, but without any [help with] Spanish.'[37] Radosh and his co-editors, who published this report without any source reference, did not manage to identify officers of the naval intelligence directorate who were with Kuznetsov (LEPANTO), while these were the future Rear Admiral Grigory Evteyevich Grischenko and the future Vice Admiral Victor Mikhailovich Gavrilov.[38]

Other officers of the military attaché staff were Boris Sveshnikov (codenamed ALCALA), the air force attaché; Dmitry Tsyurupa (codenamed FRIDO), formally Gorev's secretary but more often his representative in Albacete or Archena; and Vasili Lyubimtsev (codenamed PEDRO), a technical officer and code clerk, all of whom were accredited as diplomats. Gorev wrote about his subordinates:

JUAN [Ratner] is continuing to work a half-day on General Asensio's staff; the remaining time he takes my place to deal with various routine matters. He has worked out a plan for the PUR [Political Directorate of the RKKA], instructions for the military commissars and so on. He works a lot and well.

PEDRO [Lyubimtsev] is dealing with all the technical stuff; I have sometimes been surprised by his endurance and capacity for work in this. In the meantime, I cannot report anything but excellent testimonials about his performance.

Barbara treats our work very patiently, but even she reminds us and checks up, just in case we dirty our laundry.[39]

Noticeably, no one ever commented on this last phrase, because apparently no one, including the editors of *Spain Betrayed*, knew who this 'Barbara' was. In the Russian original it is actually 'Varvara', which stood for the War Ministry,[40] then headed by Francisco Largo Caballero. This remark is very important, as it shows the nature of relations between top Soviet military advisers and their Spanish hosts, who were grateful and friendly but watched out, not allowing the Russians to go too far.

Yet another intelligence officer, Ivan Kuzmin (DIEGO), used the cover of Soviet commercial representative in Barcelona, heading the local RU sub-station. The official diplomatic status considerably limited operational possibilities for Gorev's men, and during his first weeks and months in Spain Gorev sent numerous complains to the Director requesting a change in his own and his officers' official status[41] so that, as normal 'volunteers' rather than attachés, they could do their job more efficiently.

While only a limited number of RU officers under diplomatic cover were involved in intelligence work, there was in fact a much larger group operating outside official Soviet legations. Some of them combined jobs, being listed (and often indeed serving) as military advisers, while their principal task was to observe, assess, and report to the headquarters. Among them was Colonel Ivan Grigorievich Chusov (MURILLO), adviser to the chief of staff of the Catalan army (with cover documents in the name of 'Ivan Pilipenko', secretary of the Soviet consulate in Barcelona). One of the Catalan intelligence chiefs, Vicente Guarner, talks warmly in his memoirs of his relationship with a military adviser Colonel 'Ivan Filipenko', whose real name he did not know.[42] Other RU observers were Alexey Vasilievich Mokrousov (HORACE, in Russian 'Goratsyi'),[43] adviser to the Aragon front; Colonel Pyotr Ivanov (PIRU),[44] and Dmitry Sokolov, quite a mysterious figure, possibly hiding under the codename CID, and modestly listed as 'official of the reserve'. Other agents—SATURNINO, PATRI, and BENEDITO—remain unidentified. Many RU 'illegals' and future 'illegals' worked as interpreters, and a good example is Veniamin Abramson, whose daughters, also interpreters, Paulina and Adelina, were with their father in Spain. Other interpreters were future GRU 'illegals' Anatoly Gurevich, Fyodor Kravchenko, and Alexey Korobitsyn.

Artur Stashevsky, who succeeded Winzer as Soviet commercial attaché, was also a former intelligence officer. In 1921–4, Stashevsky was the first Soviet resident in Berlin in charge of the amalgamated INO/RU station under diplomatic cover as Secretary of the Russian Trade Delegation. But since 1925 he had been attached to the NKVT, the foreign trade commissariat, where he remained until his Spanish posting, with a short break in Torgsin ('Trade with Foreigners'), a foreign trade firm with a chain of hard currency shops that also bought diamonds and jewellery from the local populace in return for food and that earned more gold during Stashevsky's directorship there than all Soviet gold mines together.[45] It is certainly wrong, as Krivitsky (and after him Radosh and many others) claim, that

'Stashevsky was sent to manipulate the Spanish economy' or to 'put it right'. With his four years in gymnasium and a crash Red Army Commander course in 1918, Stashevsky was simply not qualified to do that. It would take considerable imagination to interpret his two letters to Moscow from Valencia, reproduced in *Spain Betrayed*, to support the thesis that Moscow's representative could influence the Spanish economy. Stashevsky simply informed Moscow that 'abnormality, disorganization, carelessness, and laxity are everywhere'; then he mentioned his conviction 'that provocation is all around and everywhere; that there is a fascist organization among the high command, which carries out sabotage and, of course, espionage', pointing a finger at General José Asensio Torrado, whose name he spelt incorrectly. Finally, Stashevsky expressed a faint hope 'that through skilful manoeuvring and persistence, we shall succeed in introducing planned development into this work, even if elementary in nature'.[46] That was it. In December 1936 another military intelligence officer, Major Grigory Grechnev (BAJO), joined Stashevsky at the trade legation.

One of Stashevsky's roles in Spain was 'to cajole, cajole, cajole all sides and demonstrate how Soviet engineers could help build up war production'.[47] Whatever Stashevsky achieved, he was recalled to Moscow in June 1937 and was never seen again. Stashevsky, one of the senior managers of the famous Torgsin, had indeed sold Russian furs, gold, and silver with some success in the early 1930s, earning the Soviet Union a lot of needed hard currency, but that was practically all he knew about the economy. Contrary to Krivitsky's sinister reading, the fact that two intelligence officers were sent as Soviet trade attachés to Spain is a good proof that Stalin was neither interested in, nor capable of, influencing the Spanish economy in any way. The third trade attaché, about whom very little is known, was Pavel Ivanovich Malkov, who was still there in November 1937.[48] Adelina Abramson remembered that in spring 1946 Malkov was sent with the Soviet delegation to Argentina to restore diplomatic and trade relations. It may be added that her father, Benjamin Abramson, had been among the first Soviets to work in the offices of Sudamtorg in Buenos Aires in the 1920s.

Another error in Krivitsky's 1939 'memoirs', written by Isaak Don Levine, caused even more historical confusion. This is the idea that Stashevsky, who reportedly was on good personal terms with Juan Negrín, influenced Negrín's decision to ship the Spanish gold reserve to the USSR. In fact, Stashevsky had not even arrived in Spain when all major discussions and the shipment itself took place. As mentioned earlier, Josef

Winzer, not Stashevsky, was Negrín's contact and acted as an intermediary between Madrid and Moscow.

Stashevsky succeeded Winzer as the commercial attaché in October, as it seems Winzer/Vinarov had more important things to do in Spain. According to some evidence, by the end of the year he had moved to Bilbao. In his own extremely vague and misleading memoirs, first published in Sofia in 1969, General Ivan Vinarov wrote that all the time (until March 1938) he 'worked in Paris helping the Spanish war effort'.[49] In November, a career Soviet diplomat, Iosif Rafailovich Tumanov,[50] was sent to Bilbao to establish a Soviet representation. Officially a councillor at the embassy, he settled there as the provisional Consul with a staff of three people occupying a large mansion. This 'consulate' was certainly a cover for Gorev's staff, whose officers were also instructed to establish good working relations with the local army commanders.[51] In spring 1937 two of them—Winzer/Vinarov and Kirill Janson (ORSINI)—were still in Bilbao, and Gorev complained to Voroshilov about some small squabbles between his people and Tumanov.[52] Soon Vinarov would move to Paris, while both Janson and Tumanov would return to Moscow to face a firing squad a year later.

In early April 1937, Berzin, Chief Soviet military adviser, also visited the Basque capital. It is hard to say whether he was interested in the city's heavy industries, wanted to check its defensive ring known as the Cinturón de Hierro, or was there in connection with the successful intelligence operations of the Red Army agents. Whatever Berzin's business in the Basque Country, on 19 June Bilbao succumbed to Franco's troops' siege.

All Red Army officers, including its intelligence personnel and interpreters, unlike their NKVD colleagues, were registered with the appropriate Spanish authorities who paid their salary. In the hands of Franco's secret services, this information turned out to be entirely useless, but it allowed modern historians to restore many names and identify almost every person who came from the Soviet Union to fight for the Republic. One of them was Fyodor Kravchenko, who served as the interpreter of 'General Pablo' or Pablo Fritz (Dmitry Grigorievich Pavlov arrived in November 1936 and commanded the 1st Armoured Brigade). Enrique Líster described him as 'Captain Antonio, his [General Pablo's] interpreter–adjutant–secretary and I don't know what else besides, whom I had known at the [International] Lenin School, where he was called Pintos, and who in his own country after the war, under the real name of Kravchenkov [sic], won the high award of Hero of the Soviet Union'.[53]

Fedor Iosifovich Kravchenko (codenamed KLEIN, MAGNAT, and PANCHO) was born in Russia in 1912 but spent his childhood in Uruguay, where he had lived for sixteen years until 1929, when his parents decided to return to the Soviet Union. No wonder Fedor spoke perfect Spanish and soon started working for the KIM, which was a usual gateway to Soviet intelligence. Accordingly, he was recruited by the Red Army intelligence in 1936 and sent to Spain, where he stayed for two years.

After his return to Moscow, Kravchenko was trained as an RU 'illegal' and soon sent to Uruguay, operating under deep cover as 'Manuel Ronsero', a businessman. Naturally, he knew the country, and it was easier for him to settle there, though his sphere of interests reportedly included other Latin American countries and even Mexico. In October 1941 Kravchenko was suddenly recalled to Moscow. After an internal investigation, he was sent behind the German lines, where he commanded one of the guerrilla detachments, earning the highest Soviet decoration—the Order of Lenin with the golden medal of the Hero of the Soviet Union. Shortly after receiving his award, in early May 1945 in Toulouse, France, Kravchenko joined Dolores Ibárruri, who was allegedly the only person informed of his clandestine mission. She provided the GRU resident with a doctored Spanish passport in the name of Antonio Martínez Serrano, and soon he became deputy chief of staff of a Spanish guerrilla unit. The group, actually the GRU 'illegal' residency, was based in Toulouse, using Société Commerciale Fernandez-Valledor as a front. From French territory, Kravchenko directed GRU operations against Franco's Spain. According to his official GRU biography, he managed to set up agent networks in Madrid, Valencia, and Barcelona. It was perhaps the only Soviet intelligence source that provided military intelligence about Spain directly from within its territory.[54] Major Kravchenko was transferred to the acting reserve in 1951 and, together with Grigulevich and other former intelligence officers, was active in the Soviet Society for Friendship and Cultural Relations with Foreign Countries (the successor of the famous VOKS), where he was vice-president of the USSR–Uruguay friendship society. Kravchenko died in Moscow aged 76 and was buried with honours at the Kuntsevo cemetery. The official army newspaper *Krasnaya Zvezda* published his obituary on 1 December 1988.

Like Kravchenko, Alexey Pavlovich Korobitsyn was the son of Jewish immigrants, and Spanish was his mother tongue. He was born in December 1910 in La Rioja, Argentina, as Alexis Moiseyevich Kantor. His mother,

Lydia Korobitsyna, together with her three sons Leon, Alejandro, and Alexis, returned to the Soviet Union in 1924. For twelve years Alexey served with the Baltic Fleet and later with the Soviet merchant marine, until he was recruited to the RU in 1936. According to his official GRU biography, in Cartagena, Korobitsyn, codenamed TURBAN, NARCISO, and LEO, served as personal interpreter of Nikolai Kuznetsov, the naval attaché, and even commanded a torpedo boat. This version is supported by Adelina Abramson,[55] and Kuznetsov himself mentioned 'Narciso' in his memoirs. In reality, Korobitsyn operated 'from a legal position' as chief of the press section of the Soviet Consulate in Barcelona, using his own name.[56] For certain specific operations, however, he went undercover, posing as the Argentinean 'Cantor Edmund'. In January 1937, for his work in Spain, Korobitsyn was awarded the Order of the Red Banner, while Kravchenko was decorated with both the Red Banner and the Red Star. After his tour of duty in Spain (October 1936–November 1937) and a training course in Moscow, Korobitsyn was sent to Mexico in 1939 as the RU 'illegal' resident, where he, together with Kravchenko, reportedly controlled several agent groups. According to another version, Korobitsyn, posing as a rich Mexican businessman, soon managed to become honorary consul general of Mexico in Cleveland, USA, and before the war was sent to the Mexican embassy in Berlin, where he was second-in-command at the consular section. This strangely coincides with Kravchenko's alleged assignment, as stated in his official GRU biography, which instructed him to penetrate the Ministerio de Relaciones Exteriores of Uruguay with the aim of getting a diplomatic post in Berlin. Reportedly, the only reason Kravchenko failed to accomplish this mission was because, without Moscow's permission, he married a general's daughter in Montevideo—the only way to avoid military service and find employment with the Foreign Ministry. Whatever the truth, like Kravchenko, Korobitsyn was also recalled to Moscow in 1941 (which would hardly have happened if he had indeed been a Mexican diplomat in Berlin), and was then parachuted behind the lines as a group leader, codenamed LEO, together with Kravchenko (PANCHO) and two Austrian anti-fascists.[57] Remarkably, Grigulevich was in Mexico at the same time and during the war mounted a large-scale sabotage operation in Argentina, Uruguay, and other Latin American countries. After the war Korobitsyn served in Bucharest, Romania, posing as a member of the Soviet Control

Commission under the alias 'A. P. Korablev' but in reality controlling a group of agents in Romania. In 1947 Major Korobitsyn returned to Moscow and was appointed section chief of the secret intelligence school. During his time there he was twice sent as an 'illegal' on undercover missions to Germany and France.[58] Until his premature death in 1966, Korobitsyn lived in Moscow, teaching Spanish at the Military Institute for Foreign Languages, one of the GRU establishments,[59] where his 'boss' was Paulina Abramson, the wife of Colonel General Mamsurov,[60] by that time the deputy director of the GRU. He also published three books of fiction under his own name, though very few people in the Soviet Union knew this writer's true history.

Another Russian émigré, Kirill Khenkin, also fought in Spain, then from 1941 served with the NKVD special troops, was selected for training as an 'illegal', and wrote a book about one of the most famous Soviet spies, 'Colonel Rudolf Abel'. Khenkin—whose mother was the daughter of a lieutenant general in the tsarist army and whose father was the son of a poor Jew from the city of Rostov in the south of Russia, an actor and singer—lived with his parents in Paris, where the family emigrated in 1923. Kirill studied at university, and in summer 1937 decided to join the International Brigades in Spain. He went to the PCF recruitment centre located at No. 7 Avenue Mathurin Moreau, where his application was promptly turned down because of his Russian passport. This refusal did not discourage the 21-year-old, and he immediately contacted Sergey Efron, a fellow Russian émigré, who, as everybody knew, had the right contacts at the Soviet Embassy in Paris. (Efron was an active NKVD agent; together with Orlov, he would soon be involved in the operation against the defector Ignatz Reiss.) With Efron's assistance, Khenkin managed to reach Valencia. From the railway station he went directly to the Hotel Metropol, where he was instructed to ask for comrade Orlov. Several cabriolet cars were parked in front of the hotel, all staffed, according to Khenkin, with well-tanned young blond men wearing military uniforms.[61] This corroborates information received from other sources that Orlov, like other Soviet intelligence chiefs in Spain, was guarded by the German communists trained in the Comintern M-School in Moscow. In the hotel lobby Khenkin noticed a group of armed Serbians in addition to several plain-clothes agents behind the reception counter. Orlov's room was on the seventh floor.

Khenkin, who wrote his book almost four decades after the events when he joined the staff of the Radio Liberty in Munich, vividly remembered their meeting. The young man was greatly impressed by an exquisite breakfast served by a servant in a white jacket. He also noticed that Orlov was carrying a Walther PPK 7.65 mm in a flat chamois leather holster (compare this detail with Ian Fleming's *Dr No* or *Goldfinger*—this 'detective model' was recommended to the creator of James Bond by a gun expert). According to Khenkin, Orlov was smoking Lucky Strike, then still in its signature green pack, and during their conversation was sitting at a considerable distance from his visitor.[62] This observation gives some extra credibility to Khenkin's account. He could not know it, of course, but Orlov was especially careful, because several months before he had been shot at point blank range by another Russian émigré who had also come from France. After the meeting, Khenkin writes, Orlov dismissed him, and he never heard from the NKVD chief again. Finally, he got to Albacete, and from there was directed to one of the International Brigades before he joined a guerrilla detachment of the XIV Cuerpo de Ejército Guerrillero where he met Ramón Mercader. At the end of the Second World War, Khenkin, who spoke fluent French and had spent four years with the elite OMSBON[63] troops of the NKVD, was invited to the intelligence school, where his radio instructors were two Germans, Rudolf Abel and Willie Fisher.

In autumn 1948 the chief of Soviet foreign intelligence, Pavel Fitin, signed an order sending Fisher on a mission to the USA, where he arrived from Canada in November, travelling through several European countries. On 26 November in New York he met Grigulevich, who provided him with forged documents and money. Fisher (codenamed MARK) was instructed to reactivate the VOLUNTEER agent network to renew the collection of atomic intelligence that had stopped at the end of the war. Lona Cohen (LESLIE) and her husband Morris Cohen (VOLUNTEER), whose photos were found in a safe-deposit box in Brooklyn that had been used by Fisher/Abel, were part of the network. A witness later told the FBI about a glaring intelligence lapse, when in 1950 the Cohens had given a dinner party at which the featured guest was their case officer, Fisher. In 1957, having established the identities of the Cohens, the FBI obtained their fingerprints and sent them to friendly security services just in case they surfaced somewhere.[64] And they did.

In June 1957, after Fisher had introduced himself as 'Rudolf Abel' to federal agents, he spent about five years in prison, and in February 1962 was exchanged for the American pilot Francis Gary Powers. Powers was shot down while flying a reconnaissance mission over the Soviet Union. Khenkin writes that, after Fisher had returned to Moscow, where he was hailed as a national hero, he and his former radio instructor often discussed Orlov, who, when Fisher was arrested by the FBI in New York, lived in the USA. For an extended period of time Orlov had been investigated by the same FBI people under Alan H. Belmont, then head of the Domestic Intelligence Division, who were dealing with Fisher/Abel, but it never came to their mind to ask him about Fisher. It is said that as soon as Fisher's photo appeared in the *New York Times* Orlov telephoned Raymond Rocca in the CIA Counter-Intelligence Division to confirm that he knew 'Colonel Abel'.[65] However, Orlov was not called upon to testify at the trial.[66]

Among many interesting personalities in Khenkin's book, the name of Korobitsyn is missing, though they both worked at the same time in one and the same Military Institute for Foreign Languages, albeit in different departments. Remarkably, Khenkin's colleague at the French faculty, teaching military translation, was Isaiah Bir, nicknamed 'Fantômas' by the Sûreté and arrested in Paris in 1927, while his department chair was Colonel Sergey Markovich, who managed to flee from France when his spy ring was uncovered there in 1934. According to Khenkin, yet another person in Moscow with whom he discussed Orlov was Lev Vasilevsky, who was helping to train guerrillas in Spain.

After guerrilla training and raids behind the lines, another area in which Soviet advisers progressed to a more hands-on operational role was in the International Brigades. The first commander of the XI (German–Austrian) International Brigade was 'General Emilio Kléber' (Manfred, actually, Moishe Stern). Stern, an Austrian Jew, was also an experienced Soviet military intelligence officer with an impressive service career.[67] In 1929–32 Stern was the RU's chief 'illegal' resident in the United States. Based in New York and operating under the cover name of 'Mark Zilbert' and sometimes 'Mr Herb', he controlled a network of sources and agents involved in the theft of military secrets. As already mentioned, in 1933–4 he served as the chief military adviser to the Chinese Communist Party Central Committee in Shanghai, working together with Otto Braun and Arthur Ewert.[68] From February to July 1934 Jonny de Graaf was his chief expert there in charge of explosives and special operations. As later in Spain, Stern operated in Shangai using the pseudonym 'Fred'. A little-known fact is that his two younger brothers, Wolfgang 'Wolf' and Leo Stern, were also military intelligence officers and took part in the Spanish campaign, together with Manfred, who in November 1936 let himself be portrayed as the 'Saviour of Madrid', which was ridiculous. Some authors name either Gorev or, more often, Stern/Kléber as Soviet generals who played a decisive role in the defence of the city, forgetting that neither of them had any experience in the commanding of troops, as both were professional intelligence officers but not soldiers. Colonel Rojo, the man who directed the defence of Madrid, complained bitterly about 'General Kléber'.[69] Stern's relationship with other military leaders and Comintern representatives was not helped by the fact that he used to organize hot nights with scantily clad demoiselles. His fall was imminent, preceded by a number of angry telegrams between Madrid and Moscow.[70]

Soon enough FRED (as Stern was codenamed in the Comintern correspondence) was recalled to Moscow, but, contrary to conventional wisdom, he was not executed on his return to the USSR in 1937. In Moscow he worked as a military adviser to Otto Kuusinen of the ECCI until he was arrested in the Comintern Hotel Lux on 23 July 1938 as a 'German spy'. In May 1939 Stern was sentenced to fifteen years in a forced-labour camp on the Kolyma River valley, a large complex called 'Dalstroy' (an abbreviation for the 'Far East Construction Site'). In 1941 and 1944 Stern applied to the 'Great Führer of the party and state, Comrade Iosif Vissarionovich Stalin', to release him and let him go to the front to fight for the fatherland as a private. This privilege was not granted. In 1952 Stern wrote to the Kremlin again, but his appeal was once more ignored. The 'Saviour of Madrid' died in the Gulag in 1954, after being sentenced to a second term. He shared the fate of over one million prisoners who perished there between 1932 and 1954. His brothers miraculously survived the repressions. Wolfgang Stern, who worked as an editor in Vienna and was part of the RU station in Spain, became a GRU colonel and after the Second World was was transferred to the East German military intelligence, which, almost until the reunification of Germany, was under the command of Lt Gen. Karl Kleinjung, personal bodyguard of Eitingon throughout the Spanish Civil War.[71] After his retirement, Wolfgang Stern was appointed director of the Institute of Military History in Potsdam. Leo Stern worked as an assistant to Professor Max Adler in Vienna between 1925 and 1932 and in 1934 spent five months in prison for his communist activities. From 1936 he was a lecturer at the International Lenin School in Moscow and also worked at the Press Department of the Comintern from where in January 1937 he was sent to Spain, returning to Moscow in April 1938. Before the war broke out he was teaching German at the Moscow Institute for Foreign Languages and in 1941 joined the Red Army. Leo Stern entered Vienna in 1945 with the storm troops of Marshal Tolbukhin's army as a lieutenant colonel and personal interpreter for the marshal. He was soon demobilized and worked as a member of the Soviet Control Commission. Dr Leo Stern was visiting professor of Vienna University during the summer semester of 1946 and in the High School for International Trade until, in 1950, he, like his brother Wolf, also moved to East Germany. He lived in Halle and in East Berlin, pursuing an academic career, and died in Halle in January 1982.[72] Among his many published works there is not a single line about his brother, Manfred Stern, 'the Saviour of Madrid'.

Whether as a result of Yezhov's intrigues, or a conclusion that Stalin made after the generals' revolt in Spain (or maybe owing to a number of complex factors), in early 1937 Stalin decided that the Red Army with its intelligence directorate had become disloyal to him and posed real danger to his power. Therefore, and especially after the Tukhachevsky trial where all defendants confessed,[73] neither personal heroism, nor previous achievements, and not even absolute conformism and obedience to Stalin's will could save ranking RU officers from execution. Many of them understood there was a sword hanging over their heads and tried to do something to survive. Amazingly, every official, not only intelligence officers, knew perfectly well what Stalin wanted to hear and often freely admitted that they had been spies, wreckers, and saboteurs, confusing some Western writers, journalists, and observers.

On 20 February 1937, the deputy chief of the RU, division commander Alexander Nikonov, who compiled the very first intelligence assessment of the Spanish situation for the Politburo, reported from Spain:

Even worse scum is the small group of counter-revolutionary Trotskyites, mainly in Catalonia and in part in the Basque country, who are carrying out vile anti-Soviet activity and propaganda against the VKP(b), its leaders, the USSR, and the Red Army. With the connivance of the 'orthodox' anarchists, the Trotskysts (POUMists) at the beginning of the war had their own special regiment with two thousand rifles on the Catalan front. This has now increased to thirty-two hundred men and has received weapons for everyone. This regiment is the rottenest unit of the entire Republican army, but it has nonetheless existed up to now and receives supplies, money, and ammunition. It goes without saying that it is impossible to win the war against the rebels if this scum within the Republican camp are not liquidated.[74]

This bloodthirsty paranoid rhetoric did not save Nikonov's life: he was executed in Moscow on 26 October 1937, sharing the fate of practically all other leaders of the Soviet military intelligence of the 1930s.

In Spain, the officers could feel what was going on in their country, especially after the February–March Plenum, where Stalin spoke about 'wreckers, saboteurs, Trotskyist-fascist spies and murderers who infiltrated all our echelons of power',[75] and two months later when he personally visited the RU headquarters, claiming that 'the whole directorate has fallen into German hands'.[76] The nucleus of Soviet military intelligence in Madrid, Valencia, and Barcelona consisted of people who had operated together in China in the late 1920s to the mid-1930s, such as Stern, Gorev, Vinarov, Salniņš, and others.[77] Both RU operatives allegedly sent to murder General Franco in 1937, Grigory Semyonov and Elli Bronina, had also been in China before going to Spain: Semyonov was working in the Military Department of the Chinese Communist Party's Central Committee in March 1927;[78] Bronina (then under her own name as Renée Marceau, a French woman) arrived in Shanghai in April 1934 as a wireless operator for the RU resident Yakov Bronin. And even Jan Berzin, one of the founders and most prominent chiefs of Soviet military intelligence, was sent from Moscow to the Far East as deputy (political) commander of the Osobaya Krasnoznamyonnaya Dalnevostochnaya Armiya (OKDVA) (Special Red-Banner Far Eastern Army) from April 1935 until May 1936. Kristaps Salniņš, who had become Brigadier Commissar by that time, served there together with Berzin as assistant intelligence chief. They all knew each other well, but the choice they were facing was either to denounce their comrades or to admit their blunders. The other tactics were to praise everybody who was around, as Gorev did intelligently in April 1937. Those few foreigners who still remained on the RU staff and were on important assignments abroad preferred not to interfere in the internal matters of the country that had given them refuge. Nothing helped.

One such officer was Colonel Johann Hermann, born in Narva, Estonia, to the German family in 1894.[79] Hermann joined the Communist Party in 1919, and four years later graduated from the Eastern Faculty of the RKKA Military Academy. Like many of his RU colleagues, he served in China from June 1923 until March 1926. Back in Moscow, Hermann occupied important posts in the 3rd (analysis and statistics) department and for three years, until February 1936, was on an undercover mission abroad. Before he arrived in Madrid in October 1936 as a controller of 'a group of agents',[80]

Colonel Hermann, alias Johnson, served at the headquarters as section chief of the Western Department, which was in charge of agent intelligence (HUMINT) in the most important Western countries: Britain, France, and the USA, but also Germany, Italy, Poland, Romania, Finland, and the Baltic states. Like other senior RU officers, Hermann was decorated with the Order of Lenin in January 1937. Upon his return to Russia in the summer of 1938 he was arrested and shot as a 'German spy'. He was exonerated in 1957.[81] Regrettably, nothing is known about Colonel Hermann's operation in Spain.

At the same time, much is written about another RU 'illegal', Anatoly Markovich Gurevich (aka Victor Sukolov, codenamed KENT), a 'small chief' of the legendary Rote Kapelle ('Red Orchestra'), who was sent by the RU to Spain in December 1937 together with two other students of the Leningrad School of Foreign Tourism, Mikhail Ivanov and Pyotr Naimushin. Their group of volunteers, consisting mainly of pilots and interpreters, left Leningrad on board the cargo ship *MV Andrey Zhdanov* and just before the New Year arrived in Havre via Antwerp. From there they went to Paris by bus and on 30 December crossed the French–Spanish border in Portbou, a small but important point for the republicans because it was one of the few places from where supplies and volunteers could get into the republican territory. In 1937 Orlov used this corridor to France many times.

After a short language course, Gurevich (alias 'Antonio González'), Semyon Pankin ('Simón Rubio'), and Ivanov ('Miguel Viñas') were transferred to Cartagena as interpreters with the Republican Navy. Soon Gurevich found himself on board a submarine C-4 commanded by Lt Cdr Ivan Burmistrov.

It was this old Soviet submarine that the sabotage and guerrilla instructor Syroyezhkin had chosen for sending his deputy Vasilevsky on a dangerous mission to Mallorca in the summer of 1938 after its Spanish crew had managed to bring the submarine from the river Garonne in Bordeaux to Cartagena. In his memoirs, *The Spanish Chronicle of Grigory Grande*, Vasilevsky devoted a whole chapter to this minor episode. He could not know then and probably never learned in his lifetime that his interpreter during this five-day mission was a future star of Soviet wartime intelligence. Gurevich stayed in Spain until July 1938 with cover documents identifying him as the Republican Navy Lt 'Antonio González', although he was officially listed as a Soviet interpreter. From Spain Gurevich returned to Moscow to study in the military intelligence school. In April 1939 he surfaced in Belgium and then in France, using an Uruguayan passport in the name of 'Vincent Sierra'. Gurevich was posing as a rich businessmen and set up a trading company named Simexco as a cover. All three legendary leaders of the Red Orchestra—Leopold Trepper (alias Jean Gilbert, known as the 'grand chef'), Alexander Rado (DORA), and Gurevich (KENT)—who miraculously survived the arrest, were all treated as traitors in the USSR. Trepper and Rado were sentenced to ten years' imprisonment in Moscow after the war. Gurevich was sentenced to twenty years in 1946, in spite of the fact that he had managed to convince his German interrogator, the chief of Sonderkommando Rote Kapelle Heinz Pannwitz, to defect to the Soviets. Pannwitz, shocked by the German defeat, accepted his prisoner's suggestion to meet his GRU chiefs and, together with two other people, surrendered to the French in the Austrian town of Bludenz. Both Pannwitz and Gurevich were soon turned over to the Soviet representatives in Paris and dispatched to Moscow by plane. In Moscow, Gurevich was immediately arrested by SMERSH agents and later sentenced to twenty years in the Gulag.

Similarly to the case of Horst Kopkow, a notorious Nazi war criminal used by British intelligence,[82] the NKVD chiefs put Pannwitz on their payroll because he could identify Gestapo informers in the liberated territories and within the Allied forces. In 1955 Rado and Trepper were cleared of treason charges, and Pannwitz was repatriated to Germany (as was Kopkow). On 8 October 1955 Gurevich was freed from the corrective labour camp in the Komi republic in north-western Russia (the infamous Syktyvkar, Vorkuta, Ukhta, and Sosnogorsk concentration camps) but rearrested by the Leningrad militia on 9 September 1958 on the grounds that the amnesty had been erroneously applied in his case. Two years later Gurevich was finally released and he was fully exonerated in 1991. It was established, according to Sudoplatov, that his only act of misconduct had been his marriage to Margarete Barcza in France without the Centre's prior agreement. In 1992 his son, daughter-in-law, and grandchildren, all of whom live in Spain, visited Gurevich in St Petersburg. He died on 2 January 2009, aged 86.

Whatever the Red Army intelligence did in Spain, they were certainly helping the Republic to win the war and their own country to defend itself against its future attackers. Unlike their military 'neighbours', the NKVD (and its successors) always played an important political role in the USSR, first as an organ of repression and only after that as an intelligence and counter-espionage service. Orlov's 1993 biography asserts that his (and, therefore, the NKVD's) larger purpose was 'to build up a secret police force under NKVD control to effect a Stalinization of Spain'. The authors also claim that the chief Soviet military adviser, Jan Berzin, complained that Orlov and the NKVD 'were treating Spain like a colony' and demanded 'that Orlov be recalled from Spain at once'.[83]

Christopher Andrew also quotes the above statement, adding that, 'from the outset, however, the NKVD was engaged in Spain in a war on two fronts: against Trotskyists within the republicans and the International Brigades, as well as against Franco and the nationalist forces'.[84] This, however, is only partly true and only in relation to a certain period of the war.

Various secret documents that became available to researchers after the collapse of the Soviet Union clearly demonstrate that the head of station, whether Kulov, Orlov, or, from August 1938, Kotov, strictly followed the instructions from the Centre, which varied according to the operational situation, Moscow's requirements, and how NKVD commissars (Yagoda, Yezhov, and Beria) interpreted what Stalin and other leaders wanted. As for the thesis that Orlov's larger purpose was 'to build up a secret police force under NKVD control', it seems unlikely, primarily because the Spanish Government never asked him or his bosses 'to build up a secret police force'. In the republican government there might have been good friends of the Soviet Union, but none of them wanted to have the second NKVD in Spain. Apart from that, Orlov was simply not the right man for this job. His previous career in the OGPU-NKVD—a junior officer in the economic directorate, unit commander of the border troops, unsuccessful INO 'illegal', and, finally, assistant chief of the transport department—promised little chance of success. Orlov's own claim that his role in Spain was 'to advise the Republican government on matters of intelligence, counter-intelligence and guerrilla warfare' is also contradicted by Juan Negrín's memoirs. This claim is also not borne out by the KGB correspondence, as shall be seen below.

As formulated by Moscow, the main task of the NKVD station in Spain, acting from the Soviet legation, was to provide the Soviet leadership with intelligence on the whole spectrum of Spanish problems, including information dealing with counter-intelligence.[85] The only way to do it was to place 'moles' and recruit agents and informers in all key government institutions.

From the first days of their arrival in Spain, the main interest of Orlov and Belyaev was, obviously, the DGS, where they were officially accredited. Until August 1937, when the, SIM was finally established within the Ministry of Defence, the NKVD representatives tried to act through the Department of Information of the DGS, which had the right to arrest and investigate and commanded a small army of well-armed policemen. At first, it was not easy, as from August 1936 Manuel Muñoz Martinez, a former Civil Governor of Cadiz (interim), was the Director General. Then from December 1936 until May 1937 Wenceslao Carrillo, a Socialist supporter of Largo Caballero and Santiago's father, headed the DGS. Later, at the end of May 1937, a Communist, Lt Col. Antonio Ortega, replaced Carrillo senior, while Communist police chiefs were appointed for the three largest cities. From that time on and until March 1939, when the SIM was disbanded, the Republican security system was thoroughly infiltrated by the Communists.[86] Their information was filtered by the NKVD and RU stations and dispatched to Moscow. However, in the tumultuous atmosphere of 1937, hardly anyone in the Soviet leadership took any notice of it. In the large volume of correspondence between the NKVD and Stalin,[87] there is not a single report from Spain.

Two persons at the NKVD Lubyanka headquarters were the recipients of most of this intelligence: Abram Sloutsky and Sergey Spiegelglass. A huge volume of records remains closed. But some KGB dispatches, declassified by Soviet foreign intelligence for a lucrative book project in the early 1990s (only part of which could be verified), made it possible to get a glimpse of intelligence operations (real or bogus) conducted or planned by the NKVD in Spain in the period between January 1937 and July 1938.

Just hours before the clock struck midnight on New Year's Eve 1937, an unnamed NKVD officer in Valencia asked his Moscow superiors to send him urgently a number of radio transmitters, explaining: 'One is needed to provide our network in Gibraltar about which I informed you. The second will be needed for the nephew of Franco's premier (K. codenamed NEPHEW) who has been sent by us to the enemy.'[88]

At that point, Franco did not have a premier, although the reference might be to Ramón Serrano Suñer. Since his brothers were murdered in Madrid, it is doubtful that one of his nephews could be a Russian agent. It is also unclear how NEPHEW planned to use his radio transmitter and remain undetected. As for Gibraltar—the British territory of slightly over 2.6 square miles—even before but especially during the war, this housed the main interception centre for Spain.[89] The importance of these intelligence activities was heightened by the fact that the Spanish Civil War proved an important testing ground for weapons and tactics that were later to be used in the Second World War. However, nothing is known so far about any secret intelligence obtained by the NKVD from this centre. It is very doubtful that the station in Valencia or Barcelona was capable of running a 'network of agents' on that small territory or that such a group ever existed. At the time, Moscow had several opportunities to receive the Gibraltar traffic from other sources. For example, important intelligence was regularly forwarded to the Western Department of the Foreign Office, where two Russian 'moles'—Donald Maclean and John Cairncross—delivered to their London NKVD handlers what Cairncross described as 'a wealth of valuable information on the progress of the Civil War in Spain'.[90]

Another cryptogram was allegedly sent on 10 January 1937. Orlov's biographers explain how 'the Centre turned a blind eye to Orlov enlisting [the Governor of Murcia] Bretel for an operation which, in January 1937, looked very promising', and how 'the Governor of Murcia had set up a six-man group' to carry out Orlov's instructions, which included the possible organization of an armed rebellion in Morocco.[91]

Stalin had already been informed about the situation. He read the 'special report' sent to him personally three months previously by Antonov-Ovseyenko, Soviet consul in Barcelona, and was against the rebellion. In the first place, Stalin had his own theory regarding 'national liberation movements'.[92] Stalin was also aware that, in spite of the 1935 Franco-Soviet Treaty of Mutual Assistance, the conservative circles in Paris were sceptical about real Soviet intentions, and he did not want to irritate them by causing problems in Spanish Morocco on the eve of the planned Franco-Soviet military negotiations. So whoever signed the telegram was bound to provoke Moscow's dissatisfaction (which was not the case with Nikolsky/Orlov, who received his Order of Lenin in January 1937).

As for the governor's name, 'Bretel' must be the result of the erroneous transliteration from Russian. The Civil Governor of Murcia from 17 January 1937 was Antonio Pretel Fernández, who had joined the PCE after a lifetime in the PSOE. As regards the mission, the Republican government had established a little known special service during the first days of the war within the Army General Staff, called the Servicio de Información de Acción Militar (SIAM), whose task was the preparation of mass uprising in rebel zones and the direction of the acts of destruction and sabotage behind the enemy lines.[93] From the very beginning it coordinated all the separate guerrilla detachments that later formed the XIV Guerrilla Corps mentioned above. It is highly improbable that the NKVD station in Spain would dare to recruit the governor and send him on a dangerous mission to Morocco. A much more feasible explanation is that the author of the report knew about such plans of the Republican SIAM and invented all the rest, presenting it as the station's operation.

Two other daring missions that appear in the KGB files were possibly planned, but almost certainly not accomplished, by Orlov. In the spring of 1937 he reported to the Centre: 'I draw your attention to the enclosed report about our connection with Lord Churchill [sic] and the valuable service he is ready to render to us. We hope with his assistance to send, through the British Fascist organizations, doctors and nurses to Franco for intelligence purposes.'[94]

Though the fact that a relative of the future British Prime Minister was ready to 'render service' to the NKVD is, without doubt, sensational news for the intelligence community and the British public, the second part of the report is extremely far-fetched. In order to carry out such an operation, it was not only necessary to have 'doctors and nurses'—trained NKVD agents—ready to go to the rebel zone to spy for the Soviets, but they also had to be trusted persons of the 'British Fascist organizations' in order to be sent to Franco. In general, there were very few British individuals helping the rebels, as Franco did not welcome foreign humanitarian aid workers.

The second attempt to infiltrate the rebels' zone, as reported by Orlov only two weeks after his 'doctors and nurses' cable, is of considerable interest to researchers. The NKVD resident informed Moscow:

About the mission of sending people to Franco's rear, both anarchists and by selecting journalists in England: KARO [unidentified] was sent by me on a mission to Paris, where she communicated the assignment to the Englishman B—E— [unidentified] to select several reliable journalists in London for sending to the other side. B—E—had been recommended to us by *our source* [emphasis added], an English journalist B, a representative of the United Press (American). On 24 May I shall have a meeting in Paris with candidates for transferring over to Franco.[95]

Only one English journalist representing the United Press International, a news agency headquartered in the United States, was in Spain at the time. His name is Burnett Bolloten. As for the Orlov's idea of selecting 'several reliable journalists in London for sending to the other side', this project was never realized. Only Philby was sent to the Franco camp, but without any involvement of Orlov. And, contrary to his promise to the Moscow superiors, Orlov did not go to Paris in May[96]—most probably because no 'candidates for transferring over to Franco' were found.

His first political report seems to point to the date when Orlov/Nikolsky finally became the NKVD chief for Spain—27 February 1937.[97] Here for the first time the NKVD representative gave his take on the political situation, at the same time as trying to analyse the strength and weaknesses of the Republican government's handling of the conflict. What is more, he allowed himself to criticize not only the chief Soviet military adviser (Berzin), who was very senior in rank and position, but also his military intelligence 'neighbour' Gorev.[98] In all probability, by that time Orlov felt sure enough that it was permissible or even encouraged to be critical. As soon as he became the chief, Orlov/Nikolsky was personally responsible for all NKVD operations in Spain. And the operations that followed had nothing to do with intelligence collection or even with the war itself. As predicted, those were 'special tasks'.

17

The Secret History of Orlov's Crimes: January 1937–July 1938

Orlov's promotion to NKVD chief for Spain in or about February 1937 coincided with the most murderous period in the whole history of the KGB. What happened inside one of the most feared repressive organs in the world (the NKVD) fully mirrored the situation in the USSR, where the 'new Red terror' took the form of mass operations of the Yezhovite secret police targeting putative enemies throughout the population, the army, the secret services, and the nomenklatura.[1] In the Red Army, the 'neighbours' (military intelligence personnel) suffered most of all from the obedient and ruthless NKVD executors.

In May, Berzin returned from Spain, was decorated and promoted, and on 3 June he was back in his former office in the old military intelligence headquarters on 19 Znamensky Lane, known to its inhabitants as the 'chocolate house'. He was certainly late to work that very day, as at 9.30 in the morning the doorbell rang and his young Spanish mistress, Aurora Sánchez, stepped into his flat. Eight days later they celebrated her twentieth birthday together and the next morning they got married.[2] Two weeks before Aurora came to Moscow for the first and last time, Stalin was also at the 'chocolate house', chairing a meeting where he declared that 'the whole [intelligence] directorate has fallen into German hands', demanding that it disband all agent networks. It was a signal for the NKVD—mass arrests started in June.[3]

The events in Russia in the spring of 1937 were also echoed in Western Europe. Not for the first time, but with an increased vigour, the NKVD carried out abductions and assassinations in several countries. In Spain, the liquidation of 'enemies of the people' and 'Trotskyite–fascist spies' became a significant part of NKVD foreign operations.[4] However, one has to be realistic in the estimates, as the number of the NKVD victims of various nationalities during the Spanish Civil War cannot be compared even remotely with that of Russia. There were no mass operations in Spain conducted by the NKVD, and every individual target was decided and approved in Moscow.

All liquidations were planned and executed under Orlov's direction. After an apparent failure to mount some sort of intelligence-gathering operations, it seems that Orlov's main preoccupation was now witch-hunting. In other words, he became primarily engaged in the persecution of those who, for different reasons, were declared enemies by Stalin and Yezhov. One of the first of Orlov's 'special operations' took place in France.

On 25 January 1937, Dmitry Navashin, a former banker, was murdered in Paris. There is good reason to think that Orlov was involved. To this day, the case remains in the archives of the French Sûreté as unsolved. Despite the intensive investigation, the killer was not found, and the motive that led to the crime could not be determined. The French criminal investigation service, the Sûreté Générale, finally decided to close the case. However, comparatively recently and quite out of the blue, KGB-related historians published the name of the assassin.[5] Without any reference to any document, they named the culprit as Panteleimon Takhchiyanov, an officer of the NKVD special reserve. Different sources give different reasons for this murder, but suffice it to say that for many years Navashin had served as the vice-director and then director of the Banque Commerciale pour l'Europe du Nord (BCEN), a Soviet banking institution operating in France under French law. Back in March 1930, Grigory Besedovsky, a Soviet defector, named Navashin as a secret agent of the OGPU who regularly wrote reports to their head of station in Paris, Vladimir Voynovich.[6] From Besedovsky's MI5 file it is not clear whether or not this is true. Anyway, the real name of the OGPU resident was Zakhar Volovich (alias 'Vladimir Yanovich'). Whether Navashin was or was not in contact with him plays a secondary role; of much greater interest is the documented fact that the Banque Commerciale pour l'Europe du Nord was the very financial institution selected by both Soviet and Spanish authorities to carry out financial transactions on behalf of the Republic in connection with the sales of Spanish gold in exchange for foreign currency. The currency equivalent of gold sold to the Gosbank for purposes other than payment of Republican debts was transferred to the Soviet bank in Paris (the BCEN), where the Republican government had opened a network of accounts. This ensured that the insurgents, as well as Western financial circles, would remain in the dark about many financial operations.[7] Navashin, who had excellent contacts in banking circles in Paris and in the NKVT in Moscow,[8] could easily learn about those secret transactions. But that would be only part of the problem. Whether or not he collaborated with Soviet intelligence at any time, the NKVD suspected Navashin of being in contact with the Secret Intelligence Service better known as MI6—that is, a double agent. In 1936 that was surely enough for a death sentence. But it was still not all.

Two previously unknown details add more mystery to this tragic case. On 5 September 1936, José Diaz, the general secretary of the PCE, reported to Moscow that, thanks to the assistance of Diego Martinez Barrio, probably the most moderate of the Republican leaders actively involved with Masonic elements (he was the Grand Master of the Grande Oriente Español before the war), a contact had been established with a French freemason in order to purchase aeroplanes. The latter demanded a direct contact with 'La Pasionaria' (Dolores Ibárruri) or another responsible comrade.[9]

It is known that Navashin was himself a prominent freemason. In Russia, he was a member of the Lodge Astrea and in 1924 joined the Lodge Grand Orient of France recommended by Anatole de Monzie, French Minister of Transportation. In the lodge, Navashin's contacts included bankers, members of the Cabinet, and senators. It is clear that, as soon as the Spanish communists had contacted French freemasons, the information could soon reach Navashin. That in itself made him a potential source of trouble, in addition to the fact that, as a former director of the BCEN, he could have access to information that might permit him to reveal this Soviet institution's operations to both British and French authorities.

On 17 January 1937, attaché Orlov applied to the French Embassy in Valencia for a short-term visa to visit France. A two-week visa was issued, and he left Spain for France on 23 January, travelling by train via the border-crossing tunnel Port-Bou–Cerbère. On Sunday morning, 24 January, he was in Gare d'Austerlitz in Paris. Navashin was murdered on 25 January, after which date Orlov quietly returned to his duties in Spain. Such coincidences happen very rarely, especially where secret services are concerned. Orlov was not the assassin in this case but almost certainly acted as an observer. His Soviet diplomatic passport and the fact that he was a diplomat from a neighbouring country would definitely be of use if a cover happened to be necessary.[10]

Another operation that involved Orlov concerned Brian Goold-Verschoyle, a young communist electrical engineer and a naive supporter of the Soviet Union. Brian was of old Anglo-Irish stock, born on 5 June 1912 as the youngest son of the family owners of the Manor House, Dunkineely, County Donegal.[11] According to some early researchers, Brian seemed unaware that he was being used as a courier for the NKVD in London. Controlled by Henri Pieck, Goold-Verschoyle (codenamed FRIEND) couriered British agents' reports, mainly from Foreign Office clerk John King, when Ignace Reif, Lev Nikolsky (Orlov), and then Theodor Maly were supervisors of agent groups in London. It was claimed that Brian had been shocked when one of King's packages came open and he discovered secret British documents inside.[12]

The declassified security service files prove that this is not correct and that this information came from Krivitsky.[13] Formally recruited in Moscow in the summer of 1933 with the help of his brother's Russian wife Olga,[14] Brian returned to London to work undercover and was photographing documents, serving as a courier and a cut-out, and meeting Soviet controllers Theodor Maly and Dmitry Bystrolyotov,[15] who were running most important agents in Britain. He actually worked full time for the NKVD.

Dmitry Alexandrovich Bystroletov, codenamed HANS and ANDREI, who had operated in the West for seventeen years, was, like Maly, one of the 'Great Illegals'. Bystroletov was born on 4 January 1901 in the Crimea. He was a strikingly handsome, multilingual extrovert, learning foreign languages while serving as a sailor. He later studied in Turkey, Czechoslovakia, and Switzerland, receiving his doctorate degree at the Medical Faculty of the University of Zurich in 1935, by which time he had already been a Soviet agent-runner and recruiter for over ten years, having started his career in or about 1923. A report quoted by Mitrokhin quaintly records that Bystroletov 'quickly reached close terms with women and shared their beds'. His first 'honey trap' for the OGPU was set up in Prague, where he had actually been recruited. In 1927 he seduced a 29-year-old secretary of the French Embassy, who, over the next two years, gave Bystroletov copies of both French diplomatic ciphers and classified communications.[16] Like Grigulevich, Bystroletov never became an NKVD/KGB officer, only a civil employee. In the late 1920s he was running Ernest Oldham, a cipher clerk of the Foreign Office, whom he had managed to recruit a year earlier, while Oldham's wife became Bystroletov's mistress. Even without coming to Britain, Bestroletov continued to recruit and run valuable sources in the

Foreign Office, including Raymond Oake and John H. King. He was also Maclean's controller when the latter became an independently acting agent, providing information about Spain and other politically important materials from the Western Department. Nevertheless, in February 1938 ANDREI was suddenly sacked from the service and in November was arrested. Unlike many others, however, Bystroletov survived the Gulag, where he became an invalid, and in 1966 he deposited 5,000 pages of his memoirs with the manuscript collection of the Public Saltykov-Schedrin Library in St Petersburg. Of this, only a very small part was published in the form of two books that are perhaps more powerful that Solzhenitsyn's world-famous *The Gulag Archipelago* but throw very little light on Bystroletov's work in Soviet intelligence.

Bystroletov's London courier, Brian Goold-Verschoyle, travelled to Russia again in May 1935, as he had also done in 1933 and 1934. Before he went, he made allusions (as his mistress wrote in a letter to the Security Service) that he might not come back. He did, however, come back and was very depressed. In the summer, when he and Lotte (Margarete Charlotte Moos, a married German exile in London who was studying at the London School of Economics) became close friends, he told her everything about his contacts with the NKVD. In November, he was summoned to Amsterdam, where he met Bystroletov, Krivitsky, and almost certainly Magdalena Werker, whom Krivitsky called 'Madeleine' in his book.[17] Though both Krivitsky and his biographer describe her as his Dutch secretary to raise his status, because his operation was so small she was his only support personnel. In the words of Krivitsky's biographer, 'she handled his messages, both ordinary and covert; scheduled his appointments, both commonplace and clandestine; made hotel reservations; answered the telephone; typed'. As many in Amsterdam, in addition to her native Dutch she spoke German, English, and French and also served as a cut-out between Krivitsky and agents. In her time, Werker visited Russia, became a Communist, was recruited by the OGPU, and had been working as an underground courier since 1928.[18] Brian said to his Lotte that 'Dr Lessner'—this is how Krivitsky introduced himself—was accompanied by an older lady with a beautiful face. That was Werker without any doubt.

In February 1936 Brian Goold-Verschoyle went back to Russia with a forged Norwegian passport and began training as a wireless operator and photographer. In mid-April Lotte joined him in Moscow. There they used to meet Bystroletov. She later identified him to the Security Service in

London only as 'John'.[19] After his training was completed, Brian was posted
to the NKVD station in Valencia in November 1936.

There exist many versions of where exactly Brian worked in Spain. Some
authors suggest that he was employed by Radio Barcelona. His mother
thought that he transmitted messages for the Soviet Ambassador in Valencia.
His NKVD prosecution file asserted that he worked 'in his profession and
instructed members of the International Brigades in his skill'.[20] Barry
McLoughlin, a historian at Vienna University, basing his judgement on
Costello and Tsarev's book, thinks that he probably served as an instructor
in the guerrilla-training base in Benimamet.[21] The study of all available
documents leads to the conclusion that Goold-Verschoyle was based at the
Soviet Embassy and worked for the NKVD station as Orlov's assistant. In
her letter to Krivitsky of 8 May 1939, Sybil, Brian's mother, revealed that he
could speak Russian, French, German, and Spanish. 'One of the difficulties
of finding him in Spain,' she wrote, 'was that we heard he had kept the
Spanish name on his passport and, as he could speak Spanish like a native
and was rather Spanish looking with dark brown eyes and dark hair—tall
and slender and he used to wear a Spanish beret while in Spain—he could
easily pass for a Spaniard'.[22]

Being able to communicate freely with all sorts of people, Brian soon
started to object to the NKVD's methods of imposing conformity,[23] as
Krivitsky's biographer put it. Orlov decided that he had become a Trotskyite and had to be removed. One day in April 1937, Brian was asked to fix
the radio transmitter on the Spanish vessel *Magallanes* moored in Barcelona
harbour. Once he came aboard, he was escorted to what he thought was the
radio cabin, and locked there. The ship docked at Feodosiya, a port in the
south of the Crimean peninsula, on 6 May 1937. Six days later Goold-
Verschoyle was in the Lubyanka prison.[24]

The formal arrest warrant was issued on 15 May. It was based on a report
from Sloutsky, Orlov's boss:

At the beginning of April 1936 Mrs Margarete Charlotte Moos arrived in
Moscow. According to Brian Goold-Verschoyle, she had had a relationship with
him since July 1935 and was the wife of Siegfried Moos, a German Communist
immigrant in England. In October 1936 Margarete Charlotte Moos returned to
London . . . Goold-Verschoyle himself was sent by us in 1936 to work in SCHWED's
[Orlov's] rezidentura. In the period when he worked for us Brian Goold-
Verschoyle was forbidden to disclose his address. Despite this, he remained in
contact with Margarete C. Moos and corresponded with her. We have learned

from this correspondence that Brian Goold-Verschoyle, Margarete C. Moos and Siegfried Moos are active Trotskyites. In addition, Brian Goold-Verschoyle was very curious about matters that had nothing to do with his own work, which is further proof he had links to a Trotskyite organisation and probably to a hostile intelligence service as well.[25]

On 4 August 1937 the Special Board ('osoboe soveschanie') of the NKVD sentenced Brian to eight years in prison on the charges of 'counter-revolutionary Trotskyite activities'.[26] According to the MI5 version, he was reportedly killed in the Soviet Union in 1941 while on board a train that was hit during a German bombing raid.[27] In reality, Goold-Verschoyle and several other foreign prisoners landed in the Solovetsky Special Purpose Camp known under the Russian acronym SLON. High-security prisoners were scattered to the four winds. One managed to leave the USSR in 1956. Another died in 1941. Yet another, together with many Austrian and German anti-fascists, was handed over to the Gestapo in 1940. Brian Goold-Verschoyle remained in prison and died in confinement in Orenburg Province on 5 January 1942.[28] His mother Sybil never learned what happened to her son and was desperately writing letters to Krivitsky in America. He could help her only by telling her about Brian's arrest by the NKVD.

As the cases of Andreu Nin and Goold-Verschoyle demonstrate, among the intelligence activities involving Orlov, several operations were related to the Kremlin's determination to eliminate Trotskyists in Spain. Just days before Goold-Verschoyle quietly disappeared in Barcelona, Marc Rein left the Hotel Continental on the Rambla de Canaletas, where he was staying, never to come back.

Mark Rein was the son of the Russian Menshevik leader Rafail Abramovich (born Rein), who managed to escape abroad on the eve of the famous Menshevik show trial of 1931. In France, Rein became a member of the French Young Socialists. He came to Barcelona on 5 March 1937 to work at the armaments factory Télécommande, while at the same time representing several leftist publications, including the *Social Demokraten*, a famous newspaper in Stockholm, and the New York Jewish daily *Forward*. On the evening of 9 April Rein left his hotel 'without either his coat or hat', as several eyewitnesses testified; two days later his friends and then his father started to search for him. As usual, it was all in vain. They were further misled by a letter addressed to Rein's friend, Nicolas Sundelewicz (arrested in July on the accusation of wanting to kill Stalin), received on 16 April.

It was a short note in Russian stating that Marc Rein had had to leave for Madrid in connection with some urgent matters.

This sort of deception—sending letters signed and sometimes even written by people who were dead by the time the letter was dispatched—was Orlov's favourite trick. As shall be seen, it became his hallmark technique, which he used several times.[29] The second letter, this time addressed to his father Abramovich, who recognized it as being written by his son, aroused many suspicions. First, it arrived in Barcelona on the same day as, according to the stamp, it had been posted in Madrid, which was simply unrealistic at that time. Secondly, Sundelewicz noticed that the obligatory censors' stamp was missing. Many of Rein's friends, among whom was future German Chancellor Willy Brandt, believed that he could have been taken back to Russia, either to make him accuse his father or as a hostage.

Willy Brandt, born Herbert Frahm, may himself be a clue to the solution of Rein's mysterious murder. After Hitler's rise to power in 1933, Brandt went into exile in Norway, where Trotsky lived from the summer of 1935 until the end of 1936. In February 1937 Brandt travelled to Spain, ostensibly as a journalist covering the civil war but also to act as liaison between Sozialistische Arbeiterpartei (SAP) members of the International Brigades and the Partido Obrero de Unificación Marxista (POUM) militia. He wrote: 'The truth of the matter is: the Comintern is determined to destroy all forces that refuse to obey its orders. It is for this reason that the whole international labour movement must rise against it.' The Communists reciprocated by denouncing Brandt as 'an agent of Franco' and 'a spy of the Gestapo'.[30]

According to Mitrokhin's notes, the earliest reference to Brandt (code-named POLYARNIK by the NKVD) in his KGB file is a description of him in 1936 as a member of the Danzig Trotskyites. There one can find fabricated claims, without doubt reports of various informers, that 'POLYARNIK had been tasked by the French Sûreté to infiltrate POUM, that he had betrayed many members of the SPD to the Gestapo and that he was involved in the murder of Marc Rein'.[31] Therefore, the logic of Moscow's order to Orlov to 'liquidate' Rein could have been either to support this allegation, or to get rid of another Trotsky sympathizer who had had personal contacts with him in Norway, and who in Barcelona continued to be on friendly terms with his former secretary.[32] In fact, the KGB never left Brandt alone until his resignation as the Chancellor of West Germany in May 1974, ironically, also in connection with the Soviet–East German espionage case.

Russian sources, closely connected with the KGB Press Service, openly state that Marc Rein was on Orlov's list of foreign 'literniks' (people condemned to be liquidated) who were to be murdered in Spain on Stalin's orders.[33] According to their version, two agents of the Grupo de información—Alfred Herz and Mariano Gómez Emperador—with the help of their secret informer S.S.I. no. 29, abducted and killed Abramovich's son. The involvement of Herz and Gómez Enperador in the abduction of Rein is convincingly proved by the German researchers Michael Ulm and Patrik von zur Mühlen. Herz's collaboration with the NKVD, and personally with Orlov, as well as with the secret N-Apparat (Nachrichtendienst—that is, intelligence service) of the KPD in Paris, is well documented. By 1935, the KPD representatives in Paris, through their Dutch bureau, had already established contact with Herz and two other German émigrés in Catalonia to do security checks on the members of the German community there.

The initial public investigation initiated by Rein's friends, Willi Müller and Paul Hertz, together with Rein's father, collected a lot of facts and details but failed to answer the main question: what was the motive for the murder? On 8 April 1937, one day before Marc Rein went missing, a police officer had visited the Hotel Continental and asked for information about guests in rooms 39 to 45 (Rein's room was 42). Some time later it was found out that the 'policeman' had been using an old type of police identity badge and therefore it was not possible to identify him.[34] It was only established that he spoke Spanish without any accent.

On 9 April someone had telephoned the hotel and asked the operator to put him through to the guest in room 42 by the name of 'Bovich', which could have been an incorrect pronunciation or a misunderstanding for the name of Rein's father, Abramovich. The caller was advised that no guest with such a name was registered at the Continental. Finally, in the evening of the same day, Marc Rein received a telephone call inviting him to an urgent meeting.[35] No one ever saw him again. The events, as they were developed after Marc Rein's disappearance and the clumsy cover-up, point to a typical Orlov-style operation.

Karl Mewis (alias 'Fritz Arndt'), who represented the KPD in the foreign service of the PSUC in Catalonia, and was also in charge of the counter-intelligence work of the KPD in Barcelona,[36] reported to the party leadership, the Comintern, and the NKVD. He received orders accordingly and started to spread disinformation alleging that Rein was a victim of the Trotskysts.

Franz Dahlem, one of the leaders of the KPD liaison group in Paris and a secretary of the ECCI, came to Spain in 1937 as head of the so-called Deutsche Büro in Valencia—that is, officially he was a KPD representative with the PCE. At the same time, Dahlem directed all counter-intelligence activities of the German Communist organization in Spain,[37] working in close contact with the NKVD. He told one of the investigators that Rein had been abducted by the POUM, because he knew about their plans to launch an armed revolt.

Simultaneously, Alfred Herz began spreading rumours that Rein had gone to the front, where it was easy to disappear.

Another rumour was spread by Leopold Kulcsar,[38] an Austrian NKVD agent who demonstrated his zeal in the Kurt Landau case later in the year. Kulcsar claimed that Rein had had a special assignment to unite all opposition against the communists, thus undermining their growing influence, and that either the POUM militia or the Anarchists had murdered him.[39] In June, Walter Ulbricht, one of the leaders of the KPD who visited Spain several times as a Comintern emissary, made an attempt to stop the investigation. He declared that both investigators, Müller and Hertz, had better put their energy into useful political work and claimed that the accusations against the KPD in Rein's case were the result of the provocations of 'spies and the Trotskyites'. Alfons Laurencic (Agent S.S.I. no. 29), acting on the orders of the Catalan government, soon found out that all evidence pointed to Alfred Herz and Gómez Emperador, whose brigade was responsible for the surveillance of the Hotel Continental.

In quest of news about his son, Abramovich arrived in Spain and was received by the Prime Minister, Juan Negrín. On 24 May 1937 the government department Information and Liaison Office ('Oficina de Información y Enlace') asked Mariano Gómez Emperador for Marc Rein's file.[40] A high-ranking official of the Interior Ministry conducted an investigation based on Laurencic's evidence, but it did not yield results. On the next day Agent S.S.I. no. 29 was arrested by the Servicio Alfredo Herz (he was apparently soon released, as his investigation reports on the 'Caso Marc Rein' followed on 27, 28, and 31 May). Laurencic had continued his investigation for another two weeks until the NKVD intervened. In January 1938 Rein's friend Sundelewicz was arrested for the second time.

After two years of meticulous research, Rafail Abramovich was able to compile a final report. Based on the best evidence that the team could collect, it stated that most probably Rein, an electro-engineer, had been asked to assist in the urgent repairs of a secret transmitter that was installed in a safe house somewhere in the area of the calle Muntaner. There was a PSUC secret private prison in its immediate vicinity.[41] Joaquín Olaso Piera, who is sometimes called the chief of the 'policía privada del PSUC and who headed its personnel department, was reported to have been in charge of this prison.

The testimony of Agent S.S.I. no. 29, revealing that Alfred Herz and his people had been shadowing the hotel where Rein stayed, as well as the orchestrated cover-up that followed the operation and the documents seen and copied by Vasili Mitrokhin in the KGB archives[42] provide enough evidence to implicate Moscow in the abduction and murder of Marc Rein. This means that Orlov, as the NKVD chief in Spain, should be held responsible.

Rafail Abramovich was of the same opinion when he arrived in America many years after the war still trying to find out what happened to his son. Unfortunately, before confronting Orlov, Abtamovich met the widow of Ignatz Reiss, Elsa Bernaut, who claimed she had met Orlov in a sanatorium near Moscow and remembered how he looked like. She recalled in her memoir:

Another Menshevik leader whom I came to like and respect was Rafael Abramovich... He knew that the head of the NKVD in Barcelona, where Rein had last been seen, had been a certain Orlov-Nikolsky, alias Shved or Lova [information she picked up from Krivitsky's book], and was sure this man would know who had been responsible for his son's disappearance. As I have mentioned, I had met Orlov and could give a fairly accurate description of him, though Krivitsky and I were both sure he must have been ordered home to Moscow from Spain and shot there with the others. One day Abramovich asked me and Juan Andrade, one of the POUM leaders, to his apartment, where he questioned us about Orlov. Neither of us had any idea of his whereabouts... When Alexander Orlov, who had been with the Soviet commercial services in Valencia, began to publish articles about the Soviet terror in Spain, Abramovich and others at first believed him to be Orlov-Nikolsky. But when Abramovich met Alexander Orlov years later in the United States it was clear from the description I had given him that this Orlov, who was slight, fair-haired, and about ten years too old, was not the man I had met near Moscow in 1932.[43]

There is no need to say that many years after the events Abramovich met that very Nikolsky-Orlov who was responsible for his son's death in Spain.

Another participant in the operation against Mark Rein, albeit much less significant than Orlov, one of the NKVD agents in Barcelona Alfred Herz, deserves attention because of a historical confusion that sometimes surrounds his name and his Spanish adventures.

With regard to the role of Herz, a bad error originated in an article by Carlo Tresca, an Italian-born American anarchist, newspaper editor, and political activist,[44] published on 28 February 1938 in the Manhattan anarchist paper *Il Martello*[45]—an error that was then picked up by several authors. In fact, it is still repeated in some modern accounts, though as early as 1988 Pierre Broué, who was one of those who had followed Tresca's false lead, reluctantly admitted in his Trotsky biography that he was probably wrong about the identity of Herz.

Tresca wrote:

This is a certain Alfred Herz who is actually the chief of the PSUC checa of Barcelona, a branch of the Communist party. His second-in-command is the one named Hermann, and at his side works his wife, three police escorts and four police agents of a brigade quartered at Puerta del Angel...A. Herz, organiser and executioner of the abduction of Marc Rein, a Socialist, is the same person who is known from another source under the name of George Mink and whom we are now going to describe.[46]

Then follows a short biography of George Mink, who is described quite accurately; even his arrest in Copenhagen in 1935 is not overlooked. The only problem is that Alfred Herz, a German, and George Mink, a Ukrainian American, were two different people.

Alfred Herz and his wife Käthe came to Barcelona from Amsterdam, where they had lived in exile, in 1934. In July 1935 Herz wrote to a friend that he had opened a small bookshop. This is a classic cover for any intelligence operative, albeit self-made. Indeed, it has been established without doubt, based on meticulous research in the German, Russian, and Spanish archives, that Herz worked for the KPD intelligence (N-Apparat) and counter-intelligence (A-Apparat) services.[47] Al least one report about the activities of Herz in Catalonia has been found in the Moscow archives.[48] Documents and written testimonies of many witnesses and participants in the events[49] confirm that, from the beginning of the war until at least July 1937, Herz was an active member of the Servicio extranjero del PSUC and had an office in the Hotel Colón on the Plaza de Catalunya in Barcelona.[50] His neighbour there was Karl Mewis (alias 'Karl or Fritz Arndt'), who until the end of the year directed the activities of the service as the KPD representative. The agents working with Herz were the German Hermann Geisen and the Pole Szaja Kinderman (aka Georg 'Jorge' Scheyer), who both took active part in the arrests and tortures of 'dissidents'. On 24 May 1937 Laurencic reported on 'Alfredo Herz', also mentioning that his wife was helping him.[51]

Hubert von Ranke also came to Barcelona in 1936. Born in Munich in 1902, he was, by the time he came to Spain, a rather experienced underground worker, recruited to the KPD M-Apparat in 1932 by the legendary Hans Kippenberger, a leader of the Hamburg Uprising. 'M' naturally stood for 'military', but the aim of this secret KPD service was decomposition of the army and law-enforcement agencies by infiltration and propaganda, as well as of other political parties opposed to the communists, and the investigation of traitors in the KPD ranks. When he had met Kippenberger, Hubert von Ranke was one of the top managers of the German Lufthansa in Berlin-Tempelhof, but now he devoted all his time to party work. When Kippenberger and his associates emigrated to Paris in October 1943, von Ranke also moved there, operating under the party name 'Moritz'. In 1934 in Paris he was one of the organizers of Ernest ('Teddy') Thälmann's escape from German prison, which failed. After Kippenberger had left Paris, being summoned to Moscow (where he was arrested and shot in 1937), von Ranke closely collaborated with Hermann Nuding and later with Willie Münzenberg. In July 1936 he returned to Paris from a short stay in Czechoslovakia, where he was sent by the party, and, after discussing the situation in Spain with Münzenberg and Herbert Wehner, he left for Barcelona with the first Communist volunteers. In Spain von Ranke was using a forged Luxembourgian passport in the name of 'Mathias Bresser'. Later, Katja Landau and Pierre Broué would mix everything up, calling him 'Moritz Bresser' (that is, putting together his party pseudonym and his passport name) and falsely accusing him of being a Comintern and GPU agent sent from Moscow.

From the end of August 1936 Hubert von Ranke was assigned first as a political commissar ('delegado politico') to Centuria Thälmann, commanded by Hans Beimler, and then sent to the Aragon front, but at the end of the year he was back in Barcelona. Here he worked first at the so-called Foreign Secretariat ('Sevicio Extranjero') of the PSUC and from June 1937 joined the Catalan directorate of the DEDIDE, which was part of the Republican Ministry of the Interior and reported to its DGS. The chief of the Republican DEDIDE was Francisco Ordóñez Peña.[52] In his memoirs von Ranke recalled that in the Hotel Colón Herz once introduced him to Orlov and another time to one 'Pedro', almost certainly Eitingon, the head of the Barcelona substation, whose codename in Spain was PIERRE. According to von Ranke, Orlov was quite direct and invited him to collaborate with the NKVD, which offer von Ranke refused. In the DEDIDE, Ranke's job was to interrogate foreign suspects, and, after May 1937, almost exclusively the followers and sympathizers of the POUM. Ranke, signing his reports to Moscow by his party pseudonym 'Moritz', informed that he was able to unmask many 'Trotskyite Gestapo agents' among the German volunteers,[53] but this information was not taken too seriously, because everybody knew that it was part of Orlov's operation against the Trotskyists and had little to do with reality. At least for Herbert Wehner, who personally recruited the first 100 volunteers, the report had no consequences.

By the end of the year, von Ranke had become seriously disgruntled on account of his disagreements with Karl Mewis, the KPD representative in Catalonia. Soon he was sacked from the government service and in November returned to Paris. There, using the communist publishing house Prométhée, he published a brochure about the Spanish Civil War, which was sharply criticized by the KPD leadership. With its title *Wir im fernen Vaterland geboren: Die Centuria Thälmann*, borrowed from a famous song of the International Brigades ('Wir, im fernen Vaterland geboren, nahmen nichts als Hass im Herzen mit. | Doch wir haben die Heimat nicht verloren, uns're Heimat ist heute vor Madrid', text written by Erich Weinert), it was signed by the pseudonym 'E. Mohr'. This forty-page brochure was quickly withdrawn from circulation and is now a great rarity. Von Ranke's authorship remained a secret until quite recently.

He completely broke with the Communist Party in spring 1938. The next year, after the Second World War broke out, he was drafted into the French army, where he served as an officer of military intelligence. When Nazi troops entered and occupied Paris, he fled first to Bordeaux and then to Northern Africa. In autumn 1940, after his demobilization, von Ranke returned to France, where he lived half-legally in the unoccupied zone using various aliases ('Henri-Georges Frank' and 'Hubert Martin') and maintaining contacts with Gertrude Stein. It must be remembered that from the beginning of the century Stein had kept a famous salon on the rue de Fleurus in Paris, visited not only by Cézanne, Monet, Renoir, Gauguin, and Picasso, who in 1906 painted her portrait, but also by the writers of the 'Lost Generation': Ernest Hemingway, Sherwood Anderson, Thornton Wilder, F. Scott Fitzgerald, John Dos Passos, T. S. Eliot, and Ezra Pound, to name but a few. Hemingway met her in 1922 and later mentioned this in his novel *A Moveable Feast*, describing days when he worked in Paris as a foreign correspondent of *Toronto Star*, which could at that time afford to have its own correspondent in Paris. Because she was an American and quite a celebrity as a writer, poet, publisher, and art collector, Hubert's interest to Stein can easily be explained.

In early 1942 von Ranke joined the French Resistance under the nom de guerre Camille. After the liberation of France in 1944, he was invited to serve as an operational officer in the intelligence department of the French Army B under General Delattre de Tassigny. He accepted the invitation and two years later was naturalized as a French citizen, 'Jean Hubert de Ranke'. Until 1960 he worked as a Bayerischer Rundfunk correspondent in Paris and then at its main editorial office in Munich. He died in his native city aged 76 and left important and interesting memoirs about his days in Spain.[54] His wife, Josepha de Campalans née Herrmann, deposited them after his death in the manuscript collection of the Munich Institute of Contemporary History.

From the documents that were discovered by German historians, it is evident that the so-called Servicio Alfredo Herz, which worked partly for von Ranke's DEDIDE and partly for the PSUC, was primarily hunting down German Trotskyists. After one report by agent S.S.I. no. 29 (Laurencic), a German interpreter was arrested for 'translating a newspaper article about Moscow show trials'.[55] Zur Mühlen states that the number of victims among the German dissident Communists in Spain reached approximately 100.[56] However, his claim that 'the executions took place in the cellars of the Hotel Colón and the corpses were later burned in the boiler-room in the basement' is based on Gorkin, whose information, as it is well known, is biased.[57] Mitrokhin's archive confirms that 'many of those selected for liquidation were lured into the building containing the crematorium and killed on the spot'.[58] This was probably the crematorium run by Stanislav Vaupshasov and the Spanish NKVD agent José Castelo Pacheco. It is not clear if it was on the site under today's offices of the Banco Español de Crédito, where Vaupshasov was giving his invaluable professional advice 'to the friendly security services of Catalonia', or another crematorium that he and Castelo Pacheco were running in Spain.

The Alfred Herz Service and the Brigada Gómez Emperador were disbanded in July 1937, but Herz and his wife continued to live in Spain. They left the country on 30 January 1939 via France and arrived in Amsterdam, where they settled in the cheap Pension Plieger at 82 Britschelei. In July, Herz wrote to his friend that they were planning to leave for Mexico.[59] Their last days are not known, and some writers suggest that perhaps they committed suicide.[60]

The Brigada Gómez Emperador was reorganized under the command of Victorio Sala, and its former chief was sent to work in Paris, where Franco's agents spotted him in August 1937.[61] From the old staff, only a Russian interpreter was taken over to the new group. While von Ranke was still in the DEDIDE, he assigned Kinderman to run a small group of agents that allegedly operated until the DEDIDE became part of the SIM in March 1938.[62] According to witnesses' testimonies, Kinderman later worked as an interrogator in the Convento de Santa Ursula in Valencia. Both he and Alfonso Laurencic remained in Spain until the end of the war. On 7 February 1938, Agent S.S.I no. 29 fell into the hands of Franco's forces, was sentenced to death, and executed in the early hours of 9 July 1939.[63]

Kinderman was interned in France in 1939, but managed to flee to Moscow. During the Second World War II served in both the Polish Armia Krajowa and the Red Army. As a matter of fact, he was born Józef Winkler on 25 October 1903 to the family of Salomon and Liba Winkler in the small ancient Polish town of Nowy Sącz. After the war, he served in the newly established Ministerstwo Bezpieczeństwa Publicznego (MBP) (Ministry of Public Security of Poland) in Warsaw as department head,[64] retiring in April 1953 with the rank of colonel.

Remarkably, Victorio Sala remained completely unnoticed by many historians and researchers.[65] In the meantime, Sala played a sinister role in the NKVD operation against the POUM, having infiltrated police informers into its ranks (one of them was Werner Schwarze, alias 'Schwitzer', a KPD member, who later worked in the Catalan directorate of the Sección Orden Público/DEDIDE and then in the SIM in Albacete and Barcelona).[66] As already noted, Nikolsky/Orlov liked Germans for their discipline, and even his personal driver and bodyguard was a young German communist. Eitingon's bodyguard was also a devoted German communist who would later become a lieutenant general in the Stasi, the Ministerium für Staatssicherheit (MfS) (the East German Ministry for State Security). Sala, according to the Russian sources, was a contact man of Grigulevich in

Barcelona.[67] The anti-POUM operation was so secret that Eitingon, the NKVD chief in Barcelona and Orlov's friend, was to be kept completely in the dark, while Orlov was organizing the whole provocation. Sala was given the codename KHOTA, and the information about him and his involvement became known because after the war he worked for the NKVD station in Mexico, whose radio traffic to Moscow was intercepted during Operation VENONA. KHOTA was mentioned in one of the telegrams.

Another Russian agent in Spain, albeit one working for the RU rather than the NKVD, was George Mink. This is the man whomTresca and others confused with Herz. Mink was a Soviet agent of long standing. He was born Godi Minkowsky, of Jewish parentage, in the city of Zhytomyr, now in the north of the western half of Ukraine, on 23 April 1899. In his Comintern biography, Mink correctly stated that he was born in Volhynia, as at that time Zhytomyr was indeed there, in a historic region straddling Poland and Russia located between the rivers Prypiat and Southern Boug. Before the war Volhynia had one of the biggest Jewish populations in the world.[68] Abandoned by his parents, in 1912 Godi was sent by his grandparents to the United States to live with relatives in Philadelphia. He wrote in 1932:

I always lived with native born Americans and I adapted myself to the life of the country, and picked up the language in a slang form ... I realized very soon that an American Native Born could get along better than an emigrant so I decided to Americanize myself, and in the year of 1916 I joined the United States Navy giving my name as George Martin Mink, born in the USA.[69]

The story goes that sailor Mink was assigned to the Boston Naval Yards when the Russian protected cruiser *Varyag* ('Viking') steamed into the port for repairs. Because he spoke some Russian, Mink was allegedly used as an interpreter and liaison with the Russian crew. 'Inspired by the Russians,' claims one report, 'Mink took every opportunity during the remainder of his career in the Navy to promote socialism and agitate against the war'.[70] This, however, is a pure invention, possibly by Mink himself, because *Varyag* was a very famous battleship in the Russian history and the story went well with Mink's future career with the Soviets.

Built by William Cramp & Sons of Philadelphia, *Varyag* had been commissioned into the Imperial Russian Navy in January 1901 and during the Russo-Japanese War of 1904–5 became famous for its crew's stoicism. In spring 1917 she was sent to Great Britain, to Cammell Laird in Birkenhead, for an overhaul, and was due to re-enter service with the Arctic squadron, but, following the Bolshevik revolution of October 1917, the sailors raised the red flag and tried to ignite the revolt, so the cruiser was stormed and seized by the British and later sold to Germany for scrap. She never visited Boston and finally sank in 1925.

George Mink became a naturalized citizen (a 1942 FBI report even listed him as born in Scranton, Pennsylvania), visited the Soviet Union in 1921 'as a sailor', according to his Profintern registration form, was appointed the International Seamen's Union (ISU) representative to the AFL Central Labour Council in Philadelphia, then joined the Industrial Workers of the World (IWW), and then was expelled from the ISU as a Communist, though at that time he was not yet a party member. Mink joined the CPUSA in late 1921 and in 1925 was sent to Philadelphia with the task of organizing a Communist fraction within the seamen's union of the IWW. There he worked briefly for the Yellow Cab Company, until, in spring 1927, he returned to the sea and left for the Soviet Union again. From the port of Novorossiisk he travelled to Moscow, where he took part in the IV Profintern Congress as a delegate from the CPUSA.[71] In various publications Mink is often linked with A. Lozovsky, General Secretary of the Profintern. An FBI report cites sources who believed that Mink was Lozovsky's brother-in-law,[72] information that cannot be independently corroborated.

In August 1930 Minsk was in Moscow, again meeting Dmitry Manuilsky,[73] head of the American Commission of the Comintern and one of the ECCI Secretaries. It is possible that after that meeting Manuilsky, who obviously liked Mink, recommended him to the OMS. Richard Krebs, one of the organizers of the ISH headquartered in Hamburg, recalled escorting Mink to the Free and Hanseatic City in 1931 after he had been given 'several thousand dollars' by Fritz Hecker, the treasurer of the Western Secretariat of the Comintern. And, if the memoirs of Krebs should be treated as biased, an FBI memo mentioned the same episode, stating that Mink had received $40,000.[74] It is possible, and it happened regularly, that from the OMS Mink was transferred to military intelligence. Remarkably, the widow of Alexander Ulanovsky, the man who succeeded Manfred Stern and Vladimir Gorev as the RU resident in North America in 1931, stated that her husband had known Mink for ten years when they met again in the United States[75]—that is, from the time of his first visit to the Soviet Union in 1921. In the USA Mink was part of the agent network controlled by

Ulanovsky that also included Whittaker Chambers, Robert Gordon Switz and his wife, Lydia Stahl, and Leon Minster. Ulanovsky was their case officer until his tour of duty was over and he returned back to Moscow. In 1935 Ulanovsky took Mink to Denmark as his assistant, and they were both arrested in Copenhagen in February.[76] They were finally expelled to the USSR, where Ulanovsky started to teach at the Frunze Military Academy, and Mink was sent to Barcelona in February 1937, arriving in early March.

In Spain, Mink's task was to spy on Anglo-American 'dissidents', primarily within the International Brigades. In December 1937, Liston M. Oak, a former member of the CPUSA, wrote in a Socialist Party paper: 'I met George Mink, American Communist, who boasted about his part in organizing the Spanish GPU [sic; all Soviet-related secret services were known as "GPU" then] and offered me a job—to put the finger on "untrustworthy" comrades entering Spain to fight against fascism such as members of the British Independent Labour Party and the American Socialist Party.'[77] In Congressional testimony ten years later, Oak identified Mink as a 'goon'— which he defined as 'a tough guy, a gangster'—in the Maritime Union. Oak testified:

I heard of Mink from time to time, from that time on, and finally I met him in a hotel in Barcelona in April 1937. He didn't know that I had become disillusioned and had resigned from the Communist Party and greeted me very cordially and invited me to his room, where he got drunk and boasted about his NKVD work, and he urged me to accept an assignment in this passport racket...[78] So I told him I would think it over and left...I knew that for my own safety I had better get out of Spain, which I did in company with John Dos Passos.[79]

Together with another American named Tony De Maio, Mink was also accused of murdering volunteers in Spain. William C. McCuistion, a former Marine Workers Industrial Union organizer and Lincoln Brigade veteran, testified under oath:

He [Mink] was officially known as a member of the military intelligence and the GPU [sic] of the Soviet Union...I saw George Mink and Tony De Maio and Captain Cohn on May 2, 1938, in a little café—one of the nicer but small cafés on the Rambla de Catalonia. I saw Tony De Maio kill two men in that café...The American that was killed at that time was going under the name of Matthews. He had a State Department passport issued under the name of Aronofsky—I think that was his correct name, but he was using the name 'Matthews' over there...The other fellow wasn't quite dead. His name was Moran, an Englishman. He was taken away to the hospital . . .

In answer to a committee question, the witness said, 'Tony De Maio shot them.'
'Why?' he was asked.
'Because they were stragglers.'[80]

Another witness, who testified before the US House of Representatives' Special Committee in May 1941, identified a photograph of George Mink taken at a 1930 conference of the ISH. The witness, the already mentioned Richard Krebs,[81] explained that 'Mink was not subjected to orders from the American party leaders. He had his own budget, that is, his own subsidy from Moscow, and operated directly under Moscow's orders.'[82] Naturally, Krebs's testimony cannot be taken for granted, like many other episodes from his book.

Noticeably, an article published by *Time* magazine contradicts McCuistion's testimony given under oath. On the same day as he claimed that he saw Mink in Barcelona, on 2 May 1938, *Time* wrote, quoting Trotskyist No. 1: 'Leon Trotsky declared in Mexico City last week, "I believe that a group of Stalin agents headed by 'The Mink' has arrived in Mexico, plotting to kill me".'[83] Trotsky based his judgement on the information collected by one of his followers, a Pole named Max Shachtman.[84] In reality, starting from May 1938, Mink's whereabouts are very difficult to establish.[85] McCuistion claimed he had contact with him in the United States in 1939, and the FBI believed, based on its informants' reports, that he was regularly travelling between the USSR and Mexico in 1940.[86] As it turned out, this information was provided by Trotsky's supporters and may or may not be true.

Today it is impossible to establish with certainly whether Mink had indeed travelled to Mexico and, if yes, in what capacity. Another former communist, Maurice L. Malkin, testified: 'A Mexican Trotskyist recognised him and he vanished. I do not know what happened. I know that plenty of American loyalists who came back [from Spain] would like to get their hands on George Mink. He was responsible for shooting many Americans in the back over there.'[87] Krivitsky's biographer Kern believes that Mink was purged in Russia in 1940, but it would probably be more correct to say that his fate remains a mystery.

With a degree of pride, KGB-sponsored publications give an account of its predecessor's role in the extermination of the Anarchists and Trotskyists in Barcelona in the spring of 1937. As usual, primary sources seldom appear, but, according to Kolpakidi and Prokhorov, who in four years published three books praising Soviet political murders abroad, among Orlov's victims were the political commissar of the Anarchist Colonna Rosselli, philosopher Camillo Berneri, editor of the newspaper *Guerra di Classe*, and his friend Francesco Barbieri, as well as Alfredo Martínez, the leader of the Libertarian Youth of Catalonia.[88]

Russian historians give an approximate and inaccurate description of what happened in the house of Berneri and they borrow deeply from the article by Carlo Tresca in *Il Martello*.[89] According to Tresca, on 4 May 1937, two representatives of the Servicio extranjero del PSUC visited the apartment at No. 2 El Portal de l'Ángel, where Berneri, his wife, Barbieri, and their comrades were having a meeting. The agents were wearing red armbands and introduced themselves as antifascists and friends. They asked Berneri not to shoot at them. Berneri and Barbieri responded that they had come to Spain to defend the revolution and that they had no reason whatsoever to shoot at other antifascists. About three o'clock in the afternoon the same people came again, made a thorough search of Berneri and Barbieri's apartment as well as of a neighbouring apartment, and confiscated documents, books, and three rifles. They forbade anybody to leave the house. On Wednesday, 5 May, at six o'clock in the morning, a group of twelve armed people entered the apartment. Six of them were police officers and . . . (words deleted by the censor). Berneri and Barbieri were arrested. On 6 May the police visited the Berneri's apartment again and assured his friends that the Anarchist leaders would be released in the afternoon. But on the same day the family learned that during the night the Red Cross had found the mutilated bodies of Berneri and Barbieri near the Palacio de la Generalitat. The autopsy revealed multiple wounds. It was established that they had been shot at point-blank range.[90] Tresca also mentioned that it was Alfred Herz, whom he calls the 'chief of the PSUC checa of Barcelona', who was responsible for the arrest and murder of the Anarchists.

It is interesting that, in spite of the KGB attempt to whitewash Orlov in a number of books, Kolpakidi and Prokhorov use the material provided by the same KGB Press Bureau to implicate him in several crimes that were certainly not Orlov's. On the positive side, they are trying to get out of Tresca's Mink–Herz muddle, providing a reasonable argument that 'Mink was in Spain under his own name as a staff officer of the intelligence department of the RKKA'.[91] Though it is true that Mink was in Spain under his own name,[92] he was certainly not an officer but an agent and even not a very trusted one after his failure in Copenhagen.

The author of the article that confused so many people, Carlo Tresca, was murdered on 11 January 1943 on New York's Fifth Avenue. He was shot dead by a gunman who has never been named, though one person was arrested.[93] There was plenty of speculation about the NKVD hand, partly because Tresca had been a member of the Dewey Commission that cleared Trotsky of charges made during the Moscow show trials. It was later established that it was certainly a mafia-related crime.

On 3 June 1937 the disaffected Soviet agent Juliet Stuart Poyntz left her office at the Women's Association clubhouse in Manhattan. She had last been seen in Moscow with George Mink at the end of 1936. Then Carlo Tresca met her again in New York in May 1937. Tresca wrote that they had known each other for twenty years and that Poyntz honestly told her friend that she wanted to break with the Soviet regime and with Communism.[94] She was never seen again. According to Kolpakidi and Prokhorov, she had been lured to her death by a former Russian lover working for the NKVD named Schachno Epstein, alias 'Joseph Berson', and her body was buried behind a brick wall in a Greenwich Village house.[95] Days before Poyntz's disappearance, they write, she and 'Berson' were seen together in New York. On 11 August 1937, Epstein/Berson left the United States on board the *Queen Mary*.[96] Their version, however, does not check with Epstein's biographical data and seems to be borrowed in full from the old book by Benjamin Gitlow,[97] who was in no position to know, because he had been expelled from the CPUSA in 1929. The book is correctly described by critics as a 'potboiler for the popular market'. The version of Krivitsky's ghost writer that Poyntz was a mistress of a Soviet military commander implicated in the Tukhachevsky trial and eventually shot—and therefore that they abducted her in order to prevent her defection—is even less reliable. Krivitsky, like Gitlow, simply could not know that.

As it turned out, the NKVD was somewhat at a loss about the fate of its former agent.[98] After reviewing the autobiography of Elizabeth Bentley, their agent and courier in the USA (until November 1945, when she started to collaborate with the FBI), the Lubyanka investigators found out that Poyntz had worked for the Profintern in Moscow from late 1929 to March 1931, before she was recruited for Serebryansky's Administration for Special Tasks. No details were given about her duties there apart from the fact that she worked for 'Yasha's Group', as it was known internally, from 1931 to

1933. The 1947 memo on Poyntz stated: 'In October 1934 [Poyntz] was recruited by the RU RKKA [military intelligence, now GRU] and in November of that year travelled to the US with an assignment to recruit agents . . . An RU representative met with Poyntz twice before her disappearance in early June 1937. The circumstances of the disappearance are not known to us.' This neither solves the mystery of Poyntz's disappearance nor gives reasons to suspect that 'she met a grim fate at the hands of GRU', as some commentators suggest.[99] At the time it seems the sole RU representative in the area was Moishe (Mikhail) Millstein, the only case officer at the Soviet Embassy in Washington. According to his memoirs, published in Moscow in 2000,[100] by the summer of 1937 all RU spy rings had been successfully destroyed as their controllers disappeared either in the Lubyanka cellars or in the Gulag camps. Millstein himself was quite busy laundering money while trying to organize arms supplies for Spain. Besides, during the Soviet times the GRU had never been involved in 'liquidations'.

The NKVD involvement in several crimes during the interwar period and especially the Spanish Civil War can, on the contrary, be established with a high degree of certainty, though in some cases direct evidence in missing.

During his comparatively short intelligence career outside Russia, Nikolsky/Orlov had dealt with agents or potential agents codenamed FRIEND at least twice. One occasion was in 1933 in Paris, where he was sent to find and recruit an unidentified officer of the Deuxième Bureau, an intelligence section of the French army general staff. The second agent was Brian Goold-Verschoyle, his wireless operator and assistant in Valencia, secretly arrested and transported to Russia for his 'suspicious views'. In the spring of 1937 Orlov and his agents had to deal with yet another 'friend'—Hans Freund—a profound anti-Stalinist and a Trostkyist and therefore a sworn enemy. Unfortunately, as often happens, no documentary proof of the Soviet involvement has surfaced to date, but the target and the way he disappeared are very similar to other cases when the NKVD under Orlov's leadership in Spain was certainly involved.

Hans David Freund was born on 12 March 1912 in the small German town of Benzlau in a Jewish family of petite bourgeoisie who emigrated to Palestine in 1933 with what became known as the Fifth Aliyah, which brought a quarter of a million Jews to the Holy Land. As a young man, Freund managed to visit the Soviet Union; he returned completely disillusioned and eager to fight against Stalinism. He then studied in Oxford, where he worked on his doctoral thesis in sociology, and in 1934 was to be found in Geneva, organizing Trotskyist fractions within the local Socialist students. Here Freund also established contacts with the Anarchists.[101]

Hans Freund left for Spain soon after the war broke out. In August, according to Katja Landau, he was doing political work in Madrid. He went as a journalist to the Guadalajara front, where he was involved in some propaganda work among the militiamen. In January 1937 he was in Paris, but was soon to return to Barcelona.[102] Early 1937 found him in the Catalan capital, where he tried to bring about a unification of various Trotskyist groups and was the main contact between the Bolshevik–Leninists and the anarchist 'Friends of Durruti' at the end of April and the beginning of May. He was with the Bolshevik–Leninists during the May Days, when their leader Grandizo Munis was in Paris, and it was Freund who wrote the leaflet distributed on the barricades that was noticed by George Orwell, who later mentioned the episode in his famous *Homage to Catalonia*, published shortly after the events.[103]

It was reported that Freund, who was also known under the pseudonyms 'Winter' and 'Moulin', had been photographed while on the barricades. He allegedly took refuge with the Anarchists. There exists no definite account as to how he met his end, because he simply disappeared. Several printed versions lack credibility.[104] As in many other similar cases in Catalonia, George Mink was suspected of being behind Freund's death in one of the secret *checas*, but again there is no evidence of Mink's involvement. Orlov, on the contrary, had a list of 'literniks', real supporters of Trotsky and his ideas, to deal with, and, if Mitrokhin's notes are correct, victims could have been disposed of in the cremation facilities. Whatever happened, from 2 August Freund was reported missing. In April 1938 his name, together with the names of several other prominent victims, appeared in the *Time* article entitled 'Stalin's Mafia'.

Among those murdered by 'Stalin's Mafia', as *Time* put it, was Ignatz Reiss, a Soviet secret agent who renounced Stalinism, and whose bullet-riddled body was found in a ditch outside Lausanne on 4 September 1937. The Reiss case has been described in detail in books and articles published in the past decades.[105] However, until this day, the role of Nikolsky/Orlov in this operation has remained completely unknown.[106] In his 1953 book and posthumously published memoirs Orlov mentioned this assassination only in passing, stressing that everything was organized so quickly that 'Reiss hadn't even had time to write his revelations',[107] which is an exaggeration, as shall be seen. As a matter of fact, Reiss was not going to write or in any other form make public any 'revelations' regarding his work for the NKVD.

Regrettably, in spite of several joint publishing projects of the early 1990s, the greater part of the substantial interwar archive, including most of the files dealing with the Spanish Civil War, has not yet been declassified by the SVR. However, what has become clear from Orlov's personal file (No. 32476, vols 1 and 2), the operational correspondence file of the NKVD station in Spain (No. 17679), selected documents from other files, as well as multiple research papers, memoirs, articles, and books that have come out during and after the civil war leads to the conclusion that, from the spring of 1937, the NKVD in Spain, headed by Orlov, concentrated its main efforts on undermining the Trotskyist movement. This meant eliminating first of all those who had ever worked for or had been in personal contact with Trotsky himself. A typical example is the death of Erwin Wolf (nickname and first political pseudonym 'Kiff', also known as 'Nicole' or 'N. Brown'), a one-time secretary of Trotsky and another naive revolutionary who, like Hans Freund, 'disappeared' without a trace on 13 September 1937.

Wolf's uncle Heinrich, President of the New York Physics Society, wrote to him in August 1933: 'I know that you are in Paris, that you have a new passport, and you could return to Germany to continue your work (studies) . . . I want to make it clear that I am neither a reactionary nor a conservative.' He further tried to dissuade his nephew from following the path he had chosen. Uncle Heinrich also said that he was not hostile to Trotskyists. In fact, he stressed, some of them were his friends, among others Max Eastman with his Russian wife (who was the sister of Nikolai Krylenko).[108] Interestingly, Orlov would later be engaged in a very active correspondence with the Eastman couple.

The last letter in the Wolf dossier in Brussels is dated 28 April 1937, a few days before he left for Barcelona. 'Going to Spain not as a volunteer-fighter, but a volunteer political worker,' writes Georges Vereeken, 'Erwin Wolf was proud that he had been able to refuse attractive proposals of a bourgeois life of comfort and ease and launch out on a dangerous and uncertain road.'[109] And dangerous it was indeed.

In the second half of July, soon after the arrest of the POUM leadership, Moulin (Hans Freund) set up a meeting in which he invited several prominent Trotskyists who were still at large. During his studies in Geneva, where he read sociology, Freund used to meet Paul Thalmann, the author of the brochure *Für die Arbeiterrevolution in Spanien*, written under the pseudonym 'Franz Heller' and smuggled to Catalonia for distribution among its sizeable German-speaking community. Thalmann, his wife Clara, and Freund came to Barcelona together. Those present at the meeting were Erwin Wolf, who was in Spain under his own name, posing as a foreign correspondent of several British newspapers, Wolf's wife, and a Spaniard whom Thalmann calls 'Munez' in his memoirs, 'a real leader of the Spanish Trotskyists'. This was quite certainly Grandiso Munis. The agenda of the urgent meeting was to discuss the political situation and chances for a revolutionary uprising after the May Days and the following arrests. Thalmann, according to his own words, painted a gloomy picture: the reign of Stalinists, hesitant behaviour of the POUMists, failure of the anarchists, and dissolution of the Control Patrols were a setback for the revolution. Wolf and 'Munez' were of the opposite opinion. According to their estimates, the political situation was favourable for a potential growth of the revolutionary forces. Moulin/Freund said that the May Days were 'the turn of the tide that would inevitably lead to a new wave'.[110] Fortunately, that never happened.

Although the conference ended without any definitive conclusion, all participants realized that to be a revolutionary had become dangerous and illegal. Thanks to Moulin's efforts, Wolf and his wife managed to rent a small apartment in the port area, and Thalmann was advised to take care, because the police were looking for the author of the brochure. On the same evening, a friend whom he calls 'Fritzchen' (Fritz) Arndt' found Thalmann and his wife in a café to warn them that their house was under surveillance and offered to move them to another place.

In the KPD registry this 'Fritz Arndt' was better known as Karl Mewis, a representative of the KPD in Catalonia who until the end of 1937 also played an important role in the 'Servicio extranjero del PSUC'.[111] Before he left for Scandinavia in March 1938, Mewis was in charge of its German section and maintained close contacts with the NKVD, and personally with Orlov, through one of his subordinates, another German named Walter Vesper (alias 'Peter Nerz').[112] Vesper was signing his reports (known as 'Informes') with the initial 'P' or sometimes 'Peter'. He was an old party cadre, attended the KPD Reichsparteischule in Berlin-Fichtenau in 1930, and together with von Ranke he took part in the raids against the POUMists.[113] It was Karl Mewis who helped Orlov to infiltrate Werner Schwarze as a 'mole' into the POUM militia—otherwise, how else would he have known about it.

It became more and more difficult to meet friends in Barcelona, as all the POUM haunts were shut down, as well as those of the 'Amigos de Durutti', but several quiet cafés in the port area were chosen for secret meetings and Thalmann kept on seeing Moulin until the latter disappeared. Soon he and his wife moved to the Wolfs' apartment and after a while decided to leave the country. They managed to obtain their exit permits, but were detained by two plain-clothes agents, after having successfully passed through the passport control at the port. They were taken to 24 Puerta del Angel and interrogated by a group of five men, who introduced themselves as a 'Spanish court'. Thalmann describes one of them as a 'Boxer' (because of the shape of his nose) who spoke Spanish with a heavy Russian accent.[114] He later learned that the 'Boxer' was the chief NKVD agent in Spain. Another man who talked to them was German.

In prison Thalmann's wife Clara met Sundelewicz and after several days they heard that Wolf had also been arrested, along with another journalist. Thalmann, whose prison conditions were rather soft, saw him in a communal cell and even managed to pass a note (for which he was promptly transferred to a much more sinister place—the Convent Santa Ursula in Valencia). Thalmann gives no dates but states that Wolf was released the following morning.[115] He himself was regularly interrogated in Santa Ursula, his investigators always asking the same questions: when was he last in Germany? when did he meet Trotsky in Norway? where was the Trotsyite Moulin? Once the 'Boxer' (Thalmann never learned that it was Orlov), accompanied by a German agent, visited him in his prison cell. After more than three weeks' confinement in Valencia, Thalmann, together with his wife, was suddenly released, and, after a quiet night at the police headquarters, two uniformed and armed bodyguards were assigned to protect them while they were placed in the Hotel Ingles. In mid-September Paul and Clara left for Barcelona, as soon as they heard that Wolf had disappeared.

According to their version, Wolf was in close contact with the Italian journalist Tioli, who, like Wolf, was sending articles to the British newspapers. The Thalmanns knew the hotel where he resided, and asked about him at reception, but did not get a clear answer and were about to leave. At that moment a strange group of three armed men in civil suits almost arrested them. Fortunately, their bodyguards were nearby and rushed to help them, showing their badges and flashing revolvers. The conflict was quickly settled after those in the hotel saw whom they were dealing with.

On the street, it was explained to Thalmann that Tioli had been kidnapped several days ago and now the police agents were detaining everybody who asked about him.

Versions of other people who knew Wolf differ in small details (Katja Landau writes that Tioli was a friend, while Georges Vereeken claims that Wolf was recommended to a certain Dr Tioli in Barcelona by Greta Finnstad, a Norwegian friend of the Socialist deputy Knudsen, whose daughter, Hjordis Knudsen, became Wolf's wife). But all agree that, after his release, Wolf came back home and, together with Hjordis, decided to return to Paris. The evening before they were due to leave, Tioli telephoned and pressed him for a rendezvous to pass on some urgent correspondence. They met in a café, and Tioli said that he had forgotten the package. He asked Wolf to wait while he went home to pick it up. But he did not come back. Instead, wrote Vereeken, a police squad arrived and immediately arrested Wolf.[116] From that day both Wolf and Tioli disappeared. The police watched Tioli's room at the Hotel Victoria for several weeks, but that did not reveal anything that could help the investigation.

Wolf's sister interceded in favour of her brother at the Spanish Embassy in Prague. On 10 October 1937 she received their reply: 'Madame, I have the honour to communicate to you that according to an official investigation of the General Security Department, of which the Ministry of the Interior has informed us, your brother, Erwin Wolf, was in prison, arrested for subversive activity. He was set at liberty on 13 September 1937.'[117] The letter shows that Wolf was rearrested but released again. On that very day he vanished, snatched from the street by those who acted on Moscow's orders. This seems the only logical explanation, as the only 'crime' committed by the young man was that he had worked for Trotsky. Remarkably, the letter of 30 August that ordered the immediate release of Thalmann (plus his and his wife's protection by the Spanish Republic) was signed by Francisco Ordóñez,[118] the chief of the DEDIDE and a friend of Prieto, the War Minister. It may be remembered that, after Prieto had dismissed Gustavo Durán, director of the SIM of Madrid, who had been vouched for by the Communists and the 'technicians' from Moscow, relations between the Minister and the Soviet advisers became strained.

On 8 February 1938 the Fournier Agency released a statement that Wolf had been transported to the USSR and shot at the same time as Antonov-Ovseyenko.[119] There are absolutely no grounds for believing this report, as it makes no sense. Wolf was one of the 'literniks' and the NKVD station in

Spain had more important things to do than to abduct a former secretary of Trotsky, imprison him and then secretly transport him to the Soviet Union just to be executed there. It is much more likely that Erwin Wolf shared the fate of Rein and others and disappeared in Vaupshasov's crematorium.

Outside Spain, the main theatre of operations for the NKVD assassins was France, where their chief targets were Trotsky's son, Lev Sedov, and the ROVS, at that time headed by General Evgeny Karlovich Miller.[120] In the summer of 1937 Orlov's counterpart in Paris, Yakov Serebryansky, devised similar plans to deal with both opposition leaders. The first stage of the operation, the penetration of their entourages, had, by the end of September, been successfully accomplished[121] by the Paris legal residency.

To put the ROVS under NKVD control, it was decided to substitute Miller with General Nikolai Skoblin. The group, under the command of Orlov's boss Sergey Spiegelgass, included the new NKVD legal resident in France, Georgy Kosenko (alias 'Kislov', codenamed FIN), and two operatives, Mikhail Grigoryev ('Alexandrov') and Veniamin Grazhul ('Beletsky').[122] On the morning of 22 September 1937 General Miller (codenamed DED by the NKVD) left his Paris headquarters never to be seen there again. Before leaving the building at 29 rue du Colisée, he deposited a letter ordering his aide to open it in case he were not to come back in a couple of hours.

This was done in the evening and the note left by General Miller read:

I have a rendezvous at half-past twelve today at the corner of the Rue Jasmin and Rue Raffet, in Auteuil, close to Bois de Boulogne, with General Skoblin, who is arranging a meeting for me with a German officer, M[onsieur] Strohmann, military attaché with a neighbouring power, and an official of the Embassy, M[onsieur] Werner. Both speak Russian fluently. Perhaps it is a trap.[123]

At one of the NKVD safe houses in Saint-Cloud, 'German representatives', played by Grigoryev and Grazhul, chloroformed the general, drugged him, and brought their victim to the Soviet steamer *Maria Uliyanova*. Soon he was registered at the Lubyanka prison as 'Number 110'.

On 30 September, eight days after the abduction of General Miller, *Pravda* published a dispatch from its special correspondent in Spain, Mikhail Koltsov. From the papers allegedly found on General Anatole Fock, captured on the Quinto (Aragon) front while fighting for Franco (but without doubt supplied by Orlov), Koltsov concluded that Miller was at loggerheads with other members of his organization over the question of how far they should go in supporting Nazi-fascism. According to Koltsov's report, a letter from Miller was found on Fock blaming him for his extreme pro-Hitler attitude. These captured documents, said *Pravda*, proved that the White guards were linked with Italian and German intervention in Spain and (the real purpose of the publication) those pro-fascist members of ROVS had an account to settle with their own chief.[124]

General Miller, a key figure of the anti-Bolshevik movement was shot in Moscow in May 1939. Skoblin was arrested by the ROVS leadership but managed to escape on the way to the police station. He had been hiding in the Soviet Embassy in Paris for almost a month under the watchful eye of the security officer named Sokolov before a special plane, chartered by Orlov, flew him to Barcelona in late October.[125] Almost certainly Spiegel-glass and Sokolov accompanied him. Although much has been written about the abduction of General Miller and his death in Moscow, there have always been plenty of blank spots in the Skoblin story.

The French investigation went no further than pointing a finger at Skoblin, who disappeared. Mireille Abbiate, whose role went undetected by the police, was reassigned to the operation against Sedov.[126] She was lucky, because other participants accept Grazhul, who was sacked from the NKVD in 1946, shared the fate of their victim. Kosenko and Grigoryev were shot in the Lubyanka prison in 1940. Tretyakov was arrested in Paris in 1942 and executed as a Soviet spy by the Nazi in 1944. Skoblin's wife, the famous Russian singer Nadezhda Plevitskaya, was brought to trial in Paris, found guilty of conspiring to kidnap General Miller, and sentenced to twenty years' hard labour. She survived her husband by only three years, dying in prison in September 1940.[127]

When on 21 January 1931 in Berlin General Nikolai Vladimirovich Skoblin handed over a signed statement to the representatives of Soviet intelligence, he could not have foreseen such an end. 'With this,' he wrote, 'I pledge my word to the Workers-Peasants' Red Army of the Union of Soviet Socialist Republics to fulfil all instructions of the Red Army intelligence representatives irrespective of the [geographical] territory. For failing to discharge my current obligations I shall be called to account in accordance with the military laws of the USSR.'[128] Signing this, he obviously did not plan a failure and quite certainly did not know the laws of the USSR—written or unwritten.

Skoblin became agent '13', also codenamed FARMER. After the abduction of General Miller, he secretly took refuge in the grey-walled Soviet

Embassy on rue de Grenelle. In late October 1937 Sloutsky's deputy, Sergey Spiegelglass, arrived in Spain. Orlov later wrote in his memoirs that Spiegelglass came unexpectedly. However, Orlov's 1993 biography reveals: 'Orlov claimed [during his CIA debriefing] that he [Spiegelglass] had arrived from Paris after being sent by Yezhov to personally direct the hunting down of Reiss. The NKVD records show that Orlov was covering up the true circumstances since Spiegelglass had been sent to Spain by Slutsky [*sic*] to arrange for Skoblin's escape by plane from France.'[129] As it happens, every disinformation has some grains of truth to it.

The former NKVD station chief in Republican Spain devoted a whole chapter of his last book to the abduction of General Miller. As it turned out, Orlov knew every tiny detail of the affair including the fact that Spiegelglass arrived in Paris on a false Austrian passport. It is hardly surprising, however, that he named all participants by their aliases and attributed the role of Skoblin's Paris warder to 'an NKVD operative by the name of Sokolov, who was officially listed on the staff of the Soviet embassy [in France] as a clerk'.[130] In reality, in the 'red book' of the Spanish Foreign Ministry an NKVD operative by the name of Sokolov was officially listed on the staff of the Soviet embassy . . . in Spain.[131]

Naturally, it was a great embarrassment for the Soviet Union that Skoblin was hiding in their embassy in Paris, which could have been stormed by the White émigrés at any moment. Had he been found there, that would obviously have led to a break of diplomatic relations between France and the USSR, and that was absolutely inadmissible in the current political situation. Therefore, Orlov in Barcelona was given a strict and urgent order to hire a small aeroplane, irrespective of the price.

On 19 October he hurried to the French consulate in Barcelona and received a visa for France valid for eight days. He soon landed at a Paris airport to pick up two passengers: Spiegelglass and Skoblin. Within a few hours Skoblin was in Barcelona under the watchful eye of Sokolov. Corroborating information about Spiegelglass's visit to Spain that October comes from his NKVD file.[132] Orlov later invented the notion that Spiegelglass had come to arrange his assassination, but it is clear from the archival documents that there had never been such an assignment. Spiegelglass was sent to Spain as part of the Skoblin rescue plan. This can be proved by a message that Orlov sent to Spiegelglass on another occasion: 'For $15,000 we could buy an airplane of the type in which you and I whisked away

FARMER.'[133] But there is a much more important telegram that directly implicates Orlov, revealing his role in Skoblin's fate:

From: MOSCOW
To: PARIS
No: ——
28 September 1937
To: SCHWED [i], YASHA [ii]
Reference nos. ——
Personal:
Your plan is accepted. The Big Boss [iii] asks to do everything possible to ensure [that the operation goes] without a hitch. The action must leave no traces. The wife [iv] should have an impression that THIRTEENTH [v] is alive and at home [vi].
    ALEKSEI [vii][134]
Comments:
    [i]   SCHWED: Lev Lazarevich Nikolsky/Orlov
    [ii] YASHA: Yakov Isaakovich Serebryansky
    [iii] BIG BOSS: Yezhov
    [iv] WIFE: Nadezhda Plevitskaya, wife of Gen. Skoblin
    [v]   THIRTEENTH: Nikolai Skoblin
    [vi] HOME: Russia
    [vii] ALEKSEI: Chief of the 7th Department GUGB NKVD, Commissar of State Security 2nd Rank Abram A. Sloutsky.

This document demonstrates that Skoblin was not only to be smuggled from France. Moscow had sent orders to SCHWED quietly to get rid of the compromised agent. And, he was instructed, 'the action must leave no traces'.

In Barcelona, Orlov placed Spiegelglass and Skoblin in the luxurious mansion that had once been the Soviet consulate at No. 15 Avenida del Tibídabo, where the NKVD station was also located. Powerful Consul-General Vladimir Antonov-Ovseyenko was recalled to Moscow in August and never came back. A well-equipped communications centre traditionally occupied the top floor of the mansion. From there Spiegelglass and Nikolsky reported to the Centre about Skoblin's safe arrival. According to the official KGB history, Skoblin perished in Barcelona in late October 1937 as a result of a bombardment of the local airfield by the Nationalist forces.[135] At the same time, it quotes a letter written by Skoblin in Spain and addressed to 'Stakh', mentioning the twentieth anniversary of the Bolshevik revolution (25 October, Old Style),[136] which has long since been celebrated on 7 November (New Style).[137] As instructed by Sloutsky, the letter was to give an impression that Skoblin was alive and well, while it is clear that the decision to liquidate him was taken by Yezhov, who correctly calculated that the agent had outlived his usefulness.

The clue to Orlov's direct involvement in this murder is hidden in a phrase from Orlov's farewell letter to Yezhov, where he stated that he had in his possession FARMER's ring (FARMER and '13' were Skoblin's code names). Possession of a man's ring is a classic symbol of its former owner's untimely death. In accordance with the old knightly code of chivalry, it was a traditional demonstration that somebody had been defeated and passed away in a battle. In the criminal underworld (which has always been closer to the Chekists), it means that somebody had been secretly murdered. The wily Chekist almost certainly mentioned this fact in his letter to the chief to remind Yezhov that he could reveal the truth about Skoblin's last days.

In his letter to Yezhov, SCHWED called his former boss Spiegelglass 'a criminal named DOUGLAS' because he had first-hand knowledge of most of the 'direct actions'. Before they bumped off their former agent, Orlov, as in several other cases described in this chapter, used his favourite 'signature' trick: he asked Skoblin 'to write a number of short undated letters for his wife containing a few encouraging words and expressions of love and devotion'.[138] Some of these letters are regularly reproduced by the Russian authors.

As expected, Orlov never admitted even the fact of Skoblin's sudden death in Spain and lied instead that, 'one evening in November 1937, Skoblin was taken out of the [Paris] embassy and smuggled aboard a Soviet cargo ship bound for Leningrad'.[139]

Another, indirect participant of this tragic affair was Walter Krivitsky. Shortly before Orlov arrived in Paris, on 6 October, the day of his scheduled departure to the USSR, Krivitsky took his family to the Hotel Bohy-Lafayette, where one of his friends had a hired limousine waiting. As his biographer put it: 'Krivitsky packed Tonya and Alek inside and departed Paris in style. Just on the outskirts of town, at the Porte d'Orleans, he asked the chauffeur, an American expatriate, to stop at a café.' Finding a pay phone, he called his faithful secretary. She picked up the receiver and heard him telling her of his break with the Soviet Union. The former illegal NKVD resident in the Netherlands was Stalin's latest defector in 1937. Spiegelglass would have to send a telegram to Yezhov and Yezhov would respond with the order to assassinate Krivitsky. But before his dead body was found in a Washington hotel, Krivitsky, according to a British intelligence source, gave testimony to the Sûreté that helped convict Skoblin's wife, a direct participant in the abduction of General Miller.[140]

The autumn of 1937 was certainly a hot season for the NKVD in Spain. On 23 September two police agents accompanied by an Assault Guard detained the Austrian Trotskyist Kurt Landau. This month-long operation that led to the arrest and murder of Landau is perhaps best of all documented by a release, albeit a small one, from the Soviet intelligence archives, testimonies of witnesses and participants, and even academic research papers. The direct involvement of Orlov may now be proved.

After the first Moscow show trial (19–24 August 1936) had reached an inglorious end, with death sentences passed on all the accused, Landau was enormously worried, because the defence of the former Bolshevik leaders, now called 'scum', 'jackals', 'hyenas', and 'mad dogs', was for him not only the duty of proletarian internationalism, but also a personal matter. One of those convicted, Valentin Olberg, was a one-time member of Landau's group in Berlin.[141] Landau was unaware that Olberg was also an agent of the INO and had worked in Germany as a secret informer among the Trotskyists. In 1930 he tried to get a post as Trotsky's secretary, one of the many attempts to penetrate Trotsky's entourage.[142] During the same year Olberg became one of Landau's followers. In 1935 he was recalled to the USSR.

'The son of a prosperous Viennese wine merchant,' writes Pierre Broué in his own short biography of Landau, 'Kurt Landau had a Bohemian student youth similar to that of many young people from the Jewish intelligentsia in the imperial capitals . . . In 1921 this educated and cultured adolescent joined the new-born Austrian Communist Party',[143] and three years later, still in Vienna, met Victor Serge. Serge was imprisoned in France for his involvement with an anarchist gang and in October 1918, thanks to the Red Cross efforts, was exchanged for Bruce Lockhart. In Russia Serge began working for the Comintern, then headed by Zinoviev, and was sent on a mission to Berlin. In November 1923 he was forced to leave after the failed Communist uprising and he moved to Vienna. By the time he and Landau met, Serge had already been associated with the so-called Left opposition led by Trotsky. Soon Landau was also in opposition to the KPÖ. In July 1929 in Vienna he met one of Trotsky's close associates and soon started corresponding with the exiled Russian revolutionary, now Stalin's enemy number one. Trotsky persuaded Landau to go and settle in

Berlin to make full use of his talents. Aged only 26, Landau was destined to become one of the leaders of the International Left Opposition—this, however, did not happen, as he was soon engaged in a bitter factional struggle, finally coming to the conclusion that Trotsky had been destroying the Left Opposition. In March 1933 he moved with his partner to Paris.

In early November 1936 Landau, also known as 'Agricola', 'Wolf Bertram', and 'Spectator', and his partner Katja (actually Julia Lipschutz, who had been living with him since 1923) arrived in Catalonia. 'He rapidly won substantial influence with the leaders of the POUM which he joined,' Broué writes, 'without abandoning his general strategy of "reforming" the Communist Parties'.[144] The POUM gave Landau the job of working with foreign journalists, writers, and ordinary militiamen. He had his own office and several staff. But the Austrian had other plans in mind. Landau expected that the impetus of the Spanish Revolution would be a beacon for the necessary reorientation of the European working class, which he had desired since the early 1930s and which he now thought a practical possibility through the medium of the POUM.

After the May Days in Barcelona, Landau did not feel safe in the suburb of Sarriá. He asked the advice of Alexander Souchy, a German anarchist, journalist, and writer, who gave him accommodation in the headquarters of the Regional Committee of the Anarcho-Syndicalist CNT in the Via Layetana. Since Souchy went abroad shortly afterwards, he advised Landau not to leave the building in the meantime.[145]

Kurt Landau's Austrian biographer, in a reference to Katja, suggests that, as a Marxist, Kurt was not made welcome in the Anarchist milieu that had given him shelter, and that he thus preferred to look for another refuge.[146] However, in a letter to his Austrian friend in July 1937, Landau wrote: 'In spite of this bloody hard situation, I feel at home like a fish in water.' Paul Thalmann, who met Souchy as soon as he arrived in Barcelona, also recalled seeing Landau in front of the Hotel Falcon hotly discussing the importance of the May Days with Max Diamant and Willy Brandt, who was defending the Popular Front policy. Because by that time the POUM was outlawed, Landau had to go into hiding. It was at that time, when he was living in the suburbs of Barcelona, on a quiet street named Carrer Montserrat de Casanovas in the house of a veteran woman activist of the opposition, that Landau wrote his article 'Bolshevism, Trotskyism and Sectarianism'. He was thinking about the revolution and the class struggle, and almost certainly did not suspect that he had been a hunted man. Although Landau's 'revolutionary' programme was naive, his fate was sealed with the death sentence written in Moscow. Accordingly, Orlov had his specific orders.

Katja Landau wrote:

On 9 October witness Charlotta Durán stepped in front of the Tribunal and made the following declaration: 'I had staying in my apartment in Barcelona a man called Kurt Landau, an Austrian by nationality, and a well-known Marxist writer. On 23 September [1937] about seven o'clock at night two police agents along with an Assault Guard came to arrest Kurt Landau. No search was carried out, but the prisoner was taken off rapidly.'[147]

A week later, the recently appointed Delegado de Orden Público in Catalonia, Paulino Gómez, officially stated that the police had had abso-lutely nothing to do with this arrest.

As she herself had been detained in order to flush him out, Katja Landau was informed of her husband's 'disappearance'. Comrades and friends made enquiries at the Comisariado General de Órden Público and at all the official prisons. It was to no avail. Even Julián Zugazagoitia, who had replaced Ángel Galarza as Minister of Interior, was unable to ascertain the whereabouts of Kurt Landau. Katja demanded a judicial inquiry, and, when the authorities were unable to clarify the fate of her husband, she led a hunger strike.[148] It was clear that Kurt Landau was arrested under the very eyes of the responsible authorities and no official knew where he was. Katja kept on asking: Were these policemen working on their own account? Were they obeying the orders of their superior, the Police Chief, Monsieur Burillo? Where was Kurt Landau taken after his arrest? What has become of him?[149]

Fifty years later, Hans Schafranek, the biographer of Landau, still had the same questions: who had planned, organized, and carried out the kidnap-ping and execution of Landau? He wrote: 'All the clues point to the GPU, but it is almost impossible to know exactly who the people involved were. The murderers knew how to cover their tracks—as they did in numerous similar cases.'[150]

Exactly one month before the arrest of Landau, Orlov reported to the Centre:

Liternoe delo [in this case, assassination operation] of Kurt Landau turned out to be the most difficult of all previous cases . . . He went deep underground and in spite of the fact that for ten days we have been keeping under vigilant surveillance a prominent female anarchist who, according to her disclosure to a source of ours [unidentified], is his courier and sees him every day, we have not so far been able to find him. Landau is without doubt a central figure in the underground organization of the POUM. That is why I suggest we should not 'pick up' Landau at the meeting, but follow him to his residence and take him later in a day or two. As you know, Landau, unlike other foreign *literniks,* has forged close links with local Trotskyite organizations.[151]

The widow of Kurt Landau, Katja, devoted a special chapter of her 1938 brochure *Stalinism in Spain* to the 'Agents of the GPU with Whom We Have Had to Deal'. Among others she named Orlov. 'He speaks German but with a strong Russian accent. He only interrogates in interesting cases; he occasionally strikes prisoners, but generally he would rather give the orders for it.'[152] Katja, who was arrested by the police twice during her husband's ordeal, names two Austrians, Leopold Kulcsar (alias 'Paul Maresch') and his wife Ilse, as the most disgusting collaborators of the NKVD who personally took part in the interrogations. She recalled how Leopold Kulcsar told her word for word:

I have come on a special assignment for the Landau case. My historic mission is to furnish proof that out of twenty Trotskyites eighteen are fascists, agents of Hitler and Franco. Perhaps subjectively you are a good revolutionary, but you are convinced that the victory of Franco would be more favourable to the realisation of your Trotskyite ideas than the victory of Stalinism.[153]

One of the Austrian veterans of the International Brigades, Hans Land-auer, in an interview with this writer, insisted that Katja Landau was wrong when she claimed that Leopold Kulcsar personally interrogated her in Barcelona. 'Papers of the Spanish Ambassador to Czechoslovakia, Luis Jiménez de Asúa, that I saw at the Archivo Histórico Nacional de Madrid,' Landauer said, 'clearly state that Kulcsar was in Spain only between the end of November and the end of December 1937'.[154] The civil war veteran was right about Kulcsar's stay in Spain but wrong about his involvement with Frau Landau. Her testimony checks on this point. The warrant for Katja's arrest ('strong suspicion of military espionage') was signed on 9 December 1937. On 18 December she was transferred to 'a semi-secret prison directly and solely responsible to the departamento'. During the night of 29/30 December 1937, at two o'clock in the morning, she was released thanks to numerous petitions presented by the French socialists, especially Marceau Pivert.[155] Corre, corre, en libertad!

The story of the Kulcsars did not start in Spain. She was born in Vienna as Ilse Pollak and was very active first in the Socialist SDAP, and then in the Communist Youth and the KPÖ. In 1922, aged 20, Ilse married Kulcsar. They had been expelled from the KPÖ in 1926 and had joined the Sozialdemokratische Arbeiterpartei Österreich (SDAPÖ) (Social Democratic Workers' Party of Austria), which had its own paramilitary organization, established in 1923 and known as Schutzbund. After the four-day-long Austrian Civil War, as skirmishes between the Schutzbund and the government forces in February 1934 became known, the Schutzbund was disbanded, and Kulcsar, with his wife, fled to Czechoslovakia, as did many other members of the SDAPÖ. In March–November 1935 Kulcsar actively corresponded with Hugh Gaitskell, a British politician and future leader of the Labour Party from 1955 until his death in 1963. They had become acquainted in Vienna, where Gaitskell had witnessed the suppression of the Marxist-oriented social-democratic workers' movement by the government of Engelbert Dolfuss. Kulcsar sent Gaitskell several letters, mainly concerning the political situation in Austria. In Prague, according to the official documents, Leopold Kulcsar quickly got a job as chief of the press and propaganda department of the Spanish Republican Embassy. But in reality his work had little, if anything, to do with press and propaganda.

Luis Jiménez de Asúa quickly realized the advantages of Prague's geographical position in the heart of Europe. Even before internal restructurings in his ministry in March 1937, when a new Political and Diplomatic Cabinet was created with Anselmo Carretero at the head of the administration of its secret service, which was called Servicio de Información Diplomática Especial (SIDE), the Republican ambassador set up his own special unit within the embassy. This unit, the Servicio de Información e Investigación (SII), headed by Leopold Kulcsar, recruited sources of information wherever it could and collected important political intelligence. The results were very impressive, and the Foreign Ministry under Álvarez del Vayo did not hesitate to cover all its financial expenses. Suffice it to say that in a few months Kulcsar and his SII controlled a wide network of agents in nine countries: Germany (28–31 agents), Czechoslovakia (31), Austria (5),[156] Hungary (1), Poland (1), Romania, Bulgaria, Yugoslavia, and Italy (1 agent for all four countries). Besides, the SII had its own counter-espionage section that used the services of five agents. The result of their work was a considerable number of operational reports, altogether 1,400, some of which had strategic importance.[157] Judging by what Kulcsar did in

Barcelona, it is likely that he had been recruited either in Vienna (where a very experienced NKVD officer named Vasili Roschin was the NKVD legal resident in 1935–8), or in Prague (where Peter Zubov headed the NKVD station in 1937–9). In November 1937 Kulcsar was sent to Spain and started working for Orlov.

Leopold ('Poldi') Kulcsar died in Paris on 28 January 1938 as a result of a kidney problem. His wife, who had been in Madrid since October 1936, had managed to get employed as a censor at the Republican Foreign Ministry's press office, then headed by Luis Rubio Hidalgo. She quickly became a mistress and deputy of her immediate boss, Arturo Barea. In April 1937, John Dos Passos visited the Foreign Press Censorship and met them both. He later remembered 'a cadaverous Spaniard and a plump little pleasant-voiced Austrian woman'.[158]

Vladimir Gorev, the RU resident, was another visitor who came to their small office virtually every morning. Gorev took a burning interest in the articles of foreign correspondents, which were all passing through the censorship.[159] Both Arturo Barea and Ilse Kulcsar had no problem in sharing the previous night's censored dispatches with a high Soviet official, hardly understanding that it was an invaluable source of information—in most cases, first-hand eyewitness accounts. For Gorev, it was an easy and legitimate way to collect intelligence and recheck the reports that he had received from other sources. Gorev was a very experienced spymaster, a former RU resident in New York with the impeccable manners of a real gentleman, according to those who knew him in America.[160] That is perhaps why his favourite articles were those by Herbert Matthews and Sefton Delmer. Ilse even believed that his liberal attitude might have caused him problems with others in the Soviet delegation.[161] Liberal attitude and good manners were, of course, part of Gorev's service duties.

After her husband's death, Ilse Kulcsar married her lover and became Ilse Barea. She and her new husband settled first in France and then moved to England, where she worked for the BBC together with another Austrian exile, George Weidenfeld (later Lord Weidenfeld). Both were employed by the new BBC Overseas Intelligence Department located at Wood Norton, a large manor house near Evesham in Worcestershire. Weidenfeld remembered Ilse only as 'the Viennese-born wife of the distinguished Spanish republican novelist'.[162] In the meantime, she was quite active publishing articles and doing translations. In 1965, Ilse, by that time widowed, returned to Austria. She later worked in Vienna for various trade-union newspapers and went on to outlive her first husband by precisely thirty-five years.

Soon after her release from prison, Katja Landau was deported to France. In Paris she met Ilse Kulcsar again. Katja wrote:

We saw her twice in the Paseo San Juan [in Barcelona], assisting in the interrogations . . . Ilse Kulcsar-Barea is spreading the story here that the Spanish government committed a grave error in releasing me, since I am very deceitful and I should have been made to talk (with the methods of Santa Ursula) because it appears that I know very well where Kurt is, in Rio de Janeiro!'[163]

Kurt Landau was certainly not in Rio. He shared the fate of other 'literniks' from Orlov's death list. One version that circulated among both administrators and inmates was that he had been put to death in the cellars of the Hotel Colón in Barcelona.[164]

In October 1938, when the leaders of the POUM were put on trial, Landau and Nin were both accused *in absentia* of having acted as agents of the Gestapo. Only sixty years later did Russian researchers find out that it was actually the NKVD that had actively collaborated with the Gestapo immediately after the Spanish Civil War.

In March 1937 Stalin himself set out to put the record straight:

The Trotskyites, who represent active elements of the subversive-wrecking and spy activities of the foreign intelligence services, have for a long time ceased to be a political trend in the working-class movement, have for a long time ceased to serve any idea compatible with the interests of the working class, and have turned themselves into an unprincipled gang of wreckers, saboteurs, spies, murderers, lacking any ideological content and working under the hire of the foreign intelligence organizations . . . In the struggle against modern Trotsyism we do not need old methods of discussion, but new methods of rooting out and extermination.[165]

Despite the vast amount of literature on the civil war in Spain, it is still necessary to stress that the Second Spanish Republic was not Stalin's Russia. No one would ever think of calling Largo Caballero or Juan Negrín 'Genghis Khan with a telegraph', a traditional despot with all the power of the modern state at his command—the epithet the great nineteenth-century dissident Alexander Herzen used to describe his fears for twentieth-century Russia. There was a civil war with its tough rules and excesses, but never a dictatorship with show trials and the opposition victims sentenced to death in batches of hundreds. And, though it is true that after the spring of 1937 the NKVD in Spain became increasingly diverted from the war against

Franco and the destruction of Trotskyists became a higher priority, the Centre was in turmoil, caught up in the paranoia of the Great Terror, with most of its officers abroad suspected of plotting with the enemy. With Stalin's Russia, Herzen's nightmare became reality.[166] But that had very little to do with the Spanish Republic.

18

The POUM Affair:
Operation NIKOLAI

In his 1992 interview with Maria Dolors Genovés, the Spanish documentary film director, Oleg Tsarev of the KGB Press Bureau said that 'Orlov was given the task of organizing a show trial: for the first time outside Russia'.[1] That was a great exaggeration, because it was simply not in Orlov's powers to organize show trials. No such trials, in fact, took place in Spain. But Orlov and his accomplices could certainly arrange a provocation. A provocation requires good knowledge of the situation inside the opposing party. This is achieved by recruiting informers and infiltrating agents inside the ranks of the opposition.

The operation against the Partido Obrero de Unificación Marxista (POUM) began with the infiltration of one Alberto Castilla into the Francoist network in Madrid under the alias 'Fernando Velasco'. He knew the ciphers, the system of communication, and the activists. He had also learnt about a number of compromising documents, including the *plano milimetrado* (a scale drawing) produced by the architect Javier Fernández Golfin, a member of the Falange, showing the exact position of the anti-aircraft batteries in the Casa del Campo. Together with other secret documents, this map was allegedly concealed at the Peruvian embassy in Madrid.[2]

On 23 May 1937, Orlov sent the following plan to be approved by Moscow:

Taking into consideration that this case [the arrest of a group of Franco agents], in connection with which the overwhelming majority have pleaded guilty, has produced a great impression on military and government circles, and that it is firmly documented and based on the incontrovertible confessions of defendants, I have decided to use the significance and the indisputable facts of the case to implicate the POUM leadership (whose [possible] connections we are looking into while conducting investigations).

We have, therefore, composed the enclosed document, which indicates the cooperation of the POUM leadership with the Spanish Falange organization—and, through it, with Franco and Germany.

We will encipher the contents of the document using Franco's cipher, which we have at our disposal, and will write it on the reverse side of the plan [*plano milimetrado*] of the location of our weapons emplacements [*sic*] in Casa del Campo, which was taken from the Falangist organization. This document has passed through five people . . . On another seized document we will write in invisible ink a few lines of some insignificant content. It will be from this document that, in cooperation with the Spaniards, we shall begin to scrutinize the document for cryptographic writing. We shall experiment with several processes for treating these papers. A special chemical will develop these few words or lines, then we will begin to test all the other documents with this developer and thus expose the letter we have composed compromising the POUM leadership.

The Spanish chief of counter-intelligence department will leave immediately for Valencia where the cipher department of the War Ministry will decipher the letter. The cipher department, according to our information, has the necessary code at its disposal. But if the department cannot decipher the letter for some reason, then we will 'spend a couple of days' and decipher it ourselves.

We expect this affair to be very effective in exposing the role POUM has played in the Barcelona uprising. The exposure of direct contact between one of its leaders and Franco must contribute to the government adopting a number of administrative measures against the Spanish Trotskyites to discredit POUM as a German–Francoist spy organization.[3]

The reasons for the Soviet and the Comintern/PCE outrage about POU-Mistas were clear: in late August 1936, the POUM publicly denounced executions in the Soviet Union of Kamenev, Zinoviev, and other old Bolsheviks. Besides, Republicans, Socialists, and Communists believed that the advocacy of revolutionary militias by the CNT and the POUM was undermining the war effort.[4] Moreover, Andreu Nin, a former Secretary of the Profintern in Moscow and leader of the POUM, invited Trotsky, then in exile in Norway, to come to Barcelona. With this, the fate of the party was sealed. The subsequent demise of the POUM and the tragic death of its leader were closely linked with the early May skirmishes in Catalonia.

Orlov's plan was eventually approved. Then Grigulevich, who could speak and write Spanish, was ordered to insert a certain text on the reverse of the scale plan of Madrid in invisible ink. This is what he wrote: 'Al Generalísimo personalmente comunico:—En complimento de su orden, fui yo mismo a Barcelona para entrevistarme con el miembro directivo del POUM, "N"(. . .) El me ha prometido enviar nueva gente a

Madrid para activar los trabajos del POUM. Con estos refuerzos, el POUM llegará a ser un firme y eficaz apoyo de nuestro movimento' [Personal communication to the Generalissimo: In executing your order, I went to Barcelona to interview a member of the leadership of the POUM, 'N'(...) He promised me to send new people to Madrid to activate the work of the POUM. With this reinforcement, the POUM will become a firm and effective supporter of our movement].[5]

Some time later Orlov decided to improve the text. This is what finally appeared as 'firm evidence' of the POUM's treacherous activities:

To the Generalissimo. I communicate personally the following: We are telling you all the information we can collect about the dispositions and movements of the Red troops; the latest information given out by our transmitting station testifies to an enormous improvement in our information services. We have 400 men at our disposal. These men are well armed and favourably situated on the Madrid fronts so that they can form the driving force of a rebellious movement. Your order about getting our men to penetrate into the extremist ranks has been successfully carried out. We must have a good man in charge of propaganda. In executing the order you gave me, amongst other things, I went to Barcelona to interview the leaders of the POUM. I gave them all your information and suggestions. The lapse of communication between them and you is explained by the breakdown of the transmitting station, which began to work again while I was there. You should already have had an answer about the most important question. N. asks that you should arrange that I should be the only person to communicate with them apart from their 'foreign friends'. They have promised me to send people to Madrid to ginger up the work of the POUM. If it is reinforced, the POUM here will become, as it is at Barcelona, a firm and effective support for our movement. We shall soon be sending you some fresh information. The organization of the action groups will be speeded up.[6]

Orlov and his agents managed to pass their forgeries to the counter-espionage service of the Comisaría General de Madrid, whose chief pre-pared a detailed report addressed to the director general of the DGS and Minister of Interior (Julián Zugazagoitia).[7] Conveniently, the Director General of Security was the recently appointed Communist, Colonel Antonio Ortega. Then Orlov asked Ortega to issue special orders to the Brigada Especial de la Comisaria General de Investigación y Vigilancia de Madrid and provide it with warrants to arrest Nin and other POUM leaders. In his memoirs, published sixteen years after the events, a former minister and member of the PCE Politburo, Jesús Hernández, wrote about Ortega's call to him immediately after Orlov's visit to the Interior Ministry and about his personal meeting with the NKVD station chief thereafter.

The version of their dialogue presented in detail in Hernández's book—as shall be proved, entirely invented by the author—helped Orlov to escape deportation from the USA in the 1950s. In the first place, Hernández's physical description of Orlov is wrong: 'He was almost two meters tall, with elegant and refined manners. He spoke Spanish with some facility. He was not more than forty-five years old.' In reality, Lev Nikolsky, who operated in Spain under the alias of Alexander M. Orlov, was about 5 feet 8 inches (less than 173 cm) tall, rather pleasant-looking, with a typical boxer nose and dark moustache. He spoke no Spanish at all and was always accompanied by his personal interpreter. In 1937 Nikolsky was 42 years old, and he looked his age.[8] In the second place, the topic of their discussion, its style, manner, and even lexica, all seem highly inappropriate and improbable.[9] If any meeting with an NKVD official indeed took place, it was perhaps with Belkin (alias Belyaev)—rather tall, elegant, with aristocratic face, good manners, and good command of French—but certainly not with Orlov.[10] One should remember that it was Belkin who was sent to Negrín after Orlov's *faux pas* in presenting the POUM case to the prime minister.

Moreover, some recently published documents show that Jesús Hernández was not exactly the person he made himself out to be in his memoirs.[11] In his book, Hernández presents himself combating Orlov:

'My friend Orlov,' I said, 'let's talk seriously. Your people want to put on a big trial against the Trotskyites in Spain, as a demonstration of the reason you shot the opposition in the USSR . . . So I understand your interest perfectly. But let's not complicate life, which is complicated enough already. If you wish, we can devote a special page in our newspapers, every day, to denounce them as a gang of enemies of the people, but let's not stage sensational spectacles, because nobody will believe them.'

'But if we have the proofs!' exclaimed Orlov.

'If I know your "apparatus", I'm aware they are able to manufacture dollars out of wrapping paper.'

'That's an absurdity—and an impermissible opinion,' muttered Orlov, obviously angry and upset.[12]

Finally, even if the discussion with any NKVD representative had taken place as described by Hernández, it would have been meaningless because, as the KGB documents clearly demonstrate, Orlov had orders from Moscow and could not have cared less about what Hernández thought.

The report to the DGS and the Ministry of the Interior specifically stressed that the whole investigation work in the POUM case should be entrusted to the police of Madrid. However, it took Ortega almost two weeks to issue appropriate orders to David Vázquez Baldominos, who was appointed Commissar General of the Cuerpo de Investigación y Vigilancia on 12 June.[13] The latter called Commissar Fernando Valentí, who commanded a squad of the mentioned Brigada Especial, and informed him of a new assignment. From that moment on, all their movements were documented and now make part of the document collection accurately filed in a blue folder entitled 'POUM Expediente' (POUM Record) at the Archivo Histórico Nacional de Madrid.[14] What has been overlooked so far is that Valentí had maintained direct contact with Orlov and 'la mujer de Casanellas' (the wife of Casanellas)[15]—that is, the Soviet illegal Maria Fortus, who lived in Barcelona and 'was planted into the Grupo de Investigación'[16] operating there as 'Julia Jiménez Cárdenas'. She, in turn, was also in contact with Grigulevich.

Officers of the Special Brigade moved from the vicinity of Madrid to Valencia in two cars, after Javier Jiménez and two other young members of the Brigade (Carlos Ramallo and Manuel Aguirre) had allegedly visited what Jiménez later called 'the General Staff (Estado Mayor) of the GPU at the Hotel Gaylord'. This episode was almost certainly invented by Jiménez, as neither he nor his young colleagues had anything to do in the Gaylord at that particular time and, as Jiménez himself admitted, were 'no dicen ni a dónde ni a qué'—that is, did not get any specific instructions about the nature of their next day's mission. From Madrid the group moved to Valencia, where Grigulevich, who, unbeknownst to them, represented the NKVD, joined the group. As usual, he had a Brazilian document identifying him as 'José Escoy' and a Spanish security service badge, and took his place in the same car as the chiefs—Commissar Valentí and Special Agent Jacinto Rossell—while Jiménez travelled with Ramallo and Aguirre.[17] From Valencia they moved on to Barcelona. The chief of the police, Lieutenant Colonel Ricardo Burillo, already knew of their arrival from a letter dispatched by Ortega. Valentí, Ramallo, and Rossell, accompanied by Grigulevich, went directly to the Soviet Consulate, while the others were quartered elsewhere to spend the night of 15 June, until the operation, of which they were not yet fully informed,[18] was given the final go-ahead. On the morning of 16 June, the Special Brigade officers[19] found out that their chiefs had spent the night at the consulate and that their task would be to arrest the POUM leaders.

On that day, Nin was very busy preparing the POUM annual conference, which was to take place three days later, and planning his party's tactics in the context of the Catalan political situation. According to his own words, at one point a young anarchist, Ramón Liarte, had warned Nin of the danger of arrest.[20] (It would be interesting to know how the young man could have learnt about it.) Nin ignored the warning. Wilebaldo Solano, one of the POUM leaders and a participant in 'Los Hechos de Mayo' (May Days), gave a detailed description of the day's sequence of events. He recalled that the meeting of the executive committee started at ten o'clock in the morning and was chaired by Nin. The committee had decided to meet, not in the party building at No. 30 Rambla de los Estudios, but in a quiet assembly hall of the Virreina Palace. Those present were Pedro Bonet, Juan Andrade, Jordi Arquer, Julián Gorkin, Enrique Gironella, Narcis Molins i Fábrega, and Solano. Josep Rovira, commander of the 29th Division, was at the front. Nin spoke first and analysed the political and military situation. Then there were three important problems to discuss: how to defend the POUM press; what remained to be done before the POUM met for its congress on 19 June; and questions related to preparations of an important international conference of independent Communists and Socialists. At about one o'clock the meeting was over, and Nin, Bonet, and others went in the direction of the POUM executive committee building. On the way, he was warned for a second time that his life was in danger. Nin laughed and said, 'They wouldn't dare!' ('No se atreveran'). Moments later he was arrested near the Virreina Palace and taken to the building of the Juventud Comunista Ibérica on the Paseo de Gracia. The last witness to see Nin at the police station was a POUM member, Teresa Carbó, who was still alive in 1992 to be interviewed by the Catalonian television team.[21]

In his testimony, Javier Jiménez Martín, a former officer of the Special Brigade, declared that Nin was then escorted first to Valencia and then to Madrid by 'los comisarios' Fernando Valentí, Jacinto Rosell, and José Escoy (Grigulevich).[22] Here he was placed at the detention centre in Atocha, which could not offer sufficient security. Then an 'old representative of foreign technicians', as the NKVD advisers were called in internal correspondence, suggested moving Nin to a house in Alcalá de Henares, where he could be interrogated in secrecy for two or three days. There is no doubt that this was Orlov. Special Agent Rosell conducted the interviews. According to the documents at the Archivo Histórico Nacional, on 18, 19, and 21 June, Nin filed four protests accusing the Communist Party of conspiracy in organizing his detention.[23]

¿Dónde está Nin? Where is Nin? This question, which became familiar in many languages, but not Russian, was asked by the whole progressive world in the days that followed. After studying all documentary material collected by Maria Dolors Genovés and her team, two Spanish historians from Alcalá de Henares concluded that, on 22 June, Nin had been transferred to the chalet that belonged to Rafael Esparza, a former Cortes deputy who had been killed in the Model Prison in Madrid in August 1936.[24]

What was the point of moving the prisoner? Orlov was sure that his plan would work and that, under duress, Nin would finally break down and sign the confession that had been prepared for him. But the POUM leader was in his own country, surrounded by his own people, the Republican police officers whom he had no reason to be afraid of. The worst thing that could happen to him would be a public trial, which could prove nothing in terms of the POUM relations with Franco, his agents, or the Fifth Column. Nin was evidently not tortured (law-enforcement officers could have never expected that their prominent detainee would be murdered, so any hostile interrogation was out of the question), contrary to what has been stated by some historians.[25] The only evidence they have are books published by Hernández and Gabriel Morón.[26] There is no documentary proof that Nin was tortured and no witnesses.

Following Nin's arrest, the NKVD station continued its dirty games. A report to Moscow mentioned the government communiqué issued after Nin's disappearance that the DGS had seized incriminating documents 'indicating that the POUM leadership, namely Andrés Nin, was mixed up in espionage'.[27]

At some point Orlov decided to resort to a trick that had been known to him since one of the NKVD station officers, Syroezhkin, took part in a top secret undercover 'false flag' operation ten years earlier. The TREST/TRUST and SINDIKAT/SYNDICATE deceptions were intended to give the anti-Bolshevik émigrés in Europe the impression that there was a strong opposition to the regime and a powerful underground movement, thus luring them into the Cheka's claws. The same trick was sometimes used inside Russia during the Great Terror, when certain selected victims were approached by the NKVD officers posing as the Gestapo or British agents in order to prove their involvement with espionage.

According to the eyewitnesses' testimonies, on the night of 22 June, between 21.30 and 22.00, in a heavy rainstorm, a group of uniformed men appeared in the chalet headed by a captain and a lieutenant, the latter speaking Spanish with a heavy foreign accent. They produced documents signed by General José Miaja and Colonel Ortega ordering the guards to hand over their prisoner to the new escort. Then the 'assailants' over-powered the guards and took Nin away. The witnesses heard the captain, a Spaniard, speaking in a very friendly manner with the POUM leader and calling him 'camarada'. Moreover, they left plenty of evidence that could easily identify the intruders as Nazi agents and Franco's supporters.

As in every KGB operation, Orlov's aim in staging the show was twofold. It was his last attempt to make Nin swallow the bait and let himself be liberated (without suspecting the true intentions of his 'liberators'), therefore confirming his affiliation with the 'fascists'; and it was intended to give credence to the additional evidence conveniently left on the scene in the form of photographs, bank receipts, and so on, of Nin's direct contacts with foreign spies. Orlov and Grigulevich sat watching from their car as Nin was escorted from the chalet. JUZIK's police badge was to protect them in case the car was stopped and searched by patrols on the road.[28] As usual, they were very well armed.

Altogether there were six men who took part in the abduction operation: Orlov (SCHWED), Grigulevich (JUZIK), Tacke (BOM), Nezhinsky (VIKTOR), and two Spaniards known only by their initials 'L' and 'A—F—'. The Spaniard 'L', possibly Lacasa, and the German Tacke were probably posing as the 'captain' and the 'lieutenant', while others were waiting for them outside the chalet. Without offering any resistance, Nin went out and took his place in the car, which drove south-east in the direction of Perales de Tajuña. After about 20 kilometres the car stopped. It is not known, and will probably never be known, what happened on the way and whether the captors and the victim exchanged any words. The group disembarked and, according to Victor, the driver, went 100 metres out into the field. It was almost certainly Grigulevich who shot Nin.[29] For him, it was not the first and certainly not the last murder.

Orlov later told the FBI that, as the American historian Stanley Payne put it, 'meanwhile Stalin issued a handwritten order, which remains in the KGB archives, that Nin be killed',[30] never admitting his role in the operation. In reality, the dictator had rarely issued verbal orders on such matters and had never ever signed any document that could incriminate him in any crime committed by the NKVD on foreign soil.

As to what Moscow planned to do with Nin and his small party, the answer can be found in the events that had been developing in Moscow at the same time. On 22 May 1937 one of the most senior military leaders of the Soviet Union, Marshal Mikhail Tukhachevsky, was secretly arrested and accused of conspiring against the state. Tukhachevsky's interrogation was personally supervised by the new chief of the NKVD, Orlov's boss and Stalin's loyal hangman, Nikolai Yezhov. Stalin wanted a full confession and an admission of guilt. And an incredible thing happened: within just a few days the famous marshal confessed that he was a German spy, a Gestapo agent, and a leader of a gang of eight other senior officers acting on Trotsky's instructions. Like Tukhachevsky, all others were broken. During the trial on 11 June they were dubbed the 'Trotskyite anti-Soviet military organization', declared guilty, and sentenced to death. All were shot on the same night. After that, could Stalin or Yezhov doubt for a minute that Nin would be quickly broken and confess that he had been an agent of Franco all along? With their perverted mentality they thought it was possible. Orlov's plan was approved, reported to the Big Boss (Yezhov), maybe even to Stalin, and agreed upon. It did not work, so there was nothing left but to murder Nin.[31] Victor, the driver, who must have remained in the car while the shooting took place, was the author of a hastily handwritten note specifying the place and the participants. The note found its separate way to the Lubyanka registry. Nin disappeared—no one was punished.

Though hundreds of people were detained, in fact, nearly 1,000, contrary to the official DGS statement,[32] there was no Stalinist show trial, and not a single defendant was accused of espionage. Even if Nin had been brought to trial, he would most certainly not have been condemned to death. He would have been tried with full legal guarantees, as in fact happened in the trials of all of his POUM comrades in October 1938. That must have been clearly understood in both Moscow and the NKVD station in Valencia, and that is what led to the tragic outcome of Operation NIKOLAI.

When the POUM leaders came to trial, the case against them collapsed. Republican ministers and ex-ministers gave evidence in the POUM's favour. Gironella, the young leader who had organized the POUM militia, addressed the prosecutor, to the general scandal, as 'Vyshinsky'. Arquer insisted on testifying in Catalan. Grandizo Munis, the only real Trotskyist, declared that the POUM were in no way Trotskyists. The judgers acquitted the POUM of treason and espionage.[33] When he was later in exile, an American journalist asked Juan Negrín why his government had not acted more steadfastly when it came to defending the interests of the Republic in court. 'Because you don't get proof,' answered Negrín. 'You couldn't get proof before the judges.' 'But surely in such a crisis you suspended normal court procedures,' the journalist suggested. 'Oh yes, we had to have special courts,' said Negrín. 'But we couldn't arrest a man on suspicion. We had to keep to the system of evidence. You can't arrest an innocent man just because you are positive in your own mind that he is guilty. You prosecute a war, yes; but you also live with your conscience.'[34]

The exact date of Nin's assassination will probably never be known beyond the fact that he obviously perished after 22 June 1937. In late July, Orlov reported to the Centre that the last participant of the operation (Grigulevich) had already departed for Moscow. That must mean that both Spaniards also left for Moscow during that period.[35]

In the last five to ten years of his life, Juan Negrín thought about writing his own personal memoirs of some of the key episodes of war, and his notes that exist in slightly different versions include the Nin case. The former Prime Minister writes that he learned that the POUM leader had disappeared while attending a farewell lunch for General Douglas (Yakov Smushkevich, senior adviser for aviation) at the Soviet Embassy—that is, on 17 June. According to his notes, after lunch Negrín went directly to the Ministry of the Interior and was surprised to learn that nobody, including the minister (Zugazagoitia) and the DGS director general (Ortega), knew anything definite about what had happened to Nin after his arrest. He then instructed the DGS chief to use all possible means to find Nin, and to keep him informed. After several days, the Prime Minister was surprised that Ortega was unable to report anything. At the Cabinet session that followed, Negrín presented the decree for Ortega's dismissal. At the same time, one of the Cabinet members (almost certainly Giral) suddenly informed Negrín that Ortega 'had fallen into the Communist Party network'. If one has to believe what the former Prime Minister writes in his memoirs, he never knew about Ortega's affiliation with the PCE.[36] Ortega's resignation was accepted on 20 July.[37]

Some weeks passed and the situation did not become clearer. Finally, the Soviet Embassy called Negrín's office and asked him to receive a visitor whom he never knew by name but who eight months earlier had been introduced to him as one 'Blackstone', an attaché responsible for the security of the 'golden cargo'. 'In his new incarnation,' writes Negrín's biographer, 'this individual turned out to be Orlov, with a briefcase full of documents proving that Nin had been taken to Madrid, then to Alcalá, that his guards had locked him in the house and gone to a bar, that Falange friends of Nin pretending to be Brigadistas had entered and taken him by an oft-used route to the Franco front'.[38] Negrín, without doubt, did not believe a word, but politely remarked that the story was too perfect to be credible. After Orlov had replied angrily that the Spanish Prime Minister was offending the Soviet Union, Negrín showed him the door.

When Sergey Marchenko, the Soviet chargé d'affaires who replaced Ambassador Rosenberg, visited Negrín's office shortly after, Negrín said he had not attached any importance to Orlov's words, to which Marchenko replied: 'It was very kind indeed of you'. In his memoirs Negrín also recalled that Marchenko assured him that the Soviets took the matter seriously and that Orlov had been removed from embassy employment,[39] which was not the case. Whether Marchenko, under the circumstances, really pronounced those words, or it was only wishful thinking on behalf of the Prime Minister, will almost certainly remain unknown, but the fact is that Orlov not only carried on as chief of the NKVD in Spain, but also continued to received from Moscow new 'special tasks'.

At the end of the day, Nin's death turned out to be profitable to many. The POUM, though banned as a political movement and with its newspaper *La Batalla* closed, became a martyr, and the Nin case echoes in many publications until this day.[40] In Madrid, the leading political parties, and not only Communists, had long been seeking to break 'libertarian Barcelona', since, as noted by Helen Graham,

it challenged the model and very validity of the liberal policy and society they were seeking to reconstruct... Faced with external embargo, it needed to mobilize its domestic economic and human resources to the maximum in order to ensure survival let alone victory. And this made urban, industrial, populous Catalonia the *sine qua non* of a successful modern Republican war effort.[41]

In Moscow, Yezhov was able to report to the Master of the House, feeling at the top of his power. A year later, asking Stalin to discharge him from his NKVD post, Yezhov, admitting many shortcomings, proudly stated: 'In spite of all, when I headed the NKVD the enemy were put to rout splendidly.'[42] Whether he had this murder in mind among many others cannot be known. At the same time, one should not be misled by the image of the Stalin secret police as a well-organized, highly disciplined intelligence service. The records reveal disorganization, fiscal and operational disaster, bootstrap techniques, double-dealing, and a striking degree of tension and internal rivalry at the highest levels of the OGPU, NKVD, and their successor organizations. The problem sprang from multiple causes, such as bureaucratic empire-building, the frustration of always working at the limit of available resources, fear, and Stalin's paranoia. But the real Achilles' heel of Soviet intelligence between the wars was that the various individuals and groups involved were under constant pressure from Moscow to achieve goals that were impossible to attain.[43] Andreu Nin became the principal *cause célèbre* in the Republican zone for the remainder of the war and for many years after it was over.

19

Murder in Lausanne

The activities of Stalin's secret police could not impact on the outcome of the civil war in Spain. Remarkably, during the same time, the NKVD abducted and murdered people in other parts of Europe. Although the case of Ignatz Reiss, a former colleague of Nikolsky/Orlov, is different from those described in the previous chapters, it was part of the same 'special tasks' that began to dominate the NKVD foreign operations in 1937.

It happened in Chamblandes near Lausanne, Switzerland, on 4 September 1937, and the victim was shot and murdered by three NKVD assassins supported by two reserve teams. Orlov never provided details of this case, mentioning it only casually once or twice mainly in connection with 'a criminal named DOUGLAS [Spiegelglass]', as he wrote in a letter to Yezhov, meaning his former boss, who was in charge of the operation against the defector.

The NKVD damage assessment after Reiss, one of their experienced recruiters and agent-runners in Europe had defected and disappeared with his family from their Paris apartment, concluded that he had probably betrayed Arnold Deutsch, Philby's recruiter, whom Reiss knew. Therefore, in November 1937 Deutsch was recalled to Moscow, not, like many others, to be shot, but because his chiefs believed Reiss and other traitors had compromised him.[1] That would indeed happen, but only three years later, when a friend of Reiss would be interviewed by MI5 in the comfort of the London Langham, Europe's first grand hotel. This friend's name was Samuel Ginsberg, better known as Walter Krivitsky, who defected shortly after Reiss had been murdered.

It is hardly surprising that until this day the successors of Stalin's secret police continue to publish tales and disseminate disinformation about Reiss. One legend claims that 'the real name of a person also known as Ignatij Stanislavovich Poretski is Natan Markovich Reiss'. Amazingly, KGB fabricators try to humiliate the defector even decades after his death.[2] Documents in the Austrian archives make it clear that this former Soviet intelligence operator, who decided to break with the NKVD in the summer of 1937, protesting against Stalin's policy, was born in Podwołoczyska on the territory of the Austro-Hungarian Empire as Ignatz Reiss, the son of Johim (Joachim) Reiss.[3] Although the Reiss operation is seemingly well known, Orlov's part in it, as well as some other important details, still remained obscure.

The Swiss NKVD agent Renate Steiner, who was the first to be detained in connection with the murder of Reiss, confessed that she had brought a box of candy—strychnine-filled candy found in the luggage of one of the assassins—from Paris, where it was given to her on 25 August by a certain 'Leo'. Two Frenchmen, Pierre Louis Ducomet and Charles Martignat, introduced her to this 'Leo'. During her interrogation Steiner testified that 'Leo' had enquired whether she could drive a car and, when she told him she had a driving licence, gave her the candy and a letter for 'Rossi' (another assassin). Rossi was meeting her in Berne.[4] Mysterious 'Leo' remains unidentified. In the meantime, this is what Orlov testified under oath to the US Senate Subcommittee:

Mr SOURWINE. Did you, at one time, have an acquaintance with an NKVD official named Alexeev?

Mr ORLOV. Yes, I knew Alexeev well.

Mr SOURWINE. Where was that and what was his position?

Mr ORLOV. I first met Alexeev in 1933 in Vienna where he worked under the command of a close friend of his. Later I met him at the beginning of 1937 in France in the French Embassy [that is, the Soviet Embassy in Paris] a number of times when I used to come from Spain on business to Paris.

Working in Spain I used to visit France on business very often. I met all of the [NKVD] officers there and I met Alexeev, I met that Alexeev there. This Alexeev was a junior officer whom I had previously met in 1933 when he worked under a close friend of mine with whom we fought in the civil war on the western front. Being a junior officer, Alexeev, as is the custom in the service, tried to ingratiate himself with me to show his usefulness because I was the man who could promote him, arrange a transfer to my office, and things like that...

Mr SOURWINE. This was in the summer of 1937?

Mr ORLOV. That was in 1937, sometime in the summer.[5]

The real name of 'Alexeyev' was Boris Afanasyev, codenamed GAMMA. He was a Soviet 'illegal' and a member of the Serebryansky Administration for Special Tasks. He was posted to Vienna in 1932–3, when Nikolsky/Orlov used to meet him. In the summer of 1937, Afanasyev was operating in Paris. Together with Roland Abbiate, Charles Martignat, and Gertrude Schildbach, he was one of the assassins of Reiss at Chamblandes. It is almost certain that 'Leo', who, according to Steiner, spoke Russian and German,[6] was Lev Nikolsky alias Alexander Orlov. Krivitsky also knew him as 'Leo'.

Orlov never mentioned the name of Abbiate and was never asked about the man. Unbeknownst to him, he could meet him in New York, where this NKVD assassin served as a TASS correspondent during the whole war. Roland Jacques Claude Abbiate was born on 15 August 1905 in London to a mixed family of a French–Italian Monegasque father and a Russian–Jewish mother whose maiden name was Mandelstamm. With a British passport issued in Nice, Abbiate arrived in the United States in December 1925. In April 1926 he was arrested for impersonating an immigration officer, jailed for two years, and then deported to the UK. According to his Russian biography, from 1929 to 1932 Abbiate lived in Nice. He was allegedly recruited to the OGPU in 1932, and five years later became a Soviet citizen with the name of 'Vladimir Sergeyevich Pravdin'. At the time of the Reiss affair he was using the alias 'Dr Benoit', but then also became known to the French police as 'François Rossi'. During the investigation of the Reiss case, a map of Mexico City and its suburbs and a duplicate of his application for a visa to visit Mexico were found in Abbiate's room. As one Trotsky sympathizer put it, the purpose of his visit was unmistakable. Although back in 1937 he was 'burned'—that is, compromised as a Soviet agent—from 1941 to 1946 Abbiate (as Pravdin) worked for the TASS news agency in New York at the same time serving as the NKVD station chief there. His wife, Olga Borisovna Pravdina, was employed by Amtorg, and identified by Elizabeth Bentley as a woman known to her only as 'Margaret' (the name of Abbiate's mother). This 'Margaret' acted as Bentley's controller. Although his KGB biography states that Pravdin was discharged from the service in 1947, the post-war Soviet defector Anatoly Golitsyn claims that he operated in post-war Austria, often passing as a Frenchman. Golitsyn, of course, was well known to both CIA and SIS stations in Vienna as a KGB officer in charge of Line EM (émigrés), but it seems Abbiate remained unnoticed. He was dismissed from what was now called the MGB in 1948, but was back at the Lubyanka headquarters between May and July 1953. MI5 kept him on their active watch list at least until 1954, noting alongside his already known alias of 'Rossi' two previously unknown cover names: 'Georges Quinn' and 'Roland Smith'.[7] According to Mitrokhin's notes, Pravdin committed suicide in Moscow in 1970.

After the body of Reiss had been found, Swiss and French police under the leadership of Robert Jacquillard in Lausanne started the hunt for the murderers. It was quickly established that a group of White Russian émigrés living in Paris had also taken part in the operation. Steiner, the young Swiss woman recruited by the NKVD in Paris a year before and arrested in connection with the Reiss case (together with Vadim Kondratyev she was part of the support group in Lausanne), named Dmitry Smirensky and Pierre Ducomet, who were subsequently arrested in Paris. Sergey Efron, the husband of Marina Tsvetayeva, one of the finest twentieth-century poets, was identified as their leader. This, in turn, led the investigators to the Union for Repatriation and the Union des Amis de la Patrie Soviétique (Union of the Friends of the Soviet Homeland), where Efron had an office. They soon found out that both organizations were used as NKVD fronts and recruitment centres. Nikolai Klepinin, Vadim Kondratyev, Vera Gouchkova (later Traill), Anatoly Chistoganov, N. V. Afanasov, and Ariadna ('Alya') Efron were active agents.

On 22 October 1937 police searched the office of Union for Repatriation and Efron's flat. They found nothing, and Tsvetayeva assured them that she was completely unaware of her husband's affiliation with the NKVD. On the request of the Swiss authorities, Lydia Grozovskaya, the wife of Reiss's NKVD supervisor, who worked with her husband for the Soviet Trade Delegation in Paris, was also detained.

The Swiss newspaper *La Revue* commented:

[The enquiry established] who were the agents of the GPU who organized the trailing of Reiss over many months... Unfortunately, as the French press had already revealed, as soon as the French police succeeded in uncovering a new accomplice, the latter disappeared precisely at the moment when it was possible for steps to be taken against him. That is the case, among others, with the three Russians, Beletsky and Grosovsky [*sic*], who went to Russia, and Serge Erfon, who went to Spain.

Although Smirensky (who lived in France as 'Monsieur Rollin') was arrested, Efron, Kondratyev, and Klepinin escaped via Spain, where they without doubt reported to Orlov before boarding a Soviet vessel 'port out, starboard home'. Naturally, Orlov never mentioned this episode in his writings. Very soon they found themselves settled in a safe house in Bol-shevo, a railway station about 16 miles away from Moscow, in the settlement called 'The New Way of Life' (Novy Byt) provided by the NKVD. In Russia Efron used the alias 'Andreyev', while Klepinin and his wife became the 'Lvovs'.

Marina Tsvetayeva and their son Georgy ('Mour') Efron returned to Moscow in June 1939 and joined the others in the house.

On 27 August 1939 Ariadna Efron was arrested. She was 27. A young man whom she loved and considered her fiancé in reality was an NKVD agent assigned to spy on the family. Sergey Efron was arrested six weeks later, on 10 October. The NKVD devoted a month of round-the-clock interrogations to get Ariadna to testify on paper that her father was a foreign agent. And they spent another nine months and eighteen interrogations on Sergey before sentencing him to death. During the investigation, Alya was persuaded to write: 'Unwilling to conceal anything from the prosecution I must report that my father is an agent of the French intelligence service'.[8] Klepinin, in order to protect himself and his family, also chose to incriminate Tsvetayeva's husband. According to one report, at his closed-door trial in 1941 Efron declared: 'I was not a spy. I was an honest agent of Soviet intelligence.' Nevertheless the sentence claimed that 'a group of the White émigrés consisting of S. Ya. Efron (Andreyev), N. A. Klepinin (Lvov), A. N. Klepinina (Lvova), E. E. Litauer and N. V. Afanasov arrived in Moscow to conduct espionage against the USSR'. Irma Kudrova, the Russian author who has studied the investigation files, writes about a web of fabrications so intricate it could almost be believed—and indeed, was believed—until Efron was officially exonerated in 1956.

Ariadna spent sixteen years in various prisons and concentration camps. In one of her letters to the KGB, asking about the fate of her father, she wrote that in Moscow she met Elisaveta Alekseyevna Khenkina, mother of Kirill Khenkin. Efron's daughter mentioned that Khenkina worked with their group in France and later Spain.

When Alya was released in 1965, she set about exonerating her parents' good name. Yet, despite her long years in the Gulag, she remained a Communist. When Ariadna Efron died in 1975, she left instructions that her mother's notebooks and most of her letters be sealed until 2000. Part of this collection was published in Moscow in 2008.

The flight of Efron and other agents inspired some bitter remarks from Robert Jacquillard, in a memo dated November 1937, addressed to the Political Authorities of the Confederation and the Canton of Vaud, Switzerland. He indulged in a full-length argument in favour of banning the Swiss Communist Party. 'In some countries the police and judicial action are to a great extent brought about after political interventions,' he stated. 'Our western neighbour, now that it is governed by the Popular Front, has shown an excessive tolerance for the activities of the political agents of its ally, the USSR, and of its terrorist henchmen.' According to Jacquillard, under the cloak of the right of asylum, France held a mass of sinister people, 'just as in the Canton of Vaud the Communist Party includes an important number of the criminal and mentally sick'. And he added that all those who had fought in Spain in the Swiss Brigade, whose return was imminent, 'would constitute a social danger which was all the greater since they had taken part in merciless war... One can perhaps reply that the outlawing of Communism, which can be done in several cantons here, should be a sufficient obstacle.'[9] Soon, the Communist Party was banned in Geneva, Vaud, and Neuchâtel, and went underground.

On 10 November 1937 Sloutsky wrote a report requesting that decorations be conferred upon a group of INO officers 'for the self-sacrificing and successful services to the Soviet government' (i.e. for the murder of Ignatz Reiss and abduction of General Miller). Three days later, a secret decree of the All-Russian Central Executive Committee named Spiegelglass S. M. to be awarded the Order of Lenin; Pravdin V. S. (Roland Abbiate), Grigoryev M. V., Kosenko G. N., Grazhul V. S., Afanasyev B. M., and Dolgorukov A. L. the Order of the Red Banner; Arsenyeva M. S. (Mireille Abbiate) the Order of the Red Star.[10] All other participants of the operation were shot.

More than half a century after the murder of Ignatz Reiss, the Soviet authorities demonstrated that they did not change much from the Stalinist times. In his official reply to the letter sent by two Swiss historians to the Commission for Rehabilitation, the public prosecutor of the USSR wrote on 8 June 1990: 'Ignace Reiss, born in 1899, was serving abroad. During 1937 he refused to return to the USSR after misappropriating a large sum of money and some highly secret documents... No legal case was opened against Ignace Reiss, and thus there is no need to begin a procedure of rehabilitation.'[11] Formally, they were, of course, perfectly right: as in the case of another Soviet defector, Georges Agabekov, Reiss has never been tried and sentenced. Like every other 'liternik', he was simply 'liquidated'. The French Ministry of Interior study 'A Soviet Counter-Espionage Network Abroad: The Reiss Case', published on 20 September 1951, stated: 'The assassination of Ignace Reiss on 4 September 1937 at Chamblandes near Lausanne, Switzerland, is an excellent example of the observation, surveillance and liquidation of a "deserter" from the Soviet secret service.'[12] Even after the collapse of the Soviet Union, such 'special operations' never stopped.

20

1938 and Beyond

The early months of 1938 were gloomy and hectic. On 1 January the California Golden Bears defeated the Alabama Crimson Tide in a Rose Bowl. In February, Sir Anthony Eden resigned as British Foreign Secretary following major disagreements with Prime Minister Neville Chamberlain. And in March German troops occupied Austria, announcing its annexation into the Third Reich. By 1938 Serebryansky's Administration for Special Tasks was by far the largest section of Soviet foreign intelligence, claiming to have 212 'illegals' operating in sixteen countries. Mitrokhin's notes from the secret KGB archives clearly show that, after Trotskyists, the largest number of 'enemies of the people' pursued by the NKVD during the Great Terror came from the ranks of Soviet intelligence services.[1] And defectors from those services were always at the top of the execution lists.

On 2 July 1930, eight years before the first government visitors appeared in Bletchley Park, the Secret Intelligence Service intercepted a telegram sent from the Moscow OGPU headquarters to its station housed at the Soviet Embassy in Berlin. At that time Nikolsky/Orlov was one of the station's officers under cover on the staff of the trade delegation, but the telegram was not for him. It was marked for a 'Comrade Veresayev', the code name assigned to the head of the Berlin station Nikolai Samsonov, alias 'Golst'.[2] An urgent message from Moscow informed him that his agent networks were now in danger as a result of the defection of a high-ranking OGPU official named Grigory Sergeyevich Arutyunov, aka Georges Agabekov. The telegram read: 'An especially dangerous situation has arisen for those comrades who were in touch with our organization in Constantinople up to the 24/6/30 [the date when Agabekov defected].' A list of ten agents followed and it was said that they were to return to Moscow at once. Three others were ordered to 'change their places of residence forthwith and temporarily cease activity'.[3] Without doubt the dictator was duly informed and made appropriate conclusions, and all necessary measures were taken to effect Agabekov's assassination—for the time being, to no avail.

Grigory Sergeyevich Arutyunov, alias 'Nerses Ovsepyan',[4] who became better known under his alias 'Georges Agabekov', an OGPU official in charge of its Eastern Section, was one of the first Soviet defectors and the author of two volumes of valuable memoirs published in the West as one small book.[5] As a matter of fact, Agabekov was the very first Soviet defector to come from the top ranks of the Soviet foreign intelligence. Those who defected before him—Yevgeny Dumbadze, a 30-year-old official of the OGPU and Comintern;[6] Boris Bazhanov, a former secretary to Stalin, and Grigory Besedovsky, a former Soviet chargé d'affaires in France—could reveal very little about the work of secret Soviet agents outside Russia. During his debriefing, Bazhanov mentioned only one or two people who were of any interest to Western intelligence services.[7] Besedovsky could reveal, with any certainty, only selected Soviet espionage operations based on his personal experiences in Vienna, Paris, and Tokyo, where he had served as a diplomat. But Agabekov had joined the Cheka in 1920, and by the time of his defection had been promoted to head its Eastern Section. He had been posted as an 'illegal' resident to Turkey responsible for operations in the Middle East and was able to blow entire networks of 'legal' and 'illegal' Soviet intelligence officers and agents in many parts of the world.

Both fans and scholars of Soviet intelligence history will remember that Agabekov had fallen in love with the youngest daughter of an Englishman 'who worked in the Constantinople offices of the Blair and Campbell Shipping Company',[8] named Isabel Streater. In January 1930 he had tried in vain to change sides, offering his services to the British diplomats in Turkey, then half a year later was seen in Paris; 'it was reported that Agabekov was assassinated in the Pyrenees Mountains on the Spanish border', while in reality he 'was killed in Paris',[9] as Pavel Sudoplatov claimed in his memoirs.

Although Gordon Brook-Shepherd, a former intelligence officer appointed the *Daily Telegraph*'s correspondent in Austria after the Second World War and Agabekov's only biographer, sharply criticized him for 'gross misinterpretations and factual errors', he himself could not avoid errors. Agabekov approached the British Embassy in Istanbul[10] in February 1930 with an offer 'to disclose the methods whereby the OGPU was tapping correspondence between the Foreign Office and Embassies and Legations in the East',[11] according to an SIS report from Paris. In his own account of events, Agabekov stated that he 'applied to one of the foreign missions in Constantinople in April asking for permission to enter the country represented by it'.[12] That is, Britain. What was clearly 'a slip of pen' (or the translator's error) is a claim that he arrived in Paris on 27 January 1930, for at that time he was still in Turkey. The first British report to London about a contact with Agabekov is dated 30 April 1930, corroborating Agabekov's statement. In the late summer of 1930, newspapers announced that the French authorities had become suspicious about Agabekov's possible further involvement with the Soviet secret police, and on 14 August he was expelled from France and forced to take up residence in Belgium.[13] With the benefit of hindsight, one can now say that these suspicions, if they really existed, were absolutely ungrounded.

Back in July, Oswald A. 'Jasper' Harker of MI5 had sent a dispatch to Captain Hue M. Miller, who at that time was working for Sir Basil Thomson's Directorate of Intelligence. Miller had jumped ship from MI5 and had an MA with first-class honours in English literature and a second class in modern languages.[14] 'In confirmation of Miss Sissmore's telephone conversation with Liddell this morning,' Harker wrote, 'I entirely concur with your view that a HOW [Home Office Warrant] on the Hotel d'Angleterre, Room 19, Rue de la Boetie, Paris, might be of considerable value, as also some observation on OVSEPIAN [Agabekov] in Paris if this could be arranged. I should be very grateful if you would let me see copies of any results of interest you may obtain from this check.'[15] After her marriage, 'Miss Sissmore' would become known as Jane Archer. She would later be leading Krivitsky's debriefing in London, while 'Liddell' was an expert on Soviet subversive activities, Guy Liddell. Liddell was Miller's Scotland Yard colleague, and together they moved to MI5 in 1931, with Miller returning to his old job and Liddell eventually becoming one of the Security Service's most distinguished deputy director generals.

The required warrant duly followed six days later. The reason was that, in spite of several earlier defections, both the Security Service and the Secret Intelligence Service had no experience of how to handle a defector and remained suspicious. 'The individual named [Agabekov], who states himself to have been a member of the Russian OGPU,' one MI5 report said, 'has made a rather theatrical "escape" from Constantinople to Paris. He has given a lurid account of orders from his former chiefs including the liquidation of recalcitrant Soviet employees. It is strongly suspected both by the War Office department concerned [M.I.1.c.—that is, SIS] and ourselves that he may be acting as agent provocateur.'[16] The file, from which this document comes, does not specify what caused these suspicions.

By 30 July both the SIS (Valentin Vivian) and MI5 (Oswald Harker) were studying Agabekov's statements, made by him in the Paris Préfecture de Police and received from the SIS station in the form of a top secret report,[17] at the same time continuing to test his reliability by extracting new information.[18] Ironically, in spite of this defector's earlier attempts to establish contacts with SIS representatives, his eagerness to share all his knowledge of the OGPU and its agents, and his love affair with a young English lady, he was expelled from France and forced to take up residence in Brussels. The French authorities gave several explanations for this strange decision, but the official reason seems, according to the French report sent to London on 18 August, that Agabekov had been expelled 'chiefly as the result of a request made by the British Counsul-General in Paris, who had intervened on behalf of Miss Streater's mother'.[19] Behind this official explanation, however, was almost certainly the decision of the Direction Générale de la Sûreté Générale, who found Agabekov evasive and uncooperative,[20] as their British colleagues were informed afterwards. There is also no doubt that in the handling of Agabekov in Paris Maurice Jeffes, a long-term SIS representative under Passport Control Office cover, was involved.

In Brussels, Agabekov and his fiancée took up rooms at No. 87 Rue Potagères, and he started to campaign for himself. He decided the best route for him was to make his case known to the press, and on 26 August, in an interview with the Paris edition of the *Chicago Tribune*, he revealed who he was and told part of his story. In the words of Brook-Shepherd, Agabekov described 'his plight as a "homeless" refugee from Bolshevism—denied entry to Britain, expelled from France, and with only a three months' permission to stay in Belgium'. This 'unkind treatment', the interview implied, was only dissuading other important OGPU men from following his example. British newspapers picked up Agabekov's lament and it echoed around Whitehall, also reaching the offices of the Military Intelligence Section 6, at that time under Admiral Hugh 'Quex' Sinclair. 'It seems to have done the trick,' writes Brook-Shepherd, 'for only twenty-four hours later the first preparatory moves were made in London to arrange for a direct contact with the defector. On 17 September 1930 in an office of the Belgian Sûreté Publique in Brussels this confrontation at long last took place.'[21] In reality, the meeting was not spontaneous and had little to do with the interview given by Agabekov in Paris shortly after his meeting with Besedovsky.

At the end of August, Captain Miller, then still an officer of Basil Thomson's Directorate of Intelligence (he would return to MI5, where he had served during the First World War), informed the interested parties (MI6 and MI5):

As regards developments subsequent to Agabekov's expulsion from France, our representative in Belgium reports that Agabekov was arrested in Liége, the economic capital of Wallonia, the French-speaking region of Belgium, on 14 August. He was shortly released but the watch has been kept on him by the Belgian authorities . . . His further movements will be reported, and the question of establishing contact with him again is being considered. Our representative reports that there is at present no idea of expelling him from Belgium.[22]

As mentioned above, the newspapers in Europe reported that Agabekov was expelled from France on the same day, 14 August, as he was detained in Belgium. And soon he would be temporarily expelled from Belgium, too.

Agabekov met SIS envoys on 17 and 18 September in one of the offices of the Belgian Sûreté Publique. HM Government was by now particularly interested in identifying a Soviet agent known only as D/3, who was gathering intelligence from inside the Foreign Office.[23] As it turned out later, this agent was Francesco Constantini (codenamed DUNCAN), who was recruited in 1924 with the help of an Italian communist. 'Despite his lowly status,' writes Christopher Andrew, 'Constantini had access to a remarkable range of diplomatic secrets'.[24]

By the time of his rendezvous with SIS officers in Brussels, Agabekov had finished working on his first important book, *GPU: Memoirs of a Chekist*, extracts of which were first published by the émigré Russian newspaper *Poslednie Novosti* ('The Latest News') in Paris in September 1930, and soon the whole book was released by the publishing house Strela ('Arrow') in Berlin.

The decision to assassinate Agabekov had already been taken in July 1930, and a Special Tasks group headed by Serebryansky and based in Paris had immediately received an appropriate order from Moscow.[25] But when Agabekov settled in Belgium, he was under police protection, enjoying especially good personal relations with Baron Verhulst, director of the Sûreté Publique,[26] so the operation was probably postponed until a better time.

On 13 October 1930, *Novoe Russkoe Slovo* ('The New Russian Word'), a Russian-language newspaper published in New York City that in April 2010 marked its centenary, ran a long article, 'OGPU—Reminiscences of the Chekist, G. Agabekov'. It was considered so important that its full text, carefully translated into English, was included in the hearings before the US House of Representatives investigating Communist activities in the United States.[27] Nevertheless, according to the strict and unchanging rules of the defector game, the Service continued to remain suspicious and distrustful of this particular source.

In spite of this attitude, which he was certainly able to feel, during his collaboration with the British authorities Agabekov provided high-grade intelligence, giving the first ever top-level account of the work of the OGPU, its methods, structure, and personnel. Among other things, he disclosed that, from 1926 onwards, the OGPU had been reading British diplomatic correspondence in Persia and other countries. Realizing that Agabekov's revelations could inflict serious damage on Soviet interests, in May 1931 the OGPU launched an operation that became known as the 'Philomena Affair', aiming to lure Agabekov to Bulgaria, abduct him there, and bring to the Soviet Union[28]—or to kill him on the spot.

In October 1931 Frank Foley, head of the SIS station in Berlin, informed the Broadway office that the OGPU resident Samsonov was being recalled to Moscow[29] because the centre thought he had been compromised. In March 1932, the SIS representative in Bucharest, Major Montague 'Monty' Chidson, reported that

in the minds of the Romanian police there is absolutely no doubt that a very genuine attempt was planned upon the life of Agabekov. For this reason they regard it as inconceivable that he should still be in Soviet pay. Moreover, they have ample confirmation of their contention in this respect as they have recently intercepted a number of letters from Kaminsky, the OGPU Representative in Constantinople, addressed to the OGPU resident agent in Bucharest . . . The letters completely confirm the Soviet intention to assassinate Agabekov.[30]

This seems to have changed Vivian's attitude to him for a while, but not dramatically and not for too long.

In the summer of 1931 Austria and the whole of Europe were shaken by the daring murder in Vienna of the former OGPU agent Georg Semmelmann, committed by another OGPU agent, Andreas Piklovič. Early in the morning of 25 July 1931, he killed Semmelmann by shooting him twice in the head and was caught red-handed. The assassin, presumed to be a member of the Hamburg OGPU station (personal number INO-VIII-9), after almost a year of the pre-trial investigation and imprisonment, appeared at the Vienna Criminal Court on 2 March 1932 to be acquitted and released from custody. Despite the fact that Agabekov recognized Piklovič from a photo shown to him in Brussels, after which the defector immediately went to Vienna to testify, he failed to appear on the witness stand because the judge ruled against it.

About a week or so before it happened, on 13 November 1931 Agabekov left his room in the Hotel Fürstenhof at No. 4 Neubaugürtel in the VII 'shopping' district of Vienna. Without delay, he went to the Federal police headquarters to announce that he would like to speak to Andreas Piklovič, who had been detained and was kept in solitary confinement. When asked, Agabekov repeated his testimony, as given previously to the Belgian Sûreté in Brussels. Agabekov insisted that, as soon as he was shown a copy of the forged Swiss passport of 'Egon Spielmann', used by Piklovič for the Vienna operation, he immediately recognized his good friend and OGPU colleague by the name of—Schulman.

The defector further stated that he had known Schulman for about ten years. However, his testimony was not accepted by the Austrian police, because 'Spielman' had already been identified by the German, Yugoslav, and Austrian security services as Piklovič, who had been expelled from Austria five years previously for communist propaganda activities.[31] As a matter of fact, the investigators should have been all ears to Agabekov's revelations, because on 7 August they intercepted a letter sent by the OGPU Vienna station and signed by Igor Vorobyov in which Volobyov praised Piklovič, whom he called 'Andrey', for his heroic behaviour in prison and criticized his OGPU colleagues in Germany for not informing the Vienna organization about the 'action'. Vorobyov also informed Moscow that he considered it wrong to involve a high-ranking INO officer in a murder and suggested that for this work rank-and-file Polish or Romanian communists would be better suited.[32] In addition to this letter, the testimony of Agabekov, a former department head of the OGPU Lubyanka headquarters, could have been of great value. But, when informed about Agabekov's presence in Vienna, the investigating judge at the II Vienna District Court for Criminal Cases banned any possible confrontation between the suspect and Agabekov, because, according to the judge, it could violate the Austrian code of criminal procedures and hinder proper identification. Agabekov was duly informed about the decision of the judge to exclude him from the witnesses list 'on political grounds'.[33] At least, what he said was written down and filed.[34] He returned to Brussels and at the end of the month left for Sofia.

After he had moved to Belgium and started travelling abroad, the OGPU Administration for Special Tasks began to set up a trap in Varna, Bulgaria. In 1931 Agabekov managed to publish his second book[35] of sensational revelations, which remained largely unnoticed in the West but was immediately dispatched to Moscow and studied at the OGPU Lubyanka headquarters. No one there was happy, and the chief of INO Stalislaw Messing was quickly replaced by Artuzov. As a result, it was decided to speed up the operation against the whistleblower.

Several months before Agabekov had arrived in Vienna, a French engineer, Alexandre August Lecoq, 'domiciled at the Hotel de Bretagne on the Rue de Richelieu in Paris, the property of his mother-in-law', as the police protocol would later put it, learned from a Russian refugee, one Nestor Filia, that Filia's wife Evdokia and daughter Anna possessed a fortune of one hundred million Swiss francs deposited in a Geneva bank.[36] The problem was, according to Filia, that both women were in Russia, and, to make them and everybody around rich and happy, they were to be smuggled out of the country. Lecoq volunteered to arrange for Evdokia's and Anna's secure travel from Nikolaev, a city in southern Ukraine where they allegedly resided, to Paris for an agreed commission.

In May 1931 Lecoq asked his friend, a Soviet agent with a Greek passport in the name of Jean Panayotis, who lived in France, and his secretary Sergey Mintz (also a Soviet agent) to help him bring both women to Paris.[37] To verify whether the bank really existed and the deposit was indeed there, Panayotis wrote to the Swiss banker Otto Jaeger in Winterthur. He received no answer but still went ahead.

On 25 July Panayotis went to Moscow, where he spent some considerable time, also visiting the southern towns of Nikolaev and Odessa. While he was away, Mintz informed Lecoq that Panayotis was a Soviet agent and that his trip to the Soviet Union had only one aim—to work out a plan to force Agabekov back to Russia. Lecoq was told that arrangements had to be made for Agabekov to go to Varna, where he was to be taken on board a Soviet vessel, which would transport him to Odessa and from there to Moscow. Then the Soviet authorities, as part of an exchange scheme, would let the Filia family be reunited in the West. Lecoq agreed to cooperate, and after some time Panayotis came back from Russia with a plan.

Whether he realized it or not, by giving his agreement the Frenchman was becoming an accomplice in the OGPU assassination plot. After his return from Moscow, Panayotis visited Jaeger, the Swiss banker, who confirmed that the deposit was in place. Jaeger would later finance the whole operation. Soon Samsonov, the OGPU station chief in Berlin, advised Panayotis to get in touch with one Stopford, an Englishman living in Paris who had wide social contacts (and with whom, according to a police report, Panayotis started a sexual relationship).

Albert Stopford, described as an 'enigmatic figure',[38] was a 72-year-old English gentleman living in one of the most prestigious addresses at 31 rue de Valois in the 1er arrondissement. He was tall, distinguished looking, and quite obviously rich and well connected. And he was a homosexual, which was how the OGPU had got a hold on him. In the middle of October Stopford arrived in Brussels, where he booked himself an expensive suite at the Grand Hotel. He met Agabekov at the lobby downstairs and introduced him to Otto Jaeger, who immediately produced a Swiss passport in that name. Jaeger explained that his function was to arrange the financial side of the deal and offered Agabekov very tempting terms,[39] which the defector was simply unable to refuse.

Although the Russian KGB historians claim that Jaeger was also an OGPU agent,[40] it is possible that he was simply duped. At one moment he was offered and signed a smart commission contract and was shown a letter of attorney issued by Evdokia Filia, in which she guaranteed that she would cover the costs of any expenses in order to get out of Russia.[41] The letter, of course, was forged by the OGPU.

At the end of September 1931, Stopford arrived in Brussels and met Agabekov in his house at 186 rue au Bois to make him an offer. There was a rich lady with a daughter, he said, who must be helped to leave Russia. A ship would be rented in Varna through the services of a professional smuggler named Dimitrov. Agabekov, with his experience in security matters, should make sure that no Soviet agent was on board. Stopford promised to pay the defector 250 francs per day for the journey and £2,000 in the event of the successful outcome of the operation.[42] Later Jaeger also visited Agabekov and confirmed their commitment. Panayotis accompanied the two on both visits but never showed himself to Agabekov. Before leaving, Agabekov received 10,000 francs from Stopford and departed for Vienna.

After he had not been allowed to see Piklovič/Schulman, Agabekov decided that, in order to obtain some useful information, he might try to see a good acquaintance of his with whom he had worked in Tehran. Konstantin Konstantinovich Yurenev was now the Soviet Plenipotentiary to Austria, and Agabekov hoped to bump into him while promenading along Reisnerstrasse in front of the Soviet Embassy. But waiting for Yurenev, he saw two other familiar faces. One was Mikhail Gorb, former head of the Central European Section of the OGPU and now the OGPU station chief in Vienna, working under the cover of a press attaché. Agabekov also recognized Gorb's companion, who he knew was Igor Lebedinsky, former personal secretary of the chief of the INO. In Vienna Lebedinsky served as Gorb's assistant, posing as chief of the consular section of the embassy under the alias 'Vorobyov'.[43] After Gorb's departure he had been appointed head of station. Quite happy that his former colleagues had not noticed him but that he had noticed and recognized them instead, Agabekov decided to get out of this place while there was still time. Later Zarubin complained that, because Agabekov had recognized Gorb in Vienna, his good friend was urgently recalled to Moscow.[44] In 1937, during the Great Terror, he was arrested and shot as 'a German spy'.

Agabekov failed to obtain a Bulgarian visa and left using a complex roundabout trip via Czechoslovakia and Romania,[45] where he managed to get a short-stay permit. He came to Sofia, but, according to his own words, was advised by the police to leave the country immediately and returned to Brussels.

Back in Belgium, Agabekov again applied for permission to travel to Sofia, explaining that he wished to disclose to the Bulgarian authorities some Bolshevik agents who, he said, he knew were operating there.[46] At that time the SIS station in Sofia had little or no official contact with the local security services[47] and Bulgaria did not have diplomatic relations with Soviet Russia, but the visa was granted. In late November 1931, Agabekov was on his way to Bulgaria via Romania for the second time, and again he was placed under tight police surveillance. The Romanian police later claimed that during his transit through the country Agabekov had multiple contacts with Russian refugees and some British officials. Upon arriving in Sofia, he went to the bank and collected another 10,000 French francs in cash. Then he visited the police directorate and introduced himself, asking for personal protection. Agabekov explained that in Brussels he had been instructed to visit one M. Dimitrov, allegedly a smuggler in Varna, who resided at 20 Ulitsa Nishka and who would help him with the vessel. The police chief confirmed that Dimitrov was really a smuggler, that the authorities knew about his contacts with the OGPU, and advised Agabekov not to go to Varna under any pretext but to return to Belgium immediately.[48] The defector became very worried.

It took Stopford and Lecoq some time to find an argument good enough to persuade him to make another trip, this time to Constantza on the Black Sea coast of Romania. They agreed to meet in Bucharest during the Christmas holidays. Agabekov instinctively trusted the Frenchman, as every Russian in exile trusts a foreigner—a trait that has long been noticed and used by the KGB as well as its predecessors and successors. In the morning of 26 December Agabekov arrived in Bucharest and checked in at the Athénée Palace (today part of Hilton chain), while Lecoq had arrived some time before and settled at the Grand Hotel. In spite of all efforts, this time Lecoq was unable to obtain Bulgarian visas for both of them and after an exchange of coded telegrams with Mintz and Stopford asked Agabekov to proceed to Constantza, a busy port with regular services to the Soviet Union and Turkey, and wait there until a ship arrived from Varna.[49]

During his two weeks' stay in Constantza, Agabekov was closely watched by both the OGPU agents and the Romanian police detectives (possibly, at the request of the British), who were also instructed to take care of his security. It was later discovered that, apart from the main group, there were also two Soviet 'illegals' probably sent to observe and report and, if necessary, act as a back-up team. One of them was using an Austrian passport in the name of 'Johann Kouril'. This genuine document had been purchased from the real Johann Kouril by an Austrian Communist Party activist and OGPU agent named Franz Wolf.[50] (In the course of several arrests and searches and during a police raid on the forgery workshop on Heiligenstädterstrasse in Vienna, hundreds of forged passports and other papers were confiscated, but many, including this one, had been 'distributed' before the raid.) The second member of the back-up team also used an Austrian identity.

On 7 January 1932 Lecoq introduced Agabekov to a Bulgarian who said his name was Geno Tzonchev and who explained that he just arrived from Varna, where one of his friends owned a ship and would be happy to do anything for money. However, Agabekov quickly found out that, in reality, the Bulgarian came from Istanbul, where the whole operation against him was planned and coordinated.

On the next day 'Kouril' received a telegram from Varna with the following text: 'The state company [OGPU] wants to close the deal immediately. I return home today. Bill.'[51] He understood that the operation must be abandoned at once and immediately left Constantza for Vienna. Two days later an unidentified person called his hotel asking for 'Mr Kouril'. Satisfied that he had left, the caller hung up.[52]

The telegram was sent by another 'illegal' who was also using a genuine Austrian passport in the name of 'Franz Zenner' during his visits to Romania and Bulgaria, though in Constantza he introduced himself as Wilhelm ('Bill') Koss. Remarkably, although it was very quickly established that his passport was in fact officially issued by the Austrian Embassy in Berlin, the Austrian authorities did not move to search for a possible Soviet mole or collaborator in their embassy.

In the meantime, the traffic of messages between the OGPU residencies in Berlin, Paris, and Istanbul and the Lubyanka head office in Moscow increased considerably.[53] In charge of the operation were Ivan Nikolaievich Kaminsky, codenamed MOND (whom Agabekov either by mistake or because he only knew his alias remembered as 'Nikolai Ivanovich Kremlevsky', the 'legal' resident in Istanbul), and Nikolai Ivanovich Dneprov, officially one of the inspectors of the Soviet Trade Delegation in Ankara.

Grigory ('Grisha') Alekseyev, a deserter from the Tsarist army now employed by the Sovtorgflot (Soviet Merchant Marine) office in Istanbul, one of Kaminsky's agents, received instructions to go to Constantza on board the SS *Elena Philomena* and organize Agabekov's abduction and transportation to Odessa. Should there be a problem, Alekseyev was instructed to use chloroform. In the last resort, he was ordered to shoot the defector after receiving a signal from another accomplice, the Bulgarian agent Tzonchev, after which he was to hide on the ship.

After Lecoq had introduced Tzonchev to Agabekov, the trio started spending a lot of time together. Upon the arrival of the steamer, the Bulgarian was to supervise the abduction operation entrusted to Alekseyev. According to the plan, another accomplice, Sava Nicolas Samuridis, a Greek businessman, was to act as an interpreter between the captain of the *Philomena* and Grisha.

Spiros Katopodis, the captain of the vessel, which was sailing under the Greek flag, was awarded a contract by the Sovtorgflot to perform freight services for a period of six months. Katopodis agreed because he hoped the contract would help get him out of his financial problems. The deal was arranged by one Caligas, a co-owner of the forwarding company Galanis & Caligas in Istanbul. Each participant was paid a tidy sum of money and instructed by Kaminsky and Dneprov about what exactly he had to do.[54] Even then, such operations were meticulously planned.

Six months after the assassination of Georg Semmelmann and less than three months before the trial of Piklovič in Vienna, the *Philomena* anchored in Constantza. Alexeyev stayed in his cabin on board, while Samuridis and Katapodis checked in at the nearby Hotel Cherica. Samuridis informed Tzonchev that he had told Agabekov about the arrival of the ship and that Agabekov and Lecoq should get ready for a journey to Bulgaria. However, Agabekov refused to step on board and proposed that the ship should go directly to Odessa, to secure Mme Filia's escape to freedom and prosperity.

It was a totally unexpected move. Samuridis, Tzoncev, and Katopodis tried to explain that they could not go to Odessa without first collecting cargo in Varna, after which Agabekov and Lecoq announced that they would leave Constantza at once. Lecoq, in the meantime, managed to telephone Mintz in Paris, and as a result a telegram signed by Stopford was soon handed to Agabekov, asking him to stay for another couple of days. He apparently agreed, but Lecoq took the train and departed for Paris. As it was clear that Agabekov had no intention of getting on board, Alexeyev left the ship and started looking for him. Tzonchev and Samuridis joined in. They found Agabekov in a restaurant enjoying his dinner. All this frantic activity in Constantza during the evening of Monday, 11 January, was under the watchful eye of the Romanian police. Tzoncev then tried to board a steamer to Istanbul, but was detained by police agents. Early next morning found Alexeyev, armed with a revolver, in the lobby of the hotel where Agabekov was staying. He was politely advised by the receptionist that the guest had left for Bucharest (this was part of a security arrangement). Somewhat disoriented, Alexeyev went looking for Samuridis to inform him that Agabekov had disappeared only to find out that both Greeks were also absent. At that moment police decided it was time to act.[55] All the plotters were detained: Alexeyev in Constanza, Spiros Katopodis and Sava Samuridis in Bucharest, Lecoq on a train at a border crossing.[56] Katopodis had spent six months in a Romanian prison, and after his release the Russians refused to pay him. He was later involved in the smuggling of arms to Republican Spain until the rebel gunboat *Canovas del Castillo* captured his ship, now renamed *Sylvia*, together with its cargo, in the Straits of Gibraltar.[57] His further fate is unknown.

After Harold Gibson, who headed the Bucharest SIS station from December 1922, departed for Riga in March 1931, his successor, Major Montagu 'Monty' Chidson, and Archie Gibson established new networks with sources in the Red Army, Soviet Navy, and industry, producing reports that were declared 'accurate time after time'. Under the new head of station, the SIS forged quite close relations with both the Romanian security police and military intelligence.[58] With or without the British help, the Constantza operation was rolled up, many Soviet agents were compromised, and until the next opportunity Agabekov was left alone.

He returned safely to Brussels, where another problem awaited him. The authorities told him that his activities during the 'Philomena Affair' were in violation of the conditions on which he had been granted temporary asylum. And, though Baron Verhulst, chief of the Sûreté Publique in Brussels, did his best to prevent the expulsion order, he was overridden by higher authority. Agabekov was therefore required to leave Belgium, though the ban was not permanent, and his British wife, whom he had married shortly before Christmas 1930, was permitted to stay. On the eve of Agabekov's departure, a working agreement was improvised that turned him, in effect, into an ad hoc agent on the British payroll,[59] which could lead to the conclusion that he was forced to leave Belgium because the SIS needed him in Germany. His new field of operation was Berlin, full of Soviet agents.

It is unclear exactly what Agabekov did there, as only one small part of his MI5 Personal File No. 4096 was released in 2006, and none at all of his SIS files. As stated above, the British Passport Control Officer in Berlin and, that is, the SIS man was the experienced Captain Frank Foley, who by the time he returned to London when the war broke out had operated in the German capital for almost twenty years.[60] In what capacity Agabekov worked for him is not known, but there is little doubt that he was used as a penetration agent helping to uncover Communist conspiracy for which Berlin was a centre and where the West European Bureau (WEB) of the Comintern was located until 1933.[61] Berlin was also a first stopover for many Soviet agents on the way from Moscow to London and Agabekov could have been very useful in spotting them. That he was actively in touch may be confirmed by the fact that three years after his arrival in Berlin the Service continued to prove his reliability. In spring 1933 an SIS source was asked to give his opinion about Agabekov's writings. In May this source reported that he had read one of Agabekov's books and, though not familiar with the territories described there, thought that a lot of it was fiction. He added that he frequently heard from his OGPU friends that the book contained many inaccuracies.[62] In reality, the informant was, wittingly or unwittingly, helping the OGPU in undermining Agabekov's image—it can now be confirmed without doubt that both Agabekov's books were a mother lode of important information, in spite of a few minor errors. According to one of the reports from his declassified MI5 file, as soon as the Nazis came to power and the WEB moved to Copenhagen, the SIS stopped all contacts with Agabekov. By the summer of 1933, Lt Colonel Claude Dansey (later ACSS), described by one of his colleague as 'a "copybook" secret service man', had already been setting up the undercover Z Organization (formally established in 1936) to carry out operations in Europe.[63] In those days Russia was certainly not a priority for C's small staff at 54 Broadway, off Victoria Street.

By April 1936, Isabel Edith Streater, now Mme Arutyunova (Agabekov married and lived in Europe under his real name), separated from her husband without a formal divorce and returned to England, where she enrolled on a secretarial course. She later worked as a shorthand typist in the offices of A. Burner & Co. in London, while her sister was employed by the Foreign Office.

In August, Monty Chidson left Bucharest and settled in The Hague, as usual using the Passport Control Office as cover for his intelligence activities. Like Henry Landau before him, Chidson thought working there was quite boring. He did not know it, of course, but in the interwar period The Hague was the second most important operational base of Soviet intelligence in operations against Britain. Chidson's neighbour there was a quiet Dutch architect, painter, and graphic artist named Henri Christiaan Pieck, whose main occupation, at the time when the new PCO was taking up his Dutch post, was to cultivate friendship with several British Foreign Office cipher clerks. Pieck was also running Captain John H. King, an important Soviet agent who was passing him over copies of Foreign Office telegraphic traffic. The intelligent-looking Austrian antiquarian, Dr Martin Lessner, whose little shop of treasures Chidson used to visit during his work in The Hague, also had a small side job: he was one of the 'illegal' residents, the OGPU supervisor operating undercover who would later become famous as Walter Krivitsky. Several Soviet agents, and among others Brian

Goold-Verschoyle, travelled from London to The Hague especially to meet their OGPU (and later NKVD) handlers. As it turned out, for quite a few people, life in this third largest city in the Netherlands was full of adventures, but at the time the SIS knew nothing about all this.

During the same year Agabekov was allowed to return to Brussels. It seems that in autumn 1936 he still tried to demonstrate his usefulness and that the Service was following his activities, restraining from any personal contact because it was not quite satisfied with his 'product' and was not sure what to do with him.[64] Moreover, in the 1930s neither the SIS nor MI5 had enough experience in handling Soviet defectors. In fact, before the war they had only one. Johnny De Graaf of the Comintern's secret service OMS seconded to the RU (Soviet military intelligence) was a walk-in mercenary who came to Frank Foley's Berlin office becoming an in-house success story and a closely guarded secret for seven decades.

In 1937 the NKVD set up their second trap. Forty years later, from the SIS summaries (none of the records has been opened for researchers so far), Gordon Brook-Shepherd learned the following:

The setting was the Spanish Civil War, then raging at its peak, with Stalin heavily committed in political and military support to the Republican side . . . What Aga-bekov now found himself drawn into was the more modest [than the Spanish gold reserve transfer to Moscow] but nonetheless lucrative operation of the looting of Spanish art treasure. The Russians had helped to organize the system whereby, whenever a church, monastery or castle fell into Republican hands, it would be stripped of pictures or any other valuables likely to find eager purchasers on the international market. These were then smuggled across the border into France, and sold up to dealers in Paris and other countries, including Brussels. An OGPU agent named Zelinsky was running the operation from the Belgian end and, early in 1937, it occurred either to him, or his superiors in Moscow, that profit might now be combined with long-delayed revenge.[65]

According to the British author, Agabekov was approached through intermediaries and offered a part in the operation on the French side, where he was to secure the dispatch of the loot to Paris dealers and auction houses. 'At the beginning of July 1937,' Gordon Brook-Shepherd writes, 'Agabekov was known to have passed through Paris on his way to the Pyrenees. And that Paris contact was the last living trace of the defector.'[66] But the famous writer was wrong. On 7 January 1937 Agabekov was arrested by the Belgian police 'on the charge of stealing by means of false keys, receiving [stolen securities], and passing under a false name. Locked up on this charge, he was released on 18 December 1937.'[67] There is no way he was in Paris in July.

Pavel Sudolpatov, who later headed the 'Special Tasks' but was not in the position to know it at the time, claims in his memoirs that 'Agabekov was killed in Paris, after being lured to a safe house where he was supposed to arrange a clandestine deal to smuggle diamonds, pearls, and precious metals belonging to a wealthy Armenian family'. According to Sudoplatov, 'the Armenian, whom he met in Antwerp, was a plant who lured Agabekov to the safe house with appeals to national feelings. In the safe house a former officer of the Turkish army, our assassin, awaited him, together with a young illegal, Aleksandr Korotkov, who would later become chief of the illegal department of the First Chief Directorate in the 1950s.'[68] Korotkov began his OGPU career as a junior assistant to Nikolsky/Orlov, going with him on a mission to Paris, where he was soon unmasked and returned to Moscow. His 'official' SVR biography is a sheer invention.[69] Sudoplatov writes that 'the Turk knifed Agabekov and killed him. Agabekov's body was stuffed into a suitcase, thrown into the sea, and never found.'[70] (In the English-language edition that preceded its Russian version by four years, neither 'the Turk' nor 'the plant' who allegedly lured Agabekov to the safe house is identified. Sudoplatov's 1998 Russian book gives the Armenian's name as 'G. Takhchianov'.[71])

In reality, he was Panteleimon Ivanovich Takhchianov, codenamed HASAN. Born in Turkey in 1906, he joined the OGPU in 1932. A year later he was sent abroad as an 'illegal' and in 1936 settled in France, documented as a Turkish *Gastarbeiter* (migrant worker). In the 1940s Takhchianov held a senior position in the Illegals' Directorate, but after the war was transferred to the Second Chief Directorate (SCD) (KGB's internal security branch).[72] There, he took part in the infamous Operation PRIBOI ('Breakers'), the deportation of the 'enemies of the people' from the Baltic Republics in March 1949, for which Colonel Takhchianov was awarded the Order of the Great Patriotic War.[73]

While Takhchianov was quite obviously the 'Turk' described by Sudoplatove, the 'Armenian' could have been Mikhail Andreyevich Allahverdov, codenamed ZAMAN.[74] Allahverdov knew Agabekov very well because in 1928 he succeeded him as the legal resident in Iran, where he worked under the cover of a consulate official in Kermanshah. When in April 1928 Agabekov was back in Moscow promoted to chief of the OGPU Near Eastern Section, Abram Osipovich Einhorn became the chief resident in

Iran. But, according to his KGB biography, while in 1933–4 Allahverdov operated undercover in Austria (Vienna), Switzerland (Zurich), and France (Paris), from July 1934 to October 1937 he was the NKVD resident in Afghanistan and from November 1937 to December 1938 he was in Turkey. There is no mention of his return to Paris in 1938, although there is a strange gap in his biography between December 1938 and June 1939. Allahverdov later worked in Sudoplatov's Special Bureau and in 1945 was sent on a top-secret clandestine operation to Switzerland.[75] In any event, there are some reasons to believe that Agabekov met his death in a totally different place and under different circumstances.

Baron Verhulst of the Belgian security police claimed that one day Agabekov was tempted to take charge of the next consignment of looted treasures directly from the Republican territory,[76] which allowed Brook-Shepherd to speculate that as soon as he crossed the border Agabekov was butchered and his remains were thrown into a ravine. By the time they were found, he writes, identification was impossible. To begin with, there is no any evidence whatsoever that this defector's remains were ever found.

There may be strong arguments that Agabekov could indeed, on whatever pretext, have been lured into the Republican territory, but he would hardly have been 'butchered' there at once. Most likely he would have been arrested and delivered to Barcelona for interrogation. His British contacts would have been of great interest to the NKVD. There would also have been another, very personal reason not to murder him at once. In October 1929, in Istanbul, one of Agabekov's subordinates was a local OGPU resident named Naum Eitingon, posing as an attaché of the Soviet Embassy (alias 'Leonid Aleksandrovich Naumov'). Now Eitingon, alias 'Leonid Kotov', was the NKVD substation chief in Catalonia, occupying a former mansion of the Soviet Consulate General at No. 15 Avenida del Tibidabo, which, from November 1937, he had been sharing with Orlov. It was almost certainly here that Agabekov was forced to write (or sign) the so-called Letter to the Soviet Authorities widely quoted by Russian historians,[77] which was later backdated as if written on 4 September 1936. The fact that he was arrested and kept in confinement in Spain for some time may also explain why so many of Agabekov's personal effects, including some old financial statements, without doubt from his abandoned apartment in Brussels,[78] later appeared in the Soviet archives. It goes without saying that Orlov never mentioned Agabekov in his memoirs.[79] He, however, was no less interested than Eitingon in interrogating the defector, because, at exactly the time he was working under the cover of the Soviet Trade Delegation in Berlin, Semmelmann was also there, listed as 'Hugo Mannhöffer', operating for the RU organization in Romania, Switzerland, Italy, Austria, Germany, and Greece. Their 'employment' at the Trade Delegation also ended at the same time—in April 1931, of which Semmelmann was informed by a letter signed by one Stern.[80] It is possible that it was Wolf Stern, a brother of Manfred Stern. Using the alias 'Wolf Goldstein', Stern had worked at the Press Department of the Soviet Embassy in Vienna from 1924 to 1927, also actively collaborating with the Intelligence Directorate of the RU from 1926. The most recent study[81] does not say what he was doing between 1927 and 1934 when he was seen in Vienna again in February 1934, but it is quite possible that during this time Stern had been employed by the Soviet Trade Delegation (Handelsvertretung) in Hamburg, from where Semmelmann received his dismissal notice. Whoever signed the latter, Semmelmann panicked and offered to sell his first-hand knowledge of Soviet espionage in Europe, first to the British diplomats in Berlin and later to the Romanian Embassy in Vienna, but he was asking such a large sum for his information that both turned him down. Finally, he moved with his young wife to Vienna and wrote a letter to the Soviet Trade Delegation asking for money and threatening court action.[82] The scandal had been unrolling from the end of April—at the time Nikolsky returned from Berlin to Moscow so he would certainly be anxious to know what had happened in Vienna and what Agabekov's role was in this case. If Agabekov had categorically refused to collaborate with his interrogators, he would probably have been transported to Moscow for further 'treatment', but it seems he agreed, and, after getting his full confession, some material proof of his treachery, and his undated repentance letter, the NKVD lost any interest in him.

On 20 February 1938 Victor Serge, a Russian revolutionary and writer born in Brussels who made a spectacular career in the Soviet Union only to return back to Belgium as a disillusioned anti-Stalinist shortly before the civil war broke out in Spain, wrote a new entry in his diary. He remembered Agabekov's first book as a very 'extraordinary document of betrayal and informing'. 'As chief of the secret service for the Near East,' Serge wrote, '[Agabekov] was living at Istanbul as an established Iranian businessman with a considerable bank account. In leaving, kept only 1,000 pounds sterling, which he considered as being due him.' Serge briefly mentioned an OGPU attempt to kidnap Agabekov in Constanza and finished his record by stating: 'Lives like a bourgeois in Brussels, adores his wife, plays stock market.'[83] This, however, turned out to be very far from reality.

Separated but not divorced, Agebekov's young wife Edith Streater became very worried when a short article from the French newspaper *Les Dernières Nouvelles* dated 16 December 1938 reached her. It was an account based on the information supplied by Vladimir Burtsev, a well-known Russian émigré who lived in Paris. Burtsev stated that he had seen Agabekov and implied that he had definite grounds to believe that Soviet agents had kidnapped and killed the defector. Therefore, she applied to the Passport and Permit Office for an exit permit and was duly interviewed there by the Security Service.[84] Enquiries, which were formally made by the French Sûreté in Paris as a result of enquiries instituted by the Foreign Office through the British Embassy, had no success. Georgy Sergeyevich Arutyunov, better known as Agabekov, had last been seen in March 1938.

Amazingly, Piklovič, whom Agabekov identified as his former OGPU colleague and who was caught red-handed in a house on Vienna's Hockegasse where he murdered Semmelmann, walked out of a courtroom a free man. Although it was quite certainly a professional assassination—one shot in the head followed by another one, for 'control'—and Pilovič admitted that he had committed the crime, five members of the jury voted 'not guilty' against seven who voted 'guilty,[85] so he was released. An important witness, Hofrat Bernhard Pollak, the chief of the Austrian State Police whose telephone number was found in the Semmelmann papers, decided not to appear before the court. Piklovič was soon back in Moscow where he died of a lung disease from which he had already been suffering in Vienna.[86] In his victim's pocket the Austrian investigators found two letters that led to one Christian Broda (later the Minister of Justice in the Bruno Kreiski cabinet and a socialist).[87] Back in 1931, Christian, like his elder brother Engelbert ('Bertl') Broda, was a young communist activist and a member of the underground communist cell in Vienna.[88] A police investigation established, however, that the letters were written not by Christian, who was only 15 at the time, but by somebody else. The family apartment at 14 Prinz-Eugen-Strasse in Vienna was used as an accommodation address where letters arrived and were sent further to another address.[89] Litzi, a former wife of Kim Philby, later also lived on Prinz-Eugen-Strasse.

Engelbert Broda arrived in London on 10 April 1938, only days after Agabekov had disappeared. Though information supplied by a reliable source convinced Special Branch that Broda was an active Communist, the Security Service was less certain. However, Broda's MI5 Personal File 46663, vol. 1, opened in January 1931, contained *The Times* and the *Daily Telegraph* accounts of the Semmelmann case as evidence against the Broda brothers.[90] According to the *Daily Telegraph* report:

The police have made a sensational discovery of a Communist news centre in the fashionable Prince Eugen Strasse. The first clues were obtained among papers taken from an ex-Communist spy named Semmelmann who was shot dead in Vienna last month by a Jugoslav Communist agent named Piklovich at the moment when Semmelmann was about to sell the secrets of the Soviet espionage system to the Yugoslav authorities. On examining Semmelmann's documents the police were surprised to find papers relating to the flat of Dr Broda [the father of Engelbert and Christian], the owner of the Prince Eugen Strasse flat and the so-called 'Five Tower Castle' in Styria.

The second clipping in the Broda's MI5 file was from *The Times* of London. Under the header '"Red" Orders Found' the newspaper wrote:

A watch was kept for several weeks on the Vienna flat, and revealed that Communist instructions were reaching this place by various means, including the post. The agent who received and re-dispatched them proved to be Christian Broda, the 14-year-old son of Dr Broda, and the lad has admitted to the police that he got them from his brother in Berlin. Dr Broda and his elder son are absent, and so far have not been traced. This Communist centre apparently dealt only with propaganda and espionage outside Austria. The police are unable to discover the moving spirits, and have been able only to arrest subordinates. Masses of Communist material were also found at Five Tower Castle.[91]

Captain Hugh Miller of the Directorate of Intelligence, who in 1931 returned to MI5, noted on the file: 'It subsequently transpired that the elder was a registered member of the Austrian Communist party. The family's town house at Prinz Eugen Strasse was also visited by the police who found communist literature and papers relating to the dissemination of communist propaganda. Neither he (Ernst) or his sons were arrested.'[92] It is not recorded how Dr Broda managed to settle the case with the Austrian police in 1931, but, remarkably, the biographies of both Engelbert Broda and his brother Christian were published in Vienna and London precisely eight decades after the events.

Another MI5 document where Broda is mentioned is an intercepted letter between two Englishmen who were of interest to the Security Service. The memo in the file reads: 'Cross reference to intercepted letter from Arthur Henry Ashford Wynn to David Haden-Guest mentioning

Engelbert Broda, Landsberg, Berlin-Grünewald, Hubertusallee 22'.[93] Both
Wynn and Haden-Guest were members of the CPGB. Wynn, codenamed
SCOTT by the NKVD, would be later identified as a recruiter of the Oxford
Spy Ring. David Guest was the son of the Labour MP Leslie Haden-Guest
and Carmel Haden-Guest, who visited the battalion and her volunteer son
at the Fontaubella Valley in the spring of 1938. She brought with her such
invaluable items as a pair of binoculars and cigarettes, always in short supply.
David, an outstanding mathematician, was killed in August of that year. The
monument to the Internationals killed on the Ebro remained undiscovered
throughout the Franco years.[94] The intercepted letter is the only MI5 entry
on Berti Broda until July 1938. At this time, instead of accepting an
invitation to what turned out to be a unique opportunity to meet Albert
Einstein socially, Berti told his son later,[95] he preferred to attend a political
event (where he was spotted by the Special Branch watches).

    Although he was briefly interned in London in 1939, during the war
Broda was cleared for the most secretive work involving the British and
American nuclear weapons programme, known in Britain as the Tube
Alloys Project and in the USA as the Manhatten Project. In December
1942, the head of the NKVD London station, Anatoly Gorsky (alias 'Gromov', codenamed VADIM), reported: 'EDITH [Edith Suschitzky/Tudor-Hart]
sent us a detailed report through MARY [Litzi Philby] on the result and status
of work on ENORMOZ [the Tube Alloys Project and the Manhattan Project
respectively], both in England and in the USA. ERIC [Engelbert Broda] had
given her this report on his own initiative to pass to the CPGB.'[96] ERIC
would become one of the most important Soviet sources on the Manhattan
Project. He later became a professor, returning to Austria in June 1947.
A month before that, he wrote to his son, who had remained in London:
'You will be interested, and please tell Mummy too, that I have now had an
invitation from the Austrian government to work in the University of
Vienna.' Naturally, Broda did not disclose his relations with Soviet intelligence but added an interesting detail. 'I shall teach in the University,' he
wrote, 'but shall be paid by the Government, namely the Ministry of
Electric Power. I shall have an office in the Ministry with a telephone and
a secretary and perhaps a carpet on the floor...'.[97] To put the record
straight, it was the Federal Ministry for Power Industry (Bundesministerium
für Elektrifizierung und Energiewirtschaft), headed at the time by the
communist minister Karl Altmann, of which Berti, who arrived in Vienna
with his second wife, also preferred not to inform his son in London. When

in November 1947 Altmann was succeeded by the Socialist Alfred Migsch, who took part in the Austrian resistance, was arrested by the Gestapo and spent a year-an-a-half in the Mauthausen, nothing changed in Broda's life. In December 1947 he wrote that he was in absolutely the right place for work and in 1948 had an opportunity to visit England. A MI5 source reported: 'He visited Cambridge and Edinburgh. The reason for the Edinburgh visit was ostensibly a series of lectures he was to give, but this seems unlikely to be the real reason since, if he had anything new and useful to report, he would certainly not pass on the information to British scientists, whom he must regard as his opponents in the next war—it seems more probable that he wanted information from them.'[98] Both Engelbert and his brother Christian Broda were buried in Vienna with honours.

Back in early 1938, planning for the abduction of Lev Sedov, the son of Trotsky and his most trusted and active European representative, was at an advanced stage, in spite of the recent furore aroused in France by the NKVD's suspected involvement in General Miller's disappearance.[99] Like his predecessor several years earlier, the head of the White Guard ROVS Eugen Karl Miller disappeared in broad daylight from a Paris safe house.

Serebryansky was personally in charge of the exfiltration supervised by Spiegelglass from Moscow Centre. A fishing boat had been hired at Boulogne and other preparations were on the way when the order arrived to abort the operation.[100] Without doubt one of the main reasons was the reappearance in Paris of Walter Krivitsky, who returned to the 'city of light' on 7 November, the anniversary of the Bolshevik coup, and soon contacted Sedov. They actually met on 11 November in an apartment on the rue d'Edimbourg. At that time, quite incredibly, Krivitsky suspected Sedov of being an NKVD agent, but he did not have much of a choice.[101]

After their first meeting, Krivitsky began paying almost daily visits to Sedov. Ironically, Mark Zborowski, one of the NKVD informers in Trotsky's inner circle, was appointed Krivitsky's 'bodyguard', while Krivitsky's application for a 'legal' resident status in France (and with it, government protection) was being processed. Naturally, Zborowski was not able to protect the defector physically, but he was assigned to accompany him everywhere and, if anything was to happen, to be a witness.[102] Contrary to the opinions of some authors, who portray him as a ruthless penetration agent, Zborowski obviously did not betray the runaway's whereabouts to the NKVD and to some degree that saved Krivitsky's life for another three years.

On 8 February 1938, Sedov was taken to hospital with acute appendicitis. Zborowski persuaded him that it would be more secure to have his appendix removed not at a French public hospital but in the private Clinique Mirabeau, a small establishment run by Russian émigrés. Like many other Russian émigrés in France, this private hospital's bosses were connected with the Union for Repatriation of Russians Abroad, an NKVD front. No sooner was Sedov on the operating table than Zborowski, as he later admitted, alerted his NKVD control. Sedov's appendectomy operation was successful and for a few days he seemed to be making a normal recovery. Then he had a sudden relapse, which baffled his doctors. Despite repeated blood transfusions, he died in great pain on 16 February at the age of 32. To date, there is no proof that the NKVD was responsible for his death.[103] According to the final autopsy and post-mortem, he had died of peritonitis. Zborowski later explained to American congressmen that, in Sedov's case, his sudden death was due to natural causes.

It remains unknown whether Sloutsky managed to report the news to Yezhov and Stalin. The day after Sedov's passing away, on 17 February, Spiegelglass was summoned to the office of the NKVD deputy chief, where he found the breathless body of his former comrade and chief.[104] The telegram of Georgy Kosenko, the Paris resident, never reached Sloutsky.

Spiegelglass was immediately appointed to take Sloutsky's place. When Spiegelglass himself was arrested, he explained during the interrogation:

In the first half of 1938 Sedov died in Paris of natural causes. I rang up Yezhov to inform him. He said, 'Come to my office.' When he read the telegram, he concluded, 'A good operation. We did a good job on him, didn't we?' I said nothing to this, but I have no doubt that he reported to the Central Committee that we had liquidated Sedov...[105]

This seems to solve the mystery of Sedov's death once and for all.

Knowing Spiegelglass well, from operations in which they had taken part together and not simply from his official biography, which he had heard several times during the *chistka* campaign,[106] Orlov was well aware that, should one day Spiegelglass receive an order to liquidate him, he would not be spared. He also realized that his German bodyguards would not help, as any of the officers of the NKVD station, including his second-in-command Eitingon, would kill him without a second thought if an order came from Moscow. Therefore, he started to prepare for his departure with care.

Edward Gazur, the FBI Special Agent who became a friend and admirer of the former NKVD spy, gives a very incriminating account of how the Orlovs prepared their escape, which certainly deserves to be quoted in full:

What Orlov did require was the financial means to make good his escape. Throughout his long service with the Soviet government, he had earned a salary well above the norm and had prudently saved and invested a portion for the rainy day that was about to come. He had first conceived a plan to save and invest during his posting to Paris in 1926 and would later open savings accounts in each of the capitals where he was later assigned.[107] Each of these savings accounts had remained untouched through the years, growing with accumulated interest, as Orlov did not feel it prudent to invest money in a shaky Communist government.[108]

Sometime during early 1938, Maria went to their bank in Paris and had all of their foreign savings accounts consolidated into the one they held there. The Orlovs were more than amazed when they learned that their savings and investments had accumulated to slightly over $13,000 in US currency [about $200.000 in 2013].[109]

Gazur continues:

Orlov's financial situation was also helped by his hobby of antique collecting, long before it became fashionable. His collection and field of experience was rare solid gold European wristwatches in the category of the Duchene Peyrot, Patek Philippe and Rolex, as well as unique American watches. While in Spain, he had also acquired a small collection of valuable Moorish daggers from the era of the 800-year occupation of the southern regions of Spain by the Mohammedan peoples of North Africa. His collection would not be left behind in Spain.

In addition to his watch and dagger collection, over the years Orlov had built up his art collection piece by piece. From their families, Orlov and Maria had inherited a number of fine antiques, including several large ornate Russian icons that were no longer fashionable in the world of Communism, as well as numerous pieces of fine furniture from the time of the Tsars. The watch and dagger collection posed no problem and could easily be transported to their next destination; however, their art collection, antique furniture and the larger inherited items were too bulky to be transported at short notice. They therefore had no choice but to sell the items that could not be taken with them as they had no idea when the time would come to flee, or the place of their final destination, or the means by which they would get there.[110]

Leiba Lazarevich Feldbin, whom Gazur calls 'General Orlov', came from a poor and very religious Jewish family from Bobruisk, and Maria Vladisla-vovna Rozhnetskaya, whom he had married in Archangel in 1921, when she was only 18, was from a poor Jewish family from Kiev joining the

Communist Party at 16. An educated analysis would find it surprising and unlikely that the family 'inherited' and then carried around the world all those 'large ornate Russian icons and numerous pieces of fine Tsarist furniture', as Gazur describes them, up to their new destination in Spain enveloped in flames of the civil war.

Maria made numerous trips to the grand auction houses of Paris [Gazur writes], which specialized in antiques, taking with her on the train those items she could handle and placing them on consignment. On her next trip to Paris, she would deposit the proceeds from the previous auction in their Paris bank account and so on. In the meantime, Orlov had established contacts in both Toulouse and Perpignan where he could dispose of the larger items, and on each of his trips from Barcelona he would go directly to the dealer with his load of the day. When they had sold all of their tangible property and put these monies into their Paris bank account, they were surprised to learn that their liquid financial asserts were in excess of $22,000 [about $338,461.00 seventy years later]. Needless to say, there were relatively few people who had $22,000 in 1938.[111]

Alas, Orlov deliberately lied to Gazur in order to cover the more nefarious sources of his wealth.

By late March, all communications with the NKVD station in Spain were signed by Zalman Passov, the new chief of INO. Orlov wrote about his boss:

Yezhov selected for that job a young officer from another department by the name of Passov, a good-looking chap, who had been very close to Yezhov's family and regularly accompanied Yezhov's wife on her vacations. Neither by experience, nor by his previous positions did Passov measure up to the highly important post of director of Soviet intelligence all over the world.[112]

Although Passov was indeed quite inexperienced in the matters of foreign intelligence and was about ten years younger than his representative in Spain, all the rest is Orlov's fantasy.[113] In any event, the lack of experience did not prevent Passov, together with Spiegelglass as his first deputy, from supervising a large-scale intelligence collection—an effort that in no way influenced Stalin's decision-making in 1938.

One of the long-term intelligence operations in Spain, about which Orlov regularly reported to his Moscow chiefs, had been codenamed NEW ENROLMENT.[114] The idea involved the vetting, recruitment, and initial training of selected volunteers from the International Brigades who represented many nationalities and could be used later against different targets in

Europe and overseas. Therefore, the Personnel Department at the IB Base in Albacete was from the very beginning staffed by officers and agents of the NKVD and RU, who selected future recruits for their respective services. For several weeks from December 1936 to January 1937 the Finnish Communist Tuure Léhen ('Marcus') headed this department, also widely known under its German name 'Kaderabteilung'. Lehén (in Moscow 'Langer')[115] was the son-in-law of Otto Kuusinen and for a long time had been in charge of the most secret military section of the Org department of the ECCI. The future star agent of the British SIS, Johann de Graaf, worked for this section as a 'special instructor'.

From the German contingent alone at least twenty-nine volunteers were directed by the KPD personnel department otherwise known as Grupo germánico or Deutsche Sprachgruppe under Wilhelm Bahnik, to the 'special service' of their Soviet friends. Bahnik (alias 'Fernando Sommer') headed the department from August to October 1937.[116] His successor there was Willi Kreikenmeyer. The department handled all German, Austrian, German-speaking Swiss, Dutch, and Scandinavian personnel. In other national sections, Josef Dycka ('Kurt Denis') and Max Stern ('Otto Glaser'), among others, were responsible for the Austrian personnel. Dycka was an RU officer, the husband of the Rote Kapelle case officer Maria Polyakova. In September 1941 he was dropped by parachute behind the German lines on the Polish border but quickly found by the security police, shot, and killed. As well as working in the personnel department, Stern also served in the republican SIM. After the Second World War he was a member of the KPÖ Press Service and from 1961 was posted as the Moscow correspondent of the communist newspaper *Volkstimme*. From 1973 in Vienna, Stern, who also wrote a book about Austrian volunteers in the Spanish war, headed the KPÖ party archive. Among other interesting personalities, Alfred Tanz was in charge of the Anglo-Saxon section[117] and Rudolf Frei of the Swiss section. Like Stern, Frei had also served in the SIM of Barcelona.[118] The last chief of the personnel department was the Bulgarian Georgi Mikhailov ('Zhelezov'), who occupied this post from November 1937 to December 1938. Under Mikhailov the department employed eighty-three staff and functioned as a separate and independent human resources division,[119] regularly sending fresh recruits to the training centres for 'special services'.

The 'New Enrolment' programme was very secret and extremely productive in terms of mass recruitment. There were several training centres or schools that prepared its 'students' for special operations behind the lines.

The RU schools were in Benimàmet, a suburb of Valencia; they trained guerrillas for the front-line operations against the Nationalists and saboteurs or wireless operators to be used outside Spain. This second, more sophisticated and discreet training was supervised by the RU personnel from Section A, and for obvious reasons each of its three *secciós* or *détachements* was headed by the German communists, staff members of the intelligence directorate of the Red Army. One of the section chiefs was the previously mentioned Richard Stahlmann (Artur Illner), and two others were Victor Priess[120] and Heinrich Fomferra.[121] Among their 'students' in Benimámet were, among others, Hans Schwarz,[122] Richard Staimer,[123] Wilhelm Fellendorf,[124] Albert Hößler,[125] and Friedrich Dickel, who later served as the Interior Minister of East Germany until the fall of the Berlin Wall. All were sent by RU headquarters on special assignments to Europe and Asia during the war. All except Dickel, who until his arrest in 1943 in Shanghai operated in Finland, were in some way supporting the work of what later became known as the Rote Kapelle, a large RU network of sources, case officers, cut-outs, support personnel, and W/T operators known as 'the pianists', which some authors, perhaps with slight exaggeration, call 'one of the most successful spying operations of the Second World War'. Of 217 members of the Red Orchestra caught by the Gestapo, 143 died.

Although some authors claim that Nikolsky/Orlov and Kotov/Eitingon were supervising all this special training,[126] in reality the NKVD was kept aloof from all these activities, which were controlled, from top to bottom, first by the head of the Soviet Military Mission, the RU resident, then in the field by one of the Section A staff officers, and finally by a senior RU agent in charge.

After Spain, in 1937 Fomferra was sent to Belgium to help Johann Wenzel set up a radio transmission network in support of the wide-scale intelligence operation supervised by the 'Grand Chef' Trepper and Kent/Gurevich. His official GRU biography, however, does not mention this important fact, saying instead that in 1937–9 Fomferra was teaching in a RU special school in Moscow. After Belgium, in April 1939, he was sent, together with Hans Schwarz, to Hungary and Slovakia, from where they transmitted coded messages to Moscow until February 1942, when both were arrested. Broken under torture by the Gestapo, they revealed a lot about their work for Soviet intelligence and in addition Fomferra said all that he knew about Wenzel's work in Belgium. Wenzel, who until his arrest in June 1942 was transmitting to Moscow top-grade intelligence received by Gurevich in Berlin from Harro Schulze-Boysen, was quickly broken by his interrogators and agreed to take part in the 'Funkspiel', a radio game with Moscow.

In the meantime, another former student of the Benimámet intelligence school Wilhelm Fellendorf, together with Erna Eifler, a former code clerk of Wilhelm Bahnik, were parachuted into German territory in May 1942.[127] Both managed to reach Berlin. It seems it was another attempt to set up a communication line for the group of Schulze–Boysen. Whatever they did in Berlin, in October they found themselves in Hamburg, hiding at the house of Viktor Priess, where his mother Katharina and brother Heinz gave them temporary shelter. On 15 October the Gestapo arrested all four of them. Fellendorf and Eifler were executed.

Albert Hössler also attended the same RU school in Benimámet. After a three-month training course he was seconded to the Hans Beimler Batallion of the XI International Brigade and seriously wounded during an operation in June 1937. He was treated first in Spain but then transferred to a Paris hospital. In 1939 Hössler was recovering in a sanatorium near Moscow. In 1941 he married Klavdia Rubtsova, his doctor. After the war with Germany had broken out, Hössler was sent to continue the training that had begun in Spain at the various special forces training facilities in Moscow, Ryazan, and Ufa, and on 5 August 1942 was dropped by parachute, together with Robert Barth, behind German lines on the border with Byelorussia. One part of their mission was to find assets—one group of agents designated station D5 and another group known as station D6—that the NKVD had left in Berlin and to establish a channel of communication for them. There would also be a second part. The problem was that, since June 1941, the NKVD had for a second time lost contact with its best agent in Berlin, Willy Lehmann, codenamed A-201 and later BREITENBACH.

After his first case officer, Pavel Kornel (alias 'Mikhalsky'), had been recalled to Moscow (only to be arrested and shot there in 1937), Lehmann's controller became the German Erich Tacke (BOM), who in June 1937 would take part in the abduction and murder of Nin in Spain. When Tacke's supervisor, Fedor Karin, decided he was about to be caught, Tacke was sent to Moscow, so control of Lehmann was handed to Hermann Klesmet (KARL), a long-time Soviet agent. He ran Lehmann and other sources until he himself had to leave Germany in the autumn of 1933. Lehmann's second Soviet case officer was Vasili Zarubin, the 'illegal' resident. After Zarubin's tour of duty in Germany was over and he had returned to Moscow in 1937, his replacement was Alexander Agayantz (RUBEN), the brother of Ivan Agayantz. Alexander headed the Paris residency from 1934 to 1937, and in May 1937 was transferred to Berlin, where he worked under diplomatic cover. In Berlin, Agayantz was replacing Boris Gordon, who had served there for two years. He ran Lehmann and other sources until November 1938, but in December died in the Berlin Charité Hospital while undergoing an operation for a perforated stomach ulcer. By that time Agayantz was the only NKVD case officer in the Berlin residency.

Lehmann was left without any contacts and naturally stopped receiving payments from his Moscow masters. But after all those years he had got used to the monthly compensation of 580 Reichsmark that the NKVD paid him in addition to his Gestapo salary. In June 1940, at considerable risk, Lehmann wrote a letter and managed to pass it over to the Soviet Embassy at 63 Unter den Linden, in which he suggested renewing relations. On that occasion he was lucky. Or so it seemed.

In August 1939 the new head of station arrived in Berlin under the cover of the 1st Secretary (later Counsellor) of the Soviet Embassy. His name was Amayak Kobulov, a poorly educated younger brother of Bogdan Kobulov, Beria's favourite. The new resident had no foreign intelligence experience, spoke no German, and was travelling abroad for the first time in his life. His appointment was deeply but silently resented by the officers of the German section. One of them was Alexander 'Sasha' Korotkov, former assistant of Nikolsky during their failed operation in Paris in 1933–4. Although Korotkov was unmasked by the French Sûreté and had to flee to Moscow, he was allegedly sent to Paris again in 1937, coming back to Moscow a year later. Here Korotkov and his wife were both fired from the NKVD, but he wrote a personal letter to Beria and was restored, to the great surprise of other officers. In May 1940 Pavel Fitin, the new chief of Soviet foreign intelligence, sent him to Berlin as Kobulov's deputy.

One sunny day in September the telephone rang on Lehmann's RSHA desk and the voice on the other end announced that Lehmann's good colleague Preuß would be happy to visit him at the office the next day. It was a phrase that Lehmann had suggested should be used in his letter to the Soviet Embassy. It sounded quite innocent, but for the agent it meant that a contact was set up for the next day, at 8.30 in the morning, near the newspaper kiosk at the Wittenbergplatz Underground Station. The 31-year-old 3rd Secretary of the Soviet Embassy, Korotkov (alias 'Alexander Erdberg'), was there to see Lehmann. Korotkov's role in handling Lehmann

and other German sources of what would later become known as the Rote
Kapelle operation is usually greatly exaggerated in both Western and Russian sources. In just a few weeks Korotkov would hand over the control of
their best German asset to another young NKVD officer with a diplomatic
passport named Boris Zhuravlev.[128] On 19 June 1941 Lehmann told Zhuravlev that Germany would attack Russia in exactly three days. An urgent
telegram was immediately sent to Vsevolod Merkulov, the head of the
NKGB, the successor of the NKVD, who reported to Stalin. Two days
before, on 17 June, Merkulov had already reported the same date and hour
for the German attack, based on the information provided by the Berlin
residency. On this report Stalin wrote his resolution 'Disinformation' and
put it aside. As predicted, in the early hours of 22 June, 'to the sole
accompaniment of croaking frogs', as one reporter put it, the Nazi troops
invaded the Soviet Union, and Stalin was shocked by 'an unparalleled act of
perfidy in the history of civilized nations'. Soon the Soviet Embassy was
withdrawn from Berlin, and both case officers departed in the direction of
Moscow, again leaving Lehmann without a contact. Before his departure,
Korotkov had managed to meet Arvid Harnack, Harro Schulze-Boysen
(STARSHINA/MASTER SERGEANT), and Adam Kuckhoff (STARIK/OLD MAN),
handing over considerable funds to finance their underground activities.
Harnack (codenamed BALT and later CORSICAN), a scientific expert in the
Reich Economic Ministry and lecturer on foreign policy at Berlin University, had been recruited by Boris Gordon, the NKVD head of station, in
1935 with the help of the former Soviet consul in Königsberg, Alexander
Hirschfeld. During the same year Naum Markovich Belkin (KADI), Orlov's
fellow worker in Madrid, Valencia, and Barcelona, was also posted to Berlin
as the 'illegal' NKVD resident, where he was running many agents from
different underground KPD 'Apparats' who would later join him in Spain.

Neither Hössler nor Barth knew about their true mission when they
landed near Bryansk. They thought they would have to re-establish contacts
with the anti-fascist resistance and specifically with the Schulze–Boysen/
Harnack group in Berlin. Pavel Fitin of the NKVD asked his RU colleague
Philip Golikov to send a group to Germany to find BREITENBACH. 'In
September 1941,' Korotkov wrote in his post-war memo, 'in response to
our question about assistance in establishing contact through the intelligence directorate of the Red Army [RU], they agreed to assist in restoring
communication with our valuable agents in Berlin'.[129] Fitin had to act as he
did, because the collaboration between the NKVD and the British SOE

regarding sending PICKAXE teams into the occupied territory had not yet been properly established.[130] So the RU sent two well-trained Germans from its reserve. Hössler was arrested at 17 Wilhelmshöher Strasse in Berlin at the end of September. It was the address of Erika Gräfin von Brockdorff, given to the 'pianists' of the Red Orchestra Berlin group. Hössler, who had received his wireless operator training in Bukovo under Willy Fisher, initially agreed to the play-back game, but, after noticing that his warning signals had not been heeded in Moscow, he refused to collaborate further and was executed.

Robert Barth, a former typesetter of the Communist *Rote Fahne* newspaper, who was parachuted into the occupied territory with Hössler, was arrested in October when he visited his sick wife at hospital. Unlike Hössler, he had agreed to take part in the Funkspiel as long as he was asked to, and soon Moscow transmitted the coded phrase to call Lehmann. Agent BREI-TENBACH was arrested in December in a sting operation conducted by his Gestapo colleagues. His interrogation protocols did not survive. He was quietly shot just before Christmas.

After Lehmann had been caught, Barth was released from Gestapo custody and sent to the Western Front as an informant. He was captured after D-Day by the US Army, together with other prisoners of war. Instead of keeping a low profile, he immediately told his CIC interrogators that he was an NKVD agent and was handed over to the Soviets. As a Gestapo collaborator, he was sentenced to death and shot in November 1945.

After the war in Spain had broken out, hardly anyone in the RU or NKVD doubted that war was imminent. And everyone understood that Germany and its satellites would be the main adversary. Until at least August 1939, it was absolutely clear to everybody. Therefore, in addition to the RU special schools, only one of which trained guerrillas to help the Republican army, a secret NKVD facility was set up near Barcelona. Known under the code name CONSTRUCTION, this first extraterritorial spy school, unlike guerrilla war, sabotage, and subversion training bases declared to the authorities, was operated clandestinely, and its existence was deliberately concealed from the Republican government.[131] The instruction from Moscow was to select and train a contingent of about seventy internationals (preferably Germans, Austrians, Scandinavians, but also Britons and Americans) who could be used in covert operations, initially as 'sleepers' but to be activated 'at the time of the major conflict'.[132] In November 1938, when it became apparent that Orlov had deserted his post and probably defected, Beria ordered the NKVD training course to be shut down. Nevertheless, almost all its former students were used by the NKVD and other Soviet services during the war.

Peter Carroll, who was researching the Spanish odyssey of the Abraham Lincoln Battalion, received an enthusiastic welcomed from the KGB while working on his book in Moscow.[133] Carroll had to admit that some evidence had survived to show that American volunteers had collaborated with Soviet intelligence during the Spanish Civil War.

Without a clear sense of their mission [Carroll writes], they left their units and entered a special training program outside Barcelona. A trusted member of the American Communist party screened the names and eliminated a few men. Then, using aliases and false identification, dressed in civilian clothes, they commenced intensive training in guerrilla tactics, sabotage and espionage under the tutelage of two Spanish instructors. They worked with explosive devices, studied cryptography, and learned radio transmission. But unlike the Spanish guerrilla team that also included Americans—[Alex] Kunslich, [Irving] Goff, and [William] Aalto being known examples—who operated behind fascist lines, this unit never went into action in Spain. Indeed, these activities were so secret that a militia unit once mistakenly arrested the entire group, requiring the direct intervention of André Marty to obtain its release.[134]

In October 1941, Aalto and Goff wrote of their experiences in Spain for the American communist magazine *Soviet Russia Today*:

Our first intimate contact with a Russian guerrilla adviser was in the spring of 1938 when our Brigade was sent to the Granada-Malaga front as an experimental group to try out new techniques . . . Our Soviet advisers not only put at our disposal their experience, but also practical aid. In our guerrilla schools, lessons from the Red Army's experience were taught to us, verbally and through Spanish translations of Red Army manuals. The mines and the trick apparatus we used in Spain were constructed from patterns given to us by our Soviet advisers . . . The whole Spanish army and especially the guerrillas were reminded of the support of the Soviet Union every time they loaded a gun—for the bullets so often were Soviet.[135]

On 10 May, Orlov sent a telegram to the Centre: 'I request that you send the prepared passports to my name marked "Strictly Personal" so that nobody will know their new surnames.'[136] The documents were intended for the graduates, who completed their training and were sent out of Spain. About one of them Carroll writes:

Another member of the special detachment . . . received orders at the end of the war to suspend all party work and 'lie low' for further instructions. A few years later, Steve Nelson [chief of the party secret service whom Orlov knew in Spain][137] saw the man and his wife in a San Francisco restaurant. When he approached them, the man tried to avoid contact. Nelson had the pleasure of telling him that he could emerge from the underground. Other members of the special unit did have the opportunity to put their espionage training into practice; after Spain, they went to work for Soviet intelligence.[138]

Indeed, most of the Austrians and Germans who were later parachuted by the SOE into occupied territories were from the CONSTRUCTION school supervised by the NKVD station officers.[139] The school also provided men for Orlov's personal bodyguard detail. Fortunately, in what concerned the PICKAXE teams dropped by the RAF between January 1942 and March 1944, MI5 did not have to rely on Orlov's testimonies, because many NKVD agents who underwent SOE training gave ample information about their background to their hosts.[140] The SOE claims to have dropped by parachute or landed by boat and submarine twenty-five NKVD agents during the war. Altogether, by the end of Operation PICKAXE thirty-four agents had arrived in Britain.[141] Though many of them were Spanish Civil War veterans, some were not. That leaves more than half of the CONSTRUCTION 'pupils' unidentified. Naturally, Orlov would have been able to provide extensive information on many of them, but chose not to.

From Orlov's testimonies to the US Congress and his interviews with the officers of the Counterintelligence Staff of the CIA or agents of the FBI,[142] the former head of the NKVD station in Spain, who was perfectly informed about everything that was going on inside Soviet foreign intelligence, preferred to invent stories whenever he got an opportunity. Orlov correctly calculated that, if America was happy to accept Stalin's secretary (Bazhanov), it would be even more happy and proud to accept Stalin's intelligence chief, the 'four-star NKVD general', as one prominent British author put it. Understanding perfectly well that the job of the FBI and CIA was to take from him his dowry of information—what Frederick Forsyth would later call 'the price of the bride'—Orlov started inventing stories that could not be easily corroborated to enhance his own importance.

Mr ORLOV. [Apart from myself] there was another person abroad who knew about the identity of that Soviet agent [Zborowski] among the Trotskyites. That man was General Lushkov, who had been, before that, Deputy to Marshal Blücher.[143]

Genrikh Samoilovich Lyushkov (his name is spelt erroneously in Orlov's testimony) had never been a general, never served under Marshal Blücher, and had no idea about the identities of the Soviet agents in Europe. Exactly one month before Orlov deserted his post, on 13 June 1938, the chief of the Far Eastern NKVD directorate, Commissar of State Security 3rd Rank Lyushkov, crossed the Manchurian border on foot, wearing his full uniform with medals. He had with him his NKVD identity card No. 83 counter-signed by Yezhov. Before he had been sent to the Far East, he had been the NKVD chief of the Azov–Black Sea province. In January 1938, Yezhov ordered his deputy Frinovsky (as he later testified) to tell Lyushkov that, if the situation became critical, he should commit suicide. The signal was to be a telegram from Moscow about his dismissal or promotion. When the telegram did arrive, Lyushkov, instead of committing suicide, escaped abroad over the Siberian–Manchurian border.[144] From there he was turned over to the Japanese military authorities, who promptly transported him to Tokyo under close escort. On 1 July the Japanese press revealed—and it was noted by all interested sides—that Lyushkov had found refuge in Japan.[145]

Though the Japanese highly valued Lyushkov as a propaganda asset, they remained realistic about his knowledge of Soviet state secrets. As a Japanese intelligence colonel noted in an interview: 'It was amazing, in fact, that Lyushkov knew so little except his own job in the NKVD. As for secret intelligence affecting the Red Army in particular, I do not think it would be excessive to say that the commissar knew absolutely nothing.'[146] And he certainly knew nothing at all about Soviet agents abroad, so Orlov was inventing 'facts' as usual.

After resignation, in his letter to Stalin (probably never sent), Yezhov stated that, because of Lyushkov's defection, he 'literally went mad'.[147] On the evening of 15 June, three days after Lyushkov's escape, Frinovsky met the Far Eastern army commander Blücher in Yezhov's office to brief him about the Lyushkov case.[148] That was the only link between Lyushkov, the local NKVD chief, and Blücher, the military commander of the Far Eastern Red Army until his arrest in October.

Commissar of State Security Lyushkov was the highest NKVD officer ever to defect. Despite the lack of any military experience, he worked for the Japanese Kwantung Army in Manchukuo and in July 1945 was trans-ferred to the Japanese military mission in Dairen. There he was allegedly shot by the head of the mission to prevent him from getting caught by the invading Soviet army. His body was cremated under the false name of a Japanese serviceman.[149] By the time of his testimony in 1953, Orlov knew from the press that Lyushkov had been long dead, so he felt free to invent anything that could not be verified.

Asked about the NKVD crimes of 1938 before his own escape from Spain, Orlov was eager to entertain his listeners with stories as long as they did not concern his own work and supported his image of an anti-Stalinist whose life was permanently in danger:

Mr ORLOV. Now, another outstanding underground chief, a Soviet Party member [*sic*] and a Soviet national, was killed under the following circumstances in Rotterdam, Holland. He was called for an appointment to a certain cafeteria to meet a Soviet intelligence man from Moscow. He came there. They sipped their coffee, had their talk, and then that man from Moscow gave him a package which ostensibly contained 3 or 4 books. He walked out first from the café, the cafeteria, and the underground Soviet agent remained at his table for about 15 minutes.

In 15 minutes he walked out, and when he was in the doorway the bomb exploded. It was in the package, and he was killed.

Those things created a double terror, and no one knew whether he would survive if he defected.[150]

Orlov correctly judged that, among the American lawmakers who listened to him, there would be no experts. In fact, in the USA there are very few such experts even today, especially where the clandestine activities of the Soviet special services in such countries as Belgium or the Netherlands are concerned. Therefore, Orlov's lies went unnoticed, while, as it turned out, that murder in Rotterdam had indeed something to do with the NKVD in Spain. Some details of this operation became known only after the collapse of the Soviet Union.

According to police protocol, shortly after midday on Monday, 23 May 1938, a 41-year-old driver, Harm de Jonge, was strolling down Coolsingel, one of the best-known streets in the city, on which Rotterdam City Hall is located. As he moved in the direction of Hofplein and crossed Aert van Nesstraat, a side street of Coolsingel, de Jonge's attention was caught by a man with a small moustache and a grey fedora. It seemed the man had just left the Atlanta Hotel, carrying a small parcel covered in yellowish-brown paper in his left hand. He was already at a considerable distance from where de Jonge stood by the time he was outside the Lumière cinema. At that moment, at fourteen minutes past twelve, according to his testimony, de Jonge saw a blue flame coming from the parcel and heard an explosion. As he later told the police: 'I saw the body of the man being blown to the right, toward the pavement, where it landed close to the litterbin at the kerb. Part of one of his legs fell in front of my feet. I picked it up carefully and put it down by the body. His blood covered my shoes.'[151] This driver probably had nerves of steel.

According to the papers found on the dead body by the police, the victim was Josef Novak, who had arrived from Berlin by night train that same morning. He had taken a taxi to the Central Hotel at the Kruiskade and at 11.30 walked to the Atlanta Hotel in Coolsingel. In the ground floor bar he ordered a sherry, speaking German with a Slavic accent. About ten minutes later another man entered the bar. He went straight up to Novak and handed him a parcel that contained a nicely packed box of chocolates— or, rather, a professionally made explosive device. The second man had a quick beer and left the hotel within five minutes. A short while later Novak also left the Atlanta, thereby, as it was correctly noted, sparing the hotel considerable damage.[152] Though missing many details and inventing others as he narrated his story, Orlov was amazingly well informed about the operation that was taking place far away from his own turf, an operation that became known to specialists only twenty years after his death.

The victim, whose real name was Yevhen Konovalets, was not a 'Soviet Party member' and even not a Soviet national, as Orlov claimed. Quite the opposite, Colonel Konovalets was a leader of the Organization of Ukrainian Nationalists (OUN) and a zealous anti-communist. With his unit, Konovalets had fought for Ukrainian independence against the Bolsheviks and against the German puppet regime in the Ukraine in 1919–20. After the defeat, he settled in Berlin and continued the struggle, setting up a Ukrainian Military Organization in 1920. After the murder of the Ukrainian leader Symon Petlyura in Paris in May 1926, Konovalets became the unchallenged leader of the Ukrainian nationalist movement,[153] and in 1929 moved from Berlin to Geneva, where it was easy to maintain links with German and Lithuanian intelligence. He was expelled by Swiss authorities in 1936 and settled in Rome.

Soon after his arrival in Italy, Konovalets should have read in the newspapers that the Swiss police had uncovered one of secret 'communications points' (punkt svyazi) established by the Comintern/OMS in Zurich and detained two foreigners, one of whom was documented as 'Karl-Peter Normann' from Poland and another as the Austrian 'Josef Strenn'. Without doubt both names were false and their passports doctored. The two men recruited the Swiss family of Ernest Planque and his two sisters. The sisters were members of their country's foreign service, one in London, the other in Belgrade and subsequently in Antwerp. During the investigation it was established that 'Normann' had ordered Planque to spy on Konovalets. As reported in Geneva's *Le Courier*, in July 1936 the case came before a court, but the only person in the dock was Planque, because his sisters had disappeared without trace and both OMS agents, 'Normann' and 'Stren', had fled abroad after being released on bail. According to the Swiss scholar Peter Huber, the Planque sisters had been in contact with Roland Abbiate since 1934.[154] As already mentioned, together with Charles Martignat, Boris Afanasyev, and Gertrude Schildbach, Abbiate was one of the assassins of Ignatz Reiss, who was shot near Lausanne. It was not far from the place where Konovalets used to live: perhaps fortunately for him, by that time he had already been living in Rome, from where he actually came to Rotterdam.

The man who had handed over the deadly parcel to Konovalets in the Atlanta Hotel had called himself 'Valyukh'. He acted as a contact between the leadership of the OUN and the Ukrainian underground in the Soviet Union. The parcel was said to contain secret messages from Russia. The suspicion that 'Valyukh' was an NKVD plant came up immediately. Investigators soon established that before February 1938 this man, without doubt a fellow Ukrainian, had already been in touch with Konovalets. As a test, during their previous meeting in February, 'Valyukh' gave him cigarettes, chocolates, and a book of songs as a present. If Konovalets had refused to take those small gifts, he would probably have been killed in a different fashion. Even then NKVD psychologists worked on the behavioural pattern (psychological profile) of a future victim, while other specialists concentrated on the appropriate weapon.

While the daily paper of the Dutch Communist Party, *Het Volksdagblad*, characteristically described the stories in the media about Stalin's hand as 'fairy tales',[155] the police were able to establish that the assassin had made several telephone calls to Vienna and Berlin from the Hoofdpostkantoor (Head Post Office) located on the very same Coolsingel before he disappeared from the scene. That was almost certainly to report that the operation had been successful and at the same time to mislead the police by providing wrong leads, as shortly after the murder 'Valyukh' left for France.

Before two Dutch researchers published the results of their investigation almost sixty years after the events, Pavel Sudoplatov admitted in his memoirs that he had blown up Konovalets on the orders of his NKVD superiors. After spending two days in a safe house in Paris, he proceeded to Barcelona.

There, he was allegedly met by Orlov's deputy Eitingon and assigned to a guerrilla unit.[156]

For obvious reasons, neither Orlov nor Sudoplatov ever admitted that they had met in Spain.[157] But it could only have been in Barcelona that Orlov could have learned the details of the Rotterdam operation and only from Sudoplatov, the assassin. There was simply nobody else to tell him. As a small reward, Sudoplatov spent three weeks in Catalonia, almost certainly not fighting with the Dąbrowski Brigade (re-formed in August 1937), as he claimed in his book, but enjoying a well-deserved rest arranged by Orlov and Eitingon. By the end of June, he had returned to Moscow to report to Passov and Spiegelglass. In a few months, Sudoplatov would succeed them both as the new chief of the Soviet foreign intelligence in charge of Special Tasks.

Sudoplatov had hardly managed to reach Moscow after the 'action' in Rotterdam, when Belgian and French papers reported another brutal assassination. For a while, comrades and friends of the victim knew nothing about it.

In Brussels, the Congress was set for 16–17 July 1938, which was a weekend. On Saturday morning the Belgian socialist Georges Vereeken received a copy of a letter from Rudolf Klement, typed in German and addressed to the founder and leader of the IV International. Vereeken later recalled that he had to read it two or three times before he could believe his eyes. The long-time supporter and comrade Klement was accusing Trotsky of having deceived him, saying that he had gradually become aware of this. When Vereeken compared the handwritten signature on the letter with other letters from Klement in his possession, there was no room for doubt, or, at least, Vereeken was quite convinced that it was certainly his signature. 'Had he gone straight over to the enemy?' Vereeken thought.[158] For him, 'the enemy' were the Stalinists.

That was the last operation in which Orlov took part before he disappeared for fifteen years.

On or about 9 July, he sent the following cryptogram to Moscow from Barcelona: 'I confirm the receipt of your telegram No. 1743. In order to be in Antwerp on 14 July, I must depart from here on 11 July, or the 12th at the latest.' Orlov asked 'to be informed, before that date, the terms of my meeting with our comrade in Antwerp'. Then he also asked whether his people (five persons) 'must, by the 14th July, be in Europe already or can they, for the time being, stay in Spain in a state of readiness?'[159] Apparently, Orlov was referring to a list of names that both he and the Centre had.

Quite possibly it was a list of his CONSTRUCTION school graduates, because those who were expected in Europe by 14 July were designated only by numbers: 5, 10, 26, 27, and 29.

He was soon informed that, 'yes', the group must be in Europe by 14 July, to which SCHWED promptly responded:

Confirm the receipt of telegram No. 1750. On 12 July, I shall register my departure and send JOURNALIST [an unidentified female agent] to Brussels and her brother [unidentified, but obviously a wireless operator] to the city of FIN [Paris where the NKVD 'legal' resident at that time was Georgy Kosenko, codenamed FIN]. On 12 or 13 one of the five people mentioned in telegram 1743 will be transferred there [i.e. to Paris]. Contact with everybody will be prearranged. Wire whether the brother must take the radio transmitter with him, whether it should be packed, whether diplomatic correspondence and inventory should be destroyed. I shall be in Antwerp on July 14.[160]

Though their names have never been disclosed by Soviet intelligence, it is possible that numbers 26 and 27 from Orlov's list were the NKVD agent of Polish–Jewish origin Szyfra Lypszyc and her brother. It is known that Szyfra, whom the French Sûreté thought to be a 'militant member' of the French Communist Party, was in Spain during the war, and that she spoke French. Szyfra Lypszyc figures in Soviet documents only as 'Hanna';[161] she had arrived in London in November 1941 using the alias 'Anna Uspenskaya', to be dropped by parachute into France. She was the first Soviet agent of the wartime Operation PICKAXE. After several attempts she finally landed by boat in Brittany on 11 January 1941 and, accompanied by a special guide who knew the area well, successfully crossed the border. She managed to come to Paris and established contact with two groups of French agents and one 'Alex' who had been left behind especially when France was occupied. The two groups were led by experienced French agents 'Rom' and 'Gustav', the latter having operated in France since the late 1920s. In addition, according to the NKVD record, two small groups were also formed in the south of France in 1940 from the agents that had earlier been sent from Spain.[162] It will be remembered that, apart from a female agent and her wireless operator brother, Orlov's group included three more graduates of the Barcelona spy school. They all moved to France on 12–13 July 1938. If indeed Szyfra Lypszyc was one of them, after the operation she went to Moscow for further training.

Those frantic activities of a special group under Orlov's command somehow remained unaccounted for, while it seems that from early July

SCHWED had been preparing a 'clearing' operation that, he knew, would be his last one in this war—an operation that was to be conducted, not in Spain, but in Paris and Brussels simultaneously.

In Brussels, Vereeken, a member of the International Secretariat of the Fourth International and one of the leaders of the Belgian Trotskyists, had the impression that Klement's letter did not ring true, but he was inclined, as he later put in his book, 'to read cowardice and treachery into it'.[163] As he had only a few hours to comply with his responsibilities, he decided to meet his trusted comrades before the Founding Congress began in Paris. When he showed them the letter, they also learned that Klement had disappeared with all the documents that were to have been used at the Congress, whose aim was to make the official proclamation of the establishment of the Fourth (Trotskyite) International.[164] That was very bad news.

On Saturday, 20 August 1938, *La Lutte Ouvrière* came out with the article covering the story. 'All Klement's acts have been checked out up to Wednesday, July 13, at 1500 hrs,' it reported. 'On [July] 15 five copies of the same letter, addressed to Trotsky, were posted in Perpignan. This letter was supposed to justify Klement's so-called split with the Fourth International and give the GPU an alibi. The text is in German . . . The letter is officially addressed to the following members: Rous, Naville, Vereeken and Sneevliet [and Molinier].'[165]

The original German text is not available. What follows is the letter, translated first into French and then into English. But even in this version it is easy to find the same expressions, arguments, and speech patterns that are in all the other documents forged by Orlov to implicate other 'literniks' with whom he had to deal.[166] It is this unmistakable style that betrays the real author of the letter.

Mr Trotsky!

You cannot deny, even after reading this letter, that I have been a loyal fighter under the banner of the Fourth International. I thought it was preparing a new destiny for the international movement and I followed its progress and its battles to the point of fanaticism. In many cases I have carried out your will blindly and without hesitation. When you were in France and you assured me, supporting your argument with historical examples, that it was necessary to make some temporary concessions to the fascist leaders in the name of the proletarian revolution and the struggle against Stalinist dictatorship, I ended up by giving way to your arguments. But I thought at that time that this bloc, which was clinched on bases which were unclear to me, could undermine the movement; and my doubts were only removed by your explanation that this bloc was only a tactical step, that in the end the Fourth International would have its Austerlitz, and that history would justify us.

I remember now that this event caused me considerable psychological disturbance, due on the one hand to my good faith and blind devotion to the Fourth International and to yourself, and on the other to the fact that what you said was using fascism meant direct collaboration with the Gestapo.

My work on the IS [International Secretariat] during the last two years, under your direction and in part under Lyova's [Sedov], awoke many doubts which tortured me incessantly and led me to the conclusion that I had to break with you. I was not the only one to suffer under your Bonapartist methods. Because of your leadership, the *Fourth International has been amputated several times and is now nothing but a mutilated corpse* [emphasis added]. Nin, Roman Well [NKVD agent] and Jacob Frank have each left us in turn. You have let the POUM be torn apart by the Stalinists. Not long ago people like Sneevliet and Vereeken who showed such political sense and wisdom on the Spanish question also left us. Molinier, Jean Bur and his group, Ruth Fischer, Maslow, Brandler and others have left us. It would be puerile to think that public opinion can be calmed down solely by explaining that they are GPU agents. The position you have taken on one of the members of the John Dewey commission, describing Bills [*sic*, Carleton Beals] as a GPU agent, has only created more confusion.

I must state with the fullest sense of responsibility that the epileptic state of the Fourth International is a direct result of your methods of command and Lyova's. You think you can save the situation by calling an international conference to strengthen the IS (and with that aim you propose, obviously on a nod from 'over there', to bring Walter Held onto it). The absence of internal unity in our sections will degenerate at the conference into a split and the Fourth International will be faced not with any Austerlitz, but with a Waterloo. This will come after the Moscow trials have aroused suspicion even among some of our own adherents. Of course, the John Dewey commission is far from having dispelled that impression. The 'Pero'–Eiffel affair was also a big blow to the organisation. You yourself know how difficult it was for Lyova, Braun and myself to assemble some not very convincing material to lessen the blow dealt by the Moscow trials.

Now that I am persuaded of the bankruptcy of the Fourth International, and that I have completely understood where collaboration with fascism leads to and totally persuaded that the present situation can only be saved by fresh concessions to the bloc, I have decided to break off all relations with you, in the conviction that the path I have long followed loyally is sown with betrayals. I have no intention of intervening publicly against you, I am tired and weary of all that. I am going, and I leave my place for Walter Held to take.

Camille[167] (one of Klement's pseudonyms)

The weird irony of the letter is the picture of the allegedly current state of the Fourth International—'amputated several times and is now nothing but a mutilated corpse'; it turned out to be the exact description of what was left of Rudolf Klement himself.[168] At the end of August 1938, the decapitated and mutilated body of the former secretary to Trotsky was recovered from the Seine at Meulan, about 20 miles from Paris.

Sudoplatov wrote in his memoirs that Alexander Korotkov killed both Agabekov and Klement with the help of a 'Turk' whom he did not identify. In the case of Klement, according to Sudoplatov, they were also assisted by a young agent, Ale Taubman, codenamed YUNETS or YOUNGSTER,[169] a former mate of Grigulevich in the Lithuanian underground.[170] Sudoplatov recalled that Taubman was Klement's assistant for a year and a half. Herschl Mendel of the Left Opposition then living in Paris knew Taubman as 'the man from Grodno named Kaufmann'. He also met him with Klement on several occasions and thought the 'assistant' was very suspicious.[171] Korotkov, as mentioned, started his foreign intelligence career as a junior member of Nikolsky's operation in Paris five years before the Klement affair. It is very unlikely, though not entirely impossible, after his failure and near arrest at that time, that he would now be sent back to France.

Sudoplatov speculates that 'one night Taubman suggested that Klement join him for dinner with his friends and led Klement to an apartment on Boulevard Saint-Michel where the Turk and Korotkov stabbed Klement to death, cut off his head, put his body into a suitcase and threw it into the Seine'.[172] Christopher Andrew, using Mitrokhin notes, writes that 'on 13 July 1938 the NKVD abducted Klement from his Paris home'.[173] According to Broué's version, 'worried not to have seen him [Klement], several of [his party comrades] went to his flat at Maisons-Alfort where he lived under the name of Roger Bertran: all was in order and the table was laid for an uneaten meal'.[174] One does not normally lay a table for a meal before going out to a friendly dinner; it is difficult to abduct someone from his home without leaving a trace; and one has to bear in mind that from the Paris suburb of Maisons-Alfort to Boulevard Saint-Michel is a very considerable distance that is not easy to cover on foot. But Klement did disappear from his flat and was later found dead in the Seine, while five typed letters received by the members of the International Secretariat in Paris with a postmark *Perpignan RP 15 VII am Pyrenees Orles*, in addition to a handwritten letter received by Trotsky two weeks later, posted from New York,[175] suggest that it was a more complex operation, probably involving more people than the trio identified by Sudoplatov.

A group, mentioned in Orlov's telegram No. 316 dated 9 July 1938 and Moscow's telegrams Nos 1743 and 1750,[176] consisting of five graduates of the Barcelona spy school plus Orlov himself, were in Paris (except the woman, who went to Brussels) on 13 July. Because the NKVD legal head of station in France, Georgy Kosenko (FIN), had been 'burned' by his direct participation in the abduction of General Miller several months before, the operational back-up had to be secured by somebody else. Orlov, with his Soviet diplomatic passport, was in an ideal position to play this role. And he was there—in the right place at the right time.

Several decades later the KGB archivists released two pages from Korotkov's personal file that represent the beginning and the end of his three-page letter to Beria dated 9 January 1939, when he was suddenly sacked from the service. Page 32 (reverse) is missing, while the previous page ends with the words 'In December 1937 I was offered to go to . . .' and then the text breaks and continues with 'used to be elected secretary of the Komsomol cell of the department'. The author of the book where the letter was published for the first time, himself a former intelligence officer, reconstructs missing paragraphs in the following way:

In December 1937 I was offered to join the underground in France [*mne bylo predlozheno vyekhat v podpolie vo Franziyu*, i.e. 'I was sent on a secret mission to France'] to take charge of a group set up to liquidate several traitors who remained abroad.

In March 1938 my group liquidated ZHULIK ('Swindler'), in July KUSTAR ('Amature'), and I was personally leading these operations and did the most unpleasant and dirty work.

From the professional point of view, it is very hard to imagine that, after he had been exposed to the DST in Paris in 1934, Korotkov would be sent there again three years later as a group leader. If indeed, because of the tremendous deficit of other experienced officers, most of whom had been executed or sent to the Gulag in the middle of the Great Terror campaign, he was sent to do the dirty work, it is more likely that he joined his former chief (Nikolsky/Orlov) in Spain, from where, using it as a base, he could operate against targets in France. This is a standard practice for Soviet intelligence: to carry out operations against one country from the neighbouring territory. Although two 'literniks' codenamed ZHULIK and KUSTAR by the NKVD have never been identified, the circumstances and timing of operations point to Agabekov and Klement.[177] After the assassination of

Klement, Orlov was to proceed to Antwerp, where, on or about 14 July, he was to meet Speigelglass on board the Soviet steamer *Svir*.

Orlov's agents from the Barcelona spy school could have been used in this operation for surveillance and as a back-up team. The already mentioned Szyfra Lypszyc, an NKVD agent who was in Spain and later operated in France, was later described by the Sûreté as 'the French Communist militant'. She eventually got into trouble and was arrested by the Gestapo because, contrary to her orders, she decided to get involved in sabotage and subversion and was caught in an attempt to burn a granary.

This last liquidation in Paris offered Orlov an ideal opportunity to say farewell to his former service. He disappeared with his family on the same day, having obtained a letter of recommendation from the Canadian Consul General. It is almost certain that he had never tried to approach the US Embassy, as he claimed, because it would have been dangerous for him for a number of reasons.[178] As the USSR and Canada did not have diplomatic relations at that time and Orlov had never visited the country, it was much more secure for him to go to Canada. Besides, the SS *Montclare* would be sailing that very evening from Cherbourg to Montreal.

The Orlovs were exceptionally well prepared for the trip. Besides the sum of $22,800 that Orlov falsely declared he had 'saved',[179] Maria carried in her hand luggage the amount of $68,000—operational funds embezzled by the former head of station from his personal safe at the Soviet consulate on Avenida del Tibídabo in Barcelona.[180] Together this came to $90,800—a handsome sum at the time (representing over $1,500,000 in 2014). This time Orlov was going to America as a rich man.

Until August, no one looked for him, as it was not unusual for an operative to lay low for a while, especially after an 'action'. His absence could have been caused by many circumstances (Eitingon and Caridad Mercader, for example, had to spend a few months in Cuba after the assassination of Trotsky, before being able to return to Moscow). The Klement operation was developing according to the plan, and two weeks later, Trotsky received a usual Orlov-style 'posthumous' letter from his former secretary (with a New York stamp), so no one worried too much about the trusted Chekist who might have had plenty of reasons not to show up. His family could also not be contacted, because no one knew their address.

Orlov was gaining time, and his calculation was correct. A letter posted from Europe to Mexico would take about two weeks to reach its destination. Posted from the United States, it would take a couple of days. Therefore, he had two weeks and perhaps a few more days until an NKVD informer in Trotsky's secretariat would be able to identify the location of the sender by the postage stamps and make the corresponding report.[181] Because he knew about Mark Zborowski in Paris, he was sure that Trotsky's household in Mexico was also infiltrated. 'There is no such thing as a man with no weak point,' he was taught. 'Find that point, press the nerve, he'll cooperate.'[182] Whether he was right or wrong about the agent, two weeks proved to be enough initially to misdirect the NKVD and prepare his blackmail letter to Yezhov.

'When I arrived in Canada from Europe, I called up my cousin Isaac Rabinowitz,' Orlov later testified. 'I asked him to contact Nathan Koornick and to send him to me in Montreal because I needed the services of Nathan Koornick.'[183] He already knew from his previous trip to New York that such services would be provided upon demand.

Leiba Feldbin (now Orlov) had become reacquainted with his Koornick cousins while visiting Rabinowitz during his trip to the United States in the autumn of 1932. Then he, Eitingon, and Serebryansky had been exploring possibilities of setting up espionage networks in the United States using their Jewish relatives. Nathan Koornick told the FBI that he 'knew and liked Feldbin's father', and this was one of the reasons why he had responded immediately by travelling from Philadelphia to Montreal. He recalled how he had checked into the Hotel Windsor as instructed by Rabinowitz. It was in the lobby that he had met Orlov, who asked him to deliver two sealed letters to the Russian embassy in Paris.[184] Koornick took it for granted that he must help his relative and returned to New York to obtain a passport for a trip abroad.

It may, of course, be a coincidence, but the dates miraculously concur. Orlov entered France on the morning of 12 July 1938 at Le Perthus.[185] Klement was murdered in the late afternoon or evening of July 13. His four letters to the French and Belgian Trotskysts were mailed from Perpignan two days later. On 21 July the SS *Montclare* docked in Montreal. Within the next two days, Koornick visited his relative in Canada, after which he returned to New York. In his exile in Mexico, Trotsky received a letter 'from Klement' shortly after Koornick had returned to the United States from Canada after his meeting with Orlov. Thus, the letter reached Trotsky two weeks after his former secretary had been murdered by the NKVD,[186] because it had been posted by Koornik in New York on Orlov's request.

Naturally, he had never been asked about it, because the Klement case had never been investigated by the American authorities.[187]

Koornick was back in Canada by the beginning of August. Almost two decades later he told the FBI in Los Angeles that at that time he gave his relative $2,000. The loan was not solicited, as his cousin 'always appeared to live well and did not appear to be in need of any money'.[188] It was according to the unwritten rules.

Koornick explained to the FBI agents that his meetings with Feldbin/ Orlov were usually arranged through a mutual cousin, Isaac Rabinowitz, now deceased. Koornick remembered that he had left Montreal for Paris on a steamship operated by the Canadian Pacific Line, the name of which he had forgotten. Following instructions, he went to the city and immediately took a taxi to the Russian Embassy. It was a holiday, so only a single clerk appeared to be on duty. Koornick gave him a parcel prepared by Orlov, after which he immediately returned to the waiting taxi, went to the post office, as instructed, and dropped off a postcard. This postcard was addressed to Yakov Suritz, the Ambassador.[189] Koornick returned to Montreal on board the *Empress of Australia* and learned that his relative had gone to the United States without giving any forwarding address. Koornick did not see Orlov again until March 1954. According to the FBI report, at that time Orlov summoned Koornick to New York City and received from him an affidavit describing the activities that Koornick had performed for him in Paris in 1938.[190] Orlov was preparing for a confrontation with the US justice system that he knew would be inevitable.

As it turned out, Koornick was given two letters. He later recalled that the letters were addressed 'one to the head of the NKVD and the other to a personal friend of Stalin for personal delivery to Stalin'.[191] In reality, there had never been 'a letter to Stalin', though Orlov/SCHWED did indeed send two packages accompanied by letters. One was addressed to 'Comrades Suritz and Biryukov', the Ambassador and 1st Secretary of the Soviet Embassy in Paris. The text read: 'Please urgently forward this package to Nikolai Ivanovich Yezhov without showing it to Kislov. I am a member of the staff [service] of Nikolai Ivanovich.'[192] The second letter was to 'Kislov' (Georgy Kosenko, the NKVD head of station in Paris), explaining that two packages had been left at the embassy, one for him and one for Ambassador Suritz, and that both must be forwarded to Yezhov without delay.

The KGB decided to declassify Orlov's farewell letter with several deletions. Names of the NKVD officers and agents as well as of clandestine operations known to Nikolsky and included in a two-page appendix, which formed the essence of his blackmail effort, remain secret until this day. The appendix, with several omissions, is given here for the first time. As there is no FOIA in Russia, during the period of instability and disorder in the KGB of the early 1990s, some snippets of information were sold to selected Western authors piece by piece, without any possibility to re-check with the original documents. It also seems important to offer a new translation of the original letter from SCHWED to the NKVD chief.

For personal eyes only

To People's Commissar
Nikolai Ivanovich Yezhov

I would like to explain to you in this letter how I, after nineteen years of irreproachable service to the Party and to Soviet power, after years of underground work, after the Party and Government awarded me the orders of Lenin and the Red Banner for my efforts for two years of full and active self-sacrifice and struggle under the conditions of ruthless war—how it could have happened that I have left you.

My irreproachable life had always been dedicated to the service of the proletarian cause and Soviet power under the firm control of the [Communist] Party and members of the staff of our *Narkomat* [People's Commissariat]. I enjoyed great trust from the Soviet leadership and the party, was respected and loved by my comrades. Every hour, every minute, my heart was beating in unison with the pulse of the whole party, all of our beautiful motherland. Now, much deeper than any time before, I feel how happy I was with you, how rich and attractive, how full of deep sense, my life was and how senseless and superfluous it has now become. Just how could it have happened?

On 9 July I received a telegram from Sergey [Spiegelglass], which lacked any operational justification. It implied that, for absolutely preposterous and entirely incomprehensible reasons, I was being led into a trap aboard the steamship *Svir*, which had obviously been sent specially to capture me. The telegram instructed me to go to Antwerp on 14 July, where I would be met on board this steamship by a comrade I knew personally.

'It is desirable,' the telegram stated, 'that the first meeting take place on board'. To 'secure the secrecy of the meeting' it was suggested that I should travel by the diplomatic car from our embassy in France accompanied by the consul general . . .

I started to analyse the telegram: why should the first meeting take place aboard the ship? Why, if not to strike me down and transport me [to Russia] as a notorious enemy? Why should I have to be accompanied by a consul general in a diplomatic car unless it was to keep me under surveillance during the journey—or, in the event of some delay near the steamship, to invoke the power of the consul general to declare me insane after suffering concussion in Spain to claim that I was being escorted back to the USSR under great care. Security was the explanation given in the telegram regarding the diplomatic car . . .

This third-rate telegram, from the operational point of view, was only a smoke screen intended to cover an insidious trap set up for a totally innocent man. It was clear to me that the chief of the department showed an excess of zeal in his purge of the apparatus and had decided to advance his career by attempting to present me . . . as a criminal, who must by all means be lured on board as an 'enemy of the people'. Then he could shout 'hurrah' in expectation of being rewarded for a well-planned and executed operation. It was clear to me that my fate had been predetermined and that death lay in store for me.

I asked myself: do I, as a member of the Party, have the right, even under a threat of inescapable death, to refuse to go back home? My comrades who worked with me know that I have many times risked my life when required for the [Communist] cause and the Party.

I repeatedly exposed myself under heavy bombardment. Together with the naval attaché I was under attack from Fascist bombs for two whole weeks when unloading munitions ships—even though it was not part of my duties. I have risked my life many times fulfilling operational tasks known to you. At a distance of three paces a White Guard who sought to kill me, a hated Bolshevik, fired at me. When I was in plaster after crushing two of my vertebrae in a car incident, despite doctor's orders, I did not give up work, but continually drove to various towns at the front in the interests of the struggle with the enemy . . .

The Party had never demanded senseless death from its members, and certainly not in the interest of criminal career-makers.

But it was not even the threat of illegal and unjust punishment that stopped me from going to that steamship. It was the realization that, after my execution, and the exile or execution by a firing squad of my wife, my 14-year-old sick girl would find herself in the streets. She would be dogged by children and adults as the daughter of an 'enemy of the people'. That this should be the fate of the daughter of the father whom she was proud to consider an honest Communist and fighter was far beyond my power.

I am not a coward. I would even accept an erroneous, unjust verdict, holding for as long as possible, unwanted by anyone, a sacrificial lamb given to the Party, but to die knowing that my sick child would have to endure such horrible suffering—that was more than I could stand.

Could I count, upon arrival in the USSR, on a just investigation of my case? No, and once again no! My rationale is as follows:

1. The very fact that I was not recalled, but that an obvious trap was set up for me on that ship explains it all. Evidently I had been listed as an enemy of the people even before I was to step on board.

2. I would have found myself in the hands of a criminal named DOUGLAS [Spiegelglass], who, until July 1938, was the deputy head of the Foreign Department. He directed the NKVD assassination squads that bumped off Ignatz Reiss,

who was shot in 1937. I would have played right into the hands of DOUGLAS, who, out of purely personal motives, had already liquidated two most honest comrades. [Nikolsky obviously meant Stanislaw Glinski, former resident in Paris, and Theodor Maly, former resident in London, both of whom he knew. He was unaware that Ignace Reif, his former chief in Copenhagen, would also be arrested soon after his defection in July 1938, and shot.]

This is not all. I know that DOUGLAS gave the order to liquidate the hero of the Spanish War Walter [Karol Swierczewski, in Spain General Walter], who voluntarily spent sixteen months at the front. The name of this Walter is one of the few names popularly known to every soldier. This order was given by DOUGLAS based on unconfirmed rumours and hearsays that he, Walter, allegedly had 'unhealthy ideas that might lead to his refusal to go back home' . . .

Honest people did not fulfil this criminal order. Soon Walter, of his own volition, went back home as light of heart as ever, believing in the Party. There are many other examples that characterize the criminal nature of the man (D.) whose careerist motives made him ready to liquidate dozens of honest people and Party members, pretending that those operations were necessary for the success of our struggle against the enemies.

In this quest for popularity, the careerist DOUGLAS, in the presence of the members of my operational staff, talked glibly about the service, revealing a number of secrets. He terrorized my men by announcing names of our former co-workers who were shot by firing squad without trial (speaking just in style of the [notorious] *Novoe Vremya* magazine).

DOUGLAS himself, as well as trustworthy officers who arrived from home, tried to figure out what grounds they had for accusing our people, who enjoyed full confidence, of espionage while their networks continued to be operating and quite intact? If P. [Glinski, codenamed PYOTR, the NKVD head of station in Paris], for example, was a spy, why were we kept working with such a man as TULIP [Zborowski], whom he had recruited? How come he did not betray TULIP?[193] Or if M. [Maly, codenamed MANN, the 'illegal' station head in London] had been a spy, why did he not betray WAISE [Maclean] or SÖHNCHEN [Philby], or others who continue to work until now?[194]

In short, these are the reasons that persuaded me, a man devoted to the Party and the USSR, not to walk into the trap prepared for me aboard that ship by the criminal careerist DOUGLAS.

I want you, as a human being [Nikolsky writes this to Yezhov, Stalin's executioner], to appreciate every stage of the tragedy that I now have to endure: a loyal Party member deprived of the Party and an honest citizen deprived of my motherland.

My sole purpose now is to survive to bring up my child until she comes of age.

Always remember that I am not a traitor to my Party or my country. No one and nothing will ever make me betray the cause of the proletariat and the Soviet power. I did not want to leave my country any more than a fish wants to leave water, but delinquent activities of criminal people have thrown me in at the deep end... From my knowledge of other cases I know that your apparatus will concentrate all their reserves on my physical liquidation. Put a stop to your people! It suffices to say that they have caused me extreme misery by depriving me of the right to live and fight within the ranks of the Party to enjoy the just rewards of long years of unselfish service. I have been deprived not only of my country, but of the right to live and breathe the same air as the Soviet people.

If you leave me alone, I will never embark on anything harmful to the Party or the Soviet Union. I have not committed, nor will I commit, anything damaging to the Party and our country.

I solemnly swear to the end of my days not to utter a word that may harm the Party that brought me up or the country in which I grew up.

SCHWED

PS I ask you to issue an order not to disturb my old mother. She is now 70; she is innocent. I am the last of her four children to survive and she is a sick and unhappy creature.[195]

The Appendix reads as follows:

1. Removal of metal. Details. [Most certainly transportation of the Spanish gold to Russia.]

2. The case of [name deleted by the censors]. The trip: ALEKSEI [Chief of the 7th Department GUGB NKVD, Commissar of State Security 2nd Rank Abram A. Sloutsky. Possibly his trip to Spain in December 1936]. [Deleted] The CZECH and his wife [deleted, possibly Korotkov]. Their present location [possibly Paris, the assassination of Klement]. A letter post restante. Failures. The last means.

[Three lines deleted]

5. Details of [deleted] adventures [deleted]. The house of [deleted]. Travels. Breakfast at [deleted]. Details of negotiations with [deleted] on this case.

6. Details about FARMER [Nikolai Skoblin]. His ring (signed), left TO KADI [Naum Belkin], is in my possession. I also have his letter to [deleted, possibly Stanislav Glinski, the NKVD officer]. The key for a talk with 13 [female agent]. The last meetings with ALEXANDER [unidentified], their trip in the car with a stranger (F) and a frank conversation. The symbolic meaning of small parcels from DOUGLAS [Speigelglass].

[Two lines deleted]

9. All the history of the case NIKOLAI and NIKOLAYEVTSY [participants of the operation NIKOLAI, i.e., the arrest and assassination of Andreu Nin and arrests of other POUMists]. I have a draft of the cryptogram written by JUZIK [Grigulevich], as well as a draft of the letter written by SIEGFRIED [unidentified], which was found later in another copy after the operation.

[Three lines deleted]

13. A detailed history of all the affairs of TULIP [Mark Zborowski]. Have at my disposal two pages of his report home [to Moscow Centre] about the possibility of his failure and those responsible for this. All his role [*sic*]. All his deeds (SNEBLIT [Henk Sneevliet], LUGWIG [Ignatz Reiss], OLD MAN [Trotsky], SON [Lev Sedov]).

[Three lines deleted]

16. The work of GAMMA [Boris Afanasyev].

17. The trip of TROYAN [unidentified]. Its objective.

18–19. All *liter* [assassination] operations (some substantial evidence, witnesses ...)

20–29. [Deleted]

30. Have photographic pictures and real surnames of the participants in the operation NIKOLAI. Those who can identify these photos. The date of their departure to the [Soviet] Union. The photos are at three consulates (Swiss, Austrian and Polish). [Deleted].

31–33. [Deleted]

34–39. All about the OLD MAN and SON [Trotsky and Sedov]. The account of the whole work of everyone including GAMMA, TULIP and others.

40. About the show trials.

[Four lines deleted]

45. All the work in the country of Grafpen [Georgy B. Grafpen, alias Gregory Blank, codenamed SAM, legal NKVD resident in London].

46. All the work in the country of FIN [Georgy N. Kosenko, alias Kislov, codenamed FIN, legal NKVD resident in Paris].

And so forth. All this will never see the light of the day! [196]

The letter came as a great shock to Yezhov. He understood that after the escape of another ranking officer, Commissar Genrikh Lyushkov, on 13 June 1938—that is, exactly one month before Nikolsky—the ground was sinking beneath him. He did not report the fact to Stalin immediately in July, hoping that SCHWED would resurface one day. Now Yezhov feared that it would be one more count in his future indictment. [197] Nikolsky had never been recalled, nor were there any reasons to suspect him, far less to investigate or execute him, so a record was entered into his personal file after the receipt of his letter in August 1938 notifying that his 'flight was regarded as a result of fear and misunderstanding'. [198] At the same time, Eitingon was appointed acting chief and ordered to search his former boss's safe. A report was sent to the centre and a certificate written out stating that a sum in excess of $60,000 was missing.[199] Naturally, other valuables that Orlov took with him to America and later mentioned to Gazur, like a collection of classic mechanical gold wristwatches or ancient Moorish daggers, were simply not listed anywhere.

That was the ignominious end to the inglorious service career of the senior major of state security named Lev Lazarevich Nikolsky, chief of the NKVD in Spain. Fifteen years later he resurfaced in the United States as the NKVD 'General Alexander Orlov'—that is, under an invented title, rank, and name, representing an organization that had long ceased to exist.

When he took Orlov's place, Eitingon wrote to head office: 'In my opinion, we should put an end, once and forever, to misleading our chiefs and must teach our officers to report things as they are in reality. I stress once again that indulging in fantasies is dangerous in our business.'[200] Did Eitingon think that his former boss in his intelligence reports was 'indulging in fantasies'? On the other hand, maybe Orlov was right to act as he did, because, as one author put it, 'when Moscow received accurate intelligence, Stalin distrusted the source'.[201] Anyway, it is a very notable remark, clearly demonstrating what this experienced NKVD veteran thought about Orlov's work.

As soon as Sergey Marchenko, the Soviet chargé d'affaires, had returned to Spain after his visit to Moscow that autumn, he was summoned to the office of the Prime Minister. Marchenko reported:

In my first conversation with him after my return, Negrín incidentally touched on the questions of the work of our neighbors [officers of secret services] in Spain. He expressed a desire that the new leader of this work, Comrade Kotov [Eitingon], not advertise himself [sic] and not acquire a wide circle of official acquaintances (by this he was emphatically alluding to the indiscreet conduct of Com. Kotov's predecessors [Orlov and Belyaev/Belkin]). He declared bluntly that he thought a connection between Com. Kotov and his workers and the Ministry of Internal Affairs and SIM was inexpedient . . .

The fact that Negrín, who is always extremely delicate with regard to our people, considered it necessary to make such a remark undoubtedly indicates the great pressure on him from the Socialist party, the anarchists, and especially the agents of the Second International concerning the 'interference' of our people in police and counterintelligence work. Unfortunately, as I once reported, a number of workers who have now been recalled [Syroyezhkin and Belkin] did not understand that it was necessary to change their methods of work in a timely fashion and not to wait for the Spanish [leaders] themselves to demand it.

I informed Com. Kotov about this conversation with Negrín, and he will come to the appropriate conclusions from this [exchange].[202]

After Nikolsky had disappeared, his former subordinates were recalled to Moscow. Belkin was dismissed from the service and Syroezhkin arrested and shot. Nikolsky/Orlov could not have cared less about the fate of his comrades in arms—in July 1938 new life awaited him, a prosperous and peaceful life in America.

PART III

The Orlov Legacy

Interlude 3
The Letter

On 2 May 1939, an interesting letter was intercepted by the Security Service in London, but it did not pay much attention to it. The letter was duly filed but remained buried in the archives for another fifteen years and even then did not attract any attention. The message read in part:

From: Earl C. Reeves, Ridgewood, New Jersey, USA
To: Mrs Marie Brett-Perring [journalist and writer posing as an officer of the French Secret Service], 12 Nevern Place, Earls Court, London SW5 9PR
Date: 21 April 1939

. . .

'For your info, Gen. W. G. Krivitsky, in April 15 Satevepost [*Saturday Evening Post*] approximately tells all about Soviet and GPU in Spain, Yagoda in it, Moscow end. And in Spain 'NIKOLSKY, alias SCHWED, alias LYOVA, alias ORLOV'. Wasn't he your friend?'[1]

In 1939, as in 1953 when he surfaced in the USA, promptly becoming a public figure, MI5 had no information at all about Nikolsky/Orlov. And it certainly did not want to spend its time investigating (which was probably right), because, as will be seen, it would not make much progress anyway and because it knew the person to whom this letter was addressed. Quite remarkably, the Security Service had started watching the adventurous Mme Perring eighteen years before, in October 1918.

From the MI5 Registry (Personal File 12296, volumes 1–7):

Marie Anne Teresa de Styczinska BRETT PERRING: British/French (of Polish origin). Mrs PERRING's espionage career began in the First World War when she was in touch with French, British, German, and (later) Russian intelligence personnel. [The Service] decided that she was not to be trusted and was probably an 'agent provocateur'. She settled in Britain in the 1930's and in 1939 she claimed to have sent flowers to Hitler. The same year she was found to be selling information to the Japanese Naval Attaché and reporting to the British Union of Fascists. During the

Second World War she offered her services unsuccessfully to a number of Allied intelligence organisations. However, she also supplied information to the International News Service (part of the Randolph Hearst group) some of it to the detriment of the Allied cause. In 1942 she was prosecuted for possessing information useful to an enemy and sentenced to three months' imprisonment, after which she was detained until 1944.[2]

Still, maybe her American correspondent's query was not quite ungrounded as only three years earlier Marie Brett-Perring had boasted in an article written for the then very popular American magazine *Liberty* that, 'as a member of the famous French Sûreté Générale', she 'gained admission into the OGPU, notorious Russian secret service, and by it was taken to Moscow for special training'.[3] And, although this is almost certainly an exaggeration, according to the records that have already been opened to the public she had been closely watched for thirty years and MI5 watchers noted that at least in London she was indeed in touch with some members of Russian intelligence. Was not Edita Suschitzka, a.k.a. Edith Tudor-Hart, whose leads helped to recruit Philby, Wynn, and a number of other spies in the UK, a friend of Maria Styczinska, a.k.a. Marie Brett-Perring? And EDITH (Tudor-Hart) was a member of the group, briefly headed by Nikolsky, then posing as an American businessman Goldin, and later living in the United States as Alexander Orlov, who indeed possessed a lot of information very useful to the Security Service. A simple letter from America? As a wise man noticed, opportunity is often difficult to recognize; we usually expect it to beckon us with beepers and billboards.[4]

While in May 1939 MI5 simply did not comprehend the importance of the intercepted telegram, an additional opportunity was presented to its FBI colleagues after it had missed Orlov, a.k.a Koornick, a.k.a Berg, several times before and during the war. It will be remembered that the Boston office conducted an exhaustive investigation throughout the United States looking for the Orlovs, who were only known to them as 'Alexander L. and Marie Berg', for whatever reason 'believed to be of German extraction and sympathies', as one FBI memo stated.[5] In May 1944, shortly before his tour of duty in the USA was over, Grigory Heifetz (sometimes spelt 'Kheifets'), the NKVD head of station in San Francisco, sent a short telegram to Pavel Fitin, the 31-year-old chief of Soviet foreign intelligence. In his telegram Heifetz, codenamed Haron (also Charon or Kharon, the mythical ferryman of Hades), asked Fitin to remind him of the surname of Orlov.[6] The telegram was a response to the earlier instruction from Moscow. It means

that, although Fitin had joined the NKVD in November 1938 after Orlov
had defected and almost certainly had never heard about him before he was
promoted to head Soviet foreign intelligence in May 1939, by the end of the
war he had some ideas regarding this defector and ordered the San Francisco
residency to find Orlov. Naturally, neither the Russian Section of the US
Army's Signal Intelligence Service at Arlington Hall nor the FBI had heard
the name Orlov before he surfaced in the USA with his articles. And,
although VENONA was a joined project, the all-important intercept at the
MI5 registry was ignored, together with Krivitsky's testimonies, when the
decryption of Soviet traffic, together with the verification of names and
aliases at Arlington Hall, began in 1946. As Orlov's wife Maria wrote in a
letter to her husband, they were terribly lucky all their life.[7] Or maybe luck
and good fortune had nothing to do with the case of Orlov, and Kim
Philby, who headed the foreign counter-intelligence Section V of MI6 at
the time, did his best to ensure that no information about this particular
person could reach America. Good luck or not, Orlov managed to remain
in hiding for fifteen years. Everything changed in 1953: Stalin died, Beria
was executed, and Fitin was discharged from the NKVD. By that time
Philby had resigned from MI6 and had been unemployed for about two
years. In April, Orlov surfaced in New York with his sensational revelations
and immediately became famous though no less secretive and cautious. The
KGB residency was able to find him in Ann Arbor only in November 1969.

21

From Trotsky to Tito

As Benjamin Disraeli put it, it is probably true that the secret of success in life is for a man to be ready for his opportunity when it comes. Sudoplatov had been ready. After his return from Rotterdam, where he had successfully blown up the leader of the Ukrainian nationalists and his three-week sojourn in Barcelona, he returned to Moscow and was immediately promoted, at the same time acquiring a reputation as a first-rate demolition expert. In March 1939 Sudoplatov received instructions personally from Stalin to kill Trotsky and on the same day was appointed deputy head of foreign intelligence. He promptly moved into his new office, No. 735 on the seventh floor of the Lubyanka building that used to be Sloutsky's quarters. Soon Eitingon, who had just returned from France, where he had moved after the Republican defeat, was introduced to Pavel Fitin, the 32-year-old new chief of foreign intelligence just promoted to this post,[1] as an officer in charge of Trotsky's assassination operation. Codenamed UTKA ('Duck'), this operation was given absolute priority over any other tasks. The plan, signed by Fitin, Sudoplatov, and Eitingon (now codenamed TOM) and typed personally by Sudoplatov in one copy only, had been ready by early July and approved by Stalin in early August 1939.[2] By that time preparations for the 'action' were already in full swing.

In 1936, en route to Mexico, Trotsky wrote: 'Stalin conducts a struggle on a totally different plane. He seeks to strike not at the ideas of the opponent, but at his skull.'[3] The KGB version of the operation claims that by April 1938 two reliable 'illegals', who had also taken part in the Spanish Civil War—'Felipe' and 'Mario'—had arrived in New York on board a Soviet ship from Novorossiysk and quickly established contact with the New York NKVD station. This must be dismissed as an invention, first because nothing has so far been heard about Soviet sailings between New York and Novorossiysk, either by commercial fleet, or indeed by cruise or passenger ship. Besides, only diplomats were permitted to travel by direct routes, while the 'illegals' were obliged (and still follow this rule) to use complex roundabout ways to reach their final destination. Indeed, both 'Mario' and 'Felipe' (the latter was Grigulevich) arrived from New York where they came from Paris. In June 1939 both were already in Mexico. But, in the previous November, Spiegelglass, who was in charge of the operation in Moscow, and Peter Gutzeit, the first NKVD head of station in New York and controller of the pair, were arrested. Accordingly, the agents were ordered to return to the United States. Grigulevich successfully landed there in July 1939, but 'Mario' is said to have been detained on the border and, after some time (and thanks to the efforts of the New York NKVD station) was expelled to Mexico.[4] The semi-official KGB historians do not say what happened to this agent thereafter, except that after the operation 'Felipe' and 'Mario', as well as several other participants, managed to leave the country. Thus David Serrano Andonegui, a militant communist and ex-major of the Spanish republican army who took an active part in the attack against Trotsky and who was accused by Don Levine of having been a trained NKVD agent, must be excluded from the list of suspects. He could not have been 'Mario', because he was soon arrested and tried. In January 1940, Grigulevich/Felipe was allegedly reporting the situation at the Lubyanka head office and by mid-February was back in New York. The KGB account also asserts, quoting the operational plan UTKA, that 'individuals who were previously to be used in the operation would not be used at this stage'.[5]

Nevertheless, Grigulevich/Felipe arrived in Mexico, again driving a 'luxurious, dark coloured car', as it was later described, and establishing his quarters in a nice house in the Acacias in Mexico City, rented from a rich landlord with perfect reputation. Not by chance, the house was conveniently close to Avenida Coyoacán. Soon Grig contacted Antonio Pujol Jiménez (codenamed JOSE), whom he later described as 'very loyal, exceptionally reliable and quite bold'.[6] Back in 1933 Pujol had become a member of the League of the Revolutionary Writers and Artists and in 1936, together with celebrated Mexican painters David Alfaro Siqueiros and Luis Arenal, had participated in the first Pan-American Congress of Artists against War and Fascism. Shortly after the congress Pujol joined the International Brigades in Spain, where he was spotted by the NKVD and agreed to cooperate. Among Grigulevich's other collaborators were his future wife, the Mexican Communist Laura Araujo Aguilar (LUISA) and both Arenal brothers, Luis and Leopoldo. In Coyoacán, one of the boroughs of the Federal District of Mexico City where Trotsky and his entourage lived, Pujol used two communist girls, Julia Barrados Hernandez and Ana Lopez Chavez, to rent an apartment that could be used to watch the house and entertain police officers who were sent by the authorities to guard the famous Russian revolutionary.

As usual, there were two different plans of action. According to the first plan, which seemed almost perfect, the attack on the Trotsky villa in Coyoacán was to be led by a group of agents drawn from the veterans of the Spanish Civil War, headed by Siqueiros, a former lieutenant colonel of the Popular Army, with Pujol and David Serrano acting as his second-in-command. Serrano had fought in Spain with the Republican forces and reportedly 'had been trained in Moscow and Spain in NKVD work for the preceding six years',[7] though there is no way to prove it. In any event, this group was directed by Grigulevich. The whole operation was controlled by Eitingon (codenamed TOM). He was also in charge of a small back-up unit (Group MOTHER) that included the Spanish Communist Caridad Mercader, who was given a code name KLAVA/CLAUDIA and her son Ramón, with an equally uncomplicated code name RAYMOND. She had been born on 31 March 1892 to a wealthy family in Santiago de Cuba as Eustacia María Caridad del Río Hernández. A mother of four, she had left her husband, the Spanish railroad magnate Pablo Mercader Marina, and fled to Paris. When the Spanish Civil War broke out, she was living in Barcelona, and together with the anarchists successfully fought against the rebels. Her eldest son Pablo was killed in action. Ramón, her middle son born in 1914, commanded a Republican army unit. The youngest son, Luis, and her beautiful daughter, Montserrat, came to Moscow in 1939 with other children of Spanish Republicans who had fled from Franco.[8] According to Kirill Khenkin, who served with him in Spain, Ramón was sent to Moscow in the summer of 1937 for formal recruitment and training.[9] However, Isaac Don Levine, who was one of the first writers to investigate the case, claimed that Lieutenant Mercader left the fortress in Barcelona's Montjuïc, where he was recovering from wounds received at the Aragon front, arriving in Moscow in December 'as a protégé of Eitingon',[10] which must be his euphemism for a 'recruit' and again may or may not be true. According to the semi-official KGB history, Ramón was recruited in 1937 and sent to Paris on a doctored Belgian passport in the name of 'Jacques Mornard' to work among the Trotskyists in early 1938. This suggests that Khenkin was probably right, because Ramón certainly needed time to take up and adapt to a new role of a Belgian playboy cum businessman, though, of course, he was born of a good family and spoke French as a Frenchman. With the help of an NKVD collaborator named Ruby Weil, who was approached with a request for assistance by a Soviet undercover agent in New York,[11] Mercader got acquainted with Sylvia Angeloff, an American Trotskyist, who played a key role in introducing him to Trotsky's inner circle. They both attended the founding conference of the Fourth International in Périgny, France, in September 1938.

From the end of 1939 Operation UTKA was simultaneously run out of the Soviet missions in Paris and New York. It was supported in Paris by Lev Petrovich Vasilevsky,[12] who had come from Spain and was now using the cover of Consul General, and in New York by the old member of the Spiegelglass–Gutzeit team named Grigory Rabinovich. He was a former Kremlin and Lubyanka physician sent on an intelligence mission posing as a representative of the Soviet Red Cross. It was decided that, as a Jew and a medical doctor, Rabinovich was best suited to penetrate Trotsky's organization. At the Lubyanka headquarters he was given the code name LUCH ('Beam'), arriving in New York in September 1934. He was recalled to Moscow in 1936 or in early 1937, only to be sent back to the United States in November 1937.[13] Now codenamed GARRI ('Harry'), Rabinovich started receiving information that finally helped to identify the Angeloff sisters as reliable leads to Trotsky's household in Mexico.[14] However, his Red Cross office was not the only base of an anti-Trotsky operation in the New York City area.

From the Soviet Consulate General, Pavel Panteleimonivich Pastelnyak was assigned to supervise the operation. Pastelnyak, documented as 'P. P. Klarin' (codenamed LUKA), was sent to New York in March 1939 as head of security of the Soviet pavilion at the New York World's Fair, where one of his assistants was the young officer by the name of Konstantin Alekseyevich Chugunov (alias 'K. A. Shabanov', later codenamed SHAH).[15] In response to a sudden summons from Moscow, the official Soviet delegation left the fair in early December, but Pastelnyak and Chugunov were assigned to the NKVD station then headed by Gaik Ovakimyan (who succeeded Gutzeit).[16] Ovakimyan (GENNADY) had already asked Moscow in August 1939 to promote Konstantin Kukin (IGOR) to his deputy and let Pastelnyak (LUKA) stay in New York.[17] Later Pastelnyak became his deputy, with a separate channel of communication with Moscow. Eitingon also spent several months in Paris preparing to leave for America and Mexico, which he finally did using an Iraqi passport.

Ramón Mercader was also in Paris. For some reasons the US Embassy was not quite satisfied with his Belgian documents and refused to grant him an entry visa, so Moscow supplied Ramón with new Canadian papers identifying him as 'Frank Jacson' (with a error in the spelling of the surname, typical of the NKVD forgers; as mentioned earlier, Maly's American and Nikolsky's Austrian passports contained similar misspellings). It seems that, as far as Operation UTKA was concerned, the Paris NKVD station was active only until the end of March 1940, when Ambassador Surits became a *persona non grata* and had to leave France—the Soviet ambassador was no longer welcome, as he had been cabling home with some harsh criticism of 'Anglo-French warmongers'. Thus, New York and Mexico City became the two most important centres for the anti-Trotsky activity and Grigulevich became one of the leading players.

It is certainly wrong to think, as some do, that a key part of the initial assault plan was the infiltration of a young American 'agent', Robert Sheldon Harte (codenamed AMUR or CUPID), pretending to be a New York Trotskyist, as a volunteer guard at Trotsky's villa.[18] Harte's role was only to open the main gate of the guarded compound on Vienna Street after the assault group had staged its surprise attack at about four o'clock in the morning of 24 May. The American was young and naive and, according to General Salazar, who headed the investigation, a devoted Stalinist, but quite surely not an agent. (At about the same time as Sheldon left for Mexico City in April 1940, a real agent, Tom Black, was given money and told by his NKVD controller in New York to go to Mexico to spy on the Trotsky household, but, he later told the FBI, he somehow neglected this assignment. A few months later Trotsky was murdered.)[19] One Nestor Sánchez, who became acquainted with Siqueiros in Paris at the time of the Spanish Civil War and who also took part in the attack on Trotsky's house, stated in his police testimony that 'Siqueiros had assured us that all would go well because one of Trotsky's guards had been bought'. He added that he (Sheldon) 'had no doubt been bribed by the French Jew',[20] which was how he described Grigulevich/Felipe. Both Siqueiros and Grig decided not to brief Sheldon Harte on what would happen after he had opened the gate. This is indirect proof that he was not an agent, as claimed in many published accounts, but a naive collaborator who was kept in the dark about the whole affair. In his account of the attack, written immediately after it, Trotsky reasonably argued that 'if Sheldon Harte were an agent of the GPU he could have killed me at night and gotten away without setting in motion 20 people

all of whom were subjected to a great risk'.[21] An even more solid corrob-
oration comes from the VENONA decrypts, where in a message from New
York to Moscow (Nos 1143–4) Robert Sheldon Harte was named by his full
name and some concern was expressed that a new investigation into his
murder was being demanded by Trotsky's widow.[22] Mexican investigators
found out that Robert spent the night of 21 May—that is, three days before
the attack on the villa—at the Hotel Europa with a prostitute, who was soon
found. She testified that Sheldon had a large sum of money on him and was
a little drunk that night,[23] without doubt after leaving the company of Grig,
who was only 25 then, two years Robert's senior.

KGB records, seen and copied by Vasili Mitrokhin, identify Grigulevich
as the leader of the assault on Trotsky's villa. The head of the Mexican secret
police, General Leandro Sánchez Salazar, described him as 'undoubtedly an
agent of the G.P.U. and the real instigator of the attack'. Like his key
witnesses, the Mexican police chief believed Grigulevich to be 'a French
Jew' partly as a result of discovering some of his underwear 'bought on the
Boulevard Saint Michel in Paris'. This is another indicator that Grigulevich
indeed operated in Paris after his ten-month assignment in Spain, as Sudoplatov recalled. From there he and 'Mario' sailed to New York. The
remaining 2,000 miles to Mexico they travelled by train.

At this stage the role of Eitingon was that of a supervisor, while the whole
organization was given to Grigulevich and Siqueiros. A much more senior
and experienced operative, Eitingon remained in the shadows, virtually
unknown to other participants. General (then Colonel) Salazar wrote that
it seemed 'all the important agents of the G.P.U. [sic] use the simplest names
(Pedro, Leopoldo, Felipe) and that their own collaborators do not know
their real identity'.[24] He identifies the Communist and Spanish Civil War
veteran Juan Zúñiga Camacho, 'one of the three people who played an
important role' in the May attack, as 'Pedro'. Remarkably, Eitingon's
documented cover name in Spain was also 'Pedro' or 'Pierre' (while he
signed his reports from Mexico as TOM). Thus, one may conclude that the
Mexican police knew little about Eitingon or had been misled by the
mixture of real and cover names. 'Leopoldo' was almost certainly Leopoldo
Arenal.

Whoever planned this operation, it was planned rather well. It addition to
a reliable and unsuspecting contact inside Trotsky's well-guarded villa
(Sheldon Harte), and about twenty armed young people in military and
police uniforms, many of them former Spanish fighters, two young and

attractive women were additionally employed to watch the villa and, if necessary, seduce members of the police force assigned by the government to guard it. Julia Barradas Hernandez, the former wife of David Serrano, and Ana Lopez Chavez, a girlfriend of another member of the Siqueiros group by the name of Mariano Herrera Vasquez, rented Apartments 11 and 13 in the tenement house at 85 Abasolo Street, a few steps from where Trotsky and his entourage resided. They expertly combined duty and fun, and by the end of May had befriended many police officers. On the night of 23/24 May the girls organized a big party, with their police friends taking part. After hearing the first shots from the villa, they disappeared.

Besides all these measures, an extra facility was also rented in the village of Santa Rosa on the Desert of the Lions road (but in reality nearly a mile off the road) on the top of the hill. It was a hut used as one of the external bases, though many people, including Grig, Siqueiros, his wife Angélica Arenal, her two brothers Luis and Leopoldo, Antonio Pujol, and a few others knew about it and either visited or stayed there for some time, which later allowed the police to find the house and learn the fate of Robert Sheldon Harte.

Harte was visibly shocked by the attack. Eitingon testified during an interrogation after his arrest in 1953, no doubt tongue in cheek, that 'Sheldon appeared to be a traitor and brought the attackers to the room where there was neither Trotsky nor his archive. As soon as they started shooting he angrily told the assault group that being an American, had he known how they would behave, he would never have let them in.' He also said that Sheldon was murdered by the Mexicans.[25] Sudoplatov, who was in charge of the whole operation, admitted, quite uninhibitedly, that Harte was taken away and shot because he knew Grigulevich and could expose him. 'And what else could we do with him!' exclaimed Grig when later asked for the reason young Sheldon was murdered. 'To hide him away and then illegally transport to Moscow would be too complicated.'[26] Harte's corpse was found in a shallow well filled with lime in a garden near the hut. The house was rented by Luis Arenal, the brother-in-law of Alfaro Siqueiros.

Regarding 'Mario', whose role in this operation remains unclear, it was the NKVD code name for Vittorio Vidali. Under the pseudonym 'Carlos Contreras', Vidali had played a crucial role in the founding of the famous Fifth Regiment[27] during the civil war in Spain. Both Siqueiros and Grigulevich briefly served in the regiment, which later became the core of the Popular Army. Among the attackers there were many veterans of the

Spanish Civil War, and it is reasonable to think that Vidali could have acted as a political instructor here, too, while Siqueiros and Grigulevich were busy with the administration. Vidali could also have served as a liaison to the Partido Comunista Mexicano (PCM, Mexican Communist Party), being one of the members of its Central Committee, because the operation required a lot of support from the PCM, including a considerable propaganda effort. Whatever his role, he managed to escape unscathed.

The failure of the first attack on the villa in May 1940, followed by the dispersal of Siqueiros's gunmen, led the second group of assassins (Eitingon, Caridad, and Ramón Mercader) to start implementing the back-up plan. In due course, Siqueiros was tracked down and arrested. Grigulevich, however, remained unidentified by the Mexican police and managed to smuggle himself, Pujol, and Laura out of the country, assisted by the Chilean Consul General in Mexico, Pablo Neruda. For a while, the trio settled in Montevideo, Uruguay, where Pujol took the name 'Abel Bertrán Bastar'. Together with his wife Ada, whom he met during his forced exile, he returned to Mexico in 1960. Another important accomplice, Juan Zúñiga Camacho, then about 28 years old, also escaped arrest.

The KGB account adds that, apart from the Felipe group, Luis and Leopoldo Arenal also managed to escape. Later Luis Arenal assisted Siqueiros in the creation of murals, and lived in Mexico City until his death in May 1985. Leopoldo Arenal and his second wife, Rose, using forged Cuban passports in the name of Francisco José Guillén y Fernández with the help of Grigulevich's friend Neruda, quickly received Chilean visas and disappeared in Santiago de Chile. It is possible, though not certain, that Leopoldo Arenal later figured in the VENONA intercepts as 'Alexander'. Remarkably, 'Mario' (who figures but is not identified either in the VENONA intercepts from New York or in the KGB history volume) never appeared in any document relating to this operation, including the award list that names all its principal participants. It seems that the role attributed to Vidali in this particular operation is greatly exaggerated in most of the published accounts both in Russia and in the West.

In late May or early June 1940, an inspector from Moscow Centre named Andrey Grigoryevich Graur (alias 'Vetrov') visited New York. In his report to Beria, Graur recommended recalling Ovakimyan as a 'politically untrustworthy person', and JUNG (Akhmerov), HARRY (Rabinovich), JUZIK (Grigulevich), and MARTINEZ (unidentified)[28] as operatives who had been enlisted by enemies of the people Yezhov and Spiegelglass.

Trotsky was killed by Ramón Mercader on 20 August 1940. The NKVD assassin, whose identity was a mystery until September 1950, had served his full term in prison, spending 19 years, 8 months, and 14 days of his life in the 'Black Palace of Lecumberri' (which now houses the Archivo General de la Nación), together with other criminals. On 6 June 1941 Beria wrote a memo to Stalin, and about a week later the Presidium of the Supreme Soviet of the USSR issued a decree that remained secret for over half a century.[29] According to it, Grigulevich was awarded the Order of the Red Star for 'exemplary performance of special tasks', according to its statute.

Beria clearly liked young Grig, and Grigulevich did his best not to disappoint his patron. It seems that in February 1941 he received a new secret order from Moscow. This time it was to do in Krivitsky in New York. Naturally, the following story told by Grigulevich to his KGB colleague Nikolai Leonov may not accurately describe what actually happened. And, just like every other KGB officer, General Leonov cannot be expected to tell the truth.[30] However, the story is important, as it may add some new details to one last episode of Krivitsky's life that still remains unclarified.

Walter Krivitsky, one of the most notable of all Soviet pre-war defectors, was not happy in New York, as he felt that Big Brothers from Moscow were watching him and setting up a trap. Several incidents were reported by Krivitsky and his friends. In the Bureau files there are indeed confessions of Soviet agents like Wally Amadeo Sabatini (codenamed NICK), veteran of the Spanish Civil War, who, interviewed by the FBI in the early 1950s, said that he had tailed Krivitsky.[31] One FBI memo states that another Soviet agent in the USA, Joseph Katz, utilized Irving Raymond Schuman and Sabatini in watching Krivitsky. Schuman and Sabatini served together in what later became known as the Lincoln Battalion. The archival records show that Sabatini, whose 'education ended at age 14', attended the International Lenin School in Moscow in 1933. In Spain, Sabatini was political commissar of the Mackenzie–Papineau Battalion and later a member of the Communist Party's Control Commission[32]—a special body established to watch and exercise discipline over International Brigade personnel. One history of the Lincolns noted an uncompromising speech by Sabatini calling for the execution of deserters. At some point, the NKVD recruited him as an agent.

This is what Grigulevich allegedly told his friend Leonov:

In early 1940s [sic], I was on an undercover mission to one of the Latin American countries. One day over a wireless transmitter there comes an order, 'Go to the

USA immediately and liquidate a dangerous traitor sentenced by the Soviet court.' So I come to the United States, buy a revolver, which was not a problem at that time, and start to prepare for the action. My operational brief suggested that the object lived in New York. I visited the hotel where I knew he had been staying and noted its telephone number. Just to be sure, I called him and said that I was a former prisoner of war, learned that he was in America, and suggested that we should continue our fight with the USSR. I offered to meet him in person and asked about his schedule. He said that he was normally busy in the morning and asked that I call in the afternoon in two or three days.

However, quite soon Grig realized that to kill a man in America required more ingenuity than he expected. First of all, he told Leonov, he had to inspect all entrances and exits of the hotel where his victim was staying, in order to decide what distraction (*imitatsiya*) should be used in this operation. (In the KGB lingo, *imitatsiya* is part of the escape technique: a sudden fire, smoke, alarm, loud explosion, or a siren outside the doors to distract attention and allow the assassin to clear the area unnoticed.) Grig further explained:

On the day I planned to do away with the traitor, I popped in a café for a cup of morning coffee. When I opened a newspaper, I could not believe my eyes—the headlines were screaming about a Russian émigré who mysteriously committed suicide in his hotel room last night. I immediately rushed to the hotel. The newspaper report was confirmed by the staff and I learned that the dead body was brought to the mortuary. So I went there and found out that it was very true indeed and that it was my man.

According to Grigulevich, this affair ended quite unexpectedly:

Upon returning to my base in a Latin American country, I radioed to the Centre that, unfortunately, there was no chance to fulfil their order as the object committed suicide. In two days there comes a cryptogram: 'Congratulations! Your mission has been very successful and you are awarded the Order of the Red Banner.'[33] I again informed Moscow that I had absolutely nothing to do with it. In their response they said they understood that after such a difficult and exhausting mission my nervous system needed rest and suggested that I go to Acapulco or elsewhere for a three-week holiday.[34]

Krivitsky was collaborating with the authorities, revealing what he knew to the enemy and, unlike Orlov, was becoming increasingly dangerous to Soviet intelligence. About a year before, Nicholas Dozenberg was imprisoned as a result of his disclosures. Dozenberg was a member of a massive spy ring set up in the United States by the RU in the mid-1920s.

Earl Browder, the CPUSA leader, whose whole family worked for the NKVD and who was personally seeing off American volunteers departing for the Republican Spain, was another victim of Krivitsky's revelations. He finally entered the federal penitentiary in Atlanta in March, but stayed only until May of the following year, when President Roosevelt pardoned him as a goodwill gesture to the American Communist Party and the Soviet Union. In January 1941, when Grigulevich presumably received his orders to go to New York and liquidate the traitor, Vernon Kell and Jane Archer of MI5 were searching for Krivitsky to ask him more questions and the Moscow Centre learned about the developments from their 'mole' in the Security Service.[35] Blunt passed his first batch of MI5 documents to the NKVD London station at exactly that time and among them was a complete copy of the previous debriefing of Krivitsky, with several useful leads.[36] At the same time, as often happens, within the Security Service itself, some people were quite sceptical about Krivitsky and his 'product'. One memo from an unidentified British official states:

Krivitski [sic] may have been thrown out of Russia by Stalin but he is still a Communist. His lawyer, Louis Waldman, is a well-known Shyster. I consider this man a traitor, liar and a dyed-in-the-wool Communist. My belief is that while he might not be unwilling to stab one of Stalin's men in the back, if it came to a showdown he would revert to type and stab us in the back.[37]

Even far away in America, the defector had every reason to worry. According to his biographer, on 5 February 1941, the day after one of his friends had left him near his subway stop in New York, Krivitsky telephoned Waldman, a Ukrainian-born lawyer and attorney for his family, telling him he was going to Washington to request FBI protection.[38] It was high time for Beria to give his final go-ahead to the assassin.

Later, the victim's cause of death would be registered as suicide. But one may argue that Krivitsky had little reason to commit a suicide. He was constantly, fiercely, fighting for his life, and succeeded in avoiding at least one NKVD trap in Paris. With great difficulty he managed to escape with his family to New York. There, under very tough circumstances, he was lucky not only to survive but also to become rather famous and make enough money to live a decent life. Finally, he was due to testify during the next Congressional hearing, which was a token of acceptance and trust. And he had a small son and a wife to take care of in America.

On the other hand, Krivitsky had never been a general, nor was he ever in charge of 'the whole Soviet military intelligence in Western Europe', as so many people believed. Krivitsky knew very little about the structure and staff of the Soviet intelligence services, even in the historic perspective.[39] He none the less managed to transform MI5's understanding of the nature and extent of Soviet intelligence operations,[40] and provided several leads that resulted in many interviews and even some arrests of Soviet intelligence assets on both sides of the Atlantic. Fully understanding that he was a hunted man, Krivitsky so feared for his life that this could have become a mania that led him to end it by his own hand—that is, if Grigulevich was not inventing and Krivitsky was not his operation.

Before the Second World War, there was no legal NKVD station in Argentina, and Moscow was convinced that the country was a major Nazi base. Though this belief was greatly exaggerated, it was shared by the FBI to such an extent that, in June 1940, J. Edgar Hoover, according to a recent report, produced his plan for a new clandestine intelligence agency, the Special Intelligence Service, to operate across Latin America to counter any threat from the Nazis. The new agency, which, ironically, was known as SIS, was headed by Assistant Director Percy E. Foxworth. The American SIS representatives operated in Brazil, Argentina, Chile, and Mexico, where there were large expatriate German communities, and even managed to establish declared outposts in Rio de Janeiro and Buenos Aires during the course of war. Such activities, of which Moscow was without doubt duly informed, reinforced Stalin's suspicions of Nazi plots in Latin America.[41] One of the main sources of information from Latin America was Grigulevich.

After the Second World War had broken out, the German merchant fleet was unable to enter Argentinean ports. Thanks to British warships and a rather large network of agents and subagents run by the local British resident, Captain Reginald 'Rex' Miller, since the spring of 1938 appointed to Montevideo with cover as Civilian Assistant to the Naval Attaché in South America, all Nazi activities in Uruguay, Chile, and Argentina were well under control. Miller reported in May 1940 that a ship-watching service had been established on the Argentine coast of Patagonia, although he complained that the task was one of 'considerable difficulty'.[42] In their turn, the Soviet network, established and headed by Grigulevich, informed Moscow in 1941 that strategic raw materials were being exported from Chile and Argentina in neutral vessels to Spain, and then secretly transported overland through France to Germany. Ordered to disrupt this export trade,

Grigulevich, assisted by the Argentinean codenamed TINTO, his wife DORA, and the Italian MARCELLO (all unidentified), recruited a sabotage team of eight Communist dockyard workers and seamen. It consisted of four Ukrainians, one Spaniard, and two Argentineans.[43] This group was led by a Ukrainian of Polish descent by the name of Felix Wierzbicki, codenamed BESSER, who in December 1941 obtained a job in the port of Buenos Aires and in his free time was assisting another recent recruit, an Argentinean with the cover name DOMINGO, to make delayed-action incendiary devices. The KGB files reveal that Grigulevich, like his British counterpart Captain Miller, also ran smaller agent groups targeting Nazi organizations in Chile and Uruguay, but, unlike British networks, these were sabotage teams. At the same time and in the same area, the RU also operated several small units headed by Spanish Civil War veterans Korobitsyn and Kravchenko. Grigulevich's agents, about seventy in number, remained the basis of Soviet intelligence operations in Latin America during the war, as well as the early years of the cold war.[44] It is, however, obvious that without great luck and the right contacts he would not have done so well.

To be able to recruit many people and obtain all necessary materials, Grig was assisted by the Communist Party underground in each country where his wartime operations brought him. In early 1941 Codovilla, whom Grigulevich met in Spain, returned to Argentina, took an active part in the pro-USSR anti-fascist campaign, and became secretary general of the CPA. He assigned Armando Cantoni, a Communist functionary in Buenos Aires, to help Grigulevich find necessary candidates for his spy network.[45] In March 1942, according to a report sent by Captain Miller of MI6 to the Head Office, Argentine was 'assuming increased importance, not so much for fear of axis internal coups but because she is almost the only remaining country where enemy agents can operate with comparative freedom'.[46] About the same time, in the spring of 1942, Brigadier General Hayes Kroner, the head of the US War Department's Military Intelligence Service, was given 'official approval and direction' to establish a secret intelligence organization, which would become known to only a few selected individuals as 'The Pond'. It was a Paris Pond agent who first reported the NKVD massacre of about 20,000 Polish officers in the Katyn Forest, information that was suppressed in 1942 'because it showed the Soviet Union in a negative light'.[47] According to the KGB files, between the beginning of 1942 and the summer of 1944 'over 150 successful incendiary attacks were mounted by Grigulevich's agents against German cargoes'. By that time the centre had instructed Grigulevich to stop all subversive activities in Argentina, so Wierzbicki was busy making grenades for the Argentinean Communist underground when he was seriously injured by an explosion in his workshop. He was later arrested, but his comrades in arms found away to free him and smuggle him to Uruguay. In 1944 Grigulevich (now codenamed ARTUR) was summoned to Montevideo, where a Soviet Embassy was by then established, to give a detailed report to his superiors on all the operations, finances, and agents of his group, starting from 1941.[48] Because Beria was still in power, he did not have much to worry about.

Based on Mitrokhin's notes, Christopher Andrew writes that 'communications between Grigulevich and the Centre were slow and spasmodic, depending on occasional couriers between Buenos Aires and the New York NKVD residency'.[49] In the VENONA decrypts, the Chilean Communist Eduardo Pecchio and a member of the Latin American section of the Columbian Broadcasting Service, Ricardo Setaro (codenamed GONETS), are mentioned as ARTUR's couriers to New York.[50] Russian sources, however, name Ricardo Veles, Argentinean journalist and movie critic, as one the most important of Grigulevich's assistants and his permanent link to the New York NKVD residency.[51]

In the meantime, Grigulevich's reputation as an expert in special operations—in other words, as saboteur, assassin, and arsonist—was rising in the minds of those few intelligence chiefs in Moscow who knew about him. This was partly because all the activities of his group during the war were well documented, but also because, with the help of two friends, Rodolfo Ghioldi and Emilio Troise, Grigulevich managed successfully to smuggle the whole archive of the NKVD 'illegal' residency in Buenos Aires to Montevideo.[52] But where there is success there are foes. And the chief among them was one of Orlov's former assistants, soon to become Grig's boss. Having served under so many chiefs, Sasha Korotkov knew how to trim the sails to the wind. After the fall of Beria, he would show it.

By late 1944, when he was finally cleared of all suspicion, Grigulevich was asked by the head of station in Montevideo to write a handbook and a lexicon based on his experience for those who would work there after him. There has been no Soviet embassies in Latin America before and during the war (and, accordingly, no 'legal' NKVD stations), so newly arriving officers, many of whom had never served abroad, needed professional tips. Grigulevich was happy to comply. He wrote about what he thought his colleagues should know.

The Creole, in Spanish Criollo, is always finely dressed irrespective of whether he is a janitor or a minister. He feels uncomfortable if he does not have a well-ironed suit, stiff collar, stylish hat known as chambergo [or gaucho: soft hat, made of wool or felt, it has a broad brim and regular crown], and polished shoes. He prefers braces to belts and fixes the long sleeves of his cambric shirt by rubber bands (and also his socks). He waxes his hair with the disgusting brilliantine called gomina. A hanky in his breast pocket and a massive finger-ring are obligatory. When it rains, a young Criollo prefers a raincoat and an older man takes an umbrella in the English style. In summer, all men wear panama hats or rancho-hats made of straw, light-coloured suits and usually black shoes. In winter, each Criollo parades in a gabardine coat and considers himself unworthy of note if he does not possess one. According to one French traveller, a typical Argentine is a slave of fashion of his own voitionl and belongs to a rare human breed where males are more beautiful than the females. Strolling along the streets, the Criollo considers it good etiquette to follow all passing women with his eyes, like in the hippodrome, and on some of them he will heap mounds of compliments-*pyropes* as if they were racing horses.[53]

Still a spy on a deep-cover mission, Grigulevich demonstrated literary talent that would later help him to become a writer and an academic. But back in the 1940s, his weapon was not a pen.

Like Grigulevich, the stocky bespectacled man who posed as Second Secretary of the Soviet Embassy in Washington by the name of 'Zubilin' and whose real name was Vasili Zarubin had to be a buccaneer to survive under such monsters as Yezhov and Beria. Nevertheless, he felt terribly uncomfortable when, during a dinner for members of the Soviet Embassy, given early in 1944 by the governor of Louisiana, he was called 'a General' and asked for his views on the Katyn massacre. Zarubin's problem was that he had personally interrogated and shot Polish officers in Kozelsk.[54] The situation was becoming embarrassing for a diplomat, though Zarubin somewhat awkwardly responded that German allegations that about 20,000 Polish prisoners of war had been shot by the NKVD were a provocation.[55] Because the question was asked by a guest who identified himself as a US military intelligence officer, Zarubin, in his subsequent report to Moscow, tried to explain this humiliation as an FBI provocation.

It is quite possible that by the end of the war the Bureau had tired of a man who so brazenly operated against the United States, which was officially declared a wartime ally. Without doubt it was encouraged by an anonymous typewritten letter in Russian received at the FBI headquarters on 7 August 1943 that identified 'Zubilin' (Zarubin) as the chief NKVD resident. But by the time the letter reached the FBI, Zarubin had moved to Washington to take overall control of the work of the New York and San Francisco stations.[56] In the meantime, the letter-writer, who was one of Zarubin's senior officers, sent a similar letter to Stalin, this time accusing his boss of collaborating with the FBI. In the summer of 1944 Zarubin was recalled to Moscow and replaced in Washington by Anatoly Gorsky, who until a few months previously had been the NKVD head of station in London. In September Gorsky took over the Washington station, while 'Vladimir Pravdin' (Roland Abbiate, now codenamed SERGEI), one of the murderers of Ignatz Reiss, was posted as the New York station deputy head, and then head from October 1941. After a brief visit to Moscow, 'Pravdin' returned to New York, where he operated from January 1944 to March 1946 using the cover of the TASS bureau chief. Back at the Lubyanka head office, Zarubin was promoted, but, contrary to some sources, he never succeeded in re-establishing his position, taking early retirement three years later while feuding and denunciations continued where he left them.

In August 1944 the newly appointed NKVD head of station in San Francisco sent a letter to Moscow denouncing his colleague in Mexico City, Tarasov (Lev Vasilevsky). Tarasov, the letter claimed, had bundled attempts to liberate Trotsky's assassin, Ramón Mercader, and had adopted a grand style. As his private residence Tarasov rented a house with grounds, employing two servants in addition to the staff allocated to him. No doubt the reporter had visited him there, as he added that Tarasov was spending too much time breeding parrots, poultry, and other birds.[57] For the time being the report was filed and no action taken. Meanwhile, when Tarasov/Vasilevsky returned from Mexico in late 1945, he was promoted to deputy chief of the Illegals Directorate and later served as department head of scientific and technical intelligence. Thanks to his experience in Spain, Vasilevsky was promoted to Sudoplatov's deputy at the 9th department (subversion and sabotage abroad). His career, like that of many others, ended with the fall of Beria.

On 23 November 1945, Gorsky received an urgent cryptogram from Moscow ordering him to cease contact with all American agents as soon as possible. The panic was caused by Elizabeth Bentley's defection. Gorsky promptly proposed liquidating the traitor and noted that Agent X (Josef Katz) could be used for the job. In his memo, sent only twenty days after Bentley's first contact with the FBI, Gorsky proposed a variety of options for murdering her, including shooting, arranging an accident, or faking a suicide. Finally, Gorsky decided that a slow-acting poison should be administered, 'something Katz could place on a pillow or handkerchief or in her food'. The Centre responded: 'No measure should be taken with regards to [Bentley]. It is arranged with Comrade Beria.'[58] For a while her life was saved.

While thirty-six sources and seven Soviet operators were compromised and whoever remained was 'put on ice' in the United States, Josef Katz was sent to Europe. On 16 August 1947, Moscow asked the NKVD head of station in Paris, Ivan Agayants (alias 'Avalov'), to meet Katz to review the prospects of eliminating Bentley, in anticipation of her acting as a government witness in any future Soviet espionage trials. Soon Agayants reported that Katz was prepared to take on the assignment.[59] In other words, the agent was prepared to return to the USA and murder Bentley.

In November 1948, Grigulevich reappeared in New York to meet William Fisher.[60] Fischer, it will be remembered, a native German born in England and better known by his alias 'Rudolf Ivanovich Abel', rose in position from a wireless operator who had once worked for Nikolsky's group in London to a star spy in the first decade of the cold war. In reality, Fischer/Abel boasted somewhat obscure achievements during his nine years in the USA. Remarkably, both Fischer and Grigulevich had no scruples about meeting Orlov in America. By the time Grigulevich had arrived in New York, the matter of Bentley's assassination had been put aside (but not entirely forgotten). The KGB archives mention an unsuccessful search for Bentley's whereabouts for as long as ten years.[61] Like Grigulevich, Josef Katz was last seen in the USA in or about 1948 before he resurfaced there again much later.

Strangely, there was a lot in common between the two. Katz was born in Lithuania in 1912; Grigulevich was born in Lithuania in 1913.[62] Katz had acquired US citizenship when his father had naturalized in 1925; Grigulevich's father had emigrated and acquired Latin American (Argentinean) citizenship in 1926. Katz was recruited into NKVD foreign intelligence for undercover work abroad in 1937;[63] Grigulevich joined the NKVD as a secret staff member in or about 1937 when he came back from Spain. Katz left the United States at some point after the war, probably in 1948 or early 1949 (Bentley identified Katz as a Soviet agent known to her as 'Jack' on 10 January 1949); Grigulevich was still in the United States in late 1948 and was documented to have set up a company in Rome in 1949. By placing a mail cover on his brother Morris in early 1949, the bureau learned that Joseph Katz was living in France. But newly discovered documents place Katz in

Italy. 'Currently in Italy,' Gorsky reported to Moscow, 'forming a company on our instruction to cover the illegal courier line between Europe and the USA'.[64] Grigulevich also lived in Italy, working for Soviet intelligence until the time he was recalled to Moscow.

There are a few other curious coincidences. One of Katz's code names was X (IKS). Copying the documents in the archives of the Soviet foreign intelligence, Mitrokhin noticed that at one time Grigulevich had had an additional code name, 'something like DAKS'.[65] The FBI was able to link Katz directly to two individuals, Robert O. Menaker and Floyd C. Miller, whom Katz had used to infiltrate the Trotskyist movement.[66] From his arrival in Spain in 1936 and until he left Mexico in 1940, Grigulevich's main task was to undermine the Trotskyist movement and eliminate its chief ideologist and leader. There are at least two documented episodes (the proofs provided by the KGB archivists) when Katz was allegedly selected to assassinate Elizabeth Bentley. But Joseph Katz was an aircraft engineer by education and an American citizen. He never had a chance to learn how to murder people and had a family in the USA whom he wanted to visit and did visit. It is hard to imagine him in the role of the NKVD assassin. Grigulevich, on the contrary, was a cold-blooded killer with long-time experience. Eventually, Katz turned out in Haifa, where he was interviewed but denied any knowledge of espionage or, in the FBI agent's words, 'denied ever having been a Soviet agent'.[67] And, although Joseph Katz and Iosif Grigulevich are two different people,[68] the similarity is truly amazing.

Perhaps one of the most remarkable public appearances ever made by a Soviet undercover operator took place on 6 November 1951. On that day a respectable Costa Rican diplomat Don Teodoro Castro attended the open- ing in Paris of the Sixth Session of the United Nations General Assembly as a trusted member of the Costa Rican delegation. Castro was, of course, Grigulevich, whose main previous expertise had been in sabotage and murder.[69] On Beria's proposal, he and his wife were now posted to Italy, launching into entirely new careers. Naturally, it was only a cover.

Experienced officers of the specialized unit of the MGB's First Chief Directorate, responsible for the tracking, acquisition, and processing of birth certificates, identity papers, cover documentation, and bogus life stories for undercover operatives, did not need to help him this time. Grigulevich managed it himself to perfection. In Santiago de Chile he recruited a Costa Rican Communist and journalist Joaquín Gutiérrez Mangel (codenamed

AMIGO), who had been working in Chile as vice-consul of Costa Rica since February 1942. Don Joaquín was happy to help his Soviet friend. He invented a story of one Teodoro Castro Bonnefil, the illegitimate son of a dead (and childless) Costa Rican notable, and managed to persuade the Consul General, Alejandro Oreamuno Beeche, that it was all true. Appropriate documents were issued, and soon Messrs Teodoro Castro and his consort left Chile, with new genuine Costa Rican documents and a letter of recommendation signed by Don Alejandro. It was in the August of 1945. The pair headed for Argentina. Several months later they turned up in Moscow.

Gutiérrez remained in his post until 6 June 1948, when, after a short civil war, a *de facto* government board took office and outlawed the Communist Party. The future professor of the University of Costa Rica, he became a correspondent of *El Siglo*, official newspaper of the Partido Communista de Chile (PCC) (Chilean Communist Party). In the early 1960s, Joaquín Gutiérrez Mangel was sent to Russia as its foreign correspondent. By that time Grigulevich's reputation as an expert and academic had been firmly established among specialists, and there was hardly anybody from Spain or Latin America whom he did not meet in Moscow.

Although Grig had been well known among his KGB colleagues for inventing stories, Yuri Paporov accepted his tale and described in his book how cordially the Costa Rican ambassador in Santiago accepted don Teodoro and how impressed he was by his alleged resemblance to his late (fictitious) father. In reality, Benjamin Odio—first Ambassador of Costa Rica to Argentina, Chile, and Uruguay, with headquarters in Buenos Aires—was appointed on 5 August 1949, when Grigulevich was already in Rome. In Chile there were only consuls in Talcahuano and Valparaiso, a vice-consul in Iquique, and a consul general and a vice-consul in Santiago, but *no* ambassador.[70]

At the beginning of 1949, Grigulevich/Castro and his wife were in Rome, where they set up a small import–export business as a front. In the autumn of 1950, 'don Castro' arranged a meeting with the members of a visiting delegation from Costa Rica that included the leading Costa Rican politician of his generation, don José Figueres Ferrer, the moderate socialist head of the founding junta of the Second Republic, as well as don Daniel Oduber and don Francisco J. Orlich, who were instrumental in establishing coffee exports to Italy.[71] This meeting was a turning point towards new opportunities.

Grigulevich's success in winning Figueres's confidence probably played a decisive role in his future diplomatic career. Hoodwinked by Grigulevich/ Castro's fraudulent account of his illegitimate birth, Figueres probably decided that they were distant relatives.[72] Thereafter, according to his KGB file, studied and partially copied by Mitrokhin, Grigulevich became a friend of the future president.

On 7 July 1951, Teodoro Castro wrote a letter to the Costa Rican foreign minister, Mario Echandi, informing the minister that Antonio Facio Ulloa, head of the Legation of Costa Rica in Italy, had offered him the post of First Secretary of the mission *ad honorem*. Soon Grigulevich received his diplomatic passport No. 2026, together with the presidential decree from San José.[73] On 9 November, Grigulevich/Castro was chosen as Counsellor to the Delegation of Costa Rica to the VIth regular session of the United Nations General Assembly in Paris. Claudio Volio, the Minister of Agriculture, headed the delegation.[74] During the plenary session at the new UN building on the riverside of the Palais de Chaillot, Castro was introduced to US Secretary of State Dean Acheson, and British Foreign Secretary Anthony Eden—but not, it seems, to Soviet Foreign Minister Andrey Vyshinsky. The day before, in his address to the United Nations, Vyshinsky, Stalin's former bloodthirsty prosecutor, had declared in the course of a lengthy diatribe, referring to President Truman's speech on arms limitation: 'I could hardly sleep last night having read that speech. I could not sleep because I kept on laughing.'[75] When he had finished and returned to his place flanked by two dark-suited individuals, hundreds of news photographers rushed to take his photo.

There was another target for Vyshinsky's sarcasm: Grigulevich. During one of the sessions, the Greek delegation demanded the return to Greece of the children evacuated to the Soviet bloc during the Greek civil war. The Costa Rican delegation supported the motion, and Grigulevich/Castro was chosen to draft a speech in favour to be delivered by one of the members, Jorge Martínez Moreno. Although he did his best to limit the offence to the Soviet delegation, Vyshinsky condemned the speech as the ramblings of a diplomatic clown.[76] His criticism, of course, was first of all directed against Moreno and the position taken by the Costa Rican delegation, but no doubt 'don Theodoro' was equally embarrassed.

As expected, Vyshinsky's denunciation did no damage to Grig's career. On the contrary, still in Paris an MGB officer posing as Vyshinsky's interpreter, Major Yuri Dashkevich, tried to pitch 'don Teodoro', as the latter related to his friends in Moscow years later. One officer of the KGB Latin American department recalled that Grigulevich described the episode to him in Moscow 'with considerable sarcasm'.[77] The story of how the MGB tried to approach him was no doubt invented by Grig, but the episode from the UN session is true.

On 15 February 1952, don Teodoro was appointed as observer for Costa Rica to the IX Congress of Agrarian Industries in Rome, and a month later to the XI Session of the International Consultative Committee for Cotton, also in Rome.

On 23 April he was promoted to Minister Plenipotentiary of Costa Rica in Italy and, according to his KGB file, was on good terms with the American ambassador, Ellsworth Bunker, and his successor, Claire Boothe Luce, and established friendly relations with the Costa Rican nuncio to the Holy See, Prince Giulio Pacelli, a nephew of Pope Pius XII (Eugenio Pacelli).[78] Later the KGB wits created a legend that, acting as Don Teodoro, Grigulevich was even awarded the Knightly Order pro Merito Melitensi of the Order of Malta for his outstanding diplomatic service. Some even claimed that they saw the cross of the Order with their own eyes.[79] This is pure fantasy, but it turned out there is no smoke without fire.

The Grand Master and the Sovereign Council of the Order of Malta during the assembly on 21 November 1953 accepted Teodoro Castro into the Order, thus making him a member (of the 3rd Class) and a Knight. It was noted that the new Knight came from a chivalrous and noble Christian family and not only was an ambassador of his country to Italy but had distinguished himself for providing considerable and gratuitous financial help to the Italians who had been victims of a major flood in early December 1951. 'A good Catholic enlivened by altruistic nobleness of spirit and behaviour,' Don Teodoro was an ideal candidate to be accepted to the Order. The only problem was that neither the Grand Master nor the Sovereign Council knew at the time that 'Teodoro Castro' was a Karaite who did not follow the Hebrew Scriptures, a Communist who had no respect for God or people, and a spy whose prime mission was to steal secrets of the foreign governments and murder those who refused to comply. Now they know.

Soviet and Russian accounts of his diplomatic service (from mid-1951 to late 1953) resemble a puzzle pieced together from fact, fancy, and improvisation. One author claims, for example, that Grigulevich was awarded 'by the Pope the Order of the Maltese Cross, which, according to its Charter, can only be given in Vatican'.[80] Alas, this is not correct. The Pope is responsible only for the Vatican decorations, such as the Order of Saint Gregory or Pro Ecclesia et Pontife. Established in 1920, the Knightly Order pro Merito Melitensi is given in recognition of those activities that have conferred honour and prestige on the Sovereign Military Order of Malta. It is awarded only by Decree of the Sovereign Council or by *motu proprio* of the Grand Master.

Amazingly, Grigulevich was not the only Soviet spy in the Costa Rican Embassy at 24 Piazza Sallustio in Rome. A young attaché, Julio Cesar Pascal Rocca, known to the NKVD in Montevideo under the code name PEGAS, worked with Grigulevich in Latin America before joining him in Italy. While in Rome, Rocca regularly wrote letters to the Foreign Ministry praising the wisdom, devotion, and high-level contacts of Don Teodoro.[81] Laura, who was known to the diplomatic corps in Rome under the name of Inelia Idalina de Castro, is said to have helped her husband a great deal. However, discussing the details of his and Castro's meetings in Rome, Minister Volio said: 'Castro and I were together at some social functions such as receptions and dinners but I never met his wife and don't know whether she was in Rome at that time.'[82] Maybe she was not, and, besides, as an accredited Costa Rican diplomat, Grigulevich could hardly collect any useful intelligence.

On 22 July 1952, Teodoro Castro was appointed Minister Plenipotentiary to Yugoslavia. Sudoplatov recalled a memo from the personal file of the 'illegal':

While fulfilling his diplomatic duties in the second half of the year 1952, [Grigulevich] twice visited Yugoslavia, where he was well received. He had access to the social group close to Tito's staff and was given the promise of a personal audience with Tito. The post held by MAKS at the present time makes it possible to use his capabilities for active measures against Tito.[83]

By 'active measures', Sudoplatov meant murder.

When Sudoplatov was reading this memo, shown to him personally by Stalin in his Kremlin office in February 1953, Grigulevich was no longer part of his Special Tasks group.[84] In 1947, he was transferred to the Fourth (Illegals) Directorate of the Komitet Informatsyi (KI) (Committee of Information), a joint intelligence service that existed from 1947 until 1951, headed at that time by Alexander Korotkov, now a general. Having made his reputation during the pre-war missions by assassinating 'traitors' abroad,

Korotkov, together with General Pitovranov, Deputy Minister of State Security, designed a plan to murder the leader of Yugoslavia. From the very beginning, it was Stalin's idea. Before Sudoplatov was summoned to the Kremlin to discuss this plan, Vasili Romanovich Sitnikov, the MVD head of station in Vienna, was instructed to organize a meeting between Grigulevich and his Moscow bosses. In a safe house outside the city, the Costa Rican diplomat was asked in what way he could be most useful taking into consideration his high post. As reported to Stalin: 'MAKS suggested an effective "direct action" against Tito. We discussed with him how he imagined this could be accomplished.'[85] As usual, 'direct action' was a euphemism for murder.

Grigulevich suggested four possible ways to assassinate CARRION CROW, as Marshal Tito was by then called in all secret correspondence. According to his plan, it was possible to:

(a) administer a lethal dose of pneumonic plague from a silent spray;

(b) obtain an invitation to the reception given in Tito's honour during his forth-coming visit to London by the Yugoslav ambassador . . . where MAKS would shoot Tito with a silenced pistol;

(c) use the same method at a diplomatic reception in Belgrade;

(d) give Tito a gift of jewellery in a booby-trapped box which would release a lethal poison gas as soon as it was opened.[86]

During the meeting, Grigulevich was asked to submit a more detailed proposal. Meanwhile, the MVD, still under full Beria's supervision, assured Stalin that there was no doubt that 'MAKS, because of his personal qualities and experience in intelligence work, is capable of accomplishing a mission of this kind'.[87] The MVD leadership then asked for Stalin's personal approval. Sudoplatov recalled that the document was returned to the Lubyanka office unmarked.

Nevertheless, on the next day Sudoplatov received a file (*liternoe delo*) that contained reports on Tito from the Belgrade station and Moscow's instruc-tions to the officers there.[88] Soon he was summoned to face a mixed team of Stalin's and Khrushchev's men, who insisted that the murder of the leader of the independent state was in the best interests of the Soviet Union.[89] Sudoplatov, an experienced operative, called the plan 'bad tradecraft', but he had in mind technicalities, not the essence.

The appointment of MAKS, a senior Costa Rican diplomat, as Tito's assassin was approved, and Grigulevich composed a farewell letter addressed to his wife to be made public should he be captured or killed during the assassination attempt.[90] Naturally, the letter was signed by his assumed name. In the same manner, a letter was composed and placed on 'Jacques Mornard' when Sudoplatov and his deputy Eitingon sent him to Mexico to murder Trotsky, an operation where Grigulevich was also playing an important role. On 1 March 1953, Beria reported to Stalin that Tito was unfortunately still alive. On the next day, after an all-night dinner at his Kuntsevo dacha, Stalin suffered a fatal stroke. Tito survived him by almost three decades.

On 25 April, at the White Palace in Belgrade, His Excellency Teodoro Castro Bonnefil presented his credentials as Minister Plenipotentiary of Costa Rica to Yugoslavia to the head of state, Marshal Josip Broz Tito. As appropriate to such occasions, they exchanged small talk but it was not in private. Together with the Costa Rican diplomat there were representatives of seven other countries, so any 'active measure' against the Yugoslav President was out of the question.

It has always been unclear when and how Grigulevich returned to Moscow. Sudoplatov thought it was in May 1953, after Orlov had begun to publish his reminiscences of Stalin and the NKVD in *Life* magazine. Vitaly Pavlov, another former KGB general who prepared the Cohens for their British mission, echoed Sudoplatov, while other authors gave their own versions,[91] none of which was based on documents. In reality, in November 1953, five months after Beria's arrest, Grigulevich/Castro was still a member of the Costa Rican delegation to the VII General Assembly of the UN Food and Agriculture Organization (FAO) headed by Claudio Volio. Only on 16 January 1954 did the government of Costa Rica formally accept his resignation as Minister Plenipotentiary in Italy. As in the case of Rocca, there is no record, however, confirming that a letter of resignation from 'Don Teodoro' had ever been sent.

'Owing to a serious illness of my wife I have to leave for Switzerland today' was the text of the telegram that the Foreign Ministry in San José received on 5 December 1953. Judging by the letters written from Rome (now in the National Archives of Costa Rica), Grigulevich left Italy on 10 December. Soon, together with his wife and baby daughter, he was in Vienna, which was still occupied by Allied troops and divided into four sectors. Evgeny Kravtsov (alias 'Kovalyov'), former chief of the German–Austrian desk at the Moscow Centre, had recently arrived to head the growing MVD Vienna station.[92]

1 & 2. Lyubov Därenthal and Alexander Dickhoff-Därenthal. In August 1924 Boris Savinkov, a fierce anti-Bolshevik, was lured to the Soviet territory and arrested, together with his mistress, named Lyubov, which means 'love' in Russian, and her husband, Alexander Dickhoff-Därenthal. Savinkov publicly repented, but this did not help him, and he conveniently died in prison despite 'a heroic attempt to save his life' by Grigory Syroyezhkin, an operations officer. A year later Syroyezhkin shot the last 'control' bullet into the chest of Sidney Reilly in a wild forest near Moscow putting a glorious end to another operation. Although Reilly used to describe Mrs Därenthal as 'a stinking Jewess with a shiny face, fat hands and thighs', which was probably not true judging by her photograph, published here for the first time, she was certainly instrumental in bringing Savinkov to Russia; Därenthal and her husband were promptly released and later lived in Moscow. Together with Orlov, Syroyezh-kin spent two years in Spain training the Republican guerrillas. (*Boris Savinkov papers, International Institute of Social History, Amsterdam*)

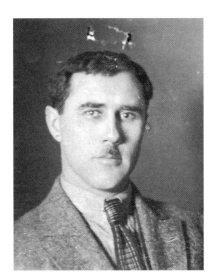

3. Victor Karpov first arrived in London in March 1930 to work, he said, at ARCOS. In December 1930 he was described as Deputy Soviet Trade Representative and Deputy Head of the Trade Delegation. He was transferred to Berlin in early 1931 but continued visiting London with his wife and children in an official capacity. Guy Liddell commented that Karpov appeared to control OGPU activity throughout Europe including London. At the time this was the role played by the OGPU illegal Berthold Ilk. (© *The National Archives, Kew, KV 2/2665*)

4. Alexander Korotkov and his wife, Maria, in Paris. Operation EXPRESS, 1933, one of
the first in a chain of unsuccessful espionage operations assigned to Lev Nikolsky (who
was not yet Orlov), was an attempt to recruit a member of the famous French Deuxième
Bureau, where Soviet intelligence had already been developing a source codenamed
JOSEPH. A group that included a young operations officer, Alexander Korotkov, posing
as a Czech student, his wife, Maria Wilkowyska (both in the picture), and Nikolsky,
posing as an American businessman, set up a base in Geneva and focused full time on
clandestinely spotting their target 'with access to vital intelligence'. Nothing came out of
it, and after several months Nikolsky deserted the operation and joined his family in
Vienna, while Korotkov was placed under surveillance by the French. (*Surveillance
photograph, French DST*)

5. No. 9 Latschka Gasse, Vienna. In 1933, a young Cambridge University graduate named Harold Adrian Russell Philby arrived in Vienna, and soon the *Daily Telegraph* and the *New York Times* Vienna bureau chief Eric Gedye introduced him as a lodger to the young woman named Alice Kohlmann who would become Philby's first wife. Together they shared an apartment at No. 9 Latschka Gasse in the comfortable IX District of the Austrian capital. (*Latschka Gasse* © *Boris Volodarsky*)

6. Former Vienna's Cottage Sanatorium for people with nerve- and metabolic disorders on 74 Sternwartestraße in 18th district. Because of its convenient geographical position and lax laws, Vienna had become the centre of Soviet espionage long before the Second World War. Then and now, Russian secret police mandarins used to spend their time in clinics and sanatoriums in and around Vienna. One such establishment, run by Dr Karl Noorden in the 1930s, was appropriated after the war by the Soviet occupation authorities. Nikolsky's wife and daughter lived in Vienna for two years 'under the care of Dr Noorden'. (*Sternwartestraße 74, Vienna-Währing* © *Boris Volodarsky*)

7. 80–86 Regent Street, London. Nikolsky spent several months of 1935 as the controller of a group of Soviet spies in London. With a genuine American passport in the name of 'William Goldin', he decided to register his American Refrigerator Company at 80–86 Regent Street in London. (© *Boris Volodarsky*)

8. Johannes de Graaf. In 1935 a large group of operatives was dispatched by Moscow to 'make a revolution' in Brazil. Among this group was Johannes 'Johnny' de Graaf, a German communist who worked for both the Comintern and Soviet military intelligence in Britain, China, and Germany. Keith Jeffery's *MI6: The History of the Secret Intelligence Service* devoted several pages to 'The Jonny Case', and unsurprisingly the book *Johnny: A Spy's Life* was published during the same year in America. But it turned out that MI5 was interested in a different 'Johnny', whose name was also Johannes de Graaf (in the photogragh) and who it suspected was a German spy. (© *The National Archives, Kew, KV 2/125*)

9. Naum Belkin. In September 1936, together with the experienced Soviet intelligence operator Naum Belkin (in the photograph), Nikolsky, alias 'Alexander Orlov', was sent to Spain as a liaison to the republican Ministry of Interior.

10. 7 November 1936, Madrid. After arranging, together with the Soviet Naval Attaché Nikolai Kuznetsov, the transfer of the Spanish gold reserve to the Soviet Union, Orlov returned to Madrid just in time to celebrate the nineteenth anniversary of the Bolshevik revolution. Although General (then Major) Mamsurov later claimed in his memoirs that it was his room at the Hotel Gaylord, in reality it was Gorev's spacious apartment at the Hotel Palace. From left to right: Paulina 'Lina' Abramson, Iosif Ratner, Mikhail Koltsov, Vladimir Gorev, Alexander Orlov, Soledad Sancha, Luis Lacasa and Hajji-Umar D. Mamsurov. This photograph was taken by Roman Karmen. Exactly the same photograph but with Karmen in her place was taken by Lina Abramson (later Mamsurova). (*Courtesy of Adelina Abramson-Kondratyeva, Cañada Blanch Centre collection*)

11. Orlov in Spain 1937. In January 1937, without doubt in recognition of the successful transfer of the Spanish gold to Moscow, Nikolsky/Orlov was awarded the highest Soviet decoration, the Order of Lenin, and in the spring of 1937 appointed the NKVD head of station in Spain. He concentrated all his efforts on the physical extermination of those whom Moscow considered Trotsky's sympathizers. (*Author's private collection*)

12. Barcelona, May Days 1937. In May 1937 the NKVD station in Spain used the situation provoked by the clashes in Barcelona between the 'revolutionary political forces' and the government supported by the PCE to discredit and dissolve the POUM, a party opposed to the Communists. The POUM leader dared to invite Trotsky to Spain, thus sealing his fate. (*Cañada Blanch Centre collection*)

13. David Crook, a good-looking young Englishman from London (in the photograph), and another British volunteer, David Wickes, were reporting to the NKVD Barcelona substation hidden at the Soviet Consulate about Orwell and his first wife, Eileen. Crook was allegedly recruited by George Soria when recovering from a bad wound. Soria, a French writer and journalist, arrived in Spain in April 1936 as a correspondent for the *Regards* magazine. Crook agreed to do 'special work for the international movement'. (*Courtesy of the David Crook family*)

14. Police photographs of Ramón Mercader after his arrest in August 1940. In 1938 Orlov deserted his post in Spain and arrived in America using his diplomatic passport to enter the country legally. From New York he sent a letter to Trotsky in Mexico, falsely warning him about the danger to Trotsky's life allegedly coming from Mark Zborowski, a Soviet informant in Trotsky's circle in Paris. In reality, the operation against Trotsky was supervised by Orlov's deputy in Spain, Naum Eitingon. Eitingon, who just like Philby had been married four times and was a great womanizer, recruited a beautiful Spanish woman named María, one of whose sons was a young officer, Ramón. In the summer of 1937 Orlov sent Ramón to Moscow for special training. Stalin's Enemy No. 1, Trotsky, was murdered by Ramón Mercader on 20 August 1940 in the course of the operation supervised by Eitingon. The NKVD assassin, whose identity was a mystery until September 1950, had served his full term in prison, spending there 19 years, 8 months, and 14 days. (*Ramón Mercader police mugs, Mexican Police Archive, Cañada Blanch Centre collection*)

15. Vasili Zarubin. During the war, while Orlov lived in America in hiding, the chief NKVD resident in charge of all operations there was Vasili Zarubin posing as the Soviet diplomat 'Zubilin'. Both Orlov and Zarubin served in the same Foreign Section of Stalin's secret police and knew each other well. Both had blood on their hands. Unsurprisingly in Putin's Russia both of them are praised as intelligence heroes. (Surveillance photograph, FBI).

16. Kim Philby. On the night of 23 January 1963, Philby, now a double agent working for both MI6 and the KGB, disappeared in Beirut, successfully exfiltrated by the Soviets. At that time Philby's former controller was in Ann Arbor, placed at the University of Michigan by the CIA. 'Our purpose in recruiting upper-class Englishmen was really not so much for their intelligence work *per se*, though that was important,' Orlov related. 'But, through the high positions they would eventually arrive at, Moscow could put in their real agents, their professionals—people who might he hired in as chauffeurs, maids, gardeners'. At that point Orlov was not lying; he really thought this was the case.

& **18.** Orlov's remains and his corner in H. Keith Melton's private spy museum. After his death, ov's last FBI minder Edward Gazur dreamt of burying his friend's remains near the Kremlin wall, ere, he thought, Orlov belonged. Fortunately, this never happened and Orlov's ashes together with ie personal belongings landed in the private spy museum of H. Keith Melton in Florida. There, ch has a whole stand devoted to Orlov. (*H. Keith Melton, private collection, courtesy H. Keith Melton*)

19. Orlov's gold-tipped Parker Vacuumatic pen made in Canada where Orlov bought it is with another American family with close ties to the CIA. According to the legend invented by Orlov and supported by all his earlier biographers, he used this pen to write a personal letter to Stalin offering a deal to the Soviet dictator: he, Orlov, would not betray any Soviet operation or asset that he knew about, and in exchange for that Stalin would leave him alone. Such a letter was in fact never written. (*The Bagley-Rocca family collection, courtesy Tennent H. Bagley*)

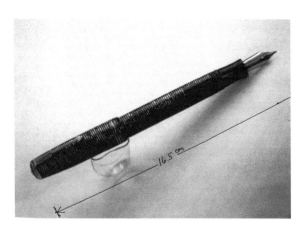

20. The Vienna house where Dr Arnold Deutsch lived. Contrary to the information disseminated by the KGB and its successors, Orlov was neither the recruiter nor the real controller of the Soviet spies Philby, Maclean, Burgess, Blunt, and Cairncross, erroneously known as the Cambridge Ring of Five, which, as this book seeks to prove, never existed. At the same time, the real spotter, assessor, developer, recruiter, and handler of intelligence assets in London, Cambridge, and Oxford was the Austrian Dr Arnold Deutsch, whose death remains a mystery until this day, and whose daughter, aged 78, this writer invited for tea in Vienna trying to find out what really happened in November 1942. (*Schiffamtsgasse 20, Vienna's 2nd district* © *Boris Volodarsky*)

Without doubt he was instructed to deal with Grig and his family personally. Grigulevich, Laura, and their daughter Esperanza/Nadezhda (according to her own words—Romanella) successfully landed in a safe house in the Soviet zone and, after receiving a new set of documents, boarded the train from Vienna to Moscow.

Back in Moscow, Grigulevich was placed in the Latin American department of the USSR State Committee for Cultural Relations with Foreign Countries, the successor of the famous VOKS. This was a KGB front organization, and Grigulevich did not complain too much. Later, discussing it with his friends— Vitaly Pavlov,[93] Yuri Paporov, another KGB colleague, and Vadim Polya-kovsky, all of whom visited Grig in his two-room Moscow apartment near the Sokol underground station—Grigulevich suggested that his recall to Mos-cow was due to Korotkov's personal antipathy. 'He [Korotkov, at that time chief of the Illegals Directorate] envied me,' Grig used to say. 'He couldn't stand it that I lived in luxury abroad. Korotkov himself even didn't finish secondary school and besides he was against me because I was a Jew. Stalin died but he was not alone in inventing the Doctors' Plot.'[94] Since the collapse of the Soviet Union, books continue to be published in Moscow about both Korotkov and Grigu-levich, praising them as heroes of Russia. In reality, after the arrest of Beria, Korotkov did his best to avoid the fate of his State Security colleagues, many of whom were arrested, dismissed from the service, and occasionally shot following Beria's fall, and he tried to avoid purges by purging Beria's cadres. Among others, Sudoplatov and Eitingon were arrested and Grigulevich recalled to Moscow.

Although formally Grigulevich was sacked from the intelligence service and moved to the MVD-KGB special reserve, he successfully defended a doctoral thesis, became a senior researcher at the Ethnographic Institute of the Soviet Academy of Sciences (where his daughter also worked), and made a new life for himself as a leading writer and academic, an expert on Latin America and an authority on ethnography and religion. Whether he ever met Luis Lacasa, a communist militant so close to the NKVD in Spain and almost certainly one of the participants in Operation NIKOLAI (murder of Nin), could not be established.[95] In the early 1960s both started travelling abroad again.

In 1980 in the KGB hospital on Pekhotny Lane in Moscow Grigulevich bumped into an old acquaintance, Naum Eitingon, whom he knew in Barcelona as 'Kotov' and who was arrested shortly before Grig returned to the USSR. At that time and until his death a year later, Eitingon was not exonerated nor restored to his general's rank, in spite of his many appeals to the Communist Party congresses and to the CPSU leaders. His crime was not the assassination of Lev Trotsky, which he supervised in 1940, nor the murder attempt on the German Ambassador to Turkey, Franz von Papen, which Eitingon organized two years later; he was accused of being too close to the previous Kremlin leadership and of knowing too much.

Grigulevich died on 2 June 1988 survived by his daughter. He was cremated, and the ashes were buried at the cemetery of the Donskoy monastery in Moscow, where many of his former friends and colleagues from the Special Tasks had found peace.

In early 2005, Nil Nikandrov, one of the co-authors, together with Tsarev, of the six volumes of essays on the history of the Russian foreign intelligence, announced that he had finished his research and would soon publish a book about 'Comrade Miguel'. The book, entitled simply *Grigulevich*, came out in Moscow in the same year as part of the famous series 'The Life of Outstanding People', known in the Soviet Union (and still popular in Russia today) as Zhe-Ze-eL, started by Maxim Gorky in 1933.[96] The book was officially presented and launched by the SVR, in February 2006.

In all Russian and many Western publications about him, Grigulevich is pictured as a veteran master spy whose first intelligence school was Spain, and as a great 'illegal' who managed to become an ambassador of a foreign country and a Knight of the Order of Malta. But the truth is that this obviously talented man was not a spy and not even an intelligence officer. His task was not to extract secrets or exert influence. Grigulevich, whose portraits and adventures fill the Internet and bookshelves, wasted a large part of his life travelling the world ready to kill for Stalin. As an intelligence operative, he was not a great 'illegal' but a great loser: his operations against Nin in Spain and against Trotsky in Mexico were intelligence failures; he was sent to New York to dispose of Krivitsky, but Krivitsky committed suicide. As a Costa Rican diplomat in Rome, Grigulevich was unable to collect intelligence of any value, and when the orders came from Moscow to murder Tito he did not have the opportunity. When Stalin died and Beria was dealt with, Grigulevich was recalled to Moscow, and the KGB ceased its relationship with him. One comedy was finished and another began. He was awarded a doctorate in history without having to defend a thesis and became a member of the Russian Academy without any academic achievement. He is said to have authored and co-authored fifty-eight books, which lost any value they had after the collapse of the Soviet Union. As a result, all his efforts only reinforced, rather than challenged, the Soviet leaders' misunderstanding of the West.

22

True Lies

Orlov's books and articles may not be as plentiful as those of his former agent cum academic, Grigulevich-Lavretsky, but they were much more influential in their effect on the readers. His legacy consists of two books written while he served in Spain, which were published under different names.[1] He is also the author of four articles for *Life* magazine under the general title *Stalin's Secrets* published when he re-emerged in April 1953 as a serialization of his book about Stalin's crimes, and of a totally phoney story *The Sensational Secret behind Damnation of Stalin*, which came out in April 1956[2] (all five make part of *The Legacy of Alexander Orlov* printed by the US Government Printing Office in 1973). Orlov's three books were published under his NKVD alias in the United States: *The Secret History of Stalin's Crimes* (1953), an international bestseller translated into many languages; *The Handbook of Intelligence and Guerrilla Warfare* (1963), commissioned by the CIA; and *The March of Time: Reminiscences* (2004), posthumous memoirs edited and published by his former FBI minder Edward J. Gazur. In addition, Orlov wrote an entirely misleading article 'How Stalin Relieved Spain of $600,000,000'[3] and another one ambitiously entitled 'The Theory and Practice of Soviet Intelligence', published in the classified CIA journal *Studies in Intelligence*, 7/2 (1963), 45–65. Even Orlov's 1968 interview with the US Professor Stanley G. Payne, which had been kept in an archive for a long time, finally came out in Germany in 2000 in the form of a pamphlet.

Besides, there are such books as *The Storm Petrels* (1977) by Brook-Shepherd with three full chapters devoted to Orlov, *Deadly Illusions* (1993) by Costello and Tsarev, as well as Gazur's *Secret Assignment* (2001), some parts of which strangely coincide with Orlov's memoirs, published by Gazur after his own book had come out.[4] There is even one thriller by Jordi Sierra i Fabra based on Orlov's *Reader's Digest* article and entitled *Camarada Orlov* (1998, 2005), plus several non-fiction works in Spanish.

This impressive library might not be worth much attention, bearing in mind that most of what Orlov said, even under oath, or during his debriefing by the US intelligence officials, or in private discussions with his friend Gazur, has by now been established as outright invention. Unfortunately, even prominent and sufficiently cautious historians of the Spanish Civil War, not to mention less prominent and accurate scholars, at least until quite recently, continued, often quite uncritically, to include Orlov's testimonies in their books, written several decades after his death.[5] Many others, who devote their works to the Soviet history, sometimes base full chapters on Orlov's 'revelations' and continue to do so.

Actually, it is quite unprecedented for one deserter's life (and inventions) to be so broadly represented in published works. On the other hand, Orlov had lived for thirty-five years in America—one of the longest records to date. The first fifteen years there he had spent in hiding, writing his book about Stalin's crimes. After he resurfaced in New York in 1953 following Stalin's death, he became a public figure, with many writers and even scholars seeking his advice.[6] In spite of, or may be because of, the great publicity around him after the publication of his articles, Orlov lived in constant fear for his life. From his personal experience he knew pretty well that, if and when his former colleagues wanted to find him, they would be able to do so. Indeed, in November 1969 and then again about two years later, in August 1971, he was visited by a KGB officer from the New York station. A reliable explanation as to why they needed him then is still missing.

By calling himself 'chief adviser of the Spanish government' and claiming that he received orders directly from Stalin,[7] Orlov managed to convince the Department of Justice and the US Congress that, although only an attaché, the lowest-ranking diplomat, he was a very important person and Stalin's personal secret envoy in Spain. Orlov's intuition had served him well, and it seems it was a fashionable trend at the time to present oneself as a person of great influence close to the dictator. Thus, Boris Bazhanov claimed that he was Stalin's personal secretary, Walter Krivitsky that he was Stalin's secret agent, and Jesús Hernández that he was Stalin's minister. When President Eisenhower took office in January 1953, the Cold War had been under way for six years. The lawmakers and all those who decided Orlov's fate were very flattered to learn that such a high-ranking Soviet official as 'General Orlov' wanted to change sides. It also gave them an inflated feeling of pride in their superiority to others. So Orlov's appearance out of the blue was quite welcome. At the end of the day, the Agency and the Bureau also hoped that the 'General' might tell them something that they did not know.

His way to America had been quite tricky, and well planned out. On 21 July 1938 he and his small family quietly disembarked in Quebec and were easily admitted to the country (with which the Soviet Union did not have diplomatic relations) by the Immigration Office of the Dominion Government. They checked into the Hotel Château Frontenac and after a few hours boarded the train for Montreal.

Three weeks were enough to contact relatives, most of whom Orlov had located back in 1932 during his first trip to the USA, to buy a gold-tipped Parker, to write and send a farewell letter to Yezhov, and to open a bank account in Maria's name, into which they placed all the proceeds from their 'antique sales' in France. On 13 August, precisely one month after he had left his post in Spain, Orlov went to the American legation in Ottawa and asked for temporary visas for himself and his family.

This is how he described the episode:

The secretary of the legation had in the past served in Spain for a number of years and he apparently was glad to see a man from those parts . . . The Ambassador asked me whether I would like to meet him and the senior members of his staff. I said I would be honoured. I was taken into a large sitting room and there I met the Ambassador and his aides. They were all, of course, interested in the Spanish Civil War. The questions they asked were intelligent and to the point. I did my best to answer all of them with the exception of those which related to military secrets of the Republican camp . . . When on leaving the legation I received our passports from the friendly secretary, I noticed that the Ambassador was gracious enough not to put any limit to the duration of our sojourn in the United States. He inscribed in the diplomatic visas, which he granted us, the word 'indefinite'.[8]

As it happened, on that very day there was no ambassador at the US Embassy to Canada. Ambassador Norman Armour had left on 15 January 1938, and the new ambassador, Daniel C. Roper, did not arrive until 19 May 1939. White, Methodist, Straight, and Democratic, according to his State Department file, chairman of the Woodrow Wilson re-election campaign in 1916, Ambassador Roper, aged 71, would hardly have cared to listen to what this Russian had to say, even if he had been there at the time. Besides, from stamps in Orlov's Soviet diplomatic passport, it is evident that on 13 August 1938 the unnamed 3rd Secretary of the American legation in Ottawa put a seal and a rubber stamp on page 26, allowing Orlov (and his family) free entrance into the United States for twelve months (!) from the date. Although the passport was officially issued and valid until 5 September 1939, this unnumbered page looks very suspicious. Besides, a text in Russian on page 25 clearly states that 'this passport has 25 numbered pages'. One may only guess as to how an extra page of a different colour appeared in Orlov's document and why he preferred to keep it in a safe deposit box in a bank far away from his home until his death.

Besides, Orlov hardly had any time for courtesies at the legation. Immediately after receiving their visas, the family rushed to the railway station and left for the Big Apple. At the border checkpoint at Rouses Point, in the State of New York, an officer confirmed their entry with a stamp admitting them on the same day, 13 August, under paragraph I section 3 of the Immigration Act of 1924 for an 'indefinite' stay. On their arrival in New York, the Orlovs checked into the Wellington Hotel on Broadway and East 55th Street as Leo, Maria, and Vera Koornicks. This is how their American adventure began.

Fleeing to the New World, Orlov left behind several corpses and a few recruits, among whom Kim Philby would probably become by far the most famous.

On 2 March 1938, while Orlov was still in Spain, General Franco personally pinned the Red Cross of Military Merit on Philby's chest. Philby later wrote:

My wounding in Spain helped my work—both journalism and intelligence work—no end. Before then there had been a lot of criticism of British journalists from Franco officers who seemed to think that the British in general must be a lot of communists because so many were fighting with the International Brigade. After I had been wounded and decorated by Franco himself, I became known as 'the English-decorated-by-Franco' and all sorts of doors opened to me.[9]

That would certainly help him later, when he was heading the Iberian territorial section of MI6's Section V (counter-intelligence), but not during the civil war.

The KGB and Philby himself cleverly invented Philby's adventures in Spain in order to demonstrate that he was sent to the Iberian Peninsula on a risky intelligence mission as a secret Soviet agent.

One such anecdote is an often-repeated story of his escaping arrest 'almost literally by the skin of my teeth', as Philby wrote in his memoirs. He recalled that two months after his arrival in Spain, in April 1937, two

Nationalist Civil Guards hammering on his bedroom door woke him up in the middle of the night. As he dressed he realized he had left his cipher, provided by his Soviet controllers in London and written on a piece of rice paper, in the pocket of his trousers. Philby describes how he masterly deceived the guards by using a simple trick that offered him a chance to crunch and swallow the compromising sheet of paper.

In reality, he did not need any 'code on a piece of paper' because he was not enciphering his messages—he was not that advanced as an agent at that time and his mission in Spain was not to collect intelligence. Instead, should he come across something valuable to report to the NKVD, he had agreed with his case officer on a simple code of communicating the information 'in every fifth word of the letter or a post-card' that he was instructed to write to 'Mademoiselle Dupont' in Paris. One would probably describe the situation as a huge flop on behalf of the experienced Dr Deutsch, who allegedly failed to notice that the address given to his young probationer coincided with that of the Soviet legation. This, if it had been noted by the censors, would certainly have ended the career of the future KGB star agent. The whole story of the letters to Paris, however, looks like another anecdote produced by Philby and his KGB mentors to entertain the readers. There were several accommodation addresses in London where he could have written.[10] There was no need at all to involve Paris in a complex scheme that makes little sense.

After Philby had been summoned to London for debriefing on the first three months of his Spanish mission, he was confronted by Deutsch. The episode is described in Orlov's biography. 'Weren't you ashamed of writing such dull letters to such a beautiful woman as Mademoiselle Dupont?' Deutsch allegedly asked Philby. He was stuttering more than usual but managed to respond: 'Try and write an interesting letter yourself when you have to communicate something serious in every fifth word'.[11] It goes without saying that not a single card reportedly sent by Philby to Paris has ever been found or reproduced.

From Maly's communications with Moscow, Philby's mission becomes crystal clear. Maly reported that he had personally briefed SÖHNCHEN (Philby's first code name) on the need to discover the system of the guards, primarily around Franco and then around other rebel leaders. Philby was instructed to report on the weak and vulnerable points in Franco's security and recommend ways to gain access to him and his staff 'by observing the control over those visiting him or his headquarters, his (their) excursions into the streets, their daily schedule, their home addresses or the locations of the places they frequent, where they sleep, where they eat (whether they eat in restaurants)—in short, all that is needed to act'. Of secondary interest was the 'number of German and Italian troops arriving in the Nationalist camp'.[12] Moscow was sufficiently well informed about them without the help of Philby, whose position in the rebel zone would not have facilitated any intelligence-gathering.

As Maly had already been shot, Deutsch thought it would do no harm to anybody if he criticized his old friend:

> This was the case when MANN [Maly], according to the Centre's order, was given the task of ordering SÖHNCHEN to assassinate Franco, although MANN knew that SÖHNCHEN would not be able to cope with this assignment. When the Centre continued to insist on this operation, he communicated the task to SÖHNCHEN, but in such a way that SÖHNCHEN saw that MANN himself did not take this assignment seriously. Such behaviour undermines the Centre's authority in the eyes of these people—the more so since they have a natural tendency to cynicism, which they have inherited from their class and the general attitude of the British intelligentsia. That is why they should always see our officers display an unshakeable confidence in the Centre, because only in this manner will they be able to overcome this attitude inherited from their bourgeois class.[13]

Another story that was often repeated in Soviet publications about Philby (from where it leaked to Western accounts) concerns Philby's alleged meetings with Orlov and other NKVD officers in France. Thus, according to Costello and Tsarev, on 4 September 1937 (when Reiss was shot dead near Lausanne), 'Deutsch eventually received specific instructions from the Centre for SÖHNCHEN personally to re-establish contact with Orlov'.[14] It is further suggested that 'ten days later Philby travelled to Biarritz—the elegant spa on the French Atlantic coast—to make his first rendezvous in two years with Orlov.[15] At the café of the Miramar Hotel they arranged that they would meet at least twice a month at Narbonne to exchange military and political intelligence according to a prearranged schedule.'[16] No one cared to specify exactly what important intelligence a young journalist and his former London controller were going to exchange so frequently and under such tremendous risk in that charming small city full of Franco spies.

That was another deliberate invention aimed at glorifying both the NKVD and their British agent. From the border-crossing stamps in his passport one can deduce that Orlov did not visit France either in June, or in September. In fact, he did not travel there until 8 October. Equally wrong is the claim in the introduction and epilogue to Orlov's last book that Philby passed on the intelligence he gathered within the Franco camp at meetings with NKVD officers across the French border at Hendaye or Saint-Jean de Luz,[17] two small towns between the Spanish border and Biarritz. In reality, a young agent had very limited opportunity to gather any intelligence, least of all military intelligence. Philby was not competent in military matters and would certainly see no difference between a platoon and a company or between a light and a heavy tank, not to mention more complicated things like new German weapons and equipment. Moreover, those one or two officers remaining in the NKVD station in Paris under the command of Kosenko[18] after the purges could not afford to travel many hours to the French–Spanish border to pick up Philby's reports, as they had their hands full with more important and urgent matters. One should not forget that a young British agent posing as a freelance journalist in the rebel zone was only a very little fish. After that most of the foreign intelligence personnel perished in Stalinist purges. Except for a handful of the most important capitals, the NKVD stations were closed down.

Philby's employment by the Secret Intelligence Service after the war broke out was his lucky chance in favourable circumstances when the recruits were taken on trust. In April 1940, on Guy Burgess's advice, Philby applied for a vacancy in Section D and subsequently met War Office intermediary Marjorie Maxse for a preliminary assessment. When they met again a few days later, Maxse was accompanied by Burgess, who had joined the same section upon its formation two years earlier in anticipation of the war and who was anxious to know her opinion of Philby's suitability. Eventually, Robert Barrington-Ward, the deputy editor of *The Times*, where Philby worked as a war correspondent, received a phone call asking whether Philby was available for war work. In this way Philby was hired as an intelligence officer.[19] Only then did his career as a Soviet 'mole' begin.

The section of the SIS in charge of special operations was formed in June 1938 as Section D run by Major (later Colonel) Laurence D. Grand of the Royal Engineers.[20] Its functions included a mixed bag of war-related tasks such as organizing and equipping resistance units, contact with and support of anti-Nazi groups and organizations in Europe, as well as sabotage, covert operations, and subversive propaganda. It seems that, when Philby's vetting was taking place, Colonel Grand was too busy to look into the matter himself, as he was right in the middle of a debacle that threatened to compromise the SIS organization in Sweden. In the summer of 1938, soon after Section D had been established and Burgess accepted as a member, an Englishman in his mid-thirties made a tour of the main ore fields of Sweden. His name was A. F. Rickman. To those who wished to know, Mr Rickman explained that he was researching a book, which indeed came out a year later. At the end of July 1939, Rickman was back in Sweden, this time as a businessman with a permanent residence in Stockholm. On 11 April 1940 he received via Brigadier Reginald Sutton-Pratt, the British military attaché to Sweden, a telegram from Colonel Grand in London ordering him to go ahead with Operation OXELÖSUND and wishing him the best of luck. Eight days later the police called upon Rickman to carry out a routine search and found a large cache of explosives and a collection of anti-Nazi propaganda leaflets. On the next day the search was extended to a cellar that Rickman was renting, and the officers were startled to find a further stock of some 33 kilos of gelignite, 57 kilos of hexogen, 8 limpet mines, and a whole range of other sabotage equipment.[21] When Philby was joining the service, Rickman was tried and sentenced to eight years' hard labour, and the chief of Section D was doing his best to get out of the embarrassing situation.

Philby's first intelligence reports probably started to reach Moscow after September 1941, when he began working for Section V, the Iberian section, in charge of Spain, Portugal, Gibraltar, and part of Africa. Before that, when Anatoly Gorsky was back in London again, as the NKVD head of station, Philby and other Cambridge recruits had lost all contact with Soviet intelligence[22]—not because of the information that they delivered or failed to deliver, but because the Soviets were not prepared to believe them.

In early 1944, a new Section IX was created within SIS 'to study past records of Soviet and Communist activity'. Again, as six years before, the service was anticipating the war, which this time would fortunately be 'cold', only occasionally turning 'hot'. Philby was promoted to head this new section with a remit for 'the collection and interpretation of information concerning Soviet and Communist espionage and subversion in all parts of the world outside British territory'. A year later, in the spring of 1945, Menzies set up a committee 'on SIS reorganisation' that he himself chaired. The day-to-day work was handled by his deputy, Maurice Jeffes, and the other members of the committee were Dick Ellis, Lieutenant Colonel J. K. Cordeaux RM (Naval Intelligence Department's representative with MI6), and Kim Philby.[23] As one of his SIS colleagues, Robert Cecil, wrote later: 'Philby at one stroke had . . . ensured that the whole post-war effort to counter Communist espionage would be known to the Kremlin. The history of espionage records few, if any, comparable master-strokes.'[24] That, however, was absolutely not the case as viewed from Moscow.

Back in October 1943 Moscow Centre informed their London station that, after a long analysis of the voluminous reports of the Cambridge Five, Elena Dmitrievna Mordzhinskaya, major of state security and deputy chief of the information section, had concluded that they were double agents working on the instructions of SIS and MI5.[25]

As far back as their years at Cambridge, Philby, Maclean and Burgess had probably been acting on instructions from British intelligence to infiltrate the student left before making contact with the NKVD. Only thus, the Centre reasoned, was it possible to explain why both SIS and MI5 were currently employing in highly sensible jobs Cambridge graduates with a Communist background. The lack of any reference to British recruitment of Soviet agents in the intelligence supplied either by SÖHNCHEN (Philby) from SIS or by TONY (Blunt) from MI5 was seen as further evidence that both were being used to feed disinformation to the NKVD. 'During the entire period that s[ÖHNCHEN] and T[ONY] worked for the British special services' [the report suggested], 'they did not help expose a single valuable ISLANDER [British] agent either in the USSR or in the Soviet embassy in the ISLAND' . . . It therefore ordered the London residency to create a new independent agent network uncontaminated by the Five.[26]

Taking their cue from the master conspiracy theorist in the Kremlin, the conspiracy theorists at the Lubyanka could explain the voluminous intelligence from the Five, consisting, in their view, of disinformation along with large amount of accurate high-grade reports, as an elaborate British game of deception. As usual, the Soviet capacity to understand the political and diplomatic intelligence it collected never approached its ability to collect that intelligence. As a result, the information that reached the Kremlin was to reinforce rather than challenge Stalin's conspiracy theories.[27] Probably without any irony, at dinner with Churchill in the Kremlin in October 1944 Stalin proposed a toast to 'the British intelligence service'.

Early in 1945, several American intelligence and counter-intelligence organizations made various approaches to MI6 on the question of collaboration in counteracting the growing Communist and Soviet expansion and espionage. On 16 July, Philby, as head of Section IX, called an informal meeting in London of liaison officers representing ONI (US Office of Naval Intelligence), G-2 (US Army Intelligence), Special Branch and OSS X-2

(Counterespionage Branch of the Intelligence Service of the Office of Strategic Services). During the meeting, Philby explained that the recent visit of the chair of the Joint Intelligence Committee (JIC), Victor Cavendish-Bentinck, to General Eisenhower and to Washington resulted in an agreement that collaboration between British and American services on the issue was desirable. As for MI6, the three American services mentioned would be involved, while the FBI would act in liaison with MI5, Sections F (Colonies & Political Parties) and B (Counter Espionage and Counter Subversion), which were handling the problem within the British Empire. As a result of those discussions it was agreed that the three American Services would approach Section IX directly (not through Section V as it had done previously), and would deal with Philby, or his deputy, Lt Colonel Rodney Dennys. Such an arrangement would continue until the United States organized a secret intelligence service of their own.[28] Without any doubt, the minutes of the meeting were reported by Philby to his controller, Boris Krötenschield,[29] who, in turn, duly informed the resident, Konstantin Kukin. In Moscow the information was duly filed, but nothing more happened because Fitin and his subordinates continued to be seriously confused about what exactly Philby and his friends were up to.[30] A memo in the file reminded their case officer that Philby and others had been recruited and at different times controlled by such traitors, spies, and enemies of the people as Reif, Maly, Bystroletov, and Nikolsky/Orlov. Of these, two had been shot, one was serving a twenty-year sentence in the Gulag, and one was in hiding somewhere in America.

Shortly after that meeting chaired by Philby, on 27 August 1945, a letter arrived at the British consulate in Istanbul. It had been written and signed by Konstantin Volkov, Soviet Vice-Consul and deputy head of the NKGB (successor of the NKVD) station in Turkey.[31] Unfortunately for him, his letter did not reach the hands of the experienced SIS station chief Cyril Machray, an old hand in Middle East affairs about whom Volkov must have been informed, but was delivered to the British Vice-Consul, C. H. Page. In his letter Volkov was requesting an urgent meeting. For whatever reason, Page did not reply. A week later, Volkov turned up at the British consulate in person and asked for political asylum for himself and his wife. In return for asylum and the sum of £50,000 (equivalent to something over £2 million in 2014), he offered important documents and high-grade insider information obtained while working on the British desk in Moscow Centre. Among Soviet agents in London, he revealed, two were in the

Foreign Office and seven (!!!) 'inside the British intelligence system', including one 'fulfilling the function of head of a section of British counter-espionage' (another recorded wording is 'fulfilling the duties of a Head of Department in British Counterintelligence').[32] This description fitted both Philby and Roger Hollis of MI5. But whatever information he possessed, there is little doubt that then, as now, his request for such financial remuneration would have been rejected by the Head Office.

Under the first heading [Brook-Shepherd reports], he [Volkov] offered to name 314 Soviet agents in Turkey and no fewer than 250 Soviet agents in Britain. Those names, Volkov said, were locked in a suitcase in an empty flat in Moscow. As a bonus, he offered to provide details about the intelligence headquarters in Moscow and about current Soviet operations in the Near East and Iran, complete with specimens of Soviet official seals, rubber-stamps and identity documents.[33]

It may be added that the majority of those 250 Soviet agents in post-war Britain remain unidentified until this day.

There was one more startling piece of information. For the past two and a half years, Volkov said, the Russians had been able to intercept all cipher traffic between the British embassy in Moscow and London. This meant that Stalin had been aware before the Teheran, Yalta, and Potsdam conferences what the Western negotiating position was or, at least, what the British thought about the situation.[34]

On 19 September Philby received a report of Volkov's meeting with Page that came from the Istanbul consulate (but not from the SIS station, with Machray remaining unaware of the Volkov affair simply because no one cared to tell him). Philby writes: 'That evening, I worked late. The situation seemed to call for urgent action of an extra-curricular nature.'[35] This probably means that he had to set up an emergency meeting with his Soviet controller. He arranged it on the next day.[36] Krötenschield immediately informed the resident and Kukin–Moscow. This time the information was acted upon promptly. On 21 September, the Turkish embassy in Moscow issued visas for two NKGB hit men, 'Andrey Boiko'[37] and 'Alexander Danilov', posing as diplomatic couriers. The Turkish consular officials were puzzled, as neither name figured on their list of regular Soviet Foreign Ministry couriers, but complied without argument. 'Boiko' was the NKGB Colonel Andrei Makarovich Otroschenko, then chief of the 5th Department (Near and Middle East) of the 1st Directorate.[38] 'Danilov', also an alias, was from Sudoplatov's Special Tasks. Philby succeeded in gaining authorization from the chief to fly to Turkey to deal personally with the Volkov case, but when he arrived in Istanbul the game was over. Volkov, for whom it was a first field posting, miscalculated his chances again by checking into Istanbul's ninety-year-old French Hospital La Paix. Two days before Philby stepped on Turkish soil, Volkov and his wife Zoya, both on stretchers, had been carried aboard a Soviet aircraft.[39] As Philby himself later admitted in his book, the Volkov case had 'proved to be a very narrow squeak indeed'.[40]

Mitrokhin's notes from the Volkov investigation file in Moscow fully corroborate this story. Under interrogation in the Lubyanka prison before his execution, Volkov confessed and admitted his guilt. What happened to his wife is not recorded. In February 1947 Philby arrived in Istanbul to replace Machray (who had been transferred to the Foreign Office's security department), as First Secretary of the embassy and SIS head of station with a staff of four officers.

It was his first overseas posting. As usual, Philby first established friendly relations with the head of the Istanbul directorate of the National Security Service (Milli Emniyet Hizmeti), the Turkish intelligence organization also responsible for security. In January 1948 this yielded results, as his contact introduced Philby to Ismail Akhmedov, a GRU defector. Philby was not only allowed to interview him alone, but was also not obliged to share the results with the Turks.[41] It is not known what Philby reported to the Head Office in London, but Akhmedov later collaborated with MI5, helping to investigate several leads provided by Gouzenko.

During the debriefing, Akhmedov immediately noticed that Philby had some difficulty in grasping the meaning of the military terms he used. As a non-military man, Philby had problems understanding such professional expressions as 'strategic echelon', 'operational depth', 'the initial period of war', and so on, so it quickly became clear to the defector that he was dealing with a civilian. One day, Philby also popped up with a question of private interest: 'Tell me, please, how the Soviets treat their double agents?'[42] He was advised that the Soviets did not like double agents.

Akhmedov's file is still classified. Brook-Shepherd, who had enjoyed some limited access to it, wrote that when at one point Akhmedov showed interest in moving on from Turkey, it only remained to dissuade him from coming to England. Philby simply declared that it was impossible.[43] Nevertheless, the 'Spycatcher' Peter Wright of MI5 invited Akhmedov to London. Then he moved to Germany and from there to the USA, where he settled in the Washington area.

With slightly less luck in Ottawa, shortly after Volkov's letter had reached the British consulate, Igor Gouzenko, a GRU cipher clerk at the Soviet embassy in Canada, would not have been able to defect., as noted by Cristopher Andrew in his Authorized History of MI5: 'With slightly more luck in Istanbul,' he adds, 'Volkov would have succeeded in unmasking Philby and disrupting Soviet intelligence operations on a much larger scale than Gouzenko was able to do'.[44]

The Canadians and their US colleagues kept the British well informed of the Gouzenko debriefing. At the receiving end in London, the 'Corby' traffic, as the Gouzenko case became known among those who needed to know, was handled primarily by Philby, who kept Moscow updated.[45] Noticeably, although Gouzenko could provide information only about the GRU network, Krötenschild immediately received a bunch of instructions to put all contacts under his control on ice. Eight cryptonyms in all were mentioned in the Lubyanka telegrams, three of which were still referred to as 'valuable sources', because they were indeed the best British agents that Moscow had. These were STANLEY [Philby], HICKS [Burgess], and JOHNSON [Blunt]. Besides, two were mentioned together as DAVID and ROSA (unidentified), plus there were three others.[46] There was a similar rise in the volume of wireless traffic between Moscow and London in connection with the Volkov case.

Both the Foreign Office and MI6 agreed that Philby had performed exceptionally well in his career, and he was soon appointed to the post that could eventually have brought him right into the chief's chair. As the new SIS head of station in Washington, and liaison with the CIA, Philby set sail for the USA in October 1949. But the great days of the Cambridge Spy Ring ended with the flight of Burgess and Maclean two years later, and the subsequent retirement of Philby from the SIS. Shortly before Christmas he was summoned to a 'special inquiry' at MI5 headquarters, 'an informal trial', which Philby later described in his memoirs. But back in December 1951 he had won his round and was acquitted. He was extremely lucky, because, during the whole rise and fall of Philby as a Soviet spy, his former short-time controller Nikolsky/Orlov was hiding in the USA without anyone knowing about it.

Philby wrote in his KGB biography:

He [Goldin? Lyova? Bill? Agent SÖHNCHEN never heard Nikolsky's real name] was recalled to Moscow at the end of the Spanish war, but instead he went to America. He lived in the States, in Canada. But he never said a single word about me, though of course he was interrogated in a tough way by the CIA and the FBI and he was in constant contact with them.[47]

What Philby wrote about Orlov he was simply not in the position to know. But it is true that, when the FBI showed Orlov Philby's photo, he denied any knowledge of the man.

Stalin died on 5 March 1953, by which time his best British agent had been unemployed for two years and without any contact with Soviet intelligence. While the late dictator's body was embalmed and placed in a glass case in Lenin's Mausoleum on Red Square, Orlov's *Secret History of Stalin's Crimes* was serialized by *Life* magazine. One of the best known and oft-quoted episodes in the book, debated until this day, is the assassination of Sergey Kirov, Stalin's party comrade and the leader of the Leningrad Communist Party organization.

This is how Robert Conquest describes what happened:

On 1 December 1934, at about four o'clock in the afternoon, the young assassin Leonid Nikolaev entered the Smolny, headquarters of the Communist Party in Leningrad. Kirov was preparing a report on the November plenum of the Central Committee from which he had just returned. He was shortly supposed to deliver it to the *aktiv* of the Leningrad Party [*sic*] now assembling in a conference room farther along on the same floor. At 4.30, he left his office and turned towards the office of the Leningrad Second Secretary [*sic*], his trusted aide, Mikhail Chudov. He had gone only a few steps when Nikolaev moved from a corner, shot him in the back with a Nagan revolver, and then collapsed beside him. At the sound of the shot Party officials came running along the corridor. They were astonished at the complete absence of guards. Even Kirov's chief bodyguard, Borisov, who according to standing instructions should have been with him, was nowhere to be seen. This killing has every right to be called the crime of the century.[48]

Whether it was indeed 'the crime of the century' is debatable, but its investigation had probably been the longest ever in the history of the Soviet Union and post-Communist Russia, taking altogether about six decades. The meticulous examination of all documents, including witnesses' testimonies, established that at about half past four, Kirov, a member of the Presidium of the Central Executive Committee of the USSR and the Secretary of the Central Committee and the Leningrad Committee of the CPSU, arrived from his home. He got out of the car and went into the heavily guarded Smolny Institute, which had been turned into the Party headquarters. Special Agent Mikhail Borisov, one of the senior members of his guard detail, was on permanent duty at the building. Borisov met his boss as usual and was walking about fifteen paces behind him in the vestibule. According to Borisov's own words, he followed Kirov at this distance up to the second floor. When he reached the first staircase, Kirov was already at the landing between the first and second floors, so Borisov followed him up to the entrance to the third floor. After getting to the corridor, he continued to follow him at a distance of about twenty paces. Another bodyguard, Nikolai Dureiko, assigned as a walking patrol on the third floor, was to meet Kirov at his aide's office. When Kirov turned into the left corridor, Borisov was still some steps behind and did not have him in sight. At 4.37 p.m., he heard a shot. While he was pulling his revolver out of its holster, Borisov heard a second shot. When he came there, he saw three people: Kirov, lying face down, an unknown individual with a revolver, and the house electrician Seliverst Platych, who was closing the glass door at the end of the corridor.[49] Nobody else was there.

Platych, 39 years old, a reserve Red Army officer and a party member since 1925, rushed towards the gunman, who had collapsed after the second shot and lay unconscious, threw aside the gun, and hit the man twice in the face with his fist. The electrician was so agitated that during the interrogation on the next day, of all the people who had been there, he could hardly remember anything.[50]

According to Orlov:

At the entrance to the corridor, which led to Kirov's secretariat, the usual guards were absent. Nikolayev [the gunman] entered the corridor without hindrance. Nobody was there except a middle-aged man by the name of Borisov, who acted as Kirov's personal attendant ... When Nikolayev entered the corridor, Borisov was preparing a tray with tea and sandwiches, which he soon carried into the conference room, where a meeting of the Bureau of the Leningrad Party Committee was in progress under the leadership of Kirov. Nikolayev waited patiently. Some time later, Borisov entered the conference room again and told Kirov that he was being called to the direct Kremlin wire. In about two minutes, Kirov got up from his chair and went out of the conference room, closing the door behind him. At that moment, a shot was heard. Not a soul was in the corridor ...[51]

The initial examination of Kirov's body revealed no signs of a pulse or breathing. As the body was being moved, Dr Halperina arrived and diagnosed facial cyanosis, detected no pulse or respiration, and found dilated pupils with no response to light. Nevertheless until 5.40 p.m. the doctors were performing artificial respiration. Kirov was finally pronounced dead, with the conclusive protocol signed at 7.55 p.m. by a large group of physicians[52]—indeed the best doctors available at the moment.

Immediately after the shooting, Kirov's personal assistant called the Kremlin and asked Stalin's secretary to put him through to Stalin because of an emergency. He was politely advised that Stalin was out of reach. Then he asked that Stalin be informed that Kirov was seriously wounded by a shot in the back of the head. A few minutes later Stalin called. After talking with Smolny, he came quickly to the Central Committee and ordered all members of the Politburo and the Central Committee secretaries to be summoned to his office. After the meeting, it became clear that Stalin, Molotov, Voroshilov, and some other people would have to leave for Leningrad immediately to conduct an investigation personally. They left that very same night[53] by a special train.

The historian Donald Rayfield describes the trip:

Stalin's train raced through the night along 700 kilometres of track guarded by thousands of NKVD men. In the morning, accompanied by the heads of every branch of the power structure . . . Stalin left the train. He was greeted by Philip Medved, head of the Leningrad NKVD and a friend of Kirov. Stalin struck him in the face and called him a wanker.[54]

According to Orlov:

The arrival of Stalin in Leningrad was a great event. A whole floor of the Smolny building was reserved for him, as well as a dozen or so rooms in the magnificent NKVD building, which were quickly isolated from the rest of the offices. Stalin set to work immediately. The first man whom he summoned to his office was Philip Medved. This evidently was just a formality because Stalin was well aware that Medved did not know anything about the murder beyond the official facts. He dismissed him quickly and asked for Zaporozhets. Stalin was closeted with him for more than an hour. After that he ordered Nikolayev brought in. Those present during Stalin's conversation with Nikolayev were: Yagoda, the chief of the NKVD, Mironov, the chief of the Economic Administration, and a trusted officer of the Operative Department who escorted Nikolayev from his cell . . .

'And where did you get the revolver?' asked Stalin.

'Why do you ask me? Ask Zaporozhets about that!' answered Nikolayev with an insolent sneer.

Stalin's face turned green with anger. 'Take him away!' he shouted . . .

As soon as the door closed, Stalin leaped to his feet, hurled Nikolayev's file into Yagoda's face and snarled: 'Bungler!' then cast a sidelong glance at Mironov . . .

Stalin knew where Borisov was. After his conversation with the assistants of Kirov, he went to the NKVD building and ordered Borisov brought before him. Stalin's talk with Borisov was very short. After that Borisov was secretly liquidated by order of Stalin. One more witness had been put out of the way.[55]

In reality, Stalin, Molotov, and Voroshilov boarded Stalin's personal coach of a special train and left for Leningrad, accompanied by the detail headed by Stalin's bodyguard Nikolai Vlasik. Yagoda, the NKVD chief, was in the same train, but Vlasik did not see Yezhov. After their arrival (Medved was not at the train station) they got into waiting limousines and went to a special residence on the island kept for top-level visitors. As General Vlasik put it: 'Stalin spent his off-time at a house on the islands and worked at Smolny.'[56]

Medved met Stalin, Voroshilov, and Molotov at the residence. Then they went to Smolny to interrogate Nikolaev. Vlasik, Stalin's bodyguard, had been staying in the waiting room the whole time without leaving. He later testified:

I recall one occasion very well when they brought Nikolayev in to Stalin, Molotov and Voroshilov at the office. Nikolayev made a very bad impression. He was small, mean looking, and so forth. Two agents were leading him by the arms, and he looked totally exhausted and said nothing. I don't remember the names of the agents who brought in Nikolayev. I can't say exactly how long Stalin, Molotov and Voroshilov interrogated Nikolayev, but he stayed in the office quite a while. I didn't hear any loud talk, screaming, or noise from the office when they were interrogating Nikolayev. I don't recall if anyone besides Stalin, Molotov and Voroshilov took part in or was present at Nikolayev's interrogation.[57]

Vlasik knew Medved well from the time they both worked in the Moscow Cheka. He also knew Medved's deputy, Zaporozhets, a former OGPU resident in Vienna. In an affidavit personally signed by Vlasik in 1965, Stalin's long-time personal bodyguard stated that he had absolutely no memory of his boss ever summoning Medved or Zaporozhets prior to Kirov's murder and had absolutely no knowledge of any personal contact between Stalin and the two chiefs of the Leningrad NKVD Directorate.[58]

Stalin also never visited the Leningrad NKVD building and never talked to Borisov. Vlasik recalled: 'I remember the following. [A guard] walked into the waiting room and told me that they were taking Borisov in a truck to be interrogated by Stalin in Smolny. There was some ice on the road, the truck got into an accident, and Borisov was taken to the hospital unconscious . . . I don't remember who told Stalin what happened to Borisov.'[59] In Vlasik's words, when Stalin heard the news, he became visibly upset in Molotov's presence and expressed extreme dissatisfaction with the men who were unable to get Borisov to Smolny safely.[60]

When the second commission was investigating Kirov's murder in 1965, Vlasik, still alive and in good form (he would die two years later aged 71), insisted that Stalin had nothing to do with it. He declared that such rumours were completely groundless. Himself one of Stalin's victims, having twice been fired from his job and placed under arrest, Vlasik, who had known Stalin personally for many years, categorically denied any possible involvement of his former master.[61]

Orlov claimed:

> I learned the secret of the Kirov case after I returned to the Soviet Union, in the fall of 1935...I learned that the former chief of the Leningrad Administration, Medved, and his deputy Zaporozhets, who were sentenced in connection with the Kirov case to imprisonment, were not in prison at all. Instead, by order of Stalin, they were appointed to leading posts in *Lenzoloto* ('Leningrad Gold'), the richest gold fields in Siberia...Before returning to Moscow, Stalin appointed Mironov for the duration of several months chief of the Leningrad Administration and virtual dictator over Leningrad.[62]

Extracts from the State Archive of the Russian Federation read:

Medved, Philip Demianovich: From 8 January 1930 to 10 July 1934—OGPU plenipotentiary in the Leningrad military district and chief of the Leningrad NKVD directorate from 15 July to 3 December 1934. Arrested in December 1934. On 23 January 1935 sentenced to three years of corrective labour and sent to Kolyma in north-eastern Siberia to work at the *Dalstroi* camp mining administration. Summoned to Moscow in May 1937, arrested on 7 September and shot. His relatives were informed that Medved died in the Gulag in October 1946. In December 1957 the Supreme Court ruled that there was no 'body of crime' (corpus delicti) in Medved's case and he was exonerated.

    Zaporozhets, Ivan Vasilievich: From 1921 joined the Cheka working in Moscow and on undercover missions in Poland, Czechoslovakia and Austria. In October 1923, chief of the 4th section (foreign trade) of the EKU [where Nikolsky/Orlov served in the 6th (financial) section from 1 May 1924]. During the same year Zaporozhets was posted to Berlin and in 1925—to Vienna as the OGPU resident agent. From 14 March 1931—chief of the Secret Political Department (SPO) at the head office; from 30 October 1931—deputy OGPU plenipotentiary in the Leningrad military district. On 23 January 1935 sentenced to three years of corrective labour though he was not in Leningrad when Kirov was murdered. Zaporozhets did not serve his sentence because he was suddenly appointed first deputy and then director of Dalstroi. Like his former boss Medved, Zaporozhets was arrested on 14 August 1937, transported to Moscow and secretly shot.

    Mironov, Lev Grigoryevich: Joined the OGPU in May 1924 [together with Nikolsky/Orlov]. Commissar of State Security 2nd Rank. From 11 August

1931—chief of the Economic Directorate (EKU), and from 1933—member of the Collegium. From 28 November 1936—chief of the Counterintelligence Department (KRO) of the Chief Directorate of State Security (GUGB) of the NKVD. Arrested on 14 June 1937, sentenced to death and shot on 29 August 1938. Not exonerated.[63]

And Mironov never served in Leningrad; he only came there to investigate Kirov's murder.

From Orlov's *Secret History*, written almost twenty years after Kirov's murder: 'I was not in the Soviet Union at that time, and my only sources of information were the official announcements of the Moscow press.'[64]

At the end of March 1990 Alexander Yakovlev, adviser to the first Soviet President Mikhail Gorbachev, addressed the Politburo Commission to request a new investigation of the Kirov assassination. An authoritative investigation team was formed. It included senior members of the Prosecutor General's investigation department, the Chief Military Prosecutor's office staff, the KGB, and the party Control Commission. This imposing panel studied all available documents in every Soviet archive and interviewed witnesses. They also rechecked evidence, documents, and the conclusions of three previous investigations. In June the panel presented a detailed forty-four-page report. It was established without any reasonable doubt that the crime had be committed by a single individual (Nikolaev) and that neither the NKVD nor Stalin had anything to do with it. But the Soviet dictator certainly used Kirov's assassination to unleash his own wave of repression, which took thousands of lives even before the Great Terror.

The final conclusion of the Yakovlev Commission sent to the last Soviet Minister of Interior, who was at the same time a Member of the Politburo, intended putting an end to this 'crime of the century':

To Comrade Pugo
NOT FOR PUBLICATION
No St-87(k)
March 26, 1990
A memorandum examined by the commission provided a comprehensive analysis of facts and documents gathered by the Central Committee commissions appointed in the 1950s and 1960s to explore the circumstances surrounding S. M. Kirov's murder. The basic conclusions of the most recent investigation were that the available evidence indicates that the act of terrorism perpetrated against S. M. Kirov was planned and committed by Nikolaev alone. In 1933–34 there was no counterrevolutionary terrorist organization in Leningrad, nor any so-called

Leningrad Centre. There is no proof on which to base any accusation that G. Ya. Biseneks [George Bisenieks, who was accused of providing a contact between the assassin and Trotsky in exile], the former consul of bourgeois Latvia in Leningrad, was involved in arranging Kirov's murder. There is also no proof of a plot to murder Kirov involving his bodyguard, M. V. Borisov, who died in an automobile accident. And finally the memorandum states that there is no evidence confirming the involvement of I. V. Stalin and the People's Commissariat of Internal Affairs [NKVD] in organizing and carrying out Kirov's murder, either in the criminal case files on Nikolayev et al., or in the documents uncovered by the investigations conducted in 1957–1967 and 1988–1989.

[signed] A. Yakovlev[65]

As mentioned, nothing new was discovered except, perhaps, for one important fact. The Politburo Commission also discussed the scope of arguments in Khrushchev's 'Secret Speech' at the XX party congress, which suggested that the assassin of Kirov was assisted from 'within the NKVD, that Nikolaev was released after he was arrested for suspicious behaviour and that the functionaries of the Leningrad NKVD were given very light sentences'. The experts noted that the source of the rumours that Stalin was behind the murder of Kirov was the text published by Alexander Orlov and entitled *The Secret History of Stalin's Crimes.*[66] After it first came out in 1953, a single chapter of Orlov's book caused three top-level government investigations.

In December 2009 the FSB declassified fourteen volumes out of fifty-six dealing with Kirov's murder. The Kirov Museum curator Tatiana Sukharnikova was the only historian allowed to study the files. Her conclusion was that Nikolaev had acted alone—but that Kirov was almost certainly shot *not* in the corridor of the Smolny Palace and *not* with the Nagant revolver that belonged to Nikolaev. The story goes on.

Together with other readers around the world, the FBI was hugely impressed by Orlov's book. They immediately started to investigate and quickly found out that during the previous fifteen years they had been on Orlov's track twice but never caught him. Naturally, when Krivitsky started to publish his revelations in 1939, no one thought of looking for Orlov in America. But in 1943 Special Agent in Charge (SAC) Edward A. Soucy of the Boston Field Division Office wrote to J. Edgar Hoover, the FBI director, that 'it is requested that the Bureau indices be checked under the name of Alexander L. Berg and Maria Orlowe [*sic*] Berg'. Soucy's suspicions were based on the fact that 'the above subjects maintain a safety deposit box at the Pilgrim Vaults, Incorporated; they have stated to vault company officials that they are aliens and refuse to list contents of their box'. He added that rolls of films had been noted in the said box and that 'subjects have not been seen since August 16, 1941 but have sent in rentals in June 1942 from New York City and in September 1943 from Pittsburg'. No return address was given, and their present whereabouts remained unknown.[67] Hoover somewhat carelessly responded that 'it appears that the subject of your communication may be identical with one Alexander Berg, who is an Honorary Consul for the Norwegian Government and who assumed his duties at San Francisco, on September 2, 1942'.[68] In June 1944 the case was closed.

Ten years later, in July 1954, the FBI Director informed the US Assistant Attorney General William F. Tompkins that the Bureau had initiated an investigation of Alexander Orlov in April 1953 based upon the *Life* articles, where 'he is described as having been at various dates a prosecutor for the USSR Supreme Court, an official of the People's Commissariat of Internal Affairs (NKVD), and a diplomat representing Stalin to the Spanish Republic during the Spanish Civil War'.[69] A judge, a ministry official, and a diplomat: Orlov was none of it, but it all sounded good and solid in America.

During this new investigation in 1953, the issue of Pilgrim Vaults came up again. The problem actually was that, as the Orlovs sometimes spoke Yiddish between themselves, and because there were rolls of film in their safe deposit box, an employee of the bank thought they were perhaps German spies. He reported the couple to the FBI, whose detectives learned that 'Mr Berg (Orlov) was permitted to remove from his safe two passports, one in the name of Alexandria Orlo [*sic*], and the other in the name of Vera Orlo [*sic*], whom the detectives thought to be the mother and sister respectfully of Mrs Berg'.[70] This information was entirely ignored later, and Orlov had never been asked why and for what reason at one point in 1941 he decided to remove his and his late daughter's Soviet passports, nor had it ever been noticed by anybody that page 20 (and, accordingly, page 21) of his diplomatic passport, containing several visas and border crossing stamps, had mysteriously disappeared.

On 29 June 1954, Joseph J. Gaudino, inspector representing the Immigration and Naturalization Service (INS), New York City office, furnished a copy of the sworn statement to Mr and Mrs Orlov, while the investigator Denton J. Kerns informed the couple that he was authorized by law to administer oaths and take testimony in connection with the enforcement of the Immigration and Nationality laws of the United States. Both were sworn in the presence of their attorney, Hugo Pollock.

Mr KERNS. Do you solemnly swear that all the statements you are about to make will be the truth, and whole truth and nothing but the truth, so help you God?

Mr ORLOV. I do.

Mr KERNS. What is your true and correct name?

Mr ORLOV. Alexander Orlov.[71]

Mr KERNS. Have you ever been known by other names?

Mr ORLOV. Yes, by the name of Nikolsky, that was my Party name in Russia.[72] I have also been known under the name of Nicolayev [sic]. This name, Nicolayev, was the name given to me by the Soviet Foreign Office when I travelled abroad.[73] I also used the name of Koornick for purpose of registering in hotels in the United States . . .

Mr KERNS. Have you ever been known by any other names, Mr. Orlov?

Mr ORLOV. No.[74]

Mr KERNS. Have you ever been known by any nicknames?

Mr ORLOV. Yes, but only in the Secret Service in the Soviet Union; that was Schwed. I used this name only in corresponding with the Central Committee of the Party . . .[75]

Mr KERNS. When and where were you born?

Mr ORLOV. On August 20, 1895 in Moscow, Russia.[76]

Mr KERNS. Of what country are you a citizen?

Mr ORLOV. I am stateless.[77]

Mr KERNS. Do you take an oath that this is a true and correct statement?

Mr ORLOV. Yes, absolutely.

Mr KERNS. And you are aware that you are under oath at the present time?

Mr ORLOV. Yes.[78]

It was not the first time that Orlov committed perjury in America. During the examination the 'FBI's KGB General' managed to lie deliberately on another twenty-five occasions. He said that from 1918 until 1920 he was in the Red Army as Commander on the south-west front of guerrilla detachments and counter-intelligence chief, which, as we saw, was not true. He claimed that from 1920 to 1921 he was Chief of Investigations and Counter-Intelligence of the Frontier Department of Northern Russia, while such a post never existed. At the time he was a junior officer in Archangel. He said that he was appointed Deputy Chief of the Economic Department of the OGPU where he 'was in charge of Control of Soviet Industry and Trade and Combating Corruption'—a complete invention. The position described by Orlov existed only in his imagination. Gazur repeated Orlov's claim that 'at the end of 1926, I was appointed Chief of the Economic Division of the Foreign Department of the NKVD in charge of Control of Foreign Trade of the Soviet Union; I remained in this post until the summer or fall of 1935; in 1935 I was named Deputy Chief of the Department for Railways and Sea Transport of the NKVD'[79] is equally untrue, as nothing of the sort ever existed. From 1926 to 1935 Nikolsky/Orlov was abroad on various undercover missions. At the same time, Orlov completely avoided speaking about his work as an OGPU–NKVD operative in Europe before and during the Spanish Civil War.

The INS investigator Kerns asked Orlov many questions about his activities in Spain, especially concerning purges and assassinations. The answer was: 'In Spain, I was an official advisor to the Republican Government of Spain on matters concerning German Counter-Espionage and had no authority whatsoever in matters of arrest, trials or repressions.'[80] For 'German Counter Espionage' he certainly got an approving nod from the official.

By 1954, the US Department of Justice (through both the FBI and INS) should have been aware that *everything* Orlov said was untrue. The FBI files contain reports from many confidential sources and eyewitnesses that Orlov had taken direct part in crimes committed in Spain.[81] In 1951, a book was published in the United States with a correct exposé of the executions outside Russia ordered by the Stalin secret police.[82] The same author also presented his version of the murder of Kirov (partly borrowed by Orlov for his own book, which came out a year later).[83] Finally, in 1955 David J. Dallin published his brilliant volume exposing Soviet espionage activities in Europe and the USA.[84] After all this, Orlov's case should at the very least have been treated with far more caution, but all evidence against him was seemingly entirely ignored by the US authorities.

A BILL
For the relief of Alexander Orlov and his wife, Maria Orlov
Be it enacted by the Senate and House of Representatives of the United States of America in Congress assembled, that for the purposes of the Immigration and Nationality Act, Alexander Orlov and his wife, Maria Orlov, shall be held and considered to have been lawfully admitted to the United States for permanent residence as of the date of the enactment of this Act, upon payment of the required visa fees. Upon the granting of permanent residence to such aliens as provided for in this Act, the Secretary of State shall instruct the proper quota-control officer to deduct the required numbers from the appropriate quota or quotas for the first year that such quota or quotas are available.[85]

An imposing looking senator, George H. Bender (R) from Ohio, intro-
duced the above Bill to the 84th United States Congress on 1 April 1955.
The Bill was read twice and referred to the Committee on the Judiciary.
After the Bill had been passed by Congress and signed by the President,
Alexander Orlov became a legal resident in America.

23
The Affair called 'Agent Mark'

O n 28 September 1955, in Room 411 of the Russell Senate Office Building in Washington, Senator James O. Eastland was presiding over the hearings. Orlov was in his element:

Mr. ORLOV. I was sent by the Politburo to Spain in September 1936. Before that I should say approximately in August during the famous Moscow trial of Zinoviev and Kamenev, [I learned] that there was a highly secret agent and highly valued agent in France, who was planted to the Trotskyites and became the closest friend of Trotsky's son, Lev Sedov.

He was so highly valued that even Stalin knew about him. His value, as I understood then, was that he would become the organizer of the assassination of Trotsky or Trotsky's son any time, because in view of the great trust Trotsky and Trotsky's son had in him that Mark could always recommend secretaries to Trotsky, guards to Trotsky, and in that way could help to infiltrate an assassin into Trotsky's household in Mexico.[1]

'Agent Mark' was Mark Zborowski, codenamed TYUL'PAN ('TULIP').

The medical anthropologist Mark Zborowski died of heart failure at San Francisco's Mount Zion Hospital on 30 April 1990, aged 82. He was born in Uman, Central Ukraine, emigrating to the United States in 1941 from France. Educated at the University of Paris, Zborowski was best known among colleagues for his ground-breaking research on the cultural mitigation of pain and his ethno-historical account of Jewish life in the Shtetls of Eastern Europe. He is also famous as the author of two important books, as well as of a good number of professional publications.

In the United States, Mark found employment as a research assistant at Harvard University, a private Ivy League research centre located in Cambridge, Massachusetts. During the war he worked as a consultant for the US Army, and after it as a consultant for the Studies in Contemporary Cultures project at Columbia University. He became an American citizen in 1947.

Dr Zborowski was also director of research on cultural components in attitudes towards pain with a grant from the United States Public Health Service. In the 1960s he moved to San Francisco and continued his research on the cultural components of the experience of human pain and helped establish Mount Zion Hospital's Pain Centre, where he spent his last days.[2]

In 1921, Mark moved with his parents to Lodz, Poland, where he completed his schooling, and in 1928 he went to France to continue his undergraduate studies. (According to one source, he had joined the Communist Party, been arrested, and fled to France to escape a prison sentence.[3]) He studied medicine at the University of Rouen and philosophy at the University of Grenoble. Although he reportedly came from a well-to-do family, young Zborowski had to work to support his studies. It was in Grenoble in 1932 that, while working as a porter in a boarding house, he was approached by Boris Afanasyev (codenamed GAMMA), an OGPU 'illegal' and member of the Serebryansky Service, who advised Mark to apply to the Soviet Embassy in Paris, asking for a repatriation visa to return to his motherland, where everything, including studies and medical care, was free. Mark liked the idea, and spent a day filling in all the necessary application forms, which M. Afanasyev promised to deliver personally to the embassy. After several months (so-called 'cultivation' is a long process), Zborowski was informed by his new friend that he should go to Paris to meet somebody who would help him with a visa. When they settled in a small café, this mysterious 'somebody' joined them. 'This man will talk to you,' Afanasyev said, introducing his colleague as 'Dmitry Mikhailovich'. Twenty-five years later, Zborowski, during his testimony at the US Senate, could remember only that the man had a Russian name. 'Ivan Petrovich or Nikolai Ivanovich', he recalled.[4]

Mark's host was the 'legal' OGPU resident, known to the French authorities as the Soviet diplomat Dmitri Michailoff' while his real name was Dmitry Mikhailovich Smirnov (codenamed VICTOR). After a few further meetings and discussions of the most general topics, Smirnov informed Zborowski that, if he wanted to be admitted to the Soviet paradise, he had to prove himself worthy of it, demonstrating his loyalty to the first land of socialism. 'Our enemies are the Trotskyites,' said the OGPU man; 'go and penetrate their gang for us'. Mark did not know how, but it was explained that membership in the Trotskyite organization was open and free and that the only thing to do would be to go to a given address and find out what those perfidious Trotskyites were doing and what their plans were.

The young man did what he was asked and soon became one of the active members of the Trotskyist organization in France. He also began supplying the OGPU with various Trotskyist documents, at the same time informing on the activities of Lev Sedov (Trotsky's son) and others. At the same time he did a great job for the Sedov organization by assisting in publishing the *Bulletin of the Opposition*, to which he contributed under the pen name 'Étienne'[5] and by maintaining contact with Trotsky's scattered followers in other countries. After the tragic death of Sedov, he became both the publisher of the *Bulletin* and Trotsky's most important contact with his European supporters. During the founding conference of the Fourth (Trotskyist) International in September 1938, Zborowski seems to have been the only representative of the Russian section, whose members, real or not, had been entirely exterminated in the Soviet Union.

Writing about Mark Zborowski and his agent work in Paris, some historians stress that 'he had done major damage to the Trotskyists in France in the late 1930s'.[6] They tend to forget that in 1933 he joined the Department of History and Sociology of the University of Paris, then entered the Institute of Ethnology of the same university, and also completed his studies at l'École des Hautes Études d'Histoire des Religions, receiving a degree in 1937 and a diploma in 1938. With such extensive studies he did not have much time for spying, and indeed his meetings with his Soviet controllers were rare. Zborowski later testified:

From 1937 on, after the first trial [Moscow show trial], I changed my entire attitude toward the NKVD and the Stalinists and Stalinist policy, and since then, since this period of time I began to miscarry the orders that I received.[7] . . . Now, after the death of Sedov, I still saw those NKVD people on very rare occasions, very rare occasions. Then, finally, after 1938, I didn't see any one of them any more.[8]

Contrary to Orlov's claims—and he did his best to show the members of the US Senate Subcommittee that he was exposing a real spy of a high calibre, 'known personally to Stalin himself'—documents that have surfaced so far demonstrate that Mark Zborowski was only one of many agents and informers infiltrated into the tiny Trotskyist movement both in Europe and the USA. Although one of Moscow's missives described Zborowski as 'a dedicated and tested operative', it was noted that 'in terms of his personality he is not energetic enough and shows little initiative. He must be systematically guided in his future work.'[9] As soon as Zborowski had arrived in the United States, a move facilitated by David J. Dallin and his wife

Lydia,[10] Moscow learned about it and instructed the 'legal' resident Vasili
Zarubin to re-establish contact. 'TULIP is of great interest regarding use of
him to cultivate Trotskyites in the US, try to find out his particulars through
the agents in the circles of the Menshevik Nikolayevsky, Sarah Weber and
Estrina [Lydia Dallin].'[11] The Centre wrote about the agent:

He was recruited in 1934[12] in France to cultivate Trotskyites. After that, on our
instructions, T[ULIP] left party work and broke off relations with the Polish Communists. In the summer of 1936 he actively began to cover Trotskyite activities. He
established contact with French Trotskyites (Rousee, Nabal and others) leaders of
the International Trotskyite Secretariat (IS), and with the Russian section headed by
Sedov, then became Sedov's first assistant in the IS's work to publish 'Bulletin of
the Opposition'. With his active participation we removed all of the secret archives
of the IS, all of Sedov's archives, and a substantial portion of the 'Old Man's
[Trotsky] archives.[13]

For the theft of Trotsky's papers, the operational group in Paris headed by
Serebryansky was awarded the Order of the Red Banner, which demonstrates the importance attached to this, as it turned out, useless act. 'The
operation', according to Christopher Andrew, 'was as pointless as it was
professional. The papers stolen from the institute (many of them press
clippings) were of no operational significance whatever and of far less
historical importance that the Trotsky archive which remained in Zborowski's hands and later ended up at Harvard University.'[14] Besides, the
'action' in Paris could easily betray Zborowski, who, together with Estrina,
had personally delivered the archive to Boris Nikolaievsky at the International Institute of Social History, of which they were both members, only
days before.

While it is probably an exaggeration that Sedov's sudden death in
February 1938 enabled the NKVD to take a leading role in the Trotskyist
organization, it was certainly well penetrated. On one occasion Zborowski
wrote to tell Trotsky that the *Bulletin of the Opposition* was about to publish
an article entitled 'Trotsky's Life in Danger' (by Max Shachtman), which
would expose the activities of NKVD agents in Mexico and which some
believe was Zborowski's way to maintain his own cover. The article was
indeed published, but it neither helped Trotsky nor exposed real NKVD
assets in Mexico, falsely concentrating on George Mink.

With the advantage of hindsight, it is now possible to say that in 1938
Trotsky's life was not really in danger. Orlov's boss Spiegelglass failed to
arrange the penetration of Trotsky's entourage in Mexico and was arrested

in November. The hunt for Trotsky's life stopped for two years. At that time Orlov was already in America looking for a lawyer with good connections who would help him legalize his status without drawing attention to his person. Thanks to the husband of one of his Koornick aunts, he obtained an introduction to John F. Finerty, a well-known civil-rights attorney who did not conceal his sympathies for the Trotsky movement. Soon the Orlovs, accompanied by Finerty, visited the Washington office of James L. Houghteling, the INS Commissioner who also dealt with Krivitsky and who referred them to his assistant, Thomas B. Shoemaker. Shoemaker agreed with Finerty that 'the best thing for Orlov to do was to avoid publicity and keep his arrival secret'.[15] As no record of the meeting was made, Finerty would later claim that his client had been officially exempted from alien registration. In late December 1938, both to win Finerty's future support and to keep his stakes high with the American authorities should he be forced to bargain for his residence permit, Orlov sent a letter to Trotsky warning him about the alleged danger to his life. By revealing 'agent Mark' to Trotsky and later the American authorities, Orlov was feathering his own nest.

As a matter of fact, Orlov wrote three letters. Two of them he sent to Trotsky's villa in Coyoacán, one by registered and one by ordinary mail addressed to Trotsky and his wife, and he left one copy for his own records. Mentioning Zborowski only by his first name 'Mark', he correctly reported that the agent had engineered the theft of archives from the Nikolaievsky Institute in Paris and warned Trotsky not to trust 'any person, man or woman, who may come to you with recommendations from this provocateur'.[16] Moscow learned about the letter only in June 1939, when Lydia Dallin returned from America and met Zborowski. She told him that the 'Old Man' had received a denunciatory report on 'Mark', with a physical description, a reference to his former membership in the Polish Communist Party, and a hint that he could have been involved in Sedov's death. Lydia added that Trotsky did not believe the report and saw it as a provocation.[17] Mark, in turn, reported the incident to his NKVD case officer. This is how Moscow learned about Orlov's letter. They should have also realized that Orlov had broken his word, given to Yezhov, but by that time Yezhov had already been arrested and placed at the sinister Sukhanovka prison 'for particularly dangerous enemies of the people', confessing to all possible crimes, including a humiliating history of sexual deviancy. Under the circumstances, no one cared about Orlov.

As mentioned above, at the end of April 1938 Trotsky declared in Mexico City that a group of Stalinist agents headed by George Mink had arrived in the country plotting to kill the founder of the Fourth International. At that time both Mink and Orlov were still in Barcelona, but there is no evidence that the two knew each other. At least, Orlov never mentioned Mink in any of his writings, testimonies, or interviews. It is remarkable, however, that the FBI had never asked him about Mink—probably considering him long gone. Thirteen years before they had first interviewed Orlov, in September 1940, Joseph Hansen, Trotsky's secretary and guard from 1937 until the day he and Charles Cornell detained Trotsky's assassin, contacted the US Consulate in Mexico City. On 14 September Hansen handed Robert G. McGregor, a Consulate official, a confidential document that identified five American citizens as agents of the NKVD. The names provided by Hansen—Nathan Witt, Lee Pressman, Hedda Gumperz (Massing), Paul Massing, and Grace Hutchins—were already known to the authorities from various sources, including the testimony of Whittaker Chambers. Two weeks later, the American Legation in Mexico City informed the State Department that Hansen was leaving Mexico for New York to conduct an independent investigation concerning Trotsky's assassination. The State Department informed the FBI, asking it to provide a confidential contact for Hansen in New York. The FBI Director, J. Edgar Hoover, himself monitored the situation. Before a planned meeting between Hansen and B. Edwin Sackett, the special agent in charge of the New York City FBI office, Hoover instructed his subordinate on how the interview was to be handled:

Information has further been supplied by the State Department to the effect that Hansen and his associates liquidated George Mink six months ago, shortly before the first attack on Trotsky in May of 1940, by tying Mink up and throwing him into a crater some thirty miles from Mexico City. Should Hansen call at the New York office, he should be handled tactfully and all information he can supply and his assistance in this investigation should be obtained. No information, of course, should be furnished him concerning the progress of the investigation by the Bureau. However, every attempt should be made to determine the truth of the report concerning George Mink.[18]

That is, exactly two years after the *Time* correspondent had reported about Trotsky fears of the Stalinist agents and George Mink in particular, in April 1940 the American diplomats in Mexico had reasons to believe that Mink had actually been found and disposed of by Trotsky's supporters.

A year later the same people from the American Socialist Workers' Party helped Zborowski to enter the United States, while Joe Hansen was serving on the SWP's National Committee and was editing the party's newspaper. Indeed, the world is small, and if Mink was really sent to Mexico in 1940, then it was not in connection with Trotsky's assassination but to help Captain Fyodor Kravchenko (KLEIN, later MAGNAT), another Spanish Civil War veteran and the RU case officer there.[19] What happened to Mink remains unknown.

In September 1955, speaking to the US Congress, Orlov greatly exaggerated the value of Zborowski as a Soviet penetration agent. 'It is my firm belief', he declared, 'that that man Zborowski, all through those years, had been in the United States as an agent of the NKVD conducting espionage on a large scale. I told the FBI man who used to come to me for information that I am afraid that the Russians might kill me.'[20] Orlov's deposition was used against Zborowski when the latter was subpoenaed to testify in February 1956.

Though he never spied against the United States, as Orlov was seeking to demonstrate, the NKVD used Zborowski to report not only on the Trotskyists but also against individual targets such as David Dallin and Victor Kravchenko, a former member of the Soviet Purchasing Commission in Washington who abandoned his post and requested political asylum in the USA in 1944.[21] In America, Zborowski's links to the NKVD were two brothers who called themselves Robert Soblen and Jack Soble. They were born in Lithuania as Ruvelis Leiba Sobolevicius (1900) and Ābrams Sobolevicius (1903). Trotsky knew Ruvelis as 'Roman Well' and Ābrams as 'Senin' (sometimes spelled Senine, in a French manner). Both were leading figures in the German branch of the Trotskyist movement before shifting their operation first to Canada and then to the United States, where they arrived in 1940. Their group included, among others, Martha Dodd, Alfred Stern, and Boris Morros. Zborowski maintained his contacts with them after the war, being unaware, as was everybody else, that one of its trusted members, Morros, had been 'turned' by the FBI in 1947.[22] But J. Edgar Hoover's subordinates learned about TULIP even before Morros agreed to collaborate and long before Orlov denounced Zborowski in December 1954 from the source so secret (signal intelligence) that sometimes they preferred to keep an agent at large rather than to divulge where their information was coming from. Thanks to this secrecy, William Weisband from Odessa, a linguist adviser at Arlington Hall known at the Lubynka as agent ZVENO ('Link'), has never been prosecuted for espionage, although he virtually killed this highly classified and compartmentalized source by betraying it to the NKVD.

In 1944, in the course of the top-secret US–British signal intelligence operation that later became known as the VENONA Project, the following message sent from New York to Moscow was intercepted and later decrypted:

In spite of measures taken, TYULPAN [TULIP/Mark Zborowski] has not so far succeeded in making KOMAR's [GNAT, the Soviet defector Victor Kravchenko] acquaintance. One cannot insist strongly to ESTRINA [Lydia Estrina, Mrs David Dallin] and DALIN [David J. Dallin] as this would arouse suspicion. In a day or so TULIP is meeting with DALIN and ESTRINA. The latter promised to have a detailed chat on the GNAT affair after which the meeting [with Zborowski] will probably take place. In the last conversation ESTRINA declared that something serious is still expected, but what they are afraid of she did not say. We shall do everything possible to find out what she is talking about and measures have been taken accordingly.

Signed MAJ [Stepan Apresyan, NKVD head of station in New York][23]

By August 1944 Zborowski had already managed to meet GNAT and report some relatively useful information about him, his contacts, and his whereabouts. He also reported that, after Kravchenko's first article in *Cosmopolitan*, this former Red Army officer (Victor Kravchenko was a captain) and Purchasing Commission official had broken with Don Levine, his ghost writer, because the latter had signed that article as co-author. In response, Don Levine accused Kravchenko of 'commercialization and pettiness' and added that the defector still had to give proof of his sincerity to the US government.[24] Victor Kravchenko was later found in his Manhattan apartment with a bullet in his head, and this sudden death has never been satisfactorily explained. Kravchenko died in February 1966. At that time Zborowski was in prison. To his great misfortune and to a certain degree thanks to Orlov's 'revelations', unlike in the Weisband case mentioned above the authorities found the way to incarcerate him.

Zborowski was tried and found guilty of perjury owing to several misleading statements he had made to the Senate Subcommittee about his work for the NKVD in America, while the VENONA decrypts proved the opposite. Though this conviction was later overturned, he was retried in 1962 and received a forty-seven-month prison sentence. In the same year, Orlov was approached by the CIA and placed in the Law School office of the University of Michigan in Ann Arbor. Though he did not do any teaching,[25] the agency seems to have been paying his salary and overheads, and he received an advance of $6,000 for a new book—an enormous chunk of money for the University of Michigan Press to bring forward at the time.[26] The book, published a year later in a small format with less than 200 pages, opened with the author's preface:

Before World War II, when I was one of the chiefs of the Soviet intelligence, I lectured at the Central Military School in Moscow on the tactics and strategy of intelligence and counterintelligence. In 1936 I wrote down the basic rules and principles of Soviet intelligence in the form of a manual which was approved as the only textbook for the newly created NKVD schools for undercover intelligence officers and for the Central Military School in Moscow.[27]

Orlov was in Spain, without coming back to Moscow, from mid-September 1936 to mid-July 1938. After that he deserted and came to the United States. At the same period of time, during the Great Terror, so many of his NKVD colleagues were unmasked as 'enemies of the people' and either shot or sent to the Gulag that the leadership decided new recruits needed some basic training. As it turned out, not only did 'the Central Military School in Moscow' never exist, but 'NKVD schools for undercover intelligence officers' were also sheer invention. According to the NKVD order no. 00648 of 3 October 1938, the very first Soviet foreign intelligence school was set up in Balashikha, near Moscow.[28] By that time Orlov was already in the USA. Known as Shkola Osobogo Naznacheniya (SHON) or Special Purpose School, the school employed (and still does) 'burned' or retired Soviet spymasters who survived purges as lecturers and it drew its recruits from the Party and Komsomol. Before the war broke out there were no manuals or textbooks of any kind. As expected, any search for Orlov's *Handbook* in the Russian archives drew a blank.

24
MI5: Secrets of Personal File 605.075

S ir Percy Sillitoe, director general of the Security Service, did not like what he called 'book-learned intellectuals'. During his last days in office he took no notice of the news about the 'NKVD general' coming from the USA. But Roger Hollis, a former banker and journalist who had just been appointed deputy director general, took a keen interest. As soon as the news of Orlov's articles and his subsequent interrogations by the FBI reached England in mid-July,[1] Evelyn McBarnet of Section D.1.A. was instructed to look into the case. She had no other way to deal with it but to rely on the assistance of the MI5 security liaison officer G. T. D. Patterson at the British Embassy in Washington.

On 29 September 1953, Patterson sent a Top Secret Personal Guard message addressed to the Director General but forwarded to Ms McBarnet. It read in part:

You may like to hear what I know about this business—although it is not very much. ORLOV came to this country in the late 1930s from Spain and I understand that the FBI knew nothing about him until his articles in 'Life' magazine appeared in April of this year. At that time the FBI did not deal with security and intelligence matters but I believe the Naturalisation and Immigration service knew about ORLOV, or at least something of his activities, when he landed. Everyone then apparently forgot about him. The Bureau interviewed him—I believe in May of this year—and extracted a lot of information from him. When this was all written up the result was an enormous report of 60 or 70 pages. I have not seen it but I can well imagine that it is extremely interesting. As far as I can discover, however, neither the report nor any of the details contained in it were made available to [the FBI representatives in London] so I do not think that either [he or his assistant] were holding out on you when they gave you what seemed to be rather a terse reply to your enquiry. The detailed ORLOV report remains closeted in the Bureau.

Although the Bureau may have their own reasons for their reticence in this matter, I cannot imagine that the report on ORLOV contains anything of sensational interest to us but I am sure it will be both of interest and of some use. I have tried to find out if it were he who preceded Paul HARDT [Teodor Maly] as the illegal resident agent in the UK and I do not think that this is so. However, as I said above I have not yet seen the [FBI] case officer. I hope to be able to send you something more useful when I write again on this matter.[2]

In connection with the recent defection of Maclean and Burgess, and a growing suspicion concerning Philby's involvement, the Security Service, however, was more than persistent in wanting to learn as much as possible about Orlov and anything he could reveal about the activities of the RIS in Britain.

Even before the letter of the security liaison officer in Washington had reached Hollis, the American Embassy in London had informed MI5:

Alexander ORLOV has admitted being an official of the NKVD in Europe up until 1938, when he defected.

ORLOV was asked, without mentioning 'Kim' PHILBY's name, whether he knew of a plan by Paul HARDT, alias MALY, to send an English journalist to Spain to assassinate Franco during the Spanish Civil War... He [Orlov] said neither of the persons mentioned was of English origin.[3]

Not knowing anything about Orlov's involvement in handling Philby, Maclean, and, partly, Burgess, the Security Service was intuitively concentrating on one of Orlov's most sacred secrets. Orlov certainly knew what happened to Maclean and Burgess and could easily deduce that during all those years they had continued to work for Soviet intelligence. His information about them, however, would be of only historic interest two years after their defection. But Philby was an entirely different case, and here Orlov's testimony could play a crucial role in exposing the traitor. MI5 were also eager to recheck information provided by Krivitsky during his January–February 1940 interviews in London. But Orlov was determined to resist all their efforts.

First of all, he had apparently read all the books written by other Soviet defectors by the time he was interrogated and knew exactly what they had revealed and where they were right or wrong. With some, like Petrov in Australia, he even maintained a steady correspondence. He was also familiar with all transcripts of Congressional hearings that had anything to do with Soviet affairs. Accepting Orlov as a bona fide defector, the FBI and MI5 were unaware that they were dealing with an experienced and cunning Chekist who had had ample time to prepare his story.

As mentioned, after the defection of his two Cambridge friends in May 1951, one of the first priorities for MI5 was Philby. They could not find a pre-war photo of the man to show to Orlov, but supplied the earliest one they could. On 27 August 1953 the FBI reinterviewed Orlov, at which time a photograph of Philby, along with a number of other unlabelled photographs, was shown to him, without providing any additional information. As expected, he 'did not recognize' his former English agent. Amazingly, despite the correct identification of 'Nikolsky@Orlov@Schwed' (which stands for 'also known as' in MI5 documents) by Krivitsky as the predecessor of Maly in London, it was decided that it was perhaps another [Konstantin] Nikolsky, who, they erroneously thought, had been the NKVD 'illegal' resident agent in Britain before Maly took over.[4] Later Orlov confirmed that Krivitsky did indeed mean him and no one else, when he described the man 'nicknamed Lyova who was sent to organize the OGPU in Spain', but he flatly denied that he had ever been in Britain. As until about 1959 MI5 was not permitted to reveal the Orlov affair to its SIS colleagues, this most valuable lead was not followed.

In due course the FBI was persuaded to share the Orlov material with the British, albeit limiting the collaboration to working only with MI5. In part, it was quite interested to do so, as it was rather inexperienced in counter-espionage matters and expected to get a lot of extra knowledge about persons and events described by Orlov. This was essentially a vain hope, as Orlov skilfully manipulated the information that he provided.

The questionnaire prepared by MI5 primarily covered four main topics: intelligence activities in England (the appropriate memorandum dated 1 October 1953 was duly furnished to the Security Service by FBI representatives in London); Russian intelligence personnel in the UK and elsewhere; Orlov's activities and the NKVD operatives and agents in Spain; and comments on Krivitsky's book, congressional testimony, and his information summarized during his London interviews.

For whatever reason, the memorandum provided by the FBI in response to the request from London remains classified. About Spain, Orlov told his usual story, stressing that he was Stalin's representative with the Spanish government, and that he met Juan Negrín and Indalecio Prieto, Minister of Marine and Air and, in the Negrín government, Minister of War, several times a week and was even allowed to issue orders in Prieto's name. He declared that his main preoccupation was counter-intelligence and guerrilla warfare and, when confronted with an accusation that he was a direct participant in the assassination of Nin, coolly responded that he was only a political attaché and therefore could not have been responsible for such things. Orlov admitted that there had been an assassination attempt on Franco's life by an NKVD agent, but said that the agent was expelled from the Nationalist zone and was not able to approach the general. Interestingly, Orlov mentioned another NKVD agent 'among Franco's closest entourage who met him on a daily basis', but did not provide any clues. Now, if Orlov did not mean Philby, who certainly had no way of meeting Franco 'on a daily basis',[5] it is extremely doubtful that such an agent ever existed.

Even more than half a century after the events, it is not easy to navigate through the mountains of Orlov's inventions, although there are several cases in which it may be possible.

On 30 September 1953 the FBI reported:

ORLOV was able to provide little further information concerning the individual KRAL with alias Krum. He stated that he remembers having seen a dark Latvian in the Russian Embassy in Paris in about 1936 and 1937. He said that since KRAL was reported to have been a Latvian, it is possible this individual whom he saw in Paris was KRAL. He described this person as probably in his thirties, height 6' 1'', built slender, characteristics narrow, long and sharp face. He said the individual was a high-strung, nervous type, said he wore no glasses and dressed in dark clothing.

ORLOV noted that KRAL was the same individual that Walter Krivitsky claimed was sent to assassinate him in France. ORLOV noted KRAL was a Latvian, but had formerly been a professional safecracker and was reported to look like a Spaniard. He said KRAL planned to obtain an audience with Franco under the pretext of being an inventor who had a special type of gas mask to sell.[6]

Orlov certainly borrowed his 'KRAL' from Krivitsky's book. During his MI5 debriefing, Krivitsky deliberated over a matter:

If a Yugoslav called KRAL is still in the OGPU service, he will undoubtedly be used for operations in the United Kingdom [this explains MI5's repeated interest in him]. KRAL speaks good English and German. He is an expert lock breaker. He is 46–49 years of age, tall, very dark and thin, in looks very like King Alfonso of Spain. His name was originally IVANOVITCH, but on entering the service of the OGPU he became KRAL.

To this Krivitsky's biographer Gary Kern added that 'Ivan Kral, a native of Sarajevo, came to Russia in 1924 and worked with Krivitsky in the 1930s. He was one of a group of four who in November 1937 attempted unsuccessfully to intercept Krivtsky at the Gare du Nord train station in Marseilles after his defection. He was purged the next year'.[7]

Orlov obviously knew nothing about Kral, and certainly had not met him, and Krivitsky's biographer failed to mention that Ivan Kral had never worked for the OGPU, as Krivitsky asserted.[8] Brigade Commissar Ivan Ivanovich Kral, born in 1902, was an RU officer and that was how Krivitsky came to know him. Kral was arrested in Moscow on 2 August 1938, sentenced in March 1939, and died on 16 November 1941. In 1937 he was 35. Taking Krivitsky's 'Kral' as a matrix, Orlov rather correctly described Grigulevich, a Lithuanian whom he met in 1936 and 1937 and of whose potential role as Franco's assassin he must have been informed. He also knew that the operation had been called off. That is why he told his FBI interrogators that, 'shortly after he entered Franco's territory, he was thrown out of the country for some reason I am not aware of'. The real Kral had never been sent to Spain.

Orlov was clearly not inclined to say anything about his own involvement or share his knowledge of any intelligence operations on the ISLAND or in the United States. So he disclosed nothing, admitting only that in 1932 he was in America on holidays. But being in a very shaky position without any status, he decided to provide some limited information that would do no harm to anybody and would lead the authorities nowhere in any case.

Thus, he recalled meeting in Spain a young Englishman known to him only as 'John' or 'Johnny', who was allegedly sent there in the spring of 1938 after having escaped from England. According to Orlov, this man had to leave the country because he was suspected of having stolen blueprints for the Soviets from an English factory where he worked. A painstaking and laborious investigation led another female MI5 officer, T. Selmes-Taylor, to one Eric Camp, whose career included a conviction in 1936 for an offence under the Official Secrets Act, which consisted of the obtention of aircraft plans from Gloucester Aircraft Company, where he worked as a draughtsman. Camp was bound over for two years on this charge. However, there was not proof that he had passed those plans to Soviet representatives. After his release and with some communist help, Camp joined the International Brigade in Spain in 1938.[9] Whether Miss Taylor was right or not, it was finally decided to drop the case.

In the course of interrogation Orlov was also asked about Boris Bazarov, whom he knew well. The Bureau learned about Bazarov from Hede Massing's book *This Deception* (1951), where she stated that Bazarov was one of her Soviet espionage superiors in the United States in 1935 (for whom she retained a warm affection). The FBI had had his name on their files since June 1939, when Krivitsky was interviewed by a representative of the US Department of State. Krivitsky's account was duly registered in the files, with this description of Bazarov:

> The chief of the Soviet military intelligence in the United States travelled on the *Normandie*, first class, from New York May 8, 1937, using a Greek passport. His real name is Boris Spaak or Spak. He is about 48 years of age, a former officer in Wrangel's army, who in 1920 went over to the Soviet intelligence work. He is a highly intelligent man and came to the United States around 1934–1935.[10]

Orlov also read the book and, true to the old Chekist habit (and contrary to Krivitsky's somewhat garbled but positive account), decided to denigrate his former colleague and belittle his successes. He invented a story that in the late 1920s Bazarov, who was operating as a counter-intelligence agent against White Russian officers in Germany, had a meeting with one of his informants, a former White Russian professor. While the agent was handing over his notes to Bazarov in his apartment, Orlov said, it was raided by the German police. The notes were hurriedly hidden inside some sheet music lying on the top of a piano, and were not located, even though the apartment was searched. Bazarov, according to Orlov, 'identified himself as a Soviet diplomat and in view of the fact that one of the two raiding German policemen was also a Soviet agent, was immediately released'. (Such tales later made up the bulk of Orlov's *Handbook*, commissioned and paid by the CIA.) Orlov further commented that, because of his Tsarist army background Bazarov was given only minor jobs in the NKVD. By the time Orlov came up with this story, the FBI section responsible for Soviet espionage has grown from seven to fifty supervisors, and had acquired considerable experience in dealing with spymasters, their agents, collaborators, defectors, and their testimonies. But neither before, nor after, him had the Bureau dealt with such an outrageous liar as Orlov.

Although it was true that Bazarov was a former White Army officer, he served under General Anton Denikin, Commander of the Armed Forces of South Russia, and in November 1920 was evacuated to Turkey together with General Wrangle's troops; all the rest was Orlov's invention. Bazarov first settled in Constantinople, but soon moved to Berlin, where in early 1921 he approached Soviet representatives asking for repatriation to Soviet Russia. As usual, the OGPU man who handled the case explained to the former tsarist platoon commander that, in order to win the honour of being admitted to the Bolshevik paradise, Bazarov was to go back to Turkey to spy on the Russian émigrés there. (In his NKVD biography written in Moscow in August 1937 Bazarov indicated that this was how he started his secret service career.) From Turkey he was sent to Vienna, from where all Balkan operations were traditionally directed. In the Austrian Außenamt's diplomatic list of 1924–6 Bazarov figures as 'SCHPAK Boris, Leiter der Kurierabteilung', where among his 'couriers' were Georg Killich, Karl Tchulenk, and Elsa Hutschnecker (Lisa Gorskaya), all prominent future Chekists. On his return to Moscow in December 1925, Shpak changed his name to Bazarov and was enlisted as a commissioned INO officer, soon promoted to head its Balkan section. In late 1928, shortly before Nikolsky/Orlov arrived there, Bazarov was in Berlin, again as one of the OGPU 'illegal' resident agents (codenamed KIN), supervising the activities of several other undercover agents.

One of the records made during Krivitsky's debriefing mentioned agent ARNO (Oldham). Krivitsky stated that 'attached to him was Orloff [sic] whose sole work was looking after ARNO'.[11] Krivitsky was wrong. As mentioned, Oldham's controller was Dmitry Bystroletov, who was part of the Bazarov cell. In 1934 Bazarov returned to Moscow and resumed his work at the Lubyanka. In December he was sent to the United States as an 'illegal' resident to replace Valentin Markin. Bazarov and his assistants, 'illegals' Iskhak Akhmerov, Norman Borodin, and A. Samsonov,[12] were operating very successfully in unusual harmony with the 'legal' station that used the cover of the Soviet Consulate General in New York and was headed by the Vice Consul Peter Davydovich Gutzeit (alias 'Gusev', codenamed NIKOLAI), the first legal resident in the USA,[13] assisted by another NKVD operative, the second Vice Consul V. P. Rumyantsev. Orlov knew them all, of course, but revealed nothing. It may also be added that the consulate in New York was headed by Leonid Mikhailovich Tolokonsky, Soviet Consul General and at the same time the RU (military intelligence directorate) resident who in 1931–3 was posted to London under the cover of 2nd Secretary and Press Officer of the embassy. From mid-August 1935 his secretary in New York was 'Mikhail Milsky', better known at the Red Army intelligence headquarters as Mikhail Abramovich Milstein. When Tolokonsky was suddenly recalled to Moscow to disappear for ever in October 1936, Milstein was promoted to head of station, managing to hold this position during the important period of the Spanish Civil War (he left New York in late July

1938, missing Orlov's arrival there by only a few days), in which he took an active, albeit indirect, part buying war materiel and transferring money to different parts of the world in order to obtain arms for Spain. The only Jew at the top of Soviet military intelligence, he also managed to survive during all the Stalinist and post-Stalinist years, rising to lieutenant general and retiring from the Soviet Army in February 1972.[14] Before he joined the staff of the USA–Canada Institute in Moscow, Milstein was known to only a few professionals in London and Washington. Upon becoming a public figure, he impressed many, among others Barry Blechman, a former official of the US Arms Control and Disarmament Agency. General Milstein, he said, was 'a Soviet patriot first, last and always, but he had enormous curiosity about, and admiration for, the United States'.[15] This is not to mention that for about six decades Milstein had conceived and administered (or taught others how to carry them out) some of the most sophisticated intelligence operations against the 'main adversary', the USA.

When Otto Steinbrück instructed Milstein before sending him to Washington, he did not tell him that an experienced intelligence officer, Regimental Commissar Boris Bukov, was already operating there without any official cover.[16] Like the 'legal' RU resident, Bukov spent a lot of time assisting the republicans in Spain by arranging supplies of arms and ammunition, but he also recruited 'helpers' from those American volunteers who returned from Spain, at the same time working with those who had already been recruited there by his RU colleagues. Bukov controlled the 'illegal' network in the USA during the whole Spanish war, from 1936 until April 1939. When he returned to Moscow, there was not a single familiar face at the headquarters. As he instructed his officers, Steinbrück could not have expected that in a few months he, Artuzov, and Bukov's chief Karin would be arrested and shot.

In March 1937 Bazarov (subsequently codenamed NORD) was promoted to a major of state security, the same rank as Orlov had had when he was sent to Spain the previous September. A capable and experienced intelligence operative who dispatched to Moscow high-grade intelligence acquired from a source 'with contacts in the circle of President Roosevelt',[17] Bazarov was then recalled to Moscow and shot on 21 February 1939 after the Great Terror was formally over.

The British Security Service was also very anxious to know about one Boris Lvovich Ermin. Krivitsky said that the real name of the person presenting himself as 'Antonio Spina', holder of the United States passport

No. 254980 issued on 10 February 1936, was really Elman, a former member of the Soviet Embassy in Rome in 1928 and 1929. Elman's details were filed in the MI5 Registry in Personal File 87282.[18]

Orlov claimed that an NKVD agent named Elman first came to his attention in Moscow in the late 1920s. At the time Elman, who was, according to Orlov, assigned to the Soviet Embassy in Rome as an NKVD operative, suddenly became famous in Moscow because he had reportedly succeeded in bribing the Italian Minister of Corporations. Orlov then invented a story about the minister, Giuseppe Bottai (in reality, deputy secretary of the Corporations, the reshaped Chamber of Deputies under Mussolini), and added that after just one week the bribe was returned in full and that Elman's venture turned into a failure.

The 'FBI's KGB General' stated that he first met Elman in Moscow in the early 1930s after Elman had come back from Rome and before he went to the United States. Orlov noted that Elman was a Rumanian national who had come to Russia around 1927 and, as the 'one who had not participated in the revolution, was looked down upon by the "old guard" of the Soviet Secret Police'. As a result, Orlov said, he was usually assigned insignificant tasks and never held a position as official of the NKVD. Orlov observed that Elman was a close friend of Gutzeit and stated that he had no idea what had become of Elman after he had returned from the United States.[19] All this was duly noted.

In reality, 'Ermin a.k.a. Elman' was Boris Davydovich Berman. Orlov knew him very well. Berman was a Russian Jew born in 1901 in eastern Siberia to a well-to-do family of a brick-manufacturer. In February 1921 Berman was already a Cheka operative in Irkutsk, and from 1924 served with Nikolsky in the EKU, where he remained until January 1928. In 1931 Berman was transferred to the INO and sent to Berlin as the 'legal' resident agent in Germany. Nikolaev/Orlov left Berlin in April 1931. In 1933 Berman was an 'illegal' resident in Rome and from June 1934 served as assistant INO chief, soon promoted to deputy and then first deputy chief of the Soviet foreign intelligence. In March 1937 Berman, Commissar of State Security 3rd rank, was appointed People's Commissar of Internal Affairs of Byelorussia, where Nikolsky/Orlov came from. When Orlov defected, Berman was chief of the 3rd Directorate of the NKVD. In Belarus, he was responsible for mass repressions.[20] In November 2011, Gerald Howson was still asking this writer about the mysterious 'Antonio Spina a.k.a. Ermin', who was to be mentioned in the second edition of Howson's famous book *Arms for Spain* then being prepared for publication. (Unfortunately, Gerald died shortly after, not being able to finish the work.)

In one of her intelligence assessments, Miss McBarnet of MI5 noticed that Orlov provided a fairly accurate description, from a Russian point of view, of an actual operation involving W. G. Walton, a junior British diplomat. Walton was a British subject of British descent, but born and educated in Russia. He was employed at the British embassy in Moscow as 3rd Secretary and translator in 1934. During the time of his employment in Moscow he reported being approached by two individuals, whom he believed belonged to the NKVD and who suggested that he might be willing to work for the Soviets. Mr Walton was transferred to London in August 1934 and was contacted on several occasions by a man whom the Security Service believed to be a representative of the RIS. The contact, however, ceased in early 1935, as the Russians probably decided at that stage that Walton was being used as a double agent.[21] Ms McBarnet's superior commented that 'it is difficult to see how this story could have reached the source [Orlov]'.[22] McBarnet could not know, of course, that Nikolsky/Orlov operated in London at the time. She suggested that, because Walton's wife was the Russian Princess Golitsyn, who presumably knew the story, it could have somehow leaked to White Russian circles, where Orlov could have heard it. She certainly missed the fact that Orlov had nothing to do with White Russian circles. In reality, he learned about the approach from either Deutsch or Reif, or possibly from Schuster, the head of station at the embassy who was almost certainly 'a man whom the Security Service believed to be an RIS representative'.

Another person who interested MI5 was 'Akhmerov alias William Grienke'.[23] Orlov gave little information about him during his debriefing. Now anyone interested may instantly access sufficient biographical data on Iskhak Abdulovich Akhmerov from the Internet (placing a careful filter on what KGB historians and former operators write about him and his work). But in 1953 the secret British Colossus computers, which was only ten years young, still had limited programmability, and the Security Service had limited resources. In any event, the following document was filed in the Orlov MI5 file:

In April 1949 a source considered reliable reported on one Robert Iskhakovich AKHMYEROV [sic], 'a junior lieutenant of the MVD' who was thought at that time to be in Palestine. AKHMYEROV's surname was said to be that of his mother who was described as BERIA's private secretary and a major general of the MGB. AKHMYEROV's father, whose surname was not given, was said by the source to have been posted in 1936 to the Soviet Consulate General in New York where he was 'employed on secret work'. AKHMYEROV himself was stated to be in New York from 1937–1938 attending school and then returned to the Soviet Union. In 1945–1947 AKHMYEROV was stationed with MVD units in Germany. As he was born about 1922 he cannot be identical with GRIENKE. The New York connection and the fact that it is just conceivable that his father may have used the name AKHMYEROV as well prompts us to forward this trace.[24]

For those familiar with Russian patronymics, it is obvious that the father of Robert Iskhakovich should be Iskhak. At the same time, the source was certainly wrong about Akhmerov senior's posting to the Soviet Consulate in New York, where his details would have been known to the authorities, which was obviously not the case. In America Akhmerov operated under-cover from April 1934 to December 1939 and from late September 1941 to 1945. His and Bazarov's recruits in the United States included several important agents in various government offices. Akhmerov later claimed that his best source was Harry Hopkins, one of President Roosevelt's closest advisers, which was an exaggeration invented either by Akhmerov himself, or by his former colleague.[25] Hede Massing, who broke with the NKVD in 1938, remembered Akhmerov as a 'Muscovite automaton', but in fact he was much less robotic than Hede claimed in her interviews with the FBI. Unknown to her, Akhmerov was engaged in a passionate love affair with his assistant, Helen Lowry, correctly described in a Bureau report as the half-niece of the American Communist Party leader Earl Browder.[26] In 1936 Lowry was recruited to serve as a courier for the legal NKVD residency in New York—that is, like Zarubina during her time in Vienna, to be officially registered as a secretary or typist but in reality doing secret work such as carrying stolen and photographed documents from Washing-ton to be wire-transmitted to Moscow from the New York NKVD station at the Consulate. However, in November 1937 she was transferred to the 'illegal position'—that is, to the undercover work. From the very beginning his new assistant impressed Akhmerov as 'a very serious, quiet and thought-ful young woman'.[27] They started an affair, and in 1939 Akhmerov appealed to Moscow for a permission to marry her. Whatever Moscow's reasons were, the permission was granted, and in December 1939 Akhmerov brought his young wife to Moscow, where she soon became Elena Ivanovna Akhmerova.

Though there was little compartmentalization in 1953, it was perhaps due to the lack of proper collaboration between the two British services and spoiled relations between the CIA, FBI, and SIS[28] that information about

Akhmerov had been so sparse by the time the Bureau learned about Orlov's existence. From the recently declassified documents it becomes clear that, as soon as Akhmerov was posted abroad, first as a Secretary of the Soviet consulate in Istanbul, where he was sent in 1928, information about him was duly noted and filed, certainly thanks to SIS efforts. It was reported that he was to some extent implicated in Comintern activities in the Middle East and was apparently engaged in 'political work' at the consulate. Akhmerov was later transferred as acting Consul General to Trebizond (now Trabzon), better known in Russia as Trapezund, a position he occupied until mid-1929, and as such would not escape attention of the SIS organization there.

According to his latest, corrected biography, the young Tatar started to work for the Soviet intelligence in Turkey.[29] At that time Agabekov headed the Eastern section of the OGPU, which oversaw operations there. Akhmerov joined the ranks of the 'clean-handed, cool-headed and warm-hearted', as the Chekists like to describe themselves, in 1930, when Agabekov was the 'illegal' resident in Istanbul, and was sent to Bukhara' where he took part in the suppression of anti-Soviet guerrillas. Upon his return in 1931, it was decided to transfer him to the INO. In 1933 Akhmerov, later codenamed YUNGA, which means 'a boy seaman, still in training' though he was already 32, was reportedly sent on his first under-cover mission to China posing as a Turkish student. It was a successful test run, and in 1934 he was posted to New York as an assistant to Valentin Markin (codenamed DAVIS), one of the 'illegal' residents.[30] Markin, alias 'Arthur Walter', was soon found in the Luxor Hotel in Manhattan, which was famous for its Turkish and Russian baths, with a serious head wound, subsequently dying in a hospital where he was taken (as the Bureau later learned, 'having contracted pneumonia after a successful surgery'). In the meantime, Akhmerov enrolled at a Columbia University English language course as a Turkish student, until Peter Gutzeit, the first 'legal' head of the NKVD station in New York, alias 'Gusev', helped him obtain an American passport, almost certainly thanks to the efforts of Jacob Golos. Twenty years later, in a lecture delivered to young KGB officers, Akhmerov recalled that switching from the status of a foreign student to that of an American in such a big city as New York was not difficult.[31] Before he was identified from the VENONA messages as the Soviet 'illegal' behind the codenames MER and ALBERT, Akhmerov was known among the officials privy to the VENONA intercepts as 'Elizabeth Bentley's Bill'. Using the alias 'William Greinke', an American clothier, he was running a fur and clothing business in Baltimore.

Nothing is known so far about his son, who was allegedly in New York while Akhmerov/Greinke was courting Miss Lowry, but it is highly doubtful that his (former) wife had ever been a high-ranking officer of the MGB, as the MI5 memo suggests. According to his official SVR biography, Akhmerov was not married before he met MADLEN (Lowry), but, of course, it cannot be taken for granted. Remarkably, Yuri Kobaladze, a Moscow businessman, who in his previous career had been the KGB general in charge of his service's Press Bureau, told the American author Herbert Romerstein that Akhmerov indeed had a son from another woman. Akhmerov junior, like his father, served with the KGB, but 'apparently died of alcoholism', Kobaladze reported. At the time that his son allegedly attended an American school, Iskhak Akhmerov was one of three assistants to Boris Bazarov, the new 'illegal' resident of the NKVD (the two others were, as mentioned, Borodin and Samsonov). In March 1937 Bazarov was promoted to a senior rank, but in the summer was recalled to Moscow for party 'cleansing' (*chistka*). He never came back, and Akhmerov took his place, running sources with the help of two female couriers, both true-born Americans—Helen Lowry and Elizabeth Bentley. By the end of 1939 all of them, including his son Robert, then 17, and his 29-year-old wife, were recalled back to the USSR, leaving Bentley in New York in the company of Golos.

After very successful and productive work in the USA, the young couple came to Russia, where Lowry/Akhmerova was trained as a Soviet 'illegal'. In December 1941 they both returned to America, settling first in New York City but later moving to Baltimore. Their mission ended in 1945 when Akhmerov's cover was blown by Elizabeth Bentley, who knew his wife only as 'Catherine'. With Bentley's defection, seven Soviet operatives and thirty-six sources were compromised.

Back in the USSR in early 1946, Akhmerov continued working for Soviet intelligence and soon rose to deputy chief of Directorate S (Illegals) of the KGB's First Chief Directorate. He retired in 1955 and died on 18 July 1976 aged 75. His wife Helen passed away in 1981.[32] At the time of writing, their daughter, Elena Akhmerova, was living in Moscow.

Orlov's next exercise in disinformation concerned Grigory Grafpen, of whom there was no trace in MI5 records in 1953. At the same time, though with some considerable delay, the Foreign Office's London Diplomatic List for 1939 mentioned one Gregory Blank as an attaché at the Soviet Embassy then located in Harrington House, 13 Kensington Palace Gardens. 'Blank' was Grafpen.

Although the FBI managed largely to fill the gap by providing reliable information about Grafpen to its British partners, some details of his service career are given here for the first time.

A review of the US Department of State records relating to non-immigrant visa applications submitted originally to the American Embassy in Moscow produced the following details on what concerns Grigory Borisovich Grafpen. A request for a visa to enter the United States was made on 26 March 1927 at the American Consulate in Berlin. The applicant was described as being 36 years old, born on 20 November 1891 in Odessa, and visiting the United States for business purposes as a representative of the firm called 'Industroy' (Industrial Development and Construction) to familiarize himself with the manufacture of industrial machinery and to interest technical experts in constructing industrial plants in Russia. It was noted that Grafpen arrived in the USA on 20 May and stayed until 20 July 1927. At that time he was almost certainly only an agent or a co-optee. On 16 December 1929, when Nikolsky/Orlov was in the German capital working under the cover of the Soviet Trade Delegation, a visa was requested for Grafpen at the American Consulate in Berlin. In the embassy's note, delivered to the consulate by Nikolsky, it was stated that Grafpen desired to visit North America for business purposes and to resume his duties as general manager of the Amtorg Trading Corporation. He arrived in the United States by *the SS Paris*.

Before he left Europe, Grafpen had to submit a Declaration of Non-Immigrant Alien about to depart for the United States, which he did in Berlin. He stated that he had been working for the past two years as general manager of Amtorg and at the time of application was still so employed. His domicile, he wrote, was at 12 Nikitsky Boulevard, Moscow. As references, he listed Amtorg, New York City, and the Russian Trade Delegation in Berlin, where Nikolsky/Orlov worked at the time. As a relative in the United States, Grafpen listed Dr Penn, his brother, who lived in Philadelphia, Pennsylvania.[33]

In 1930 it was established that in New York Grafpen was an office manager heading the administrative staff known as a secret OGPU department within Amtorg. A confidential source employed by Amtorg in New York City from 1926 to 1933 told the FBI that the staff of this Russian trade organization numbered about 800 persons at its peak and was reduced to about 40 during the Depression. Of these, 'about 75 per cent were sent from Russia, and most of them were communists, most of them OGPU agents'.

The source also reported that the most arrogant of these was Grafpen, who was denied a renewal of his visa in 1931—that is, after four years in the USA.[34] (According to his SVR biography, Grafpen joined the OGPU in September 1931.) In 1937 Grafpen surfaced in London as the Russian diplomat 'Gregory Blank' to handle Maclean. It will be remembered that Nikolsky/Orlov recommended him as the best choice to substitute himself in London in February 1935. He also mentioned Grafpen by name in his farewell letter to Yezhov.

Orlov produced two extensive reviews of the Krivitsky material at the request of the FBI/MI5. While one of them is surprisingly accurate and reasonable, another is tendentious and marred by Orlov's evident dislike of Krivitsky. As already mentioned, in January 1940 Krivitsky was interviewed at some length by MI5. The results of these interviews were incorporated in an eighty-one-page monograph. Orlov was interviewed on 3 and 28 March, and on 9 June 1955, regarding individuals and other information in the MI5 monograph. His comments cover twenty-three densely typed pages, but the whole effort can now be assessed as a complete waste of time. Orlov knew very little about Soviet military intelligence, and Krivitsky, as an RU employee during his entire espionage career, had only a vague idea about the structure of both services. To his credit, he had a good memory, was eager to help, and had learned a lot of useful details from 1935, when he joined the NKVD, until he defected in 1937.

Orlov was not lying when he said he was not familiar with the general organization of the Red Army military intelligence directorate. He assumed the information furnished by Krivitsky was correct, though it can now be stated it was not. During an interview Orlov suddenly recalled that in 1933, when he was in Artuzov's office, Artuzov, then head of the foreign department, 'ordered an experienced OGPU agent to France where he was to work in the underground; his job was to crack the French Military Staff and to obtain French military intelligence information'. Orlov said he was unable to recall who this agent was. It is no surprise that his memory failed on this occasion, because it was none other than Nikolsky/Orlov himself.

Concerning the shipments of arms to Spain for use in the Spanish Civil War, Orlov stated that 'not one rifle' arrived there through the efforts of a group or groups such as those described by Krivitsky. On this account he was right, and Krivitsky's information turned out to be nothing but invention and self-praise.

Asked about the channels of communication, Krivitsky commented that, in organizing the ship's crews as a courier system, valuable help was obtained from Edo Fimmen, head of the Seamen and Transport Workers Union in Hamburg in 1926, of which Orlov had no knowledge, since it was an RU operation. Fimmen, also known under his pseudonym 'Nel Jaccard', a leader of the International Transport Workers' Federation (ITF), certainly played a key role in organizing international courier services for the Comintern and Soviet military intelligence. Although Edo Fimmen was a bona fide trade-union leader and a friend of Willi Münzenberg, he himself was quite anxious to know what Krivitsky had to say and kept Krivitsky's article 'My Flight from Stalin', published by the *Saturday Evening Post*, among his personal papers.[35]

As reflected in the MI5 monograph (p. 26), Krivitsky stated that he knew how Shanghai, China, was a regular meeting place for IV Directorate[36] agents in the Far East. He said Agnes Smedley had also 'made her headquarters there though she was strictly an OGPU agent'. Orlov's comment, this time justified, was that he knew nothing about Agnes Smedley's work and did not know her to be an OGPU agent. Indeed, she was not, but it is rather strange that Krivitsky knew so little about her.

Smedley reached the Sino-Soviet border at the end of 1928, travelling from Moscow through the whole of Siberia and the Russian Far East. According to her latest biographer,[37] it was an OMS mission, but her initial contacts there, first of all with Arthur Ewert, Otto Braun, and Richard Sorge, and her later circle of friends that included Ursula Kuczynski and Ozaki Hotsumi, indicate that she came to China as an agent of the IV Directorate of the Red Army then under Berzin. Smedley moved to Shanghai in May 1929, having spent several months in Harbin, Mukden, and Nanking, capital of Chiang Kai-shek's China, where she arrived in March. Although, contrary to many claims, she had never been a Communist Party member, there is little doubt that she worked for the Soviet military intelligence, and it was Smedley who introduced Sorge to the Japanese intellectual Ozaki Hotsumi (she was a mistress of them both and had a string of other lovers). 'Out here,' she wrote to one of her female friends, 'I've had a chance to sleep with all colours and shapes'.[38] Hotsumi, who was very well connected and later served as an adviser to the Japanese prime minister, became Sorge's best Japanese informant. In September 1947, General Douglas MacArthur's Far East Command sent to Washington a memo, based on captured Japanese records, that rather accurately described Smedley's involvement in Sorge's spy ring during Agnes's early years in China. In January 1930, 'under the direction of the 4th Bureau of the Red Army General Staff', it read, Sorge was sent to China with two other members of the bureau, posing as a correspondent of the German *Soziologische Magazin*. In Shanghai the three men joined two other operatives, who were mentioned only by their code names, according to the report. Within six months, it claimed, Sorge was directing a unit in Shanghai that included five Japanese, three Germans, four Chinese, two operatives of unknown origin, and 'Agnes Smedley, the well-known American Communist [*sic*] journalist who was acting as correspondent for the *Frankfurter Zeitung*'.[39] In May 1948, with a reference to MacArthur's intelligence chief, Major General Charles A. Willoughby, an article in an American magazine was quoting the report that Agnes Smedley had served 'Stalin's secret service in the Far East', operating as a recruiting officer and courier for the Soviet spy Richard Sorge. 'If the Communists could do this in Japan,' the author of the article continued, 'it staggers the imagination to try to figure out what they have probably succeeded in doing here in our country . . . If thirty of them could penetrate the intelligence service of the Japanese Army in China, how many must have been planted in the security branches of our defence establishments at home and abroad? How many Communist spies were there in the US Foreign Service and in the State Department?'[40] In 1952, two years after her death in London on the way to China, the FBI closed their investigation, but a year later they were still interested in her role, posing questions to Orlov for their own files and for the British services, whom Smedley always accused of 'watching' her.[41] But Orlov knew nothing about Smedley.

Orlov was also asked to comment on Krivitsky's statement that, while he (Krivitsky) was still in the service, the head of the British section of the INO was a man called REIFF (*sic*), who had been a representative of the OGPU in England from 1931 to 1934. Orlov said he had never heard the name.

In the meantime, Ignaty Reif, alias 'Max Wolisch', was Nikolsky/Orlov's boss when he was posted as the 'illegal' resident agent to Britain from April 1934 until February 1935. When the Home Office did not prolong his residence permit, Reif/Wolisch had to leave the country, and Nikolsky/Orlov took over the running of several of Reif's recruits, including Philby. From May 1938, when Nikolsky/Orlov was still in the service, Reif was in charge of the British desk at the 5 Department (foreign intelligence) of the NKVD Security Directorate (GUGB).

Among others, Krivitsky mentioned Dr Arnold Deutsch as a highly successful OGPU 'military and naval espionage agent' operating in England. Orlov stated bluntly that he did not know this individual. Before Krivitsky had 'fingered' him, the Security Service had never heard this name. Needless to say, Deutsch was Nikolsky's assistant in London and the recruiter of what became known as the Cambridge Five.

Krivitsky named Anton Schuster as the 'legal' resident agent in London and suggested that, at the time when he was interviewed by MI5, the head of station might have been Ivan Popov. Orlov stated that he never knew either Schuster or Popov.

Krivitsky was perfectly right about Schuster, who, before London, had also been the 'legal' NKVD head of station in Vienna and taken care of Nikolsky/Orlov and his family there. Nothing definite is known about Popov, 3rd Secretary in 1938. Popov was promoted to 2nd Secretary when Grafpen was posted to London as an attaché. He was still in London a year later with attachés Alexander Lepekhin and 'Anatoly Gromov' (real name Gorsky) as his subordinates and had probably been the acting head of station for some time and Gorsky's boss before the residency was closed down.

According to Krivitsky, after 1928 or 1929 several 'illegals' had operated in England posing as American businessmen. He said this was also the cover used by Nicolski [sic], Hardt's predecessor in London. Nicolski, he said, was later sent to Spain to help with the organization of the OGPU there. Krivitsky recalled that Nikolsky was the man's real name, and not the name under which he obtained the American passport that he used for his British operation. It was key evidence and very important information fully implicating Orlov of committing espionage against Britain.

Orlov admitted that, since he was the only individual who used the name 'Nicolsky' and who had established the OGPU in Spain during the Spanish Civil War, he was certain that Krivitsky's spoke about him. But he stated he wished to make it clear again that he had never worked with Maly, alias 'Paul Hardt', had never operated in England, had never used the cover of an American businessman, and certainly did not have an American passport.

After studying Orlov's comments, R. T. Reed of MI5's D Branch concluded: 'I have thanked the FBI for their efforts but unless I have missed something there appears to be nothing at all of value in the report. Compared with KRIVITSKY, ORLOV knew very little that is of interest to us.'[42]

Nevertheless, on 28 March 1956, an FBI liaison in London called MI5 to report the result of his request to Washington to interview Orlov again. The idea was to find out whether Orlov knew any details of NKVD or RU recruitment from the ranks of British and American volunteers who had served in the International Brigades during the Spanish Civil War.

The FBI representative stated that Orlov was currently under a deportation order in the USA and that, until he knew his fate, he was not prepared to talk. At the time the request was made, the FBI had still not managed to interrogate Orlov in detail about his service in Spain.[43] During the same year, 1956, Roger Hollis replaced Sir Dick White as director general of MI5, and any further inquiries into the Orlov case were stopped. The question of whether Hollis was a GRU asset, in such a high position that the Security Service has been too embarrassed to admit it all those years, is still being debated, although Andrew's *Authorized History of MI5* gives him a clean bill of health. And during an interview Akhmedov (GRU) had clearly indicated that ELLI was a female agent in London.

In spite of the Bill adopted by the US Congress in April 1955 granting Orlov and his wife permanent residence status, nobody could interview him properly for the next eighteen years, which he was lucky enough to spend in America in peace and comfort under full government protection. Only in 1964 did another opportunity occur, because the French DST became interested in what Orlov had written in his *Handbook*, commissioned by the CIA and published the year before.

One of the last public shows with Orlov at the centre of everybody's attention took place in 1971, two years before Orlov's death. He was invited to deliver a formal lecture to a group of US military attachés in training before their deployment to the USSR and several East European countries. It took place at the old Defence Intelligence School (now the National Intelligence University). The audience's interests were not in history but in current operations and developments in the then Warsaw Pact. Few of them had a background in KGB not to mention NKVD operations from the past, and they did not ask those kinds of questions. In his lecture, Orlov addressed the issue of KGB assassinations, his favourite topic. This was the time of the Oleg Lyalin defection,[44] so assassinations were a hot and timely item. A US government official who was present at that lecture recalled that Orlov gave the impression of being a very engaging individual, adding: 'His lecture to the attachés was meant to give them an understanding into the KGB's mind-set and operational style—mostly generalities. I will say that my friend Ray Rocca had regularly insisted that Orlov withheld a lot of information.

Ray always had a deep and nuanced understanding of and relations with former KGB officers.'[45] Orlov had never been invited to talk to MI5 or MI6.

Orlov's Personal File No. 605.075 was last consulted by the Security Service on 11 July 2006. It was then partly declassified and in August 2008 released to The National Archives in Kew, becoming a public record. But the Orlov case is not yet closed.

25
KGB in the Law Quad

On 26 August 1963, the Special Agent in Charge from the New York Field Office reported to the FBI Director J. Edgar Hoover that the Bureau was advised Alexander Orlov [and his wife] now resided at Apartment 704, 400 Maynard Street, Ann Arbor, Michigan, and had a landline telephone number 665–4871. He was employed at the University of Michigan.[1]

Several months later the deputy chief for counter-intelligence of the KGB Washington station reported the same information to his Moscow head office based on information received from his confidential source.[2]

Helen Betts, former Law School registrar at the University of Michigan, remembered Orlov as 'a nondescript man of average height; always pleasant, courteous, well dressed'. 'I knew who he was, but that's all,' she said. 'I was told by Dean Smith not to talk about him. He was paid out of a special account. He didn't teach but he had an office on the seventh floor of the legal Research Building.'[3]

In 1962, while the Orlov file was getting dusty somewhere on the MI5 registry shelf under the watchful eyes of the Registry Queens,[4] the FBI and CIA were still uncertain about how much Orlov was *not* telling them. So it was decided to place him at a university and engage him in writing, this time not about Stalin's crimes but about the theory and practice of guerrilla warfare. Before American involvement in the Vietnam War had reached its peak, some thought it could be useful if a person sent by Stalin to advise the Republicans in Spain on guerrilla warfare combat operations shared his knowledge and experience, which might be helpful in understanding the fighting tactics used by the Viet Cong. They still remembered that, under Stalin's direction, Soviet doctrine on guerrilla warfare expanded with *The Russian Partisan Directive of 1933*, which stressed the political, economic, and psychological significance of guerrilla operations in addition to the strictly military objectives.[5]

They forgot that Orlov's first-hand knowledge of such operations dated back to 1920, and that four decades later all such doctrines had become obsolete.

Orlov was happy to comply. The University of Michigan in Ann Arbor was chosen, and Allan Smith, then the dean of the UM Law School and later the acting president of the university, was contacted. 'It was my one affair with intrigue,' said Smith, speaking years later to Al Slote of the *Ann Arbor Observer*, 'and I worried about it a good deal. I remember worrying whether we really should get involved with this sort of thing.'[6]

It was Edward Meader, an intelligence officer based in Detroit, who arranged for Orlov's cosy transfer to Ann Arbor. Meader was well connected here: he lived near the Smiths in Ann Arbor Hills, and his brother, Michigan congressman George Meader, was a 1931 UM Law alumnus. Naturally, Meader was not acting on his own initiative—a CIA colleague from Washington, Morse Allen, called asking for a favour.[7]

Allan Smith recalled years later:

I was told that the CIA had an important Russian defector they wanted to place so they could continue to try to find out what he could tell them about Russian espionage. I thought hard about this and decided my justification for having Orlov here would be that he might be able to tell us something about the Russian criminal justice system at the time of the revolution, and also he'd be willing to do a little writing. He didn't do any teaching. The man himself was very cool, a mild sort of fellow, calm, reserved, slight—a little guy. I remember thinking he'd be a perfect spy. According to Meader, the CIA didn't get much out of him, but I guess they were still hoping. He was, I guess, acting as a sort of consultant to them.[8]

What sort of 'consultations' Orlov provided during the critical years of the Vietnam War can be traced through his now unclassified article in the CIA journal *Studies in Intelligence* entitled 'The Theory and Practice of Soviet Intelligence' (Spring 1963),[9] his *Handbook of Intelligence and Guerrilla Warfare* (1963),[10] and several interviews conducted by Raymond Rocca of the CIA counter-intelligence operations, which may be obtained thanks to the Freedom of Information Act (FOIA).[11] But it hardly makes sense to analyse them—to paraphrase Jane Austen,[12] in all his ways Orlov was as false and deceitful as he was inventing.

In the meantime, in Ann Arbor, Bev and Pat Pooley lived directly below the Orlovs in Maynard House. Pat Pooley recalled:

We'd just come back from two years in Africa, and I was very pregnant. One day I was carrying a big load of wash into the elevator to take down to the basement to the washing machines. Mrs Orlov was in the elevator. She took one look at me and at the basket of wash and said: 'I am going to denounce you to your husband.'

She was a doctor [but in reality, had studied for less than four semesters at the 2nd Moscow Medical School] and told us quite proudly that she too had held the rank of general—I would guess on a medical staff. She was tall and stern. He was short and had twinkly blue eyes and looked like an angel . . .

He was proud of how he had duped the Spanish government out of their gold and loved to recount that adventure in great detail. He told me how he used his knowledge of surreptitious methods to get out of Spain secretly, pick up his wife and daughter in France, and get all of them safely to Montreal . . .

In reality, on the morning of 13 July 1938, Orlov had crossed the Spanish–French border in his service limousine, accompanied by his German chauffeur and bodyguard, picked up his family from a luxury French hotel, where they had been residing for the previous few weeks, and made the rest of his trip to Paris by train travelling first class.

'Orlov and I talked about Philby [Bev Pooley also recalled]. His escape to Moscow and confession that he was a long-time Soviet agent had made headlines. Orlov told me that their purpose in recruiting upper-class Englishmen was really not so much for their intelligence work *per se*, though that was important. But through the high positions they would eventually arrive at, Moscow could put in their real agents, their professionals—people who might he hired in as chauffeurs, maids, gardeners.

'And these people,' Orlov told Pooley, his blue eyes twinkling as he relished the moment, 'these people are still there'. Orlov also said he would never go back to England, because, he claimed, 'I wouldn't last twenty-four hours there'.[13] Regrettably, no one learned about those remarks until thirty years later.

At the same time, Orlov's words demonstrate that this 'NKVD General' could never think strategically and failed to understand his former assistant's approach to the selection of potential sources. Dr Deutsch's brilliant theory that had worked so well in the case of the Cambridge and Oxford Spy Ring was that developing upper-class targets—that is, 'young radical high-fliers from leading universities before they entered the corridors of power',[14] would eventually bring success because of their strong potential to becoming highly placed sources. And these assets would become valuable because of their access to secret intelligence and their position of influence, and not, as Orlov thought, because some 'professionals' could be placed as their maids or gardeners.

A professional review of Orlov's *Handbook* appeared in the same CIA's journal that published Orlov's classified article. The anonymous reviewer wrote:

Orlov declares that the purpose of his book is to recreate an espionage handbook that he composed for the Soviets back in 1936. Fortunately for us, however, he has done no such thing... The weakest section of this book is the final chapter on guerrilla warfare; here the dated quality of Orlov's information is most clearly shown. His elementary generalizations on guerrilla activity are drawn from personal experience limited to the Russian and Spanish Civil Wars. Soviet guerrilla experience in World War II, which importantly influenced present-day guerrilla doctrine, is covered in only a page or two. Post-war guerrilla activities are not mentioned.[15]

Orlov's fantasies, and specifically his stories about the adventures of Soviet 'illegals', which make up the core of his *Handbook*, have, unfortunately, been picked up, not only by Orlov's biographers but also by many academic and even intelligence historians and authors.

MI5 records on 'Paul and Lydia Hardt' were opened in May 2002 and are now available to a researcher. Maly, who during his British assignment was using the alias 'Paul Hardt', never operated, overtly or covertly, in Austria and Germany, as claimed in books based on Orlov's fantasies, but in France, Holland, and Britain. The so-called flying or mobile squads, mentioned in Orlov's *Handbook*, are Orlov's inventions. There was indeed a so-called Special Tasks group that operated from Paris, but Maly was never its member and had never been given any of such special tasks. As mentioned above, he began his career as a linguist at the Special (Cipher) Department and was then transferred to the INO, operating in Europe as an undercover recruiter and agent-runner. Maly's arrival in Britain was noted by the authorities, because MI5 had a penetration agent within the Woolwich Arsenal spy ring. Maly's passport in the name of 'Paul Hardt', as well as that of his wife, had never been suspected,[16] as the declassified documents demonstrate. It has now been established that it was a trio of Ignace Reif, Arnold Deutsch, and Teodor Maly who should be credited with the recruitment and running of the Cambridge, Oxford, and other Soviet espionage spy rings in Britain in 1934–7.[17]

In his preface to Orlov's 1993 biography, John Costello wrote: 'While I have not personally met archivists of the Russian Intelligence Service whose unseen efforts have made this book possible, I can vouch for the unique contribution that has been made.' He also claimed that 'Joseph Gormley and Joanna Rubira of the University of Michigan provided information relating to Orlov's time at the Ann Arbor campus'.[18]

Looking for 'Mr Gormley' and 'Mrs Rubira' turned out to be quite an adventure: neither name was listed in the University of Michigan staff directories of 1990–3. Finally, Joanna Rubiner, a publicist at the UM Press, was found. 'In early 1993,' she recalled, 'I did get calls from a guy with a British accent'—quite obviously Costello. And she did indeed answer questions about the campus.[19] But later, she was greatly surprised to read:

On Friday, 14 November 1969, a passenger wearing a dark grey overcoat alighted from the morning Chicago train at Ann Arbor station and hailed a taxi. At the intersection of State and South University Streets the cab stopped. The man got out and joined the students hurrying to classes on the sprawling University of Michigan campus. The icy wind blasted snow flurries in from *Lake Huron*, rattling the bare branches of the trees on the sidewalk outside Lorch Hall as he entered through the glass swing doors of the *six-storey* Law and Economics building. No one paid any special attention to the short figure whose coat was a bit too stylishly cut—although he conspicuously did not fit in with faculty or students. Pausing before the notice board posting the day's classes, he scanned the list then set off along the ground-floor corridor.

In one of the lecture rooms, an elderly man was addressing the class of students . . .[20]

Like any experienced Midwesterner, Joanna Rubiner knew that Michigan weather arrives from the west, not the north-east. More glaringly, the Legal Research Building, where Orlov's office was, on the seventh floor, is an entirely separate building from Lorch Hall, which is located across Tappan Street. In addition, in 1969 Lorch Hall still housed the UM School of Art; the economics department did not move in until the 1980s.[21]

According to Al Slote, who interviewed her at the end of 1993 when Orlov's biography was published in the USA, Rubiner had no idea where the authors of *Deadly Illusions* got their information about the proximity of Lake Huron to Ann Arbor, or how they managed to combine the Law Quad and Lorch Hall. Moreover, she certainly did not provide them with any 'information relating to Orlov's time at the Ann Arbor campus'. Rubiner was born in 1969, the year the Orlovs moved to another place, after an officer from the KGB New York station, Mikhail Feoktistov, who worked at the United Nations and had no travel restrictions, visited them for the first time. Surprisingly, when offered the chance to return to Moscow after more than thirty years of self-exile, Orlov agreed. At that time Oleg Kalugin, who would soon be promoted to head KGB foreign counter-intelligence operations, was deputy head of station in Washington. He recalled in his memoirs:

Shortly afterward, I returned to Moscow on vacation and asked my superiors what had happened with the Orlov case. They said the decision on his fate had been kicked all the way up to the Politburo, whose members finally decided that the old defector wasn't worth the fuss. The Politburo said it would be foolish to treat a traitor as a hero, and he was too old and the case too stale to trick him into coming back and then put him on trial. No, our leaders said, leave him alone. And so we did, after wasting an enormous amount of time and money hunting for the Stalin-era spy.[22]

And Orlov never lectured at the University of Michigan.

26

In and Out of the Direction de la Surveillance du Territoire

Whether the letter from Mr Reeves of Ridgewood to Marie Brett-Perring in London, posing as a representative of the French secret service,[1] was a wild guess or a stroke of genius would for ever remain a mystery. What knowledge Ms Brett-Perring had about Nikolsky/Orlov would also be very hard to establish now. However, it is quite certain that in 1939 both French and British security services had no file on him. Therefore, as soon as Paris learned about his existence and his obvious ties with the CIA after the publication of his second book, they turned to James Jesus Angleton for help. In April 1965, in response to their request, Orlov was interviewed by Raymond Rocca, Angleton's deputy at the Counter-Intelligence Staff about some events and individuals who were of particular, albeit historical, interest to the DST, a directorate of responsible for counter-espionage and thus Angleton's counterparts, so their request was granted.

Orlov started with the story of his hurried departure from France in the spring of 1934. He said he had been operating as an 'illegal' in Paris and was staking out the headquarters of the Deuxième Bureau at number 2 bis Avenue de Tourville when he was suddenly approached by a former colleague. He claimed that he had immediately returned to Moscow, where it was decided to put him on ice for a while, and he was assigned to the 4th Transportation Directorate. It was because this directorate's assets would have been involved in the collection and transportation of Spanish gold, Orlov continued, that he was assigned the position there, from which he defected.[2] His answers to other questions were similar to this one. Therefore, it is perhaps to the benefit of the scholars and intelligence historians that neither this DST questionnaire nor Orlov's comments to it have ever been published, as they are full of inaccuracies, misleading statements, and inventions.

On the other hand, there is now an opportunity to correct for the historical record all the distortions and half-truths contained in Orlov's answers.

The French security service turned to Orlov for help because it had a problem. All its archives had been taken out of France during the war. First, the Nazis had managed to seize them in 1940, and then the Soviets recaptured the invaluable boxes when they occupied Germany. For years Moscow had denied any knowledge of this unique collection of documents belonging to the Sûreté Nationale. After the collapse of the Soviet Union, a deal was struck, and the bulk of this pre-war collection was gradually transferred to Paris after it had been copied in Russia. The archival holdings that were repatriated represented more than 10,000 boxes covering the period 1880–1940, with the majority of the papers relating to the second half of the 1930s. These included secret files on over 600,000 individuals in 7,586 boxes.[3] But all that happened at the end of the twentieth century. Therefore, it is no wonder that in 1965 the French were anxious to get any insider information they could about Soviet intelligence operations in France, especially in the interwar period, since their archives were missing, and they expected Orlov to fill in some gaps in their historical records.

The sixty-four-page DST file (plus attachments entitled 'Documents in English') is based entirely on Orlov's *Handbook*, from which the French were able to draw sixteen cases that concerned France. Additionally (and very discreetly), Orlov was asked whether the names Pierre Cot and Guy La Chambre meant anything to him.[4] Both were prominent French politicians suspected of being Soviet agents. Whether Orlov had any information, he preferred to keep it to himself.

From the first days of the Civil War in Spain, Cot, French Minister for Air, became one of the leading supporters of the Republican course. In early August 1936 he arranged for several deliveries of modern French aeroplanes to Barcelona and, as one report put it, 'used to hand over to the Soviet Union secret information he had obtained in his capacity as Aviation Secretary'.[5] In early March 1938 Pierre Cot was still Minister for Air and then again briefly after the Second World War. Following the Nazi occupation of France, Cot emigrated first to Great Britain and then to the United States.

In New York, Cot quickly established a contact with Earl Browder of the CPUSA, who reported their meeting to Moscow at the end of November 1940. This message was intercepted in the course of Operation MASK. Among other things, Browder informed Dimitrov (and automatically

Beria and the NKVD Foreign Intelligence chief Fitin) that 'COT wanted the leaders of the Soviet Union to know about his willingness to perform any of our assignments, for which (purpose) he would even be ready to break faith with his position'.[6] According to the radio traffic partially deciphered in the course of another counter-intelligence operation, now known as VENONA, Beria and Fitin followed up on Browder's message.

After a thorough background check and consultations with the 'Instan-syia' (Party leadership), Cot was approached by the sub-resident of the NKVD in New York Roland Abbiate (alias 'Vladimir Pravdin'), who was operating under cover as head of the local TASS bureau. Moscow's tele-gram reminded him 'about signing on of Pierre COT (henceforth DAEDALUS [DEDAL]).[7] It also asked for details about Cot's wife, including information regarding her social status and contacts. The last mention of Cot in VENONA decrypts is dated 12 December 1944 when SERGEJ (the codename of Abbi-ate/Pravdin) reported about his repeated but unsuccessful efforts to contact DAEDALUS' wife. The NKVD resident was obviously not informed that Madame Cot had left New York in October. During the same year as Orlov surfaced in America, in 1953, the Soviets awarded Pierre Cot the Lenin Peace Prize. Ten years later, DST questions may be explained by MASK and VENONA intercepts, by that time partially shared with the French.

Two pages of Orlov's DST file, pages 61 and 62, form a partial list of 'illegals' and 'legals', which, according to the CIA, he was able to recon-struct. It was rather short and very imprecise. Orlov remembered Yuri Praslov (alias KEPP), Pavel Sirkin [sic],[8] Alexander Korotkov, Adolf Chapsky, Dmitry Smirnov, Yury Makovsky, Naum Eitingon, Stephan Uzdanski-Elensky, whom he called 'Yelanskiy' alias 'Bernstein', Anistar Rigin [sic],[9] Vladimir Voinovich [sic],[10] Stanislaw Glinski, and his last contact in Paris, Georgy Kosenko., One of his principal assistants in 1937–8, Orlov added, was Sokolov (written down as 'SOKOROV' in the interview transcript). This was not true, and Orlov knew it because from July 1937 one Sokolov (a real name) was on the staff of the Soviet Embassy in Spain.[11]

Finally, the interviews covered several individuals and separate cases, such as the abductions of Generals Miller and Kutepov in Paris, relations between Zborowski and Dallin, Zarubin and Eitingon, and even the activities of Ángel Baza, the first chief of the Republican SIM during the civil war in Spain, who figures in the questionnaire as BOEZA. Orlov later included almost all his answers, one way or another, in his memoirs, edited and published by Gazur. In addition, there are several short Biographic Statements (sic) at the

end of the file that may be of some interest to a historian. They begin with
what the French called the 'Madam d'AEHRENTHAL' case.

SUBJECT: Mrs d'AEHRENTHAL, wife of d' AEHRENTHAL, secretary to SAVINKOV (TRUST
Operation).

Mrs d'AEHRENTHAL, the wife of SAVINKOV's secretary, had become SAVINKOV's
mistress. She had been recruited in Paris by the Soviet services by playing on her
love of money.

It was Mrs d'AEHRENTHAL who finally persuaded SAVINKOV to go to the USSR.
Carrying out instructions from the service, she worked on SAVINKOV in order for
him to find his place in history and insisted on going with him (and her husband) on
an assignment in the USSR. For this work she asked for and received from the GPU
a 5,000-dollar advance. Her request to be paid in advance "cut the bridges" and she
was then treated by the service with the utmost distrust and greatest bluntness. She
was refused permission to return to Paris.[12]

In reality, Lyubov Efimovna Därenthal was the wife of Alexander Dickhoff-Därenthal, a personal friend of Boris Savinkov, who joined him in Paris
after the Bolshevik revolutions. Savinkov was the leader of the anti-Bolshevik military organization called the People's Union for Defence of
Motherland and Freedom, inspiring and leading several armed uprisings
against the Soviets. At the end of 1921 Savinkov went to London, where he
had several meetings with Winston Churchill, a newly appointed Secretary
of State for the Colonies. A short time before, however, Churchill had been
Secretary of State for War and a staunch advocate of foreign intervention,
especially against the Bolsheviks. Among those whom Savinkov met in
London were also the Lord Chancellor, Lord Birkenhead, and even the
Prime Minister, Lloyd George. The KGB version that the meetings were
organized by Sidney Reilly, then working for SIS, seems unjustified, for the
Passport Control Office in Paris (the original SIS station coded '27000' and
headed by Maurice Jeffes) had been told to refuse Savinkov a visa.[13]
Churchill himself was primarily interested in getting hold of Savinkov,
inducing him to enter into a plan of reconciliation with Moscow, and 'C'
was informed about Savinkov's secret meeting with the Soviet envoy Krasin
through Sidney Reilly. Whether the Cheka was notified by Dickhoff-
Därenthal or his wife is not known.

Described by Reilly as a 'stinking Jewess, with a shiny face, fat hands and
thighs',[14] Mrs Därenthal, according to Reilly's biographer, became Savinkov's
mistress. She was instrumental in persuading her lover that an underground
army was waiting for him to return to Russia and 'take up the mantle of

leadership'. After several weeks Savinkov finally succumbed to temptation, despite Reilly's advice. In August 1924 he, his mistress and her husband were arrested near Minsk as a result of a complex disinformation operation master-minded by Artuzov and known as SINDIKAT-2, and were later jailed in Moscow. While Savinkov was almost certainly murdered in prison in May 1925, as Christopher Andrew suggests, by Orlov's comrade-in-arms in Spain Syroyezhkin, who took an active part in this operation, Dickhoff-Därenthal and his wife had already been released in 1924. He later became the editor of the information bulletin for VOKS, an intelligence front also used for propaganda. Five years later, in 1929,[15] Dickhoff-Därenthal was still there, occupying the same position, but in 1937 he was arrested and shot, together with other 'enemies of the people'. What happened to his wife after her release from the Lubyanka prison is not recorded, although it was reported that she worked for a women's magazine. The Därenthals are not even mentioned in the *Ocherki* essay about the OGPU operation against Savinkov. In his memoirs, Besedovsky wrote that Lyubov Därethal remained Savinkov's mistress for some time before his trial,[16] but this information cannot be independently corroborated.

Unsurprisingly, Besedovsky, who defected from the Soviet Embassy in Paris and lived in France, was also of interest to the French service. According to Orlov's DST File,

BESSEDOVSKIY [*sic*] [whose Biographical Statement follows that of the Därethals] was a very close friend of ORLOV's during the latter's period in Paris. ORLOV had left Paris before BESSEDOVSKIY's resounding defection in October 1929.' During his interviews with the CIA in 1965, Orlov claimed that the case was bungled by the Paris OGPU resident Yanovich, whom he calls his successor at this post, and stated that 'the person who was at first mainly responsible for having precipitated the defection was a former longshoreman, named ROISENHAN [*sic*].[17]

The correct name of the official was 'Boris Roisenmann', who, contrary to Besedovsky's claims, was not a member of the OGPU Collegium.[18] Without any doubt, in America Orlov read Besedovsky's memoirs published in English in 1931.[19] What is pertinent to this story is the last phrase from the Biographic Statement No. 2: 'During ORLOV's assignment in Spain, until some time in 1937, he and BESSEDOVSKIY met by chance in a Paris street. BESSEDOVSKIY obviously recognized ORLOV, but turned his head away. ORLOV himself had no desire to reopen contact so they said nothing to each other.'[20] The above statement fully supports this writer's version that it was

Besedovsky whom Nikolsky met in Paris during Operation EXPRESS in 1934. As mentioned, he immediately reported to the Centre, inventing a story that he had been recognized by a defector and was forced to abandon his mission. From Paris, Nikolsky/Orlov travelled to Austria and joined his family in Vienna. The authors of Orlov's 1993 biography state that in Paris he occasionally bumped into one Vernik, 'a Soviet official who had defected to the French and who had worked with Orlov when the latter was on a legal assignment in France in 1928–29'.[21] While Vernik does not figure on the list of Soviet defectors, the KGB files show that there was indeed one Vernik, a member of the EXPRESS group, probably from support staff, as he did not have any cover name and was paid to get a French (and international) driving licence.[22] Orlov himself never mentioned neither Vernik nor Besedovsky in his writings.

The story of Besedovsky does not end here. At one point both SIS and MI5 considered using him as an agent. They later agreed 'that in all probability as an agent he would be undesirable'.[23] Perhaps they were right. In July 1930 the Romanian government refused to grant permission to Besedovsky, who was invited to Bucharest for a lecture tour, because his information was considered highly unreliable.[24]

Besedovsky remained in France during the war and was reportedly involved in the French Resistance, one of whose leaders was Jean Moulin, once chief of cabinet of Pierre Cot's Air Ministry. For his wartime activities, Besedovsky was pardoned by the Soviets, and after the war the Service suspected that his talents, which had previously been devoted to producing anti-Stalinist material, might now be promoting Soviet-inspired propaganda. The suspicions turned out to be justified.[25] In March 1953, the Security Service's Legal Adviser, Bernard A. Hill, wrote in a memo: 'When asked his motive for fabricating material of that sort, BESSEDOVSKI [sic] said it was just the sort of information the public liked to read.'[26] Some of Besedovsky's fabrications were sophisticated enough to deceive even such a celebrated Soviet scholar as E. H. Carr.[27] In 1955, a scandal that seriously damaged Carr's reputation was connected with his contributing a foreword to Notes for a Journal attributed to the former foreign commissar Maxim Litvinov, which was shortly afterwards exposed as a forgery written by Besedovsky.

The subject of the next Biographic Statement was Walter Krivitsky. Orlov did his best to discredit Krivitsky and belittle the value of his testimonies. He told the CIA about the problems that allegedly arose with

Krivitsky's transfer from military intelligence to the NKVD around mid-1935. According to Orlov: 'Krivitsky was in favour of the transfer and tried to get a captain's rank; it was refused.'[28] (Elsa Bernaut, who became better known by her Russian alias 'Elizabeth Poretsky', stated that Krivitsky, like her murdered husband Ignatz Reiss, had the NKVD rank and pay of a captain.)[29] In fact, both were not commissioned and worked first for the Red Army intelligence and were then transferred to the NKVD without any rank,[30] as Krivitsky correctly stated during his interview on Ellis Island. Wishing to undermine Krivitsky's information given earlier to MI5 about his work in Britain, Orlov went as far as claiming that, owing to Krivitsky's contacts with Zborowski and 'a group under Soviet control', as he put it, Krivitsky was obviously fed 'deception material for as long as the channel was in existence'.[31] Even long after Krivitsky's tragic death Orlov felt great animosity towards the defector.

Of the next two subjects of the DST questionnaire, one was a certain Lagrange and the other what was called the LONONOVSKY Operation. Under 'Lononovsky', Orlov probably meant Mieczyslaw Loganowski, the OGPU resident in Vienna mentioned earlier in this book, and 'Lagrange' is an invented name from an unsuccessful operation in Paris in 1934 described in detail in previous chapters. This Lagrange, an NCO according to Orlov, allegedly told him that the chief of the Deuxième Bureau was in his, Lagrange's, pocket. Lagrange was, without doubt, another invention of Orlov.

This is what Orlov recalled about his much more experienced and successful senior colleague who succeeded him in London and was instrumental in recruiting and handling of important sources (this is Biographic Statement No. 6).

Theodor Maly, alias Paul Hardt, explained Orlov, 'was an old hand in counterespionage who considered the others in the INO (Foreign Department) as amateurs. He was a remarkable man, very straightforward. Notaryev, alias "Nikitin" handled several operations with Hardt in Paris and reported to me about his favourable opinion of Hardt's work'.[32] Orlov said he saw Hardt for the last time in Paris in January 1938, although in his *Secret History* he wrote that Maly was arrested in November 1937.

Among the INO officers who operated in Paris in the interwar period, the name of 'Notaryev alias Nikitin' does not figure. Among the many inventions of Orlov that sounded good enough to mislead several authors and even intelligence historians, several were about Maly. For example, according to Orlov, Maly, when recalled to Moscow, made a stopover in Paris and was reported as saying: 'I know that as a former priest I haven't got a chance. But I've decided to go there so nobody can say: "That priest might have been a real spy after all."'[33] All this text was in Orlov's imagination only. As mentioned, Orlov could not have met Maly in Paris in January 1938, because after his return to Moscow in the summer of 1937 Maly was banned from travelling abroad. He was shot in September 1938, two months after Orlov's defection.

The very brief Biographic Statement No. 7 is about Orlov's wife and her work for the NKVD. He said his wife lived alone in Paris in 1928 because she was sick, while he was on his way to his new assignment in Berlin. Orlov further claimed that Maria joined him in due time 'and found employment as a secretary in the Trade Delegation'. 'She was also elected a member of the Party Committee in the Service,' he added.[34] When they lived in Ann Arbor, Maria herself used to tell her neighbours that, just like her husband, she was also a general.

After living in America for three decades, Orlov realized that some of his information would be rather difficult or impossible to check. Concerning his wife's membership in the NKVD Party Committee, this was only wishful thinking—in fact, Maria had never been a member of the service.[35]

Biographic Statement No. 8 deals with one episode that Orlov imentioned in his *Handbook*, and the DST was interested in learning more about the identity of the person unnamed by Orlov, because Paris figured in the narration and because they had no doubt that such a valuable and well-informed defector was telling the truth. 'An officer of the NKVD intelligence,' Orlov wrote, 'who for the first time in his career was assigned to underground work, was supposed to pass in Italy as an Austrian citizen. His false Austrian passport waited for him in Paris. For the trip from Russia to Paris he was given a "temporary" Romanian passport.'[36] It is clear that because of this temporary Romanian passport the officer would later get into a mess. Asked about the identity of that young illegal, Orlov said that it was [Ignace] Reif [REIFF].

Naturally, nothing of the sort really happened. Reif, as will be remembered, was an experienced NKVD intelligence officer, Orlov's superior in London and Copenhagen who later headed the British desk at the Centre. As usual, Orlov continued to play 'the NKVD general' with his interviewers and traditionally did not speak too favourably about his more successful senior colleagues. In the summary of his answer, it is noted that 'the last news from REIFF to reach ORLOV in Spain was in a letter dated 1937 in which REIFF asked ORLOV to take him on in Spain. ORLOV gave REIFF no encouragement because he felt REIFF was too obsequious and timid'. Orlov also added that Reif's parents and sister were living in Poland: 'for that reason, he was considered, from a social point of view, to be a foreigner in the service.' Orlov described Reif as 'not very tall, about 1m65 (5' 5"). He had a round face, a chubby build, apprehensive and obsequious manner, hazel eyes, brown hair, regular features, wore flashy clothes, was a womanizer though married, and had had a small boy who was about five years old in 1934–35.'[37] Although Orlov was talking about Reif, this description perfectly fits his friend Eitingon, who indeed had a small son named Vladimir from his first marriage to Anna Schulmann, was proud of his dark hair and soft brown eyes, liked to wear flashy clothes on foreign assignments, and was a terrible womanizer. Reif was very serious, blond, had grey-blue eyes, and wore round spectacles.

Perhaps not by chance, the first and the last of Orlov's 'Biographic Statements' concerned the large-scale disinformation Operation TREST ('Trust'). The operation is still a classic. Unsurprisingly, when he was interviewed for the DST, little was known about early KGB operations and almost no literature existed on the subject (the first Soviet propaganda film about TREST was made in 1967, forty years after the operation). Orlov was asked to provide some details although this counter-intelligence operation was launched in 1921, long before Nikolsky, now Orlov, joined the OGPU, and was terminated in early 1927.

It seems Orlov had only a superficial knowledge about TREST in spite of the fact that he could have learned about it from Grigory Syroyezhkin, who was one of the leading participants. Syroyezhkin was a senior member of Orlov's residency in Spain and was recalled to Moscow and shot together with Reif when Orlov defected.

The only thing Orlov was able or willing to say to the DST at the time was that 'YAKUCHEV, alias FYODEROV, one of the main leaders in Operation TREST, worked in Paris on the penetration of White Russian circles'. The shorthand secretary who was writing after him misspelled both the name and the alias. Orlov also added that another important OGPU participant was Puzitsky (whose name was also misspelled) and whose 'personal address in Moscow had been given to FYODEROV as an accommodation address. A simple check on the address in Moscow would have revealed that it involved the number of a high-level member of the security services. Everyone knew it, since he went to and came from his work in a special car,'[38] he said.

Several years later, writing his memoirs that would only be published by Gazur thirty years after Orlov's death, Orlov presented a rather detailed account of Operation TREST as well as several other parallel and follow-up operations whose targets and most celebrated victims were Boris Savinkov, the Russian anti-Bolshevik terrorist who had briefly served as deputy minister of war and Sidney Reilly, the Russian Jew cum self-fashioned British 'ace of spies'. Remarkably, Gazur's and Orlov's accounts of the operation contain the same details and errors.[39] Today, the story of TREST is well known. Orlov's opinion about Operation TREST is formulated by Gazur based on Orlov's words:

TRUST was nothing more than the old 'cat-and-mouse' game [Gazur relates]. In this case, the cat was the Great Powers: England, France and America, and the mouse was the newly emerging Soviet Government, which possessed limited power assets, no leverage with which to be in a position to broker their demands, and an absence of international recognition. However, it was the mouse which was manipulating the cat.[40]

The OGPU case file No. 302330, which specifies operational details of TREST and names all its participants, comprises about forty volumes. It was opened in November 1921 when the Cheka agents intercepted a letter sent by a former Tsarist officer named Artamonov to one of the monarchist leaders in Berlin. Artamonov worked as interpreter for the British Passport Control Office in Tallinn headed by Commander Ernest Boyce. The experienced SIS officer Boyce had been the Service representative in Moscow in 1918, and from 1920 served as head of station in Helsinki and Tallinn.

The letter described the meeting between Artamonov and one Alexander Yakushev, who used to be a lecturer at the Imperial Alexander Lyceum in Tsarskoe Selo near Saint Petersburg and later served in the Railway Ministry with the rank of Acting State Councillor. Artamonov was one of his former pupils and in his letter to Berlin described Yakushev as a staunch monarchist and talented administrator who had an idea of directing all anti-Bolshevik monarchist organizations in the West from one underground centre in Moscow. According to the implausible current version of events of the SVR (successor of the KGB foreign intelligence directorate), Artur Artuzov, then the OGPU counter-intelligence chief, liked the idea[41] because he thought that would allow his organization to control all those activities. In reality, Arturov was appointed to that post only in July 1922. His two deputies were Vasili Ulrich and Romuald Pillar. Sergey Puzitsky, mentioned by Orlov as an active participant, became Artuzov's deputy six months later.[42] In any event, neither Artuzov nor Puzitsky had the luxury of service cars bringing them home, as Orlov claimed.

By the time Artuzov headed this operation, Reilly had practically broken all contacts with SIS, only occasionally visiting its Vienna representative when he was in Austria and maintaining friendly ties with Boyce. In January 1922 the Vienna station asked London whether Reilly was still 'part of the show' and was assured by Bertie Maw from the Head Office 'that Reilly is not a member of our office and does not serve C and that he is not receiving any pay from us'.[43] In November 1921, after Yakushev had returned from Tallinn, he was arrested and quickly turned. The Cheka established a bogus Monarkhicheskaya Organizatsyia Tsentralnoi Rossii (MOTsR), headed by a former Tsarist general who now served the Soviets. Yakushev never used an alias mentioned by Orlov and served as chairman of its Political Council under his own name. Among his subordinates in that council were Lieutenant General Nikolai Potapov, a former military intelligence officer, and an OGPU operator who became know as 'Opperput' but whose real name was Edward Otto Staunits. He was placed as Yakushev's deputy in charge of the organization's finances.

Although SIS kept track of Reilly over the next years, he was out of touch, getting more and more involved with Savinkov and his plans. In July 1924 Artuzov's assistant Andrey Pavlovich Fedorov visited Savinkov in Paris and persuaded him to send a trusted representative to Russia to negotiate with the non-existent anti-Soviet underground. Fedorov also met Reilly and his new wife, a London musical comedy star Pepita Bobadilla. Savinkov agreed and sent his trusted aide, Colonel Sergei Pavlovsky, who had also been turned and was later used to lure Savinkov to Russia. On 15 August Savinkov crossed the Russian border. His confession at the show trial put an end to Savinkov's organization. After spending eight months in prison with an OGPU 'snitch' who was surreptitiously debriefing him over the details of his anti-Bolshevik activities,[44] Savinkov fell from an upper window, quite possibly pushed by Syroyezhkin, who, the KGB records say, 'attempted to save him'.[45]

SIS had been informed of the TREST since 1922 thanks to their chief agent in Finland named Nikolai Bunakov (codenamed 21028). The agent had been 'deputed to keep an eye on [TREST], with the aim of ascertaining its activities and, potentially, exploiting it for intelligence on the Soviet Union'.[46] While Fedorov was sent to Paris, in July 1924 Yakushev, accompanied by 'Schyukin', introducing himself as a former colonel of the Tsarist army, 'illegally' crossed the border and met Harry Carr, Boyce's assistant in Helsinki. In 1925 Boyce decided to use his old friend Reilly to penetrate the organization. Following the advice given by Yakushev, Boyce asked Bunakov to arrange a meeting in Finland between Reilly and MOTsR. In order to stimulate Reilly, who was in the USA to make a transatlantic trip, Boyce wrote him a letter in which MOTsR was described as 'a reliable underground organization in whose active work the office [SIS] is much interested'.[47] As a result, Reilly came to Helsinki, was easily lured across the Soviet border, and never came back. In a Leningrad apartment, 'Schyukin', whose role was successfully played by Syroyezhkin, introduced him to Vladimir Styrne, his future chief interrogator at the Lubyanka prison.

Reilly's resistance after his arrest did not last long. At the end of October he wrote a letter to Dzierżyński where he promised to reveal all he knew about British and American intelligence and the activities of the Russian émigré organizations in the West. On 5 November he was taken for a walk in the woods near Moscow and shot. According to an OGPU report, Reilly 'let out a deep breath and fell without a cry'.[48] Later Boyce had to take some of the blame for the tragedy. Back in London, as recalled by Harry Carr, he was 'carpeted by the "Chief" for the role he had played in this unfortunate affair'.[49]

The TREST deception was finally exposed in 1927 when Opperput/Staunits broke with the OGPU and fled to Finland with General Kutepov's niece Maria Zakharchenko. Both were later killed during a suicide terrorist mission in Russia.

The KGB credits the success of this operation, an international scam that at the time became a major embarrassment for the intelligence services of Britain, France, Poland, Finland, and the Baltic states, to Artuzov, Puzitsky, Pillar, Styrne, Syroyezhkin, Fedorov, Yakushev, and Alexander Langovoy, a Red Army officer who for a certain period of time had been posing as an assistant chief of staff of MOTsR. Of all these men, only the ex-Tsarist General Potapov and Langovoy managed to survive. All others were arrested and shot during the Great Terror. After the operation Yakushev returned to the Railway Ministry, but in 1934 was sentenced 'for counter-revolutionary activities' to ten years in the Gulag, where he died three years later.

Orlov wrote about Fedorov:

In the early 1930s, after he had earned two decorations, Fedorov was appointed chief of the foreign department of the Leningrad NKVD, and on my trips abroad through Leningrad I made it a point to have a chat with him and listen to his past exercises in applied psychology. He disclaimed any special talents, but said that he owed his success mainly to human frailty, which makes men believe what they want to believe.[50]

Some fifteen years before, when he was younger and in better shape, all that Orlov could reveal to the DST about that operation was that there acted one 'Yakuchev', alias 'Fyoderov'.

Operation TREST was to set an important precedent. From that time on, disinformation and deception started to play a more and more important role in Soviet intelligence operations in the West. Unsurprisingly, the situation did not change, even after the collapse of the Soviet Union.

27

Comrade Walter

O rlov's posthumous memoirs consist of two parts.[1] The first describes the writer's heroic deeds during the Bolshevik revolution and the civil war in Russia, while the second deals exclusively with Spain. Several pages are devoted to Karol Świerczewski, known there as 'General Walter'.

'One of the most outstanding commanders of the International Brigades was Karol Świerczewski,' Orlov wrote.

He was serving as a colonel in the Red Army in 1936, when the Spanish Civil War broke out. Because of his Polish background and knowledge of the Polish language, he was picked as a "volunteer" for the International Brigade. He first travelled with a false Polish passport to France, where he recruited a large group of Polish miners for Spain. After he had successfully carried out that assignment, he left for Albacete, Spain. There, Karol Świerczewski assumed the pseudonym of Walter, a name which left a mark on the history of the Spanish Civil War.[2]

Orlov added that he knew General Walter very well personally.

In the Comintern archive of the former Moscow Institute of Marxism-Leninism (now Rossiisky gosudarsvennyi arkhiv sotsyalno-politicheskoi istorii, (RGASPI) the file 'Karol Świerczewski' contains his autobiography written on a single sheet of paper and signed 'Walter'. It is dated 1931. At the time Świerczewski, a graduate of the Frunze Military Academy, served as chief military instructor at the Kommunistichesky Universitet Natsionalnykh Menshinstv Zapada (KUNMZ) (Communist University of the National Minorities of the West), a training school for 'revolutionaries' and future communist leaders. It was located in Klimentovsky Lane off Pyatnitskaya Street in Moscow next to a cathedral. Comrade Walter had taught there until his departure to Spain. Based on Vaupshasov's memoirs,[3] many Russian sources claim that Świerczewski commanded the XIII

International Brigade named after Jarosław Dąbrowski, a Polish general who died fighting for the Paris Commune. In reality, in December 1936[4] Colonel Świerczewski, aged 39, arrived from Paris, where he had spent three months supervising the recruitment of the international volunteers. In Spain, Świerczewski formed and headed the XIV International Brigade with volunteers mainly from France and Belgium. Later, he commanded the 35th International Division. In January 1938 the division suffered heavily in the Battle of Teruel from aerial bombardments as well as from shortages of ammunition and a total lack of discipline. This becomes quite clear from the letter that Świerczewski, the Division Commander, sent to Vladimir Čopić, who commanded the XV International Brigade with Major Robert Hale Merriman, an American professor of economics at the University of California, as his chief of staff, from his base in Tortejada on 14 January.[5] Świerczewski held it against Čopić that a month after the battle for Teruel had begun (and only three days before the Francoist forces started an advance on the city) the new line of defence was entirely unprepared. The commanding officers did not know their tasks, Świerczewski wrote, were ill informed about the situation in general, and had done nothing to prepare for the action. As we know, in spite of the moral support (Ernest Hemingway, Herbert Matthews of the *New York Times*, and Jay Allen, who used to be a foreign correspondent for the *Chicago Tribune*—all these luminaries accompanied the Republican troops entering Teruel[6] during the Republication advance and the siege) the Battle of Teruel would be lost. In early December 1937 a future British prime minister, Clement Attlee, a left-wing Labour politician Ellen Wilkinson, and a future Labour government official and diplomat Philip Noel-Baker, all representing the party's executive committee, visited a British unit at Mondéjar accompanied by General Walter/Świerczewski.[7] In spite of all the efforts, the Republican defences were broken, and the rebels finally recaptured Teruel on 22 February 1938, with the Republicans suffering heavy losses.

Some time in the early spring of 1938 [continued Orlov] I received a letter from Moscow inquiring how real was the possibility that, if recalled, Walter might refuse to return to Russia. The letter explained that the NKVD had received information from the Fourth Department [*sic*] of the General Staff of the Red Army that Walter was in a 'very unhealthy mood', which might result in his defection. They asked me to give my opinion about the matter.[8]

He further claimed:

I decided to do everything I could to save Walter ... Next day I wrote a letter to
Yezhov personally. I told him that the denunciation against Walter was without
any foundation, that for eighteen months he had been fighting in the trenches even
though his tour of duty had ended many months before, and that his only daughter,
whom he would never abandon, was living in Moscow. I added that my four
assistants shared my opinion about Walter.[9]

Orlov's 1993 biography supports this version adding a few colourful details:

Orlov wrote a personal plea to Yezhov that was countersigned by all *five* of his
deputies. It asserted not only that Svertchevsky's [*sic*] loyalty was above reproach,
but also that he was immensely popular with the Spanish public. They made their
case by enclosing the silver box, which had been a gift to the General from the
Spanish Young Communist League. Its lid, engraved with a map of Spain, was
inset with rubies to mark the sites of the military victories won by Svertchevsky.
Inside Yezhov found letters attesting to the General's bravery and skill on
the battlefield. It was one of the rare recorded instances when the NKVD
chief was persuaded to spare one of his victims. Svertchevsky was exonerated,
but the 'Dwarf's' vengeance was redirected towards Orlov, who noted that
it was shortly afterwards, on 9 July 1938, that he received his own recall to
Moscow.[10]

According to the semi-official history of the Russian foreign intelligence,
in spring 1938 Orlov was ordered to report on Świerczewski after the Battle
of Teruel had been lost. Moscow learned that the general was in low spirits
because of the recent arrest in Moscow of three Comintern officials from
Poland who were accused of spying. Orlov duly informed Moscow:

The leader of the Polish internationalists [Świerczewski] has an embittered, hostile
mood. He openly contests the grounds for the charges against those arrested. He
claims that he has known these people for twenty years and does not believe that
they could be the enemies of the people.[11]

As if sensing that the NKVD man was reporting on him, General Walter
wrote from Spain:

We should learn a lot from the Spanish without giving unnecessary advice and
without a domineering tone (as Orlov afforded himself when speaking with
Modesto). It is equally inadmissible, however, to be lazy or to show fear. One
should not emphasize one's ego; put all victories down to one's achievements and
the lack of fortune explain by somebody else's mistakes.[12]

Contrary to what Orlov claimed in his memoirs, Świerczewski's tour of duty in Spain ended in May 1938, when he was recalled to Moscow and placed in the reserve of the People's Commissariat of Defence.[13]

In September 1938, Świerczewski was politically 'cleared' of all suspicions, not because but rather in spite of Orlov's report. One reason for this was certainly the fact that by that time Orlov had already deserted his post (and, accordingly, all his 'negative' reporting automatically became 'positive'). On 27 September Orlov's former chief, Nikolai Yezhov, personally forwarded to Stalin his first 'special report' on Mikhail Koltsov.[14] On the first page of the file Stalin wrote: 'To summon Koltsov'. Whether he had in mind to summon him to his own office or to another place is impossible to say, but on 13 December 1938 Mikhail Koltsov was arrested in Moscow. The previous summer Koltsov, one of Russia's most successful writers and journalists, had been elected to the Supreme Soviet of the Russian Socialist Federal Soviet Republic.

It was a reward for a distinguished career [Paul Preston writes], which included an active, and indeed daring, role during the Spanish Civil War. His chronicles from Spain, published daily in *Pravda*, from 9 August 1936 to 6 November 1937, had been devoured avidly by the Russian public. During the spring and summer of 1938, his vivid diary of the Spanish exploits was serialized to enormous acclaim. He was at the apogee of his popularity. In the autumn of the same year, one evening at the Bolshoi, Stalin invited him to his box and told him how much he was enjoying the Spanish diary. The dictator then invited Koltsov to give a lecture to present the History of the Bolshevik party, which he himself had edited. It was a notable token of official favour. Two days before the lecture, yet another honour came Koltsov's way—he was made a corresponding member of the Academy of Sciences. In the late afternoon of 12 December, a beaming Koltsov fulfilled his promise to Stalin and gave a warmly received lecture at the Writers' Union about Stalin's book.[15]

Later that night, shortly after he had arrived at his *Pravda* office, the NKVD took him away.[16] Świerczewski's younger daughter Martha remembered that earlier Koltsov had called Świerczewski asking for help with some Spanish material that he had been working at, and that her father, who had been unemployed for a year, duly called, but it turned out that Koltsov had been arrested the night before.[17]

Although his brother Maximilian Świerczewski was purged and spent a year in the Gulag, at the end of September 1938 the NKVD had no compromising material against 'General Walter'. A day after Yezhov sent his 'special report' to Stalin, Georgi Dimitrov wrote in his diary, referring to the telegram he sent to Manuilsky and Moskvin. 'If the Polish Walter [Świerczewski] is politically clean,' the Comintern leader suggested, 'he should be used for work in the Polish network'.[18] It is unclear what exactly Dimitrov meant by this remark but Świerczewski's official GRU biography notes that, after had he graduated from the Frunze Military Academy in 1927, Świerczewski served in the Intelligence Department of the Byelorussian military district and from 1931 to 1936 headed the secret military–political school of the ECCI.[19] Świerczewski's file in the Polish Institute of National Remembrance (Instytut Pamięci Narodowej) goes even further, stating that during his tour of duty in Spain Świerczewski was 'involved in actions ordered and supervised directly by the Soviet foreign intelligence'.[20] Naturally, his three daughters, who remained in Moscow and later wrote a book about their father, knew nothing about it.

In 1939 Świerczewski began teaching at the Frunze Military Academy. From June 1941 he was fighting on the front in the rank of major general of the Red Army, together with his brother Maximilian. His 248th Infantry Division was surrounded by the Nazi troops under the town of Vyazma, but both brothers managed to break out. At that moment Maximilian was killed in action, while Karol successfully reached the Red Army headquarters of Konstantin Rokossovsky, another Pole. Only a short time previously, on 22 March 1940, Rokossovsky had been released from the infamous Kresty prison in Leningrad, where he had served a sentence as a 'Polish spy'. The Rokossovsky family were members of the Polish nobility and they helped General Świerczewski, who, instead of being shot, was sent to Siberia. Eventually, Rokossovsky rose from a disgraced officer and a former prisoner charged with treason through the rank of colonel to become a Marshal of the Soviet Union and a Marshal of Poland. It was there, in Achinsk, on the Trans-Siberian Railway about 200 kilometres west of Krasnoyarsk, that Świerczewski remained until 1943, when Stalin appointed him to the Soviet-controlled Polish Armed Forces in the east. Świerczewski's personal file notes that 'his constant alcoholism and related disregard for life and health of his soldiers stirred conflicts with Zygmunt Berling, commander of the 1st Polish Army. Also for this reason he has been removed from the command on several occasions. Świerczewski's alcoholism-related orders gained criticism from other Polish generals as well.'[21] After the war Świerczewski was appointed Poland's deputy defence minister. Orlov wrote in his memoirs:

In 1947, I read in the papers that Karol Swierczewski, who had acquired fame in Spain as General Walter, had been ambushed and killed in Poland by anti-Communist partisans...I took this piece of news with a grain of salt. Walter was too experienced and clever to be outwitted by partisans. I didn't exclude the possibility that those who had intrigued against him in Spain had finally succeeded under different circumstances in arousing Stalin's suspicion against him.[22]

Remarkably, it seems that nobody except Orlov himself 'had intrigued' against Walter in Spain.

Vlada Pechocka, Świerczewski's Polish mistress (he also had a mistress in Spain and a wife in Russia), recalled that in December 1946 General Świerczewski was urgently summoned to Moscow. Stalin, together with Beria, received him in the Kremlin and offered him a post as national security minister. Pechocka testified that the general refused.[23] Świerczewski's daughter Martha said in a recent interview that during the same year her father met Vyacheslav Molotov, then the Foreign Minister, when they were both on an official visit to Washington, and begged the Soviet leader (Molotov served as Chairman of the Council of People's Commissars from 1930 to 1941 and as First Deputy Premier in Stalin's cabinet) to allow him to return to Russia.[24] It should be added that, apart from wearing a Polish military uniform, Świerczewski remained an officer of the Red Army according to Stalin's decree of 15 January 1945 'about the secondment of the Red Army officers to Wojsko Polskie'.

On 28 March 1947 Karol Świerczewski was reportedly killed in a Ukraińska Powstańcza Armia (UPA) (Ukrainian Insurgent Army) ambush on a road to Cisna near Baligród in the south-east of Poland. It is possible that this time Stalin's hands were clean, though Świerczewski's elder daughter was convinced that it was the NKVD who had finally settled accounts with the general.[25]

The departure of Orlov, only two months after 'General Walter' had returned to Moscow, effectively put an end to NKVD operations in Spain. Syroyezhkin and Belkin were recalled to Russia, William Fisher, who became better known under his self-invented alias 'Colonel Rudolf Abel' and who worked briefly with Nikolsky/Orlov in London, was sacked from the service. As mentioned above, Świerczewski was not formally dismissed from the service but remained unemployed for a year. After a long deliberation in Moscow, Naum Eitingon was ordered to take Orlov's place as an acting head of station. In August 1938, he had to travel to France,[26] probably still looking for Orlov but also to meet Guy Burgess, who, like other young recruits of the future Cambridge Spy Ring, had stayed without any contact with his Soviet controllers for nearly ten months.

28

Conclusion: Behind Closed Curtains

In the first decade of the twenty-first century, many academic historians acknowledge the significance of intelligence, realizing that they cannot ignore it in their studies. However, the activities and role of Soviet intelligence services are still surrounded by speculation, and most of the accounts are full of factual errors. The explanation is simple: espionage is a secretive business. 'It is rare', as the authors of the 2009 book on Soviet espionage during the 1930s and 1940s note, 'that the agents engaged in it or the agencies they serve speak honestly and openly about what they have done because the incentives to lie, dissemble, and continue to deceive are so strong for all concerned'.[1]

For several decades our knowledge of clandestine Soviet operations in Spain during the civil war was based on the books and articles written by two former Soviet intelligence operators, Walter Krivitsky and Alexander Orlov, and on the biography of Orlov based on the documents carefully selected by the KGB archivists and approved by the Service's leadership. As we have seen, this was largely a disinformation operation. It is no wonder, as the whole purpose of governments is not to document but to hide the facts related to their secret activities, while access to the primary sources in Russia was and still remains very limited. This book seeks to set the record straight and present an accurate picture of Soviet intelligence operations in Europe and America in the inter-war period and during the Spanish Civil War, revealing its methods, failures, and frustrations as its operators strove to follow orders sent from Moscow. It also tries, based on all available documentary sources, to provide information on men and women—officers, civil employees, agents, and collaborators—who took part in those operations. It is the first work in English[2] entirely devoted to the intervention of

Soviet intelligence services in the Spanish Civil War, and, as every first work, it cannot hope to cover all aspects of Soviet involvement in the Spanish conflict. But it attempts to provide a base for future historians, who should be able to expand the frontiers of research in this direction.

One example concerns the history of signal intelligence (SIGINT), which still remains understudied. Even after the revelation of the ULTRA secret in 1973 (Operation ULTRA, the surveillance of high-level German communications that began at Bletchley Park in 1938), as Christopher Andrew notes, 'it took another fifteen years before any historian raised the rather obvious questions of whether there was a Russian ULTRA', and, if so, when it began.[3] At the same time, the British interception operation codenamed MASK that had been launched before and continued during the Spanish Civil War is only partially covered in the literature,[4] while its Spanish part is presented in this work for the first time.

There is even less about secret intelligence in the most recent books in either Russia or the West on Stalin and his inner circle. This is understandable for the period from the mid-1920s until 1943, when even TRIPLEX, a code word that refers to an exceptionally sensitive British intelligence source in wartime London, could not deliver information about Moscow's decision-making. Starting from 1943 and during the initial period of the cold war, the VENONA Project was an important source of information on Soviet intelligence-gathering activity, especially when it was concluded that 'the Soviet Union should be "the first charge on our intelligence resources" in terms of its war-making capacity and warlike intentions',[5] but what information do we have about the processes behind the Kremlin walls? At the same time, as late as 1949, a production conference in the London SIS headquarters noted the continuing ban on 'clandestine operations of any kind on Moscow'. For a period of time the head of the Moscow SIS station was not allowed to do any secret work, and perhaps the lack of literature shows the lack of actual intelligence, illustrating 'the immense difficulty faced by any Western intelligence organization seeking to penetrate the Soviet Union'[6] during Stalin's reign.

While there are some excellent histories of the Soviet foreign intelligence operations and of the Spanish Civil War, it is difficult to think of any that devotes as much as a sentence to the volume and quality of SIGINT generated by the NKVD and Razvedupr (the future GRU) in the interwar period.[7] At the same time, this research confirms previously released information that the Red Army alone sent 101 wireless operators and signal intelligence

464 THE ORLOV LEGACY

specialists and 54 code clerks to Spain.[8] As recently as 1982, Professor Preston wrote, 'In 1968, Ricardo de la Cierva, the official historian of the Franco regime, produced a virtually unusable bibliography of the Spanish Civil War. Despite its shameful errors and omissions, the bibliography was nevertheless remarkable for listing nearly 15,000 titles [...] In the intervening fourteen years, the flow of books on the subject has continued unabated.'[9] Because the interest remains, by now the number of titles has probably tripled. But how many of those works devote a word to the signal intelligence or other secret Soviet operations? In several Western studies of Soviet foreign policy, the KGB is barely mentioned. Professor Andrew notes that 'the bibliography of a recent academic history of Soviet foreign relations from 1917 to 1991 (published in 1998), praised by a British authority on the subject as "easily the best general history of Soviet foreign policy", contains—apart from a biography of Beria—not a single work on Soviet intelligence among more that 120 titles'.[10] One may add that a recently published volume of another British authority on the Russian history in the chapter entitled 'Soviet Agents' gives not a single name of a Soviet agent.

Though such aberrations by leading historians are due partly to the overclassification of intelligence archives (especially in Russia under Putin), they derive at root from what psychologists call 'cognitive dissonance'—the difficulty we all have sometimes in grasping new concepts that disturb our existing view of the world.[11]

Even when books are written by Western intelligence professionals and are entirely devoted to the KGB and its predecessors, one may find passages like:

Will espionage targeted against the former Soviet empire be considered necessary in the future? What was once secret in the old Communist monolith is openly discussed, travel abroad is free, and discussion is relatively unrestricted. The president of Russia is now elected, Russian troops have been evacuated from Eastern Europe, and nuclear weapons previously deployed in Belarus, Kazakhstan and Ukraine have been returned to Russia. It is tempting to conclude that the threat posed by Russia to the United States and its European allies has changed in character so much as to make espionage an anomaly.[12]

A new generation of academics, less disoriented than most of their predecessors by the influence of intelligence and its use (or abuse) by policy-makers, should concentrate more effort on intelligence studies.[13] In the words of

Winston Churchill: 'The further backwards you look, the further forward you can see.'

Another example of possible interest for historians is the work of 'illegals'—officers and agents of various nationalities trained by Soviet intelligence agencies and sent abroad to operate under cover. The most recent examples are eleven Russian 'illegals' unmasked in the USA in June 2010 and the 'Anschlag' couple apprehended in Germany in October 2011. Some of the Soviet 'illegals' are mentioned in this work, but many, pertinent to the period it covers, remain in the shadow. A group of identified and unidentified Soviet 'illegals' of different nationalities on assignments from both the NKVD and RU operated in Spain during the war. With only a few exceptions, their activities remain largely unknown. Although it seems certain that Soviet military intelligence was primarily interested in Franco's troops as well as German and Italian units, their weapons, technology, and battle tactics, research work on the 'illegals' and their operations in any period of Soviet and post-Soviet history is a fascinating subject still awaiting exploration.

Among other related topics that remain insufficiently studied are the fates of the Spaniards, recruited by Soviet intelligence during or shortly after the civil war who either perished in Stalin's Gulag camps or fought on the front and operated behind the enemy lines within various guerrilla formations— or were sent abroad as undercover operators ('illegals'). And, while the numbers are not large, they are sufficient to merit a separate book. There have been one or two attempts to write such histories by various writers and scholars, but these do not provide a historian of the Spanish Civil War with reliable material. The same concerns Spanish and international guerrillas trained by Soviet advisers. The guerrilla warfare in Spain during the civil war is insufficiently studied, in spite of several publications.[14]

Many of the Soviet intelligence officers, diplomats, military commanders, and interpreters named in this book were then arrested and shot in the Soviet Union. One of Stalin's closest comrades-in-arms, Vyacheslav Molotov, tried to explain those mass executions several decades later.

Nineteen thirty-seven was necessary. If you consider that after the revolution we were slashing left and right, and we were victorious, but enemies of different sorts remained, and in the face of impending danger of fascist aggression they might unite. We owe the fact that we did not have a fifth column during the war to '37. After all, even among Bolsheviks there were those who were fine and loyal when everything was going well, when the country and party were not threatened with danger. But if something started, they would falter and switch sides. I think a lot of the military who were repressed in '37 should not have been rehabilitated. [. . .] These people probably were not spies, but they had ties to [foreign?] intelligence services, and, most importantly, you could not count on them at a time of crisis.[15]

However, if one studies this large group, which included heroes of the Soviet Union, chiefs of military intelligence, ranking NKVD officers, ambassadors and consuls, famous journalists and writers, repressions against them can hardly be explained by Stalin's paranoia, fear, and the lack of trust. Remarkably, among the Soviet personnel who served in Spain, there was not a single known defection with the exception of Orlov, the NKVD chief, who deserted. With such devotion, what was the reason for annihilating so many people?

One of the possible answers is that, after a few months in the West, Soviet people became different. In Britain, France, and Holland, and even in Spain, in spite of the civil war, they saw a bourgeois democratic parliamentary regime with many political parties and absolute freedom of speech. This made them potentially dangerous to the Stalinist regime. This is especially true about the Spanish Civil War. Everybody who was in Spain would never forget it. Some Soviet veterans are still living on these memories.

Even those who had never been there did not remain aloof from the conflict. Thanks in large part to the foreign correspondents and documentary film-makers, millions of people who knew little about Spain came to feel in their hearts that the Spanish Republic's struggle for survival was somehow their struggle. But the governments of Britain, France, and the United States chose to ignore the fact that Hitler and Mussolini were sending unstinting help to the rebels, as both felt that the issue of the Spanish Civil War would decide the ultimate success of their own schemes for the world order. Despite the fact that it was normal practice under international law to permit an established friendly government to purchase arms and supplies, Western powers denied this right to the Spanish Republic. Neither Anglo-French non-intervention nor the American 'moral' embargo and the subsequent extension of the 1935 Neutrality Act to encompass Spain (the Act related only to international wars and did not force the US government to invoke an embargo in a civil war) was neutral in its consequences. As a result, they limited the Republic's capacity to defend itself and threw it into the arms of the Soviet Union.[16]

Not only did the democracies refuse to assist and defend a friendly European state with a legally elected government, but they used the Spanish situation as a proving ground to test their military doctrines and make estimates in the interests of their armed forces, correcting their strategies, making adjustments to field service regulations and war plans. In London, the intelligence reports from Spain were of interest to the Admiralty, the Director of Naval Intelligence, and Air Staff Intelligence and were much sought after by the Home Office and its Air Raid Precautions Committee.[17] Wing Commander C. E. H. Medhurst, the RAF representative on the Joint Intelligence Committee, asked the Foreign Office in November 1936 to help the RAF in its information-gathering. He declared that the experience in Spain represented the first time since 1918 that such material was available. Medhurst also explained to the Foreign Office that Spain was 'a laboratory for the study of air warfare' and modified the initial survey to include 'questions concentrating on information regarding attacks on railways, roads, gas, power, water facilities, the penetration of buildings and type of buildings hit, effects of incendiaries, flares and gas bombs'.[18] He asked the Western Department of the Foreign Office to distribute the secret questionnaire to George Ogilvie-Forbes, the British chargé d'affaires in Madrid.[19]

At the same time, the Commander-in-Chief of the Home Fleet, Sir Roger Backhouse, believed that, if the Spanish government won the war, the result would be catastrophic. He reported in January 1937:

The adoption of an entirely neutral attitude to both sides, which has been our policy up to date, becomes, I submit, open to criticism should the ultimate end of the war lead to a Communistic State. The alternative, brought about by a military revolt, may be unattractive to our views, but it may be far safer to Europe, and better for Spain. Also, it seems that we are much more likely to remain friendly with Germany and Italy by taking a more sympathetic attitude to their point of view. Another consideration is that, if the Civil War ends in Communism or Anarchy, all British interests are likely to be lost, as they were in Russia, whereas, if the Insurgents win, there is hope of law and order being established and of trade being revived.[20]

In Washington, the US War Department had established a special group within G2 Military Intelligence Division to collate and assess all intelligence regarding Spain. One such confidential report regarding Russian volunteers was received by the US Military Attaché from the British Air Attaché in Paris. Among other things, the report stated that 'by now [22 March 1938] most Red Army personnel had left Spain', stressing that 'the Republicans "were glad they were gone" because they resented foreigners directing their war'.[21] In the French Perpignan, French intelligence set up an observation post that reported to the Army and Navy staff about all activities of the Soviet personnel still in Spain in March 1939.[22]

From the early days of the Soviet intervention, the activities of Soviet advisers were regulated by Stalin's directive as follows from letter No. 3780/ L dated 9 December 1936 and signed by Maxim Litvinov, People's Commissar of Foreign Affairs. The letter was addressed to Ambassador Rosenberg and Chief Military Adviser Berzin:

Your duty is to explain to our military representatives that they should in no way establish themselves as substitute for the Spaniards. They must behave in such a way that the Spanish General Staff, commanders of the units, etc., do not feel that problems are solved behind their backs. As a general rule, the advices of military–operational or organizational nature should first of all be given to the person who is directly in charge (but not to his superior), while any such advice must be well grounded and its expediency patiently explained. You should also explain to our people that, when they fail to get their recommendation accepted, they must not turn to the politically harmful method of giving orders and shouting commands insisting on having it their own way. Comrades Rosenberg and Grishin [Berzin] must strive for getting this order carried out. If one of our representatives does not fulfil the instruction and continues using command methods, he should be recalled.[23]

From all available documents, one may conclude that the Republican government was grateful to the Soviet advisers for their help and that their contribution to the struggle with the Fascist powers and rebel forces was greatly appreciated.

All Soviet advisers came to Spain only after Stalin had decided to intervene. 'Special reports' received by Soviet intelligence agencies from their stations abroad and forwarded to Stalin, only a portion of which have been discussed in the preceding chapters, demonstrate that, at least starting from 1935, the Soviet leader had been sufficiently well-informed about the international situation and the position of Western governments and their intelligence services, as well as about their views of how this situation should develop. It now seems likely that he was also informed about the intentions of the reactionary Spanish generals. Soviet intelligence had well-placed sources, mentioned in this work, who delivered high-grade intelligence from Germany, Italy, France, Portugal, and the United States, with a large volume of secret political information coming from Donald Maclean in the Foreign Office, the FO cipher clerks, and the British Embassy in Rome. There is little doubt that Stalin knew much more than previously thought, but during the first weeks of war was reluctant to intervene, owing to a number of factors.

These factors were political, technological, and financial. At the time, the Soviet Union did not have sufficient hard-currency resources to allow itself a widescale intervention, with substantial extra costs arising out of the fact that Spain was a faraway destination. There were also serious problems with Soviet technological development. When compared with their Western counterparts, the Soviets lagged behind in the production of tinplate and galvanized steel. This, in turn, was much related to the backwardness in rolling technology that characterized the entire Soviet steelmaking industry.[24] These were dangerous shortcomings, because the whole Soviet industry was in essence a war industry. Using new archival documentation, the experts now speak about the Soviet economic crisis of 1936–40. Politically, Stalin's decisions were constrained by his search for Western allies against Hitler.[25] Regarding Spain, it was only after the Fascist powers had decided to intervene at the end of July 1936, that Stalin began to contemplate his own moves in response to the Republican appeal for help. But even before any final decision was taken, Soviet intelligence services sent their officers and agents to the Iberian Peninsula. In order to move further, Stalin needed a lot of first-hand information. The MASK traffic, encrypted wireless exchange between Moscow and numerous Comintern representatives abroad, could not substitute professional intelligence assessments. Even they were not enough for Stalin, who realized the importance of the Spanish events in the changing international situation. That is why, apart from intelligence officers and undercover operators, experienced diplomats, foreign trade officials, journalists, and film-makers were in Madrid even sooner than the Red Army advisers. They were Stalin's agents-in-place, his eyes and ears in Spain and elsewhere.

Perhaps the most striking point to emerge from this research is the quantity of Soviet intelligence personnel in Spain. Although it is true that all four Soviet intelligence agencies—the NKVD, RU, Naval Intelligence and the Comintern/OMS—sent their representatives, at any given period their presence in Spain was minimal. As this work demonstrates, from the autumn of 1936 to approximately the same period of 1938 there were about ten NKVD officers in Spain. Five of them—Nikolsky/Orlov,

Belkin/Belyaev, Syroezhkin/Pancho, Eitingon/Kotov, and Vasilevsky/
Grebetsky—were on a permanent assignment, while others came on a
tour of duty of several months to one year. There were also three NKVD
'illegals': Fortus, Grigulevich, and Tacke; the last two left in July 1937 and
Maria Fortus in September 1938. These figures represent compelling evidence that the so-called overall presence of the NKVD in Spain is a myth.

    Another important point to emerge from this book is that the RU had
many more personnel in Spain than the NKVD. In addition to the fully
staffed RU station at the Soviet Embassy, and at least three officers in the
consulates in Barcelona (Ivan Kuzmin) and Bilbao (Ivan Vinarov and Kirill
Janson), and one at the trade delegation in Madrid (Grigory Grechnev),
there were also intelligence officers at the headquarters of the Chief Military
Adviser, at the General Staff of the Spanish People's Army, and on every
front, at the Base of the International Brigades in Albacete plus Service 'A'
officers assigned to various guerrilla units. One officer of the intelligence
directorate of the Soviet Navy (Leonid Bekrenev) served at the Spanish
Armada Naval headquarters. The Red Army Intelligence Directorate also
had a group of illegals controlled by experienced senior officers (one of
whom was Major, later Colonel Johann Hermann). However, in spite of
this seemingly impressive contingent, their tour of duty in Spain was rarely
more than one year, and the staff was rotated on a regular basis. The main
task of the RU personnel was to act as intelligence advisers supporting
combat operations, help in setting up Republican military intelligence and
counter-intelligence services, and to collect intelligence about German and
Italian capabilities, their arms, ammunition, and tactics. The RU officers
assigned as advisers to different fronts were also encouraged to report
directly to Moscow assessing the military–political situation in their areas
of operation. All these military advisers, as well as those from the Navy
intelligence, could not and did not interfere with the internal affairs of the
Spanish Republic. The only known and documented case is an attempt to
place Gustavo Durán, a Communist, as chief of the SIM in Madrid—he was
dismissed after only a few weeks.

    For obvious reasons, the work of both the RU and NKVD 'illegals' is
advertised least of all. The tradition of using 'illegals' goes back to the
Bolshevik times.[26] Their identities and operations are so secret that only a
few most trusted officers of the Illegals Directorate in Moscow Centre
know them. This work, for the first time, not only identifies three
NKVD and a number of the RU 'illegals' who operated in Spain, but also

provides a detailed account of the role played by one of them in the operation against the POUM. This 'illegal', Iosif Grigulevich, previously known to the experts only as 'José Ocampo' and ARTUR, whom even the VENONA analysts failed to identify, played a sinister role in the Spanish events. He was in charge of one of the Special Brigades in Madrid, a police unit that was involved in arrests, tortures, and murders. It played a direct part in the abduction and subsequent murder of Andreu Nin, the POUM leader. That Iosif Grigulevich was one of the active participants in this operation is now fully documented. Since Grigulevich's name as a Soviet 'illegal' was first mentioned in a 1992 Russian publication,[27] he became a true KGB role model, with many articles and books devoted to his heroic deeds. However, his work as a diplomat and then ambassador of Costa Rica in Rome and Belgrade, based on the diplomatic documents of the Costa Rican Foreign Ministry exclusively provided to this author, is presented in this work for the first time.

Another, much more important, although less secretive, figure receives an entirely new interpretation as a result of this research. The role played by Major of State Security Lev Nikolsky, alias 'Alexander Orlov', in interwar operations of the NKVD has until now remained obscure. Some books present him as an NKVD general, whom Stalin personally sent to Spain to help the Republican government in their struggle against Fascism. Others paint Orlov as the chief organizer of mass arrests, persecutions, and shootings of the Trotskyists. Orlov himself stated many times that in Spain he was a modest political attaché who nevertheless advised the Prime Minister and Minister of National Defence on the most important issues of national security and guerrilla warfare. He also claimed that 'he was frequently consulted personally by Stalin [sic] on actual operations during 1936'[28] and received personal orders from him to transport the Spanish gold to Russia. In reality, Orlov/Nikolsky was a mediocre intelligence officer, who operated in Europe in the 1930s as an 'illegal', twice interrupted his assignments (in Paris and London) because he was unable to carry them out, for which he was finally transferred from the foreign to the transport department and demoted to assistant chief.[29] Nikolsky became 'Orlov' in September 1936, when the NKVD leadership decided to send him to Spain. Until the February–March 1937 Plenum in Moscow, when Stalin named the Trotskyists the worst enemies of the people, wreckers, saboteurs, spies, terrorists, and murderers responsible for all problems in the USSR, Orlov served as a liaison to the Republican Interior Ministry, unsuccessfully trying to help the

PCE in setting up its own intelligence and security apparatus. Such a service, created with the help of the Soviet advisers in the 1920s, effectively operated as a secret arm of the KPD. In Spain, its members were very active in both the International Brigades and the Republican special services. Before spring 1937, Orlov also tried to 'advise' the DGS, which he partially managed to penetrate by placing Grigulevich in charge of one of its Special Brigades. From the deposition of Tomás Duran Gonzalez given to the Causa General prosecutors, it follows that another 'illegal', Maria Fortus, was planted into the Grupo de Investigación in Barcelona. Unfortunately, nothing is known about the activities in Spain of the third 'illegal', Erich Tacke.[30] However, this work establishes for the first time that he also took part in the operation against Nin.

The abduction and murder of the POUM leader was not the only crime the NKVD committed in Spain. However, in the course of this research, it became clear that there were no mass repressions, as in Russia, that Orlov and his subordinates concentrated their efforts on the literniks, foreign Trotskyists whose fate was sealed in Moscow, and that Nin was almost certainly one of the very few Spaniards (two others were possibly José Robles and Alfredo Martínez, general secretary of the Catalonian Libertarian Youth, both of whom disappeared) who became their victims. No one is going to acquit the NKVD of their crimes, but this work makes it clear that in many accounts the number of victims was greatly exaggerated. As a consequence of the May Days in Barcelona, and subsequently the death of Nin and the arrest of other POUM activists, the hostility between the Communists and the forces of revolution became bitter and violent. It would be further intensified by the determination of the Soviet representatives to emulate the Moscow show trials.[31] But the Republican authorities ensured that show trials were never staged in Spain.

The Trotskyists in Russia and abroad were not the only targets. Writers, journalists, Red Army officers, technical advisers—all were being watched and the reports sent to Moscow. The remarkable degree of control was achieved by using informers, usually among interpreters and the technical staff, anonymous volunteers, and the OMS agents who eagerly collaborated with both the NKVD and RU. All these reports were filed, indexed, and kept until further notice. In many cases they were used during preliminary investigations as incriminating material. We now know that 'operational documents' or 'signals'—a euphemism for denunciation letters and other negative reports—from Spain were used in cases of such prominent figures as Berzin, Gorev, and Koltsov, all arrested about the same time. From the KGB documents quoted in the preceding chapters, one may deduct that sometimes Orlov compiled such reports personally—in his correspondence from Valencia, for example, he critically mentions Berzin and Gorev, and from Barcelona he mentions Świerczewski. Although in his memoirs Orlov calls Koltsov his friend, in the latter's investigation file one finds a lot of 'signals' received from 'confidential sources' close to Koltsov in Spain, so Marty was not the only one who reported on the writer.

In several cases, based on reports, letters, personal characteristics, and other useful information received from its agents and informants, the Centre decided to start cultivation of individuals that figure in these documents. Thus, África de las Heras (PATRIA) and several other Spanish women were recruited in Spain, while two Americans—Ernest Hemingway (ARGO) and Morris Cohen (VOLUNTEER)—became agents in the USA. The journalist, and later historian, Burnett Bolloten was also mentioned as 'our source' in the NKVD correspondence, and, according to Paul Preston, who discussed this problem with Bolloten, the NKVD approached him in Mexico. One of the British volunteers, Charles Oliver Green, who agreed to collaborate with the NKVD, was reactivated by the RU in Britain, while a big group of the former Spanish fighters, including the guerrilla commander Domingo Ungría and Captain Peregrin Pérez Galarza, became commissioned officers of the Red Army Intelligence Directorate in Moscow.[32] When German troops invaded the Soviet Union, Spanish veterans living there volunteered to form a Spanish Battalion of the NKVD Special Brigade (OMSBON).

Pavel Sudoplatov was the NKVD chief of foreign intelligence and later of its 'special operations' who personally knew many of those recruits. It was also Sudoplatov who, following Stalin's personal orders, sent Ramón and Caridad Mercader to Mexico to assassinate Trotsky in 1940. Sudoplatov wrote in his memoirs: 'The Spanish Republicans lost, but Stalin's men and women won.'[33] It is difficult to agree with the old general. The Republican experiment inspired many Spaniards and foreigners. Despite shortages, rationing, and privations of all kinds, the sense that the Republic was worth fighting for survived well into 1938.[34] One may add that the sense that the Republic was worth fighting for survived well into our time. There are many people who continue to fight for Republican Spain while the war goes on in books, lecture halls, and Internet forums.

And what about Stalin's men and women, mentioned by Sudoplatov? Not too many of them survived. The war in Spain coincided with the Great

Terror campaign in the Soviet Union, the most ruthless political repression in its whole post-revolutionary history. It was Stalin's politics that did a lot of harm to the whole Europe and to Russia itself. The Western powers chose to support Franco, because they were afraid of the 'red menace'. It was also one of the reasons why Hitler and Mussolini decided to intervene. Russian assistance to the Republic brought many complications. Stalin's witch-hunt against Trotskyists ended the lives of many people.

But did secret intelligence help Stalin 'to reveal the cards in his adversary's hands'?[35] Less than five months after the end of the Spanish Civil War, Molotov and Ribbentrop signed the Nazi–Soviet Pact in Moscow, rendering war inevitable. Exchanging toasts with Ribbentrop, Stalin told him: 'I can guarantee, on my word of honour, that the Soviet Union will not betray its partner.'[36] They traded further toasts, with Stalin proposing a toast to Hitler's health and the Nazi proposing a toast to Stalin. When Hitler attacked Russia in June 1941, Stalin was unprepared although forewarned. Three years later, in 1944, the Assistant Secretary of State, Sumner Welles, recognized that, 'of all our blind isolationist policies, the most disastrous was our attitude on the Spanish Civil War', and, 'in the long history of the foreign policy of the Roosevelt Administration, there has been, I think, no more cardinal error than the policy adopted during the civil war in Spain'. Roosevelt was a statesman and at least he felt regret.[37] For him and other Western allies with the means to assess intelligence and the judgement to use it wisely, revelation of the cards in Hitler's hand helped shorten the Second World War.[38] Stalin was a policy-maker but not a statesman. For him intelligence played a subordinate role. For the Soviet dictator, the most important thing was his own intuition. There is no record of Stalin ever expressing regret over the defeat of the Spanish Republic, where the first battle with Fascism was lost.

The Orlovs, posing as 'Alexander L. Berg' and 'Marie Berg', spent the war in America, where he was enrolled on the Business Administration course at Dyke College, Cleveland, Ohio, from which he graduated on 15 June 1945.[39] During all those years the FBI frantically searched for these 'two unidentified Russian aliens', as the Orlovs were often referred to in FBI reports.[40] The irony of the situation was that exactly at that time, Dyke College and the Cleveland Division of the FBI were both located in the Standard Building on 1370 Ontario Street and St Clair Avenue. The college was on the third floor and the FBI office on the ninth. As the war saw the division expand in resources and responsibilities, as their official site explains, 'Cleveland personnel provided extensive security checks, tracked rumours of enemy agents, investigated sabotage matters, and kept up with a wide variety of other matters'.[41] But they never paid any attention to the mature student who had long figured on the FBI's most wanted list and who rode the elevators with them every day.

Two decades after Orlov's death and five years after the collapse of the Soviet Union, in 1996, the SVR, a successor of the KGB's foreign intelligence directorate, issued a CD-ROM in both Russian and English, with the title *Russian Foreign Intelligence: VChK [Cheka]-KGB-SVR*, which claimed to give 'for the first time . . . a professional view on the history and development of one of the most powerful secret services in the world'.[42] The aim was to emphasize the direct link between the Soviet KGB and its three present-day successors: SVR, FSB, and FSO (Federalnaya Sluzhba Okhrany (Federal Protective Service)). The photo of the monumental statue of Felix Dzierżyński removed from the square named after him (and subsequently renamed the Lubyanka Square) decorates the cover of the CD-ROM. But at least the Cheka founder known in Russia as the 'Iron Felix' is dead and buried and his ghost hardly ever visits even the memorial complex in his native Belarus dedicated to him.

Unlike his former Cheka boss, Orlov had never been laid to rest following his death in April 1973. May be that explains the mystery of why books and articles written by him and about him continue to come out.

For the lack of peace Orlov should be grateful to his friend, former FBI Special Agent Edward Gazur, a first-generation American whose family emigrated from Austria, where Orlov's family spent so much time. Gazur writes:

At the time Orlov was cremated, I asked Tommy Corrigan to separate and box a small portion of Orlov's ashes from the bulk of ashes that were in the process of being prepared for shipment to Mount Auburn Cemetery. In turn, I gave the small box of ashes to my colleague, who agreed to make the shipping arrangements to the USSR and final burial.[43]

Gazur's secret plan was to bury Orlov's ashes not far from the Kremlin wall in Moscow, where, in his view, Orlov truly belonged. Fortunately, others in the US intelligence community were much more sombre minded.

After Orlov's death, the CIA headquarters in Langley sent Paul Hartman to Cleveland to catalogue the contents of Orlov's apartment and close it up. Orlov's hats, his and Maria's fountain pens, plus a small box containing part

of his cremated remains were turned over to the counter-intelligence staff
deputy chief who had been handling the interviews with Orlov for about a
decade and whose name was Raymond Rocca, Angleton's deputy.When
this imposing man, who looked more like a theatre actor than a high-
ranking CIA officer, passed away, his son Gordon inherited the ashes and a
few other items. Gordon later explained that he did not really know what to
do with them until H. Keith Melton—a famous collector of spy parapher-
nalia and one of the founders of the International Spy Museum—came
along and asked to make them part of his private collection.[44] So instead of
the Gorky Park, as Gazur wanted, Orlov's ashes landed in Florida in a glass-
sided cabinet.

   Orlov's thick Parker pen is still in the Rocca family, reminding them
about a larger-than-life figure who had been much too lucky for far too
long. The family story goes that it is the same pen Orlov used to write a
personal letter to Stalin.

   Though the RIS would never bring itself to accept it, its legend of the
master spy 'Alexander Mikhailovich Orlov' crumbled never to be revived.
In the new history of MI5, this 'recruiter of the Cambridge Five' is not even
mentioned.

   In April 2012, a spokesman for the Moscow city government confirmed
to the Agence France-Press (AFP) that the statue of the feared 'Iron Felix'
was on a list of cultural objects designated for restoration.[45] 'I have raised a
monument more permanent than bronze...'[46] Plans are to designate this
15-ton iron monument as an object of cultural heritage. In the words of
Christopher Andrew, 'nothing better illustrates the continuity between the
Soviet and Russian foreign intelligence services than the attempt by the SVR
to reclaim its KGB past'.[47] In the twenty-first century, the future of 'one of
the most powerful secret services in the world' will be difficult to predict.

Dr Arnold Deutsch

Every author knows how notoriously hard it is to ensure accuracy, truth, and objectivity in writing about any aspect of history, but nowhere is it harder than in the field of secret intelligence and counter-intelligence. There the whole purpose of governments is not to document but to hide the facts, and there, too, witnesses are unlikely to know the full truth underlying even the events in which they have personally participated. As a result, the interpretation of these secret doings can quickly coagulate into false patterns. Writers deprived of access to fresh facts and original documents tend to copy what others have written, though that may be largely guesswork, misinformation, and speculation.[1] Unfortunately, even authors dealing with genuine documentary material sometimes allow inaccuracies, misinterpretations, and false judgements to creep into their texts. This is what exactly happened with the biography of Dr Arnold Deutsch, one of the so-called Great 'Illegals' of the Soviet intelligence history.

Unlike Orlov, Deutsch was the real recruiter and first runner of the Cambridge and Oxford spy rings. He was also a classic example of an 'illegal', because he was always engaged in undercover work, disguising his true affiliation, although he operated under his own name—that is, when he was dealing with authorities. Deutsch's recruits knew him only as 'Otto' or 'Stefan'. He operated independently from Soviet diplomatic and trade missions and his immunity from arrest was not guaranteed by a diplomatic passport, which is the principal difference between 'legal' and 'illegal' operators. His full name, even if we apply the Eastern Slavic naming custom of using a patronymic, was Arnold Joachimovich (not 'Genrikhovich') Deutsch. From December 1928 to January 1932 Deutsch worked for the Comintern OMS in Vienna, where he was identified by the Austrian police as an OGPU agent and had to flee to Moscow. His wife was Josefine (and not 'Fini Pavlovna', as some authors claim), born Rubel, and she indeed undertook training as a wireless operator at the KUNMZ, which is the Russian acronym for the Communist University for the National Minorities of the West. Deutsch had never been an NKVD officer, but was a civil employee of the Service. Finally, among the intelligence officers with whom he used to work, Karin's name was Fyodor, not 'A.F.'. 'O. G. Müller', or, to be more precise, Miller, was Georg Killich, a former courier of the Soviet Embassy in Vienna and later one of INO's passport forgers. 'R. Gurt', mentioned in several accounts, seems to be nothing other than an erroneous transliteration from Russian of 'Paul Hardt', which was one of the aliases Theodor Maly used in London.

Arnold Deutsch was born in Vienna, Austria, on 21 May 1904 to the family of Joachim and Katalin (née Eisler) Deutsch, both Austrian Jews of Slovak origin. From 1910 to 1915 he attended primary school and from 1915 to 1923 a Realgymnasium[2] at No. 2c Kleine Sperlgasse in the II (Orthodox Jewish) District of Vienna where he lived. The school is still there. On 23 June 1923 Deutsch successfully passed his exams, which enabled him to apply to the University of Vienna in the autumn of the same year. He was accepted to the Faculty of Philosophy's Department of Chemistry and Physics, where his tutor was Professor Dr D. Späth.[3]

In 1922 Deutsch joined the Austrian Communist Youth organization, where he worked directly under Richard Schüller and indirectly under Johann Koplenig, general secretary of the KPÖ. Later Deutsch also worked in the Austrian section of Münzenberg's MOPR. In December 1928 both Schüller and Koplenig recommended him to the OGPU.[4]

In his 1938 biography written for the NKVD, Deutsch named Koplenig, a well-known party functionary and a Soviet collaborator, but used Schüller's cover name KONRAD instead of his real name. Richard Hugo Schüller, a leader of the Austrian Komsomol, had been known to MI5 since April 1927 when he was reported to have attended secret meetings in Britain. In 1928 he was arrested in Paris on suspicion of being a Soviet agent and later deported.[5] Unlike Schüller, Deutsch had never been suspected in England and never arrested or detained, although in Nazi Germany he was once caught by the Gestapo escaping, almost literally, by the skin of his teeth.

All Austrian comrades with whom Deutsch worked in Vienna in the late 1920s and whom he named in his NKVD biography—Koplenig, Schüller, Siegfrid Fürnberg, Friedrich Hexmann, and ten or twenty selected others—later lived in comfort in the Hotel Lux on Gorky Street in Moscow,[6] while other members of the 1,000-strong Austrian Schutzbund contingent of immigrants in the USSR shared communal flats in the workers' districts of many Russian provincial towns.

In spring 1928 Deutsch completed his doctorate thesis 'Über Silber- und Quicksilbersalze des Amidobenzothiazols, sowie eine neue Methode zur quantitativen Silberbestimmung' ('On Silver and Mercury Salts of Amidobenzothiazols and a New Method of Quantative Silver Analysis'), accepted on 18 May 1928 with a favourable resolution 'die Arbeit ist immerhin genügend zur Zulassung zu den strengen Prüfungen'.[7] That meant that his dissertation was considered submitted and after about a month he was scheduled to defend it in front of a jury.

On 19 July 1928, less than five years after entering Vienna University and shortly after his twenty-fourth birthday, Deutsch was awarded the degree of Doctor of Philosophy with distinction.[8] His work was published as a separate brochure and can still be ordered at the Vienna University library under the Signatur D-1197.

Throughout his time at Vienna University, Deutsch described himself in his curriculum vitae as Jewish both by religion (*mosaisch*) and by ethnic origin (*jüdisch*). His intellectual progression from Orthodox Judaism to Marxist materialism cannot be traced with certainty. But, as Christopher Andrew notes in his earlier history of

Soviet intelligence operations, 'Deutsch's attraction to Schlick's vision of a world in which joy would replace suffering seems to have been accompanied, and in the end overtaken, by his growing commitment to the Communist International's vision of a new world order that would free mankind from exploitation and alienation'.[9] In the late 1920s, parallel to his underground liaison and courier work for the OMS in Vienna, Deutsch joined the 'sex-pol' (sexual politics) movement founded by the Viennese Jewish psychologist Wilhelm Reich, which ran clinics designed to bring birth control and counsel on sexual problems to workers and their wives. Deutsch also founded Münster Verlag, a small publishing house, located at 29 Obere Donaustrasse (also in II District where he lived) that published Reich's work and other 'sex-pol' literature.[10] When the Nazis came to power in Germany, Dr Reich left immediately for Vienna, then moved to Scandinavia, travelling to the United States in 1939. In his works he tried to reconcile Marxism and psychoanalysis and promoted open relationships outside marriage. Deutsch's involvement in the 'sex-pol' movement and his role in publishing some of Reich's work in Vienna brought his small publishing house to the attention of the 'anti-pornography' section of the Austrian police,[11] but he himself figured in the police files as a Communist agent.

In his NKVD biography Deutsch noted that in October 1931, 'because of the bad work of some of the members of our apparatus, we were discovered'.[12] This was not about his 'sex-pol' activity but a result of his underground work for Moscow. Indeed, in May 1932, exchanging information on 'subversive elements' with the Royal Yugoslav police, the Austrian authorities mentioned Deutsch's name among other OGPU agents in Vienna, together with the 'legal' resident 'Igor Vorobyov' (real name Igor Lebedinsky).[13] Unbeknownst to Deutsch, his future had been decided.

In January 1932 Dr Deutsch was summoned to Moscow. He arrived there with his wife, Josefine, whom he had married on 12 March 1929;[14] he called her both 'Fini' and 'Sylvia' in his writings.

Although in Moscow he came into conflict over his work in Vienna with Alexander Abramov-Mirov,[15] an experienced intelligence officer and at the time the OMS chief, and was even threatened to be placed in a factory job, Deutsch was finally invited to join the OGPU thanks to some friendly help from Killich, who was already working in its foreign department. Killich and Deutsch had known each other in Vienna where Killich worked at the Soviet legation.

In the INO Deutsch was recommended for work abroad, and in January 1933 went to Paris to help Karin (codenamed JACK), one of the 'illegal' residents.

Until October 1933 Deutsch operated in Paris very successfully, assisting Karin in every way. There he seems to have made his first recruitments. Deutsch later wrote: 'I invited comrade Luxy, the adopted daughter of the Hungarian revolutionary writer A. Gabor and the daughter of the literary translator Olga Galperina, to join in our work. Both are now in Moscow.'[16] Andor Gábor was a member of the Béla Kun revolutionary government in 1919. After its failure he emigrated to Vienna, from where, in 1924, he made a number of trips to Paris and northern France for the Communist Party. These political activities led to his banishment from Austria. Gábor moved to Berlin and started working for the *Rote Fahne* and also as a Berlin correspondent of *Ogonyok* and *Pravda*. In 1934 he joined his family in Moscow. His wife, also known as Olga Halpern-Gábor (born in 1886), a member of the KPD, came to Moscow via Czechoslovakia in 1933, as soon as the Nazis had seized power in Germany. In 1945 she moved with her husband to Budapest.[17] In July 1950, among several other foreign writers, they were both guests of the East German President Wilhelm Pieck. The fate of 'comrade Luxy', their daughter, is not known, but for a certain period in 1935 she worked for Deutsch in London. The only daughter of Andor and Olga was named Magda Gábor. She died in 1967.

'In February 1934 I went to London alone,' Deutsch recalled in his NKVD biography, 'where I recruited Edith [Edith Tudor-Hart], whom I had already known in Vienna.'[18] This seems to be another slip of memory. Edith, born in Vienna in 1908 and first noted by the Security Service in London in January 1930,[19] was not formally recruited until much later (see Appendix II). It is true, however, that in 1934 she actively assisted Deutsch in finding new recruits for his spy networks.

Judging by the documents in several Security Service files,[20] she was very active in London among the Communists and without doubt talent-spotted Philby, as Edith was a friend of Philby's first wife Alice, known to everybody as Litzi. Philby described (as usual, misleadingly) his first contact with Deutsch in the written confession obtained in 1963 in Beirut by a friendly SIS officer Nicholas Elliott,[21]

Litzi came home one evening [Philby wrote] and told me that she had arranged for me to meet a 'man of decisive importance'. I questioned her about it but she would give me no details. The rendezvous took place in Regent's Park. The man described himself as Otto. I discovered much later from a photograph in MI5 files that the name he went by was Arnold Deutsch.[22]

However, Philby was writing this 'confession' tongue in cheek because he was trying to conceal the identity of an important agent who was still living in Britain (Edith Tudor-Hart, who died in 1973). Litzi, his first wife—like Phily she was married several times—repeatedly stated that it was not she, as many authors suggested, but her good friend Edith who introduced her former husband to the Soviet spymaster in London.[23] And Deutsch seems to have been a true spymaster.

As mentioned above, Philby returned to England in May 1934, three months after Deutsch's arrival in London. In June, he was cultivated by Deutsch, who at that time worked as Reif's assistant, to be finally recruited in December. Reif, the 'illegal' resident, reported the results of the first meeting:

In future, Philby will be called SYNOK. Through Edith who is known to you, who had worked for some time under ZIGMUND [possibly Lebedinsky] in Vienna, we have established that the former Austrian [Communist] party member [Litzi], who had been recommended to Edith by our former Vienna comrades, has arrived in Britain from Vienna, together with her husband, an Englishman. He is also known to Arnold [Deutsch]. Edith has checked their credentials and has received recommendations from her Vienna friends. I have decided to recruit the fellow without delay—not for 'the organization' [Soviet intelligence], it is too early for that, but for anti-Fascist work [Comintern]. Together with Arnold and Edith, I worked out a plan for Arnold to meet with SÖHNCHEN before SÖHNCHEN moved to his father's flat. Arnold Deutsch's meeting with SÖHNCHEN took place with precautions. The result was his full readiness to work for us.

The report was signed by Reif's code name MAR.[24] This information is fully corroborated by the memo written later by Deutsch for the Maclean file (see Part I). In early January 1935, Moscow informed Nikolsky in Vienna: 'The son of the Anglo agent Philby, Ibn Saud's counsellor, has been recruited by the [London] group.'[25] Nikolsky, the future Orlov, needed to know it because he was going to London.

Deutsch lived in Moscow using the alias 'Stefan Lang', but in Britain he was registered under his real name and nationality, probably so that his cousin Oscar Deutsch, the millionaire owner of the Odeon cinema chain, could provide him with a reference for any possible application to the Home Office.[26] Operating under his real name, Deutsch could also make good use of his academic credentials to mix in academic circles and do some postgraduate work at London University, which provided ideal cover for his activities as a talent-spotter and recruiter. Another aim was to exploit sexual theories that he had learned from his 'sex-pol' tutor and use the results for the benefit of Soviet intelligence.

Actually, the idea was rather simple and was based on the popular contempt of young Europeans for bourgeois sexual morality. Deutsch's belief, based on Wilhelm Reich's teachings that political and sexual repression went together, commended him to all his recruits, men and women, most of whom were sexual perverts or paraphiliacs of one sort or another.

The 'homintern' movement in the leading British universities has been much written about. At a time when homosexual acts even between consenting adults in private were still illegal, it was the perfect ground for recruitment, masterfully used by Deutsch on a massive scale for the first time in the history of Soviet foreign intelligence (the Tsarist Okhrana widely practised this method, as, for example, in the case of Colonel Alfred Redl).[27] Dr Deutsch, however, went much further, and it seems that his success was due to his theory that recruitment of young people from good families would eventually lead not only to their taking 'useful' posts in the British Establishment (in that case he would have had almost exclusively Oxford and Cambridge students as his recruits) but in picking up individuals, irrespective of age or class, who were passionate proponents of a libertine lifestyle. The libertines, a covert movement that has been developing in Britain for centuries and is still quite popular today, were ideally suitable for clandestine work. This was almost certainly the key to Deutsch's incredible success among teachers, students, workers, housewives, and politicians.

John Cairncross, a member of the Cambridge Five, devoted two of his books to libertines: *Molière: Bourgeois et Libertine* and *After Polygamy Was Made a Sin*—dealing with the social history of polygamy. Philby and his first wife, Litzi, would be good examples for his writings.

Alice 'Litzi' Kohlmann was born on 2 May 1910 in Vienna. Her first husband was Karl Friedmann, an Austrian Zionist whom she had married at the age of 18 and divorced fourteen months later. Friedmann finally settled in Israel. Before she met Kim, recommended to her as a lodger by the *Daily Telegraph*'s Vienna correspondent Eric Gedye, she was a mistress of Gábor Péter, a communist activist from Hungary who would one day become the chief of the Allamvedelmi Osztaly (AVO), the Hungarian secret police under the Communist regime.[28] As one KPÖ document later admitted, in 1933–4 Alice Kohlmann was engaged in illegal work for the Communist Party in Vienna and was arrested.[29] To avoid another arrest, she had to flee abroad. So she seduced Kim, and soon Mrs Alice Philby found herself in London. Some time later both of them were recruited by the sweet-talking Dr Deutsch to work for the Comintern underground. Edith Tudor-Hart assisted him in both cases.

In October 1936 Deutsch recruited Arthur Wynn (codenamed SCOTT), a radio expert educated at Oundle and Trinity College, Cambridge, who was employed as a design engineer at the Highbury works of the important British valve manufacture named Cossor. Deutsch reported to the Centre:

Though EDITH we obtained SÖHNCHEN [Philby]. In the attached report you will find details of a second SÖHNCHEN who, in all probability, offers even greater possibilities than the first. Edith is of the opinion that [Wynn] is more promising than SÖHNCHEN. From the report you will see that he has very definitive possibilities. We must haste with these people before they start being active in university life.[30]

The last sentence did not mean the students' union or any other legal form of student's life, Deutsch had in mind underground Communist cells where a young candidate for cultivation and recruitment could come to the attention of the Security Service, as so often happened.

Wynn met Margaret 'Peggy' Moxon, probably his first recruit, later codenamed BUNNY, who introduced him to the Oxford Communist network. In January 1937, Theodor Maly, the 'illegal' resident agent in London since April 1936, who took control over Deutsch's spy rings in both Oxford and Cambridge, reported to Moscow: 'SCOTT. I wrote to you about him in my last letter. Through him we acquired BUNNY. He has given me about 25 leads [candidates for recruitment]. Most of these are raw material, but there are 4–5 among them who have already been studied and on whom we have already started working.'[31]

Arthur married Peggy in 1938. They had three sons and a daughter. When Wynn died in September 2001, aged 91, she survived him, as did their children. In May 2009, *The Times* published an article about Wynn calling him 'recruiter of Oxford spies'.[32] The article reported that Wynn had been recruited before Philby, which is wrong, but that the development of the Oxford ring began later, in spring and summer 1937, with Deutsch using the Cambridge model.[33] which is right.

In February 1937 Philby was sent by Maly to Spain and his wife departed for France. There, Litzi lived in luxury, occupying an atelier apartment on Paris's posh Quai d'Orsay and entertaining her guests in a country house in Grosrouvre, about one hour's drive from the capital, all at the expense of the NKVD. Officially, she was supposed to meet her husband, serving as his reserve contact channel (according to her oral memoirs they did indeed meet in Biarritz, and it is known from Maly's correspondence with the Centre that she was once sent to Lisbon to collect Kim's Spanish visa at the so-called Franco Agency there),[34] but most of the time Mme Philby spent partying, dancing, drinking, and sleeping with her lover, Pieter, a Dutch sculptor, and probably a few others. Litzi later recalled that in the house in Grosrouvre they lived in a group of twelve people, 'all strongly sympathizing with the Spanish republic, Léon Blum and the People's front'.[35] In Spain, Philby also did not lose time, and during his second posting in 1937 acquired as a mistress a Canadian actress, Frances 'Bunny' Doble, the divorced wife of Sir Anthony Lindsay-Hogg, an English baronet and an ardent royalist. 'Bunny was good company,' Tom Burns, from 1940 press attaché to newly appointed British Ambassador Sir Samuel Hoare, later recalled. He remembered a flirtatiously nostalgic meal with her in Philby's absence later described by his son, Jimmy, in a book,[36] which read more like a novel than a historical account.

The defection of Reiss and Krivitsky, both of whom knew Philby's recruiter, effectively put an end to Deutsch's successful work in London. Nevertheless, he took a considerable risk by coming back again in November 1937 to sort out problems with the agents. Arnold Deutsch, whose role as a Soviet recruiter was not discovered by the Security Service until 1940, well after he had left England for the last time,[37] was identified by Krivitsky only during his MI5 debriefing.[38] This, however, could not help to unmask Philby and others.

Still in France, Deutsch wrote a letter to the Centre.

Comrade DUCHE [Spiegelglass] told me that I should put on record all I know about GROLL [new code name given to Krivitsky after his defection]. GROLL met my wife before I myself met him. He knew the name of my wife's mother from the Vienna days. In June 1936, when I was in Paris, MANN [Maly] first introduced me to him. He asked me to give him a cover address in Paris and also to find an Austrian communist girl who could help him in his work. I introduced him to Luxy [unidentified, possibly Margo Gábor] and her husband. When I lost contact with him, he rang me up in my hotel presumably having got my address from MANN. GROLL was slightly aware of the nature of our work in London: he knew that we worked with young people and he knew about the man in the FO [King]. Signed STEFAN.[39]

Soon Deutsch returned to Moscow. Thus, already in 1937 the Centre was informed that their agent's life or, rather, freedom was in danger but did nothing. Two years later King was sentenced to ten years in jail. His trial in camera at the Old Bailey in October 1939 was kept secret for the next seventeen years.

In 1938–9 Litzi (codenamed MARY) and Edith (EDITH) were used by Burgess and perhaps others as couriers to make contact with the NKVD. But in July 1939

Gorsky, the only NKVD representative to remain in London, reported to the Centre:

MARY announced that, as a result of a four-month hiatus in communications with her, we owe her and MÄDCHEN [Burgess] £65. I promised to check at home [Moscow] and gave her £30 in advance, since she said they were in material need... MARY continues to live in [France] for some reason, she says on our orders, maintains a large flat and so on there.

To which the Centre replied: 'At one time, when it was necessary, MARY was given orders to keep a flat in Paris. That is no longer necessary. Have her get rid of the flat and live more modestly, since we will not pay.'[40]

Thus, in 1939 Litzi had to abandon her merry life in France and return to London. Some time before, in Paris, she had met Maclean, who was chasing Melinda Marling while living with his Soviet courier, Kitty Harris. Though Litzi later claimed that she severed her relations with Soviet intelligence at the beginning of the Second World War, Blunt admitted during his interrogation that, for over a year after Deutsch's departure from London 'the Ring remained in limbo, out of touch and apparently abandoned' until Burgess and Philby re-established contact with the Russians through Litzi. According to Blunt, the ring was run through a complex chain of couriers: from Litzi messages passed to Edith Tudor-Hart and thence to Bob Steward, the CPGB official responsible for liaison with the Russian embassy.[41] However, sometimes a reverse chain was in action, as a message below demonstrates. Alice Kohlmann was officially divorced from Philby in 1942, though after four decades she could hardly remember the date.

As has already been mentioned, in December 1942 the NKVD London station informed Moscow that Edith Tudor-Hart had sent a detailed report through MARY (Litzi Philby) on the result and status of work on ENORMOZ, both in England and in the USA, and that Engelbert Broda had given her this report on his own initiative.[42] At the embassy the report landed on the residency desk of a young officer named Vladimir Barkovsky (GLAN), who had arrived in London in February 1941 under cover of an attaché. Vladimir was the only officer there with technical education, having recently graduated from a Machine Tool Institute and one year at an intelligence school. In a later interview Barkovsky recalled that by the end of September 1941 the resident Gorsky had obtained a set of documents from an agent in the British S-1 Uranium Committee and that the first cryptograms about works on atomic bomb using uranium were dispatched to Moscow on 23 September and 3 October.[43] It may be added that Beria dismissed this intelligence as disinformation and only after Broda's reports had reached Stalin was it decided to establish a special laboratory (Lab. No. 2) under the direction of Igor Kurchatov, who would eventually become 'the father of the Soviet atomic bomb'.

As mentioned above, Broda arrived in Britain on 10 April 1938. The Home Office file states: 'Wishes to stay 3 weeks, first to attend a congress of the Faraday Society at Bristol University from 11th to 13th instant, and later to visit British chemists at London University. He left Austria on 20th ultimo, and since has been doing research work at Zürich University. He claims that he is not a refugee and will eventually return to Austria. In possession of £70 [about £3,300 in 2013].'

Contrary to his claims, Broda's obvious aim was to stay in London, and he already made contact with Esther Simpson at the Society for the Protection of Science and Learning (SPSL) in May 1938. Berti, as he was known to his Austrian friends, also had established contacts with the Austrian Centre. The Security Service files show that it was regarded as deeply suspect. Those left-wingers who were running the Centre were friends of Berti from Vienna days, including the communist Eva Kolmer as secretary (and Broda's personal assistant). By the July the Security Service knew that Broda was the leader of a clandestine Austrian Communist party cell in London.[44] The service also knew that Edith Tudor-Hart had been delegated by the CPGB to liaise with Broda, and, as his address had been kept secret from all, even from her, Edith had only his telephone numbers to contact him when necessary.[45] During the war she was serving as Broda's courier, providing a second channel of information between London and Moscow in what concerned the top-secret atomic research programme (the first channel had been secured by military intelligence).

A letter from the FBI liaison at the American Embassy in London to MI5 on 3 March 1955 demonstrates that the American counter-intelligence had by this time been rather well informed about Broda's activities.

Since his own field demands knowledge of nuclear physics he knows a great deal about it, but he is not and does not consider himself an expert on nuclear physics. Broda is a member of the Austrian Communist Party and a convinced, idealistic Communist. He is an extremely hard worker and has never been known to be objectionable in the presence of his university colleagues who do not share his political beliefs...In 1933 he was arrested by the Nazis because he was the leader of the Communist Party Students' union in Berlin and had organised a similar group in Frankfurt-am-Main...It is also believed that Broda has been and may be at present connected with Soviet Technical Intelligence as a supervisor of a group of Austrian scientists working in the field of nuclear energy. Certain reports, which to date have not been fully substantiated, speak of Broda as a key man in the transmission of secret atomic data from the United States, Canada and Great Britain to the Soviets.[46]

The Security Service, in return, shared its information on Broda by listing some of his Austrian contacts. Among those named were Edith Tudor-Hart and Ilona Suschitzky, the wife of Edith's brother Wolfgang. She was said to have taught in a Moscow school in 1931–6. There were also Jacob Wolloch, former husband of Eva Kolmer; Franz Karl West (Weintraub, cover name 'Thaler'), a communist functionary who returned to Vienna in 1945; and Paul Löw-Beer, a leading chemist in a pharmaceutical company in London and after 1949 an eminent Austrian businessman and industrialist. He and his wife Alice were prominent Austrian communists and Paul first came to the attention of the Security Service in 1939 when a Special Branch report on the Council of Austrians in Great Britain listed him as a leading member. Löw-Beer soon emerged as a financial adviser to the Austrian Centre as well. As early as 1940, MI5 sources suggested that he was 'a direct agent of Stalin'.[47] The focus of the lengthy MI5 investigation was to determine if there was substance to these allegations, and, though there was no doubt in Löw-Beer's political sympathies, no evidence was discovered to show that he was such an agent.[48] But, then again, no evidence had ever been discovered about Broda's connections with Soviet intelligence. Paul Löw-Beer, together with his communist friend Engelbert Broda, came from Vienna to study at the Friedrich-Wilhelms University in Berlin and they both had to leave it in 1933. It was Löw-Beer who was arrested together with Broda, and after two weeks detention both were expelled from Germany.

By 1955 the Americans seem to have known, but Austrian and British security services seem to have been unaware that Broda secretly visited the Soviet Union, residing in a house near Moscow for nine months. He never mentioned it in any of his CVs and, as his son put it, plainly wanted it to remain generally unknown.[49] It is possible that Broda was recruited by the very capable and active NKVD Vienna resident Yakov Fedorovich Tischenko (alias 'Vasili Petrovich Roschin') who operated in Vienna from May 1935 to February 1938. There is, of course, no direct evidence of it, but Berti went to Moscow by a complex route, staying in Prague for a while from where he travelled to Moscow via Poland in December 1935. His wife Hilde joined him there in June 1936, and the couple travelled to the Black Sea coast. She soon fell ill and promptly left Russia. His letters to her from Moscow were always sent through a mailbox in Prague and never mentioned the Soviet Union or anything related to it. In one of Broda's 1936 letters he wrote, 'I'm very proud to speak fluent Czech [sic]. I have already often given lectures', although his trip there was not academic and he was not a lecturer, telling his son later that he had worked in laboratories associated with two factories. By 'Czech' he obviously meant Russian and 'lectures' could have been lessons in tradecraft. Interestingly, another atomic spy, Alan Nunn May who later married Broda's wife Hilde, also visited Moscow in 1936.

According to Barbara Honigmann, Litzi's daughter, in Britain Mrs Philby 'took a war job at an armaments company as a trainee and even got a diploma, the only one she ever had in her life'.[50] Whether this was done on Moscow's instructions has never been revealed, but according to one source Litzi had a long affair with a senior MI6 officer, a colleague of Kim, who was therefore forced to resign.[51] In 1946 she left England and soon settled on Wildensteinstrasse in East Berlin, marrying another Soviet collaborator, Georg Honigmann, with whom she worked in the Soviet news agency, he as an editor and she as a censor. Soon a daughter, Barbara, was born, and the couple moved to a house in Karlshorst, a large area in East Berlin known as Russo-City, where the biggest European MGB/KGB operational base was established after the war. Soon Georg Honigmann started dating Litzi's best friend Olga, who soon became his mistress, and Litzi acquired 'Uncle Wito' as a lover. Uncle Wito was divorced from his third wife, but was sometimes living with his former family and even used to take little Barbara to spend time with her quasi-grandparents-in-law, Käthe and Ferdinand.

They, in turn, were an interesting couple of former actors. During the war they happily lived in a ménage à trois and sometime also à quatre, until Käthe's lover was arrested by the Gestapo for his involvement with what became known as the Rote Kapelle.[52]

Having spent fifty years in exile, Litzi Kohlman–Friedmann–Philby–Honigmann returned to Vienna. She rented a flat near the Belvedere, between the Soviet Embassy and the Trade Delegation, where Prinz-Eugen-Strasse and Rennweg join to form a famous square known as Schwarzenbergplatz, with an impressive monument to an unknown Soviet Soldier as the Liberator of Austria from Fascism. The local Russian community call him 'Alyosha'. Litzi never had a nameplate on the door, just 'Dr John', perhaps a former occupant. Was it part of her habitual tradecraft, known in Russian as *konspiratsiya*? She died in 1991, three years after Kim, in a Jewish home for the elderly in a quiet part of the Austrian capital. Philby's Russian wife, Rufina, survived them both. Later, together with Hayden Peake of the CIA and Mikhail Lyubimov of the KGB (who was a one-time resident in London before he was expelled), she wrote a book about her English husband—as his own memoirs, full of anecdotes and inventions supplied by the KGB, especially in what concerns Orlov and his role in Philby's life. When, several decades later, questioned by this writer whether her mother had any contact with Litzi in Vienna, the daughter of Arnold Deutsch hesitated to give a definite answer.

The life of Arnold Deutsch, Philby's recruiter, was not as long and smooth as that of his British agents. Unlike many of his INO colleagues, Deutsch was not arrested but simply dismissed from the service. There were several attempts, however, to reactivate him. In December 1937 Sloutsky suggested to Yezhov that STEFAN should be sent to the USA as an 'illegal' resident. A second, similar minute was sent on 15 March 1938 by Spiegelglass to the NKVD Deputy Commissar Mikhail Frinovsky. In October, the new chief of foreign intelligence, Zalman Passov, sent a minute to Lavrenty Beria asking for his agreement 'to finding work for comrade Lang [Deutsch] outside our organization',[53] as by this time both Arnold and Josefine had become Soviet citizens with internal Soviet documents identifying them as Stefan and Josephina Lang.

Deutsch spent twenty-one months without work. He arranged for a personal meeting with Pavel Fitin, who became chief of all Soviet foreign intelligence at the age of 32 and who wrote to Beria in December 1940 insisting that STEFAN should be sent to the USA as an 'illegal' resident agent.[54] By this time the only remaining NKVD station in America outside the embassy (the 'illegal' residency) was long defunct after its single operative Akhmerov had been recalled to the Soviet Union in December 1939. Remarkably, in April 1940 Fitin and his staff prepared, and Beria approved, a detailed plan to re-establish the 'illegal' station with a new head and case officers sent from Moscow. But for unknown reasons, perhaps because they did not have too many candidates to choose from, the NKVD never implemented the plan. Nine months later Fitin made another attempt. Beria again approved the proposal providing a generous budget and designating Deutsch as the new head of station.[55] Moscow designed a complex and elaborate scheme to move Deutsch and his family, including his Austrian mother who, for that reason, was successfully exfiltrated from Austria to establish them as legal immigrants in the USA disguised as refugees from Latvia.

According to West and Tsarev, the decision to use Deutsch again as an 'illegal' was taken by the GUGB leadership after Anthony Blunt had passed his report on Deutsch's MI5 personal file to the NKVD resident Gorsky in March 1941. If this is really so, the KGB archive (now ASVR RF) remains the only place where one can learn something about this file.[56] Anyway, it must have been quite thin and full of errors, as the only source of MI5's information about Deutsch was Krivitsky's 1940 debriefing, where the defector claimed, absolutely erroneously, that Deutsch had been an assistant of one Adam Purpis, who, according to Krivitsky, was the NKVD London resident between 1931 and 1934. As shown in this book, this is sheer invention.

As the decision to give Deutsch the role of the chief undercover NKVD agent in America was approved, one should presume there was nothing damaging in the documents that Blunt handed over to the Soviets—that is, Deutsch was absolutely 'clean' and given the green light to travel abroad. During his trip to America he was to be accompanied by Boris Krötenschild (alias 'Krotov'), who would eventually become Philby's controller in London. They were to renew contact with the sources 19th (Laurence Duggan), NIGEL (Michael Straight), and MORRIS (Abraham Glasser), and to recruit new agents.[57] Fortunately, Deutsch never reached the United States.

He departed for America, travelling through the Indian Ocean on the SS *Kayak*, but when the Pacific War broke out in early December 1941, with a series of successful Japanese attacks and invasion of several countries, Deutsch was stuck in Bombay and had to return to Moscow via Teheran, arriving there on 1 April 1942. Deutsch and his wife certainly had grounds to consider that he had been very lucky, because he very narrowly escaped the Indian Ocean raid, a sortie by the Imperial Japanese Navy launched just one day day before he arrived in the Soviet capital. It turned out to be a warning that was overlooked or neglected, because the second attempt to get him to the USA ended badly. According to the information provided by Oleg Tsarev, in November the freighter *Donbass*, with Deutsch on board, was sunk by a U-boat in the Atlantic.[58] There are, however, some serious problems with this version.

To begin with, the *Donbass* was a tanker (Captain V. E. Tsilke, 8,052 t) that without any cargo was going from Archangel to Reykjavik. She was lost in combat in the Barents Sea, which is part of the Arctic Ocean, on 7 November 1942 as part of the German operation HOFFNUNG. Two days before, the German flagship cruiser *Admiral Hipper* and the 5th Destroyer Flotilla composed of four warships began patrolling for Allied ships in the Arctic. When the cruiser's floatplane located the *Donbass*, the pilot reported to Vice Admiral Oscar Kummetz, who commanded the German squadron. Kummetz dispatched the destroyer *Z27* to sink the tanker (*Donbass*) and its escort, the auxiliary warship *BO-78*.[59] According to recent Russian research, forty-nine members of the crew were killed in the attack, while the captain and fifteen men were taken prisoners.[60] There are doubts that Dr Deutsch was among the tanker's crew.

Not unusually, this is where the next chapter of Deutsch's adventures begins.

On 21 March 1944 the general secretary of the KPÖ, Comrade Kolpenig, who lived in the comfort of the Hotel Lux in Moscow during the most turbulent years of his country's political history, wrote to Georgi Dimitrov in reference to *Genossin* Lang (Josefine Deutsch): 'Wir erhielten beiliegendes Telegramm von der Frau des Genossen Lang [Arnold Deutsch], die sich in *Lesnoj Kurort* befindet. Die Genossin hat vor der Evakuierung im Lux gewohnt. Da sich der Genosse Lang auf Kommandierung befindet, ersuchen wir um Ihre Anweisung, dass die Familie wieder ein Zimmer im Lux bekommt.'[61] Thus, in March 1944 Dimitrov wrote that Deutsch was 'currently on a tour of duty' and petitioned for the family to get back their room in the Lux upon their return from the sanatorium. In 1947 Josepine Deutsch with her daughter Nina moved to Vienna and settled in the Soviet zone of occupation in an apartment provided by the Soviet authorities on the same street as Arnold Deutsch used to have his small publishing house.

A year later, Dr J. Sabaditsch, head of Department 48 of the Vienna district court, issued the following official certificate:

According to the application of the spouse, Josefine Deutsch, Vienna II, Obere Donaustrasse Nr. 19/33, it was established in the course of the official investigation:

Dr Arnold Deutsch, born on 21 May 1904 in Vienna...died in the autumn of 1942 while parachuting in the vicinity of Möllersdorf, Lower Austria...This conclusion is based on the testimony of reliable witnesses, Erwin Zucker and Friedrich Hexmann, who made their statements in writing on 23 October 1947...

Dr Arnold Deutsch, who in 1934 lived in Paris and from 1940 in Moscow, used to be a member of the Communist Party and in the autumn of 1942 was sent by plane to Austria to lead the illegal [*sic*, underground] Communist work here. About two months after the departure of Dr Arnold Deutsch from Moscow, the leadership of the [Austrian] Communist Party there received a message sent by a wireless transmitter reporting that Dr Arnold Deutsch, immediately upon his landing by parachute in the vicinity of Möllersdorf, Lower Austria, was arrested by the Gestapo and shot. Shortly after sending this message, the informant, Hermann Köhler, a former leader of the Austrian Communist Party, was arrested and later died in the Mauthausen concentration camp.

There is no reason to doubt the veracity of the dispatch transmitted to Moscow by Hermann Köhler and now confirmed by [witnesses] Erwin Zucker and Friedrich Hexmann. Had Dr Deutsch been alive he would without doubt have come back to Austria, where not only his wife lives but where he would evidently have played a leading role in his party's work.

Therefore, the court finds the evidence of Dr Arnold Deutsch's death absolutely reliable and unambiguous. The jurisdiction of this court is based on the decision of the Supreme Court in Vienna of 27 April 1948, [No.] 1 Nd 182/48-2 according to §28...

Vienna, Palace of Justice, 24 November 1948

Signed, sealed[62]

Both 'reliable witnesses', Zucker and Hexmann, were not only active Communists but, as it turned out, NKVD collaborators.[63] Therefore the value of their statements is nil.

First of all, it is absolutely unrealistic that Pavel Fitin, chief of the Soviet foreign intelligence, after a long fight for his most experienced and reliable recruiter and agent-runner who demonstrated such great success in London, would suddenly decide to get rid of Deutsch by transferring him to Sudoplatov's department. Secondly, and this is even more important, there is no documentary proof that Deutsch had even been sent to Austria during the war. Today we know that Operation PICKAXE—that is, the parachuting of Soviet agents in Western Europe and Austria in particular—was part of the NKVD–SOE agreement of September 1941.[64] The topic is studied sufficiently enough to state that Deutsch's name or his landing in Möllersdorf do not figure in any German, Austrian, British, or Russian documents that have surfaced to date. It seems secure to conclude that Deutsch's mission in Lower Austria is another invention.

The final act of this KGB disinformation operation was staged in November 1953. The Communist Austrian newspaper *Der neue Mahnruf* reported that memorial plaques were opened in Vienna to commemorate outstanding freedom fighters, Dr Alfred Klahr, Fritz Hedrich, and Dr Arnold Deutsch.[65] The inscription on the plaque reads: 'In diesem Haus lebte Dr Arnold Deutsch. Während der Nationalsozialis-tischen Herrschaft wurde er im Alter von 38 Jahren im November 1942 von den SS-Faschisten ermordet' (In this house lived Dr Arnold Deutsch, who was murdered by the SS-fascists during the National Socialist rule in November 1942 at the age of 38). The second part of the inscription is even more cynical and deceitful than the first one: 'Er kämpfte für ein freies, demokratisches Österreich, für den Frieden, und für das Glück der Menschheit' (He was fighting for free, democratic Austria, for peace and happiness of the humanity). In reality, this prominent NKVD spymaster put time, effort, and talent into undermining Western democracies, including his native Austria, for Stalin and world Communism. Neither the present-day inhabitants of the house nor tourists of many nationalities who visit the site have the slightest idea that here lived the man whom KGB files credit with the recruitment of many secret agents for Stalin, Yezhov, and Beria—all of them documented mass murderers with an estimated death toll numbering tens of millions.

Oleg Tsarev and his British co-authors convincingly prove in several published accounts that the Vienna court was misled by false evidence.[66] Maybe the city authorities of Vienna should reconsider the decision 'to commemorate the hero', taken during the post-war occupation of Austria?

After the war, Josefine and her daughter Nina Deutsch came to live in Austria. When questioned later by a Security Service officer in Vienna, Deutsch's widow recalled several important details concerning her husband's work on the ISLAND,[67] but she was hardly able or eager to reveal much. Despite the efforts, we know only a few names of the agents and suspected agents recruited in Britain by Dr Arnold Deutsch and his NKVD colleagues before the war.

One of the OGPU–NKVD officers who successfully operated in London when both Nikolsky/Orlov and Deutsch were there was one Victor Karpov, an entirely mysterious personality who does not figure in any history of the Soviet espionage in Britain. In the meantime, Karpov, who, like Ilk, was based in Berlin, attracted the attention of the Security Service in 1932. In his MI5 personal file it is stated that Karpov was a key figure in Soviet espionage work in Britain, running the OGPU operation from a base in Germany. He used to visit London either as a clerk for ARCOS or attached to the Soviet Embassy, in which case he was accompanied by his family, with all his movements duly observed by the Special Branch watchers. In his recently declassified file, now available to researchers in The National Archives, there is a Security Service assessment of Karpov and his role from which one may conclude that MI5 thought Karpov controlled all 'GPU activities in this country'.[68] Remarkably, according to the documents in the file, Karpov operated in Britain, when, as we now know, Mitskewicz, Schuster, Grafpen, and Gorsky were heads of station hidden at the embassy, while Ilk, Reif, Nikolsky–Deutsch, and Maly controlled all undercover networks. Thus, the true role of Karpov, who, as his file puts it, 'disappeared in January 1939', remains absolutely unclear. His name does not appear in any KGB-related document that has become known so far. It seems there is still plenty of work for historians and writers.

Soviet Agents, Suspected Agents, Collaborators, and Sympathizers

Now that so much has been written about the Cambridge Spy Ring, pompously referred to in Moscow as the 'Magnificent Five', it has become obvious how insufficient and contradictory is our knowledge regarding these and other Soviet agents and collaborators. Some people despise them, but there are also those who are truly impressed by the traitors. At the same time, the newly declassified FBI files on the 'heroes' show that Burgess was 'a louche, foul-mouthed gay with a penchant for seducing young hitchhikers' and Maclean liked to dress in women's clothes. Philby's biographer, Anthony Cave Brown, called him 'quite possibly the greatest unhanged scoundrel in modern British history'.

On the other hand, with very few exceptions, Anthony Blunt was popular with the staff at all levels of the Security Service, as its official historian testifies[69] (which, much later, did not stop a KGB officer describing Blunt as an 'ideological shit').[70] Guy Liddell, as head of counter-espionage, was so impressed by Burgess, who recruited by Blunt as an MI5 agent, that he wanted to have him in his staff, and as a result Burgess had been seconded to the service for two years. In the SIS head office, Kim Philby was highly respected by the leadership and rank-and-file members. When he was posted abroad, Liddell was 'profoundly sorry' to see him go, according to Christopher Andrew's history of the Service. All five, although not exactly a 'spy ring', as it has been referred to for the past decades, remained unsuspected until 1951, and the investigation of the case was not fully resolved until almost half a century after Philby's recruitment.[71] Even a joint British–Russian documentary based on the KGB material,[72] one of the very first perestroika and glasnost products, gives a completely inaccurate story of the recruitment and work of the Cambridge spies.

This appendix lists Soviet spies and suspected spies as well as collaborators of the 1930s according to their KGB file numbers and dates of recruitment when they are known. Those who do not have file numbers and code names or whose personal file numbers are unavailable might have been KGB collaborators or sympathizers. Those who became known only by their code names remain unidentified (at least, to the public) until this day.

CODE NAME UNKNOWN [Douglas Springhall aliases 'Springy', 'Peter', 'Dave Miller'] File No. —— recruited in [between 1929 and 1931] in Moscow.

CODE NAME UNKNOWN [Alexander Ethel Tudor-Hart alias 'Harold White'] File No. —— recruited in [between 1932 and 1933] in [? Moscow].

GRIMM [unidentified] File No. —— recruited in or about 1932 by ——_ in Berlin but since 1934 worked in London.

FRIEND [Brian Goold-Verschoyle] File No. —— recruited in July or August 1933 by the OGPU in Moscow.

LUXI [unidentified, possibly Magda Gábor] File No.—— recruited in or about 1933 by Deutsch in Paris, later worked for him in London.

PFEIL/STRELA/GRETA [unidentified, possibly Margarete Charlotte Moos] File No. ——recruited in the autumn of 1933 by Deutsch in Paris.[73]

JOHN [unidentified] File No.—— recruited in October 1933 by Deutsch.

ERIC [Engelbert Broda] File No. 82702 possibly recruited in Vienna in 1934 by Tischenko/Roschin.

INSPECTOR [unidentified, possibly George Whomack] File No.—— recruited in or before June 1934 by Reif.

GOT [Percy Glading] File No. 837—— recruited in or before June 1934 by Reif.

PROFESSOR [unidentified, possibly Maurice Dobb] File No.——recruited in or before June 1934 by Reif.[74]

YEGOR [unidentified] File No. —— recruited in or before June 1934 by ——. Leontine Williams, used as an accommodation address in London in June 1934 by Deutsch.

CODE NAME UNKNOWN [unidentified female agent with access to secret documents] File No. —— recruited in or before June 1934 by Reif.

DOLLY [James MacGibbon] File No.—— recruited in 1934 by ——.

SÖHNCHEN [Philby] File No. 83790 contacted in London in May–June 1934 by Deutsch with the assistance of EDITH but recruited in or about December.

LYRIC and WAISE [Maclean] File No. 83791 recruited in December 1934 by Reif with the help of Philby.

MÄDCHEN [Burgess] File No. 83792 'initiated' to work for Soviet intelligence in January 1935 by Deutsch with the help of Maclean but was formally recruited later.[75]

SHAKH [unidentified] File No. 83793.[76]

MAG [John Herbert King] File No.—— recruited in —— 1935 by Pieck.[77]

MER [Klugman] File No. ——[78] recruited in —— 1935 by Deutsch.

JACK [Olga Neyman] File No. —— recruited in —— 1935 by Deutsch.

CODE NAME UNKNOWN [Alistair Watson] File No.—— recruited in —— 1935 by Deutsch.[79]

MARY [Alice 'Litzi' Kohlmann-Philby] File No. 8379— recruited in 1935 by Deutsch with the help of Edith Tudor Hart.[80]

27 unidentified agents between SHAKH and EDITH TUDOR HART (according to the file numbers). Note, this is an NKVD list which does not mention Russian Military Intelligence agents/collaborators such as Ernst David Weiss, Frederick William Meredith (and Margaret), Joseph Garber who served in the International Brigades in Spain, Ilse Steinfeld and Francis Claud Cockburn who, under the name of 'Frank Pitcairn' reported on the Spanish Civil War for the *Daily Worker*.[81]

EDITH [Edith Suschitzky/Tudor Hart] File No. 83820 recruited in —— 193? by Deutsch.

NELLI [Jane Stowman] File No. —— recruited in —— [between 1935 and early 1936] by Deutsch.

SCOTT [Arthur Wynn] File No. —— recruited in or about October 1936 by Deutsch with the assistance of EDITH.

BUNNY [Margaret 'Peggy' Moxon-Wynn] File No. —— recruited in January 1937 by Maly with the assistance of SCOTT.

75 agents between EDITH and TONY

TONY/JOHNSON/JAN [Anthony Blunt] File No. 83895 recruited early in 1937 by Deutsch assisted by Burgess.[82]

MOLIÈRE AND LIST [John Cairncross] File No. 83896, talent spotted in Cambridge by Klugmann, cultivated by both Burgess and Blunt and finally recruited in or about May 1937 by Deutsch.

JIM [Alexander Foote] File No. —— recruited by —— in 1937 soon after his return from Spain.

JACK [Bill Philips] File No. —— recruited by —— in 1937 soon after his return from Spain.

CODE NAME UNKNOWN [Oliver Charles Green] File No. —— recruited by —— in Spain in 1937.

CODE NAME UNKNOWN [David Wickes] File No. —— recruited by —— in Spain in 1937.

CODE NAME UNKNOWN [David Crook] File No. —— recruited in March 1937 in Spain by Nikolsky/Orlov and Belkin/Belyaev with the help of Georges Soria.[83]

CODE NAME UNKNOWN [Phoebe Pool], Blunt's courier during the 1930s, recruited by ——.

RALPH [Leo Long] File No. —— recruited in May 1937 by ——. In one of his reports Blunt wrote: 'As you already know the actual recruits whom I took were Michael Straight and Leo Long.'[84]

NIGEL and NOMAD [Michael Straight] File No. 58380 (US line registry) recruited in September 1937 by Akhmerov in the USA (Straight was successfully cultivated in London by Maly, Deutsch, Burgess, and Blunt until January 1937).[85]

MOLA and TINA [Melita Sirnis-Norwood], recruited in —— 1937 by ——, previously having been talent spotted by Andrew Rothstein, who worked for the Russian Telegraph Agency (ROSTA), in 1935.

BÄR [unidentified], recruited in —— 193? by Deutsch.

BRAUT/BRIDE [unidentified], recruited in —— 193? by Reif to cultivate ATILLA.

ATILLA [unidentified, high-ranking official at the Foreign Office], recruited in —— 193? by Deutsch.

NACHFOLGER, ATILLA's son [unidentified],[86] recruited in —— 193? by Reif.

CODE NAME UNKNOWN [Jennifer Fisher Williams-Hart], approached by Deutsch, but, in her own words, was recruited by Bernard Floud, the fact not supported by the *Authorized History of MI5* written by Christopher Andrew. According to her testimony, she 'gave up meeting Otto [Deutsch] when she joined the Home Office in 1938'.

CODE NAME UNKNOWN [Oliver Charles Green, see above][87] File No. —— reactivated in England in 1939 by ——.

DREAM [Jack Jones] File No. —— recruited in Spain by —— but had worked since the same year in London.

FLEET and GROSS [Goronwy Rees] File No. —— recruited in 1938 by —— with the help of Blunt.

O'BRIAN [Hugh O'Donnell] File No. —— recruited in —— in Britain or Spain.

PETER AND PAUL [Peter Rhodes] File No. —— recruited before 1939 (either in Oxford, or in Paris) by ——.

ABO [Peter Smolka] File No. —— recruited in —— 1939 by —— with the help of Kim and Litzi Philby.

CHARLIE [Cedric Belfrage] File No. —— recruited in —— 194? by Golos.

ELLI [unidentified], a GRU 'mole' inside MI5.

Charles Howard (Dick) Ellis (SIS)

Celia Luke (MI5)

Ormond Uren (SOE)

Ray Milne (SIS)

Olive Sheehan (Air Ministry)

Ann Gresson

Evelyne Jones

Stephen J. Wheeton

William Morrison

Alice Holland

Paddy Ayriss

Albert Williams

Nellie Williams

George Whomack

Sir Andrew Cohen

Peter Floud

Herbert Eichholzer (KPÖ)

Kurt Doberer

Margaret Mynatt aka Bianca Minotti

Documents

1 & 2. Orlov's diplomatic passport (NARA)

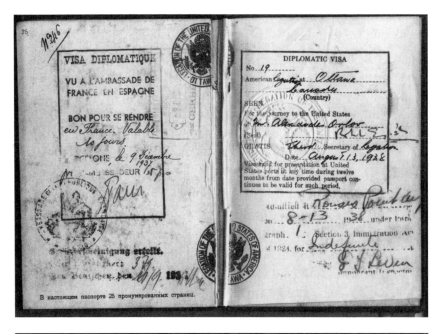

1 & 2. Continued

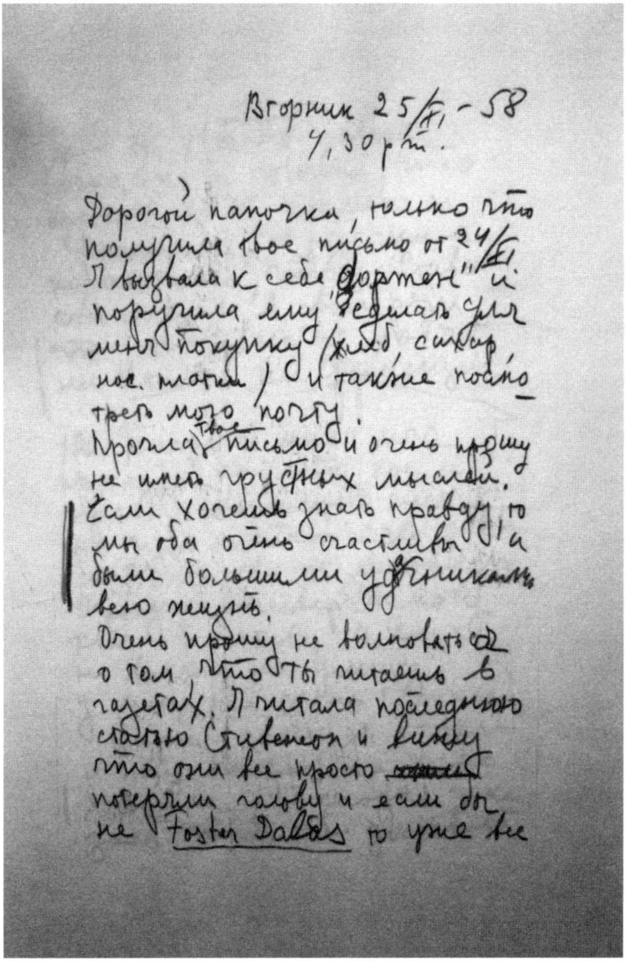

Вторник 25/XI - 58
4,30 pm.

Дорогой папочка, только что
получила твое письмо от 24/XI.
Я вызвала к себе "Фортен" и
поручила ему "сделать для
меня покупку (хлеб, сахар,
нос. платки) и также посмо-
треть мою почту.
Прочла твое письмо и очень прошу
не иметь грустных мыслей.
Сам хочешь знать правду, то
мы оба очень счастливы и
были большими удачниками
всю жизнь.
Очень прошу не волноваться
о том, что ты читаешь в
газетах. Я читала последнюю
статью Стивенсон и вижу
что они все просто ~~[illegible]~~
потеряли голову и если бы
не Foster Dallas то уже все

3. Maria's letter to Orlov, 25 November 1958

Пиру приехал в Мадрид для помощи в организации информации и разведки. Занимаясь этим делом, он одновременно посылался мною советником в бригады, когда они вели бой, был прикреплен к целому участку обороны Мадрида, занимался интербригадами и т.п. В тех отраслях работы, которые ему поручались, показал себя хорошим командиром.

К концу этого периода все советники мадридской группы завоевали себе достойное положение на тех участках, где они работали. Все трое показали себя хорошими товарищами и хорошими командирами.

Из группы советников, которые прибыли на мадридский фронт позже, тоже выдвинулся ряд отличных командиров, о которых я Вам своевременно доносил.

Считаю долгом отметить ту помощь, которую мне оказывал во всей работе по обороне Мадрида советник посольства тов.Гайкис, который пользовался исключительным авторитетом в Мадриде, и во время его пребывания там освобождал меня от всей работы по гражданской линии и по политическим комбинациям. Его мнение и советы я всегда считал особенно ценными и заслуживающими внимания.

Присланный по линии большого дома тов.Лаур вынес на своих плечах всю работу по организации транспорта, который питал гражданское население Мадрида и фронт. Ему лично в значительной степени обязан Мадрид тем, что он еще держится.

Следует отметить работу соседей во главе с тов.Орловым, которые много сделали для того, чтобы обеспечить от восстания изнутри. Со стороны тов.Орлова я всегда встречал самое лучшее отношение, товарищескую поддержку и лойяльное выполнение всех требований, связанных с обороной города.

Самое трудное время первых дней обороны города с нами были тов.Кольцов и Кармен, которые вполне лойяльно выполняли все мои поручения, связанные с обороной города.

В общем, конечно, было бы неправильно считать, что город удержан в результате работы небольшой группы советников, летчиков и танкистов. Массы Мадрида, которые первые дни обороны полностью находились под руководством компартии, остатки войск, отходящих к Мадриду, в которых уже отмечался перелом к лучшему, офицеры и командиры, которые встали во главе этих войск и обороны, - были готовы дать бой наступающим батальонам Франко. Им нужно было помочь организоваться, придать некоторую уверенность и подсказать правильное решение. Это и было сделано той группой командиров, которые провели всю оборону Мадрида. Мадрид удержали добровольцы милиционеры, мадридское население, коммунистическая партия и летчики и танкисты, которые в самый трудный момент прикрыли армию и подавили техническое превосходство противника.

4. A page from Gorev's report to Moscow dated 5 April 1937 (RGVA)

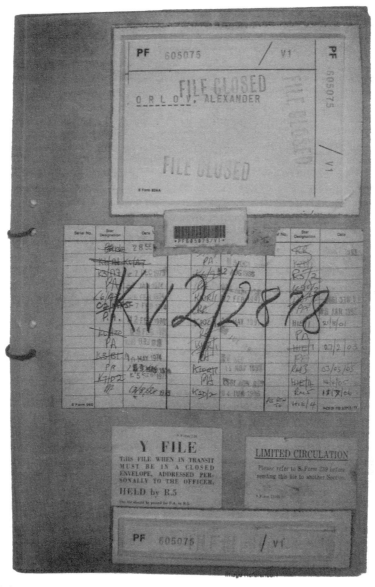

5. Orlov's MI5 file at the National Archives in Kew, Richmond

Archives

ÖNBB	Bildarchiv der Österreichische Nationalbibliothek
ÖStA	Österreichisches Staatsarchiv:
	AdR Archiv der Republik
	BKA Bundeskanzleramtsarchiv
	KA Kriegsarchiv
	NPA Neues Politisches Archiv
	PA Politisches Archiv
SWZ	Simon Wiesenthal Zentrum, Vienna
UW	Universität Wien, FB—Fachbibliothek Zeitgeschichte
UWA	Universitätsarchiv, Universität Wien
WSLA	Wiener Stadt- und Landesarchiv

BELARUS

| AKDB | Arkhiu Kamiteta Dziarzhaunai Byaspeki Respubliki Belarus (Belarus KGB Archives) |

COSTA RICA

| IMMP | Ministerio de Relaciones Exteriores y Culto, Instituto del Servicio Exterior Manuel María de Peralta, Biblioteca Don Fernando VII |

FRANCE

| AdP | Archives de Paris, Direction Générale de la Sûreté Nationale |
| SHD | Service Historique de la Défense, Paris-Vincennes |

GERMANY

BAK	Bundesarchive Koblenz
BStU	Die Bundesbeauftragte für die Unterlagen des Staatssicherheitsdienstes der ehemaligen Deutschen Demokratischen Republik, Berlin
IFZ	Archiv des Instituts für Zeitgeschichte, Munich
SAPMO	Stiftung Archiv der Parteien und Massenorganisationen der DDR im Bundesarchive Berlin
WZB	Wissenschaftszentrum Berlin für Sozialforschung

GREAT BRITAIN

| TNA: PRO | The National Archives, Public Records Office, Kew |

HUNGARY

OSA   Open Society Archives at Central European University, Budapest

ITALY

AOM   The Magistral Library and Archives of the Order of Malta, Rome

THE NETHERLANDS

IISG   Internationaal Instituut voor Sociale Geschiedenis, Amsterdam

SPAIN

AHN   Archivo Histórico National, Madrid
AHN-SGC   Archivio Histórico National-Sección Guerra Civil, Salamanca
AMAE   Archivio de Ministerio de Asuntos Exteriores
SHM   Servicio Hístorico Militar/Archivio de la Guerra de Liberación, Madrid

SWITZERLAND

SGAB   Zentralbibliotherk Zürich, Bestand Studienbibliothek zur Geschichte der Arbeiterbewegung, Nachlass Interessengemeinschaft ehemaliger Schweizerischer Spanienkämpfer
SSA   Schweizerisches Sozialarchiv:
       OH   Onori Hanspeter, Protokolle von Gesprächen über Schweizer im Spanischen Bürgerkrieg
       SB   Kleindokumente Spanischer Bürgerkrieg

USA

AAO   Ann Arbor Observer Archives, Ann Arbor, Michigan
AOP/GUL   Alexander Orlov Papers, Georgetown University Manuscripts, Georgetown University Special Collections Research Center, Washington, DC
CIA   Declassified documents pertaining to the Orlov case
       Orlov DST File (English and French)
FBI   Orlov File Bureau No. 105-22869, unclassified
       Krivitsky File Bureau No. 100-11146, unclassified

ARCHIVES

Eastman MSS	Manuscript Department, Lilly Library, Indiana University, Bloomington, Indiana
HIWRP	Hoover Institution on War, Revolution and Peace, University of Stanford
NARA	National Archives at College Park, College Park, MD
RLP/GUL	Robert J. Lamphere Papers, Manuscripts Collection, Special Collections Division, Georgetown University Library, Washington, DC
SC&A	Special Collections & Archives, George Mason University, Fenwick Library, Fairfax, VA
TL/NYU	Tamiment Library/Robert F. Wagner Labor Archives, New York University
US State	Confidential U.S. State Department Central Files, Spain, Part I, Internal Affairs, 1930–39. University Publications of America, Frederick, MD

Endnotes

CHRONOLOGY

1. For details about the service and its chief, Lt Gen. Victor Zolotov, see Boris Volodarsky, *The KGB's Poison Factory: From Lenin to Litvinenko* (London: Frontline Books, 2009), 224–54.

FOREWORD

1. Quoted in David Stafford, *Churchill and the Secret Service* (New York: Overlook Press, 1998).

INTRODUCTION

1. See Gordon Brook-Shepherd, Preface to Edward P. Gazur, *Secret Assignment: The FBI's KGB General* (London: St Ermin's Press, 2001), p. xiii.
2. See Alexander Vassiliev, White Notebook No. 2, Wilson Center Digital Archive, Vassiliev Notebooks, translation (2009), 397.
3. Peter Maurice Wright was a high-ranking MI5 officer appointed chairman of FLUENCY Working Party in 1964. Among other things, Wright claimed in his book (Peter Wright with Paul Greengrass, *Spycatcher: The Candid Autobiography of a Senior Intelligence Officer* (Richmond, Victoria: William Heinemann, 1987) that Hollis associated frequently with Agnes Smedley and was the highest traitor in MI5.
4. Paul Monk, 'Christopher Andrew and the Strange Case of Roger Hollis', *Quadrant*, 54/4 (April 2010), 37–45.
5. Christopher Andrew, *The Defence of the Realm: The Authorized History of MI5* (London: Allen Lane, 2009); and Keith Jeffery, *MI6: The History of the Secret Intelligence Service 1909–1949* (London: Bloomsbury Publishing, 2010).
6. Quoted in Christopher Andrew and Visili Mitrokhin, *The Mitrokhin Archive: The KGB in Europe and the West* (London: Allen Lane The Penguin Press, 1999), 29.

CHAPTER I

1. The Lazarevsky Institute of Oriental Languages was founded in Moscow in 1815 by a rich Armenian family of Lazarev (Lazaryan). Arabic, Persian, Turkish, Armenian, and Azerbaijani languages were taught there from 1827 until 1919, when it was transformed into the Armenian Institute. In 1921 it became the Moscow Institute of Oriental Studies.

2. Zinovy Borisovich Katsnelson was also born in Bobruisk, in 1892, and, after leaving a gymnasium in Moscow, studied law at Moscow University. Together with Feldbin, Katznelson attended the Lazarevsky Institute (August 1915– October 1916) and the 2nd Warrant Officer School (June 1916–October 1917) in Moscow. Katznelson joined the Cheka, predecessor of the NKVD-KGB, in June 1918. See N. V. Petrov and K. V. Skorkin, *Kto rukovodil NKVD 1934–1941* (Moscow: Zvenia, 1999), 228–9.

3. ORLOV FBI File, Bureau (105-22869), SAC, New York (105-6073), Serial 163, 2 October 1954.

4. A majority faction of the Marxist Russian Social Democratic Labour Party (RSDRP), later to become the Communist Party of the Soviet Union.

5. John Costello and Oleg Tsarev, *Deadly Illusions* (London: Century, 1993), 16. See also Gazur, *Secret Assignment*, 3.

6. In July 1917, after Piłsudski had forbade his soldiers to swear an oath of loyalty to the Central Powers, he was arrested by the Germans and put into prison. On 8 November 1918, three days before the Armistice, Piłsudski and his colleague were released from their Magdeburg internment and—like Lenin before them—placed on a train bound for Warsaw, as the Germans hoped that Piłsudski would be on their side.

7. The conference, which founded the Comintern, was held in Moscow on 2–6 March 1919. The convention was attended by thirty-four delegates with decisive votes and eighteen delegates with consultative votes. Russia was represented by Lenin, Trotsky, Zinoviev, Stalin, Nikolai Bukharin, and Grigory Chicherin; Germany by Hugo Eberlein (alias 'Max Albert'); Balkan Federation by Christian Rakovsky; Poland by Józef Unszlicht; Finland by Otto Kuusinen; and Austria by Karl Stenhardt (alias 'I. Gruber'). See John Riddell (ed.), *Founding the Communist International: Proceedings and Documents of the First Congress, March 1919* (New York: Pathfinder Press, 1987), 41–3. Some of the founding members were later working for the Soviet secret services.

8. The whole story reproduced by Costello and Tsarev (*Deadly Illusions*, 18) is a pure invention. During a CIA debriefing on 26 January 1965, Orlov claimed that 'Sosnowski [erroneously spelt SAZNOVSKIY] was one of the numerous Poles recruited into the Cheka by Dzierżyński, who was himself a Pole' (ORLOV DST File, p. 63). As has been documentarily established, Ignaty Sosnowski (Dobrżyński) joined the Cheka under this name in 1922—i.e. two years before

Nikolsky/Orlov. The GPU administrative order No. 14/228 of 5 December 1922 approved the staff of the organization, headed by Feliks Dzierżyński, where Sosnowski was named chief of the 6th Section (fighting against the counter-revolutionary organizations of Savinkov, Wrangel, the monarchists, and so on). Throughout his career Sosnowski was deputy head of the OO OGPU/NKVD (from 8 January 1934), and by the time of his arrest in November 1936 he was the NKVD deputy chief in the town of Saratov. His arrest was followed by that of others from Poland, Germany, Austria, and elsewhere, whom Yezhov suspected of being 'foreign agents'. See Marc Jansen and Nikita Petrov, *Stalin's Loyal Executioner: People's Commissar Nikolai Ezhov, 1895–1940* (Stanford: Hoover Institution Press, 2002), 60, 62, 64, 77. Sosnowski was sentenced to death on 15 November 1937 and shot on the same day.

9. Jansen and Petrov, *Stalin's Loyal Executioner*, 64. The Special (*Spetsial'ny otdel*) department was already functioning within the Cheka in 1921. Boky was its head from July 1921 until May 1937. One should not, however, confuse it with the department (*Osoby otdel*) headed by M. I. Gai, also translated from Russian as 'special', which dealt with security matters in the armed forces. The Special (*Spetsial'ny otdel*) department was organized within the Vserossiiskaya Chrez-vychainaya Komissiya (VChKa) (All-Russian Checka, the immediate successor of the Cheka and predecessor of the OGPU) on 28 January 1921 by administrative order No. 22 and was tasked with cryptographic communications and secret records keeping. The department consisted of first five, and later seven, sections, whose functions changed within the years. Only three sections were charged with cryptographic work: the 2nd Section developed new ciphers, the 3rd Section did the cipher work for the Cheka itself, and the 4th Section was trying to decipher enemy communications. The functions of other sections were: the 1st Section was overseeing secret work in all government institutions, the 5th Section was in charge of radio interception, the 6th Section produced forged documents, and the 7th section was busy with chemistry, photography, and graphology. According to the government decree of 5 May 1921, Spetsotdel was also charged with supervising the cipher work of all cipher services of the RSFSR. The post of department chief was considered so important that on 12 July 1921 Gleb Ivanovich Boky became a member of the Cheka Collegium and was eventually promoted to Commissar of State Security 3rd Rank (October 1935). See Petrov and Skorkin, *Kto rukovodil NKVD 1934–1941*, 114.

10. Gazur, *Secret Assignment*, 11.

11. In July 1922, the Collegium of the GPU planned serious changes and great expansion of its Economic Directorate (EKU). Suffice it to say that the EKU was headed by the Cheka's top brass: Pole Jósef Unszlicht, one of the Comintern founders, was put in charge of its foreign trade department; the other departmental heads were as follows: Viacheslav Menzinsky, Dzierżyński's deputy: agricultural department, Jekabs Peterss: industrial department;

Romuald Pillar (Baron Romuald Pillar von Pilchau): information department; Grigory Blagonravov: transport department; and Nikolsky's cousin Zinovy Katsnelson: financial department (Katznelson was acting EKU chief from June to September 1922, and then its chief until April 1925). In August, however, the idea of creating such a monstrous structure was abandoned. According to the GPU Administrative (*upravlenie delami* (UD)) order No. 160 of 15 September 1922, Katznelson was appointed head of the EKU, which consisted of the departments of industry, foreign and internal trade, general, information, and finance. See Alexander Kokurin and Nikita Petrov, 'OGPU (1929–1934)', *Svobodnaya mysl*, 7 (July 1998), 112.

12. Kokurin and Petrov, 'OGPU (1929–1934)', 119–20. According to the administrative–organizational directorate (AOU) OGPU order No. 11 of 14 January 1924, the new structure of the Economic Directorate (EKU) was established with Katznelson as its head, his two deputies A. A. Ivanchenko and V. I. Witlizki, assistant Ya. I. Keppe, Secretary A. E. Sorokin, plenipotentiary of the EKU head, S. Ya. Gagarin, and chief of chancellery K. A. Duntz. At the time EKU consisted of eight sections: (1) heavy industry and fuel (A. L. Molochnikov); (2) light industry (I. M. Ostrovsky); (3) internal trade and cooperatives (A. N. Prokofiev); (4) agriculture and food industry (S. I. Lebedinsky); (5) foreign trade (L. G. Mironov, from May 15); (6) finance (S. M. Kogenman succeeded by Nikolsky on 1 May); (7) general (acting chief A. A. Ambein); and (8) information and agents (S. A. Bryantsev).

13. See Alexander Kokurin and Nikita Petrov, 'GPU–OGPU (1922–1928)', *Svobodnaya mysl*, 7 (1476), (July 1998), 119–20.

14. See Alexander Orlov, *The March of Time: Reminiscences*, foreword Edward P. Gazur, introduction and epilogue Phillip Knightley (London: St Ermin's Press, 2004), 34–42.

15. See Petrov and Skorkin, *Kto rukovodil NKVD 1934–1941*, 229.

16. For details, see Jansen and Petrov, *Stalin's Loyal Executioner*, 40.

17. During his testimony in February 1957 Orlov lied under oath that in the Caucasus in 1926 he had been Beria's senior. See Alexander Orlov, *The Legacy of Alexander Orlov* (Washington, DC: US Government Printing Office, 1973), 74.

18. Orlov, 'The Legacy of Alexander Orlov', 87. For over six decades most of the historical interpretations of Kirov's murder would be based on Orlov's 1953 articles in the magazine *Life*, books, and witness testimonies before various US Senate committees.

CHAPTER 2

1. AP RF, f. 3, op. 24, d. 408, ll. 144–67, in V. Haustov, V. Naumov, and N. Poltnikova (eds), *Lubyanka: Stalin i Glavnoe Upravlenie Gosbezopasnosti NKVD 1937–1938* (Moscow: Materik, 2004), 531. See also 'Davydov Yakov Khristoforovich', official biography <http://svr.gov.ru/history/dav.htm> (accessed 5 February 2014).

2. According to Agabekov, one of the very first OGPU defectors to work with Davtyan in Persia, Davtyan was tall and handsome with dark hair and perfect manners. Unlike many other Soviet officials, he made a very favourable impression on everybody. See Georgii Agabekov, *Sekretnyi terror* (Moscow: Terra-Knizhnyi klub, 1998), 178–80.

3. See his interview with a TASS correspondent before his departure for Tehran, published in *Izvestia*, 8 September 1927. See also Miron Rezun, *Soviet Union and Iran: Soviet Policy in Iran from the Beginnings of the Pahlavi Dynasty until the Soviet Invasion in 1941* (Norwell, MA: Kluwer Academic Publishers, 1981), 128–9.

4. Richard Helms with William Hood, *A Look over my Shoulder* (New York: Random House, 2003), 145. Helms served as DCI from June 1966 to February 1973, the year Orlov died.

5. Dmitry Mikhailovich Smirnov, alias 'Dmitri Mikhailov', codenamed VIKTOR. In his 1955 and 1957 testimonies and his memoirs *The March of Time*, Orlov erroneously calls him 'Nikolai Smirnov, chief Rezident of the NKVD in France', in January 1937 (p. 388).

6. Zakhar Ilyich Volovich was born in 1900 in the village of Kobelyaki, near Poltava in the Ukraine, to the family of a trader. After serving in the Red Army, in 1923–4 he attended university, but then dropped out, having been recruited by the OGPU. Volovich was first sent to Turkey, but from February 1928 he was posted to Paris under the cover of clerk of the Consulate General. In 1930 he was promoted to INO section chief. As deputy chief of the Operational Department (from 1935), senior major of state security Volovich was arrested on 22 March 1937 and shot on 14 August. In Andrew and Mitrokhin, *The Mitrokhin Archive*, the reference to 'Vladimir Voinovich' as the Paris resident is incorrect.

7. Costello and Tsarev, *Deadly Illusions*, 47.

8. See Nigel West and Oleg Tsarev, *The Crown Jewels: The British Secrets at the Heart of the KGB Archives* (New Haven and London: Yale University Press, 1999), 5–6.

9. Andrew and Mitrokhin, *The Mitrokhin Archive*, 46.

10. Jan Antonovich Berzin (not to be confused with Jan Karlovich Berzin, who headed Military Intelligence and was in Spain during the Civil War) presented his diplomatic credentials on 15 June 1925 and served in Vienna until September 1927.

11. Loganowski returned to Moscow as Trilisser's deputy at the INO before moving to the NKID. Together with Davtyan, former INO chief appointed ambassador to Persia, Loganowski was posted to the same embassy as councillor. See Agabekov, *GPU: Zapiski Chekista*, 137–8.

12. Frederick S. Litten, 'The Noulens Affair', *China Quarterly*, 138 (June 1994), 511.

13. Yakov Rudnik was the first resident agent in France supervising the united RU–GPU station from February 1921. Ten years later he and his 'wife', who worked for the INO, became the main protagonists of the so-called Noulens's affair in Shanghai that lasted from June 1931 until July 1939. For details, see Litten, 'The Noulens Affair', 492–512. This experienced intelligence officer later took part in the Second World War and became a lecturer at the Moscow Institute of International Relations, an *alma mater* for the Soviet diplomats and spies. Rudnik died in 1963.

14. After Vienna, Karl Volk (alias 'Robert') moved to Berlin, where he was the chief of the KPD press service from 1926. After the Nazis came to power in Germany in 1933, Volk had to flee to France, where he broke with the communists in 1938 as a result of the Moscow Show Trials. During and after the Second World War Karl Volk lived in the USA, where he was considered a Soviet expert almost certainly collaborating with The Pond, a semi-official and top-secret US intelligence organization. He died in New York in March 1963. For details, see Hermann Weber and Andreas Herbst, *Deutsche Kommunisten: Biographisches Handbuch 1918 bis 1945* (Berlin: Karl Dietz Verlag, 2004), 821.

15. The official list of all Soviet Embassy employees, including the technical staff, dated 20 August 1925, as presented to the Federal Chancellor's office, Foreign Ministry, Administration of Public Security, and the Federal police, ÖStA/NPA, Box 667.

16. See the documents from the ÖStA/NPA, 1918–38, quoted in this chapter and in Appendix I.

17. Serebryansky was sent to Palestine as deputy resident to Yakov Blyumkin, who arrived there in December 1923 under the name of 'Moisey Gurfinkel'. When Blyumkin was recalled to Moscow in June 1924 to head the OGPU border troops in Transcaucasia, where Nikolsky later served, Serebryansky became the resident, with the task of infiltrating the Zionist movement and military organizations such as the Haganah ('defence' in Hebrew). He fulfilled his task brilliantly and in 1925 left for Paris, where he was one of INO's 'illegal' residents. Serebryansky headed the Administration of Special Tasks from 1926 until his arrest in Moscow on 20 November 1938. See his biography on the site for Sluzhba Vneshnei Razvedki (SVR) (Foreign Intelligence Service) (in Russian) and on the Documents Talk site <www.documentstalk.com/wp/serebryansky-yakov-isaakovich> (accessed 5 February 2014). See also Andrew and Mitrokhin, *The Mitrokhin Archive*, 54, 756 n. 88; Vadim Abramov, *Evrei v KGB: Palachi i Zhertvy* (Moscow: Yauza/EKSMO, 2005), 292–7.

18. Cremet became active in the French Communist Party propaganda campaign against the Rif War in French Morocco in 1925 after a trip to Russia, which earned for him a judicial condemnation. But he was only one small cog in the system of Soviet espionage in France that attracted attention of the French security service in the early 1920s. First reports of the communist espionage conspiracy in French arms industries date from December 1921; see Service

Historique de l'Armée de Terre (SHAT), 7N 2570, quoted in Douglas Porch, *The French Secret Services: A History of French Intelligence from the Dreyfus Affair to the Gulf War* (London: Macmillan, 1996), 122.

19. David J. Dallin, *Soviet Espionage* (New Haven: Yale University Press, 1955).

20. David Dallin, *Shpionazh po-sovetski: Ob'ekty i agenty sovetskoi razvedki* (Moscow: Tsentropoligraf, 2001), 40.

21. Roger Faligot and Rémi Kauffer, *As-tu vu Cremet?* (Paris: Fayard, 1991).

22. Porch, *The French Secret Services*, 120; Valery Kochik, 'Sovetskaya voennaya razvedka: Struktura i kadry (1921–1924)', *Svobodnaya mysl*, 7 (July 1998), 107; Vladimir Pyatnitsky, *Osip Pyatnitsky i Komintern na vesakh istorii*, ed. A. E. Taras (Minsk: Harvest, 2004), 304–5.

23. For details, see Merle Fainsod and Jerry F. Hough, *How the Soviet Union is Governed* (Cambridge, MA: Harvard University Press, 1979), 111.

24. Cf. Isaac Deutscher, *Stalin* (London: Penguin Books, 1970), and *The Prophet Outcast: Trotsky 1929–1940* (London: Oxford University Press, 1970). See also Dmitry Volkogonov, *Trotsky* (Moscow: Novosti, 1992), ii. 65–6, and E. H. Carr, *The Russian Revolution from Lenin to Stalin* (Houndmills, Basingstoke: Palgrave Macmillan, 2003).

25. Porch, *The French Secret Services*, 123.

26. ÖStA/NPA, BKA/AA, Box 667, Verzeichnis der Mitglieder und Mitarbeiter der Gesandschaft und der Handelsvertretung der Union der Sozialistichen Sowjet-Republiken in Österreich, 1924/5.

27. Kochik, 'Sovetskaya voennaya razvedka', 108. Uzdanski returned to the USSR in 1931. In 1932–3 and 1934–5 he served as section chief of the 3rd Department of the IV Directorate (military intelligence). In 1933 he was awarded the Order of the Red Banner 'for heroism and bravery'. In 1935–6 he was first assistant and then deputy chief of the 1st (espionage operations in the West) department. Uzdanski was arrested by the NKVD in the summer of 1936, sentenced to death on 3 November 1937, and shot on the same day.

28. After serving only two months, Duclos was permitted to attend a session of parliament. He fled into hiding and spent the next months in Moscow and Spain (1930), exerting 'discipline' on the Spanish communist movement. He returned to France in 1931 and, protected by his parliamentary immunity, resumed his party work.

29. Porch, *The French Secret Services*, 127.

30. Pavel Vladimirovich Stuchevsky was born in Poltava, Ukraine, in 1890, and before the First World War studied in Geneva, where he perfected his French to the extent that the French police were unable to recognize that he was Russian. He took part in the Soviet–Polish war and was then a secretary of the Southern Bureau of the Comintern. He moved to Moscow in 1922 and was sent on diplomatic postings to Albania (Tirana) and Manchuria (Mukden) from November 1924 to May 1927. He joined the INO in 1926, but in 1927 was transferred to the RU of the Raboche-Krestyanskaya Krasnaya Armiya (RKKA)

(The Workers–Peasants Red Army), and sent as an 'illegal' resident to Paris, where he was arrested in April 1931 and sentenced to three years in jail. He returned to Moscow in 1934 and became a functionary of the Comintern/ OMS. In 1935 Stuchevsky and his wife played an important role in organizing a communist uprising in Brazil. For details, see V. M. Lurie and V. Ya. Kochik, *GRU: Dela i Lyudi* (St Ptersburg: Neva; Moscow: Olma Press, 2002), 471.

31. Paul L. Kesaris (ed.), *The Rote Kapelle: The CIA's History of Soviet Intelligence and Espionage Networks in Western Europe, 1936–1945* (Washington, DC: University Publications of America, 1979), 342.

32. For details, see Rita T. Kronenbitter, 'Paris Okhrana 1885–1905', *Studies in Intelligence*, 10/3 (Summer 1966), 55–66.

33. Arthur Illner was born on 15 October 1891 in Königsberg; he was a prisoner of war during the First World War, and in 1919 became a member of the KPD. In 1923 Illner headed the AM-Apparat in East Prussia, and a year later immigrated to the USSR and became a Soviet citizen. He received his military–political training in the so-called M (for 'military') Comintern school supervised by both Red Army intelligence and the OGPU (personally by Otto Steinbrück, then chief of the 8th 'German' section of the Kontr-razvedyvatelnyi otdel (KRO) (Counter-Intelligence Department)) in 1924–5 and was sent by the RU to Czechoslovakia and France on secret missions. In 1928 Illner, now 'Stahl- mann', returned to Germany, where he was one of the organizers and leaders of the AM-Apparat. From 1931 to 1932 Illner/Stahlmann was a student of the International Lenin School (ILS) in Moscow. In 1933 IV Directorate (military intelligence) sent him on a clandestine mission to China, from where he returned to Moscow in 1934. During the Spanish Civil War 'Richard Stahl- mann' was a commander of the 'Servicio especial', a secret special forces unit. For more details, see Patrik von zur Mühlen, *Spanien war ihre Hoffnung: Die deutsche Linke im Spanischen Bürgerkrieg 1936 bis 1939* (Bonn: Verlag J. H. W. Dietz, 1985), 233, 267; Weber und Herbst, *Deutsche Kommunisten*, 752–3; and Erich Wollenberg, *Der Apparat: Stalins Fünfte Kolonne* (Bonn: Bundesministerium für gesamtdeusche Fragen, n.d. [1952]), 11–19.

34. Alexander Barmin, 'Testimony of Alexander Gregory Barmine, New York, NY', in *Institute of Pacific Relations, United States Senate, Hearings Before the Subcommittee to Investigate the Administration of the Internal Security Act and Other Internal Security Laws of the Committee on the Judiciary*, 31 July 1951 (Washington, DC: US Government Printing Office, 1951), 192. Barmin defected on 18 July 1937 and asked for a political asylum in France, which was granted. From 1940 he lived in the USA, where, from 1953, he worked for the Russian Service of the Voice of America. Barmin was married to Edith Kermit Roosevelt, the granddaughter of President Roosevelt. Their daughter Margot Roosevelt is an American journalist.

CHAPTER 3

1. Who operated in France using the alias 'Vladimir Borisovich Yanovich'.
2. The stranger, later identified as the Swiss businessman Giovanni de Ry, offered to sell Italian ciphers for 200,000 French francs. The wife of Voinovich, who, as already mentioned, worked with him, photographed the ciphers in a back room, and then her husband returned them to de Ry, denouncing them as forgeries. See Andrew and Mitrokhin, *The Mitrokhin Archive*, 58.
3. His name was Ernest Holloway Oldham. Volovich/Yanovich first refused to see Oldham, believing him to be an agent provocateur. A month later Oldham called again, bringing some secret FO material to which he had access. On the basis of this, the OGPU resident, though still suspicious of Oldham, arranged with him for further supplies in return for substantial cash payments. See 2878/808. There will be more about Oldham in subsquent chapters.
4. Cf. Dmitry Prokhorov, *Skolko stoit prodat Rodinu* (St Petersburg: Neva, 2005), 146–8. Several authors (e.g. Vladimir Burtsev, Paul W. Blackstock), including Prokhorov, claim that both Arens, the embassy councillor responsible for contacts with the PCF, and Helfand, Second Secretary responsible for the liaison with the Russian émigré organizations and their press, were directly involved. According to Prokhorov, Helfand was an OGPU agent recruited in 1926 when he was sent to Paris. Without documents, it is impossible to say whether Helfand was or was not an agent, but he was certainly a co-optee. In 1926 he was sent to Paris to learn French and get some experience in diplomatic work. In May he married a Russian-American actress, Sonia Moore, and after six months was appointed Vice Consul at the Soviet legation. Soon he was promoted to Second Secretary and moved with Sonia to the legation premises. Prokhorov claims that Arens left Paris on 26 January 1930—i.e. immediately after the abduction—and Helfand on 28 January. Other independent sources (see, e.g., Felicia Hardison, 'Stanislavski's Champion: Sonia Moore and her Crusade to Save the American Theatre', *Theatre History Studies*, 1 June 2004) confirm that they came to Moscow in February 1930, and this quick retreat from Paris after the Kutepov operation does not look too good for Helfand. However, in Moscow he served as assistant director of the Anglo-Romance department of the NKID and in 1935 was appointed First Secretary of the Soviet Embassy in Rome. There, he and his American wife spent four years secretly preparing for defection. In the meantime, he was promoted to Chargé d'Affaires, and in 1940 they both managed to defect to the United States, where Helfand changed his name to Leon Moore. Born on 29 December 1900 near Poltava in central Ukraine, Lev Borisovich Helfand/Leon Moore became an adviser to Allen Dulles when he was the Director of Central Intelligence. Sonia Moore, the founder and leader of the American Center for Stanislavsky Theatre Art and the Sonia Moore Studio of the Theatre, died in May 1995 at her home in Manhattan. She was 92. In their book review of *The Secret Road to World War Two: Soviet Versus Western*

Intelligence, 1921–1939 by Paul W. Blackstock, the Agency states that 'Helfand never had anything to do with the OGPU'. See CIA's *Study of Intelligence*, 14/1 (1969).

5. Administrative order No. 12 of 12 January 1930 confirmed a new staff of the INO—ninety-four officers—and set up eight operative sections. For some time Sloutky continued to fulfil the functions of EKU assistant chief. See Petrov and Skorkin, *Kto rukovodil NKVD 1934–1941*, 383.

6. Samsonov, using the alias 'Golst', served as the head of station in Berlin from 1929 to 1931.

7. Gazur, *Secret Assignment*, 471.

8. Costello and Tsarev, *Deadly Illusions*, 57.

9. See Alexander Orlov, 'Stalin's Secrets: The Man Himself', *Life*, 27 April 1953. See also Orlov, *The Legacy of Alexander Orlov*, 129–30.

10. Orlov, *The Legacy of Alexander Orlov*, 5–6.

11. Orlov, *The Legacy of Alexander Orlov*, 129.

12. Orlov, *The Legacy of Alexander Orlov*, 131. Alliluyev died from heart failure in his office when he returned from holidays to discover that all his colleagues in the Directorate of Automated Armoured Units had been arrested. The only Russian newspaper in America at the time was *Novoe Russkoe Slovo*, which was anti-Soviet and did not publish obituaries of the Communist leaders and Red Army commanders.

13. The economic data are from *The New Encyclopædia Britannica*, xx (Michigan: University of Chicago Press, 1990), 120.

14. The Archive of the NKVT, f. Special sector, op. 6066, d. 233, l. 129, 203, quoted in Sergei A. Gorlov, *Sovershenno sekretno: Moskva–Berlin, 1920–1933: Voenno-politicheskie otnosheniya mezhdu SSSR i Germaniei* (Moscow: IVI/ Rossiiskaya Akademiya Nauk, 1999), 284. See also Lev Besymenski, 'Die sowjetisch-deutschen Verträge von 1939', *Forum* (Zentralinstitut für Mittel- und Osteuropastudien), 2. Jahrgang (1998), Heft 2. See also Paul N. Hehn, *A Low Dishonest Decade: The Great Powers, Eastern Europe, and the Economic Origins of World War II, 1930–1941* (London: Continuum International Publishing Group, 2003), 212.

15. Béla Kun and his 'people's commissars' fled to Austria, arriving in Vienna's Ostbahnhof by a special train on 2 August 1919. Besides Kun himself, there were Josef Pogany, Jenö Varga, Gyula Lengyel, Bela Vago, Ferenc Rákosi, Emil Madarosz, and families. Commissar Matthias Rákosi arrived the next day by car and settled at the Grand Hotel. On 4 August, they were all transported to Karlstein. ÖStA/BKA-Inneres, Kart. 1, Pr. 11406/3.

16. 'Vorobyov' was an alias. His real name was Igor Lebedinsky, a former personal secretary of the chief of the INO, Mikhail Trilisser.

17. WOSTWAG was established in Berlin on 24 October 1923; its director up to September 1933 was David Rosenblitt. In 1929 an SIS report on the methods used by the Comintern for transferring funds to local Communist parties

named WOSTWAG, Germany, as being involved in these transfers, and mentioned David Rosenblitt as the company's liaison with the Comintern. For details, see 2878/1902 and KV 2/2566. Unfortunately, most of the information provided by the Soviet defector Walter Krivitsky and found in the MI5 files is imprecise. From 1928, the whole WOSTWAG network that had offices or daughter companies in such countries as Britain, USA, France, Germany, and China was headed by Stefan Iosifovich Mrochkovsky (until his arrest in Paris in 1939). See also Raymond W. Leonard, *Secret Soldiers of the Revolution: Soviet Military Intelligence, 1918–1933* (Westport, CT, and London: Greenwood Press, 1999), 58, but the book is not based on the primary sources and contains substantial errors, as much as its French 'sister': Pierre de Villemarest en collaboration avec Clifford A. Kiracoff, *GRU: Le Plus Secret des services soviétiques, 1918–1988* by (Paris: Stock, 1988), which should be neglected as a source.

18. These underground groups were created by Soviet advisers who prepared the 1923 uprising. There were M-Apparat (military, which dealt with all military matters and cadres); N-Apparat (intelligence, which collected information about the 'enemy'); Z-Apparat (subversion but actually penetration into the army, police, and security service). Some short time later the MP-Apparat (military-political, for the general preparation of the uprising) was established in Berlin under the command of a Red Army officer, a *kombrig*, until recently known only under his aliases 'Peter Alexandrovich Skoblevsky', 'Gorev', and 'General Rose'. In reality, his name was Voldemar Rudolfovich Roze, born 11 March 1987 in Riga as Voldemārs Roze (courtesy of Dr Jacques Mayer of Humboldt University, Berlin, whose brilliant research resulted in an essay 'Skoblewsky-Rose: Anmerkungen zur Biographie: Berichtigte und erweitere Fassung", available online). Under Rose's supervision yet another T-Apparat was established, commanded by Felix Neumann, where 'T' stood for 'terror'. Many leaders of the 'Apparats' finished different military schools and courses in Moscow. Some of them became staff officers of either the RU or the NKVD and very many were sent to Spain in 1936–7. Among those were Anton Ackermann, Wilhelm Bahnik, Hans Beimler, Hans Coppi, Franz Dahlem, Heinrich Fomferra, Theodor Lothar Hofmann, Arthur Hübner (as a staff GRU officer operated in Sweden, Norway, and Denmark) Artur Illner alias 'Richard Stahlmann', Otto Katz, Karl Kleinjung, Karl Mewis, Erich Mielke, Herbert Müller, Willi Münzenberg (who did not participate in fighting but took an active if not the leading part in the pro-Republican propaganda campaign together with Otto Katz). Hermann Nuding (helped the Republican war effort from the KPD foreign secretariat in Paris), Heinrich 'Heiner' Rau, Albert Schreiner, Kurt Schulze, Hans Schwarz alias 'Franz Schreck', Hermann Siebler, Gustav Szinda, Richard Staimer, brothers Manfred, Wolf, and Leo Stern, Erich Tacke, Franz Vehlow, Ernst Wollweber (during the war headed a sabotage group in Norway and Denmark), Bruno Wendt, Johann Wenzel (as a staff GRU officer prepared and couched radio operators), and Wilhelm

Zaisser. Some of them were killed in battle, others perished in the Soviet Gulag or were shot, but many became key figures in the intelligence and security structures of the DDR. For details, see Part II of this book. About the 'Apparats', see Wollenberg, *Der Apparat*, and 'Der Hanburger Aufstand und die Thälmann Legende', *Schwarze Protokolle*, 6 (October 1973); Heinz Höhne, *Der Krieg im Dunkeln: Die Geschichte der deutsch–russischen Spionage* (Bindlach: Gondrom, 1993).

19. Dallin, *Soviet Espionage*, ch. 3. See also Wollenberg, *Der Apparat*, 14–15.

20. CIA, Orlov's DST File, Document 'David and Lydia Dallin', 15–16 April 1965, para. 14: 'In [Orlov's] opinion, Mrs DALLIN knew all along ZBOROVSKIY's true status as a Soviet agent, and in his opinion she herself was a Soviet agent. During one of their conversations, [ORLOV] said that he sprung at her very rapidly the question: "Do you know BRUNN?" She immediately became flustered and confused and acknowledged: "Yes, I know him. He comes from the same town as I do." BRUNN, [Orlov] said, was the NKVD case officer in Paris handling émigré affairs and, in his opinion, BRUNN was Lydia DALLIN's case officer.' Para 15: 'DALLIN himself, [Orlov] stated—at least in Berlin—was a Soviet agent. [Boris] BAZAROV was his case officer and DALLIN may have been working for the Soviets against the émigrés at that time. For BAZAROV, DALLIN was running a source in the First Section of the German Foreign office.' Now it is possible to say that, while Lydia Dallin (née Lilia Estrina) might have had contacts with Soviet intelligence, at least through her friendship with Mark Zborowski, there has never been any ground to suspect her husband. For the real identity of 'BRUNN' (Berthold Karl Ilk), see n. 28 and Chapter 6.

21. Gazur, *Secret Assignment*, 13. The author refers to his personal discussions with Orlov.

22. Valery Kochik, 'Sovetskaya voennaya razvedka: Struktura i kadry (1924–1936)', *Svobodnaya mysl*, 8 (August 1998), 73.

23. Pavel Sudoplatov, *Spetsoperazii Lubyanka i Kreml 1930–1950 gody* (Moscow: Olma Press, 2003), 44.

24. See Petri Lehto and Mihkel M. Tombak, 'Consolidations and the Sequence of Acquisition to Monopoly', Discussion Paper FS IV 97–22 (Berlin: Wissenschaftszentrum, 1997), 4–5. While this work was in progress, a new book about Ivar Kreuger has been published: Frank Partnoy, *The Match King: Ivar Kreuger and the Financial Scandal of the Century* (London: Profile Books, 2009), but it does not mention any of his contacts with the Soviets or, for that matter, with the White Russians, which could have led to some interesting discoveries, as, for example, all the anti-Bolshevik ROVS money was invested in Ivar Kreuger's enterprises.

25. Petri Lehto and Mihkel M. Tombak, 'Consolidations and the Sequence of Acquisition to Monopoly', *Discussion Paper FS IV 97–22*, Wissenschaftszentrum Berlin, 1997, 4–5. This is what the Soviet writer Iliya Ehrenburg wrote

about Krueger: 'Ivar Krueger built his empire on matchboxes. He advised [Raymond] Poincaré how to stabilize the French franc, and helped the Poles implement rehabilitation measures. He was considered to be the most gifted businessman on Wall Street, and besides, he was a gentleman, a sample of integrity, tranquillity, and noble sentiments. In Chile he shut down all the factories that produced matches and threw their workers onto the street. In Germany he persuaded Social Democrats to ban the import of matches in order to save the workers from unemployment: during the inflation he bought up German factories in bulk. [Theodoros] Pangalos, the Greek dictator, was rather to his liking, but Pangalos refused to give him monopoly on matches, and Krueger managed to get him deposed in a coup [by his own Republican Guard]. He also helped overthrow the government of Bolivia. He hated the Russians because they dared not only to produce matches on their own but to export them abroad as well. He was quite a man of the world, and could discuss the works of [Sigmund] Freud and [Oscar] Wilde. In 1930 I published a book about the Match King—different from my other books of the period. *The Common Front* is a novel that requires a clue to be understood. Krueger is presented as Sven Olsson. I do not know why but I decided to kill the Match King; he died after discussions with the French Premier [André] Tardieu. The book was translated into many languages. It was 1931 when the world crisis was approaching its peak. Krueger became irritable; he tried to explain to the public that his shares were falling because of Bolshevik plotting. Several newspapers published articles accusing me of wishing to destroy the Match King. It was so stupid that I could not even feel proud of such attention. French governments changed, but Tardieu was still the Premier when Ivar Krueger shot himself in 1932. His secretary, Baron von Drachenfels, wrote in his memoirs that the day before the suicide he saw my book on the Match King's night table' (Ilya Ehrenburg, *Sobranie sochinenii v devyati tomakh* (Moscow: Gosudarstvennoe izdatelstvo khudozhestvennoi literatury, 1962–7), viii. 531; this extract trans. by this author).

26. In his essay about Berlin, Ehrenburg wrote, somewhat eerily, that 'ten years ago it was still possible to reveal an abscess but now history would have to cut rotten meat into pieces'. See Iliya Ehrenburg, 'Berlin, Yanvar 1931', in *Sobranie sochinenii v devyati tomakh*, vii. 350.

27. Andrew and Mitrokhin, *The Mitrokhin Archive*, 50.

28. Berthold Karl Ilk was born in 1896 as Brun Günzberg. Brothers Brun and Mauryki had an Austrian father and a Russian mother. Mauryki (born 1899) joined the Cheka in 1921 and changed his name to 'Mikhail Vasilievich Umansky'. He worked as an 'illegal' in France and helped to smuggle arms to Spain during the Civil War. He was arrested in April 1937, and shot in June. Brun graduated from the Imperial Export Academy in Vienna, joined the Austrian Communist Party in 1920, and was arrested for his propaganda work in Hungary in 1925. He escaped from prison and emigrated to the USSR. In

June 1926, like his younger brother, he joined the INO and took the surname Ilk. Using the alias 'David Fuchs', he operated undercover in Hamburg as an 'illegal' resident posing as a toy factory owner. From May 1935, after his return to Moscow, he was promoted to head of the 10th section of the counter-intelligence department in the GUGB NKVD. He was arrested in April 1937, and shot in June. Then, according to Krivitsky's biographer, Gary Kern, 'Fedia—the oldest boy—later took the name of "Fedin", then Alfred Kraus; he joined the Red Army and made his way into its intelligence division, and several of his friends followed his lead. They were Willy Stahl, known as "the Bear" for his powerful build; who later introduced Sorge to his future wife Maximova; Ignatz Reiss; and Samuel Ginsberg—the future Krivitsky . . . Actually the whole merry old "gang of Podwoloczyska" was wiped out' (*A Death in Washington: Walter G. Krivitsky and the Stalin Terror*, intro. Nigel West (New York: Enigma Books, 2004, 14). Unfortunately, this writer was not able to check the authenticity of Kern's information.

29. West and Tsarev, *The Crown Jewels*, 47.
30. ASVRR, File No.17698 (Correspondence with Group No. 1), p. 89, as quoted by West and Tsarev, *The Crown Jewels*, 47, 350.
31. The decision to send Hutschnecker to Berlin was made by Artur Khristiano-vich Artuzov, the new deputy chief of Soviet foreign intelligence. Artuzov (born Arturo Frauchi) came from a good Swiss–Italian family. For new appointments, see Administrative Order No. 12 signed on 12 January 1930 but coming into effect on 1 January. At the same time Artuzov continued to be assistant chief of the Secret Operational Directorate (SOU). See Kokurin and Petrov, 'OGPU (1929–1934)', *Svobodnaya mysl*, 8 (August 1998), 98. See also N. Petrov and K. Skorkin, *Kto rukovodil NKVD, 1934–1941* (Moscow: Zvenia, 1999), 93–4.
32. Kedrov and Nikolsky served together in Archangel, where, in the words of Donald Rayfield, Kedrov slaughtered schoolchildren and army officers with such ruthlessness that he had to be taken into psychiatric care. See Rayfield, *Stalin and his Hangmen* (London: Viking, 2004). 68.
33. After the Treaty of Rapallo, where the Weimar Republic and Soviet Russia agreed to 'co-operate in a spirit of mutual goodwill in meeting the economic needs of both countries', two joint-stock companies, Bersol and Metalchim, were registered in Moscow specifically for ordering military equipment in Germany. At the same time, forbidden by the Treaty of Versailles to modern-ize its forces, Germany obtained several secret facilities,such as 'Tomka', for experimenting with chemical weapons, 'Lipetsk', for training its air force, and 'Kama', a tank school in Kazan for its armoured forces. As part of the military collaboration plan, Soviet officers studied in German military academies and German instructors were assigned to the Red Army. See Kochik, 'Sovetskaya voennaya razvedka', 77.

34. At the OGPU headquarters, the Austrian Otto Steinbrück of the 8th (German) section of the counter-intelligence department was dealing with all aspects of Soviet–German collaboration.

35. Kochik, 'Sovetskaya voennaya razvedka', 74.

36. See Victor Suvorov, 'Who was Planning to Attack whom in June 1941, Hitler or Stalin', *Journal of the Royal United Services Institute for Defence Studies*, 130/2 (June 1985), 51.

37. From 1926 to 1934 Soviet Military Intelligence was known as IV Directorate—that is, IV Directorate of the Staff of the Worker and Peasant Red Army.

38. Kochik, 'Sovetskaya voennaya razvedka', 76–7. The 5th (cipher) department was then headed by Pavel Kharkevich, who had previously worked in the NKID and OGPU, and the 5th (sigint) section by Yakov Faiwusch. Before, IV Directorate had consisted of the 1st department (reconnaissance), 2nd (agent or human intelligence (humint), 3rd (information and statistics), and 4th (external relations).

39. Cf. Christopher Andrew and Oleg Gordievsky, *KGB: The Inside Story from Lenin to Gorbachev*, paperback (New York: Harper Perennial, 1991), 174.

40. The Politburo Decree of 8 December 1926. It was based on the Memorandum signed on 8 August 1921 by the Comintern (Zinoviev and Pyatnitsky), Cheka (Unszlicht), and Razvedka (Zeibot), which defined the roles of all three agencies. For details, see Vladimir Pyatnitsky, *Osip Pyatnitsky i Komintern na vesakh istorii*, 297–8.

41. Anon., 'Pas de mise a liberté provisoire', *L'Ouest-Eclaire*, 15 May 1927, p. 3.

42. Ivan Vinarov, *Boitsy tikhogo fronta* (Moscow: Iz-vo Ministerstva Oborony SSSR, 1971), 110–22. Vinarov notes that Vasili Kolarov, one of the leaders of the Bulgarian uprising, who at the time was in Vienna together with Georgi Dimitrov, had been informed about Vinarov's arrival (p. 111) although Vinarov was sent to Vienna by the Intelligence Directorate of the Red Army (then headed by Berzin).

43. Lurie and Kochik, *GRU*, 416.

44. Kokurin and Petrov, 'OGPU (1929–1934)', 103. In several otherwise reliable accounts it is erroneously stated that the head of INO was Artur Artuzov. In reality, Artuzov became the chief only on 1 August 1931. A day before he was appointed a member of the OGPU Collegium.

45. Comprehensive research in the Central Archive of the Federalnaya Sluzhba Bezopasnosti (FSB) (Federal Security Service) (successor of the OGPU–NKVD–KGB) by two Russian intelligence historians Nikita Petrov and Konstantin Skorkin also demonstrated that Nikolsky had never occupied any prominent position in the OGPU–NKVD hirarchy. See Petrov and Skorkin, *Kto rukovodil NKVD 1934–1941*. Gazur claims that 'Orlov was called back to Moscow where he was appointed Chief of the Economic Department for Foreign Trade of the KGB' (*Secret Assignment*, 14). Costello and Tsarev write that Nikolsky was appointed 'head of the Section VIII in charge of industrial

espionage' (*Deadly Illusions*, p. x). The authors refer to 'Orlov Legacy page 6' based on Orlov's inventions. According to the internal order (Administration Directorate order No. 12 of 12 January 1930), the Foreign Department consisted of eight sections: 1: 'illegals', headed by L. G. Elbert; 2: arrivals and departures to and from the USSR, headed by I. A. Babkin; 3: intelligence work in capitalist countries, headed by M. G. Molotkovsky; 4: intelligence work in Lithuania, Latvia, Estonia, Poland, and Finland, headed by A. P. Nevsky; 5: counter-intelligence operations against Russian émigrés, the so-called 'White Line', headed by A. P. Fyodorov; 6: intelligence work in the Middle East, headed by K. S. Baransky; 7: foreign counter-intelligence, mainly, the security of Soviet personnel abroad, headed by A. A. Neiman; 8: scientific and technical intelligence, which was vacant.

46. Gazur, *Secret Assignment*, 13; Costello and Tsarev, *Deadly Illusions*, 55. The authors do not reproduce a photocopy of this passport.

47. A copy of the document is at the documentary collection of the LSE's Cañada Blanch Centre.

48. See Gazur, *Secret Assignment*, 14–15.

49. Cecil F. Melville, *The Russian Face of Germany: An Account of the Secret Military Relations between the German and Soviet–Russian Governments* (London: Wishart, 1932).

INTERLUDE I

1. ÖStA/AdR, BKA/AA, Geschäftszahl 201.905/15/32, Verbal Note No. 52/a.

2. On 24 January 1938 Yezhov opened an NKVD conference in Moscow. At its conclusion, on 27 January in the Kremlin, a large group of NKVD chiefs were handed government decorations by the Chairman of the Supreme Soviet Mikhail Kallinin. Among them was Nikolai N. Fedorov. See *Izvestia*, 28 January 1938.

3. Upon his arrival in Vienna, Schuster handed Nikolsky an Austrian passport in the name of 'Leo Feldbiene' (incorrectly spelt French version of 'Feldbin', his name at birth). As 'Feldbiene' he was registered in Vienna at Löwengasse 32/4/14 from 7 to 16 September 1932. His registration card reads that 'Feldbiene' was born on 7 August 1895 in Brody, Poland. Businessman, married, domiciled in Gloggnitz, ditrict of Neunkirchen, Lower Austria. WSLA, MA8-M2711-13/2003H, 4 June 2003.

4. ÖStA/AdR, BKA/AA, Zl. 208.101/15/32. It is interesting to note that this verbal note did not even have a number. The handwritten comment on the case cover sheet clearly shows that Schuster delivered it personally on 15 September. Next morning he gave notice to the authorities that 'Feldbiene' was moving out. Indeed, Nikolsky was moving away, but not from Vienna; he was moving away from Berlin, and this time not as 'Feldbiene', but again as 'Nikolaev'.

5. ORLOV, Record of Sworn Statement, US Department of Justice, INS, File Nos. A2 472 619-620-620 (T), 29 April 1954. Investigator: Denton J. Kerns, Place: 70 Columbus Avenue, New York, in ORLOV FBI File, Bureau 105-22869, New York 105-6073, Serial 237, p. 40.
6. Gazur, *Secret Assignment*, 552.
7. Gazur, *Secret Assignment*, 19.
8. For details, see Carl Tobien, *Dancing under the Red Star* (London: WaterBrook Press, 2006).
9. Eitingon, who would eventually become Orlov's friend and successor in Spain, was a good recruiter. According to his chief Sudoplatov, Eitingon recruited as 'sleeper-agents', and then left on the West coast, two Polish Jews, who remained under deep cover for more than ten years. In his memoirs Sudoplatov wrote that one of these agents, codenamed CHESSPLAYER, was a dentist with a French medical degree that the OGPU had subsidized. At the end of 1941, Moscow learned that these agents were close to members of Robert Oppenheimer's family, and an American NKVD courier (Kitty Harris) was tasked to locate them. To date CHESSPLAYER remains unidentified. For details, see Jarold L. Schecter and Leona Schecter, *Sacred Secrets: How Soviet American Operations Changed American History* (New York: Brassey's, 2003), 62.
10. Einhorn's mission in America was to obtain industrial secrets. In the semi-official history of the Russian foreign intelligence he is even credited with laying the basis for OGPU industrial espionage operations in the USA. Surprisingly, his name is not mentioned either in John Earl Haynes, Harvey Klehr, and Alexander Vasiliev, *Spies: The Rise and Fall of the KGB in America* (New Haven and London: Yale University Press, 2009), which deals with Soviet espionage there in the 1930s and 1940s, nor in Andrew and Mitrokhin, *The Mitrokhin Archive*, nor, one may add, in any other Western publication. Einhorn's Russian biography (in English) may be found at <http://www.documentstalk.com/wp/einhorn-abram-ossipovich-1899-1955>.
11. About Jacob Golos and his American operations, see John Earl Haynes and Harvey Klehr, *Venona: Decoding Soviet Espionage in America* (New Haven and London: Yale University Press, 1999); Kathryn S. Olmsted, *Red Spy Queen: A Biography of Elizabeth Bentley* (Chapel Hill, NC: University of North Carolina Press, 2002); Lauren Kessler, *Clever Girl: Elizabeth Bentley, the Spy who Ushered in the McCarthy Era* (New York: Harper Perennial, 2003); and Haynes, Klehr, and Vassiliev, *Spies*. The best biography of Golos is on the Russian DocumentsTalk site <http://www.documentstalk.com/wp/golos-jacob> (accessed 5 February 2014), though it probably needs some comment. Jacob's father was almost certainly Naum Davidovich Reisen and his mother's name was Golosenko, from which comes 'Golos', but 1915 he was naturalized in America as Joe N. Raisin, which was an uneducated American spelling of his German-Jewish name.

CHAPTER 4

1. Sophia Poznánska was born in June 1906 in Kalisz, Poland, to a well-to-do family. She joined a local branch of Hashomer Hatzair (a socialist–zionist younth movement of the boy scouts type) and in August 1925 with one of its groups emigrated to Palestine, where her brother Olek (Alexander) had already settled in a kibbutz. In 1926 she moved to Tel Aviv, leaving behind both Kibbutz Dalet and Hashomer Hatzair for ideological reasons and joining the Ihud, a communist cell organized by Leopold Trepper. At the end of 1926 she returned to Poland to visit her family there, and stayed near Kalisz for quite a while, living with a young man who in the meantime started working for the communist underground in Poland. In November 1927 Poznánska returned to Tel Aviv and resumed her work in the Palestine Communist Party (PCP). Here she received her first secret assignment: Trepper found her work as a maid for a British police officer who was known for harassing communists, so that she could find his list of suspects in his pockets and warn them in time.

2. Neri Livneh, 'A Woman Called Zosha', *Haaretz*, 5 December 2009.

3. Cut-outs know only the source and the destination of the information that they transmit and thus ensure that a controller and a source do not come into direct contact. This increases security, because the controller, especially if he or she is a member of the embassy, may be under constant surveillance and so can compromise the source. An intermediary or cut-out helps to reduce the risk.

4. 'Le Complot Fantomarx', *Le Figaro*, 15 June 1932.

5. Porch, *The French Secret Services*, 127–8; Alexander Ivanovich Kolpakidi, *Entsyklopedia voennoi razvedki Rossii* (Moscow: Astrel, 2004), 433–4. Vladimir Pyatnitsky, who also describes the Fantômas case in some detail (Pyatnitsky (son of Osip Pyatnitsky), *Osip Pyatnitsky i Komintern na vesakh istorii*, ed. A. E. Taras (Minsk: Harvest, 2004), 309), practically copies Kolpakidi's text without any reference to the source.

6. Livneh, 'A Woman Called Zosha'.

7. Porch, *The French Secret Services*, 128.

8. See Leopold Trepper (in collaboration with Patrick Rotman), *The Great Game: Memoirs of a Master Spy, Leader of the Red Orchestra* (London: Michael Joseph, 1977), 80, and Kolpakidi, *Entsyklopedia voennoi razvedki Rossii*, 435–6.

9. Rayfield, *Stalin and his Hangmen*, 184–5.

10. Rayfield, *Stalin and his Hangmen*, 184–5. Upon his death in 2003, Christopher Hill, the famous Marxist historian of the English Civil War, was accused of being a Soviet spy. In the following chapters we shall discuss whether there were indeed grounds for such accusations.

11. Valentin Nalivaichenko to LB.ua, 14 January 2010 <http://lb.ua/news/2010/01/14/19793_nalivaychenko_nazval_kolichestvo_zh.html> (accessed 5 February 2014).

12. Kokurin and Petrov, 'OGPU (1929–1934)', 106–7. At the time the EKU was headed by Lev Mironov and his deputy Mark Gai, with two assistants, A.Minayev-Tsykhanovsky and D. Dmitriev; section 1: machine-building, fuel and energy (Ya. Rzhavsky); 2: black and non-ferrous metallurgy (Ya. Dashevsky); 3: rubber, chemical, and construction industry plus Gosplan, the state planning organization (Ya. Rybalsky); 4: war industry (vacant); 5: light industry (N. Schaslivtsev); 6: supplies and cooperation (I. Ilitsky); 7: foreign trade (D. Dmitriev, assistant chief); 8: agriculture (D. Apresian); 9: finances and credits (Ya. Love); 10: technical intelligence (M. Sokolov); and 11: special equipment (A. Goryanov-Gornyi). For the INO structure, see below.

13. As a matter of fact, until 1936 there was not a single department or section in the OGPU, and later in the NKVD, targeting foreign intelligence or security services and/or the armed forces. By the NKVD Order No. 00383 of 28 November 1936 such a unit (3rd department, counter-intelligence) was established within the Glavnoe Upravlenie Gosudarstvennoi Bezopasnosti (GUGB) (Chief Directorate of State Security), replacing the economic department.

14. Russian sources often give incorrect and misleading accounts of Korotkov's biography. The book by Teodor Gladkov, *Korol nelegalov* [Alexander M. Korotkov] (Moscow: Gaia eterum, 2000), devoted to Korotkov's 'heroic' life, is full of false hagiography and factual errors. Some interesting facts are in Pavel Sudoplatov and Anatoli Sudoplatov, with Jerrold L. Schecter and Leona P. Schecter, with Foreword by Robert Conquest, *Special Tasks: The Memoirs of an Unwanted Witness: A Soviet Spymaster Pavel Sudoplatov* (London: Little, Brown and Company, 1994). Unfortunately, Kesaris (ed.), *The Rote Kapelle*, published by the CIA in 1979, although otherwise useful, provides incorrect information about Korotkov; on pp. 275–8 there is a short biography of 'Alexander Erdberg', whom the contributors thought could possibly be 'identical with Sergei Kudrayavtsev [*sic*], who was involved in the Corby case in Canada in 1946 and who in 1969 was Soviet Ambassador to Cambodia'. (Sergey M. Kudryavtsev also served as an ambassador to Cuba in 1962.) This led to a similar error in Christopher Andrew and Oleg Gordievsky, *KGB: The Inside Story from Lenin to Gorbachev*, paperback (New York: Harper Perennial, 1991), 255. In reality 'Erdberg' was one of the aliases of Alexander Mikhailovich Korotkov, who would become a general and a chief of Directorate S (Illegals) of the KI. For Korotkov, see Part III. In Kesaris (ed.), *The Rote Kapelle*, he is erroneously credited with the recruitments of Arvid Harnak (codenamed CORSICAN) and Harro Schulze-Boysen (codenamed STARSHINA).

15. See Costello and Tsarev, *Deadly Illusions*, 96.

16. Their registration documents in the Austrian archives clearly show that from April 1933 to October 1934 Maria and Vera Nikolsky stayed in Austria, often changing addresses and identities (e.g. 'Nikolaeff, Feldbiene'). See n. 43.

17. Costello and Tsarev, *Deadly Illusions*, 96.

18. Sudoplatov et al., *Special Tasks*, 244 n. 9.

19. Andrew and Mitrokhin, *The Mitrokhin Archive*, 61–2. See also Anthony Adamthwaite, 'French Military Intelligence and the Coming of War', in Christopher Andrew and Jeremy Noakes (eds), *Intelligence and International Relations 1900–1945* (Exeter: University of Exeter, 1987), 193.

20. See Sinclair McKay, *The Secret Life of Bletchley Park* (London: Aurum Press, 2010), 43.

21. Andrew and Mitrokhin, *The Mitrokhin Archive*, 62, 760 n. 34. As already mentioned, before the war France had six intelligence services. The most important and the best known was the intelligence division of the army general staff. It had two sections, the SR and the Deuxième Bureau. The SR gathered intelligence, which the Bureau evaluated and forwarded to the general staff (see Adamthwaite, 'French Military Intelligence and the Coming of War', 191). Under normal circumstances, both of these services should have been the target of the Razvedupr (military intelligence), for whom Reiss had worked until recently, rather than the OGPU.

22. WSLA, MA8-M2711-13/2003, 4 June 2003.

23. ÖStA/AdR, BKA/AA, ZL. 145.867/15/33. Here for the first time, references are made to files nos 147.715/15/33 and 148.100-G.D.l. 1933; the latter signifies that the case belongs to the Generaldirektion für die öffentliche Sicherheit (GD) (Austrian Counter-Intelligence Service), an Austrian equivalent to the French DST.

24. ÖStA/AdR, Verbalnote No. 14, 19 April 1933.

25. The Austrian Embassy in Moscow had already reported the upcoming appointment of Petrovsky in February. In a 'Strictly Confidential' letter to Chancellor Dolfuss, the embassy characterized the new ambassador as a 'Polish Jew, old communist and militant party member'. It was noticed that Petrovsky had no academic education and for a long time had served as secretary of the Commissar for Foreign Affairs. The author of the report noted that, as his predecessor in Vienna, Petrovsky had previously served as Soviet Ambassador to Iran and compared the very different *modus operandi* used by Soviet diplomacy in the East and West, which naturally determined the choice of people for appropriate diplomatic posts. In this respect it was observed that the Soviet Union viewed Austria as the gate to the Balkans, and so diplomats with 'Eastern' skills and habits were sent to Vienna. Petrovsky himself, asked by an Austrian diplomat in Moscow why he had been chosen, responded that he suffered from some form of kidney decease and needed an urgent medical operation, for which he was seeking help and advice from Austrian doctors. ÖStA/NPA, Kart. 55, Zl. 8/P, Moskau, 3 February 1933. Before the arrival of the new ambassador in Vienna at the end of March 1933, the embassy staff consisted of only four members: Pavel Nekunde, 1st Secretary and Consul; Anton Schuster, 2nd Secretary (OGPU); Nikolai Fyodorov, Vice-Consul (OGPU); and Nikolai Popov, trade representative. *Corps Diplomatique à Vienne* (February 1933), 39.

26. Cited in Erika Weinzierl-Fischer, *Die österreichischen Konkordate von 1855 und 1933* (Vienna: Verlag für Geschichte und Politik, 1960), 213.

27. At the time of the terrible famine in the Soviet Union, its main exports to the UK were wheat, butter, oil, furs, timber, and eggs. 'In 1932,' Gareth Jones reported, 'the United Kingdom bought £32,179,000 worth of goods from the Soviet Union, and sold goods in return to the value of only £9,044,000' (see Gareth Jones, 'Soviet Dwindling Trade', *Western Mail*, 6 April 1933).

28. Vinarov was chief GRU resident in Austria from 1930 to 1933. According to a memo from his personal file, he 'established intelligence groups [*sic*] at several Czech military factories including Škoda Works that manufactured the world's first triple-barrelled gun turrets for the battleships of the Austro-Hungarian navy and also produced LT-35 and LT-38 tanks for the Czechoslovak army, which are better known under their German labels Panzer 35(t) and Panzer 38 (t). He managed to obtain top-grade intelligence about aviation industry. Thanks to his efforts the intelligence directorate got 17 Greek passports. From his sources in Bucharest, Belgrade, Athens and Sofia, Vinarov also received intelligence of strategic importance...' (Lurie and Kochik, *GRU*, 363).

29. Belev (codenamed AUGUST) was born on 5 March 1908 in the village of Gorno Brodi, then part of the Ottoman Empire (but from 1913 part of Greece). He began his literary career in 1923 and became an activist in the Bulgarian Communist Party. He was arrested in 1926 and sentenced to death, but the verdict was changed to fifteen years in prison. He was released under the amnesty declared in 1932 (his official biography in Bulgaria claims that he escaped), and in August of that year he went to Amsterdam to take part in the international anti-war congress. He worked for the GRU in Vienna, Paris, and Bucharest (1933–4), where he was arrested again and imprisoned for two years. In 1936–9 he continued working for the GRU in Europe, spending a year in Spain, where he was sent in 1937. At the end of 1939, following instructions from the Soviet military attaché (and GRU resident) in Bulgaria I. F. Dergachev, Belev set up an undercover group. After the war he became a well-known writer in Bulgaria. Krstio Belev died in Sofia on 25 January 1978. See Lurie and Kochik, *GRU*, 497–8. See also *Encyclopaedia Bulgaria*, i (Sofia: Izdatelstvo na BAN, 1978), 242.

30. Nicholas Dozenberg, US Congress, Executive Session Testimony, 21 May 1940, pp. 580–1.

31. See Lurie and Kochik, *GRU*, 464; Kolpakidi, *Entsyklopedia voennoi razvedki Rossii*, 369–70; Hans Schafranek (ed.), *Die Betrogenen: Österreicher asl Opfer stalinistischen Terrors in der Sowjetunion* (Vienna: Picus Verlag, 1991), 79–80. Two years before their arrest by the NKVD in 1938, both Arnaldo Silva and Karl Nebenführ were promoted to the rank of 'battalion commissar', equal to major.

32. Damiano Signorini, 'Italian Communists inside Stalin's Gulag', trans. from *Prometeo* 15 (June 2007) <http://www.leftcom.org/en/articles/2008-03-01/italian-communists-inside-stalin%E2%80%99s-gulags> (accessed 5 February 2014).

33. Kern, *A Death in Washington*, 45.

34. Anulov (alias 'Akulov') was born in Moldavia on 28 July 1897 as Leonid Abramovich Moskovichi. According to his GRU biography, he joined the Red Army in 1918. From 1919 he was in military intelligence, where he was promoted to section chief. In 1929–32 he was in China. In January 1937 Anulov was awarded the Order of Lenin, allegedly for Spain. He returned to Moscow through France, and in June 1937 was dismissed from the service (his GRU biographers claim that he was resident in Switzerland, Spain, and France). He was sentenced to fifteen years 'corrective labour' in May 1939, and exonerated in 1955. He died in Moldavia in September 1974. See Lurie and Kochik, *GRU*, 334–5.

35. Like Anulov, Major (1935) Isaak Elkunovich Rosenberg was a Jew from Moldavia, born in Kishinev in 1902. He worked for the OMS in Austria (October 1923–July 1924) and France (August 1924–July 1925) using the alias 'Kunov'. A GRU officer from 1932, he was awarded the Order of Lenin in 1937. He was arrested, sentenced to death, and shot in April 1938, but then exonerated in September 1956 (Lurie and Kochik, *GRU*, 460). His biography published in Russia says nothing about his work in Switzerland.

36. See W. G. Krivitsky, *In Stalin's Secret Service: Memoirs of the First Soviet Masterspy to Defect* (New York: Enigma Books, 2000), 140 ff.; Kern, *A Death in Washington*, 46–53; Kolpakidi, *Entsyklopedia voennoi razvedki Rossii*, 119; Barry McLoughlin, Hannes Leidinger, and Verena Moritz, *Kommunismus in Österreich 1918–1938* (Vienna: StudienVerlag, 2009), 406–7, 473–4.

37. Konstantin Mikhailovich Basov was born Jan Ābeltiņš in Latvia on 25 September 1896. After a short spell in the Latvian Cheka (1918–20), he joined the registration directorate (military intelligence) in Siberia. In 1922 he was transferred to its Moscow headquarters. Basov was one of the RU 'illegal' residents in Germany in 1927–30, where he recommended Richard Sorge for recruitment (Sorge and his then wife Christine came to Moscow in 1924; his career as a Soviet agent had begun in Shanghai in 1929). After the intelligence failure in Austria, Basov served at the headquarters. He graduated from the Stalin Academy of Mechanized and Motorized services in 1935. In his MI5 deposition Krivitsky called him 'Serge Bassoff', claiming that Basov was his courier and inventing a story about meeting him in New York in 1940. In reality, Basov was arrested and shot in December 1937. See Lurie and Kochik, *GRU*, 343–4. In his book *Stalin i GRU* (Moscow: Yauza, 2010), Yevgeny Gorbunov claims that Basov's group was released with the help of Richard Protze, until 1938 head of Abwehr III-F.

38. For example, Vera Alexandrovna Guchkova, the daughter of the founder, born in 1907, was an NKVD agent who visited Moscow in 1937 and on the day of the murder of Ignatz Reiss went back to Paris to pay 10,000 francs to the assassins. 'Ezhov worshipped me,' wrote Vera in one of her recently found letters. 'He had a small but graceful face, like that of an icon or a statuette, with a kind smile, an honest and open look in his dark eyes . . . And he saved my life' (see Dmitry Sezeman, 'Iz vospominanii', *Literaturnaya gazeta*, 47, 21 November 1990; However, the text of the letter of Vera Guchkova was omitted in the publication. It is quoted only in Arkady Vaxberg's comments 'Pravda o "platnom agente"', published in the same issue). Vera Guchkova married a Scottish linguist, Robert Traill, who was killed during the Spanish Civil War, and after Hitler had occupied France she was arrested in Paris with other foreign communists, including her friend Arthur Koestler. During the early months of the Occupation, still in internment, she conducted an intense clandestine romance with a German officer—an episode she later described in her autobiographical novel *The Cup of Astonishment*, published under the pseudonym Vera T. Mirsky. After further adventures, she arrived in London in 1941. There is little doubt that she continued to serve as a Soviet agent there. She regularly visited Moscow for the annual film festival as a film-reviewer for the *Observer*. Vera Traill died in Cambridge, UK, in 1987. Her obituary was published in the *Daily Telegraph* on 30 April 1987.

39. William L. Shirer, *The Rise and Fall of the Third Reich: A History of Nazi Germany*, paperback (London: Pan Books, 1964), 278.

40. Kolpakidi, *Entsyklopedia voennoi razvedki Rossii*, 118–19.

41. Natalia Vladimirovna Zvonaryova (May 1901—October 1994) joined military intelligence in 1924. After her return from Vienna, Zvonaryova worked at the headquarters. From January 1935 to January 1936 she was Berzin's secretary, and then until July 1938 continued to serve at the secretariat. In November 1938 she was dismissed from the service and almost certainly arrested, but was soon exonerated and restored to her rank. She took part in the war. From 1946 Zvonaryova served as an inspector in the Soviet Commandant's office in Berlin. She retired from the army as lieutenant colonel with many high decorations for bravery.

42. Costello and Tsarev, *Deadly Illusions*, 98.

43. Costello and Tsarev write that 'she [Maria] travelled with her Austrian passport made out for Marguerite Feldbin' (*Deadly Illusions*, 97). In another chapter (p. 143) they give her alias as 'Maria Feldbeine'. Both these aliases are wrong. The Austrian archival documents show that (*a*) the Nikolskys travelled on their Russian passports as members of the family of the Soviet *Handelsvertretung* (Trade Mission in Berlin) official 'Leo Nikolaev' (the alias of Lev Nikolsky at the time); (*b*) Maria used her Austrian passport only once, between 15 September and 3 October 1934, when she and Vera lived in Vienna at No. 4 Ungargasse; (*c*) the name was spelt as 'Margareta Feldbiene'. The bearer was

identified as 'née Kochowska, born on 20 May 1904 in Gródek', southern
Poland, widowed, arrived from Gloggnitz, Lower Austria. From Vienna, she
and Vera allegedly moved to Graz. WSLA, MA8-M2711-13/2003, 4 June
2003.

44. In 1945–55, when Austria was occupied by Allied troops, and later during the
cold war, several Soviet spies and collaborators like former Major Hans Nielke,
who worked in the State Archive; former Oberleutnant Franz Kraft, diplomatic courier; Alois Kahr, cipher clerk at the Foreign Ministry, and others
robbed the archives taking away any documents related to Soviet espionage.
Having conducted research in the Austrian archives for many years, this writer
has first-hand evidence of such 'mopping-up' when a lot of valuable documents were removed. See also Nikolaj Chochlow, *Recht auf Gewissen* (Berlin:
Deutsche Verlagsanstalt, 1959), 138.

45. ÖStA/AdR, BKA/Generaldirektion für die öffentliche Sicherheit, Zl. 148100
G.D.l./1933, Bundes-polizeidirektion Wien, Abteilung für Gefangenhaus-
Angelegenheiten (Penitentiary Department of the Vienna Police Directorate),
Case 'Leo Nikolajew' no. Zl. G 5700/33, and 'Maria Nikolajew' no. Zl. G
5741/33, dated 26 April 1933.

46. ASVRR, Personal File SCHWED, No. 32476, vol. 2, p. 170, telegram, 13 June
1933, quoted by Costello and Tsarev, *Deadly Illusions*, 98.

47. WSLA, MA8-M4337-39/05, 26 August 2005.

48. In addition to Costello and Tsarev, authors of Orlov's KGB-sponsored biog-
raphy, there is a former FBI Special Agent Edward Gazur and another fellow
Special Agent William E. Duff, author of *A Time for Spies: Theodore Stepanovich
Mally and the Era of the Great Illegals* (Nashville and London: Vanderbilt
University Press, 1999). But contrary to Gazur, who dismisses the book by
Costello and Tsarev as fabrication, Duff writes about Orlov basing his infor-
mation on Tsarev's 'revelations'.

49. 'The Shameful Years: Thirty Years of Soviet Espionage in the United
States', House Report No. 1229, *Committee on Un-American Activities US
House of Representatives* (Washington, DC: US Government Printing Office,
1952), 5:29.

CHAPTER 5

1. Vladimir Petrov and Evdokia Petrov, *Empire of Fear* (London: Andre Deutsch,
1956), 126–7. The Special (Cipher) Department of the OGPU, where Petrov
started working in 1933, was headed by Gleb Boky. His first impression of
what he saw there and the above description, however, refer to the sister
organization, the Military Intelligence Section headed by Pavel Kharkevich,
who explained to Petrov: 'The people whom you see here and with whom
you will work are engaged in deciphering the codes used in communications
between foreign countries and their embassies here in Moscow. You will

realize how important this work is. Our socialist homeland is isolated and is surrounded by capitalist countries, who, by their very nature, must be continually plotting to destroy the achievements of the Socialist Revolution which spells their doom' (p. 126).

2. Costello and Tsarev, *Deadly Illusions*, 98.

3. Until 4 July 1933 Maria and Vera lived in Vienna on Pelikangasse 15/1/48 and then moved to the IX District and took a room at the Hotel Atlanta, where they stayed from 27 August 1933 to 25 April 1934. WSLA, MA8-M2361-63/2003, 14 May 2003. See also ÖStA/AdRR, BKA/AA, Zl. 145.867/1933–47 PS Russland, Radiogramm No. 153, dated 31 October 1933 and registered at the Austrian Federal Chancellery under No. 231100.

4. See, e.g., an article in *Time* magazine '"Idealist" on "Bloodsuckers"'', 29 April 1935, where Stahl is called 'Master Spy'.

5. 2878/1586, Personal File SWITZ-TILLEY.

6. Dallin, *Soviet Espionage*, 60.

7. In his native Latvian, Alfreds Tiltiņš; see TNA: PRO KV 2/1899. She was born in 1896 in Latvia as Maria-Emma Schul. In 1919 she joined the Bolshevik party, and in 1920 the Red Army intelligence section. According to her official biography, from April 1921 to August 1922 she operated in Europe and in 1922 was posted as a typist and cipher clerk to the Soviet Embassy in Prague. In 1923 she was transferred to Paris, where she assisted the 'illegal' resident Alfred Tilton, her future husband. In 1926 they both moved to Germany, operating there for a year before moving to the United States in 1927. In 1930 Maria Tilton returned to the headquarters, where, documented as 'Maria Uspens-kaya', she worked as section head under the Latvian intelligence chief Jan Berzin. In February 1931 Maria was promoted and sent as an 'illegal' resident to Finland, where she was allegedly running thirty agents. She was arrested, together with her agents, and in April 1934 sentenced to eight years of hard labour. See Lurie and Kochik, *GRU*, 55, 477.

8. Jan Alfred Tilton was born on 4 March 1897 to a peasant family. He took part in the Russian civil war and in 1921–2 attended a course at a military academy before joining military intelligence on Berzin's invitation. Upon his return to the Soviet Union, Tilton served in various command capacities in the Red Army. From 1932 to 1936 he even commanded a mechanized brigade in Borisov, Byelorussia. His GRU biography claims that from 1936 to November 1937 Tilton served as a Soviet military adviser in Spain but this information is not corroborated by other sources. Noticeably, he was awarded the Order of Lenin, the highest Soviet decoration, in 1936 in addition to three orders of the Red Banner received in the 1920s for his operations in Europe. Tilton's good fortune came to an end in November 1937 at the peak of purges in the Red Army. In 1940 he was sentenced to fifteen years of hard labour and in December 1942 died in the Gulag.

9. Nicholas Dozenberg, Executive Session Testimony of 21 May 1940, in House Committee on Un-American Activities, *Investigation of Un-American Propaganda Activities in the United States: Executive Hearings* (Washington, DC: US Government Printing Office, 1941), ii. 571.

10. Filip Samoilovich Rosenbliett was born in 1888 in the town of Mogilev-Podolsk. Some time before the revolution his Jewish family managed to immigrate to the USA, where he became a naturalized US citizen and was educated as a dentist. In 1925 he was recruited by the Razvedupr (military intelligence) and before returning to Russia in 1935 was a trusted contact of the GRU 'illegal' residents Werner Wolf, Janis Tilton, Arnold Ikal, Alexander Ulanovsky, and Boris Bukov, his services mainly being that of a safe-house keeper. From 1935 to 1937 Rosenbliett was in Moscow, where he arrived with his wife. (Chambers was almost certainly wrong when he wrote that 'Dr Philip Rosenbliett left for Moscow around the summer of 1936'. (See Whittaker Chambers, *Witness* (Chicago: Henry Regnery Company, 1952), 397.) Once there, he took Soviet citizenship and was commissioned by the Red Army Medical Corps as medical officer 2nd rank. In 1937, he was dispatched to the United States with a special assignment and returned to Moscow by the end of the same year. Rosenbliett was arrested in Moscow in January 1938 and sentenced to eight years' imprisonment on 17 September 1939. In April 1949, at the height of a new wave of Stalinist repression, Rosenbliett was exiled on the charge of belonging to a 'Trotskyite-espionage' organization. No further information on his fate has been discovered to date. See Lurie and Kochik, *GRU*, 460.

11. 'Hearings Regarding Communist Espionage', *Hearings before the Committee on Un-American Activities*, House of Representatives, Eighty-First Congress, First and Second Session, 8 November, 2 December 1949; 27 February and 1 March 1950 (Washington, DC: Government Printing Office, 1951).

12. Tilton was arrested in November 1937 but did not plead guilty. After more than three years of interrogations, he was sentenced to fifteen years in the Gulag on 15 December 1940. So one of the best and most experienced GRU 'illegals' died in the labour camp in February 1942. See M. Alekseyev, A. Kolpakidi, and V. Kochik, *Entsyklopaedia voennoi razvedki, 1918–1945* (Moscow: Kuchkovo pole/Voennaya kniga, 2012), 773–4.

13. TNA: PRO KV 2/1901, Serial 241b, Personal File TILTON-SCHUHL.

14. 'Finland: Spy from Michigan', *Time* magazine, 7 May 1934. The *Time* correspondent was not very precise, because the *Cornell Daily Sun* had already reported the same news on 24 April (see 'Finnish Courts Convict Yankee', p. 6). According to some Russian sources, Maria Tilton died in prison in or about 1938.

15. Dallin, *Soviet Espionage*, 64.

16. Most of Lydia Stahl biographies, including a Wikipedia compilation and the 'official' GRU version, contain plenty of errors and do not say what happened

after her arrest (sixteen months before the trial) and sentencing in April 1935. The American military historian Douglas Porch, who erroneously claims that she 'was given a ten-year prison sentence' (Porch, *The French Secret Services*, 124), relates, with reference to Faligot and Kauffer, that Stahl started collaborating with the Abwehr and subsequently worked for them in Central Europe. After Hitler's defeat, according to Porch, she fled to South America. Her GRU biography does say that she died in Argentina, but refrains from any further comment.

17. Trepper, *The Great Game*, 80–1.
18. Kolpakidi, *Entsyklopaediya voennoi razvedki*, 435–6.
19. Andrew Meier, *The Lost Spy: An American in Stalin's Secret Service* (New York and London: W. W. Norton & Company, 2008), 163.
20. '"Idealist" on "Bloodsuckers"', *Time*, 29 April 1935.
21. See TNA: PRO KV 2/1417, No. 2939, J. A. Cimperman to J. M. Marriott, 9 March 1950, Twenty years after his Paris adventure, Robert Gordon Switz continued to collaborate with the Bureau. See, e.g., Rosenberg et al., FBI File No. 65-15330, 8 June 1950, PDF, p. 76, where his name is mentioned alongside such government witnesses/former Russian agents as Louis Budenz, Paul and Hede Massing, and Elizabeth Terrill Bentley. In his 1952 autobiography *Witness*, Whittaker Chambers described Gorev as his first Soviet handler 'Herbert', which was a slip of memory. In reality, 'Herbert' was Gorev's successor in the USA by the name of Valentin Markin.
22. After the USA, Minster was sent to Shanghai, where his cover was the manager of a radio shop. In Shanghai his superior was again Manfred Stern, who served as the Comintern's military adviser to the Jiangxi Soviet. In China, Minster and his wife operated under their own names as Mr and Mrs Minster, residing in apartment 6 at No. 20, Route Camille Lorioz. MI5 opened a file on Minster on 23 July 1934 (see TNA: PRO KV 2/2962). The Security Service knew that Minster also used the aliases 'Minter' and 'Charlie Barton' but were unaware that in Moscow he was better known as Grigory Ivanovich Schneider. Schneider was born in Russia to a Jewish family in 1898 but married an American woman named Mary Minster, becoming a naturalized American citizen in 1919. His official GRU biography states that he joined the Red Army in 1925 and was transferred to its Intelligence Directorate in 1926, having operated in the USA, Finland, and Spain. There is no mention of his mission in Shanghai. The official biography also states that he was promoted to quartermaster 3rd rank in 1936 and was awarded the combat Order of the Red Star in January 1937. However, in December he was suddenly discharged from the military service. Minster died in Moscow in 1968. One of his distant relatives is currently researching a book about Leon Minster.
23. TNA: PRO KV 2/1586.
24. ASVRR, Personal File SCHWED, No. 32476, vol. 2, pp. 164–5, quoted by Costello and Tsarev, *Deadly Illusions*, 102.

25. For Pieck's personal file, see TNA: PRO KV 2/809–814. For details of his operations, see Andrew, *The Mitrokhin Archive* and *The Defence of the Realm*. See also, F.A.C. Kluiters, 'Bill Hooper and Secret Service'.

26. ÖStA/AdRR, BKA/AA, Zl. 145.867/1933–47 PS Russland, Légation de l'Union des Républiques Socialistes Soviétiques en Autriche, Verbalnote No. 52, 30. October 1933.

27. ÖStA/AdRR, BKA/AA, Zl. 145.867/1933–47 PS Russland, Radiogramm No. 153.

28. See 'Wer ist Wer', *Lexikon Österreichischer Zeitgenossen* (Vienna, 1937), 252.

29. ÖStA/AdRR, BKA/AA, Zl. 145.867/1933–47 PS Russland, Radiogramm No. 366, dated 10 November 1933.

30. *Testimony before the US Senate Subcommittee to Investigate the Administration of the Internal Security Act and Other Internal Security Laws of the Committee of the Judiciary*, 15 February 1957, pp. 66–9. In *Deadly Illusions* Costello and Tsarev claim that Orlov testified before a 'Senate Internal Security Sub-Committee on 14 September 1957', while it was in February that he described to the grateful audience the 'sixth line of Soviet intelligence consists of paving the way for the Soviet Foreign Office in ticklish international manipulations'. Later, commissioned by the CIA to write a book about Soviet intelligence, he paraphrased this wonderful formula into 'the sixth line of Soviet intelligence consists of influencing decisions of foreign governments through secret agents in important positions within the councils of the foreign states' (Alexander Orlov, *Handbook of Intelligence and Guerrilla Warfare* (Ann Arbor: University of Michigan Press, 1963), 27).

31. Orlov, *Handbook*, 81.

32. See Giordano B. Guerri, *Giuseppe Bottai* (Rome: Bompiani, 2010), and Giuseppe Bottai, *Diario 1935–1944* and *Diario 1944–1948*, ed. Giordano Guerri (Milan: Biblioteca Universale Rizzoli, 2001).

33. See *Bolscevismo e capitalismo: [scritti di] Iosif Stalin, V. Molotov, V. Kuibyscev, G. F. Grinko*. Con un'avvertenza di Giuseppe Bottai (Florence: G. C. Sansoni, 1934).

34. Costello and Tsarev, *Deadly Illusions*, 443n. 33.

35. Andrew and Mitrokhin, *The Mitrokhin Archive*, 61.

36. Expenses of the EXPRESS group in France, 1 February 1934, n/file reference. Author's archive.

37. Mark Zborowski was approached by the OGPU 'illegal' Boris Afanasyev (GAMMA) in Grenoble, France, in 1932, and given the code name B-138. For details see Mark Zborowski, 'Testimony of Mark Zborowski Accompanied by Herman A. Greenberg, Esq., His Attorney', *Hearing before the Subcommittee to Investigate the Administration of the Internal Security Act and Other Internal Security Laws of the Committee on the Judiciary*, United States Senate, Eighty-Fourth Congress, Second Session on Scope of Soviet Activity in the United States, 29 February 1956, pt 4 (Washington, DC: GPO, 1956), 81. His recruitment was completed in 1934, almost certainly by the station chief Stanislav Glinsky.

38. See Costello and Tsarev, *Deadly Illusions*, 111–12; cf. Mikhail Bulgakov, *The Master and Margarita*, trans. Mirra Ginsburg, paperback (New York: Grove Press, 1995), 3.

39. Cf. Andrew and Mitrokhin, *The Mitrokhin Archive*, 59.

40. In April–March 1934 the group consisted of SCHWED (Nikolsky), DLINNY (Korotkov), JEANNE (Korotkov's wife Maria), Source 205 (unidentified), JOSEPH, and one Vernik (proper name). Noticeably, by that time 'Arnold Finkelberg', the American courier, was not with the group, possibly replaced by Vernik. Together with other documents from the Orlov KGB file declassified for the *Deadly Illusions* project, the report is to be found at the LSE Cañada Blanch Centre.

41. He was actually leaving for Vienna. Describing the episode, Costello and Tsarev (*Deadly Illusions*, 111–13) refer to his long letter of 8 May 1934 (ASVRR, Personal File SCHWED, No. 32476, vol. 2, pp. 290–4, SCHWED to the Centre; Costello and Tsarev, *Deadly Illusions*, 444–5 nn. 59–62), but part of this report they attribute to Korotkov: 'SCHWED ran across Vernik by chance. He asked where and what SCHWED was doing. SCHWED has decided to leave Paris for a while to see how things will turn out' (allegedly page 294 of the report). But on page 290 of the same letter Nikolsky had already informed the Centre: 'Today, according to your instruction, I am leaving for Switzerland,' so a reference to Korotkov's note makes no sense and is probably an invention.

42. Orlov's biography was published first in English in June 1993. Nelson died in December 1993, six months after the first edition of *Deadly Illusions* had appeared in Britain and the USA, which explains why his name is not mentioned there.

CHAPTER 6

1. Cf. Andrew and Mitrokhin, *The Mitrokhin Archive*, 77–8. Interestingly, Orlov is not even mentioned in Andrew, *The Defence of the Realm*. This is how the author explains it: 'The book [*Authorized History*] does not have enough room for a full history of the KGB as well as MI5. It contains numerous cross-references to *Mitrokhin Archive*, which has numerous references to Orlov and was reissued by Penguin on publication of *The Defence of the Realm*' (Professor Andrew to author, 4 May 2013).

2. Guy Liddel diary, 1 November 1942.

3. 'The Work of Arcos', *Russian Information and Review*, 1/1 (October 1921), 19.

4. For details, see TNA: PRO KV 5/1.

5. TNA: PRO KV 2/799, Yakov Georgievich Zhilinsk.

6. TNA: PRO KV 2/643, Leonid Ivanovich Vladimirov.

7. TNA: PRO KV 2/642, Ivan Mikhailovich Orekhov.

8. TNA: PRO KV 2/640, Vasili Vasilievich Barabanov.

9. TNA: PRO KV 2/639, Isaak Lvovich Groushko.

10. TNA: PRO KV 2/1410–1415, Nikolai Klementievich Klyshko,. Several decades later, MI5 concluded assessing Klyshko's role in the 1920s: 'It is virtually impossible at this distance of time to determine with any accuracy what Klishko's [sic] role was in relations to the Russian intelligence service and the Comintern; certainly contemporary assessments, suggesting that he was the OGPU "Resident" or the UK representative of the Third International, are misleading. Klishko was not a trained intelligence officer; what he had to offer the Soviet regime in the post-Revolution period were his contacts [here] and an experience of conspiratorial work in the UK before the revolution... Although we have detailed evidence of their own activities from both Allen and Kirchenstein... the part played by Klishko remains somewhat obscure. It would be misleading to suggest that he controlled these operations; he was probably the channel through which much of the communications and reporting to Moscow passed, but his main role would seem to have been one of providing support and above all as paymaster' (TNA: PRO KV 2/1415, 'Klishko', section V (conclusions), 4 January 1972, p. 17).

11. See Ivy Litvinov papers, 1911–97, Hoover Institution Archives, Collection number 87075.

12. Probably anticipating HM Government's hostile action, the Politburo decided to recall Klyshko; see RGASPI, f. 17, op. 3, d. 346, l. 1.

13. TNA: PRO KV 2/1016 and Cabinet Papers, CAB 24/129, C.P. 3410, Home Office Directorate of Intelligence, 'Foreign Support of Communist Agitators in the United Kingdom', 11 October 1921. See also Andrew, *The Defence of the Realm*, 145. Victor Madeira writes about William Norman Ewer, known as 'Trilby' to his co-conspirators, that he was probably the very first Cambridge graduate recruited by the Russians as early as in 1919. For details, see Victor Madeira, 'Moscow's Interwar Infiltration of British Intelligence, 1919–1929', *Historical Journal*, 46/4 (December 2003), 915–33.

14. See Hansard, The Case of Nicholas Klishko [sic], House of Lords Debates, 17 November 1931, vol. 83, cc. 49–53.

15. See Andrew Thorpe, 'Comintern "Control" of the Communist Party of Great Britain, 1920–43', *English Historical Review*, 113/452 (June 1998), 647. Mikhail Markovich Borodin operated in Glasgow on behalf of the Comintern as 'George Brown'. He was the father of Norman Borodin, a Soviet 'illegal'.

16. TNA: PRO KV 2/648. The other person standing court with Macartney was a German, Georg Hansen, described as a student. In the indictment the charge against McCartney was that between 1 March and 17 November 1927 'he solicited, invited, and endeavoured to persuade George Monkland, for a purpose prejudicial to the safety and interest of the State, to obtain, collect, and communicate to him information calculated to be useful to an enemy'. See 'Evidence Given In Camera', *The Times*, 18 January 1928.

17. TNA: PRO KV 3/35.

18. Contrary to what is stated in his official GRU biography, which mentions his regular visits to Britain between 1920 and 1924, Kirchenstein gained employment with the Arcos Steamship Company in 1924; see TNA: PRO KV 3/17. Interception of his correspondence and that of his colleagues began in May 1924.

19. Bronisław Bortnowski, another Pole who at that time was assistant RU director, reported to Voroshilov that in Britain working conditions were very difficult and financial expenses high. In his report Bortnowski stressed that, although the results were indeed rather poor, RU personnel in the UK was highly professional and responsible. He reminded the commissar that until 1926 Britain was not considered as a priority target.

20. Hansard, The House of Commons debates, 2 June 1927, vol. 207, cc. 523–4.

21. TNA: PRO KV 3/17. For the Security Service records on Koling, see KV 2/807.

22. TNA: PRO KV 3/17. See also Harriette Flory, 'The Arcos Raid and the Rupture of Anglo-Soviet Relations', *Journal of Contemporary History*, 12/4 (October 1977), 707–23; Jennifer Betteridge, 'The Rupture of Diplomatic Relations with Russia, May 1927 and the Political Purposes of Surveillance', unpublished paper, Leeds University, 2006; and Gill Bennett, *Churchill's Man of Mystery: Desmond Morton and the World of* Intelligence (Abingdon and New York: Routledge, 2007), ch. 5. During the Politburo meeting in connection with the Arcos raid, its members came to the same conclusions as Kirchenstein. Paragraph 8 of the secret protocol No. 102 of 13 May 1927 instructed all Soviet plenipotentiaries abroad to destroy all secret materials in their possession 'that are not absolutely necessary for the current work of the legation as well as that of the OGPU, RU and Comintern'. The same instructions concerned Soviet trade delegations. RGASPI, f. 17, op. 162, d. 5, ll. 7–8. This time Yagoda (OGPU), Berzin (RU), and Pyatnitsky (OMS) were added to the distribution list and received an extract from this secret Politburo protocol.

23. RGASPI, f. 76, op. 3, d. 379, l. 63.

24. 'The Work of Arcos', *Russian Information and Review*, 1/1 (October 1921), 19.

25. See, e.g., Jan Valtin, *Out of the Night* (London: William Heinemann, 1941), 285–9, though this author's evidence should be taken with a pinch of salt. See also Thorpe, 'Comintern "Control"', 647–8.

26. Early in 1930, naval and military intercept stations began picking up what was described as 'a mass of unusual and unknown transmissions, all in cipher except for "operators" chat'. Analysis of the transmissions revealed that they were messages exchanged between the Comintern in Moscow and a worldwide network of clandestine radio stations. The operation, codenamed mask, to identify, locate, and decrypt the Comintern messages, was launched during the same year. For details, see Andrew, *The Defence of the Realm*, 175–8.

27. For details, see Keith Jeffery, *MI6: The History of the Secret Intelligence Service 1909–1949* (London: Bloomsbury Publishing, 2010), 230–1. The name 'false

flag' was borrowed by secret services from naval warfare operations. In intelligence, recruitments or approaches are called false-flag operations if they seek to hide the real government agency or agent behind the operation.

28. Andrew and Gordievsky, *KGB*, 111–12. Rosengoltz was arrested on 7 October 1937, then sentenced to death and shot on 15 March 1938.

29. About Reiss's activities in Amsterdam, see Elizabeth K. Poretsky, *Our Own People: A Memoir of 'Ignace Reiss' and his Friends* (London: Oxford University Press, 1969), 72–85. One has to bear in mind, however, that these are memoirs written by the widow thirty years after the events and that therefore the book does contain factual and judgemental errors. See also Peter Huber, 'Sowietische und parteikommunistische Nachrichtkanäle in der Schweiz (1937–1944)', in Hans Schafranek und Johannes Tuchel (eds), *Krieg im Äther: Wiederstand und Spionage im Zweiten Weltkrieg* (Vienna: Picus Verlag, 2004).

30. Aliases Vasili L. Spiru, Anton Tauber, Julius Pober, codenamed HOFMANN.

31. ASVRR, File No. 17698, vol. 1, pp. 3–4, telegram from Moscow dated 7 August 1930, as quoted in West and Tsarev, *The Crown Jewels*, 51–3.

32. West and Tsarev, *The Crown Jewels*, 52–3.

33. West and Tsarev, *The Crown Jewels*, 54–5. Charles Duff, about whom one of his friends wrote that he 'knew Spain inside out and actually resigned his Foreign Office job when he realised how the establishment was almost solidly pro-fascist and was prepared to sacrifice not just Spain but Britain to fascism' (see Albert Meltzer, 'I couldn't Paint Golden Angels', AK Press, 1996, ch. 2), was almost certainly not an agent. A fluent Spanish speaker, after he retired he taught linguistics and languages and wrote books. Noticeably, one of them, written in collaboration with Dmitri Makaroff, was *Russian for Beginners* (1962).

34. West and Tsarev, *The Crown Jewels*, 47, 55.

35. West and Tsarev, *The Crown Jewels*, 56.

36. TNA: PRO KV2/983–8, Personal File 'Fredrick Robert Kuh', and KV 2/1099–1101, 'Federated Press of America'. According to the MI5 files, the Press, based at 50 Outer Temple, was a cover organization for Soviet intelligence. It was set up in 1923 by William Ewer to provide cover for Russian espionage activity in the UK. Similar organizations, as, for example, the Russian News Agency ROSTA in Vienna, were opened in other countries. Until its closure in March 1928 the Press was the nerve centre of communist espionage in Britain, providing a place of employment for agents and a clearing house for Soviet money going to agents throughout Western Europe. About William Norman Ewer (his name is spelt incorrectly in *The Crown Jewels*), alias 'Kenneth Milton', see TNA: PRO KV 2/1016–17. See also Madeira, 'Moscow's Interwar Infiltration of British Intelligence, 1919–1929'. Rado's Vienna team also included such famous names as György Lukács, a former member of the Hungarian Soviet government, Charles Reber of the Communist *Humanité*, Gerhard Eisler, who would spy for the Soviet Union in the USA and later head

East German Radio and Television, and Konstantin Oumansky, a future Soviet Ambassador to the United States who was also appointed chief NKVD resident in North America codenamed REDAKTOR/EDITOR. See Sándor Radó, *Codename Dora* (London: Abelard-Schuman, 1976), p. xii.

37. Sources designated as OS/42–46 were people working for this news agency. See West and Tsarev, *The Crown Jewels*, 56–7.

38. West and Tsarev, *The Crown Jewels*, 54–5. On 21 October 1930 Charles Duff despatched a private letter of recommendation to Sir Geoffrey Faber written on the official Foreign Office letterhead advising him to meet Joseph Lahodny. Thus, the Soviet agent was able to establish contacts with the publishing firms Faber & Faber, Geoffrey Bles, and Jonathan Cape.

39. West and Tsarev, *The Crown Jewels*, 59–60.

40. West and Tsarev, *The Crown Jewels*, 59–60.

41. UWA, Akte 5909. Her official SVR biography erroneously claims that she graduated from Vienna University with a diploma in foreign languages (French, German, and English). According to one Russian source, in 1920 Esther left the Romanian gymnasium and was admitted to the Faculty of History at the Universitatea Regele Carol I din Cernăuți, as it was then known, now Chernivtsi State University, romanized after the dissolution of the Austro-Hungarian monarchy after the First World War. She did not study in the wonderful red-brick university building that was erected after she had moved to France, where this future Soviet 'illegal' allegedly continued her education at the University of Paris. In 1922 she relocated to Vienna.

42. WSLA, MA8, 23 January 2004.

43. Lisa Zarubina (née Esther Rosenzweig) was born on 31 December 1900 in a small Jewish village in the Chernowitz region of Northern Bukovina, formerly part of the Austro-Hungarian Empire, then Romania and now Ukraine. When Hutschnecker was in Romania, she studied at university and was active in the Komsomol.

44. West and Tsarev, *The Crown Jewels*, 52.

45. West and Tsarev, *The Crown Jewels*, 60.

46. If one is to believe the KGB-sponsored *Ocherki*, the Ilk–Weinstein organization covered fifteen countries and included about fifty agents and sources (see Primakov et al. (eds), *Ocherki*, ii. 213–14).

47. Moritz Iosifovich Weinstein, alias 'Guchkov', was a Latvian Jew born in 1901. In 1924 he graduated from the Law Faculty of Moscow University and joined the OGPU. As deputy head of station, Weinstein controlled a group of agents in Germany, the network in Britain, and the so-called Jewish line (recruitment of confidential contacts among the Jewish community in different countries— a practice later borrowed by the Mossad).

48. West and Tsarev, *The Crown Jewels*, 62.

49. Centre to KIN, 16 September 1931, signed by Otto Steinbrück. Reproduced in Vladimir Sergeyev, 'Da Vinci sovetskoi razdedki', *Nezavisimaya gazeta*, 6 October 2006.

50. In his own memoirs, published in Moscow in 1996, Bystroletov wrote that the inscription on the gun read 'For intrepidity and relentlessness'; see Dmitri Aleksandrovich Bystrolyotov, *Puteshestvie na krai nochi* (Moscow: Sovremennik, 1996), 36. However, his memory did not serve him right. In reality, the OGPU order No. 1042/c of 17 November 1932 stated that 'For successful recruitment operations of great operational value while demonstrating exceptional persistence—I award: BYSTROLYOTOV D. A., an OGPU INO operative, a firearm with the inscription "for the relentless struggle against the counterrevolution. From the OGPU Collegium". Signed: OGPU Deputy Chairman Balitsky.' The order was classified TOP SECRET. Who could have suspected that, in less than five years, with Stalin's approval, the former heads of Foreign Intelligence Artuzov and Messing, the former chiefs of NKVD departments Karl Pauker, Georgi Prokofyev, Alexander Shanin, Pilyar (actually, the only aristocrat in the 'organs', Baron Romuald Pillar von Pilchau), Georgy Molchanov, Ignaty Sosnowski, Gleb Boky, Filipp Medved, former residents Bazarov, Maly, and Chapsky, as well as the former OGPU Deputy Chairman Vsevolod A. Balitsky, would all be shot as 'conspirators'. For details, see Jansen and Petrov, *Stalin's Loyal Executioner*, 64.

51. Two of Bystroletov's books were published in Russia in the mid-1990s: *Pir Besstrashnykh* ['The Feast of the Fearless'] (Moscow: Granitsa, 1993) and *Puteshestviye na krai nochi* ['Trip to the Night's End']. They are written in very powerful prose, maybe even better than Solzhenitsyn's famous *The Gulag Archipelago* (first published in the West in 1973). Unfortunately, however good, there is almost nothing in Bystroletov's books about the author's work as a Soviet 'illegal' abroad.

52. TNA: PRO KV 2/1241–2, Personal File Charlotte Magrarete MOOS, No. 42470/V1–V2, Serial 64, p. 7.

53. For details of the Oldham story, see Andrew and Mitrokhin, *The Mitrokhin Archive*, 59–64. See also West and Tsarev, *The Crown Jewels*, 71–3.

54. TNA: PRO KV 2/808.

55. Dr Nick Barratt, 'Casebook: Spies like Us', *Your Family History*, 1/1 (2010). I am grateful to Victor Madeira for the reference.

56. Andrew and Mitrokhin, *The Mitrokhin Archive*, 64. See also TNA: PRO KV 2/809–10, Personal File PIECK. Pieck was interviewed by MI5 in 1950.

57. For his MI5 personal file, PF 47813, vol. 2 (vol. 1 was destroyed), see TNA: PRO KV 2/815–16.

58. Bazarov was soon sent to the United States to take over a group of three other 'illegals', NKVD officers Akhmerov, Borodin, and Samsonov, each of whom was running important sources, because the resident Valentin Markin was found dead in New York. In March 1937 Bazarov was promoted to major of state security, but several weeks later was recalled to Moscow for 'cleansing' (*chistka* or party purge). Bazarov was arrested on 3 July 1938. On 21 February 1939 he was accused of high treason, sentenced to death, and shot.

59. See West and Tsarev, *The Crown Jewels*, 81.

60. From the Personal File MAG (John King) No. 21870, vol. 1, p. 3, dated 8 October 1934, as quoted in West and Tsarev, *The Crown Jewels*, 81. Interestingly, Andrew and Mitrokhin, quoting a secondary source, offer a rather different characteristic of King: 'Pieck cultivated King with patience and skill. On one occasion he and his wife took King and his lover for an expensive touring holiday in Spain, staying at the best hotels. Mrs Pieck complained that the whole holiday had been a "real ordeal" and that King and his mistress were "incredibly boring".'

61. Andrew and Mitrokhin, *The Mitrokhin Archive*, 65.

62. For the details of King's case, see TNA: PRO KV2/815–16.

63. Andrew and Mitrokhin, *The Mitrokhin Archive*, 65. There are a few minor inaccuracies in Mitrokhin's otherwise precise notes that perhaps deserve a comment. First, contrary to what is stated on page 65, in 1934 Abram Sloutsky was only deputy chief of the INO. In May 1934 Artuzov, the chief, was summoned to Stalin and after a long discussion was appointed first deputy chief of Military Intelligence, then known as IV Directorate commanded by Semyon Petrovich Uritsky. Until May 1935 Artuzov controlled both NKVD and GRU operations abroad. Sloutsky was appointed chief of the V Department of the GUGB NKVD (foreign intelligence, successor of the INO) on 21 May 1935. Secondly, Agabekov indeed mentioned that Akselrod was traveling on an Austrian passport in the name of 'Friedrich Keil', but he referred to his and Akselrod's activities in Constantinople in 1929 (together with the legal resident Naum Eitingon alias 'Naumov') while Akselrod was preparing for a special mission in Egypt. Actually, it is hard to establish which passport Akselrod used for his new mission in Italy. But it is known that he had his first meeting with Constantini in January 1935 and that he stayed in Rome until August 1937. Akselrod was then recalled to Moscow, where he first worked at the Lubyanka headquarters before being promoted in 1938 to deputy director of the Shkola Osobogo Naznacheniya (SHON) (Special Purpose School), which trained operatives for the INO. On 16 October 1938 he was arrested and charged with counter-revolutionary activities. On 20 February 1939 Akselrod was sentenced to death and shot on the same day.

64. Andrew, *The Defence of the Realm*, 265.

65. Lurie and Kochik, *GRU*, 534. From April 1933 until his transfer to the NKVD Krivitsky was deputy director of the Institute of Military Industry in Moscow.

66. TNA: PRO KV 2/802–5. See also W. G. Krivitsky, *MI5 Debriefing and Other Documents on Soviet Intelligence*, ed. Gary Kern, paperback (Riverside, CA: Xenos Books, 2004), 117.

67. Parparov was born on 23 November 1893 in the Pskov district in Russia. He graduated from the Legal Department of Moscow University in 1924 and joined the OGPU in February 1925. He was soon sent to Berlin to work under cover of the Soviet Trade Delegation, returning to Moscow in

1929 (i.e. he worked in Berlin together with Nikolsky for more than a year). After special 'illegal' training in Moscow, Parparov was again sent to Germany, this time with a Romanian passport. His official SVR biography claims that he later obtained Costa Rican passports for himself and his wife. After Hitler came to power, Parparov was able to recruit sources, one of whom was Arvid Harnack, in 1935 a lecturer at the University of Berlin. He was recruited in August and assigned the code name BALT. During the Spanish Civil War and until his recall in early 1938 Parparov supplied Moscow with high-grade political intelligence from Germany. One of his sources, codenamed MARTA (but also YUNA and AUGUSTA), was the wife of a German diplomat, and she regularly informed Parparov about her husband's work. Soon after his arrival in Moscow Parparov was arrested but released after a year-long investigation in June 1939. He was reinstated in the NKVD foreign department with the rank of major of state security and in 1940 sent to Estonia to handle one of his sources from the German Foreign Ministry, now working in the embassy in Tallinn. In October 1941 Parparov was sent to Iran, as his official biography claims, to move from there to Switzerland in order to control important agents there and in France (nothing is known about such agents so far). However, he did not manage to get a Swiss visa, and in 1943 returned to Moscow, joining Sudoplatov's 4th Department. After the war he resigned from the NKVD to chair a military sub-faculty of Moscow University. Parparov died in Moscow in 1960.

68. TNA: PRO KV 2/2572.

69. See TNA: PRO KV 2/805. In 1930-4 the structure of the RU departments at the headquarters did not change. Only in 1931 a new 5th (cipher) department was formed under Pavel Kharkevich and the 5th (signal intelligence, sigint) section under Yakov Faiwusch. Other departments were 1 (reconnaissance) headed by Victor Lutskevich and then Afanacy Trifonov; 2 (human intelligence, humint): Ruben Tairov, Boris Melnikov, Vasili Davydov; 3 (information and statistics): Ivan Klochko, Alexander Nikonov; 4 (external relations): Fedor Sudakov, Ivan Rink, Vasili Sukhorukov, Vasili Smagin, Anatoly Gekker. See Lurie and Kochik, *GRU*, 51.

70. Krivitsky's MI5 debriefing (TNA: PRO KV 2/804-5) is partly reproduced without comments in Nigel West, *MASK: MI5's Penetration of the Communist Party of Great Britain* (London: Routledge, 2005), but the best published source is Krivitsky, *MI5 Debriefing*, ed. Kern.

71. On 27 November 1935 the People's Commissar of Defence approved the new organization of the Red Army Intelligence Directorate, still known as the Razvedupr (RU). The reformed directorate consisted of twelve departments. The first, headed by Otto Steinbrück (who had, together with Artuzov, been transferred from the NKVD), was in charge of all Soviet military espionage in the Western hemisphere. It was divided into five sections and employed thirty-six officers. The second, headed by Fyodor Karin, directed intelligence operations in the East,

it was also divided into five sections and had the staff of forty-three officers. The third, headed by Oscar Stigga, dealt with military and technical intelligence. The fourth, under Vasili Bogovoy, supervised the activities of the intelligence departments of the Soviet military districts and fleets. The fifth, headed by Col. Pavel Kharkevich, was in charge of signal intelligence and ciphers; and the sixth department, headed by Anatoli Ilyich Gekker (see Krivitsky's London debriefing: 'The head of the department for relations with foreign powers was up to 1937, and may still be, a man called Heckert' [sic] (West, MASK, 252)), was in charge of the Razvedupr's foreign relations. RGVA, f. 4, op. 15, d. 80; op. 14, d. 1479, pp. 296–301. Other departments were of less importance and were not directly engaged in operational work abroad.

72. Kern, *A Death in Washington*, 50.
73. For his very short but authoritative biography, see Lurie and Kochik, *GRU*, 534.
74. Kern, *A Death in Washington*, 271.
75. Melita Sirnis, better known as Norwood, who was catapulted into the public eye in September 1999 as both the most important British female agent in KGB history and the longest serving of all Soviet spies in Britain. See Andrew and Mitrokhin, *The Mitrokhin Archive*, 152.
76. West, MASK, 206.
77. Putna was arrested on 20 August 1936 as a member of the 'military-fascist plot' in the Red Army. Together with others, he was sentenced to death and shot on 11 June 1937. After Sirkov and during the war, Colonel (later Major General) Ivan Andreyevich Sklyarov, codenamed BRION, was the 'legal' resident of the Intelligence Directorate of the Raboche-Krestyanskaya Krasnaya Armiya (RKKA) (The Workers–Peasants Red Army) in Britain and the Soviet military and air attaché.
78. SONYA was Ursula Kuczynski, a.k.a Ruth Werner, Ursula Hamburger, and Ursula Beurton, the sister of Jurgen Kuczynski. SERGEY was a code name of Nikolai Aptekar.

CHAPTER 7

1. As told to MI5 by Walter Krivitsky; see TNA: PRO KV 2/805. See also Chapter 14.
2. See Costello and Tsarev, *Deadly Illusions*, 114–15, 445.
3. The KGB archivists made a note here that JEANNE was Nikolsky's wife Maria, but other documents prove that she did not come to London until autumn 1934. In the financial report drafted by Deutsch and dated 1 July 1935, JEANNE is not mentioned (see Chapter 12).
4. According to Andrew (*The Defence of the Realm*, 183), Norwood was recruited as a Soviet agent in 1937. However, her name was already in a short list of Glading's trusted contacts by January 1936. One of the earlier reports also

pointed to 'a certain amount of mystery that seems to surround her actual Communist party activities' (*The Defence of the Realm*, 182).

5. If 'a female employee' was Norwood, née Sirnis, a secretary in the British Non-Ferrous Metals Research Association (BNFMRA), who had first come to the attention of the Security Service in 1933 (Andrew, *The Defence of the Realm*, 182–3), the material was from the BNFMRA. This recruitment would turn out to be very important for the Soviets, as she not only became the Soviet Union's longest-serving British agent but at the end of the war was supplying Moscow with some of the crucial secrets of the British atomic-bomb project.

6. The full text is published here for the first time. ASVRR, Personal File SCHWED, No. 32476, vol. 2, p. illegible. Author's archive. A copy can be found at the Cañada Blanch Centre of the LSE.

7. Yevgeny Petrovich Mitskewicz, SVR, official biography, 2009. Mitskewicz was born on 24 December 1893 in Ukraine. He took part in the Civil War in 1919–20 and was awarded the Order of the Red Banner for 'liquidations of armed gangs' in Byelorussia. Nikolsky/Orlov was there at the same time, engaged in the same activities. They both joined the OGPU in 1924. As an INO officer, in 1925 Mitskewicz was sent to Germany to run a spy ring in Hamburg. In November 1927 he was moved to Rome, Italy, where he stayed until 1930 controlling an underground group. After a tour of duty in Britain (his KGB biography does not specify whether he was a 'legal' or an 'illegal' resident; although his name is not in the London diplomatic roster of 1931–3, he could have operated under an alias), Mitskewicz was sent to the USA in 1934 and from there to China. In both countries he acted as an 'illegal' resident. In 1937 Mitskevicz returned to the USA, again as the controller of a group of 'illegals'. At the end of the war he was sent to Italy. Mitskevich retired from the service in 1953 and died in Russia in 1959.

8. Andrew, *The Defence of the Realm*, 166–7.

9. See Philip H. J. Davies, *MI6 and the Machinery of Spying* (London: Frank Cass, 2004), 67–75. For the scope of the SIS activities in Russia at the time, see Keith Jeffery, *MI6: The History of the Secret Intelligence Service 1909–1949* (London: Bloomsbury, 2010).

10. Both Whomack and Williams were known communists; see TNA: PRO KV 2/1003, Albert Henry Edward Williams, and KV 2/1237–8, George Whomack.

11. ASVRR, File No. 89113, vol. 1, p. 123, History of the London Rezidentura, as quoted by West and Tsarev, *The Crown Jewels*, 122.

12. Group leader, or *gruppovod* in Russian, is 'an operational intelligence officer or an experienced agent who on instructions from the Central Organization directs the intelligence work of a number of agents enrolled in a group' (Vasiliy Mitrokhin (ed. and intro.), *KGB Lexicon: The Soviet Intelligence Officer's Handbook*, paperback (London and Portland, OR: Frank Cass, 2002), 28). For

assignments planned for Zarubin, Deutsch, and Wolisch, see Erwin Stawinski, *Zarubiny: Semeinaya rezidentura* (Moscow: Olma Press, 2003), 209.

13. Fyodor Yakovlevich Karin (born Todres Yankelevich Krutyansky in 1896) joined the Cheka in 1919 and in 1921 was transferred to the INO. It is reported that from 1922 to 1924 Karin operated 'from illegal positions' in Romania, Austria, and Bulgaria, but he was probably running agents there while based in Vienna. In 1924 he was posted to Harbin, China, under the cover of a consular official. From 1927 to early 1934 he was an 'illegal' resident in the United States, without doubt under the cover of Amtorg, then in Germany, and finally in France, where his assistant was Arnold Deutsch. In early 1934 Karin returned to Moscow to be promoted to INO's first section head. Together with Artuzov and Steinbrück, two experienced and high-ranking INO officers, Karin was transferred to the RU and in January 1935 became chief of its 2nd (Eastern Hemisphere or Oriental) department. As a result of Stalinist purges in the RU, Karin was arrested in May and executed in August 1937. See Abramov, *Evrei v KGB*, 205–6.

14. ASVRR, Personal File STEFAN, No. 32826, vol. 1, pp. 24–7, as quoted by West and Tsarev, *The Crown Jewels*, 106.

15. See Appendix I.

16. The London *rezidentura* expenses report written by Deutsch for the period of June–July 1935 mentions LUXI among other agents who received 'operational payments'. ASVRR, file and volume unspecified, p. 123. Author's private archive with a copy at the LSE.

17. ASVRR, Personal File STEFAN, No. 32826, vol. 1, pp. 24–7, as quoted by West and Tsarev, *The Crown Jewels*, 106.

18. Chancellerie Fédérale, Departement des Affaires Ètrangeres, Corps Diplomatique à Vienne (July 1930).

19. ASVRR, Personal File STEFAN, No. 32826, vol. 1, pp. 24–7, as quoted by West and Tsarev, *The Crown Jewels*, 106. 'Edith' is without doubt Edith Suschitzky who became Mrs Tudor Hart, having married the Englishman and fellow Communist Dr Alexander Tudor Hart in August 1933 in Vienna. Regarding her recruitment at the time, it was perhaps a pun rather than an error or slip of memory. In Russian, the expression *privlekat k sotrudnichestvu* (to co-opt an individual) and *verbovat* (to recruit) can often substitute one another. Edith was indeed co-opted to carry out Soviet intelligence assignments while in Vienna but was formally recruited as an agent much later (see Appendix II). Nigel West's statement that 'Alex Tudor Hart . . . had been recruited by the NKVD *rezident* in Barcelona, Alexander Orlov' (*MASK*, 202) is certainly not correct; see TNA: PRO KV 2/1603.

20. Dr Arnold Deutsch was registered at No. 1 Freyung (Hof 3, Stiege 1, Wohnung 19), at the very heart of Vienna I, where he lived until 31 January 1934. WSLA, MA8, 12 December 2003.

21. On 1 April 1933, following Artuzov's proposals, the INO was reorganized. Instead of six sections it now had eight departments (*otdeleniya*). Artuzov remained the chief, with Sergey Vasilievich Puzitsky as his PA and Abram Aronovich Sloutsky as deputy. Department 1 (headed by 'Leonid Alexandrovich Naumov'/alias of Naum Isaakovich Eitingon) was in charge of 'illegals' and their operations; department 2 (Yakov Mikhailovich Bodesko) controlled all visits to and foreign trips from the USSR; department 3 (Otto Steinbrück) was responsible for political intelligence in the capitalist countries of the West; department 4 (Kazimir Stanislavovich Baransky) collected political intelligence in Lithuania, Latvia, Estonia, Finland, and Poland; department 5, White émigrés, headed by Andrey Pavlovich Fedotov, ran agents and sources in various Russian émigré communities abroad; department 6 (Iliya Gedeonovich Gert, acting chief) collected intelligence and mounted covert 'black' operations in the countries of the Middle East, East Asia, and Far East; department 7 (Ernst Yakovlevich Furman) was in charge of economic intelligence and security of Soviet colonies abroad; and department 8 (Pyotr Davydovich Gutzeit) was focused on scientific and technical intelligence. A. Kokurin and N. Petrov, 'OGPU (1929–1934)', *Svobodnaya Mysl*, 8/1477 (1998), 107.
22. Stawinski, *Zarubiny*, 209.
23. Tsarev and Costello, *Rokovye illyuzii* (Moscow: Mezhdunarodnye Otnosheniya, 1995), 101. Cf. Costello and Tsarev, *Deadly Illusions*, 114.
24. Stawinski, *Zarubiny*, 209. Their children, Zoya and Peter, helped to research the book devoted to their parents.
25. WSLA, MA8–M2763-64/2003, 6 June 2003.
26. According to his official biography, Ignace Hiel (Ignaty Yakovlevich Reif), captain of state security, was born in 1902 in Kowel and lived in Warsaw until 1915. He did some work for the Communist Party in Ukraine in 1918. In 1920 he joined the Red Army. From 1922 until 1924 he worked in the Soviet Embassy in Berlin as an archivist and librarian developing contacts with the German Communists in the Berlin–Brandenburg area who were preparing the uprising. In 1924 Reif returned to Moscow and joined the staff of *Pravda*. In 1925 he was recruited by the OGPU, where he worked in the EKU and INO departments. In April 1934 Reif was sent as the 'illegal' resident agent to London via Austria using the alias 'Max Wolisch'. (In reality, Reif was sent to Britain in August 1933, travelling via Vienna and arriving in London in mid-September; his initial role was not 'illegal' resident but assistant resident based in Copenhagen.) In February 1935 Wolisch was given 'the unwanted alien' status and soon had to leave England. Upon his return to Moscow, Reif worked as deputy chief of the British section of the INO. He was arrested on 29 July 1938. On 28 August he was sentenced to death as a 'member of a terrorist organization' and shot on the same day.
27. Stawinski, *Zarubiny*, 209. One may speculate that it could have been William Norman Ewer. Ewer, alias Kenneth Milton, was the foreign editor of the *Daily*

Herald, and, according to the Security Service documents, from about 1919 to 1929 was a prime mover in a Russian intelligence organization in London. See TNA: PRO KV 2/1016–17.

28. Stawinski, *Zarubiny*, 210.

29. In 1926 Stalin asked Menzhinsky to stage a show trial that would swing public opinion at home and abroad. According to Donald Rayfield, the motives behind the Shakhty trial related to the disparity between promised prosperity and the actual penury of the country. This had to be blamed on someone, and 'foreign saboteurs' were named as culprits. Moreover, Stalin loathed foreign specialists and wanted Soviet citizens to shun them. Nikolsky's former boss, Nikolai Krylenko, together with Andrei Vyshinsky, who would eventually become the Prosecutor General, were chosen by Stalin to conduct a formal investigation. The Shakhty trial was Vyshinsky's first public test. Rayfield, *Stalin and his Hangmen*, 140, 156, 158–9, 210.

30. Stawinski, *Zarubiny*, 211–12.

31. In July 1937 Glinsky (alias V. V. Smirnov, codenamed PETER or PYOTR in Russian) was recalled to Moscow and shot. He became a victim of Yezhov's campaign against the Poles.

32. Maly's MI5 file released to The National Archives is rather poor. See TNA: PRO KV 2/1008–9, Paul Hardt. After the 1933 reorganization, Maly was appointed assistant chief of the INO's 3rd department headed by Steinbrück.

33. Stawinski, *Zarubiny*, 212–13.

34. Lehmann's file was unclassified by the RIS on 29 June 2009. It emerged that Lehmann was a 'walk-in' who offered his services to Soviet intelligence. He chose not to go to the Soviet Embassy himself but sent a friend, a former policeman named Ernst Kuhr, with some secret documents. Soon the OGPU started working directly with Lehmann. For details, see Chapter 22.

35. The interview of 15 December 1957. For details, see Herbert Romerstein and Eric Breindel, *The Venona Secrets: Exposing Soviet Espionage and American Traitors* (Washington, DC: Regnery Publishing, 2000), 89–90. See also Uwe Klussmann, 'Nachricht aus der Apotheke', *Der Spiegel*, 40, 29 September 2009, pp. 50–2.

36. During his years as a Soviet agent, Glading used aliases Edgar Upton, Butch Morgan, R. Cochrane, James Brownlie, and Percy Clark. TNA: PRO KV 2/1022. See also Richard C. Thurlow, 'Soviet Spies and British Counter-Intelligence in the 1930s: Espionage in the Woolwich Arsenal and the Foreign Office Communications Department', *Intelligence and National Security*, 19/4 (Winter 2004), 610–31. Glading had been in the MI5's watch-list since 1932.

37. In both *The Mitrokhin Archive* and TNA: PRO KV 2/1603, Edith Tudor-Hart is said to be sharing a joint code name STRELA/PFEIL with her husband Alexander. However, further research revealed that PFEIL and EDITH were recruited at different times and in different places; besides, in the balance sheet of the London NKVD station of June–July 1935 both PFEIL and EDITH are mentioned as receiving payments for their foreign travel.

38. West and Tsarev, *The Crown Jewels*, 124. They spell the code name of the unidentified agent as ATTILA, but in the original KGB documents in Russian in possession of this writer it is ATTILLA. Interestingly, the authors refer this 1934 report to the same file, volume, and page as the 1933 report of Mitskewicz (File 89113, vol. 1, p. 123 (*The Crown Jewels*, 352)).

39. ASVRR, File No. 83791, vol. 1, p. 72, Memo to the file WAISE/SIROTA, dated 13 July 1935, signed MAR. Author's archive.

40. See Interlude 2.

41. See, e.g., Valtin, *Out of the Night*. The Danish journalist Jakob Andersen, who collaborated with Oleg Gordievsky for his book *De røde spioner* (Copenhagen: Høst & Søn, 2002), gives a more sober and convincing assessment of the Soviet intelligence operations in Denmark in the interwar period. In his autobiography, *Next Stop Execution* (London: Macmillan, 1995), Gordievsky presents a first-hand account of his intelligence work in the country in the 1960s and early 1970s.

42. For the travel dates, see Costello and Tsarev, *Deadly Illusions*, 141, 449n. 3.

INTERLUDE 2

1. ASVRR, Personal File SCHWED, No. 32476, vol. 2, p. 4. Author's archive.

2. 'MAR [Reif] reports that SÖHNCHEN has contacted his friend [Maclean], the latter has agreed to work, wants to come into direct contact with us. MAR asks for consent' (Cryptogram to Centre No. 55/4037 from the NKVD *rezident* in Copenhagen, 26 August 1934).

3. He stayed in Vienna for only a few days, while he arranged modest but clean accommodation for his family on Ungargasse, where they settled on 15 September.

4. From 15 September to 3 October 1934 Maria and Vera lived in Vienna at No. 4 Ungargasse near the Soviet Embassy as 'Margareta und Veronika Feldbiene'. WSLA, MA8-M-2711-13/2003, 4 June 2003.

5. I am grateful to H. Keith Melton, an intelligence historian, author, and the largest private collector of spy memorabilia in the world for providing access to his unique collection.

6. Agent ATILLA was an important NKVD source in the Cabinet Office. In April 1940 Zarubina was sent to London to contact him but learned upon arrival that he was abroad with a government delegation.

7. ASVRR, Personal File SCHWED, No. 32476, vol. 3, p. 5 (p. 9 of the letter, which was written on both sides of the sheet of paper), SCHWED to the Centre, 24 February 1935. Author's archive.

8. STEFAN's memo, undated. The KGB archivists refer it to 'File DEUTSCH, No. 63791, vol. 1, page unknown', but it seems likely to be an extract from ASVRR, Personal File LYRIC (later WAISE), No. 83791, vol. 1.

9. ASVRR, Personal File STEFAN, No. 32826, Autobiography, December 1938 (erroneously referenced by West and Tsarev as File No. 32626 (*The Crown Jewels*, 352)).

10. In his report from London dated 12 July 1935 SCHWED wrote that 'in each and every letter you repeat your orders not to maintain personal contact with [my] assistant [deleted]. I have never told you about such an intention. It is certainly much healthier and better for [our] work . . .' (ASVRR, Personal File SCHWED, No. 32476, vol. 3, instruction from the Centre, p. 21).

11. Cf. Andrew, *Authorized History*, 180, 835.

CHAPTER 8

1. Costello and Tsaarev, *Deadly Illusions*, 445 n. 3.

2. ASVRR, Personal File SCHWED, No. 32476, vol. 3, p. 15, SCHWED to the Centre, 24 January 1935, quoted by Costello and Tsarev, *Deadly Illusions*, 147, 451 n. 17.

3. See Barbara Honigmann (Litzi's daughter), *Ein Kapitel aus meinem Leben* (Munich and Vienna: Carl Hanser Verlag, 2004), 62.

4. Genrikh Borovik, *The Philby Files: The Secret Life of the Master Spy Kim Philby—KGB Archives Revealed*, ed. with an intro. Phillip Knightley (London: Little, Brown and Company, 1994), 70. The author, one of the trusted Soviet 'international correspondents' and a relative of a former KGB chairman, was given a surrogate Philby file to write a hagiography, which came out edited and with an introduction by Phillip Knightley.

5. Remarkably, this information, also reproduced in Andrew and Mitrokhin, *The Mitrokhin Archive* (pp. 80–1), comes not from the notes made by Vasili Mitrokhin in the KGB archives, but from *Deadly Illusions*. There is no reference to it in Andrew, *Authorized History*, and no related documents have ever been released by the Home Office or the Metropolitan Police Aliens Registration Office to The National Archives.

6. ASVRR, Personal File SCHWED, No. 32476, vol. 3, p. 13, SCHWED to the Centre, 24 February 1935, quoted by Costello and Tsarev, *Deadly Illusions*, 144–5.

7. As already mentioned, 'Wolisch' was legally registered in Vienna in August 1933. WSLA, MA8-M2763-64/2003, 6 June 2003.

8. ASVRR, Personal File SCHWED, No. 32476, vol. 3, p. 41, undated (February–March 1935), quoted by Costello and Tsarev, *Deadly Illusions*, 145. The 'control' letter with the information that his wife had left was sent on 19 March.

9. ÖStA/NPA, Kart. 278, Bundespolizeidirektion Wien, Zl. 22114/13, 2 May 1932. This document was sent by the Security Department (GD1), where it was registered under No. 158.057-G.D.1-1932 on 31 May 1932 to the Royal Yugoslav embassy in Vienna in response to the latter's enquiry. It names Vorobyov, Tshchembrovsky, Kolosov, Rine, Gordeyev, Deutsch, Litvak,

Grünberg, Godner, Geodor, Jordanov, and Gromov and a group of nine GPU and Comintern agents.

10. See Andrew, *Authorized History*, 180.

11. ÖStA/NPA, Kart. 19, Bundespolizeidirektion Wien, Zl. IV-4978/190/31, 4 February 1932. The 'Klose und Kommunistische Passfälscherwerkstätte' (Communist Passport Forgery Workshops) file fills several volumes. See also NARA, File No. 841.00/1631, Records of the Department of State relating to Internal Affairs of Austria, 1930–9, Decimal File 863, Microfilm Publication M1209, Roll 7. Hede Massing, aka Hede Gumperz, née Hedwig Thune in Vienna, Austria, on 6 January 1900, is commonly described as the first wife of Gerhard Eisler (see, e.g., 'The Judiciary: Woman with a Past', *Time*, 19 December 1949, or a Wikipedia entry), which is wrong. Regarding their life together in Vienna and then Berlin in the early 1920s, Eisler testified that they had never been married but simply cohabitated together briefly in 1921–2 and later split (RGASPI, f. 495, op. 205, d. 154, l.82, Einvernahmeprotokoll von 23. Juli 1951). As a matter of fact, in 1923 he married Hede's younger sister Elli Thune, a stenographer of the Russian Trade Delegation in Berlin, where Nikolsky later served. During his time in Berlin, Eisler was part of the KPD Pressapparat, having previously edited the Comintern's propaganda journal *Kommunismus* published in Austria for South and Eastern Europe (its office was housed at the then KPÖ Zentrale on 69 Alserstrasse, 1090 Vienna). Hede, who later married Paul Massing, then an agricultural scientist, testified against Eisler during her collaboration with the FBI in 1947. For details, see Robert J. Lamphere and Tom Shachtman, *The FBI–KGB War: A Special Agent's Story* (New York: Random House, 1986). For a certain period of time Hede Massing operated as an NKVD agent (codenamed REDHEARD), first as a courier and then as a recruiter. In the United States her sources and collaborators were her husband Paul, then Laurence Duggan of the State Department, and Franz Leopold Neumann of the OSS, who later served as First Chief of Research of the Nuremberg War Crimes Tribunal. In the USA, Massing reported to the 'illegal' resident Boris Bazarov (NORD). See her reminiscences, Hede Massing, *This Deception* (New York: Duell, Sloan and Pearce, 1951). However, one should bear in mind that this is cold war literature and not everything in the book is true and correct.

12. Report of 9 October 1934; see West and Tsarev, *The Crown Jewels*, 116.

13. Report of 24 April 1935; see West and Tsarev, *The Crown Jewels*, 117.

14. Complaining about the possible problems of unreliable documents, particularly passports, Maly wrote to the Centre in 1935, describing how two other operatives, MANOLY (possibly, Evgeny Kavetsky) and RAYMOND (Reiss), had been thoroughly searched when travelling from Holland to France.

15. Orlov, *Handbook*.

16. Orlov, *Handbook*, 64–5. There is no mention of the incident in the Austrian police records.

17. I thank Herbert Koch of the WSLA, MA8 for providing this information. WSLA, MA8-M277-13/2003, Mr Koch to author, 4 June 2003.

18. ASVRR, Personal File SCHWED, No. 32476, vol. 3, Nikolsky's letter, p. 9, §10. Author's archive.

19. Orlov's travel schedule, part of which is reproduced in his KGB-sponsored biography, suggests that his permanent stay in London lasted only from June to September 1935 (see Chapter 12). According to *Deadly Illusions*, 'Orlov's "William Goldin" American passport that he used for his English trips contains a visa issued at the British Consulate in Stockholm dated 11 July 1934. The first incoming immigration stamp 25 July indicates he spent only ten days during his first visit to England. [This must an error—his *incoming* immigration stamp was issued on 15 July. On 25 July Nikolsky was in Moscow, i.e., he spent even less than ten days in England during his first visit.] The next incoming stamp was issued in Newhaven for 18 September 1934, indicating that he must have taken the cross-Channel ferry. Then he appears to have left the country again the following month [October 1934], because there is an immigration stamp for Plymouth, suggesting that his third arrival was again across the Channel by way of Cherbourg. [It is hard to imagine that anyone would think of travelling to London via Cherbourg and Plymouth when Cherbourg–Portsmouth is a much shorter and more convenient route.] There is an alien registration stamp given by the Bow Street police station on 14 January 1935 and two additional Harwich Immigration Office incoming stamps for 13 March and 26 April 1935, indicating a North Sea crossing from Esbjerg in Denmark' (Costello and Tsarev, *Deadly Illusions*, 450–1 n. 3).

20. See Costello and Tsarev, *Deadly Illusions*, 155. BRIDE is unidentified, but was certainly one of the CPGB libertine activists.

21. ASVRR, Personal File SCHWED, No. 32476, vol. 3, pp. 113–15, SCHWED to the Centre, 24 April 1935, as quoted by Costello and Tsarev, *Deadly Illusions*, 155.

22. Orlov, *Handbook*, 97.

23. Handwritten endorsement on SCHWED's report of 24 April 1935 (Costello and Tsarev, *Deadly Illusions*, 155, 452 n. 41).

CHAPTER 9

1. This must have been a pretext. The assault on a maid was allegedly made on 5 February but she declared it to the police only two weeks later. Another strange circumstance accompanying the arrest was a thorough search of the hotel room.

2. David Aleksandrovich Uger (codenamed REMI) was born in Kiev on 30 October 1895. In 1918 he joined both the Communist Party and the Red Army. He graduated from the Zhukovsly Military Engineering Academy and was invited to the RKKA Intelligence Directorate. He worked in Amtorg in

the USA under the cover of an engineer in the aviation department and then in the headquarters (May 1930–December 1933). In early 1935 he was again sent abroad. After his release from arrest in Copenhagen, he commanded the RKKA armour testing facility (November 1935–June 1937). He was arrested and shot. See Lurie and Kochik, *GRU*, 478–9. His official GRU biography says nothing about his arrest.

3. Max Germanovich Maksimov (real name Max Friedmann, alias Hans Grünfeld, codenamed BRUNO) was born in Poland in 1894. Before his arrest in Copenhagen he was stationed in Holland and from 1933 until February 1935 in Germany. After Copenhagen, he worked at the RU headquarters in Moscow, preparing for an assignment in the USA. He was arrested by the NKVD in May 1937 and shot in November.

4. David Oskarovich Lvovich was born in 1898 and joined Soviet military intelligence in 1921. He served as Soviet Consul in Georgia, Azerbaijan, Persia, and Turkey (1922–9). From 1932 he was section chief at the RU headquarters; from 1935 he was the 'illegal' resident agent in Germany. During the Spanish Civil War he was a member of the military attaché staff (see Part II). After his return, he was sentenced to fifteen years' 'corrective labour'. He died in 1939.

5. Jerry King et al. *We Accuse* [From the Record] (New York: privately printed, 1940), quoted in Herbert Romerstein and Stanislav Levchenko, *The KGB against the 'Main Enemy': How the Soviet Intelligence Service Operates against the United States* (Lexington, MA: Lexington Books, 1989), 131–2. See also Jakob Andersen with Oleg Gordievsky, *De røde spioner* (Copenhagen: Høst & Søn, 2002), 129–31.

6. The CPSU Central Committee's resolution of 8 December 1926 forbade the recruitment of local communists for intelligence work.

7. See *Istoricheskii arkhiv*, 6 (1994), 39.

8. RGASPI, f. 17, op. 162, d. 11, l. 46.

9. No. 053, RGVA, f. 4, op. 15, d. 5, l. 101.

10. TNA: PRO HW 17/19–22, MASK decrypts, London–Moscow. See also TNA: PRO KV 2/1180, Robert Stewart.

11. Ayriss was born in 1903 and died in 2000. She was also known under her marital names of Hardy and Garman and her party alias Jessie Miles. Before she went to Moscow in 1927, Jessie worked as secretary to Albert Inkpin, the first General Secretary of the CPGB and head of the party's Friends of Soviet Russia. TNA: PRO KV 2/2330, 'Jessie Emma GARMAN'.

12. See *Testimony of William McCuiston*, US House of Representatives, 1939.

13. Alexander Ivanovich Kolpakidi and Dimitri P. Prokhorov, *Imperia GRU* (Moscow: Olma Press, 2000), i.

14. For details, see Andersen with Gordievsky, *De røde spioner*.

CHAPTER 10

1. ASVRR, Personal File SCHWED, No. 32476, vol. 3, document, p. 8, §VII, SCHWED to the Centre, 12 July 1935. Author's archive.

2. ASVRR, File MANN, No. 9705, vol. 1, pp. 41, 48, as quoted by West and Tsarev, *The Crown Jewels*, 117.

3. West and Tsarev, *The Crown Jewels*, 88. The authors erroneously state that Krivitsky operated at that time under the code name GROLL. In reality, the NKVD codenamed him GROLL, which means 'rancour' in German, only after his defection in November 1937. Before that, his code name was WALTER.

4. Hoover Institution: Papers of Bertram D. Wolfe. Alexander Orlov, 'Answers to the Questionnaire of Prof. S. G. Payne'.

5. Soviet military intelligence was known as IV Directorate of the Staff of the Red Army in the period between 1926 and 1934.

6. Kern, *A Death in Washington*, 54.

7. Earl M. Hyde Jr, 'Still Perplexed about Krivitsky', *International Journal of Intelligence and Counterintelligence*, 16/3 (July 2003), 428, 437. The author is described as a 'CIA officer for thirty years with the first half of his career spent in the Intelligence Directorate, doing analysis of East European matters; the next fifteen years were spent abroad in the Operations Directorate, as well as in counterintelligence'.

8. Helms with Hood, *A Look over my Shoulder*, 144. Krivitsky's FBI file contains more than 500 pages that were declassified, and 300 that at the time of writing absurdly remain classified.

9. See West and Tsarev, *The Crown Jewels*, 89, 115.

10. Tom Bower, *The Perfect English Spy: Sir Dick White and the Secret War 1935–90* (London: Heinemann, 1995), 34.

11. About Krivitsky's debriefing, see Andrew, *The Defence of the Realm*, 263–8. See also Krivitsky, *MI5 Debriefing*, ed. Kern.

12. As already mentioned, Deutsch was supervising ATILLA and his son, and Nikolsky was supervising Philby and Maclean, both of whom did nothing as agents at the time, though occasionally learning bits and pieces of tradecraft from Deutsch. Two other agents controlled by Nikolsky were BÄR, about whom nothing is known, and PROFESSOR, who was probably used as a talent-spotter working without any pay. As will be seen, there were also support personnel, who included couriers and access agents.

13. As Goldin/Orlov came for only short stays during September 1934–April 1935 and had no meetings with agents or known Communists, he was of no interest to the Security Service. In fact, it learned about 'Orlov' only from Krivitsky and after the FBI had started to talk to him in America (see Part III). In one of his reports to Moscow, answering §7 of the enquiry, SCHWED stated that 'we have nothing whatsoever to do with [deleted] and never violated your

instructions. During several months there were only two cases that obliged me to contact him, both extraordinary' (ASVRR, Personal File SCHWED, No. 32476, vol. 3, letter, p. 17). Author's archive.

14. See, e.g., Vin Arthey, *The Kremlin's Geordie Spy: The Man they Swapped for Gary Powers*, paperback (London: Biteback, 2010); and Nikolai Dolgopolov, *Abel-Fisher* (Moscow: Molodaya Gvardiya, 2011).

15. 'Polkovnik Abel o Sebe', *Trud* (February 1966).

16. See Costello and Tsarev, *Deadly Illusions*, 154.

17. Nigel West's claim in *MASK* (p. 213) that 'it is likely that HEIR [English translation of the German code name NACHFOLGER] was Charles Munday, a 22-year-old assistant chemist employed at the Arsenal' has absolutely no ground.

18. ASVRR, Personal File SCHWED, No. 32476, vol. 2, p. 123. Author's archive.

19. As expected, nuggets of information coming from different KGB-related sources tend to mask the identity of this particular agent. In West and Tsarev, *The Crown Jewels*, we read that Percy Glading introduced Deutsch to ATILLA in August or September 1934. In Costello and Tsarev, *Deadly Illusions*, ATILLA is referred to as a British government agent and in Stawinski, *Zarubiny*, Lisa is described as having been sent to London in April 1940 to re-establish contact with ATILLA, who was put on ice by Deutsch in 1937. He missed several prearranged meetings at Madame Tussauds, and Lisa soon found out that he had been sent as a British embassy staff member to an unspecified country.

20. ASVRR, Personal File SCHWED, No. 32476, vol. 3, p. 112, SCHWED to the Centre, quoted by Costello and Tsarev, *Deadly Illusions*, 228.

21. Costello and Tsarev, *Deadly Illusions*, 227.

22. ASVRR, Personal File SCHWED, No. 32476, vol. 3, p. 112, SCHWED to the Centre, quoted by Costello and Tsarev, *Deadly Illusions*, 228; they do not provide a date, but it must be 12 July 1935 (see *Deadly Illusions*, 452 n. 30, 462 n. 18).

23. ASVRR, Personal File SCHWED, No. 32476, vol. 4, p. 51, SCHWED to the Centre, 7 July 1935, quoted by Costello and Tsarev, *Deadly Illusions*, 225.

24. Andrew and Mitrokhin, *The Mitrokhin Archive*, 80.

25. ASVRR, Personal File SCHWED, No. 32476, vol. 3, letter, p. 20, SCHWED to the Centre, 12 July 1935. Author's archive. See Volodarsky Papers at the Cañada Blanch Centre, LSE.

26. ASVRR, Personal File WAISE, No. 83791, vol. 1, p. 72, Reif's (MAR) Memorandum for the file, 13 July 1935. Author's archive/LSE.

27. ASVRR, Personal File SCHWED, No. 32476, vol. 3, letter, p. 21, Report from London of 12 July 1935 (possibly, the archivist was not quite sure). Author's archive. Cf. Costello and Tsarev, *Deadly Illusions*, 230–1. Interestingly, the authors do not reproduce but quote from this report, source-referencing it to Philby's KGB Memoir, p. 37.

28. See Costello and Tsarev, *Deadly Illusions*, 230–1.

29. Andrew and Mitrokhin, *The Mitrokhin Archive*, 709.

30. See Elizabeth Hill, *In the Mind's Eye: The Memoirs of Dame Elizabeth Hill*, ed. Jean Stafford Smith (Sussex: Book Guild, 1999), 171–2.
31. Martin Kitchen, 'SOE's Man in Moscow', *Intelligence and National Security*, 12/3 (July 1997), 95.
32. Hill, *In the Mind's Eye*, 52–3.
33. Dame Elizabeth Hill (or 'Lisa', as she was known to her many acquaintances), was born in Russia in 1900, but emigrated with her family to Britain in 1917. After an early career as a school teacher and freelance lecturer, and after having gained an honours degree and her Ph.D. at the School of Slavonic and East European Studies in London, she was appointed lecturer in Russian at Cambridge University in 1936. From 1945 she ran a course of Russian for members of the armed services, and in 1948 became Cambridge's first ever Professor of Slavonic Studies, a post that she held until her retirement in 1969. She continued to lead an active life, travelling widely and researching, until her death at the age of 96. I am grateful to the staff of Cambridge University Library for their help in researching 'The Papers of Dame Elizabeth Hill (1900–1996)'.
34. TNA: PRO KV 2/3049–50. Galton continued to work at the School of Slavonic and East European Studies after the war and obtained a powerful position there. A case summary form 1954 (serial 140a) notes the dangers of her having access to the names of every serviceman who attended the Joint Services School of Language courses at the School.
35. Andrew and Mitrokhin, *The Mitrokhin Archive*, 80. According to the memoirs of two other Soviet spies and friends of Burgess (see Goronwy Rees, *A Chapter of Accidents* (London: Chatto & Windus, 1971); and Michael Straight, *After Long Silence* (London: Collins, 1983)), he built up a remarkable range of contacts among the continental 'Homintern'. One of them was Edouard Pfeiffer, chef de cabinet to Edouard Daladier, French war minister from January 1936 to May 1940, and prime minister from April 1938 to March 1940. Interestingly, during the Spanish Civil War the NKVD in Moscow received high-grade reports from their source CHANCELLOR (possibly Pfeiffer) in the French cabinet office. See Part II.
36. Cf. Costello and Tsarev, *Deadly Illusions*, 229, 463 n. 27.
37. Cf. Andrew, *The Defence of the Realm*, 170.
38. Andrew and Mitrokhin, *The Mitrokhin Archive*, 75.
39. See part of her MI5 file PF 63349 in TNA: PRO KV 2/1013. She and Alexander Tudor-Hart married in 1933 at the British Consulate in Vienna. Ironically, the passport control officer presiding over the ceremony was none other than Captain Thomas ('Tommy') Kendrick, a long-term SIS representative in Austria, who 'had a separate office from those of the Legation and Consulate, and no diplomatic or consular status', according to a former colleague. When Alexander Tudor-Hart left for Spain in 1936, leaving Edith with her newly born son Tommy, surveillance of her flat and photographic

studio, which she shared with her artist friends Pearl Binder and James Fitton, continued. See also Kenneth Benton, 'The ISOS Years: Madrid 1941–3', *Journal of Contemporary History*, 30/3 (July 1995), 360–2; and Barry McLoughlin, 'Proletarian Cadres en route: Austrian NKVD Agents in Britain, 1941–3'. *Labour History Review*, 62 (1997), 296–317.

40. ASVRR, Personal File STEFAN, No. 32826, vol. 1, pp. 24–7, quoted by West and Tsarev, *The Crown Jewels*, 106.

41. West and Tsarev, *The Crown Jewels*, 87, SCHWED to the Centre, 8 September 1935. For the full text of the letter, see West and Tsarev, *The Crown Jewels*, 108.

42. See Costello and Tsarev, *Deadly Illusions*, 157. Reference is made to ASVRR, Personal File SCHWED, No. 32476, vol. 3, p. 147.

43. Costello and Tsarev, *Deadly Illusions*, 158.

44. Andrew and Mitrokhin, *The Mitrokhin Archive*, 81.

45. Philby, *My Silent War*, 12, 17.

46. ASVRR, Personal File SCHWED, No. 32476, vol. 2, pp. 89–90, SCHOR to the Centre, 9 October 1935, as quoted by Costello and Tsarev, *Deadly Illusions*, 159. See also Centre to SCHWED, telegram of 10 October 1935. SCHOR is unidentified, but is possibly William Fisher, better known as Col. Rudolf Abel.

47. Cf. Andrew, *The Defence of the Realm*, 185.

CHAPTER 11

1. See West and Tsarev, *The Crown Jewels*, 117.

2. Andrew and Mitrokhin, *The Mitrokhin Archive*, 81–2.

3. See, e.g., Sudoplatov, *Spetsoperazii*, 45, and Stawinski, *Zarubiny*, 213.

4. See Costello and Tsarev, *Deadly Illusions*, 457 n. 33.

5. Orlov, *The Legacy of Alexander Orlov*, 6.

6. See Costello and Tsarev, *Deadly Illusions*, 200–1.

7. On 25 March 1936 Maly (MANN) reported that MAG had delivered 'seventy separate documents (telegrams) and dailies for the 14, 18, 19 and 21 March are being forwarded from him with this mail' (West and Tsarev, *The Crown Jewels*, 94).

8. ASVRR, Personal File WAISE, No. 83791, vol. 1, p. 75, Memo to file, 22 March 1936 (?!), quoted by Costello and Tsarev, *Deadly Illusions*, 196.

9. SVR, the official biography of Adolf Sigizmundovich Chapsky, 18 September 1892–4 November 1937.

10. For details, see Appendix II. According to their personal files numbers, 105 were recruited between Philby and Blunt.

11. Haynes, Klehr, and Vassiliev, *Spies*, 46.

12. Andrew and Mitrokhin, *The Mitrokhin Archive*, 84.

13. Fritz Molden married Ms Dulles in 1948. About *Die Presse* and its post-war history, see Christa Zöchling's story in the Austrian magazine *Profil* of 18 April 2009.

14. See George Weidenfeld, *Remembering My Good Friends: An Autobiography* (London: HarperCollins Publishers, 1994), 145.

15. About Smolka–Smollett, see Andrew and Gordievsky, *KGB*, 325–6. See also Andrew and Mitrokhin, *The Mitrokhin Archive*, 111, 158.

16. See West and Tsarev, *The Crown Jewels*, 157. It seems strange, however, that the source reference for Philby's 1980 story of this recruitment is to the personal file of Burgess: ASVRR, Personal File MÄDCHEN, No. 83792, vol. 1, p. 216.

17. See 'The Strange Case of the Vienna Correspondent', *Catholic Herald*, 20 May 1949. See also TNA: PRO FO 953/857.

18. Timothy Garton Ash, 'Orwell's List', *New York Review of Books*, 25 September 2003.

19. Andrew and Mitrokhin, *The Mitrokhin Archive*, 158.

20. See Ash, 'Orwell's List'.

21. Charles Beauclerk, 13th Duke of St Albans, born 16 August 1915, was a successful officer, achieving the rank of colonel in the Intelligence Corps before the age of 30.

22. Weidenfeld, *Remembering My Good Friends*, 145.

23. See Michael Shelden, 'Revealed: George Orwell's Big Brother Dossier', *Electronic Telegraph*, 27 June 1998.

24. Angelo M. Codevilla, 'Political Warfare: A Set of Means for Achieving Political Ends', in J. Michael Waller (ed.), *Strategic Influence: Public Diplomacy, Counterpropaganda and Political Warfare* (Washington, DC: Institute of World Politics Press, 2010), 220. Angelo Codevilla is a professor of international relations at Boston University. He served as a US Navy officer, a foreign service officer, and professional staff member of the Select Committee on Intelligence of the United States Senate.

25. TNA: PRO HS4/334, Agreed Record of Discussions between British and Soviet Representatives on the Question of Subversive Activities against Germany and her Allies, Copy No. 6, 30 September 1941.

26. TNA: PRO HS4/334, Circular from Gubbins, 22 August 1944. For details about the NKVD–SOE Pickaxe missions, see Barry McLoughlin, 'Proletarian Cadres en route: Austrian NKVD Agents in Britain 1941–43', *Labour History Reviews*, 62/3 (Winter 1997), 296–317.

27. Ferdinand Mount, 'Stalin's Ghost Sits Too Easily among Us', *Sunday Times*, 9 March 2003.

28. The book was published as K. E. Holme, *The Soviets and Ourselves: Two Commonwealths* (London: Harrap, 1945).

29. Barry McLoughlin and Kevin McDermott, *Stalin's Terror: High Politics and Mass Repression in the Soviet Union* (Houndmills, Basingstoke: Palgrave Macmillan, 2003), 141.

30. Michael Ellman, 'Stalin and the Soviet Famine of 1932–33, Revisited', *Europe–Asia Studies*, 59/4 (June 2007), 663–93.

31. Quoted in James Hannam, 'The Last of Stalin's Foot Soldiers', *First Things*, 8 October 2012.

32. Cf. Martin Kettle, 'Christopher Hill: Obituary', *Guardian*, 26 February 2003.

33. TNA: PRO KV 2/1667–9, James MacGibbon/Jean Margaret MacGibbon. He was never brought to trial and his name is missing in Christopher Andrew, *The Defence of the Realm*. See also Michael Evans and Magnus Linklater, 'Death-Bed Confession of the Spy who Got away', *The Times*, 30 October 2004, and Hamish MacGibbon, 'Diary', *London Review of Books*, 33/12, 16 June 2011, pp. 40–1.

34. See *Labour Review of Books*, 9/12, 25 June 1987, pp. 3–5.

35. ASVRR, Personal File TONY, No. 83895, vol. 1, p. 240, quoted by Costello and Tsarev, *Deadly Illusions*, 246.

36. Wright, *Spycatcher*, 221.

37. Andrew and Mitrokhin, *The Mitrokhin Archive*, 184.

38. See Jeffery, *MI6*, 664. However, the author incorrectly states that in March 1939 Cowgill was a colonel (p. 486), while in reality he was still lieutenant colonel when in May 1947 he was awarded the American Legion of Merit. See TNA: PRO WO 373/148.

39. From March 1935 the Transport Department was headed by Commissar of State Security 2nd Rank Alexander Shanin. For details about the NKVD structure in 1936, see Alexander Kokurin and Nikita Petrov, 'NKVD (1934–1938)', *Svobodnaya mysl*, 6 (June 1997), 110–17.

40. Ivan Krekmanov was born in Bulgaria in 1895. He joined the Communist Party in 1919. After 1925 he emigrated to Yugoslavia, where he worked as Dimitrov's secretary before the authorities expelled him to Austria in 1927. From 1929 he operated as the RU case officer and cell supervisor (*rezident*) in Czechoslovakia (1930–3), where he operated with a forged Dutch passport. In 1932 in Switzerland he reported about his agent network in the Czechoslovak military industry to Berzin. The Czech communist leader Klement Gotwald assisted Krekmanov in his intelligence work. After one year at the headquarters, Krekmanov was sent to Germany, from where he was recalled in 1938 and sent to the Gulag. However, Dimitrov, General Secretary of the Comintern from 1934, asked the authorities for his release. From 1941 Krekmanov fought with the Otdelnyi Motostrelkovyi Batalion Osobogo Naznacheniya (OMS-BON) (Special Motorized Battalion), and was sent on a short secret assignment to Turkey. In 1945 he returned to his native Bulgaria, where he died in October 1976.

41. Arvo Vercamer and Jason Pipes, 'German Military in the Soviet Union 1918–1933' <http://www.feldgrau.com/articles.php?ID=23> (accessed 13 December 2013).

42. For biographical details, see Hans-Ulrich Seidt, *Berlin, Kabul, Moskau: Oskar Ritter von Niedermayer und Deutschlands Geopolitik* (Munich: Universitas Verlag, 2002).

43. TsA FSB RF, ASD No. R-9000, Tukhachevsky et al., vol. 'Court procedures', Supreme Court's Military Collegium ruling No. 4n-0280/57 of 11 January 1957, p. 236, as quoted in Julia Kantor, *Voina i mir Mikhaila Tukhachevskogo* (Moscow: Izdatelsky dom 'Ogonyok'/Vremya, 2005), 379.

44. See TNA: PRO HW 17/27, MASK decrypts Moscow–Madrid–Moscow.

45. APRF, f. 3, op. 24, d. 224, l. 130, $39, pos. 244, 'To the NKVD for fulfilment'.

46. Most of these reports are published and to be found in Haustov et al. (eds), *Lubyanka: January 1922–December 1936*.

47. Rayfield, *Stalin and his Hangmen*, 267–71.

48. ASVRR, MANN to Centre, 24 May 1936, Personal File WAISE, No. 83791, vol. 1, p. 71, MANN to Centre, 24 May 1936, quoted by and Costello and Tsarev, *Deadly Illusions*, 200. There must be an error in the reference. Maly's telegram to the Centre of Sunday, 24 May 1936, could not have been stitched in the same file before Nikolsky's memo of 22 March. For details about the archives, see Oleg Gordievsky, 'The KGB Archives', *Intelligence and National Security*, 6/1 (January 1991), 7–14.

49. A memorandum from the Western Department (23 June) warned that 'the chances of Parliamentary Government surviving are becoming very slight' and 'the Communists have at the same time been busy arming themselves and strengthening their organization'. On 6 July, the Foreign Secretary referred to the weakness of Spain in a meeting of the cabinet. TNA: PRO FO 371, Records of the Foreign Office, General Correspondence, file 20522, documents W4919 and W5693; Records of the Cabinet Office, Cabinet Minutes and Conclusions, file 85.

50. See Enrique Moradiellos, 'British Political Strategy in the Face of the Military Rising in Spain', *Contemporary European History*, 1/2 (July 1992), 123–37. See also B. J. C. McKercher, 'The Foreign Office, 1930–39', *Contemporary British History*, 18/3 (Autumn 2004), 87–109.

51. ASVRR, Personal File WAISE [MacLean], No. 83791, vol. 1, p. 75, MANN to the Centre, 24 May 1936, quoted in Costello and Tsarev, *Deadly Illusions*, 204.

52. Foreign Office to Phipps, 11 March 1938, Phipps Papers, Churchill College Archives Centre, Cambridge, PHPP 2/21, quoted in Andrew and Gordievsky, *KGB*, 219.

53. ASVRR, Personal File STEFAN, No. 32826, vol. 1, pp. 24–7, and Deutsch's biography of 15 December 1938, quoted by West and Tsarev, *The Crown Jewels*, 106.

54. West and Tsarev, *The Crown Jewels*, 107.
55. On 11 October 1938 the new head of Foreign Intelligence, Zalman Passov (28 March–22 October 1938), sent a memo to Beria: 'At the end of 1937 an eminent recruiter for the illegal apparatus, the temporary employee Comrade Lang, Stefan Georgievich [Deutsch], was summoned back to the Soviet Union. His recall was connected with the treachery of RAIMOND [Ignatz Reiss]' (ASVRR, Personal File STEFAN, No. 32826, vol. 1, p. 214, quoted by West and Tsarev, *The Crown Jewels*, 112.
56. This happened on 20 September 1938, two months after Orlov had defected.
57. Alexander Orlov, *The Secret History of Stalin's Crimes* (New York: Random House, 1953), 230–1. See also Andrew and Mitrokhin, *The Mitrokhin Archive*, 102. In his book Orlov wrote that Maly told this to 'a friend in Paris', but then how could Orlov know? Andrew decided that Maly spoke to Orlov.
58. At the time, the Chief Directorate of State Security of the NKVD (GUGB) consisted of ten departments: 1st (Guards: protection and bodyguards—K. Pauker), 2nd (Operod: operational—N. Nikolayev-Zhurid), 3rd (KRO: counter-intelligence—L. Mironov), 4th (SPO: secret-political—V. Kursky), 5th (OO: special, i.e. state security in the Red Army—I. Leplevsky), 6th (TO: transport—A. Shanin), 7th (INO: foreign intelligence—A. Sloutsky), 8th (URO: registration and records—V. Tsesarsky), 9th (Spets: secret communications and interception—G. Boky), and 10th (Penitentiary: prisons—Ya. Weinstock). The above-mentioned scientific and technical section was part of the INO, but the work was still in its infancy. In 1939 Gaik Ovakimyan, the legal resident, was the first to demonstrate the enormous potential for S&T in the United States (Andrew and Mitrokhin, *The Mitrokhin Archive*, 140), but then again he was quite unusual among INO officers, as he held a science doctorate from the Moscow Higher Technical School (later widely known as the MVTU named after N. E. Bauman). The S&T line started to develop in earnest in connection with atomic espionage. See also Katherine A. S. Sibley, 'Soviet Industrial Espionage against American Military Technology and the US Response, 1930–1945', *Intelligence and National Security*, 14 (Summer 1999), 94–123.
59. West, *MASK*, 26.
60. Haynes, Klehr, and Vassiliev, *Spies*, 382–3.
61. TNA: PRO KV 2/2880. One Home Office document (Serial 78a) in the file wrongly states that Volodarsky was born in Tcherkask on 22 January 1903. See a copy of his Soviet passport in the same file.
62. TNA: PRO KV 2/2880, Letter of Colonel Sir Vernon Kell to the American Embassy dated 7 January 1933, Serial 79a.
63. 'BRIT was supposed to have worked on economic espionage. His task had been to establish a network to shed light on oil concerns.' However, his work in the United States expanded beyond oil; BRIT was also overseeing a source, Abraham Glasser (codenamed MAURICE), in the US Justice Department (Haynes,

Klehr, and Vassiliev, *Spies*, 382). In April 1938 Volodarsky/Feldman disappeared, having moved to Canada, where in November 1940 he was arrested by
the Royal Canadian Mounted Police. Under threat to be deported to the
USSR, Volodarsky agreed to provide some information to the FBI, becoming,
in the words of one former RCMP counter-intelligence officer, 'not a double,
but a dropout turned informant or defector source'. As during those years and
especially before the VENONA intercept the FBI was at a loss about the identities
of Soviet intelligence personnel in the United States, and especially about the
station chiefs, Volodarsky's information was good enough to identify Gaik
Ovakimyan as the most senior NKVD representative, who was tailed round
the clock and subsequently arrested on 5 May 1941. Volodarsky/Armand
Feldman named Dr Maurice Bacon Cooke, a specialist in the fractional
distillation of crude petroleum, as one of Ovakimyan's recent recruits, codenamed OCTANE. In April Cooke was used in the FBI operation to trap Ovakimyan. Because of his collaboration with the authorities, his case was closed
and Volodarsky remained in Canada. His former NKVD colleagues looked for
him until 1945, when they managed, with the help of Judith Coplon (SIMA),
to obtain a copy of his FBI investigation file. See 'Reference on the Feldman
case', Alexander Vassiliev, White Notebook no. 1, p. 155.

64. The Brandes couple has never been fully identified by MI5; see TNA: PRO
KV 2/1004.

65. In the book written by Zoya Voskresenskaya and Eduard Sharapov, *Taina Zoi
Voskresenskoy* (Moscow: Olma-Press, 1998), Zoya Zarubina, the daughter of
Vasili Zarubin, recalls that Mikhail Borovoy was arrested, spent some time in
prison, but was released (p. 392), thanks to her father.

66. Tsarev was interviewed by William Duff; see William Duff, *A Time for Spies*
(Nashville and London: Vanderbilt University Press, 1999), 142.

67. See Costello and Tsarev, *Deadly Illusions*, 459 n. 63. Accounts of the fate of
Dmitri Bystroletov in *Deadly Illusions* and *The Mitrokhin Archive* differ considerably. Mitrokhin's notes reveal that, when Bystroletov refused to confess to
imaginary crimes, he was brutally beaten, two of his ribs were broken and a
lung was smashed; his skull was also fractured and his stomach muscles were
torn by repeated kicks by his interrogators. He was finally sentenced to twenty
years' imprisonment in 1939, but was rehabilitated during the Second World
War (Andrew and Mitrokhin, *The Mitrokhin Archive*, 106). Tsarev and Costello
write that Bystroletov was sent to a labour camp, released in 1954, and
rehabilitated in 1956. In Bystroletov's memoirs, published by his grandson in
Moscow in 1996, the inserts between pages 544 and 545 reproduce several
documents, namely, Bystroletov's arrest warrant No. 3957 signed by Beria on
17 September 1938, his 'guilty' verdict (page 303 of his personal file) of 8 May
1939, sentencing him to twenty years of hard labour, his concentration camp
release note No. 0034109 of 20 October 1954, and his exoneration certificate
No. 4n01443 of 22 March 1956, signed by Colonel V. Borisoglebsky of the

Military Collegium of the Supreme Court of the USSR. Bystroletov died in Moscow in 1975. His official biography is accessible on the SVR site. A book about Bystroletov in English was written by Emil Draitser, *Stalin's Romeo Spy: The Remarkable Rise and Fall of the KGB's Most Daring Operative* (Evanston, IL: Northwestern University Press, 2010). Unfortunately, it contains factual errors.

68. There seems to be an error in Andrew and Mitrokhin, *The Mitrokhin Archive* (p. 107), when the authors state that 'in April 1938 a new resident, Grigory Grafpen, arrived to take charge', with a reference to Costello and Tsarev, *Deadly Illusions*, 207. As a matter of fact, the arrival date of Gravpen is not mentioned either on page 207 or on any other page, but on page 208 it is said that in April 1938 Grafpen took over the spy networks. His name as 'Attaché Gregory Blank' appeared in the London Diplomatic List published in June 1939, which means that he arrived either in late 1937 after Schuster/Chapsky had been recalled in the summer, leaving all work to Gorsky/Gromov, or in early 1938, but almost certainly before April. Costello and Tsarev write that in April 1938 he took over responsibilities of running the Cambridge network and Deutsch's Oxford recruits, which is certainly an exaggeration. They describe the newcomer as 'a strong-willed NKVD officer whose cultivated manner and smart suits helped him pass for one of the Soviet diplomats in the gloomy Victorian mansion overlooking Kensington Gardens that served as the USSR's embassy' (Costello and Tsarev, *Deadly Illusions*, 207–8). Where all these details come from is not specified. At the time the Soviet Embassy was in Harrington House, 13 Kensington Palace Gardens, W8.

69. ASVRR, Personal File STEFAN, No. 32826, vol. 1, pp. 239–40, quoted by West and Tsarev, *The Crown Jewels*, 110–11.

70. Some authors mention 'a young and apparently inexperienced female NKVD officer codenamed NORMA' (Andrews and Mitrokhin, *The Mitrokhin Archive*, 107). According to others, 'NORMA is not identified ... The Centre had selected a young female agent in her late twenties to be his [Maclean's] control officer ... A dark-haired and attractive woman, she was only four years older than her charge' (Costello and Tsarev, *Deadly Illusions*, 208–9). A former KGB general claimed that 'NORMA [was] an attractive dark-haired woman, only four years *younger* than lyric [Maclean]' (Vitaly Pavlov, *Zhenskoe litso razvedki* (Moscow: Olma Press, 2003), 119).

71. 'Altogether,' writes Nigel West, 'Kitty handled Maclean for *four years* [emphasis added; in reality from April 1938 until June 1940], but after their last hurried rendezvous in Paris in June 1940, when the Wehrmacht were less than fifty miles from the city, they never saw each other again' (West, MASK, 202).

72. Genrikh Borovik (*The Philby Files*, 124) writes that by 1940 KAP (Gorsky) had been shot as a Polish spy, which, as we shall see further, is not true.

73. See Philby, *My Silent War*, 14.

74. Andrew and Mitrokhin, *The Mitrokhin Archive*, 107–9.

75. ASVRR, *History of the London Rezidentura*, File No. 89113, vol. 1, p. 434, quoted by West and Tsarev, *The Crown Jewels*, 144.

76. See Gorsky, Anatoly Veniaminovich, the official SVR biography, 2009. Gorsky left the USA on 7 December 1945 after the NKVD had learned about the defection of their important agent, Elizabeth Bentley, and in 1946 was promoted to head 1 (American) Department of the NKVD foreign intelligence. He was sent abroad on short-term intelligence assignments in 1947–50, but it is unclear what happened to him after those years. Gorsky was born in 1907, and died in Moscow in 1980.

77. Andrew and Mitrokhin, *The Mitrokhin Archive*, 183.

78. Even Russian sources admit that Sloutsky was poisoned. For details about KGB poison laboratories, see Boris Volodarsky, *The KGB's Poison Factory: From Lenin to Litvinenko* (London: Frontline Books, 2009), ch. 3. On 6 April 1938 Stalin appointed Yezhov to an extra position, making him People's Commissar for Water Transport in addition to his NKVD job.

79. TsA FSB, Archival investigation case of Mikhail Frinovsky, Yezhov's first deputy, No. 15301, vol. 3, pp. 117–22, quoted by Jansen and Petrov, *Stalin's Loyal Executioner*, 68. The second deputy who took part in the poisoning was Leonid Zakovsky.

80. See Orlov, *The Secret History of Stalin's Crimes*, 232.

81. Jansen and Petrov, *Stalin's Loyal Executioner*, 68.

82. Regrettably, many dates are given inaccurately, even in the most reliable sources. Cf., e.g., Andrew and Gordievsky, *KGB*, app. B, p. 649; West and Tsarev, *The Crown Jewels*, Chiefs of the Foreign Department at Moscow Centre, p. xi; Andrew and Mitrokhin, *The Mitrokhin Archive*, app. B, 'Heads of Foreign Intelligence, 1920-99', 739. The updated list of Soviet Foreign Intelligence chiefs follows: December 1920–January 1921: Yakov Khristoforovich Davtyan (alias Davydov), acting head VChK; January–April 1921: Ruben Pavlovich Katanyan VChK; April–August 1921: Yakov Khristoforovich Davtyan VChK; August 1921–March 1922: Solomon Grigoryevich Mogilevsky VchK, from February 1922 GPU; March 1922–October 1929: Meer Abramovich Trilisser, from July 1923 OGPU; December 1929–July 1931: Stanislav Adamovich Messing; August 1931–May 1935: Artur Khristianovich Artuzov, from July 1934 GUGB NKVD; May 1935–February 1938: Abram Aronovich Sloutsky, 7th Department GUGB NKVD; 17 February–28 March 1938: Sergey Mikhailovich Spiegelglass, acting head; 28 March–22 October 1938: Zalman Isaevich Passov, 5th Department of the First Directorate NKVD; 22 October–2 December 1938: Pavel Anatolyevich Sudoplatov, acting head; 2 December–May 1939: Vladimir Georgievich Dekanozov; May 1939–June 1946: Pavel Mikhailovich Fitin. The post-war chiefs are listed accurately in Andrew and Mitrokhin, *The Mitrokhin Archive*, though the list ends in 1996 when Vyacheslav Ivanovich Troubnikov succeeded Yevgeny

Maksimovich Primakov as head of Russian Foreign Intelligence. As Troubnikov was one of Primakov's men, President Putin replaced him with his own protégé shortly after he was elected as President of Russia. In May 2000 Sergey Nikolaevich Lebedev was appointed head of the SVR. He was dismissed by Putin in October 2007 and sent to Minsk to a lowly CIS post. Probably the reason was the unfavourable anti-Russian campaign unleashed by the media in connection with the brutal assassination in London of Alexander Litvinenko, who was poisoned by Russian agents on 1 November 2006. Lebedev was replaced by Mikhail Yefimovich Fradkov, who remained in office when this book was sent to press.

83. Pavel Sudoplatov and Anatoli Sudoplatov with Jerrold L. Schecter and Leona P. Schecter, *Special Tasks: The Memoirs of an Unwanted Witness: A Soviet Spymaster Pavel Sudoplatov* (London: Little, Brown and Company, 1994), 45.

84. Costello and Tsarev, *Deadly Illusions*, 253.

85. APRF, f. 3, op. 74, d. 20, l. 51. Angel Viñas, who researched the topic, gives a detailed and well-documented account of the situation and the initial Soviet reaction on the Spanish conflict. Angel Viñas, *La soledad de la República: El abandano de las democracies y el viraje hacia la Unión Soviética* (Barcelona: Crítica, 2006), 86; see also pp. 85 ff. and 93ff.

86. On 23 July 1936 the ECCI Secretariat met to discuss the Spanish situation, and, after hearing a report by Ernö Gerö, a Comintern official responsible for Spain, drafted instructions to the PCE, which were sent, with Dimitrov's note, for Stalin's approval. For the text and details, see Boris Volodarsky, 'Soviet Intelligence Services in the Spanish Civil War, 1936–1939', Ph.D. thesis, London School of Economics, July 2010; and Alexander Dallin and F. I. Firsov (eds.), *Dimitrov and Stalin 1934–1943: Letters from the Soviet Archives* (New Haven and London: Yale University Press, 2000), 45–118.

87. Roman Karmen, *No Pasaran* (Moscow: Sovetskaya Rossiya, 1972), 227–43. Cf. Daniel Kowalsky, *Stalin and the Spanish Civil War* (New York: Columbia University Press, 2004), ch. 2, 'Soviet Diplomacy and the Spanish Civil War').

88. As shall be discussed further in the following chapters, in the first weeks of war Ehrenburg sent several key confidential dispatches to Moscow through Ambassador Rosenberg, which had a marked impact on the Kremlin policy in Spain.

89. Mark Zuehlke, *The Gallant Cause: Canadians in the Spanish Civil War, 1936–1939* (Vancouver and Toronto: Whitecap Books, 1996), 35.

90. For Politburo appointments, see RGASPI, f. 17, op. 3, d. 980, l. 308 and d. 981, l. 213, protocols of the meeting of 21 August 1936.

91. Rosenberg was married to Marianna Yaroslavskaya, the daughter of Yemelian Yaroslavsky, a prominent member of the Central Committee. In 1918 and 1920 Rosenberg was one of the first Soviet representatives in Berlin and Kabul. After his return to Moscow and until 1926 he headed a special section at the NKID that assessed all intelligence that was coming from the OGPU and RU. After working on the staff of the Central Party Committee in 1926–30 as coordinator of all

Soviet intelligence services, in 1930 he was sent to Italy as a councillor to the Soviet plenipontiary there. A year later he was appointed Soviet chargé d'affaires in France in September 1934 moving to Geneva elected Deputy Director General of the League of Nations representing the Soviet Union. From 27 August 1936 was in Spain serving as the first Soviet plenipotentiary to the Republican government. From February until December 1937 he was the NKID's representative in Georgia. He was arrested and then shot on 5 March 1938.

92. Kowalsky, *Stalin and the Spanish Civil War*, incorrectly lists the first Soviet representatives in Spain; see ch. 2, 'Stalin's Diplomats in the Republic'.

CHAPTER 12

1. See Ángel Viñas, 'Francoist Myths in Democratic Spain', Keynote address, Association of Contemporary Iberian Studies, 2012 Annual Congress, London, September 2012.
2. Cf. Gaynor Johnson, 'Introduction' in Gaynor Johnson (ed.), *The International Context of the Spanish Civil War* (Newcastle upon Tyne: Cambridge Scholars Publishing, 2009), p. vii. Speaking about the 'conspiracy' one has to admit that neither the KGB and its successors, nor MI5 or MI6, declassified any documents related to the Spanish Civil War. The official and semi-official histories of MI5 and MI6 contain practically no information about the wartime operations, their results, the intelligence that was collected, and its influence on the decision-making.
3. Paul Preston, *We Saw Spain Die: Foreign Correspondents in the Spanish Civil War* (London: Constable, 2008), 3; and Viñas, 'Francoist Myths', 9.
4. Preston, *We Saw Spain Die*, 3–4.
5. Preston, *We Saw Spain Die*, 3–4.
6. Viñas, 'Francoist Myths', 9.
7. Preston, *We Saw Spain Die*, 4; and 'Spain's October Revolution and the Rightist Grasp for Power', *Journal of Contemporary History*, 10/4 (October 1975), 555. See also Viñas, 'Francoist Myths', 9.
8. Carlos Jerez Farran and Samuel Amago, *Unearthing Franco's Legacy: Mass Graves and the Recovery of Historical Legacy in Spain* (Notre Dame, IN: University of Notre Dame Press, 2010), 61.
9. Preston, *We Saw Spain Die*, 4. Helen Graham, *The Spanish Civil War: A Very Short Introduction*, paperback (Oxford: Oxford University Press, 2005), 16; and Gabriel Jackson, *The Spanish Republic and the Civil War, 1931–1939* (Princeton: Princeton University Press, 1967), 160.
10. Preston, *We Saw Spain Die*, 4.
11. See Ángel Viñas, 'Una sublevación military con ayuda fascista', *El Pais*, 17 July 2012.
12. Preston, *We Saw Spain Die*, 5.
13. Paul Preston, *The Spanish Holocaust: Inquisition and Extermination in Twentieth-Century Spain* (London: Harper Press, 2012), p. xii.
14. Preston, *The Spanish Holocaust*.

15. *El Correo Gallego*, 20 April 1922, as quoted by Preston, *The Spanish Holocaust*, p. xii.

16. Juan de Iturralde, *La guerra de Franco, los vascos y la Iglesia*, 2 vols (San Sebastian: Publicaciones del Clero Vasco, 1978), i. 433.

17. See Zara Steiner, *The Triumph of the Dark: European International History 1933–1939* (Oxford: Oxford University Press, 2011), 181.

18. Preston, *The Spanish Holocaust*, pp. xiii–xiv.

19. Preston, *The Spanish Holocaust*, p. xv.

20. Jeffery, *MI6*, 284.

21. See Peter Day, *Franco's Friends: How British Intelligence Helped Bring Franco to Power in Spain* (London: Biteback, 2011), ch. 1, 13–14.

22. Jeffery, *MI6*, 285. At the same time, no one observed the activities of an opposing side. On 3 June 1935, Mussolini's son-in-law and the future foreign minister of Italy, Galeazzo Ciano, ordered his embassy in Paris to begin subsidizing the founder of the Spanish Falange, José Antonio Primo de Rivera, with 50,000 lire ($4,000) a month, a very generous retainer. After December, however, this subsidy was halved and for whatever reason Primo de Rivera did not claim the payments for the early months of 1936. After his imprisonment in March these payments stopped. See John F. Coverdale, *Italian Intervention in the Spanish Civil War* (Princeton: Princeton University Press, 1975), 57–8.

23. See Michael Alpert, *A New International History of the Spanish Civil War* (Houndmills, Basingstoke: Palgrave Macmillan, 2004), 10.

24. Alpert, *A New International History of the Spanish Civil War*.

25. Jeffery, *MI6*, 271–86.

26. But, as correctly noted by Anthony Adamthwaite, 'in practice Britain and France were far from democratic, especially in the making of foreign policy' (Anthony Adamthwaite, 'The Spanish Civil War Revisited: The French Connection' in Gaynor Johnson (ed.), *The International Context of the Spanish Civil War*, 1–17).

27. Johnson, 'Introduction', p. vii.

28. Johnson, 'Introduction', pp. x–xi. According to the British historian Michael Alpert, 'Its failure had been evident since the early 1930s, largely because the United States was not a member... Germany's leaving the League a few months after Hitler took power in 1933, the withdrawal of Japan in the same year, and the absence of the Soviet Union until 1934 were further factors in the League's weakness... When the League of Nations and the quest for disarmament seemed to have failed, only collective security against aggression was left' (Alpert, *A New International History of the Spanish Civil War*, 6).

29. Alpert, *A New International History of the Spanish Civil War*, 11.

30. Falange Española de las Juntas de Ofensiva Nacional Sindicalista, or the Spanish Phalanx of the Assemblies of the National Syndicalist Offensive, founded by José Antonio Primo de Rivera. His sister, Pilar, founded the women's section of the Falange.

31. Ignacio Hidalgo de Cisneros, *Cambio de rumbo (memorias)*, 2 vols (Bucharest: Colección Ebro, 1964), ii. 135–6, and Preston, *Spanish Holocaust*, 126–7.

32. Julián Zugazagoitia, *Guerra y vicissitudes de los españoles*, 2 vols (Paris: Libería Española, 1968), i. 28–32; Ian Gibson, *La noce en que mataron a Calvo Sotelo* (Barcelona: Plaza y Janés, 1986), 15–22; Preston, *Spanish Holocaust*, 126–7.

33. TNA: PRO HW 17/27, nos 254–9, LUIS to MAYOR, 13 July 1936. Decrypts of MASK messages Moscow–Madrid–Moscow in Volodarsky, 'Soviet Intelligence Services', 34.

34. TNA: PRO HW 17/27, nos 254–9.

35. *Diario de Sesiones de las Cortes (DSC)*, 15 July 1936.

36. Cf. Helen Graham, ' "Against the State": A Genealogy of the Barcelona May Days (1937)', *European History Quarterly*, 29/4 (1999), 485–7. For a detailed analysis of the factors that led to the civil war, see Ángel Viñas, *La conspiración del general Franco: Y otras revelaciones acerca de una guerra civil desfigurada* (Barcelona: Crítica, 2011), 373–80.

37. See Coverdale, *Italian Intervention*, 60.

38. Viñas, 'Una sublevación military'. Professor Viñas writes: 'Without the constant interplay of the Monarchists (bent upon the restoration of the monarchy) and fascist Italy and the promises made before the coup and fulfilled afterwards, the rebellion might have lost some of its most fundamental assets: the availability of modern aircraft and the support of Mussolini's Italy' (Viñas to author, 2 August 2012).

39. By Professor Ángel Viñas.

40. Ambassador von Stohrer received his accreditation in July 1936 but did not arrive before August 1937. From November 1936 Nazi Germany's representative in Salamanca was Wilhelm Faupel.

41. See Coverdale, *Italian Intervention*, 63 n. 75. See also Ángel Viñas, *La Alemania nazi y el 18 de Julio* (Madrid: Alianza Editorial, 1977), 255–346.

42. TNA: PRO, Records of the Foreign Office, General Correspondence (FO 371), file 20522, documents W4919 and W5693; Records of the Cabinet Office, Cabinet Minutes and Conclusions, file 85.

43. Coverdale, *Italian Intervention*, 60.

44. Alpert, *A New International History of the Spanish Civil War*, 18.

45. Steiner, *The Triumph of the Dark*, 203.

46. Douglas Little, *Malevolent Neutrality: The United States, Great Britain and the Origins of the Spanish Civil War* (Ithaca and London: Cornell University Press, 1985), p. 196; Steiner, *The Triumph of the Dark*, 202; Viñas, *La conspiración*, 373–80.

47. Enrique Moradiellos, 'The Gentle General: The Official British Perception of General Franco during the Spanish Civil War' in Paul Preston and Ann L. MacKenzie, *The Republic Besieged: Civil War in Spain 1936–1939* (Edinburgh: Edinburgh University Press, 1996), 7.

48. Ministero degli affair esteri (MAE), Politicas, b. 9, Report 1536/665 of 28 May 1936, as quoted in Coverdale, *Italian Intervention*, 62.

49. Juan de la Cierva y Codorníu was a Spanish aeronautical engineer. His most famous accomplishment was the invention of a single-rotor aircraft that came to be called 'autogyro'. Five years after de la Cierva had made his important invention, in 1925 he moved to England, where he established a private aviation company. In London Juan de la Cierva joined a group of 'friends' of the Nationalist course, the so-called Spanish Committee in London, founded by Sir Charles Petrie, which also included Marqués del Moral, José Antonio de Sangróniz or the Duke of Alba, the Tory MP Victor Raikes, the British businessman Arthur F. Loveday, Douglas Jerrold, and Luis Bolín. Their secretary was Kenneth de Courcy, a friend of Stewart Menzies, then deputy chief of MI6. De la Cierva died in an air accident in Croydon on 9 December 1936 aged 41.

50. Graham D. Macklin, 'Communication: Major Hugh Pollard, MI6, and the Spanish Civil War', *Historical Journal*, 49/1 (March 2006), 277–80. Luis Bolín's account is in *Spain: The Vital Years* (Philadelphia and New York: J. B. Lippincott Company, 1967), chs 1–5. See also Hugh Thomas, *The Spanish Civil War* (London: Eyre & Spottiswoode, 1961), ch. 13; Paul Preston, *Franco: A Biography* (London: Basic Books, 1994), 140–3; and Antonio González-Betes, *Franco y el Dragón Rapide* (Madrid: Rialp, 1987), perhaps the most complete account of the affair. In, *La conspiración*, 23–188, Viñas offers a detailed analysis of Bolín's version and suggests a totally different interpretation of events based on his own research and on Day, *Franco's Friends*.

51. TNA: PRO HS 9/1200/5, Major Hugh Bertie Campbell Pollard.

52. Apart from Macklin, 'Communication: Major Hugh Pollard', these include Jeffery, *MI6*; Hugo Garcia, *The Truth about Spain: Mobilising British Public Opinion, 1936–1939* (Eastbourne: Sussex Academic Press, 2010); Day, *Franco's Friends* (2011) and Viñas, *La conspiración*.

53. *Life*, 18 January 1938.

54. For Pollard's background, see Macklin, 'Communication: Major Hugh Pollard'.

55. Viñas, *La conspiración*, 45.

56. Moradiellos, 'British Political Strategy', 123–37; McKercher, 'The Foreign Office', 87–109.

57. *Guardian*, 25 June 1966.

58. Bolín, *Spain: The Vital Years*, 40.

59. See Luis Suárez Fernández, *El general de la Monarquía, la Republica y la Guerra civil* (Madrid: Actas, 1999), 315.

60. *Diario de Las Palmas*, 11 May 1907.

61. Viñas, *La conspiración*, 85–6.

62. Jeffery, *MI6*, 285–6.

63. At the time of writing Graham Macklin was also a research fellow at the University of Huddersfield, UK.

64. William Mackenzie, *The Secret History of SOE: The Special Operations Executive, 1940–1945* (London: St Ermin's Press, 2000), 32, as quoted by Macklin, 'Communication: Major Hugh Pollard', 279.

65. Hillgarth, born Hugh Evans, was an officer, adventurer, writer, and spymaster. He was a military adviser to the Spanish Foreign Legion in Morocco, served as a British Vice Consul in Majorca during the civil war, monitoring the activities of the Francoist forces and receiving an OBE for his various services, and was made naval attaché in Madrid in August 1939. Here he built up a network of spies to monitor the activities of the Axis marine. In 1943 Hillgarth was appointed Chief of British Intelligence in the Far East. See Duff Hart-Davis, *Man of War: The Secret Life of Captain Alan Hillgarth—Officer, Adventurer, Agent* (London: Century, 2012), which does not mention Pollard.

66. For details, see Viñas, *La conspiración*, 180–5. However, the London auction house Bonhams, which sold his nine military medals in 2003, recorded the following: 'Temporary Captain 25.6.1942 Intelligence Corps.' After the liberation of Austria, which was divided into four Allied Occupation Zones, the SIS task was monitoring and penetrating the KPÖ and the Soviets. The head of station in Vienna, George Young, had a staff of over twenty officers and secretaries reporting to London in August 1946. He was worried that this number of staff would be too large for satisfactory embassy cover, but the head office thought differently, and soon five more officers, six women secretaries, and '2 British handymen' arrived in Vienna. It is quite possible that Hugh Pollard was one of them. However, in 1947 SIS activities in Austria were disrupted by fears of Soviet penetration (Jeffery, *MI6*, 669–70) and that could have been the reason for Pollard's recall to Britain in June 1947.

67. Johnson, 'Introduction', pp. vii–xi.

68. Johnson, 'Introduction', pp. vii–xi.

69. Johnson, 'Introduction', pp. xiii–xiv.

70. Johnson, 'Introduction', pp. xiii–xiv.

71. Johnson, 'Introduction', pp. xiii–xiv.

72. Viñas, 'Francoist Myths', 10.

73. Johnson, 'Introduction', pp. xiii–xiv.

74. See Steiner, *The Triumph of the Dark*, 185.

75. Alpert, *A New International History of the Spanish Civil War*, 198.

76. Cf. Viñas, *La conspiración*, 376.

CHAPTER 13

1. Later, all naval intelligence on Spain was summed up in a classified series of publications *Navy in the Civil War*, 1–17 (Moscow: GRU, 1937–8). Unlike the staff of secret services of other countries, Abram Sloutsky, who finally succeeded Artuzov as the INO chief after the latter had moved to the RU in May 1935, had excellent opportunities to present a good report. His lack of agents-in-place was substituted by a very valuable source in the Gestapo Berlin headquarters—SS Hauptsturmführer Willy Lehmann (BREITENBACH), recruited in 1929. Other sources who supplied Moscow with a mass of important FO documents were the already mentioned cipher clerks of its Communications department, Maclean in the Iberian section of the Western Department, and the brothers Constantini in the British Embassy in Rome. In 1937 Bystroletov was sent on a mission to Berlin to contact a Soviet agent on the Reichswehr general staff, recruited earlier. 'Be proud that we have given you one of our best sources,' Yezhov reportedly told him (Andrew and Mitrokhin, *The Mitrokhin Archive*, 106).

2. Before his appointment to the OMS, Melnikov headed RU's 2nd department (agent networks).

3. Soon after he graduated from the International Lenin School in Moscow, in 1931 Gerö joined the staff of the Latin Secretariat of the ECCI headed by S. Minev ('Stepanov') and D. Manouilsky. As a member of the Secretariat Gerö was sent on missions abroad to control the work of the PCF (1931–2), the Belgian Communist Party (he spent seven months in Brussels in 1932), and the Communist Party of Italy, and for a year (1934–5) Gerö was on a secondment to the PCE, acting there as instructor. From 1931 both Togliatti and Gerö held important positions in the ECCI. In October 1932 the PCE leadership was summoned to Moscow, their policy was condemned, and they were summarily expelled from the Party and Comintern. Replacing José Bullejos and the other renegade figures at the command of the PCE was a hand-picked group of pro-Soviet Spaniards of the younger generation selected by the Orgburo and approved by the Secretariat. All of them had spent many years in the International Lenin School in Moscow and the special military–political school of the ECCI Organizational Department located at the village of Bakovka. These included José Díaz, Jesús Hernández, Vicente Uribe, Antonio Mije, Manuel Hurtado, Dolores Ibárruri, and Enrique Líster. See Kowalsky, *Stalin and the Spanish Civil War*, ch. 1. Two years after the purge, in October 1934 the Comintern leaders Dimitrov and Manuilsky sent Togliatti to Paris to organize the international solidarity campaign with the Spanish proletariat and support Spanish communists. See Aldo Agosti et al., *Le Komintern: L'Histoire et les hommes. Dictionnaire biographique de l'Internationale Communiste en France, à Moscou, en Belgique, au Luxembourg, en Suisse (1919–1943)* (Paris: Les Éditions de l'Atelier, 2001), 304–5, 543–4. See also Gerö's report to Dimitrov, dated April

1936, about the opposition 'fractions' in the Spanish Socialist Youth and other relevant documents in S. Pozharskaya and A. Saplin (eds), *Komintern i grazhdanskaya voina v Ispanii* (Moscow: Nauka, 2001). See also Aldo Agosti (ed.), *Togliatti negli anni del Comintern, 1926–1943* (Rome: Carocci, 2000); Elena Aga-Rossi and Victor Zaslavsky, *Togliatti e Stalin: Il PCI e la politica estera staliniana negli archivi di Mosca* (Bologna: Mulino, 2007); and Giorgio Bocca, *Palmiro Togliatti* (Rome: Laterza, 1973). On a personal level, Gerö was fluent in both Castilian and Catalan and was one of the very first Comintern emissaries to be sent to Spain in 1936.

4. The GRU had a network of highly placed German agents: still unnamed Captain K (codenamed '18') in the Abwehr, Harro Schulze-Boysen (STARSHINA) in the Air Transport Ministry, Gerhard Kegel (HWZ) in the Foreign Ministry, Rudolf Herrnstadt (ARBIN), Ilsa Stöbe (ALTA), and Kurt Welkisch (ABC) in Warsaw, Klara Schabbel and Johann Wenzel in Berlin, and Oskar von Niedermayer, the former Reichswehr liaison in Moscow, at Berlin University. Kegel was recruited as a GRU agent by Rudolf Herrnstadt in 1933 when he worked as foreign correspondent. In 1945 Kegel crossed the front line, deserting to the Red Army and later made an excellent career in East Germany. His last post was his country's permanent representative at the UNO headquarters in Geneva. Herrnstadt also recruited Stöbe and Kegel's friend Welkisch before immigrating to the USSR in 1939. In Moscow he worked at the GRU headquarters and the Comintern, occupying important posts in East Germany after the war. Like Herrnstadt, Stöbe worked in Warsaw for *Berliner Tageblatt* (later she was appointed Cultural Attaché) and Welkisch for *Breslauer Neues Nachrichten*, a job Kegel helped him to get. Later Kegel, Stöbe, and Welkisch worked at the Nazi Foreign Ministry. Another unnamed important GRU source in Germany was one ARNO recruited in 1936. There were also at least three sources in Italy— SIGO, LEONARDO, and ALBERTI—who supplied intelligence specifically on the Spanish problem.

5. Regiment Commissar Dr Evgeny Sigiznumdovich Iolk was born in Riga on 1 August 1900. He joined the Red Army in 1926 and for a year served on the staff of Mikhail Borodin, chief Soviet political adviser in China. Iolk also lectured at the ILS and the Institute of Red Professors. In 1935 he defended his doctoral thesis in economics. In February–August 1937 Iolk was sent on a special mission to Spain, for which he was awarded the Order of the Red Star. After his return to Moscow, in August 1937, he was expelled from the party and sacked from the service, then arrested and shot (see Lurie and Kochik, *GRU*, 398). Nikonov was arrested, sentenced to death, and shot on 26 October 1937. Shubin was also arrested and shot in December 1937.

6. For the Politburo meeting of 21 August 1936, see RGASPI, f. 17, op. 3, d. 980, l. 308 and d. 981, l. 213, quoted in Kowalsky, *Stalin and the Spanish Civil War*, ch. 2, n. 21.

7. *Dokumenty vneshnei politiki SSSR* (Moscow: Politizdat, 1974), t. 19, dok. 249.

8. See M. T. Mescheryakov, 'SSSR i grazhdanskaya voina v Ispanii', *Otechestven-naya istoriya*, 3 (1993), 5.

9. Iosif Markovich Ratner (1901–53) was born in the Mogilev district in Byelo-russia. He joined the Red Army in 1919 and eventually graduated from the Frunze Military Academy in 1929. He spoke German, French, and Polish. From September 1936 he was Gorev's secretary and personal assistant in Madrid. In November 1937 Ratner was transferred to the same post in China. From October 1939 he served at the headquarters, and lectured at the Frunze academy. He became a major general in 1944. See Lurie and Kochik, *GRU*, 288–9.

10. Hajji Umar Dzhiorovich Mamsurov (1903–68) served in the Red Army from 1918, first in the North Caucasus. In 1935 he completed a special military intelligence course and from December was an officer (at that time—*sekretny upolnomochennyi*, i.e. secret operative) of the Special Section A (special oper-ations) at the headquarters. In Spain Mamsurov served as senior military adviser on subversive operations and guerrilla warfare from August 1936 to October 1937. His interpreter there was Paulina ('Lina') Abramson, whom he eventu-ally married. After his return to Moscow Mamsurov was appointed chief of the Special Section A (1938–40). He also took part in the Russo-Finnish war as the commander of the Special Ski Brigade, operating in the rear, and finished the Second World War as the deputy chief in charge of intelligence matters of the Central Partisan Staff. He was nominated as a hero of the Soviet Union in 1945. He was the first deputy chief of the GRU (1957–68), and colonel general. RGVA, personal fund No. 41131. See also Lurie and Kochik, *GRU*, 126–7. For Paulina's memoirs about her husband and many others who served in Spain, see Paulina Abramson and Adelina Abramson, *Mosaico Roto* (Madrid: Compa-ñía Literaria, 1994).

11. Wendt was born in 1895. He served as sailor in the German Navy and later as radio officer in the Merchant Marine. Joined the RU in 1929. He was Sorge's first radio operator in Japan. According to one source, 'Wendt proved slow at building radio sets and fearful about sending out messages. Sorge had him recalled' (James Gannon, *Stealing Secrets, Telling Lies: Spies and Codebreakers* (Dulles, VA: Brassey's, 2002), 141).

12. Slavomir Vukelić returned from Spain to Moscow in June 1938 and settled at the Hotel Savoy where he was soon arrested. He died during a medical operation in the Lefortovo prison in spring 1939.

13. According to the border-crossing stamp in his diplomatic passport, a copy of which is at the LSE Cañada Blanch Centre.

14. Krivitsky, *In Stalin's Secret Service*, 71–2. This text must have been ghost-written by Isaac Don Levine, since during his debriefing in London in 1940 Krivitsky did not know Nikolsky's first name, nor was he aware that Nikolsky had been sent to Spain under the alias 'Alexander Mikhailovich Orlov'. All that

Krivitsky could recall *after* his book had been published was: 'Nikolski, OGPU, predecessor of Mally [*sic*] as OGPU illegal resident in the United Kingdom. Nikolski was his real name; he was in England under another name posing as a businessman and holding a US passport. He was subsequently sent to Spain to organise an OGPU organisation there' (see TNA: PRO KV 2/804–5). By 'an OGPU organisation' Krivitsky apparently meant the NKVD station. It is absolutely amazing that this information, received by MI5 in 1940, never reached the CIA or the US Department of Justice (FBI and INS), whose officers were dealing with Nikolsky's (Orlov's) case in the United States thirteen years later.

15. Georgi Dimitrov, *The Diary of Georgi Dimitrov 1933–1949*, ed. Ivo Banac (New Haven and London: Yale University Press, 2003), 32, 14 September 1936.

16. APRF, f. 3, op. 74, d. 20, l. 87. The document is quoted in full in Yuri Rybalkin, *Operatsyia 'X': Sovetskaya voennaya pomosch respublikanskoi Ispanii, 1936–1939* (Moscow: AIRO-XX, 2000), 28–9.

17. Costello and Tsarev (*Deadly Illusions*, ch. 10, which is entitled 'Keep Out of Range of Artillery Fire', the title borrowed from Krivitsky (*I Was Stalin's Agent*, 93)) refer to Krivitsky's words that 'the decision to send him [Orlov] to Spain was taken by a special meeting of the Politburo on 14 September 1936'. Then they write: 'In an interrogation with the FBI in 1954, Orlov corrected the assertions of Walter Krivitsky as "pure invention". The fact that he was in Spain by 9 September appears to confirm Orlov's account...'. Nikolsky/Orlov could not have been in Spain by 9 September for the simple reason that, according to the stamp on page 11 of his diplomatic passport, he crossed the Soviet–Polish border at Stolpce (now Stolbtsy) only on 10 September.

18. Alias 'V.V. Smirnov', codenamed PYOTR.

19. See, e.g., Gazur, *Secret Assignment*, 339.

20. Gazur, *Secret Assignment*, 44. The same date Orlov specified in his answers to the questionnaire put to him by Professor Stanley Payne in 1968.

21. See Georgi Dimitrov, *The Diary of Georgi Dimitrov 1933–1949*, ed. Ivo Banac (New Haven and London: Yale University Press, 2003), 27. Interestingly, there is no mention of this important meeting in Pozharskaya and Saplin (eds), *Komintern i grazhdanskaya voina v Ispanii*, a very important collection of documents from the Russian archives.

22. RGASPI, Osobaya Papka ('Special Folder'), Protocol No. 42, 29 August 1936, §395, f. 17, op. 162, d. 20, l. 62

23. Gazur, *Secret Assignment*, 45, 47.

24. See Petrov and Petrov, *Empire of Fear*, 157. A brilliant description of how OGPU officials did all they could to get a foreign posting and how much 'shopping' (a euphemisms for foreign goods) they brought back with them to Russia can be found in Agabekov, *Sekretny terror*, 243–7. Unfortunately, this

chapter, entitled 'Chekisty naiznanku' (The Chekists Inside Out), is completely missing in the English translation that is currently available.

25. Protocol (A) No. 13 of the meetings of the ECCI Presidium of 16 and 17 September 1936, RGASPI, f. 495, op. 2, d. 232, as quoted in Antonio Elorza and Marta Bizcarrondo, *Queridos camaradas: La International Comunista y España, 1919–1939* (Barcelona: Planeta, 1999), 303.

26. Extract from the Protocol of the 23 Session of the Politburo of 20 September 1936, SAPMO-BArch, RY 1/12/3/292, p. 3, quoted in Michael Uhl, *Mythos Spanien: Das Erbe der Internationalen Brigaden in der DDR* (Bonn: Dietz, 2004), 66.

27. Müller was born on 13 September 1900 in Ludwigshafen, joining the KPD at the age of 19. He was first arrested in 1924 after the Communist uprising and then again in May 1933, as secretary of the KPD in Baden-Pfalz. Released in April 1935 from his internment in the Dachau concentration camp, Müller escaped to France. He would then come to Spain as deputy of Franz Dahlem in charge of the IB personnel section for the German, English, Scandinavian, and Austrian units. After Spain he returned to France and until the end of the Second World War was a responsible KPD functionary there. After the war, having returned to Germany, he joined the SPD. Herbert Müller died in his native town aged 94 as Honourable Citizen. See Weber und Herbst, *Deutsche Kommunisten*, 517–18.

28. Hausladen was born in Bavaria on 19 January 1901. At the age of 20 joined the KPD active in its different organizations in Germany. First arrested in March 1933, he was thrown into the concentration camp Sonneburg and tortured. Upon release, Hausladen emigrated to France. In 1937 he went to the Soviet Union, where he worked for the Comintern under the alias 'Henry Jakob'. He was arrested by the NKVD. Though Wilhelm Pieck allegedly intervened, asking Dimitrov to release Hausladen, four months later, on 30 August 1938, Hausladen was shot as a 'German spy'. See Weber und Herbst, *Deutsche Kommunisten*, 292–3.

29. Uhl, *Mythos Spanien*, 66–7.

30. ASVRR, File No. 17679 Operational Correspondence, Spain, vol. 1, p. 20, 15 October 1936, quoted in Costello and Tsarev, *Deadly Illusions*, 255–6.

31. Evgeny M. Primakov, Vadim A. Kirpichenko, et al. (eds), *Ocherki istorii Rossiiskoi vneshnei razvedki*, 6 vols (Moscow: Mezhdunarodnye otnosheniya, 2003), iii. 139. No file reference, no date.

32. Costello and Tsarev, *Deadly Illusions*, 255.

33. After the outbreak of the Spanish Civil War (and until its end), the ministers were:

1. General Sebastián Pozas Perea/Military (19 July–4 September 1936); 2. Ángel Galarza Gado/PSOE (4 September 1936–17 May 1937), Subsecretary Wenceslao Carrillo Alonso/PSOE (until mid-December 1936, succeeded by Carlos Rubiera Rodrígez); 3. Julián Zugazagoitia Mendieta/PSOE (17 May

1937–5 April 1938), Subsecretary Carlos Rubiera Rodrígez, until 3 June 1937, succeeded by Juan Simeón Vidarte Franco-Romero; the Basque Socialist and Delegado de Orden Público Paulino Gómez Sáiz was on the same day named the representative of the government in Catalonia (*Gaceta*, 4 June 1937, no. 155, p. 1058), succeeding in this post José Echevarría Novoa; 4. Paulino Gómez Sáiz (9 April 1938–1 April 1939).

34. Group within a country secretly aiding an enemy attacking from without.

35. Julio de Antón, 'Las checas policiales', 11 February 2008 <http://historianovel. blogspot.co.at/2008/02/las-checas-policiales-segn-julio-de.html> (accessed 16 December 2013>.

36. AHN, Causa General de Madrid, Caja 1520, Exp. 1, pp. 17–52, Declaración de Agapito García Atadell (fo. 10). For the latest research, see Preston, *The Spanish Holocaust*. See also Julius Ruiz, 'Defending the Republic: The García Atadell Brigade in Madrid, 1936', *Journal of Contemporary History*, 42/1 (2007), 97–115.

37. *Gaceta de Madrid*, 7 October 1936.

38. There was nothing new in this idea. In 1923, when the KPD planned an insurrection in Germany, Soviet intelligence advisers were sent, as described above, to create and effectively to run several underground 'Apparats' that functioned as intelligence, security, and counter-intelligence services of the Party (at the same time providing a pool of new recruiters for the OGPU and Soviet military intelligence). Likewise, the Siecherheitsdienst (SD) became the first Nazi party intelligence organization that was administered as an independent office until 1939.

39. For details, see Volodarsky, 'Soviet Intelligence Services', ch. 2, where the telegrams are published and analysed for the first time. These pleas were certainly supported by Gerö, the Comintern 'controller' of the PCE who worked at the Manuilsky Secretariat, which was nothing other than the internal security service of the ECCI.

40. RGASPI, f. 17, op. 3, d. 981, l. 50, 11 October 1936, §43, pos. 258.

41. In Orlov's 1993 biography, Costello and Tsarev describe a visit to Orlov paid by the KGB officer Mikhail Feoktistov (codenamed GEORG) on Moscow's instruction in 1971. According to the authors, 'Orlov, who had fondly recalled Eitingon, his deputy in Spain and his friend Sudoplatov, brightened visibly on hearing that they were both alive and well' (p. 384). In reality, Orlov hardly knew Sudoplatov who was released from prison in August 1968, a year before Feoktistov's first visit to Orlov, and was only exonerated in January 1992. Costello and Tsarev also mention that Orlov had asked Feoktistov 'about Lev Mironov, his former colleague [in reality—his boss] in the Economic Department whom he had written in his book had fallen victim to Stalin's purges. He was surprised to learn, 'Costello and Tsarev write, 'that Mironov had not only survived but that until 1964, he had been head of the Administrative Department of the Central Committee of the Communist Party' (p. 384). Commissar of State Security 2nd Rank Lev Grigoryevich Mironov was arrested

in June 1937, while Orlov was still in Spain and was duly informed about his arrest, and shot at Kommunarka on 29 August 1938, soon after Orlov's escape. 'I do not believe he was not executed,' Orlov interrupted Feoktistov, according to Costello and Tsarev. 'Like myself, he was too fond of telling the truth' (p. 384).

42. ASVRR, File No. 17679, vol. 1, p. 20(?), Correspondence with Rezidentura, Spain, 15 October 1936, quoted in Costello and Tsarev, *Deadly Illusions*, 281 (without any reference). The report further stated: 'The anarchists with a hint of instruction will get rid of the POUM leaders. "The masses" (about seven thousand people) have in most cases by chance strayed into this organization and can easily be involved into a number of other political organizations. This is the view of Iliya Ehrenburg who knows Catalonia well' (Costello and Tsarev, *Deadly Illusions*, 468).

43. Graham, *The Spanish Civil War*, 40–1.

44. See Ángel Viñas, 'La decisión de Stalin de ayudar a la República: Un aspecto controvertido en la historiografía de la Guerra Civil', *Historia y Política*, 16 (2006), 78–84. Professor Viñas offers a graphic sequence based on archival documents. The first step towards full-scale Soviet help was the creation of the 'X' section within the RU on 8 August 1936. The next was Stalin's telephone call from his dacha in Sochi to the deputy Foreign Minister Nikolai Krestinsky on 14 August ordering him to speed up the Spanish operation. That was followed by a decision of the Politburo three days later authorizing a visit of Spanish delegation to get acquainted with Soviet military facilities. At the same time an oil tanker (the *Remedios*) was redirected to transport 6,000 tons of Soviet fuel to Spain. Another important decision on 21 August was to open an embassy and send Soviet advisers to assist the PCE in its efforts to organize a coherent resistance to the rebels. Finally, an extraordinary meeting of the Politburo on 26 August made a decision to permit the Comintern to start organizing International Brigades using volunteers from all over the globe.

45. Gerald Howson, *Arms for Spain: The Untold Story of the Spanish Civil War* (London and New York: John Murray, 1998), pp. 125–6.

46. According to Howson, the arms were an assortment of old and ancient rifles and machine guns, all nearly worn out. There were also 240 German grenade-throwers and six, but only six, Vickers light howitzers, which were indeed useful. See Howson, *Arms for Spain*, 126.

47. Julio Álvarez del Vayo, *The Last Optimist* (London: Putnam, 1950), 281.

48. In his posthumous memoirs, Orlov described him as 'one Winzer, a pleasant man of about forty-eight who acted as our trade representative' (Orlov, *The March of Time*, 215). It is difficult to disagree, as Vinarov/Winzer was indeed only acting. In October 1936 he was 40.

49. See, e.g., Lurie and Kochik, *GRU*, 363–4. Kolpakidi (*Entsyklopaediya voennoi razvedki*, 259), writes that Vinarov controlled a group in Portugal. Vinarov was dismissed from the army in June 1938 but not purged, and in 1940 was invited as a lecturer to the Frunze Military Academy. During the war he was one of the

guerrilla instructors, took part in operations behind the lines, and was sent on a mission to Turkey. In 1944 Vinarov returned to Bulgaria, where he occupied top government posts. General Vinarov died on 25 July 1969.

50. See Vinarov, *Boitsy tikhogo fronta*. Sisters Paulina and Adelina Abramson in their memoirs also state that Vinarov 'operated non far from Spain' (see Paulina Abramson and Adelina Abramson, *Mosaico Roto* (Madrid: Compañía Literaria, 1994), 227).

51. Ángel Viñas, 'Gold, the Soviet Union, and the Spanish Civil War', *European Studies Review* (Sage), 9 (January 1979), 111.

52. See General Archive of the Bank of Spain (ABE), in Madrid, *Agencia de Paris*, legajo 4416. The decision to ship Spanish gold reserves to Russia was taken by the government on 6 October—i.e. only three days before it became known in London and Paris.

53. FBI, 8 February 1955, from the legal attaché, US Embassy, Madrid, to Director (FBI, Alexander ORLOV 105-22869), Serial 262, unclassified.

54. Orlov, *The March of Time*, 237. All this is pure invention, as it was Largo Caballero himself who informed Rosenberg about the decision on 15 October. See Ángel Viñas, *El oro español en la guerra civil*, paperback (Madrid: Instituto de Estudios Fiscales, 1976), 190–1.

55. Costello and Tsarev, *Deadly Illusions*, 258–9. The only difference is that, according to Orlov's biographers, he received the telegram from Stalin on 20 October, which is certainly more accurate than Orlov's 12 October, and that he received it at the Hotel Gaylord.

56. Álvarez del Vayo, *The Last Optimist*, 285–6.

57. The first connection between the Spanish gold and Winzer is in Álvarez del Vayo, *The Last Optimist* (first published in 1950). In Orlov's memoirs, *The March of Time*, Winzer is mentioned twice.

58. All information contained in Krivitsky, *In Stalin's Secret Service*, ch. III, 'Stalin's Hand in Spain', pp. 65–100, must be disregarded as well as the whole bunch of books whose authors used it as a serious source. Some articles about Krivitsky and his adventures—e.g. Jean Monds, 'Krivitsky & Stalinism in the Spanish Civil War', *Critique*, 9 (Spring–Summer 1978), 7–35; Hyde, 'Still Perplexed about Krivitsky'; or Raymond J. Batvins's review of Krivitsky's book in *Intelligence and National Security*, 19/2 (Summer 2004), 388–90—are truly appalling, while Gary Kern's biography of Krivitsky (Krivitsky (author) and Kern (ed.), *MI5 Debriefing*) deserves a lot of praise.

59. Stalin, Telegram to CC CPSp (15 October 1936), in Stalin, *Works* (London: Red Star Press, 1978), xiv. 149.

60. The letter to the Comintern's Bureau was sent by the PSUC, as justly noted by Hugh Thomas, 'a pseudonym for the communists in Catalonia'.

61. Reproduced in French in Elorza and Bizcarrondo, *Queridos camaradas*, 363.

62. Preston, *The Spanish Civil War*, 252–4; Hugh Thomas, *The Spanish Civil War*, paperback (London: Penguin Books, 2003), 507–8.

63. See Mary-Kay Wilmers (a relative of Eitingon), *The Eitingons: A Twentieth-Century Story* (London: Faber and Faber, 2009), 266.

64. Sudoplatov and Sudoplatov, *Special Tasks*, 34. Sudoplatov had been Eitingon's friend and immediate superior for many years.

65. For details about Eitingon and his family, see Wilmers, *The Eitingons*, where ch. 23, 'Spain', should unfortunately be disregarded—what Mrs Williams writes about her distant relative Naum, as well as about Orlov and their operation in Spain, is simply incorrect. About Eugenia Puzyriova, whose name is transliterated erroneously in most of the accounts where she is mentioned, see Fundación Pablo Iglesias (ed.), *Los rusos en la Guerra de España 1936–1939*, Catálogo (Madrid: Fundación Pablo Iglesias, 2009), 289. In Spain Puzyriova was decorated with the medal 'Al mérito militar' and would become the only NKVD female officer to receive a British military medal for her role in providing assistance to convoys from Britain to the Soviet Union during the war. Sudoplatov notes, however, that, simultaneously, she was part of the support team for the Cambridge ring (Sudoplatov and Sudoplatov, *Special Tasks*, 36).

66. Antonov-Ovseyenko was appointed on 21 September and arrived in Barcelona via Paris, where he met and discussed the Spanish situation with Ehrenburg, on 1 October. See Protocol of the Politburo meeting of 21 September 1936, RGASPI, p. 17, op. 3, d. 981, l. 213, quoted in Kowalsky, *Stalin and the Spanish Civil War*, ch. 2, p. 20, n. 34. About Antonov-Ovseyenko, his earlier career and his role in Spain, see Volodarsky, 'Soviet Intelligence Services', 89–94.

67. There are several books and even scholarly articles written about Eitingon—e.g. Wilmers, *The Eitingons*; Eduard Sharapov, *Naum Eitingon: Karayushchy mech Stalina* (St Petersburg: Neva, 2003); Ilya Kuznetsov, 'KGB General Naum Isakovich Eitingon (1899–1981), *Journal of Slavic Military Studies*, 14/1 (2001), 37–52. Unfortunately, all of them are very unreliable. The best source is *Kto rukovodil organami gosbezopasnosti 1941–1954* (Moscow: Zvenia, 2010), written by the intelligence historian Dr Nikita Petrov, as well as his earlier work, *Kto rukovodil NKVD 1934–1941*, written in collaboration with Konstantin Skorkin. In October 1921, after a heavy wound and recovery, Eitingon was transferred to Ufa, Bashkortostan, and in 1923 was transferred to Moscow, where from March 1923 to December 1925 he served in different sections of the OGPU Eastern Department. In 1925–6 Eitingon was posted to Shanghai as a 'legal' resident; in 1926–7 he served in Beijing under the cover of Consul General, and later, from 1927 to 1929, in Harbin. From May to July 1929 Eitingon was in Moscow and then, until June 1930, was posted to Istanbul using the alias 'Leonid Alexandrovich Naumov' (codenamed BUR) and the 'legal' cover of an attaché. Agabekov described him and his work in Turkey in detail in his book *GPU: Zapiski chekista* (Berlin: Strela, 1930), 214–15, partially translated into English as *OGPU: The Russian Secret Terror* (New York: Bretano's, 1931), 207–8. From June 1930 to July 1931 Eitingon served as deputy chief of the Administration for Special Tasks under Yakov Serebryansky. Then, after only

four months in Moscow, he was sent to hunt Agabekov in France and Belgium, where he remained until November 1932. From December 1932 to October 1933 he headed INO's 1st Section ('Illegals') and then himself was sent to the USA as an undercover supervisor ('illegal' resident). In October 1936 Eitingon was sent to Barcelona using the alias 'Leonid Alexandrovich Kotov'. After Orlov's desertion, Kotov became acting head of station, also known as 'General Kotov', though in reality he was not a general at that time. See Petrov, *Kto rukovodil organami gosbezopasnosti 1941–1954*, 951–2. Contrary to many accounts, including that of Orlov, Eitingon did not perish during Stalin's purges, but died in the comfort of the Kremlin clinic in May 1981, after spending some twelve years in prison (he was arrested in 1953) and later working as editor of the Moscow publishing house International Relations, whose staff he joined in 1965.

68. Howson, *Arms for Spain*, 126.

69. Jānis Bērziņš (13 November 1889–29 July 1938), in Russia Jan Karlovich Berzin, born in Pēteris Ķuzis, Latvia. Berzin was Chief of Soviet Military Intelligence for over eleven years from March 1924 until April 1935 and then again after his return from Spain in June 1937. In 1907, aged 18, Bērziņš was sentenced to eight years of hard labour for the murder of a policeman. Berzin joined military intelligence in December 1920, rising to the rank of the Army Commissar 2nd Grade (15 June 1937). In Spain, he was known under his *nom de guerre* 'Grishin'. Berzin appears in the VENONA decrypts as STARIK (Romerstein and Breindel, *The Venona Secrets*, 119), Russian for 'old man', a nickname by which he was indeed known to many of his subordinates; however, his official code name in Spain was DONIZETTI. A staunch Stalinist, he was nonetheless executed during the Moscow Trials. On the night of 27–8 November 1937 Berzin was arrested as a 'Trotskyite' and shot near Moscow.

70. For the dates of hers and Berzin's arrival, see Fundación Pablo Iglesias (ed.), *Los rusos*, 266, 280. Noticeably, La Pasionaria knew Berzin's interpreter by her real name; see Dolores Ibárruri, *El único camino* (Madrid: Instituto de la Mujer, 1992), 481.

71. Siebler was born in Hindenburg on 26 August 1901. He joined the KPD in 1921, and from 1927 was on a mission in Berlin for the RU as part of the group headed by Arthur Hübner. His small shop on Blücherstrasse, used as a cover, sold radios. He emigrated to Moscow in 1930, where he was trained as a radio operator. From the autumn of 1931 he worked in Norway, and then in Manchuria, where he was Sorge's courier. In 1935 he was recalled to Moscow and sent to Switzerland and from there to Spain. He returned to Moscow in August 1937, was purged but survived, and in 1967 moved with his family to East Berlin. See Lurie and Kochik, *GRU*, 508–9.

72. Petrov and Petrov, *Empire of Fear*, 57.

73. One of the junior officers of the NKVD *rezidentura* in Spain was Inna Natanovna Belenkaya. When Orlov deserted, she was recalled to Moscow, where she committed suicide before she could be arrested. See Primakov et al.,

Ocherki, vol. iii, ch. 11, p. 144. According to Russian sources, Inna Belenkaya was the wife of Samuel Perevoznikov, member of the Yasha [Serebryansky] Group, and the sister of Serebryansky's wife, Polina Belenkaya.

74. Graham, *The Spanish Civil War*, 40.

75. Preston, *The Spanish Civil War*, 163–4.

76. Orlov's biographers write: 'The only official whom journalist Louis Fischer found at the Hotel Gaylord was *General* [emphasis added] Orlov, who advised the American reporter, "Leave as soon as possible. There is no front. Madrid is the front"' (Costello and Tsarev, *Deadly Illusions*, 465 n. 21). Costello and Tsarev not only deliberately exaggerated Orlov's rank, but referenced this quotation to a non-existing work ('Fischer, *The War in Spain*, New York, 1941, p. 369'). In reality, the only work by Louis Fischer entitled 'The War in Spain' was an article published in the *New Statesman* in London on 20 August 1938.

77. Louis Fischer, *Men and Politics* (London: Jonathan Cape, 1941), 364.

78. About Soledad Sancha, see Soledad Fox, *Constancia de la Mora in War and Exile: International Voice for the Spanish Republic* (Brighton and Portland: Sussex Academic Press/Cañada Blanch Centre for Contemporary Spanish Studies, 2007); and Javier Juárez, *Patria: Una española en el KGB* (Barcelona: Debate, 2008), 86 n. 9. Born in Madrid in 1911, Soledad Sancha joined the PCE at the age of 20. During the civil war she worked at the Soviet Embassy, according to the author, most of the time as Orlov's personal interpreter. After the war she lived in exile in the USSR with the Communist architect Luis Lacasa. A year after his death in 1966, Sancha returned to Spain. Notably, in his detailed account of this celebration on 7 November 1936, Karmen (*No Pasaran!*, 261) mentioned Gorev, Ratner, Mamsurov (whom he described incorrectly), Lina, Koltsov, and himself, completely 'forgetting' others, which was certainly not the result of dementia. The present author is in possession of two photos from Karmen's Moscow archive, one taken by Karmen himself, and another by Lina, which clearly show all participants whose names were noted by Karmen. Both photos are reproduced in Fundación Pablo Iglesias (ed.), *Los rusos*, 161, with a full caption, and in the memoirs of Abramson and Abramson, *Mosaico Roto*, 252–3.

79. Cf. Isaac Don Levine, *Die Psyche des Mörders: Der Mann der Trotzki tötete* (Vienna, Frankfurt, and Zurich: Europa Verlag, 1970), 30.

80. Unpublished memoirs of José Fernández Sánchez.

81. See Ángel Viñas, *La soledad de la República*; *El escudo de la República: El oro de España, la apuesta soviética y los hechos de mayo de 1937* (Barcelona: Crítica, 2007); *El honor de la República: Entre el acoso fascista, la hostilidad británica y la política de Stalin* (Barcelona: Crítica, 2009); and, with Fernando Hernández Sánchez, *El desplome de la República* (Barcelona: Crítica, 2009). See also Preston, *We Saw Spain Die* and *The Spanish Holocaust*, as well as Howson, *Arms for Spain*. Howson is now working on a new, updated version of his book.

82. RPA, f. 3, op. 65, d. 223, ll. 90, 141–2, 146, quoted in Oleg V. Khlevniuk, *Master of the House: Stalin and his Inner Circle* (New Haven and London: Yale University Press, 2009), 173.

83. Among several excellent studies in German, see zur Mühlen, *Spanien war ihre Hoffnung*; Peter Huber und Michael Uhl, 'Politische Überwachung und Repression in den Internationalen Brigaden (1936–1938)', in Nikolaus Lobkowicz, Leonid Luks, Donal O'Sullivan, and Alexei Rybakov (eds), *Forum für osteuropäische Ideen- und Zeitgeschichte* (Cologne: Böhlau Verlag, 2001), ii. 121–59; Uhl, *Mythos Spanien*; Ralph Hug, *St Gallen–Moskau–Aragón: Das Leben des Spanienkämpfers Walter Wagner*, ed. Peter Huber, paperback (Zurich: Rotpunktverlag, 2007); and Peter Huber and Ralph Hug, *Die Schweizer Spanienfreiwilligen: Biografisches Handbuch* (Zurich: Rotpunkverlag, 2009). See also Hans Landauer with Erich Hackl, *Lexikon der österreichischen Spanienkämpfer 1936–1939* (Vienna: Verlag der Theodor Kramer Gesellschaft, 2003). An interesting episode is in Paul Thalmann, *Wo die Freiheit stirbt: Stationen eines politischen Kampfes*, paperback (Oloten und Freiburg im Breisgau: Walter Verlag, 1974), 206–8, where the author, not knowing the name, accurately describes Orlov as 'der Boxer' or 'Boxernase', the chief GPU agent in Spain, who took part in his interrogations.

84. See Jesús Hernández, *Yo fui un ministro de Stalin* (Madrid: G. del Toro, 1974), 78–183.

85. Krivitsky, *In Stalin's Secret Service*, 88.

86. See Volodarsky, 'Soviet Intelligence Services'. See also 'Lista de las personas Rusas para inscribir en las filas de las tropas Españolas', in Enrique Moral Sandoval, Aurelio Martín Nájera, and Augustín Garrigós Fernández (eds), *Obras completas de Largo Caballero*, viii. *Notas históricas de la guerra de España (1917–1940) y otros escritos* (Madrid: Fundacion Francisco Largo Caballero; Barcelona: Instituto Monsa de Ediciones, 2009).

87. See, e.g., Reiner Tosstorff, *El POUM en la revolució espanyola* (Barcelona: Editorial Base, 2009), 30–1. See also Stanley G. Payne, *The Spanish Civil War, the Soviet Union, and Communism* (New Haven and London: Yale University Press, 2004), 196, to which Helen Graham comments: 'That such intervention occurred is clear. But given Antonov-Ovseenko was suggesting a political direction which all Catalan liberals were in any case keen to take, it makes no sense to argue that their decision was purely the product of Soviet "duress". What the Soviet diplomat offered Companys was a largely superfluous reminder of the liberal Republic's precarious international position. Nor did Companys need to be reminded that the POUM's presence in the Generalitat was an additional obstacle to liberal normalization' (Graham, '"Against the State"', 507).

88. Antonov-Ovseyenko's reports to the Politburo from Barcelona, a collection of documents named 'The Diary of Antonov-Ovseyenko', became known only in spring 2010. RGASPI, f. 17, op. 120, d. 263. For details, see Volodarsky, 'Soviet Intelligence Services', 90–1.

89. Ehrenburg, *Sobranie sochinenii v 9-ti tomakh*, ix. 114–18.

90. Published in Robert Radosh, Mary R. Habeck, and Gregory Sevostianov (eds), *Spain Betrayed: The Soviet Union in the Spanish Civil War* (New Haven and London: Yale University Press, 2001), documents 11, 12, and 13, pp. 25–32.

91. Ehrenburg, *Sobranie sochinenii v 9-ti tomakh*, ix. 118.
92. His name is spelt incorrectly in Fundación Pablo Iglesias (ed.), *Los rusos*, 267. Before Spain, Bekrenev headed the intelligence department of the Black Sea Navy Chief of Staff.
93. No file reference, no date, quoted in Primakov et al. (eds), *Ocherki*, iii. 132.
94. One should differentiate between NKVD informants and agents. Informants are normal citizen who work elsewhere and who, in whatever circumstances, report to their case officers on more or less anything that happens around them. An agent is a person who operates in a hostile environment (e.g. among the Trostkyists), fulfilling specific tasks and achieving results. According to the Russian 'Memorial' historian Dr Nikita Petrov, whose informed opinion is based on archival documents, by the end of the Second World War there were about one million informers and several hundred thousand agents in the USSR. See Nikita Petrov, 'Stalin i NKVD', interview in *Echo Moskvy*, 20 June 2009.
95. Manuel Uribarri, *El S.I.M. de la República*, vol. ii of *La Quinta Columna Española* (La Habana, Cuba: Tipografia la Universal, 1943), 11.
96. Graham, *The Spanish Civil War*, 110.
97. Kevin McDermott and Jeremy Agnew, *The Comintern: A History of the International Communism from Lenin to Stalin* (Houndmills, Basingstoke: Palgrave Macmillan, 1996), 140.
98. Established on 12 June 1937, *La Vanguardia*, 13 June 1937, p. 6.
99. Khlevniuk, *Master of the House*, 174.
100. From the speech on the February–March 1937 Plenum, RGASPI, f. 558, op. 11, d. 772, ll. 14 and 88, quoted in Khlevniuk, *Master of the House*, 175. For the full Russian text, see *Voprosy istorii*, 3 (1995), 3–15, and Haustov et al., *Lubyanka, 1937–1938* , 95–109.
101. 'Decision of the Presidium of the ECCI on the Work of the Communist Party of Spain', *Communist International*, 14/2 (February 1937), 136–8.
102. Franz Borkenau, *Spanish Cockpit: An Eye-Witness Account of the Political and Social Conflicts of the Spanish Civil War* (London: Faber and Faber, 1937), 240. The author, who visited Spain twice during the civil war, may be wrong about Spain and the Spaniards, but the above quoted observations are certainly correct.
103. RGVA, f. 33987, op. 3, d. 960, ll. 27–8, cited by Radosh et al. (eds), *Spain Betrayed*, document 30, pp. 118–19.
104. Very few published sources are devoted to the Russian émigré volunteers in the Spanish Civil War (one of the best is probably Judith Keene, *Fighting for Franco: International Volunteers in Nationalist Spain during the Spanish Civil War, 1936–39* (London and New York: Leicester University Press, 2001)), and there are still major gaps in our knowledge of the Russian volunteers from Europe and America fighting for the Republic.
105. Cf. Andrew and Mitrokhin, *The Mitrokhin Archive*, 72.

CHAPTER 14

1. 'Rebels for a Cause', Letters, *Vanity Fair* (November 2001), 36.
2. Schafranek, 'Kurt Landau', *Revolutionary History*, 4/1–2 (Winter–Spring 1992).
3. Sam Tanenhaus, 'Innocents Abroad', *Vanity Fair* (September 2001).
4. See Radosh et al. (eds.), *Spain Betrayed*. The German historian Frank Schauff, mentioning the book in a review article, notes: 'Certainly, the documentation is correct, but the editors of the archival material are ideologically biased in their comments and the reader often asks oneself, why these comments say virtually the contrary from what can be read from documents [that are translated and reproduced] . . . Nonetheless, this documentation is certainly a very important source of information' (Frank Schauff, 'A Comment on Recent Literature on Soviet and Comintern Involvement in the Spanish Civil War', *Iberoamericana: America Latina–España–Portugal*, ns 29 (March 2008), 206–7). Only a few years passed and what seemed 'explosive new revelations' turned into a mess. Not to mention Alexander Matveyevich Nikonov being called 'the deputy chief of the GRU in Spain, Anatoly Nikonov' (p. 121), while the Red Army Intelligence Directorate was not known as GRU before 1943. Nikonov had only been in Spain for about two months on an inspection tour. Or 'the GRU established secret prisons' (p. xvii)—absurdities that misinform the reader. There are many misleading errors, analysis of which can itself produce a thick volume. Here are only two minor ones. Document 14, which the editors for whatever reason call André Marty's 'Remarks about the CP of Spain', which the document is *not*, represents Marty's report about the situation in Spain dated 14 October 1936. Radosh and his co-author, Mary R. Habeck, who did the translations, suggest the following version: 'I was very surprised on my arrival in Madrid by the work of Codo[villa]. There is no other term for this than "ka" [*sic*]. He does everything himself . . . Before his arrival in September, he wrote many of the editorials for *Mundo Obrero* himself' (pp. 37–8). The original of the document, which is part of the Moscow RGASPI collection, reads as follows: 'I was very surprised on my arrival in Madrid by the work of Codo. There is no other term for this than "ca" [that is, 'cacique' meaning a bigwig or a big shot in French]. He does everything himself . . . Until his *departure* in September [emphasis added], he wrote many of the editorials for *Mundo Obrero* himself' (for comparison, see Pozharskaya and Saplin (eds.), *Komintern*, doc. 38, p. 174.) Radosh and his co-editors write further: 'Thus, for example, Com. Checa, upon whom has been laid responsibility for organising the police, spends three-quarters of his day signing passes, searching rooms, and dealing with petty problems' (p. 39), while the original reads: 'Thus, for example, Com. Checa, upon whom the responsibility for organizing the police has been entrusted, spends three-quarters of his day signing passes, *looking for rooms* [emphasis added] and settling minor matters.' Perhaps the only consolation is that the translation of the same document suggested by Antonio Elorza and published in *Centre and Periphery* is even worse, and that in the Russian version published in Moscow one full line of the text is completely missing. It is also amazing that all three sources give a

different source reference to Marty's report. Many more principal errors contained in *Spain Betrayed* are discussed in Viñas's trilogy, which he himself calls 'a demolition work of a profoundly mendacious work'.

5. Norman Markowitz, 'Book Review Essay: Spain Betrayed by Ronald Radosh', *Political Affairs*, 18 June 2004.

6. Costello and Tsarev write that 'Orlov's KGB file reveals that it was he who personally selected, trained and recruited Morris Cohen, a Jewish American from Brooklyn who had volunteered to fight with the Abraham Lincoln Battalion in Spain' (*Deadly Illusions*, 276). This is another attempt to enhance Orlov's image. According to the testimony of Jack Bjoze, the American Communist who fought in Spain and who personally recommended his friend Cohen to Soviet intelligence, Cohen was not recruited by Orlov and not even during the Spanish Civil War. According to Mr Bjoze's testimony, 'during the World's Fair [in 1939 in New York], a Russian came to me … They needed people they could trust. I recommended a number of veterans who fought in Spain, and Morris was one of them' (see 'A complete and unedited interview with Jack Bjoze, dated 1–17 August 1999, portions of which were utilized in The Red Files PBS broadcast'). From the World's Fair Cohen was transferred to Amtorg, where he was recruited by Semyonov. He and his wife later operated in the USA and Britain, where they were arrested in January 1961 as part of the Portland spy ring. Morris Cohen, who had a Ukrainian father and a Lithuanian mother, died in Moscow on 23 June 1995. The obituary, published by the *Volunteer* (17/2 (1995), 6) is very inaccurate. In his KGB memoirs, written in Moscow in December 1978, Cohen recalled that, after he had been released from hospital, he was sent to the 'Barcelona School for Political Studies', where he got acquainted 'with Soviet comrades who offered me to work in Soviet intelligence'. It is possible that Cohen had started his collaboration with the NKVD in Spain and was then formally recruited in the USA. Some additional information about the Cohens can be found in their FBI File, 100-406659, which is now declassified.

7. For Browder's and his family involvement with Soviet intelligence, see James G. Ryan, 'Socialist Triumph as a Family Value: Earl Browder and Soviet Espionage', *American Communist History*, 1/2 (December 2002), 125–42. See also John Earl Haynes, Harvey Klehr and James G. Ryan, 'Correction to "Helen Lowry and Earl Browder"', *American Communist History*, 8/1 (2009), 135–6.

8. While scholars and intelligence professionals may find enough literature on Fyodor Karin and Vasili Zarubin's family (his sister Anna also worked for the intelligence service), there is very little on Erich Tacke, a veteran Soviet intelligence officer who in most of the accounts is presented as an innocent victim of Stalin's purges. So far, Tacke has been mentioned in several books: Reinhard Müller, *Menschenfalle Moskau: Exil und stalinistische Verfolgung* (Hamburg: Hamburger Edition, 2001); Igor Damaskin with Geoffrey Elliott, *Kitty Harris: The Spy with Seventeen Names* (London: St Ermin's Press, 2001); Stawinski, *Zarubiny*; and Primakov et al. (eds), *Ocherki*, iii. Damaskin borrows heavily from the Zarubins' memoirs, still making many errors (as, e.g., his statements that Yunona was Tacke's wife in Harbin in

1928, which she was not; that Vasilevsky, alias Tarasov, was 'Yuri', while in fact he was Lev Petrovich, and so on). Reinhard Müller, a history professor from Hamburg, on the contrary, works exclusively with the Soviet archival material, mainly from the Russian State Archive of Social-Political History (RGASPI), where fund 495 contains Tacke's Personal Comintern File No. 6620. On page 13 one finds his autobiography, which makes no mention at all of his involvement with Soviet intelligence. Erich Tacke (Comintern pseudonym 'Albert', code-named BOM by the NKVD) was born on 18 February 1894 in Bad Lauterberg/Harz in Lower Saxony, Germany. Interestingly, according to his NKVD Investigation File No. 3618, Tacke was born in 1894 in Riga, Latvia. (According to the immigration records of Ellis Island, New York, Tacke was born in 1899 and at the time he left Germany was living in Wietze near Hanover.) His school friend and future NKVD colleague was Werner Rakow (Inkov). From 1910 until 1914 Tacke studied banking and then found employment in different banks. In March 1914, together with Rakow, he went to St Petersburg as a German correspondent of the Russo-Asian Bank. During the First World War he was interned in Russia as a civil PoW. He was released in 1918 and returned to Germany, where he was sentenced by a military court in Hanover. Because of his good command of Russian, Tacke was sent to the Berlin school of military interpreters. In October 1918 Tacke tried to desert to Moscow but was detained in Kovno (now Kaunas, Lithuania). Back in his garrison in Wolfenbüttel, in early 1919 he joined the KPD. From 1921 Tacke was a member of the secret KPD M-Apparat. It seems that in spring 1923 Tacke, together with his elder sister Dora, went to New York to join their many relatives who resided there (Bernard Tacke had arrived in 1893, Christina Tacke in 1897, Barney Tacke in 1902, Chas and August Tacke in 1906). According to the official passenger record, Erich Tacke arrived in New York on 11 March 1923 on board the *York*, coming from Bremen, manifest line number 0028. It is not known how long Tacke stayed in the United States, but in 1927 he was already working in the Soviet consulate in Harbin, together with Vasili Roshchin and Vasili Zarubin. Vasili Petrovich Roshchin (real name Yakov Fyodorovich Tishchenko) was on a mission in Harbin, first as a Red Army intelligence officer from late 1925 until 1926, and then as an INO operative until November 1930. In the summer of 1932 he arrived in Berlin as a deputy of Boris Berman, the legal OGPU resident, taking Tacke with him. Roshchin was one of ten operational officers assigned to the Berlin station. In Berlin Tacke was in charge of a small undercover cell that included himself; his wife, Yunona Sosnovskaya; Karl Gursky, a *gruppovod* (supervisor of a small group of agents); his wife and two couriers, Margaret Browder and Kitty Harris. Because of the failure of an agent in Paris, all group members were recalled to Russia. However, as a native German speaker and an experienced agent, Tacke, together with Yunona, was sent back to Berlin in 1934 with the task of penetrating one of the secret services. Though his mission was independent and secret, he soon started meeting Vasili Zarubin, the 'illegal' NKVD resident—or, at least, Zarubin's biographer claims that they met. After an unsuccessful approach to his former friend, now a member of the NSDAP and the SS, Tacke was recalled to Moscow. In his Comintern autobiography Tacke wrote that from the end of 1932 he worked in Moscow in the German section of the Verlaggenossenschaft ausländischer Arbeiter (Publishing Association of Foreign Workers). According to the German historian Reinhard Müller, on 22 April 1936 Tacke was arrested and in June 1936, together with Herbert Berndt and Kreszentia ('Zenzl') Mühlsam, charged with espionage. The indictment was changed at the last moment into 'preparations to carry out anti-Soviet agitation and propaganda' according to the Article 58-11 of the Criminal Code. Bernd and Mühlsam were finally sentenced to different (short) terms, and Tacke was released. According to this author's information, in April 1937 Tacke was sent to Spain to join Orlov. He certainly took part in the operation against Andreu Nin in June 1937 (see Personal File SCHWED, No. 32476, vol. 1, p. 101), after which he was recalled to Moscow. In his book Reinhard Müller states that 'on 2 September 1937 Erich Tacke was sentenced to death by the Military Collegium of the Supreme Court [of the USSR] and shot' (*Menschenfalle Moskau*, 253 n. 11). When contacted by this author, Müller responded: 'You found a correctable error. Tacke was shot dead [on] 31.3.1938' (Reinhard Müller to author, 24 November 2005). A 'correctable error' in Müller's account occurred because Tacke and his wife were arrested in September 1937. See RGASPI, Personal File TACKE, f. 495, op. 205, d. 6620. See also Michael Buckmiller und Klaus Meschkat (eds.), *Biographisches Handbuch zur Geschichte der Kommunistischen Internationale: Ein deutsch-russisches Forschungsprojekt* (Berlin: Akademie Verlag, 2007), 408, where the date of his execution is also given incorrectly. But, contrary to what Müller writes, it is stated that Tacke was sentenced not by the Military Collegium but by the Special Ordinance ('Osoboe Postanovlenie'), which is a rare and rather exceptional case demonstrating special importance and secrecy. About Tacke in Spain, see Stawinski, *Zarubiny*, 292. See also Weber und Herbst, *Deutsche Kommunisten*, 777, based on Müller's biography.

A well-documented work on the American Abraham Lincoln Brigade, as the surviving group of veterans called their unit after the war, is still to be written. A number of books that are dealing with the subject—e.g. Marion Merriman and Warren Lerude, *American Commander in Spain: Robert Hale Merriman and the Abraham Lincoln Brigade* (Reno, NV: University of Nevada Press, 1986); Peter Carroll, *The Odyssey of the Abraham Lincoln Brigade: Americans in the Spanish Civil War*, paperback (Stanford, CA: Stanford University Press, 1994); or Alvah Cecil Bessie, *Alvah Bessie's Spanish Civil War Notebooks* (Lexington, KY: University Press of Kentucky, 2001)—all contain errors of different nature, sometimes important. There is a brilliant critical article by Harvey Klehr, 'The Myth of "Premature Anti-Fascism"', *New Criterion*, 21/1 (September 2002), 19, which analyses many discrepancies of Carroll's account.

9. Personal questionnaire of Israel Pickett Altman (Morris Cohen), August 1937, RGASPI, f. 545, op. 3, d. 509. Cohen's passport in the name of 'Altman' was

obtained through the good services of the Soviet 'illegal' Yakov Golos. As a leading member of the CPUSA and a Soviet resident agent, Golos was involved in sending American volunteers to Spain. A considerable number of American volunteers received their travel documents through the firm financed by the Party and run by Golos in New York: World Tourist Inc. Many of them later landed in Moscow and were used to document Soviet 'illegals'.

10. Personal questionnaire of Israel Altmann (Morris Cohen), 31 January 1938, IB Archive, Moscow, f. 856, op. 6, doc. 78. The original was in English, hand-written by Altman. A copy of this document is at the ALBA archive, Tamiment Library/Robert F. Wagner Labor Archives, New York University. I am grateful to Gail Malmgreen for help in locating this and other valuable sources.

11. Born Voldemārs Ozols in Byelorussia in 1884, Waldemar Ozols was a Latvian officer who took part in the First World War. Several Russian biographies describe him as a Soviet officer who served in Spain as a general with an International Brigade. According to his MI5 file, Ozols, codenamed ZOLA, also known as 'the General', was part of the Rote Kapelle network in France during the war whose radio transmitter (call name 'Marianne') was later used by the Germans in a playback operation. See TNA: PRO KV 2/2069.

12. Israel Altman's personnel card at the International Brigades Base in Albacete, filed on 3 April 1938. TNA: PRO KV 2/2069, document 77.

13. Morris Cohen, 'KGB Memoirs, December 1978', in Vladimir Chikov, *Razvedchiki-nelegaly* (Moscow: Exmo/Algoritm-kniga, 2003), 421.

14. According to his official KGB biography, Yatskov joined the NKVD in 1939, and two years later was sent to New York. Yatskov was Harry Gold's handler, and, together with his NKVD colleague, Alexander Feklisov, managed to penetrate the Manhattan Project. Harry Gold and Lona Cohen served as cut-outs and couriers to the star source within the project, the German physicist Klaus Fuchs (codenamed REST and CHARLES), previously recruited by the GRU in London. Fuchs moved to New York in 1943 as part of the British research team known as MSN-12. Among Yatskov's American 'assistants' who helped him to collect important scientific and technical intelligence were Julius Rosenberg, Morton Sobell, and David Greenglass. Two of his important US sources, BLOCK, recruited in 1942, and PERSEUS, recruited in 1944, remain unidentified. In 1946 Yatskov was transferred from New York to Paris, where he served as the NKVD station head under cover of 2nd Secretary of the Soviet Embassy. Colonel Yatskov died in Moscow in March 1993. Fifty-seven years after his arrest, in 2008, having spent almost twenty years behind the bars, Morton Sobell said in an interview: 'Now, I know it was an illusion. I was taken in.' See Sam Roberts, 'Figure in Rosenberg Case Admits to Soviet Spying', *New York Times*, 11 September 2008, p. A1.

15. Andrew and Mitrokhin, *The Mitrokhin Archive*, 194.

16. Andrew and Mitrokhin, *The Mitrokhin Archive*, 194. See also Archivo Carlos Esplá, JARE, Libros de Actas.

17. TNA: PRO, KV 2/2203, Oliver Charles GREEN, Personal File 46438, vol. 1, Serial 90a, 21 September 1942.

18. Recently unclassified MI5 files reveal that, in June 1941, Special Branch opened an inquiry into McCartney, who, as they put it, 'might interest himself in obtaining information for the Soviet Union' (TNA: PRO KV 2/68, Lee MILLER.

19. Wilfred McCartney, *Walls Have Mouths*, with Prologue, Epilogue and Comments at the end of the majority of the chapters by Compton Mackenzie (London: Victor Gollancz, 1936).

20. Thomas, *The Spanish Civil War*, 574 n. 1.

21. Richard Baxell, *British Volunteers in the Spanish Civil War: The British Battalion in the International Brigades, 1936–1939* (Abersychan, Wales: Warren & Pell, 2007), 72.

22. John Halstead and Barry McLoughlin, 'British and Irish Students at the International Lenin School, Moscow, 1926–37', a paper given during a conference at Manchester University in 2001 (Barry McLoughlin to author, 18 December 2013). A more detailed study is in Barry McLoughlin with John McIlroy, Alan Campbell, and John Halstead, 'Forging the Faithful: The British at the International Lenin School, 1926–37', *Labour History Review*, 68/1 (April 2003), 99–128; and 'British Students at the International Lenin School: The Vindication of a Critique', *Twentieth Century British History*, 16/4 (2005), 471–88.

23. TNA: PRO KV 2/1594, based on his MI5 Personal File 37634, vol. 1.

24. David Crook, another Soviet agent, recalled that, at the time of Springy's release (1949), the Chinese Communist Party requested the CPGB to send four people to polish, as they put it, but in reality to sub-edit, the English translation of some of their Communist writings. Springhall was one of them. From China he was sent to Moscow in 1952 for treatment. See David Crook, 'That Valley in Spain Called Jarama (1936–38) (1990; Crook family©2004). For the details of his MI5 investigation, see TNA: PRO KV 2/1594–1596, 'Douglas springhall'.

25. Like Foote and Philips, Beurton worked in Brigade transport, driving a lorry from the battalion cookhouse. When his car was hit by shellfire near Jarama in February 1937 and almost completely destroyed, Leonard and his passenger, Captain George Nathan, miraculously escaped injury. See Baxell, *British Volunteers*, 79.

26. TNA: PRO KV 6/44.

27. Alexander Foote, *Handbook for Spies* (London: Museum Press, 1949), 41–2.

28. TNA: PRO KV 2/2203, Oliver Charles GREEN.

29. ASVRR, Personal File TONY (Blunt), No. 83895, vol. 1, pp. 231–40, as quoted in West and Tsarev, *The Crown Jewels*, 142. Cf. Costello and Tsarev, *Deadly Illusions*, 464 n. 74.

30. Interview with Douglas Eggar, in Baxell, *British Volunteers*, 121.

31. About Gibbons and Smith, see Halstead and McLoughlin, 'British and Irish Students'.

32. Grigory Sergeevich Syroezhkin was born on 25 January 1900 to a peasant family. He received no formal education. In about 1917 he took and passed exams for four classes of the gymnasium. From 1921 worked in the Cheka, took part in Operation SYNDICATE against Boris Savinkov. Under the alias 'Serebryakov', Syroezhkin had a number of operative contacts with Polish intelligence and counter-intelligence that would later be remembered and used against him. In 1925 he took part in Operation TRUST, aimed to lure Sydney Reilly to Russia. Here Syroezhkin acted under the alias 'Schyukin', a militant of the fictitious anti-Soviet Monarchist Organization of Central Russia. Syroezhkin was highly decorated by the Soviet government: he was a cavalier of the Order of Lenin, Order of the Red Banner, and received commemorative gold watches and arms engraved with his name. After the desertion of Orlov, Syroezhkin was recalled to Moscow. On 8 February he was arrested and on 26 February 1939 he was accused of espionage for Poland. He was sentenced to death and shot on the same day. Syroezhkin was exonerated in 1958.

33. In the 1920s Vasilevsky worked in counter-intelligence in Georgia, then until 1936 he was in the OGPU–NKVD of Transcaucasia, a region immediately south of the peak of the Caucasus mountains, and consisting of Georgia, Azerbaijan, and Armenia. In 1939–41 he was the 'legal' NKVD resident in France and in 1941–2 deputy legal resident in Ankara, Turkey. During much of the period of the Manhattan Project, in 1943–5, Vasilevsky was the resident in Mexico City, where Kitty Harris (codenamed ADA and NORMA) was his courier. In 1945, for his contribution in handling atomic spies in the United States, Vasilevsky was appointed deputy head of Department S ('Illegals'). In 1953 he was one of Sudoplatov's deputies in the 9th Department of the MVD (subversion, terror, and assassinations abroad). Although Vasilevsky was fired from the service in 1953, together with his chiefs Sudoplatov and Eitingon (who were subsequently arrested and spent long terms in prison), he remained at large, and in 1959 was reinstated as a Communist Party member. Vasilevsky wrote many books about the Spanish Civil War, but, alas, none of any historic value. One of the books, entitled *Ispanskaya khronika Grirogiya Grande* [*Spanish Adventures (Chronicles) of Gregory Grande*] (Moscow: Molodaya gvardiya, 1985) is dedicated to his friend, Grigory Syroezhkin. Vasilevsky died in 1979.

34. See Stanislav Alekseevich Vaupshasov, *Na trevozhnykh perekryostkakh: Zapiski chekista* (Moscow: Politizdat, 1988), ch. 'Partisan Corps'.

35. See Jesús Hernández, 'How the NKVD Framed POUM', published by Robert Pitt in May 1996 <http://www.whatnextjournal.org.uk/Pages/Pamph/NKVD.html> (accessed 17 December 2013). See also Jesús Hernández, *Le Grand Trahison* (Paris: Fasquelle, 1953).

36. Kirill Prokofyevich Orlovsky (1895–1968) was born in the village of Myshko-vichi in the Mogilev district of Byelorussia to a peasant family. He attended the

parochial school for four years. In 1915 he was drafted into the Tsarist army. In 1918 he returned to Myshkovichi. Here he joined the Bolsheviks and organized the partisan movement in Bobruisk (where Nikolsky came from). He became an operative of the Bobruisk Cheka (December 1918–May 1919). In1919–20 he attended a military school. While still a cadet, he took part in the Soviet–Polish war. From May 1920 until May 1925 he took part in the guerrilla warfare in Western Byelorussia. Orlovsky studied in KUNMZ in 1925–30. He worked in the OGPU personnel department in Minsk in charge of recruitment and training of volunteers for guerrilla operations. In 1937–8 he was on a special assignment in Spain. From January 1938 till February 1939 he studied at the NKVD high school in Moscow. From March 1941 to May 1942 he was on a tour of duty in China. Upon his return he became an officer of the 4th Department (NKVD) for Special Tasks and Guerrilla Warfare under Pavel Sudoplatov. In October 1942 he parachuted into Byelorussia. Heavily wounded, he retired from the NKVD as colonel. He returned to Myshkovichi and was appointed chairman of the local collective farm. Honours included Hero of the Soviet Union, Hero of the Socialist Labour, five Orders of Lenin, two Orders of the Red Banner. Like all other NKVD officers, Orlovsky is not mentioned in the official list of Soviet advisers (see Fundación Pablo Iglesias (ed.), *Los rusos*).

37. Alexander Markovich Rabtsevich (1887–1961) was born in a village near Bobruisk to a peasant family. In 1918 he fought as a partisan, then in the Red Army. He was a guerrilla fighter in Western Byelorussia (1921–4), then an OGPU officer. In 1937–8 he was on a special assignment in Spain. After Spain Pabtsevich worked in the NKVD of Byelorussia in Minsk. During the Second World War he served with the Sudoplatov's Special Motorized Brigade, known as OMSBON, and then was sent behind the German lines to the occupied territory of Byelorussia. He was named Hero of the Soviet Union. After the war he continued to serve in the Byelorussian NKVD and MGB until 1952. He died in Minsk in April 1961.

38. Vasili Zakharovich Korzh (13 January 1899–5 May 1967), also known under his partisan *nom de guerre* 'Komarov', was a Byelorussian communist activist and Soviet Second World War hero. A collective farm chairman, NKVD officer, and volunteer with the Republican forces in the Spanish Civil War, he is best remembered for organizing and leading one of the first Soviet partisan units during the 1941–4 occupation of the Byelorussian Soviet Socialist Republic by Nazi Germany. On account of his partisan service, Korzh was made a major-general in the Soviet military in 1943 and was awarded the honorary title Hero of the Soviet Union in August 1944. See Sergey Kvitkevich, 'Zhyve imya legendarnaga kambryga', *Minskaya Prauda*, 11 February 2009.

39. Nikolai Arkhipovich Prokopyuk (1902–75), NKVD colonel, was born into the family of a joiner. He went to a parochial school and worked as a farm labourer. In 1916 he took and passed exams for six classes of the gymnasium. In

1921 he joined the Cheka. From 1924 till 1931 he served with the frontier guards in Byelorussia. In 1935 Prokopyuk was transferred to the INO (Foreign Intelligence) in Moscow, and in 1937 was assigned to the NKVD Barcelona sub-station under Eitingon. (When the Soviet KGB approached Orlov in the United States in November 1969, it produced a letter from Prokopyuk. According to the former FBI Special Agent Gazur, Orlov categorically denied to the US authorities any knowledge of the man (see Gazur, *Secret Assignment*, 369, 370, 373; Costello and Tsarev, *Deadly Illusions*, 3, 377.) In spite of his denial, Orlov had mockingly demonstrated that his memory served him well by mentioning to Gazur that his former subordinate (he gave Gazur an invented name) 'had formerly been an officer of the KGB [*sic*] Frontier Guards'. When Orlov deserted, Prokopyuk was recalled to Moscow and demoted in rank and pay. Before the Second World War he was on a tour of duty to Helsinki, but not as a case officer (he had a lowly administrative function). In the summer of 1941 Prokopyuk's former resident in Finland, E. T. Sinitsyn, recommended that he should be restored to the Party membership and sent to the German front. Consequently, Prokopyuk became an officer of the Sudoplatov's 4th Department and was sent behind the lines. He was named Hero of the Soviet Union in 1944. After the Second World War, together with Vaupshasov, Prokopyuk went to China and took part in the first phase (August 1945–end 1946) of the Chinese Civil Wa). In China Prokopyuk was in charge of guerrilla warfare. After China he was assigned to the Soviet Military Administration in Germany as a Special Tasks officer. According to SVR-related sources, he took part in various clandestine operations. Prokopyuk retired in 1950 because of poor health.

40. Artur Karlovich Sprogis, according to Vaupshasov, was a one-time guardsman of the Kremlin Guards (the so-called Latvian Riflemen). Sent to Spain in November 1936, he served as an adviser in the XIV *Cuerpo de Guerrilleros* that was part of the XI International Brigade (German–Austrian) concerned with disguised reconnaissance and sabotage at the front. In Spain Sprogis met Elisaveta Parshina, who, according to the Russian sources, was there on a special mission as a GRU 'illegal' under the alias of Josefa Pérez Herrera (in reality, she was the interpreter for Sprogis). Together with him, she returned to Moscow in November 1937. During the Second World War Sprogis was in charge of the *aktivka* (active measures—i.e. sabotage and subversion behind enemy lines) in military unit No. 9903 in Zhavoronki near Moscow, training saboteurs, while Parshina was engaged in the counter-intelligence work in the Caucasus. In 1943 she gave birth to their son, Leonid. Parshina and the child were sent on a mission to Czechoslovakia under false identities in 1946, to return to Moscow only in 1953. Parshina died in 2002. One of her books, *La brigadista*, was published in Spain in the same year with the foreword by Sprogis. Karl Kleinjung, future head of the DDR Stasi Military Intelligence, was one of Sprogis's 'pupils' in Spain. For more about Kleinjung, see Boris

Volodarsky, *Nikolai Khokhlov ('Whistler'): Self-Esteem with a Halo*, paperback (Vienna: Borwall Verlag, 2005); and *The KGB's Poison Factory*. About Artur Sprogis, see G. Osipov, *Tovarishch Artur, kto vy?* (Moscow: Politizdat, 1989).

41. Vaupshasov, *Na trevozhnykh perekrestkakh*, ch. 'Partisan Corps'.

42. Radosh et al., *Spain Betrayed*, 291.

43. It has always been a tradition of the Soviet intelligence officers' memoirs not to disclose real names and dates except for people and cases that were widely publicized by the KGB for propaganda purposes. This concerns personalities named by Vaupshasov in his book—almost all of them, like himself, became Heroes of the Soviet Union, long celebrated for their daring exploits behind the enemy lines during the Second World War.

44. Andrew and Mitrokhin, *The Mitrokhin Archive*, 97.

45. Andrew and Mitrokhin, *The Mitrokhin Archive*, 97.

46. Andrew and Mitrokhin, *The Mitrokhin Archive*, 770 n. 34.

47. Cf. Andrew and Mitrokhin, *The Mitrokhin Archive*, 54, 95.

CHAPTER 15

1. Vaupshasov, *Na trevozhnykh perekryostkakh*, ch. 'Rytsari svobody'.

2. Alias 'Maksimov', codenamed YUZ, ARTUR, MAKS, and FELIPE.

3. All Soviet and Russian sources, without exception, give Grigulevich's nationality as Karaite (Nil Nikandrov, 'Ryadovoi Kominterna po klichke Migel', *Latin America*, 1 (1999), 29; I. K. Shatunovskaya, 'Vsya zhizn—podvig: uchenogo ... i razvedchika', *Latin America*, 3 (1993), 69; E. Bai, 'Spion po osobym porucheniyam Kremlya', *Izvestiya*, 5 May 1993; Primakov et al. (eds.), *Ocherki*, iii. 154), while in reality Karaite is a member of a Jewish religious movement known as Karaism, also spelled Karaitism. In dismissing the Talmud as manmade law substituted for the God-given Torah, Karaism set itself in direct opposition to rabbinic Judaism. The movement began in eighth-century Persia. Though its members were never numerous, it spread to Egypt and Syria and later into Europe by way of Spain and Constantinople. During the ninth or tenth century, the name Karaites was adopted to underscore the group's emphasis on a personal reading of the Bible.

4. Sudoplatov and Sudoplatov, *Special Tasks*, 193. Yuri N. Paporov, a former KGB officer, who served in Mexico (1957) and Cuba (1964), and knew Grigulevich well, recalled that Juzik told him that he had personally shot one and almost strangled another police provocateur while in the Communist underground in Vilnius. See Yuri Paporov, 'Sudba peresmeshnika', *Sovershenno Sekretno*, 2/129 (2000), 10–11. Ale Taubman, another future NKVD 'illegal', was with Grigulevich in the Lithuanian youth underground.

5. Iosif Friedgut, who changed his name to Nikolai Samoilovich Friedgut, was born in 1905 and joined the OGPU in 1929. In 1938 he was dismissed from the service and sent to the Gulag. In July 1941 he was released on Sudoplatov's

written request (together with Ya. Serebryansky, S. Apresyan, I. Kaminsky, P. Zubov, and R. Sobol) and sent on a mission to Afghanistan, where he died in the line of duty a year later. See Abramov, *Evrei v KGB*, 67.

6. See Nikolay S. Leonov, former KGB general, one of the leading specialists in Latin America, interviewed by Shatunovskaya ('Vsya zhizn—podvig', 65). See also Andrew and Mitrokhin, *The Mitrokhin Archive*, 130. The fact that Grigulevich was recruited by Friedgut is mentioned in Sudoplatov, *Spetsoperazii*, 270. It can be found only in the Russian 2003 edition, and the officer's name, spelt 'Josef Friedgood' by the American editors, is named in the earlier American edition only in connection with the war victims among Sudoplatov's staff.

7. See, e.g., Augustín Guillamón, 'La NKVD et SIM en Barcelona', *Balance*, No. 22, November 2001.

8. See Nikandrov, 'Ryadovoi Kominterna', 35–6. Nikandrov worked in the 1 Latin American Department of the Soviet Foreign Ministry in the 1980s.

9. Codovilla was born in 1894 in Italy. Late in 1912 he emigrated to Argentina. From 1921 and until his death Codovilla was a member of the PCA's Central Committee and the Politburo. From 1931 and until August 1937 Codovilla, known under various pseudonyms (luis, medina, and thomas), was a Comintern emissary in Spain. In early 1941 he returned to Argentina, participated in the pro-USSR anti-fascist campaign and was appointed secretary general of the Argentine Communist Party, a post he held until March 1963, when he became president of the party. Codovilla was a staunched Stalinist and remained loyal to the Soviet Union after Stalin's death, frequently attending major Communist gatherings in Moscow. It is possible that Codovilla secretly worked for the same Special Tasks group of the NKVD as Grigulevich, but no documentary proof had ever been published, only indirect references. Codovilla died in Moscow in April 1970.

10. Ghioldi, born in 1897, son of a labourer, became a teacher and a militant in the Argentine socialist movement. In the summer of 1921 Ghioldi went to Moscow for instructions. Later that year he represented the Comintern at the founding congress of the Chilean Communist Party. From 1928 to 1934 he was secretary general of the Argentine Communist Party. In 1934 Ghioldi came to Moscow again and was elected an alternate member of the ECCI. In November 1935, on Soviet instructions and assisted by Soviet advisers, almost all of whom were German Communists affiliated with the RU, he and Prestes attempted to start an insurrection in Brazil against President Getúlio Vargas, for which they were arrested and tried; Ghioli was sentenced to four and a half years in prison. After the Second World War he returned from Uruguay to Argentina, where in 1945 he lost the elections to become a senator from Buenos Aires, but in spite of that in 1951 he was the only Communist candidate in the country's presidential elections. In the following two decades Ghioldi often lived abroad and visited Moscow several times. There is little

doubt that he fully cooperated with Soviet intelligence during his entire career. In March 1969 he opened the XIII Congress of the Argentine Communist Party and then in June of the same year was heading the Argentine delegation at the international conference of Communist parties in Moscow. It was the year when foreign Communist leaders were instructed by the International Department of the CPSU, successor of the Comintern/OMS and the KGB, successor of the NKVD, on how to deal with their own 'velvet revolutions'. Until his death in 1985 Ghioldi remained a member of the Argentine Comunist Party Politburo. For details, see N. P. Kalmykov et al. (eds), *Komintern i Latinskaya Amerika* (Moscow: Nauka, 1998), 373–4.

11. For a detailed story of the coup based on the Comintern archives, see William Waack, *Camaradas—Nos arquivos de Moscou—A história secreta da revolução brasileira de 1935* (São Paulo: Companhia das Letras, 1993). By May 1935, long before the victories of the Popular Front governments in Spain and France, the ECCI Political Commission had already sent a telegram to Prestes categorically protesting against his changing the revolutionary slogan from 'All Power to the National Alliance' to 'All Power to the Soviets' or even 'All Power to the Communist Party', as he wanted. The telegram, signed by Dimitrov, Van Min, Pyatnitsky, Otto Kuusinen, and Manuilsky, advised Prestes to use 'all temporary allies, including those representatives of the national bourgeoisie, who supported anti-imperialist struggle'. The victory of the National Liberation Alliance at this stage, it was explained to Prestes, would lead to the establishment of the power of the Soviets at the next stage of the revolution. RGASPI, f. 495, op. 184, d. 53, ll. 13–14, outgoing correspondence, 13 May 1935. In November, when Prestes and his Soviet advisers thought the revolution was ripe, the ECCI Secretariat instructed the PCA Politburo to start the insurrection when they considered it appropriate; to secure the support of the insurgents in the army by workers and peasants; and to do everything possible to protect Prestes from arrest. The PCA was informed that the amount of $25,000 was transferred urgently by wire to their account and asked to keep Moscow updated on the events. RGASPI, f. 495, op. 184, d. 53, l. 77, outgoing correspondence, 26 November 1935. The telegram was signed by, among others, Ercoli (Togliatti), Manuilsky, Moskvin (Trilisser), Marty, and Wilhelm Pieck.

12. In 1940 Ghioldi was released from prison and returned to Argentina, to be arrested there again in 1943. From there he went to Montevideo to lead the foreign bureau of the Argentine Communist Party. Here he would meet Grigulevich, who, after his second secret mission in Buenos Aires, was temporarily located at Montevideo, where the 'legal' NKVD residency was set up within the newly opened Soviet embassy.

13. See, first of all, Michael Smith, *Frank Foley: The Spy who Saved 10,000 Jews* (London: Hodder & Stoughton, 1999), 53–61; and Jeffery, *MI6*, 267–71. See also Nigel West, *At Her Majesty's Secret Service: The Chiefs of Britain's Intelligence*

Agency MI6 (London: Greenhill Books, 2006), 45–6; and Richard Colin Thurlow, 'The Historiography and Source Materials in the Study of Internal Security in Modern Britain', *History Compass*, 6/1 (2008), 147–71.

14. Thurlow, 'Historiography and Source Materials'.

15. Nigel West, *MASK: MI5's Penetration of the Communist Party of Great Britain* (London and New York: Routledge, 2005), 23.

16. Jeffery refers to *Ottawa Citizen* of 4 February 1954, see Jeffery, *MI6*, 267–71.

17. See R. S. Rose and Gordon D. Scott, *Johnny: A Spy's Life* (University Park, PA: Pennsylvania State University Press, 2010). The publication was accompanied by the following description: 'Johann Heinrich Amadeus de Graaf, known as Johnny all his life, was born on 11 May 1894, in Nordenham, near Bremerhaven in northwest Germany. He died at age 86 on 2 December 1980, in Brockville, Ontario, where he and his wife ran a tourist lodge. That he lived as long as he did is miraculous considering that he had spent many years acting as a double agent, pretending to work for Soviet intelligence while really functioning as an operative for Britain's MI6. His life had many twists and turns, and murder, treachery, intrigue, and violence were never far from his doorstep. Eventually joining the Spartacus Bund in 1919, which evolved into the German Communist Party, he later became a staunch anti-Communist and played a key role in undermining the efforts of Communists in Brazil to oust the government of Getulio Vargas in 1935. After retiring from MI6, he even volunteered his services to J. Edgar Hoover in 1950. Based on documents from multiple government archives as well as many interviews, the most important of which was a series that Gordon Scott [one of the authors] conducted with Johnny in 1975–6, this story of the life of a spy who hid behind sixty-eight different aliases during the course of his colourful career is a gripping tale of espionage and counterespionage during a critical period of the political history of the twentieth century.' Upon close examination, the biography appears to contain so many inventions and fantasies that Johnny, who the authors say was interviewed, seems to have been as big a storyteller as Orlov.

18. See Waack, *Camaradas*, 342.

19. Weber and Herbst, *Deutsche Kommunisten*, 258–9.

20. Ewert was born on 13 November 1890 in Heinrichswalde, Germany. He joined the KPD in 1920 after having spent a year in jail as a political prisoner. Five years later, in 1925, Ewert was elected to its Central Committee, Politburo, and Secretariat. In June 1934 he became a member of the ECCI and, under the alias 'Harry Berger', was sent to Brazil to head its South American Bureau there and direct the Communist Party of Brazil. His wife, Elise Saborowski, followed him. After the November 1935 uprising they were both arrested in Rio de Janeiro. Tortured for eleven months, the strongly built Ewert lost 50 kg, and was sentenced to thirteen years in jail. His wife was extradited and handed over to the Gestapo. She died in 1939 in the concentration camp at Ravensbrück. He was amnestied in May 1945 and returned to

Germany, where he was immediately placed, first in the Berlin Charité clinic and then in a sanatorium for mentally unstable patients. Ewert died in Eberswalde in July 1959. His former close associate and friend Gerhard Eisler, with whom he worked in China, was appointed by the Party to make the funeral oration. For his biography, see David P. Hornstein, *Arthur Ewert: A Life for the Comintern* (Lanham, MD, New York, and London: University Press of America, 1993). See also Manuel Caballero, *Latin America and the Comintern, 1919–1943* (Cambridge: Press Syndicate of the University of Cambridge, 1986), 117–20.

21. See Chapter 2. Stuchevsky was sent by Jan Berzin, the RKKA intelligence director, to Paris as their 'illegal' resident in 1927, was arrested there in April 1931 and sentenced to three years' imprisonment. He returned to Moscow in 1934 and joined the OMS. In November 1935, under the alias 'Leon Jules Vallée' (his other aliases were 'Paul' and 'René'), together with his wife, Sofia Margulyan, he was sent to Brazil, travelling on a Belgian passport. The Comintern team's well-equipped radio operator was Victor Allen Barron, an American communist who was 26 years old when he left Moscow. His genuine US passport identified him as Victor Allen George. Victor's father was Harrison George, a leading personality of the CPUSA, who at one time lived conjugally with Earl Browder's sister Margaret, NKVD courier in Europe in the 1930s. Victor was raised by his mother, whose second husband, a man named Barron, adopted him. Arrested after the failed coup, Victor Barron died in prison. Arrested in Rio in January 1936, Stuchevsky managed to return to Moscow, where he died in 1944. He is buried in the Novodevichie cemetery.

22. Locatelli (aliases 'Ezio' and 'Walter'), was born in 1901, and in 1924 joined both the Italian and French Communist parties. In 1926–8 he worked for the OMS in France, Switzerland, and Germany (Berlin). From 1928 to 1935 he was in Moscow, from where he was sent to Brazil. He returned to the USSR in 1936, and after the civil war had broken out, he was sent by the OMS/RU to Spain. In 1940 he operated as an 'illegal' in France.

23. Ghioldi was using the aliases 'Autobelli', 'Luciano Busteros', 'Indio', and 'Quiroga'.

24. Guralsky was born on 10 April 1890 in Riga as Abraham Yakovlevich Heifetz. He was also known as 'A. Guriy', 'Juan de Dios', 'Rústico', El Viejo, August Klein, and, finally, 'Professor Arnold Blanco'. His nephew was Grigory Markovich Heifetz, an OGPU–NKVD officer who operated in the United States. An old Bolshevik, first arrested for revolutionary activities in 1914 and then released on bail, Guralsky escaped to Vienna. From the end of 1919 Guralsky was the ECCI representative in Germany, from where he was expelled a year later. In 1923 he was there again preparing the Communist uprising as chairman of the 'Revolutionary Committee'. In 1934 he was deputy head of the Länder Secretariat for South and Carribean Americas. In Brazil, Guralsky was also accompanied by his wife, Ines Tulczynska. After their return

to Moscow in 1936, he was expelled from the Party and sentenced to eight years, almost certainly for the failure of the 'November Revolution', but he was suddenly released in 1938. During the war Guralsky was engaged in the propaganda campaign among the German PoWs, acting under the alias 'Professor Arnold'. He died in 1960. See Kalmykov et al. (eds), *Komintern i Latinskaya Amerika*, 375–6. See also M. M. Panteleyev, 'Avantyurist ili politicheskiy deyatel?', *Voprosy Istorii*, 9 (September 1998), 121–30.

25. Olga Benario (née Gutmann) was born in Munich on 12 February 1908. A 16-year-old girl and Communist activist, Olga, who at that time worked as a typist at the Soviet Trade Delegation in Berlin, met Otto Braun, a legendary chief of all 'special secret work' of the KPD. Braun was married, and the young woman became his mistress. In 1926 Braun was arrested, but, with Olga's help, the underground Apparat managed to organize his escape. On 11 April 1928 five armed militants stormed the Berlin Moabit prison when she visited him there in preparation for the show trial, and not only released their former leader, but also managed to smuggle Braun and his mistress across the border. They both went to Moscow, where he received professional military education, later graduating with honours from the Frunze Military Academy, and she was elected to the KIM Central Committee. At the same time, in 1930, she was reportedly recruited to the RU. The pair separated in 1931, and in April 1932 Braun was sent to Harbin, China, as the 'illegal' RU resident and military adviser to the ECCI representative, who was Arthur Ewert at the time. Although in 1933 the chief military adviser Manfred Stern arrived, Braun remained in China until late 1939. Olga Benario continued to work for the RU in Europe under aliases 'Frida Leuscher' and 'Ana Baum de Revidor', visiting Britain, France, and Belgium in 1931. In the autumn of 1934, when she was sent to Brazil as 'Maria Villar', personal assistant to Luis Carlos Prestes. In Rio she became his wife, was arrested, together with him, in March 1936, and extradited to Nazi Germany, where she died in a concentration camp in Bernburg on 5 April 1942. Otto Braun spent the war in the Soviet Union, getting Soviet citizenship and becoming one of the Soviet writers. In 1954 he relocated to East Germany. Otto Braun died during a holiday trip to Varna, Bulgaria, on 15 August 1974. See Lurie and Kochik, *GRU*, 498; Kolpakidi, *Entsyklopaediya voennoi razvedki*, 314–15; Weber and Herbst, *Deutsche Kommunisten*, 122–3, which does not include a separate biographical entry on Benario. See also Fanny Edelman, *Banderas, Pasiones, Camaradas* (Buenos Aires: Ediciones Dirple, 1996), 50; Hornstein, *Arthur Ewert*, 189–207.

26. See Waack, *Camaradas*, 107.

27. Hornstein, *Arthur Ewert*, 189–235.

28. TNA: PRO HO 334/161/17678. Naturalisation Certificate: John Henry De Graaf. From Germany. Resident in London. Certificate AZ17678, issued 29 October 1945.

29. Jeffery, *MI6*, 664. Strangely, Jeffery, discussing the period, writes about an SIS station at Bad Salzuflen as well as various SIS German units at Hamburg and Düsseldorf, and about Simon Galliene as senior SIS officer in Germany at the time, but does not even mention Bad Oeynhausen. Moreover, he says nothing about the Intelligence Bureau there, which was located in the same building and headed by Lieutenant Colonel Felix Cowgill, who until his retirement in 1944 headed Section V in MI6.

30. Rose and Scott, *Johnny*, 370.

31. Rose and Scott, *Johnny*, 385.

32. Jeffery, *MI6*, 271.

33. Weber and Herbst, *Deutsche Kommunisten*, 258–9.

34. Hans Schafranek unter Mitarbeiten von Natalja Mussijenko, *Kinderheim No. 6: Österreichische und deutsche Kinder im sowjetischen Exil* (Vienna: Döcker Verlag, 1998), 71–2.

35. See TNA: PRO KV 2/125, Johannes de graaf. Amazingly, neither Jonny nor his case is mentioned in Andrew, *The Defence of the Realm*, although there is a small trace of him in the monthly 'Most Secret Report on Activities of Security Service' submitted to the Prime Minister in the spring of 1943, whose draft was prepared by Anthony Blunt. The report stated: 'de graaf. This Canadian traitor, of Dutch parentage, was detected by our interrogation staff on entering this country. He confessed to having worked for the German Secret Service for more than two years, during which he had insinuated himself into an Allied escape organisation for our prisoners of war which he is believed to have betrayed to the enemy. He was in addition a well-trained saboteur' (see Andrew, *The Defence of the Realm*, 290).

36. Nikandrov, 'Rydovoi Kominterna', 42–3. See also Edelman, *Banderas*, 27–8.

37. Alexander Kolpakidi and Dmitry Prokhorov, *KGB: Vsyo o vneshnei razvedke* (Moscow: Olimp, 2002), 168. In 1930 Vidali came to Moscow, where he was indoctrinated not only in Communist ideology, but most certainly in intelligence matters as well. Like Codovilla, Vidali actively collaborated with the NKVD, possibly working for the same Special Tasks Group, first headed by Serebryansky and later by Sudoplatov, like several other Comintern functionaries, such as Alexander Avigdor (real name Yahel Kosoi), Naum Leschinski (Nadav), and Wolf Averbuch. See Dmitry Prokhorov, *Spetzsluzhby Izrailya* (St Petersburg: Neva; Moscow: OLMA Press, 2002), 229–30. See also Joel Beinen, 'The Palestine Communist Party 1919–1948', *MERIP Reports*, 55 (March 1977), 3–17. According to some Russian sources, Vidali's NKVD code name was MARIO. His book (Vittorio Vidali, *Diary of the Twentieth Congress of the Communist Party of the Soviet Union*, paperback (Westport, CT: Lawrence Hill; London: Journeyman Press, 1974)), published twenty years after Stalin's death, relates a lot about Spain but nothing about the NKVD.

38. Grigulevich, interviewed by Shatunovskaya, 'Vsya zhizn—podvig', 62. There is one interesting nuance that should not be left unnoticed. Further in the

interview (p. 63) Grigulevich suddenly reveals that his boss in Madrid was one Müller. 'As it turned out,' says Grig, 'he was German, a party member from before the revolution, and was shot in the USSR in 1939'. A professional swindler, Grig was obviously cheating his future readers. In reality, 'Müller' was Boris Melnikov, indeed a Bolshevik party member from 1916. who served both in military intelligence and as a diplomat. From 1935 to 1937 Melnikov/ Müller headed the OMS. He was arrested and executed in Moscow in 1938. Therefore, Grig's remark may mean that when he arrived in Valencia he was still working for the OMS.

39. Shatunovskaya, 'Vsya zhizn—podvig', 63. According to Spanish and Russian sources, Grigulevich arrived in Madrid with Brazilian documents in the name of 'José Ocampo'. See Alexander Kolpakidi and Dimitri P. Prokhorov, *KGB: Prikazano likvidirovat'* (Moscow: Yauza/Exmo, 2004), 294. Also see *Causa General, La dominación roja en España: Avance de la información instruida por el ministerio público*, 2nd rev. edn (Madrid: Ministerio de Justicia, 1943), ch. IX, '*Manifestaciones de la influencia Soviética*': 'Unos delegados de la G.P.U. [*recte* NKVD], que se hacen llamar camaradas Coto, Pancho y Leo, secundados por un individuo que usaba el nómbre de José Ocampo y varias mujeres intér-pretes, instalados todos ellos en el Hotel Gaylord, de la calle de Alfonso XI...orientan durante el año 1937 las actividades de la Policía marxista madrileña' (Representatives of the GPU, who called themselves comrades Coto [Eitingon], Pancho [Syroyezhkin] and Leo [Vasilevsky], accompanied by an individual using the name José Ocampo and several female interpreters... were directing the activities of the Marxist police of Madrid).

40. Andrew and Mitrokhin, *The Mitrokhin Archive*, 391.

41. As soon as Santiago Carrillo received his passport to travel to Russia, he rushed to Moscow to be there by 3 March. After about three weeks, he, together with Trifon Medresso Lherba [Trifón Medrano Lherba], Frederico Melchor Fernández [Federico Melchor Fernández], Felipe Mennos Arconada [Felipe Muñoz Arconada], Juan Ambai Bermet [Juan Ambou], and J. L. Entralgo [José Laín Entralgo] (the last two received their Spanish passports in Warsaw), applied for transit visas to Austria at the Austrian Embassy in Moscow. Visas were granted, and they crossed the country, travelling by train, on 28 March. ÖStA/AdR, NPA, Karton 693, Zl. R 452/379 Durchreise spanischer Kommunisten durch Österreich. Österrichische Botschaft in Moskau, am 21. April 1936 an das Bundeskanzleramt, Auswärtige Angelegenheiten, Wien. All personal names are reproduced according to the original Austrian documents, where they were clearly transliterated from Russian by a German speaker. The correct spelling is given in brackets. On 21 March 1936 the report from Feldkirchen informed that Arconada, Medrano, and Melchor had crossed the Austrian–Swiss border on the way from Moscow. The security service reported that altogether 165 visas were required for such Spanish travellers. ÖStA/AdR, NPA, Karton 693, G.D.321-089-St.B. 'Durchreise spanischer Kommunisten von Russland durch Österreich nach Spanien'.

42. Andrew and Mitrokhin, *The Mitrokhin Archive*, 390–1.

43. The informer CARMEN was probably the German representative in the KIM, who was hated in the JSU for her dogmatism and was best known to Spaniards as *Carmen la gorda* ('Carmen the Fat'). She later became the wife of Col. Martínez Cartón of the PCE leadership (see David Wingeate Pike, *In the Service of Stalin: The Spanish Communists in Exile, 1939–1945* (Oxford: Oxford University Press, 1993, 16).

44. Early in 1977, through a KGB agent in the PCE leadership, the Madrid KGB residency received the draft of Carrillo's forthcoming book, *'Eurocommunismo' y Estado*, which would be published by Critica later that year. According to Mitrokhin's notes, the Centre was scandalized by the criticism of the Soviet Union that they found in this work.

45. *Boletín Oficial de la Junta de Defensa de Madrid*, 1, 13 November 1936. The five were Luis Rodríguez Cuesta (secretary of the Council), Segundo Serrano Poncela (representative at the DGS), Fernando Claudín Pontes (representative at the Press Cabinet), Alfredo Cabello (representative at the Emisión Radiofónica), and Federico Melchor (representative in charge of the forces of Security, Assault and the Republican National Guard).

46. Almost certainly this is an error. November makes more sense, because it was at a meeting on 19 November that the Junta resolved to stake out the Finnish premises and to proceed to arrest the individuals responsible for various incidents. This is probably the meeting mentioned.

47. L. Vorobyov, 'Nachalo boevogo puti Maksa', in Primakov et al. (eds), *Ocherki*, iii. 152–3, ch. 1.

48. 'There can be no doubt', writes Paul Preston, 'that many of the activities attributed to "Miguel Martínez" were Koltsov's'. At the same time he acknowledges the likelihood that some of the activities attributed to 'Miguel Martínez' may not have been carried out by Koltsov (but, for example, by Grigulevich, Gorev, Orlov, Mamsurov, or even perhaps a Spanish Communist, a member of the Fifth Regiment, like Luis Lacasa, about whom more will be heard). In his memoirs of the siege of Madrid, Vicente Rojo, the Republican Chief of Staff, writes of knowing 'Miguel Martínez' and of his work with the Quinto Regimiento. It is certainly the case that Koltsov knew Rojo, and he wrote about him on more than one occasion. See Preston, *We Saw Spain Die*, 179.

49. Helen Graham, *Socialism and War: The Spanish Socialist Party in Power and Crisis, 1936–1939* (Cambridge: Cambridge University Press, 1991), 63–4.

50. Mikhail Koltsov, *Ispanskii dnevnik* (Moscow: Sovetsky pisatel, 1957), 233; Primakov et al. (eds), *Ocherki*, iii. 152.

51. Koltsov, *Ispanskii dnevnik*, 245.

52. Koltsov, *Ispanskii dnevnik*, 245.

53. M. E. Koltsov, *Ispaniya v ogne* (Moscow: Politizdat, 1987), vol. 1, bk 2, November, p. 227.

54. 'V Madride ya rukovodil gruppoi, kotoroi polzovalsya dlya samykh raznykh del'—Grigulevich, interviewed by Shatunovskaya ('Vsya zhizn—podvig', 63).

55. These details point to one of the special brigades of the already mentioned Checa de la Agrupación Socialista de Madrid, situated on the calle Fuencarral. It was commanded by the police chief in charge of the Soviet Embassy security detail by the name of Anselmo Burgos Gil, together with David Vázquez Baldominos. In June 1937 Vázquez Baldominos would be appointed Comisario general del Cuerpo de Investigación y Vigilancia in Madrid (see *Gaceta de la República*, 164, 13 June 1937, p. 1198).

56. Katja Landau, 'Stalinism in Spain', *Revolutionary History*, 1/2 (Summer 1988), 40–55.

57. Grigulevich to Shatunovskaya: '[Upon my arrival in Spain] I started working as an interpreter at our embassy and soon became an adviser and the right hand of Carrillo who was then in charge of public order at the *Junta de Defensa de Madrid* (Committee for the Defence of Madrid). His father—a right-wing Socialist—was the head of the state security of the whole [Republican] Spain' (Shatunovskaya, 'Vsya zhizn—podvig', 63).

58. For the full text of this declaration, which reflected the decisions of the Junta of 13 November, see *ABC*, 14 November 1936, p. 13.

59. Both Carrillo and Melchor would be among the leadership of the PCE forty years after the events, in 1977 (see *La Vanguardia Española*, 10 May 1977, p. 12).

60. Ian Gibson, *Paracuellos: Cómo fue. La verdad objetiva sobre la matanza de presos en Madrid en 1936* (Madrid: Ediciones Temas de Hoy, 2005), 58–9.

61. Ramón Torrecilla Guijarro, declaration of the witness, 11 November 1939, 26–7.

62. According to the British Foreign Office files, three agents posing as anti-Communists entered Spain early in 1937 'with the object of assassinating General Franco'. TNA: PRO FO 371/21285 W3393, Sir H. Chilton to Foreign Office, 16 February 1937.

63. Kolpakidi, *Entsyklopaediya voennoi razvedki*, 267. According to a more reliable source, Semenov arrived in Spain in the autumn of 1936, together with other RU personnel. See Lurie and Kochik, *GRU*, 463–4. The latter account seems more precise, because Semenov was sentenced to death and shot on 11 February 1937.

64. Kolpakidi, *Entsyklopaediya voennoi razvedki*, 267. Yakov Grigorievich Bronin (real name Liechtenstein) was born in 1900 in Latvia and joined the RKKA in 1922. He served as an RU 'illegal' in Germany (1930–3) and was then Sorge's successor in Shanghai (1933–5). In April 1934 his new radio operator arrived from Moscow. She was a young and very attractive French woman named René Marceau, who soon became Bronin's wife. In November 1935 Bronin was arrested in Shanghai and sentenced to fifteen years while his wife managed to escape to Russia. After two years in jail, in December 1937, Bronin was exchanged for the son of Chiang Kai-shek, Chiang Ching-kuo (aka Nikolai

Vladimirovich Yelizarov), and came to Moscow. After his return, he worked at the headquarters and was the chair of the foreign languages faculty at the Stalin Military Academy. In September 1949 he was arrested and sentenced to ten years in the Gulag, but after Stalin's death was released and in April 1955 was exonerated. Bronin later worked in the Institute for the World Economy and International Relations (IMEMO), a Soviet think-tank that became a retirement harbour for many former intelligence officers. In 1964, under the pseudonym 'Ya. Gorev', he published a book *Ya Znal Sorge* ('I Knew Sorge'). Bronin died in Moscow in September 1984. See Lurie and Kochik, *GRU*, 354–5.

65. Samuil Bronin, *Istoriya moei materi* (Moscow: Sphera, 2004).
66. According to several authoritative accounts of the Legion's history, none of its air squadrons was in training in Portugal. See, e.g., Raymond L. Proctor, *Hitler's Luftwaffe in the Spanish Civil War* (Westpoint, CT: Greenwood Press, 1983).
67. According to the author, they travelled via London and Hull, a strange route, as there was no direct ferry connection between Hull and any port in Denmark. See Bronin, *Istoriya moei materi*, chs 12–14.
68. Bronin, *Istoriya moei materi*, chs 12–14. According to her official biography, Bronina left the service in 1940, successfully defending an M.Phil. thesis in medicine nine years later. When her husband was arrested in September 1949, she immediately lost her job. In an almost unprecedented move, Bronina left the Communist Party of her own volition in 1978, aged 65. Lurie and Kochik, *GRU*, 355.
69. Lurie and Kochik, *GRU*, 62.
70. ASVRR, File No. 5581, vol. 1, p. 38, MANN to the Centre, 24 January 1937, quoted by Costello and Tsarev, *Deadly Illusions*, 165 n. 75. The original text of the cryptogram is not reproduced. The authors state only that 'it was intended to get Philby into the heart of Franco's entourage where Moscow was planning to use him to set up the assassination of the General [Franco]'.
71. ASVRR, File No. 5581, vol. 1, p. 45, MANN to the Centre, 24 May 1937: 'The fact is that söhnchen has come back [from Spain] in very low spirits. He has not even managed to get near to the 'interesting' objective. But I think or rather feel from my talks with him that, even if he had managed to make his way through to Salamanca, even if he had managed to get near Franco, then—in spite of his intention—he would not have been able to do what was required of him. Though devoted and ready to sacrifice himself, he does not possess the physical courage and other qualities necessary for this [assassination] attempt.'
72. See Viñas, *El honor de la República*, 320–2.
73. Sudoplatov, *Spetsoperazii*, 60. This text is omitted in the English-language edition.
74. About the attempted assassination on the Yugoslav leader Iosip Broz Tito, see Chapter 21.

75. See Ivo Banac (ed.), *The Diary of Georgi Dimitrov 1933–1949* (New Haven and London: Yale University Press, 2003), 38–40.
76. Andrew and Gordievsky, *KGB*, 158. The authors do not refer to an archival source but quote Jonathan Haslam, *The Soviet Union and the Struggle for Collective Security* (London: Macmillan, 1984), 116.
77. TNA: PRO HW 17/27, mask traffic Madrid–Moscow–Madrid.
78. Grigulevich, interviewed by Shatunovskaya in 1986 (Vsya zhizn—podvig', 63). As usual, Grigulevich was inventing his stories but used real facts. Indeed, on 8 March 1921, Eduardo Dato, the President of Alfonso XIII's Council, was murdered by CNT terrorists near his Madrid home. One of the killers, Ramón Casanellas Lluch, took refuge in Moscow, later returning to Spain, where he headed the Partit Comunista de Catalunya. Grigulevich could have learned his real story because the Ukrainian wife of Ramón Casanellas was an experienced OGPU–NKVD 'illegal' who operated in Catalonia in 1930–4 as 'Julia Jiménez Cárdenas'. She was in Spain again from October 1936 to September 1938 using both her real name, Maria Fortus, and her Spanish alias. For details, see Volodarsky, 'Soviet Intelligence Services'.
79. Andrew and Mitrokhin, *The Mitrokhin Archive*, 114.
80. Primakov et al. (eds), *Ocherki*, iii. 153.
81. Thalmann, *Wo die Freiheit stirbt*, 137, quoted by Hans Schafranek in his English-language summary of his own biography *Das Kurze Leben des Kurt Landau: Ein österreichischer Kommunist als Opfer der stalinistischen Geheimpolizei* (Vienna: Verlag für Gesellschaftkritik, 1988). Max Diamant and Herbert Frahm (better known by his pseudonym 'Willi Brandt') were the SAP delegation to Spain.
82. Primakov et al. (eds), *Ocherki*, iii. 153.
83. Helen Graham, *The Spanish Republic at War, 1936–1939*, paperback (Cambridge: Cambridge University Press, 2002), 287–8.
84. Since then, this writer has managed to obtain a copy of the original document from the KGB archives, which has only a page number. Cf. Costello and Tsarev, *Deadly Illusions*, 291. The authors give the reference of the report as ASVRR, Personal File SCHWED, No. 32476, vol. I, p. 101, SCHWED to the Centre, 24 July 1937.
85. A copy of this document is in this writer's archive. Cf. Costello and Tsarev, *Deadly Illusions*, 292. The authors erroneously transliterate Spanish geographical names from Russian.
86. For example, one report from Barcelona published by the leading Spanish newspaper *El Pais* states: 'The documents . . . [filmed by M. Dolors Genovés's group] prove, for the first time, the theory that Nin was murdered by the Soviet political police [*sic*]. Five men murdered him: Alexander Orlov and Juzik, both NKVD members, and three Spaniards only revealed by the initials L., A.F., I.L. [*sic*]. Along with them, as spectators and dismal accomplices, were another NKVD agent [*sic*], the Hungarian Ernö Gerö and his driver, the latter only known by the name Victor, probably an alias' (Enric Company, 'Nin esta enterrado cerca de Madrid', *El Pais*, 6 November 1992).

87. For details, see Volodarsky, 'Soviet Intelligence Services', 151–2.

88. For example, Burnett Bolloten wrote, quoting Krivitsky: 'The Soviet Union seemed to have a grip on Loyalist Spain, as if it were already a Soviet possession' (Bolloten, *The Spanish Civil War: Revolution and Counterrevolution* (Chapel Hill, NC: University of North Carolina Press, 1991), 221).

89. Sudoplatov and Sudoplatov, *Special Tasks*, 74.

CHAPTER 16

1. A book with this title was written by Jordi Serra i Fabra: *Camarada Orlov* (Madrid: Bronce, 2005).

2. RGASPI, f. 558, op. 11, d. 188, ll. 99–102. The document in reproduced in full in Vladimir Haustov et al. (eds), *Lubyanka*, 79–81.

3. RGASPI, f. 558, op. 11, d. 188, ll. 103–4. The document in reproduced in full in Haustov et al. (eds), *Lubyanka*, 81–2.

4. 'Compte rendu du général Schweisguth sur un entretien avec M. Léger', 9 October 1936, SHA 7N 3143, quoted by Michael Jabara Carley, 'Five Kopecks for Five Kopecks: Franco-Soviet Trade Negotiations, 1928–1939', *Cahiers du monde russe et soviétique*, 33/1 (January–March 1992), 48.

5. 'Compte rendu du général Schweisguth sur un entretien avec M. Léger', 9 October 1936, SHA 7N 3143, quoted by Carley, 'Five Kopecks for Five Kopecks', 48. TNA: PRO FO 371 20583, W 14793/9549/41, N. Lloyd Thomas, British chargé d'affaires in Paris, to R. Vansittart, private and confidential, 26 October 1936.

6. TNA: PRO FO 371 20583, W 14793/9549/41, N. Lloyd Thomas to Anthony Eden, British Foreign Secretary, No. 1310, 14 October 1936; and including 'Notes on the attitude of the French general staff towards the Franco-Soviet Pact' by Colonel F. Beaumont-Nesbitt.

7. TNA: PRO FO 371 20583, W 14793/9549/41, Ambassador Potemkin to Narkomindel, 9 November 1936, *Dokumenty Vneshnei Politiki*, vol. XIX, p. 549; 'Record of the conversation...with the minister of state of France Chautemps', V. P. Potemkin, 19 January 1937, pp. 43–6; Potemkin, then deputy Commissar of Foreign Affairs, to Ya. Z. Surits, Soviet ambassador in Berlin, 4 May 1937, pp. 227–8; André-Charles Corbin, French ambassador in London, 17 April 1937, MAE RC, Russie/2057, dos. 3. TNA: PRO FO 371 20702, C3620/532/62, note by R. Vansittart, 13 May 1937. In April 1937 Potemkin succeeded Nikolai Krestinsky as deputy Commissar of Foreign Affairs and Surits replaced him as Soviet ambassador in Paris, while Marcel Rosenberg was recalled from Valencia to Moscow. Foreign embassies immediately informed their ministries about the changes, citing details of Potemkin's colourful biography. Born in 1876, Potemkin was first arrested and spent time in prison aged 23; he joined the Communist Party in 1919 and until 1921 was the chief of the political section of the Red Army on different fronts; first

included in the official Soviet delegation in Marseilles as representative of the Red Cross in 1922–3; a year later Potemkin was appointed Consul General in Istanbul, where he remained until October 1926; he then served as Councillor of the embassy there and in 1929 moved to Greece as the Soviet plenipotentiary; from 1932 until December 1934 he was ambassador in Rome and then in Paris. ÖStA/NPA, Kart. 668, Zl. 19/P, Report of the Austrian Embassy in Moscow to Dr Guido Schmidt, state secretary for foreign affairs, Moscow, 7 April 1937.

8. Carley, 'Five Kopecks for Five Kopecks', 49. TNA: PRO FO 371 20702, C3620/532/62, untitled note by E. Rowe-Dutton, British Embassy, Paris, 17 June 1937.

9. David Shearer, 'Social Disorder, Mass Repression and the NKVD during the 1930s', in Barry McLoughlin and Kevin McDermott, *Stalin's Terror: High Politics and Mass Repression in the Soviet Union* (Houndmills, Basingstoke: Palgrave Macmillan, 2003), 102.

10. Shearer, 'Social Disorder, Mass Repression and the NKVD'. Among others, the GUGB included internal security, counter-intelligence, anti-sabotage, and foreign intelligence departments.

11. Mentioned in Orlov, *The March of Time*; otherwise never listed in any other sources and unidentified.

12. See, e.g., Ministerio de Defensa Nacional, Administración Central, Pagaduría General de Campaña, which lists all payments received by Soviet personnel in Spain. Thus, Orlov is listed in the July 1938 salary statement as receiving the general's compensation of 2,596.66 pesetas.

13. This was not the 'VICTOR' who took part in the murder of Andrés Nin.

14. Prokopyuk was assigned to a special guerrilla detachment in Almería, Andalusia, while Vasilevsky was with a 150-men-strong unit located in the Sierra de Guadarrama—to be exact, in the Sierra de la Mujer Muerta—where their commissar was Peregrín Pérez Galarza. In Barcelona, Vaupshasov was an adviser with the Seguridad and Orlovsky operated deep behind the Franco lines.

15. Hajji-Umar Dzhiorovich Mamsurov (1903–68) served in the Red Army from 1918, first in the North Caucasus. In 1935 he completed a special military intelligence course and from December served as an officer (at that time *sekretny upolnomochennyi*, i.e. secret operative) of the Special Section A at the headquarters. In Spain, Mamsurov served as a senior military adviser on subversive and special operations from October 1936 until September 1937. There his interpreter was Paulina Abramson, whom he eventually married. After his return to Moscow, Mamsurov was appointed chief of the Special Section A (1938–40). He also took part in the Russo-Finish war as the commander of the Special Ski Brigade, operating in the rear, and finished the Second World War as the deputy chief in charge of intelligence matters of the Central Partisan Staff. Hero of the Soviet Union (1945). First deputy chief of the GRU (1957–68), colonel general. See RGVA, Personal File No. 41131.

16. Mamsurov was the first, and Kharitonenkov was the last, senior RU adviser from Service A. He is mentioned as 'Jaritonenkov' in Fondación Pablo Iglesias (ed.), *Los rusos*, 274.

17. Nikolai Kirillovich Patrakhaltsev was born in 1908 and joined the Red Army in 1931. He had a one-year military training as a junior commanding officer. He was sent to Spain as an officer of the RU Service A. Here Patrakhaltsev was awarded his first Order of the Red Banner (he received his second for special operations behind the lines during the Finnish War in 1940). In December 1940–June 1941 he served as assistant military attaché in Romania. During the Second World War Petrakhaltsev was training groups to be deployed behind the German lines. In October 1950 he was appointed chief of the 5th GRU Directorate (Spetsnaz) and promoted to major general in February 1963. Patrakhaltsev died in 1998, with the obituary published by the *Krasnaya Zvezda*, the official Soviet army newspaper, on 22 October. See also Lurie and Kochik, *GRU*, 450. His name is spelt as 'Patrajalsev' in Fondación Pablo Iglesias (ed.), *Los rusos*, 286.

18. Vasili Avraamovich Troyan (1906–March 1973) joined the RKKA in 1928 and the party in 1930. In Spain, Troyan was one of the officers of Section A and after his return to Moscow headed one of the sections of the new, expanded Special Department A (reconnaissance and subversion). He was at the RU headquarters in the Second World War and was in action with guerrilla units in Greece and Yugoslavia. Colonel Troyan was awarded the Order of Lenin, two Orders of the Red Banner, the Order of the Great Patriotic War 1 Class, the Order of the Red Star, and many medals.

19. Andrei Emilev was born on 4 April 1904 in Romania as Sava Draganov Kontrov to a peasant Bulgarian family. He joined the Bulgarian Communist Party in 1923 and a year later moved to Austria to study chemistry at the University of Graz. Having spent six years in Austria, he also became a member of the KPÖ, and in 1930 was recruited to Soviet military intelligence. Draganov/Emilev operated in various 'illegal' residencies in Europe under the leadership of Vinarov. From February 1936 (until June 1938) he was a member of the RU Service A and one of its longest-serving officers in Spain, where he was awarded the Order of the Red Banner in November 1937. From July 1939 to September 1930 he was section chief at the Central Officer Training School of the (RU) of the RKKA General Staff and later was a course chief at the 3rd faculty of the High Intelligence School of the General Staff. During his last years (Emilev died in 1970) he was deputy chair at the Department of Rare Languages of the high courses for foreign languages of the Soviet Foreign Ministry. See Lurie and Kochik, *GRU*, 493.

20. Maria Fortus was a legendary Soviet intelligence officer who began her work with the Ukrainian Cheka in 1919. Maria was probably the first Soviet 'illegal' in Spain in 1930–4, arriving in Barcelona with a forged Uruguayan passport in the name of 'Julia Jiménez Cárdenas' to work with her husband, Ramón

Casanellas Lluch, the leader of the Communist Party of Catalonia. When he died in a car accident in 1933, she continued working. Their son, also Ramón, born in 1920, was sent by the KIM to Spain four months before the war and died in action as a pilot. Maria was in Spain under her own name and also as 'Julia Jiménez Cárdenas' from October 1936 to September 1938, combining the work of interpreter with that of a deep cover 'illegal'. In his testimony, the former SIM member Tomás Duran Gonzalez stated: 'I knew another woman whose name was Iliya [in reality 'Julia' = Maria Fortus], I am not sure I pronounce her name correctly, who lived in Barcelona and went to Madrid where she stayed at the Hotel Gaylord. She was planted into the Grupo de Investigación and was a polyglot speaking castellano though with some difficulty. She was assigned as a technical adviser to the Catalan police' (AHN, Causa General, Ramo separado no. 37: Policia (Tomos I y II)). For the original Spanish version, see Volodarsky, 'Soviet Intelligence Services', 158 n. 15.

21. Parshina would also become an 'illegal' and would be sent to Prague after the Second World War as 'Maria Kovalikova'.

22. Lydia Kuper was born in Poland in 1914, lived with her parents in Odessa, and studied philosophy and letters in Madrid. Here, at the age of 21, she became the wife of Gabriel León Trilla, one of the founders of the PCE. During the Spanish Civil War Lydia worked as an interpreter at the General Staff. After the war she lived in exile in the Soviet Union and could return to Spain only in 1957. She became a translator and translated into Spanish many Russian classics. Lydia Kuper died in February 2011. For her obituary, see Marcos Rodríguez Espinosa, 'Lydia Kúper, veterana traductora del ruso', *El Pais*, 12 February 2011.

23. If not a coincidence, then it must be Maria Iosifovna Polyakova, an experienced GRU 'illegal' and future controller of both the Rote Kapelle (Trepper) and the Rote Drei (Rado). According to Fondación Pablo Iglesias (ed.), *Los rusos*, 288, Polyakova (the interpreter) was born in 1902 and served in Spain from 20 October 1937 to 18 November 1938. In the Russian-language biography of Polyakova (the intelligence officer, born 1908) in Vladimir Lota, *'Alta' protiv 'Barbarossy'* (Moscow: Molodaya Gvardiya, 2005), it is exactly this period that is not covered. According to Lota, Polyakova was recalled to Moscow from her clandestine mission in Switzerland 'at the end of 1937'. Then 'she was summoned to the then RU chief Ilyichev at the end of 1938', so it is quite possible that all this time she was in Spain. Her official GRU biography states that Polyakova was born on 27 March 1908, was an 'illegal' resident in Switzerland in 1936–7, and was awarded the Order of the Red Star in June 1937 (Lurie and Kochik, *GRU*, 452), which was typical for an assignment in Spain. Polyakova's husband, another Soviet 'illegal', the Austrian Joseph Dicka, was in Spain from late 1936 until December 1937.

24. Almost certainly the wife of Rudolf Leitner; see n. 57.

25. Simona Isaakovna Krimker, only 19 years old in Spain, would become the wife of the Soviet 'illegal' Vladimir Vasilievich Grinchenko. Together with a group of Spaniards, Soviet agents, she will take part in a special operation in Lithuania in February 1944. The group, named 'Guadalajara', apart from Krimker included José Garcia Granda (Volodya), Vicente de Blas (Ivan), Sebastián Piera (Kolya) and Rafael Pelayo (Sergey).

26. Dobrova arrived in Spain on 14 November 1937 and left on 13 August 1938. Fondación Pablo Iglesias (ed.), *Los rusos*, erroneously gives the date as August 1939. It is obvious that she was on an intelligence mission, because she was awarded a combat Order of the Red Star.

27. For example, in his book *A History of Modern Russia: From Nicholas II to Putin* (London: Penguin Books, 2003), Robert Service writes that 'thousands of anti-fascist fighters were arrested and executed [in Spain] at the behest of the Soviet functionaries' (p. 230).

28. Andrew and Mitrokhin, *The Mitrokhin Archive*, 95–6. As the Mitrokhin documents were translated from Russian, this training camp was erroneously trans-literated as 'Argen' in the book. The NKVD 'watcher' there was Sergeant of State Security Bolotnikov.

29. For one of the earlier reports, describing all the difficulties of his own work and that of his subordinates, see, e.g., SANCHO to the Director, 16 October 1936, No. 30, Document 19 (Radosh et al. (eds), *Spain Betrayed*, 66–70, source unnamed).

30. 'Spain because of its democratic and pacifistic spirit lacked these [military intel-ligence] services to which it accorded an importance of a secondary order but, with the outbreak of the war and having only just realised the nature of the latter, it leads us to reflect on the essential need to reorganise or rather to create them with the necessary size and importance' (*Proyecto de Organización del Servicio Secreto del Estado Mayor de la Junta Delegada de la Defensa de Madrid*, AHPCE, Collection Military Documents of the Civil War, High Command of the Red Army [Soviet Military Mission], Bundle 28, quoted in Diaz, 'Spanish Intelligence'.

31. Vladimir Efimovich Gorev, aka Vysokogorets (October 1900–June 1938), was born into a Byelorussian peasant family. He joined the Red Army in 1917 and soon took part in the civil war. After several months at the Eastern Faculty of the Red Army Military Academy, he was sent to China as a military adviser. Gorev worked there under the aliases 'Nikitin' and 'Gordon'. For two semesters he read a course at the Frunze Military Academy in 1928, after which he joined the RU in January 1930. From January 1930 to May 1933, Gorev was posted as an 'illegal' resident of the RU in New York. It is, perhaps, a noticeable coincidence that, exactly like Zarubin in Germany, Gorev intro-duced himself to his American contacts as 'Herbert'. At least this is what Whittaker Chambers recalled in his 1952 autobiography *Witness* (New York: Random House), describing his first Soviet handler. Indeed, it was Gorev who recruited Chambers as a Soviet agent with the codename SOTYI ('100th'). Back in the USSR, Gorev was named the *voenkom* (military commissar) of the 31 brigade of the Leningrad military district. From August 1936 to 3 October 1937

he was Soviet military attaché in Spain. Upon his return to Moscow he was promoted to the rank of division commander and placed in the Chief Directorate of the Command Personnel of the Red Army. He was arrested on 25 January 1938 and shot on 20 June 1938, but was then exonerated posthumously in October 1956. See Lurie and Kochik, *GRU*, 231–2; Kolpakidi, *Entsyklopaediya voennoi razvedki*, 262. See also Frank Schauff, *Der verspielte Sieg: Sowietunion, Kommunistische Internationale und Spanischer Bürgerkrieg 1936–1939*, paperback (Frankfurt/Main: Campus Verlag, 2004), 204.

32. For Lvovich, see Chapter 9. Lvovich was in Spain from November 1936 until May 1938 as a 'military intelligence adviser'. See also Ehrenburg, *Sobranie sochinenii v 9-ti tomakh*, ix. 138–40.

33. Schauff (*Der verspielte Sieg*, 204) mentions his CV, possibly of August 1936, and refers it to RGVA, f. 4, op. 19, d. 18 l. 61, calling him 'Bruno Bundt'. In Fondación Pablo Iglesias (ed.), *Los rusos*, he is erroneously transliterated as 'Bruno Vent' (p. 299).

34. Abramson and Abramson, *Mosaico Roto*, 63.

35. Leonid Konstantinovich Bekrenev (spelt 'Brekreniov' in Fondación Pablo Iglesias (ed.), *Los rusos*, 267) was a naval intelligence officer who headed the intelligence department of the Black Sea Fleet. He served in Spain from 29 December 1936 to 9 May 1937.

36. Nikolai Petrovich Annin, born in Kronstadt, joined the Communist Party and the Red Army in 1918. As a volunteer at the southern front, he commanded a detachment of reconnaissance cavalry, was one of those who ruthlessly suppressed the Kronstadt rebellion in 1921, and then served as a naval officer with the Amur military flotilla. Annin came to Spain in September 1936. For his ten-month service in Spain, he was awarded the Order of Lenin and the Order of the Red Banner. Later Annin commanded the northern group of the Belomor military flotilla. See Ivan D. Papanin, *Lyod i plamen* (Moscow: Politizdat, 1977). See also Fondación Pablo Iglesias (ed.), *Los rusos*, 264.

37. Radosh et al. (eds), *Spain Betrayed*, 69.

38. According to Fondación Pablo Iglesias (ed.), *Los rusos*, 273, Grischenko was in Spain from October 1936 to June 1937. During the Second World War, Grischenko was Bekrenev's successor as the chief of the intelligence department of the Baltic Fleet. Starting from October 1936, a large group of Soviet naval officers arrived in Spain. That included chief naval advisers N. G. Kuznetsov, V. A. Alafuzov, P. A. Pitersky, V. A. Tsypanovich, G. A. Zhukov (not to be confused with Marshal Zhukov); advisers at the Naval General Staff N. E. Basisty and S. G. Sapozhnikov; senior advisers to fleets A. P. Alexandrov, V. P. Drozd, S. D. Soloukhin, and I. D. Eliseyev. Several officers such as N. P. Annin, I. N. Bykov, G. E. Grischenko and P. L. Karandasov served directly with the battleship crews; others, like I. A. Burmistrov, N. P. Egipko (MATISS), V. A. Egorov, M. V. Grachev, G. Yu. Kuzmin, and S. Lisin, commanded the submarines; and a group of captains, including A. P. Batrakov, V. I. Belov, V. A. Larionov, and

S. A. Osipov, commanded torpedo boats. See V. M. Lurie, *Admiraly i generaly Voenno-Morskogo flota SSSR, 1946–1960* (Moscow: Kuchkovo Pole, 2007).

39. Quoted in Radosh et al. (eds), *Spain Betrayed*, 67.

40. Erroneously called 'the Military Ministry' in Radosh et al. (eds), *Spain Betrayed* (p. 68).

41. SANCHO to the Director, No. 30, of 16 October 1936. The telegram (Document 19) is reproduced, but completely misinterpreted, by Radosh et al. (eds), *Spain Betrayed*, 57, 66–70.

42. See Vicente Guarner, *Cataluña en la Guerra de España, 1936–39* (Madrid: Ed. G. del Toro, 1975), 256–7.

43. In Fundación Pablo Iglesias (ed.), *Los rusos*, 301, 'Horacio' is identified as one Yushkevich, division commander and adviser to the Eastern Front, which this writer believes is incorrect.

44. Pyotr Ivanovich Ivanov (August 1897–August 1938), alias 'Ivanichev', graduated from the main faculty of the Frunze Military Academy in 1927 and soon joined the intelligence directorate. He served in Poland as assistant military attaché (November 1928–October 1929) and then at the headquarters. His official GRU biography does not mention Spain, saying only that from August 1933 to April 1938 Ivanov served as the Soviet military attaché in Finland. This, however, is not correct, as, according to the Spanish archival documents, he was in Spain from October 1936 to August 1937 (see Fundación Pablo Iglesias (ed.), *Los rusos*, 274). Colonel Ivanov was arrested in Moscow and shot in April 1938. See Lurie and Kochik, *GRU*, 249. Ivanov's namesake, Nikolai Petrovich Ivanov, was another intelligence officer who served in Spain as adviser to the General Staff of the Frente del Este from April 1937. He returned to Moscow in late April or early May 1938, and in July was appointed Soviet military attaché to China. This Ivanov, alias 'Grigoriev', was later promoted to a general and died in Moscow in 1975.

45. Artur Stashewski (born Hirschfeld), son of Karol (24 December 1890–July/August 1937) completed four classes of the gymnasium. He was active in the Social Democratic movement in 1906–12 and worked as a factory worker in Paris and London in 1908–17. Stashevsky came to Russia in 1918 and joined the Communist Party. In the same year, he attended short courses at the Lefortovo Military School for Red Commanders and was sent to the Western front. He was promoted to brigade commissar and then division commissar. Finally, he joined the military intelligence department of the Red Army and was sent to Berlin as Soviet commercial attaché, alias 'Verkhovsky' (1921–4), in reality heading one of the first RU stations abroad then known as the Berlin Command Centre. In 1922 Stashevsky was one of the first Soviet military intelligence officers to be awarded the Order of the Red Banner. In Berlin, Stashevsky also represented the INO. In 1924–5 he was appointed a member of the Managing Council of the Soviet merchant marine. From 1925 till 1935 Stashevsky was a high-ranking official of the Narkomintorg, and a managing

director of the important Soviet foreign trade firm Torgsin in 1932–3, making a serious contribution to the restoration of the Russian fur trade with the West and at the same time undertaking research in the technology of fur dyeing. He was recalled to Moscow in July 1937. On the way back he travelled through Paris, where his French wife and daughter lived, but did not have time to see his family. A month later he wrote a letter asking his wife to join him in Moscow, which she did. Stashewski was arrested on 8 July and executed on 21 August 1937. His official GRU biography incorrectly states that he was a Soviet trade representative (*torgpred*) in Spain from June 1936 to April 1937. See Lurie and Kochik, *GRU*, 185. See also Kolpakidi, *Entsyklo-paediya voennoi razvedki*, 201; Alexandr Kochański (ed.), *Księga polaków uczest-ników Rewolucji Październikowej, 1917–1920, Biografie* (Warsaw: Książka i Wiedza, 1967), 795. See also Elena Osokina, *Zoloto dlya industrializatsyi: Torgsin* (Moscow: ROSSPEN, 2009).

46. See Radosh et al. (eds), *Spain Betrayed*, document 25, pp. 90–2.
47. Ángel Viñas to author, 7 February 2006.
48. See Abramson and Abramson, *Mosaico Roto*, 32.
49. See Vinarov, *Boitsy tikhogo fronta*, 289–99.
50. In *La soledad de la República* Angel Viñas writes: 'Este comportamiento nos hace pensar que Tumanov no era diplomático professional por lo que nuestra interpretación es que se trataría de un agente del GRU o, más verosímilmente, del INO' (p. 163). Tumanov (born Rosenblum), an old Bolshevik, who started his career in the Red Army, could have been a military intelligence officer in 1921–3, when he served in Turkey as an assistant to the Soviet military attaché, but he should have left the service and joined the NKID at the period when he was a chairman of the Delegation of the Soviet–Turkish border commission (1924–5). Indeed, in Moscow and abroad he occupied responsible, OGPU-related posts (head of the consular service, chief of the personnel department, member of the Collegium, 1931–5), but there are still grounds to believe that he was a straight diplomat. Agabekov's memoirs partially corroborate this version, as the defector mentions Tumanov as an old party member and an acting *polpred* (ambassador) in Persia who had to report to the Central Control Commission in Moscow in charge of the Soviet personnel abroad because of minor violations of the Bolshevik 'ethics'. Agabekov, a one-time head of the Eastern Department of the OGPU and a chief of station in Persia and Turkey, where Tumanov also served, was definitely in a position to know and gives plenty of names of the officers and agents of both OGPU and the RU, but mentions Tumanov as a diplomat (Agabekov, *Sekterny terror*, 279–80; *Cheka za rabotoi* (Berlin: Strela, 1931), 272–3). For Tumanov's career highlights, see Schauff, *Der verspielte Sieg*, 352–3. Tumanov was shot on 28 August 1938 on the shooting grounds of the State Farm Kommunarka not far from Moscow, 'reserved' especially for prominent victims.

51. There is little doubt that the consulate served as cover for the RU personnel. 'Tumanov did not hurry to visit his Bilbao offices staffed at the time by the military attaché, one Jansson [*sic*], and the secretary, Struganoff,' Ángel Viñas writes, quoting the local press of the period (see *La soledad de la República*, 163). 'One Jansson' was Kirill Ivanovich Janson, born in 1894 in Latvia. Brigadier ('Kombrig') Janson joined the Red Army in 1918 and received the best possible education, having graduated from the Academy of the General Staff and then from the special faculty of the Frunze Military Academy. From August 1925 to April 1928 Janson served as the Soviet military attaché in Italy. In October 1936 he was sent to Spain, where he stayed until May 1937. Like many of his RU colleagues there, Janson was awarded the Order of Lenin. Although he took part in the October revolution and later served with the Latvian riflemen unit that guarded Lenin, a special honour in the Soviet Union, Janson was arrested in Moscow in December 1937, sentenced, and shot on 22 August 1938, six days before his former consul, Tumanov. See Lurie and Kochik, *GRU*, 328.

52. For Gorev's report of 23 May 1937, see Radosh et al. (eds), *Spain Betrayed*, 276–8.

53. Enrique Líster, *Nuestra Guerra, aportaciones para una historia de la guerra civil 1936–1939* (Paris: Colleción Ebro, Ed. de la Librairie du Globe, 1966), 100. Líster was right and Kravchenko, whom he called 'Kravchenkov', eventually became Hero of the Soviet Union on 3 May 1945. Among many Spaniards of his group in Toulouse, there was Domingo Ungría, who had formerly commanded the XIV Partisan Corps of *guerrilleros* in Spain. Ungría's former adviser and the corps' instructor Ilya Starinov helped him to join the intelligence department of the Red Army after Ungría's involvement in guerrilla warfare in Russia in 1941–2. Ungría survived two wars only to die in Spain at the end of 1945 while on an 'illegal' assignment trying to cross the border.

54. Lurie and Kochik, *GRU*, 413–14. For details, see also Vladimir Lota, 'Bez sanktsii na lyubov', *Sovershenno Sekretno*, 12 (2003).

55. See Abramson and Abramson, *Mosaico Roto*, 122.

56. See 'El XIX aniversario de la Revolución rusa', *La Vanguardia*, 8 November 1936, p. 2; and Frank Mintz, *Autogestión y anarcosindicalismo en la España revolucionaria* (Madrid: Traficantes De Sueños, 2006), 102 n. 39.

57. According to Vladimir Vaschenko, who calls Korobitsyn 'my first teacher in intelligence work', the two were 'I. Steiner (TARAS) and M. Leitner (MAXIM)'. They may be identical with Josef Steiner (born 23 December 1902), who had been fighting in Spain with the XIII International Brigade since February 1937, was wounded in September, and ended the war in France in 1939. Steiner was parachuted by the Red Army behind the German lines, got caught, and was interrogated by the Gestapo in Salzburg in May 1941, and was then placed in the concentration camp at Dachau, from where he was released in April 1945; he later lived in Bischofshofen. The second Austrian was probably Rudolf Leitner (born 13 March 1914). In May 1934 Leitner left Austria for

Czechoslovakia and then the Soviet Union. After completing the Red Army Airborne Induction Training program in Ryazan, Leitner was sent to Spain in July 1937, where he served with the XI International Brigade, being promoted to the rank of lieutenant. In April 1939 he returned to the Soviet Union. In September 1940 Leitner volunteered to be sent on a secret mission to the German Reich, was arrested by the Gestapo in October 1940, and, after six months of interrogation in Vienna, was also placed in Dachau and later Buchenwald. In May 1944 he managed to flee, was caught, but pretended to be a Russian soldier, and was placed in a forced labour camp. Leitner managed to survive and after the war lived in Innsbruck, where he died in 1992. The Austrian DÖW keeps records on both of them.

58. See Vice Admiral Vladimir Vaschenko, 'Byvshikh razvedchikov ne byvaet', *Literaturnaya Rossiya*, 17, 25 April 2008.

59. Lurie and Kochik, *GRU*, 410. See also RGVA, f. 37837, op. 3, d. 179, ll. 3, 5, 17.

60. See Abramson and Abramson, *Mosaico Roto*, 123–4.

61. Kirill Khenkin, *Okhotnik vverkh nogami* (Frankfurt am Main: Posev Publishing House, 1981), 19.

62. Khenkin, *Okhotnik vverkh nogami*, 21.

63. Motorized Special Brigade.

64. See Lamphere and Shachtman, *The FBI–KGB War*, 276–7.

65. Costello and Tsarev, *Deadly Illusions*, 371–2; and Gazur, *Secret Assignment*, 435–6.

66. For details, see James B. Donovan, *Strangers on a Bridge: The Case of Colonel Abel* (New York, NY: Atheneum, 1964). See also Jeffrey Kahn, 'The Case of Colonel Abel', address to an international conference on criminal law, A. Herzen Russian State Pedagogical University in St Petersburg, 6–8 October 2010. An article with the same title, based on this address, was published in *Journal of National Security, Law and Policy*, June 2011.

67. About Manfred Stern, see Walerij Brun-Zechowoj, *Manfred Stern—General Kleber. Die tragische Biographie eines Berufsrevolutionärs (1896–1954)* (Berlin: Trafo Verlad Dr. Wolfgang Weiss, 2000); Lurie and Kochik, *GRU*, 492; Viñas, *La soledad de la República*; Dallin, *Soviet Espionage*; Mark Zuehlke, *The Gallant Cause: Canadians in the Spanish Civil War, 1936–1939* (Vancouver: Whitecap, 1996); Herbert L. Matthews, 'Canadian Leader Praises Spaniards', *New York Times*, 12 December 1936. See also 'The Shameful Years: Thirty Years of Soviet Espionage in the United States', House Report No. 1229, *Committee on Un-American Activities, US House of Representatives* (Washington, DC: US Government Printing Office 1952); and TNA: PRO HW 17/27 MASK Traffic Spain, Nos 58, 59–62, 86.

68. For details, see Otto Braun, *Chinesische Aufzeichnungen, 1932–1939* (Berlin: Dietz Verlag, 1973), 40–1.

69. Vicente Rojo Lluch, *Así fue la defensa de Madrid* [Aportacion a la historia de la Guerra de España/1936–39] (Mexico: Ediciones Era, 1967), 214. Rojo, however, praised Gorev, calling him 'an extraordinary intelligent man, correct, discreet, active, sincere and loyal'.

70. For details, see Volodarsky, 'Soviet Intelligence Services', 169–71.

71. About Karl Kleinjung, see Volodarsky, *Khokhlov*, 5–7.

72. Helmut Meier (ed.), *Leo Stern (1901–1982): Antifaschist, Historiker, Hochschullehrer und Wissenschaftspolitiker* (Berlin: trafo Verlag, 2002). See also Landauer with Hackl, *Lexikon der österreichischen Spanienkämpfer 1936–1939*, 219; and Weber and Herbst, *Deutsche Kommunisten*, 763.

73. In 1935 Mikhail Nikolaievich Tukhachevsky was made a Marshal of the Soviet Union aged only 42. At the same time he was deputy Commissar of Defence. In this capacity in January 1936 Tukhachevsky visited Britain, France, and Germany—a rather strange route nevertheless approved by Stalin. However, and especially after the military insurrection in Spain, Stalin came to the conclusion that when properly supported by foreign powers the generals may be successful in overthrowing even democratically elected government. At one point he decided that the Soviet military was the only institution that could oppose his quest for absolute power and, as a preventive measure, set out to 'liquidate' Tukhachevsky and a group of other senior commanders. Several authors, including the British historian Robert Conquest and the former chief of Nazi intelligence Walter Schellenberg (see *The Labyrinth: Memoirs of Walter Schellenberg* (Cambridge, MA: Da Capo Press, 2000), 25–8) suggested that the Nazi leaders wishing to weaken the Red Army forged documents implicating its best-known commander in a conspiracy to seize power and used the then President of Czechoslovakia Edvard Beneš to get them to Stalin. According to yet another researcher, a Soviet agent in the ROVS military organization in Paris, General Nikolai Skoblin, played a key role in the operation against Tukhachevsky (see Igor Lukes, *Czechoslovakia between Stalin and Hitler: The Diplomacy of Eduard Beneš in the 1930s* (Oxford: Oxford University Press, 1996), 95). However, after the collapse of the Soviet Union it became clear that the plan to get rid of young Red Army leaders capable of overthrowing Stalin's dictatorial regime was concocted personally by Stalin and carried out by the NKVD. The most recent research in the NKVD archives by the Russian historian Julia Kantor clearly demonstrates that it was Stalin's plot, while not a single document from the so-called 'voluminous dossier assembled by Heydrich to implicate Tukhachevsky' was found either in Stalin's personal archive (AP RF) or in the multi-volume investigation file on Tukhachevsky in the NKVD archive (TsA FSB). See Chapter 13.

74. Radosh et al. (eds), *Spain Betrayed*, 133, document 33 (20 February 1937, No. 51418).

75. The full text of Stalin's speech is in *Voprosy istorii*, 3 (1995), 3–15.

76. TsA FSB, without any reference, quoted in Gorbunov, 'Voennaya razvedka v 1934–1939 godakh', *Svobodnaya mysl*, 3 (March 1998), 57. Shortly after Stalin's visit to the RU headquarters, on 22 May 1937 the NKVD arrested Tukhachevsky and seven other senior commanders. Their June trial was dubbed the 'Case of Trotskyite Anti-Soviet Military Organization'.

77. Salniņš operated in Harbin in 1921, posing as a German businessman 'Christopher Vogel', and all four were part of General V. K. Blücher's mission to China in 1924. He was again in Shanghai in 1927, this time as an American 'Christopher Lauberg', with Vinarov as his assistant. Salniņš headed a group of Soviet guerrillas sent by General Blücher behind the Chiang Kai-shek lines during Soviet–Chinese border clashes of 17–20 November 1929.

78. The decision to send Semyonov to China was taken during a secret session of the CPSU Central Committee on 3 March 1927. See *VKP(b), Comintern and China*, vol. III, pt 1, p. 633. There his task was to organize Communist military underground and the so-called *Fünfergruppen*—5-man sabotage groups, a homage to German workers' secret groups of underground fighters.

79. Estonia was occupied by a religious order of German nobles in the thirteenth century. They stayed in power when Estonia was occupied by Sweden four centuries later and by Russia in the eighteenth century. Many Germans lived in Estonia, even after it had become independent in 1920.

80. See Fundación Pablo Iglesias (ed.), *Los rusos*, 273. Although largely based on archival documents, this exhibition catalogue inaccurately gives the date of Hermann's arrival as 'May 1936' and incorrectly transliterates his name as 'Guerman'.

81. Lurie and Kochik, *GRU*, 371–2. Another foreigner and high-ranking officer (of the NKVD), a successor of Nikolsky/Orlov as the London 'illegal' resident, shared the fate of his RU colleague: Theodor Maly, one of the best Soviet 'illegals' and and agent runners, who sent Philby to Spain, was recalled to Moscow in 1937 and shot in 1938.

82. See Sarah Helm, 'The Gestapo Killer who Lived Twice', *Sunday Times*, 7 August 2005. In Reichssicherheitshauptamt, Chief Directorate of Security, Kopkow headed Department IV A 2 (Sabotage).

83. Costello and Tsarev, *Deadly Illusions*, 267. But, interestingly, concerning this latter statement, the reference is made not to any archival source but to Krivitsky's book, which, as this work seeks to demonstrate, is highly unreliable and in major part is the product of the imagination of Krivitsky's ghostwriter.

84. Andrew and Mitrokhin, *The Mitrokhin Archive*, 95.

85. Primakov et al. (eds), *Ocherki*, iii. 132.

86. Juan Simeón Vidarte, the undersecretary of Interior at the time, admitted in his book that the security service was full of 'nests of spies and confidants of the GPU' (*Todos fuimos culpables: Testimonio de un socialista español*, 2 vols (Barcelona, Buenos Aires, and Mexico: Grijalbo, 1978), 751. Gabriel Morón Diaz, a Civil Governor of Almeria and a socialist, who was appointed deputy

Director General and Inspector General of the DGS in June 1937, found this organization too thickly infested with Communists to make any major changes. See Gabriel Morón, *Política de ayer y política de mañana: Los socialistas ante el problema español* (Mexico City: Talleres Numancia, 1942), 100–5.

87. Haustov et al., *Lubyanka, January 1922–December 1936*, and *Lubyanka, 1937–1938*. There are, however, reports about the situation in Spain from other countries.

88. ASVRR, File No. 17679, vol. 1, p. 52. Cf. Costello and Tsarev, *Deadly Illusions*, 272. The KGB archivists attribute this report to Orlov, though it could have been Belkin or Eitingon. Costello and Tsarev place it in the same mixed pile of intelligence reports of 29 December 1929, which also contained information about the French Deuxiéme Bureau's documents cache, and two pages before the report that follows.

89. For whatever reason, Jeffery, *MI6*, never mentioned this fact.

90. TNA: PRO FO 371/21287, Spain, Code 41, Minute by Cairncross, 23 March 1937. Cf. Andrew and Mitrokhin, *The Mitrokhin Archive*, 85.

91. ASVRR, File No. 17679, vol. 1, p. 54. Cf. Costello and Tsarev, *Deadly Illusions*, 274, 467 n. 21.

92. See Stalin, 'Marxism and the National Question' and 'The National Question and Leninism', both in *Works* (Moscow: Foreign Languages Publishing House, 1954), ii and xi, respectively. Stalin distinguished between socialist nations and bourgeois nations, the only 'two types of nations known to history'. Stalin spoke for the critical, proletarian, Leninist approach to the national question and was categorically opposed to non-proletarian movements of national liberation.

93. See Diaz, 'Spanish Intelligence'.

94. ASVRR, File No. 17679, vol. 1, p. 161, dated 4 May 1937, quoted by Costello and Tsarev, *Deadly Illusions*, 273–4. In reality, it was Viscount Victor Churchill, a cousin of Sir Winston Churchill. Victor Churchill was a treasurer of the Spanish Medical Aid in Barcelona; see Howson, *Arms for Spain*, 222–3.

95. The authors of *Deadly Illusions*, who also quote this telegram, source reference it to ASVRR, File No. 17679, vol. 1, p. 15 (see p. 237). However, there must be some confusion, as the above-mentioned report of 4 May 1937 is referenced to the same file and volume, but p. 161. Cf. Costello and Tsarev, *Deadly Illusions*, 273–4 n. 20.

96. This author is in possession of the copies of all pages of Orlov's diplomatic passport that he used in Spain (and later for entering Canada and the USA) with visas, exit permissions and border stamps. Orlov left Barcelona for France on 28 May 1937 through the border-crossing Port-Bou but returned on the same day (passport pages 17–18). He was almost certainly visiting his family.

97. The report is reproduced in full in Costello and Tsarev, *Deadly Illusions*, 265–6. However, this writer has doubts about the accuracy of the source reference (File No. 17679, vol. 1, p. 28), as a similar report said to belong to the same file

and allegedly sent on the same day is referenced to pp. 60–1 (see *Deadly Illusions*, 466 nn. 45, 46).

98. 'Gorev has no military experience. In war affairs he is a child. Grishin [Berzin] is a good party member, but he is not an expert' (Orlov's report of 27 February 1937).

CHAPTER 17

1. Barry McLoughlin, 'Mass Operations of the NKVD, 1937–8: A Survey', in Barry McLoughlin and Kevin McDermott (eds), *Stalin's Terror: High Politics and Mass Repression in the Soviet Union* (Houndmills, Basingstoke: Palgrave Macmillan, 2003), 118.

2. See a transcript of her 1987 interview in O. A. Gorchakov, *Jan Berzin— komandarm GRU* (St Petersburg: Neva, 2004), 113.

3. The Politburo dismissed Berzin on 1 August. He was arrested on 27 November and, after prolonged interrogations at the Lubyanka, confessed to being a German spy, to preparing the assassination of Stalin and other leaders, and to taking part in the fascist–espionage organization of nationalist Latvians. He was shot on 29 July 1938 in the village of Butovo.

4. Cf. Andrew and Mitrokhin, *The Mitrokhin Archive*, 116.

5. See Stanislav Lekarev, '"Gasan": Chelovek-kinzhal', *Argumenty nedeli*, 25, 26 October 2006. See also Alexander I. Kolpakidi and Dmitri P. Prokhorov, *KGB: Spetsoperatsyi sovetskoi razvedki* (Moscow: Olimp/Astrel/AST, 2000), 368–76.

6. Grigorij Bessedowsky, *Den Klauen der Tscheka Entronnen: Erinnerungen* (Leipzig and Zurich: Grethlein & Co., 1930), 294. The German editors incorrectly spell the name as 'Newaschin'.

7. Ángel Viñas, 'The Financing of the Spanish Civil War', in Paul Preston (ed.), *Revolution and War in Spain, 1931–1939* (London: Methuen, 1984), 270. The Republicans asked their Soviet counterparts to be allowed to use the bank in October–November 1936.

8. For example, one of Navashin's good friends at the NKVT was Semyon Borisovich Chlenov, who worked in Paris in the 1920s as an expert of the Soviet legation. Back in the USSR he was appointed chief legal adviser of the NKVT. Chlenov was arrested shortly before the murder of Navashin.

9. TNA: PRO HW 17/27, MASK decrypts, Spain, No. 29. For the full text of the telegram, see Volodarsky, 'Soviet Intelligence Services', 198.

10. Boris Volodarsky, 'Murder Convictions', *History Today*, 60/3 (March 2010), 66.

11. See Barry McLoughlin, *Left to the Wolves: Irish Victims of Stalinist Terror* (Dublin: Irish Academic Press, 2007), 117. This is the latest and without doubt the best account of Brian Goold-Verschoyle's life and death. The only disadvantage is that, besides using excellent primary sources from both Russian and British

archives, the author also relied on the KGB-sponsored biography of Orlov and on Krivitsky's writings.

12. Andrew and Gordievsky, *KGB*, 218. With regard to Goold's alleged consternation when Foreign Office documents fell out of a parcel he was handling in London, the incident was discussed during his interrogation in Moscow. Brian responded that he had no recollection of such an incident and was, in any case, informed of the contents by a senior officer in the London 'illegal' *rezidentura* (see McLoughlin, *Left to the Wolves*, 184, based on the investigation file).

13. TNA: PRO KV 2/817, Brian Goold-Verschoyle, KV 2/1801, Hamilton Niall Stuart Goold-Verschoyle, and KV 2/1241–1242, Margarete Charlotte Moos.

14. TNA: PRO KV 2/1801, Hamilton Niall Stuart Goold-Verschoyle, Serial 42b, the Security Service PF 41.426, Extract.

15. TNA: PRO KV 2/1242, Serial 98a.

16. For Bystroletov, see Chapters 4, 6, and 11. See also Andrew and Mitrokhin, *The Mitrokhin Archive*, 57–64. However, the authors erroneously state that he was 'the illegitimate son of a Kuban Cossak mother and—Bystroletov later persuaded himself—the celebrated novelist Aleksei Tolstoy' (p. 57). In reality, his mother was a teacher, Klavdia Dmitrievna Bystroletova, and his father Count Alexander Nikolayevich Tolstoy, an official of the State Property Ministry. The most recent biography of Bystroletov (Draitser, *Stalin's Romeo Spy*) is unreliable in several places, as the author relied heavily on the KGB-sponsored biography of Orlov.

17. See Krivitsky, *In Stalin's Secret Service*, 219, 228–30. For details about Krivitsky's Dutch milieu, see Igor Cornelissen, *De GPOe de Overtoon: Spionnen voor Moscou 1920–1940* (Amsterdam: Van Gennep, 1989).

18. Kern, *A Death in Washington*, 55.

19. TNA: PRO KV 2/1242, Serial 64, Personal File Margarete Charlotte MOOS.

20. See McLoughlin, *Left to the Wolves*, 170.

21. McLoughlin, *Left to the Wolves*, 170.

22. TNA: PRO KV 2/804, Serial 7a, Personal File Walter KRIVITSKY, mother's letter, 8 May 1939.

23. Kern, *A Death in Washington*, 258. McLoughlin, *Left to the Wolves*, 168–75.

24. McLoughlin, *Left to the Wolves*, 175, 177.

25. McLoughlin, *Left to the Wolves*, 175, 177. The author is quoting Brian's NKVD investigation file.

26. McLoughlin, *Left to the Wolves*, 186.

27. TNA: PRO KV 2/817, Personal File Brian GOOLD-VERSCHOYLE. In his book *A Death in Washington* Gary Kern writes: 'A surprisingly large body of literature has grown up around Goold-Verschoyle since Krivitsky gave his account. It reveals that he was Irish, not English, and that his brother Neil was a translator of Brecht. One account states that he asked his commander in Barcelona to be relieved of service, as he wanted to fight for a Republican, not a Communist,

Spain. He was arrested in the manner described by Krivitsky and shipped to Sevastopol, then sent to Moscow, where he received an eight-year sentence. Another account reports that he died in the Gulag, and that Neil remained a dedicated Communist nevertheless' (p. 259).

28. McLoughlin, *Left to the Wolves*, 177–95.

29. In operations against Rein, Agabekov, Skoblin, and Klement.

30. Willy Brandt, *My Road to Berlin* (London: Peter Davies, 1960), chs 2–4, quoted in Andrew and Mitrokhin, *The Mitrokhin Archive*, 575.

31. Andrew and Mitrokhin, *The Mitrokhin Archive*, 575.

32. The KGB file on Brandt (POLYARNIK), which covers about forty years of his life and political activities, also shows that, while back in Stockholm during the war, Brandt passed on information to the NKVD residency, and was also in touch with British and American intelligence officers. In 1962, when he was Mayor of West Berlin, the KGB embarked on an operation to force Brandt to cooperate, threatening to reveal his wartime dealings with Soviet intelligence. According to Andrew and Mitrokhin, the attempted blackmail failed. Nevertheless, in 1974 Chancellor Brandt had to resign as a result of what became known as the Guillaume Affair. For details, see Markus Wolf with Anne McElvoy, *Man without a Face* (London: Jonathan Cape, 1997).

33. See, e.g., Kolpakidi and Prokhorov, *KGB: Prikazano likvidirovat'*, 288–9.

34. Here and hereafter, zur Mühlen, *Spanien war ihre Hoffnung*, citing Willi Brandt, *Links und frei: Mein Weg 1930–1950* (Hamburg, 1982), who in his turn refers to the *Bericht über die Nachforschungen im Falle Mark Rein in Spanien vom 1.–10. Juli* (Investigation report).

35. Zur Mühlen, *Spanien war ihre Hoffnung*.

36. See fully documented account of his activities in Spain in Uhl, *Mythos Spanien*, 76–95, and zur Mühlen, *Spanien war ihre Hoffnung*, 167–73. Karl Mewis was born on 22 November 1907 in Lower Saxony, Germany, to the workers' family. He was with first the Sozialistische Arbeiter-Jugend (SAJ) (Socialist Workers Youth) and then the Kommunistischer Jugend Verband Deutschlands (KJVD) (Young Communist League of Germany), before joining the KPD. From autumn 1932 to 1934 he was a student of the ILS in Moscow using the alias 'Meinhard'. From summer 1934 he operated in the German communist underground under the alias 'Köbes'. In 1935 Mewis took part in the VII World Congress of the Comintern and then in the 'Brussels KPD Conference' in Moscow, where he was elected to the KPD Central Committee. From 1935 to 1936 he again operated in the German communist underground under the alias 'Karl Arndt'. In 1936 Mewis immigrated to Denmark, where in Copenhagen he headed the Northern Bureau of the KPD (Außen Leitstelle Nord). In December 1936 he came to Paris and from there was sent to Spain. From January 1937, under his old party name 'Karl Arndt' but also responding to the name 'Fritz', Mewis served as the KPD representative with the Catalonian communists, residing in the hotel Colón in Barcelona and playing an

active role in the Servicio extranjero del PSUC. Because Franz Dahlem was the official KPD representative to the PCE, Mewis was responsible for Catalonia, with its concentration of German immigrants. It was reported that Mewis and his Servicio were actively involved in policing non-communists. In December Dahlem was summoned to Moscow to report and Mewis was promoted to his place as the KPD representative with the PCE Central Committee. In April 1938 he returned to Denmark via Esbjerg 'to open the second front', as he later wrote in his memoirs (Karl Mewis, *Im Auftrag der Partei: Erlebnisse im Kampf gegen die faschistische Diktatur* (Berlin: Dietz Verlag, 1972), 169, 175), 169, 175). According to his most recent biography, in May 1938 he was heading the underground AL Mitte in Prague, which, when the Nazi troops entered the city, moved first to Malmö and then to Stockholm. In autumn 1939 Mewis was summoned to Moscow to report on the situation. Back in Sweden, he was arrested and was held for a year in an internment camp. After the war he lived in East Germany, occupying several high posts, including that of an ambassador to Poland. Karl Mewis died in East Berlin on 16 June 1987 (Weber and Herbst, *Deutsche Kommunisten*, 501), when winds of change were already blowing though the city.

37. Zur Mühlen, *Spanien war ihre Hoffnung*, 132–5.
38. IISG, Nachlaß Paul Hertz, Leitzordner 1b; Korr.-Mappe R, Schreiben Kulcsars vom 12.11.1937 an Otto Bauer und Schreiben Paul Hertz' und Willi Müllers vom 1.11.1937 an Fritz Adler.
39. Zur Mühlen, *Spanien war Ihre Hoffnung*, 170.
40. AHN, Sección P.S. Barcelona, carpeta 804, in zur Mühlen, *Spanien war ihre Hoffnung*, 71. Request dated 24 May 1937.
41. There were actually two *checas* in this area: one on the calle Muntaner no. 321, where later the Prefectura of the SIM in Barcelona was located, and another on Muntaner no. 388.
42. See Andrew and Mitrokhin, *The Mitrokhin Archive*, 575, with reference to the document k-26, 88.
43. Elizabeth K. Poretsky, *Our Own People: A Memoir of 'Ignace Reiss' and his Friends* (London: Oxford University Press, 1969), 258–9.
44. Tresca was first a Bolshevik supporter, but after the destruction of the anarchist movement in Catalonia and Aragon he became an outspoken opponent of the Soviet Union.
45. It was later reprinted in the French translation as Document No. 10 in the *Cahier Leon Trotsky Numéro special Les process de Moscou dans le monde* (July–September 1979).
46. Document No. 10, *Cahier Leon Trotsky Numéro special Les process de Moscou dans le monde* (July–September 1979).
47. See, e.g., Huber and Uhl, 'Politische Überwachung', ii. 13–14.
48. The report of 'Moritz' (Hubert von Ranke), RGASPI, f. 545, op. 2, d. 145, l. 63.

49. For example, Hubert von Ranke's still unpublished memoirs 'Erinnerungen, Spanien' (Emigration in Paris, 1933–45), Munich, Institut für Zeitgeschichte, Nachlässe und Sammlungen, Sig. ED 161), and Antonia Stern's unpublished 1939 memoirs in IISG, 'Hans Beimler: Dachau—Madrid. Ein Dokument unserer Zeit', 1–301.

50. In *Spanien war ihre Hoffnung* (p. 153), with reference to two sources—Gorkin's *Stalins langer Arm*, 202, and a report of a Nazi informer 'Pat' (Bundesarechiv Koblenz, Akten des Reichssicherheitshauptamtes R58, Akt 590), zur Mühlen mentions one 'Carmen', who acted as an NKVD liaison and had been seen in Herz's entourage, concluding that she could possibly be Gertrude Schildbach, a long-time OGPU–NKVD agent who took part in the assassination of Ignatz Reiss. This was definitely not the case, as in 1936–7 Schildbach was in Italy and Switzerland and after the Reiss operation in September 1937 fled to Moscow. By this time Herz had also been released from his duties. One possible candidate could have been 'Carmen la gorda', an NKVD agent already mentioned. She later became the wife of Colonel Martínez Cartón of the PCE leadership.

51. AHN, Sección P. S. Barcelona, carpeta 13. I am very grateful to Professor Jesús Fernando Salgado Velo of the University of Santiago de Compostela for finding in the archives, and sending me, a series of valuable reports compiled by Agent S.S.I. no. 29 in May 1937.

52. He was a leader of the Federación Universitaria Escolar (FUE) and in September 1934, together with Gabriel Morón, took an active part in the preparation of a general strike and a rebellion by socialists and anarchists in Asturias on 6 October. In 1936 Ordóñez took part in the assassination of Calvo Sotelo. From 12 February 1937 Ordóñez served as 2nd Secretary of the Spanish Embassy in Moscow, where he remained until 30 June—that is, more than two weeks after the DEDIDE had been established. In early 1938, having headed the most important counter-intelligence service of the Republic for only about half a year, Ordóñez was again sent to Moscow to the same junior post and remained there until April 1938. After his return and until January 1938 he served in the Foreign Ministry and was then transferred to the Ministry of National Defence.

53. See Fritjof von Meyer, 'Einsamer Wolf unter Wölfen', *Der Spiegel*, 12/1993.

54. Hubert von Ranke, Munich, Institut für Zeitgeschichte, Archiv, Bestand ED 161.

55. Zur Mühlen (*Spanien war ihre Hoffnung*, 160) refers to the agent's report of 27 May 1937. A copy of this report is in this author's archive. Agent S.S.I. no. 29 informed about the 60-year-old German academic Gustav Schlosser, who lived half of his life in Barcelona and who so imprudently allowed himself to translate reports about Moscow's anti-Trotskyite show trials.

56. Zur Mühlen, *Spanien war ihre Hoffnung*, 161.

57. Julian Gorkin, *Stalins langer Arm* (Berlin: Kiepenheuer & Witsch, 1984), 235.

58. Mitrokhin, vol. 5, ch. 7, in Andrew and Mitrokhin, *The Mitrokhin Archive*, 97.

59. IISG, Nachlaß Hans Stein, Persönliche Korrespondenz, Mappe 77, Alfred Herz.

60. David Pike mentions another couple with a similar fate: the already mentioned Joaquín Olaso Piera (alias 'Martin', alias 'Emmanuel'), who had served as inspector-general of public order in Catalonia and later in the SIM, and earned the nickname of 'the eye of Moscow', and his girlfriend, Dolorès Garcia Echevarieta, about whose *mort troublante* the press reported in 1954. See Pike, *In the Service of Stalin*, 31.

61. SMH, legajo 280, carpeta 17, SIFNE, Nota de esta oficina: espionaje rojo, 31 August 1937.

62. *Gaceta de la República*, 87, 28 March 1938.

63. For the detailed report from the trial, see 'El constructor de las "checas" comparace ante un consejo de guerra', *La Vanguardia Española*, 13 June 1939, p. 5. See also Rafael López Chacón, *Por que hice las chekas de Barcelona? Laurencic ante el Consejo de Guerra*, paperback (Barcelona: Editorial Solidaridad Nacional, 1939), 10.

64. First oddział IV of wydział II, and then wydział V and III of Departament VII. See Biuletyn Informacji Publicznej Polski Instytut Pamięci Narodowej. Funkcjonariusze organów bezpieczeństwa PRL.

65. Hugh Thomas mentions Sala only once in a footnote, writing: 'The chief Catalan police agent acting for Gerö, Victorio Sala, once a member of the POUM, later broke with the communists, whom he has since accused of atrocious crimes' (Thomas, *The Spanish Civil War*, paperback (London: Penguin, 2003), 681 n. 2).

66. Personalliste, SAPMO-BArch, SgY11/V237/4/29, in Huber and Uhl, 'Politische Überwachung', 152. In 1939–40 Schwarze worked in the KPD foreign organization in Belgium. In 1940–5 he was interned in France but managed to escape. At the end of the Second World War Schwarze joined the American Office of Stratigic Services (OSS), was trained by them as a secret agent, and then parachuted into the Rhein area still occupied by the Wehrmacht troops. He later lived in East Germany. For details, see Mewis, *Im Auftrag der Partei*, 151.

67. Nil Nikandrov, *Grigulevich: Razvedchik, kotoromu vezlo* (Moskva: Molodaya gvardiya, 2005), 63–4.

68. RGASPI, Personal files of the CPUSA members, f. 495, op. 261, d. 1667, ll. 1–6, George Mink Autobiography. See Vernon L. Pedersen, 'George Mink, the Marine Workers Industrial Union, and the Comintern in America', *Labor History*, 41/3 (2000), 307–20. Correctly quoting from Mink's Comintern autobiography, Pedersen incorrectly claims that Minkowsky was born 'in the Russian village of Zittomir Volyan' (p. 308).

69. Pedersen, 'George Mink', 308.

70. Pedersen, 'George Mink', 309.

71. Pedersen, 'George Mink', 309.

72. FBI, Custodian Detention Report, 26 December 1942, p. 15.

73. RGASPI, f. 495, op. 37, d. 73, minutes of a meeting between Comrade Manuilsky and American comrades, 31 August 1930.

74. FBI, Report of 26 December 1942, p. 4, in Pedersen, 'George Mink', 314.

75. See Nadezhda Ulanovsky and Maya Ulanovsky, *Istoriya odnoi sem'i* (*The History of One Family*) (New York: Chalidze Publications, 1982), 120.

76. About the Copenhagen affair, see John Earl Haynes, 'The American Communist Party as an Auxiliary to Espionage: From Asset to Liability', 2005 Raleigh International Spy Conference paper, pp. 5–7. Ulanovsky was on the MI5 watch list from January 1925 until long after the war. The Service knew that Ulanovsky operated in Holland under a variety of aliases in the 1920s and was arrested in Denmark. For his personal file with photos, see TNA: PRO KV 2/1417, which is part of his PF 4251, vol. 1.

77. Liston M. Oak, 'I am Exposed as a Spy', *Socialist Call*, 18 December 1937, as cited by Romerstein and Levchenko, *The KGB against the 'Main Enemy'*, 137.

78. In March 1935, Copenhagen police arrested Mink after a hotel chambermaid complained of a rape attempt. Police found that he had in his possession four American passports, one in his name, one fraudulent passport with his photograph but in the name of Al Gottlieb, one for Harry H. Kaplan, and one for Abraham Wexler. The Kaplan passport was authentic; when American authorities asked Harry Kaplan how his passport had got into Mink's hands, Kaplan stated that it had been stolen from him. The Wexler passport was also authentic; Wexler claimed it had been stolen but he could not say when, where, or by whom. Wexler was a member of the small Marine Workers' Industrial Union, of which Mink was the first national chairman, and Kaplan was an associate of Mink. The obvious implication was that both had turned their passports over to Mink for later alteration by insertion of new photographs. A Danish court convicted Mink of espionage, and he served eighteen months in prison. He was then deported to the USSR. See Chapter 10. Genuine passports of American volunteers were delivered from Spain to Moscow in large quantities, to be used later by the Soviet 'illegals'.

79. US House of Representatives, Special Committee on Un-American Activities, *Hearing Regarding Leon Josephson and Samuel Liptzen*, 69–74. See also Romerstein and Levchenko, *The KGB against the 'Main Enemy'*, 136–7.

80. Testimony of William C. McCuistion, *Investigation of Un-American Propaganda Activities in the United States*, Hearing before a Special Commission on Un-American Activities, House of Representatives, 76th Congress, 1st Session, vol. 11, pp. 6551–640.

81. Richard Krebs is better known as Jan Valtin, author of the bestselling *Out of the Night* first published at the time of his congressional testimony, a work that had been ghost-written by Isaac Don Levine. Richard Krebs should not be confused with another Krebs, whose real name was Werner Rakow (aka Vladimir Inkov, aka Felix Wolff, aka Krebs and, erroneously, Kreps), who worked for the RU in Vienna in the mid-1920s and was a Soviet military intelligence

'illegal' resident in the USA in 1925–7. For more about Richard Julius Hermann Krebs, see TNA: PRO KV 2/1102. See also Ernst von Waldenfels, *Der Spion, der aus Deutschland kam: Das geheime Leben des Seemanns Richard Krebs* (Berlin: Aufbau-Verlag, 2002).

82. US House of Representatives, Special Committee on Un-American Activities (Dies Committee), vol. 14, pp. 8512–3. See Romerstein and Levchenko, *The KGB against the 'Main Enemy'*, 137–9.

83. Anon., 'The Mink', *Time*, 2 May 1938.

84. Shachtman wrote: 'An international assassin is en route to Mexico. He sailed early this week from the port of Galveston, Texas, for the port of Vera Cruz, Mexico, to carry out the mission assigned to him by his gangster overlords: TO ORGANIZE THE MURDER OF LEON TROTSKY. In this country he is known to certain circles by the name of George Mink—known to the Philadelphia police as a petty larceny crook—subsequently known to the workers on New York's waterfront as the financially well-heeled boss of the late "Marine Workers Industrial Union" organized nine years ago by the Communist Party. In Moscow, after the inevitable collapse of his "Union" he was known as an associate of Juliet Stuart Poyntz in the Red International of Labor Unions, where he worked in reality as an agent of the GPU, especially charged with surveillance over American communists and other visitors to Moscow's hotels' (Max Shachtman, 'Comrade Trotsky's Life is Menaced', *Workers' International News*, 1/5 (May 1938), 1–2).

85. See Kern, *A Death in Washington*, 465 n. 626. However, in Fondación Pablo Iglesias (ed.), *Los rusos*, 283, it is stated that Mink died in action during an intelligence mission on 4 March 1937, which is certainly incorrect.

86. Pedersen, 'George Mink', 318–19.

87. Dallin, *Soviet Espionage*, 410.

88. Kolpakidi and Prokhorov, *KGB: Prikazano likvidirovat'*, 290–1. For more details, see René Revol, 'Procès de Moscou en Espagne', *Cahiers Leon Trotsky*, 3 (July–September 1979), 122.

89. Carlo Tresca, 'En fustigeant sans trêve ni peur toutes les dictatures, nous accomplissons notre devoir', *Il Martello*, 28 February 1938, repr. in *Cahiers Leon Trotsky*, 3 (July–September 1979), 189–95), trans. from the Italian by Annie Scattolon. In his turn, Tresca quotes the *Solidariad Obrera* of 11 May 1937.

90. Tresca, 'En fustigeant sans trêve', 190.

91. Kolpakidi and Prokhorov, *KGB: Prikazano likvidirovat'*, 290–1.

92. According to the Spanish sources (Fondación Pablo Iglesias (ed.), *Los rusos*, 283), Mink also used cover names 'Norman' and 'Berman'.

93. A mass of circumstantial evidence led police to arrest Carmine Gallante as the triggerman. But Galante, who later became head of one of New York's mafia families before his own execution in 1979, was never prosecuted. The question of who hired a killer has never been resolved. See Dorothy Gallagher, *All the*

Right Enemies: The Life and Murder of Carlo Tresca (Fredericksburg, PA: Rutgers University Press, 1988). See also Mauro Canali, 'Tutta la verità sul caso Tresca', *Liberal* (February–March 2001).

94. Carlo Tresca, 'Où est Juliet Stuart Poyntz?' *Modern Monthly* (March 1938), *Il Martello*, 26 April 1938, repr. in *Cahiers Leon Trotsky*, 3 (July–September 1979), 196–8, trans. from the Italian by Annie Scattolon.

95. Tresca, 'Où est Juliet Stuart Poyntz?', *Cahiers Leon Trotsky*, 197. Andrew and Gordievsky, *KGB,* 161. The KGB-sponsored sources state that Alexander Borisovich Epstein (literary pseudonym 'Shakhno Epstein') was born in 1881 in Lithuania, the son of a rabbi. In 1903 he joined the Bund and took part in revolutionary activities in Poland. After his second arrest there in 1907, Epstein came to Vienna, from where he moved over to Geneva. In 1910–17 he lived in the US publishing articles in the Jewish press. In 1917 Epstein returned to Russia and in 1919 joined the Communist Party, starting working for Agitprop. In May 1921 he was sent by the OMS to the USA, where he worked undercover for two years. Altogether he had lived in America for fourteen years, finally coming to Moscow in 1928. In January 1929 the CPUSA reported to the ECCI that Epstein, who for the past five years had worked there as 'Joseph Berson', took an active part in the Communist Party work as a member of its Central Committee and associate editor of a daily Yiddish language newspaper *Morgen Freiheit*, the largest of nine daily newspapers in the USA affiliated with the Communist Party. After his return from the USA, Epstein reportedly worked in Kharkiv, Ukraine, and from 1942 in Moscow, where he died in 1945. See Kolpakidi and Prokhorov, *KGB: KGB: Spetsoperazii sovetskoi razvedki,* 435–6.

96. Tresca, "Où est Juliet Stuart Poyntz?" *Cahiers Leon Trotsky*, 197. According to the same Russian sources, Epstein returned to the Soviet Union, where he became the executive secretary of the Jewish Antifascist Committee. He died on 21 July 1945.

97. See Benjamin Gitlow, *The Whole of their Lives: Communism in America—A Personal History and Intimate Portrayal of its Leaders* (New York: Charles Scribner's Sons, 1948).

98. See Haynes, Klehr, and Vassiliev, *Spies*, 535.

99. See Haynes, Klehr, and Vassiliev, *Spies*, 535. According to Vassiliev's notes from the KGB files, in December 1944 the American Department of the GRU informed their Lubyanka colleagues that Poyntz was not in their network 'and nothing was known about her'.

100. Mikhail Millstein, *Skvoz gody voin i nischety* (Moscow: ITAR-TASS, 2000), 39.

101. 'Freund dit Moulin', *Cahiers Léon Trotsky*, 3 (July–September 1979), 135.

102. Katja Landau, 'Stalinism in Spain'.

103. See 'Hans Freund: Letters from Madrid', *Revolutionary History*, 4/1–2 (2009). Ssigned by his pseudonym 'Moulin', these letters were dated 24 August and

27 September 1936 and were published by the Information and Press Service of the Fourth International in its bulletins No. 7 of 4 September and No. 12 of 21 October 1936; they were reproduced in *Revolutionary History*. Orwell's book was first published in the UK in April 1938 and the episode is mentioned on p. 148.

104. See the editorial introduction to 'Hans Freund: Letters from Madrid', *Revolutionary History* (2009).

105. Elsa Reiss, 'Ignace Reiss: In Memoriam', *New International*, 4/9 (September 1938), 276–8; Peter Huber, Daniel Künzi, and Jean-Marie Argelès, 'L'Assassinat d'Ignace Reiss', *Communisme: Revue d'études pluridisciplinaires*, 26–7 (1990), 5–28; Kern, *A Death in Washington*; Andrew and Mitrokhin, *The Mitrokhin Archive*, to name but a few.

106. The Reiss case and Orlov's role in it are analysed in Chapter 19.

107. Orlov, *The March of Time*, 319.

108. According to Georges Vereeken (*The GPU in the Trotskyist Movement* (London: New Park Publications, 1976), 168–74), Wolf lived in Brussels and left some documents, which he must have regarded as very important, with an old member of a Trotskyite organization. The quoted letter of 22 August 1933 was among them. Max Eastman, author, and Elena ('Eliena') Vassilyevna Krylenko-Eastman, artist, later actively corresponded with Orlov in the United States. This correspondence can be found in the Eastman MSS, Manuscript Dept, Lilly Library Indiana University, Bloomington, Indiana. The subject is dealt with in Part III of this work.

109. See Vereeken, *The GPU in the Trotskyist Movement*, 170.

110. Thalmann, *Wo die Freiheit stirbt*, 198–200.

111. Zur Mühlen, *Spanien war ihre Hoffnung*, 133.

112. Huber und Uhl, 'Politische Überwachung', 141. Remarkably, the authors of the most recent reference book (Weber und Herbst, *Deutsche Kommunisten*, 2004) do not say much about the underground activities of Karl Mewis.

113. Weber and Herbst, *Deutsche Kommunisten*, 815–16. See also Michael Uhl, 'Die internationalen Brigaden im Spiegel neuer Dokumente', *IWK*, 4 (1999), 486–518. After the war Vesper lived illegally in France, where he was interned in 1940 but managed to escape. After that he was one of the leaders of the KPD Bureau in occupied France and from 1942 took part in the Resistance. After the Second World War he lived for a while in West Germany and was a deputy of the German Bundestag. In 1952 Vesper and his wife moved to the DDR, where from 1959 he worked at the Foreign Ministry as ambassador in Hungary and Czechoslovakia. Vesper died in East Berlin in 1978 and was commemorated by a DDR postal stamp of 1987.

114. Thalmann, *Wo die Freiheit stirbt*, 206–8, 227.

115. According to Katja Landau, the Italian *Corriere della Serra* of 29 July 1937 noted that on 27 July Erwin Wolf and another journalist were taken to the Security Police prison at 24 Puerta del Angel to open a preliminary investigation into their political activity. See Katja Landau, 'Stalinism in Spain'.

116. Vereeken, *The GPU in the Trotskyist Movement*, 173.

117. Katja Landau, 'Stalinism in Spain'.

118. Thalmann, *Wo die Freiheit stirbt*, 239.

119. René Dazy, *Fusillez ces chiens enragés: Le Genocide des trotskistes* (Paris: O. Orban: 1981), 198. Two months later, on 25 April 1938, the already mentioned *Time* article reported that Erwin Wolf, Czech secretary to Trotsky during his exile in Norway, had 'disappeared' while serving in Spain as a volunteer.

120. General Miller was the uncle of Lisa Hill of the London School of Slavonic Studies, whose mother, née Louisa Maria Wilhemina Sophia Miller, married Frederick William Hill.

121. Andrew and Mitrokhin, *The Mitrokhin Archive*, 98.

122. Kolpakidi and Prokhorov, *KGB: Prikazano likvidirovat'*, 333. Captain of state security Grigoryev was arrested in Moscow on 2 November 1938, sentenced to death, and shot on 28 January 1940.

123. Reproduced in Hugo Dewar, *Assassins at Large: Being a Fully Documented and Hitherto Unpublished Account of the Executions outside Russia Ordered by the GPU* (Westport, CT: Hyperion Press Inc., 1981; repr. of 1952 edn published by Beacon Press, Boston), 3. See also Primakov et al. (eds), *Ocherki*, iii. 118.

124. Dewar, *Assassins at Large*, 15.

125. 'For $15,000 we could buy an airplane of the type in which you and I whisked away farme' (ASVRR, Operational Correspondence File [DOP] No. 19897, vol. 3, p. 121, SCHWED to Spiegelglass, 10 May 1938, quoted by Costello and Tsarev, *Deadly Illusions*, 472 n. 15). See also Part III of this work.

126. Andrew and Mitrokhin, *The Mitrokhin Archive*, 99.

127. Primakov et al. (eds), *Ocherki*, iii. 118.

128. ASVRR, Personal File '13', No. 13016. The copy of the document is reproduced in Primakov et al. (eds), *Ocherki*, ii, insert. According to the Russian sources, Skoblin was registered as agent EZh-13, codenamed farmer. Interestingly, contrary to all previous accounts, it is evident from this statement that Skoblin thought he was dealing with the Red Army intelligence, and not the OGPU. Thus, it is possible that he was initially recruited under the 'false flag', as was his recruiter Peter Kowalski, the INO OGPU officer.

129. Costello and Tsarev, *Deadly Illusions*, 299.

130. Orlov, *The March of Time*, 202–3.

131. See the entry for the Soviet Union in the heading 'Lista del Cuerpo Diplomático extranjero', July 1937, pos. 6, Archivio de Ministerio de Asuntos Exteriores (AMAE), courtesy of Professor Ángel Viñas.

132. See File No. 21746, vol. 1, pp. 198–9. The authors of *Deadly Illusions* refer to this file as SPIEGELGLASS Investigation File (p. 472 n. 20 and 474 n. 51), which means that it was opened after 2 November 1938, when Spiegelglass was arrested. Unfortunately, Costello and Tsarev reproduce only some scrappy pieces from this file.

133. ASVRR, Operational Correspondence File No. 19897, vol. 3, p. 121, 10 May 1938, quoted by Costello and Tsarev, *Deadly Illusions*, 472 n. 15.

134. Nikita Petrov and Natalia Gevorkyan, 'Konets agenta 13', *Moskovskie novosti*, 46 (1995). The telegram is also reproduced in Kolpakidi and Prokhorov, *KGB: Prikazano likvidirovat'*, 338. It is published in English for the first time.

135. See Primakov et al. (eds), *Ocherki*, iii. 118.

136. Kolpakidi and Prokhorov, *KGB: Prikazano likvidirovat'*, 337–8. Stakh, to whom Skoblin addressed his letter, was a former 'legal' resident in Paris, Stanisław Glinski, son of Martin (1894–1937). It is clear that Skoblin was led to believe that Glinski was alive and in Moscow, therefore he mentioned Glinski's successor in Paris, Georgy Kosenko, but still appealed to 'Stakh'. In reality, Glinski was arrested in Moscow on 30 August 1937 and, after torture, shot on 9 December.

137. A year before, in the same building, Consul Antonov-Ovseyenko had given a formal reception to the local dignitaries on 7 November, inviting all Catalan officials, including the President of the Generalidad, to celebrate the XIX anniversary of the Bolshevik revolution. Iliya Ehrenburg was also present. For the media report, see *La Vanguardia*, 8 November 1936, p. 2.

138. Orlov, *The March of Time*, 207.

139. Orlov, *The March of Time*, 207.

140. Kern, *A Death in Washington*, 144, 166; TNA: PRO KV 2/805, Personal File KRIVITSKY.

141. Hans Schafranek, 'Kurt Landau', *Cahiers Léon Trotsky*, 5 (January–March 1980), 71–95, translated from French by Ted Crawford with the English version published in *Revolutionary History*, 4/1–2 (Winter–Spring 1992).

142. About Olberg, see Rita T. Kronenbitter, 'Leon Trotsky, Dupe of the NKVD', *Studies in Intelligence*, 16/1 (special edition 1972), 15–61.

143. Pierre Broué, 'Kurt Landau', *Revolutionary History*, 9/4 (2008), 229–36.

144. Broué, 'Kurt Landau', 229–36.

145. Schafranek, 'Kurt Landau'.

146. See Schafranek, *Das kurze Leben des Kurt Landau*.

147. Katja Landau, 'Stalinism in Spain'.

148. Cf. Paul Preston, *We Saw Spain Die: Foreign Correspondents in the Spanish Civil War*, postscript to the paperback edn (London: Constable, 2009), 439–43.

149. Katja Landau, 'Stalinism in Spain'. In fact, Colonel Ricardo Burillo was Director General of Security (Jefe superior de la Dirección General de Seguridad) in Catalonia from May 1937.

150. Schafranek, 'Kurt Landau'.

151. ASVRR, Personal File SCHWED, No. 32476, vol. 1, pp. 91–2, SCHWED to the Centre, 25 August 1937, quoted by Costello and Tsarev, *Deadly Illusions*, 286.

152. Katja Landau, 'Stalinism in Spain'. Unfortunately her passionate document is full of errors and the editors' comments to its English edition are even more unsatisfactory. In one of the editions of his famous book, Hugh Thomas even

noted that the horrible stories the brochure contains remain in doubt (Thomas, *The Spanish Civil War*, 3rd edn (1977), 703 n. 2). Katja mentioned 'Georg Scheyer, alias Sanja Kindermann', in reality the already mentioned Szaja Kinderman. In a letter to *Revolutionary History*, 6 July 2003, Reiner Tosstorff comments: 'Georg Scheyer alias Sanja (correctly Schaja or Szaja— for Izchaak) Kinderman was a Polish Jew, living as a refugee in Barcelona, a Stalinist, who took the chance to make a career after 19 July. It seems, although I have no possibility to prove this oral information, that he played a major roIe in the Polish state security after 1945, but was expelled in 1968. He is supposed to be living in Sweden now.' About Szaja Kinderman, whose real name was Józef Winkler, see this chapter. 'Karl Meives alias Karl Arndt', in reality Karl Mewis, is also mentioned in this chapter, alias 'Fritz and Karl Arndt'. 'Seppi Kappalanz, the wife of GPU agent Moritz Bressler', was in reality Josepha (Seppel) Campalans, the widow of the former Catalan Socialist politician Rafael Campalans i Puig. She was born Herrmann in 1907 in Königstein/Taunus. After the general elections of 1931, her husband was elected deputy for Barcelona and occupied this post until his death in 1933. Seppel Campalans worked as a translator of the KPD *Abteilung für Abwehr und Gegnerarbeit* in Barcelona, headed by Hubert von Ranke, alias 'Moritz' (two others were Hermann Geisen and Minna Artz-Neubeck). '[Alfred] Herz— another name for the Lithuanian Stalinist George Mink'—is also discussed in this chapter. 'Franz Feldman: without doubt the sinister Stalinist hatchet man Ernö Gerö': this is certainly not the case, as Gerö was a Comintern representative to the PSUC, and, as correctly noticed by Reiner Tosstorff in the above-mentioned letter, it is hardly imaginable that he was at the same time occupied with such 'minor' activities. As far as Pauline Dobler is concerned, at least the name is correct. Dobler did not belong to any party or political group, and between 1929 and 1936 travelled a lot as a governess visiting England, Spain, and Italy. The last time Dobler came to Spain was in December 1936. Until her arrest on 8 July 1937 she occupied a technical position in the POUM Secretariat. Hubert von Ranke in his unpublished memoirs recalled that he and his deputy 'Peter Nerz' (that is, Walter Vesper) paid Dobler 600 pesetas—after she was released, having been 'turned' during the interrogations. In 1939 Pauline Dobler was working with Gorkin in Paris when she was uncovered as a Stalinist mole. See also Reiner Torsstorff, letter to *Revolutionary History*, 6 July 2003. The latest research shows that Paula, also Paulina Dobler (Zurich, 21 April 1910–Zurich, 15 September 1987), was interrogated on 24 April 1937, as some 'Trotskyite/POUM material' had been found in her possession. She was arrested on 8 July 1937 'for spying' (Verhaftung wegen Spionage), and at the time when Landau was arrested Dobler was herself interrogated (23 September and 25 September 1937, RGASPI: f. 495, op. 183, d. 12; BAR E 2001 (D) 1, Bd. 65). In October 1943 Dobler left France for Switzerland and 'lay low' in Geneva. See Huber and Hug, *Die Schweizer Spanienfreiwilligen*, 168, 464.

153. Katja Landau, 'Stalinism in Spain'.
154. Hans Landauer to author, Vienna, 9 November 2005. He made the same claim in his book, Landauer and Hackl, *Lexikon der österreichischen Spanien-kämpfer 1936–1939*, 146–7. Luis Jiménez de Asua's papers are not at the AHN but at the Fundacion Pablo Iglesias archives.
155. Katja Landau, 'Stalinism in Spain'. See also Broué, 'Kurt Landau'.
156. One of the agents was Otto Bauer, a famous Austrian politician. A prisoner of war in Russia during the First World War, he led the left wing of the Social Democratic Party when he returned, and was appointed Minister of Foreign Affairs in the new Austrian republic (1918). Following the failure of the Schutzbund uprising in February 1934, Bauer was forced into exile. He first lived in Brno and then in Paris, where he died in July 1938, aged 56. Though his strong Austro-Marxist views were no secret to anybody, no one ever knew that Otto Bauer was a mercenary agent of the Spanish Republican secret service. For the documentary reference, see reports 31 and 32, 25 June 1937, Anexo 13, Historia del Servicio, AMAEC, caja RE 60, quoted in Ángel Viñas (dir.), *Al servicio de la República: Diplomáticos y la Guerra Civil* (Madrid: Marcial Pons Historia, 2010), 230 n. 40.
157. About Kulscsar in Prague, see Viñas (dir.), *Al servicio de la República*, 229–32.
158. See Preston, *We Saw Spain Die*, 40.
159. Preston, *We Saw Spain Die*, 39.
160. See Ulanovsky and Ulanovsky, *The History of One Family*, 101.
161. Preston, *We Saw Spain Die*, 39.
162. Weidenfeld, *Remembering My Good Friends*, 96–7. Ilse Barea-Kulcsar returned to Austria in 1965 to work for the Österreichischer Gewerkschaftsbund (ÖGB) (Austrian Trade Union Federation) and the Socialist Party. She died in Vienna on 1 January 1973. Among other figures mentioned in George Weidenfeld's memoirs, are Soviet spies and collaborators Peter Smollett, Guy Burgess, Anthony Blunt and Moura Budberg. Moura Budberg (née Maria Ignatyevna Zakrevskaya) was the Ukrainian-born wife of Count Johann Benckendorff. Later she was briefly married to Baron Nikolai von Bud-berg-Bönningshausen, and was at various times the mistress of Sir Robert H. Bruce Lockhart, Maxim Gorky and H. G. Wells. She had been called 'the Mata Hari of Russia'. One of her friends in London was Guy Burgess who used to be a regular guest at her flat in Knightsbridge. There's a comment in Moura's MI5 file dating August 1950 that someone in Burgess' position should not mix with her. That was, of course, before Burgess was exposed as a Soviet spy a year later. After the spy scandal broke out, she reportedly told the Security Service that Sir Anthony Blunt, to whom Burgess' was most devoted, was a member of the Communist Party. Blunt only confessed of spying in 1963. For Marie (Moura) Ignatievna Budberg personal file, see TNA: KV 2/979–981. See also, Nina Berberova, *Moura: The Dangerous Life of the Baroness Budberg* (New York, NY: New York Review Books, 2005).

163. Katja Landau, 'Stalinism in Spain'. Katja's bitterness is understandable, but Paul Preston convincingly explains why she saw Ilse Kulcsar twice during interrogations. The book *We Saw Spain Die* had already been published, but Professor Preston wrote a gripping epilogue for the paperback edition entitled 'Love, Espionage and Treachery' (*We Saw Spain Die* (2009). Katja was first released on 29 November. However, on 8 December, she was rearrested by a special squad in an unmarked car and taken to a detention centre in the Passeig de Sant Joan. There she was interrogated by Leopold Kulcsar, who told her that she would never leave the building alive. It was during these interrogations, according to Preston, that Katja twice saw Ilse and concluded that she too was an NKVD agent involved in the persecution of the foreign anti-Stalinists. In fact, although Katja's account of what happened to her was exact, her interpretation of what she saw can be seen to be erroneous when contrasted with Arturo Barea's explanation of Ilse's presence in Barcelona.

164. Hans Landauer to author, Vienna, 9 November 2005. Professor Grover Furr from Montclair State University seeks to prove that the strange disappearance of Kurt Landau, Hans Freund, Erwin Wolf, Marc Rhein, José Robles, and others had nothing to do with the NKVD. 'There is no evidence', he writes, 'that a single one of these people was "executed or tortured to death in Communists prisons", or killed by Communists. Not one!' See his publications 'Fraudulent Anti-Communist Scholarship from a "Respectable" Conservative Source: Prof. Paul Johnson' <http://msuweb.montclair.edu/~furrg/pol/pauljohnsonfraud.html> and 'Evidence of Leon Trotsky's Collaboration with Germany and Japan' <http://clogic.eserver.org/2009/furr. pdf> (both accessed 9 January 2014). In contrast to Professor Furr, the British historian Paul Johnson asserted in one of his bestselling books that 'during the rest of 1937 and well into 1938, many thousands of POUM members, and indeed other Leftists of all descriptions, were executed or tortured to death in Communist prisons. They included a large number of foreigners' (Paul Johnson, *Modern Times: The World from the Twenties to the Eighties* (New York: HarperCollins, 1983), 334–5).

165. Stalin, 'O nedostatkakh partiinoi raboty i merakh likvidatsyi trotskistskikh i inykh dvurushnikov' ('About the Deficiencies in the Party Work and Measures of the Liquidation of the Trotskyite and other Double-Dealers'), *Voprosy istorii*, 3 (1995), 3–15.

166. Cf. Andrew and Mitrokhin, *The Mitrokhin Archive*, 87–8, 708.

CHAPTER 18

1. María Dolors Genovés, *Especial Andreu Nin: Operació Nikolai*, Televisió de Catalunya, SA, 1992.

2. George Soria, *Trotskyism in the Service of Franco: A Documented Record of Treachery by the POUM in Spain* (New York: International Publishers,

1938), 9. There are reasons to believe that this pamphlet was prepared by Orlov, who provided forged proofs of the POUM's espionage, which were then put together and signed by the NKVD agent Georges Soria. Its production was financed by the CPGB from the Comintern funds.

3. ASVRR, SCHWED to the Centre, 23 May 1937, Operational Correspondence File No. 17679, vol. 1, pp. 154–6, quoted by Costello and Tsarev, *Deadly Illusions*, 288–9.

4. Preston, *We Saw Spain Die*, paperback (2009), 439.

5. AHN, Causa General, Caja 1741, Exp. 20. Further investigation revealed that Castilla was chosen because he was the only one who knew the cipher ('porque era el único que conocia el lenguaje cifrado') (Causa General, Caja 1539, Exp. 1).

6. Soria, *Trotskyism in the Service of Franco*, 9–10.

7. The full text of this report of 1 June 1937 is reproduced in Viñas, *El escudo*, 690–3.

8. This writer is in possession of a large collection of photos of Nikolsky, including documentary footage from May 1937 showing 'Orlov' with volunteers.

9. See Hernández, *Yo fui un ministro de Stalin*, 78–183.

10. Gabriel Jackson, a scholar who studied and copied the memoirs of Juan Negrín for his book about the former Republican Prime Minister, in both the Paris and Las Palmas archives where they are preserved, notes that Negrín rejected Jesús Hernández's book as 'invención folletinesca' (feuilletonic invention). Jackson also recalls that on pp. 30–2 of the memoir Negrín relates that Ambassador Marchenko, who by that time had succeeded Rosenberg, sent him an elegant, French-speaking Soviet agent named Belaief (Belyaev). See Gabriel Jackson, *Juan Negrín: Spanish Republican War Leader* (Brighton, Portland, and Toronto: Sussex Academic Press/Cañada Blanch Centre, 2010), 94, 96.

11. During a meeting of the Council of Ministers of 15 July 1937, Hernández made a special declaration on the question of relations with the Soviet Union and with the Russian advisers. He said: 'We are tired of the constant anti-Soviet attacks of several organs of the press, we protest against the Jesuitical relations with the Russian comrades when something isn't okay—blame is heaped on the Russians, on the people who came here at your request, who are sacrificing their lives for Spain. For example, the affair of the liberation of Nin (as you probably know, the arrested Nin was freed from prison by a group of armed raiders—C.): instead of searching for the criminals who had freed Nin, you caved in to the slanderous allusions against the Russian comrade (a rumor was going around that the Russians, supposedly, abducted Nin—C.). On the matter of the theft of the ciphers, which took place as a result of the irresponsibility or treachery of criminal elements—once again insinuations against the Soviet comrades are being dragged in. The party demands that you put an end to these dirty intrigues against the Soviet Union' (RGVA, Agent CID [unidentified] to the Director, 22 July 1937, f. 35082, op. 1, d. 190, ll. 171–81, cited by Ronald Radosh, Mary R. Habeck, and Grigory Sevostianov (eds),

Spain Betrayed: The Soviet Union in the Spanish Civil War (New Haven and London: Yale University Press, 2001), document 45, p. 216.

12. Jesús Hernández, 'How the NKVD Framed the POUM', a translation of the relevant passages from *Yo fui un ministro de Stalin* <www.marxists.org/history/spain/writers/hernandez/persecution_of_poum.html> (accessed 10 January 2014).

13. *Gaceta de la República*, 164, 13 June 1937, p. 1198.

14. AHM, POUM, Caja 663, Exp. 1. In the Russian RGASPI there are also interesting documents regarding the activities of the POUM. See RGASPI, f. 495, op. 183 (POUM) and f. 545, op. 2, d. 148.

15. AHN, FC-Causa General, Caja 1520, Exp. 1, p. 87, Deposition of Pedrero, 9 December 1939, Folio 121.

16. AHN, FC-Causa General, Ramo separado no. 37, Deposition of Tomás Duran Gonzalez.

17. See Maria Dolors Genovés, 'Operació Nikolai: L'Assasinat d'Andreu Nin', in *Història política, societat i cultura dels països catalans*, ix (Barcelona: Edicions 62, 1998), 305–7.

18. Javier Jiménez Martín, a former Special Brigade officer and probably a participant in Operation NIKOLAI, to M. Dolors Genovés in the documentary 'Operación Nikolai'. According to César Vidal (*Checas de Madrid* (Barcelona: Carroggio/Belacqva, 2005), 199), Ortega's orders to arrest Nin, Gorkin, Andrade, Gironella, Arquer, and 'todos cuantos elementos del POUM' were transformed to Burillo by teletype by Antonov-Ovseyenko and Stashevsky. This is definitely incorrect. Even though Antonov-Ovseyenko Jr admitted to M. Dolors that his father was the NKVD co-optee, the Soviet Consul General was not in a position to act on behalf of the NKVD, not to mention the Spanish authorities, and to give orders, as Vidal and several other authors assert.

19. According to Javier Jiménez, apart from José-Grigulevich, there were also five police officers who came from Madrid to arrest Nin, and indeed some researchers mention names, such as Andrés Zurreyo, Pedro de Buen, Ángel Aparicio, and Cipriano Blas in connection with this operation (see, e.g., Professor Pelai Pagès i Blanch, 'El asesinato de Andreu Nin, más datos para la polemica', *Ebre 38: Revista Internacional sobre la guerra civil*, 4 (2010), 57–76, and Ángel Viñas, 'La garra de Moscú'.

20. Ramón Liarte in the documentary 'Operación Nikolai'.

21. Victor Alba in the documentary, 'Operación Nikolai'. See Wilebaldo Solano, 'El ultimo día con Andreu Nin', *El Periodico*, 16 June 1987.

22. Javier Jiménez Martín in the documentary 'Operación Nikolai'. See also 'Andres Nin: El troskista que se fue al frío', *Cambio 16*, 305, 16 October 1977, p. 39.

23. Maria Dolors Genovés, 'Operació Nikolai: L'Assasinat d'Andreu Nin'.

24. M. Dolors Genovés to author, 20 October 2005. The commonly held view is that Nin was taken to a chalet belonging to or rented by Constancia de la Mora and Ignacio Hidalgo de Cisneros, but to the best of this author's knowledge this version has not been confirmed by any documents.

25. For example, George Esenwein writes: 'Acting on the orders of Alexander Orlov and other agents of the NKVD, the Soviet security police, communists in the governments' security forces began gaoling POUM leaders...Nin himself was taken to a prison on the outskirts of Madrid, where, under torture, he was murdered by his communist captors' (*The Spanish Civil War: A Modern Tragedy*, paperback (New York and London: Routledge, 2005), 205).

26. Gabriel Morón Díaz, former Civil Governor of Almería, appointed deputy director and Inspector General of the DGS on 3 June 1937 (*Gaceta* of 4 June), claims in his book that, during the investigation of the Nin case, he said to the Minister Zugazagoitia: 'Now that the Prime Minister is determined to know the truth, you can tell him, the truth is that the kidnapping of Andreu Nin was planned by the Italian Codovilla, by el comandante Carlos [Vidali], Togliatti and the directors of the Communist Party, including Pepe Díaz. The order to torture him was given by Orlov, and all of them acted in response to the great interest that Stalin had in the disappearance of the secretary and confidant of the creator of the Red Army' (Morón, *Política de ayer y política de mañana*, 732; the above passage translated by Gabriel Jackson). Morón's writings should be rejected as an 'invención folletinesca'. At the same time, Angel Viñas argues: 'Although torture is not mentioned anywhere in the acts, it is unlikely that it was not practised [in Nin's case]. It was habitual for the Soviets to use torture during the interrogations' ('La garra de Moscú', 40).

27. AVRR, File No. 7862 ASSISTANT (Nin's NKVD codename), vol. 1, pp. 234, 240 (Costello and Tsarev, *Deadly Illusions*, 289, 470 n. 56).

28. ASVRR, SCHWED Personal File No. 32476, vol. 1, p. 101, SCHWED to the Centre, 24 July 1937, quoted by Costello and Tsarev, *Deadly Illusions*, 291.

29. In very similar circumstances three years later, after the unsuccessful attack on the Trotsky's villa in Mexico, Grigulevich took away and shot a young American, Robert Sheldon Harte, to prevent him revealing what had happened.

30. Payne, *The Spanish Civil War*, 228.

31. All documents that have become known to date suggest that the idea of the operation was to implicate Nin and the POUM in collaboration with the Germans and the Francoists. This bizarre attempt failed, so Nin had to die. The shameful censorship of the archives has misled historians of international relations in a variety of ways, as Professor Andrew correctly notes. In the case of Nin it is impossible to make definite conclusions until all pertinent secret documents in Moscow are declassified. It would only be for the benefit of history and the Spanish people if the Spanish government demanded appropriate actions from the Russian authorities.

32. The defendant of the accused, Benito Pabón y Suárez de Urbina, the Cortes deputy, stated on 2 July 1937 that, though the DGS declared 300 people had been arrested, in fact the figure was about 1,000. AHN, legajo 1741, expediente 20, quoted in Viñas, *El escudo*, 611 n. 9.

33. See Thomas, *The Spanish Civil War* (2003), 842. Two of the accused were absolved and five given prison sentences. All escaped from Spain at the end of the war. See Preston, *The Spanish Civil War*, 263.

34. John T. Whitaker, 'Prelude to World War: A Witness from Spain', *Foreign Affairs*, 21/1 (October 1942), 118.

35. One of the Spaniards who possibly also took part in Operation NIKOLAI was Juan Cobo Garcia, a 28-year-old mechanic born in Jaen who had been a member of the Communist Party since 1935. According to the records found by the Spanish Centre in Moscow, he was head of the special services in Valencia. Cobo left Spain for the Soviet Union in 1937. He worked in Kolomna, Kokand, and as master and head of a tyre workshop in Moscow. See Ángel Luis Eucinas Moral, *Fuentes históricas para el estudio de la emigración española a la U.R.S.S., 1936–2007* (Madrid: Exterior XXI, 2008). Whether he indeed took part in the operation against Nin is hard to state with certainty, but in the autumn of 1936 Juan Cobo was one of the leading members of the checa de Marqués de Riscal no. 1 under the orders of the Minister of Interior, Galarza, officially as Primera Compañía de Enlace del Ministerio de Gobernación. From 1934 Cobo served as Comisario Jefe of the police and later as special agent of the DGS. He later immigrated and lived in the Soviet Union. I am grateful to his grandson, Jorge Dieguez Cobo, for this information.

36. Jackson, *Juan Negrín*, 94.

37. See *Gaceta*, 19 July 1937; and *ABC*, 20 July 1937, Edicion de la mañana, p. 9.

38. Jackson, *Juan Negrín*, 95.

39. Juan Negrín, draft of his interpretation of the Nin case and other matters of repression of dissident forces within the Republican zone, p. 67, as quoted by Jackson, *Juan Negrín*, 95–6.

40. See, e.g., Angel Viñas, 'Los Hechos de Mayo, Desmitificados', *La Aventura de la Historia* (May 2007), 22–8; and 'La garra de Moscú: Junio de 1937. El assesinato de Nin', *La Aventura de la Historia* (June 2007), 34–41. Ironically, when this book was still being researched, Reiner Tosstorff of the Johannes-Gutenberg University in Mainz, Germany, had been preparing for a conference in Bristol with the paper 'Case Closed: The Assassination of Andreu Nin, the Persecution of the POUM and its Background'. Fortunately, as Dr Tosstorf told this author, he did not go to the conference. The case of Andreu Nin is not closed.

41. Graham, '"Against the State"', 531.

42. RGASPI, f. 17, op. 3, d. 1003, ll. 34, 82–4, Yezhov to Stalin, 23 November 1938.

43. Cf. Pedersen, 'George Mink', 320.

CHAPTER 19

1. See Andrew and Mitrokhin, *The Mitrokhin Archive*, 103.

2. Yet another, probably honest but erroneous, version is that his real name was 'Nathan Markovich Poretsky' (Abramov, *Evrei v KGB*, 274–5).

3. UWA, student's questionnaire No. B-1465 for the winter semester 1918–19, filled in personally by Reiss, then a student of the Faculty of Law. Though born in the Jewish family with Yiddish as his mother tongue, Reiss used different spellings of his first name depending of what geographical location he wanted to show he was coming from: Austrian, Polish, or Ukrainian. The German version was 'Ignatz' and the Polish–Ukrainian 'Ignacy'.

4. Steiner, Renate, Interrogation protocol of 10 November 1937, ArP, Rapport de l'Inspecteur Borel of 30 January 1938, pp. 23–7, as cited by Peter Huber, *Stalins Schatten in die Schweiz. Schweizer Kommunisten in Moskau: Verteidiger und Gefangene der Komintern* (Zurich: Chronos-Verlag, 1994). See also Poretsky, *Our Own People*, 239.

5. 'Testimony of Alexander Orlov', *Committee on the Judiciary*, US Senate, Eighty-Seventh Congress, 28 September 1955, pp. 2–3.

6. Steiner, Interrogation protocol of 10 November 1937, ArP, Rapport de l'Inspecteur Borel, 30 January 1938.

7. For details, see TNA: PRO KV 2/2389, Olga and Vladimir Pravdin, which is part of the MI5 Personal File 86046.

8. KGB of Belarus dossier, author's collection. Efron was shot on 16 October 1941.

9. Peter Huber, 'Shoot the Mad Dogs', trans. by Ted. Crawford of 'Fuzillez ces chiens enragés', *Rouge*, special edition for the 50th anniversary of Trotsky's death (Summer 1990), 10.

10. Nikita Petrov, 'Ubijstvo Ignatiya Reissa', *Moskovskie novosti*, 63, 17–24 September 1995.

11. Petrov, 'Ubijstvo Ignatiya Reissa'. The appeal was written by Peter Huber and Daniel Künzi, co-authors of 'L'Assassinat D'Ignace Reiss'.

12. Frank J. Rafalko (ed.), *A Counterintelligence Reader* (Washington: NACIC, 1998) <http://www.fas.org/irp/ops/ci/docs/ci1/ch4b.htm> (accessed 10 January 2014).

CHAPTER 20

1. Andrew and Mitrokhin, *The Mitrokhin Archive*, 89, 100.

2. Nikolai Grigorievich Samsonov was born in 1896 in Nizhny Novgorod, Russia. He studied at a university but dropped out to pursue a military career. In 1917 he graduated from a military school and joined the army. From May 1920 Samsonov was a member of the VChK. In 1924–5 worked under cover on the staff of the Soviet repatriation commission in Constantinople; in 1925–30 as 2nd and then 1st Secretary of the Soviet Legation in Prague, where he recruited Bystroletov. In both Prague and, from November 1929, Berlin, where he worked under cover of the press attaché, Samsonov used the alias 'Golst'. From 1931 he worked at the Centre, promoted to major of state security and Sloutsky's assistant at the INO. From February to August 1937 Samsonov was posted as the INO resident to Harbin, China, but on 16 August was arrested and shot.

3. Gordon Brook-Shepherd, *The Storm Petrels: The First Soviet Defectors, 1928–1938* (London: Collins, 1977), 129.
4. There is certain confusion in the Security Service files regarding Agabekov. Even his recently declassified MI5 file TNA: PRO KV 2/2398, which, in fact, is a part of his Personal File No. 4096 V. 1, is entitled 'Nerses OVSEPIAN, aliases George AGABEKOV, George ARUTIUNOV', which is wrong. His real name, as stated, was Georgy Sergeyevich Arutyunov, born on 15 January 1895 in Ashgabat, Turkmenistan, and he used aliases 'Azadov' in Bokhara (Bukhara), 'Georges Agabekov' when he worked in Afghan and Persia, and 'Nerses Ovsepyan' when he operated as an 'illegal' resident in Istanbul. One of the reports about Agabekov's career claims in one and the same document: '(8) In 1927 Agabekov was posted to the Soviet legation in Tehran, where he took over the duties of OGPU representative from one Kazas,' and a little further: '(10) In 1926 he became Resident of the OGPU in Tehran, with the official title of Attaché to the Embassy, where he remained until May 1928.' See TNA: PRO KV 2/2398 Serial 15a (20a) Enclosure B.
5. Agabekov, *OGPU.* In a rare act of literary and historical barbarism, the publisher and especially the translator, who translated not from the original Russian text but from a French edition, omitted whole chapters and totally restructured the original work. As a result, academic historians and scholars, as well as Western intelligence professionals, have been deprived of much of Agabekov's excellent material for all these years.
6. Like Agabekov, Dumbadze operated in Turkey. He defected in June 1928 and soon arrived in Paris, where he published a book (E. Dumbadze, *Na sluzhbe Cheka i Kominterna* (Paris: Mishen, 1930), with an introduction written by Vladimir Burtsev), where Dumbadze described his work and that of the OGPU in detail. Nevertheless, it seems neither the French nor the British authorities took any interest in him.
7. Among them was Reza Shah's Court Minister, Abdul Hossein Khan Teymourtash. For details, see Boris Volodarsky, 'Unknown Agabekov', *Intelligence and National Security* (2013).
8. Brook-Shepherd, *The Storm Petrels*, 111.
9. Sudoplatov and Sudoplatov, *Special Tasks*, 48.
10. In Brook-Shepherd's version, Constantinople. After the creation of the Republic of Turkey in 1923, various alternative names besides Istanbul were abolished by the government. With the Turkish Postal Service Law of 28 March 1930, the Turkish authorities officially requested foreigners to cease referring to the city with their old non-Turkish names (such as Constantinople, Tsarigrad, etc.) and to adopt Istanbul as the sole name of the city. See Stanford J. Shaw and Ezel Kural Shaw, *History of the Ottoman Empire and Modern Turkey* (Cambridge: Cambridge University Press, 1977), ii. 386. Besides, Brook-Shepherd wrote the day of Agabekov's final decision to defect was 5 January 1931. See Brook-Shepherd, *The Storm Petrels*, 112. At the same time he referred to unspecified

police records that 'conclusively show that on 27 June 1930 Agabekov arrived in Paris following his English fiancée'—that is, half a year *before* he decided to defect. An SIS report mentioned below gives the date as 26 June 1930.

11. TNA: PRO KV 2/2398, secret report from Paris dated on or about 4 July 1930.
12. Agabekov, *OGPU*, 247–8.
13. ÖStA/NPA, Box 671, Case Pr. Zl. IV-5303/2/30, Report of 16 October 1931, Attachment '*Neues Wiener Abendblatt* vom 14. August 1930', with a reference to the telegram from Paris of the same date. There was speculation that Paris had acted under pressure from Moscow. That was in part corroborated by the account by Victor Serge ('Agabekov', *New International* (January–February 1950), 51–7), though Brook-Shepherd insisted that it was the result of a request made by the British Consul General in Paris (*The Storm Petrels*, 117). This is again wrong: as seen from Agabekov's personal file, the British consul was not in a position to influence such a decision, in spite of the pressure from Ms Streater's relatives, and the expulsion was caused mainly by the fact that the French thought Agabekov suspicious, perhaps even a double agent, not entirely collaborative and generally a nuisance, so after the interrogation they wanted to get rid of him as soon as possible. See TNA: PRO KV 2/2398, SIS reports from Paris. According to *The London Gazette* of 13 June 1970, Isabel Edith Streater, Personal Assistant, United Kingdom Mission to the United Nations in New York, was awarded the MBE.
14. Andrew, *The Defence of the Realm*, 118. 'With Thomson's dismissal,' the Official Historian of the Security Services writes, 'the Directorate of Intelligence disappeared [...] The Secret Service Committee was initially sceptical of the need to preserve MI5 at all but eventually concluded that, because of increasing espionage by a number of powers and the threat of Bolshevik subversion in the army and navy, MI5 should continue, on a reduced scale, to have responsibility for counter-espionage in the armed forces' (p. 120).
15. TNA: PRO KV 2/2398 OVSEPIAN (Agabekov), Serial 9a, 21 July 1930.
16. TNA: PRO KV 2/2398 OVSEPIAN (Agabekov), Serial 12a.
17. TNA: PRO KV 2/2398 OVSEPIAN (Agabekov), Serial 14a, CX/12650/2205.
18. The SIS representative in Paris was sent ten photographs of suspected OGPU agents in Europe allegedly acting against the British interest for Agabekov's identification, followed on 30 July 1930 by another two. Agabekov recognized a person on photo no. 3 as an OGPU agent whom he knew and who, according to Agabekov, was of some importance, though he gave an incorrect name. According to the security service files, on the photo was 'Lev Gillairovich ELLERT', a suspected OGPU agent who operated in Europe in the 1930s (see TNA: PRO KV 2/2398 and ELLERT's file TNA: PRO KV 6/59). In reality, it was Lev Gilyarovich Elbert, a prominent Chekist and a member of the GPU from December 1923. From January until May 1926 ELBERT worked in Greece under the cover of attaché of the Soviet Embassy in Athens. In 1929 he was a member of the Soviet Embassy in Paris and, according to some sources, took

part in the abduction of General Kutepov in January 1930. In November 1945 ELBERT was in Berlin, where he died the next year from a heart problem. It is on the record that, when in Moscow, ELBERT used different aliases—the poet Mayakovsky, with whom Elbert was friendly, also knew him as Heifetz.

19. Brook-Shepherd, *The Storm Petrels*, 117.

20. Brook-Shepherd suggests that behind the expulsion order there might have been the French Deuxième Bureau 'who had interrogated Agabekov during July' (*The Storm Petrels*, 117), but this writer found no proof to this claim.

21. Brook-Shepherd, *The Storm Petrels*, 118.

22. TNA: PRO KV 2/2398 OVSEPIAN (Agabekov), CX/12650/2205, dated 20 August 1930.

23. TNA: PRO KV 2/2398 OVSEPIAN (Agabekov), CX/12650/2205, Serial 20a. The Security Service was quite well informed about the activities of the Soviet agents in London and kept files and tracks on many of them. Thus, agent B-1 was known to have been William Norman Ewer (see TNA: PRO KV 2/1016–1017, Personal File EWER), foreign editor of the *Daily Herald*. Ewer (codenamed herman) was receiving information that he then sent to the OGPU London station from his many sub-sources. Among those were GINHOVERN, JANE, and DALE from the Special Branch of Metropolitan Police, as well as journalists George Edward Slocombe (alias Nathan Grünberg), a Briton who was the Paris correspondent of the *Daily Herald*, as well as Frederick Robert Kuh, a Federated Press of America (FPA) representative in Berlin. If one is to believe West and Tsarev, Ewer had at least two sub-sources, one in the Foreign Office and one in the Home Office. It is difficult to say whether Agabekov was able to provide leads to any of them. Besides, again according to West and Tsarev, two highly placed old Etonians in the Foreign Office were Ewer's contacts: Sir Arthur Willert and John D. Gregory. At that time Willert, as Head of the News Department, was the press officer at the Foreign Office, while Gregory, a former British chargé d'affaires in Bucharest, was an Assistant Secretary. For more details, TNA: PRO KV 2/485, Personal File SCOLOMBE; TNA: PRO KV 2/983-988, Personal File KUH; TNA: PRO KV 2/1099-1101, Personal File FEDERATED PRESS OF AMERICA. See also West and Tsarev, *The Crown Jewels*, 9–12.

24. Andrew and Mitrokhin, *The Mitrokhin Archive*, 46.

25. Kolpakidi and Prokhorov, *KGB: Prikazano likvidirovat'*, 244.

26. See Brook-Shepherd, *The Storm Petrels*, 120.

27. *Hearings before a Special Committee to Investigate Communist Activities in the United States of the House of Representatives*, Seventy-First Congress, Third Session pursuant to H. Res. 220 providing for an investigation of Communist propaganda in the United States. Part I–Volume No. 5, December 1930 (Washington, DC: GPO, 1931).

28. The first account of the 'Philomena Affair' is in Brook-Shepherd, *The Storm Petrels*, 130–46, without any reference to any source or archive.

29. TNA: PRO M.I.1.c. 20.10.31, 450/Germany 30a, in TNA: PRO KV 2/2398, OVSEPIAN (Agabekov), Serial 65a.

30. TNA: PRO CX/12650/2205, dated 15 March 1932, in TNA: PRO KV 2/2398, OVSEPIAN (Agabekov), Serial 86a.

31. It was stated that Piklovič worked in Moscow in the OGPU KRO's 4th section (counter-intelligence, Eastern Europe) and that he was known under this name as a student in Vienna in 1922. Those familiar with the OGPU practices of the time will agree that there is nothing strange or unusual for a secret service operative to use different names when travelling or living abroad, so Agabekov could indeed have known him in Russia as Schulman.

32. ÖStA/BKA/Inneres, PDW, Berichte, Karton 17, Beilage zum Bericht Pr. Zl. 3412/16/31.

33. IfZG, Gerichtsakt Semmelmann, Amtsvermerk, 14 November 1931.

34. ÖStA/NPA: Box 671, Case Pr. Zl IV-5338/31. Report of 24 November 1931.

35. Georges Agabekov, *Cheka za rabotoi* (Berlin: Strela, 1931).

36. TNA: PRO KV 2/2398, OVSEPIAN (Agabekov), General Direction of Police, Corps of Detectives, report dated 25 January 1932, Serial 80b. See also Brook-Shepherd, *The Storm Petrels*, 131. The author names the bank as the Banque Fédérale in Geneva and refers to an unspecified version of the story in which the sum of Swiss Francs 400 million is named.

37. ÖStA/NBA, Box 671, Document *Die Affaire Arutiunov-Agabecov: Das Komplott von Constantia, 1931–1932*, Romanian police headquarters, Ministry of Interior, 1932. In the British document the name is given as PANAYOTTI, a Greek subject born in Odessa, Russia, and his supposed secretary in named SERGIUMINTZ (clearly an error; *recte* Sergey or Serge Mintz), both domiciled in Paris.

38. Brook-Shepherd, *The Storm Petrels*, 132.

39. Brook-Shepherd, *The Storm Petrels*, 134.

40. Kolpakidi and Prokhorov, *KGB: Prikazano likvidirovat'*, 244.

41. TNA: PRO KV 2/2398, OVSEPIAN (Agabekov), General Direction of Police, Corps of Detectives, report dated 25 January 1932, Serial 80b. See also ÖStA/NBA, Box 671, Document *Die Affaire Arutiunov-Agabecov: Das Komplott von Constantia*.

42. Brook-Shepherd, *The Storm Petrels*, 134.

43. TNA: PRO KV 2/2398, OVSEPIAN (Agabekov), Serial 82a. At the time MI5 and Scotland Yard were able to confirm this information only partially. They also shared it with their Austrian colleagues. Documents found by this writer in the Austrian and Soviet archives fully corroborate Akabekov's story. In 1930 Mikhail Gorb became deputy chief of Artur Artuzov, who succeeded Meier (Mikhail) Trilisser as chief of the Foreign Section (INO), a post Artuzov held in 1930–5 (OGPU administrative order no. 12, dated 12 January 1930, confirming the new staff of the INO—ninety-four officers—and setting up eight operational sections). When Agabekov saw him in Vienna, Gorb, the OGPU resident, was posing as Press Attaché with a diplomatic passport issued in the name of 'Konstantin Komarovsky'. Igor Lebedinsky, alias Vorobyov, was later the OGPU 'legal' resident in Austria who handled both Dr Arnold Deutsch and Edith Sushitzky, the future recruiters of Kim Philby in London. See also ÖStA/NPA, Box 671, Bundespolizeiamt-Inneres, Case Pr. Zl. IV-3412/4/31.

44. Stavinsky, *Zarubiny*, 153.
45. For Agabekov's personal account of the events, see TNA: PRO KV 2/2398, OVSEPIAN (Agabekov), Serial 82a.
46. TNA: PRO KV 2/2398, OVSEPIAN (Agabekov), General Direction of Police, Corps of Detectives, report dated 25 January 1932, Serial 80b.
47. Jeffery, *MI6*, 274.
48. TNA: PRO KV 2/2398, OVSEPIAN (Agabekov), General Direction of Police, Corps of Detectives, report dated 25 January 1932, Serial 80b.
49. For Agabekov's personal account of the events, see TNA: PRO KV 2/2398, OVSEPIAN (Agabekov), Serial 82a.
50. ÖStA/NPA, Box 671, Case Pr. Zl. IV-743/32, Report of the Vienna Police Directorate to the Foreign Ministry of 8 March 1932. This episode was part of the large-scale document forgery operation conducted by the OGPU in Austria and Germany in the late 1920s–early 1930s. David Dallin describes the case in his book *Soviet Espionage*, 92–103. It became known as the Klose Affair.
51. 'Kouril' and 'Zenner', Soviet 'illegals' based in Vienna, made up a second team in Operation PHILAMENA. They both escaped to Austria and had never been identified. See ÖStA/NBA, Box 671, Case Pr. Zl. IV-742/32, Report of the Vienna Police Directorate of 19 March 1932.
52. According to the police record, the telephone call to the Grand Hotel in Constanza, where 'Kouril' was staying, was made from the Post Office (Telegraphenamt) on Laurenzberg in Vienna's I district on 10 January at 1.30 p.m. See ÖStA/NPA, Box 671, Case Pr. Zl. IV-742/32, Report of the Vienna Police Directorate to the Foreign Ministry, 8 March 1932.
53. ÖStA/NBA, Box 671, Document *Die Affaire Arutiunov-Agabecov: Das Komplott von Constantia*.
54. ÖStA/NBA, Box 671, Case Pr. Zl. IV-742/6/32, Report of the Vienna Police Directorate, 19 March 1932.
55. Agabekov's own version differs in some details. According to him, Alexeyev tried to kill him on Monday, 11 January, shortly after Tzonchev had left him in a restaurant and while he was still finishing his dinner. Alexeyev was allegedly arrested by the Romanian police near the restaurant's window with a Mauser pistol in his hand. See TNA: PRO KV 2/2398, OVSEPIAN (Agabekov), Serial 82a.
56. ÖStA/NBA, Box 671, Case Pr. Zl. IV-742/6/32, Report of the Vienna Police Directorate, 19 March 1932. Shortly after the operation had collapsed, Jean Panayotis went to Vienna, where he stayed from 21 February to 2 March 1932 at the hotel Stadt Triest, and then left for Paris. See ÖStA/NPA, Box 671, Case Pr. Zl. IV-742/32, Report, 8 March 1932. Nothing more was heard of him.
57. Howson, *Arms for Spain*, 194–5.
58. Jeffery, *MI6*, 271–2.
59. See Brook-Shepherd, *The Storm Petrels*, 146.

60. For details about Foley's activities in Berlin, see Smith, *Frank Foley*. See also Henry Landau, *All's Fair: The Story of British Secret Service behind German Lines* (New York: Putnam, 1934); and *Spreading the Spy Net: The Story of a British Spy Director* (London: Jarrods, 1938). Captain Landau was Foley's predecessor in Berlin. The latter took over as head of station in 1920 and remained at his post until 1939. He was then transferred to Oslo.

61. For the West European Bureau in Berlin (1919–33), see RGASPI, f. 499, op. 1. Four others were the Amsterdam Bureau, the Vienna (South-Eastern) Bureau, the Caribbean (Central American) Bureau, and the South American Bureau.

62. TNA: PRO KV 2/2398, OVSEPIAN (Agabekov), Cross-Reference, dated 29 May 1933, Serial 88b.

63. For details, see Jeffery, *MI6*, 314–16.

64. TNA: PRO KV 2/2398, OVSEPIAN (Agabekov), Cross-Reference, 3 December 1936, Serial 96a: 'On 30.11.36 S.I.S. forwarded under CX/12650/2205/V a translation of a letter from Georgi Agabekov with regard to the G.P.U [*sic*, from 1934 it was NKVD] and the general situation in the U.S.S.R. Agabekov stated that, with the knowledge of the local Sûreté, he had been in contact for about three months with the representative of the Opposition group of the Bolsheviks-Zinoviev-ists, who held a responsible diplomatic post in the Soviet Embassy in Brussels. S.I.S. reported that they had not been in contact with agabekov since 1933, and were not altogether satisfied with the accuracy of the statements made in the above-mentioned letter. Taking full account of the possibilities of provocation, S.I.S. were not encouraging any closer association' (original in S.F. 420/1, Vol. 5, Serial 197a). It may be added that the work with the earlier defector Grigory Besedovsky, who defected to France, was as unsuccessful as the work with Agabekov. The situation was beginning to change in 1940 when Jane Sissmore (by then Archer), one of the leading Soviet experts of MI5, was given an opportunity to debrief Krivitsky, who defected to France and later moved to the USA.

65. Brook-Shepherd, *The Storm Petrels*, 148–9.

66. Brook-Shepherd, *The Storm Petrels*, 149.

67. TNA: PRO KV 2/2398, OVSEPIAN (Agabekov), Serial 96b, Extract for File P.F. R. 4096, V. 2, Serial 33a, 14 January 1939.

68. Sudoplatov, *Spetsoperatzii*, 80–1.

69. See <http://svr.gov.ru/history/kor.htm> (accessed 3 January 2014).

70. Sudoplatov and Sudoplatov, *Special Tasks*, 48.

71. Sudoplatov, *Spetsoperatzii* , 80–1.

72. His son Sergey was born on 1 January 1935. See Stanislav Lekarev, 'Hasan: Chelovek-kinzhal', *Argumenty Nedeli*, 25–26 October 2006. A document from the Russian archives confirms that in April 1949 Colonel Takhchianov acted as chief of Department 2d of the SCD of the Soviet Ministry of State Security (MGB). The decree to award a large group of the MGB officers for the

deportation of people from the Baltic Republics, Moldavia, and the Black Sea coast of the Caucasus was issued on 24 August 1949.

73. RGVI, Ukazy o nagrazhdenii sotrudnikov NKVD 1940s. Decree of 24 August 1949.

74. He is mentioned in Sudoplatov, *Special Tasks*, book only once (erroneously, as 'A. M. Alakhverdov') and in connection with a different episode.

75. His official SVR biography is at <http://svr.gov.ru/history/al.htm> (accessed 3 January 2014).

76. This is also hearsay. Baron Verhulst allegedly said it to Boris Bazhanov, and the latter, four decades later, to Gordon Brook-Shepherd. See Brook-Shepherd, *The Storm Petrels*, 149 n. 1.

77. See, e.g., Kolpakidi and Prokhorov, *KGB: Spetsoperatsyi sovetskoi razvedki*, 362; Lt Colonel Deryabin, ' "Petrov", "Grisha" on zhe Agabekov', *Krasnaya Zvezda*, 23 May 1990.

78. Besides the above-mentioned penitential 'Letter to the Soviet authorities', the NKVD appeared to have been in the possession of several of Agabekov's private documents, including the manuscript of his memoirs (286 typed pages, 26 chapters) in the Central State Archive of the October Revolution in Moscow that allegedly got there from a Prague archive after the war. See Victor Bortnevsky, 'Oprichnina: Nevozvrashchenets Grigorii Agabekov i sekretnaya sluzhba Stalina', *Sobesednik*, 34 (August 1989). The same document is referred to in Kolpakidi and Prokhorov, *KGB: Spetsoperatsyi sovetskoi razvedki*, 617, as from GARF, f. 5881, op 1, d. 701a. Also mentioned is his original receipt, dated 8 May 1933, for 9,000 French francs, which he received in Brussels from an unnamed person or organization.

79. Orlov's American biographer, Gazur, was led to believe that the defector was murdered in Brussels in early 1938. See Gazur, *Secret Assignment*, 166. In her turn the biographer of Eitingon, Mary-Kay Wilmers, somehow came to the conclusion that the murder of Agabekov was masterminded by Eitingon. See Wilmers, *The Eitingons*, 345.

80. For the text of the letter and other details of the 'Semmelmann Affair', see McLoughlin et al., *Kommunismus in Österreich*, 452–70.

81. Dieter Hoffmann et al., *Wer war wer in der DDR? Ein Lexikon ostdeutscher Biographien* (Berlin: Christoph Links Verlag, 2010).

82. See McLoughlin et al., *Kommunismus in Österreich*, 457. See also 'Der Mord in der Hockegasse', *Neue Freie Presse*, 24017 (Vienna, Sunday, 26 July 1931), S. 11.

83. Serge, 'Agabekov', 6.

84. Report of Interview, 9 May 1940, in TNA: PRO KV 2/2398, OVSEPIAN (Agabekov), Serial 103a.

85. *Neue Freie Presse*, Vienna, Saturday, 5 March 1932, p. 2. According to the Austrian law of the time, a two-third majority was needed in order to convict the defendant.

86. *Neue Freie Presse*, Abendblatt, 4 March 1932, pp. 3–4.

87. See 'Fememord in Gersthof', *Die Presse*, 22 May 2009.

88. For Engelbert Broda's full biography, see his son's book Paul Broda, *Scientist Spies: A Memoir of my Three Parents and the Atom Bomb* (Leicester: Matador, 2011).

89. Maria Wirth, *Christian Broda: Eine politische Biographie* (Vienna: V&R unipress/ Vienna University Press, 2011), 58–60.

90. See TNA: PRO KV 2/2349, 'Engelbert BRODA', Personal File, 46663, Vol. 1, Serial 1.

91. Both extracts are quoted in Broda, *Scientist Spies*, 37–8.

92. Broda, *Scientist Spies*, 38.

93. TNA: KV 2/2349 (1931–40), Serial 1a, 12 July 1932.

94. Richard Baxell, *Unlikely Warriors: The British in the Spanish Civil War and the Struggle Against Fascism* (London: Aurum, 2012), 333, 335.

95. See Broda, *Scientist Spies*, 38.

96. Haynes, Klehr, and Vassiliev, *Spies*, 65–66.

97. Broda, *Scientist Spies*, 237–9.

98. Broda, *Scientist Spies*, 240–1. See also Andrew Brown, 'The Viennese Connection: Engelbert Broda, Alan Nunn May and Atomic Espionage', *Intelligence and National Security*, 24/2 (April 2009), 173–93.

99. Andrew and Mitrokhin, *The Mitrokhin Archive*, 99.

100. Andrew and Mitrokhin, *The Mitrokhin Archive*, 99.

101. See Kern, *A Death in Washington*, 151, 433 n. 258.

102. Testimony of Mark Zborowski, *Committee on the Judiciary*, US Senate, Eighty-Fourth Congress, Second Session, part 4, 29 February 1956, 95.

103. Andrew and Mitrokhin, *The Mitrokhin Archive*, 99.

104. Gazur writes about Spiegelglass: 'He was not a professional KGB [*sic*] officer but a crony of Yezhov. When Yezhov became chairman of the KGB [*sic*] in 1936, he brought about 300 of his trusted friends and associates from the Central Committee of the Communist Party into the KGB, and chose his personal friend Spiegelglass to head the Mobile Groups' (Gazur, *Secret Assignment*, 490). In reality, Sergey Spiegelglass was a professional and high-ranking OGPU and later NKVD officer, who joined the Cheka in 1919. He was born in April 1897 in the village of Mosty in the Grodno district of Byelorussia in an intelligent Polish–Jewish family. In 1900 the family moved to Warsaw, where Sergey entered primary school. From 1912 Spiegelglass helped his family by giving private lessons and soon joined the revolutionary movement. In 1914 he was detained by police for taking part in a revolutionary cell. In 1915 Spiegelglass finished school and managed to enter the Faculty of Mathematics of Moscow University. In 1917 he was drafted to the student batallion of the Tsarist army in Nizhny Novgorod and then sent to the officers' school in Peterhof, from which he graduated and was transferred as an ensign to Melitopol. In February 1918 Spiegelglass came to Moscow and soon joined

the Red Guard—namely, its military counter-intelligence department. In January 1919, when the Military Department of the VChK and the counter-intelligence department of the army were joined to form one Osoby (special) Department of the VChK, Spiegelglass wrote an application to Artur Artuzov to join. Artuzov, the son of an Italian–Swiss cheese-maker, who had settled in Russia, and the nephew of Mikhail Kedrov, headed the new counter-intelligence department, the KRO. Artuzov wrote on Spiegelgallss application: 'To Comrade Kedrov. I think he should be accepted.' Thus Spiegelglass became an inspector of the Osoby Otdel (OO). About Kedrov it must be added that he was a semi-qualified doctor and virtuoso pianist, who would slaughter schoolchildren and army officers in northern Russia with such ruthlessness that he had to be placed into psychiatric care. Kedrov was relieved of his post of the chief of the OO, which he headed from 1 January to 18 August 1919, also being a member of the VchK Collegium since 27 March. At that point, after re-enacting the drownings of the French Revolution with captive White officers, he prepared to exterminate the inhabitants of Vologda and other northern towns. Kedrov suffered from hereditary madness; his father, a violinist, had died in a lunatic asylum. The son spent some time in psychiatric care before re-emerging to work, just as cruelly, for the Cheka near the Caspian Sea. He retired from the Cheka after the civil war and was head of a neurosurgical institute when Beria arrested him in 1939 (see Rayfield, *Stalin and his Hangmen*, 80–1). In spite of the fact that the Supreme Court acquitted Kedrov on 9 July 1941, he was shot on 17 October of that year. Together with Kedrov, Spiegelglass took part in the so-called Kedrov expedition to the north. In Archangel he supposedly met Nikolsky, who was posted there at the beginning of 1921 to serve in the OO, whose first chief was Mikhail S. Kedrov (Primakov et al. (eds), *Ocherki*, ii. 9; Costello and Trarev, *Deadly Illusions*, 25–6). According to Russian sources (Kolpakidi and Prokhorov, *KGB: Spetsoperatsyi sovetskoi razvedki*, 549–53), Spiegelglass personally took part in many executions. His sister also worked in the Cheka. In 1921 Spiegelglass was sent to Minsk, Byelorussia, as a ranking member of the local Cheka, but he was soon recalled to Moscow to become chief of the 6th counter-intelligence section of the OGPU. From 1924 Spiegelglass worked in Soviet foreign intelligence. His first foreign posting was in Mongolia. His work there was considered very successful, and, upon returning to Moscow, Spiegelglass was appointed deputy chief of INO. During his ten years in this post he was sent on many foreign assignments, including two PCS tours to Manchuria (north-east China) and France. He also visited the United States under cover. In September 1936 Spiegelglass was promoted to deputy chief of what soon became known as the 7th Department of the GUGB NKVD from 25 December 1936 (Soviet foreign intelligence). He was in charge of all foreign operations of the so-called White line (against the White émigrés) and against Soviet defectors. In 1937 Stalin made him personally responsible for the liquidation (assassination) of Lev Trotsky. Owing to the desertion of Orlov in July 1938, the operation was rolled up, as he knew many of the participants. It must be mentioned that Mark Zborowski, codenamed tulip and kant, was never part of the operation. From February to April 1938 Spiegelglass was acting chief of Soviet foreign intelligence. He was arrested on 2 November 1938 and accused of failing to fulfil an important party order (the murder of Trotsky). According to Costello and Tsarev, he started giving evidence only on 31 May 1939 after 'strong pressure'—a euphemism for torture (*Deadly Illusions*, 469). Spiegelglass was convicted of treachery on 28 November 1940 and executed on 29 January 1941. In December 2005 Byelorussian newspaper *Beloruskaya Delovay Gazeta* devoted a front-page article to the Cheka hero.

105. ASVRR, Operational Check File douglas [Spiegelglass], No. 21476, vol. 1, p. 99, as quoted by Costello and Tsarev, *Deadly Illusions*, 469–70.

106. In Russian, the term *chistka*, or purge, means clearing out party ranks. It refers to the removal of dead wood from the party and therefore, as a rule, from the service. During a party meeting a candidate for a purge had to stand up and recount the story of his life.

107. That is, Paris, Berlin, and London. Not only was this activity highly risky as there is always a chance that the agent will never be sent to the same country again, a standard practice in any intelligence service; more importantly, it was a pursuit strictly forbidden in the Soviet intelligence services, both because of its capitalist nature and for fear that foreign currency would be saved in order to fund an escape to the West. Any such saving, if it ever became known to anybody in the service, would immediately be reported, and the officer recalled and most certainly arrested and shot.

108. Gazur, *Secret Assignment*, 181–3. Nikolsky/Orlov could definitely not avoid investments in 'the shaky Communist government', as the government held regular drawings of the state lottery seeking cash to finance industrialization, and it was actually a duty of every NKVD officer and party member to buy this lottery, thus 'investing' in the state.

109. This is a complex, even if possible, operation even today. Moreover, in 1938 in Spain Maria had a passport in the name of 'Orlova'; in the summer of 1926 in Paris she was the wife of the Soviet trade delegation employee 'Leon Nikolayev' and, accordingly, 'Maria Nikolayeva', as she was in Berlin in January 1928. She was 'Margareta Feldbiene' in London in 1934, and in Russia her (true) name was Maria Nikolskaya. How she managed, with such a variety of identities and without any knowledge of French, to 'consolidate all foreign savings accounts into one' in Paris remains a mystery.

110. Gazur, *Secret Assignment*, 181–3.

111. Gazur, *Secret Assignment*, 181–3.

112. Orlov, *The March of Time*, 370.

113. Zalman Isayevich Passov (erroneously named 'Zelman' by Mitrokhin) was born in April 1905. He joined the Red Army in 1919 and the GPU in May 1922. In the autumn of 1928 Passov was sent to study at the High School of the OGPU Border Guards, a one-year course also aimed to train officers of KRO and OO departments of the OGPU. In 1929 Passov worked at the KRO and in September 1930 was transferred to the OO, formally headed by Olsky. In the summer of 1937 he was deputy chief of military counter-intelligence within the OO, and was awarded the Order of Lenin for his role in the purge of the Red Army command. ('On 6 May 1937 a former Red Army air defence commander was arrested on Yezhov's orders. The interrogators were instructed in the following way: "Let him testify about the existence of a military conspiracy in the Red Army with as many participants as possible." Later, during the same month, the Deputy People's Commissar of Defense, Marshal Tukhachevsky, was arrested, together with a number of other "conspirators". They were tortured until they confessed' (Jansen and Petrov, *Stalin's Loyal Executioner*, 69). Thus, knowing Passov well and having confirmed his loyalty, Yezhov appointed him chief of the 5th Department of the First Directorate of the NKVD (foreign intelligence), a decision approved by the Politburo on 28 March 1938. By 22 October he had been arrested and put into prison. As the investigation was under way, Senior Major of State Security Passov was asked to start working on a handbook of *zakordonnaya* (foreign) intelligence for the NKVD school, the kind of book Orlov claimed he had written (see Part III of this work). On 14 February 1940 Passov was executed.

114. Primakov et al. (eds), *Ocherki*, iii. 144, ch. 11.

115. Lehén graduated from the Military Academy of the RKKA in 1924 and in 1925–6 was sent to Germany as an undercover 'special instructor' of the military M-Apparat of the KPD using the alias 'Langer'. He also worked in Austria and Czechoslovakia and from 1927 headed all military work of the ECCI in Moscow. Lehén, alias 'Marcus', came to Spain in the autumn of 1936 as a guerrilla instructor in Albacete, but was soon appointed chief of the personnel department (from December 1936 to January 1937). After that he served as a military adviser of the XI Brigade (Rapport vom Marty, 9 October 1937, RGASPI, f. 517, op. 3, d. 25. Another report, without title and date, f. 545, op. 2, d. 101, l. 5, quoted in Huber and Uhl, 'Politische Überwachung', ii. 136). Lehén would later become Finnish Minister of Internal Affairs in the provisional government imposed by the Soviet Union in December 1939 and headed by Kuusinen, his former father-in-law.

116. Wilhelm Bahnik was born on 15 May 1900 in Gnesen/Posen, Germany. In 1923 he joined the KPD. From 1925 he was in AM-Apparat. From 1930 to 1931 Bahnik studied in the Comintern Military School in Moscow, after which he was sent to Germany as an employee of the KPD Centrall Committee, working in the staff of Hans Kippenberger. To some comrades he was

known only as Theo, Martin, or Ewald. In 1935 Bahnik emigrated to Moscow and was sent to the special forces school in Ryazan, from where in October 1936 he was posted to Spain. In autumn 1937 Bahnik was sent to the front with a special mission. On 12 March 1938, during an operation together with the Edgar André Battalion, he was seriously wounded and committed suicide to avoid capture. See Huber and Uhl, 'Politische Überwachung', 136–7; Weber and Herbst, *Deutsche Kommunisten*, 71.

117. Alfred Tanz would later be recruited by the NKVD in New York as agent AMIGO. Tanz joined the CPUSA in 1935 and served with the Lincoln Battalion. IB records contain a 1937 memo written in Russian, and labelled 'top secret', that identifies Tanz as a 'reliable' comrade and a candidate for undefined 'organisational-technical work' (Haynes, Klehr, and Vassiliev, *Spies*, 295–6). Other persons in charge of the English section were Hercules Avgherinos, Alex Cummings, Ben Gardner, Conrad Caye, Bob Kerr, Jerry Klein, Eric Parker, Arnold Reisky, and Mayer Saul Shapiro (Huber and Uhl, 'Politische Überwachung', 138).

118. Huber and Hug, *Die Schweizer Spanienfreiwilligen*, 184–5.

119. RGASPI, f. 545, op. 2, d. 101, 'A tous les collaborateurs du service du personnel' (January 1938).

120. Viktor Priess was born on 21 July 1908 in Hamburg. In 1925 he joined the KPD and from 1928 was a member of its AM-Apparat. In 1930–1 Priess was educated in the Comintern Military School in Moscow and was later responsible for the security of Ernst Thälmann and organized deliveries of the Soviet arms to China. In winter 1933 Priess managed to emigrate to Oslo and from there to Copenhagen, where Hans Kippenberger asked him to keep a watchful eye on Walter Ulbricht and his circle. This led to Priess's expulsion from the KPD, but in or about December 1936 he was sent to Spain. Here Franz Dahlem informed him that his party membership would be restored. In 1939 Priess was interned in France but managed to escape to Algeria and in 1942–3 even served in the British Army. In 1943, together with thirty others, Priess was allowed to come to the Soviet Union. He was probably on a special assignment all along, because in Moscow he immediately started working at the RU headquarters. But Ulbricht did not forget him, and Priess was again expelled from the KPD and in March 1947 arrested. Sentenced to twenty-five years for anti-Soviet activity, he remained in the Gulag until 1956, when he managed to return to Germany. Priess did not stay in the DDR, but went to live in his native town, Hamburg, where he died in 1999. See Weber and Herbst, *Deutsche Kommunisten*, 577.

121. Heinrich Fomferra was born on 19 November 1895 in Essen and from 17 years of age was active in politics as a militant. Fomferra was sentenced and served eighteen months for taking part in the burglary at a tram depot and later again received an eighteen months' suspended sentence after being convicted of involvement in explosives offences. In 1929–30, together with

Johann Wenzel, he was among the first cadets of the Comintern Military School in Moscow, after which he worked at the AM-Apparat in Ruhr. Fomferra was also one of the couriers of the OMS. After the Second World War Fomferra worked in the Stasi, for a long time heading the secretariat of the Minister Wilhelm Zaisser. In Spain Zaisser was known as 'General Gomez', first commander of the XIII International Brigade and later of the Base in Albacete. For his wartime collaboration with the Gestapo, Fomferra was temporarily discharged from the service in 1952, but a year later was restored in the ranks, and during his last years served at a secret department of the DDR People's Army. He died in East Berlin in 1979.

122. Born on 9 November 1909 in Berlin, Schwarz joined the KJVD and later the KPD. In 1933 he was chosen to work in the AM-Apparat. Soon he received an order to murder a confidential informant of the Gestapo named Alfred Kattner. Together with Kurt Granzow, Schwarz successfully fulfilled the order on 1 February 1934 and was sent to the Comintern Military School in Moscow (1934–5). In 1936 he was sent to Spain but soon returned to continue his special training in the Soviet Union. In 1942 he was sentenced to twelve years in jail, but in 1944 was freed by the partisans. On 2 September 1944 Hans Schwarz was killed in action. Weber and Herbst, *Deutsche Kommunisten*, 724.

123. Richard Saimer, born 25 January 1907, joined the KPD in 1925 at the age of 18. In 1931 he was sent to the Military School in Moscow and two years later emigrated to the Soviet Union and studied at the KUNMS. In September 1936, together with the first RU contingent, Staimer was sent to Spain, returning back to Moscow in 1938. From there, after additional training, he was sent to support Sandor Rado's Rote Drei network in Switzerland but was arrested there in December 1939, spending two years in prison. Through Italy, Staimer returned to the Soviet Union, where he worked as political instructor until 1945. In July he was sent to Berlin, later occupying various high posts in the DDR. He passed away aged 75. See Weber and Herbst, *Deutsche Kommunisten*, 754.

124. Wilhelm Fellendorf was born on 8 February 1903 in Hamburg. He was active in the paramilitary Rotefrontkämpferbund of the KPD and in 1933 had to emigrate first to Sweden, and from there to Denmark, and finally to the Soviet Union. In Spain he had the rank of a lieutenant and attended the RU school in Benimamet, whose cadets were known as 'tank men'. See Günther Nollau and Ludwig Zindel, *Gestapo ruft Moskau: Sowjetische Fallschirmagenten in 2. Weltkrieg* (Munich: Blanvalet Verlag, 1979), 19–20.

125. Hössler (11 October 1910 Mühlau–22 December 1942, Berlin) was active in the KJVD Communist Youth movement and between 1932 and 1935 was detained by the police several times. Together with Karl Kleinjung, Hössler was one of the organizers of the KJVD congress in Holland in 1935, when both he and Karl were arrested and interned in Fort Honsswijk. From there

650   NOTES TO PAGES 325–330

they managed to flee to Belgium and the Soviet Union. From October 1935 to January 1937 Hössler attended the ILS and from there was posted to Spain, where he attended the RU training course in Benimamet together with Fellendorf, while Kleinjung was at the NKVD spy school, and until February 1939 was a member of Eitingon's bodyguard unit.

126. See, e.g., Uhl, 'Die internationalen Brigaden', 486–518.

127. Erna Eifler from Berlin and Charlottenburg had worked for the BB-Apparat and then for the Comintern, using the alias 'Gerda', and in 1936 came to Vienna together with her partner, the chemist Walter Caro. They travelled with doctored passports as 'Käthe and Kurt Glanz'. According to their passports, she was born on 5 June 1909, and he on 11 February 1906, both in Litzelsdorf in the Austrian Burgenland. In reality he was born on 19 June 1906 in Berlin. It was reported that from Vienna they moved to Shanghai and that she later operated in England (see Nollau and Zindel, *Gestapo ruft Moskau*, 20) but it is possible that she was part of Orlov's undercover network in Spain. In one of the 1937 messages to Moscow there is mention of a female agent codenamed karo who was sent to Paris to contact an Englishman.

128. It was Boris Nikolayevich Zhuravlev, codenamed NIKOLAI. At the same time his namesake in Moscow, Pavel Mikhailovich Zhuravlev, headed the 1st (German) section of the 5th (Foreign) Department of the GUGB. He was the 'legal' OGPU resident from December 1927 to February 1931 in Prague, from February 1931 to November 1932 in Ankara, and from January 1933 to January 1938 in Rome.

129. ASVRR, File No. 34118, vol. 2, p. 120, quoted in Costello and Tsarev, *Deadly Illusions*, 396.

130. For the details about this collaboration, see Donal O'Sullivan, *Dealing with the Devil: Anglo-Soviet Intelligence Cooperation during the Second World War* (New York, Vienna, and Oxford: Peter Lang, 2010).

131. ASVRR, Operational Correspondence File [DOP] No. 19897, vol. 3, p. 118, quoted by Costello and Tsarev, *Deadly Illusions*, 275–6.

132. Primakov et al, *Ocherki*, iii. 144–5.

133. Boris Labusov of the KGB Press Bureau arranged for Carroll's interview in Moscow with Morris Cohen and Percy Ludwich. Carroll calls Labusov a 'press officer of the Russian Intelligence Service'. Boris Nikolaevich Labusov, who headed the SVR Press Bureau from March 1999 (to September 2006) succeeding General Yuri Kobaladze, was recruited by the KGB while still a student of the Minsk Pedagogical Teachers Training Institute. He was commissioned in 1978 and spent one year learning tradecraft in the Minsk KGB school only metres away from his alma mater. In Moscow, Labusov was a member of the First Chief Directorate (foreign intelligence). In 1979–80 he was at the American desk and, according to Gordievsky, was sent as a deputy station chief to Washington, DC (head of PR Line). From 1988 to 1992 Colonel Labusov was the KGB station head in Brussels, and upon return to

Moscow was transferred to the SVR Press Bureau, which he was promoted to head seven years later.

134. Carroll, *The Odyssey of the Abraham Lincoln Brigade*, 196–7.

135. William Aalto and Irwing Golf, 'Guerrilla Warfare: Lessons in Spain', *Soviet Russia Today* (October 1941), 22. *Soviet Russia Today* was published by Jessica Smith, who had been married to Harold Ware, founder of a Soviet spy ring in the US government. After Ware's death, she married John Abt, a member of the ring.

136. ASVRR, Operational Correspondence File [DOP] No. 19897, vol. 3, p. 118, quoted by Costello and Tsarev, *Deadly Illusions*, 276.

137. When Nelson's book about the Spanish Civil War (Steve Nelson, *The Volunteers* (New York: Masses & Mainstream, 1953)) came out, the author's official address was Allegheny County Prison, Pittsburgh. In the book, except for praise for Lenin, not a single Russian name or any contact with any secret service is mentioned. Nelson was recruited in Moscow, where he studied in the International Lenin School together with his wife from 1930 to 1933 and before his arrest in 1950 was probably the most important liaison between the NKVD/KGB and the CPUSA. About Nelson, see also Haynes, Klehr, and Vassiliev, *Spies*.

138. Carroll, *The Odyssey of the Abraham Lincoln Brigade*, 197.

139. Personally involved were Nikolsky/Orlov, Eitingon/Kotov, Syroezhkin/Grande, and Vasilevsky/Grebetsky.

140. See TNA: PRO KV 2/2827.

141. TNA: PRO CAB 102/650, War Cabinet and Cabinet Office, Historical Section, SOE, W. J. M. Mackenzie, unpublished history. See also Dónal O'Sullivan, 'Dealing with the Devil', *Journal of Intelligence History*, 2/2 (Winter 2004), 53.

142. See Part III of this work.

143. Orlov, *The Legacy of Alexander Orlov*, 39.

144. Jansen and Petrov, *Stalin's Loyal Executioner*, 143–5. For details about Genrikh Lyushkov, see Alvin D. Coox, '*L'Affaire* Lyushkov: Anatomy of a Defector', *Soviet Studies*, 19/3 (January 1968), 405–20; Alvin Coox, *The Anatomy of a Small War: The Soviet–Japanese Struggle for Changkufeng/Khasan, 1938* (Westport, CT: Greenwood Press, 1977); Dirk Thomas Kunert, *General Ljuschkows Geheimbericht: Über die Stalinsche Fernostpolitik 1937/38* (Bern: Schweizerisches Ost-Institut, 1977); Diana P. Koenker and Ronald D. Bachman (ed), *Revelations from the Russian Archives* (Washington, DC: Library of Congress, 1997), 120–1; Rayfield, *Stalin and his Hangmen*. Lyushkov is supposed to have been executed by the Japanese in Manchuria in August 1945 in order to prevent his falling into Soviet hands.

145. Coox, *The Anatomy of a Small War*, 2.

146. Coox, '*L'Affaire* Lyushkov', 414.

147. APRF, f. 57, op. 1, d. 265, ll. 16-26-ob, cited in Jansen and Petrov, *Stalin's Loyal Executioner*, 145.

148. APRF, f. 57, op. 1, d. 265, ll. 16-26-ob, cited in Jansen and Petrov, *Stalin's Loyal Executioner*, 145.

149. See Petrov and Skorkin, *Kto rukovodil NKVD 1934–1941*.

150. Orlov, *The Legacy of Alexander Orlov*, 76.

151. Rotterdam Police, Department ID, Report concerning the murder of Konovalets written by police inspectors P. W. Schoemaker and J. P. Bontenbal, Rotterdam, 20 June 1938, folder 7, p. 14, quoted in Marc Jansen and Ben de Jong, 'Stalin's Hand in Rotterdam: The Murder of the Ukrainian Nationalist Yevhen Konovalets in May 1938', *Intelligence and National Security*, 9/4 (October 1994), 676.

152. Algemeen Rijksarchief (ARA), Secret Chronological Archive of the Ministry of Justice, box 16811, 13-10-1938-5804, in Jansen and de Jong, 'Stalin's Hand in Rotterdam', 678.

153. ARA, Secret Chronological Archive of the Ministry of Justice, box 16811, 13-10-1938-5804, in Jansen and de Jong, 'Stalin's Hand in Rotterdam', 678.

154. ARA, Secret Chronological Archive of the Ministry of Justice, box 16811, 13-10-1938-5804, in Jansen and de Jong, 'Stalin's Hand in Rotterdam', 680.

155. See *Het Volksdagblad*, 1 June 1938.

156. Sudoplatov and Sudoplatov, *Special Tasks*, 31.

157. In America, Orlov was least of all interested to reveal that he had had anything to do with the NKVD assassin in Spain. In his turn, Sudoplatov, a two-star general and one of the chiefs of the NKVD intelligence by the time Orlov testified in the US Congress, was equally uninterested to remember his contact with the traitor who had deserted his post during the Spanish Civil War.

158. Vereeken, *The GPU in the Trotskyist Movement*, 306–7.

159. ASVRR, SCHWED to the Centre, undated, Personal File SCHWED, No. 32476, vol. 1, p. 120, quoted by Costello and Tsarev, *Deadly Illusions*, 302.

160. ASVRR, SCHWED to the Centre, 10 July 1938, Personal File SCHWED, No. 32476, vol. 1, p. 121, quoted by Costello and Tsarev, *Deadly Illusions*, 302.

161. Vyacheslav I. Trubnikov, Vadim A. Kirpichenko, Yu. Zhuravlyov, and L. Zamoisky (eds), *Ocherki istorii Rossiiskoi vneshnei razvedki* (Moscow: Mezhdunarodnye otnosheniya, 2003), iv. 237–8. Until summer 1942 'Hanna' operated quite successfully in Paris reporting about the location of the German troops but then overstepped her orders and, as taught at the school, got engaged in sabotage. She was arrested attempting to burn a granary. Agents 'Rom' and 'Hanna' were later executed.

162. Trubnikov et al., *Ocherki*, iv. 236–7.

163. See Vereeken, *The GPU in the Trotskyist Movement*, 307.

164. Vereeken, *The GPU in the Trotskyist Movement*, 307.

165. Vereeken, *The GPU in the Trotskyist Movement*, 310–11.

166. As Hugo Dewar correctly notes: 'The dogmatic character of Stalinist ideology, combined with the Communist Party method of organisation, army-like discipline and fundamental lack of democratic freedom of thought, has a peculiar result. It results in the creation of a special type of person, using a special jargon with a marked style of speaking and writing. It is impossible for anyone who has been thoroughly trained in the Stalinist school to disguise this fact if he has remained faithful to its teachings (and often even if he hasn't)' (*Assassins at Large*, ch. IV).

167. Vereeken, *The GPU in the Trotskyist Movement*, 307–9.

168. Rudolf Alois Klement was born in 1908. Originally active in the KPD, he studied philosophy at Hamburg University and from 1932 was active in the Left Opposition when the leader of the local group asked him to go to Prinkipo to replace Jan Fraenkel and then Otto Schüssler at about the same time that Jean van Heijenoort went there. Klement could already speak five languages and immediately started to learn Russian: six months later he could do German translations from Russian, including particularly difficult pieces, which Trotsky thought good quality. He arrived in Prinkipo at the beginning of May 1933 and left with the Old Man in mid-July, since he was allowed to stay in France with Trotsky. He stayed with him for the whole of the latter's legal residence in France, first in the village of Saint-Palais and afterwards in the villa Ker-Monique at Barbizon. Klement did not accompany Trotsky after he had left France, but stayed in Paris, with a short break in Brussels before coming back to the French capital to take over the headquarters of the International Secretariat, of which he had become the administrative secretary, frequently changing his pseudonyms (Frédéric, Ludwig, Walter Steen, Camille, Adolphe). Klement did a huge amount of work in translating, corresponding with the sections, keeping the files, and writing articles for the press and internal bulletins. See Pierre Broué, 'Rudolf Klement', *Revolutionary History*, 1/1 (Spring 1988). As much as Lev Sedov, Trotsky's son, Klement was surrounded by NKVD agents, one of whom, by the name of Kaufmann (in reality, Ale Taubman), had been his close friend and secretary for over a year.

169. Sudoplatov and Sudoplatov, *Special Tasks*, 48; Sudoplatov, *Spetsoperazii*, 81.

170. Sudoplatov, *Spetsoperazii*, 293.

171. See Broué, 'Rudolf Klement'. Hersch Mendel (1890–1968), also known as Katz, Nathan, Belman, etc., was a Jewish revolutionary from Poland. He founded the Left Opposition there in 1932. He had lived for a time in Paris and returned just before Klement's murder. He later emigrated to Israel, where he wrote his autobiography, *Memoirs of a Jewish Revolutionary* (London: Pluto, 1988).

172. Sudoplatov and Sudoplatov, *Special Tasks*, 48.

173. Andrew and Mitrokhin, *The Mitrokhin Archive*, 100.

174. Broué, 'Rudolf Klement'.

175. Vereeken, *The GPU in the Trotskyist Movement*, 312–13.

176. ASVRR, Personal File SCHWED, No. 32476, vol. 1, p. 120, quoted by Costello and Tsarev, *Deadly Illusions*, 302, 473 n. 30.

177. This conclusion is collaborated by a remark in Sudoplatov and Sudoplatov, *Special Tasks*: 'During two years as an illegal in France he [Korotkov] supervised a Turkish assassin in liquidating important Trotskyites and other defectors, including Rudolf Klement and Georgi Agabekov' (p. 244 n. 9). In the 1940s, Sudoplatov notes, Korotkov used his high position to send the Turk back to Ankara as an 'illegal' resident to get rid of him. The Turk was recently identified as Panteleimon Takhchiyanov (codenamed HASSAN), who was born in Turkey, served in the OGPU-NKVD-KGB, and took part in 'sensitive' operations in Paris during the Spanish Civil War (Stanislav Lekarev, '"Gasan"—chelovek-kinzhal', *Argumenty nedeli*, 25, 26 October 2006). In 1943–5 he headed the KGB in Turkmenistan.

178. He had already visited the United States as a Soviet trade representative under a different identity (Leo Nikolaev). Besides, to apply for a US visa with his diplomatic passport, he needed an official note from the Soviet Foreign Ministry.

179. On 25 August 1955, Mr Max Weinman, Hearing Examiner, INS, furnished a copy of the transcript of the INS hearing at which ORLOV and his wife testified on 27 June 1955. Mr. Weinman also furnished a copy of an INS report in the ORLOV case dated 13 July 1995, by Investigator Sidney E. Mason. Both documents are part of the ORLOV FBI File, Director, Bureau (105-22869), SAC, New York (105-6073) Doc. No. 12, serial 303, unclassified.

180. ASVRR, Personal File SCHWED, No. 32476, vol. 1, p. 170, as quoted by Costello and Tsarev, *Deadly Illusions*, 304. The authors mention the amount of 'about $60,000' while the semi-official KGB history states that the funds amounted to $68,000 (Primakov et al. (eds), *Ocherki*, iii 146).

181. To the best of this writer's knowledge, there was no penetration of the Trotsky secretariat in Mexico. The NKVD agent codenamed PATRIA, who was later commissioned and promoted to colonel, failed to get close to the Trotsky entourage as planned. See Raúl Vallarino, *Mi nombre es Patria: La novela de la espía española del KGB* (Barcelona: Suma de Letras, 2008); and Juárez, *Patria*.

182. See Frederick Forsyth, *The Fist of God* (New York: Bantam Dell Publishing Group, 1994), 308–9.

183. ORLOV FBI File, Director, Bureau (105-22869), SAC, New York (105-6073), Doc. No. 12, serial 303, unclassified.

184. Report from SAC Los Angeles concerning the interview with [Nathan Koornick, name deleted] on 8 October 1954, ORLOV FBI File, Bureau (105-22869), Los Angeles (105-1608), serial 246.

185. See Orlov's diplomatic passport, p. 9.

186. Regarding the dates, see Vereeken, *The GPU in the Trotskyist Movement*, 313.

187. But even before 'Orlov' had surfaced in the USA, the Klement case was analysed by a former British Communist now Trotskyist Hugo Dewar, in his

book *Assassins at Large* (1951). Dewar writes: 'The name of Carleton Beals was mentioned in the letter, and it was written "Bills", that is, in the manner in which a Russian not familiar with English spelling would write it, using the English 'i', which a Russian would tend to pronounce as 'ee'. Having met and spoken with Klement, the author can testify to the fact that his knowledge of English was sufficient for him not to have made such an elementary mistake. Moreover, whoever had written the letter had sent out three copies, each of which had been signed in a different way—Klement, Adolphe and Frederic. Adolphe and Frederic were two of the three pseudonyms used at one time by Klement. But his third pseudonym, Camille, and the one that he had been using for the two years previous to his disappearance, was on none of the letters. The recipients of the copies naturally wondered why none of them had been signed "Camille". The conclusion they drew was that the writer of the letter wished to emphasise its genuineness by thus demonstrating his knowledge of the pseud-onyms used a considerable time before. But why should Klement have resorted to this, when it would have been so much simpler and more effective to hand over two of the letters to his French comrades in person? Or why not at least on one of the letters make use of the current pseudonym? If, that is, the writer knew of it . . . Since the letter was typewritten, with only the date and the signature in ink, it was not possible to declare it a forgery from a comparison of handwriting, but Klement's friends nonetheless refused to accept it as having been voluntarily written by him. Their reaction, however, may very well be put down to the desire not to admit a grave defection on the part of a leading member of their organisation. But the contents of the letter itself unquestionably gave strong support to their contention that the letter was phoney.'

188. See a seven-page report from Los Angeles SAC concerning an interview with Nathan Koornick on 8 October 1954, ORLOV FBI File, Bureau (105-22869), Los Angeles (105-1608), serial 246.

189. Suritz was appointed Soviet ambassador in Paris on 5 April 1937. With the same decree he was relieved of his duties as Soviet ambassador to Nazi Germany, in which capacity he had served from 1934. From August 1936 Suritz and the Soviet Trade Representative in Germany David Kandelaki were involved in what became known as the second phase of Kandelaki's mission, which was the intensification of trade with Germany. On 12 January 1937 the Soviet ambassador spoke with the Reich Minister of Economics, Hjalmar Schacht. Suritz reported to Moscow: 'Essentially, the discussion was about the Comintern and he [Schacht] said that everybody, including us, should leave Spain alone' (AVP RF, f. 5, op. 17, p. 126, d. 1, l. 17).

190. ORLOV FBI File, Bureau (105-22869), Los Angeles (105-1608) serial 246: interview with Nathan Koornick on 8 October 1954.

191. ORLOV FBI File, Bureau (105-22869), Los Angeles (105-1608) serial 246: interview with Nathan Koornick on 8 October 1954.

192. A copy of the letter in Russian is in this author's archive and can be viewed at the Cañada Blanch Centre of the LSE.
193. This part of the letter shows that Nikolsky knew the TULIP case well and was speaking tongue in cheek when telling the Americans his 'agent Mark' story.
194. The text clearly demonstrates that, even though knowing 'other operational sources' in the UK, Nikolsky was unaware of other members of the Cambridge Spy Ring, because they were all recruited after he had left London.
195. ASVRR, Operational Record File No. 76659, vol. 1, pp. 245–58, which is quoted by Tsarev and Costello (*Deadly Illusions*, 308–12) as Correspondence of the Rezidentura in Spain, File No. 76659, vol. 2, pp. 85–98. See also Tsarev and Costello, *Rokovye illyuzii*, 353–7. In the Russian edition the reference is given to the File orlov (incorrect), No. 76659, vol. 1, p. 98.
196. ASVRR, File No. 76659, vol. 1, p. 301, front and reverse. Author's archive.
197. Jansen and Petrov, *Stalin's Loyal Executioner*, 147.
198. ASVRR, Personal File SCHWED, No. 32476, vol. 1, p. 170, quoted by Costello and Tsarev, *Deadly Illusions*, 305.
199. Costello and Tsarev, *Deadly Illusions*, 304. As already noted, other sources give a figure of $68,000.
200. ASVRR, PIERRE [Eitingon] to the Centre, summarizing work of the *rezidentura* in Spain for the year 1938, undated, File No. 17679, vol. 1, page unspecified; see Primakov et al. (eds), *Ocherki*, iii. 140, ch. 11.
201. O'Sullivan, *Dealing with the Devil*, 294.
202. Top Secret No. 91/ss, 10 November 1938, incoming to the S[ecretariat of] Narkom No. 31/os of 17/11/38. RGVA, f. 33987, op. 3, d. 1081, l. 16, cited by Radosh et al., *Spain Betrayed*, document 78, p. 496.

INTERLUDE 3

1. TNA: PRO KV 2/2878, File No. 139.424, Name: Nikolsky, Serial 77a, extracted from file on 31 January 1951.
2. TNA: PRO KV 2/1094-1097. See also TNA: PRO HO 45/25765. She was convicted at Bow Street Police Court on 9 October 1942 and sentenced to three months' imprisonment, but was subsequently detained under defence regulation 18B. Four years after her release Ms Styczinska was still on the MI5 watch list. It seems no one cared to ask her about Nikolsky/Orlov. In the meantime, according to at least one British researcher, 'Marie Brett-Perring, undoubtedly an intelligence agent of some kind', long before the German attack on Russia, 'over a period of months had been feeding the British Security Services with information concerning German military activities in Eastern Europe, particularly in Poland and the Ukraine. Marie Brett Perring was surprisingly accurate (Robin O'Neil, 'Extermination of the Jews of Galicia', unpublished PhD thesis, University College, London, ch. 1 n. 33).

3. See Marie Brett-Perring, 'Is Moscow Ready to Reach Out for France', *Liberty*, 1 August 1936, p. 59.
4. The 'wise man' was William Arthur Ward.
5. See Orlov's FBI file 105-22869 X to X-18, 3 April 1942–31 August 1945.
6. VENONA, San Francisco to Moscow, No. 259 of 17 May 1944. Comments state that Orlov is the only occurrence, therefore unidentified.
7. Intercepted letter of Maria to her husband in New York hospital, Baker Pavillion, 528 East 68th Street, room 1220, dated Tuesday, 25 November 1958, 4.30 p.m.

CHAPTER 21

1. Fitin, born 1907, completed his graduate studies as an agricultural engineer in 1932 and, after serving one year as a private in the Red Army, was invited to take a course at the Central NKVD School (March–August 1938). Immediately after that he was accepted by the GUGB as a junior operative, and by the following October wahad been promoted to deputy chief of its 5th department (foreign intelligence). Fitin, codenamed VICTOR in all secret correspondence, was appointed chief of Soviet foreign intelligence on 13 May 1939 and occupied this post until June 1946, ending his career as lieutenant general; for a year and a half he was Minister of State Security of Kazakhstan. Fitin was sacked from the service after Stalin's death and ended up as director of the photo laboratory of the Soyuz Sovetskikh Obshchestv Druzhby i Kulturnoi Svyazi s Zarubezhnymi Stranami (SSOD) (Union of Soviet Societies for Friendship and Cultural Relations with Foreign Countries,), for which he was surely extremely grateful. See Petrov and Skorkin, *Kto rukovodil NKVD 1934–1941*, 423. See also VENONA/BRIDE, Mexico City–Moscow, 3 June 1944, No. 461.
2. L. Vorobiov, 'Operatsiya "Utka"', in Primakov et al. (eds), *Ocherki*, iii. 93. The KGB/SVR account published in the third volume of the semi-official history of the service should be taken with a pinch of salt, as it is largely based of two early Western accounts: the book written by the chief Mexican investigator, General Leandro A. Sánchez Salazar, ex-chief of Secret Service of the Mexican police, with the collaboration of Julian Gorkin (whom the essay accuses of being an FBI and DST agent since 1938), entitled *Murder in Mexico: The Assassination of Leon Trotsky* (London: Secker & Warburg, 1950); and a well-known book by Isaac Don Levine, *The Mind of an Assassin* (London: Weidenfeld & Nicolson; New York: Farrar, Straus and Cudahy, 1959). Both books were written and published too early to become a good, reliable source, though they contain a lot of useful, albeit sometimes faulty information. The *Ocherki* version, admitting that the archival material pertaining to the operation has been at least partially destroyed, makes use of a very limited number of the NKVD–KGB documents, limiting itself to some snippets from the operational plan dated

August 1939 and quoting extracts of the interrogation protocol of Eitingon dated March 1954, when he was already in the Butyrka prison. Among other things, the essay claims, improbably, that the initial budget of the operation was $31,000 for six months. Interestingly, the author(s) of the *Ocherki* piece completely disregard research made by General Volkogonov shortly after the collapse of the Soviet Union and based partially on the NKVD archival material, the two above-mentioned early books, and interviews with, among others, Sudoplatov.

3. Leon Trotsky, *Writings of Leon Trotsky [1936–37]* (London: Pathfinder Books Ltd, 1978), 51.
4. Primakov et al. (eds), *Ocherki*, iii. 94.
5. Primakov et al. (eds), *Ocherki*, iiii. 93.
6. Andrew and Mitrokhin, *The Mitrokhin Archive*, 114.
7. Don Levine, *The Mind of an Assassin*, 83. Mary-Kay Wilmers, one of distant relatives of Eitingon and the editor of the *London Review of Books*, calls Don Levine 'the most lurid of Cold War historians' (see *The Eitingons*, 273).
8. Sudoplatov and Sudoplatov, *Special Tasks*, 70. Luis Mercader del Río Hernández was born in Barcelona in 1923. He later became a professor specializing in telecommunications. Among other books, he also published memoirs about his brother, Luis Mercader, Germán Sánchez, and Rafael Llanos, *Rámon Mercader, mi hermano: Cincuenta anos despues* (Madrid: Espasa-Calpe, 1990).
9. Khenkin, *Okhotnik vverkh nogami*, 208.
10. Don Levine, *The Mind of an Assassin*, 37.
11. Either Grigory Rabinovich or Jacob Golos.
12. Alias 'Lev Aleksandrovich Tarasov', codenamed YURI.
13. On 13 November 1937 Sloutsky informed the Central Committee: 'We are sending Comrade Rabinovich back to the USA to his previous job' (RGASPI, f. 17, op. 97, d. 1231, l. 10).
14. Rabinowich was recalled to Moscow in December 1939, ending his part in the operation. In New York, neglecting all guidelines of espionage tradecraft, he used to meet Golos several times a week every week. After Rabinovich had left New York, the resident Ovakimyan became Golos's controller.
15. Chugunov stayed in New York until February 1945, and his work there can be assessed from the cables between New York and Moscow decrypted in the course of Operation VENONA, where SHAH is identified as 'Konstantin Alexeevich Shabanov'. Chugunov was fired in 1953 in the purge of the Soviet state security following the arrest of Lavrenty Beria, and was transferred to VOKS as head of its American department. Here Chugunov would work, together with Grigulevich, who returned from his last foreign mission and settled in Moscow in early 1954. In the 1970s Chugunov became a rather well-known translator from English and died in March 1991 still working closely with the Russian literary journal *Inostrannaya Literatura* ('Foreign Literature').

16. Ovakimyan, born in August 1898, was a rather well-educated Soviet Armenian (he was a chemical engineer), who, like Nikolsky/Orlov and many other colleagues, worked at the OGPU Economic Directorate before moving to foreign intelligence in 1931. From March 1931 to August 1932, Ovakimyan was posted to Berlin, where he succeeded Nikolsky as assistant 'lega'l resident under the cover of the Soviet Trade Mission. In June 1933 Ovakimayn came to New York as Gutzeit's deputy in charge of scientific and technical intelligence and, after the recall of Gutzeit in October 1938, he was promoted to head of station. He operated in America until his arrest by the FBI on 5 May 1941. This was possible only because, carelessly, he was sent to America under the cover of Amtorg rather than that of a diplomatic mission. Released on $25,000 bail, he was never tried and was soon able to leave for Moscow, departing from San Francisco quite legally on 23 July 1941 (AVP RF, f. 0129 'Referentura po USA', correspondence regarding the arrest of Gaik Ovakimyan, op. 25a, d. 6, ll. 39–132). Back at headquarters, Ovakimyan became involved with atomic intelligence, rising to major general. According to the semi-official KGB history (Primakov et al. (eds), *Ocherki*, iv.. 401, 408–15), Ovakimyan took part in the meeting with the American delegation, visiting Moscow at the end of 1943, posing as 'Colonel Osipov'. Indeed, William J. Donovan's 'Memorandum on Conversation at the NKVD' of 27 December 1943 names one 'Col. Ossipov, Head of the Section Conducting Subversive Activities in Enemy Countries'. According to the CIA comments to the document, Colonel Osipov was soon promoted. As a commentator put it: 'Shortly after the war the two Russians [who took part in that December meeting] were identified in the press as Lt. Gen. P. M. Fitin and Maj. Gen. Aleksandr P. Osipov. As late as 1950 they were still publicly reported to be associated with each other, as chief and deputy respectively of Section 12 (foreign intelligence services) of the MVD, successor to the NKVD' ('Memoranda for the President: OSS-NKVD Liason', CIA, Centre for the Study of Intelligence, Studies Archive Indexes, vol. 7, no. 3). It must be added that, according to Robert Lamphere, the FRI had voluminous files on Ovakimyan (Lamphere and Shachtman, *The FBI–KGB War*, 25).

17. In the same telegram, dated 4 August 1939, GENNADY (Ovakimyan) asked to be assigned to his station GLAN (N. N. Yershov), LAVR/LAUREL (F. S. Novikov), and TWEN/TWAIN (S. M. Semyonov), who had completed their postgraduate technical studies and courses of English to work in XY line (scientific and technical intelligence). He also asked for BLERIO (Stanislav Shumovsky) to be moved from the West Coast to the East, where he had better sources. Shumovsky was engaged in aviation espionage. All of these young NKVD officers were registered in New York as members of the Soviet Purchasing Commission. GLAN was also the codename of Vladimir Barkovsky in London during the war (1941–6). Later Barkovsky served as deputy resident in charge of Line S & T in Washington, DC.

18. See Andrew and Mitrokhin, *The Mitrokhin Archive*, 114.
19. See Lamphere and Shachtman, *The FBI–KGB War*, 168.
20. Salazar and Gorkin, *Murder in Mexico*, 48–9.
21. Leon Trotsky, 'Stalin Seeks my Death', *Fourth International*, 2/7 (August 1941), 201–7, written in Coyoacán on 8 June 1940.
22. See VENONA (at the time BRIDE), New York–Moscow, 10 August 1944. Among other things, the New York NKVD station reported: 'The latter [Trotsky's widow Natalia Sedova] intends to demand a renewal of the investigation of the effects of Robert Sheldon HART who was murdered [sixty-three groups unrecoverable].'
23. Salazar and Gorkin, *Murder in Mexico*, 48–9.
24. Salazar and Gorkin, *Murder in Mexico*, 55.
25. Primakov et al. (eds), *Ocherki*, iii. 101.
26. As recalled by a former KGB colleague, Yuri Paporov, in *Izvestiya*, 5 May 1993.
27. See Preston, *The Spanish Holocaust*, 350.
28. Chikov (*Razvedchiki-nelegaly* (Moscow: Exmo/Algoritm kniga, 2003), 267), quoting this undated report, identifies MARTINEZ as 'Antonio Martínez from the Comintern'.
29. RGASPI, f. 17, op. 163, d. 1316, ll. 45–7. The same decree awarded Caridad Ramonovna Mercader and Naum Isaakovich Eitingon the Order of Lenin; Lev Petrovich Vasilevsky and Pavel Anatolievich Sudoplatov the Order of the Red Banner; Iosif Romualdovich Grigulevich and Pavel Panteleimonovich Pastelnyak the Order of the Red Star.
30. Leonov was Fidel Castro's closest Russian adviser and one of the KGB's best experts on Latin America; until September 1991 he headed Directorate RI (intelligence analysis and assessment) in Yasenevo.
31. See Kern, *A Death in Washington*, 319.
32. Tamiment Library, ALB Archives, File Wally Amadeo Sabatini, Italian–American, born 1909, YCL member from 1924.
33. Given for heroism in combat or for other extraordinary accomplishments of military valour.
34. Shatunovskaya/Leonov, interview with Grigulevich, *Latinskaya Amerika*, 3 (1993), 65. Grigulevich was in Uruguay, where he escaped after an attempt on Trotsky's life. In the story, related to Leonov, he deliberately changed the date of the operation, since at that time he was on another special mission in New York. However, this mission was so important that he could not possibly have combined it with the occasional murder of a traitor. On 26 November 1948 Grigulevich had a secret meeting in New York with William Fisher, the Soviet 'illegal' better known as 'Colonel Rudolf Abel'. Grigulevich gave Fisher $1,000 and three documents in the name of Emil Robert Goldfus. The real Goldfus, born in New York on 2 August 1902, had died at the age of only fourteen months. Fisher's file, seen by Mitrokhin, records that his birth certificate had been obtained by the NKVD in Spain at the end of the Spanish

Civil War, at a time when it was collecting identity documents from members of the International Brigades for use in illegal operations. See Andrew and Mitrokhin, *The Mitrokhin Archive*, 193.

35. For details, see Kern, *Death in Washington*, 325–8.

36. For the summaries of the interviews, largely conducted by Jane Archer of MI5 in Krivitsky's room at the Langham Hotel, London, in January–February 1939, see TNA: PRO KV 2/804–5. Much is reproduced in Krivitsky, *MI5 Debriefing*. See also West, MASK, 247–312, app.2.

37. Reproduced in Chris Hastings and Charlotte Edwardes, 'MI5 Thought Churchill Nephews Were Spies', *Daily Telegraph*, 23 June 2002.

38. Kern, *A Death in Washington*, 323. When Gary Kern wrote his biography of Krivitsky, he knew little or nothing about Grigulevich's special assignment in New York. In discussing the case with this writer, he mentioned that 'without any question Krivitsky pulled the trigger; but he may have been prompted by a threat against his family to do so or by something we will never know... Maybe someday the KGB file on Krivitsky will be opened – then everything will be revised. The death, however, will probably remain a mystery' (Gary Kern to author, April–May 2006).

39. According to a post-war MI5 report, Krivitsky provided the Security Service 'for the first time with an insight into the organization, methods and influence of the Russian Intelligence Service' (Andrew, *Authorized History*, 265).

40. Andrew, *Authorized History*, 268.

41. Cf. Andrew and Mitrokhin, *The Mitrokhin Archive*, 131. Wartime Soviet agents with access to US policy documents on Argentina included Laurence Duggan, a Latin American expert in the State Department, and Maurice Halperin, chief of the Latin American Division in the OSS R&A Branch. See Hayden B. Peake, 'OSS and the Venona Decrypts', *Intelligence and National Security*, 12/ 3 (July 1997), 22, 25, 26. There were also sources in the OSS. For details, see Haynes, Klehr, and Vassiliev, *Spies*, chs 4–5.

42. See Jeffery, *MI6*, 456–7.

43. The semi-official Primakov et al. (eds), *Ocherki* (iv. 376), identifies them as Grigory Furdas, Grigory Yaremchuk, Pavel Borisyuk, and one Yakov. The Spaniard had a cover name MATISS and the Argentineans were FLORINDO and BONITO.

44. Primakov et al. (eds), *Ocherki*, iv. 376.

45. See Nikandrov, *Grigulevich*, 36.

46. Jeffery, *MI6*, 461.

47. See Mark Stout, 'The Pond: Running Agents for State, War and the CIA', *Studies in Intelligence*, 48/3 (2004).

48. Andrew and Mitrokhin, *The Mitrokhin Archive*, 131–2.

49. Andrew and Mitrokhin, *The Mitrokhin Archive*, 131–2.

50. Andrew and Mitrokhin, *The Mitrokhin Archive*, 132, 778. VENONA decrypts, 2nd release, p. 26; 3rd release, vol. 2, p. 101.

51. See Nikandrov, *Grigulevich*, 34.
52. Nikandrov, *Grigulevich*, 40. According to Yuri A. Markov, who worked as secretary of the Secret Department of the Comintern in Moscow, and then in the 4th department of the NKVD under Sudoplatov, where he was in charge of the sabotage operations in Latin America, with the help of Troise the archives were brought from Buenos Aires to Montevideo in the diplomatic pouches of the Foreign Ministry of Uruguay. Troise was introduced to the NKVD operative by Rodolfo Ghioldi before the latter was arrested in Buenos Aires in 1943.
53. Nikandrov, *Grigulevich*, 41. *The New Encyclopædia Britannica* is more laconic: 'Creole, originally, in the 16–18 century, any white person born in Spanish America of Spanish parents, as distinguished from an American resident who had been born in Spain. The term has since been used with various meanings, often conflicting or varying from region to region . . . In such countries as Peru, the adjective creole describes a certain spirited way of life. Important expressions of this way of life are the abilities to speak wittingly and persuasively on a wide range of topics, to turn a situation to one's advantage, to be masculine (*macho*), to exhibit national pride, and to participate in fiestas and other sociable activities with a certain gusto—in sum, to be *muy criollo* ("very creole").'
54. Cf. Andrew and Mitrokhin, *The Mitrokhin Archive*, 163.
55. After the collapse of the Soviet Union, Russian President Boris Yeltsyn officially admitted this crime of Stalin, committed by the NKVD—only a small episode among many.
56. For details about the letter, see Ben Fisher, '"Mr Guver": Anonymous Soviet Letter to the FBI', CIA Center for the Study of Intelligence, *Studies in Intelligence*, 7 (1997).
57. VENONA decrypts, 4th release, part 4, pp. 115–16.
58. ASVRR, File No. 70545 (probably Operational Correspondence File), vol. 1, pp. 420–2, quoted by Allen Weinstein and Alexander Vassiliev, *The Haunted Wood* (New York: Random House, 1998),108.
59. ASVRR, File No. 70545 (probably Operational Correspondence File), vol. 1, pp. 420–2, quoted by Weinstein and Vassiliev, *The Haunted Wood*, 108.
60. See Andrew and Mitrokhin, *The Mitrokhin Archive*, 193.
61. The KGB reports mention an unsuccessful search for Bentley's whereabouts as late as 1955. See Weinstein and Vassiliev, *The Haunted Wood*, 108.
62. For Katz's date of birth, see the FBI SILVERMASTER GREGOR File No. 65-56402, vol. 147 (October 1948–March 1949), Serials 3691-2730, Ladd to Fletcher, 12 January 1949, pdf, p. 37.
63. A late 1943 memo described Katz as 'a secret staff member of the NKGB of the USSR'—that is, like Reiss, Krivitsky, and indeed Grigulevich, he was a civil employee of the service. See Alexander Vassiliev, White Notebook No. 1, p. 151, citing File No. 70994, which is almost certainly an Operational Correspondence File.

64. Alexander Vassiliev, Black Notebook, 'Failures in the USA (1938–1948)' by Anatoly Gorsky, p. 78. It must be said that the FBI files and Robert Lamphere's account place Katz continuously in Paris from 1948 to 1951.

65. Andrew and Mitrokhin, *The Mitrokhin Archive*, 212.

66. See Nigel West, VENONA: *The Greatest Secret of the Cold War* (London: HarperCollins, 1999). 164.

67. See Lamphere and Shachtman, *The FBI–KGB War*, 280–2. Robert Lamphere recalled: 'I found his brother's telephone number quite easily, and called and asked for Joseph. His sister-in-law was a bit surprised, but put Katz on the line. His voice was more guttural than I expected—given Bentley's description of it as being typically Brooklyn-accented—but he said he was Joseph Katz. I identified myself as a former FBI agent, long since out of the Bureau, and said I was writing a book and that he was in it. Katz was a bit taken aback at the idea' (p. 296).

68. This is how one Bureau document describes Joseph Katz: 'Elizabeth Terrill Bentley has made a tentative identification of a photograph of Joseph Katz as the unknown subject, with alias Jack, for whom she worked in the fall of 1944, as a Soviet espionage agent. According to information previously furnished by Bentley, she had for a short time furnished to Jack material which had been obtained in Washington by members of the Soviet espionage network operating in agencies of the US Government . . . It might be noted that the physical description of Jack and Joseph Katz coincides in every respect to the extent that they both walk with a limp, are Lithuanian jews, have blue eyes, thin lips, dark blond hair receding at the temples, lines from the nose to the corners of the mouth, speak the Luthuanian, Russian, English and Spanish languages' (FBI SILVERMASTER File No. 65-56402-3720, vol. 147, pdf, p. 38). These were also the languages spoken by Grigulevich.

69. Andrew and Mitrokhin, *The Mitrokhin Archive*, 212.

70. I am greatly indebted to Professor Dr Jorge Saenz for this and other valuable information from the Costa Rican diplomatic archives.

71. Costa Rica's most serious political crisis since 1917 came in 1948. A faction containing alleged Communists tried to prevent the seating of the president-elect, Otilio Ulate. José Figueres Ferrer, a socialist landowner, put down the rebellion and turned the government over to Ulate. On 6 June 1948 the new government 'accepted the resignation' of many public officers, including Communists. In 1953 Figueres was elected in his own right. He was elected again in 1970, having meanwhile established his Partido de Liberación Nacional (PLN) as the dominant group in the Legislative Assembly. In 1974 Daniel Oduber of the same PLN succeeded Figueres as president. In their second volume, Andrew and Mitrokhin reveal that José Figueres took $300,000 in KGB money to help finance his political activities. His only concession, according to the authors, was to establish diplomatic relations with the Soviet Union after he became president in 1953. However, Figueres, codenamed

KASIK, agreed to occasional meetings with KGB representatives, which means that his personal file in the SVR archives may contain more surprises. See Andrew and Mitrokhin, *The World Was Going Our Way: The KGB and the Battle for the Third World* (New York: Basic Books, 2005), 67–9, 117–18.

72. Andrew and Mitrokhin, *The Mitrokhin Archive*, 212.

73. IMMP, Papers 'Teodoro Castro'. On 14 July 1951 don Teodoro (Grigulevich) was appointed First Secretary *ad honorem* to the Legation of Costa Rica in Rome, Italy.

74. Fifty years later, Don Claudio Volio recalled: 'I remember Teodoro Castro as an educated, well informed man. Apart from the meeting, Castro and I were briefly together in some social events. He seemed to be a witty, kind and most charming person, even sweet in his manners. I never had the slightest hint that he was someone or something different from what he pretended to be' (Claudio Volio to author, 24 August 2006). I am grateful to Ms Alejandra Volio and Dr Jorge Saenz for their cooperation.

75. Dean Acheson, *Present at the Creation: My Years in the State Department* (New York: Norton, 1969), 580–1; Andrew and Mitrokhin, *The Mitrokhin Archive*, 213. See also Andrey Yanuaryevich Vyshinsky, 'On Measures against the Threat of Another World War and for Strengthening Peace and Friendship among Other Nations', in *Speeches of A. Y. Vyshinsky at the Plenary Session of the UN General Assembly, Paris, 8 and 16 November 1951* (London: Soviet News, 1951).

76. Andrew and Mitrokhin, *The Mitrokhin Archive*, 213.

77. Paporov, 'Sudba peresmeshnika', 11. Yuri Paporov was assigned to Mexico City under cover as the cultural attaché at the Soviet embassy in mid-1950s.

78. Andrew and Mitrokhin, *The Mitrokhin Archive*, 213–14.

79. Nikolai S. Leonov, former KGB adviser to Fidel Castro. See interview with Shatunovskaya, *Latinskaya Amerika*, 3 (1993), 65; Yuri N. Paporov, *Akademik nelegalnykh nauk* [Iosif Grigulevich] (St Petersburg: Neva, 2004), 137. See also Georgy Chernyavsky, 'Grigulevich Iosif Romualdovich: razvedchik, uchyonyi, pisatel', *Nezavisimaya gazeta*, 17 May 2001.

80. According to the Foreign Ministry of Costa Rica, Teodoro B. Castro never had any foreign or Costa Rican awards during his government service. I am very grateful to Señora Carmen Claramunt Garro, Jefe del Departamento Diplomático, Ministerio de Relaciones Extériores y Culto, República de Costa Rica, and Don Jorge Saenz Carbonell, Embajador, Director Alterno para cuestiones de historia diplomática, Instituto del Servicio Exterior Manuel Maria de Peralta, San José, Costa Rica, for their extraordinary help during this author's research.

81. IMMP, Papers 'Julio Cesar Pascal Rocca', courtesy of don Jorge Saenz, Embajador, Director Alterno para cuestiones de historia diplomática, parte académica investigaciones y museo diplomático. The Soviet 'illegal' was appointed as Civil Attaché to the Costa Rican Legation in Italy on 12 December 1951. On

21 April 1952, together with Castro, Julio Cesar Pascal Rocca was appointed as observer for Costa Rica to the XI Session of the International Consultative Committee for Cotton in Rome. A few months after Castro/Grigulevich was appointed as Minister Plenipotentiary, Rocca was promoted to Second Secretary of the Legation in Italy and appointed as Second Secretary in Yugoslavia. On 10 November 1953 he became a member of the Costa Rican delegation to the VII General Assembly of the Food and Agriculture Organization (FAO) of the United Nations, headed by Minister of Agriculture Claudio Volio. I am grateful to former minister don Claudio Volio for his personal impressions about Teodoro Castro and Julio Rocca. On 16 January 1954 Rocca was appointed Costa Rican Chargé d'Affaires *ad interim* in Italy because of don Castro's resignation. In February the Costa Rican government appointed a new Chargé d'Affaires *ad interim* in Italy, Fernando Montes de Oca y Gomez. On 5 March 1954, his appointment was declared void, and a new Chargé d'Affaires, Cesar Valverde, was appointed instead. Valverde's resignation was accepted on 16 March 1954. Montes de Oca was again appointed to this post on 5 April. On 15 July 1954 the government of Costa Rica accepted Mr Pascale Rocca's resignation as Second Secretary in Italy. However, there is no record confirming that there was actually any letter of resignation from him. I am grateful to Jorge Saenz for this information.

82. Claudio Volio to author, 28 August 2006.
83. Sudoplatov and Sudoplatov, *Special Tasks*, 336. As mentioned before, at least until the death of Stalin, 'active measures' always stood for 'murder'.
84. From its formation in 1926, the Administration for Special Tasks underwent many changes and reorganizations as well as renaming. After the defection of Oleg Lyalin, the Line F officer of the KGB London station, to the British in September 1971, Department V, which he represented and which was a modified Administration for Special Tasks, was formally disbanded. In reality, it had existed until mid-1990s as the 8 Department of the SVR Directorate S. At the time of writing, it still exists, reporting directly to the DDO (operations).
85. Sudoplatov and Sudoplatov, *Special Tasks*, 336.
86. Quoted from Volkogonov's article in *Izvestiya*, 11 June 1993.
87. Sudoplatov and Sudoplatov, *Special Tasks*, 337.
88. *Liternoe delo* is a letter-coded file. In the Sudoplatov Service, *liternoe delo* always meant assassination. Mitrokhin in his *KGB Lexicon* (p. 62) gives a similar but much broader interpretation of the term.
89. The gathering in the Kremlin included General Semyon Ignatyev, Minister of State Security (MGB) from 1951 to 1953; General Yevgeny Pitovranov, who from 1952 to 1953 headed IV Directorate (special operations) of the MGB; General Ivan Serov, First Deputy Interior Minister from 1947 to 1954 and later first chairman of the KGB; General Sergey Savchenko, from 1951 until March 1953 chief of Soviet foreign intelligence (First Chief Directorate of the MGB);

General Vasili Ryasnoy, from February 1952 deputy minister of State Security, and chief of foreign intelligence from 11 March to 28 May 1953; and General Alexey Yepishev, a former Ukrainian CP functionary suddenly appointed Deputy Minister of State Security in 1951 (dismissed in March 1953, days after the death of Stalin).

90. Andrew and Mitrokhin, *The Mitrokhin Archive*, 465–6.
91. See Sudoplatov and Sudoplatov, *Special Tasks*, 355; Vitaly Pavlov, *Operatsiya 'Sneg'* (Moscow: Geya, 1996); Paporov, 'Sudba peresmeshnika', and *Akademik*, 151–2; Marjorie Ross, *El secreto encanto de la KGB: Las cinco vidas de Iósif Griguliévich* (San José, Costa Rica: Farben/Norma, 2004).
92. In the 1950s the list of MVD operatives in Austria, without those attached to the Central Group of Forces in Baden bei Wien (the Special Tasks group headed by Col. Evgeny Ivanovich Mirkovsky) or those in Vienna's Palais Epstein, which housed the Soviet *kommendatura* ('commandant's office') and not counting Smersh personnel, included twenty-five case officers and one interpreter (Valentina Gavrilova). Some of them would become well known in the following years. Among those are Boris Nalivaiko, Anatoly Golitsyn, Petr Deryabin, Sergey Kondrashev, and Saul Okun, the latter of the Special Tasks Group. Author's archive.
93. Pavlov joined the NKVD in late 1938. He was posted as head of station in Ottawa (1942–6) and Vienna (alias 'Nikolai Kedrov', from 1966). In 1947 he was transferred to the newly established 'illegals' directorate, where he worked until 1961, the last thee years as its chief. Noticeably, before his retirement in 1990, Lieutenant General Pavlov's job included investigating the cases (and archival records) of defectors from the late 1930s to the late 1980s.
94. Paporov, *Akademik*, 155.
95. The only way to ascertain this was to ask Nadezhda Grigulevich, who did not respond to this writer's query, made in August 2011 when the book was being prepared for publication.
96. Gorky had plagiarized it from a pre-revolutionary publisher, F. Pavlenkov.

CHAPTER 22

1. One is *Trotskyism in the Service of Franco* published simultaneously in London (Lawrence and Wishart) and New York (International Publishers) in 1938 by the publishing houses associated with the CPGB and CPSU and signed with the name of the NKVD agent Georges Soria. Both editions were manufactured by a small family printer Purnell and Sons based in Somerset. Forty years later, in a work about the Spanish Civil War (Soria, *Guerra y revolución en España 1936–1939* (Barcelona: Grijalbo, 1978), 78–9) Soria, without mentioning the book, stated that 'the charge that the POUM leaders were "agents of the Gestapo and Franco" was no more than a fabrication, because it was impossible to adduce the slightest evidence'. Another book is *Espionaje en España*

(Barcelona: Ediciones 'Unidad', 1938), signed with the pseudonym 'Max Rieger' (Prefacio de José Bergamín). There is no doubt that Orlov's figure stands firmly behind both books, which contain forgeries produced by him, although it is possible that neither was actually drafted by Orlov. While for the first publication Soria simply compiled the material provided by Orlov, the second book is attributed by experts to a collective work of the very same Georges Soria and the Spanish Communist intellectual Wenceslao Roces, supervised by the special envoy of the ECCI in Spain, Stoyan Minev alias 'Stepanov'. It seems that the book was initially written in French and then translated into Spanich by Lucienne and Arturo Perucho. In any case, both books were to support Orlov's operation against the POUM.

2. Alexander Orlov, 'The Sensational Secret behind Damnation of Stalin', *Life* magazine, 23 April 1956, pp. 34–8, 43–5.

3. Alexander Orlov, 'How Stalin Relieved Spain of $600,000,000', *Reader's Digest* (November 1966), 37–8, 41–8.

4. Ironically, in spite of some criticism of this book in previous chapters, Orlov's life in America is described best of all in Gazur's book, especially when it is based on the Department of Justice documents. That said, Gazur's subtitle— *The FBI's KGB General*—is completely unjustified, and everything dealing with the life and adventures of Orlov and his family before they settled in the USA is unreliable, as this work seeks to demonstrate. Orlov had never been a general and had never served in the KGB, the Service that was established in March 1954, almost twenty years after Orlov's desertion.

5. See, e.g., Graham, *The Spanish Republic at War 1936–1939*; Payne, *The Spanish Civil War*.

6. Remarkably, Robert Lamphere who was at the heart of major Soviet espionage investigations on behalf of the FBI when Orlov's name became known and was actively interviewed by the Bureau does not even mention Orlov in his famous book.

7. ORLOV FBI File, Director, FBI, letter to Assistant Attorney General William F. Tompkins, 16 July 1954, unclassified.

8. Orlov, *The March of Time*, 377–8.

9. Andrew and Gordievsky, *KGB: The Inside Story*, 222. In the book there is no reference to this quotation, which probably comes from Gordievsky's recollections of reading KGB archival documents.

10. As already mentioned, one was at 16 Brixton Hill, SW2, in Brixton, and another at 4 Castletown Road, W14, in Hammersmith (File SCHWED No. 32476, vol. 2, author's archive). To send postcards that could contain only minimal information from Spain to Paris and from there to London would be an unnecessary chore.

11. ASVRR, Philby KGB Memoir, p. 53, quoted by Costello and Tsarev, *Deadly Illusions*, 167–8.

12. Costello and Tsarev, *Deadly Illusions*, 165. Unfortunately, no reference to the KGB file is given. Other documents show that it should have been File No. 5581, opened on the attempt to assassinate Franco.

13. Deutsch's memorandum, early 1939, ASVRR, Personal File STEFAN No. 32826, vol. 1 p. 349, quoted by Costello and Tsarev, *Deadly Illusions*, 169.

14. Costello and Tsarev, *Deadly Illusions*, 170.

15. According to Philby's KGB-sponsored biography edited, forwarded and highly praised by Phillip Kightley, 'the first [meeting with his Soviet controller] would take place rather quickly, just two or three weeks after his arrival, as Kim remembered it, on the first Sunday in June [6th]. He had to take the train from Bayonne to Narbonne and meet the man there' (Borovik, *The Philby Files: The Secret Life of the Master Spy—KGB Archives Reveal*, 117–18).

16. Costello and Tsarev, *Deadly Illusions*, 171.

17. Knightley, *Philby*, ch. 5, cited by Andrew and Gordievsky, *KGB: The Inside Story*, 223.

18. Stanislav Glinsky, the head of station, was recalled in July 1937. In September 1937 the Paris NKVD station was headed by captain of state security Georgy Kosenko assisted by Mikhail Grigoryev. In October there arrived Ivan Agayants, to be posted first to the Trade Delegation and later to the Consulate.

19. Morris Riley, *Philby: The Hidden Years* (London: Janus Publishing, 1999), 2–3.

20. TNA: PRO HS 8/214.

21. For details, see C. G. McKay, 'Iron Ore and Section D: The Oxelösund Operation', *Historic Journal*, 29/4 (December 1986), 975–8.

22. In February 1940 the Centre issued orders for all contacts with Philby to be terminated. Contact with Burgess was broken off at about the same time. Mitrokhin notes indicate: 'In 1940, when there was no contact with Burgess, he handed over material for the CPGB through MARY [Litzi Philby] and EDITH [Edith Tudor-Hart]. In the summer of 1940 Burgess told Michael Straight: "I've been out of touch with our friends for several months"' (Andrew and Mitrokhin, *The Mitrokhin Archive*, 112, 772 n. 99).

23. See Jeffery, *MI6*, 622–3. The author names 'Bill Cordeaux' as a committee member.

24. Quoted in Andrew and Mitrokhin, *The Mitrokhin Archive*, 165–6. An interesting point of view on Philby and his Cambridge friends as Soviet agents is in S. J. Hamrick, *Deceiving the Deceivers: Kim Philby, Donald MacLean and Guy Burgess* (New Haven and London: Yale University Press, 2004).

25. Cf. Andrew and Mitrokhin, *The Mitrokhin Archive*, 157.

26. Andrew and Mitrokhin, *The Mitrokhin Archive*, 157–9. Missive to the London station of 25 October 1943.

27. Andrew and Mitrokhin, *The Mitrokhin Archive*, 71, 156–9.

28. Memorandum to Commodore Shelley, US Navy, 17 July 1945, NARA, Record Group 38, CNSG Library, Box 78, 386014/4. Those present at this meeting were Lt Commander, USNR, William C. Ladd, representing ONI,

who undersigned the memorandum, Lt Colonel Calfee and his relief, Major Stone, representing Special Branch, and Mr Pearson, representing X-2. On that very day, 16 July 1945, following Cavendish-Bentinck's recommendation that 'SOE should become a wing of the SIS' and under pressure from Sir Stewart Menzies, the chief of SOE Sir Colin Gubbins accepted the fusion of the two organizations (Stephen Dorril, *MI6: Fifty Years of Special Operations*, paperback (London: Fourth Estate, 2001), 27.

29. Alias Krotov, codenamed KRECHIN.

30. Cf. Andrew and Mitrokhin, *The Mitrokhin Archive*, 159.

31. Although the Volkov case is well known, it has been misinterpreted in many accounts. Thus, for example, Brook-Shepherd states that his name was Konstantin Petrovich Volkov (*Storm Birds*, 40), Andrew writes that he was Konstantin Dmitrievich Volkov (*The Mitrokhin Archive*, 182), while the story is completely missing in Keith Jeffery's history of MI6 published in 2010.

32. The most reliable account of this episode remains Brook-Shepherd, *Storm Birds*, ch. 4, which corrects a number of Philby's inventions.

33. Brook-Shepherd, *Storm Birds*, 41–2.

34. Brook-Shepherd, *Storm Birds*, 41–2. As we now know, the Kremlin was very well informed, thanks to many moles within British and US government offices.

35. Philby, *My Silent War*, 115.

36. Primakov et al. (eds), *Ocherki*, v. 69. Russian sources do not specify how he managed to do it, and the authors of *The Crown Jewels* (p. 174) suggest that Philby wrote a letter to the Russians with a summary of the Volkov defection attempt handing it over to Burgess for an urgent delivery to Krötenschild.

37. Brook-Shepherd, *Storm Birds*, 44. The name was spelt incorrectly by Brook-Shepherd.

38. Otroschenko was born on 19 August 1902 in Tashkent. He joined the OGPU in June 1924. From May 1925 he was Agabekov's assistant at the Eastern Section (Near and Middle East) and after Agabekov's defection was sent first as deputy head of station (from March 1931) and then head of station (from 1934) to Iran under the cover of the Soviet Consulate General in Meshkhed. From August 1953 to August 1955 Otroschenko was the MVD-KGB resident in Tehran using the alias 'A.M. Boiko'. In April 1956 Otroschenko was fired from the service; he died in Moscow in 1993.

39. Andrew, *Authorized History*, 344–5.

40. Philby, *My Silent War*, 113.

41. Cf. Brook-Shepherd, *Storm Birds*, 48–9.

42. Ismail Akhmedov, *In and Out of Stalin's GRU* (London: Arms & Armour Press, 1984), 195.

43. Brook-Shepherd, *Storm Birds*, 49–50.

44. Andrew, *Authorized History*, 345. Christopher Andrew interviewed Mrs Gouzenko and her daughter (both of whom live under assumed names) in Canada

in November 1992. In 1948 Gouzenko published a book about his life entitled *Iron Curtain*. In 1954 he published a novel *The Fall of a Titan*, called by the *Time* magazine 'one of the most important novels of the century', which was translated into forty-four languages with over 200,000 hardcover copies sold.

45. See Jeffery, *MI6*, 657.

46. Wright with Greengrass, *Spycatcher*, 183. For the album of photographs of Soviet agents involved in the case provided by the Royal Canadian Mounted Police (RCMP) from October 1948, see TNA: PRO KV 2/1424.

47. ASVRR, Philby KGB Memoir, p. 213, quoted by Costello and Tsarev, *Deadly Illusions*, 455 n. 108.

48. Robert Conquest, *The Great Terror: Stalin's Purge of the Thirties* (London: Macmillan, 1968), 43. Although a new edition of the book exists (*The Great Terror: A Reassessment* (London: Hutchison, 1990)) it was decided to use the original first version, because the author writes in the 1990 edition: 'The new information available since I wrote of the murder in the *Great Terror* validates the story then given in all points of substance, and I have had to amend it, there and here, only as to certain details' (p. 38).

49. The interrogation protocol of Operations Commissar Borisov of the Leningrad *Oblast* NKVD compiled by interrogator Molochnikov, 1 December 1934, Archives Case File No. OS-100807, vol. 25, for Nikolaev et al., cited in Diana P. Koenker and Ronald D. Bachman (eds), *Revelations from the Russian Archives* (Washington, DC: Library of Congress, 1997), 79.

50. Testimony of Seliverst Alekseevich Platych given to Lev Mironov of the GUGB NKVD on 2 December 1934, Archives Case File No. OS-100807, vol. 25 (with a notarized copy in vol. 15) for Nikolaev et al., cited by Koenker and Bachman (eds), *Revelations from the Russian Archives*, 79–81.

51. Orlov, *The Secret History of Stalin's Crimes*, 18–19.

52. Protocol signed by Professor Bogen et al. on 1 December 1934, cited by Koenker and Bachman (eds), *Revelations from the Russian Archives*, 74–5.

53. Written testimony of A. Poskrebyshev, former head of the Special Section of the CC to the Party Control Commisssion (N. M. Shvernik) of the CC CPSU on 28 July 1961, cited by Koenker and Bachman (eds), *Revelations from the Russian Archives*, 73–4.

54. Rayfield, *Stalin and his Hangmen*, 242.

55. Orlov, *The Secret History of Stalin's Crimes*, 21–4.

56. General Vlasik's written statement to the party commission of the CC CPSU of 17 March 1965, cited by Koenker and Bachman (eds), *Revelations from the Russian Archives*, 78.

57. General Vlasik's written statement to the party commission of the CC CPSU of 17 March 1965, cited by Koenker and Bachman (eds), *Revelations from the Russian Archives*, 78.

58. Affidavit in the file, recording the interview with General Vlasik on 17 February 1965, in Koenker and Bachman (eds), *Revelations from the Russian Archives*, 77.

59. General Vlasik's written statement to the party commission of the CC CPSU of 17 March 1965, in Koenker and Bachman (eds), *Revelations from the Russian Archives*, 78.

60. Affidavit in the file, recording the interview with General Vlasik on 17 February 1965, in Koenker and Bachman (eds), *Revelations from the Russian Archives*, 77.

61. Affidavit in the file, recording the interview with General Vlasik on 17 February 1965, in Koenker and Bachman (eds), *Revelations from the Russian Archives*, 77.

62. Orlov, *The Secret History of Stalin's Crimes*, 8.

63. Petrov and Skorkin, *Kto rukovodil NKVD, 1934–1941*, 295–6, 300–1.

64. Orlov, *The Secret History of Stalin's Crimes*, 5.

65. Alexander Nikolaevich Yakovlev, academician, member of the Politburo (at the time of signing the document), 'Some Thoughts on the Results of the Inquiry into the Circumstances Surrounding the Murder of S. M. Kirov', cited by Koenker and Bachman (eds), *Revelations from the Russian Archives*, 70–1. A copy of the final document of the 1990 investigation 'The memo of the Office of Public Prosecutor of the USSR and the KGB Investigation Department regarding the minute of A. N. Yakovlev "Some thoughts on the results of the inquiry into the circumstances surrounding the murder of S. M. Kirov"' of 14 June 1990 (in Russian) is in this author's files.

66. P. N. Pospelov, 'Materials on the Question of the Murder of S. M. Kirov', intro. Vijay Singh, *Revolutionary Democracy*, 2/1 (April 1996) <http://www.revolutionarydemocracy.org/rdv2n1/kirov.htm> (accessed 16 January 2014). See also Petr Nikolaevich Pospelov, 'Zapiska P. N. Pospelova ob ubiystve Kirova', *Svobodnaya Mysl*, 8 (May 1992), 64–71.

67. ORLOV FBI File Bureau 105-22869, Boston 62-1246-X7, of 11 September 1943, declassified. The case actually originated in Boston (File No. 100-12458), and, in his report to the Bureau dated 18 August 1942, SAC, Los Angeles, stated that 'investigation concerning Subject's residence in Los Angeles was requested of the Los Angeles Police Department, and they have advised as follows: [the owner] of the apartment house at 3360 West 9th Street, LA, has no tenants by subjects' name and her records do not indicate any in the past' (ORLOV FBI File Bureau 105-22869-XI, declassified).

68. ORLOV FBI File Bureau 100-91869 of 4 October 1943, declassified.

69. Director, FBI, letter to Assistant Attorney General William F. Tompkins, 16 July 1954, unclassified.

70. orlov FBI File Bureau 105-22869, New York 105-6073-186 of 29 April 1954, p. 10, unclassified.

71. This was his cover identity only in Spain.

72. Orlov certainly had in mind Lenin, Stalin, Trotsky, and other Bolshevik leaders, all of whom used 'party names' instead of their real names, but his case had nothing to do with the Party. Like most of the Chekists of Jewish origin, he had officially changed his name, from Leiba Lazarevich Feldbin to Lev Lazarevich Nikolsky.

73. The NKID had nothing to do with Nikolsky's trips abroad. The present writer is in possession of a copy of his passeeport pour l'étranger No. 104290 PB 23/38 in the name of Léon Nikolaeff (in Russian Lev Leonidovich Nikolaev) issued on 27 October 1933. The document was issued, not by the NKID, but by the OGPU, and signed personally by Yagoda. The destination of the trip was Austria.

74. Nikolsky was known and actively travelled with an Austrian passport in the name of Leo Feldbiene and an American passport in the name of William Goldin. Moreover, in the United States he often registered under the name of Alexander L. Berg or Igor Berg.

75. SCHWED was Nikolsky's regular code name in the OGPU and later the NKVD; and he never corresponded with the Central Committee.

76. Leiba Feldbin aka Lev Nikolsky aka Alexander Orlov was born on 21 August 1895 in Bobruisk, Byelorussia.

77. Nikolsky had never been deprived of his Soviet citizenship, nor had he ever appealed to the Soviet government denouncing it; his diplomatic passport had never been revoked; he also never applied to the American authorities asking to grant him the citizenship.

78. Record of sworn statement, File No. A2 472 619 in the ORLOV FBI File Bureau 105-22869, New York 105-6073-237, of 23 August 1954, pp. 34–47, declassified.

79. Record of sworn statement, File No. A2 472 619 in the ORLOV FBI File Bureau 105-22869, New York 105-6073-237, of 23 August 1954, pp. 34–47, declassified.

80. Record of sworn statement, File No. A2 472 619 in the ORLOV FBI File Bureau 105-22869, New York 105-6073-237, of 23 August 1954, p. 51, declassified.

81. See ORLOV's Bureau File 105-22869, where there is plenty of evidence against Orlov.

82. Hugo Dewar, *Assassins at Large* (London and New York: Wingate, 1951).

83. See Dewar, *Assassins at Large*, 144–63, ch. 'Who Killed Kirov'. Hugo Dewar was born in 1908 in Leyton. Joining the Independent Labour Party in 1928, he subsequently co-founded, with F. A. Ridley, the Marxist League. In 1931 he joined the Communist Party of Great Britain, to support its Balham group then battling against Stalinist policies, but was expelled in the following year. He took part in the founding of the Communist League, the first Trotskyist group in Britain, and continued to be active in 'Left Opposition' groups until he was drafted into the army in 1943. On his discharge, he became a tutor in adult

education, also writing many books and articles exposing Stalinism. He held firmly to his faith in revolutionary socialism until his death in June 1980. See Hugo Dewar Papers (MS 206), Modern Records Centre, University of Warwick.

84. Dallin, *Soviet Espionage*.

85. ORLOV FBI File Bureau 105-22869, New York 105-6073-286, of 8 June 1955, declassified.

CHAPTER 23

1. Testimony of Alexander Orlov, US Senate, 87th Congress, 28 September 1955, p. 2.

2. See David Price, 'Obituary for Mark Zborowski, 1908–1990', *Anthropology Newsletter*, 39/6 (1998), 31; Testimony of Mark Zborowski, US Senate, 84th Congress, Second Session on Scope of Soviet Activity in the United States, 2 March 1956, p. 123, Exhibit No. 5. Zborowski was survived by his wife, Regina Levy Zborowski, and their son George.

3. See John Earl Haynes and Harvey Klehr, *Early Cold War Spies: The Espionage Trials that Shaped American Politics* (New York: Cambridge University Press, 2006), 212.

4. Testimony of Mark Zborowski, US Senate, 84th Congress, Second Session, 29 February 1956, pt 4, p. 83.

5. It was not his 'espionage alias' as some authors suggest. See, e.g., papers of Susan Weissman of Saint Mary's College of California, USA, Henry Kasson's article in the *New Leader*, and Frank Fox, 'Mark Zborowski, the Spy who Came out of the Shtetl', *East European Jewish Affairs*, 29/1–2 (Summer 1999), 119–28.

6. Haynes, Klehr, and Vassiliev, *Spies*, 479.

7. Testimony of Mark Zborowski, US Senate, 84th Congress, Second Session, 29 February 1956, pt 4, p. 90.

8. Testimony of Mark Zborowski, US Senate, 84th Congress, Second Session on Scope of Soviet Activity in the United States, 2 March 1956, p. 104.

9. Haynes, Klehr, and Vassiliev, *Spies*, 479.

10. Born Lilia Estrina in Russia, codenamed SOSEDKA or NEIGHBOUR by the NKVD.

11. Haynes, Klehr, and Vassiliev, *Spies*, 479.

12. With reference to a report in Zborowski's KGB file (ASVRR, TULIP File No. 31660, vol. 1, p. 1), Costello and Tsarev claim that he was recruited in 1933 by an NKVD agent B-138 whose code name was JUNKER (*Deadly Illusions*, 322). In reality, Zborowski himself was agent B-138.

13. Haynes, Klehr, and Vassiliev, *Spies*, 479.

14. Andrew and Mitrokhin, *The Mitrokhin Archive*, 93. Moscow instructed its agents to photograph the Harvard papers and to obtain other documents

belonging to Trotsky, as they hoped to find tips about a possible Trotskyist conspiracy in Russia.

15. ORLOV FBI File, Bureau (105-22869), Serial 30, Finerty's deposition.

16. A copy of the letter signed 'Stein' and dated 27 December 1938 was later submitted as part of his testimony and is reproduced in full in Orlov, *The Legacy of Alexander Orlov.*

17. Costello and Tsarev, *Deadly Illusions*, 320-1, quoting the report of the Paris chief Georgy Kosenko (FIN) to Moscow of 25 June 1939, ASVRR, File tulip No. 31660, vol. 1, pp. 262-4.

18. Director Hoover to SAC New York, 1 October 1940, reproduced in Alan Gelfand, *The Gelfand Case: A Legal History of the Exposure of US Government Agents in the Leadership of the Socialist Workers Party* (Detroit, MI: Mehring Books, 1985), i. 233-5.

19. Kravchenko was deputy RU resident in Latin America from 1939 to December 1941 working in Mexico, Brazil, Peru, Ecuador, and Uruguay.

20. Orlov's testimony of 25 September 1955, in Orlov, *The Legacy of Alexander Orlov.*

21. For details, see Gary Kern, *The Kravchenko Case: One Man's War on Stalin*, paperback (New York: Enigma Books, 2007).

22. Costello and Tsarev, *Deadly Illusions*, 359; Haynes, Klehr, and Vassiliev, *Spies*, 480. See also Arthur Spencer, 'A Strange Interlude: A Footnote to the Soblen Case', *Survey* (October 1963). After Morros had agreed to become a double agent, for the next ten years the FBI was able to monitor the activities of the Soble ring before they rolled up the network in 1957.

23. VENONA, New York to Moscow, No. 594 of 1 May 1944.

24. BRIDE (one of the names of what later became known as VENONA), New York to Moscow, No. 1145 of 10 August 1944.

25. See Chapter 25.

26. See Al Slote, 'The Spy in the Law Quad', *Ann Arbor Observer* (December 1993), 81. Al further writes, 'But the real smoking gun is a letter in the [University of Michigan] Press's files. Dated November 29, 1960, it was written by the late Fred Wieck, then director of the Press. Wieck states that "Mr Alexander Orlov has just agreed to write for us a Soviet intelligence handbook... We have in turn agreed to make him an advance against royalties in the amount of six thousand dollars. Mr Orlov will deliver his manuscript in approximately thirteen months." The letter is addressed to Morse Allen, CIA, Washington, DC.' The present author's efforts to recover a copy of this letter were not successful. I am grateful to John Hilton of the *Ann Arbor Observer* for his help.

27. Orlov, *Handbook*, preface.

28. See Andrew and Mitrokhin, *The Mitrokhin Archive*, 117. The school was opened in November 1938 and in 1943 became the first Soviet Intelligence School of the NKVD. In September 1948 it became the High Intelligence School, later known as School 101, which was renamed the Red Banner

Institute in 1968 and the Andropov Institute after the deah of Yuri Andropov in 1984. At the end of 1994, after the collapse of perestroika, the Institute was upgraded to the Russian Foreign Intelligence Academy.

CHAPTER 24

1. From John Edgar Hoover, Director, FBI, to Legal Attaché, London, England, dispatched by Secret Air Courier, 16 July 1953. Subject: Espionage. 'Alexander Orlov,' the letter informed, 'wrote a series of four articles in the April, 1953, issue of "Life" magazine. He has since been interviewed and has admitted being an official of the NKVD in Europe up until 1938, when he defected.' The rest of the letter is blackened by the censor. FBI, 100-374183.

2. TNA: PRO KV 2/2878.

3. TNA: PRO KV 2/2878, extract for File No. n/n (later PF 605.075), Name: Orlov, Alexander, Serial 346b, vol. 7, date 24 July 1953.

4. This confusion was based on the fact that in 1929 one Konstantin Nikolsky applied for a British visa in Moscow with the intention of joining the Soviet Embassy staff in London; he was thought to be an OGPU agent.

5. Although Philby's articles from Spain were published by *The Times* without revealing the name of the author, Orlov could have learnt that SÖHNCHEN was sent to the rebel zone.

6. TNA: PRO KV 2/2878, FBI to MI5, No. 4624-65-745, 30 September 1953.

7. Krivitsky (author) and Kern (ed.), *MI5 Debrieifing*, 160.

8. Some Russian sources erroneously claimed, following Krivitsky, that Kral was an INO NKVD operative.

9. TNA: PRO KV 2/2879, PF 605.075, ORLOV, Minute Sheet, §62: T. Selmes Taylor, D.I.B. to R. T. Reed, D.I.A., 9 July 1955. After the 1953 re-organisation of the Security Service, D Branch became the division responsible for counter-espionage. Before he was promoted to Deputy Director of MI5 under Roger Hollis in 1956, Graham Mitchell had been in charge of D Branch. See also his declassified MI5 file, TNA: PRO KV 2/2029, PF 45251, vols 1–2 covering 1936–8. Both Eric Joseph Gardner CAMP and his wife Edith Joan CAMP were Communists. 'Also of concern was Eric Camp,' Richard Baxell, an expert on the British volunteers, writes, 'who had declared himself to be an aircraft designer from London when he volunteered for Spain. R. W. "Robbie" Robson, responsible for recruiting and vetting volunteers, was later reported as stating that he believed that Camp was a bad type who, "wanted to go to Spain, principally so that his wife would get an allowance" (TNA: PRO KV 2/2030, Eric Joseph Gardner Camp and Edith Joan Camp, Serial 281). In Spain, Camp quickly made himself unpopular with his superiors and was believed to be guilty of stealing cigarettes. Arthur Ollorenshaw, an instructor at the officer training school at Pozorubio, wrote a highly critical report of Camp's propensity for "telling tales", believing that Camp's descriptions of having passed

documents to the USSR and of being a professional crook were invented. Ollorenshaw believed that Camp was quite possibly mentally unhinged and should unquestionably "be excluded from the Party" (RGASPI, f. 545, op. 6, d. 113, l. 37). Others agreed; in a note signed "J.B." (probably the American Jim Bourne, who served as political commissar to the British Battalion in September 1937), Camp was described as having "no capacity for self-criticism. He deludes himself as well as others. Has illusions of self-importance and grandeur" (RGASPI, f. 545, op. 6, d. 113, l. 32). Camp deserted from the battalion on 20 September 1938, though he did later return. He was, unsurprisingly, assessed as being "weak and a bad type" (RGASPI, f. 545, op. 6, d. 113, l. 37). Back in Britain after his Spanish experiences, Camp registered for employment as an aircraft draughtsman, but the 1936 court case meant that no employer was prepared to offer him work. Besides, MI5 were obviously very strongly in favour of black-listing him from this type of work. As a result, Camp remained unemployed, and on 6 May 1941 Special Branch suggested reregistering him under a different employment (TNA: PRO KV 2/2030, Serial 211). In September 1942, still unemployed, Camp joined the RAF. Not surprisingly, he was very discreetly kept under observation, as MI5 were aware that if Camp knew he was being watched he may well become disgruntled and create trouble for the authorities (Letter from C. H. Sargant of MI5 to Squadron Leader Elliott of the Air Ministry, 31 March 1943, TNA: PRO KV 2/2030, Serial 285a). In April 1943 Camp was arrested and charged with forging a cheque. A suggestion to discharge Camp from the RAF was deferred, in order to give him a second chance, perhaps because his commanding officer's report stated that, though Camp openly admitted holding Communist views, he was an exemplary soldier and did not engage in spreading propaganda. However, Camp was barred from any confidential work, as he was deemed to be completely financially untrustworthy. Following Camp's arrest, his description of his earlier arrest in 1936 and his domestic situation began to unravel. After his marriage to a Mildred Todd in 12 April 1943, it was discovered that Camp was still married to his first wife, Edith, and the Metropolitan Police brought charges of bigamy against him. In his witness statement Camp confessed that he had, indeed, been passing aircraft information to the Russians via his wife (who was a Party member) when he was arrested in 1936. He also admitted to having passed on more documents to her at the end of February 1943, though he recanted this in a later statement made on 24 February 1944. However, all the witness reports, including his wife's, contradicted Camp's story of his supposed espionage, and the British authorities eventually reached the same conclusion that Ollorenshaw and Bourne had in Spain: that Camp was a serial fantasist (Special Branch theorized that the several anonymous letters they had received over the years, accusing Camp of various activities, might, in fact, have been sent by Camp himself; see TNA: PRO KV 2/2030, Serial 328a). Additional charges of "effecting a public mischief at common law" and "doing an act likely to mislead" were added, and Camp was eventually sentenced to nine months in prison (TNA: PRO KV 2/2030 Serial 340a). When the possibility of Camp being an undercover member of the Communist Party was raised, a sardonic assessment by the Security Services concluded: "We have little evidence to show that he has been any more faithful to the Party than he has been to his wife" (TNA: PRO KV 2/2030, Serial 267)' (Dr Baxell to author, 28 August 2012).

10. J. Edgar Hoover to the FBI liaison (Legal Attaché or legat) in London John A. Cimperman, 28 April 1948, in Krivitsky's FBI File No. 100-11146, part 2 of 4, PDF, p. 18.

11. See TNA: PRO KV 2/2878, extract from Note for File No. 605.075, dated 23 January 1940–25 January 1940.

12. Borodin was born in Chicago in 1911 in the family of Mikhail Gruzenberg, party name 'Borodin'. Borodin senior worked for the Comintern in Mexico, the USA, and Britain in 1919–22, and was the Comintern's chief political adviser in China in 1923–7. While in Britain, Borodin was arrested in Glasgow in August 1922 and put in Barlinnie Prison before he was deported to Moscow in February 1923. For details, see Dan N. Jacobs, *Borodin: Stalin's Man in China* (Cambridge, MA: Harvard University Press, 1981). For the only account of his father to appear in Russian, see Norman Borodin, 'Kto byl Mikhail Borodin', *Otchizna*, 8 (1971), 9–11. Norman Borodin, whose brother Fred was also born in the USA, joined the OGPU in March 1930, and in 1931 was sent as an 'illegal' resident to Oslo, Norway. He was later transferred to Germany and after the Nazis had come to power moved to Paris. Upon his return to Moscow in 1934, Norman attended the resident course at the Red Army Chemical Academy before he was sent to the USA in 1935. There, codenamed granit and operating under the alias 'George Ryan', he was credited with running three important sources. Nevertheless, three years later, in 1938, Borodin was recalled to Moscow and in September transferred to the censorship agency known as Glavlit. According to the Soviet sources, but without any documented reference, during the war Borodin was on an undercover mission in Berlin posing as a foreign member of the Swiss Red Cross Mission, but no further details are known. In 1955 in the KGB he headed the department dealing with foreign correspondents in Moscow, and from 1961 Colonel Borodin worked at the Agency Press News ('Novosti'), a KGB front, where one of his subordinates was a young apprentice, Yuri Bezmenov, who later defected to the USA and settled in Canada. Norman Borodin died in 1974. About A. Samsonov there is no information.

13. Gutzeit, born in 1901, served together with Nikolsky/Orlov in the Economic Directorate before he was transferred to the INO in 1933, where, from March, he headed its 8th section. After the establishment of diplomatic relations with the USA, he was sent to New York as the first NKVD station chief under the

cover of Vice-Consul at the Soviet Consulate General. In 1938 he returned to Moscow and was promoted to head the scientific and technical section of the 5th (foreign intelligence) GUGB Department. Gutzeit was arrested in October 1938, sentenced, and shot in February 1939.

14. Milstein operated in New York, first as a member, and then suddenly as the head of the RU station from 1935 to 1938 using the alias 'Milsky', and then, under the same alias, he was on an alleged inspection tour visiting Canada, the United States, and Mexico in the summer of 1944. For details about his activities in the USA during the Spanish Civil War, see Boris Volodarsky, *Between Stalin and Franco: Soviet Intelligence Services in the Spanish Civil War, 1936–1939* (forthcoming).

15. 'Topics of the Times: A Model Soviet General', *New York Times*, 20 November 1992.

16. Bukov, born Altmann, was another high-ranking officer of Jewish extraction who managed to survive Stalin's purges. Before America, Bukov was posted to Germany (1920–8), where he also operated 'from the illegal position'. In 1935, using a complex route, he was again sent abroad, passing through several countries before arriving in New York. As soon as the Spanish Civil War broke out, he was appointed 'illegal' resident. After his successful return from the USA, he was given a three-month holiday, then in July 1939 he was invited to lecture at the Central School for the Chiefs of Staff and from 1940 was teaching tradecraft at the High Intelligence School of the Red Army. When the Nazi troops attacked Russia in June 1941, Bukov was transferred to the 2nd Moscow Institute of Foreign Languages, where he headed the Department of Geography. Many military interpreters and intelligence officers graduated from this institute.

17. Vladimir Sergeyev, 'Da Vinci sovetskoi vneshnei razvedki', *Nezavisimoe voennoe obozrenie*, 10 June 2006. Bazarov's official SVR biography claims that one of his sources was the congressman Samuel Dickstein, a Jew born in Lithuania. A well-known book, *The Haunted Wood* by Weinstein and Vassiliev, also claims that Dickstein was allegedly paid $1,250 a month by the NKVD from 1937 to early 1940. But, as already mentioned, in June (or early July) 1937 Bazarov was recalled to Moscow for a Communist Party *chistka* that lasted until March 1938. Although he was 'cleared', he never returned to the USA, was arrested on 3 July 1938, and later shot. It is doubtful that Dickstein could have been his source, although we saw that during the early period of the Spanish Civil War important intelligence from the US administration was indeed regularly reported to Stalin by the NKVD. This was, of course, thanks to the activities of at least three sources in the US Department of State, codenamed erich, kiy, and 19 (Laurence Duggan). For Bazarov's autobiographies written for the Party Control Commission in August and October 1937, see RGASPI, f. 17, op. 97, d. 76, pp. 3–5, 9–18, 20–4.

18. For STOTT, see TNA: PRO KV 2/2878, p. 7, 26 October 1953. The acronym STOTT, which for whatever reason is not explained or even mentioned (except for one footnote) in Jeffery's *MI6*, stands for a British intelligence station within an embassy in a foreign country. 'When we needed information from abroad on our developing cases,' writes Robert Lamphere, 'we'd send a memo to STOTT, our acronym for the British intelligence office in Washington, which would give copies of our requests to both the MI5 and MI6 reps' (see Lamphere and Schachtman, *The FBI–KGB War*, 131).

19. Lamphere and Schachtman, *The FBI–KGB War*, 7–8.

20. Petrov and Skorkin, *Kto rukovodil NKVD, 1934–1941*, 107–8.

21. TNA: PRO KV 2/2878, Alexander ORLOV: Comments and Questions, E. McBarnet, D.1.A., 17 November 1953.

22. TNA: PRO KV 2/2878, PF 605.075, ORLOV, Minute Sheet, Minute 10, §7, 6 November 1953.

23. About Akhmerov, codenamed YUNGA, MER, ALBERT, and GOLD, who was also known as Michael Green, Michael Adamec, and Bill Grienke, see Andrew and Mitrokhin, *The Mitrokhin Archive*, and Haynes, Klehr, and Vassiliev, *Spies*.

24. TNA: PRO KV 2/2878, File Alexander ORLOV, PF 128.288, GRIENKE, Correspondence,

25. For an authoritative opinion regarding Harry Hopkins and his relations with Soviet intelligence, read Verne W. Newton, 'A Soviet Agent? Harry Hopkins?' *New York Times*, 28 December 1990.

26. SAC Kansas City to Director FBI, 15 November 1962, Serial 790; SAC Baltimore to Director FBI, 28 March 1963, Serial 818, Akhmerov's FBI file No. 65-57905. See John Earl Haynes, James G. Ryan, and Harvey Klehr, 'Helen Lowry and Earl Browder: The Genealogy of a KGB Agent and her Relationship to the Chief of the CPUSA'; *American Communist History*, 6/2 (December 2007), and, by the same authors, 'Correction to "Helen Lowry and Earl Browder"', *American Communist History*, 8/1 (June 2009). See also Andrew and Mitrokhin, *The Mitrokhin Archive*, 138, and Massing, *This Deception*, 155.

27. Alexander Vassiliev's notes on 'YUNG to the Centre, 9 November 1937'. Yellow Notebook, no. 2, p. 21.

28. Relations between US and British services seriously deteriorated in 1951, owing to the defection of Maclean and Burgess and subsequent recall of Philby from Washington.

29. Akhmerov's official SVR biography (<http://svr.gov.ru/history/ah.htm>) is a typical hagiography full of factual errors. Its improved version, based exclusively on the KGB sources, is at <http://www.documentstalk.com/wp/akhmerov-iskhak-1901-1976> (accessed 16 January 2014).

30. From 1926 to 1929 Markin, who was described by Whittaker Chambers as a man of 'three particular passions—intrigue, the piano and Germany', operated in Germany on behalf of the IV Directorate (intelligence) of the Red Army.

Walter Krivitsky knew him as 'Oskar'. From 1930 to 1932 he completed his university education in Moscow, at the same time heading the propaganda section of the KIM (youth branch of the Comintern) Executive Committee. In 1932 Markin moved from the Chocolate House (RKKA intelligence head-quarters) to the Lubyanka INO offices and was promptly sent as an 'illegal' resident to the United States. In New York Chambers knew him as 'Herman'. The FBI learned about Markin's existence only thirteen years after his death in New York in August 1934.

31. See Weinstein and Vassiliev, *The Haunted Wood*, 36. As demonstrated by the arrests of ten Russian 'illegals' in the USA in June 2010, this is equally easy even now.

32. Information by V. S. Antonov, SVR's Historical Collection.

33. Leo Graff Penn, a pharmacist born in Odessa, arrived in the United States in May 1906. His father was indicated as Bernard Penn, and his mother as Valerie Penn, both born in Russia.

34. TNA: PRO KV 2/2878, Memo: Gregory Borisovich Grafpen, with aliases, 29 January 1954.

35. IISG, Stukken betreffende E. Fimmen in archief ITF, Edo Fimmen personal correspondence 159/6/12, dossier 1.

36. That he notoriously kept on calling 'Fourth Department' in all his testimonies and publications.

37. See Ruth Price, *The Lives of Agnes Smedley* (New York: Oxford University Press, 2005), chs 8–10. Sadly, there are several errors in this otherwise very interesting book, mainly concerning the activities of the Soviet intelligence personnel as well as their personal names. Thus, Berzin's name and patronym-ics were Jan Karlovich, and not 'Ian A.', as stated by the author, who confused the intelligence chief with his namesake, Jan Antonovich Berzin, a diplomat. Kuczynski, a GRU operator and Smedley's rival for a place in Sorge's bed, was Ursula, not Sonja. Mironov, mentioned by both Louis Gibarti and Max Klausen, was almost certainly not 'Jakob Mirov-Abramov', as the author suggests, but rather Lev Mironov, NKVD counter-intelligence chief, while 'Jakob Mirov-Abramov' was in reality Jakov Abramov-Mirov, a professional military intelligence officer. The Comintern never had a 'central committee' (p. 7), its educational establishment was known as International Lenin School (ILS), not 'Institute' (p. 170), while the Comintern and 'purely Soviet intelli-gence' never 'officially merged' as asserted in the book (p. 170).

38. Price, *The Lives of Agnes Smedley*, 191.

39. 'Summary of Information: Smedley Agnes', 19 September 1947, ID 923289, RG 319, quoted in Price, *The Lives of Agnes Smedley*, 382–3.

40. Alfred Kohlberg, 'Soviet-American Spy Prodigies', *Plain Talk*, 2/8 (May 1948), 21.

41. 'It is not that I fear anything at all, or fear the final outcome,' she noted in a letter. 'It is simply that the report in Manchuria showed so definitely that it came from the British Secret Service, and that the American Consul was cooperating with them in "watching" me. I don't want to be watched, even when I am doing perfectly legitimate things as I am in China' (Smedley to Roe, 12 April 1929, Gilbert Roe Papers, quoted in Price, *The Lives of Agnes Smedley*, 183).

42. TNA: PRO KV 2/2879, PF 605.075, ORLOV, Minute Sheet, §131, 24 August 1955.

43. TNA: PRO KV 2/2879, PF 605.075, ORLOV, Note for File, Serial 64a, dated 28 March 1956.

44. Oleg Adolfovich Lyalin was a KGB officer of what was then Department V (like 'victory') responsible for abductions, assassinations, and other special operations on foreign soil, a successor of Serebryansky's 'Yasha Group' and Sudoplatov's Special Tasks. Accordingly, a Line F officer, Lyalin, was sent to London in the 1960s, posing as an official of the Soviet Trade Delegation. After a while, he began an affair with his secretary, Irina Teplyakova, and started drinking. All this led to his recruitment as a defector-in-place by MI5 in the spring of 1971. On 30 August Lyalin was arrested near Warren Street tube station with Irina in the car. It was already late evening. He was brought to the police station, charged with driving while drunk, and kept in custody until morning. At 9.00 a.m. he was transported to the court for hearing and quickly released on bail. But, instead of returning to his duties, Lyalin decided to stay in Britain. He had provided details of Moscow's sabotage plans in London, Washington, Paris, and other Western capitals. As a result, British authorities expelled 105 Soviet officials suspected of being KGB and GRU operatives on 25 September 1971. Many of those individuals concerned had been known to the Security Service for some time, but over the period of his secret collaboration Lyalin had confirmed a number of probable identifications and, because officers were rotated on a regular basis, added new names. Lyalin was given a new identity and an appropriate accommodation. He continued working with MI5 until his death on 12 February 1995, aged 57. 'Though the British government released few details about Lyalin after his defection,' Christopher Andrew writes, 'the Attorney General told the Commons that he was charged with "the organization of sabotage within the United Kingdom" and "the elimination of individuals judged to be enemies of the USSR"'. The KGB was caught completely off-guard by Lyalin's defection. Two days after the expulsion, Brezhnev cut short a tour of Eastern Europe for an emergency Politburo meeting, which led to a mass recall of Line F officers from the foreign capitals.

45. John 'Jack' Dziak to author, 26–7 February 2013.

CHAPTER 25

1. See Orlov FBI file, from SAC New York (105–6073) to the Director, FBI (105–22869) dated 26 August 1963.
2. See Costello and Tsarev. *Deadly llusions*, p. 483*n* 18. This source remains unidentified. The author of this book visited the place in October 2013.
3. Slote, 'The Spy in the Law Quad', 75.
4. Female staff who run the files and keep them up to date.
5. See Ernesto Guevara, Brian Loveman, and Thomas M. Davies, *Guerrilla Warefare* (Lincoln: University of Nebraska Press, 1985), 8.
6. Slote, 'The Spy in the Law Quad', 79.
7. Slote, 'The Spy in the Law Quad', 79.
8. Slote, 'The Spy in the Law Quad', 79.
9. See Orlov, 'The Theory and Practice of Soviet Intelligence', *Studies in Intelligence*, 7/2 (Spring 1963). The article was declassified thirty years later.
10. Orlov, *Handbook of Intelligence and Guerrilla Warfare* (Ann Arbor: University of Michigan Press, 1963), with two follow-up editions in 1965 and 1972. In 1969 the same publisher would publish Elsa Poretsky's memoirs about her husband Ignace Reiss, and Babette Gross's recollections about Willi Münzenberg in 1974.
11. See also a World Association of International Studies (WAIS) 2013 discussion <http://waisworld.org/go.jsp?id=02a&o=77481> (accessed 16 January 2014).
12. Jane Austen, *Pride and Prejudice*, ch. 47.
13. See Boris Volodarsky, *EL caso Orlov* (Barcelona: Critica, 2013), 231 and 447 n. 121.
14. Cf. Andrew and Mitrokhin, *The Mitrokhin Archive*, 75. The files noted by Mitrokhin, comments Professor Andrew, make clear that Deutsch was the first to devise this recruitment strategy (p. 764).
15. Anonymous, 'Handbook of Intelligence and Guerrilla Warfare by Alexander Orlov', *Studies in Intelligence* (1963), A28–A29, unclassified.
16. See TNA: PRO KV 2/811. See also KV 2/1021 'Percy Eded Glading', vols 1–6; KV 4/228, 'Report on the Operations of F.2.C. in Connection with Russian Intelligence during War 1939–1945'; KV 4/227, History of the Operations of M.S. during the War 1939–1945, 'Percy Glading'; KV 4/185–196, 'Liddell Diaries'.
17. Costello and Tsarev claim: 'Until the KGB archive files were released... the assumption had been that Maly was the *éminence grise*. This incorrect inference had first been argued by co-author Costello in his book on the Blunt case, *Mask of Treachery*... Two years later Christopher Andrew and Oleg Gordievsky, in their book, *Inside the KGB*, pp. 156–9, advanced the same theory, supposedly on the authority of the latter author's recollections of his service with the First Chief Directorate. It has been established by Costello and Tsarev in conversations with Gordievsky that his failure to appreciate Orlov's true role

was because neither he nor anyone else in the KGB below the highest level had seen Orlov's operational files until the summer of 1990 when the Russian author was given special access. Since it was Orlov's successor whose portrait was hung alongside Maly's in the memorial room, Gordievsky gave Maly the credit for being the mastermind behind the Cambridge network' (Costello and Tsarev, *Deadly Illusions*, 453, n. 65).

18. Costello and Tsarev, *Deadly Illusions*, p. ix.
19. Slote, 'The Spy in the Law Quad', 77.
20. Costello and Tsarev, *Deadly Illusions*, 1; emphases added. The authors further note: 'Though he had aged heavily, his features were easily recognized by the visitor from the photographs in a thirty-year-old administrative file, which described him as: "Medium height, athletic build, nose slightly broken, balding head, hair turning grey. Wears a short moustache, also grey. Very resolute features and manners. Walk, gestures and speech sharp; steady eyes. Has an excellent command of English with an American accent. Speaks German more or less fluently, can express himself in French and Spanish."' Costello and Tsarev give the reference for this description (p. 431, n. 2) as the KGB File No. 76659, 'ALEXANDER ORLOV', vol. 1, p. 2, and add that the photos and description of Orlov had originally been prepared by the NKVD in July 1938, before the cancellation of the search for him after his flight to the United States. Judging by many photos and even video footage of Orlov in Spain in the period of 1937–8, his hair was dark and his moustache black, *not* grey. His eyes were *not* steady, as testified by many who knew him in 1938 and later. He spoke very little German, could hardly express himself in French and Spanish, and, contrary to Louis Fischer's recollections (*Men and Politics* (London: Cape, 1941), 343), did *not* speak English well until much later. Finally, the KGB file reference, as well as the file name, also seems to be incorrect.
21. See Slote, 'The Spy in the Law Quad', 77.
22. Oleg Kalugin, *Spymaster: My 32 Years in Intelligence and Espionage against the West* (rev. edn; New York: Basic Books, 2009), 109.

CHAPTER 26

1. See Chapter 23.
2. The information was provided by a source that cannot be identified.
3. This unique collection is now available for researchers at Les Archives Nationales in Paris and Fontainebleau.
4. CIA, Orlov DST File, p. 6.
5. Haynes and Klehr, *Venona*, 211.
6. RGASPI, Secretariat of Dimitrov, f. 495, op. 73, 74, and 75; Beria to Comrade Dimitrov, 29–30 November 1940, N 5170/b (RGASPI, f. 495, op. 74, d. 478, l. 1; Fitin to Dimitrov, ibid, l. 3).
7. VENONA, KGB Moscow–New York, No. 424 of 1 July 1942.

8. It was certainly Albert Joachimovich Syrkin (Sirkin), alias 'Bernardi', who served in the press section of the Soviet Embassy in Italy in 1924 and joined the OGPU in 1925 (according to other sources, 1926). Syrkin was an INO officer and operated as an illegal in Italy, France and Germany. In September 1937, Syrkin became deputy of Yakov Serebryansky in what was known as Yasha's Group for Special Tasks in Paris. As a member of this special unit, Syrkin took part in the abduction of General Kutepov in January 1930. Syrkin and his wife, Vera Syrkina, were in close friendly relations with NKVD officers Umansky, Chapsky, Ilk, Spiegelglass, Karin and others mentioned in this work. Both Syrkin and his wife were arrested on 10 November 1938 on Beria's personal orders. Albert Sirkin was shot in March 1940.

9. Almost certainly Aristarkh Aristarkhovich Rigin (alias 'Rylsky'), born 1887. Rigin was a commissioned INO officer from 1922, with numerous foreign postings: as attaché in China (1922–4), Denmark (1924–5), 2nd Secretary in Japan (1925), 2nd Secretary of the Soviet Embassy in France (1925–7), when Nikolayev/Orlov was on his first foreign mission there accredited with the Commercial Delegation, in Italy (1927–8), again in China (1935–6), and then was transferred to the military intelligence directorate and promoted to Brigadier-Commissar. Rigin's last assignment was in Paris (1936–7). While stationed in Spain, Orlov was a regular guest at the Soviet Embassy in Paris, where he certainly met his old colleague. Rigin was arrested in Moscow in September 1937, and shot a year later.

10. This is another proof that Orlov almost certainly read books written by Besedovsky and published in Berlin, Paris, and London in 1929–31 (see Bibliography). The real name of the officer was Zakhar Ilyich Volovich, alias 'Vladimir Borisovich Yanovich'.

11. See Boris Volodarsky, *El caso Orlov* (Barcelona: Crítica, 2013), 231, 447 n. 121.

12. CIA, Orlov DST File, p. 52.

13. See Jeffery, *MI6*, 182. Jeffery cautiously writes: 'Cumming declined to help organise a visa for him after the Foreign Office had refused to issue one.'

14. Andrew Cook, *On His Majesty's Secret Service: Sidney Reilly Codename ST1* (Brimscombe: Tempus, 2002), 208.

15. See GARF, VOKS, f. 5283, op. 1, d. 126, l. 9. See also International Institute of Social History (IISG), Amsterdam, Boris Victorovič Savinkov Papers, 1917–24.

16. Besedowsky, *Den Klauen der Tscheka Entronnen*, 86–94.

17. CIA, Orlov DST File, p. 53.

18. See Grigory Besedovsky, *Revelations of a Soviet Diplomat* (London: Williams and Norgate, 1931), and *Sydney Morning Herald*, 5 October 1929, p. 17. In November 1930, Arthur Henderson, then Foreign Secretary, stated in the House of Commons that members of the OGPU were permitted to enter Britain. As an example it was claimed that 'Moses Roisenman arrived in England in June 1930 under a false name'. He was erroneously believed to be 'the chief of the

Foreign Section of the OGPU'. The *Daily Mail* even reported that Roisenman 'is known to have been in touch with a number of military spies, English and foreign, in order to obtain information *re* latest types of tanks, armoured cars and big guns' (5 July 1930). See also Lt Col. Arthur Henry Lane, *The Alien Menace: A Statement of the Case* (London: Boswell Publishing Co., 1933). In reality, Boris Anisimovich Roisenman was a member of the Presidium of the Central Control Commission and at the same time of the Collegium of the People's Commissariat of the Workers–Peasants' Control responsible for the personnel of Soviet representations abroad and for their proper functioning. See Leonid Mlechin, *MID: Ministry Inostrannykh Del—tainaya diplomatiya Kremlya* (Moscow: Tsentropoligraf, 2011).

19. See Besedovsky, *Revelations of a Soviet Diplomat* .
20. CIA, Orlov DST File, p. 53.
21. For the Vernik episode, see Costello and Tsarev, *Deadly Illusions*, 111–13.
22. No file reference. Document 16, Expenses of EXPRESS GROUP in France, 1 February 1934, in this author's archive. The copy of the file is at the Cañada Blanch Centre of the LSE.
23. TNA: PRO, Personal File Grigoriy BESEDOVSKIY, KV 2/2670-2671, Serial 32a, of October 1929.
24. *Jewish Telegraphic Agency*, 1 August 1930.
25. Christopher Andrew notes: 'During the early Cold War, the Paris residency also appears to have been the most successful promoter of active measures designed to influence Western opinion and opinion-formers' (Andrew and Mitrokhin, *The Mitrokhin Archive*, 601–2).
26. TNA: PRO, Personal File Grigoriy BESEDOVSKIY, KV 2/2670-2671, Serial 111a, 19 March.1953.
27. Andrew and Mitrokhin, *The Mitrokhin Archive*, 602.
28. CIA, Orlov DST File, p. 54.
29. See her book Elisabeth K. Poretsky, *Our Own People: A Memoir of 'Ignace Reiss' and his Friends* (Ann Arbor: University of Michigan Press, 1969).
30. Surprisingly, even such a well-researched account as Haynes, Klehr, and Vassiliev, *Spies*, states that 'Poretsky (often known by his pseudonym, Ignace Reiss)' was 'a senior GRU officer' (pp. 5, 230).
31. CIA, Orlov DST File, p. 54.
32. CIA, Orlov DST File, p. 57.
33. Orlov, *The Secret History of Stalin's Crimes*, p. 230-1. See also Andrew and Gordievsky, *KGB* (1992); Andrew and Mitrokhin, *The Mitrokhin Archive* (1999); and Andrew, *The Defence of the Realm* (2009), p. 183.
34. Orlov's DST File, p. 58.
35. Because of the Communist Party role in the Soviet society, the Party Committee, alongside the Collegium, belonged to the governing bodies of the NKVD. Maria Nikolskaya, as seen from the documents, had never been a member. See N. Petrov and K. Skorkin, *Kto rukovodil NKVD, 1934–1941*

(Moscow: Zvenia, 1999); N. Petrov and A. Kokurin (eds), *Lubyanka, 1917–1991* (Moscow: Materik, 2003).

36. Alexander Orlov, *Handbook of Intelligence and Guerrilla Warfare* (Ann Arbor: University in Michigan Press, 1963), 53.
37. Orlov's DST File, p. 59.
38. Orlov's DST File, p. 60.
39. See Orlov, *The March of Time*, 124–62 (ch. 6 'Sidney Reilly—Britain's Intelligence Ace'); Gazur, *Secret Assignment* (ch. 26 'Reilly, Ace of Spies'). It is possible that later Orlov learned the details of the operation from the book by Paul W. Blackstock, *The Secret Road to World War Two: Soviet Versus Western Intelligence, 1921–1939* (Chicago: Quadrangle Books, 1969), which contains plenty of inaccuracies.
40. Gazur, *Secret Assignment*, 503–4.
41. See Primakov et al. (eds), *Ocherki*, ii. 113.
42. Artuzov served as head of KRO OGPU from 13 June 1922 to 22 November 1927 (Administrative Order UD GPU No. 102 of 7 July 1922); see Petrov and Skorkin, *Kto rukovodil NKVD, 1934–1941*, 94. About Puzitsky, see Administrative order AOU No. 14/228 of 5 December 1922.
43. Jeffery, *MI6*, 182–3.
44. Andrew and Mitrokhin, *The Mitrokhin Archive*,45.
45. Costello and Tsarev, *Deadly Illusions*, 35.
46. Jeffery, *MI6*, 182.
47. Primakov et al. (eds), *Ocherki*, ii. 122.
48. Andrew and Mitrokhin, *The Mitrokhin Archive*, 46.
49. Jeffery, *MI6*, 184.
50. Orlov, *The March of Time*, 139.

CHAPTER 27

1. Orlov, *The March of Time*, edited by Phillip Knightley.
2. Orlov, *The March of Time*, 342.
3. See Vaupshasov, *Na trevozhnykh perekryostkakh*, ch. 'Rytsari svobody'.
4. Instytut Pamięci Narodowej, Warszawa, Karol Świerczewski 'Walter' (1897–1947).
5. RGASPI, Special collection. For a full text of the letter, see Pozharskaya and Saplin, *Komintern i grazhdanskaya voina v Ispanii*, 390–2.
6. For details, see Preston, *We Saw Spain Die*, 315–17. Jay wrote to Carlos Baker: 'At Teruel, where it was bitterly cold, EH saved my eardrums when we were on a granite hilltop with no place to hide and being bombed to hell by tri-motor Savoias by showing me how to hold my mouth open by means of a pencil between my teeth.'
7. Baxell, *Unlikely Warriors*, 301–2. In the evening of 6 December, as Attlee himself recorded, the volunteers were paraded to greet the Labour Party

leaders. To loud cheers, Baxell writes, No. 1 Company was renamed the Major Attlee Company in his honour, and the visitors were greeted by a volley of shots 'in welcome and in memory of the fallen'. Fred Copeman introduced the visiting delegation to the members of the battalion. During the same month Professor J. B. S. Haldane took Copeman's advice to go home but returned to visit the British fighters at Mas de las Matas on the Teruel front with Harry Pollitt. And on Christmas Eve the American singer Paul Robeson sang for the Internationals (pp. 302–3).

8. Baxell, *Unlikely Warriors*, 344.
9. Baxell, *Unlikely Warriors*, 346.
10. Costello and Tsarev, *Deadly Illusions*, 300–1; emphasis added. No documentary source is given to support this claim.
11. Primakov et al. (eds), *Ocherki*, iii. 143–4.
12. V. Kardin, 'Pan Walter' *Sovershenno sekretno*, 7 (July 2000), 26–7 <sovsekretno.ru> (accessed 17 January 2014).
13. Instytut Pamięci Narodowej, Warszawa, Karol Świerczewski 'Walter' (1897–1947).
14. Special Report to Stalin by N. I. Yezhov and L. P. Beria with the attachment of investigation material on M. E. Koltsov, 'Top Secret', No. 109103, 27.9.1938. APRF, f. 3, op. 24, d. 366, ll. 55–64.
15. Preston, *We Saw Spain Die*, 173.
16. Preston, *We Saw Spain Die*.
17. Interview with Martha Świerczewska, Radio *Ekho Moskvy*, 18 April 2010.
18. See Dimitrov, *The Diary of Georgi Dimitrov*, 75, telegram to Manuilsky and Moskvin, 28 September 1938. Very noticeable is Manuilsky's response (Dimitrov's diary entry of 24 October), which the editor of its English version interpreted as 'a perceptive letter from Manuilsky in which he anticipates Soviet strategy after the German attack in 1941' (p. 75). In reality, in his letter of 19 October 1938, Manuilsky wrote: 'The unity of the international workers' movement . . . creates the conditions for a successful war against fascist Germany, Italy, and Japan' (p. 87).
19. Lurie and Kochik, *GRU*, 179–80.
20. Instytut Pamięci Narodowej, Warszawa, Karol Świerczewski 'Walter' (1897–1947): 'Realizował tam działania zlecone i nadzorowane bezpośrednio przez sowiecki wywiad zagraniczny.'
21. Instytut Pamięci Narodowej, Warszawa, Karol Świerczewski 'Walter' (1897–1947).
22. Orlov, *The March of Time*, 346.
23. Kardin, 'Pan Walter'.
24. Interview with Martha Świerczewska, Radio *Ekho Moskvy*, 18 April 2010.
25. Paul Preston met her in the late 1990s. Preston to author, 29 May 2013.
26. After the forced departure of Maly and Deutsch from London in the second half of 1937, their agents' network ceased to exist, while the purges led to

general chaos in the Moscow Centre and its foreign stations, with 70% of operatives shot, imprisoned, or dismissed from the service. When Eitingon met Burgess in Paris in August 1938, the latter complained he was afraid that Cairncross, 'a novice, might drop out altogether feeling isolated' (ASVRR, File list/Cairncross, No. 83896, vol. 1, p. 42, quoted by West and Tsarev, *The Crown Jewels*, 209). Burgess himself was quite uncertain what to do as at the time he was unsuccessfully trying to get employed by MI6. Eitingon's report about the meeting is in his personal file PIERRE, dated 9 August 1938, File No. 33797, vol. 1, pp. 104–7, quoted by Costello and Tsarev, *Deadly Illusions*, 237.

CHAPTER 28

1. Haynes, Klehr, and Vassiliev, *Spies*, 541.
2. Volodarsky, *El caso Orlov*, focuses on Soviet intelligence operations in Spain, but is in Spanish.
3. Andrew and Mitrokhin, *The Mitrokhin Archive*, 707.
4. West, MASK.
5. Jeffery, *MI6*, 649.
6. Jeffery, *MI6*, 705–9.
7. Andrew and Mitrokhin, *The Mitrokhin Archive*, 707–8.
8. According to Dr Kowalsky (*Stalin and the Spanish Civil War*, ch. 13), 167 wireless operators, interception specialists, and signallers from the USSR served in Spain between November 1936 and March 1939 (RGVA, f. 33987, op. 3, d. 1143, l. 127). On 22 February 1937 Uritsky (the GRU Director whom Kowalsky calls 'section X chief') reported to People's Commissar of Defence Voroshilov: 'In November 1936 a group of our officers organized a SIGINT detachment for the Spanish army. Work began in December 1936 with the deployment of intercept centres in Rocafort (8 km north-west of Valencia), a northern group in Barcelona, a southern group in Villaflora (6 km north-west of Murcia), and a reserve group in Torrejon de Ardos . . . The radio intelligence service sends reports to the general staff approximately twice each day. According to the communiqués of our advisers, these reports provide highly reliable intelligence on the enemy' (RGVA, f. 33987, op. 3, d. 1010, l. 199).
9. Paul Preston, 'Reading History: The Spanish Civil War', *History Today*, 32/11 (November 1982), 45–7.
10. Andrew and Mitrokhin, *The Mitrokhin Archive*, 707–8. See Caroline Kennedy-Pipe, *Russia and the World, 1917–1991* (London: Arnold, 1998).
11. Andrew and Mitrokhin, *The Mitrokhin Archive*, 708.
12. John Limond Hart, *The CIA's Russians* (Annapolis, MD: Naval Institute Press, 2003), 20.
13. Cf. Andrew and Mitrokhin, *The Mitrokhin Archive*, 708.
14. See, e.g., Francisco 'Quico' Martínez Lopet, *Guerrillero contra Franco: La guerrilla antifranquista de León 1936–1951* (León: Instituto Leones de Cultura, 2002);

and Àngel Prieto Prieto, *Guerrilleros de la libertad: Resistencia armada contra Franco* (Madrid: Oberón, 2004).

15. F. Chuyev, *Sto sorok besed s Molotovym* (1990), in Khlevniuk, *Master of the House*, 174.

16. Preston, *We Saw Spain Die*, 364–5. On 6 January 1937 the US Congress quickly passed Pittman Bill for mandatory arms embargo in Spanish conflict.

17. For details, see TNA: PRO GC&CS. Naval, Air and Military sections. Air Staff Intelligence reports on the Spanish Civil War. Events leading up to the Spanish revolution, 01 January 1936–02 May 1938, HW 22/1, and Reports on Spanish Military and Civilian Activity, 03 May 1937–06 May 1938, HW 22/2.

18. FO 371/220550/W16575/62/41, letter from Medhurst to Roberts, 18 November 1936, as quoted by Greg Kennedy, 'The Royal Navy, Intelligence and the Spanish Civil War: Lessons in Air Power', *Intelligence and National Security*, 20/2 (June 2005), 243.

19. Kennedy, 'The Royal Navy', 241–3.

20. TNA: PRO ADM 116/3514/M.01479/37, 3/2/37, Report of HMS NELSON visit to Palma, 30 January 1937, as quoted by Kennedy, 'The Royal Navy', 245.

21. NARA, Washington, DC: Records of the Military Intelligence Division (MID) 2657-S-144, Record Group 165, Military Attaché Paris to Assistant Chief of Staff G-2, 22 March 1938, Report No. 24125-W; see George F. Hofmann, 'The Tactical and Strategic Use of Attaché Intelligence: The Spanish Civil War and the US Army's Misguided Quest for a Modern Tank Doctrine', *Journal of Military History*, 62/1 (January 1998), 120.

22. An intelligence report dated 4 March 1939, 'Personnel et matériel russes en Espagne républicaine', 5 copies to the EMA–SR (État-Major d'Armée–Service de Renseignement) and 1 copy to the SR/4 Marine, Cañada Blanch Centre, LSE, this author's papers.

23. TsAMO, f. 132, op. 2642, d. 77, l. 44 (Rybalkin, p. 54).

24. See Ronald Amman, Julian Cooper, and R. W. Davies, *The Technological Level of Soviet Industry* (New Haven and London: Yale University Press, 1977), 117.

25. Paul Preston, *The Spanish Civil War: Reaction, Revolution & Revenge*, paperback (London: Harper Perennnial, 2006), 244.

26. 'Illegals' have always been used by Soviet and then Russian intelligence services for the most secret operations. The last known case dates back to 2011, when a Russian couple with Austrian passports was arrested in Germany.

27. 'Terakty', *Moskovsky Komsomolets*, 2 August 1992. See also publications about Grigulevich in *Latinskaya Amerika* journal in 1973, 1983, and 1986, where he was mentioned only as a specialist in Latin America. His intelligence career was covered briefly for the first time by Shatunovskaya (*Latinskaya Amerika*, 3 (1993), 61–72, 109). See also Mikhail Yuriev, 'Samyi nelegalny nelegal', *Sovershenno Sekretno*, 12/2010, 16–17.

28. Costello and Tsarev, *Deadly Illusions*, 249.

29. In his later interviews with Raimond Rocca of the CIA, Orlov claimed that, 'while operating as an illegal in Paris and staking out the headquarters of French intelligence, he was approached by a former colleague and immediately returned to Moscow, where it was decided to put him on ice for a while, assigning him to the 4th Transportation Directorate [*sic*] where he served until reassigned to Spain. In Spain, 4th Transportation Directorate assets would have been involved in the taking of the Spanish gold. Subsequently, he was assigned the position there from which he defected' (Rocca to a source that cannot be named).

30. Otherwise, Tacke's intelligence work is well documented; see Volodarsky, *El caso Orlov*, chs 5, 8.

31. Preston, *The Spanish Civil War*, 244.

32. For details about Spaniards in the Soviet intelligence services, see Volodarsky, *Comintern and the Spanish Civil War* (forthcoming).

33. Sudoplatov and Sdoplatov, *Special Tasks*, 31.

34. Preston, *The Spanish Civil War*, 245.

35. Sir Horace Rumbold, as quoted by Christopher Andrew in Andrew and Noakes (eds), *Intelligence and International Relations*, 6.

36. Quoted in Robert Leckie, *Delivered from Evil: The Saga of World War II* (New York: Harper & Row, 1987), 92.

37. Preston, *We Saw Spain Die*, 364–5.

38. Andrew and Noakes (ed), *Intelligence and International Relations*, 6.

39. Gazur, *Secret Assignment*, 298–9.

40. See Bureau, 105-22869 X–X18 Serial.

41. <http://www.fbi.gov/cleveland/about-us/history> (accessed 17 January 2014).

42. Andrew and Mitrokhin, *The Mitrokhin Archive*, 735.

43. Gazur, *Secret Assignment*, 589–90.

44. Rocca family to author, 24 November 2005.

45. IPOT News, Moscow, 16 April 2012.

46. Horace, *Third Book of Odes*, III.30 'Exegi monumentum aere perennius'.

47. Andrew and Mitrokhin, *The Mitrokhin Archive*, 735.

APPENDIX

1. Volodarsky, *Khokhlov*, p. xiv.

2. The gymnasium, in the German education system, is a type of secondary school with a strong emphasis on academic learning, comparable with the British grammar school system or with prep schools in the United States.

3. Vienna University Archive (UWA), Philosophische Fakultät der Universität Wien, Rigorosenakt Nr. 9929 des Arnold Deutsch, 2/V-1928, Z. 1098, S. 2 'CV'. There were only three faculties at the University of Vienna: Faculty of Philosophy, Faculty of Medicine, and Faculty of Law.

4. ASVRR, Personal File STEFAN, No. 32826, pp. 24–7, Deutsch's autobiography of 15 December 1938, quoted by West and Tsarev, *The Crown Jewels*, as File No. 32626.
5. TNA: PRO KV 2/594, 'Richard Hugo Schueller'.
6. For details, see Ruth von Mayenburg, *Hotel Lux* (Munich: C. Bertelsmann Verlag, 1978). The author herself was a GRU operator who spent seven years at the Lux.
7. UWA, Rigorosenakt Nr. 9929 des Arnold Deutsch: 'The work is at any rate sufficient to apply for permission to sit a strict examination.'
8. UWA, Nationale für ordentliche Hörer der philosophischen Fakultät, entries for Arnold Deutsch 1923–1927; Rigorosenakt No. 9929 des Arnold Deutsch, 'Beurteilung der Dissertation', Vienna, 18 May 1928; records of Deutsch's Ph.D. examination 1928.
9. Andrew and Gordievsky, *KGB*, 201–2.
10. Andrew and Gordievsky, *KGB*, 201–2.
11. DÖW, Akte 5547, Bundes-Polizeidirektion Wien, Beschlagnahme des Buches 'Geschlechtsreife, Enthaltsamkeit, Ehemoral' von Dr Wilhelm Reich, erschienen im Münster-Verlag, Zl. 38.Z. g. P. /34, Vienna, 27 April 1934 (Austrian court decision of 17 April 1934 to confiscate the print run of the book by Reich entitled *Sexual Maturity, Abstinence and the Morals of Marriage*, published by Deutsch). See also Andrew, *Authorized History of MI5*, 170, and Andrew and Gordievsky, *KGB*, 202–3.
12. Deutsch's autobiography of 15 December 1938 (West and Tsarev, *The Crown Jewels*, 105).
13. ÖStA/NPA, Kart. 278, Bundespolizeidirektion Wien, Zl. 22114/13, 2 May 1932. See also Part I of this work.
14. Record No. RZ. 26, 1929, in the Trauungsbuche der Israelischen Kultusgemeinde Wien. Same record at MA8, Wiener Stadt- und Landesarchiv. Deutsch's statement 'we married in 1924', quoted in *The Crown Jewels*, 107, should thus be considered a slip of memory.
15. In 1937, both Abramov–Mirov, who worked in turn in the RU and OMS, and Iosif Pyatnitsky, the former Secretary of the Comintern Executive Committee in charge of all international work of the Comintern during the 1920s and 1930s, were arrested. Mirov–Abramov was shot in November 1937 and Pyatnitsky a year later.
16. For the 1938 KGB biography of Deutsch, see West and Tsarev, *The Crown Jewels*, 106.
17. For her short biography, see Zhidong Yang (ed.), *Klara Blum* (Vienna: Böhlau Verlag, 2001), 617–18.
18. West and Tsarev, *The Crown Jewels*, 106.
19. TNA: PRO KV 2/1012–14, 'Edith Tudor-Hart'. According to her MI5 file, Edit Suschitzky, a Polish–Austrian Jewess, was a communist who first came to the UK around 1925. Expelled in 1931 on account of her political activities,

she got married in Vienna in August 1933 to Dr Alexander Ethel Tudor-Hart, an Englishman and a fellow communist. The couple returned to London together several weeks later, but separated when Dr Hart went to Spain as a medical volunteer to the International Brigades. In 1947 Edith Tudor-Hart told a reliable source that she had worked for the OGPU in Austria and Italy in 1932–33. She became a naturalized British subject and set herself up as a professional photographer. Having joined the CPGB in 1927, she remained associated with the Communist Party for the rest of her life.

20. See, e.g., TNA: PRO KV 2/1012–14, 'Edith Tudor-Hart', KV 2/1603, 'Alexander Ethel Tudor-Hart', KV 2/1241–2, 'Margarete Charlotte Moos'; and KV 2/817, 'Brian Goold-Verschoyle'.

21. As correctly stated in his very well-written obituary (see *Independent*, 18 April 1994), Elliott's was 'a distinguished career, publicly and unluckily marked by two notorious events, the death of Commander Lionel Crabb and the flight of Kim Philby to Moscow. Elliott and the Service suffered criticism in both cases and he felt this deeply to the end of his life.' Though he was an operational officer and his SIS colleagues say pen-pushing and detailed analysis were not for him, Elliott left two excellent books of memoirs, *Never Judge a Man by his Umbrella* (1991) with a chapter about Philby, and *With My Little Eye* (1994). In this last book, the obituary recalls, Elliott wrote: 'The successful Field Officers will be generally found to have three important characteristics. They will be personalities in their own right. They will have humanity and a capacity for friendship and they will have a sense of humour which will enable them to avoid the ridiculous mumbo-jumbo of over-secrecy' that typically characterized his own style.

22. Andrew, *The Defence of the Realm*, 169.

23. Honigmann, *Ein Kapitel aus meinem Leben*, 78–9. Litzi stated that 'daß alles zwar in Wien begonnen, aber erst in London richtige, feste Formen angenommen hat, die Anwerbung und der Eintritt in den sowjetischen Geheimdienst'.

24. Costello and Tsarev, *Deadly Illusions*, 137. It seems strange, however, that Reif used the real name of Deutsch in his correspondence. The authors mention Reif's cryptonym as MARR, while in the KGB files in both typed and handwritten documents it is spelled as MAR.

25. Costello and Tsarev, *Deadly Illusions*, 115. See also Part I.

26. Cf. Andrew, *The Defence of the Realm*, 171.

27. For the most recent account, see Verena Moritz and Hannes Leidinger, *Oberst Redl: Der Spionage Fall, der Skandal, die Fakten* (St Pölten: Rezidenz Verlag, 2012).

28. His short biography can be accessed on <http://www.findagrave.com/cgi-bin/fg.cgi?page=gr&GRid=15052816> (accessed 17 January 2014).

29. KPÖ letter dated 28 October 1980.

30. West and Tsarev, *The Crown Jewels*, 274. The KGB co-author had not identified SCOTT as Arthur Wynn to West when the book was published.

31. West and Tsarev, *The Crown Jewels*, 274.

32. Ben Macintyre and Steve Bird, 'Civil Servant Arthur Wynn Revealed as Recruiter of Oxford Spies', *The Times*, 13 May 2009. The article contains a number of errors. Thus, Pavel Fitin was not 'the KGB's head of counter-intelligence', but head of Foreign Intelligence (1939–46) of the Chief Directorate of State Security of the NKVD. In 1941 Wynn was not 35 years old, but 31 (born 22 January 1910). Wynn did *not* graduate from Oxford. He was recruited, not by Maly, who was not in London in October 1934, but by Deutsch (STEFAN) in or about January 1937. See Appendix II.

33. See Costello and Tsarev, *Deadly Illusions*, 247.

34. Almost surely a reference to the liaison office run in the Portuguese capital by Franco's brother Nicolás.

35. Honigmann, *Ein Kapitel aus meinem Leben*, 83.

36. Jimmy Burns, *Papa Spy: A True Story of Love, Wartime Espionage in Madrid, and the Treachery of the Cambridge Spies* (London: Bloomsbury, 2011), 41. In reality, the true story of the wartime espionage in Madrid is a little-known article by Kenneth Benton, 'The ISOS Years: Madrid 1941–3', *Journal of Contemporary History*, 30/3 (July 1995), 359–410.

37. Andrew, *Authorized History of MI5* 169.

38. TNA: PRO KV 2/804, Krivitsky's debriefing, October 1939–April 1940; KV 2/805, Jane Archer's summary of the debriefing.

39. ASVRR, Personal File STEFAN, No. 32826, vol. 1, p. 207, dated 23 October 1937, quoted by West and Tsarev, *The Crown Jewels*, 110.

40. Andrew and Mitrokhin, *The Mitrokhin Archive*, 110.

41. Wright with Greengrass, *Spycatcher*, 228.

42. Haynes, Klehr, and Vassiliev, *Spies*, 65–6. Amazingly, the authors failed to identify mary as Litzi Friedmann in their book.

43. Anon., 'Uchyonye i razvedchiki delali obshee delo' (interview with V. Barkovsky), *Nezavisimaya gazeta*, 21 July 1999.

44. All Broda's 'extremist' and communist activities in Britain were duly registered in his MI5 file, PF 46663. Nevertheless, during the war he was cleared for the most secretive work involving the British and American atomic bomb research and development.

45. Until mid-July 1938 the telephone number was Primrose 3456, whose subscriber was Edward Alexander Newmark, married to the Austrian woman née Kalisch. From the second half of July Broda used the number Paddington 5443, belonging to Jack Rapoport. The latter came under the notice of Special Branch in 1935 and 1936, when he was in relations with Margaret Charlotte Moos. At that time Moos, who was married to the fellow countryman Siegfried Moos, actively associated with Edith Tudor-Hart and her husband Alexander, also being a mistress of Brian Goold-Verschoyle, a courier of the Soviet spy ring controlled by Teodor Maly (Moos MI5 file, PF 42470, vol. 2, serial 23a).

46. Broda, *Scientist Spies*, 258–9.
47. TNA: PRO KV 2/2181, Serial 6c, January 1940.
48. See TNA: PRO KV 2/2181–90.
49. Broda, *Scientist Spies*, 56.
50. Honigmann, *Ein Kapitel aus meinem Leben*, 106–7.
51. Wright with Greengrass, *Spycatcher*, 324.
52. Honigmann, *Ein Kapitel aus meinem Leben*, 22.
53. West and Tsarev, *The Crown Jewels*, 111–12.
54. West and Tsarev, *The Crown Jewels*, 112.
55. Haynes, Klehr, and Vassiliev, *Spies*, 501.
56. West and Tsarev, *The Crown Jewels*, 113. Andrew, *Authorized History of MI5*, states that the Home Office file of Deutsch does not survive.
57. Haynes, Klehr, and Vassiliev, *Spies*, 501.
58. West and Tsarev, *The Crown Jewels*. We also read in Costello and Tsarev, *Deadly Illusions*: 'Deutsch survived the purges because he did not even figure in evidence extracted from his colleagues... In mid-Atlantic on 7 November 1942 the freighter [*Donbass*] was torpedoed by a U-boat. Eyewitness reports describe Deutsch's courage when, fatally wounded on deck, he continued to bravely encourage and help others to abandon ship' (p. 458).
59. Jürgen Röhwer, *Chronology of the War at Sea, 1939–1945: The Naval History of World War Two* (Annapolis: US Naval Institute Press, 2005).
60. Andrey Nelogov, 'Soviet Merchant Marine Losses in WWII' (in progress) <shipsnostalgia.com> (accessed 17 January 2014).
61. 'We received the attached telegram from the wife of Comrade Lang [Arnold Deutsch], who is currently in the *Lesnoy* health resort. Comrade Lang [Josefina Deutsch] used to live in the Lux before the evacuation. As Comrade Lang [Arnold Deutsch] is away on an assignment, we are seeking your instructions for the family [Deutsch] to get an apartment in the Lux again' (Barry McLoughlin and Hans Schafranek (eds), *DÖW, Österreicher im Exil: Sowjetunion 1934–1945* (Vienna: Deuticke, 1999), 680).
62. DÖW, Akte 20000/d 58 ARNOLD DEUTSCH, Erkenntnis über den Beweis des Todes.
63. In the autumn of 1945 Hexmann was presiding over the repatriation of his countrymen on behalf of the KPÖ leadership with his office in the Hotel Lux. According to many witnesses, he behaved like a typical Stalinist henchman. For details, see Hans Schafranek, '"Angehörigen von Volksfeinden können wir nicht helfen": Das Schicksal der Familie Nebenführ', in Hans Schafranek (ed.), *Die Betrogenen: Österreicher as Opfer stalinistischen Terrors in der Sowjetunion* (Vienna: Picus Verlag, 1991), 92.
64. See O'Sullivan, 'Dealing with the Devil'; Barry McLaughlin, 'Proletarian Cadres en Route: Austrian NKVD Agents in Britain, 1941–43', *Labour History Review*, 62/3 (Winter 1997), 296–317; Hans Schafranek, 'In Hinterland des Feindes: Sowjetische Fallschirmagenten im Deutschen Reich 1942–1944',

DÖW, *Jahrbuch 1996*, pp. 10–40; Hans Schafranek, 'Die Anfänger der Operation Pickaxe 1941/42', *Journal for Intelligence, Propaganda and Security Studies*, 2/1 (2008), 7–22; Primakov et al., *Ocherki*, iv (1941–5).

65. *Der neue Mahnruf*, 11 (November 1953), 4.

66. See, e.g., Costello and Tsarev, *Deadly Illusions*, 457 n. 37; West and Tsarev, *The Crown Jewels*, 113.

67. Andrew, *Authorized History of MI5*, 184. Later Professor Andrew also managed to find and interview Ninette Elizabeth, born in London in May 1936 (Christopher Andrew to author, 18 October 2007). In Austria. Ninette Elizabeth married the son of an Austrian communist and changed her name to Nina Jakl. This writer interviewed her in Vienna in May 2014.

68. TNA: PRO KV 2/2665, 'Victor Karpov', October 1932, serial 74a.

69. Andrew, *The Defence of the Realm*, 836.

70. See Charles Saumarez Smith's review of Miranda Carter' book about Blunt, 'Scholar, Gentleman, Prig, Spy', *Observer*, 11 November 2001.

71. Andrew, *The Defence of the Realm*, 836–7.

72. *Comrade Philby*, Walberry Production in cooperation with Soyuztelefilm/ Channel 4, Directors: Victor Viktorov, Frances Berrigan, Script: Rostislav Andreyev, 1990.

73. The Security Service, which kept extensive files on Moos, part of them now declassified (PF 42470, vols 1–3), and who interviewed her several times, believed that she was not a Soviet agent but only an unfortunate mistress of Brian Goold-Verschoyle, spending some months with him in Moscow. Moos lived in Paris when Deutsch was there until October 1933. She moved to London in December 1933, soon after Deutsch had been informed that he was going to Britain. Deutsch arrived there three months later. In London Moos maintained an active contact with Edith Tudor-Hart, and had intimate relations with Jack Rapoport, the subscriber to one of the telephones used by Engelbert Broda, the leader of the covert Austrian Communist cell in London and future top spy in the British atomic project. Moos's second lover was Brian Goold-Verschoyle, another Soviet spy with whom she secretly went to Moscow.

74. In 1920 Dobb joined the Communist Party and in the 1930s was central to the burgeoning Communist movement at the university. One of his disciples was Kim Philby (Dobb was 'Philby's economics supervisor and an important influence on him'). It has been suggested that Dobb was a talent-spotter for the Comintern and Soviet intelligence. See Phillip Knightley, *The Life and Views of the KGB Masterspy* (London: André Deutsch, 1988), 30–1, 36–7, 45. Knightley interviewed Philby in Moscow in 1988. 'It was to Dobb that Kim Philby turned on his last day in Cambridge for advice on how best to devote his life to the Communist cause,' Christopher Andrew writes. In July 1934 'a Security Service report . . . noted that the Soviet ambassador, Ivan Maisky, and members of his staff were "making mysterious motor-car drives to Cambridge and other neighbouring towns"' (*Authorized History of MI5*, 167–8).

75. The statement in West and Tsarev, *The Crown Jewels*, about 'the recruitment of Guy Burgess at the end of 1934' (p. 127) is an error. Though Burgess was most probably given the pseudonym MÄDCHEN after his meeting with Deutsch in December 1934, in mid-July 1935 the Centre still ordered Nikolsky and Deutsch not to proceed with the recruitment.

76. This file number is given by West and Tsarev (*The Crown Jewels*, 356) in reference to the agent codenamed SHAH (Harry Houghton). Here is an evident discrepancy. Judging by the file number, Houghton should have been recruited immediately after Burgess in the second half of 1935, but according to several reliable sources he was recruited only after 19 January 1952 in Warsaw with Moscow learning about him in March. There are two possibile explanations: either the KGB played a foul game with the British co-author (as they did with Costello), giving him a false file number (this could be an unidentified spy's file, for example), or Houghton was recruited in 1935, which is unlikely.

77. There is another inconsistency. West and Tsarev write in *The Crown Jewels* (pp. 82–3) that Captain King was recruited in February 1935. This, however, is impossible, as the numbers of Philby's and Maclean's personal files are now known, as well as the dates of their recruitment. Between the two there was no recruitment, so King must have been recruited either before Philby or after Burgess.

78. It is possible that File No. 83793, erroneously referring to SHAKH, may be the personal file of Klugman or Watson or King.

79. Contrary to what Peter Wright believed at the time, when he was involved in the post-war investigation of the Cambridge spies, Watson should have been recruited, not in 1938 but even before Blunt, whom Wright interrogated about his former friend.

80. From her own KGB file number it follows that Edith herself had not become a fully-fledged agent until some time later, contrary to what Borovik claims in *The Philby Files*: 'From the archives, it seems that Edith Tudor-Hart was recruited by Arnold Deutsch ("Stefan") in 1929. In 1934 she recruited Litzi Friedmann ("Mary") and recommended Kim Philby for recruitment' (p. 301 n.).

81. See also, Paul Preston, *We Saw Spain Die* (2008): 42, 51–2, 177, 200–3, as well as John William 'Jack' Reid, a sub-agent for Oliver Charles Green.

82. This clearly contradicts claims made by Costello and Tsarev, *Deadly Illusions*: 'The fourth man, Anthony Blunt, the fifth man, Michael Straight, and the sixth man, John Cairncross' (p. 220), a 'sequence of recruitment according to the NKVD records' (461 n. 1).

83. See the autobiography of David Crook, 'That Valley in Spain Called Jarama' (1936–38), entry of 14 March 1937, David Crook 1990/Crook family©2000.

84. ASVRR, Personal File TONY, No. 83895, vol. 1, p. 240, quoted by Costello and Tsarev, *Deadly Illusions*, 246.

85. The information in Haynes, Klehr, and Vassiliev, *Spies* ('Burgess in February reported that Blunt had successfully carried out Straight's recruitment' (p. 245)), must not be understood literally. Actually, an agent must be signed up by a Service employee or an officer and not by another agent, who may talent spot or suggest a candidate, but the decision is always taken in Moscow and carried out in place by a member of the station. This also explains why Straight was filed as a US line agent.

86. Contrary to Nigel West's guess in *MASK*, p. 213, it is unlikely that NACHFOLGER, known as HEIR in English, was a 22-year-old assistant chemist, Charles Munday, employed at the Woolwich Arsenal.

87. Judging by the documents in his personal file, see TNA: PRO KV 2/2203–4, at least in the UK Green was almost certainly an agent of the Soviet military intelligence.

Bibliography

PRIVATE DOCUMENT COLLECTIONS

Dr T. H. Bagley, Belgium
H. Keith Melton, USA
Prof. Ángel Viñas, Belgium

UNPUBLISHED TYPESCRIPTS

Betteridge, Jennifer, 'The Rupture of Diplomatic Relations with Russia, May 1927 and the Political Purposes of Surveillance', Leeds University, 2006.

Kluiters, F.A.C., 'Bill Hooper and secret service', 30 pages.

Mayer, Jacques, 'Skoblewsky-Rose: Anmerkungen zur Biographie. Berichtigte und erweitere Fassung', 15 typed pages courtesy of Dr Jacques Mayer of Humbold University, Berlin, 7 March 2012.

MI5, 'D.3 Survey of Russian Espionage in the United Kingdom 1935–1955', SF441-0302-8/V1, The National Archives, Kew, KV3/417.

O'Neil, Robin, 'Extermination of the Jews of Galicia', unpublished Ph.D. thesis, University College, London.

Ranke, Hubert von, Papers, Bestand ED 161, Archiv des Instituts für Zeitgeschichte, Munich.

Spencer, David E., 'Alexander Kunslich in Spain', Tamiment Library, New York University, New York.

Stern, Antonia, 'Hans Beimler: Dachau–Madrid. Ein Dokument unserer Zeit', IISG, undated (1939), 301 pages.

Viñas, Ángel, 'Francoist Myths in Democratic Spain', Keynote address, Association of Contemporary Iberian Studies, 2012 Annual Congress, London, September 2012. Whaley, Barton, 'Biographical Index of Soviet Intelligence Personnel', Appendix C, Soviet Clandestine Communication Nets, AD705665, Air Force Office of Scientific Research (AFOSR), Arlinton, VA, 70-1139 TR, declassified.

Whaley, Barton, 'Soviet Guerrillas in the Spanish Civil War', Center for International Studies, Massachusetts Institute of Technology, Cambridge, MA, September 1969, 143 typed pages.

Wohl, Paul, 'A Caliostro of the Underground, or The Real Story of Soviet Agent Krivitsky', undated (1940), 32 typed pages.

AUTHOR'S INTERVIEWS

Bagley, Tennent H., former high-ranking CIA official.
Dziak, John J., former senior intelligence officer and executive in the Office of the Secretary of Defence and in the Defence Intelligence Agency.
Gordievsky, Oleg, former spy.
Landauer, Hans, a veteran of the Spanish Civil War and a curator of the Dokumentationsarchiv des Österreichischen Widerstand.
Peake, Hayden, curator of CIA's Historical Intelligence Collection.

DOCUMENTARIES AND BROADCASTS

Berrigan, Frances, Victorov, Victor, Andreyev, and Rostislav (script), *Comrade Philby*, Walberry Production (UK) with Soyuztelefilm/Channel 4, 1990.
Berrigan, Frances, Victorov, Victor, Andreyev, and Rostislav (script), *Comrade Philby*, Walberry Production (UK) with Soyuztelefilm (USSR), 1991.
Genovés, María Dolors, *Especial Andreu Nin: Operació Nikolai*, aired by the Televisió de Cataluny, 6 November 1992.
A complete and unedited interview with Jack Bjoze, dated 1–17 August 1999, portions of which were utilized in 'The Red Files' PBS broadcast.

PUBLISHED DOCUMENTS

Adibekov, G. M., Adibekova, Zh. G., Rogovaya, L. A., and Shirinya, K. K. (eds), *Politburo TsK RKP(b)–VKP(b) i Komintern, 1919–1943. Dokumenty* (Moscow: ROSSPEN, 2004).
Adibekov, G., Di Biagio, A., Gori, F., Dundovich, E., Conti, K., Kosheleva, L., Narinsky, M., Pons, S., Rogovaya, L., Filitov, A., and Khlevniuk, O. (eds.) *Politburo TsK RKP(b)–VKP(b) i Evropa: Resheniya 'osoboi papki', 1923–1939* (Moscow: ROSSPEN, 2001).
Akten zur deutschen auswärtigen Politik, 1918–1945: Serie D (1937–1945), iii. *Deutschland und der spanische Bürgerkrieg* (1936–1939) (Baden-Baden: Imprimerie Nationale, 1951).
Asholt, Wolfgang, Reinecke, Rüdiger, und Schlünder, Susanne (eds), *Espana en la corazón: Der Spanische Bürgerkrieg: Medien und kulturelles Gedächtnis* (Bielefeld: Aisthesis Verlag, 2008).
Barmin, Alexander, 'Testimony of Alexander Gregory Barmine, New York, NY', in *Institute of Pacific Relations, United States Senate, Hearings Before the Subcommittee to Investigate the Administration of the Internal Security Act and Other Internal Security Laws of the Committee on the Judiciary*, 31 July 1951 (Washington: US Government Printing Office, 1951).
Bayerlein, Bernhard H. (ed.), and Hadeler, Wladislaw (trans.), *Georgi Dimitroff: Tagebücher 1933–1943* (Berlin: Aufbau-Verlag, 2000).

Bennett, G., and Hamilton, K. A. (eds), *Documents on British Foreign Policy*, series 3, vol. 1: *Britain and the Soviet Union, 1968–1972* (London: The Stationery Office, 1998).

Benson, Robert Louis, and Warner, Michael (eds.), VENONA: *Soviet Espionage and the American Response 1939–1957* (Washington, DC: NSA and CIA, 1996).

Causa General. La dominación roja en España. Avance de la información instruida por el ministerio público, 2nd rev. edn (Madrid: Ministerio de Justicia, 1943).

Cotterill, David J. (ed.), and Enzenberger, Maria (trans.), *The Serge–Trotsky Papers*, paperback (London: Pluto Press, 1994).

Dallin, Alexander, and Firsov, F. I. (eds), *Dimitrov and Stalin, 1934–1943: Letters from the Soviet Archives*, Russian documents trans. Vadim A. Staklo (New Haven and London: Yale University Press, 2000).

'Decision of the Presidium of the E.C.C.I. on the Work of the Communist Party of Spain', *Communist International*, 14/2 (February 1937), 136–8.

Dimitrov, Georgi, *The Diary of Georgi Dimitrov 1933–1949*, ed. Ivo Banac (New Haven and London: Yale University Press, 2003).

Documents on German Foreign Policy 1918–1945, Series C (1933–1937), vol. 3, 14 June 1934–31 March 1935 (Washington, DC: US Government Printing Office, 1959).

Dokumenty veshnei politiki SSSR, T. 19, 1 January–31 December 1936 (Moscow: Politizdat, 1974); T. 20, 1 January–31 December 1937 (Moscow: Politizdat, 1976); T. 21, 1 January–31 December 1938 (Moscow: Politizdat, 1977).

Haustov, V. N., Naumov, V. P., and Plotnikova, N. S. (eds), *Lubyanka: Stalin i Glavnoe Upravlenie Gosbezopasnosti NKVD 1937–1938* (Moscow: Materik, 2004).

Haustov, V. N., Naumov, V. P., and Plotnikova, N. S. (eds), *Lubyanka: Stalin i NKVD-NKGB-GUKR 'Smersh' 1939–March 1946* (Moscow: Materik 2006).

Haustov, V. N., Naumov, V. P., and Plotnikova, N. S. (eds), *Lubyanka: Stalin i VChK-GPU-OGPU-NKVD January 1922–December 1936* (Moscow: Materik, 2003).

'Hearings Regarding Communist Espionage', *Hearings before the Committee on Un-American Activities*, House of Representatives, Eighty-First Congress, First and Second Sessions, 8 November, 2 December 1949, 27 February, and 1 March 1950 (Washington: GPO, 1950).

Henderson, Loy W., Memorandum of conversation [with General Krivitsky], 15 March 1939, six typed pages, in Michael Warner, *VENONA: Soviet Espionage and the American Response, 1939–1957* (Walnut Creek, CA: Aegean Park Press, 1996).

Institut zur Geschichte der Arbeiterbewegung (ed.), *In den Fängen des NKWD: Deutsche Opfer des stalinistischen Terrors in der UdSSR* (Berlin: Dietz, 1990).

Kalmykov, N. P., Yanchuk, I. I., Korablyova, L.Yu., Larin, E. A., and Heifets, L. S. (eds), *Komintern i Latinskaya Amerika* (Moscow: Nauka, 1998).

Kesaris, Paul L. (ed.), *The Rote Kapelle: The CIA's History of Soviet Intelligence and Espionage Networks in Western Europe, 1936–1945* (Washington: University Publications of America, 1979).

Khlevnyuk, Oleg, Kvashonkin, A., Kosheleva, L., and Rogovaya, L. (eds), *Stalins-koe politburo v 30e gody*. Collection of documents (Moscow: AIRO-XX, 1995).

Koenker, Diana P., and Bachman, Ronald D. (eds), *Revelations from the Russian Archives* (Washington, DC: Library of Congress, 1997).

Kokurin, A. I., and Petrov, N. V. (eds), *Lubyanka: organy VChka-OGPU-NKVD-NKGB-MGB-MVD-KGB, 1917–1991*. Spravochnik (Moscow: Mezhdunarod-nyi fond 'Demokratiya', 2003).

Koltai, Ferenc (ed.), *László Rajk and his Accomplicies before the People's Court* (Buda-pest: Budapest Printing Press, 1949).

Kozlov, V. A., and Mironenko, S. V. (eds), *Prikazy NKVD SSSR 1934–1941 gg. Katalog rassekrechennykh dokumentov Gosudarstvennogo arkhiva Rossiiskoi Federatsyi* (Novosibirsk: Sibirskii khronograf, 1999).

Kravchenko, Victor, 'Testimony of Victor A. Kravchenko Regarding Communism', *Hearings before the Committee on Un-American Activities*, House of Representatives, 22 July 1947 (Washington, DC: US Government Printing Office, 1947), 1–30.

Kravchenko, Victor, 'Testimony of Victor A. Kravchenko Regarding Communism', *Hearings before the Committee on Un-American Activities*, House of Representatives, 7 March 1950 (Washington, DC: US Government Printing Office, 1950), 1175–94.

Krivitsky, W. G., *MI5 Debriefing and Other Documents on Soviet Intelligence*, ed. Gary Kern, paperback (Riverside, CA: Xenos Books, 2004).

Krivitsky, Walter, 'Testimony of Walter G. Krivitsky, Former member, Soviet Military Intelligence, through an Interpreter, Boris Shub', Wednesday, 11 October 1939, *Investigation of Un-American Propaganda Activities in the United States, Hearing before a Special Committee on Un-American Activities*, House of Representatives, Seventy-Six Congress (Washington, DC: US Government Printing Office, 1939).

Lambert, The Hon. Margaret, Breuning, E. C. M., Duke, K. H. M., Stambrook, F. G., and Watt, D. C. (eds), *Documents on German Foreign Policy 1918–1945*, Series C (1933–1937), vol. VI, 1 November 1936–14 November 1937 (London: HMSO, 1983).

László Rajk und Komplizen vor dem Volksgericht (Budapest: Government Printing Office, 1949).

Lenin i VChK: Collection of Documents, 1917–1922 (Moscow: Izdatelstvo politiches-koi literatury, 1987).

Lih, Lars T., Naumow, Oleg, und Chlewnjuk, Oleg (eds), *Stalin: Briefe an Molotow, 1925–1936*. Mit einer Einführung von Robert C. Tucker (Berlin: Siedler, 1996).

'Lista de las personas Rusas para inscribir en las filas de las tropas Españolas', in Enrique Moral Sandoval, Aurelio Martín Nájera, and Augustín Garrigós Fernández (eds), *Obras completas de Largo Caballero*, viii. *Notas históricas de la guerra de España (1917–1940) y otros escritos* (Madrid: Fundacion Francisco Largo Cabal-lero; Barcelona: Instituto Monsa de Ediciones, 2009).

Los Russos en la Guerra de España 1936–1939 (Madrid: Fundación Pablo Iglesias, 2009).

Narinski, Mikhail, and Rojahn, Jürgen (eds), *Centre and Periphery: The History of the Comintern in the Light of New Documents* (Amsterdam: International Institute of Social History, 1996).

Non-Intervention and Intervention, Seeds of Conflict, Series 3, The Spanish Civil War, 1936–1939 (Nendeln: Kraus Reprint, 1975).

Orlov, Alexander, *The Legacy of Alexander Orlov* (Washington, DC: US Government Printing Office, 1973).

Petrov, Nikita, *Die Sowjetischen Geheimdienstmitarbeiter in Deutschland* (Berlin: Metropol, 2010).

Petrov, Nikita, *Kto rukovodil organami gosbezopasnosti, 1941–1954* (Moscow: Zvenia, 2010).

Petrov, N. V., and Skorkin, K. V., *Kto rukovodil NKVD, 1934–1941* (Moscow: Zvenia, 1999).

Politburo TsK RKP(b)–VKP(b) i Evropa: Resheniya 'osoboi papki', 1923–1939 (Moscow: ROSSPEN, 2001).

Pons, Silvio, 'The Papers on Foreign and International Policy in the Russian Archives: The Stalin Years', *Cahiers du Monde Russe*, 40/1–2 (January–June 1999).

Pozharskaya, S. P., and Saplin, A. I. (eds.), *Komintern i grazhdanskaya voina v Ispanii* (Moscow: Nauka, 2001).

Radosh, Ronald, Habeck, Mary R., and Sevostianov, Grigory (eds), *Spain Betrayed: The Soviet Union in the Spanish Civil War* (New Haven and London: Yale University Press, 2001).

Sekrety Polskoi Politiki 1935–1945: Rassekrechennye dokumenty SVR (Moscow: Ripol Klassik, 2010).

Sotskov, Lev (ed.), *Agressiya: Rassekrechennye dokumenty sluzhby vneshnei razvedki Rossiiskoi Federatsyi 1939–1941* (Moscow: Ripol Klassik, 2011).

The Intelligence War in 1941 (Washington, DC: CIA Centre for the Study of Intelligence, 1991).

'The Shameful Years: Thirty Years of Soviet Espionage in the United States', House Report No. 1229, *Committee on Un-American Activities, US House of Representatives* (Washington, DC: US Government Printing Office, 1952).

Vakhaniya, Vladimir, *Lichnaya sekretnaya sluzhba I. V. Stalina*. Sbornik dokumentov (Moscow: Svarog, 2004).

Zborowski, Mark, 'Testimony of Mark Zborowski, Accompanied by Herman A. Greenberg, Esq., His Attorney', *Hearing before the Subcommittee to Investigate the Administration of the Internal Security Act and Other Internal Security Laws of the Committee on the Judiciary*, United States Senate, Eighty-Fourth Congress, Second Session on Scope of Soviet Activity in the United States, Wednesday, 29 February 1956, pt 4 (Washington, DC: GPO, 1956).

Zborowski, Mark, 'Testimony of Mark Zborowski, Accompanied by Herman A. Greenberg, Esq., His Attorney', *Hearing before the Subcommittee to Investigate the Administration of the Internal Security Act and Other Internal Security Laws of the*

Committee on the Judiciary, United States Senate, Eighty-Fourth Congress, Second Session on Scope of Soviet Activity in the United States, Friday, 2 March 1956, Part 5 (Washington, DC: GPO, 1956).

Zeman, Z. A. B. (ed.), *Germany and the Revolution in Russia, 1915–18*. Documents from the Archives of the German Foreign Ministry (Oxford: Oxford University Press, 1958).

SECONDARY SOURCES: BOOKS AND ARTICLES

Aalto, William, and Goff, Irving, 'Guerrilla Warfare: Lessons in Spain', *Soviet Russia Today* (October 1941), 22–3.

Abramov, Vadim, *Evrei v KGB: Palachi i Zhertvy* (Moscow: Yauza/EKSMO, 2005).

Abramson, Paulina, and Abramson, Adelina, *Mosaico roto* (Madrid: Compañía Literaria, 1994).

Abse, Tobias, 'Togliatti: Loyal Servant of Stalin', *What Next*, 25 (2003), 51–65.

Acheson, Dean, *Present at the Creation: My Years in the State Department* (New York: Norton, 1969).

Adamthwaite, Anthony, 'French Military Intelligence and the Coming of War', in Christopher Andrew and Jeremy Noakes (eds), *Intelligence and International Relations 1900–1945* (Exeter: Universityof Exeter, 1987).

Adamthwaite, Anthony, 'The Spanish Civil War Revisited: The French Connection', in Gaynor Johnson (ed.), *The International Context of the Spanish Civil War* (Newcastle upon Tyne: Cambridge Scholars Publishing, 2009), 1–17.

Adibekov, G. M., Shakhnazarova, E. N., and Shirinya, K. K., *Organizatsionnaya struktura Kominterna, 1919–1943* (Moscow: ROSSPEN, 1997).

Agabekov, G. S., *Cheka za rabotoi* (Berlin: Strela, 1931).

Agabekov, G. S., *GPU: Zapiski chekista* (Berlin: Strela, 1930).

Agabekov, Georges, *OGPU: The Russian Secret Terror*, trans. from the French by Henry W. Bunn (New York: Bretano's, 1931; Westport, CT: Hyperion Press, 1975).

Agabekov, Georgii, *Sekretnyi terror* (Moscow: Terra-Knizhnyi klub, 1998).

Aga-Rossi, Elena, and Zaslavsky, Victor, *Togliatti e Stalin: Il PCI e la politica estera staliniana negli archivi di Mosca* (Bologna: Il Mulino, 2007).

Agostegui, Julio, and Martinez, Jesús A., *La Junta de Defensa de Madrid* (Madrid: Comunidad de Madrid, 1984).

Agosti, Aldo (ed.), *Togliatti Negli Anni del Comintern, 1926–1943* (Roma: Carocci, 2000).

Agosti, Aldo, Broué, Pierre, Dreyfus, Michel, Gotovitch, José, Huber, Peter, Lemarquis, René, Narinski, Mikhail, Panteleiev, Mikhail, Pennetier, Claude, Studer, Brigitte, Wehenkel, Henri, and Wolikow, Serge, *Le Komintern:*

L'Histoire et les hommes: Dictionnaire biographique de l'Internationale Communiste en France, à Moscou, en Belgique, au Luxembourg, en Suisse (1919–1943) (Paris: Les Éditions de l'Atelier, 2001).

Aizpuru, Mikel, *El informe Brusiloff: La Guerra Civil de 1936 en el Frente Norte vista por un traductor ruso* (Irun: Alberdania, 2009).

Akhmedov, Ismail, *In and Out of Stalin's GRU* (London: Arms and Armour Press, 1984).

Alba, Victor, and Schwartz, Stephen, *Spanish Marxism versus Soviet Communism: A History of the P.O.U.M. in the Spanish Civil War*, paperback (London: Transaction Publishers, 2009).

Albers, Patricia, *Shadows, Fire, Snow: The Life of Tina Modotti*, paperback (Berkeley and Los Angeles: University of California Press, 2002).

Alekseyev, M., Kolpakidi, A., and Kochik, V., *Entsyklopaedia voennoi razvedki, 1918–1945* (Moscow: Kuchkovo pole/Voennaya kniga, 2012).

Alexander, Robert, *The Anarchists in the Spanish Civil War* (London: Janus Publishing Company, 1999).

Alexeyev, Kirrill Mikhailovich, 'Was Ambassador Oumansky Murdered?', *Saturday Evening Post*, 3 July 1948, pp. 20 ff.

Alexeyev, Mikhail, *Voennaya razvedka Rossii: Ot Ryurika do Nikolaya II*, 2 vols (Moscow: Russkaya Razvedka, 1998).

Alpert, Michael, *A New International History of the Spanish Civil War* (Houndmills, Basingstoke: Palgrave Macmillan, 2004).

Álvarez del Vayo, Julio, *The Last Optimist* (London: Putnam, 1950).

Álvarez, Santiago, and Cabra Loredo, Dolores, *Historia política y militar de las Brigadas Internacionales* (Madrid: Compañía Literaria, 1996).

Amman, Ronald, Cooper, Julian, and Davies, R. W., *The Technological Level of Soviet Industry* (New Haven and London: Yale University Press, 1977).

Andersen, Jakob, in collaboration with Oleg Gordievsky, *De røde spioner* (Copenhagen: Høst & Søn, 2002).

Andrew, Christopher, 'F. H. Hinsley and the Cambridge Moles: Two Patterns of Intelligence Recruitment', in Richard Langhorne (ed.), *Diplomacy and Intelligence during the Second World War: Essays in Honour of F. H. Hinsley* (Cambridge: Cambridge University Press, 1985), 22–40.

Andrew, Christopher, *Secret Service: The Making of the British Intelligence Community* (London: Sceptre, 1987).

Andrew, Christopher, 'Intelligence, International Relations and "Under-Theorization"', *Intelligence and National Security*, 19/2 (Summer 2004).

Andrew, Christopher, *The Defence of the Realm: The Authorized History of MI5* (London: Allen Lane, 2009).

Andrew, Christopher, and Dilks, David, *The Missing Dimension: Governments and Intelligence Communities in the Twentieth Century* (Chicago: University of Chicago Press, 1984).

Andrew, Christopher, and Gordievsky, Oleg, *Instructions from the Centre: Top Secret Files on KGB Foreign Operations 1975–1985* (London: Hodder & Stoughton, 1990).

Andrew, Christopher, and Gordievsky, Oleg, *KGB: The Inside Story from Lenin to Gorbachev*, paperback (New York: Harper Perennial, 1991).

Andrew, Christopher, and Gordievsky, Oleg, *More Instructions from the Centre: Top Secret Files on KGB Global Operations 1975–1985* (London: Frank Cass, 1992).

Andrew, Christopher, and Harold, James, 'Willi Münzenberg, the Reichstag Fire, and the Conversion of Innocents', in David Charters and Maurice Tugwell (eds), *Deception in East–West Relations* (London: Pergamon, Brassey, 1990).

Andrew, Christopher, and Mitrokhin, Vasili, *The Mitrokhin Archive: The KGB in Europe and the West* (London: Allen Lane The Penguin Press, 1999).

Andrew, Christopher, and Mitrokhin, Vasili, *The World Was Going Our Way: The KGB and the Battle for the Third World* (New York: Basic Books, 2005).

Andrew, Christopher, and Noakes, Jeremy (eds), *Intelligence and International Relations 1900–1945* (Exeter: University of Exeter, 1987).

Anonymous, 'Kto ubil Valtera Krivitskogo?' *Literaturnaya Gazeta*, 4, 24 January 1990, p. 14 (editorial compilation based on Flora Lewis's 1966 article).

Ansó, Mariano, *Yo fui ministro de Negrín* (Barcelona: Planeta, 1976).

Antonov-Ovseyenko, Anton V., *The Time of Stalin: Portrait of a Tyranny* (New York: Harper & Row, 1981).

Argenteri, Letizia, *Tina Modotti: Between Art and Revolution* (New Haven and London: Yale University Press, 2003).

Ash, Timothy Garton, 'Orwell's List', *New York Review of Books*, 25 September 2003.

Ashkenazi, F. M., and Marshalova, N. V. *Sovetskoe ugolovnoe pravo: Bibliografiya, 1917–1960* (Moscow: Gosjurizdat, 1961).

Bagley, Tennent H., *Spy Wars: Moles, Mysteries, and Deadly Games* (New Haven and London: Yale University Press, 2007).

Baikalov, Anatoly V., *In the Land of the Communist Dictatorship: Labour and Social Conditions in Russia Today* (London: J. Cape, 1929).

Bajanov, Boris (Bazhanov), *Avec Stalin dans le Kremline* (Paris: Les Éditions de France, 1930).

Barmin(e), Alexander, *One Who Survived: The Life Story of a Russian under the Soviets*, intro. Max Eastman (New York: G. P. Putnam's Sons, 1945).

Barron, John, *The Secret Work of Soviet Secret Agents*, paperback (London: Hodder and Stoughton, Corgi edition, 1979).

Barron, John, *KGB Today: The Hidden Hand*, paperback (London: Hodder and Stoughton, Coronet edition, 1985).

Barruso Báres, Pedro, *El Frente Silencioso: La Guerra Civil española en el Sudoeste de Francia (1936–1940)* (Alegia/Gipuzkoa: Hiria, 2001).

Baxell, Richard, *British Volunteers in the Spanish Civil War: The British Batallion in the International Brigade, 1936–1939* (Abersychan, Wales: Warren & Pell, 2007).

Baxell, Richard, *Unlikely Warriors: The British in the Spanish Civil War and the Struggle against Fascism* (London: Aurum, 2012).

Bazhanov, Boris, and Doyle, David W. (Contributor), *Bazhanov & the Damnation of Stalin* (Athens, OH: Ohio University Press, 1990).

Bearse, Ray, and Read, Anthony, *Conspirator: The Untold Story of Tyler Kent* (New York: Doubleday, 1991).

Beaune, Danièle, *L'Enlèvement du Général Koutiepoff* (Aix-en-Provence: Publications de l'Université de Provence, 1998).

Bennett, Gill, *Churchill's Man of Mystery: Desmond Morton and the World of Intelligence* (Abingdon and New York: Routledge, 2007).

Benson, Robert Louis, *The VENONA Story*, paperback (Washington, DC: National Security Agency, Center for Cryptologic History, 2001).

Benton, Kenneth, 'The ISOS Years: Madrid 1941–3', *Journal of Contemporary History*, 30/3 (July 1995), 359–410.

Bérard, Ewa, *La Vie tumulteuse d'Ilya Ehrenburg: Juif, Russe et Soviétique* (Paris: Éditions Ramsay, 1991).

Berberova, Nina, *Moura: The Dangerous Life of the Baroness Budberg* (New York: New York Review Books, 2005).

Besedovsky, Grigory Z., *Revelations of a Soviet Diplomat* (London: Williams & Norgate, 1931).

Besedovsky, Grégoire, *Oui, j'accuse! Au service des Soviets* (Paris: Libraire der la Revue Française, 1930).

Besedowsky, Grigorij, *Im Dienste der Soujets* (Leipzig and Zurich: Grethlein & Co., 1929).

Besedowsky, Grigorij, *Den Klauen der Tscheka entronnen: Erinnerungen* (Leipzig and Zurich: Grethlein & Co., 1930).

Bethell, Nicholas, *The Great Betrayal: The Untold Story of Kim Philby's Biggest Coup* (London: Hodder, 1984).

Binder, David, 'K.G.B. Aide Tells of Defector who was Kim Philby's Handler', *New York Times* (International), Wednesday, 26 June 1991, A11.

Birchall, Ian, 'The Success and Failure of the Comintern', in Keith Flett and David Renton (eds), *The Twentieth Century: A Century of Wars and Revolutions?*, paperback (London: Rivers Oram Press, 2000).

Birstein, Vadim J., *SMERSH: Stalin's Secret Weapon* (London: Biteback Publishing, 2011).

Blyton, Enid, *Greene, H. Secret Agent in Spain: An Englishman's Cloak and Dagger Operation*, paperback (London: Pan, 1999).

Boadle, Donald, 'Vansittart's Administration of the Foreign Office in the 1930s', in Richard Langhorne (ed.), *Diplomacy and Intelligence during the Second World War: Essays in Honour of F. H. Hinsley* (Cambridge: Cambridge University Press, 1985), 68–84.

Bocca, Giorgio, *Palmiro Togliatti* (Roma: Laterza, 1973).

Bohlen, Charles, *Witness to History 1919–1969* (London: Weidenfeld & Nicolson, 1973).

Bolín, Luis, *Spain: The Vital Years* (Philadelphia and New York: J. B. Lippincott Company, 1967).

Bolloten, Burnett, *The Grand Camouflage: The Spanish Civil War and Revolution, 1936–39*, intro. H. R. Trevor-Roper (New York, Washington, DC, and London: Frederick A. Praeger; second printing 1968).

Bolloten, Burnett, *The Spanish Civil War: Revolution and Counterrevolution* (Chapel Hill, NC: University of North Carolina Press, 1991).

Bonamusa, Francesco, *Andreu Nin y el movimiento comunista en España 1931–1937* (Barcelona: Anagrama, 1977).

Bondarev, N. V. 'Moskovskie gody Iosipa Broza Tito: Predystoriya partizana' (article), Rossiiskii Institut Strategicheskikh Issledovanii, Moscow, 6 July 2010.

Borkenau, Franz, *Spanish Cockpit: An Eye-Witness Account of the Political and Social Conflicts of the Spanish Civil War* (London: Faber and Faber, 1937).

Borovik, Genrikh, *The Philby Files: The Secret Life of the Master Spy Kim Philby: KGB Archives Revealed*, ed. with an intro. Phillip Knightley (London: Little, Brown and Co., 1994).

Bortnevsky, Victor, 'Oprichnina: Nevozvrashchenets Grigorii Agabekov i sekret-naya sluzhba Stalina', *Sobesednik*, 34 (August 1989).

Bortnevsky, V. G., *Zagadka smerti generala Wrangelya: Neizvestnye materially po istorii Russkoi emigratsii* (St Petersburg: St Petersburg University Publishing, 1996).

Bottai, Giuseppe *Diario 1935–1944* and *Diario 1944–1948*, ed. Giordano Guerri (Milan: Biblioteca Universale Rizzoli, 2001).

Bower, Tom, *The Red Web: MI6 and the KGB Master Coup* (London: Aurum Press, 1989).

Bower, Tom, *The Perfect English Spy: Sir Dick White and the Secret War 1935–90* (London: Heinemann, 1995).

Bowers, Claude G., *My Mission to Spain: Watching the Rehearsal for World War II* (London: Victor Gollancz, 1954).

Bowker, Gordon, *George Orwell*, paperback (London: Abacus, 2003).

Boyarsky, Vyacheslav, *Diversanty zapadnogo fronta: Artus Sprogis i drugie* (Moscow: Krasnaya zvezda, 2007).

Brackman, Roman, *The Secret File of Joseph Stalin: A Hidden Life* (London: Routledge, 2000).

Brandt, Willy, *My Road to Berlin* (London: Peter Davies, 1960).

Braun, Otto, *Chinesisches Aufzeichnungen 1932–1939* (Berlin: Dietz Verlag, 1975).

Brenan, Gerald, *The Spanish Labyrinth: An Account of the Social and Political Background of the Spanish Civil War*, paperback (Cambridge: Cambridge University Press, 2000).

Brett-Perring, Marie, 'Is Moscow Ready to Reach Out for France?' *Liberty*, 1 August 1936, p. 59.

Breuer, William B., *Top Secret Tales of World War II* (New York: John Wiley & Sons, 2000).

Bridges, Peter, 'George Kennan Reminisces about Moscow in 1933–1937', *Diplomacy & Statecraft*, 17 (2006), 283–93.

Brigada Internacional ist Unser Ehrenname. Erlebnisse ehemalige deutscher Spanienkämpfer 2 vols (Berlin: Militätverlag der DDR, 1974).

Brockway, Fenner, *The Truth about Barcelona* (London: ILP, 1937).

Brockway, Fenner, *Towards Tomorrow: The Autobiography of Fenner Brockway* (London: Hart-Davis, 1977).

Broda, Paul, *Scientist Spies: A Memoir of my Three Parents and the Atom Bomb* (Leicester: Matador, 2011).

Brodsky, Joseph, 'Collector's Item' [Orlov and Philby], in Joseph Brodsky, *On Grief and Reason*, paperback (London: Penguin Books, 1995).

Bronin, Samuil, *Istoriya moei materi* (Moscow: Sphera, 2004).

Brook-Shepherd, Gordon, *The Storm Petrels: The First Soviet Defectors, 1928–1938* (London: Collins, 1977).

Brook-Shepherd, Gordon, *The Storm Birds: Soviet Post-War Defectors* (London: Weidenfeld and Nicolson, 1988).

Brook-Shepherd, *Iron Maze: The Western Secret Services and the Bolsheviks* (London: Macmillan, 1998).

Broué, Pierre, 'The "May Days" of 1937 in Barcelona', trans. into English by John Archer, *La Verité* (January 1988).

Broué, Pierre, 'Rudolf Klement', *Revolutionary History*, 1/1 (Spring 1988).

Broué, Pierre, *The German Revolution, 1917–1923*, paperback (London: Haymarket Books, 2006).

Broué, Pierre, 'Kurt Landau', *Revolutionary History*, 9/4 (2008), 229–36.

Broué, Pierre, and Témime, Emile, *La Revolution et la guerre d'Espagne* (Paris: Les Éditions de Minuit, 1961).

Brown, Anthony Cave, *Treason in the Blood: H. St John Philby, Kim Philby, and the Spy Case of the Century* (Boston: Houghton Mifflin Co., 1994).

Brown, Andrew, 'The Viennese Connection: Engelbert Broda, Alan Nunn May and Atomic Espionage', *Intelligence and National Security*, 24/2 (April 2009), 173–93.

Brunovsky, Vladimir, *The Methods of the OGPU* (London: Harper & Brothers, 1931).

Brun-Zechowoj, Walerij, *Manfred Stern: General Kleber. Die tragische Biographie eines Berufsrevolutionärs (1896–1954)* (Berlin: Trafo Verlad Dr Wolfgang Weiss, 2000).

Buchanan, Tom, 'A Far Away Country of which We Know Nothing? Perceptions of Spain and its Civil War in Britain, 1931–1939', *Twentieth Century British History*, 4/1 (1993).

Buchanan, Tom, *Britain and the Spanish Civil War* (Cambridge: Cambridge University Press, 1997).

Buchanan, Tom, 'The Death of Bob Smillie, the Spanish Civil War and the Eclipse of the Independent Labour Party', *Historical Journal*, 40/2 (June 1997), 435–61.

Buchanan, Tom, 'Edge of Darkness: British "Front-Line" Diplomacy in the Spanish Civil War, 1936–37', *Contemporary European History*, 3/3 (2003), 279–303.

Buckley, Henry, *The Life and Death of the Spanish Republic: A Witness to the Spanish Civil War*, intro. Paul Preston (London and New York: I. B. Tauris, 2013).

Buckmiller, Michael, und Meschkat, Klaus (eds), *Biographisches Handbuch zur Geschichte der Kommunistischen Internationale: Ein deutsch-russisches Forschungsprojekt* (Berlin: Akademie Verlag, 2007).

Budenz, Louis Francis, *This is my Story* (New York: Whittlesey House, McGraw-Hill Book Company, 1947).

Budkevich, L. S., *'Delo Sorge': Sledstvie i sudebnyi protess* [based on Japanese sources] (Moscow: Nauka, 1969).

Bulgakov, Mikhail, *The Master and Margarita*, trans. Mirra Ginsburg, paperback (New York: Grove Press, 1995).

Burke, Colin, 'Kim Philby, the American Intelligence Community, and OP-20-G: The Fox Built the Hen-House and Took the Keys', *Cryptologia*, 25/2 (April 2001).

Burns, Jimmy, *Papa Spy: A True Story of Love, Wartime Espionage in Madrid, and the Treachery of the Cambridge Spies* (London: Bloomsbury, 2011).

Bystroletov, Dmitri Aleksandrovich, *Pir Besstrashnykh* (Moscow: Granitsa, 1993).

Bystroletov, Dmitri Aleksandrovich, *Puteshestvie na krai nochi* (Moscow: Sovremennik, 1996).

Callaghan, John, and Morgan, Kevin, 'The Open Conspiracy of the Communist Party and the Case of W. N. Ewer, Communist and Anti-Communist', *Historical Journal*, 49/2 (2006), 549–64.

Canali, Mauro, 'Tutta la verità sul caso Tresca', *Liberal* (February–March 2001).

Carew-Hunt, Robert N., 'Willi Münzenberg', in David Footman (ed.), *International Communism*, St Anthony's Papers IX (Oxford: Chatto & Windus, 1960).

Carley, Michael J., 'Five Kopecks for Five Kopecks: Franco-Soviet Trade Negotiations, 1928–1939', *Cahiers du monde russe et soviétique*, 33/1 (January–March 1992), 23–57.

Carley, Michael J., *1939: The Alliance that Never Was* (London: House of Stratus, 2000).

Carley, Michael Jabara, 'Resurgent France or Decadent France? War Origins Once Again', *Canadian Journal of History* (University of Saskatchewan), 37/2 (August 2002), 311–17.

Carley, Michael Jabara, 'Caught in a Cleft Stick: Soviet Diplomacy and the Spanish Civil War', in Gaynor Johnson (ed.), *The International Context of the Spanish Civil War* (Newcastle upon Tyne: Cambridge Scholars Publishing, 2009), 151–81.

Carley, Michael Jabara, *Silent Conflict: A Hidden History of Early Soviet–Western Relations* (Lanham, MD: Rowman & Littlefield, 2014).

Carr, E. H., 'The Origin and Status of the Cheka', *Soviet Studies*, 10/1 (July 1958), 1–11.

Carr, E. H., *The Comintern and the Spanish Civil War*, ed. Tamara Deutscher (London: Macmillan, 1984).

Carr, E. H., *The Russian Revolution from Lenin to Stalin* (Houndmills, Basingstoke: Palgrave Macmillan, 2003).

Carrillo, Santiago, 'Réplica de Santiago Carrillo', *El Pais*, 28 October 2005.

Carroll, Peter N., *The Odyssey of the Abraham Lincoln Brigade: Americans in the Spanish Civil War*, paperback (Stanford, CA: Stanford University Press, 1994).

Carter, Miranda, *Anthony Blunt: His Lives* (New York: Farrar Straus Giroux, 2002).

Castells, Andreu, *Las Brigadas Internacionales de la Guerra de España* (Barcelona: Ed. Ariel, 1974).

Castillo-Puche, José Luis, *Hemingway in Spain* (New York: Doubleday & Company, 1974).

Castro Delgado, Enrique, *Hombres made in Moscu* (Mexico: Publicaciones Mañana, 1960).

Cattell, David T., *Communism and the Spanish Civil War* (Berkeley and Los Angeles: University of California Press, 1955).

Cattell, David T., *Soviet Diplomacy and the Spanish Civil War* (Berkeley and Los Angeles: University of California Press, 1957).

Cecil, Robert, *Hitler's Decision to Invade Russia 1941* (London: Davis-Poynter, 1975).

Cecil, Robert, 'The Cambridge Comintern', in Christopher Andrew and David Dilks (eds), *The Missing Dimension: Governments and Intelligence Communities in the Twentieth Century* (London: Macmillan, 1984).

Cecil, Robert, 'C's War', *Intelligence and National Security*, 1/2 (May 1986).

Cecil, Robert, *A Divided Life: A Personal Portrait of the Spy Donald Maclean* (New York: William Morrow, 1989).

Cecil, Robert, 'Philby's Spurious War', *Intelligence and National Security*, 9/4 (October 1994).

Chacón, Rafael López, *Por que hice las chekas de Barcelona? Laurencic ante el Consejo de Guerra*, paperback (Barcelona: Editorial Solidaridad National, 1939).

Chambers, Whittaker, *Witness* (Chicago: Henry Regnery Company, 1952).

Chaminade, Marcel, 'Soviet Influence in Spain 1919–1936', *Catholic Mind*, 863 (8 December 1938), 449–62.

Charodeev, Gennady, 'Nevypolnennoe zadanie razvedchika Philby', *Izvestiya*, 14 November 2001.

Charters David A., and Tugwell, Maurice A. J. (eds), *Deception Operations: Studies in the East–West Context* (London: Brassey's, 1990).

Chase, William J., *Enemies within the Gates? The Comintern and the Stalinist Repression, 1934–1939* (New Haven and London: Yale University Press, 2001).

Chertoprud, Sergey, *Nauchno-tekhnicheskaya razvedka ot Lenina do Gorbacheva* (Moscow: Olma Press, 2002).

Chinsky, Pavel, and Werth, Nicolas, *Staline: Archives inédites, 1926–1939*, paperback (Paris: Berg International, 2001).

Chochlow, Nikolaj, *Recht auf Gewissen* (Berlin: Deutsche Verlagsanstalt, 1959).

Clark, Katerina, *Moscow, the Fourth Rome: Stalinism, Cosmopolitanism and the Evolution of Soviet Culture, 1931–1941* (Cambridge, MA: Harvard University Press, 2011).

Claudín, Fernando, *La Crise du movement communiste du Komintern au Kominform II* (Paris: Masperó, 1972).

Claudín, Fernando, *The Communist Movement: From Comintern to Cominform*, paperback (Harmondsworth: Penguin Books/Peregrine Books, 1975).

Clough, Bryan, *State Secrets: The Kent–Wolkoff Affair* (Hove: Hideaway Publications Ltd, 2005).

Codevilla, Angelo M., 'Political Warfare: A Set of Means for Achieving Political Ends', in J. Michael Waller (ed.), *Strategic Influence: Public Diplomacy, Counterpropaganda and Political Warfare* (Washington, DC: Institute of World Politics Press, 2010).

Cohen, Morris, 'KGB Memoirs, 27 December 1978', in Vladimir Chikov, *Razvedchiki-nelegaly* (Moscow: Exmo/Algoritm-kniga, 2003).

Coleman, Peter, 'Willi Münzenberg', *Quadrant* (Australia), 48/7 (July–August 2004).

Comisión del PCE presidida por Dolores Ibarruri y compuesta por Manuel Azcárate, Luis Balaguer, Antonio Cordón, Irene Falcón, and Jose Sandoval, *Guerra y Revolución en España*, 3 vols (Moscow: Editorial Progreso, 1966).

Connolly, Cyril, *The Missing Diplomats* (London: Queen Anne Press, 1952).

Conquest, Robert, *The Great Terror: Stalin's Purge of the Thirties* (London: Macmillan, 1968).

Conquest, Robert, *Inside Stalin's Secret Police: NKVD Politics, 1936–1939* (Stanford, CA: Hoover Institution Press, 1985).

Conquest, Robert, *Stalin and the Kirov Murder*, paperback (Oxford: Oxford University Press, 1990).

Conquest, Robert, *The Great Terror: A Reassessment* (London: Hutchinson, 1990).

Cook, Andrew, *On His Majesty's Secret Service: Sidney Reilly Codename ST1* (Brimscombe: Tempus, 2002).

Coox, Alvin D., 'L'Affaire Lyushkov: Anatomy of a Defector', *Soviet Studies*, 19/3 (January 1968), 405–20.

Coox, Alvin D., *The Anatomy of a Small War: The Soviet–Japanese Struggle for Changkufeng/Khasan, 1938* (Westport, CT: Greenwood Press, 1977).

Coppi, Hans (jun.), 'Die "Rote Kapelle" im Spannungsfeld von Widerstand und nachrichtendienstlicher Tätigkeit: Der Trepper Report vom Juni 1943', *Vierteljahrshefte für Zeitgeschichte*, 3 (July 1996) (Munich: Institut für Zeitgeschichte), 431–58.

Coppi, Hans, und Andersen, Geertje (eds), *Dieser Tod paßt zu mir: Harro Schulze-Boysen—Grenzgänger im Widerstand. Briefe 1915 bis 1942* (Berlin: Aufbau Verlag, 1999).

Cornelissen, Igor, *De GPOe de Overtoon: Spionnen voor Moscou 1920–1940* (Amsterdam: Van Gennep, 1989).

Costa-Amic, Bartomeu, *León Trotsky y Andreu Nin: Dos asesinatos del stalinismo (aclarando la historia)* (San Pedro Cholula, Puebla, Mexico: Altres-Costa-Amic, 1994).

Costello, John, and Tsarev, Oleg, *Deadly Illusions* (London: Century, 1993).

Cotterill, David J. (ed.), and Enzenberger, Maria (trans.), *The Serge–Trotsky Papers*, paperback (London: Pluto Press, 1994).

Courtois, Stephane, and Kriegel, Annie, 'La Seconde Mort de Willi Muenzenberg', *Communisme*, 38–9 (1994).

Courtois, Stéphane, and Panné, Jean-Louis, 'The Shadow of the NKVD in Spain', in Stéphane Courtois et al., *The Black Book of Communism: Crimes, Terror, Repression* (Cambridge, MA, and London: Harvard University Press, 1999).

Courtois, Stéphane, Werth, Nicolas, Panné, Jean-Louis, Paczkowski, Andrzej, Bartosek, Karel, and Margolin, Jean Louis, *The Black Book of Communism: Crimes, Terror, Repression* (Cambridge, MA, and London: Harvard University Press, 1999).

Coverdale, John F., *Italian Intervention in the Spanish Civil War* (Princeton: Princeton University Press, 1975).

Cox, Soledad, *Constancia de la Mora in War and Exile: International Voice for the Spanish Republic* (Brighton: Sussex Academic Press, 2007).

Cross, J. A., *Sir Samuel Hoare, a Political Biography* (London: Jonathan Cape, 1977).

Cuadriello, Jorge Domingo, *El exilio republicano español en Cuba* (Madrid: Siglo XXI de España, 2009).

Dahlem, Franz, 'The Military–Political Work of the Eleventh International Brigade', *Communist International*, 25/5 (May 1938), 445–54.

Dahlem, Franz, *Weg und Ziel des antifaschistischen Kampfes. Ausgewählte Reden und Aufsätze* (Berlin: VVN-Verlag, 1952).

Dahlem, Franz, *Am Vorabend des zweiten Weltkrieges 1938 bis August 1939: Erinnerungen*, i (Berlin: Dietz Verlag, 1977).

Dallin, David J., *Soviet Espionage* (New Haven: Yale University Press, 1955).

Dallin, David, *Shpionazh po-sovetski: Ob'ekty i agenty sovetskoi razvedki* (Moscow: Tsentropoligraf, 2001).

Damaskin, Igor, with Elliott, Geoffrey, *Kitty Harris: The Spy with Seventeen Names* (London: St Ermin's Press, 2001).

Danilov, S. Yu., *Grazhdanskaya voina v Ispanii* (Moscow: Veche, 2004).

Davies, Philip H. J., *MI6 and the Machinery of Spying* (London: Frank Cass, 2004).

Davina Croll, Kirsteen, 'Soviet–Polish Relations, 1919–1921', Ph.D. thesis, University of Glasgow, Department of Central and East European Studies, University of Glasgow, September 2008.

Davis, Philip H. J., *MI6 and the Machinery of Spying*, paperback (London: Frank Cass, 2004).

Day, Peter, 'Love in a Cold War Climate' [The Life of Aino Kuusinen], *National Interest* (Summer 1995).

Day, Peter, *Franco's Friends: How British Intelligence Helped Bring Franco to Power in Spain* (London: Biteback, 2011).

Dazy, René, *Fusillez ces chiens enragés: Le Genocide des trotskistes* (Paris: O. Orban: 1981).

De la Fuente, Inmaculada, *La roja y la falangista: Dos hermanas en la España del 36* (Barcelona: Planeta, 2006).

Del Vayo, Álvarez, *Freedom's Battle* (London: William Heinemann, 1940).

Deriabin, Peter S., with Evans, Joseph C., *Inside Stalin's Kremlin: An Eyewitness Account of Brutality, Duplicity, and Intrigue* (Washington, DC: Brassey's, 1998).

Deriabin, Peter, and Bagley, T. H., *The KGB: Masters of the Soviet Union* (London: Robson Books, 1990).

Deriabin, Peter, and Gibney, Frank, *The Secret World* (London: Arthur Barker, 1959).

Deutscher, Isaac, *Stalin* (London: Penguin Books, 1970).

Deutscher, Isaac, *The Prophet Outcast, 1929–1940*, paperback (London: Oxford University Press, 1970).

Deutscher, Tamara, 'The Purges Recalled', *New Left Review*, London (November–December 1969).

Dewar, Hugo, *Assassins at Large* (London and New York: Wingate, 1951).

Dewar, Hugo, *Assassins at Large: Being a Fully Documented and Hitherto Unpublished Account of the Executions outside Russia Ordered by the GPU* (Westport, CT: Hyperion Press, 1981, repr. of the 1952 edn published by Beacon Press, Boston).

Diaz, Antonio, 'Spanish Intelligence during the Second Republic and the Civil War: 1931–1939', *Journal of Intelligence History*, 6/1 (Summer 2006), 41–65.

Díaz Fernández, Antonio M., *Los servicios de inteligencia españoles: Desde al guerra civil hasta el 11-M. Historia de una transición* (Madrid: Alianza Editorial, 2005).

Dilks, David, 'Flashes of Intelligence: The Foreign Office, the SIS and Security before the Second World War', in Christopher Andrew and David Dilks, *The Missing Dimention: Governments and Intelligence Communities in the Twentieth Century* (Chicago: University of Chicago Press, 1984).

Dingle, Reginald J., 'Russia's Work in Spain', London, 1939, in *Non-Intervention and Intervention*, Seeds of Conflict, Series 3, The Spanish Civil War, 1936–1939 (Nendeln, Liechtenstein: Kraus Reprint, 1979), ch. 19, pp. 1–20.

Dobrin, S., 'Some Questions of Early Soviet Legal History', *Soviet Studies*, 7/4 (April 1956), 353–71.

Dolgopolov, Nikolai, *Abel-Fisher* (Moscow: Molodaya Gvardiya, 2011).

Don Levine, Isaac, *The Mind of an Assassin* (London: Weidenfeld & Nicolson; New York: Farrar, Straus and Cudahy, 1959).

Don Levine, Isaac, *Die Psyche des Mörders: Der Mann der Trotzki tötete* (Vienna, Frankfurt, and Zurich: Europa Verlag, 1970).

Doombadze, Evgeny Vasilyevich, *Na Sluzhbe Cheka i Kominterna* (Paris: Michel, 1930).

Dorril, Stephen, *MI6: Fifty Years of Special Operations*, paperback (London: Fourth Estate, 2001).

Dos Passos, John, *The Fourteenth Chronicle: Letters and Diaries of John Dos Passos*, ed. with a biographical narrative by Towsend Ludington (Boston: Gambit Inc., 1973).

Drabkin, Ya. S., Babichenko, L. G., and Shirinya, K. K. (eds), *Komintern i ideya mirovoi revolyutsyi*. Documents (Moscow: Nauka, 1998).

Draganov, Dragomir, 'La causas de la derrota de la República' [Stoyan Minev's reports to the Comintern leadership], *Cuadernos Republicanos*, 55 (Primavera/Verano 2004), Madrid: Centro de Investigación y Estudios Republicanos (CIERE), 33–47.

Driberg, Tom, *Guy Burgess: A Portrait with Background* (London: Weidenfeld & Nicolson, 1956).

Droz, Jaques, *Willi Münzenberg (1889/1940). D'Erfurt à Paris: Un homme contre*, Actes, colloque international, 26–29 March 1992 (Aix-en-Provence and Montpellier: La Bibliothèque Méjanes and Maison de Heidelberg, 1993).

Dullin, Sabine, *Diplomates et diplomatie sovietique en Europe (1930–1939): Structures et methodes d'une politique extérieure sous Staline* (Paris: Univ. 1, Diss. 1998).

Dullin, Sabine, 'Litvinov and the People's Commissariat of Foreign Affairs: The Fate of an Administration under Stalin, 1930–39', in Silvio Pons and Andrea Romano (eds), *Russia in the Age of Wars* (Milan: Feltrinelli Editore, 2000).

Dullin, Sabine, *Men of Influence: Stalin's Diplomats in Europe, 1930–1939* (Edinburgh: Edinburgh University Press, 2008).

Dumbadze, E., *Na sluzhbe Cheka i Kominterna* (Paris: Id-vo 'Mishen', 1930).

Duran, Juan Garcia, *Bibliography of the Spanish Civil War, 1936–1939* (Montevideo: Editorial El Siglo Ilustrado, 1964).

Durgan, Andy, 'Freedom Fighters or Comintern Army? The International Brigades in Spain', *International Socialism Journal*, 84 (1999), 1–16.

Eastman, Max, *Einstein, Trotsky, Hemingway, Freud and Other Great Companions* (New York: Collier Books, 1962).

Edelman, Fanny, *Banderas, Pasiones, Camaradas* (Buenos Aires: Ediciones Dirple, 1996).

Ehrenburg, Ilya, *No Pasaran* (London: Malik Verlag, 1937).

Ehrenburg, Ilya, *Sobranie sochinenii v devyati tomakh* (Moscow: Gosudarstvennoe izdatelstvo khudozhestvennoi literatury, 1962–7).

Ellman, Michael, 'Stalin and the Soviet Famine of 1932–33, Revisited', *Europe–Asia Studies*, 59/4 (June 2007), 663–93.

Elorza, Antonio, 'Codovilla en Paracuelos', *El Pais*, Saturday, 1 November 2008.

Elorza, Antonio, 'Le Front populaire espagnole à travers les archives du Komintern', in Serge Wolikow (ed.), with Maurice de Carrez, Michel Cordillot, and Jean Vigreux, *Une histoire en revolution? Du bon usage des archives, de Moscou et d'ailleurs* (Dijon: Publications de l'Université de Bourgogne, 1996).

Elorza, Antonio, and Bizcarrondo, Marta, *Queridos camaradas: La International Comunista y España, 1919–1939* (Barcelona: Planeta, 1999).

Encyclopaedia Bulgaria (Sofia: Izdatelstvo na BAN, 1978).

Erickson, John, *The Soviet High Command: A Military–Political History, 1918–1941* (London: Routledge, 2001).

Ericson, Edward E., *Feeding the German Eagle: Soviet Economic Aid to Nazi Germany, 1933–41* (Westport, CT: Greenwood Press, 1999).

Esenwein, George, 'Zum Tode von Burnett Bolloten', *Tranvia: Revue der Iberischen Halbinsel* (Berlin), 8 (March 1988), 65–6.

Esenwein, George R., *The Spanish Civil War: A Modern Tragedy*, paperback (New York and London: Routledge, 2005).

Esenwein, George, 'The Cold War and the Spanish Civil War: The Impact of Politics on Historiography', in Brian D. Bunk, Sasha D. Pack, and Carl-Gustaf Scott (eds), *Nation and Conflict in Modern Spain: Essays in Honour of Stanley G. Payne* (Madison: University of Wisconsin/Parallel Press, 2008), 175–89.

Eucinas Moral, Ángel Luis, *Fuentes históricas para el estudio de la emigración española a la U.R.S.S., 1936–2007* (Madrid: Exterior XXI, 2008).

Ezhenedelnik sovetskoi justitsii (1922).

Fainsod, Merle, and Hough, Jerry F., *How the Soviet Union is Governed* (Cambridge, MA: Harvard University Press, 1979).

Faligot, Roger, and Kauffer, Rémi, *As-tu vu Crémet?* (Paris: Fayard, 1991).

Faligot, Roger, and Kauffer, Rémi, 'Du nouveau sur Malraux, la Chine & le Komintern', *Asie Extrême*, published by the Centre d'Etude et de Recherches Asie Orientale (CERAO), (University of Rennes II, Rennes, Haute Bretagne, 1991).

Fernández Cuesta, Raimundo, *Testimonio, recuerdos y reflexiones* (Madrid: Dyrsa, 1985).

Fernández, Rodrigo, 'Una española, espía en el KGB' [África de las Heras], *El Pais*, 30 March 2008.

Fernándo Sánchez, José, 'Los últimos consejeos rusos en España', *Historia*, 16 (April 1984), 25–7.

Feuchtwanger, Lion, *Moskau 1937: Ein Reisebericht für meine Freunde* (Amsterdam: Querido Verlag NV: 1937).

Feuchtwanger, Lion, *Moskva 1937* (Moscow: Goslitizdat, 1937).

Firsov, Fridrikh I., 'Dimitrov, the Comintern and Stalinist Repression', in Barry McLoughlin and Kevin McDermott (eds), *Stalin's Terror: High Politics and Mass Repression in the Soviet Union* (Houndmills, Basingstoke: Palgrave Macmillan, 2003).

Firsov, Friedrich, 'Geheimtelegramme der Komintern im Spanischen Bürgerkrieg', *Forum für osteuropäische Ideen- und Zeitgescichte* (ZIMOS, Eichstätt, Katholische Universität Ingolstadt), i (1999).

Firsow, Fridrich, 'Die Komintern und die "Große Säuberung"', in Michael Buckmiller und Klaus Meschkat (eds), *Biographisches Handbuch zur Geschichte der Kommunistischen Internationale: Ein deutsch-russisches Forschungsprojekt* (Berlin: Akademie Verlag, 2007), 361–77.

Fischer, Ben, ' "Mr Guver": Anonimous Soviet Letter to the FBI', *The CIA Centre for the Study of Intelligence Newsletter*, 7 (1997), 10–11.

Fischer, Ernst, *Trotsky Unmasked* (New York: Workers' Library Publishers, 1937).

Fischer, Louis, *Men and Politics* (London: Cape, 1941).

Fischer, Markoosha, *My Lives in Russia* (New York: Harper & Brothers, 1944).

Flory, Harriette, 'The Arcos Raid and the Rupture of Anglo-Soviet Relations', *Journal of Contemporary History*, 12/4 (October 1977), 707–23.

Fomin, Fyodor Timofeyevich, *Zapiski starogo chekista* (Moscow: Politizdat, 1964).

Fondación Pablo Iglesias (ed.), *Los rusos en la Guerra de España 1936–1939*, Catalogue (Madrid: Fondación Pablo Iglesias, 2009).

Foote, Alexander, *Handbook for Spies* (London: Museum Press, 1949).

Forsyth, Frederick, *The Fist of God* (New York: Bantam Dell Publishing Group, 1994).

Fox, Soledad, *Constancia de la Mora in War and Exile: International Voice for the Spanish Republic* (Brighton and Portland: Sussex Academic Press/Cañada Blanch Centre for Contemporary Spanish Studies, 2007).

Fradkin, Viktor, *Delo Koltsova* (Moscow: Vagrius, 2002).

From *The Times* own correspondent, 'Fleeing from the Purge: Soviet Diplomat's Appeal: "My Own Death Warrant"', *The Times*, 8 December 1937, p. 16.

Fuensanta, José Ramón Soler, 'Mechanical Cipher Systems in the Spanish Civil War', *Cryptologia*, 28/3 (July 2004).

Fuente, Inmaculada de la, *La roja y la falangista* (Barcelona: Planeta, 2006).

Fyrth, Jim, *The Signal was Spain: The Spanish Aid Movement in Britain, 1936–39* (London: Lawrence and Wishart, 1986).

Gallagher, Dorothy, *All the Right Enemies: The Life and Murder of Carlo Tresca* (Fredericksburg, PA: Rutgers University Press, 1988).

Gannon, James, *Stealing Secrets, Telling Lies: Spies and Codebreakers*, paperback (Dulles, VA: Brassey's, 2002).

Gannon, Paul, *Colossus Bletchley Park's Greatest Secret* (London: Atlantic Books, 2006).

Garcia, Hugo, *The Truth about Spain: Mobilising British Public Opinion, 1936–1939* (Eastbourne: Sussex Academic Press, 2010).

Garcia Perez, Rafael, *Franquismo y Tercer Reich* (Madrid: CEC, 1994).

Garosci, Aldo, *Gli intellettuali e la guerra di Spagna* (Torino: Giulio Einaudi editore, 1959).

Gazur, Edward P., *Secret Assignment: The FBI's KGB General* (London: St Ermin's Press, 2001).

Gelfand, Alan, *The Gelfand Case: A Legal History of the Exposure of US Government Agents in the Leadership of the Socialist Workers Party* (Detroit, MI: Mehring Books, 1985).

Gellately, Robert, *Stalin and Hitler: The Age of Social Catastrophe* (London: Jonathan Cape, 2007).

Genovés, Maria Dolors, 'Operació Nikolai: L'Assasinat d'Andreu Nin', in *Història política, societat i cultura dels països catalans*, ix (Barcelona: Edicions 62, 1998), 305–7.

Getty, J. Arch, *Origins of the Great Purges: The Soviet Communist Party Reconsidered, 1933–1938*, paperback (Cambridge: Cambridge University Press, 1987).

Getty Arch J., 'The Politics of Repression Revisited', in Arch John Getty and Roberta Thompson Manning (eds), *Stalinist Terror: New Perspective*, paperback (Cambridge: Cambridge University Press, 1993).

Getty, Arch John, and Manning, Roberta Thompson (eds), *Stalinist Terror: New Perspective*, paperback (Cambridge: Cambridge University Press, 1993).

Getty, J. Arch, and Naumov, Oleg V., *The Road to Terror: Stalin and the Self-Destruction of the Bolsheviks, 1932–1939*, trans. Benjamin Sher (New Haven and London: Yale University Press, 1999).

Gibson, Ian, *La noce en que mataron a Calvo Sotelo* (Barcelona: Plaza y Janés, 1986).

Gibson, Ian, *Paracuellos: Cómo fue. La verdad objetiva sobre la matanza de presos en Madrid en 1936* (Madrid: Ediciones Temas de Hoy, 2005).

Gide, André, *Return from the USSR* (New York: Knopf, 1937).

Gieseke, Jens, with Doris Hubert, *The GDR State Security: Shield and Sword of the Party* (Berlin: Die Bundesbeauftragte für die Unterlagen des Staatssicherheitsdienstes der ehemaligen Deutschen Demokratischen Republik, 2004).

Gil, Javier Cervera, *Madrid en Guerra: La Ciudad Clandestina, 1936–1939* (Madrid: Alianza Editorial, 2006).

Gill, Anton, *A Dance between Flames: Berlin between the Wars* (London: John Murray, 1993).

Gitlow, Benjamin, *The Whole of their Lives: Communism in America—A Personal History and Intimate Portrayal of its Leaders* (New York: Charles Scribner's Sons, 1948).

Glees, Anthony, *The Secrets of the Service: British Intelligence and Communist Subversion 1939–1951* (London: Cape, 1987).

Godicheau, François, 'La Légende noire du Service d'Information Militaire de la République dans la guerre civile espagnole, et l'idée de contrôle politique', *Le Mouvement Social*, 201 (October–December 2002).

Godman, Peter, *Der Vatikan und Hitler: Der geheimen Archive* (Munich: Droemer Verlag, 2004).

Goldin, V. I., *Rossiiskaya voennaya emigratsyia i sovetskie spetzsluzhby v 20e gody XX veka* (St Petersburg: Iz-vo Poltorak/Solti, 2010).

Goldman, Albert, *The Assassination of Leon Trotsky: The Proofs of Stalin's Guilt* (New York: Pioneer Publishers, 1940).

González-Betes, Antonio, *Franco y el Dragón Rapide* (Madrid: Rialp, 1987).

Gorbunov, Yevgeny Aleksandrovich, 'Voennaya razvedka v 1934–1939 godakh', *Svobodnaya mysl*, 2 (February 1998), 98–109; 3 (March 1998), 54–61.

Gorbunov, Yevgeny, *Stalin i GRU* (Moscow: Yauza/Eksmo, 2010).

Gorchakov, O. A., *Jan Berzin—komandarm GRU* (St Petersburg: Neva, 2004).

Gordievsky, Oleg, 'The KGB Archives', *Intelligence and National Security*, 6/1 (January 1991), 7–14.

Gordievsky, Oleg, *Next Stop Execution* (London: Macmillan, 1995).

Gordievsky, Oleg, 'Unrewarded Loyalty to the Wrong Cause', *Spectator*, 26 May 2001.

Gordievsky, Oleg, and Volodarsky, Boris, 'Untangling the Web of Deception', *Spectator*, 19 May 2007, pp. 38–40.

Gori, Francesca, Guercetti, Emanuela, and Dundovich, Elena, *Reflections on the Gulag: With a Documentary Appendix on the Italian Victims of Repressions in the USSR*, paperback (Milan: Feltrinelli, 2003).

Gorkin, Julian, *Stalins langer Arm* (Berlin: Kiepenheuer & Witsch, 1984).

Gorlov, Sergey A., *Sovershenno sekretno: Moskva–Berlin, 1920–1933* (Moscow: Rossiiskaya Akademiya Nauk, 1999).

Gorlov, Sergei A., *Sovershenno sekretno: Moskva–Berlin, 1920–1933. Voenno-politicheskie otnosheniya mezhdu SSSR i Germaniei* (Moscow: IVI/Rossiiskaya Akademiya Nauk, 1999).

Gorodetsky, Gabriel, 'Geopolitical Factors in Stalin's Strategy and Politics in the Wake of the Outbreak of World War II', in Silvio Pons and Andrea Romano (eds), *Russia in the Age of Wars* (Milan: Feltrinelli Editore, 2000).

Gould, Jonathan S., 'The OSS and the London "Free Germans"', *Studies in Intelligence*, 46/1 (2002), 11–29.

Gouzenko, Igor, *The Iron Curtain* (New York: E. P. Dutton, 1948).

Gouzenko, Igor, *This Was My Choice* (Montreal: Palm, 1968).

Graham, Helen, *Socialism and War: The Spanish Socialist Party in Power and Crisis, 1936–1939* (Cambridge: Cambridge University Press, 1991).

Graham, Helen, 'War, Modernity and Reform: The Premiership of Juan Negrín 1937–1939', in Paul Preston and Ann L. Mackenzie (eds), *The Republic Besieged: Civil War in Spain 1936–1939*, paperback (Edinburgh: Edinburgh University Press, 1996).

Graham, Helen, '"Against the State": A Genealogy of the Barcelona May Days (1937)', *European History Quarterly*, 29/4 (1999), 485–542.

Graham, Helen, *The Spanish Civil War: A Very Short Introduction*, paperback (Oxford: Oxford University Press, 2005).

Graham, Helen, *The Spanish Republic at War 1936–1939*, paperback (Cambridge: Cambridge University Press, 2002).

Greene, Herbert, *Secret Agent in Spain: An Englishman's Cloak and Dagger Operations for the Republicans* (London: Robert Hale, 1938).

Grey, Marina, *Le Général meurt à minuit: L'Enlèvement des généraux Koutiépov (1930) et Miller (1937)* (Paris: Plon, 1981).

Grimalt, José, 'Operación Nikolai', *Levante*, 15 January 1993.

Gross, Babette, *Willi Münzenberg: A Political Biography* (Ann Arbor, MI: Michigan University Press, 1974).

Gross, Babette, *Willi Münzenberg: Eine politische Biographie*. Mit einem Vorwort von Arthur Koestler (Stuttgart: Deutsche Verlags-Anstalt, 1967).

Guadarrama, Dr P., et al., *Stripped of all Fetish: Authenticity of Marxist Philosophy in Latin America* (Las Villas: INCC University of Columbia, Central University of Las Villas, UCLV, 1999).

Guarner, Vicente, *Cataluña en la Guerra de España, 1936–39* (Madrid: Ed. G. del Toro, 1975).

Guerri, Giordano B., *Giuseppe Bottai* (Rome: Bompiani, 2010).

Guevara, Ernesto, Loveman, Brian, and Davies, Thomas M., *Guerrilla Warefare* (Lincoln: University of Nebraska Press, 1985).

Guillamón, Augustín, *Barricadas en Barcelona* (Barcelona: Espartaco Internaacional, 2007).

Hall, Allan, 'Stalin's Secret Files on Hitler', *The Scotsman*, Wednesday, 16 March 2005.

Hammant, Thomas B., 'Some Incidents in the 1930s', *Cryptologia*, 25/1 (January 2001), 61–3.

Hamrick, S. J., *Deceiving the Deceivers: Kim Philby, Donald MacLean and Guy Burgess* (New Haven and London: Yale University Press, 2004).

Hansen, Joseph, 'The Attempted Assassination of Leon Trotsky', *Fourth International*, 1/4 (August 1940), 85–91.

Harding, Luke, 'The Woman who Kept Spy Secrets of the "Third Man"', *Observer*, Sunday, 7 November 2004.

Hardison, Felicia, 'Stanislavski's Champion: Sonia Moore and her Crusade to Save the American Theatre', *Theatre History Studies*, 1 June 2004.

Hart, John Limond, *The CIA's Russians* (Annapolis, MD: Naval Institute Press, 2003).

Hart-Davis, Duff, *Man of War: The Secret Life of Captain Alan Hillgarth—Officer, Adventurer, Agent* (London: Century, 2012).

Hastings, Chris, and Edwardes, Charlotte, 'MI5 Thought Churchill Nephews Were Spies', *Daily Telegraph*, 23 June 2002.

Haustov, Vladimir, and Samuelson, Lennart, *Stalin, NKVD i repressii, 1936–1938 gg.* (Moscow: ROSSPEN, 2009).

Haynes, John Earl, 'The American Communist Party as an Auxiliary to Espionage: From Asset to Liability', 2005 Raleigh International Spy Conference paper, pp. 5–7.

Haynes, John Earl, and Klehr, Harvey, *Venona: Decoding Soviet Espionage in America* (New Haven and London: Yale University Press, 1999).

Haynes, John Earl, and Klehr, Harvey, *Early Cold War Spies: The Espionage Trials that Shaped American Politics* (New York: Cambridge University Press, 2006).

Haynes, John, and Klehr, Harvey, *In Denial: Historians, Communism, & Espionage* (New York: Encounter Books, 2003).

Haynes, John Earl, Klehr, Harvey, and Vassiliev, Alexander, *Spies: The Rise and Fall of the KGB in America* (New Haven and London: Yale University Press, 2009).

Hedeler, Wladislaw, 'Ezhov's Scenario for the Great Terror and the Falsified Record of the Third Moscow Show Trial', in Barry McLoughlin and Kevin McDermott (eds), *Stalin's Terror: High Politics and Mass Repression in the Soviet Union* (Houndmills, Basingstoke: Palgrave Macmillan, 2003).

Hehn, Paul N., *A Low Dishonest Decade: The Great Powers, Eastern Europe, and the Economic Origins of World War II, 1930–1941* (London: Continuum International Publishing Group, 2003).

Heiberg, Morten, y Agudo, Manuel Ros, *La trama oculta de la Guerra Civil: Los servicios secretos de Franco, 1936–1945* (Barcelona: Crítica, 2006).

Helms, Richard, with Hood, William, *A Look over my Shoulder* (New York: Random House, 2003).

Herbst, Josephine, *The Starched Blue Sky of Spain*, paperback (New York: Harper Perennial, 1992).

Herman, Carol, 'Last Days in the Abyss' [Marina Tsvetayeva], *Washington Times*, 15 February 2004.

Hernández, Jesús, *Le Grand Trahison* (Paris: Fasquelle, 1953).

Hernández, Jesús, *Yo fui un ministro de Stalin* (Madrid: G. del Toro, 1974).

Hernández Sánchez, Fernando, *Comunistas sin partido: Jesús Hernández, ministro en la Guerra Civil, disidente en el exilio* (Madrid: Editorial Raices, 2007).

Hernández Sánchez, Fernando, *Guerra o revolución: El Partido Comunista de España en la Guerra civil* (Barcelona: Crítica, 2010).

Hidalgo de Cisneros, Ignacio, *Cambio de rumbo (memorias)*, 2 vols (Bucharest: Colección Ebro, 1964).

Hill, Elizabeth, *Why Need We Study the Slavs? An Augural Lecture* (Cambridge: Cambridge University Press, 1951).

Hill, Elizabeth, *In the Mind's Eye: The Memoirs of Dame Elizabeth Hill*, ed. Jean Stafford Smith (Sussex: Book Guild, 1999).

Hill, George A., *Go Spy the Land: Being the Adventures of I.K. 8 of the British Secret Service* (London: Cassell, 1932).

Hinsley, F. H., and Simkins, C. A. G., *British Intelligence: Security and Counter-intelligence*, iv (London: HMPO, 1990).

Hoare, Geoffrey, *The Missing Macleans* (London: Cassell & Co, 1955).

Hoffmann, Dieter, Müller-Enbergs, Helmut, Wielgohs, Jan, Herbst, Andreas, Kirschey-Feix, Ingrid, and Reimann, Olaf W., et al., *Wer war wer in der DDR? Ein Lexikon ostdeutscher Biographien* (Berlin: Christoph Links Verlag, 2010).

Hofmann, George F., 'The Tactical and Strategic Use of Attaché Intelligence: The Spanish Civil War and the US Army's Misguided Quest for a Modern Tank Doctrine', *Journal of Military History*, 62/1 (January 1998), 101–33.

Höhne, Heinz, *Der Krieg im Dunkeln: Die Geschichte der deutsch–russischen Spionage* (Bindlach: Gondrom, 1993).

Honigmann, Barbara, *Ein Kapitel aus meinem Leben* (Munich and Vienna: Carl Hanser Verlag, 2004).

Hopkins, James K., *Into the Heart of the Fire: The British in the Spanish Civil War* (Stanford, CA: Stanford University Press, 1998).

Hornstein, David P., *Arthur Ewert: A Life for the Comintern* (Lanham, MD, New York, and London: University Press of America, 1993).

Houghteling James L., *A Diary of the Russian Revolution* (New York: Dodd, Mead & Co., 1918).

Howson, Gerald, *Arms for Spain: The Untold Story of the Spanish Civil War* (London and New York: John Murray, 1998).

Hubbard, L. E., *Soviet Money and Finance* (London: Macmillan, 1936).

Huber, Peter, 'Shoot the Mad Dogs', trans. by Ted. Crawford of 'Fuzillez ces chiens enragés', *Rouge*, special edition for the 50th anniversary of Trotsky's death (Summer 1990), 9–10.

Huber, Peter, 'Die Ermordung des Ignaz Reiss in der Schweiz (1937) und die Verhastung dissidenter Schweizer Spanienkämpfer durch den Geheimapparat der Komintern', in *Kommunisten verfolgen Kommunisten: Stalinischer Terror und 'Säuberungen' in den Kommunistischen Parteien Europas seit des dreissiger Jahren* (Berlin: Akademie Verlag, 1993).

Huber, Peter, *Stalins Schatten in die Schweiz. Schweizer Kommunisten in Moskau: Verteidiger und Gefangene der Komintern* (Zurich: Chronos-Verlag, 1994).

Huber, Peter, and Kunzi, Daniel, 'Paris dans les années 30: Sur Serge Efron et quelques agents du NKVD', *Cahiers du Monde russe et soviétique*, 32/2 (1991), 285–310.

Huber, Peter, and Uhl, Michael, 'Politische Überwachung und Repression in den Internationalen Brigaden', in Nikolaus Lobkowicz, Leonid Luks, Donal O'Sullivan, and Alexei Rybakov (eds), *Forum für osteuropäische Ideen- und Zeitgeschichte* (Cologne: Böhlau Verlag, 2001), ii. 121–59.

Huber, Peter, and Hug, Ralph, *Die Schweizer Spanienfreiwilligen: Biografisches Handbuch* (Zurich: Rotpunkverlag, 2009).

Huber, Peter, Künzi, Daniel, and Argelès, Jean-Marie, 'L'Assassinat d'Ignace Reiss', *Communisme: Revue d'études pluridisciplinaires*, 26–7 (1990), 5–28.

Hug, Ralph, *St Gallen–Moskau–Aragón: Das Leben des Spanienkämpfers Walter Wagner*, ed. Peter Huber, paperback (Zurich: Rotpunktverlag, 2007).

Humbert-Droz, Jules, *Memoires: Dix ans de lutte antifasciste, 1931–1941*, iii (Neuchatel: A la Baconniere, 1972).

Ibárruri, Dolores, *El único camino* (Madrid: Instituto de la Mujer, 1992).

Ibárruri, Dolores, Azcárate, Manuel, Balaguer, Luis, Cordón, Antonio, Falcón, Irene, and Sandoval, José (eds), *Guerra y revolución en España*, 4 vols (Moscow: Ed. Progreso, 1966–71).

Iglesias, Ignacio, *Experiencias de la Revolución: El POUM, Trotski y la intervención Soviética* (Barcelona: Laertes, 2003).

Institut zur Geschichte der Arbeiterbewegung (ed.), *In den Fängen des NKWD: Deutsche Opfer des stalinistischen Terrors in der UdSSR* (Berlin: Dietz, 1990).

International Committee of the Fourth International, *How the GPU Murdered Trotsky: The Indictment that Remains Unanswered* (London: The Committee, 1976).

Irving, David, *Uprising* (London: Focal Point, 2001).

Iturralde, Juan de, *La guerra de Franco, los vascos y la Iglesia*, 2 vols (San Sebastian: Publicaciones del Clero Vasco, 1978).

Jackson, Angela, *British Women and the Spanish Civil War*, paperback (Barcelona: Warren & Pell/Cañada Blanch Centre for Contemporary Spanish Studies, 2009).

Jackson, Gabriel, *The Spanish Republic and the Civil War, 1931–1939* (Princeton: Princeton University Press, 1967).

Jackson, Gabriel, *Juan Negrín: Spanish Republican War Leader* (Brighton, Portland, and Toronto: Sussex Academic Press/Cañada Blanch Centre for Contemporary Spanish Studies, 2010).

Jacobs, Dan N., *Borodin: Stalin's Man in China* (Cambridge, MA: Harvard University Press, 1981).

Jansen, Marc, and De Long, Ben, 'Stalin's Hand in Rotterdam: The Murder of the Ukrainian Nationalist Yevhen Konovalets in May 1938', *Intelligence and National Security*, 9/4 (October 1994), 676–94.

Jansen, Marc, and Petrov, Nikita, *Stalin's Loyal Executioner: People's Commissar Nikolai Ezhov, 1895–1940* (Stanford, CA: Hoover Institution Press, 2002).

Jeffery, Inez Cope, *Inside Russia: The Life and Times of Zoya Zarubina* (New York: Eakin Publications, 1999).

Jeffery, Keith, *MI6: The History of the Secret Intelligence Service 1909–1949* (London: Bloomsbury Publishing, 2010).

Jerez Farran, Carlos, and Amago, Samuel, *Unearthing Franco's Legacy: Mass Graves and the Recovery of Historical Legacy in Spain* (Notre Dame, IN: University of Notre Dame Press, 2010).

Jiménez, Javier (interview with), 'Andrès Nin: El trotskista que se fué al frio', *Cambio 16*, 305, 10–16 October 1977.

Johnson, Gaynor (ed.), *The International Context of the Spanish Civil War* (Newcastle upon Tyne: Cambridge Scholars Publishing, 2009).

Johnson, Paul, *Modern Times: The World from the Twenties to the Eighties* (New York: HarperCollins, 1983).

Juárez, Javier, *Comandante Durán: Leyenda y tragedia de un intelectual en armas* (Barcelona: Debate, 2009).

Juárez, Javier, *Patria: Una española en el KGB* (Barcelona: Debate, 2008).

Kalugin, Oleg, *Spymaster: My 32 Years in Intelligence and Espionage against the West* (rev. edn.; New York; Basic Books, 2009).

Kalugin, Oleg, with Montaigne, Fen, *Spy Master: My 32 Years in Intelligence and Espionage against the West* (London: Smith Gryphon Publishers, 1994).

Karmen, Roman, *No Pasaran* (Moscow: Sovetskaya Rossiya, 1972).

Kantor, Julia, *Voina i mir Mikhaila Tukhachevskogo* (Moscow: Izdatelsky dom 'Ogonyok'/Vremya, 2005).

Kardin, V., 'Pan Walter' [General Karol Swierczewski], *Sovershenno sekretno*, 7 (July 2000), 26–7.

Karpov, V. (SVR Press Bureau), 'Neizvestnyi razdevchik Glinski', *Novosti razvedki i kontrrazvedki*, 2/83 (1997), 5.

Karpov, V. (SVR Press Bureau), 'Sudba rezidenta' (Was the author of *The Secret History of Stalin's Crimes* really a traitor?), *Novosti razvedki i kontrrazvedki*, 23–4/56–7 (1995), 8–9.

Kasson, Henry, 'The Zborowski Case: A Veteran Soviet Secret Agent is Uncovered in New York', *New Leader*, 25 November 1955.

Katz, Otto, *The Nazi Conspiracy in Spain*, by the editor of *The Brown Book of the Hitler Terror*, trans. from the German manuscript by Emile Burns (London: Gollancz, 1937).

Kaufmann, Bernd, Reisener, Eckhard, Schwips, Dieter, and Walther, Henri, *Der Nachrichtendienst der KPD 1919–1937* (Berlin: Dietz Verlag, 1993).

Keene, Judith, *Fighting for Franco: International Volunteers in Nationalist Spain during the Spanish Civil War, 1936–39* (London and New York: Leicester University Press, 2001).

Kennedy, David, *Freedom from Fear: The American People in Depression and War, 1929–1945* (New York: Oxford University Press, 1999).

Kennedy, Greg, 'The Royal Navy, Intelligence and the Spanish Civil War: Lessons in Air Power', *Intelligence and National Security*, 20/2 (June 2005), 238–63.

Kennedy-Pipe, Caroline, *Russia and the World, 1917–1991* (London: Arnold, 1998).

Kerbs, Diethart (ed.), *Willi Münzenberg* (Berlin: Edition Echolot, 1988).

Kern, Gary, *A Death in Washington: Walter G. Krivitsky and the Stalin Terror*, intro. Nigel West (New York: Enigma Books, 2004).

Kern, Gary, *The Kravchenko Case: One Man's War on Stalin*, paperback (New York: Enigma Books, 2007).

Kerr, Sheila, 'KGB Sources on the Cambridge Network of Soviet Agents: True or False?', *Intelligence and National Security*, 11/3 (July 1996).

Kerr, Sheila, 'Investigating Soviet Espionage and Subversion: The Case of Donald Maclean', *Intelligence and National Security*, 17/1 (March 2002), 101–16.

Kersten, Kurt, 'Das Ende Willi Münzenbergs. Ein Opfer Stalins und Ulbrichts', *Deutsche Rundschau* (Baden Baden), 83/5 (May 1957).

Kessler, Lauren, *Clever Girl: Elizabeth Bentley, the Spy who Ushered in the McCarthy Era* (New York: Harper Perennial, 2003).

Khenkin, Kirill, *Okhotnik vverkh nogami* [*Hunter Upside Down: The Case of Rudolf Abel*] (Frankfurt am Main: Posev Publishing House, 1981).

Khlevnyuk, Oleg, 'Istoriya "Tainoi istorii"', *Svobodnaya mysl*, 3 (1996), 114–19.

Khlevnyuk, Oleg, *Politburo: Mekhanizmy politicheskoi vlasti v 30-e gody* (Moscow: ROSSPEN, 1996).

Khlevniuk, Oleg, 'Party and NKVD: Power Relationships in the Years of the Great Terror', in Barry McLoughlin and Kevin McDermott (eds), *Stalin's Terror: High Politics and Mass Repression in the Soviet Union* (Houndmills, Basingstoke: Palgrave Macmillan, 2003).

Khlevniuk, Oleg V., *Master of the House: Stalin and his Inner Circle* (New Haven and London: Yale University Press, 2009).

King, Jerry, et al., *We Accuse* [From the Record] (New York, privately printed, 1940).

Kippenberger, Hans (als A. Neuberg), Tuchatschewski, M. N., and Ho Chi Minh, *Der bewaffnete Aufstand: Versuch einer theoretischen Darstelling*. Eingeleitet vom Erich Wollenberg, paperback (Frankfurt am Main: Europäische Verlagsanstalt, 1971).

Kitchen, Martin, 'SOE's Man in Moscow', *Intelligence and National Security*, 12/3 (July 1997), 95–109.

Klehr, Harvey, 'The Myth of "Premature Anti-Fascism"', *New Criterion*, 21/1 (September 2002), 19.

Klehr, Harvey, Haynes, John Earl, and Firsov, Fridrikh Igorevich, *The Secret World of American Communism* (New Haven and London: Yale University Press, 1995).

Klussmann, Uwe, 'Nachricht aus der Apotheke', *Der Spiegel*, 29 September 2009, pp. 50–2.

Knightley, Phillip, *The Life and Views of the KGB Masterspy* (London: André Deutsch, 1988).

Kochański, Aleksandr (ed.), *Księga polaków uczestników Rewolucji Październikowej, 1917–1920, Biografie* (Warsaw: Książka i Wiedza, 1967).

Kochik, Valery, 'Sovetskaya voennaya razvedka: Struktura i kadry (1917–1918)', *Svobodnaya mysl*, 5 (May 1998), 94–103; '(1918–1921)', 6 (June 1998), 88–103; '(1921–1924)', 7 (July 1998), 97–109; '(1924–1936)', 8 (1998), 68–94; '(1936–1941)', 9–12 (1998), 98–122.

Kochik, Valerii, *Razvedchiki i rezidenty GRU: Za predelami Otchizny* (Moscow: Exmo, 2004).

Kocho-Williams, Alastair, 'The Soviet Diplomatic Corps and Stalin's Purges', *Slavonic and East European Review (SEER)*, 86/1 (January 2008), 90–110.

Koenker, Diana P., and Bachman, Ronald D. (eds), *Revelations from the Russian Archives* (Washington: Library of Congress, 1997).

Koestler, Arthur, *Spanish Testament* (London: Collins with Hamish Hamilton, 1938).

Koestler, Arthur, *Darkness at Noon* (London: Collins with Hamish Hamilton, 1940).

Koestler, Arthur, *The Invisible Writing*, being the second volume of *Arrow in the Blue* (London: Collins with Hamish Hamilton, 1954).

Kokurin, Alexander, and Petrov, Nikita, 'GPU–OGPU (1922–1928)', *Svobodnaya mysl*, 7 (July 1998), 110–25.

Kokurin, Alexander, and Petrov, Nikita, 'OGPU (1929–1934)', *Svobodnaya mysl*, 8 (August 1998), 95–114.

Kolpakidi, Alexander Ivanovich, *Entsyklopaediya voennoi razvedki Rossii* (Moscow: Astrel, 2004).

Kolpakidi, Alexander Ivanovich, and and Prokhorov, Dmitri P., *Imperia GRU* (Moskva: Olma-Press, 2000).

Kolpakidi, Alexander Ivanovich, and Prokhorov, Dmitri P., *KGB: Vsyo o vneshnei razvedke* (Moscow: Olimp, 2002).

Koltsov, Mikhail, *Ispanskii dnevnik* (Moscow: Sovetsky pisatel, 1957).

Koltsov, M. E., *Ispaniya v ogne* (Moscow: Politizdat, 1987).

Konieczny, Kazimierz, and Wiewióra, Henryk, *Karol Swierczewski Walter* (Warsaw: Nasza Księga, 1971).

Konoplitsky, Vladimir, 'The Hero of the Soviet Intelligence Died in Disgrace' [Vasili Zarubin], *Pravda*, 11 February 2003.

Köstenberger, Julia, 'Die Internationale Lenin-Schule (1926–1938)' in Michael Buckmiller und Klaus Meschkat (eds), *Biographisches Handbuch zur Geschichte der Kommunistischen Internationale: Ein deutsch-russisches Forschungsprojekt* (Berlin: Akademie Verlag, 2007).

Kowalsky, Daniel, *Stalin and the Spanish Civil War* (New York: Columbia University Press, 2004).

Krasikov, Anatoly, *From Democracy to Dictatorship: Spanish Reportage* (Oxford: Pergamon Press, 1984).

Krasnov, Vladislav, *Soviet Defectors: The KGB Wanted List* (Stanford, CA: Hoover Institution Press, 1986).

Kravchenko, Viktor A. (plaintiff), *Kravchenko versus Moscow: Report of Famous Paris Case* (London: Wingate, 1950).

Kravchenko, Viktor A., *I Choose Freedom: The Personal and Political Life of a Soviet Official* (Garden City, NY: Garden City Publishing, 1947).

Kravchenko, Viktor A., *I Chose Justice* (New York: Scribner's, 1950).

Krivitsky, W. G., 'Stalin's Hand in Spain', *Saturday Evening Post*, 211/42, 15 April 1939, pp. 5–7, 115–22.

Krivitsky, Walter, *Ya byl agentom Stalina*, ed. A. Kolpakidi, Glossary compiled by A. Kolpakidi and V. Lurie (Moscow: Sovremennik, 1996).

Krivitsky, W. G., *In Stalin's Secret Service: Memoirs of the First Soviet Masterspy to Defect* (New York: Enigma Books, 2000).

Kronenbitter, Rita T., 'Paris Okhrana 1885–1905', *Studies in Intelligence*, 10/3 (Summer 1966), 55–66.

Kronenbitter, Rita T. 'The Sherlock Holmes of the Revolution', *Studies in Intelligence*, 11/4 (Autumn 1967), 83–100.

Kronenbitter, Rita T., 'Leon Trotsky, Dupe of the NKVD', *Studies in Intelligence*, 16/1 (special edition 1972), 15–61.

Kudrova, Irma, *The Death of a Poet: The Last Days of Marina Tsvetaeva*, intro. Ellendea Proffer, trans. from the Russian by Mary Ann Szporluk (New York: Overlook Press, 2004).

Kuhns, Woodrow J. (ed.), *Assessing the Soviet Threat: The Early Cold War Years*, paperback (Washington, DC: CIA Centre for the Study of Intelligence, 1997).

Kunert, Dirk Thomas, *General Ljuschkows Geheimbericht: Über die Stalinsche Fernostpolitik 1937/38* (Bern: Schweizerisches Ost-Institut, 1977).

Kuusinen, Aino, *Der Gott stürzt seine Engel* (Vienna: Verlag Fritz Molden, 1972).

Kuusinen, Aino, *Before and after Stalin: A Personal Account of Soviet Russia from the 1920s to the 1960s* (London: Michael Joseph, 1974).

Kuusinen, Aino, *The Rings of Destiny: Inside Soviet Russia from Lenin to Brezhnev* (New York: William Morrow, 1974).

Kuzichkin, Vladimir, *Inside the KGB: Myth & Reality*, intro. Frederick Forsyth, trans. Thomas B. Beattie (London: André Deutsch, 1990).

Lamphere, Robert J., and Shachtman, Tom, *The FBI–KGB War: A Special Agent's Story* (New York: Random House, 1986).

Landau, Henry, *All's Fair: The Story of British Secret Service behind German Lines* (New York: Putnam, 1934).

Landau, Henry, *Spreading the Spy Net: The Story of a British Spy Director* (London: Jarrods, 1938).

Landau, Katja, 'Stalinism in Spain', *Revolutionary History*, 1/2 (Summer 1988), 40–55.

Landauer, Hans, 'Wien–Moskau–Madrid: Die Odyssee Österreichischer Schutzbündler 1934–1945', *DÖW, Jahrbuch 1990* (Vienna: DÖW, 1990).

Landauer, Hans, with Hackl, Erich, *Lexikon der österreichischen Spanienkämpfer 1936–1939* (Vienna: Verlag der Theodor Kramer Gesellschaft, 2003).

Langhorne, Richard (ed.), *Diplomacy and Intelligence during the Second World War: Essays in Honour of F. H. Hinsley* (Cambridge: Cambridge University Press, 1985).

Laqueur, Walter, *Stalin: The Glasnost Revelations* (New York: Scribner's, 1990).

Last, Jef, *Lettres d'Espagne* (Paris: Gallimard, 1939).

Lazitch, Branko, in collaboration with Drachkovitch, Milorad M., *Bibliographical Dictionary of the Comintern* (Stanford, CA: Hoover Institution Press, 1973).

Lebedev, Sergey N., Kirpichenko, Vadim A., Zhuravlyov, Yu., and Zamoisky, L. (eds), *Ocherki istorii Rossiiskoi vneshnei razvedki* (Moscow: Mezhdunarodnye otnosheniya, 2003), v.

Lebedev, Sergey N., Kirpichenko, Vadim A., Zhuravlyov, Yu., and Zamoisky, L. (eds) *Ocherki istorii Rossiiskoi vneshnei razvedki* (Moscow: Mezhdunarodnye otnosheniya, 2003), vi.

Leckie, Robert, *Delivered from Evil: The Saga of World War II* (New York: Harper & Row, 1987).

Leguina, Joaquín, and Jiménez, Lorenzo Hernandés, 'Andreu Nin: Muerto sin sepultura', *Claves de Razón Práctica*, 187 (October 2008), 42–6.

Lehto, Petri, and Tombak, Mihkel M., 'Consolidations and the Sequence of Acquisition to Monopoly', Discussion Paper FS IV 97–22 (Berlin: Wissenschaftszentrum, 1997).

Leites, Nathan, and Bernaut [Poretsky], Elsa, *Ritual of Liquidation: Bolsheviks on Trial* (Clencoe, IL: Free Press, 1955).

Leitz, Christian, *Economic Relations between Nazi Germany and Franco's Spain, 1936–1945* (Oxford: Clarendon Press, 1996).

Lekarev, Stanislav, '"Gasan": Chelovek-kinzhal', *Argumenty nedeli*, 25, 26 October 2006.

Leo, Gerhard, *Frühzug nach Toulouse* (Berlin: Verlag der Nation, 1988).

Leo, Gerhard, *Frühzug nach Toulouse* (Berlin: edition q, 1992).

Leonard, Raymond W., *Secret Soldiers of the Revolution: Soviet Military Intelligence 1918–1933* (Westport, CT, and London: Greenwood Press, 1999).

Leonidov, Vladimir, 'Kto vy, gospodin Erdberg?' *Novosti razvedki i kontrrazvedki*, 1/58 (1996), 9.

Levine, Isaac Don, *Eyewitness to History: Memoirs and Reflections of a Foreign Correspondent for Half a Century* (New York: Hawthorn, 1973).

Levytsky, Boris, *The Uses of Terror: The Soviet Secret Police 1917–1970*, trans. H. A. Piechler (New York: Coward, McCann & Geoghegan, 1972).

Lewis, Flora, 'Who Killed Krivitsky?' *Washington Post*, Sunday, 13 February 1966.

Líster, Enrique, *Memorias de un luchador: Los primeros combates* (Madrid: G. del Toro, 1977).

Líster, Enrique, *Nuestra Guerra, aportaciones para una historia de la guerra civil 1936–1939* (Paris: Colleción Ebro, Ed. de la Librairie du Globe, 1966).

Litten, Frederick S., 'The Noulens Affair', *China Quarterly*, 138 (June 1994), 492–512.

Little, Douglas, *Malevolent Neutrality: The United States, Great Britain, and the Origins of the Spanish Civil War* (Ithaca, NY, and London: Cornell University Press, 1985).

Livneh, Neri, 'A Woman Called Zosha', *Haaretz*, 5 December 2009.

Lockhart, R. H. Bruce, *Memoirs of a British Agent* (London: Putnam, 1932).

Longo, Luigi, *Internatsyonalnye brigady v Ispanii* (Moscow: Voennoe iz-vo Ministerstva Oborony, 1960).

Lota, Vladimir, 'Bez sanktsii na lyubov' [Fedor Kravchenko], *Sovershenno Sekretno*, 12 (2003), 28–30.

Lota, Vladimir, *GRU i atomnaya bomba* (Moscow: Olma Press, 2002).

Luengo Teixidor, Félix, *Espías en la Embajada: Los servicios de información secreta republicanos en Francia durante la Guerra Civil* (Bilbao: Servicio Editorial Universidad del País Vasco, 1996).

Lukes, Igor, *Czechoslovakia between Stalin and Hitler: The Diplomacy of Eduard Beneš in the 1930s* (Oxford: Oxford University Press, 1996).

Lurie, V. M., *Admiraly i generaly Voenno-Morskogo flota SSSR, 1946–1960* (Moscow: Kuchkovo Pole, 2007).

Lurie, V. M., and Kochik, V. Ya., *GRU: Dela i Lyudi* (St Petersburg: Neva; Moscow: Olma Press, 2002).

Lustiger, Arno, *Schalom Libertad! Juden im spanischen Bürgerkrieg* (Berlin: Aufbau Taschenbuch Verlag, 2001).

McCartney, Wilfred, *Walls Have Mouths*, with Prologue, Epilogue and Comments at the end of the majority of the chapters by Compton Mackenzie (London: Victor Gollancz, 1936).

McDermott, Kevin, and Agnew, Jeremy, *The Comintern: A History of the International Communism from Lenin to Stalin* (Houndmills, Basingstoke: Palgrave Macmillan, 1996).

McGovern, John, *Terror in Spain: How the Communist International has destroyed Working Class Unity, Undermined the Foght against Franco and Suppressed the Social Revolution* (London: Independent Labour Party, 1938).

Macintyre, Ben, *Operation MINCEMEAT: The True Spy Story that Changed the Course of World War II* (London, Berlin, and New York: Bloomsbury, 2010).

Macklin, Graham D., 'Communication: Major Hugh Pollard, MI6, and the Spanish Civil War', *Historical Journal*, 49/1 (March 2006), 277–80.

McKay, Sinclair, *The Secret Life of Bletchley Park* (London: Aurum Press, 2010).

McKercher, B. J. C., 'The Foreign Office, 1930–39', *Contemporary British History*, 18/3 (Autumn 2004), 87–109.

McKnight, David, *Espionage and the Roots of the Cold War: The Conspiratorial Heritage* (London: Frank Cass, 2002).

MacLean, Fitzroy, *Eastern Approaches* (London: Jonathan Cape, 1949).

McLoughlin, Barry, 'Proletarian Cadres en route: Austrian NKVD Agents in Britain 1941–43', *Labour History Reviews*, 62/3 (Winter 1997), 296–317.

McLoughlin, Barry, 'Mass Operations of the NKVD, 1937–8: A Survey', in Barry McLoughlin and Kevin McDermott (eds), *Stalin's Terror: High Politics and Mass Repression in the Soviet Union* (Houndmills, Basingstoke: Palgrave Macmillan, 2003), 118–52.

McLoughlin, Barry, *Left to the Wolves: Irish Victims of Stalinist Terror* (Dublin: Irish Academic Press, 2007).

McLoughlin, Barry, and McDermott, Kevin, 'Rethinking Stalinist Terror', in Barry McLoughlin and Kevin McDermott (eds), *Stalin's Terror: High Politics and Mass Repression in the Soviet Union* (Houndmills, Basingstoke: Palgrave Macmillan, 2003), 1–18.

McLoughlin, Barry, and McDermott, Kevin (eds), *Stalin's Terror: High Politics and Mass Repression in the Soviet Union* (Houndmills, Basingstoke: Palgrave Macmillan, 2003).

McLoughlin, Barry, and Schafranek, Hans, *DÖW, Österreicher im Exil – Sowjetunion 1934–1945* (Vienna: Deuticke, 1999).

McLoughlin, Barry, Leidinger, Hannes, and Moritz, Verena, *Kommunismus in Österreich 1918–1938* (Vienna: StudienVerlag, 2009).

McLoughlin, Barry, Schafranek, Hans, and Severa, Walter (eds), *Aufbruch-Hoffnung-Endstation: Österreicherinnen und Österreicher in der Sowjetunion, 1922–1945* (Vienna: Verlag für Gesellschaftskritik, 1997).

McLoughlin, Barry, McIlroy, John, Campbell, Alan, and Halstead, John, 'Forging the Faithful: The British at the International Lenin School, 1926–37', *Labour History Review*, 68/1 (April 2003), 99–128.

McLoughlin, Barry, McIlroy, John, Campbell, Alan, and Halstead, John, 'British Students at the International Lenin School: The Vindication of a Critique', *Twentieth Century British History*, 16/4 (2005), 471–88.

McMeekin, Sean, *The Red Millionaire: A Political Biography of Willi Münzenberg, Moscow's Secret Propaganda Tsar in the West* (New Haven and London: Yale University Press, 2003).

McNeish, James, *The Sixth Man: The Extraordinary Life of Paddy Costello* (London: Quarter Books, 2008).

Madeira, Victor, 'Moscow's Interwar Infiltration of British Intelligence, 1919–1929', *Historical Journal*, 46/4 (December 2003), 915–33.

Mader, Julius, Stuchlik, Gerhard, and Pehnert, Horst, *Dr Sorge funkt aus Tokyo* (Berlin: Deutsche Militärverlag, 1965).

Main, Steven J., 'The Red Army and the Future War in Europe', in Silvio Pons and Andrea Romano (eds), *Russia in the Age of Wars* (Milan: Feltrinelli Editore, 2000), 171–86.

Mairer, Petra Maria Julia, 'Wilhelm Münzenberg und die Editions du Carrefour im Französischen Exil', Leopold-Franzens-Universität Innsbruck (Zeitgeschichte), Hausarbeit, 2008, Archivnummer V131705.

Maisky, Ivan, *Spanish Notebooks* (London: Hutchinson, 1966).

Malai, Vera V., *Grazhdanskaya voina v Ispanii 1936–1939 godov i Evropa* (Moscow: Nauka, 2011).

Mallett, Robert, 'The Anschluss Question in Italian Defence Policy, 1933–37', *Intelligence and National Security*, 19/4 (Winter 2004), 680–94.

Marchenko, Anatoly, *My Testimony* (New York: Dutton, 1969).

Marenches, Count de, and Ockrent, Christine, *The Evil Empire: The Third World War Now* (London: Sigdwick & Jackson, 1988).

Massing, Hede, *This Deception* (New York: Duell, Sloan and Pearce, 1951).

Matthews, Herbert Lionel, *Half of Spain Died: A Reappraisal of the Spanish Civil War* (New York: Scribner, 1973).

Mayenburg, Ruth von, *Blaues Blut und rote Fahnen: Ein Leben unter vielen namen* (Vienna and Munich: Molden-Taschenbuch Verlag, 1969).

Mayenburg, Ruth von, *Hotel Lux* (Munich: C. Bertelsmann Verlag, 1978).

Meier, Andrew, *The Lost Spy: An American in Stalin's Secret Service* (New York and London: W. W. Norton & Company, 2008).

Meier, Helmut (ed.), *Leo Stern (1901–1982): Antifaschist, Historiker, Hochschullehrer und Wissenschaftspolitiker* (Berlin: trafo Verlag, 2002).

Melgounov, Sergei Petrovich, *The Red Terror in Russia* (London: J. M. Dent, 1925).

Melville, Cecil F., *The Russian Face of Germany: An Account of the Secret Military Relations between the German and Soviet–Russian Governments* (London: Wishart, 1932).

Mercader, Luis, Sánchez, Germán, and Llanos, Rafael, *Ramón Mercader, mi hermano: Cincuenta anos despues* (Madrid: Espasa-Calpe, 1990).

Merridale, Catherine, *Ivan's War: The Red Army 1939–45* (London: Faber & Faber, 2005).

Merriman, Marion, and Lerude, Warren, *American Commander in Spain: Robert Hale Merriman and the Abraham Lincoln Brigade* (Reno, NV: University of Nevada Press, 1986).

Mewis, Karl, *Im Auftrag der Partei: Erlebnisse im Kampf gegen die faschistische Diktatur* (Berlin: Dietz Verlag, 1972).

Meyers, Jeffrey, *Hemingway: A Biography*, paperback (Cambridge: DaCapo Press, 1999).

Millstein, Mikhail, *Skvoz gody voin i nischety* (Moscow: ITAR-TASS, 2000).

Mínev, Stoyán, *Las causas de la derrota de la República Española: Informe elaborado por Stoyán Mínev (alias Stepánov y Moreno), delegado en España de la Komintern durante los años 1937–1939*. Edición, traducción directa del original ruso a notas por Ángel Luis Encinas Moral (Madrid: Miraguano Ediciones, 2003).

Mintz, Frank, *Autogestión y anarcosindicalismo en la España revolucionaria* (Madrid: Traficantes De Sueños, 2006).

Miravitlles, Jaume, *Los comunicados secretos de Franco, Hitler y Mussolini* (Barcelona: Plaza & Janes Ed., 1977).

Mitrokhin, Vasiliy (ed.), *KGB Lexicon: The Soviet Intelligence Officer's Handbook*, paperback (London and Portland, OR: Frank Cass, 2002).

Mlechin, Leonid, *Osobaya papka SVR* (Moscow: Yauza/Exmo, 2004).

Modesto, Juan, *Soy del Quinto Regimento* (Barcelona: Laia, 1978).

Möller, Horst (ed.), *Der Rote Holocaust und die Deutschen: Die Debatte um das 'Schwarzbuch des Kommunismus'* (Munich and Zurich: Piper, 1999).

Monds, Jean, 'Krivitsky & Stalinism in the Spanish Civil War', *Critique*, 9 (Spring–Summer 1978), 7–35.

Monk, Paul, 'Christopher Andrew and the Strange Case of Roger Hollis', *Quadrant*, 54/4 (April 2010), 37–45.

Moorehead, Alan, *The Traitors* (London: Harper & Row, 1953).

Mora, Constancia de la, *In Place of Splendor: The Autobiography of a Spanish Woman* (New York: Harcourt, Brace and Company, 1939).

Moradiellos, Enrique, 'British Political Strategy in the Face of the Military Rising in Spain', *Contemporary European History*, 1/2 (July 1992), 123–37.

Moradiellos, Enrique, 'The British Image of Spain and the Civil War', *International Journal of Iberian Studies*, 15/1 (2002), 4–13.

Morgan, Kevin, Gidon, Cohen, and Flinn, Andrew (eds), *Agents of the Revolution: New Bibliographical Approaches to the History of International Communism in the Age of Lenin and Stalin* (Bern: Peter Lang, 2005).

Moritz, Verena, and Leidinger, Hannes, *Oberst Redl: Der Spionage Fall, der Skandal, die Fakten* (St Pölten: Rezidenz Verlag, 2012).

Morón, Gabriel, *Política de ayer y política de mañana* (Mexico City: Talleres Numancia, 1942).

Müller-Enbergs, Helmut, and Otto von Dietz, Wilfriede, *Wilhelm Zaisser: Spanien-kämpfer–MfS-Chef–Unperson* (Berlin: Dietz, 2008).

Müller, Reinhard, *Menschenfalle Moskau: Exil und stalinistische Verfolgung* (Hamburg: Hamburger Edition, 2001).

Murphy, David E., *What Stalin Knew: The Enigma of Barbarossa* (New Heaven and London: Yale University Press, 2005).

Narinski, Mikhail, 'Otnosheniya mezhdu SSSR i Frantsiei, 1933–1937 god', in A. Yu. Melville, M. M. Narinski, and A. O. Chubarian (eds), *SSSR, Franstsiya I evolutsiya Evropy v 30-e gody* (Moscow: MGIMO, 2003), 69–103.

Naumov, Leonid, *Stalin i NKVD* (Moscow: Novyi khronograf, 2010).

Navarro Bonilla, Diego, *Derrotado, pero no sorprendido: Reflexiones sobre la información secreta en tiempo de guerra* (Madrid: Plaza y Valdés Editores, 2007).

Nekhamkin, Sergey, 'Za Abelem letopisets ne khodil' [Vadim Kirpichenko about Abel/Fisher], *Izvestiya*, 11 July 2003.

Nelson, Steve, *The Volunteers* (New York: Masses & Mainstream, 1953).

Nikandrov, Nil, 'Ryadovoi Kominterna po klichke Migel', *Latin America*, 1 (1999), 25–44.

Nikandrov, Nil, *Grigulevich: Razvedchik, kotoromu vezlo* (Moscow: Molodaya gvar-diya, 2005).

Nollau, Günther, and Zindel, Ludwig, *Gestapo ruft Moskau: Sowjetische Fallschirma-genten in 2. Weltkrieg* (Munich: Blanvalet Verlag, 1979).

Nørgaard, Erik, *Truslen om krig: Komintern, Folkerfront og 5. Kolonne* (Lynge: Bogan's Forlag, 1985).

Nollau, Günther, with a Foreword by Leonard Schapiro, *International Communism and World Revolution: History & Methods* (New York: Frederick A. Praeger, Publishers, 1961).

Novikov, M. V., *SSSR, Comintern i grazhdanskaya voina v Ispanii 1936–1939*, 2nd edn (Yaroslavl: Yaroslavl State Pedagogical University, 2007).

Novikov, M. V., 'Sovetskiy Soyuz i grazhdanskaya voina v Ispanii 1936–39', *Rossiiskaya istoriya* (Moscow), 5 (2009), 51–63.

Olaya, Francisco, *El oro de Negrín* (Móstoles: Ed. Tierra Madre, 1990).

Ollivier, Marcel, *Le Guépéou en Espagne: Les Journées sanglantes de Barcelone du 3 au 9 mai 1937* (Paris: Spartacus, 1937).

Olmsted, Kathryn S., *Red Spy Queen: A Biography of Elizabeth Bentley* (Chapel Hill, NC: University of North Carolina Press, 2002).

Olshansky, A., *Zapiski agenta Razvedupra* (Paris: Mishen, 1930).

Olson, James M., 'The Ten Commandments of Counterintelligence', *Studies in Intelligence*, 11 (Fall–Winter 2001), 81–7.

Orlov, Alexander, *The Secret History of Stalin's Crimes* (New York: Random House, 1953).

Orlov, Alexander, 'The Ghastly Secrets of Stalin's Power', *Life*, 6 April 1953, pp. 110–12.

Orlov, Alexander, 'Inside Story of How Trials Were Rigged', *Life*, 13 April 1953, pp. 160–2.

Orlov, Alexander, 'Treachery to His Friends, Cruelty to Their Children', *Life*, 20 April 1953, pp. 142–4.

Orlov, Alexander, 'Stalin's Secrets: The Man Himself', *Life*, 27 April 1953.

Orlov, Alexander, 'The Sensational Secret behind Damnation of Stalin', *Life*, 40/17, 23 April 1956, pp. 34–8, 43–5.

Orlov, Alexander, *Handbook of Intelligence and Guerrilla Warfare* (Ann Arbor: University of Michigan Press, 1963).

Orlov, Alexander, 'The Theory and Practice of Soviet Intelligence', *Studies in Intelligence*, 7/2 (Spring 1963), 45–65.

Orlov, Alexander, 'How Stalin Relieved Spain of $600,000,000', *Reader's Digest* (November 1966), 37–8, 41–8.

Orlov, Alexander, *Tainaya istoriya Stalinskikh prestuplenii* (Moscow: Vsemirnoe slovo, 1991).

Orlov, Alexander, *The March of Time: Reminiscences*, foreword Edward P. Gazur, introduction and epilogue Phillip Knightley (London: St Ermin's Press, 2004).

Orlov, Boris, 'Nakanune bolshogo terrora: Armiya i oppozitsyiya', *Cahiers du monde Russe et Soviétique*, 32/3 (July–September 1991).

Orlov, Vladimir, 'Marina Tsvetaeva', in Marina Tsvetaeva, *Izbrannye proizvedeniya* (Moscow: Sovetsky pisatel, 1965).

Orwell, George, *Orwell in Spain*, ed. Peter Davison (London: Penguin Books, 2001).

Osipov, G. O., *Tovarishch Artur, kto vy?* (Moscow: Politizdat, 1989).

O'Sullivan, Donal, 'Dealing with the Devil: The Anglo-Soviet Parachute Agents (Operation "Pickaxe")', *Journal of Intelligence History*, 4 (Winter 2004), 33–63.

O'Sullivan, Dónal, *Dealing with the Devil: Anglo-Soviet Intelligence Cooperation during the Second World War* (New York, Vienna, and Oxford: Peter Lang, 2010).

Otto, Wilfriede, *Erich Mielke: Biographie. Aufstieg und Fall eines Tschekisten* (Berlin: Dietz, 2000).

Page, Bruce, Leitch, David, and Knightly, Phillip, *Philby: The Spy who Betrayed a Generation* (London: André Deutsch, 1968).

Pagès i Blanch, Pelai, 'El asesinato de Andreu Nin, más datos para la polemica', *Ebre 38. Revista Internacional sobre la guerra civil*, 4 (2010), 57–76.

Paillole, Colonel Paul, *Fighting the Nazis: French Intelligence and Counterintelligence 1935–1945* (New York: Enigma Books, 2003).

Panteleyev, M. M., 'Avantyurist ili politicheskiy deyatel?', *Voprosy Istorii*, 9 (September 1998), 121–30.

Papanin, Ivan D. *Lyod i plamen* (Moscow: Politizdat, 1977).

Paporov, Yuri N., 'Sudba peresmeshnika', *Sovershenno Sekretno*, 2/129 (2000), 10–11.

Paporov, Yuri N., *Akademik nelegalnykh nauk* [Iosif Grigulevich] (St Petersburg: Neva, 2004).

Parshina, Elizaveta Aleksandrovna, *Dinamit dlya seniority* (Moscow: Sovetsky pisatel, 1989).

Parshina, Elizaveta, *La brigadista: Diario de una dinamitera en la Guerra Civil*, Prologue by Artur Sprogis (Madrid: La Esfera de los Libros, 2005).

Partnoy, Frank, *The Match King: Ivar Krueger and the Financial Scandal of the Century* (London: Profile Books, 2009).

Pastor Petit, Domingo, *Espionaje (España 1936–1939)* (Barcelona, Bogotá, Buenos Aires, Caracas, and Mexico: Editorial Bruguera, 1977).

Pastor Petit, Domingo, *Los dossiers secretos de la guerra civil* (Barcelona: Editorial Argos, 1978).

Payne, Stanley G., *The Spanish Civil War, The Soviet Union, and Communism* (New Haven and London: Yale University Press, 2004).

Payne, Stanley G., *El colapso de la República: Los orígenes de la Guerra Civil (1933–1936)* (Madrid: La Esfera de los Libros, 2005).

Payne, Stanley (questions), and Orlov, Alexander (answers), *The NKVD in Spain*, intro. Frank Schauff, paperback (Cologne, Weimar, and Vienna: Böhlau Verlag, 2000).

Paz, Armando, *Los Servicios de Espionaje en la Guerra Civil Española, 1936–1939* (Madrid: Libreria Editorial San Martin, 1976).

Peake Hayden B., 'OSS and the Venona Decrypts', *Intelligence and National Security*, 12/3 (July 1997), 14–34.

Peake Hayden B., 'Soviet Espionage and the Office of Strategic Services', in Warren F. Kimball (ed.), *America Unbound: World War II and the Making of a Superpower* (New York: St Martin's Press, 1992), 107–38.

Pech, Karlheinz, 'Ein neuer Zeuge im Todesfall Willi Münzenberg', *Beiträge zur Geschichte der Arbeiterbewegung*, 1 (Berlin: Dietz Verlag, 1995).

Pedersen, Vernon L., 'George Mink, the Marine Workers Industrial Union, and the Comintern in America', *Labor History*, 41/3 (2000), 307–20.

Peirats, José, *Los anarquistas en la crisis política española* (Buenos Aires: Editorial Alfa, 1964).

Peirats, José, *Los anarquistas en la Guerra Civil Española* (Madrid: Ediciones Júcar, 1976).

Penchienati, Carlo, *Brigate internazionali in Spagna: Delitti della 'Ceka' comunista* (Milan: Edizione del Secolo, 1950).

Pérez Salas, Jesús, *Guerra en España (1936 a 1939). Bosquejo del problema militar español. De las causas de la guerra y del desarollo de la misma* (Mexico: Grafos, 1947).

Petrov, Nikita, 'Ubijstvo Ignatiya Reissa', *Moskovskie novosti*, 63, 17–24 September 1995.

Petrov, Nikita, *Die soujetischen Geheimdienstmitarbeiter in Deutschland: Der leitende Personalbestand der Staatssicherheitsorgane der UdSSR in der Soujetischen Besatzungszone Deutschlands und der DDR von 1945–1954*. Biografisches Nachschlagewerk (Berlin: Metropol, 2010).

Petrov, Nikita, *Kto rukovodil organami gosbezopasnosti 1941–1954* (Moscow: Zvenia, 2010).

Petrov, Nikita, and Gevorkyan, Natalia, 'Konets agenta 13', *Moskovskie novosti*, 46 (1995).

Petrov, Nikita, and Roginskii, Arsenii, 'The "Polish Operation" of the NKVD, 1937–8', in Barry McLoughlin and Kevin McDermott (eds), *Stalin's Terror: High Politics and Mass Repression in the Soviet Union* (Houndmills, Basingstoke: Palgrave Macmillan, 2003), 153–72.

Petrov, N. V., and Skorkin, K. V., *Kto rukovodil NKVD 1934–1941* (Moscow: Zvenia, 1999).

Petrov, Vladimir, and Petrov, Evdokia, *Empire of Fear* (London: André Deutsch, 1956).

Philby, Rufina, and Peake, Hayden, with Lyubimov, Mikhail, *The Private Life of Kim Philby* (New York: Fromm International, 2000).

Pike, David Wingeate, *In the Service of Stalin: The Spanish Communists in Exile, 1939–1945* (Oxford: Oxford University Press, 1993).

Pike, David Wingeate, *Spaniards in the Holocaust: Mauthausen, the Horror on the Danube* (London and New York: Routledge, 2000).

Pisón, Ignacio Martínez de, *Enterrar a los muertos* (Barcelona: Editorial Seix Barral, 2005).

Pollitt, Harry, 'In Memory of the British Comrades who Have Fallen in Spain', *Communist International*, 14/2 (February 1937), 142–5.

Pons, Silvio, 'The Papers on Foreign and International Policy in the Russian Archives: The Stalin Years', *Cahiers du Monde russe*, 40/1–2 (January–June 1999), 235–50.

Pons, Silvio, *Stalin and the Inevitable War, 1936–1941* (London: Routledge, 2002).

Pons, Silvio, and Romano, Andrea (eds), *Russia in the Age of Wars* (Milan: Feltrinelli Editore, 2000).

Porch, Douglas, *The French Secret Services: A History of French Intelligence from the Dreyfus Affair to the Gulf War* (London: Macmillan, 1996).

Poretsky, Elisabeth K., *Our Own People: A Memoir of 'Ignace Reiss' and his Friends* (London: Oxford University Press, 1969).

Pospelov, Petr Nikolaevich, 'Zapiska P. N. Pospelova ob ubiistve Kirova', *Svobodnaya mysl*, 8 (May 1992), 64–71.

Pozharskaya, Svetlana, 'Comintern and the Civil War in Spain', *Ebre*, 38 (May 2003), 47–56.

Pozharskaya, Svetlana, *Fransisko Franko i ego vremya* (Moscow: Olma Media Group, 2007).

Pozniakov, Vladimir, 'Soviet Military Intelligence in the Inter-War Period and its Forecasts of Future War, 1921–41', in Silvio Pons and Andrea Romano (eds), *Russia in the Age of Wars* (Milan: Fondazione Giangiacomo Feltrinelli, 2000).

Preston, Paul, 'Spain's October Revolution and the Rightist Grasp for Power', *Journal of Contemporary History*, 10/4 (October 1975), 555–78.

Preston, Paul, 'Reading History: The Spanish Civil War', *History Today*, 32/11 (November 1982), 45–7.

Preston, Paul (ed.) *Revolution and War in Spain 1931–1939* (London: Methuen, 1984).

Preston, Paul, *Franco: A Biography* (London: Basic Books, 1994).

Preston, Paul, *A Concise History of the Spanish Civil War* (London: Fontana, 1996).

Preston, Paul, *Doves of War: Four Women of Spain*, paperback (London: Harper-CollinsPublishers, 2003).

Preston, Paul, 'Failure of the Brave New Spain', *The Times*, 17 June 2006.

Preston, Paul, *The Spanish Civil War: Reaction, Revolution & Revenge*, paperback (London: Harper Perennnial, 2006).

Preston, Paul, *We Saw Spain Die: Foreign Correspondents in the Spanish Civil War* (London: Constable, 2008).

Preston, Paul, *We Saw Spain Die: Foreign Correspondents in the Spanish Civil War*, paperback (London: Constable, 2009).

Preston, Paul, *The Spanish Holocaust: Inquisition and Extermination in Twentieth-Century Spain* (London: Harper Press, 2012).

Preston, Paul, *El zorro rojo: La vida de Santiago Carrillo* (Madrid: Debate, 2013).

Preston, Paul, and Mackenzie, Ann L. (eds), *The Republic Besieged: Civil War in Spain 1936–1939* (Edinburgh: Edinburgh University Press, 1996).

Price, David, 'Obituary for Mark Zborowski, 1908–1990', *Anthropology Newsletter*, 39/6 (1998).

Price, Ruth, *The Lives of Agnes Smedley* (New York: Oxford University Press, 2005).

Priess, Heinz, *Spaniens Himmel und keine Sterne: Ein deutsches Geschichtsbuch. Erinnerungen an ein Leben und ein Jahrhundert* (Berlin: Ed. Ost, 1996).

Prieto, Indalecio, 'Remembrances and Perspectives', Speech, Barcelona, 28 August 1938 (S.I., 1938).

Prieto, Indalecio, *Yo y Moscu* (Madrid: Editorial NOS, 1955).

Prieto, Indalecio, *Cómo y por qué sali del Ministerio de Defensa National: Intrigas de los rusos en España* (Barcelona: Fundación Indalecio Prieto/Planeta, 1989).

Prieto, Indalecio, *Entresijos de la guerra de España: Colección de artículos sobre intrigas de alemanes, italianos y rusos* (Barcelona: Fundación Indalecio Prieto, 1989).

Primakov, Evgeny M., Kirpichenko, Vadim A., Podgornov, L., Zhuravlyov, Yu., and Zamoisky, L. (eds), *Ocherki istorii Rossiiskoi vneshnei razvedki* (Moscow: Mezhdunarodnye otnosheniya, 2003), i–iii.

Proctor, Raymond L., *Hitler's Luftwaffe in the Spanish Civil War* (Westpoint, CT: Greenwood Press, 1983).

Prokhorov, Dmitry, *Spetzsluzhby Izrailya* (St Petersburg: Neva; Moscow: OLMA Press, 2002).

Prokhorov, Dmitry, *Skolko stoit prodat Rodinu* (St Petersburg: Neva, 2005).

Puschkin, Juri, *GRU in Deutschland—Die Aktivitäten nach der Wende* (Düsseldorf: Barett Verlag, 1992).

Pyatnitsky, Vladimir I., *Zagovor protiv Stalina* (Moscow: Sovremennik, 1998).

Pyatnitsky, Vladimir I. (son of Osip Pyatnitsky), *Osip Pyatnitsky i Komintern na vesakh istorii*, ed. A. E. Taras (Minsk: Harvest, 2004).

Quirosa-Cheyrouze y Muños, Rafael, *Gariel Morón Diaz (1896–1973): Trayectoria política de un socialista español* (Almería: Editorial Universidad de Almería, 2013).

Radó, Sándor, *Dora meldet* (Berlin: Militärverlag der DDR, 1974).

Radó, Sándor, *Codename Dora* (London: Abelard-Schuman, 1976).

Radosh, Ronald, 'But Today the Struggle', *New Criterion*, 5/2 (October 1986), 5–15.

Radosh, Ronald, Habeck, Mary R., and Sevostianov, Grigory, *Spain Betrayed: The Soviet Union in the Spanish Civil War* (New Haven and London: Yale University Press, 2001).

Radzinsky, Eduard, *Stalin: The First In-Depth Biography Based on Explosive New Documents from Russia's Secret Archives*, paperback (New York: Anchor, 1997).

Rayfield, Donald, *Stalin and his Hangmen* (London: Viking, 2004).

Razumovsky, Maria, *Marina Tsvetayeva: A Critical Biography*, trans. from Russian by Aleksey Gibson (Newcastle upon Tyne: Bloodaxe Books, 1995).

Rees, Jenny, *Looking for Mr Nobody: The Secret Life of Goronwy Rees* (London: Weidenfeld and Nicolson, 1994).

Regler, Gustav, *Das Ohr des Malchus* (Cologne and Berlin: Kiepenheuer & Witsch, 1958).

Regler, Gustav, *The Great Crusade*, with a preface by Ernest Hemingway, trans. Whittaker Chambers and Barrows Mussey (New York: Longman's Green, 1940).

Reich, Rebecca, 'Lost in Time' [Marina Tsvetayeva], *Moscow Times*, 6 February 2004.

Reilly, Pepita, *The Adventures of Sydney Reilly* (London: Ellis, Matthew & Marot, 1931).

Reiss, Elsa, 'Ignace Reiss: In Memoriam', *New International*, 4/9 (September 1938), 276–8.

Retzlaw, Karl [Karl Gröhl], *Spartakus: Aufstieg und Niedergang. Erinnerungen eines Parteiarbeiters* (Frankfurt: Verlag Neue Kritik, 1972).

Reverte, Jorge M., 'Paracuellos, 7 de noviembre de 1936', *El Pais*, 5 November 2006.

Revol, René 'Procès de Moscou en Espagne', *Cahiers Leon Trotsky*, 3 (July–September 1979), 121–32.

Rezun, Miron, *Soviet Union and Iran: Soviet Policy in Iran from the Beginnings of the Pahlavi Dynasty until the Soviet Invasion in 1941* (Norwell, MA: Kluwer Academic Publishers, 1981).

Riddell, John (ed.), *Founding the Communist International: Proceedings and Documents of the First Congress, March 1919* (New York: Pathfinder Press, 1987).

Riding, Allan, 'Composing the Work an Ill-Fated Poet Never Began' (Marina Tsvetayeva), *New York Times*, 31 March 2005.

Rieger, Max (pseud.), *Espionaje en España*, preface by José Bergamín, trans. Lucienne Perucho and Arturo Perucho (Barcelona: Ediciones 'Unidad', 1938).

Riley, Morris, *Philby: The Hidden Years* (London: Janus Publishing, 1999).

Roberts, Geoffrey, 'The Fascist War Threat and Soviet Politics in the 1930s', in Silvio Pons and Andrea Romano (eds), *Russia in the Age of Wars* (Milan: Feltrinelli Editore, 2000), 147–58.

Rocca, Pablo, 'Ensayo sobre Felisberto: Una suma de saberes', *El Pais Cultural* (Montevideo, Uruguay), 22 December 2000.

Rodrígez de la Torre, Fernando, *Bibliografía de las Brigadas Internacionales y de la participación de extranjeros a favor de la República (1936–1939)* (Albacete: Instituto de Estudios Albacetenses 'Don Juan Manuel', 2006).

Roewer, Helmut, *Die Rote Kapelle und andere Geheimdienstmythen: Spionage zwischen Detschland und Russland im Zweiten Weltkrieg 1941–1945* (Graz: Ares Verlag, 2010).

Röhwer, Jürgen, *Chronology of the War at Sea, 1939–1945: The Naval History of World War Two* (Annapolis: US Naval Institute Press, 2005).

Rojo Lluch, Gen. Vicente, *Así fue la defensa de Madrid* [Aportacion a la historia de la Guerra de España/1936–39] (Mexico: Ediciones Era, 1967).

Romanov A. I., *Nights are Longer There: SMERSH from the Inside*, trans. Gerald Brooke (London: Hutchinson, 1972).

Romerstein, Herbert, and Breindel, Eric, *The Venona Secrets: Exposing Soviet Espionage and America's Traitors*, paperback (Washington, DC: Regnery Publishing, 2000).

Romerstein, Herbert, and Levchenko, Stanislav, *The KGB against the 'Main Enemy': How the Soviet Intelligence Service Operates against the United States* (Lexington, MA: Lexington Books, 1989).

Rosenfeld, Niels Erik, *Stalin's Secret Chancellery and the Comintern Evidence about the Organizational Patterns* (Copenhagen: C. A. Reitzels Forlag, 1991).

Rosmer, Alfred, 'A Fictionized Version of Trotsky's Murder', *Fourth International*, 10/3 (March 1949), 91–4.

Ross, Marjorie, *El secreto encanto de la KGB: Las cinco vidas de Iósif Griguliévich* (San José, Costa Rica: Farben/Norma, 2004).

Rufat, Ramón, 'Le Service d'espionage de l'Armée républicaine pendant la guerre civile espagnole de 1936–1939', *Materiaux pour l'histoire de notre temps*, 3–4 (July–December 1985), 68–70.

Rufat, Ramón, *Espions de la République* (Paris: Éditions Allia, 1990).

Ryan, James G., 'Socialist Triumph as a Family Value: Earl Browder and Soviet Espionage', *American Communist History*, 1/2 (December 2002), 125–42.

Rybalkin, Yuri, *Operatsiya 'X': Sovetskaya voennaya pomosch respublikanskoi Ispanii, 1936–1939*, paperback (Moscow: AIRO-XX, 2000).

Safrian, Hans, 'Sozialgeschichte, Hintergründe und Motive österreichischer Spanienkämpfer', in *Jahrbuch 1982* (Vienna: Domentationsarchiv des Österreichischen Widerstandes, 1989).

Sánchez, Germán, 'El misterio de Grigolèvich: Rastro biográfico del agente de Stalin acusado de dirigir la fase final contra Andreu Nin', *Historia 16*, 233 (1995), 115–22.

Sanchez, Paco, 'Las ceutíes en la Guerra Civil', *El Faro* (Ceuta/Melilla), 19 March 2006, p. 15.

Sánchez Salazar, General Leandro A., with the collaboration of Julian Gorkin, *Murder in Mexico: The Assassination of Leon Trotsky* (London: Secker & Warburg, 1950).

Sanford, George, 'The Katyn Massacre and Polish–Soviet Relations, 1941–43', *Journal of Contemporary History*, 41/1 (January 2006), 95–111.

Savich, Ovidiy, *Lyudi internationalnykh brigad* (Moscow: Pravda, 1938).

Savich, Ovidiy, *Dva goda v Ispanii, 1937–1939* (Moscow: Sovetskii pisatel, 1981).

Sawatsky, John, *Gouzenko: The Untold Story* (Toronto: Macmillan, 1985).

Scammell, Michael, *Koestler: The Indispensable Intellectual* (London: Faber & Faber, 2010).

Schafranek, Hans, *Das kurze Leben des Kurt Landau: Ein österreichischer Kommunst als Opfer der stalinistischen Geheimpolizei* (Vienna: Verlag für Gesellschaftskritik, 1988).

Schafranek, Hans, 'Österreichische Spanienkämpfer in den Gefängnissen und Konzentrationslagern des Franco-Regimes', in *Jahrbuch 1982* (Vienna: Domentationsarchiv des Österreichischen Widerstandes, 1989).

Schafranek, Hans, *Zwischen NKWD und Gestapo: Die Auslieferung deutscher und österreichischer Antifaschisten aus der Sowjetunion an Nazideutschland 1937–1941* (Frankfurt/Main: ISP-Verlag, 1990).

Schafranek, Hans, '"Angehörigen von Volksfeinden können wir nicht helfen": Das Schicksal der Familie Nebenführ', in Hans Schafranek (ed.), *Die Betrogenen: Österreicher as Opfer stalinistischen Terrors in der Sowjetunion* (Vienna: Picus Verlag, 1991).

Schafranek, Hans, 'Kurt Landau', *Cahiers Léon Trotsky*, 5 (January–March 1980), 71–95; Eng. trans. *Revolutionary History*, 4/1–2 (Winter–Spring 1992).

Schafranek, Hans, 'Die Anfänger der Operation Pickaxe 1941/42', *Journal for Intelligence, Propaganda and Security Studies*, 2/1 (2008), 7–22.

Schafranek, Hans, unter Mitarbeit von Mussijenko, Natalja, *Kinderheim No. 6: Österreichische und deutsche Kinder im sowjetischen Exil* (Vienna: Döcker Verlag, 1998).

Schafranek, Hans, and Tuchel, Johannes (eds), *Krieg im Äther: Wiederstand und Spionage im Zweiten Weltkrieg* (Vienna: Picus Verlag, 2004).

Schauff, Frank, 'A Comment on Recent Literature on Soviet and Comintern Involvement in the Spanish Civil War', *Iberoamericana: America Latina–España–Portugal*, ns 29 (March 2008), 205–14.

Schauff, Frank, *Der verspielte Sieg: Sowietunion, Kommunistische Internationale und Spanischer Bürgerkrieg 1936–1939*, paperback (Frankfurt/Main: Campus Verlag, 2004).

Schecter, Jarold L., and Schecter, Leona, *Sacred Secrets: How Soviet American Operations Changed American History* (New York: Brassey's, 2003).

Scheel, Heinrich, *Vor den Schranken des Reichskriegsgerichts—mein Weg in den Widerstand* (Berlin: Edition q, 1993).

Schellenberg, Walter, *The Labyrinth: Memoirs of Walter Schellenberg* (Cambridge, MA: Da Capo Press, 2000).

Schlachterman, Vladimir, 'Krestnitsa Sorge', *Sovershenno sekretno*, 5 (2007), 22–5.

Schlachterman, Vladimir, 'Kto vy, tovarishch Kent?', *Sovershenno sekretno*, 8 (2007), 28–31.

Schlayer, Felix, *Diplomat im rotten Madrid* (Berlin: F. U. Herbig Verlagsbuchhandlung, 1938).

Schliemann, Jörgen, 'The Life and Work of Willi Münzenberg', *Survey*, 55 (April 1965), 64–91.

Schlögel, Karl, *Moscow 1937* (London: Polity Press, 2012).

Schulz, Heinrich E., Urban, Paul K., and Lebed, Andrew I., *Who Was Who in the USSR* (London: Methuen, 1972).

Schwarz, Stephen, 'The NKVD in the Spanish Civil War: The Case of Andreu Nin', VI International Council for Central and East European Studies (ICCEES) World Congress, 31 July 2000, Tampere, Finland.

Scott, E. J., 'The Cheka', *Soviet Affairs* (St Antony's Papers), 1 (London: Chatto & Windus, 1956).

Seale, Patrick, and McConville, Maureen, *Philby: The Long Road to Moscow* (London: Hamish Hamilton, 1973).

Sedova (Trotsky), Natalia, 'How it Happened', written in Coyoacán, Mexico, in November 1940 (Natalia Sedova Internet Archive, December 2001).

Seidt, Hans-Ulrich, *Berlin, Kabul, Moskau: Oskar Ritter von Niedermayer und Detschlands Geopolitik* (Munich: Universitas Verlag, 2002).

Serge, Victor. Agabekov', *New International* (January–February 1950), 51–7.

Sergueiev, Lily, *Secret Service Rendered: An Agent in the Espionage Duel Preceding the Invasion of France* (London: William Kimber, 1968).

Sergueiew, Lily, *Seule face à l'Abwehr* (Paris: Flammarion, Éditions J'ai Lu, 1966).

Serra i Fabra, Jordi, *Camarada Orlov* (Madrid: Bronce, 2005).

Serrallonga i Urquidi, Joan, 'El aparato provincial durante la segunda República: Los gobernadores civiles, 1931–1939', *Hispania Nova*, 7 (2007), 139–92.

Sevostianov, Grigory N., *'Sovershenno sekretno': Lubyanka–Stalinu o polozhenii v strane, 1922–1934 gg*, 8 vols, 14 bks (Moscow: Institut RossiiskoiIstorii, 2001–8).

Sezeman, Dmitry Vasilievich, 'Iz vospominanii: Bolshevskaya dacha', *Literaturnaya gazeta*, 47, 21 November 1990.

Shainberg, Maurice, *Breaking from the KGB: Warsaw Ghetto Fighter... Intelligence Officer... Defector to the West* (New York, Jerusalem, and Tel Aviv: Shapolsky Publishing of North America, 1986).

Shatunovskaya, I. K. 'Vsya zhizn—podvig: uchenogo... i razvedchika', *Latin America*, 3 (1993), 61–72.

Shaw, Stanford J., and Shaw, Ezel Kural, *History of the Ottoman Empire and Modern Turkey* (Cambridge: Cambridge University Press, 1977).

Shearer, David, 'Social Disorder, Mass Repression and the NKVD during the 1930s', in Barry McLoughlin and Kevin McDermott (eds), *Stalin's Terror: High Politics and Mass Repression in the Soviet Union* (Houndmills, Basingstoke: Palgrave Macmillan, 2003), 320–70.

Shirer, William L., *The Rise and Fall of the Third Reich: A History of Nazi Germany* (London: Pan Books, 1964).

Sibley, Katherine A. S., 'Soviet Industrial Espionage against American Military Technology and the US Response, 1930–1945', *Intelligence and National Security*, 14/2 (Summer 1999), 94–123.

Singh, Vijay, 'Materials on the Question of the Murder of S. M. Kirov', *Revolutionary Democracy*, 2/1 (April 1996).

Skidmore, Thomas E., 'Failure in Brazil: From Popular Front to Armed Revolt', *Journal of Contemporary History*, 5/3 (1970), 137–57.

Skoutelsky, Rémi, 'André Marty et les Brigades internalionales', *Cahiers d'histoire, revue critique d'histoire*, 67 (1997), 103–24.

Skoutelsky, Rémi, *L'Espoir guidait leurs pas: Les Volontaires français dans les Brigades internationales 1936–1939* (Paris: Grasset, 1998).

Skoutelsky, Rémi, *Novedad en el frente: Las Brigadas Internacionales en la guerra civil* (Madrid: Temas de Hoy, 2006).

Skripnik, O., *Ukrainsky slid u rozvidzi* [Maria Fortus] (Kyiv: Yaroslaviv Val, 2009).

Slote, Alfred, 'The Spy in the Law Quad', *Ann Arbor Observer* (December 1993).

Slusser, Robert M., 'Recent Soviet Books on the History of the Secret Police', *Slavic Review*, 24 (1965), 90–8.

Smedley, Agnes, *China's Red Army Marches* (London: Lawrence and Wishart, 1936).

Smedley, Agnes, *Chinese Destinies* (Beijing: Foreign Languages Press, 2003).

Smirnov, V. P., 'Le Komintern et le Parti communiste français pendant la "Drôle de Guerre", 1939–1940 (D'après les archives du Komintern)', *Revue des études slaves*, 65/4 (1993), 671–90.

Smith, Michael, *Frank Foley: The Spy who Saved 10,000 Jews* (London: Hodder & Stoughton, 1999).

Smith, S. A., 'The Comintern, the Chinese Communist Party and the Three Armed Uprisings in Shanghai, 1926–1927', in Tim Rees and Andrew Thorpe (eds), *International Communism and the Communist International 1919–1943* (New York: Manchester University Press, 1998).

Smyth, Denis, 'The Politics of Asylum, Juan Negrín and the British Government in
1940', in Richard Langhorne (ed.), *Diplomacy and Intelligence during the Second
World War: Essays in Honour of F. H. Hinsley* (Cambridge: Cambridge University
Press, 1985), 126–46.

Snegiryov, Vladimir, 'Ubiistva zakazyvalis v Kremle', *Trud*, 24–5 July 1992.

Soboleva, Tatyana A., 'Some Incidents in the 1930s', trans. and ed. Thomas
R. Hammant, *Cryptologia*, 25/1 (January 2001), 61–3.

Soboleva, Tatyana A., *Istoriya shifrovalnogo dela v Rossii* (Moscow: Olma Press,
2002).

Soboleva, Tatyana A., *Tainopis v istorii Rossii* (Moscow: Mezhdunarodnye otnosheniya, 1994).

Sokolsky, George, 'These Days', *Times Herald* and *New York Journal American*, 30
October 1953, p. 10.

Solano, Wilebaldo, 'El ultimo día con Andreu Nin', *El Periódico*, 16 June 1987.

Solomon, G. A., *Sredi krasnykh vozhdei*, 2 vols (Paris: Mishen, 1930).

Solomon, Georgij Aleksandrovic, *Unter den roten Machthabern: Was Ich in Dienste d.
Soujets persönlich sah und erlebte* (Berlin: Verlag für Kulturpolitik, 1930).

Soria, Georges, 'Le P.O.U.M.: Organisation de terrorisme et spionnage au service
de Franco', *L'Humanité*, 25 October 1937.

Soria, George, *Trotskyism in the Service of Franco: A Documented Record of Treachery by
the POUM in Spain* (New York: International Publishers, 1938).

Soria, Georges, *Guerra y revolución en España, 1936–1939*, 5 vols (Barcelona: Grijalbo,
1978).

Southworth, Herbert, Letter to the Editor, *Times Literary Supplement*, 17 November
1978.

Southworth, Herbert Rutledge, '"The Grand Camouflage": Julian Gorkin, Burnett Bolloten and the Spanish Civil War', in Paul Preston and Ann L. Mackenzie
(eds), *The Republic Besieged: Civil War in Spain 1936–1939*, paperback (Edinburgh:
Edinburgh University Press, 1996), 260–310.

Southworth, Herbert R., *Conspiracy and the Spanish Civil War: The Brainwashing of
Francisco Franco* (London: Routledge/Cañada Blanch Studies in Contemporary
Spain, 2001).

Southworth, Herbert R., *El mito de la cruzada de Franco*, Edición y prólogo de Paul
Preston, paperback (Barcelona: Random Hause Mondadori, 2008).

Soler Fuensanta, Ramón, José, and López-Brea Espiau, F. J., *Soldados sin rostro: Los
servicios de información, espionaje y criptografia en la Guerra Civil española* (Barcelona:
Debate, 2008).

Souchy, Augustin, *Nacht über Spanien: Bürgerkrieg und Revolution in Spanien* (Darm-
stadt-Land: Verlag die freie Gesellschaft, n.d. [1955]).

Soutou, Georges-Henri, Frémeaux, Jacques, and Forcade, Olivier (eds), *L'Exploitation du Renseignement en Europe et aux États-Unis des années 1930 aux années 1960*,
Actes du colloque international tenu aux Écoles militaries de Saint-Cyr Coëtquidan, organisé par le Centre de recherche des Écoles de Saint-Cyr Coëtquidan,

le Centre d'histoire de l'Europe et des relations internationals au XXe siècle et le Centre de l'Islam contemporain (Paris IV–Sorbonne) le 3 et 4 juin 1998 avec le concours de l'AASSDN (Paris: Institut de Stratégie Comparée Ephe IV–Sorbonne/Economica, 2001).

Sovetskoe pravo (1922–30).

Spencer, Arthur, 'A Strange Interlude: A Footnote to the Soblen Case', *Survey*, 49 (October 1963), 113–28.

Spiegelhagen, Franz (pseudonym of Otto Katz), *Spione und Verschwörer in Spanien: Nack offiziellen nationalsozialistischen Dokumenten* (Paris: Éditions du Carrefour, 1936).

Stalin, *Works* (Moscow: Foreign Languages Publishing House, 1954).

Stalin, *Works* (London: Red Star Press Ltd., 1978).

Starinov, A. K. [Anna K. Obrucheva], *Behind Fascist Lines: A Firsthand Account of Guerrilla Warfare during the Spanish Revolution*, paperback (New York: Ballantine Books, 2001).

Starinov, Col. I. G., *Over the Abyss: My Life in Soviet Special Operations*, paperback (New York: Ballantine Books, 1995).

Starinov, Ilya Grigoryevich, *Zapiski diversanta*, Kniga 1 (Moscow: Almanakh 'Vympel', 1997).

Starinov, Ilya Grigoryevich, *Miny zamedlennogo deystviya: razmyshleniya partisana-diversanta*, Kniga 2 (Moscow: Almanakh 'Vympel', 1999).

Stawinski, Erwin, *Zarubiny: Semeinaya rezidentura* (Moscow: Olma Press, 2003).

Stead, Philip John, *Second Bureau* (London: Evans Brothers Limited, 1959).

Steiner, Zara, *The Triumph of the Dark: European International History 1933–1939* (Oxford: Oxford University Press, 2011).

Stout, Mark, 'The Pond: Running Agents for State, War and the CIA', *Studies in Intelligence*, 48/3 (2004).

Suárez Fernández, Luis, *El general de la Monarquía, la Republica y la Guerra civil* (Madrid: Actas, 1999).

Sudoplatov, Pavel, *Spetsoperazii Lubyanka i Kreml 1930–1950 gody* (Moscow: Olma Press, 2003).

Sudoplatov, Pavel, and Sudoplatov, Anatoli, with Schecter, Jerrold L., and Schecter, Leona P., with Foreword by Robert Conquest, *Special Tasks: The Memoirs of an Unwanted Witness: A Soviet Spymaster Pavel Sudoplatov* (London: Little, Brown and Company, 1994).

Sulzberger, Cyrus Leo, *A Long Road of Candles* (London: Macdonald, 1969).

Sutherland, John, *Stephen Spender: A Literary Life* (Oxford: Oxford University Press, 2005).

Suvorov, Victor (pseud. of Vladimir Rezun), *Inside Soviet Military Intelligence* (London: Macmillan, 1984).

Suvorov, Victor, 'Who was Planning to Attack whom in June 1941, Hitler or Stalin', *Journal of the Royal United Services Institute for Defence Studies*, 130/2 (June 1985), 50–5.

Suworow, Viktor (pseud.), *Marschall Schukow* (Berlin: Pour le Mérite, 2002).

Tabouis, Geneviève, *They Called Me Cassandra* (New York: Da Capo Press, 1973).

Tanenhaus, Sam, *An Un-American Life: The Case of Whittaker Chambers* (London: Old Street Publishing, 2007).

Tascón, Julio, 'International Capital before "Capital Internationalization" in Spain, 1936–1959', Minda de Gunzburg Center for European Studies (Harvard University) Working Paper Series No. 79, November 2001.

Thalmann, Paul, *Wo die Freiheit stirbt: Stationen eines politischen Kampfes*, paperback (Oloten and Freiburg im Breisgau: Walter Verlag, 1974).

The Intelligence War in 1941 (Washington, DC: CIA Centre for the Study of Intelligence, 1991).

The New Encyclopædia Britannica, 36 vols (Michigan: University of Chicago Press, 1990).

Thomas, Hugh, *The Spanish Civil War* (London: Eyre & Spottiswoode, 1961).

Thomas, Hugh, *The Spanish Civil War*, 3rd edn (London: Harper & Row, 1977).

Thomas, Hugh, *The Spanish Civil War*, paperback (London: Penguin, 2003).

Thorpe, Andrew 'Comintern "Control" of the Communist Party of Great Britain, 1920–43', *English Historical Review*, 113/452 (June 1998), 637–62.

Thurlow, Richard C., 'Soviet Spies and British Counter-Intelligence in the 1930s: Espionage in the Woolwich Arsenal and the Foreign Office Communications Department', *Intelligence and National Security*, 19/4 (Winter 2004), 610–31.

Thurlow, Richard Colin, 'The Historiography and Source Materials in the Study of Internal Security in Modern Britain', *History Compass*, 6/1 (2008), 147–71.

Tobien, Carl, *Dancing under the Red Star* (London: WaterBrook Press, 2006).

Torchikov, V. A., and Leontyuk, A. M. (eds) *Around Stalin: Bibliographical Dictionary* (St Petersburg: Neva, 2000).

Tosstorff, Reiner, 'Ein Moskauer Prozeß in Barcelona: Die Verfolgung der POUM und ihre internationale Bedeutung', in Hermann Weber and Dietrich Staritz (eds), *Kommunisten verfolgen Kommunisten: Stalinistischer Terror und 'Säuberungen' in den Kommunistischen Parteien Europas seit den 30er Jahren* (Mannheim: Akademie Verlag GmbH, 1993).

Tosstorff, Reiner, *El POUM en la revolució espanyola* (Barcelona: Editorial Base, 2009).

Trepper, Leopold (in collaboration with Patrick Rotman), *The Great Game: Memoirs of a Master Spy, Leader of the Red Orchestra* (London: Michael Joseph, 1977).

Tresca, Carlo, 'En fustigeant sans trêve ni peur toutes les dictatures, nous accomplissons notre devoir', *Il Martello*, 28 February 1938, repr. in *Cahiers Leon Trotsky*, 3 (July–September 1979), 189–95, trans. from the Italian by Annie Scattolon.

Tresca, Carlo, 'Où est Juliet Stuart Poyntz?' *Modern Monthly* (March 1938), *Il Martello*, 26 April 1938, repr. in *Cahiers Leon Trotsky*, 3 (July–September 1979), 196–8, trans. from the Italian by Annie Scattolon.

Trevor-Roper, H. R., *The Philby Affair: Espionage, Treason, and the Secret Service* (London: William Kimber, 1968).

Trotsky, Leon, *My Life* (New York: Charles Scribner's Sons, 1930).

Trotsky, Leon, 'The Comintern and the GPU: The Attempted Assassination of May 24 and the Communist Party of Mexico', *Fourth International*, 1/6 (November 1940), 148–63.

Trotsky, Leon, 'Stalin Seeks My Death', *Fourth International*, 2/7 (August 1941), 201–7.

Trotsky, Leon, 'The Comintern and the GPU: The Attempted Assassination of May 24 and the Communist Party of Mexico', *Fourth International*, 1/6 (November 1940), 148–63.

Trotsky, Leon, *Writings of Leon Trotsky [1936–37]* (London: Pathfinder Books Ltd, 1978).

Trubnikov, Vyacheslav I., Kirpichenko, Vadim A., Zhuravlyov, Yu., and Zamoisky, L. (eds), *Ocherki istorii Rossiiskoi vneshnei razvedki* (Moscow: Mezhdunarodnye otnosheniya, 2003), iv.

Tsarev, Oleg, 'Soviet Intelligence on British Defence Plans 1945–1950', in Lars Christian Jenssen and Olav Riste (eds), *Intelligence in the Cold War: Organisation, Role, International Cooperation* (Oslo: Norwegian Institute for Defence Studies, 2001).

Tsarev, Oleg, 'Aleksandr Orlov, russkii razvedchik', *Echo Moskvy*, interview with Yev. Kiselev, 15 June 2008.

Tsarev, Oleg, and Costello, John, *Rokovye illyuzii* (Moscow: Mezhdunarodnye otnosheniya, 1995).

Tsarev, Oleg, and West, Nigel, *KGB v Anglii* (Moscow: Zentrpoligraf, 1999).

Tsvetayeva, Marina, *Vivre dans le feu: Confessions*, ed. with a preface by Tzvetan Todorov, trans. Nadine Dubourvieux (Paris: Robert Laffont, 2005).

Tudor-Hart, Edith, *The Eye of Conscience*, text by Wolf Suschitzky (London: Dirk Nishen Publishing, 1987).

Tudor-Hart, Dr Julian, 'Alex Tudor-Hart, MRCS LRCP', Obituary, *Socialism & Health* (December 1992).

Uhl, Michael, 'Die internationalen Brigaden im Spiegel neuer Dokumente', *IWK*, 4 (1999), 486–518.

Uhl, Michael, *Mythos Spanien: Das Erbe der Internationalen Brigaden in der DDR* (Bonn: Dietz, 2004).

Ulanovsky, Nadezhda, and Ulanovsky, Maya, *Istoriya odnoi sem'i* (New York: Chalidze Publications, 1982).

Ulbricht, Walter, *Zur Geschichte der deutschen Arbeiterbewegung: Aus Reden und Aufsätzen*, ii. *1933–1946* (Berlin: Dietz, 1968).

Unfried, Berthold, 'Foreign Communists and the Mechanism of Soviet Cadre Formation in the USSR', in Barry McLoughlin and Kevin McDermott (eds), *Stalin's Terror: High Politics and Mass Repression in the Soviet Union* (Houndmills, Basingstoke: Palgrave Macmillan, 2003).

Unzueta, Patxo, 'El honor de Carrillo', *El Pais*, 27 October 2005.

Uribarri, Manuel, *El S.I.M. de la República*, vol. ii of *La Quinta Columna Española* (La Habana, Cuba: Tipografía la Universal, 1943).

Utrilla, Daniel, 'Dinamitera en La Guerra civil' [Parshina], *El Mundo*, 329, 3 February 2002.

Vallarino, Raúl, *Nombre clave: PATRIA. Una espía del KGB en Uruguay* (Montevideo: Editorial Sudamericana, 2006).

Vallarino, Raúl, *Mi nombre es Patria: La novela de la espia española del KGB* (Barcelona: Suma de Letras, 2008).

Valtin, Jan (pseud. of Richard Julius Hermann Krebs), *Out of the Night* (London: William Heinemann, 1941).

Van Doorslaar, Rudi, 'Anti-Communist Activism in Belgium, 1930–1944', *Socialist Register*, 21 (1984), 114–27.

Van Heijenoort, Jan, *With Trotsky in Exile: From Prinkipo to Coyoacan* (Cambridge, MA: Harvard University Press, 1978).

Vasilevsky, Lev Petrovich, *Ispanskaya khronika Grigoriya Grande*, paperback (Moscow: Molodaya gvardiya, 1985).

Vasilevsky, L. P., 'Fashistskii "Legion Kondor" v Ispanii v 1936–1939 gogakh', *Voenno-istoricheskii zhurnal*, 12 (1960), 118–19.

Vassiliev, Mark, 'Dnevnik sovetskogo voennogo konsula v Barcelone (1936)', *Alternativa*, 3 (2000) <http://scepsis.net/library/id_475.html> (accessed 20 January 2014).

Vaupshasov, Stanislav Alekseevich, *Na trevozhnykh perekryostkakh: Zapiski chekista* (Moscow: Politizdat, 1988).

Vázquez-Rial, Horacio, *El soldado de porcelana* [Biography of Gustavo Durán], paperback (Barcelona: Ediciones B, 1998).

Vereeken, Georges, *The GPU in the Trotskyist Movement* (Clapham: New Park Publications, 1976).

Vidal, César, *Checas de Madrid* (Barcelona: Carroggio/Belacqva, 2005).

Vidal, César, *Paracuellos—Katyn* (Madrid: Libroslibres, 2005).

Vidali, Vittorio, *Diary of the Twentieth Congress of the Communist Party of the Soviet Union*, paperback (Westport, CT: Lawrence Hill; London: Journeyman Press, 1974).

Vidarte, Juan-Simeón, *Todos fuimos culpables: Testimonio de un socialista español*, 2 vols (Barcelona, Buenos Aires, and Mexico: Grijalbo, 1978).

Vikin, Andrei, 'Zhena generala Eitingona', *Novosti razvedki i kontrrazvedki*, 23–4/56–7 (1995), 14.

Villemarest, Pierre de (avec collaboration de Clifford A. Kiracoff), *GRU: Le Plus Secret des services soviétiques, 1918–1988* (Paris: Stock, 1988).

Vinarov, Ivan, *Boitsy na tikhiya front: Spomeni na razuznavacha*, recorded and edited by Stefan Zhelev (Sofia: Izdatelstvo NABKP, 1969).

Vinarov, Ivan, *Boitsy tikhogo fronta* (Moscow: Iz-vo Ministerstva Oborony SSSR, 1971).

Viñas, Ángel, *El oro español en la guerra civil*, paperback (Madrid: Instituto de Estudios Fiscales, 1976).

Viñas, Ángel, *La Alemania nazi y el 18 de Julio* (Madrid: Alianza Editorial, 1977).

Viñas, Ángel, *El oro de Moscú: Alfa y omega de un mito franquista* (Barcelona and Buenos Aires: Ediciones Grijalbo, SA, 1979).

Viñas, Ángel, 'Gold, the Soviet Union, and the Spanish Civil War', *European Studies Review* (Sage), 9 (January 1979), 105–28.

Viñas, Ángel, *Política commercial exterior en España, 1931–1975* (Madrid: Banco Exterior de España, Servicio de Estudios Económicos, 1979).

Viñas, Ángel, 'The Financing of the Spanish Civil War', in Paul Preston (ed.), *Revolution and War in Spain, 1931–1939* (London: Methuen, 1984), 266–83.

Viñas, Ángel, 'The Gold, the Soviet Union and the Spanish Civil War', in Martin Blinkhorn (ed.), *Spain in Conflict, 1931–1939: Democracy and its Enemies* (London: Sage Publications, 1987), 224–43.

Viñas, Ángel, *En las garras del águila: Los pactos con Estados Unidos, de Francisco Franco a Felipe Gonzáles, 1945–1995* (Barcelona: Editorial Crítica, 2003).

Viñas, Ángel, *Negotiating the US-Spanish Agreements, 1953–1988: A Spanish Perspective* (Miami, FL: Jean Monnet Chair, University of Miami, 2003).

Viñas, Angel, 'La decisión de Stalin de ayudar a la República: Un aspecto controvertido en la historiografía de la Guerra Civil', *Historia y Política*, 16 (2006), 65–108.

Viñas, Ángel, *La soledad de la República: El abandano de las democracies y el viraje hacia la Unión Soviética* (Barcelona: Crítica, 2006).

Viñas, Ángel, *El escudo de la República: El oro de España, la apuesta soviética y los hechos de mayo de 1937* (Barcelona: Crítica, 2007).

Viñas, Ángel, 'La garra de Moscú', *La aventura de la historia*, 104 (June 2007), 34–41.

Viñas, Ángel, *El honor de la República: Entre elacoso fascista, la hostilidad británica y la política de Stalin* (Barcelona: Crítica, 2009).

Viñas, Ángel (dir.), *Al Servicio de la República: Diplomáticos y la Guerra Civil* (Madrid: Marcial Pons Historia, 2010).

Viñas, Ángel, *La conspiración del general Franco: Y otras revelaciones acerca de una guerra civil desfigurada* (Barcelona: Crítica, 2011).

Viñas, Ángel, *La república en Guerra: Contra Franco, Hitler, Mussolini y la hostilidad británica* (Barcelona: Crítica, 2012).

Viñas, Ángel, 'Una sublevación military con ayuda fascista', *El Pais*, 17 July 2012.

Viñas, Ángel, and Hernández Sánchez, Fernando, *El Desplome de la República* (Barcelona: Crítica, 2009).

Viñas, Ángel, and Seidel, Carlos Collado, 'Franco's Request to the Third Reich for Military Assistance', *Contemporary European History*, 2/2 (2002), 191–210.

Viñas, Ángel, Viñuela, Julio, Eguidazu, Fernando, Pulgar, Carlos Fernandezm, and Florensa, Senen, *Politica Comercial Exterior en España (1931–1975)* (Madrid: Banco Exterior de España, 1979).

Viñas Martín, Ángel, González Calleja, Eduardo, Hernández Sánchez, Fernando, Ledesma, José Luis, Aróstegui Sánchez, Julio, Raquer Suñer, Hilari, Sánchez Pérez, Francisco, Puell de la Villa, Fernando, Nuñes Seixas, and Xosé, Manuel, *Los mitos de 18 de julio* (Barcelona: Crítica, 2013).

Vinogradov, V. K. (ed.), *VCheka upolnomochena soobshchit . . .* (Moscow: Kuchkovo pole, 2004).

Vital, David, 'Czechoslovakia and the Powers, September 1938', *Journal of Contemporary History*, 1/4 (October 1966), 37–67.

Vitale, Ida, 'Las mujeres de Felisberto', *Letras Libres* (June 2003), 84–6.

Volkogonov, Dmitri, *Stalin: Triumph and Tragedy* (London: Grove Press, 1991).

Volkogonov, Dmitry, *Trotsky*, 2 vols (Moscow: Novosti, 1992).

Volkogonov, Dmitri, *Trotsky: The Eternal Revolutionary* (London: Free Press, 1996).

Volkogonov, Dmitri, *The Rise and Fall of the Soviet Empire: Political Leaders from Lenin to Gorbachev* (London: HarperCollins, 1998).

Volodarsky, Boris, *Nikolai Khokhlov ('Whistler'): Self-Esteem with a Halo*, paperback (Vienna: Borwall Verlag, 2005).

Volodarsky, Boris, 'Looking back on the Spanish Civil War', Letter to the Editor, *Times Literary Supplement*, 14 June 2006.

Volodarsky, Boris, *The KGB's Poison Factory: From Lenin to Litvinenko* (London: Frontline Books, 2009).

Volodarsky, Boris, 'Murder Convictions', *History Today*, 60/3 (March 2010), 66.

Volodarsky, Boris, 'Soviet Intelligence Services in the Spanish Civil War, 1936–1939', Ph.D. thesis, London School of Economics, July 2010.

Volodarsky, Boris, 'Kim Philby: Living a Lie', *History Today*, 60/8 (August 2010), 39–45.

Volodarsky, Boris, 'The KGB in Ann Arbor', *American Intelligence Journal*, 30/1 (2012), 39–45.

Volodarsky, Boris, *El caso Orlov: Los servicios secretos soviéticos en la Guerra civil española* (Barcelona: Crítica, 2013).

Volodarsky, Boris, 'Unknown Agabekov', *Intelligence and National Security* (2013), 890–909.

Waack, William, *Camaradas—Nos arquivos de Moscou—A história secreta da revolução brasileira de 1935* (São Paulo: Companhia das Letras, 1993).

Wahlback, Krister, 'Sweden: Secrecy and Neutrality', *Journal of Contemporary History*, 2/1 (January 1967), 183–91.

Waldenfels, Ernst von, *Der Spion, der aus Deutschland kam: Das geheime Leben des Seemanns Richard Krebs* (Berlin: Aufbau-Verlag, 2002).

Waller, J. Michael (ed.), *Strategic Influence: Public Diplomacy, Counterpropaganda and Political Warfare* (Washington, DC: Institute of World Politics Press, 2010).

Wark, Wesley K., 'British Intelligence on the German Air Force and Aircraft Industry, 1933–1939', *Historical Journal*, 25/3 (September 1982), 627–48.

Wark, Wesley K. 'Baltic Myths and Submarine Bogeys: British Naval Intelligence and Nazi Germany, 1933–1939', *Journal of Strategic Studies*, 6/1 (March 1983), 60–81.

Wark, Wesley K., *The Ultimate Enemy: British Intelligence and Nazi Germany, 1933–39* (London: I. B. Tauris & Co., 1985).

Wark, Wesley K., 'Coming in from the Cold: British Propaganda and the Red Army Defectors 1945–1952', *International History Review*, 9/1 (February 1987), 48–72.

Wark, Wesley K., 'British Intelligence and Small Wars in the 1930s', *Intelligence and National Security*, 2/4 (October 1987), 67–87.

Wark, Wesley K. 'Three Military Attachés in Berlin in the 1930s: Soldier-Statesmen and the Limits of Ambiguity', *International History Review*, 4 (November 1987), 586–611.

Wark, Wesley K., 'Something Very Stern: British Political Intelligence, Moralism and Strategy in 1939', *Intelligence and National Security*, 5/1 (January 1990), 150–70.

Wark, Wesley K. (ed.), *Espionage: Past, Present, Future?* (Abingdon: Frank Cass, 1993).

Watson, Derek, 'The Politburo and Foreign Policy in the 1930s', in E. A. Ress (ed.), *The Nature of Stalin's Dictatorship: The Politburo, 1924–1953* (Houndmills, Basingstoke: Palgrave Macmillan, 2004), 135–47.

Watt, Donald Cameron, 'British Intelligence and the Coming of the Second World War in Europe', in Ernest R. May (ed.), *Knowing One's Enemies: Intelligence Assessment before the Two World Wars* (Princeton: Princeton University Press, 1986).

Weber, Hermann, and Herbst, Andreas, *Deutsche Kommunisten: Biographisches Handbuch 1918 bis 1945* (Berlin: Karl Dietz Verlag, 2004).

Weber, Mark, 'The Roosevelt Legacy and The Kent Case', *Journal of Historical Review*, 4/2 (Summer 1983), 173–203.

Weidenfeld, George, *Remembering My Good Friends* (London: Harper Collins Publishers, 1994).

Weinstein, Allen, and Vassiliev, Alexander, *The Haunted Wood* (New York: Random House, 1998).

Weinzierl-Fischer, Erika, *Die österreichischen Konkordate von 1855 und 1933* (Vienna: Verlag für Geschichte und Politik, 1960).

Weissman, Susan, 'The Banality of Cowardice: Marc "Etienne" Zborowski, Stalin's Master Spy in the Left Opposition', VI International Council for Central and East European Studies (ICCEES) World Congress, 31 July 2000, Tampere, Finland.

Weissman, Susan, 'Marc Zborowski, Stalin's Agent in Parisian and American Leftist Circles', Brown Bag Lunch Seminars, Saint Mary's College of California, 2 April 2001.

Weissman, Susan, 'Marc Zborowski: Stalin's Spy in the International Left', 32nd Annual Convention, American Association for the Advancement of Slavic Studies (AAASS), Washington, DC, 7 November 2001.

Werner, Ruth [Ursula Kuczynski], *Sonjas Rapport* (Berlin: Verlag Neues Leben, 1977/5; Auflage, 1979).

Wessel, Karl, '"... hat sich offenbar selbst umgebracht". Untersuchungsprotokoll zum Auffinden der Leiche Willi Münzenbergs am 17. Oktober 1940', *Beiträge zur Geschichte der Arbeiterbewegung*, 1 (Berlin: Dietz Verlag, 1991).

Wessel, Harald, *Münzenbergs Ende: Ein deutscher Kommunist im Widerstand gegen Hitler und Stalin: Die Jahre 1933 bis 1940* (Berlin: Dietz, 1991).

West, Nigel, *The Illegals: The Double Lives of the Cold War's Most Secret Agents* (London: Hodder & Stoughton, 1993).

West, Nigel, *VENONA: The Greatest Secret of the Cold War* (London: HarperCollins, 1999).

West, Nigel, '"Venona": The British Dimension', *Intelligence and National Security*, 17/1 (Spring 2002), 117–34.

West, Nigel, *MASK: MI5's Penetration of the Communist Party of Great Britain* (London: Routledge, 2005).

West, Nigel, *At Her Majesty's Secret Service: The Chiefs of Britain's Intelligence Agency MI6* (London: Greenhill Books, 2006).

West, Nigel, and Tsarev, Oleg, *The Crown Jewels: The British Secrets at the Heart of the KGB Archives* (New Haven and London: Yale University Press, 1999).

Whaley, Barton, *Guerrillas in the Spanish Civil War* (Cambridge, MA: Institute of Technology, 1969).

Whealey, Robert H., 'Economic Influence of the Great Powers in the Spanish Civil War: From the Popular Front to the Second World War', *International History Review*, 5/2 (May 1983), 229–54.

Whitaker, John T., 'Prelude to World War: A Witness from Spain', *Foreign Affairs*, 21/1 (October 1942).

Whitwell, John, *British Agent*, intro. Wesley K. Wark (Abingdon: Frank Cass, 1997).

Whymant, Robert, *Stalin's Spy: Richard Sorge and the Tokyo Espionage Ring* (London: I. B. Tauris & Co. Ltd, 2006).

Wilhelm, John Howard, 'The Orlov File', *Johnson List* No. 7022, 17 January 2003.

Wilkinson, David, 'Malraux, Revolutionist and Minister', *Journal of Contemporary History*, 1/2 (April 1966), 43–64.

Wirth, Maria, *Christian Broda: Eine politische Biographie* (Vienna: V&R unipress/ Vienna University Press, 2011).

Wolf, Markus, with McElvoy, Anne, *Man without a Face* (London: Jonathan Cape, 1997).

Wolfe, Bertram D., 'The Swaddled Soul of the Great Russians', *New Leader*, 29 January 1951.

Wolikow, Serge (dir.) avec la collaboration de Carrez, Maurice, Cordillot, Michel, et Vigreux, Jean, *Une histoire en révolution?* *Du bon usage des archives, de Moscou et d'ailleurs* (Dijon: Publications de l'Université de Bourgogne [*sic*], 1996).

Wolin, Simon, and Slusser, Robert M. (eds), *The Soviet Secret Police* (New York: Frederick A. Praeger, 1957).

Wollenberg, Erich, *The Red Army* (London: Secker & Warburg, 1938).

Wollenberg, Erich, *Der Apparat: Stalins Fünfte Kolonne* (Bonn: Bundesministerium für gesamtdeutsche Fragen, n.d. [1952]).

Wolton, Thierry, *Le KGB en France*, paperback (Paris: Graseet, 1985).

Wolton, Thierry, *Le Grand Recrutement* [Henri Robinson], paperback (Paris: Grasset, 1993).

Woytak, Richard A., *On the Border of War and Peace: Polish Intelligence and Diplomacy in 1937–1939 and the Origins of the Ultra Secret* (New York: Columbia University Press, 1979).

Wright, Peter, with Greengrass, Paul, *Spycatcher: The Candid Autobiography of a Senior Intelligence Officer* (Richmond, Victoria: William Heinemann, 1987).

Yang, Zhidong (ed.), *Klara Blum* (Vienna: Böhlau Verlag, 2001).

Young, Robert J., 'French Military Intelligence and Nazi Germany, 1938–1939', in Ernest R. May (ed.), *Knowing One's Enemies: Intelligence Assessment before the Two World Wars* (Princeton: Princeton University Press, 1986).

Ypsilon (pseudonym of Karl Volk and Jules Humbert-Droz), *Pattern for World Revolution* (Chicago and New York: Ziff Davis Publishing Co., 1947).

Zavala, José María, *En busca de Andreu Nin: Vida y muerte de un mito silenciado de la Guerra Civil*, Prólogo Stanley G. Payne (Barcelona: Plaza y Janés, 2005).

Zborowski, Mark, 'The Children of the Covenant', *Social Forces*, 4 (1951).

Zborowski, Mark, *People in Pain* (San Francisco: Jossey-Bass, 1969).

Zborowski, Mark, and Herzog, Elizabeth, *Life is with People: The Jewish Little-Town of Eastern Europe* (New York: International Universities Press, 1962).

Zipperstein, Steven J., 'Underground Man: The Curious Case of Mark Zborowski and the Writing of a Modern Jewish Classic', *Jewish Review of Books*, 2 (Summer 2010), 38–42.

Zuehlke, Mark, *The Gallant Cause: Canadians in the Spanish Civil War, 1936–1939* (Vancouver and Toronto: Whitecap Books, 1996).

Zugazagoitia, Julián, *Guerra y vicisitudes de los españoles*, 2 vols (Paris: Libería Española, 1968).

Zugazagoitia, Julián, *Los trabajos clandestinos*. Prólogo de José María Villarías Zugazagoitia (Madrid: Viamonte, 2005).

Zur Mühlen, Patrik von, *Spanien war ihre Hoffnung: Die deutsche Linke im Spanischen Bürgerkrieg 1936 bis 1939* (Bonn: Verlag J. H. W. Dietz, 1985).

Zur Mühlen, Patrik von, *Fluchtweg Spanien-Portugal: Die deutsche Emigration und der Exodus aus Europa 1933–1945* (Bonn: Verlag J. H. W. Dietz Nachf., 1992).

ADDITIONAL SOURCES

Antonov, Vladimir, 'Polkovnik África', *Nezavisimoe voennoe obozrenie*, 3 November 2006.

Arthey, Vin, *The Kremlin's Geordie Spy: The Man they Swapped for Gary Powers*, paperback (London: Biteback, 2010).

Beevor, Anthony, *The Battle for Spain* (London: Weidenfeld & Nicolson, 2005).

Blunt, Anthony, and Pool, Phoebe, *Picasso: The Formative Years, a Study of his Sources* (New York: New York Graphic Society, 1962).

Blunt, Anthony, 'From Bloomsbury to Marxism', *Studio International* (November 1973).

Boyar, Jane, and Boyar, Burt, *Hitler Stopped by Franco*, paperback (Los Angeles, CA: Marbella House, 2001).

Brackman, Roman, *The Secret File of Joseph Stalin: A Hidden Life* (London and New York: Routledge, 2001).

Brossat, Alain, *Agents de Moscou* (Paris: Gallimard, 1988).

Cairncross, John, *Molière: Bourgeois et libertin* (Paris: A. G. Nizet, 1963).

Cairncross, John, *After Polygamy Was Made a Sin: The Social History of Christian Polygamy* (London: Routledge & Kegan Paul, 1974).

Cairncross, John, *The Enigma Spy: The Story of the Man who Changed the Course of World War Two* (London: Century, 1997).

Cairncross, John, *An Agent for the Duration* (London: Little, Brown & Co., 1998).

Chernyavsky, Georgy, 'Grigulevich Iosif Romualdovich: razvedchik, uchyonyi, pisatel', *Nezavisimaya gazeta*, 17 May 2001.

Chikov, Vladimir, *Razvedchiki-nelegaly* (Moscow: Exmo/Algoritm kniga, 2003).

Chikov, Vladimir, *Russkie nelegaly v USA* (Moscow: Exmo/Algoritm kniga, 2003).

Damaskin, Igor A., *Stalin i razvedka* (Moscow: Veche, 2004).

Dienko, A. (ed.), *Razvedka i kotrrazvedka v litsakh*. Entsiklopedicheskii slovar Rossiiskikh spetssluzhb (Moscow: Russkii mir, 2002).

Dolgopolov, Nikolay, *Oni ukrali bombu dlya Sovetov* (Moscow: XXI vek-Soglasie, 2000).

Dolgopolov, Nikolay, *S nimi mozhno idti v razvedku* (Moscow: Voskresenye, 2002).

Dolgopolov, Nikolay, *Genii vneshnei razvedki* (Moscow: Molodaya Gvardiya, 2004).

Draitser, Emil, *Stalin's Romeo Spy: The Remarkable Rise and Fall of the KGB's Most Daring Operative* (Evanston, IL: Northwestern University Press, 2010).

Drozdov, Yuri, *Vymysel isklyuchen*, paperback (Moscow: Vympel, 1997).

Elliott, Geoffrey, and Shukman, Harold, *Secret Classroom: A Memoir of the Cold War*, paperback (London: St Ermin's Press, 2003).

Fischer, Markoosha, *The Nazarovs* (Whitefish, MT: Kessinger Publishing, 2005).

Fox, Frank, 'Mark Zborowski, the Spy who Came out of the Shtetl', *East European Jewish Affairs*, 29/1–2 (Summer 1999), 119–28.

Freemantle, Brian, *KGB* (London: Michael Joseph/Rainbird: 1982).

Gladkov, Teodor, *Korol nelegalov* [Alexander M. Korotkov] (Moscow: Gaia eterum, 2000).

Hill, Christopher, *Lenin and the Russian Revolution* (London: Hodder & Stoughton, 1947).

Houghton, Harry, *Operation Portland: The Autobiography of a Spy* (London: Rupert Hart-Davis, 1972).

Hyde, Earl M., Jr, 'Still Perplexed about Krivitsky', *International Journal of Intelligence and Counterintelligence*, 16/3 (July 2003), 428–41.

Karpov, Vladimir (ed.), *Rassekrecheno vneshnei razdedkoi* (Moscow: Olma Press, 2003).

Katamidze, Slava, *Loyal Comrades, Ruthless Killers: The KGB and the Secret Services of the USSR, 1917–1991* (Staplehurst: Spellmount, 2003).

Khrapachevsky, Roman, 'Ispanskoe zoloto Kremlya', *Russkii Focus*, 7 (May 2001).

Kiselyov, Aleksandr, *Vneshnyaia razvedka: Otdel spetsialnykh operatsyi* (Moscow: Yauza/Exmo, 2004).

Knight, Amy, *Who Killed Kirov? The Kremlin's Greatest Mystery* (New York: Hill & Wang, 2000).

Koch, Stephen, *The Breaking Point: Hemingway, Dos Passos, and the Murder of Jose Robles* (Washington, DC: Counterpoint, 2005).

Kolosov, Leonid Sergeevich, *Sobkor KGB: Zapiski razvedchika i zhurnalista* (Moscow: Tsentrpoligraph, 2001).

Kolpakidi, Alexander Ivanovich, *Entsyklopediya Sekretnykh sluzhb Rossii* (Moscow: AST, 2004).

Kolpakidi, Alexander I., and Prokhorov, Dmitri P., *KGB: Spetsoperatsyi sovetskoi razvedki* (Moscow: Olimp/Astrel/AST, 2000).

Kolpakidi, Alexander I., and Prokhorov, Dmitri P., *KGB: Prikazano likvidirovat'* (Moscow: Yauza/Exmo, 2004).

Kolpakidi, Alexander I., and Prokhorov, Dmitri P., *Vneshnyaia razvedka Rossii* (Moscow: Yauza/Exmo, 2004).

Krasilnikov, Rem Sergeevich, *KGB protiv MI6: Okhotniki za shpionami* (Moscow: Zentrpoligraf, 2000).

Kun, Miklós, *Stalin: An Unknown Portrait* (Budapest: Central European University Press, 2003).

Kurz, Hermann, *OGPU: In der Hölle der Tscheka* (Leipzig: Tauber-Verlag, 1932).

Kuznetsov, Ilya I., 'KGB General Naum Isakovich Eitingon (1899–1981)', *Journal of Slavic Military Studies*, 14/1 (2001), 37–52.

Lainer, Lev, *VENONA: Samaya sekretnaya operatsiya amerikanskikh spetssluzhb* (Moscow: Olma Press, 2003).

Lyubimov, Mikhail, *Blesk i nischeta shpionazha* (Moscow: Astrel, 2005).

Marks, John D., *The Search for the Manchurian Candidate*, paperback (New York: W. W. Norton & Company Inc., 1979).

Martirosyan, A. B., *Zagovor marshalov: Britanskaya razvedka protiv SSSR* (Moscow: Veche, 2003).

Medvedenko, Anatoly, 'Prikazyval li Stalin ubit Franco?', *Ekho planety*/ITAR-TASS, 11, 14–20 March 2003.

Naumov, Leonid, *Bor'ba v rukovodstve NKVD v 1936–38 gg.* (Moscow: Samizdat, 2003).

Newton, Verne W., *Cambridge Spies: The Untold Story of McLean, Philby, and Burgess* (Silver Spring, MD: Madison Books, 1991).

Osokina, Elena A., *Zoloto dlya industrializstsyi: Torgsin* (Moscow: ROSSPEN, 2009).

Patenaude, Bertrand M., *Stalin's Nemesis: The Exile and Murder of Leon Trotsky* (London: Faber and Faber, 2009).

Pavlov, Vitaly, *Operatsiya 'Sneg'* (Moscow: Geya, 1996).

Pavlov, Vitaly, 'Operatsiya SCHWED', in Vitaly Grigoryevich Pavlov, *Sezam, otkroisya!* (Moscow: TERRA-Knizhnyi klub, 1999).

Pavlov, Vitaly, *Zhenskoe litso razvedki* (Moscow: Olma Press, 2003).

Peshchersky, Vladimir L., *Krasnaya Kapella: Sovetskaya razvedka protiv abvera i gestapo* (Moscow: Zentrpoligraf, 2000).

Philby, Kim, *My Silent War: The Autobiography of a Spy* (London: Panther, 1976).

Platoshkin, Nikolai Nikolayevich, *Grazhdanskaya voina v Ispanii, 1936–1939 gg.* (Moscow: Olma Press, 2004).

Rees, Goronwy, *A Chapter of Accidents* (London: Chatto & Windus, 1971).

Rogovin, Vadim Z., *1937* (Moscow: Izdatelstvo Moskva, 1996).

Rose, R. S., and Scott, Gordon D., *Johnny: A Spy's Life* (University Park, PA: Pennsylvania State University Press, 2010).

Schafranek, Hans (ed.), *Die Betrogenen: Österreicher asl Opfer stalinistischen Terrors in der Sowjetunion* (Vienna: Picus Verlag, 1991).

Schild und Flamme: Erzählungen und Berichte aus der Arbeit der Tscheka (Berlin: Militärverlag der Deutschen Demokratischen Republik, 1973).

Sharapov, Eduard P., *Naum Eitingon: Karayushchy mech Stalina* (St Petersburg: Neva, 2003).

Smolensky, Alexander P., and Krasnyansky, Eduard, *Zalozhnik: Operatsiya 'Memorandum'* (Moscow: Vagrius, 2006).

Sobell, Morton, *On Doing Time* (New York: Charles Scribner's Sons, 1974).

Soria, Georges, *Comment vivent les Russes* (Paris: Éditeurs franais runis, 1949).

Soria, Georges, *Le Ballet Moisseiev* (Paris: Éditions Cercle d'art, 1955).

Soria, Georges, *Les 300 Jours de la revolution russe* (Paris: Lafont, 1967).

Soria, Georges, *Guerre en Espagne, 1936–1939* (Paris: Lafont, 1977).

Sotskov, Lev, *Kod operatsyi 'Tarantella'* (Moscow: Molodaya gvardiya, 2007).

Straight, Michael, *After Long Silence* (London: Collins, 1983).

Suvorov, Victor, *The Chief Culprit: Stalin's Grand Design to Start World War II* (Annapolis, MD: Naval Institute Press, 2008).

Tolstoy, Nikolai, *Stalin's Secret War* (London: Jonathan Cape, 1981).

Tolz, Vladimir, 'Naum Eitingon: deti shpionov', *RFE/RL*, transcript, 29 September 2002.

Tsarev, Oleg, 'Bez durakov', *Echo Moskvy*, interview with S. Korzun, 23 February 2006.

Vasilevsky, L[ev] P[etrovich], 'Fascistskii "Legion Kondor" v Ispanii v 1936–1939 godakh', *Voenno-Istoricheskii Zhurnal*, 12 (1960), 118–19.

Vaxberg, Arkady, 'Pravda o "platnom agente"', *Literaturnaya gazeta*, 21 November 1990.

Vinarov, Ivan, *Boitsy tikhogo fronta* (Moscow: Voennoe izdatelstvo Ministerstva oborony, 1971).

Vorobyov, Evgeny, *Zemlya do-vostrebovaniya* [Lev Manevich] (Moscow: Izvestiya, 1973).

Wilmers, Mary-Kay, *The Eitingons: A Twentieth-Century Story* (London: Faber and Faber, 2009).

Yuriev, Mikhail, 'Samyi nelegalnyi nelegal' [Grigulevich], *Sovershenno Sekretno*, 12/259 (December 2010), 16–17.

Zenkovich, Nikolay A., *Na KGB rabotali i STAR i MLAD* (Moscow: Olma Press, 2003).

Zeutschel, Walter, *Im Dienst der kommunistischen Terror-Organisation (Tscheka-Arbeit in Deutschland)* (Berlin: J. H. W. Dietz Nachfolger, 1931).

Zubok, Vladislav, 'Stalin's Plans and Russian Archives', *Diplomatic History*, 21/2 (Spring 1997).

Zubov, Oleg, 'Takoi vot strannyi shpion' [Orlov], *Novyi mir*, 12 (1996).

Index